International Handbook of Research on Conceptual Change

Conceptual change research investigates the processes through which learners substantially revise prior knowledge and acquire new concepts. Tracing its heritage to paradigms and paradigm shifts made famous by Thomas Kuhn, conceptual change research focuses on understanding and explaining learning of the most difficult and counter-intuitive concepts. Now in its second edition, the *International Handbook of Research on Conceptual Change* provides a comprehensive review of the conceptual change movement and of the impressive research it has spawned on students' difficulties in learning.

In 31 new and updated chapters, organized thematically and introduced by Stella Vosniadou, this volume brings together detailed discussions of key theoretical and methodological issues, the roots of conceptual change research, and mechanisms of conceptual change and learner characteristics. Combined with chapters that describe conceptual change research in the fields of physics, astronomy, biology, medicine and health, and history, this handbook presents writings on interdisciplinary topics written for researchers and students across fields.

Stella Vosniadou is Professor of Cognitive Psychology in the Department of Philosophy and History of Science at the National and Kapodistrian University of Athens, Greece. She is the current chair of the interdisciplinary graduate program in Cognitive Science between the University of Athens and the Economic University of Athens, and director of the Cognitive Science Laboratory at the University of Athens.

Educational Psychology Handbook Series
Series Editor: Patricia A. Alexander

International Handbook of Research on Conceptual Change
Second Edition

Edited by
Stella Vosniadou

Routledge
Taylor & Francis Group

NEW YORK AND LONDON

Second edition published 2013
by Routledge
711 Third Avenue, New York, NY 10017

Simultaneously published in the UK
by Routledge
2 Park Square, Milton Park, Abingdon, Oxon OX14 4RN

Routledge is an imprint of the Taylor & Francis Group, an informa business

© 2013 Taylor & Francis

First edition published 2008 by Routledge

Library of Congress Cataloging-in-Publication Data
International handbook of research on conceptual change / edited by Stella Vosniadou.
    p. cm. — (Educational psychology handbook series)
    Includes bibliographical references.
  1. Concept learning—Research. 2. Concepts—Research. I. Vosniadou, Stella.
  LB1062.I58 2008
  370.15′23—dc22   2007041601

ISBN: 978–0–415–89882–9 (hbk)
ISBN: 978–0–415–89883–6 (pbk)
ISBN: 978–0–203–15447–2 (ebk)

Typeset in Minion
by Keystroke, Station Road, Codsall, Wolverhampton
Printed and bound in Great Britain by TJ International Ltd, Padstow, Cornwall

This book is dedicated to Giyoo Hatano,
whose work in conceptual change was an inspiration to all of us

CONTENTS

ACKNOWLEDGMENTS

This book is dedicated to Giyoo Hatano, whose work in conceptual change was an inspiration to all of us. Giyoo was one of the original editors of this volume and instrumental in its conception. His untimely death did not allow him to complete the project. We have reprinted in this volume Chapter 7 from his book with Kayoko Inagaki entitled "Young children's naïve thinking about the biological world." I am indebted to Kayoko Inagaki for her permission to reprint this chapter in the Handbook and to Naomi Miyake for her extensive discussion of Giyoo's work in her chapter.

I would like to thank Patricia Alexander, who suggested to me the idea of editing a Handbook in this area and who supported it all along as the series editor for Educational Psychology. I would also like to express my thanks to the editorial director of the series, Lane Akers, who has been extremely helpful and supportive all along the many months it took to complete this project. All the authors who contributed chapters for the Handbook were very cooperative and willing to make the required changes in their chapters. I would like to thank them for that. Last but not least, I thank my secretary Spyridoula Efthimiou who has spent hours formatting and correcting manuscripts and references for this book.

CONCEPTUAL CHANGE RESEARCH: AN INTRODUCTION

Stella Vosniadou, National and Kapodistrian University of Athens

Research on conceptual change investigates how concepts change with learning and development in different subject matter areas with a focus on explaining students' difficulties in learning the more advanced and counterintuitive concepts in these areas. Some researchers are not persuaded that there is a need to distinguish "conceptual change" processes from learning in general. We argue, however, that while conceptual change is undeniably a form of learning, it is important to differentiate it from other types of learning because it requires fundamental changes in the content and organization of existing knowledge as well as the development of new learning strategies for deliberate knowledge restructuring and the acquisition of new concepts. In fact, it is our contention that the problem of conceptual change is one of the major reasons behind students' widespread failure to understand counterintuitive concepts, mostly (but not only) in science and mathematics. We also argue that, to a large extent, the general ineffectiveness of instructional interventions in these areas could be attributed to the inadequate attention that has been given so far to the problem of conceptual change (Vosniadou, Vamvakoussi, & Skopeliti, 2008).

The problem of conceptual change first became apparent to philosophers and historians of science in their attempts to explain how scientific theories change. According to Kuhn (1970), normal science operates within sets of shared beliefs, assumptions, commitments, and practices that constitute "paradigms." Discoveries emerge over time that cannot be accommodated within the existing paradigm. When these anomalies accumulate, science enters a period of crisis which is eventually resolved by a revolutionary change in paradigm. Many scientific revolutions, such as the Newtonian theory in physics, the Copernican theory in astronomy, and the Darwinian theory of evolution in biology can be seen as the products of radical conceptual change. In these cases new theories are generated to explain known and new phenomena, and new concepts are formed (Thagard, 1992).

Ideas about conceptual change from the history and philosophy of science were soon brought to developmental psychology through the work of Susan Carey (1985) and to science education through the work of Michael Posner and his colleagues (Posner, Strike, Hewson, & Gertzog, 1982). Research in science education in the 1970s had shown that students bring to the science education task alternative frameworks, preconceptions, or misconceptions, some of which are rather robust and difficult to extinguish through teaching (e.g., Driver & Easley, 1978; Viennot, 1979). In some cases these alternative frameworks appeared to be similar to earlier theories in the history of science, such as the impetus theory[1] in mechanics (McCloskey, 1983). Posner et al. (1982) drew an analogy between the concepts of normal science and scientific revolution offered by philosophers of science such as Kuhn (1970) and Piaget's (1970) concepts of assimilation and accommodation, and derived from this analogy an instructional theory to promote "accommodation" in students' learning of science. According to Posner et al. (1982), students need to undergo a radical conceptual change when it comes to learning scientific concepts such as *force, heat,* and *energy.*

Over the years, a significant body of research emerged to investigate the processes of conceptual change, the learning mechanisms involved in the generation of new concepts, and the instructional strategies that can promote it. The theoretical and methodological discussions that have taken place in this process have been some of the most interesting in the field of learning and instruction, raising important questions about the nature of knowledge, its organization, and its revision. Although the beginnings of conceptual change research can be traced to scientific discovery in physics and physics education, this research is by no means restricted to physics but makes a larger claim about learning that transcends many domains of knowledge and can apply, for example, to biology (Inagaki & Hatano, 2002), psychology (Wellman, 2002), history (Leinhardt & Ravi, 2008), political science (Voss & Wiley, 2006), medicine (Kaufman, Keselman, & Patel, 2008), environmental learning (Rickinson, Lundholm, & Hopwood, 2009), and mathematics (Vosniadou & Verschaffel, 2004).

The second edition of the *International Handbook of Research on Conceptual Change* updates the first volume, published in 2008, and includes additional chapters that further clarify the role of conceptual change processes in the acquisition of subject matter knowledge and the instructional interventions that can promote it. Overall, this edition of the Handbook presents in a cohesive manner the results of an impressive body of research conducted in recent years in the area of conceptual change.

A ROADMAP TO THE BOOK

The Handbook is divided into five parts. The first part is entitled *Theoretical Issues in Conceptual Change Research.* It consists of five chapters that focus on fundamental theoretical issues in conceptual change research, such as the definition of concepts and of conceptual change, the specification of the different kinds of conceptual changes that can take place, the coherence versus fragmentation debate, as well as some methodological issues. In the first chapter, Vosniadou argues that naïve physics is a "framework theory" that constrains the acquisition of scientific concepts and that the learning of science is difficult because it requires fundamental changes in students' ontological and epistemological knowledge and the creation of new representations. These conceptual changes happen in a slow and gradual manner as the constraints of naïve physics are gradually lifted, creating in the process fragmentation and misconceptions. Vosniadou goes on to demonstrate how fragmentation and misconceptions can result from the use of constructive, enrichment types of mechanisms used by students to incorporate scientific information to incompatible existing knowledge.

In the next chapter, diSessa explains and advocates a "knowledge in pieces" approach to conceptual change. In it he enriches and redefines the debate between "coherence" and "fragmentation" views, discussing three main issues: (a) the grain size of elements necessary to understand conceptual change, (b) the very meaning of coherence, and (c) the problem of accounting for empirically evident sensitivity to context. diSessa argues that two of the characteristic strengths of the knowledge in pieces approach are in dealing with the "long road" to competence and in treating evident diversity across students, across domains, and across contexts within a domain.

Chi in her chapter argues that conceptual change requires an understanding of the ways new knowledge conflicts with what is already known, and addresses the differences between incorrect knowledge versus misconceived conflicting knowledge. She offers a theoretical framework that lays out two different kinds of conceptual change as a function of how conflicting knowledge is defined, postulates the processes by which such conflicting knowledge can be changed, and speculates on the kind of instruction that might achieve such change. Halldén, Scheja, and Haglund, on the other hand, propose a theoretical and methodological approach to analyzing personal meaning making based on intentional analysis. This approach focuses on learners' interaction with the learning material and with their surroundings, emphasizing the potentialities of learning. In the last chapter, Siegler and Svetina describe a method – the microgenetic/cross-sectional design – that they believe can yield data that can resolve the theoretical disputes regarding the nature of the processes of change that take place during learning and development. Experiments using this method support Vygotsky's and Werner's position that short-term and long-term change have many similarities, including progress through similar sequences of qualitatively distinct knowledge states.

Part II is entitled *Conceptual Change in the Content Areas*. It consists of 12 chapters that describe the processes of knowledge acquisition and conceptual change in different subject matter areas such as physics, astronomy, matter, biology, medicine, history, and mathematics. In the first chapter Brown and Hammer present their own theoretical perspective to account for conceptual change in physics – a complex systems account. They argue that in a complex systems account, structure and coherence can emerge out of a dynamic system of simpler agents and, because of that, this perspective has the potential to integrate findings from previous work. In the second chapter, Siler, Klahr, and Matlen describe changes in the way children think about a small, but essential, part of middle school science instruction – experimental design, otherwise known as the "control of variables strategy." The two chapters that follow, by Smith and Wiser, and Wiser and Smith, provide a detailed description of the long progression involved in the learning of the concepts of matter and materials. They argue that students not only have difficulties in understanding the atomic–molecular theory of matter which is taught at school but also have considerable difficulties understanding the macroscopic concept of matter and its relationships to certain other key concepts in this area, such as the concepts of weight, density, volume, solid, liquid, and gas. They go on to provide a very interesting account of the conceptual changes that are needed in this area and to show how they interrelate with changes in mathematical and epistemological understanding.

The next two chapters deal with conceptual change in biology. The chapter by Inagaki and Hatano is a reprint of Chapter 7 of their book *Young Children's Naïve Thinking about the Biological World*. They describe the conceptual changes that take place in the course of the development of biological knowledge, paying particular attention to outlining some of the mechanisms of conceptual change. The second chapter on biology is written by E. Margaret Evans, who reviews the empirical research on the Darwinian theory of evolution, particularly that conducted in diverse religious and cultural contexts. She argues that the theory of evolution is counterintuitive because of initial constraints on cognition. These constraints give rise to cognitive biases or intuitive theories that appear to limit humans' view of nature. The core question is the extent to which the human mind is capable of conceptual change when confronted with scientific evidence that appears to flatly contradict such a self-serving view of the world.

The domain of medicine is discussed in the next chapter by Kaufman, Keselman, and Patel. The authors examine cross-cultural research pertaining to lay understanding and reasoning, using as examples research on nutritional disorders and HIV-related issues. They also discuss the kinds of interventions that can be designed to promote conceptual change in these areas. They argue that lay understanding of health concepts has a bearing on consumer health decisions and behavior and that conceptual understanding of health issues gives individuals the power to derive better predictions and explanations of health-related phenomena, which can then be applied in decision making.

The next three chapters address the problem of conceptual change in history and the social sciences. Leinhardt and Ravi trace the ways in which history as a domain has undergone a conceptual shift. They also examine some of the literature that exists to see if and how students manage these shifts in considering what history is. The accounts of student knowledge show that students can and do attend to ideas such as authorship and do move from an accuracy-driven definition to a criterion-driven understanding of historical phenomena. Carretero, Castorina, and Levinas, on the other hand, focus on the concept of "nation" because of its pivotal role in historical accounts in numerous countries. They argue that students have an essentialist idea of nation as an immutable political object whose historical origin is misunderstood, and that these ideas remain stable until adulthood. The chapter by Lundholm and Davies examines conceptual change in economics and the political domain. The authors emphasize the importance of students' sense of self and values in these domains, and point out that questions about how societies should be constituted in terms of equity and distribution of resources are more central to the social sciences compared to the natural sciences.

The last two chapters in this section look at mathematics from a conceptual change point of view. Vamvakoussi, Vosniadou, and Van Dooren discuss how the framework theory approach to conceptual change can be applied in the case of mathematics learning and teaching. They argue that the framework theory not only explains a great deal of the evidence on students' systematic errors, but also generates novel predictions regarding the specific areas in mathematics that students are going to find difficult to understand during the conceptual change process. Blair, Tsang, and Schwartz investigate the transition from natural numbers to integers (which include zero and the negative numbers) using multiple methodologies ranging from fMRI to classroom instruction.

The third part of the book is entitled *Conceptual Change in the Philosophy and History of Science* and consists of two chapters. The first, by Arabatzis and Kindi, provides information about the roots of the conceptual change approach in the philosophy and history of science, including a critical analysis of Thomas Kuhn's more recent work in which he attempted to address some of the difficulties faced by his original account of conceptual change and to articulate further his key philosophical notion of incommensurability. In the second chapter, Paul Thagard examines three central concepts in biology, psychology, and medicine, namely the concepts of life, mind, and disease. He argues that all three concepts have undergone a progression that involved shifts in theoretical understanding from the theological to the qualitative to the mechanistic. He attempts to show how concepts with a mechanistic underpinning differ from theological and qualitative ones, and discusses some of the psychological impediments to students' acquisition of mechanistic understanding of life, disease, and mind.

Part IV includes five chapters that focus on *Learner Characteristics and Mechanisms for Conceptual Change*. Sinatra and Mason try to capture the "warming trend" in conceptual change research (Murphy & Mason, 2006; Sinatra & Pintrich, 2003). They review current theory and research on how key constructs such as achievement goals, epistemic motives, interest, self-efficacy, and affect might influence the change process. In the next chapter, Nersessian draws on literature across the "mental models framework" to support the idea that internal and external representations are "coupled" in reasoning processes. She argues that analogical, imagistic, and simulative modeling are productive means of conceptual change in that they involve abstractive reasoning processes by means of which truly novel combinations of unrepresented structures and behaviors can emerge. In his chapter, Clement discusses two traditional approaches to promote conceptual change through instruction: the use of dissonance-producing strategies such as cognitive conflict, and the use of constructive strategies, involving, for example, analogies. He goes on to argue that these seemingly disparate approaches can be combined successfully in a model evolution approach that includes many cycles of model evaluation and revision.

The role of collaboration and reflection as social mechanisms that promote conceptual change is examined in the chapter by Miyake, while Martin and Schwartz examine the role of dynamic transfer and innovation. They argue that most transfer situations involve similarity transfer, which occurs when people are able to recognize that they have well-formed prior ideas that can be profitably used to describe another situation in a new way. Dynamic transfer, on the other hand, occurs when component competencies are coordinated through interaction with the environment to yield novel concepts or material structures. The two types of transfer can work together so that people can transfer the idea of being innovative when it is appropriate to do so.

Part V, on *Instructional Approaches to Promote Conceptual Change*, includes six chapters that provide different ideas about how to promote conceptual change in the classroom. In the first chapter, Duit, Treagust, and Widodo argue that there is a large gap between what is known in research about conceptual change and what happens in practice in normal science classes. Most teachers hold views about teaching and learning that are limited when seen from recent conceptual change perspectives. Consequently, their instructional repertoires are also far from teaching based on conceptual change perspectives. These authors argue that attention should be paid to the problem of familiarizing teachers with the recent state of conceptual change research and changing their instructional practices. In the next chapters, Bereiter and Scardamalia point out some of the educational benefits of viewing conceptual change in terms of self-organizing systems, while Clark and Linn highlight the knowledge integration perspective and its implications for education. Chinn, Duncan, Dianovsky, and Rinehart discuss core features of inquiry-based approaches to conceptual change and examine some of the empirical evidence bearing on their efficacy. In the next chapter, Tytler and

Prain argue that the guided construction of representations productively constrains students' reasoning and learning of science concepts and processes and promotes conceptual change. Jonassen and Easter focus on the advantages of model-based reasoning for conceptual change. They argue that model building is a powerful strategy for engaging, supporting, and assessing conceptual change in learners because models scaffold and externalize internal, mental models and provide multiple formalisms for representing conceptual understanding and change. In Part VI, *Reflections*, Murphy and Alexander's chapter summarizes some of the themes that run through the volume while also pointing at some important areas of inquiry that require deeper investigation, particularly for classroom instruction, such as "text," "talk," and "transfer."

NOTE

1   In the Middle Ages, an interesting theory was proposed known as the "impetus theory." The most articulated view of the theory was that of Buridan (1300–1388). According to Buridan, when an object is set in motion an "impetus" (or "vis" and "forza" in Latin) is imparted into the object. This "impetus" keeps the object in motion for some time after it has lost its contact with the agent. As the impetus gradually dissipates, the object slows down, until it finally stops or falls to the ground due to its weight (Franklin, 1978). The impetus theory resembles a common misconception found in children and adults that there is a force within inanimate objects that have been set in motion even when the objects have lost their contact with the original mover. This force gradually dissipates and finally runs out as the object slows down and stops.

REFERENCES

Carey, S. (1985). *Conceptual change in childhood.* Cambridge, MA: MIT Press.

Driver, R., & Easley, J. (1978). Pupils and paradigms: A review of literature related to concept development in adolescent science students. *Studies in Science Education, 5,* 61–84.

Franklin, A. (1978). Inertia in the middle ages. *The Physics Teacher, 16*(4), 201–208.

Inagaki, K., & Hatano, G. (2002). *Young children's thinking about the biological world.* New York, NY: Psychology Press.

Kaufman, D. R., Keselman, A., & Patel, V. L. (2008). Changing conceptions in medicine and health. In S. Vosniadou (Ed.), *International handbook of research on conceptual change* (pp. 295–327). New York, NY: Routledge.

Kuhn, T. S. (1970). *Structure of scientific revolutions.* Chicago, IL: University of Chicago Press.

Leinhardt, G., & Ravi, A. K. (2008). Changing historical conceptions of history. In S. Vosniadou (Ed.), *International handbook of research on conceptual change* (pp. 328–341). New York, NY: Routledge.

McCloskey, M. (1983). Intuitive physics. *Scientific American, 248*(4), 122–130.

Murphy, P. K., & Mason, L. (2006). Changing knowledge and beliefs. In P. A. Alexander & P. H. Winne (Eds.), *Handbook of educational psychology* (pp. 305–324). Mahwah, NJ: Lawrence Erlbaum Associates.

Piaget, J. (1970). *The science of education and the psychology of the child.* New York, NY: Grossman.

Posner, G. J., Strike, K. A., Hewson, P. W., & Gertzog, W. A. (1982). Accommodation of a scientific conception: Towards a theory of conceptual change. *Science Education, 66,* 211–227.

Rickinson, M., Lundholm, C., & Hopwood, N. (Eds.). (2009). *Environmental learning: Insights from research into the student experience.* Amsterdam, The Netherlands: Springer Verlag.

Sinatra, G. M., & Pintrich, P. R. (Eds.). (2003). *Intentional conceptual change.* Mahwah, NJ: Lawrence Erlbaum Associates.

Thagard, P. (1992). *Conceptual revolutions.* Princeton, NJ: Princeton University Press.

Viennot, L. (1979). Spontaneous reasoning in elementary dynamics. *European Journal of Science Education, 1*(2), 205–221.

Vosniadou, S., & Verschaffel, L. (2004). Extending the conceptual change approach to mathematics learning and teaching. In L. Verschaffel and S. Vosniadou (Guest Eds.), Conceptual Change in Mathematics Learning and Teaching, Special Issue of *Learning and Instruction, 14*(5), 445–451.

Vosniadou, S., Vamvakoussi, X., & Skopeliti, I. (2008). The framework theory approach. In S. Vosniadou (Ed.), *International handbook of research on conceptual change* (pp. 3–34). New York, NY: Routledge.

Voss, J. F., & Wiley, J. (2006). Expertise in history. In K. A. Ericsson, N. Charness, P. Feltovich, & R. R. Hoffman (Eds.), *The Cambridge handbook of expertise and expert performance* (pp. 569–584). Cambridge, UK: Cambridge University Press.

Wellman, H. M. (2002). Understanding the psychological world: Developing a theory of mind. In U. Goswami (Ed.), *Handbook of childhood cognitive development* (pp. 167–187). Oxford, UK: Blackwell.

Part I

Theoretical Issues in Conceptual Change Research

1

CONCEPTUAL CHANGE IN LEARNING AND INSTRUCTION

The Framework Theory Approach

Stella Vosniadou, National and Kapodistrian University of Athens

Conceptual change research investigates learning requiring the substantial revision of prior knowledge and the acquisition of new concepts, usually under conditions of systematic instruction (Hatano & Inagaki, 2003; Vosniadou & Ioannides, 1998). The term "conceptual change" was first introduced by Thomas Kuhn (1962) to indicate that the concepts embedded in a scientific theory change their meaning when the theory (paradigm) changes. Posner and his colleagues (Posner, Strike, Hewson, and Gertzog, 1982; see also McCloskey, 1983a, 1983b) were instrumental in seeing the relevance of the problem of conceptual change for the learning of science and the extinction of students' misconceptions. They drew an analogy between Piaget's (1970) concepts of assimilation and accommodation, and the concepts of normal science and scientific revolution offered by philosophers of science such as Kuhn (1962), and derived from this analogy an instructional theory to promote "accommodation" in students' learning of science. According to Posner et al. (1982) there are four fundamental conditions that need to be fulfilled before conceptual change can happen: (1) there must be dissatisfaction with existing conceptions, (2) there must be a new conception that is intelligible, (3) the new conception must appear to be plausible, and (4) the new conception should suggest the possibility of a fruitful program.

This theoretical framework, known as the *classical* approach to conceptual change, became the leading paradigm that guided research and instruction in science education for many years. In the classical approach, misconceptions are incorrect alternative theories that need to be replaced by the correct scientific views. Students are seen to be very much like scientists who will be led to the scientific view when they become dissatisfied with their existing conceptions and realize the fruitfulness of the new conception. In this context, dissatisfaction with the prior conception became an important prerequisite for conceptual change, making *cognitive conflict* the major instructional strategy for producing it.

Over the years practically all of the above tenets of the classical approach were subjected to serious criticism. Researchers argued that conceptual change is a slow and gradual affair and not a dramatic gestalt-type shift (Caravita & Halden, 1994; Vosniadou & Brewer, 1992); that misconceptions are not inaccurate or misconceived theories but that they should be reconceived as faulty extensions of productive knowledge (Smith, diSessa, & Roschelle 1993); that not only cognitive/rational but also affective and motivational factors have an important role to play in conceptual change processes (Pintrich, Marx, & Boyle, 1993; Sinatra & Pintrich, 2003); and that conceptual change is significantly influenced by social and situational factors (Hatano & Inagaki, 2003).

Smith et al. (1993) criticized the use of cognitive conflict on the grounds that it is inconsistent with the ideas of constructivism and that it presents a narrow view of learning that focuses only on the mistaken qualities of students' prior knowledge, ignoring their productive ideas that can become the basis for achieving a more sophisticated scientific understanding. According to Smith et al. (1993), instruction that "confronts misconceptions with a view to replacing them is misguided and unlikely to succeed" (p. 153).

diSessa (1988, 1993) put forward a different proposal for conceptualizing the process of conceptual change in the learning of science that emphasized the continuity between prior knowledge and scientific understandings. He argued that the knowledge system of novices consists of an unstructured collection of many simple elements known as phenomenological primitives (*p-prims* for short) that originate from superficial interpretations of physical reality. P-prims appear to be organized in a conceptual network and to be activated through a mechanism of recognition that depends on the connections that p-prims have to the other elements of the system. According to this position, the process of learning science is one of collecting and systematizing these pieces of knowledge into larger wholes. This happens as p-prims change their function from relatively isolated, self-explanatory entities to become integrated in a larger system of complex knowledge structures such as physics laws. In the knowledge system of the expert, p-prims "can no longer be self-explanatory, but must refer to much more complex knowledge structures, physics laws, etc. for justification" (diSessa, 1993, p. 114).

We agree with diSessa (1993) and Smith et al. (1993) that a theory of conceptual change should provide an account of the knowledge acquisition process that captures the continuity one expects with development. We also agree with them in that we need to move from thinking of conceptual change as involving single units of knowledge to systems of knowledge that consist of complex substructures that may change gradually and in different ways. Finally, we agree with Smith et al.'s (1993) recommendation to researchers to "move beyond the identification of misconceptions" toward research that focuses on the evolution of expert understandings and particularly on "detailed descriptions of the evolution of knowledge systems over much longer durations than has been typical of recent detailed studies" (p. 154).

For a number of years now we have been involved in such a program of research that attempts to provide detailed descriptions of the development of knowledge in various areas of the physical sciences, such as observational astronomy (Vosniadou & Brewer, 1992, 1994; Vosniadou & Skopeliti, 2005; Vosniadou, Skopeliti & Ikospentaki, 2004, 2005; Samarapungavan, Vosniadou, & Brewer, 1996), mechanics (Ioannides & Vosniadou, 2002), geology (Ioannidou & Vosniadou, 2001), biology (Kyrkos & Vosniadou, 1997), and more recently in mathematics (Vosniadou & Verschaffel, 2004; Vamvakoussi, Vosniadou,

& Van Dooren, this volume). Our studies are mostly cross-sectional developmental studies investigating the knowledge acquisition process in subjects ranging from five to 20 years of age. We have also conducted several text comprehension studies and other instructional interventions in which the results of our research were used to develop instructional materials to be used in schools in Greece (Vosniadou, Ioannides, Dimitrakopoulou & Papademitriou, 2001; Vamvakoussi & Vosniadou, 2012; Vosniadou & Skopeliti, submitted a, submitted b). The results of this research have led to the development of the framework theory approach to conceptual change (Vosniadou, Baltas & Vamvakoussi, 2007; Vosniadou, Vamvakoussi & Skopeliti, 2008). In the pages that follow we outline the basic principles of this approach and describe its similarities and differences to other theoretical positions on conceptual change in learning and instruction.

THE FRAMEWORK THEORY APPROACH: BASIC PRINCIPLES

The framework theory is based on cognitive/developmental research and attempts to provide a broad theoretical basis for understanding how conceptual change is achieved in the process of learning science. At the heart of the framework theory is the idea that young children start the knowledge acquisition process by developing a naïve physics that does not consist of fragmented observations but forms a relatively coherent explanatory system – a framework theory. Learning science requires fundamental ontological, epistemological and representational changes in naïve physics. After all, currently accepted science is the product of a long historical process characterized by radical theory changes that have restructured our representations of the physical world. Because learners use additive, enrichment types of learning mechanisms to assimilate scientific information to existing but incompatible knowledge structures, the process of learning science and mathematics is slow and gradual and characterized by fragmentation and misconceptions, many of which can be interpreted as "synthetic models." In the pages that follow the main principles of the framework theory will be explicated with reference mainly to the domain of natural science.

Naïve Physics is a Framework Theory

The human child is a complex organism capable of engaging in quick and efficient learning immediately after birth. Cognitive developmental research has provided substantial empirical evidence to support the view that children organize the multiplicity of their sensory experiences under the influence of everyday culture into narrow but relatively coherent domains of thought from early on (Baillargeon, 1995; Carey & Spelke, 1994; Gelman, 1990). At least four well-defined core knowledge domains can be distinguished and considered roughly as "framework theories" – physics, psychology, mathematics, and language.

Framework theories are skeletal structures that ground our deepest ontological commitments in terms of which we understand the world. They are very different from scientific theories in that they are not explicit, well-formed, socially shared constructs; they lack the explanatory power and internal consistency of scientific theories; they are not subject to metaconceptual awareness; and they are not systematically tested for confirmation and/or falsification. Nevertheless, they are called "theories" because they are relatively coherent and principle-based systems characterized by a distinct ontology and causality and are generative in that they can give rise to prediction and explanation.

For example, it appears that infants use the criterion of self-initiated movement to distinguish animate from inanimate entities, thus creating two fundamentally different ontological domains – naïve psychology and naïve physics. Naïve physics and naïve psychology are also distinguished in terms of their causality. Naïve physics obeys the laws of mechanical causality while naïve psychology is governed by intentional causality. Once categorized as a physical or psychological object, an entity inherits all the characteristics and properties of the other entities that belong to the same category. Knowledge acquisition proceeds from a very broad and relatively explanatorily weak set of structures to more detailed and explanatorily rich categorizations with better fit to the world (see also Keil, 1981).

A great deal of cognitive developmental and science education research has shown that children and lay adults who have not been exposed to much science answer questions about force, matter, heat, the day/night cycle, etc. in a relatively consistent way, revealing the existence of initial conceptions rooted in a framework theory of naïve physics (Baillargeon, 1995; Carey & Spelke, 1994; Gelman, 1990; Vosniadou & Brewer, 1992, 1994). Some of the many examples are the following: Categorization studies in astronomy have shown that young children categorize the "earth" as a physical object (as opposed to an astronomical – physical – object) and apply to it all the characteristics of physical objects in general, such as solidity, stability, and up–down gravity (Vosniadou & Skopeliti, 2005). Similarly, children as well as lay adults categorize concepts such as force, energy, and heat as properties of objects that can be possessed, transferred, and dissipated (Chi, 2008; Ioannides & Vosniadou, 2002). In the case of the concept of "matter," preschool children group solids, liquids, and powders together as consisting of some kind of stuff, distinguishing them from gases (air) and non-material entities (heat, electricity), or mental entities (ideas, wishes). In other words, material entities are things that can be seen, touched, and felt, and produce some kind of physical effects. They find atoms very strange because they have almost none of the properties of macroscopic objects – they are too small to be seen, they are not colored, they are neither hard or soft, they are never created or destroyed, etc. (Wiser & Smith, this volume; Carey, 1991). Finally, Evans (this volume; see also Mayer, 1985; Wellman & Gelman, 1998) argues that evolutionary concepts are counterintuitive because they challenge two entrenched biases of naïve physics, namely the belief that living things are separate, stable, and unchanging (*essentialism*) and that animate behavior is goal-directed (*teleology*) and intentional (*intentionality*).

Conceptual Change Requires Fundamental Changes in Students' Ontological and Epistemological Commitments and in their Representations

Understanding the scientific concept of the earth requires children to re-categorize the earth from the ontological category "physical object" to the ontological category "physical–astronomical object." Such re-categorizations happen in the conceptual system of elementary school children between third and sixth grades (Vosniadou & Skopeliti, 2005). Similar re-categorizations are made in many other domains. The concepts of force, energy, and heat, which are categorized as entities or substances in the initial conceptual system of novices, are re-categorized as processes or interactions in the conceptual system of experts (Chi, 2008; Wiser & Smith, 2008). Plants are categorized as inanimate in the conceptual system of the preschooler but are later re-categorized as living things. In this process new ontological categories are formed while old ones might be radically reorganized (Carey, 1985; Hatano & Inagaki, 1997).

Such re-categorizations are accompanied by significant epistemological and representational changes. As shown in Figure 1.1, categorizing the earth as an astronomical object allows it to be represented as a spherical, rotating planet in space as opposed to a flat, solid and stable ground with the solar objects above its top. While such new representations are often constructed with the help of external, cultural models and artifacts, they nevertheless depend crucially on the development of children's perspective-taking abilities and their epistemological sophistication. Children must understand how the earth can appear flat from the perspective of someone on the earth but spherical from the perspective of someone who views the earth from the moon. These developments require the ability to make distinctions between "appearance" and "reality" and to understand that what appears evident through the senses may in fact be subject to different interpretations.

Similar ontological, epistemological, and representational changes are required in all subject-matter areas of science. The epistemological knowledge necessary to make sense of the atomic matter theory, for example, includes the nature of scientific models and their relation to observed objects and events, as well as the understanding that many macroscopic properties of matter are emergent (Wiser & Smith, this volume). Understanding the microscopic model of matter requires children to understand the distinction between perceptual and physical properties and how they are linked. In recent years a number of experimental studies have shown high correlations in students' performance in conceptual change tasks and epistemic belief tasks (Mason & Gava, 2007; Mason, Gava, & Boldrin, 2008; Stathopoulou & Vosniadou, 2007a, 2007b; Kyriakopoulou & Vosniadou, 2012).

Conceptual Change is a Slow Process during which Fragmentation and Misconceptions can be Created

The abovementioned ontological, representational, and epistemological changes do not happen overnight. We argue that conceptual change, at least initially, is achieved gradually as constructive, enrichment types of mechanisms are used, to add new but incompatible information to existing conceptual structures. In fact, the particular strength of the framework theory approach is that it can explain the formation of misconceptions and of fragmentation as the result of the application of constructive types of mechanisms on incompatible knowledge structures. More specifically, it is claimed that when learners use the usual constructive, enrichment types of mechanisms to incorporate scientific information to naïve physics, the product can either be an internally inconsistent – fragmented – conception or a misconception.

Fragmentation can be produced when learners simply add scientific information to their naïve physics without concern for internal consistency and coherence. For example, many children who believe that night is caused because the sun goes down behind the mountains simply add the scientific information that the earth turns to their original but incompatible explanation, thus creating an internally inconsistent, fragmented response (Vosniadou & Brewer, 1994; Vosniadou & Skopeliti, submitted a, submitted b).

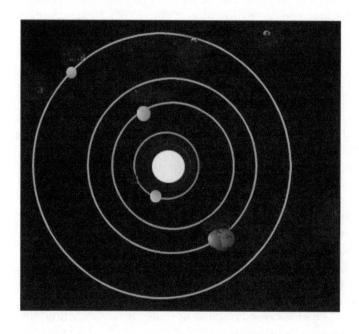

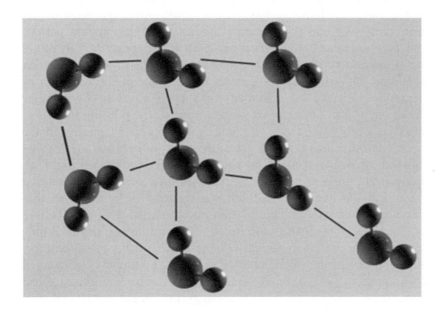

Figure 1.1 Changes in the representation of the concepts of "earth" and of "matter"

Misconceptions, on the other hand, can be produced when learners, in the search for coherence and internal consistency, incorporate scientific information to their incompatible prior knowledge, distorting it and creating what we call a "synthetic" conceptions or model. Such "synthetic" constructions can often provide incorrect but nevertheless creative solutions to the problem of incommensurability between initial conceptions and scientific information. For example, some children who believe that night is caused because the sun goes down behind the mountains distort the scientific information that the earth turns (which they find very counterintuitive), coming up with the new idea that it is the sun and the moon that turn around the earth (every 24 hours). These children have created a new – synthetic – explanation that retains part of their original conception (that it is the sun and moon that move) but also changes it in a way (from up–down movement to rotational movement). By assimilating the scientific information these children have managed to avoid internal inconsistency, creating a distortion which however has some limited explanatory power (Vosniadou & Skopeliti, submitted a).

Synthetic conceptions represent an intermediate state of knowledge, a bridge between the initial concept and the scientific perspective that is not yet available to the student. As such they provide an intermediate state of illusionary coherence that conceals the conflict between inconsistent beliefs and allows for the student to deal with the tasks at hand and move on in the acquisition process. Although incorrect, such hybrid conceptions can often represent progress, enabling the student to move on in the process of conceptual change.

Although it is possible that a number of different cognitive mechanisms could model this process, we have conceptualized it to involve the gradual lifting of the beliefs and presuppositions of the framework theory, allowing the formation of more sophisticated conceptions until full conceptual change has been achieved. Although most of the evidence comes from cross-sectional developmental studies, the developmental pattern is clear. For example, our studies of children's ideas about the shape of the earth have shown that children usually start with models of a square, rectangular or disc earth which is supported, stable, and flat, where space is organized in term of the direction of "up–down," where gravity operates in an "up–down" fashion, and where the sky and solar objects are located above its top. These initial models meet all the presuppositions of the earth categorized as a physical object. The models of the hollow sphere and the truncated sphere, on the other hand, which are more sophisticated and are formed usually by older children, show that some of the abovementioned presuppositions have been lifted. The model of the hollow sphere, for example, presupposes an understanding that the earth is spherical and not supported, but it is constrained by the belief that gravity operates in an up–down fashion. The children who construct this model believe that people live on flat ground inside the earth because they would fall "down" if they lived on the surface of the spherical earth. Similarly, the up–down gravity presupposition constrains the understanding of the spherical earth in children who have constructed a flattened or truncated sphere, who also believe that people live on flat ground above the top of the earth. These children can see the earth as a spherical, suspended, and sometimes rotating object but they still organize space and gravity in terms of the directions of up–down.

These alternative representations of the earth are not rare. In fact, only 23 of the 60 children in the Vosniadou and Brewer (1992) study had constructed the culturally accepted representation of the earth as a sphere. The remaining children either provided synthetic models or gave fragmented responses. These findings have been confirmed by many cross-cultural studies (e.g., Blown & Bryce, 2006; Diakidoy, Vosniadou & Hawks, 1997; Hayes, Goodhew, Heit, & Gillan, 2003; Mali & Howe, 1979; Samarapungavan et al., 1996; Vosniadou, Skopeliti & Ikospentaki, 2004, 2005).

A number of additional experimental studies in our lab have confirmed the gradual process of conceptual change and the formation of synthetic conceptions. For example, Figure 1.2 shows the synthetic models of the layers and composition of the earth's interior revealed in the drawings and verbal explanations of students in Grades 1, 6, and 11 (Ioannidou & Vosniadou, 2001). Most first graders believe that the earth contains only solid materials (i.e., ground and rocks) arranged in flat layers. When the students are instructed about the existence of magma inside the earth, they seem to think that the magma is placed at the bottom, rather than in the center, of the spherical earth. It is only later that the circular layering appears in their drawings, with the magma placed in the

Frequency of Models of the Layers and Composition of the Earth by Grade

		1st Grade	6th Grade	11th Grade
Spherical Layers *Magma in the layer below the surface*	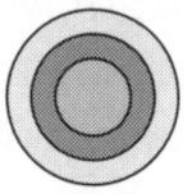	0	1	1
Spherical Layers *Magma in the center of the earth*		2	15	12
Spherical Layers *Solid Materials*		0	1	1
Flat Layers *Magma in different places inside the earth*	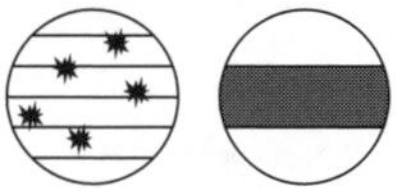	0	0	0
Flat Layers *Magma in the bottom of the earth*		2	0	2
Undetermined Layers *Solid Materials*	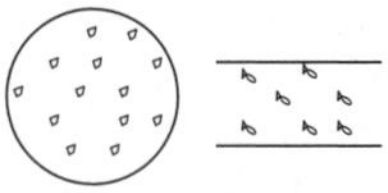	4	0	0
Flat Layers *Solid Materials*		14	5	3
Total		**24**	**24**	**24**

Figure 1.2 Frequency of models of the layers and composition of the earth by grade

center of the spherical earth. Even the 11th grade students (as well as most undergraduate prospective teachers) believe that magma is located very deep in the center of the earth, rather than relatively close to its surface, and have difficulties understanding the scientific explanations of volcanoes and earthquakes.

In another study (Kyrkos & Vosniadou, 1997), we investigated students' understanding of plant development and the concept of photosynthesis, which has been shown to be difficult for students to understand (Barker & Carr, 1989; Haslam & Treagust, 1987; Wandersee, 1983). From the perspective of the framework theory approach, students' difficulties arise from the incommensurability between the scientific and naïve explanatory frameworks of plant development. As is shown in Table 1.1, most first graders consider plants in the context of a psychological framework theory, explaining plant development through an analogy to animals. More specifically, they think that plants take their food (i.e., water and other nutrients) from the ground through their roots and that they grow as food accumulates in small pieces inside them. As instruction about photosynthesis comes in, this initial explanation becomes fragmented, and a number of different synthetic models are formed. Some of them are shown in Table 1.2. In the first synthetic model students still claim that plants grow through feeding, but add to it the information, coming from photosynthesis, that plants also "breathe" – plants take in dirty air; they clean it and give out clean air. Another synthetic model claims that plants take food and water from the ground through their roots, but they also take food from the air and light through their leaves. A more advanced synthetic model of photosynthesis develops in older children who understand that plants make food by themselves but still think of it in terms of mixing elements and not as a chemical process.

Summary

To sum up, the framework theory meets all the criticisms of the classical approach made by different researchers and can also account for fragmentation (Smith et al., 1993). First, we are not describing unitary, faulty conceptions but a knowledge system consisting of many different elements organized in complex ways. Second, we make a distinction

Table 1.1 Initial and scientific explanations of plant development (photosynthesis)

Initial explanation	Scientific explanation
Plants take their food from the ground (water or other nutrients) through their roots.	Plants create their own food through the process of photosynthesis.
Plants grow as food accumulates in small pieces inside them.	Photosynthesis is a chemical process during which solar energy is used to transform water + CO_2 into organic materials like glucose. Oxygen is also formed and stored in the plant or released in the atmosphere.
Plants do not breathe.	Plants take in CO_2 from the atmosphere and use it in the process of photosynthesis. To this extent "breathing" in plants is related to growth and development.

Synthetic models

Table 1.2 Synthetic models in photosynthesis (Kyrkos & Vosniadou, 1997)

1. Initial explanation – analogy to animals	Plants take food from the ground through their roots. Food accumulates inside the plant and makes it grow. They do not breathe.
2. Photosynthesis as breathing, separate from feeding	Plants take food from the ground through their roots. Photosynthesis is about breathing and it does not affect the initial explanation of feeding. Plants take in dirty air, clean it, and give out clean air.
3. Photosynthesis as a revised feeding process	Plants take food from the ground and from water through their roots. They also take food from the air and light through their leaves (O, CO_2).
4. Photosynthesis as a revised feeding process	Plants take food from the ground and from atmosphere and also use water and O or CO_2 to make the food in their leaves through the process of photosynthesis (no understanding of photosynthesis as a chemical process).

between initial explanations prior to instruction and those that result after instruction, some of which are synthetic models. Synthetic models are not stable but dynamic and constantly changing as children's developing knowledge systems evolve. Our theoretical position is a constructivist one that shows how constructive types of mechanisms can create fragmentation and misconceptions when scientific information is built on existing but incompatible knowledge structures. Finally, the theory provides a comprehensive framework within which meaningful and detailed predictions can be made about the knowledge acquisition process.

SIMILARITIES TO AND DIFFERENCES FROM OTHER APPROACHES

The "Classical Approach" to Conceptual Change

Unlike the classical approach, the framework theory approach makes a fundamental distinction between *preconceptions* and *misconceptions* and considers many misconceptions to be synthetic conceptions or models. Preconceptions are considered to be children's initial ideas about the physical world and explanations of physical phenomena constructed on the basis of everyday experience in the context of lay culture *before they are exposed to school science*, while misconceptions result from students' erroneous interpretations of the scientific concepts *after they are exposed to school science*.

Unlike the classical approach, the framework theory does not claim that conceptual change can be achieved through some kind of sudden replacement of initial conceptions with a scientific concept when students become dissatisfied with it. Conceptual change is usually a slow process not only because it involves a large network of interrelated concepts but also because it requires the construction of completely new, conceptual, representations that require radical changes in the ontology and epistemology of naïve physics.

Last but not least, an important difference between the framework theory and the classical approach is that the former does not claim that students' misconceptions should be treated as wrong conceptions, to be replaced with the correct scientific view. Rather, we claim that learning science requires the creation of new ontologies and new representations and the ability to flexibly move among them. In other words, learning science requires the ability to understand that the same phenomenon can be explained from different perspectives and some of these perspectives have greater explanatory power than others. This is an area where the framework theory also differs from another influential approach to conceptual change, the one proposed by Chi and her colleagues (Chi, 1992, 2008; Chi, Slotta & de Leeuw, 1994). Chi (2008) defines conceptual change as the kind of learning required when the new, to-be-learned, information requires changing prior, *misconceived*, knowledge. The most difficult-to-change misconceived knowledge, according to Chi (2008), involves the assignment of a concept to a wrong ontological category.

The "Knowledge in Pieces" View

The framework theory is not inconsistent with aspects of the knowledge-in-pieces approach, and particularly with the view that we need to focus on rich knowledge systems that are composed of many constituent elements, p-prims being one of them. Arguably, many components of children's initial concepts are experientially based, building on the multiplicity of perceptual and sensory experiences that are obtained via observation and interaction with physical objects. But it is assumed that these are integrated from early on into larger conceptual structures under the influence of lay culture and language, and later on through systematic instruction. In other words, from the framework theory point of view, to the extent that knowledge elements such as p-prims could be postulated to operate in our conceptual system, they become organized in conceptual structures much earlier than it is claimed by the knowledge in pieces approach.

A common mistake about the framework theory is to interpret it as claiming that students are always coherent and theory-like. This is not the case. As explained earlier, students create fragmented or synthetic conceptions all the time. The framework theory explains these conceptions not as random mistakes but as the product of the use of constructive mechanisms on incompatible knowledge structures. Unlike diSessa (1993, 2008), who argues for a learning process that proceeds from fragmentation to coherence under the influence of instruction, we believe that the need and search for coherence is more an initial condition of the cognitive system and that fragmentation and inconsistency can be the product of instruction, in cases when a rather coherent, but incompatible, structure is already established.

On the other hand, like Smith, diSessa, and Roschelle (1993), we do not expect students to hold unitary, isolated, and context-independent misconceptions. Synthetic conceptions are situational models often constructed on the spot to deal with the demands of specific situations. Although we expect these conceptions to have some minimal internal consistency and explanatory power, we might still find that students change them depending on the affordances of the specific contexts to which they are exposed. We also agree with diSessa (2008) that the individual student's personal learning history is unique – there are probably no two students with exactly the same understanding across contexts.

In the first edition of this handbook Brown and Hammer (2008) proposed a complex systems perspective which they claim can integrate various findings from previous work, and within which "the differences in diSessa's and Vosniadou's models mostly disappear" (p. 135). Their argument is that the knowledge system should be seen as consisting of dynamic cognitive structures that arise from the interactions of smaller conceptual elements. Some of these dynamic cognitive structures can be rather stable and similar across a variety of contexts but others may dissipate and reform quickly in different contexts.

The "Theory Theory" Approach

The framework theory approach has many similarities with "theory theory" approaches, all of which claim that concepts are embedded in larger theoretical structures that constrain them and that conceptual change happens when a concept is reinterpreted in the context of a new theory (Carey, 2008; Gopnick & Meltzoff, 1997). The framework theory approach differs from the "theory theory" approaches, however, in that it does not make a commitment as to the origins of framework theories and more specifically as to whether they are present at birth, are built on what Carey (2009) calls "core cognition," or have some other origins. Rather, it focuses on older children and situations that require the reorganization of prior knowledge as a result of systematic instruction. Second, it considers conceptual change as a slow and gradual process of knowledge revision and not as the sudden change from one coherent theory to another. It is, furthermore, claimed that this gradual revision can be achieved, at least in part, through the operation of the same constructive, enrichment types of mechanisms used in regular knowledge acquisition processes.

According to Carey (1985, 2008), conceptual change cannot be achieved through the use of enrichment types of mechanisms but is made possible by bootstrapping mechanisms, similar to those described in the philosophy and history of science (Gopnik & Meltzoff, 1997). Bootstrapping usually involves some kind of analogical transfer of information from a different domain of thought. For example, changing conceptions of number (from natural number to rational number) are thought to depend on the construction of mappings between number and physical objects as the child learns measurement. Similarly, the development of scientific, mechanistic biology and psychology requires mappings from the domain of physics. We also believe that bootstrapping can be a powerful mechanism for conceptual change. However, the results of many empirical studies show that many conceptual changes happen as a result of the use of enrichment types of mechanism to incorporate scientific information to initial conceptual structures. The advantage of the framework theory over other "theory theory" approaches is that it offers a constructivist account that can explain the creation of fragmentation and misconceptions.

Sociocultural Approaches

Criticisms from sociocultural theorists point out that conceptual change is not an individual, internal, cognitive process, as it is often seen from a purely cognitive perspective, but should be considered as a social activity that takes place in complex sociocultural settings that involve the use of symbolic languages, tools, and artifacts. We also believe that it is important to consider the role of sociocultural practices, tools, and artifacts in conceptual change processes. However, this should not be done without consideration of the crucial role individual minds play in intellectual functioning. As Hatano (1994) aptly states, "although understanding is a social process, it also involves much processing by an active individual mind. It is unlikely that conceptual change is induced only by social consensus. The post-change conceptual systems must have not only coherence but also subjective necessity. Such a system can be built only through an individual mind's active attempts to achieve integration and plausibility" (p. 195).

Conceptual Change in Mathematics

The application of the conceptual change approach to mathematics learning and teaching is a relatively new attempt. Although there has been a great deal of research in the tradition of misconceptions during the 1970s and 1980s, the mathematics education community has been reluctant to adopt the conceptual change approach, which was developed mainly in the context of physical sciences. This is because mathematics has been traditionally regarded as a discipline with particular characteristics that differentiate it from the physical sciences. Thomas Kuhn himself exempted mathematics from the pattern of scientific development and change presented in *The Structure of Scientific Revolutions* (see Mahoney, 1997). He did this because mathematics is based on deductive proof and not on experiment, is proven to be very tolerant to anomalies, and does not display the radical incommensurability of theory before and after revolution. Unlike science, the formulation of a new theory in mathematics usually carries mathematics to a more general level of analysis and enables a wider perspective that makes possible solutions that have been impossible to formulate before (Corry, 1993; Dauben, 1984).

However, from a learning point of view, it appears that students are confronted with similar situations when they learn mathematics and science. As it is the case that students develop a naïve physics on the basis of everyday experience, they also develop a naïve mathematics that appears to consist of certain core principles or presuppositions (such as the presupposition of discreteness in the number concept) that facilitate some kinds of learning but inhibit others (Gelman, 2000; Lipton & Spelke, 2003). Such similarities support the argument that the framework approach to conceptual change can be fruitfully applied in the case of mathematics learning. In fact, in recent years a systematic attempt has been made to test the predictions of the framework theory approach in the learning of mathematics concepts, and particularly in explaining students' difficulties with rational numbers. This research is presented in detail in the chapter by Vamvakoussi, Vosniadou, and Van Dooren (this volume) and for this reason it is not going to be given a full presentation in this chapter. The basic ideas are, however, the following.

Students form an initial understanding of number roughly as natural number. This initial concept then stands in the way of understanding the concept of rational number presented through instruction. Understanding the mathematical concept of rational number requires fundamental ontological, epistemological, and representational changes in the initial concept of number. This does not happen easily. Students need to realize that certain presuppositions, such as the discreteness of numbers, are valid only in specific contexts. Also, learning about rational numbers requires students to construct meanings for new symbolic notations – fractions and decimals – not encountered before (Stafylidou & Vosniadou, 2004). In addition to the difficulty of interpreting decimal and fractional notation in its own right, students have to realize that different symbolic notations refer to the same object; i.e., that decimals and fractions are interchangeable representations of rational numbers, and not different kinds of numbers (Vamvakoussi & Vosniadou, 2010).

The empirical evidence from a series of studies that explicitly tested the predictions of the framework theory supported the hypothesis that students use enrichment types of learning mechanisms to add rational number information to natural number. These mechanisms create fragmentation and "misconceptions" of the rational number concept which can be explained as "synthetic models." One of these synthetic models is to conceptualize the rational numbers set as consisting of three different and unrelated "sets" of numbers: whole numbers, decimals, and fractions. As they come to understand the principle of density through instruction, students then apply this principle additively to the different "sets" of numbers. As a result, students come to think differently for integers, decimals, and fractions in terms of their structure (discrete vs. dense). They also become reluctant to accept that there might be fractions between two decimals, or vice versa (Vamvakoussi & Vosniadou, 2010).

Implications for Instruction

A large body of empirical evidence has been accumulated in the past 20 or so years pointing to the problem of conceptual change, particularly in the areas of science and mathematics. Nevertheless, the relevant findings and results have not yet found their way into everyday classroom practices. This is true for both science teaching (Duit, 2007; Duit, Treagust, & Widodo, this volume) and mathematics (see also Greer, 2004, 2006; Resnick, 2006). Researchers and teachers often associate instruction for conceptual change with the use of cognitive conflict (Posner et al., 1982), and they are disappointed when they find out that misconceptions are not extinguished easily even when the students realize that they are wrong. Although limited use of dissonance-producing strategies can be useful in instruction, they can only produce dissatisfaction with existing ideas. They do not do the job of building the enormous amount of new knowledge that needs to be built.

From a constructivist point of view there is clearly a learning paradox involved in teaching for conceptual change. Constructivist theories argue that new knowledge should be built on what students already know. Conceptual change research on the other hand points out that prior knowledge can sometimes stand in the way of understanding new scientific information. What is then to be done?

Unlike "theory theory" approaches, the "framework theory" approach argues that enrichment types of mechanisms can bring about a gradual knowledge revision of prior knowledge that can lead toward conceptual change. Care needs to be exercised, however, in the use of enrichment mechanisms because they can also lead to fragmentation and misconceptions when the new, to-be-acquired information is incompatible with prior knowledge. For this reason, Vosniadou and her colleagues propose the careful design of research-based curricula, based on students' learning progressions, which can identify the areas of students' prior knowledge on which new, scientific information can be built while at the same time highlighting the areas that need to be revised. This often requires taking a long-term perspective in curricula design as well as in everyday teaching practices, carefully planning the sequence of concepts to be taught (see Vosniadou, Ioannides, Dimitrakopoulou, & Papademetriou, 2001).

When areas of knowledge revision are identified it is often not very useful to tell students that they are wrong. It might be more fruitful to design instructional activities to help students understand that the scientific point of view represents a larger perspective that has more explanatory power. For example, usual instruction in observational astronomy for young children often consists of showing them the globe and telling them that this is a model of the earth. This type of instruction is inadequate because it does not explain to students how it is possible for the earth to be spherical when it appears to our senses to be flat, and of how it is possible for people and objects to stand on the surface of this spherical earth without falling down. When instruction does not provide explanations that answer students' problems of understanding the scientific point of view from the students' perspective, it can lead to fragmentation and the formation of synthetic models. In the instruction we have designed, various demonstrations and models are used to help children understand how the earth can simultaneously appear to be flat from the point of view of someone on the earth but spherical from the point of view of someone in space.

Model-based instruction can be very useful in helping students gradually understand that things are often different from what they appear to be and that our beliefs are subject to hypothesis testing and can be falsified. Epistemological and representational growth and flexibility are necessary requirements for conceptual change. Regardless of how far one can go in knowledge acquisition relying on social-constructivist types of approaches that build on prior knowledge, the problem of conceptual change requires that teachers also teach students how to use mechanisms for knowledge restructuring, such as model-based reasoning, the deliberate uses of analogies, and cross-domain mappings. Instructional interventions should also pay attention to the development of students' metaconceptual awareness, epistemological sophistication and intentional learning skills that will allow them to engage in meaningful, long-term learning (Sinatra & Pintrich, 2003; Wiser & Smith, this volume; Vosniadou, 2003).

We agree with Hatano and Inagaki (2003) that considerable social support is required for this type of instruction. One way teachers can provide the sociocultural environment to encourage metaconceptual awareness is to ask students to participate in dialogical interaction, which is usually whole-class discussion. Whole-classroom dialogue can be effective because it ensures on one hand that students understand the need to revise their beliefs deeply instead of engaging in local repairs (Chinn & Brewer, 1993), and on the other that they spend the considerable time and effort needed to engage in the conscious and deliberate belief revision required for conceptual change.

It is probably clear by now that teaching and learning for conceptual change requires substantial amounts of effort on the part of the teacher, as well as on the part of the learner. For this effort to be invested, there should be an environment within which this is both necessary and appreciated. That is, for teachers to design relevant and meaningful activities (Vosniadou et al., 2001), and for students to be actively engaged, there should be a broader educational community that recognizes and is capable of assessing this kind of effort.

CONCLUSIONS

We argued that science and mathematics concepts are difficult to learn because they are embedded in initial, framework theories of physics and mathematics, which are different explanatory frameworks from those that are now scientifically accepted. These naïve framework theories are not fragmented observations but form a relatively coherent explanatory system that is based on and continuously re-confirmed by everyday experience. Students are not aware of these differences and employ the usual enrichment mechanisms to add scientific and mathematical information to existing knowledge structures, destroying their coherence and creating internal inconsistency and misconceptions that are "synthetic models."

In order to foster conceptual change through instruction, we can consider the design of curricula and instruction that reduce the gap between students' expected initial knowledge and the to-be-acquired information, so that learners can use their usual constructive, enrichment types of learning mechanisms successfully. It is also important to develop in students the necessary metaconceptual awareness, epistemological sophistication, hypothesis testing skills, and the top-down, conscious, and deliberate mechanisms for intentional learning that will prepare them for meaningful, life-long learning. Instruction for conceptual change requires not only the restructuring of students' naïve theories but also the restructuring of their modes of learning and reasoning. This cannot be accomplished without substantial sociocultural support.

REFERENCES

Baillargeon, R. (1995). A model of physical reasoning in infancy. In C. Rovee-Collier & L. P. Lipsitt (Eds.), *Advances in infancy research* (Vol. 9, pp. 305–371). Norwood, NJ: Ablex.

Barker, M., & Carr, M. (1989). Teaching and learning about photosynthesis. *International Journal of Science Education, 11*(1), 48–56.

Blown, E. J., & Bryce, T. G. K. (2006). Knowledge restructuring in the development of children's cosmologies. *International Journal of Science Education, 28*(12), 1411–1462.

Brown, D., & Hammer, D. (2008). Conceptual change in physics. In S. Vosniadou (Ed.), *The international handbook of research on conceptual change* (pp. 127–154). New York, NY: Routledge.

Caravita, S., & Halden, O. (1994). Re-framing the problem of conceptual change. *Learning and Instruction, 4*, 89.

Carey, S., & Spelke, E. (1994). Domain-specific knowledge and conceptual change. In L. A. Hirschfeld and S. A. Gelman (Eds.), *Mapping the mind: Domain specificity in cognition and culture*. Cambridge, UK: Cambridge University Press.

Carey, S. (1985). *Conceptual change in childhood*. Cambridge, MA: MIT Press.

Carey, S. (1991). Knowledge acquisition: Enrichment or conceptual change? In S. Carey & R. Gelman (Eds.), *The epigenisis of mind: Essays on biology and cognition*. Hillsdale, NJ: Lawrence Erlbaum Associates.

Carey, S. (2008). Math schemata and the origins of number representations. *Behavioral and Brain Sciences, 31*(6), 645–646.

Carey, S. (2009). *The origin of concepts*. New York, NY: Oxford University Press

Chi, M. T. H. (1992). Conceptual change within and across ontological categories: Examples from learning and discovery in science. In R. Giere (Ed.), *Cognitive models of science: Minnesota Studies in the Philosophy of Science* (pp. 129–186). Minneapolis, MN: University of Minnesota Press.

Chi, M. T. H. (2008). Three types of conceptual change: Belief revision, mental model transformation, and categorical shift. In S. Vosniadou (Ed.), *International handbook of research on conceptual change* (pp. 61–82). New York, NY: Routledge.

Chi, M. T. H., Slotta, J. D., & de Leeuw, N. (1994). From things to processes: A theory of conceptual change for learning science concepts. *Learning and Instruction, 4*, 27–43.

Chinn, C. A., & Brewer, W. F. (1993). The role of anomalous data in knowledge acquisition: A theoretical framework and implications for science instruction. *Review of Educational Research, 63*, 1–49.

Corry, L. (1993). Kuhnian issues, scientific revolutions and the history of mathematics. *Studies in History and Philosophy of Science, 24*, 95–117.

Dauben, J., (1984). Conceptual revolutions and the history of mathematics: Two studies in the growth of knowledge. Originally appeared in E. Mendelsohn (Ed.), *Transformation and tradition in the sciences: Essays in honor of I. Bernard Cohen*, (pp. 81–103). Cambridge, UK: Cambridge University Press. Reprinted in D. Gilies (Ed.), *Revolutions in mathematics* (pp. 15–20). Oxford, UK: Oxford University Press, 1992.

Diakidoy, I. A., Vosniadou, S., & Hawks J. (1997). Conceptual change in astronomy: Models of the earth and of the day/night cycle in American-Indian children. *European Journal of Psychology of Education, XII*, 159–184.

diSessa, A. A. (1988). Knowledge in pieces. In G. Forman & P. B. Pufall (Eds.), *Constructivism in the computer age* (pp. 49–70). Hillsdale, NJ: Lawrence Erlbaum Associates.

diSessa, A. (1993). Toward an epistemology of physics. *Cognition and Instruction, 10*(2/3), 105–225.

diSessa, A. A. (2008). A bird's-eye view of the "pieces" vs. "coherence" controversy (from the "pieces" side of the fence). In S. Vosniadou (Ed.), *International handbook of research on conceptual change* (pp. 35–60). New York, NY: Routledge.

Duit, R. (2007). Science education research internationally: Conceptions, research methods, domains of research. *Eurasia Journal of Mathematics, Science & Technology Education, 3*(1), 3–15.

Gelman, R. (1990). First principles organize attention to and learning about relevant data: Number and animate–inanimate distinction as examples. *Cognitive Science, 14,* 79–106.

Gelman, R. (2000). The epigenesis of mathematical thinking. *Journal of Applied Developmental Psychology, 21,* 27–37.

Gopnik, A., & Meltzoff, A. N. (1997). *Words, thoughts, and theories.* Cambridge, MA: MIT Press.

Greer, B. (2004). The growth of mathematics through conceptual restructuring. *Learning and Instruction, 14*(5), 541–548.

Greer, B. (2006). Designing for conceptual change. In J. Novotná, H. Moraová, M. Krátká, & N. Stehlíková (Eds.), *Proceedings of the 30th Conference of the International Group for the Psychology of Mathematics Education* (Vol. 1, pp. 175–178). Prague, Czech Republic: PME.

Haslam, F., & Treagust, D. F. (1987). Diagnosing secondary students' misconceptions of photosynthesis and respiration in plants using a two-tier multiple choice instrument. *Journal of Biological Education, 21*(3), 203–211.

Hatano, G. (Guest Ed.). (1994). Introduction: Conceptual change – Japanese perspectives. Special Issue of *Human Development, 37*(4), 189–197.

Hatano, G., & Inagaki, K. (1997). Qualitative changes in intuitive biology. *European Journal of Psychology of Education, XII,* 111–130.

Hatano, G., & Inagaki, K. (2003). When is conceptual change intended? A cognitive–sociocultural view. In G. M. Sinatra & P. R. Pintrich (Eds.), *Intentional conceptual change* (pp. 407–427). Mahwah, NJ: Lawrence Erlbaum Associates.

Hayes, B. K., Goodhew, A., Heit, E., & Gillan, J. (2003). The role of diverse instruction in conceptual change. *Journal of Experimental Child Psychology, 86,* 253–276.

Ioannidou, I., & Vosniadou, S. (2001). The development of knowledge about the composition and layering of the earth's interior. *Nea Paedia, 31,* 107–150 (in Greek).

Ioannides, C., & Vosniadou, S. (2002). The changing meanings of force. *Cognitive Science Quarterly, 2*(1), 5–62.

Keil, F. C. (1981). Constraints on knowledge and cognitive development. *Psychological Review, 88,* 197–227.

Kuhn, T. (1962). *The structure of scientific revolutions.* Chicago, IL: University of Chicago Press.

Kyriakopoulou, N., & Vosniadou, S. (2012). *The relation between conceptual change in physical science, theory of mind and personal epistemology and implication for science instruction.* Paper presented at the 8th International Conference on Conceptual Change, Trier, Germany, 1–4 September.

Kyrkos, Ch., & Vosniadou, S. (1997). *Mental models of plant nutrition: A study of conceptual change in childhood.* Poster presented at the Seventh European Conference for Research on Learning and Instruction, Athens, Greece.

Lipton, J. S., & Spelke, E. S. (2003). Origins of number sense: Large number discrimination in human infants. *Psychological Science, 14*(5), 396–401.

Mahoney, M. S. (1997). *Revolution in mathematics* (Unpublished manuscript).

Mali, G. B., & Howe, A. (1979). Development of earth and gravity concepts among Nepali children. *Science Education, 63*(5), 685–691.

Mason, L., & Gava, M. (2007). Effects of epistemological beliefs and learning text structure on conceptual change. In S. Vosniadou, A. Baltas, & X. Vamvakoussi (Eds.), *Reframing the conceptual change approach in learning and instruction* (pp. 165–196). Oxford, UK: Elsevier.

Mason, L., Gava, M., & Boldrin, A. (2008). On warm conceptual change: The interplay of text, epistemological beliefs, and topic interest. *Journal of Educational Psychology, 100*(2), 291–309.

Mayer, R. E. (1985). Implications of cognitive psychology for instruction in mathematical problem solving. In E. A. Silver (Ed.), *Teaching and learning mathematical problem solving: Multiple research perspectives* (pp. 123–138). Hillsdale, NJ: Lawrence Erlbaum Associates.

McCloskey, M. (1983a). Naïve theories of motion. In D. Gentner & A. Stevens (Eds.), *Mental models.* Hillsdale, NJ: Lawrence Erlbaum Associates.

McCloskey, M. (1983b). Intuitive physics. *Scientific American, 248*(4), 122–130.

Piaget, J. (1970). *Structuralism.* New York, NY: Basic Books.

Pintrich, P. R., Marx, R. W., & Boyle, R. B. (1993). Beyond cold conceptual change: The role of motivational beliefs and classroom contextual factors in the process of conceptual change. *Review of Educational Research, 63,* 167–199.

Posner, G. J., Strike, K. A., Hewson, P. W., & Gertzog, W. A. (1982). Accommodation of a scientific conception: Towards a theory of conceptual change. *Science Education, 66,* 211–227.

Resnick, L. B. (2006). The dilemma of mathematical intuition in learning. In J. Novotná, H. Moraová, M. Krátká, & N. Stehlíková (Eds.), *Proceedings of the 30th Conference of the International Group for the Psychology of Mathematics Education* (Vol. 1, pp. 173–175). Prague, Czech Republic: PME.

Samarapungavan, A., Vosniadou, S., & Brewer, W. F. (1996). Mental models of the earth, sun, and moon: Indian children's cosmologies. *Cognitive Development, 11,* 491–521.

Sinatra, G. M., & Pintrich, P. R. (Eds.). (2003). *Intentional conceptual change.* Mahwah, NJ: , Lawrence Erlbaum Associates.

Smith, J. P., diSessa, A. A., & Roschelle, J. (1993). Misconceptions reconceived: A constructivist analysis of knowledge in transition. *Journal of the Learning Sciences, 3,* 115–163.

Stafylidou, S., & Vosniadou, S. (2004). Students' understanding of the numerical value of fractions: A conceptual change approach. *Learning and Instruction, 14,* 503–518.

Stathopoulou, C., & Vosniadou, S. (2007a). Conceptual change in physics and physics-related epistemological beliefs: A relationship under scrutiny. In S. Vosniadou, A. Baltas, & X. Vamvakoussi (Eds.), *Reframing the conceptual change approach in learning and instruction* (pp. 145–163). New York, NY: Elsevier.

Stathopoulou, C., & Vosniadou, S. (2007b). Exploring the relationship between physics-related epistemological beliefs and physics understanding. *Contemporary Educational Psychology, 32,* 255–281.

Vamvakoussi, X., & Vosniadou, S. (2010). How many decimals are there between two fractions? Aspects of secondary school students' reasoning about rational numbers and their notation. *Cognition and Instruction, 28*(2), 181–209.

Vamvakoussi, X., & Vosniadou, S. (2012). Bridging the gap between the dense and the discrete: The number line and the 'rubber line' bridging analogy. *Mathematical Thinking and Learning, 14*(4), 265–284.

Vosniadou, S. (2003). Exploring the relationships between conceptual change and intentional learning. In G. M. Sinatra & P. R. Pintrich (Eds.), *Intentional conceptual change* (pp. 377–406). Mahwah, NJ: Lawrence Erlbaum Associates.

Vosniadou, S., Baltas, A., & Vamvakoussi, X. (Eds.). (2007). *Reframing the conceptual change approach in learning and instruction.* Oxford, UK: Elsevier.

Vosniadou, S., & Brewer, W. F. (1992). Mental models of the earth: A study of conceptual change in childhood. *Cognitive Psychology, 24,* 535–585.

Vosniadou, S., & Brewer, W. F. (1994). Mental models of the day/night cycle. *Cognitive Science, 18,* 123–183.

Vosniadou, S., & Ioannides, C. (1998). From conceptual development to science education: A psychological point of view. *International Journal of Science Education, 20*(10), 1213–1230.

Vosniadou, S., Ioannides, C., Dimitrakopoulou, A., & Papademetriou, E. (2001). Designing learning environments to promote conceptual change in science. *Learning and Instruction, 11,* 381–419.

Vosniadou, S., & Skopeliti, I. (2005). Developmental shifts in children's categorization of the earth. In B. G. Bara, L. Barsalou, & M. Bucciarelli (Eds.), *Proceedings of the XXVII Annual Conference of the Cognitive Science Society* (pp. 2325–2330). Mahwah, NJ: , Lawrence Erlbaum Associates.

Vosniadou, S., & Skopeliti, I. (submitted a). Children's erroneous inferences in the comprehension of counter-intuitive science text. *Learning and Instruction.*

Vosniadou, S., & Skopeliti, I. (submitted b). Instructional analogies in conceptual restructuring processes. *Cognitive Psychology.*

Vosniadou, S., Skopeliti, I., & Ikospentaki, K. (2004). Modes of knowing and ways of reasoning in elementary astronomy. *Cognitive Development, 19,* 203–222.

Vosniadou, S., Skopeliti, I., & Ikospentaki, K. (2005). Reconsidering the role of artifacts in reasoning: Children's understanding of the globe as a model of the earth. *Learning and Instruction, 15,* 333–351.

Vosniadou, S., Vamvakoussi, X., & Skopeliti, I. (2008), The framework theory approach to the problem of conceptual change. In S. Vosniadou (Ed.), *International handbook of research on conceptual change.* New York, NY: Routledge.

Vosniadou, S., & Verschaffel, L. (2004). Extending the conceptual change approach to mathematics learning and teaching. *Learning and Instruction, 140,* 445–451.

Wandersee, J. H. (1983). Students' misconceptions about photosynthesis: A cross-age study. In H. Helm & J. D. Novak (Eds.), *Proceedings of the International Seminar: Misconceptions in Science and Mathematics* (pp. 441–446). Ithaca, NY: Cornell University.

Wellman, H. M., & Gelman, S. A. (1998). Knowledge acquisition in foundational domains. In D. Kuhn & R. Siegler (Eds.), *Cognition, perception and language. Volume 2 of the Handbook of child psychology* (5th edn., pp. 523–573). New York, NY: Wiley.

Wiser, M., & Smith, C. L. (2008). Learning and teaching about matter in grades K-8: When should the atomic–molecular theory be introduced? In S. Vosniadou (Ed.), *The international handbook of research on conceptual change* (pp. 205–239). New York, NY: Routledge.

2

A BIRD'S-EYE VIEW OF THE "PIECES" VS. "COHERENCE" CONTROVERSY (FROM THE "PIECES" SIDE OF THE FENCE)

Andrea A. diSessa, University of California at Berkeley

The central principle of conceptual change research is the constructivist idea that "old" ideas constrain learning. In classroom-relevant study, conceptual change research has laid blame for difficulties at the feet of "entrenched naïve ideas." In physics, naïve ideas said to be like the medieval impetus theory of motion must give way to counterintuitive Newtonian ideas (McCloskey, 1983). Similarly, developmental studies seek to find the great intellectual accomplishments of childhood in dramatic revisions to the way domains are construed. Childhood biology has been claimed to be psychological (Carey, 1985) or "vitalistic" (Inagaki & Hatano, 2002), in stark contrast to adult or scientific ideas about living things.

Roughly three decades after the beginnings of modern conceptual change research, one would think that the basic nature of naïve ideas should be settled. Old ideas, of course, are different in content from new ones. But what in their nature, or in their relation to new ideas, makes them entrenched, difficult to change, requiring extended experience or exceptional instruction? It is puzzling and ironic, given its centrality, that no consensus exists on this issue.

This chapter looks at a critical fault line concerning the nature of naïve ideas. On one hand, naïve ideas have been described as coherent, systematic, or even theory-like – similar enough to scientists' carefully laid out *theories* to deserve the same term. On the other hand, naïve ideas have also been described as many, diverse, and displaying limited integration or coherence. I believe that the fragmentary vs. coherent issue is manifestly epistemologically and empirically fundamental. Our very sense of the nature of knowledge and how it changes is at stake. If we cannot settle on a broad characterization of naïve knowledge, how can we expect to settle other, more subtle issues, such as tracking conceptual change in detail? I believe that the state of the art in theoretical sophistication and empirical methodology has advanced far since the early days of conceptual change research. It is time to push toward a consensus on the nature of naïve ideas.

THE CHAPTER'S INTENT

This chapter is part of my larger agenda to promote a consideration of "coherent vs. fragmentary" as central, and to help foster a sensible resolution. I aim here to avoid technical theoretical considerations and detailed empirical argument, although some of that will be referenced for illustration. Instead, I want to take seriously the possibility that, in addition to technical issues and data, basic feelings of sensibility drive researchers' predilections. I work here at the level of researchers' own persistent intuitions, motivations, and perspectives. In a sense, this strategy reflects the epistemological orientation of my basic claims about naïve, intuitive knowledge. In particular, the strategy assumes that conviction is distributed in nature, and thus I assume that multiple arguments that can be quickly reached and relatively briefly treated may have surprising effects, alongside in-depth and more "rigorous" arguments.

Many of the issues treated here arise informally and are somewhat disconnected from focused scientific give-and-take. In particular, many of the questions I treat are near-transcriptions of comments that have come to me after talks, for example, or in "final words" of reviewers of journal articles. Questioners or reviewers often acknowledge force in the presented arguments, but voice residual feelings concerning implausibilities with the pieces position.

Despite the less formal nature of the questions and responses here, I want to exert due diligence concerning a few issues close to the core of the debate. In particular, I want to note that my main concern has been conceptual change in physics. Conceptual change in physics, mechanics in particular, has some special characteristics that may not be true in all domains. In particular, physical intuition is built from a huge and critically important phenomenology – living every day in the physical world and having to negotiate it effectively in order to survive and flourish. To take a contrast case, children's cosmologies certainly make interesting study from a conceptual change point of view (for example, Vosniadou & Brewer, 1992). But it is unclear that uninstructed ideas in this domain are nearly as rich and experientially founded as intuitive physics. Biology probably constitutes an intermediate domain – not so salient and instrumentally important in young children's lives as physics, but still grounded in everyday observations that children make concerning living things. I believe that insights from the "fragmentary" position apply to most, if not all domains, more so to the extent that the domains are rich and experientially founded. Still, I take physics as a prototype to avoid unnecessary complexity.

In sum, domain differences constitute a caveat that I mark but will not pursue. Other "due diligence" issues, central to this chapter, are treated in the next section.

WHAT IS AT ISSUE?

I characterized the debate as concerning whether naïve ideas consist of relatively independent fragments or whether they are coherent wholes. I use the phrase "knowledge in pieces" to describe the general position of fragmentation. On the coherence side, those who advocate the "theory theory" (e.g., Gopnik & Wellman, 1994; McCloskey, 1983) – that students' "old" ideas are systematic enough to be called a theory – are staking out an extreme version of the coherence position. Some of the more prominent if less extreme coherence advocates are Susan Carey (e.g., Carey, 1999) and Stella Vosniadou (e.g., Vosniadou, 2002). "Less extreme" refers to explicit acknowledgment of aspects of intuitive theories that are different from professional science, such as being less articulately espoused, absence of meta-conceptual awareness, and a lesser degree of coherence, smaller breadth of coverage, and so on.

Slogans such as "theory theory" or "knowledge in pieces" are good for drawing attention to positions in a debate, but they are not sufficient even for the rough and ready treatment here. The real debate begins in the issue of grain size: At what grain size and level of detail must we describe intuitive ideas so as to have characterized them adequately to understand conceptual change?

While grain size is seldom discussed explicitly, one can get a good gestalt simply by looking at researchers' descriptions of naïve ideas. How much and what kind of things are said to characterize the naïve state? Coherence advocates appear to think that a paragraph of natural language text, or a few compact principles (each a sentence or two in length), suffices. Of course, researchers say much more in terms of motivation, implications, and certainly in terms of empirical validation. But descriptions of naïve ideas are seldom elaborate. Early descriptions of "intuitive theories" of mechanics were often in terms of a single phrase or sentence, and seldom more than a paragraph. For example, Vosniadou (2002) describes a claimed-to-be-complete range of meanings of force – sufficient to cover students' ideas from kindergarten to ninth grade – in a one-page chart, using a sentence or two to describe each meaning. In contrast, in one paper (diSessa, 1993) I describe more than three dozen elements of intuitive knowledge in mechanics, using about a paragraph each, while making clear that the descriptions are partial, and that the listing is not by any means complete.

Grain size entails two subsidiary considerations that are equally important. The first consideration is *structure*. If one has many knowledge elements, one must ask how they relate to one another. What is the structure of naïve physics?

Anticipating later argument, I think the coherence position has a salient theoretical problem right here. While coherence is a vague word, one important core meaning has inherently to do with relations; that is, the meaning of coherence requires an articulation of structure. What are the relations among parts of, for example, intuitive theories, and how can we even make an overall judgment of "coherent" without the articulation of structure? Definitions of coherence and specifications of relations are usually missing or minimal in accounts by coherence advocates.

My early work on intuitive ideas aimed mainly to establish a sensible grain size at which to think about naive knowledge as a precursor to describing structure (including "systematics" or coherence). To cut a long story very short, I believe it is important and possible to track intuitive ideas at a sub-conceptual grain size ("smaller" and more numerous than scientific concepts). Some of my more recent research aimed to establish the architecture (specific relational structure) of normative scientific concepts at a grain size consistent with what we see in naïve knowledge (see, for example, diSessa & Wagner, 2005). So, the *fact* that relational structure exists is not the issue. How to describe it, and whether and how one can make a judgment of "coherent," is the point.

The second consideration is *contextuality*. When do children or students use what particular ideas? With more elements, it is strongly likely there is a much greater contextuality.

In contrast to structure, contextuality provides a fairly easy empirical window. Do children always say things that are aligned with descriptions of their intuitive ideas, or, in contrast, is it easy to ask questions about slightly different situations that elicit different responses? A fair amount of my empirical work demonstrates circumstances and questions that elicit answers that cannot be covered by the kind of sparse descriptions of naïve ideas offered by coherence advocates. Contextuality depends not only on whether we have covered the range of ideas students actually have, but also on whether our descriptions of student knowledge are precise enough that we know when that knowledge should actually be used.

To summarize, I claim that the debate about coherence should be construed, more precisely, as concerning the grain size of mental entities. From a knowledge in pieces point of view, "intuitive theories," if they exist, are highly aggregated; we will not be able to describe conceptual change at all perspicuously from such a high level. Only with a more appropriate grain size can we describe the structure (and, in consequence, define and evaluate coherence) of naïve ideas. Only at that level can we track the building of naïve elements into normative concepts.

Having refined what is at stake – from "pieces vs. coherence" to "grain size" and related issues – I begin exposition in earnest by responding to a set of common questions that reveal prejudices against, or misunderstanding of, the pieces perspective. I begin by elaborating issues related to those discussed just above.

QUESTIONS ABOUT KNOWLEDGE IN PIECES

More or Less

What is all the fuss about? Isn't the dispute just a matter of degree?

No one can believe that people are 100% coherent and consistent, and no one can believe people have nothing more than a completely incoherent jumble of ad hoc ideas. Might the dispute here be an issue of "half full" vs. "half empty"?

First, note that the relevant question of coherence, as construed here, is distinct from the issue of whether people can track a coherent line of reasoning. Instead, it is about the relational structure of the totality of domain-relevant knowledge. For example, it is conceivable that people could always track coherent lines of reasoning, and yet, in terms of the totality of ways of thinking, they might track different and incommensurable lines on different occasions.

Metaphorically speaking, on a 10-point scale, we can safely rule out 1 (complete incoherence) and 10 (complete coherence). However, after that, what is a good estimate? Given still fairly sketchy empirical results, why should anyone make such a fuss about whether one's predilection puts an estimate in the upper or lower half of the coherence scale?

The flaw in such temporizing is that there is a prior, unaddressed issue, before we can even get to disputes about quantitative measures. We must ask what is the legitimate grain size at which we should begin to formulate a measure – or even a conception – of coherence. Here, the positions of "pieces" and "coherence" are asymmetrical. "Pieces" advocates agree that concepts and theories define legitimate foci. However, I also believe that there exists an entire other universe of sub-conceptual elements that must be tracked in order to see the construction of concepts and theories – that is, in order to understand conceptual change.

Assessing coherence requires yet another step beyond agreeing, even roughly, on grain size. We need to describe the relations among elements that we examine in order to determine coherence. We must consider *structure*. For example, mathematicians might insist that coherence means deductive coherence. Pursuing this line, we could characterize deductive coherence as follows:

> Elements are either propositions or terms; terms may be undefined, or defined; propositions are either axioms or they must be proven; and the relation "proven" is highly restrictive in the usual way.

No one that I know supports the axiomatic version of coherence for naïve ideas, which is very nearly categorical (either you have it or you don't). However, neither do they deny it, nor are there forthcoming specific proposals as to what relations coherence does entail.

Contrast a different sort of relation by which one might assess coherence. Let us say that two ideas are coherent if one vaguely seems to imply the other, or even if they merely seem related in some unspecified sense. That is a very different kind of coherence, and probably has very different consequences for conceptual change. The bottom line is that I do not believe coherence can be assessed *at all* until we have a better agreement on what grain size, what kind of elements are at issue (their ontology; e.g., "propositions," "axioms," or "p-prims"), *and* what sort of relations are relevant (e.g., "provable," or "vaguely related"). My work puts forward several different kinds of relations one might investigate in naïve or expert knowledge systems, such as mutual plausibility, mutual use, and common abstractions (see the Systematicity section of diSessa, 1993). Each would support a different judgment about the level of coherence in a knowledge system. More recent work (e.g., diSessa & Wagner, 2005) proposes a categorical criterion of coherence, called *alignment*, which I believe to be important in assessing fully developed scientific concepts.

Even without agreements on elements and relations, I believe empirical and theoretical work from the pieces community provides decent constraints on levels of coherence. For example, in listing dozens of elements that seem to have, at best, sketchy relations of any sort with one another, future more definitive assessments of coherence seem bounded. The mere fact of a large number of elements makes a very high level of coherence implausible, whatever the relational measure. Furthermore, my theory of the development of intuitive elements (diSessa, 1993) suggests largely independent developmental trajectories, which makes a high degree of coherence improbable.

To sum up, the underlying important issues are primarily grain size and, then, structure (e.g., relational coherence). Until we make progress on these, discussion about the level of coherence is crude, heuristic, and uncertain. In view of this, the dispute between pieces and coherence is not so much a matter of degree. I believe that there is a large family of sub-conceptual elements – multiple elements that play a role in the construction of scientific concepts – and the structure of that family of elements and their contributions to instructed concepts must be charted in order to understand conceptual change. Coherence advocates, to the extent they do not recognize or articulate any sub-conceptual structure, are simply playing a different game.

Partisanship

Aren't partisans driving toward extremes in the debate between pieces vs. coherence? Isn't the resolution – and more sensible research – likely somewhere in the middle?

"Pieces vs. coherence" is the banner I've chosen in the deeper disputes about grain size and such. There is no easy middle to retreat to. Conceptual change researchers, in my view, must get down to brass tacks, define and defend their choices of grain size, ontology, and relational structure. My own takes are undoubtedly wrong or incomplete to some degree. But I stand for the need to articulate sub-conceptual architectures.

Forests and Trees

Isn't the "pieces" point of view wallowing in a "fine and esoteric level of detail," while the big picture of conceptual change is missed?

Coherence is (should be) a content-independent measure of a system of knowledge. That is, very different ways of thinking about the universe might still each be internally coherent. The "forests and trees" question seems to admit that cognition is complex (who could deny that?), but it focuses on something like a schematic or structural core that explains important aspects of conceptual change. Coherence advocates presumably want to maintain that the core is coherent, even if the noisy fringe is not.

In responding to this important and interesting question, I sketch a set of issues that should be treated. Secondarily, I sketch the kind of data that supports the "pieces" position on these issues. The full set of issues constitutes a critical framework that, I argue, should be systematically applied to claims concerning the existence of core-and-coherent conceptual systems.

The first issue is whether core schematizations exist at all. As social scientists, we should be well aware that easy generalizations – stereotypes – can be asserted, but they often turn out to be unreliable.

Conceptual change research has spent a huge amount of time finding questions that evoke "interesting" and somewhat uniform responses. The reverse enterprise of evaluating the actual contextual range of such schematization is thinly populated. Hence, there are easy opportunities to critique proposed "core schematizations."

In diSessa, Gillespie, and Esterly (2004), we took a characterization of children's meanings of force by Ioannides and Vosniadou (2002) and used a simple strategy. We identified features of situations that we had good reason to believe would affect student responses, and then we validated that changes in these aspects made substantial differences in response. The differences in responses constituted a contexuality that Ioannides and Vosniadou's conceptions of force could not account for, since their models simply did not mention the features that we manipulated. The main judgment Ioannides and Vosniadou looked at in subjects was whether or not a force existed in a situation. We found that the existence and magnitude of forces that subjects saw depended on things such as whether a block is seen as leaning on another block, or as being leaned on. It also depended on whether a ball moving in a circle was doing so because it was tied by a string to a center, or, in contrast, guided by a circular tube. In another case, we found a significant number of students who saw that a struck bell emits a force (disconnected from the bell itself), which violated the stated contexts in which students were supposed to see forces, and also the basic nature of force, according to Ioannides and Vosniadou.

Our study design was straightforward. Almost all of the critical attributes that we used to test judgments of force were previously documented (e.g., diSessa, 1993), although not in large N studies. Data on complexities and contextualities are easy to come by, if one tries! Forgoing easy tests of generality seems an example of the fact that coherence advocates are "confirmation biased." They have ignored potential contextualities even when they are well documented in the literature.

DiSessa et al. (2004) also found a more direct problem with the generalities claimed by Ioannides and Vosniadou. As part of preliminary work for our study, we performed a near replication of their experiment, with dramatically different results ($p < .00001$). We found little or no trace of systematic answers that display coherent and consistently applied meanings of force. Clark, D'Angelo, and Schleigh (2011) replicated failure to replicate Ioannides and Vosniadou's results across five different countries, different languages, and multiple coding schemes.

Even if a proposed "core conceptual structure" can be robustly validated, I think a second criterion is important and often neglected. "Core" should mean "important." Yet many studies of conceptual change name features of naïve knowledge without demonstrating their importance at the same time that they ignore what I take to be important aspects. (Examples appear in the following two paragraphs.) Thus, the dismissive reference to "esoteric detail" by coherence advocates is pre-judgmental, and also ironic. Establishing importance is a little-recognized consideration that, I believe, dogs claims about so-called core conceptual structures.

Ioannides and Vosniadou (2002) vs. diSessa et al. (2004) also illustrates the issue of importance. Ioannides and Vosniadou focused nearly exclusively on the sheer existence of a force. However, we argued that conceptual competence involves many issues other than existence. Students may give completely normative answers concerning when a force exists, and even its magnitude, but they may still draw critically flawed inferences. One of the oldest and most robust findings in conceptual change in physics is that students infer speed from the existence of a force (Clement, 1982); they do not infer, as $F = ma$ would have, acceleration. The very emblem, $F = ma$, reminds us of the central importance of relations, not just what Ioannides and Vosniadou investigated. Can claims of "core structures" be valid if they make no reference at all to central parts of what a concept is supposed to do for us? Which side, here, is ignoring "core" issues?

"Trust that generalities might appear, despite the 'noise of details,'" is an orientation of coherence advocates with not a great deal of empirical validation. Mere assertions (a) that a "core structure" organizes a lot of data (from a database selected to demonstrate "the core"), (b) that claimed structure is core to the whole family of ideas that children display, and (c) that such structure poses the central problem of conceptual change will not suffice.

A third element of critique exists, even if we give away "existence" and "importance" of a simple, coherent core. That is, might a "pieces" explanation of "core structures" be more perspicuous than a "coherence" explanation? In this case, what I have in mind is explaining high-level regularities from a sub-conceptual point of view.

One of the best known intuitive conceptualizations is the idea that, in throwing an object up in the air, we impart an internal force to it. The force gradually dies out, allowing other forces, such as gravity, to "take over." McCloskey (1983) first popularized this "naïve theory," and Ioannides and Vosniadou's (2002) "acquired force" meaning is essentially the same idea.

In diSessa (1988), I conjectured the possibility that this so-called theory is actually a compound construction involving roughly six sub-conceptual elements that happen to apply to situations like tossing a ball into the air. The core of this conjecture is that a conflict – an object going up while being pulled down by gravity – is intuitively evident in a toss. A conceptually critical part of the toss, the peak, shows a typical intuitive pattern, called "overcoming" (diSessa, 1993), where a weakening influence is overcome by another (or a constant influence is overcome by a strengthening one). The upward "impetus" force may be invented to provide a weakening influence that is overcome by gravity at the peak of the toss.

The potential advantages of such a decomposition are these: (a) The assembly of a core conceptualization out of independently validated elements provides a good sketch of how such a "theory" could have come about. (b) The core conceptualization's properties are a consequence of the properties of independently validated elements. (The "theory" follows from joint use of a number of "principles," in the way that physicists sometimes use several basic principles together to solve a problem.) (c) Contextuality may be better handled by the "pieces" decomposition. That is, on many occasions students use the pieces, whereas they do not invoke the "full theory." High school and college students seldom (never, in my interviewing experience) use impetus to explain the fall from rest of a dropped object, where there is no conflict between motion and a known force, gravity. If a push from a hand imparts a force in a toss, should not gravity in a drop also impart one? The pieces perspective easily explains this: no conflict implies little chance of impetus use.

Years after conjecturing the decomposition of McCloskey's impetus theory, I was lucky enough to catch on video the apparent construction of the impetus theory on the fly (diSessa, 1996). The student, called J, exhibited the following behaviors: (a) She began to construct the theory only after showing apparently competent use of the corresponding Newtonian analysis. (b) The initiating event was the interviewer's pointing out the peak of the toss for analysis, where, I conjectured, overcoming and conflict is salient and should initiate the search for an "opponent" to gravity. (c) J initially tried a different "opponent" to gravity, air resistance, to fill the needed niche for overcoming; she came up with impetus only as a second try. This last shows the quasi-independence of elements (impetus does not *always* go together with overcoming), and also that construction of the impetus theory may be piecemeal. While catching construction events like this is undoubtedly extremely rare, these data show, in a case, the possibility of construction as conjectured, consistent with a multiple pieces interpretation.

To sum up this section, my belief is that coherence advocates trust that they will find core, coherent structures far beyond what is empirically warranted. (a) They ignore "noise," seldom test the contextual breadth of the constructions, and almost never deliberately challenge the existence of their proposed core structures. (b) They trust the importance of core structure, without explicit argument or validation. (c) And finally, they seldom or never consider that the decomposition of "core structure" might be exceptionally illuminating of its conceptual and contextual properties, and of the way in which it might have come to exist.

Parsimony

Scientific theories should be parsimonious. Isn't the pieces view just like the epicycles that were proposed arbitrarily to explain details of planetary motion before Kepler and Newton created a simplifying explanation? You can always explain anything if you allow any number of parameters.

Despite the fact that there are many "parameters" in the pool of sub-conceptual pieces of knowledge that I conjecture to explain naïve physics, each of these pieces is motivated by data and subject to empirical validation. They are not arbitrary.

The larger issue is: When are we forced to accept complexity as part of science? Plenty of historical precedents exist for the ultimate scientific story being much more complicated than older scientific or non-scientific explanations. The four elements of the Greeks turned into over a hundred. Consider evolution. Explaining the nature of present biological organisms simply requires a lot of time and a lot of detail. Part of the reason for the complexity is that present-day organisms developed over a long period of time, and their current forms express much historical detail, including "accidents" of history that are simply not given by simple, rational rules, or necessity. The conceptual ecology of humans is, in my view, similarly dependent on a complex history. In a nutshell, the complexities of a long historical development seldom or never admit a simple, "rational" reconstruction.

Passions run high among coherence advocates concerning basic expectations about the complexity of human thought. For example, a reviewer of a paper of mine who was, on the whole, positive said that, "The subjective impact of the study is disturbingly 'anarchistic.'" Why should complexity be disturbing? Another, published characterization of knowledge in pieces portrays it, obviously negatively, as holding that naïve knowledge is a "fragmented, inconsistent jumble" (Samarapungavan & Wiers, 1997, p. 170).

In the end, dispositions that "estimate" the complexity of answers to scientific questions must acquiesce to growing empirical and theoretical arguments. Arguments based on *a priori* dispositions either in favor of or in opposition to a complex, sub-conceptual knowledge system in humans are weak.

Robustness

How can a large collection of "fragile," random pieces account for the obvious robustness of intuitive ideas?

"Fragile" and "random" are prejudiced descriptors that do not capture much of my view of knowledge in pieces. Elements of intuitive knowledge are contextual in that there are many of them, and they each have quite specific contextual boundaries. The region of applicability of an element might, however, be quite broad. For example, the idea that "increased effort" begets "greater results" applies across the physics/psychology boundary, which professional physical ideas such as "force" do not cross.

None of the more important elements are "random" in any reasonable sense. They are important to humans' understanding the world, and are often if not always productive in everyday thinking. They are reliably activated by situations within their span of applicability; reliable activation, in fact, is critical to their empirical tractability. Productivity, indeed, explains a "resistance" to change that the conventional idea of "misconceptions" misses. If ideas are just wrong, why would people hold tightly to them? Even more, conceptual change is more difficult because, used in the proper context, many intuitive ideas will be productive *in normative physics* as well; they are constituents of correct science.

The need for shifting contextuality in the course of learning is much more characteristic of difficulty than the fact of contextuality *per se*. Even when intuitive elements are used in normative physics, they are used in new contexts and in new ways. Creating that contextuality in students' use of those ideas is not easy. And the ultimate problem is that multiple changes in the contextuality of multiple elements must all be coordinated to create a workable successor to old ways of thinking.

Consider my analysis of the "impetus theory" in a toss. The intuitive elements, such as balancing (the "tipping point" where one force overcomes another), and so on, *are not wrong!* Students will be doing a lot of balancing of forces and balancing equations when they come to solve physics problems correctly. Furthermore, I have conjectured that balancing will become an important part of conservation of energy (diSessa, 1993). So, in net, learning that "balance is wrong" is simply not appropriate. It is just that balancing is not a productive way of thinking about tossing a ball.

Scientific concepts are complicated and take extended construction. Knowledge in pieces explains – in many ways – why change is difficult. Elements need to be recontextualized, not erased, and many coordinated changes are necessary. These explanations are not tautological, as an unanalyzed appeal to "entrenchment," for example, is. The systems view of knowledge in pieces can also explain why change is easy in some instances: Say, a single, weak intuitive element is the problem, and alternative intuitive analyses exist that are in line with normative physics. In general, knowledge in pieces emphasizes how change is possible, and even sometimes easy (see the discussion of "narratives" in diSessa, 1996). In contrast, strong coherence theories seem much less interested in the details of success cases. It might be that they are incapable of explaining success.

Complexity in Instruction

Isn't the pieces point of view too complicated to be useful in instruction? How is a teacher supposed to make sense of "hundreds or thousands" of intuitive knowledge elements?

The issue of instructional implications of knowledge in pieces is huge, and it deserves a chapter on its own. Here, I make a few general points.

First, facts about the world are not beholden to us to make our lives easier. If, in fact, naïve conceptual architectures involve thousands of elements, we need to learn to deal with it. In responding to a previous question, I noted that simplicity is attractive, but it must be accountable to the facts of the matter. In similar manner, claims that have easy practical implications are also attractive. But, again, that attractiveness has little to do with validity. Educationally oriented researchers would love to have conceptual change turn out such that we can easily teach better. But that is no basis for evaluating theories or data.

A second issue is explaining complex and maybe unsettling scientific results to teachers and other professionals. This issue is important and challenging to deal with. Again, however, judging science by how easy it is to explain to non-scientists is not a valid strategy.

Preliminaries aside, what are the implications of knowledge in pieces for instruction? What can teachers do in view of those facts of the matter?

1. *Deep learning just takes time.* There are several ways to motivate the idea that, if we are to achieve deep results from instruction, we need to take adequate time to do it. However, I believe knowledge in pieces is both fundamentally correct and has the implication that, to draw out useful intuitive ideas and to assemble a good, normative concept, we cannot instructionally escape time and effort. Clark (2006) takes the issue of the amount of time it takes to create an integrated understanding head-on.

2. *Deep learning requires learning in many contexts.* Complex contextuality is a fact of the matter in a knowledge in pieces perspective. Scientific understanding unifies contexts that are "plainly" (in naïve eyes) different. That takes specific attention, it takes many contexts of use, and it takes time (see, for example, diSessa & Wagner, 2005).

3. *Students have a richness of conceptual resources to draw on. Attend to their ideas and help them build on the best of them.* I am not at all sure that teachers have the same negative reaction to the idea that students have a lot of ideas that some researchers do. In fact, I believe that attending to students carefully in a classroom lends more experiential cogency to knowledge in pieces, compared to the idea of a core and coherent structure. I think it is a powerful and useful lesson for teachers to attend to nuances in student ideas and to try to figure out how to use them productively.

   Given the fact of many ideas in intuitive knowledge ecologies, I believe it is a losing strategy to focus a lot of energy on teaching students that some particular ideas they have are just wrong. In the early days of conceptual change research, "elicit and confront" (prove to students that their intuitive theories are inadequate) was probably the most widely drawn instructional implication. I believe the strategy of confrontation has diminished visibility mainly because it does not work reliably. Knowledge in pieces provides a principled explanation of why it must fail: Pieces, one at a time, are not true or false; assemblies are the relevant scale; normative assemblies often re-use naïve knowledge, although with different contextualities. So, "dismissing" naïve knowledge categorically is a poor strategy.

4. *Coaching students meta-conceptually is very different from a knowledge in pieces perspective.* In recent years, the influence of students' ideas about knowledge and learning has come, more and more, to be considered influential. For example, students who think learning is unproblematic and fact-by-fact appear to be at a significant disadvantage (see Hofer & Pintrich, 2002, for representative state-of-the-art work). Naturally, our theoretical and empirical views of the nature of knowledge, both naïve and expert, and how expert knowledge is produced will strongly influence what we can and should cultivate in our students' views of knowledge. Hammer and Elby (2002) represent the knowledge in pieces perspective concerning students' meta-conceptual knowledge.

5. *Conceptual change in science is different for different students.* "One theory fits all" does not work. In general, learning researchers need to attend to diversity more adequately than they have in the past. Coherence views do not provide good leverage for dealing with diversity. Only with a more complex view of knowledge can we understand students' diversities and produce instruction that is well adapted to individuals or classes of students. The ability to track real-time learning from a knowledge in pieces perspective (e.g., Kapon & diSessa, 2012) is showing exactly how students are different, and how that results in their success or failure at learning.

6. *Assessment is a completely different matter from a knowledge in pieces perspective.* Strongly coherent, monolithic prior ideas can easily be monitored by any of a wide range of indicators; there is only one thing to test for. Assessing the presence, relative strength, and contextuality of a diverse collection of elements is more difficult, but (I claim) more valid and more informative. If normative ideas are as strongly coherent as naïve ones (see below), then success at conceptual change is similarly much easier to assess, compared to a more distributed view of expertise. Along the road to competence, a knowledge in pieces perspective allows textured formative assessment of individuals who might take different tracks to competence. Minstrell's "facet" methodology of assessment (e.g., Hunt & Minstrell, 1994) demonstrates how fine-grained, element-by-element assessments can guide teachers.

Aside from advice to teachers, fine-grained tracking of learning can be immensely helpful to the design of instructional materials. Designers know that the magic is often in the details. Coarse-grained views of conceptual change just cannot help with that.

Validation in Instruction

Hasn't research validated the power of teaching against "misconceptions" or "naïve theories"?
To be sure, there are instructional methods developed by people who believe in coherence and naïve theories. But the modest success of those instructional interventions does not provide definitive validation of their authors' theories. To begin, there is an increasing literature from knowledge in pieces advocates that shows significant effectiveness in instruction that they develop. The work of Marcia Linn (2006) and Jim Minstrell (Hunt & Minstrell, 1994) is emblematic. Second, I think that the very simple idea of engaging students' ideas is surprisingly powerful, independent of particular theoretical direction. So, many of the good properties of conceptual-change-inspired instruction come independent of specific theories of students' ideas. Third, many instructional methods are sensible within both theoretical perspectives. Most contemporary researchers of whatever theoretical persuasion believe that classroom discussion and visual, manipulable models can be powerful. Finally, detailed tracking of conceptual change in students through an instructional process, such as what would be necessary to validate one or another view of conceptual change, is, as mentioned, almost non-existent. Standard "before and after" tests may show *the fact* of conceptual change, but not how it happened.

Demeaning of Children

Isn't the pieces point of view dismissive of children as incoherent thinkers?
It is proper to criticize many researchers for undervaluing students' naïve knowledge. Worse, it is temptingly easy to "explain" students' problems (without really explaining) by saying that they have poor-quality knowledge. I have attended too many talks where researchers deride or even ridicule students' knowledge, using deprecating terms such as "pseudo-concepts" and comparing "misconceptions" to phenomena such as intransigent ignorance or backwardness.

Although attitudes to students do not follow strictly from theoretical orientations, I take knowledge in pieces to be a highly positive view of students' naïve knowledge. The most central part of this positive view is that many naïve pieces, although not all, actually become part of high-quality technical competence. The rich naïve cognitive ecology constitutes a generative pool of resources. In contrast, for most coherence advocates, especially theory theorists, new "good" knowledge must be generated *ab initio* by general processes such as analogy or abstraction, if any explanation of the generation of good knowledge is given at all. Most theory theorists, I believe, are only constructivist in the negative sense; naïve knowledge provides problems with which we need to deal. They have no account of content resources in naïve knowledge that are productive in attaining normative understanding.

Knowledge in pieces also provides a different view of expertise. Expert understanding is not monolithic, homogeneous, and logically consistent, either (Toulmin, 1972). Instead, it is in some respects fragmentary, often heuristic, and surprisingly more amenable to error that most expect. This is not a denigrating view of the best knowledge that human beings can produce; it is just a realistic and analytical view. As a side-effect of this recalibration of professional knowledge, students' knowledge looks much more like scientists' knowledge.

Western people *prefer* to think of themselves as rational, logical, and consistent. It is an assumed standard for good knowledge. But this is a bias based on terms that are not scientifically defined or empirically validated. Improved theory and sound empirical work will prepare for valid judgments of this sort, if any are forthcoming. These are not reliable assumptions going in.

KEY RESEARCH QUESTIONS AND MOTIVATING PHENOMENA

Research programs are often thought to be defined by theories and empirical results. However, especially in early stages, it is important to look at the central questions that researchers ask and the phenomena that motivate their inquiry.

Charting the Long Path to Competence

In terms of central research questions, almost all conceptual change researchers are concerned with the difficulty of acquiring particular concepts. Almost all researchers also agree that the path to conceptual change is long and difficult. However, explicitly charting that long path is much more characteristic of knowledge in pieces researchers. The idea of knowledge in pieces, itself, provides a first approximation model of what happens in the extended development of a new concept. A great number of elements must be collected and joined in appropriate ways to produce working, normative concepts or theories.

Charting the long path to competence is a non-negotiable focus of attention for conceptual change research. Implausible, bordering on impossible, alternatives include that, during the long period of "learning," nothing happens for a long time. Then, for some reason, conceptual change happens. I also believe that the long path of change is not a question that we can or should put off for future research. I am less concerned about how one charts gradual change of state than that we must begin to hypothesize and validate paths.

Here is an illuminating possibility for "how the long and difficult path to conceptual change" may be conceptualized. I can imagine a gradual change in parameters of a system that keeps it in a stable working mode. (For example, a tower of blocks might be stable as one gradually slides the upper blocks to the side.) But eventually, at a tipping point, a fairly rapid shift occurs to a new working mode. (The blocks, eventually, fall.) Physical scientists might call this a phase shift (e.g., after a long process of cooling, water becomes ice at a particular temperature). If conceptual change worked like this, it would validate a more coherence-oriented theory than I prefer. Still, with such a model, there is a locus of change (e.g., internal parameters of some sort) that is theoretically focused and (one should require) empirically tractable. Creating *any models at all* of the progress that is happening on "the long road to conceptual change" is the proximal goal that I am advocating just here, more important than judgments of pieces or coherence. Of course, once we get started seriously on the modeling enterprise, criteria for adequacy of models will become much more important.

An important and growing trend in pieces research is tracking real-time data in student conceptual change. I have no space to elaborate, but see, for example, Parnafes (2005), Levrini and diSessa (2008), and diSessa (in press).

In contrast, coherentists do almost exclusively diachronic or before/after studies. The grain size of their theories and many of their methodologies are unsuited to theorizing or tracking incremental change. None of us are done working out the long path to conceptual change. But some of us are seriously focused on it.

The Meaning of Coherence

A second key question that is characteristic of the knowledge-in-pieces perspective has already been discussed at some length: What is the meaning of "coherent," and how should it be empirically determined? As discussed, coherence advocates tend not to ask this question, as if "coherence" were self-evident, or they provide what I regard as unhelpful answers.[1]

Micro-development; Complex Contextuality; Multiple Strands of Conceptual Change

Turning from basic questions to phenomenological focus, there is a longer list of distinctive considerations. I start with three related foci: *micro-development, contextuality*, and *multiple strands* of development. First – as alluded to a couple of times – knowledge in pieces advocates attend to micro-developmental phenomena. Of the relatively few micro-genetic studies of conceptual change, aiming to track moment-by-moment changes in knowledge, essentially all of them are by knowledge-in-pieces advocates. Note that I am focusing here on phenomena, not on how one accounts for them. If one could account for the sort of phenomena I am pointing to here with a coherence-based framework, excellent! But the first step is to attend to those phenomena.

Micro-developmental work also highlights the importance of tracking the related phenomenology of the complex, delicate contextual dependencies of ideas, showing that a wide breadth of application of "the same idea" comes slowly, almost one context at a time (see Wagner, 2006). That work also tracks the influence of ideas as components of concepts, which is theory-characteristic of knowledge in pieces. For example, the idea of "representativeness" (to paraphrase, "bigger samples are more representative of reality") occurs to one subject only late in her learning of the law of large numbers, and it makes a demonstrable difference in terms of the range of contexts in which that subject could confidently apply the law.

I mentioned before that in my own work I have used the phenomenon of unexpected contextuality to challenge coherence-inspired work (diSessa et al., 2004). One of my prior extended case studies (of subject J, again) showed that she maintained two contradictory (to expert eyes) models of a toss – the impetus model and the correct model – through an extended interview and instructional process (diSessa, 1996; diSessa, Elby, & Hammer, 2002). The mere fact of students' use of multiple models is downplayed in most coherence research, and it is not the focus of systematic empirical study.

In general, careful study of micro-developmental phenomena leads to a focus on *multiple strands* of a "single" conceptual change. The case study of J showed important development in the student's normative model of a toss with instruction, but this did not affect her use of and confidence in her naïve model! One of the critiques we offered of coherence accounts of conceptual change concerning "force" is that aspects of it seem quite separable. For example, in diSessa et al. (2004), we charted a dramatic developmental shift *from correct to incorrect*, of children's expectation of the effect of a force in cases of circular motion. The details are not relevant, but see Table 2.1 for the numbers. Our contention is that this shift is important and that no simple "coherent" account of conceptual change can include both the general advance in sophistication of meanings of force that is conjectured, and, at the same time, this "backward" trajectory with respect to the important issue of the motion implications of the existence of a force.

"Out of the Shadows Learning"

Although it has not received a lot of empirical attention, a phenomenon I call *out of the shadows learning* is critically important and theoretically diagnostic. "Out of the shadows" refers to a situation where a minor intuitive idea, or one simply not connected by novices to the phenomenology of an expert domain, becomes importantly involved in developing an expert conception. This is, of course, a completely expectable phenomenon from a knowledge in pieces perspective. It is central to the assumption of generativity in intuitive knowledge, which I discussed in defending knowledge in pieces against claims that it demeaned children's or students' knowledge. Wagner's "representativeness" might constitute an example of out of the shadows learning. A much more dramatic possibility, which I have written about in several places, is that a "small" contextually bound idea that force can flow (diSessa et al., 2004), could become a central organizing concept in learning mechanics (diSessa, 1980). Finally, diSessa (in press) tracks several "minor" intuitive ideas in a group of students' construction of a normative law of thermal equilibration.

Table 2.1 Responses to an item asking for the effect of an off-center force on a circular object. Does the object move in the direction of the force, or opposite to it?

	Aligned (correct)	Opposite (incorrect)
High school	0%	100%
Middle school	17%	83%
Elementary school	50%	38%
Pre-school	62%	38%

Other Things Students Say

A focus of attention related to the "out of the shadows" phenomenon is making sense of the huge range of things students and children say that do not relate to the theories or coherent conceptions attributed to them. Even the most die-hard theory theorist must admit that children have a wide variety of things to say about domains (physics, biology, psychology) that are not easily assimilable to their core "theories." This is often treated as "noise" in coherence advocates' studies. Noise is often eliminated by tuning the instruments of investigation. But conceptual noise is often signal for pieces advocates. Even if it is unimportant (which I contest), it is a legitimate focus of study, and coherence advocates, in general, have nothing whatsoever, theoretically or empirically, to say about it. Of course, I expect that the "noise" will yield to analysis in the same terms that "theories" and "concepts" will – that is, in terms of pieces that form part of new concepts and theories. Before we have a definitive resolution to such issues, it is still illuminating that coherence advocates minimize and ignore "other things students say," while pieces advocates seek to understand them and bring them under the umbrella of a more powerful, general, theory of concepts and conceptual change.

I propose a "walk around" test, similar to the Turing test. Walk around your house with a child, pushing, prodding, tossing, dropping, bouncing, and watching things. Definitely include splashing and floating (since most studies of intuitive physics have essentially ignored liquids)! How much can be brought under the umbrella of any existing coherence model of physics knowledge? Or, talk with a child for an hour about her friends and family. How much of that can be brought under the umbrella of a naïve theory of mind? I believe we must eventually come to understand the diversity of things children do say, independent of whether they fit some "core theory." Coherentists seem uninterested in this.

Diversity

In my view, coherence approaches to conceptual change inevitably simplify complexities in learning and conceptual performance in the search for single, easy-to-say conceptions. In contrast, a knowledge in pieces perspective focuses on exposing and understanding *diversity* of several kinds in conceptualization. First, as mentioned, I do not think one should presume that all conceptual change works in the same way. Different domains, or even different concepts in the same domain, might be quite different. While mapping out the dimensions of this diversity and validating implications has not proceeded far, it deserves continuing attention.

Diversity in the way people handle concepts across different contexts has already been extensively discussed here, as *contextuality*. *Individual diversity* – how different students approach conceptual change differently (and, presumably, need different kinds of help in instruction) – has essentially no representation in coherence approaches to conceptual change. Case studies, almost unique to the knowledge in pieces perspective, are one way to get at diversity across individuals. The case of J, which I have used in several ways here, revealed remarkable, if not unique, individual characteristics (diSessa et al., 2002). In particular, J's persistence in using her intuitive model of a toss across several months, despite direct countering and despite also learning more about the normative model, was extremely unusual, if not unprecedented. In contrast, another case study (unpublished) showed a student with the same initial model, who spontaneously changed her model to the normative one – explicitly renouncing her old model – during one protocol segment of less than 10 minutes' duration.

Of these forms of diversity, contextual diversity has had the most empirical attention. However, the whole package of forms of diversity (individual, contextual, domain-relative) is important and expected from a knowledge in pieces perspective. None of them are typically mentioned within the coherence community.

CONCLUSION

The differences between coherence and fragmentary views of conceptual change are not just some narrow, technical issue of "how coherent are students' naïve ideas?" I hope to have exposed myriad differences that may properly be described as a difference in paradigm. However, unlike Kuhn's (1970) take, the chapter is also dedicated to the possibility that we can speak across and settle these differences.

ACKNOWLEDGMENTS

I thank the Boxer Research Group, UC Berkeley, for early critique of this chapter. David Brown provided helpful, pointed commentary. Productive comments by Stella Vosniadou are acknowledged. Joseph Wagner and Karen Chang provided specific and helpful editorial suggestions. The Spencer Foundation's support of my current work (grant numbers MG-200500036 and MG-201100101) and past conceptual change work is also gratefully acknowledged.

NOTE

1   One can find bizarrely unhelpful definitions of coherence in the literature, even by well-respected researchers. One is that coherence is the state of having no contradictions. Thus, any system of elements that *have no relation whatsoever with one another* is coherent. Equally unhelpful is that coherence amounts to a system that is well interconnected, begging the fundamental question of *what sort of connections?*

REFERENCES

Carey, S. (1985). *Conceptual change in childhood.* Cambridge, MA: MIT Press/Bradford Books.

Carey, S. (1999). Sources of conceptual change. In E. Scholnick, K. Nelson, S. Gelman, & P. Miller (Eds.), *Conceptual development: Piaget's legacy* (pp. 293-326). Mahwah, NJ: Lawrence Erlbaum Associates.

Clark, D. B. (2006). Longitudinal conceptual change in students' understanding of thermal equilibrium: An examination of the process of conceptual restructuring. *Cognition and Instruction, 24*(4), 467–563.

Clark, D. B., D'Angelo, C., & Schleigh, S. (2011). Comparison of students' knowledge structure coherence and understanding of force in the Philippines, Turkey, China, Mexico, and the United States. *Journal of the Learning Sciences, 20*(20), 207–261.

Clement, J. (1982). Students' preconceptions in introductory mechanics. *American Journal of Physics, 50*(1), 66–70.

diSessa, A. A. (1980). Momentum flow as an alternative perspective in elementary mechanics. *American Journal of Physics, 48*, 365–369.

diSessa, A. A. (1988). Knowledge in pieces. In G. Forman and P. Pufall (Eds.), *Constructivism in the computer age* (pp. 49–70). Hillsdale, NJ: Lawrence Erlbaum Associates.

diSessa, A. A. (1993). Toward an epistemology of physics. *Cognition and Instruction, 10*(2–3), 105–225.

diSessa, A. A. (1996). What do "just plain folk" know about physics? In D. R. Olson and N. Torrance (Eds.), *Handbook of education and human development: New models of learning, teaching, and schooling* (pp. 709–730). Oxford, UK: Blackwell.

diSessa, A. A. (in press). The construction of causal schemes: Learning mechanisms at the knowledge level. *Cognitive Science.*

diSessa, A. A., Elby, A., & Hammer, D. (2002). J's epistemological stance and strategies. In G. Sinatra and P. Pintrich (Eds.), *Intentional conceptual change* (pp. 237–290). Mahwah, NJ: Lawrence Erlbaum Associates.

diSessa, A. A., Gillespie, N., & Esterly, J. (2004). Coherence vs. fragmentation in the development of the concept of force. *Cognitive Science, 28,* 843–900.

diSessa, A. A., & Wagner, J. F. (2005). What coordination has to say about transfer. In J. Mestre (Ed.), *Transfer of learning from a modern multi-disciplinary perspective* (pp. 121–154). Greenwich, CT: Information Age Publishing.

Gopnik, A., & Wellman, H. M. (1994). The theory theory. In L. A. Hirschfeld & S. A. Gelman (Eds.), *Mapping the mind: Domain specificity in cognition and culture* (pp. 257–293). New York, NY: Cambridge University Press.

Hammer, D., & Elby, A. (2002). On the form of a personal epistemology. In B. K. Hofer & P. R. Pintrich (Eds.), *Personal epistemology: The psychology of beliefs about knowledge and knowing* (pp. 169–190). Mahwah, NJ: Lawrence Erlbaum Associates.

Hofer, B., & Pintrich, P. (2002). *Personal epistemology: The psychology of beliefs about knowledge and knowing.* Mahwah, NJ: Lawrence Erlbaum Associates.

Hunt, E., & Minstrell, J. (1994). A cognitive approach to the teaching of physics. In K. McGilly (Ed.), *Classroom lessons: Integrating cognitive theory and classroom practice* (pp. 51–74). Cambridge, MA: MIT Press.

Inagaki, K., & Hatano, G. (2002). *Young children's naïve thinking about the biological world.* New York, NY: Psychology Press.

Ioannides, C., & Vosniadou, S. (2002). The changing meanings of force. *Cognitive Science Quarterly, 2,* 5–61.

Kapon, S., & diSessa, A. A. (2012). Reasoning through instructional analogies. *Cognition and Instruction, 30*(3), 261–310.

Kuhn, T. S. (1970). *The structure of scientific revolutions* (2nd edn.). Chicago, IL: University of Chicago Press.

Levrini, O., & diSessa, A. A. (2008). How students learn from multiple contexts and definitions: Proper time as a coordination class. *Physical Review Special Topics: Physics Education Research, 4,* 010107.

Linn, M. C. (2006). The knowledge integration perspective on learning and instruction. In R. K. Sawyer (Ed.), *The Cambridge handbook of the learning sciences* (pp. 242–264). Cambridge, UK: Cambridge University Press.

McCloskey, M. (1983). Naïve theories of motion. In D. Gentner & A. Stevens (Eds.), *Mental models* (pp. 299–324). Hillsdale, NJ: Lawrence Erlbaum Associates.

Parnafes, O. (2005). *The development of conceptual understanding through the use of computer-based representations.* Unpublished doctoral dissertation, University of California at Berkeley.

Samarapungavan, A., & Wiers, R. (1997). Children's thoughts on the origin of species: A study of explanatory coherence. *Cognitive Science, 21*(2), 147–177.

Toulmin, S. (1972). *Human understanding* (Vol. 1). Oxford, UK: Clarendon Press.

Vosniadou, S. (2002). On the nature of naïve physics. In M. Limón & L. Mason (Eds.), *Reconsidering conceptual change: Issues in theory and practice* (pp. 61–76). Dordrecht, The Netherlands: Kluwer Academic Publishers.

Vosniadou, S., & Brewer, W. (1992). Mental models of the earth: A study of conceptual change in childhood. *Cognitive Psychology, 24,* 535–585.

Wagner, J. F. (2006). Transfer in pieces. *Cognition and Instruction, 24*(1), 1–71.

3

TWO KINDS AND FOUR SUB-TYPES OF MISCONCEIVED KNOWLEDGE, WAYS TO CHANGE IT, AND THE LEARNING OUTCOMES

Michelene T. H. Chi, Arizona State University

CONCEPTUAL KIND OF LEARNING

Learning of complex material, such as concepts encountered in science classrooms, can occur under at least two different conditions of prior knowledge. In one case, a student may have some prior knowledge of the to-be-learned concepts, but it is *incomplete.* In this incomplete knowledge case, learning can be conceived of as gap filling, and Carey (1991) had referred to this case of knowledge acquisition as the enriching kind. In a second case, a student may have already acquired some naive ideas, either in school or from everyday experiences, that are "in conflict with" the to-be-learned concepts (Vosniadou, 2004). It is customary to assume that the naive "conflicting" knowledge is incorrect, by some normative standard. Thus, learning in this second case is not adding missing knowledge or gap filling; rather, learning is changing naive conflicting knowledge to correct knowledge. This chapter focuses on this conceptual change kind of learning.

Although this definition of conceptual change appears straightforward, learning via conceptual change entails several complex, non-transparent, and interwoven issues. The existence of decades of research on conceptual change speaks to the complexity of these issues. We pose some of the key non-transparent questions as follows: (a) In what ways does naïve knowledge "conflict with" the to-be-learned materials? That is, why is conflicting knowledge *misconceived* and not merely *incorrect?* We will address the difference between incorrect knowledge versus misconceived conflicting knowledge. (b) Is misconceived knowledge always resistant to change, or is some misconceived knowledge more easily changed? (c) How should instruction be designed to promote conceptual change? This chapter hopes to add clarity to some of these questions by offering a theoretical framework that lays out two different kinds of conceptual change, with two sub-types for each kind, as a function of how conflicting knowledge is defined. Furthermore, we postulate the processes by which such conflicting knowledge can be changed, and speculate on the kind of instruction that might achieve such change.

FOUR TYPES OF MISCONCEIVED KNOWLEDGE AND HOW THEY MIGHT BE CHANGED

Superficially, the notion of misconceived knowledge seems easy to define objectively, in that it is incorrect from the perspective of the correct to-be-learned material. However, characterizing misconceived knowledge as incorrect is simplistic because it cannot explain why misconceived knowledge is often so resistant to change. To understand why misconceived knowledge is resistant to change, we propose that there are two kinds of incorrectness: (1) knowledge can be "*inaccurate*" compared to correct information or to reality, such as in having an incorrect value on an appropriate property or dimension, or (2) knowledge can be "*incommensurate*" with correct information in not having the appropriate dimensions. "Dimension" is used here to refer to a plausible property of a concept in general, rather than the specific value on a dimension. For example, living things have the capacity (or dimensions) to "move on their own volition," "be responsive," and "reproduce," whereas artifacts (non-living things) cannot even have these dimensions. In contrast the value of a dimension is a specific feature or attribute. For the dimension of "reproducing," the specific attribute for fish is to lay eggs, while the specific attribute for dogs is to give birth to live young. Thus, to say that *a whale is the same size as a salmon* is *inaccurate*, whereas to say that *a whale is a fish like a salmon* is *incommensurate*.

Based on these two kinds of incorrectness (*inaccurate* and *incommensurate*), conflicting knowledge can be examined in terms of four sub-types, in terms of representations of knowledge that are commonly discussed in the cognitive science literature, such as individual propositions or statements, mental models, categories, and schemas. Corresponding to these four types of representations, we refer to prior conflicting knowledge as either *false beliefs* (at the statement level), *flawed mental models* (at the mental model level), *category mistakes* (at the categorical level), or *missing schemas* (at the schema level). *False beliefs* and *flawed mental models* kinds of conflicting knowledge are "inaccurate," whereas *category mistakes* and *missing schemas* kinds of conflicting knowledge are "incommensurate." Although our framework does not necessarily commit to any notions of hierarchy in the grain sizes of these representations, what is critical is our proposal that the grain size at which conflict is defined (between incorrect knowledge and the to-be-learned correct material) determines how instruction should be designed to change misconceptions.

Using these four different representational formats, we examine the key questions of: In what ways do students' naïve ideas conflict with the to-be-learned materials, the ease with which such conflicting knowledge can be changed, and the type of instruction or confrontation that might trigger conceptual change. In the discussion below, our examples will be drawn primarily from science domains for three reasons. First, it is relatively easy to agree on what is considered correct or normative scientific information, and thus to contrast it with misconceived knowledge, which, by definition, implies prior knowledge that is incorrect as compared to some normative or scientifically based information. Second, misconceptions historically were recognized largely in science domains. Third, we draw our examples from science domains for which we have some data, primarily taken from concepts such as the human circulatory system and diffusion. For the headings of the three sections below, the first segment serves as a label for how knowledge is misconceived, the second segment describes the kind of conceptual change that can occur, and the third segment refers to the kind of confrontation and/or instruction that may produce conceptual change.

FALSE BELIEFS: BELIEF REVISION FROM REFUTATION

Students' naive knowledge can be represented at the grain size of a single idea, corresponding more or less to information specified in a single sentence or statement. We will refer to single ideas as "beliefs," and, when they are incorrect, as *false beliefs*. With respect to the human circulatory system, false beliefs might be knowing that "the *heart* is responsible for re-oxygenating blood" or that "*all* blood vessels have valves." Such false beliefs are incorrect because it is the *lungs* that are responsible for oxygenating blood and only *veins* but not arteries have valves (Chi, de Leeuw, Chiu, & LaVancher, 1994; Chi & Roscoe, 2002). So in what sense do these false beliefs conflict with correct information? One can think of understanding a system (such as the circulatory system) as forming a complete schema or mental model with slots (or dimensions) and features/values for each slot/dimension, such as that there is an organ (or an agent) that is responsible for oxygenation. That is, *having an agent as the cause* of oxygenation is the dimension, and the specific *organ* is the property on that dimension. Thus, the false belief that "the *heart* is responsible for re-oxygenating blood" is compatible with the dimension of having an organ as the responsible agent. Therefore, the naïve belief about the *heart* as the responsible agent is simply *false* on the same dimension, in the sense that it is *inaccurate* or *contradictory*. The correct knowledge is that it is the *lungs* and not the *heart* that oxygenate blood.

If false beliefs and correct information contradict each other on the same dimension, then one would expect that designing instruction that is targeted at *refuting* false beliefs might succeed at correcting them, resulting in *belief revision*. It appears that this is true (Broughton, Sinatra, & Reynolds, 2007; Guzzetti, Snyder, Glass, & Gamas, 1993). That is, false beliefs for some topics can be corrected when learners are explicitly confronted with the correct information by direct contradiction or explicit refutation, and even implicit refutation. Direct refutation would be saying something in the text such as, *The heart does not oxygenate blood*, and implicit refutation may simply be not mentioning *the heart* as oxygenating blood, and only mentioning *the lungs* as oxygenating blood. We have reported evidence obtained by de Leeuw (in Chi & Roscoe, 2002) for the success of both explicit and implicit types of refutations. The successful outcome of refutation can be called belief revision (see column 1, Figure 3.1).

However, there are many other incorrect beliefs in other domains that are not so readily revised by refutation, even though they can be stated at the grain size of a single idea. Consider, for example, conflicting beliefs such as *a thrown object acquires or contains some internal force* or *coldness from the ice flows into the water, making the water colder*. Although students can readily learn by adding new beliefs about "internal force," such as the equation for its relation to mass and acceleration, the definition of acceleration, and so on, these newly added beliefs cannot correct a student's conflicting belief that *a thrown object acquires or contains some internal force*. Moreover, such conflicting beliefs cannot be easily denied or refuted by contradiction. For example, stating that "a thrown object does not acquire or contain internal forces," or stating that "a thrown object contains some other kind of forces" will not succeed in helping students achieve correct understanding because these two examples of refutation contradict the conflicting beliefs on the same dimension, whereas the conflicting belief is incorrect in that it should not have that dimension at all; that is, the incorrect dimension and the correct dimension are *incommensurate*. That is, it does not make sense to talk about an object as containing or not containing forces because forces cannot be contained in objects. Thus, some

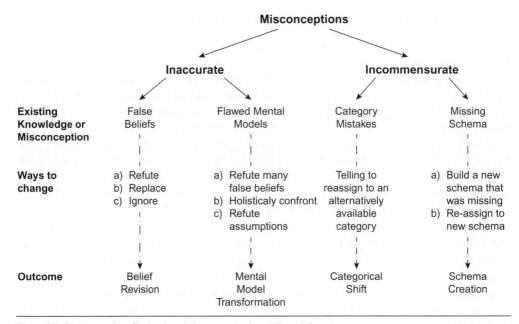

Figure 3.1 Four types of conflicting knowledge, ways to change it, and the outcome

conflicting beliefs are not incorrect in the *false* or *inaccurate* sense, therefore they cannot be explicitly or implicitly refuted. Rather, they are incorrect in the *incommensurate* sense, to be addressed in a later section below.

FLAWED MENTAL MODELS: MENTAL MODEL TRANSFORMATION FROM ACCUMULATION OF BELIEF REVISIONS

An organized collection of individual beliefs can be viewed as forming a mental model. A mental model is an internal representation of a concept (such as the *earth*), or an interrelated system of concepts (such as the *circulatory system*) that corresponds in some way to the external structure that it represents (Gentner & Stevens, 1983). Mental models can be "run" mentally, much like an animated simulation, to depict changes and generate predictions and outcomes, such as the direction of blood flow. A mental model can also have some underlying assumptions, in much the same way that an external model can.

A mental model can be so sparse and incomplete that learning would begin by *adding* and *filling-in gaps* in knowledge. However, adding and gap-filling a mental model would not constitute conceptual change. Therefore, in what other ways can mental models be incorrect so that learning is the conceptual change kind and not merely the enriching kind? Mental models can conflict with the normative correct model in being *flawed*. We define *flawed* to mean that the core assumptions of the *flawed model* are not only incorrect but also *coherent* in that they do not contradict each other, even though they may contradict the assumptions of the correct model. Moreover, students can use their naïve but coherent *flawed* mental model to offer similar and consistently incorrect explanations and predictions in response to a variety of questions. Thus, a *flawed mental model* is an incorrect naïve model that has *coherence* among its assumptions and *consistency* in its predictions and explanations.

We can capture the structure of a student's flawed mental model by examining the pattern and consistency of the generated explanations and predictions (Chi, 2000; Chi, Slotta, & de Leeuw, 1994; Vosniadou & Brewer, 1992, 1994). The accuracy of the flawed mental model can be further validated by predicting and testing how that student will respond to additional questions. For example, about half of the participants in our studies had an initial "single-loop" model of the human circulatory system. According to this flawed model, blood goes to the heart to be oxygenated, then it is pumped to the rest of the body, then back to the heart. (In contrast, the correct "double-loop" model has two paths. One path leads from the heart to the lungs, where blood is oxygenated before returning to the heart. The second path leads from the heart to the rest of the body and back to the heart.) In order to confirm that our assessment of the flawed single-loop model is accurate, we can design additional questions to see if students will respond as expected, on the basis of the single-loop model.

In what way does a flawed single-loop model conflict with the correct double-loop model? We propose that the flawed model conflicts with the correct model in that their core underlying assumptions contradict each other. For example, the three fundamental assumptions underlying a flawed single-loop model are that it is the *heart* that oxygenates blood, therefore there is only *one loop*, and that lungs serve no special purpose other than as a *destination* to which blood has to deliver oxygen. In contrast, the correct double-loop model holds three contradictory assumptions, that it is the *lungs* that oxygenate blood, that there are *two loops*, and that lungs play an important role as the *site of oxygenation*.

These different core assumptions result in different predictions about where blood goes after it leaves the heart, different explanations with respect to where blood is oxygenated, and different elements in terms of whether or not lungs play an important role in oxygenation. Thus, in an alternative way to characterize the differences in the underlying assumptions of the two models, one could instead say that two models are "in conflict with" each other because they (a) make different predictions, (b) generate different explanations, and (c) use different elements in their explanations. Notice that these criteria of conflict – different predictions, different explanations containing different elements – are the ones mentioned by Carey (1985) as compatible with the notion of *incommensurate* from the philosophy of science. In our framework here, we propose that these two conflicting models are *not incommensurate* because their underlying assumptions contradict each other on the same dimensions, even though the different assumptions do generate different predictions, explanations, and elements. Instead, we would reserve the term *incommensurate* for knowledge that is "in conflict" either laterally or ontologically, to be discussed in a following section.

Likewise, Vosniadou and Brewer (1992) have shown that young children have flawed mental models of the earth, such as a flattened square disk model. Based on what children say, one could infer that the fundamental assumption underlying a flattened disk model is that the shape of the earth is flat and finite in size, therefore predictions from such a "flat earth" model would be that one should look down to see the earth and that there is an edge from which people can potentially fall off. In short, flawed mental models are *coherent* in the sense that their underlying assumptions do not contradict each other, and *consistent* in that students retrieve and use them repeatedly to answer questions and make predictions, allowing researchers to capture the structure of their mental models by analyzing the systematicity in the pattern of their responses (see also McCloskey, 1983; Samarapungavan & Wiers, 1997; Vosniadou & Brewer, 1992; Wiser,

1987). Thus, a flawed mental model is "in conflict" with the correct model in the sense that the two models hold different assumptions, thus generating different predictions and explanations.

We refer to successful modification of a flawed mental model as mental model *transformation*. But how should we design instruction to induce mental model transformation? There are three ways. First, one could refute many false beliefs in the same way one would refute a single false belief, as discussed in the previous section. Cumulatively, the many belief revisions can change the flawed model to the correct model. A second method is to confront the naïve flawed model holistically. And a third method might be to refute the basic assumptions. There is scant evidence supporting these instructional approaches and they are briefly described next.

Accumulation of Many Individual Belief Revisions

Although we have described conflicting mental models at the mental-model level (such as a flat earth vs. a spherical earth and a single-loop vs. a double-loop), traditional instruction typically consists of a description of the correct model one sentence at a time, ignoring what individual students' flawed models are. This means that a learner's flawed model is confronted with a description of the correct model presented one sentence at a time, such that each sentence can either refute (explicitly or implicitly) an existing belief or not, as discussed in the preceding section on belief revision.

From the perspective of a mental model, there are two possible outcomes when instruction is presented sentence-by-sentence. In the first case, information presented in a given sentence or sentences may not refute (explicitly or implicitly) any of the learner's prior beliefs. Instead, the information might be new or more elaborate than what the learner knows. In such a case, the learner can assimilate by embedding or adding the new information from the sentences into her existing flawed model, so that her mental model is enriched, but continues to be flawed. For example, in the case of a single-loop flawed model, learners assume that blood from the heart goes to the rest of the body to deliver oxygen. Such models lack the idea that blood also goes to the lungs, not to deliver oxygen but to receive oxygen. Upon reading a sentence such as "The right side [of the heart] pumps blood to the lungs and the left side pumps blood to other parts of the body," students with a single-loop model may not find it to contradict any beliefs in their flawed single-loop model, since they interpret the sentence to mean that the right side pumps blood to the lungs to deliver oxygen (rather than to receive oxygen), just as it does to the rest of the body. Therefore, even though at the mental-model level, the sentence conflicts with the learner's flawed model, at the belief level, the sentence does not directly contradict the learner's prior beliefs. Thus the learner does not perceive a conflict, and the new information is assimilated into the flawed model (Chi, 2000). In short, assimilation of new information occurs when a learner does not perceive a conflict at the belief level, even though from the researcher's perspective, the new information is in conflict with the learner's flawed mental model.

The second possible outcome of sentence-by-sentence instruction is that new information presented does refute a learner's false beliefs and the learner recognizes the contradiction. Under such circumstances, as described in the preceding section, false beliefs that are explicitly or implicitly refuted (or ignored) do predominantly get revised (de Leeuw, 1993). The relevant question with respect to mental models is: Does the accumulation of numerous belief revisions eventually result in the transformation of a student's flawed mental model to the correct model? The answer is yes, by and large.

According to our data, by reading and self-explaining a text passage about the human circulatory system, five of eight students (62.5%) with a prior flawed single-loop model transformed their flawed models to the correct model. Similarly, in Vosniadou and Brewer's (1992) data, 12 of 20 children (60%) developmentally acquired the correct spherical model of the earth by the fifth grade, suggesting that their flawed mental models had undergone transformation. In short, again, for domains such as the circulatory system and the earth, coherently flawed mental models can be successfully corrected and transformed into the correct model, in over 60% of the population, with either relatively brief instruction from text (in the case of the circulatory system) or from general development and learning in school (in the case of the earth). Thus, conceptual change can be achieved in that conflicting flawed mental models can be transformed into the correct model when false beliefs within a flawed model are refuted by instruction and recognized by students as contradictions, so that the students can self-repair their flawed mental models (Chi, 2000) by revising their individual false beliefs.

Holistic Confrontation

Since flawed models and the correct model conflict at the mental-model level (flat earth vs. spherical earth; single-loop vs. double-loop), an instructional method based on holistic confrontation may induce successful model transformation. One way to design a holistic confrontation is to have students examine a visual depiction (e.g., a diagram) of their own flawed mental model, then compare and contrast it with a diagram of the correct model. We conducted a study using holistic confrontation in the following way. We pre-selected college students who had a flawed single-loop model of the circulatory system. Prior to reading a text passage about the circulatory system, we had them compare and contrast a diagram of the flawed single-loop model, which they agreed was their model, with the diagram of the correct double-loop model. We compared their learning gains with a control group who self-explained a diagram of the correct double-loop model only. We found the compare-and-contrast group to learn more than the self-explain group (Gadgil, Nokes, & Chi, 2011). So holistic confrontation might be a feasible way to achieve mental model transformation.

Refuting the Underlying Core Assumptions

A third method to transform a flawed mental model might be to refute the underlying assumptions. Although a flawed mental model is composed of many correct and many false beliefs, it appears that the core assumptions are the most critical in determining the extent to which a model is flawed. For example, across the various studies for which we have assessed students' initial mental models of the circulatory system, we found 22 students (about 50%) to have the flawed single-loop model prior to instruction. The number of correct beliefs held by these 22 students varied widely, ranging from five to 35. For example, five students held between 10 and 15 correct beliefs, and four students held between 25 and 35 correct beliefs, yet the false beliefs are all embedded within the flawed single-loop model (see Figure 2 in Chi & Roscoe, 2002). This variability suggests that knowing and learning many correct beliefs does not guarantee successful transformation of a flawed mental model to the correct model, unless the false assumptions are revised. We know of no study that has attempted to refute the underlying assumptions directly. However, we do know that when the core assumptions are not refuted, then mental model transformation is not successful. For example, when young children are told that the earth is round, they then think that the earth is round and flat like a pancake. Thus, such instruction does not violate their core assumption that the earth is flat, therefore their revised mental model continues to be flawed (Vosniadou & Brewer, 1992).

To recap, students' knowledge can consist of an interrelated system of false beliefs and correct beliefs, forming a flawed mental model. A flawed mental model can be said to conflict with a normative model if it is incorrect but coherent, in the sense that the underlying assumptions do not contradict each other, and the model consistently leads to incorrect predictions and explanations and contains elements different from the elements of a correct model. During instruction, when a specific sentence contradicts a false belief through explicit or implicit refutation, the accumulation of multiple belief revisions through refutations can lead eventually to a transformation of a flawed mental model to the correct model for over 60% of the students, either through direct instruction (in the case of the circulatory system) or from exposure to everyday experiences (as perhaps in the case of the earth). There may be other ways to design instruction, such as through holistic confrontation, or direct refutation of the underlying assumptions, that may encourage revision and reduce the likelihood of assimilation or adding to a flawed model, so that successful transformation can be achieved by all students. These ideas are shown in column 2 of Figure 3.1.

CATEGORY MISTAKES: CATEGORICAL SHIFT FROM AWARENESS AND AVAILABLE KNOWLEDGE

The preceding sections described two types of conflicting knowledge for which conceptual change can be achieved relatively successfully, mainly because conflicting knowledge, as *false beliefs* and *flawed mental models*, is incorrect in being *inaccurate*. For these two types of conflicting knowledge, the incorrectness is a matter of *inaccurate* values on some appropriate dimensions or properties. Thus, refutations that contradict the values were successful at achieving conceptual change.

However, we have also mentioned above that there are numerous *false beliefs* about concepts such as *force-and-motion* or *heat-and-temperature* across a variety of domains for which conceptual change cannot be achieved. The robustness of such misconceptions has been demonstrated in literally thousands of studies, about all kinds of science concepts and phenomena, beginning with a book by Novak (1977) and a review by Driver and Easley (1978), both published over three decades ago. By 2008, there were over 8,000 publications describing students' incorrect ideas and instructional attempts to change them (Confrey, 1990; Driver, Squires, Rushworth, & Wood-Robinson, 1994; Duit, 2008; Ram, Nersessian, & Keil, 1997), indicating that conceptual understanding in the presence of misconceptions remains a challenging problem. We propose the operational definition that certain misconceptions are robust and difficult to change because they have been mistakenly assigned to an inappropriate "lateral" category.

By a "lateral" category, we mean a category that is not hierarchically related to the category to which the concept belongs; instead it is parallel to the category to which the concept belongs. For example, *artifacts* can be considered a lateral category more or less "parallel" to *living beings*. *Artifacts* does not include the sub-categories of *living beings*, such as *animals*, *reptiles*, or *robins*. Instead, *artifacts* includes a different set of sub-categories, such as *furniture* and *toys*, and *furniture* includes sub-categories such as *tables* and *chairs* (see Figure 3.2). In short, *artifacts* and *living beings* can be thought of as occupying different branches of the same hierarchical tree (Thagard, 1990), in this case the *Entities* tree. We will refer to categories on different branches as "lateral" (vs. "hierarchical") categories, and when lateral categories occur at about the same level within a tree, we will refer to them as "parallel."

Although *artifacts* and *living beings* can both be sub-sumed under the higher-level category of *objects* and therefore share many higher-level dimensions of *objects* such as "having shape" and "can be thrown," *artifacts* and *living beings* do have distinct and mutually exclusive dimensions as well. For example, *living beings* have the capacity to "move on their own volition," be "responsive," and "capable of reproducing," whereas *artifacts* cannot.

Lateral categories can sometimes be referred to as ontologically distinct, in that they conflict by definition in *kind* and/or *ontology*. This means that conceptual change requires a shift across lateral or ontological categories. In order to support this claim that robust misconception is miscategorization across lateral/ontological categories, we have to characterize the nature of misconceptions and the nature of correct information to see whether they in fact belong to two categories that differ either in kind or in ontology, and thereby are "in conflict."

The Lateral Categories to which Misconceptions and Correct Scientific Conceptions are Assigned

In order to characterize the nature of robust science misconceptions in terms of the category to which they have been mistakenly assigned, and also to characterize the nature of scientific conceptions in terms of the category to which they should be assigned, we analyzed students' misconceptions for a variety of science concepts, consolidated researchers' findings on misconceptions, and examined the history and philosophy of science literature, to induce the properties of both the mistaken category and the correct category. The two broad conflicting categories appear to be *Entities* (the misconceived view) and *Processes* (the correct view).

How are Entity-based misconceptions in conflict with scientific conceptions? Our initial conjecture was that scientists view many of these concepts as *Processes* rather than *Entities*. *Processes* can be conceived of as an ontological tree distinct from *Entities*, verifiable by the predicate test indicating the inappropriateness of some dimensions (see Figure 3.2). For example, *heat* or the sensation of "hotness" is the speed at which molecules jostle: the higher the speed, the "hotter" the molecules feel. Thus, heat is not "hot molecules" or "hot stuff" (an *Entity*), but more accurately, the speed of molecules (a *Process*).

Entities are *objects* or *substances* that have various attributes and behave in various ways (see Figure 3.2, the *Entities* tree). For example, a ball is a physical *object* with attributes such as mass, volume, shape, and behaviors such as bouncing and rolling. On the basis of our analyses across four science concepts – force, heat, electricity, and light – we arrived at the commonality that students mistakenly categorize these concepts as *Entities*

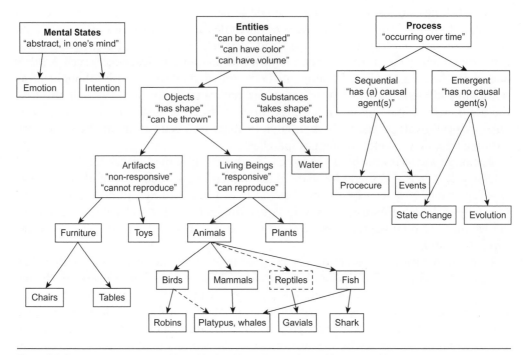

Figure 3.2 Distinct ontological trees: hierarchical and lateral categories within a tree and between trees

(Reiner, Slotta, Chi, & Resnick, 2000). For example, many students view force as a *substance* kind of *Entity* that can be possessed, transferred, and dissipated. Students often explain that a moving *object* slows down because it has "used up all its force" (McCloskey, 1983), as if force were like a fuel that is consumed. Similarly, students think of heat as physical *objects* such as "hot molecules" or a material *substance* such as "hot stuff" or "hotness" (Wiser & Amin, 2001), as indicated by phrases such as "molecules of heat" or expressions such as "Close the door, you're letting all the heat out." The misconception is that heat can be "contained," as if it were *objects* like marbles or *substances* like sand or water. In either case, heat is misconceived as a kind of *Entity*.

Misconceiving a concept such as *force* or *heat* as a kind of *substance or Entity* is serious because *Entities* and *Processes* essentially share no common dimensions. *Entities* have dimensions such as "can be contained," "can have color," and "can have volume," while *Processes* have dimensions such as "occurring over time." Thus, no *Process*, whether it's an *event* such as a baseball game, a *procedure* such as baking a cake, or a *state change* such as melting, can have the dimensions of "having volume," "having color," or "can be contained," whereas no *Entity*, such as a cake or a ball, can have the dimension of "having certain duration," such as lasting two hours. (Of course, while *Entities* don't occur through time, the *Process* of living for *living beings* can have duration.) Thus, each tree might be considered an "ontology," (and its name will be capitalized) in that the trees have mutually exclusive dimensions. This is the definition of ontology used in this framework. Generally, philosophers use the term "ontology" to refer to a system of taxonomic categories for certain existences in the world (Sommers, 1971). However, in this chapter, we will refer to categories that occupy different trees as different "ontologically" (Chi, 1997, 2005), and categories that occupy parallel branches within a tree as different "laterally" or in "kind" (Gelman, 1988; Schwartz, 1977). Unlike categories on different trees, parallel categories within a tree do share overlapping dimensions (for example, the parallel categories *artifacts* and *living beings* share the dimensions of *objects*, such as "having shape" and "can be thrown" – see Figure 3.2 again).

We claim that this is why some misconceptions are so robust – because the naïve conceptions are miscategorized into an ontologically distinct tree. Such Entity-based misconceptions not only occur for a variety of concepts across a variety of disciplines, but they are held across grade levels, from elementary to college students (Chi et al., 1994), as well as across historical periods (Chi, 1992). They may even account for barriers that were only overcome by scientific discoveries (Chi & Hausmann, 2003). In short, robust misconceptions of the ontologically miscategorized kind are extremely resistant to change, so that everyday experiences encountered during developmental maturation and formal schooling seem powerless to change them, even when students are confronted with their misconception. (This is in contrast to the greater success with which flawed mental models can be transformed from everyday experiences or formal schooling, as described above.)

Telling Students to Shift Categories

How can instruction facilitate shifts across lateral or ontological categories? If misconceptions occur as the result of category mistakes, then instruction needs to focus at the categorical level. When students' misconceived ideas conflict with correct ideas at the lateral category level, then refutation at the belief level will not promote conceptual change. This is because refutation at the belief level can only cause local revisions of the features/attributes/values of certain dimensions, whereas conceptual change of category mistakes requires changing the dimensions, which may require a categorical shift. Consider the misconception that "coldness from the ice flows into the water, making the water colder." Essentially, this misconception assumes that ice contains some "cold substance" like tiny cold molecules (the reverse of hot objects, which are often misconceived as containing "hot molecules"), and that this "cold substance" can flow into the surrounding water, which then makes the water colder. We cannot treat this misconception as a *false belief* and refute it by pointing out that *ice does not contain a cold substance*, that *coldness does not flow*, or that *water does not get colder because it gains coldness*. Refutation only works when a false belief and the correct conception contradict each other on the same dimension. So how can a misconception like "ice contains cold substances" be changed, then? Should a student expect ice to contain an alternative kind of substance if not a "cold" substance? According to our theoretical framework, the change that a student must make has to do with refuting the dimension of "being containable," not changing the feature of "coldness" or any other kind of sensation or substance. To change the dimension "containable" means that students have to be confronted at the ontological/categorical level, since "containable" is a dimension of *Entities*, and not a dimension of *Processes*. Thus, we propose that, in order to achieve radical conceptual change, we need students to make a category shift by reassigning a concept to an alternative lateral category so that a concept can inherit the dimensions of this alternative category. To achieve such reassignment, we need to confront students at the categorical level.

Conceptually, the idea of shifting across or reassigning a concept from one lateral/ontological category to another seems, in principle, to be straightforward and easily achievable, if students were told to shift. Let's consider the example of a *whale*. Suppose a young child sees a whale in the ocean and believes it to be a kind of *fish*, since whales possess many perceptual features of a *fish*, such as looking like sharks and swimming in water. Based on that mistaken categorization, the child will likely assume that whales, like other *fish*, breathe through gills by osmosis (a conceptual attribute). To promote conceptual change, we can just tell the child that a whale is a *mammal* (essentially telling the child to re-categorize or reassign *whale* to the correct category *mammals*), perhaps along with providing justification, such as pointing out that whales do not breathe through gills, but through a blowhole. The fact that most children eventually learn that whales are *mammals* suggests that lateral categorical shifts can occur readily for some misconceptions. This case of reassigning category by telling is shown in the third column of Figure 3.1.

But why is categorical shift not easily achieved for robust misconceptions for *Processes* such as *heat* and *force*? A closer examination of the relative ease of categorical shift for the *whale* example suggests that two conditions are needed in order to overcome barriers to conceptual change for robust misconceptions. First, students have to be made aware that they have made a category mistake, which requires that their ideas be confronted at the categorical level; and second, students must be knowledgeable about the correct category to which a concept actually belongs. If these two conditions are met, then conceptual change can be made with success even if it requires categorical shifts. We briefly discuss these two conditions below.

Lack of Awareness

We propose that part of the difficulty of shifting categories for many science concepts has to do with a lack of awareness, in that students do not realize that they have to shift their assignment of a concept to a different category. This is because reassigning a phenomenon or concept from one kind to another kind is rare in everyday life. That is, students do not routinely need to re-categorize, such as shifting a whale from *fish* to *mammal*, since, in our everyday environment, our initial categorizations are mostly correct. Occasionally, we might over-generalize and categorize at a higher superordinate category, but over-generalization is not incorrect and does not require conceptual change. For example, when we identify a furry object with a wagging tail that responds to our commands as a live dog (thus *a living being*), we are almost never wrong, in the sense that we might mistakenly identify it as a stuffed dog (thus an *artifact*). The fact that these category mistakes rarely occur in real life makes it difficult for learners to recognize that the source of their misunderstanding of new concepts originates from a category mistake. As with metaphors, the rarity of category mistakes is a ploy that is sometimes used in stories and films, to produce interest drama, and suspense, such as in the children's novel *Velveteen Rabbit*. Moreover, if people do make category mistakes, especially across ontological trees, such as confusing reality (either *Entities* or *Processes*) with imagination (*Mental States*), it is considered bizarre and perhaps a sign of psychological illness.

The rarity of category mistakes in real life is also consistent with findings showing the strength of commitment to the original category to which a concept is assigned, as well as to the boundary between lateral categories (Carey, 1985; Chi, 1988). The commitment to a particular category occurs even as early as age five. For example, once a concept is categorized, young children are extremely reluctant to change the category to which it is assigned. Keil's work (1989) has shown that, no matter what physical alterations are made to an object (e.g., a live dog), such as shaving off its fur or replacing its tail, five-year-olds will not accept such changes as capable of transforming a live dog to a toy dog (thus crossing the boundary between lateral categories *living beings* and *artifacts*). However, they will agree that, with appropriate alterations such as replacing black fur with brown fur, one can transform a skunk into a raccoon. This is because skunks and raccoons belong to the same *mammal* category. Thus, once assigned, even five-year-olds honor the boundary between kinds and remain committed to the category to which they have assigned a concept.

In short, shifting across lateral categories *per se* is not a difficult learning mechanism from a computational perspective and from everyday evidence, as illustrated by the *whale* example above and by the ease with which people can understand metaphors. Metaphors often invoke a predicate or dimension from one category and a concept from a lateral category, often from different ontological trees. For instance, *anger* (an *emotional Mental State*) is often treated as a *substance* (an *Entity*) that can be contained, as in "He let out his anger" or "I can barely contain my rage" (Lakoff, 1987). Thus, once students are made aware that they have committed category mistakes, shifting across categories can be undertaken readily when students are told or instructed to do so, as in the *whale* example, or when adults intentionally use metaphors by borrowing properties and values from a dimension of a lateral category.

Knowledge of Alternative Category Available

However, we propose that category mistakes are readily changed primarily when the alternative category is available to the learner who is shifting. Thus, this is the second condition that must be met in order for such category shifts to occur readily when instruction merely tells the students to shift. This type of misconception and ways of changing it are shown in the third column of Figure 3.1. When the alternative category is not available, then misconceptions are tenacious, as explained below.

MISSING SCHEMAS: CREATING THE MISSING ALTERNATIVE SCHEMA

In the preceding section, we proposed that category mistakes, those misconceptions that have been incorrectly assigned to a lateral category, can be changed when students are made aware of the need to shift, and if they know about the alternative category. This section explains why some misconceptions are so tenaciously robust and resistant to change, primarily as caused not only by students' lack of awareness for the need to change, but most importantly, because they have no knowledge of the alternative category to which a concept belongs. Because we will be addressing more complicated concepts of processes, we will refer to the alternative category as a *schema*. We begin with an example of failure to transform a flawed mental model successfully, illustrating succinctly what tenacious misconceptions mean, and how they are persistent and resistant to change.

Tenacious Misconception: An Example

Law and Ogborn (1988) carried out a study in which students were asked to use Prolog to design and build a computational model of their own understanding of force and motion. The Prolog programming required students to express their ideas in propositional rule-based statements, which we can consider to be analogous to beliefs. Building and running such a model forced students to externalize and formalize their ideas, making them explicit, explorable, and capable of offering explanations. Students assessed their models by running their programs, then made modifications based on program results or feedback from their instructor. Since programs could be run, allowing students to make predictions and observe outcomes, we can consider such a program to be analogous to an externalized mental model.

As with our circulatory system data, only some students had clear structural frameworks based on a core set of hypotheses about various aspects of motion that the researchers could identify. We can consider these students as having flawed mental models in that their underlying hypotheses are coherent and consistent. Other students had no clear conceptualization, and these students can be deemed to have sparse and incomplete models. For students with flawed but coherent mental models, the question is, can they change their flawed mental model? One way to determine whether they change their mental models is to see whether they change their implicit core hypotheses. One student's set of core hypotheses about force-and-motion is shown below. These hypotheses (for example, hypothesis b that *Force is an entity*), can be inferred from their rules (to be described below), and are compatible with various other analyses of students' misconceptions about force and motion in the literature (e.g., Reiner et al., 2000):

a. Force is the deciding factor in determining all aspects of motion;
b. Force is an entity that can be possessed, transferred, and dissipated;
c. All motions need causes;
d. Agents cause and control motion by acting as sources that supply force;
e. Sources that supply force can be internal or external, and the supplied force is referred to as an internal or external force;
f. Weight is an intrinsic property of an object (even though gravity is conceptualized as an external factor that pulls harder on heavier objects).

The advantage of the Prolog programming environment is that it allowed students to explore the consequences of their externalized beliefs or rules. For example, one student who held the core hypothesis d, that there is a source that supplies the force for every motion, wrote the following Prolog rules for determining the cause of motion:

1. object motion-caused-by itself if _object force-supplied-by _object
2. object motion-caused-by machine if _object force-supplied-by machine
3. object1 motion-caused-by _object2 if _object1 force-supplied-by _object2
4. object motion-caused-by gravity if not (_object under-the-influence-of other-external- force).

She then tested her program for the cause of a falling apple, expecting the computer to say that the motion was caused by gravity (her fourth rule). The reason was that in one of her earlier sessions, she included weight as an external supply of force, along with other forces such as friction and air current. The program's outcome can be thought of as providing explicit refutation or confrontation of her fourth rule.

When she did not get the result she expected, she modified her fourth rule by excluding gravity as an external force. After this patching, the computer still did not give her the expected answer of gravity as a cause of the apple's fall, since anything placed in air would be affected by air current, since air current is an external force. She then revised her fourth rule again to read: _object motion-caused by gravity if not (_object motion-caused-by _something). Her problems continued even after various patchings of her other rules.

This example illustrates clearly the point that, despite numerous revisions of this student's rules in response to refutations from the outcome of the Prolog program, the revisions and the accumulation of multiple revisions to her rules did not transform her flawed mental model into a correct model, because the underlying core hypotheses of her program were not changed. That is, she still assumed that *all motions need causes* (hypothesis c), that *agents cause and control motion by acting as sources that supply force* (hypothesis d), and so forth. What she did change was the value or attribute on the same dimensions, such as changing the agent that was responsible for supplying force. Thus, even though the rules are at the same grain size as a statement of *false belief*, and the set of rules is comparable to the grain size of a *flawed mental model*, clearly these misconceptions cannot be considered *false beliefs* and *flawed mental models*, because their incorrectness is not on the same dimensions, and they cannot be changed by using a refutation method.

As this example also illustrates, the student was not resistant to change *per se*, since she readily revised her rules, but the multiple belief revisions she undertook did not add up to a correct model transformation since the revisions did not change her underlying core hypotheses themselves, but only the values of the hypothesized dimensions. There are occasions, of course, when students themselves resist making changes by dismissing the feedback or explaining it away. The point here is that, even with the best of intentions and willingness to change, this student could not transform her misconceived view.

In short, there are many concepts like force and motion, for which one's initial flawed mental model is not transformed to the correct model despite repeated corrections or patchings of the underlying rules, because it is the dimensions of the flawed model themselves that need to be changed. Even though the student willingly modified individual rules (corresponding to false beliefs) as a result of external feedback (or explicit refutation from the program's outcomes), the revised rules did not transform the flawed mental model into the correct model, because the implicit underlying core hypotheses were still incorrect from a dimension perspective. Thus, the flawed model was resistant to change. What should we conclude? This suggests that some misconceptions are extremely tenacious only because their refutations occurred at the value level, and not at the dimension level.

Conflict between a Misconceived Schema and a Missing Schema

Findings of tenacious misconceptions, similar to the Law and Ogborn's (1988) study, have been documented for several decades, in that the misconceptions not only are "in conflict" with the correct scientific conceptions but, moreover, they are almost never revised, so conceptual change is not achieved. Although we were able to explain a good deal of robust misconceptions as *category mistakes* involving the ontological trees *Entities* and *Processes* (Chi, 1997), our explanation for the tenaciousness of many misconceptions was incomplete. Regardless of whether or not students conceive of heat as an *Entity*, most students nevertheless do recognize that *heat transfer* is a *Process* because they have experienced the apparent movement of "hotness" from one location to another, for example from a warm cup to cold hands. Thus, characterizing heat misconceptions merely as *Entity*-based does not adequately explain why students have difficulty understanding *heat transfer*, even though they know *heat transfer* is a *Process*.

To explain the latter kind of misconceptions, we had to propose conflicts between two additional kinds of lateral categories within the *Process* tree, which we have called *sequential* and *emergent* (Chi, 2005). Our claim is that students misconceive of some processes as the *sequential* kind when in fact they are the *emergent* kind. *Sequential* processes require a *direct* kind of causal explanation, whereas *emergent* processes require an *emergent* kind of causal explanation.

Briefly, the most explicit distinction between a *sequential* kind of process and an *emergent* kind is that a *sequential* process usually has an identifiable agent that causes some outcome or displayed pattern in a more direct (or indirect) way (indirect means mediated by an intermediate agent or event), whereas an *emergent* kind of process has no identifiable agent that directly (or indirectly) causes the displayed pattern. We will describe an everyday example, a less familiar example, and a scientific example, for each kind of process, highlighting with each example properties of *emergent* and *sequential* processes, as listed in Table 3.1 and Table 3.2. The properties in Table 3.1 and Table 3.2 are different in the following way. Table 3.1 lists the attributes characterizing the inter-level causal explanations of the relationships between the behavior/interactions of the agents and the pattern displayed at the macro level. Table 3.2 lists the "second-order interaction features" characterizing some agents' interactions relative to other agents' interactions. More detailed descriptions can be found in Chi, Roscoe, Slotta, Roy, and Chase (2012).

Table 3.1 Five attributes characterizing the inter-level causal explanations relating the agents' interactions (at the micro level) and the pattern (at the macro level) for emergent and sequential processes

Emergent causal explanations for emergent processes	Direct causal explanations for sequential processes
1. The entire collection or all the agents together "cause" the observable global pattern	1. A single agent or a sub-group of agents can "cause" the global observable pattern
2. All agents have equal status with respect to the pattern	2. One or more agents have special status with respect to the pattern
3. Local events and the global pattern can behave in disjointed non-matching ways	3. Local events and the global pattern behave in a corresponding matched way
4. Agents interact to intentionally achieve local goals; ignorant of the global pattern	4. Some agents interact to intentionally achieve the global goal and direct their interactions at producing the global pattern
5. Mechanism producing the global pattern: proportional change (collective summing across time)	5. Mechanism producing the global pattern: incremental change (additive summing across time)

Sequential example 1. In the familiar process of a baseball game, the final outcome might be explained as being due to the excellent work of the pitcher, thus attributing the outcome directly to a single agent (Sequential attribute #1, Table 3.1), thus elevating this single agent with special status (Sequential attribute #2). Moreover, the behavior of local events within the game corresponds to or aligns with the global outcome. For example, a team with many home runs in a game is more likely to win. Thus, the more home runs align with the higher scores (Sequential attribute #3).

Sequential example 2. A slightly less familiar example is seeing multiple airplanes flying in a V-formation. This V-pattern is intentional, created by the lead pilot telling the other pilots where to fly in order to achieve the global goal (Sequential attribute #4).

Sequential example 3. A sequential process from biology is cell division, which proceeds through a sequence of three stages. The first, interphase, is a period of cell growth. This is followed by mitosis, the division of the cell nucleus, and then cytokinesis, the division of the cytoplasm of a parent cell into two daughter cells. In each phase, the cells behave in distinct ways, either growing or dividing (Sequential feature #1, Table 3.2). Such a process has a definite sequence, in which some events cannot occur until others are completed (Sequential features #3 & #4, Table 3.2).

In contrast, emergent processes have neither an identifiable causal agent or agents nor an identifiable sequence of stages. Rather, the outcome results from the collective and simultaneous interactions of all agents. Let's consider three examples here as well.

Emergent example 1. The process of a crowd forming a bottleneck, as when the school bell rings and students hurry to get through the narrow classroom door, is an everyday example of an emergent process. Although there is an external trigger (the school bell), the global outcome of forming a bottleneck cannot be attributed to any single agent or group of agents, and the process is not sequential. Instead, all the students (Emergent attribute #1, Table 3.1) simultaneously (Emergent feature #3) rush toward the door at about the same speed (Emergent feature #1), shoving and bumping randomly into whichever student happens to be in the way (Emergent feature #2). See Table 3.2.

Emergent example 2. A slightly less familiar example is migrating geese flying in a V-formation. In contrast to the airplane example, the V-pattern is not caused by the leader goose telling other geese where to fly. Instead, all the geese are doing the same thing, flying slightly behind another goose because instinctually they seek the area of least resistance.

Table 3.2 Five "second-order interaction features" characterizing the relationships between some agents' interactions relative to other agents' interactions

Interactions among agents in emergent processes	Interactions among agents in sequential processes
1. All agents behave in more or less the same uniform way	1. Agents behave in distinct ways
2. All agents interact randomly with other agents	2. Agents can interact with predetermined or restricted others
3. All agents interact simultaneously	3. Agents interact sequentially
4. All agents interact independently of one another	4. Agents' interactions depend on other agents' interactions
5. Interactions among agents are continuous	5. Agents' interactions terminate when the pattern-level behavior stops

Thus, they are pursuing the local goal of flying with minimal effort (Emergent attribute #4), ignorant of the pattern they form. When all the geese do the same thing at the same time, collectively, a V-pattern emerges (Emergent attributes #1, #2, and emergent features #1 and #3).

Emergent example 3. An emergent process from biology is the diffusion of oxygen from the lungs to the blood vessels. This process is caused by all the oxygen and carbon dioxide molecules moving and colliding randomly with and independently of each other (Emergent features #1, #2, #3, #4). From such random collisions, a greater number of oxygen molecules are likely to move from the lungs to the blood than from the blood to the lungs, simply because there are a greater number of them in the lungs than in the blood. The reverse is true for carbon dioxide molecules. Since all molecules interact by colliding randomly, both kinds of molecules move in both directions, so that some oxygen molecules do move from the blood to the lungs, and some carbon dioxide molecules do move from the lungs to the blood. Thus, the local movements of individual molecules may not match the direction of the movement of the majority of the molecules (Emergent attribute #3). Nevertheless, despite local variations, the majority of oxygen molecules end up moving from the lungs to the blood, and the majority of carbon dioxide molecules end up moving in the opposite direction, without any specific intention to move in that global direction (Emergent attribute #4).

The Source of Tenacious Misconceptions

We said above that to change at the lateral categorical level, one approach is to tell students directly to shift categorically. However, an intervention of direct telling would not work between the *sequential* process category and the *emergent* process category, because we assume that students have no knowledge of the emergent category or emergent schema. If students have no knowledge of an emergent category, how can instruction facilitate conceptual change? Two major steps are required. First, students must learn to differentiate the two kinds of processes, and second, students must build knowledge of an emergent schema. We elaborate these instructional challenges below.

Differentiating the Two Kinds of Processes

The preceding examples illustrate that many phenomena in science look and act like they belong to one category rather than another. For example, heat flowing into a cool room feels like water flowing down a stream. However, the causal explanations for the similar (heat and water) patterns are distinctly different. Thus, learners can be misled by perceptual similarities at the pattern level and treat such pairs of phenomena as having the same causal explanations, resulting in miscategorization of one but not the other. Therefore, students must be made aware of their miscategorization, and in addition, must learn to discriminate between the two kinds of phenomena and to generate a correct causal explanation for the behavior at the pattern level. In short, the lack of awareness of the need to shift categories laterally is due to the low frequency of such shifts in the real world and to superficial pattern-level similarities among many phenomena. As in the case of other category mistakes, instruction aimed at promoting such shifts must begin by making students aware that they have committed category mistakes. This requires that instruction help students overlook superficial perceptual similarities at the pattern level that cause students to misconceive two kinds of processes as the same kind when in fact they are different kinds requiring different kinds of causal explanations.

But how can instruction facilitate a discrimination of two different kinds of processes? An obvious answer might be to look at the agent level, and see how the interactions among the agents are different for the two processes. But can we discriminate *sequential* from *emergent* processes just by examining the way the agents interact? For example, with close scrutiny, the interactions of the molecules in the process of *heat transfer* do look slightly different from the interactions of the water molecules in the process of *water flowing* downstream. Water flowing downstream is a *sequential process*, caused by the water molecules in one area of the stream being pushed by molecules in the area above it, so that the molecules that are being pushed move downstream a little, and then push the molecules next to them to an even lower area, and so on. In contrast, the sensation of hotness moving from one area to another area (heat flowing) is not a *sequential* process in that the sensation of hotness moving is not caused by hot molecules moving from one location to another. Rather, heat flowing or transfer is caused by the collisions of faster jostling "hotter" molecules into slower-moving molecules. That is, when faster-moving molecules collide with slower-moving molecules, the collisions cause the faster-moving molecules to slow down (thus decreasing their hotness) and the slower-moving molecules to move faster (thus increasing their hotness). This is how hotness is transferred. Thus, heat transfer is an *emergent* process. See Figure 3.2 again.

Thus, *heat transfer* and *water flowing* do have different interaction mechanisms at the agent level. Unfortunately, differences in the interactions at the agent level do not, by themselves, distinguish between *sequential* and *emergent* processes, because interactions of many *emergent* processes can also differ among themselves (and the same is true for *sequential* processes). For example, the interactions of molecules in a *diffusion* process is one of random collisions, whereas the interactions of birds and moths in the process of *natural selection*, in which moths got darker over time in industrialized England, is one of birds eating moths. Thus, the two sets of interactions are quite different, even though both processes (*diffusion* and *natural selection*) are *emergent*. Thus, looking at the mechanism of the interactions *per se* cannot help students discriminate between *emergent* and *sequential* processes.

One solution to helping students discriminate between *sequential* and *emergent* processes, even though they look similar at the perceptual pattern level, is to point out second-order relational differences. For example, Table 3.2 lists "second-order interaction features" characterizing the relationships between some agents' interactions relative to other agents' interactions. By second-order, we mean the relational differences, comparing the nature of one interaction with another interaction. Feature #1 (in Table 3.2), for example, refers to the point that the interactions of two agents of a sequential process are different (or *distinct*) from the interactions of two other agents of the same process. In contrast, the interactions between two agents in an emergent process are the same (*uniform*) as the interactions of two other agents in the same process. Thus, even though the interacting mechanism of birds eating moths in the process of natural selection is different from the interacting mechanism of molecules colliding with each other in the process of diffusion, they share the same second-order feature of *uniformity*, meaning that all molecules interact in the same way, colliding with each other; and similarly, all birds and moths interact in the same way, being eaten or not being eaten by birds. Thus, these two processes can both be categorized as *emergent*. On the other hand, in the *sequential* baseball game example mentioned above, the interactions of some of the agents (let's say between the pitcher and the batter) are obviously different from the interaction between the pitcher and the catcher who stands behind the batter. Thus, the interactions among the agents in a sequential process are not uniform. In short, by looking at the second-order interaction features, one can discriminate a *sequential* process from an *emergent* process.

Creating the Missing Schema

In contrast to the whale example, in which it seemed relatively easy for children to shift categories simply by being told that whales are *mammals*, would science students find it easy to shift categories if we simply told them that *heat transfer* is an *emergent* rather than a *sequential* process? The answer is obviously no, because students are ignorant of ideas about emergence. Thus, we assume that the second challenge of changing tenacious misconceptions of the emergent kind is that an *emergent* process category is not familiar and available to students and therefore they cannot shift and use it to assimilate novel concepts. This missing schema situation is tractable and suggests an instructional approach of building such a schema. Thus, in the case of tenacious misconceptions, instruction to promote categorical shift must also include instruction to help students first build a schema about emergence. The term "schema" is more appropriate than the term "category" for describing knowledge of emergent processes because schema is a more encompassing term, including ways of generating causal explanations for under-standing emergent processes. Our prediction is that, to achieve successful conceptual change for tenaciously misconceived concepts and phenomena, we need to first teach students the properties of such an *emergent* schema, which is uniquely distinct from the *direct* schema for *sequential* processes, with which they are familiar and to which they have mistakenly assigned concepts. Once students have successfully built such an alternative schema with its distinct set of properties (as shown in Tables 3.1 and 3.2), they can begin to assimilate new instruction (for example, about *heat transfer*) into the category. Preliminary successes using this instructional method have been shown in Slotta and Chi (2006), and Chi et al. (2012). This intervention method is shown in the last column of Figure 3.1.

SUMMARY

This chapter addresses the problem of learning for which prior knowledge conflicts with the to-be-learned information. This kind of learning is considered the conceptual change kind rather than the enrichment kind. We propose that prior knowledge can conflict with to-be-learned information in two basic ways: Prior knowledge can be incorrect in contradicting correct information on the same dimension, or prior knowledge can be incorrect in the dimensions themselves. In the former case, conceptual change can be achieved by refutation (implicitly or explicitly), either at the belief level or at a mental model level; and at both levels, conceptual change can be successfully achieved. The success of these types of refutations for false belief and flawed mental models hinges on the assumption that the misconception and the correct conception are assigned into the same category or hierarchical categories, so that they share the same dimensions as defined by their categorical membership. Therefore, the incorrect prior knowledge conflicts in an *inaccurate* sense. However, in the latter case in which incorrect prior knowledge conflicts with correct knowledge in an *incommensurate* sense, in that the source of misconceptions arises from a mis-assignment between categories on lateral branches or ontological trees, conceptual change requires a categorical shift. Such a shift necessitates that the learner is aware that the shift is needed and that the correct category is available. For many tenacious misconceptions in science, the lateral category or schema to which misconceptions have to be reassigned, *emergent processes*, does not exist in students' knowledge base, so instruction has to build a new schema. Because *emergent* and *sequential* processes are different in kind, with mutually exclusive properties, confrontation needs to reject the mis-assigned *direct* schema for interpreting emergent processes, and build the alternative *emergent* schema, perhaps through direct instruction using contrasting cases. Of course, the original *direct* schema needs to remain, as it is important for understanding other sequential processes.

A preliminary attempt at helping students build the missing *emergent* schema is discussed in Chi et al. (2012). Thus, this chapter has provided a theoretical framework that offers definitions of four different ways that prior misconceived knowledge can conflict with correct knowledge, explained why some type of misconceptions are more robust than others, and prescribed various instructional intervention methods to remove misconceptions as a function of their specific type.

ACKNOWLEDGMENTS

The author is grateful for funding and support provided by the Spencer Foundation (Grant No. 200100305 and Grant No. 200800196) and comments from Dongchen Xu.

REFERENCES

Broughton, S. H., Sinatra, G. M., & Reynolds, R. E. (2007). *Refutation text effect: Influence on learning and attention.* Paper presented at the Annual Meeting of the American Educational Researchers Association, Chicago, IL.

Carey, S. (1985). *Conceptual change in childhood.* Cambridge, MA: MIT Press.

Carey, S. (1991). Knowledge acquisition: Enrichment or conceptual change? In S. Carey & R. Gelman (Eds.), *The epigenesis of mind* (pp. 257–291). Hillsdale: NJ: Lawrence Erlbaum Associates.

Chi, M. T. H. (1988). Children's lack of access and knowledge reorganization: An example from the concept of animism. In F. Weinert & M. Perlmutter (Eds.), *Memory development: Universal changes and individual differences* (pp. 169–194). Hillsdale, NJ: Lawrence Erlbaum Associates.

Chi, M. T. H. (1992). Conceptual change within and across ontological categories: Examples from learning and discovery in science. In R. Giere (Ed.), *Cognitive models of science: Minnesota Studies in the Philosophy of Science,* (pp. 129–186). Minneapolis, MN: University of Minnesota Press.

Chi, M. T. H. (1997). Creativity: Shifting across ontological categories flexibly. In T. B. Ward, S. M. Smith, & J. Vaid (Eds.), *Conceptual structures and processes: Emergence, discovery and change* (pp. 209–234). Washington, DC: American Psychological Association.

Chi, M. T. H. (2000). Cognitive understanding levels. In A. E. Kazdin (Ed.), *Encyclopedia of psychology* (Vol. 2, pp. 146–151). Washington, DC: American Psychological Association.

Chi, M. T. H. (2005). Common sense conceptions of emergent processes: Why some misconceptions are robust. *Journal of the Learning Sciences, 14,* 161–199.

Chi, M. T. H., de Leeuw, N., Chiu, M. H., & LaVancher, C. (1994). Eliciting self-explanations improves understanding. *Cognitive Science, 18,* 439–477.

Chi, M. T. H., & Hausmann, R. G. M. (2003). Do radical discoveries require ontological shifts? In L. V. Shavinina (Ed.) *International handbook on innovation* (pp. 430–444). Oxford, UK: Pergamon.

Chi, M. T. H., & Roscoe, R. (2002). The processes and challenges of conceptual change. In M. Limon & L. Mason

(Eds.), *Reconsidering conceptual change: Issues in theory and practice* (pp. 3–27). Dordrecht, The Netherlands: Kluwer.

Chi, M. T. H., Roscoe, R., Slotta, J., Roy, M., & Chase, C. C. (2012). Misconceived causal explanations for emergent processes. *Cognitive Science, 36,* 1–61.

Chi, M. T. H., Slotta, J. D., & de Leeuw, N. (1994). From things to processes: A theory of conceptual change for learning science concepts. *Learning and Instruction, 4,* 27–43.

Confrey, J. (1990). A review of the research on student conceptions in mathematics, science and programming. In C. B. Cazden (Ed.), *Review of research in education.* Washington, DC: American Educational Research Association.

de Leeuw, N. (1993). Students' beliefs about the circulatory system: Are misconceptions universal? In *Proceedings of the Fifteenth Annual Conference of the Cognitive Science Society* (pp. 389–393). Hillsdale, NJ: Lawrence Erlbaum Associates.

Driver, R., & Easley, J. (1978). Pupils and paradigms: A review of literature related to concept development in adolescent science students. *Studies in Science Education, 5,* 61–84.

Driver, R., Squires, A., Rushworth, P., & Wood-Robinson, V. (1994). *Making sense of secondary science.* London, UK: Routledge.

Duit, R. (2008). *Bibliography – CTCSE: Students' and teachers' conceptions and science education.* Available at: www.ipn.uni-kiel.de/aktuell/stcse/stcse.html (retrieved June 1, 2009).

Gadgil, S., Nokes, T. J., and Chi, M.T.H. (2011). Effectiveness of holistic mental model confrontation in driving conceptual change. *Learning and Instruction, 22,* 47–61.

Gelman, S. (1988). The development of induction within natural kind and artifact categories. *Cognitive Psychology, 20,* 65–95.

Gentner, D., & Stevens, A. L. (Eds.). (1983). *Mental models.* Hillsdale, NJ: Lawrence Erlbaum Associates.

Guzzetti, B. J., Snyder, T. E., Glass, G. V., & Gamas, W. S. (1993). Promoting conceptual change in science: A comparative meta-analysis of instructional interventions from reading education and science education. *Reading Research Quarterly, 28,* 116–159.

Keil, F. (1989). *Concepts, kinds, and cognitive development.* Cambridge, MA: MIT Press.

Lakoff, G. (1987). *Women, fire, and dangerous things: What categories reveal about the mind.* Chicago, IL: University of Chicago Press.

Law, N., & Ogborn, J. (1988). Students as expert system developers: A means of eliciting and understanding commonsense reasoning. *Journal of Research on Computing in Education, 26,* 497–514.

McCloskey, M. (1983). Naïve theories of motion. In D. Gentner & A. L. Stevens (Eds.), *Mental models* (pp. 299–324). Hillsdale, NJ: Lawrence Erlbaum Associates.

Novak, J. D. (1977). *A theory of education.* Ithaca, NY: Cornell University Press.

Ram, A., Nersessian, N. J., & Keil, F. C. (1997). Special issue: Conceptual change. *Journal of the Learning Sciences, 6,* 1–91.

Reiner, M., Slotta, J. D., Chi, M. T. H., & Resnick, L. B. (2000). Naïve physics reasoning: A commitment to substance-based conceptions. *Cognition and Instruction, 18,* 1–34.

Samarapungavan, A., & Wiers, R. W. (1997). Children's thoughts on the origin of species: A study of explanatory coherence. *Cognitive Science, 21,* 147–177.

Schwartz, S. P. (1977). Introduction. In S. P. Schwartz (Ed.), *Naming, necessity and natural kinds* (pp. 13–41). Ithaca, NY: Cornell University Press.

Slotta, J. D., & Chi, M. T. H. (2006). The impact of ontology training on conceptual change: Helping students understand the challenging topics in science. *Cognition and Instruction, 24,* 261–289.

Sommers, F. (1971). Structural ontology. *Philosophia, 1,* 21–42.

Thagard, P. (1990). Concepts and conceptual change. *Synthese, 82,* 255–274.

Vosniadou, S. (2004). Extending the conceptual change approach to mathematics learning and teaching. *Learning and Instruction, 14,* 445–451.

Vosniadou, S., & Brewer, W. F. (1992). Mental models of the earth: A study of conceptual change in childhood. *Cognitive Psychology, 24,* 535–585.

Vosniadou, S., & Brewer, W. F. (1994). Mental models of the day/night cycle. *Cognitive Science, 18,* 123–183.

Wiser, M. (1987). The differentiation of heat and temperature: History of science and novice–expert shift. In S. Strauss (Ed.), *Ontogeny, phylogeny, and historical development* (pp. 28–48). Norwood, NJ: Ablex.

Wiser, M., & Amin, T. (2001). "Is heat hot?" Inducing conceptual change by integrating everyday and scientific perspectives on thermal phenomena. *Learning and Instruction, 11,* 331–353.

4

THE CONTEXTUALITY OF KNOWLEDGE

An Intentional Approach to Meaning Making and Conceptual Change

Ola Halldén, Max Scheja, and Liza Haglund, Stockholm University

Looking across the research on learning and conceptual change, it would probably be fair to say that there has been a tendency to adhere to what Rommetveit (1978) has called a "negative rationalism". Such negative rationalism is characterized by a predominant focus on students' shortcomings, difficulties and general fallibility in relation to learning tasks confronting them in various settings. At a research meeting held in Britain, Perkins (2005) used the phrase "theories of difficulty" to label and characterize a good portion of the research concerned with learning and development in educational settings. This phraseology captures fittingly the main thrust of the work carried out within the Alternative Framework Movement (Gilbert & Watts, 1983) and other research concerned with students' cognitive development and learning: to study obstacles to student learning. As Säljö (1991a) has pointed out in his critique of constructivist research on children's counting competencies, by adopting such a negative perspective on human learning and development we run the risk of constraining our thinking and hampering the discourse on cognition and learning:

> Children (and adults) are constantly portrayed as lacking in abilities and situationally appropriate and perfectly rational modes of quantifying and handling problems . . . are marginalized in the experiment (or in the formal setting). Other modes of reasoning, usually academic and formally elegant, are given priority as if they were "better", irrespective of what the actor is attempting to achieve.
>
> (Säljö, 1991a, p. 123)

This normative critique asserts that research systematically tends to underestimate the competencies of the learner. However, constructivist research programmes have also been critiqued on methodological grounds. In particular, it has been argued that knowledge should be viewed as contextualized within discursive practices and that it is misleading to describe beliefs, conceptions, or conceptual structures in isolation from such discursive practices; knowledge is always situated and so any attempt to account for an individual's knowledge structures must take this situatedness into account (Resnick, 1991). It is difficult to raise objections against such a methodological claim. However, sometimes this critique takes the form of an ontological statement, saying that knowledge is socially constructed and transpires only in social practices (Lave, 1991). That is to argue for the social character of knowledge, for verbal communication as being a continuous process of joint construction of meanings (Marková, 1990, p. 136). From such a vantage point interviewing provides an example of such joint construction of meaning. According to Fontana and Frey (2005) interviewing is "inextricably and unavoidably historically, politically, and contextually bound" (p. 695), and is best described as a "negotiated text" (p. 716). The outcome of an interview depends as much on the interviewer as on the interviewee, and on their interaction within a socio-historical setting at a particular point in time. So, interviews are not neutral tools for collecting data but rather "active interactions between two (or more) people leading to negotiated, contextually based results" (Fontana & Frey, 2005, p. 698).

Any research program seriously intent on contributing to the theoretical discourse on cognition and learning would need to explicate its position in respect of the concern for negative rationalism mentioned above. It would also have to employ methods for studying conceptual frameworks that can stand up against the methodological critique put forward by the sociocultural research paradigm. This chapter makes an effort to present such a theoretical stance, drawing on earlier conceptualizations and findings from a number of research projects that have considered the nature and process of conceptual change across a variety of settings. This does not mean that the research programme proposed here adheres to the ontological claims made within sociocultural approaches. On the contrary, it holds firmly to the idea that people harbour beliefs and that these beliefs form structures, and the aim of this chapter is to propose a method for interpretation that renders the description of such belief structures an intellectually sound enterprise.

Departing from Piaget's early work, the chapter begins by describing a basic constructivist model for conceptual change. It then proceeds to consider two different, but related, strands of research growing out of constructivist research on students' alternative frameworks – one focused on the nature of alternative frameworks, and the other focused on the process of conceptual change. Against the background of this brief overview we offer an alternative view on conceptual change which takes into account the intentional character of learning. In essence, this alternative view continues the early work by Marton and Säljö (1976a, 1976b; see also Marton, Hounsell, & Entwistle, 1997) which emphasized a content-related view of learning; that is, that learning always involves someone learning something, a particular content, and that the outcome of student learning is functionally related to what the students are trying to achieve in relation to a particular learning task in a particular teaching–learning environment.

A BASIC MODEL FOR CONCEPTUAL CHANGE

In the early twentieth century, when Piaget published his works on children's conception of the world and the moral reasoning in the child (Piaget, 1929, 1932), his focus was *not* on the deficiencies in the child's reasoning but rather on *how* the child set about reasoning. Piaget's objective was not to test the child's abilities or to differentiate among children with regard to their abilities. Rather, he sought to describe their shared meanings and the processes by which they constructed meaning from their experiences. So the question of interest was not what was lacking in the child's reasoning, but rather what this reasoning was like. In a sense, Piaget gave children a voice of their own; it was the children's conceptions of the world that were put to the fore and explored.

Piaget (1970) was interested in the growth of intelligence as a common feature of human beings and, in his earlier writings, the construction of our view of the world. In *The Child's Conception of the World* (Piaget, 1929) this interest is reflected in studies of how children change their conceptions of phenomena such as dreams, thoughts, the origin of the moon, cause, and the nature of the night. The pattern of conceptual change thus described was that of a conception (A) being exchanged for another conception (B) (see Figure 4.1).

This model describes a linear and hierarchical conceptual development in which primitive conceptions are successively replaced by more advanced conceptions, ultimately resulting in a conceptual repertoire corresponding to that held by a particular culture in a particular society at a given time. Research carried out within such a linear model often displays negative rationalist tendencies; there are rights and wrongs, and the concern is to explore how the individual proceeds from the wrong conception to the correct one; that is, to ascertain how the individual exchanges primitive conceptions for more advanced and culturally endorsed ones. So far the model describes a process in which the individual is socialized into an existing culture of shared meanings. However, the aim of Piaget's studies was primarily to explore the development in the child from an initial practical solipsism to the gradual construction of a world that includes herself or himself as an element. So, the focus in these studies by Piaget was not on the erroneous conceptions in themselves, but rather on the underlying structures producing these conceptions. For example, a small child often has difficulties in distinguishing between the self and events in the surrounding world. This results in a continuing process in which the child incorporates events that appear to exist in the world, dreams for instance, into her or his self, and a counter-directed process in which omnipotent egocentric ideas, such as the creation of nature, are gradually alienated into the external world.

However, there is also a normative side to this matter. The discrepancies between how children usually view the world and what may be regarded as culturally accepted views raise the question of how it is possible to help children to abandon their naïve conceptions in favour of more advanced and culturally accepted conceptions. Piaget's aim was to describe this process as an aspect of human cognition and development. Educational science, however, took it upon itself to address the normative side of the matter, focusing on how it is possible to influence this process so as to facilitate conceptual change in line with the conceptual understanding communicated in the teaching.

The 1970s saw a rapid growth of research on conceptual change in the sciences aimed at resolving this question. When Driver and Easley (1978) published their seminal paper

A ⟶ B

Figure 4.1 A linear model of conceptual change

on conceptual development in adolescent students, they pointed out that when students come up with erroneous answers to questions posed in school, these answers should not primarily be seen as misunderstandings; they could equally well be seen as coming from a perspective alternative to that used by the teacher. A central distinction was thus made between misconceptions, on one hand, and alternative frameworks on the other. While misconceptions could be seen as incorrect ideas resulting from misunderstandings of theories or models presented in the teaching, alternative frameworks could be viewed as students' "autonomous frameworks for conceptualising the physical world" (Driver & Easley, 1978, p. 62). Such alternative frameworks would prompt learners to describe and explain events in ways alternative to those endorsed in the science classroom. Moreover, alternative frameworks could also lead students to interpret information communicated in the teaching in ways other than intended. When we study history we are always trying to understand a culture and a way of perceiving the world that differ from our personal viewpoint. Similarly, students studying science are trying to grasp a scientific culture or a particular way of perceiving the world that may differ from their already established ways of viewing the world around them. The students are, as it were, approaching "one framework of ideas from within another" (Lee, Dickinson, & Ashby, 1998, p. 234). For the teacher the problem becomes one of helping the learner adopt the most appropriate point of view, and to acquire a scientifically valid conceptual understanding of the topics studied. In other words, the teacher's task is to help the learner switch from the inadequate concept (A) to the scientifically approved concept (B) (see Figure 4.1).

Two interdependent lines of research were to be developed from this idea. One was all about mapping the A's, as it were, that is, about describing the learners' alternative frames of reference. The other was about trying to describe and explain the process of conceptual change. These two strands of research are interdependent in the sense that mappings are construed with the aim of accounting for the process, and when the processes are described, they point toward specific kinds of mappings. However, for the purposes of this chapter we will describe them as two separate research strands.

RESEARCH ON THE NATURE OF ALTERNATIVE FRAMEWORKS

The 1980s and 1990s saw a rapid growth of research describing learners' conceptions of central concepts within the natural sciences (for a bibliography, see Duit, 2006). For instance, Watts (1983) described eight different ways of understanding meanings of force in physics, and Stewart (1982, 1983) documented different ways of understanding heredity in biology. Brumby (1979, 1984) foregrounded interpretations of the concept of natural selection, and Deadman and Kelly (1978) explored students' understandings of evolution and heredity prior to instruction.

While an abundance of research was being carried out within the natural sciences, the research on alternative frameworks within the humanities and the social sciences was languishing. Of course, there were studies looking at naïve conceptions, but this research was primarily concerned with describing phases or stages in learners' conceptual development (e.g., Berti, 1994; Furnham, 1994; Torney-Purta, 1994). However, in parallel with the alternative framework movement, there were other studies focusing on the learning and teaching of history. For instance, Dickinson, Gard, and Lee (1986) explored how the notion of evidence was used in history and in a classroom setting, respectively. Halldén (1986, 1993, 1994, 1998) also used history as an example in exploring student learning with the explicit aim of discussing the notion of alternative frameworks. In parallel with Halldén's approach, Marton (1981) and colleagues developed a conceptualization of learning involving rich empirical descriptions of students' conceptions of learning material in relation to teaching and learning in school and higher education. Within this phenomenographic (Marton, 1981, 1992) research tradition, Dahlgren (1978) explored students' approaches to studying and learning economics. The findings showed that students, regardless of their having taken a basic course in economics involving teaching of the fundamental principle that "price" is a function of supply and demand for a certain article of trade, insisted on explaining, for instance, the price of a bun as a result of the cost of producing that bun.

Alternative frameworks have been described in several different ways. For instance, Osborne, Bell, and Gilbert (1983), talked about "children's science", meaning "the views of the world and meanings for words that children tend to acquire before they are formally taught science" (p. 1). Posner, Strike, Hewson, and Gertzog (1982) described a "conceptual ecology," characterised by: Anomalies, analogies and metaphors, epistemological commitments, metaphysical beliefs and concepts and other knowledge (Posner et al., 1982, p. 214ff.; cf. Strike & Posner, 1982, 1992). So conceptions have been seen as something embedded in a larger conceptual system. Such systems have been explicated in various ways. In proposing that conceptions are embedded in theories, Vosniadou (1994) described a hypothetical conceptual structure involving a framework theory built on ontological and epistemological presuppositions, and a specific theory comprising information about the target conceptions. On this basis, students form specific beliefs or mental models in order to solve specific problems in practical situations.

An alternative way of describing conceptual structure was offered by Tiberghien (1994), who suggested that alternative frameworks involve different levels. Using a view of modeling in physics, Tiberghien (1994) distinguished between a theory level, a model level, and a level of experimental field of reference. The theory level describes paradigms, principles, laws, and so forth. The model level involves formalisms, relations between physical quantities and qualitative aspects associated with observable phenomena. The level of experimental field of reference, finally, involves experimental facts, experimental devices, measurements, and similar phenomena. Along a similar theoretical vein, Caravita and Halldén (1994) suggested that alternative frameworks may be understood in relation to three different levels – a theoretical, a conceptual, and an empirical – stressing that differences between common-sense beliefs and the descriptions and explanations given in science may occur at all three levels simultaneously.

In the wake of this research on the structure of conceptual systems, a debate arose on the context dependence of alternative conceptions. In studying students' beliefs as to whether acquired characteristics are inherited or not, Engel Clough and Driver (1986) demonstrated that students' beliefs were dependent on whether they were talking about the Arctic fox or caterpillars. Later, Taber (2000) argued that there are several alternative and stable conceptions that can be used in similar situations, and that it is:

possible to study conceptual development in terms of the changing extent to which the alternatives are selected over time as the learner develops both the conceptual frameworks themselves, and judgements about the contexts in which they are best applied.

(Taber, 2000, p. 414)

This view of "multiple alternative frameworks" has received support from a range of research studies, showing how students tend to use a variety of understandings in tackling learning tasks in a variety of different settings, and that such variations in ways of understanding learning tasks may be found both within and between students in various educational settings (see, e.g., Caravita & Halldén 1994; Halldén, 1999; Maloney & Siegler, 1993; Petri & Niedderer 1998; Taber 1995; 1997; Taber & Watts 1997; Tytler 1998; Watson, Prieto & Dillon, 1997; cf. Jovchelovitch 2002).

QUESTIONING THE NOTION OF ALTERNATIVE FRAMEWORKS

While most of the research has proposed elaborations, refinements and clarifications within this idea of stable alternative frameworks, there have also been attempts to radically shift the theoretical position, and move away from the notion of alternative frameworks altogether. DiSessa (1988), for instance, has proposed that learners' knowledge is better understood as "knowledge in pieces."

However, the most serious critique of alternative framework research has come from the sociocultural theory of learning. In critically reviewing and appraising the research on cognitive development and learning sociocultural commentators have levelled critique against constructivist research in general – including research on alternative frameworks and conceptual change – for not paying sufficient attention to the communicative and situational aspects of learning. Findings from a range of studies carried out within the sociocultural research tradition have demonstrated the strong impact that the learning environment has on learning in instructional settings. Säljö (1991b), for example, has shown that students' abilities to solve problems vary as a direct result of how learning tasks are presented, which suggests that conceptions should be seen not as fixed cognitive entities, but rather as socially constituted through continuous interaction with the teaching–learning environment (see also Säljö, 1994; Säljö, Schoultz, & Wyndhamn, 2001; Säljö & Wyndhamn, 1990; Wyndhamn, 1993). This criticism of research for not taking sufficient account of contextual influences on learning has not only struck the research on conceptual change. Phenomenographic research (Marton, 1981; Marton & Booth, 1997) has also been criticized for not giving sufficient attention to how situational aspects might influence learners' conceptions of aspects of various phenomena, and thus for giving a decontextualized account of students' conceptions (Säljö, 1994; cf. Bowden, 1995). Moreover, Säljö (1997) has argued that using research interviews as the primary source of information about individuals' mental lives does not really provide access to people's conceptions, but rather to specific discourses as they unfold in particular communicative practices, notably the interview. In particular, Säljö (1997) leveled critique against the common practice of viewing answers given by interviewees in interviews as indicators of existing conceptions or "ways of experiencing" the world; such a view, he argued, obstructs alternative interpretations of functional mechanisms of why people talk the way they do.

> This circularity prescribes a logic to the research process that in unnecessary ways restricts the potential significance of its outcome: we could learn much more about actors' definitions of the world if we viewed their accounts primarily as attempts at communicating in situated practices rather than as ways of experiencing.
>
> (Säljö, 1997, p. 188)

So it is important to realize that the interview, as indeed any institutionalized form of communication, involves specific social constraints that influence the interaction between interviewer and interviewee and thus shape both the form and the content of their interchange (Jönsson, Linell, & Säljö, 1991; Säljö, 1997). Indeed, the dynamics of a dialogue between interlocutors forms "part of a continuous process in verbal communication in which the speaker and the listener jointly construct the meaning of a linguistic item" (Marková, 1990, p. 136). And even though dialogues are reciprocal by their very nature, they are also inherently asymmetrical (Marková & Foppa, 1991, p. 260), and so in obtaining information about cognitive processes from interviews or other dialogically generated data, a crucial task will be to account both for situational influences and for the cognitive content of the dialogue. In other words, to arrive at a more complete understanding of the phenomenon under study any interpretation of data has to take account of cognitive as well as situational aspects of that phenomenon.

Critique of this kind has sparked discussion about the theoretical status of the construct of alternative frameworks (the A in Figure 4.1) and how this theory should be brought to bear on issues relating to teaching and learning.

RESEARCH ON THE PROCESS OF CONCEPTUAL CHANGE

As mentioned earlier, the other strand of research growing out of considerations of how learners' conceptual development may be facilitated focused on the process of conceptual change; in other words, on the transformative properties of the arrow in Figure 4.1. Drawing on Piagetian developmental psychology, the history of science, and the notion of conceptual ecology, Posner and co-workers (1982) argued that there are four necessary conditions that need to be fulfilled in order for conceptual change to occur: (1) There has to be an initial dissatisfaction with an existing conception; (2) a new and intelligible conception must present itself; (3) this conception must be plausible; and (4) it must suggest possibilities for a fruitful research programme. Posner and co-workers (1982) described the process of conceptual change as an entirely rational process, with the learner acting like a "little scientist."

In the early 1980s, Gilbert and Watts (1983) reviewed the research within the alternative framework movement and described three different models for conceptual change in relation to three different perspectives on the concept of "conception": (1) the "stepped-change model," involving an all-or-nothing view on conceptions as a set of "logical atoms" that the individual either has or does not have, (2) the "smooth-change model," which took a linear view of conceptual change involving gradual changes over an extended period of time, and (3) the "catastrophe theory model", the model preferred by Gilbert and Watts (1983), drawing on a comprehensive view of conceptual change allowing both gradual changes in conceptions and more instantaneous change processes to occur. A central idea in this model was that it allowed a cost–benefit analysis in relation to conceptual change: What do I gain if I acquire a new concept and what do I lose if I abandon my established way of conceptualizing the phenomenon in question?

Despite the apparent differences in views on how conceptual change occurs, these models have something in common: They outline a profile of conceptual change as a process moving from a conception (A) to a conception (B), but reveal little about the active components of this process; the models do not reveal much about what is involved in conceptual change or what obstacles there might be for conceptual change to occur.

As already mentioned, Vosniadou (1994) described a conceptual structure comprising a framework theory built on ontological and epistemological presuppositions together with a related set of beliefs, a specific theory, about the target conception; that is, the conception that is supposed to change. Conceptual change, then, may involve a gradual suspension and revision of the presuppositions of the framework theory ultimately allowing restructuring of beliefs within the specific theory resulting in a conceptual change. This can make the process of conceptual change a relatively slow one, sometimes involving the construction of *synthetic models* as intermediate steps towards genuine conceptual change. So, from this perspective, the core problem of conceptual change is not the direct transition from a conception A to another conception B. Rather, "It is the presuppositions that are difficult to change and resistant to instruction and not the misconceptions *per se*" (Vosniadou, 1994, p. 65). Undoubtedly this is still a causal model of conceptual change, but it is perhaps better described in a "non-linear" fashion (cf. diSessa, 2002) (Figure 4.2).

Quite a different way of looking at the process of conceptual change was introduced by diSessa and Sherin (1998), who described "conceptions", in terms of *coordinating classes*, as "systematically connected ways of getting information from the world" (p. 1171). In fact, they did away with the concept of "conception" altogether, and talked about different ways of "seeing" the world. Taking their theory to be a theory of perception, it implies that we are not bound by discursive practices and cultural tools in explaining the surrounding world. Nor are we bound by previously established conceptual structures. We are, however, constrained by particular strategies for obtaining information and particular strategies for seeing. In taking this view, diSessa and Sherin (1998) moved away from much of the prior work on conceptual change, proposing that the core problem of conceptual change is "shifting the means of seeing" (p. 1171). diSessa and Sherin's (1998) theory brings to the fore the processes involved in concept formation when students are presented with scientifically relevant learning tasks. Rather than focusing on erroneous conceptions as a barrier to acquiring new conceptions, diSessa and Sherrin (1998) introduced more of a systems theory approach, pointing up the role of coordination activities in the learner. And in connecting the students' performances in relation to learning tasks and the processes apparently guiding those performances, this theory makes an original alternative to the research perspectives adopted within the alternative framework movement which, as has been argued above, often hold an A → B view of the process of conceptual change.

This summary of research on alternative frameworks and the process of conceptual change illustrates some of the variations and tensions in theoretical approaches and conceptualizations. However, looking across the different research strands also reveals a pervading pattern implying a *causal view of conceptual change*. Almost invariably the research seeks to explain deficiencies in the conception A that force the learner to conceptual change, or to explain difficulties in achieving an understanding of B (conceptual change), by referring to constraining conditions within or around A (see Figure 4.1). However, if we view learners as individuals who intentionally try to realize

A 〜⌒⟶ B

Figure 4.2 A non-linear model of conceptual change

certain goals, the shortcomings observed in A do not become antecedents in a causal relationship. Rather, they become arguments in a *teleological* explanation of why learners explain things as they do. In taking the intentional character of learning into account, the present research builds on and follows through on the research initiative originally proposed by Marton and Säljö (1976a, 1976b) in their influential studies on the relations between learning processes and learning outcomes. Next, an attempt will be made to clarify this intentional view on learning and conceptual change.

A DISTINCTION BETWEEN "TASK" AND "PROBLEM"

In a series of early research studies (Halldén, 1982; Wistedt, 1987) the observation was made that students who were assigned learning tasks by their teacher often ended up working on different problems than the ones the teacher had expected them to work on (cf. Bennet, Desforges, Cockburn, & Wilkinson, 1984; Doyle, 1979a, 1979b). Essentially it seemed as if the students were trying to learn something different from what they were being taught. Extensive analyses of how the students tackled various tasks in different subjects made it clear that the difficulties that they had in coping successfully with subject matter requirements could be understood with reference to their personal interpretations of tasks that confronted them in various settings. Accordingly, an explicit distinction was introduced between "task" and "problem," defining "task" as: *what is presented to the [students] by the teacher with the intention that they are to do something and/or that they are to learn something* (Halldén, 1988, p. 125) and "problem" as the student's personal *interpretation of the task given* (Halldén, 1988, p. 125). Methodologically, this distinction between task and problem described a shift from a teacher-oriented to a student-oriented perspective on the learning that occurs in a particular teaching–learning environment (Entwistle, 1996; Entwistle & Ramsden, 1983). Moreover, and importantly, this distinction involved the recognition that students who were confronted with the same learning task might end up working on what amounts to different problems. While much of the previous research had been focused on students' mistakes and difficulties – thus adhering to what Rommetveit (1978) called the "negative scholarly rationalism" – an important question became what sort of learning activities students do, in fact, engage in when they are confronted with learning tasks in different settings, and what these activities imply in terms of opportunities for students' learning.

Two studies (Halldén, 1999; Scheja, 2006) on students' conceptions of statistical probability provide an example of this research stance. In both studies a sample of undergraduates taking a basic course in education were invited to participate in a problem session presenting them with the following task, originally used by Kahneman and Tversky (1982) in their investigations into decision making and judgment under uncertainty:

Linda is 31 years old, single, outspoken, and very bright. She majored in philosophy. As a student, she was deeply concerned with issues of discrimination and social justice, and also participated in anti-nuclear demonstrations.

Which of the following two statements about Linda is more probable?

A) Linda is a bank-teller.
B) Linda is a bank-teller and is active in the feminist-movement.

When the students had studied the task and decided on one of the two alternatives, they were also encouraged to comment on their choices. For a statistician, the obvious answer would be that A is the more probable statement since it is a principle of probability theory that the probability of a particular statement or an event P (e.g., that Linda is a bank-teller) is always higher than the probability of P in conjunction with another statement Q (e.g., that Linda is a bank-teller *and* is active in the feminist movement). In both studies, and in the original study by Kahneman and Tversky (1982), the majority of the students responded that B was the more probable statement. Looking solely at the quantitative distribution of the students' responses, one way of accounting for this fallacy would be to see it as a result of shortcomings in the students' knowledge of probability theory. However, while this is often the conclusion drawn, the later studies by Halldén (1999) and Scheja (2006) went beyond the quantitative pattern of responses to produce an alternative explanation of the outcome, taking account of the students' reasons for picking one statement before the other. By way of example, some students had great difficulty in choosing between the two statements. One student, who picked B, described the dilemma as follows:

> First, I thought [about choosing] A, according to the rules for determining the probability of a true statement, but then I thought I was supposed to draw conclusions from the text describing Linda, and so I chose B. But now I realize I was wrong!

For this student the task seemed to present two very different notions of "probability". The task may be seen as a problem of statistical probability, in which case the rules of probability theory may be applied. Or it may be seen as a problem involving the construction of a "good-reason assay"; that is, a rationale through which information about a person (here "Linda") can be used to reach a probable, in terms of being sensible or realistic, conclusion about that person, given the circumstances (e.g., that "Linda is a bank-teller and is active in the feminist movement"). In everyday life individuals often make decisions about probability by construing a good-reason assay and look for the rationality in observed behaviors (for an explication of this argument, see Halldén, 1999 and Scheja, 2006). The student in the excerpt above gave her answer according to her interpretation of what she thought she was supposed to do. This conclusion may seem trivial, but is nevertheless of crucial importance for understanding the personal rationality guiding the student's learning activity in relation to the task. The student tackled the task in view of her own understanding of the setting in which the task was presented; she thought she was supposed to draw conclusions from the information presented in the task, including the description of "Linda," and so tried to produce a good-reason assay arguing for the alternative that best mapped onto that description. So far, it would seem that the reasons for the student's picking statement B rather than statement A may be explicated solely with reference to the "social rules" or the discursive practice pervading the setting in which the task was presented. However, a close reading of the transcript makes it clear that the student did not draw exclusively on her knowledge (or lack of knowledge) about the situation or of the social practice as such (*"But now I realize I was wrong!"*). Her interpretation of the task also included a variation in ways of looking at probability as, on one hand, a construct of probability theory and, on the other, a historical account relying on the presumed rationality embodied in the description of the person "Linda". This analysis makes it clear that the student's understanding of the task as a problem to be solved involves not just an adjustment to perceived discursive requirements; it also involves the actualization of a repertoire of beliefs among which the student picks the belief that is perceived as being the most appropriate in the setting.

So, in solving the task the student considers the discursive requirements of the setting in which she finds herself and, in doing so, draws on her previous repertoire of beliefs and experiences to evaluate which sort of knowledge would fit the perceived requirements of that setting. From this deliberation a particular strategy for action is formed, which manifests itself in a particular way of tackling the learning task. Such a rationale for explaining students' activities has some affinity with how von Wright (1971) explained the interpretation of an action. To understand why people act the way they do in various situations it is necessary to ascribe meaning to their behavior; that is, to regard it as intentional. It is in the light of a person's intentions that her behavior becomes meaningful, can be understood in terms of action. From such an intentional perspective, to explain an action involves identifying circumstances within or around the agent that can clarify why the act was undertaken. In short: "Behavior gets its intentional character from being seen by the agent himself or by an outside observer in a wider perspective, from being set in a context of aims and cognitions" (von Wright, 1971, p. 115; cf. von Wright, 1979, 1980). Setting students' behavior into an explanatory framework involving aims and cognitions evokes two kinds of contexts: one involving the students' beliefs about how to reach certain ends and another comprising their beliefs about the type of situation and demands put on them by that particular setting, as well as beliefs about opportunities for acting in these circumstances (Figure 4.3).

This model, and the thinking that flows from it, has proved helpful in explaining variations in students' ways of dealing with learning tasks across a variety of course settings (e.g., Halldén, 1999; Lundholm, 2005; Nilsson, 2006; Petersson, 2005; Ryve, 2006; Scheja, 2002; Wistedt, 1994a, 1994b). By focusing on students' idiosyncratic ways of understanding learning tasks confronting them in various settings, it is possible to rationalize their way of dealing with these tasks with reference to their *competence-oriented* and *discourse-oriented resources* for acting on the tasks. Competence-oriented resources refer to the abilities, wants, and desires, as well as to the beliefs that an individual holds, irrespective of situation. But any interpretation of students' activities also has to take account of how the students perceive the situation in hand. Accordingly, discourse-oriented resources allow explanation of students' ways of acting on a learning

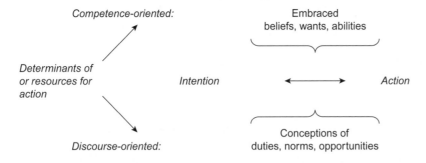

Figure 4.3 A model for rationalizing action (modified from Halldén, 1999, and based on von Wright, 1971, 1974, 1979, and 1980. Reprinted with permission from Elsevier)

task with reference to their conceptions of duties, norms, and opportunities. This is performed in a way that takes into consideration the students' beliefs about the actual setting as well as cultural norms for acting in that particular setting (Halldén, 1999). In view of this explication of the model it may be argued that it incorporates not only a cognitive dimension but also a dimension of discursive practice, albeit without explicitly addressing the matter of participation and the discursive nature of human communication brought to the fore in sociocultural theory (e.g., Rogoff, 2003; Rommetveit, 1988).

To recap, the theoretical stance described here offers an explanatory framework for rationalizing students' actions which takes account of both cognitive and sociocultural dimensions of the interaction with a particular teaching–learning setting. Students' ways of dealing with learning tasks, or more broadly, with their studies, can be explained by describing their personal understanding of the conceptual aspects of learning material; that is, with reference to competence-oriented resources. But it can also be explained with reference to discourse-oriented resources, in terms of the students' understanding of the situational constraints for dealing with their studies. In fact, competence-oriented and discourse-oriented resources can be seen as providing complementary perspectives for analyzing individual students' understanding of topics brought to the fore in a teaching–learning environment (Scheja, 2002).

So, for the researcher, the concepts of competence-oriented and discourse-oriented resources of action become important analytical categories that can help to procure a nuanced understanding of the object of study. In particular, the model described above allows reflection on the data from different viewpoints: from a cognitive outlook focusing on students' wants, beliefs, and desires in relation to the content of a learning task, and from a sociocultural viewpoint focusing on the constraints and affordances for acting in a certain setting, as these are perceived by the students in the circumstances (Figure 4.4).

This description of the analytical activity of the researcher, shown in Figure 4.4, in terms of a movement between different aspects of interpretation resembles the process of learning as it has been described in research on concept formation, where learners construct their conceptual understanding of a given task with reference to interpretations at a meta level of the subject matter as a whole (Halldén, 1988, pp. 134ff.). By analogy with this, the researcher too must construct her or his knowledge of what is to be

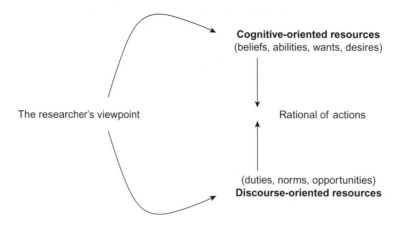

Figure 4.4 The variation in viewpoints involved in the rationalization of an action

explained, and in doing so has to draw on both cognitive and sociocultural data in order to form valid explanations of students' learning activities. Thus it is by shifting between these two different realms for interpretation – the cognitive and the sociocultural – that it is possible to reach an understanding of the meaning-making processes in which individuals involve themselves.

COHERENCE AS A PREREQUISITE FOR INTERPRETATION

Of course, these considerations of the researcher's role in rationalizing individuals' meaning-making processes raise questions relating to the ontological assumptions underlying an interpretive act of the kind described above. Arguments for systematically ascribing rationality to individuals' behaviors can be found in contemporary philosophical discussions about "radical interpretation." It has, for instance, been argued that any effort that tries to make sense of other people's utterances must rest on an assumed maxim of coherence that forms part of a wider *principle of charity* (Davidson, 2001). In essence, this principle implies that the researcher, to make sense of individuals' ways of acting on a particular situation, has to assume that these actions rely on a certain degree of coherence and cogency. In other words, the researcher has to assume that it is possible to understand other individuals. In fact, Davidson (2001) described interpretation as an adjustment between what seems to stand out as salient features for individuals and the coherence in their meaning-making processes. This implies that individuals, to some extent, overlap in how they view the world, and that this shared world-view enables intersubjectivity and mutual understanding. Salience, then, is to be regarded as a relational phenomenon; what is perceived as salient for an individual is contingent on the situation in hand and on prior experiences (cf. Roth, 2001).

So, in research on individuals' meaning-making processes the challenge becomes one of "optimizing agreement" between the individual's view and the interpretation proposed as an explication of the meaning-making activities that the individual engages in. Assuming coherence and cogency can thus be seen as a prerequisite of maximizing the intelligibility of an individual's actions. Such an assumption provides a common background against which deviations from the assumed coherency may first be recognized, and then rationalized by being set in a context of individual intentions and cognitions explicating the observed meaning-making processes from the individual's own point of view. Formally, such an intentional explication may be captured in the form of a practical syllogism (for examples, see Halldén, Haglund, & Strömdahl, 2007; Scheja, 2002).

To simply assume coherence may be regarded as a bit straightforward, considering the lively debate on coherence in conceptual structures (cf. e.g., diSessa, this volume; Engel Clough & Driver, 1986; Taber, 2000; Tytler, 1998). But this debate has focused exclusively on the conceptualizations of, for instance, science concepts. The main question has had to do with to what extent laypeople coherently use conceptualizations alternative to those used in science. However, in the present chapter, the question of coherence relates to the coherence within individuals' conceptual structures and between such structures and the individuals' interpretations of the situation to hand. In short, instead of focusing on coherence across situations the research stance presented here is concerned with the coherence identified within particular situations. Below an attempt will be made to clarify this theoretical position, drawing on ongoing empirical research into the process of conceptual change. These examples will serve to illustrate not just our theoretical stance, but also what this position can add to the research in terms of explaining the process of conceptual change.

INFERRING CONCEPTIONS FROM ACTIONS –
CREATING RELATIONSHIPS

In an ongoing study aimed at describing four- and five-year-old children's emerging understanding of the word "earth" (Larsson & Halldén, 2010), an attempt has been made to identify what kinds of problem children encounter. Besides referring to earth as "soil," the children seem to perceive the earth as a circular object up in the sky. Thus, the connotations evoked by "earth" seem to emanate not from physical experience, but rather from experiences that the children have gained in their social lives. In addressing the problem of where people live across the earth, the children talked about earth as "ground." So, in the interviews the children were talking on one hand about the "earth" in the sky and, on the other, about the "earth" on the ground where people live. However, they used different labels to refer to these two "earths." Some of the children, apparently realizing that people live on the earth located in the sky, had to try to unite the two meanings of "earth." In doing so, they were confronted with several problems. For instance, if people live on top of a spherical body they might easily fall off (cf. Vosniadou, 1994; Vosniadou, Skopeliti, & Ikospentaki, 2005). There was also the question of how it is possible to breathe on an earth located high up in the sky or in space. Some of the children who were faced with these problems tried to solve them by creating a picture of the earth as inhabiting people on a circular disc surrounded by a hollow sphere (this model has been reported in several studies on children's conception of the earth, see, e.g., Nussbaum, 1979, 1985; Vosniadou, 1994). This hollow sphere model of the earth solved the initial problem of grasping the earth as being at the same time a circular body in the sky and the "ground" where people live and lead their lives. It also solved related problems of what is up and what is down on the earth, as well as the problem of the availability of oxygen or air. This *compounded model* (Halldén et al., 2002; Larsson & Halldén, 2010) can be seen as an alternative to the synthetic model described by Vosniadou (1994). The compounded model is not a synthesis between an initial model and a scientific model but rather a model that collects information from a range of different sources and incorporates this information into a coherent system. It should also be noted that such a model does not prescribe a recipe for a correct modeling of the earth. It is simply a way for an individual to create coherence and meaning from a range of different, and sometimes contradictory, facts. In respect of questions relating to the shape of the earth the compounded model meets the requirements both of flat models of the earth, such as maps, and of astronomical models of the earth, for example the globe. In process terms the model captures a conceptual transformation that can be described in terms of two conceptions A and B being combined into a compounded conception AB (Figure 4.5).

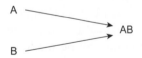

Figure 4.5 Two conceptions are combined into one conception

In a sense, this model illustrates Vosniadou's (1994) point that new information "is assimilated into the existing conceptual structure creating synthetic models or misconceptions" (p. 56). The creation of a compounded or synthetic model makes it possible to assimilate new information into this model. But the process of constructing a compounded model is rather a question of accommodation in the Piagetian sense of the word (Piaget, 1970); the model is an original product of the child's constructing activity which enables further assimilation of new information. So the construction of a compounded model is prompted by an intention to relate disparate pieces of information to make sense of the world. The model can be seen as the child's invention used to solve specific problems that do not always have their roots in presuppositions. Ultimately this meaning-making process, involving the connection of disparate pieces of information to one another in an attempt to make sense of the world, is an essential ingredient in learning and understanding.

The above provided an example of relating two contradictory bits of information to each other. However, to be able to relate more complex amounts of data to one another it is also necessary to construct some sort of coherent whole that can act as a frame of reference for these relating processes. Half a century ago, Miller (1956) argued that an individual's memory capacity is limited to bits of information ranging between five and nine. To extend this capacity it is necessary to organize different bits of information into units or chunks. Since the memory span is a fixed number of chunks it is possible to increase the number of bits of information that it contains by continuously creating larger chunks. It follows that to effectively make use of one's memory capacity and to fathom the events in an increasingly complex surrounding world, it is necessary to construct personal contexts for the information. Another study (Sternäng & Halldén, 2011) carried out within our research group provides an illustration of this process of constructing coherent wholes of information belonging to different problem areas.

The study, which focused on students' understandings of environmental problems and the intensified greenhouse effect in "green schools" in China, illustrates how the teaching in these schools confronts the student with information about pollution, the intensified greenhouse effect, the depletion of the ozone layer, the melting of the ice at the poles, and technical information on why the ozone layer is destructed, and so forth. The challenge for these students is not to relate two parameters to each other, but rather to make meaning of a huge amount of information derived from a variety of different conceptual contexts and used in several different communicative genres (Mäkitalo, Jakobsson & Säljö, 2007). The study illustrates how the students try to relate these quite diverse information bits and events to one another. And, in being asked to explain what is meant by the intensified greenhouse effect the students make an effort to construct models that allow the incorporation of most of the information given into an all-embracing model.

One such model is described in an interview with a girl called Zhu. Zhu's modeling of the intensified greenhouse effect consists of holes in the atmosphere, as a result of the depletion of the ozone layer; these holes allow the sunlight to reach the earth and to heat it up. The model also implies impossibility for the heat to escape out into space from other places on the earth where there are no holes in the atmosphere, because of the pressure of the atmosphere itself. Moreover, the melting of the ice at the poles means that the earth suffers the loss of the ice's cooling effect. A similar description of "holes" in the atmosphere was provided by a boy, Hao, who pointed out that the gases that destroy the ozone layer stay at the polar regions because "the north and the south poles are at the tops of the earth" and that is why the ozone layer is thinnest at the polar regions and the sun is able to shine right through at the earth.

Clearly these students were constructing compounded models, although these compounded models brought together more disparate information than was the case with the children's modeling of the earth. Moreover, the modeling of the intensified greenhouse effect illustrated above could hardly be regarded as a compromise or mesh of scientifically endorsed and naïve models. Of course, it may be argued that these apparently erroneous ideas should not be regarded as models in the first place, but are perhaps better described as aspects of *romancing* in the Piagetian sense of the word (Piaget, 1929). Nevertheless, they illustrate a particular way of constructing meaning from a great deal of facts and this meaning-making process may potentially be seen as a step toward a more complete, and perhaps scientifically valid, conceptualization of the phenomena involved. The point we wish to make here is that regardless of how correct or erroneous these models were in relation to a given school norm or in relation to academic science, they nevertheless made sense from the individual's point of view, and carried with them a personal rationality imbued in the coherence offered by the compounded models.

A recent investigation into a group of students studying history provides yet another example of how individuals' meaning-making processes involve the creation of compounded models. In their efforts to contextualize the vast amount of information presented during a visit to a museum, the students conformed either to a narrative or to a structural view (Björk, 1983) on historical description (Haglund, in preparation). In particular, the students seemed to construct alternative ways of accounting for the information provided – alternative, that is, in relation to the models sought in the teaching. The analysis of data made it clear that for the students the challenge was about structuring the information provided and to group it into one or several contexts for interpretation that would render the information meaningful.

In sum, the examples presented above provide an illustration of how relationships are created between disparate and sometimes contradictory pieces of information by relating these bits and pieces to a coherent whole. Essentially, this is a description not only of alternative frameworks but also of the construction of such alternative frameworks. Importantly, a compounded model of the sort described here does not imply a compromise being made between common-sense thinking and scientifically approved models. Since the learner does not have access to the complete scientific model in the first place, there can be no real compromise. Rather, the compounded model is a solution to problems that the learner faces in relation to being presented with disparate or contradictory information. Thus, the compounded model is the construction of a common context that can be used for understanding and explaining a variety of information.

In effect, the compounded model can be looked upon as an explication of the competence-oriented resources in Figure 4.4. It describes what makes assimilation (Piaget, 1952) or enrichment (Vosniadou, 1994) possible and points up the resources on which the learner draws in acting on a particular situation. As mentioned earlier, such a model can be described as involving different levels (Caravita & Halldén, 1994). There is an empirical level that states what is seen as data or evidence in a description or an explanation; this empirical level thus defines what there is to be noticed or potentially to be seen. Going back to the study on students' conceptions of probability exemplified above, it can be noted that the personal details provided by the task description on the person "Linda" are not really relevant in calculating the probability of the two statements; the information needed to reach a probability theoretical solution is rather the number of propositions made about Linda. It follows that the empirical level is constituted by a conceptual level determining what should be regarded as salient features at the empirical level. However, and as pointed out earlier, conceptions are linked to one another according to overarching principles and beliefs to be found at a theoretical or meta level.

To illustrate, in a study (Halldén, 1998) on students' understanding of the Darwinian theory of evolution it was found that students' difficulties in understanding and giving scientific explanations of, for instance, natural selection had to do with their views on what really counts as a scientific explanation (Halldén, 1998; for examples from the understanding of history see Halldén, 1986, 1998; compare the idea of presuppositions in Vosniadou, 1994). This differentiation between different levels of frameworks has important implications for the conceptualization of conceptual change. Radical conceptual change or restructuring, as opposed to enrichment (Vosniadou, 1994), would involve changes at all three levels simultaneously. Conceptual change is likely to occur when reflection at the theoretical level and tentative interpretations made at the empirical level are calibrated and brought together into a coherent conceptual pattern (Halldén, 1997) transferring the learner into an entirely new or different conceptual context (cf. Ehrlén, 2009; Österlind, 2005; cf. also Entwistle, 2010, for a related discussion on "knowledge objects").

The stability of compounded models will not be dwelt on further here. It is still an empirical question to what extent such models are momentary constructions in a specific situation and to what extent they form stable representations used for explaining phenomena in different situations.

EXPLICATING COHERENCE AS A PREREQUISITE FOR INTERPRETATION

Earlier it was mentioned that, from a methodological point of view, assuming coherence and cogency is a prerequisite of understanding an individual's meaning-making processes. In particular, it is by setting an individual's utterances and behavior in a context of aims and cognitions that it is possible to explicate this behavior in terms of meaning-making processes that make sense in the circumstances. So, methodologically, to arrive at such an understanding of an individual's meaning-making activities, it is necessary to put these activities into context. Moreover, meaning making itself, in the sense it has been exemplified here, involves putting bits and pieces into context. So, in modeling the process of conceptual change, the notion of context seems to take on added importance. The concept of context, as it is used here, refers not to the physical or discursive situation in which individuals find themselves, but to the individuals' personal framings of that situation – framings within which they think about learning material; for example, science concepts (cf. Cobb, 1986, 1990). This constructivist definition of context allows the study of meaning making in terms of individuals' contextualizations of information that is presented in a particular setting. The compounding of information into broad, but seemingly coherent, models illustrates this contextualization process and also points to the variation of contexts potentially involved in such a process.

In relation to the study of meaning making and conceptual change, different forms of context have been brought to the fore. First there is the conceptual context, which involves individual beliefs about, for instance, science concepts. An individual's conception of a science concept, of course, may differ a great deal from the ideas captured in the scientific definition of that concept. The concept of force, for example, has its place within a scientific framework that gives a particular meaning to force as something that changes the direction or velocity of an object. An individual's conception of force, however, may be "something that makes an object move." The difference between these accounts falls back on how the concept in question is contextualized by an individual in a particular situation. The situation is important because it can provide the individual with cues for how the information presented, for instance in a teaching–learning setting, should be dealt with. So apart from a conceptual context there is also a situational context that can influence how an individual understands and deals with a particular piece of information. The study presented earlier, in which students were confronted with the task of deciding on the probability of two statements in relation to a description of a person "Linda," provides a clear example. In deciding on one of the alternatives the student considered the situational framing of the task to be an important indication of how the task should be tackled.

It was described (Figure 4.4) above from a methodological point of view how competence-oriented and discourse-oriented resources can be used as complementary perspectives in trying to arrive at an understanding of individuals' meaning-making activities. Similarly, from an empirical viewpoint the conceptual and situational contexts that individuals form as a result of trying to make sense of diverse pieces of information can be seen as working together in shaping the individuals' understandings of topics brought to the fore in different settings (Scheja, 2002). This combination of conceptual and situational contexts suggests a multidimensional structure of an individual's meaning-making process in relation to tackling learning tasks in an instructional setting. In line with the distinction introduced earlier between task and problem, students may be confronted with one and the same learning task, but may end up working on quite different problems as a result of having – both situationally and conceptually – contextualized the task in different ways.

An investigation into mathematics learning (Wistedt, 1994b) is illustrative in this regard. In the study 11-year old students were asked, in groups of three to four students, to divide a piece of wood into three equally big pieces and to express this division in decimal form. From the analyses of the students' interactions it was clear that some students had contextualized the task as an everyday problem of dividing a real piece of wood, where "equally big pieces" was interpreted as "equally big, so the difference doesn't show." Others had contextualized the task as a theoretical problem where "equally big" took on quite a different and more abstract meaning, leading the students toward considering the problem of infinity. This example illustrates the shaping of a problem context, in which situational and conceptual contextualizations provide a frame of reference for thinking about a perceived problem. From the researcher's viewpoint, in the interpretation of data several different contexts need to be taken into account: the hypothesized conceptual structure of the individual (the conceptual context) and the individual's perception of the actual setting (the situational context). Of course, the situational context may also include cultural norms and presuppositional beliefs that the individual acts on habitually (Ehrlén, 2008; Halldén, 1999). However, it is also necessary to take the problem context into consideration; that is, the context in which individual learners situate a particular problem that they set themselves to solve. By studying these individually constructed contexts it is possible to achieve an understanding of the rationality of the learners' actions from the viewpoint of the learners themselves.

COMPOUNDED MODELS AND DIFFERENTIATION

Going back to the question of the process of conceptual change, above it was illustrated that individuals, confronted with information from a variety of different sources, form compounded models in an attempt to bring coherence to this jumble of information (Figure 4.4). Needless to say, however, this process of combining conceptions into compounded models only account for part of the process of conceptual change. In what follows, and drawing on the constructivist notion of context explicated above, we would argue that if conceptual compounding reflects one step in the meaning-making process, another important step involves *differentiation* within and between such compounded models.

Looking at the now rather well-researched problem of conceptions of the earth, the problem addressed in research up to now has been not how children come up with a hollow sphere model, but rather, why it is so difficult for them to abandon the hollow sphere in favor of the more scientifically accurate spherical model. The hollow sphere model covers what is culturally accounted for by, for instance, maps that can be used to navigate in a city, or globes that can be used in calculations of long distance trips or as a model for the earth as an astronomical body. Similarly, looking at the research on conceptions of the intensified greenhouse effect, the problem addressed by the research has been, not why students blend ideas about the depletion of the ozone layer with ideas about the greenhouse effect, but rather how this merger acts as an obstacle for students in achieving a scientifically valid understanding of the intensified greenhouse effect. The examples provided in this chapter serve to illustrate how learners who are confronted with learning material in a particular setting try to put this information into context, and as a result construct conceptual contexts for interpretation. Sometimes these conceptual contexts may be deemed inadequate in relation to the demands put on the students by the teaching–learning environment. However, the point is that students, as part of their development of a conceptual understanding, differentiate between different contexts, and realize that while it is possible to use a single model to account for a range of different phenomena, it may be preferable and more effective to use two models, for example in relation to the earth, or several different models to account for, for instance, the ozone layer, the intensified greenhouse effect, and environmental pollution.

DIFFERENTIATION BETWEEN CONTEXTS

What has just been described basically amounts to a model of conceptual change in which individuals who are confronted with information in a particular setting contextualize this information in ways that enable them to (1) combine information of the conceptions provided into a single compounded model and (2) differentiate between available contexts for interpretation and use ways of conceptualizing the information that correspond to these different contexts and to the current situation (Figure 4.6).

As illustrated by the empirical examples provided in this chapter, this process of compounding and differentiating involves a process of deliberation where the individual draws on cognitive-oriented and discourse-oriented resources, involving both personal

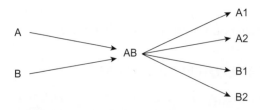

Figure 4.6 The process of conceptual change as a process of compounding and differentiating contexts

beliefs about how the information should be understood and the social framing – such as discursive rules, norms and opportunities – that may support this contextualization process.

On the face of it, this way of describing conceptual change as a process involving deliberation may conjure up an image of an intentional conceptual change in terms of deliberate attempts to radically change from one conceptual system to another (e.g., Sinatra & Pintrich, 2003). It should, however, be noted that the model proposed here involves intentionality not as a motivational and psychological background factor prompting an individual's actions but rather as an analytical construct ascribed to the individual's actions and inferred from the ways in which the individual tackles the situation in hand. To put it differently, intentions here are not to be viewed as "prior intentions" (Searle, 1969, 1983) in a causal chain of events, but as "intentions in action" (Searle, 1969, 1983) inferred within a teleological explanative framework (Davidson, 2001; von Wright, 1971). It is by ascribing an intentionality to individuals' behaviors (e.g., utterances) that makes these behaviors meaningful and reasonable in the circumstances that it is possible to arrive at an understanding of what these individuals are trying to achieve.

Such an approach differs from a sociocultural research stance in that it focuses on the individual and the individual's apparent interpretation of the setting, not – as in most sociocultural analyses – on the setting itself or on the discursive practices constituting that setting. And while sociocultural research strives to account for activities occurring within such discursive practices in terms of ways of talking or of engaging in tool-mediated action (Wertsch, 1998, cf. Vosniadou et al., 2005 with regard to their critique of sociocultural research), the intentional approach proposed here puts an effort into inferring conceptions and conceptual structures from individuals' ways of acting in a particular setting.

Moreover, and importantly, an intentional approach of the kind described here obviates at least some of the critique from sociocultural research concerning the difficulty in gaining access to people's conceptions of the world (Säljö, 1997). The research stance proposed here focuses on individuals' learning activities in a particular setting, and on the meanings that can be ascribed to those activities. In view of this focus on meaning making, the intentional approach is perhaps best described not as a psychology but rather as methodology for understanding and explaining individuals' meaning-making activities and conceptual change. However, as illustrated by the empirical examples presented above, the application of this methodology nevertheless has generated findings that point toward a theoretical model offering a view of the process of conceptual change alternative to those typically followed in research on conceptual change.

CONCLUDING REMARKS

At the outset of this chapter it was argued that much of the research on learning and conceptual change has adhered to a negative rationalism (Rommetveit, 1978) focusing on students' shortcomings and difficulties. The present chapter has outlined a methodology that does not seek to judge students' reasoning in terms of how well they do in relation to a given task. In contrast, the intentional approach proposed here actively moves away from a negative rationalist view, toward what might be called a "positive pedagogy" focusing on learners' potentiality for learning through exploring the opportunities for learning that arise in the learners' interaction with the learning material and with their surroundings. Adopting an approach to conceptual change that emphasizes potentiality rather than fallibility has important implications for teaching. From such a perspective, guiding students' efforts to develop conceptual understanding in different subject areas does not mean accepting or ignoring apparent mistakes or misconceptions. It means taking them seriously enough to look for ways to help students extend and develop these efforts within contexts that allow important salient features of the learning material to be recognized as crucial ingredients in understanding those concepts. Such a perspective, which reveals students' ways of contextualizing concepts and learning tasks, enables teachers to engage not only with students but also with students' efforts to understand. In that sense it also provides a crucial pathway for linking the students' personal conceptions to ways of thinking endorsed within the discipline.

REFERENCES

Bennet, N., Desforges, C., Cockburn, A., & Wilkinson, B. (1984). *The quality of pupil learning experiences.* Mahwah, NJ: Lawrence Erlbaum Associates.

Berti, A. E. (1994). Children's understanding of the concept of the state. In M. Carretero and J. F. Voss (Eds.), *Cognitive and instructional processes in history and the social sciences* (pp. 49–76). Mahwah, NJ: Lawrence Erlbaum Associates.

Björk, R. (1983). *Den historiska argumenteringen. Konstruktion, narration, och kolligation. Förklaringsresonemang hos Nils Ahnlund and Erik Lönnroth* [The historical argumentation. Construction, narration and colligation]. Stockholm, Sweden: Almqvist & Wiksell.

Bowden, J. (1995). Phenomenographic research: Some methodological issues. *Scandinavian Journal of Educational Research, 15,* 144–155.

Brumby, M. N. (1979). *Students' perceptions and learning styles associated with the concept of evolution by natural selection.* Doctoral dissertation, University of Surrey, Guildford, UK.

Brumby, M. N. (1984). Misconceptions about the concept of natural selection by medical students. *Science Education, 68,* 493–503.

Caravita, S., & Halldén, O. (1994). Reframing the problem of conceptual change. *Learning and Instruction, 4,* 89–111.

Cobb, P. (1986). Context, goals, beliefs, and learning mathematics. *For the Learning of Mathematics, 6,* 2–9.

Cobb, P. (1990). Multiple perspectives. In L. P. Steffe & T. Wood (Eds.), *Transforming children's mathematics education* (pp. 200–215). Mahwah., NJ: Lawrence Erlbaum Associates.

Dahlgren, L.-O. (1978). *Effects of university education on the conception of reality.* Paper presented at the 4th International Conference on Improving University Teaching, Aachen, Germany, July 26–29.

Davidson, D. (2001). *Inquiries into truth and interpretation* (2nd edn.). Oxford, UK: Oxford University Press.

Deadman, J. A., & Kelly, P. J. (1978). What do secondary school boys understand about evolution and heredity before they are taught the topics? *Journal of Biology Education, 12,* 7–15.

Dickinson, A. K., Gard, A., & Lee, P. J. (1986). Evidence in history and the classroom. In A. K. Dickinson & P. J. Lee (Eds.), *Historical teaching and historical understanding* (pp. 1–20). London, UK: Heinemann.

diSessa, A. A. (1988). Knowledge in pieces. In G. Forman & P. Pufall (Eds.), *Constructivism in the computer age* (pp. 49–70). Mahwah, NJ: Lawrence Erlbaum Associates.

diSessa, A. A. (2002). Why conceptual ecology is a good idea. In M. Limon & L. Mason (Eds.), *Reconsidering conceptual change – Issues in theory and practice* (pp. 29–60). New York, NY: Springer.

diSessa, A. A., & Sherin B. L. (1998). What changes in conceptual change? *International Journal of Science Education, 20*, 1155–1191.

Doyle, W. (1979a). Classroom tasks and students' abilities. In P. L. Peterson & H. L. Walberg (Eds.), *Research on teaching: Concepts, findings, and implications* (pp. 183–209). Berkeley, CA: McCutchan.

Doyle, W. (1979b). Making managerial decisions in classroom. In D. L. Duke (Ed.), *Classroom management* (pp. 42–74). Chicago, IL: University of Chicago Press.

Driver, R., & Easley, J. (1978). Pupils and paradigms: A review of literature related to concept development in adolescent science students. *Studies in Science Education, 5*, 61–84.

Duit, R. (2006). *Bibliography: Students' and teachers' conceptions and science education database.* Kiel, Germany: University of Kiel.

Ehrlén, K. (2008). Children's understanding of globes as a model of the earth: A problem of contextualizing. *International Journal of Science Education, 30*(2), 221–238.

Ehrlén, K. (2009). Understanding of the earth in the presence of a satellite photo: A threefold enterprise. *European Journal of Psychology of Education, 24*(3), 281–292.

Engel Clough, E., & Driver, R. (1986). A study of consistency in the use of students' conceptual frameworks across different task contexts. *Science Education, 70*, 473–496.

Entwistle, N. (1996). Recent research on student learning and the learning environment. In J. Tait & P. Knight (Eds.), *The management of independent learning.* London, UK: Kogan Page.

Entwistle, N. (2010). Knowledge objects and the nature of academic understanding. In C. Lundholm, G. Petersson, & I. Wistedt (Eds.), *Begreppsbildning i ett intentionellt perspektiv* [An intentional perspective on concept development] (pp. 51–67). Stockholm, Sweden: Stockholms univeristets förlag.

Entwistle, N., & Ramsden, P. (1983). *Understanding student learning.* London, UK: Croom Helm.

Fontana, A., & Frey, J. (2005). The interview: From neutral stance to political involvement. In N. K. Denzin & Y. S Lincoln (Eds.), *The Sage handbook of qualitative research* (pp. 695–727). London, UK: Sage.

Furnham, A. (1994). Young people's understanding of politics and economics. In M. Carretero and J. F. Voss (Eds.), *Cognitive and instructional processes in history and the social sciences* (pp. 17–48). Mahwah, NJ: Lawrence Erlbaum Associates.

Gilbert, K. G., & Watts, D. M. (1983). Concepts, misconceptions and alternative conceptions: Changing perspectives in science education. *Studies in Science Education, 10*, 61–98.

Haglund, L. (in preparation). *Making meaning of historical events.*

Halldén, O. (1982). *Elevernas tolkning av skoluppgiften* [The learners' interpretation of the school task]. Doctoral dissertation, Stockholm University, Stockholm, Sweden.

Halldén, O. (1986). Learning history. *Oxford Review of Education, 12*, 53–66.

Halldén, O. (1988). Alternative frameworks and the concept of task: Cognitive constraints in pupils' interpretations of teachers' assignments. *Scandinavian Journal of Educational Research, 32*, 123–140.

Halldén, O. (1993). Learners' conceptions of the subject matter being taught: A case from learning history. *International Journal of Educational Research, 19*, 317–325.

Halldén, O. (1994). Constructing the learning task in history instruction. In J. Voss & M. Carretero (Eds.), *Cognitive and instructional processes in history and the social sciences* (pp. 187–200). Mahwah, NJ: Lawrence Erlbaum Associates.

Halldén, O. (1997). Conceptual change and the learning of history. In J. F. Voss (Ed.), Explanation and understanding in learning history. *International Journal of Educational Research* [Special issue], 27, 201–210.

Halldén, O. (1998). Personalization in historical descriptions and explanations. *Learning and Instruction, 8*, 131–139.

Halldén, O. (1999). Conceptual change and contextualisation. In W. Schnotz, S. Vosniadou, & M. Carretero (Eds.), *New perspectives on conceptual change* (pp. 53–65). Mahwah, NJ: Lawrence Erlbaum Associates.

Halldén, O., Haglund, L., & Strömdahl, H. (2007). Conceptions and contexts: On the interpretation of interviews and observational data. *Educational Psychologist, 42*, 25–40.

Halldén, O., Petersson, G., Scheja, M., Ehrlén, K., Haglund, L., Österlind, K., et al. (2002). Situating the question of conceptual change. In M. Limon & L. Mason (Eds.), *Reconsidering conceptual change – Issues in theory and practice* (pp. 137–148). Dordrecht, The Netherlands: Kluwer Academic Publishers.

Jönsson, L., Linell, P., & Säljö, R. (1991). Formulating the past: On remembering in police interrogations. *Multidisciplinary Newsletter for Activity Theory, 9*(10), 5–11.

Jovchelovitch, S. (2002). Re-thinking the diversity of knowledge: Cognitive polyphasia, belief and representation. *Psychologie & Société*, 5, 121–138.

Kahneman, D., & Tversky, A. (1982). On the study of statistical intuitions. In D. Kahneman, P. Slovic, & A. Tversky (Eds.), *Judgment under uncertainty: Heuristics and biases* (pp. 493–508). New York, NY: Cambridge University Press.

Larsson, Å., & Halldén, O. (2010). A structural view on the emergence of a conception: Conceptual change as radical reconstruction of contexts. *Science Education*, 94, 640–664.

Lave, J. (1991). Situating learning in communities of practice. In L. Resnick, J. Levine, & S. Teasley (Eds.), *Perspectives on socially shared cognition* (pp. 63–82). Washington, DC: American Psychological Association.

Lee, P. J., Dickinson, A., & Ashby, R. (1998). Researching children's ideas about history. In J. F. Voss & M. Carretero (Eds.), *Learning and reasoning in history. International review of history education, Vol. 2.* (pp. 227–251). London, UK: Woburn Press.

Lundholm, C. (2005). Learning about environmental issues: Postgraduate and undergraduate students' interpretations of environmental contents in education. *International Journal of Sustainability in Higher Education*, 6, 242–253.

Mäkitalo, Å., Jakobsson, A., & Säljö, R. (2007). Learning to reason in the context of socioscientific problems: Exploring the demands on students in 'new' classroom activities. In K. Kumpulainen, C. E. Hmelo-Silver, & M. Cesar (Eds.), *Investigating classroom interaction: Methodologies in action.* Rotterdam, The Netherlands: Sense Publishers.

Maloney, D. P., & Siegler, R. S. (1993). Conceptual competition in physics learning. *International Journal of Science Education*, 15, 283–295.

Marková, I. (1990). A three-step process as a unit of analysis in dialogue. In I. Marková & K. Foppa (Eds.), *The dynamics of dialogue* (pp. 129–146). London, UK: Harvester Wheatsheaf.

Marková, I., & Foppa, K. (1991). Conclusion. In I. Marková & K. Foppa (Eds.), *Asymmetries in dialogue* (pp. 259–273). London, UK: Harvester Wheatsheaf.

Marton, F. (1981). Phenomenography – Describing conceptions of the world around us. *Instructional Science*, 10, 177–200.

Marton, F. (1992). Phenomenography and "the art of teaching all things to all men". *Qualitative Studies in Education*, 5, 253–267.

Marton, F., & Booth, S. (1997). *Learning and awareness.* Mahwah, NJ: Lawrence Erlbaum Associates.

Marton, F., Hounsell, D., & Entwistle, N. (Eds.) (1997). *The experience of learning: Implications for teaching and studying in higher education* (2nd edn.). Edinburgh, UK: Scottish Academic Press.

Marton, F., & Säljö, R. (1976a). On qualitative differences in learning I. Outcome and process. *British Journal of Educational Psychology*, 46, 4–11.

Marton, F. & Säljö, R. (1976b). On qualitative differences II. Outcome as a function of the learner's conception of the task. *British Journal of Educational Psychology*, 46, 115–127.

Miller, G. A. (1956). The magical number seven plus or minus two: Some limits on our capacity for processing information. *Psychological Review*, 63, 81–97.

Nilsson, P. (2006). *Exploring probabilistic reasoning: A study of how students contextualise compound chance encounters in explorative settings.* Doctoral dissertation, Växjö University, Växjö, Sweden.

Nussbaum, J. (1979). Children's conceptions of the earth as a cosmic body: A cross age study. *Science Education*, 63, 83–93.

Nussbaum, J. (1985). The earth as a cosmic body. In R. Driver, E. Guesne, & A. Tiberghien (Eds.), *Children's ideas in science.* Milton Keynes, UK: Open University Press.

Osborne, R. J., Bell, B. F., & Gilbert, J. K. (1983). Science teaching and children's views of the world. *European Journal of Science Education*, 5, 1–14.

Österlind, K. (2005). Concept formation in environmental education: 14-year olds' work on the intensified greenhouse effect and the depletion of the ozone layer. *International Journal of Science Education*, 27, 891–908.

Perkins, D. (2005). *Teaching to encourage thinking dispositions and understanding.* Paper presented at the British Journal of Psychology Conference, Edinburgh, UK, May 19–20.

Petersson, G. (2005). Medical and nursing students' development of conceptions of science during three years of studies in higher education. *Scandinavian Journal of Educational Research*, 49, 281–296.

Petri, J,. & Niedderer, H. (1998). A learning pathway in high-school level quantum atomic physics. *International Journal of Science Education*, 20, 1075–1088.

Piaget, J. (1929/1951). *The child's conception of the world.* Savage, MD: Littlefield Adams Quality Paperbacks.

Piaget, J. (1932/1965). *The moral judgement of the child.* London, UK: Free Press.

Piaget, J. (1952). *The origins of intelligence in children* (2nd edn.). New York, NY: International Universities Press.

Piaget, J. (1970). *Genetic epistemology.* New York, NY: Columbia University Press.

Posner, G. J., Strike, K. A., Hewson, P. W., & Gertzog, W. A. (1982). Accommodation of a scientific conception: Toward a theory of conceptual change. *Science Education, 66,* 211–227.

Resnick, L. B. (1991). Shared cognition: Thinking as social practice. In L. B. Resnick, J. Levine, & S. Teasley (Eds.), *Perspectives on socially shared cognition* (pp. 1–20). Washington, DC: American Psychological Association.

Rogoff, B. (2003). *The cultural nature of human development.* Oxford, UK: Oxford University Press.

Rommetveit, R. (1978). On the negative rationalism in scholarly studies of verbal communications and dynamic residuals in the construction of human intersubjectivety. In M. Brenner, P. Marsh, & M. Brenner (Eds.), *The social contexts of method* (pp. 16–32). London, UK: Croom Helm.

Rommetveit, R. (1988). On literacy and the myth of literal meaning. In R. Säljö (Ed.), *The written world: Studies in literate thought and action* (pp. 13–40). Berlin, Germany: Springer-Verlag.

Roth, W. M. (2001). Situation cognition. *Journal of the Learning Sciences, 10,* 27–61.

Ryve, A. (2006). *Approaching mathematical discourse: Two analytical frameworks and their relation to problem solving interactions.* Doctoral dissertation, Mälardalen University, Eskilstuna, Sweden.

Säljö, R. (1991a). Piagetian controversies, cognitive competence, and assumptions about human cognition. *Educational Psychology Review, 3,* 117–126.

Säljö, R. (1991b). Learning and mediation: Fitting reality into a table. *Learning and Instruction, 1,* 261–272.

Säljö, R. (1994). Minding action: Conceiving of the world versus participating in cultural practices. *Journal of Nordic Educational Research, 14,* 71–80.

Säljö, R. (1997). Talk as data and practice – A critical look at phenomenographic inquiry and the appeal to experience. *Higher Education Research & Development, 16,* 173–190.

Säljö, R., Schoultz, J., & Wyndhamn, J. (2001). Heavenly talk: A discursive approach to conceptual knowledge and conceptual change in children's understanding of elementary astronomy. *Human Development, 44,* 103–118.

Säljö, R., & Wyndhamn, J. (1990). Problem-solving, academic performance, and situated reasoning: A study of joint cognitive activity in the formal setting. *British Journal of Educational Psychology, 60,* 245–254.

Scheja, M. (2002). *Contextualising studies in higher education: First year experiences of studying and learning in engineering.* Doctoral dissertation, Stockholm University, Stockholm, Sweden.

Scheja, M. (2006). *Contextual variation and conceptual understanding in higher education.* Paper presented at the SIG Symposium on Conceptual Change, Stockholm, Sweden, May 14–17.

Searle, J. R. (1969). *Speech acts.* Cambridge, UK: Cambridge University Press.

Searle, J. R. (1983). *Intentionality.* Cambridge, UK: Cambridge University Press.

Sinatra, G. M. & Pintrich, P. R. (Eds.). (2003). *Intentional conceptual change.* Mahwah, NJ: Lawrence Erlbaum Associates.

Sternäng, L., & Halldén, O. (2011). Learning as a process of integration: Students' meaning making of the enhanced greenhouse effect. In L. Sternäng (Ed.), *Ethical and normative reasoning on climate change: Conceptions and solutions among students in a Chinese context.* PhD thesis, Department of Education, Stockholm University Stockholm, Sweden.

Stewart, J. H. (1982). Difficulties experienced by high school students when learning basic Mendelian genetics. *American Biology Teacher, 44,* 80–89.

Stewart, J. H. (1983). Student problem-solving in high school genetics. *Science Education, 67,* 731–749.

Strike, K. A., & Posner, G. (1982). Conceptual change and science teaching. *European Journal of Science Education, 4,* 231–240.

Strike, K. A., & Posner, G. (1992). A revisionist theory of conceptual change. In R. Duschl & R. Hamilton (Eds.), *Philosophy of science, cognitive psychology, and educational theory and practice* (pp. 147–176). Albany, NY: State University of New York.

Taber, K. S. (1995). Development of student understanding: A case study of stability and lability in cognitive structure. *Research in Science & Technological Education, 13,* 87–97.

Taber, K. S. (1997). *Understanding chemical bonding – The development of A level students' understanding of the concept of chemical bonding.* PhD thesis, University of Surrey, Guildford, UK.

Taber, K. S. (2000). Multiple frameworks? Evidence of manifold conceptions in individual cognitive structure. *International Journal of Science Education, 22,* 399–417.

Taber, K. S. & Watts, M. (1997). Constructivism and concept learning in chemistry –Perspectives from a case study. *Research in Education, 58,* 10–20.

Tiberghien, A. (1994). Modelling as a basis for analysing teaching–learning situations. *Learning and Instruction, 4,* 71–88.

Torney-Purta, J. (1994). Dimensions of adolescents' reasoning about political and historical issues: Ontological switches, developmental processes, and situated learning. In M. Carretero & J. F. Voss (Eds.), *Cognitive and instructional processes in history and the social sciences* (pp. 103–122). Mahwah, NJ: Lawrence Erlbaum Associates.

Tytler, R. (1998). Children's conceptions of air pressure: Exploring the nature of conceptual change. *International Journal of Science Education, 20,* 929–958.

von Wright, G. H. (1971). *Explanation and understanding.* Ithaca, NY: Cornell University Press.

von Wright, G. H. (1974). *Lecture given at Stockholm University,* Stockholm, Sweden, March 5.

von Wright, G. H. (1979). Reasons, action, and experience. In H. Kohlenberger (Ed.), *Essays in honour of Raymond Klibanshy* (pp. 107–119). Hamburg, Germany: Felix Meiner Verlag.

von Wright, G. H. (1980). Freedom and determination. *Acta Philosophica Fennica, 1*(31).

Vosniadou, S. (1994). Capturing and modeling the process of conceptual change. *Learning and Instruction, 4,* 45–70.

Vosniadou, S., Skopeliti, I., & Ikospentaki, K. (2005). Reconsidering the role of artefacts in reasoning: Children's understanding of the globe as a model of the earth. *Learning and Instruction, 15,* 333–351.

Watson, R., Prieto, T., & Dillon, J. S. (1997). Consistency of students' explanations about combustion. *Science Education, 81,* 425–444.

Watts, D. M. (1983). A study of schoolchildren's alternative frameworks of the concept of force. *European Journal of Science Education, 5,* 217–230.

Wertsch, J. V. (1998). *Mind as action.* Oxford, UK: Oxford University Press..

Wistedt, I. (1987). *Rum för lärande* [Latitude for learning]. Doctoral dissertation, Stockholm University, Stockholm, Sweden.

Wistedt, I. (1994a). Everyday common sense and school mathematics. *European Journal of Psychology of Education, 9,* 139–147.

Wistedt, I. (1994b). Reflection, communication and learning mathematics: A case study. *Learning and Instruction, 4,* 123–138.

Wyndhamn, J. (1993). *Problem-solving revisited: On school mathematics as a situated practice.* (Linköping Studies in Arts and Science, 98). Linköping, Sweden: Linköping University.

5

RELATIONS BETWEEN SHORT-TERM AND LONG-TERM CONCEPTUAL CHANGE

*Robert S. Siegler and Matija Svetina, Carnegie Mellon University/
Beijing Normal University and University of Ljubljana*

The relation between short-term and long-term change (aka learning and development, microgenetic and macrogenetic change) is among the enduring issues in developmental psychology. Classic theories of cognitive development have taken strong stances on this issue; indeed, part of the reason that these theories are considered classic is that they include clear and well-argued positions about the relation of short-term and long-term change. The stances that have been taken by the classic theorists, however, vary considerably.

Werner (1948, 1957) and Vygotsky (1934/1962) viewed short-term change as a speeded-up version of long-term change. That is, they believed that the two involved the same qualitatively distinct understandings, that the understandings emerged in the same order, and that they emerged through the same underlying processes. Learning theorists (e.g., Bijou & Baer, 1961) also viewed short- and long-term change as fundamentally similar but, unlike Werner and Vygotsky, they viewed both as occurring through gradual incremental processes and not including qualitatively distinct stages. Piaget (e.g., 1964, 1970) expressed a third perspective; he viewed the two types of change, which he referred to as learning and development, as fundamentally dissimilar. In his view, development created new cognitive structures; learning merely filled-in the details of specific content. The contrast among these positions is evident in the following quotations from Vygotsky, Piaget, and Bijou:

This (microgenetic) analysis permits us to uncover the very essence of the genetic (developmental) process of concept formation in a schematic form, and thus gives us the key to the understanding of the process as it unfolds in real life.

(Vygotsky, 1962, p. 69)

By contrast [with development], learning under external reinforcement (e.g., permitting the subject to observe the results of the deduction he should have made or informing him verbally) produces either very little change in logical thinking or a striking momentary change with no real comprehension.

(Piaget, 1970, p. 714)

development reflects the convergence of the basic principles of behavior analysis.

(Bijou & Ribes, 1996, p. 10)

The relation of short-term to long-term change continues to be of major interest within contemporary theories: dynamic systems (Fischer & Bidell, 2006; Thelen & Smith, 2006; van Geert, 1998), neo-Piagetian (Case, 1998; Karmiloff-Smith, 1992; Liben, 1987), sociocultural (Cole, 2006; Gauvain, 2001), and information processing (Munakata, 2006; Rogers & McClelland, 2004; Siegler, 2006). However, a lack of empirical data directly relevant to comparing the two types of changes has prevented understanding from proceeding very far.

In this chapter, we describe an approach that can help advance understanding of the relation between short- and long-term change: combining microgenetic designs with closely parallel cross-sectional or longitudinal designs. The purpose of this approach is to provide maximally similar information about change at varying time scales. To convey the main characteristics and uses of the approach, we first describe the microgenetic method for obtaining data about short-term change, then describe how it can be combined with standard cross-sectional or longitudinal designs, and then describe findings from some studies in which we have used this approach. The studies document surprisingly close parallels between short-term changes elicited by directly relevant experiences and long-term changes elicited by the combination of maturation and the myriad tangentially relevant experiences that occur in the course of children's everyday lives.

THE MICROGENETIC METHOD

Over the past 25 years, microgenetic designs have been used increasingly often to study cognitive development (for a review of research using the approach, see Siegler, 2006). The main reason for the increasing use of such designs is the precise descriptions of changing competence that they often yield. The microgenetic method is defined by three main characteristics.

1. Observations span the period of rapidly changing competence.
2. The density of observations within this period is high relative to the rate of change of the knowledge or skills of interest.
3. The observations of changing performance are analyzed intensively, with the goal of inferring the representations and processes that gave rise to them.

The second characteristic is especially important. Intensively examining performance while it is changing provides the high temporal resolution needed to describe the process of change. The detailed data about changes yielded by such studies also allow us to discriminate between alternative underlying mechanisms. Many mechanisms could potentially produce changes of a general sort (e.g., moving from not understanding X at five years to understanding X at seven years). However, far fewer mechanisms could give rise to the highly specific data about changes in strategy use, particular errors, solution times, and breadth and rate of generalization that can emerge from microgenetic studies. In other words, the detailed data generated by microgenetic studies constrain the range of mechanisms that could produce the changes.

Microgenetic methods have proved useful for testing predictions of a wide variety of theoretical approaches and for studying a wide variety of topics and age groups. They have been used to test predictions from diverse theoretical approaches: information processing (Alibali, 1999; Chen & Siegler, 2000), dynamic systems (Spencer, Vereijken, Diedrich, & Thelen, 2000; van Geert, 2002), neo-Piagetian (Pine & Messer, 2000; Thornton, 1999), and sociocultural (Duncan & Pratt, 1997; Forman & MacPhail, 1993). They also have been used to study development in a wide range of content areas: language (Gershkoff-Stowe & Smith, 1997), memory (Schlagmüller & Schneider, 2002), attention (Miller & Aloise-Young, 1995), locomotion (Thelen & Ulrich, 1991), mathematics (Goldin-Meadow & Alibali, 2002), theory of mind (Amsterlaw & Wellman, 2006), biology (Opfer & Siegler, 2004), and physics reasoning (Perry & Lewis, 1999), among them. Moreover, they have proved applicable to a wide range of populations: infants (Adolph, 1997), toddlers (Chen & Siegler, 2000), preschoolers (Johnson & Mervis, 1994), school-age children (Schauble, 1996), adolescents (Kuhn, Garcia-Mila, Zohar, & Anderson, 1995), and adults (Granott, 1998).

In addition to this broad applicability, microgenetic studies have suggested a conceptual framework for thinking about cognitive growth (Siegler, 1996). This framework distinguishes among five dimensions of growth: its path, rate, breadth, sources, and variability. The *path of change* concerns distinct knowledge states through which children progress while gaining competence. The *rate of change* involves the amount of time and experience needed to produce initial use of an approach and the amount of time and experience separating initial use of an approach from consistent use of it. The *breadth of change* involves how widely the new approach is generalized to other problems, contexts, and related capabilities. The *sources of change* are the causes that set the change in motion. The *variability of change* involves differences among children on the other dimensions of change.

An especially encouraging characteristic of microgenetic studies is that despite the diversity of theoretical approaches, content areas, and populations associated with their use, they have yielded rather consistent findings regarding these dimensions of change (Chinn, 2006; Kuhn, 1995; Miller & Coyle, 1999; Siegler, 2006). A common finding regarding the path of change is that just before discovery of a new approach, children shift from relatively consistent use of a single incorrect approach to more variable incorrect behavior (Alibali, 1999; Goldin-Meadow, 2001; Graham & Perry, 1993; Siegler, 1995). The rate of change tends to be gradual, with less sophisticated, earlier emerging approaches continuing to be used well after more sophisticated approaches also are used (Amsterlaw & Wellman, 2006; Bjorklund, Miller, Coyle, & Slawinski, 1997; Kuhn et al., 1995). The breadth of change often is fairly narrow, though some generalization to conceptually related tasks also is common (Kuhn et al., 1995; Schauble, 1990, 1996; Siegler, 2002). Variability of learning tends to be high; children learn via different paths, at different rates, and with differing degrees of generalization. Finally, certain sources of cognitive growth, such as encouragement to explain observations of physical phenomena or other people's reasoning, operate over a wide age range and in diverse content domains (Calin-Jageman & Ratner, 2005; Pine & Messer, 2000; Siegler, 2002).

The inherent importance of understanding how change occurs, together with the information that microgenetic studies have yielded about change, have led to widespread agreement that such studies are useful for understanding children's learning. There also is widespread agreement that at a general level, the short-term changes that are seen in microgenetic studies resemble the longer term changes that are seen in cross-sectional and longitudinal studies (e.g., Fischer & Bidell, 1998; Granott, 1998; Miller & Coyle, 1999). There is much less agreement, however, as to the level of specificity of the parallels. Miller and Coyle (1999), Pressley (1992), and Kuhn and Franklin (2006) have all noted that the degree of similarity between microgenetic and age-related change is uncertain, both at the level of the descriptive course of change and at the level of underlying mechanisms. They also have noted that the conditions used to elicit change in micro-genetic studies often differ from those that elicit it in the everyday environment. Even when the eliciting events are basically similar, the higher density of relevant experiences and the more consistent feedback in the laboratory setting could result in the changes being quite different in their specifics. These issues led Miller and Coyle (1999, p. 212) to conclude: "Although the microgenetic method reveals how behavior *can* change, it is less clear whether behavior typically *does* change in this way in the natural environment" (emphasis in original). The goal of the microgenetic/cross-sectional approach is to pro-vide maximally comparable circumstances in which to address this issue.

THE MICROGENETIC/CROSS-SECTIONAL DESIGN

The basic logic that underlies this design is that combining cross-sectional and micro-genetic components should yield maximally comparable data (Siegler & Svetina, 2002, 2006). The cross-sectional component of the design involves presenting the same tasks and measures to children of different ages. The microgenetic component involves ran-domly selecting a subset of children from the youngest group of the same population, presenting them with an experience that is designed to promote improvement on the task of primary interest, and then comparing their performance on a post-test to that of peers who did not receive the experience.

Assuming that the experimental condition produces significant improvement on the task of greatest interest, the next step is to identify an age range within the cross-sectional part of the design over which comparable amounts of growth occur on the task. This step involves selecting a global measure of performance on the task of interest, such as percent correct answers, and then locating within the cross-sectional sample two comparison groups, one for performance at pretest and one for performance at post-test. Age peers who were not assigned to the experimental condition ordinarily provide the pretest comparison group. The post-test comparison group is the age group within the cross-sectional sample whose performance on the global measure was most similar to the post-test performance of children in the experimental condition. Identification of cross-sectional and microgenetic samples that showed comparable global change (e.g., from 25% to 75% correct) allows analysis of the degree of similarity of the pattern of changes on the finer grain measures and thus of the degree of similarity of the patterns of short-term and long-term change. Choosing a comparison age range over which comparable overall change occurred is essential, because the crucial issue is the degree of similarity of the *pattern* of microgenetic and age-related change when the overall amount of change is equated. The pattern of change can involve whether the same qualitatively distinct knowledge states occur, whether these knowledge states emerge in the same order, whether the same types of errors are most common, and whether the same quantitative measures reveal change or absence of change. All of these aspects of the pattern of change were examined in the present studies.

A MICROGENETIC/CROSS-SECTIONAL STUDY OF MATRIX COMPLETION

In one microgenetic/cross-sectional study, Siegler and Svetina (2002) examined the development of matrix completion. The matrix completion task that we presented was modeled on one used by Inhelder and Piaget (1964). As illustrated in Figure 5.1, each problem involved a 2 × 2 matrix. Objects were present in the top row and in the left column; the bottom right square was empty. Six alternative responses that could complete the matrix were presented alongside it. The task was to choose the response alternative that, if inserted into the empty square, would result in the two objects at the bottom being related in the same way as the two objects at the top, and the two objects on the right being related in the same way as the two objects on the left. All objects in the problems varied along four dimensions: form, size, color, and orientation (facing left or right). Thus, one way of thinking about the item in Figure 5.1 is: "A large, gray mouse facing right is to a large gray bird facing right, as a small gray mouse facing left is to a ___." The child could then search for a small, gray, bird facing left and select the response alternative that matched that description.

This task was of interest for several reasons. It assesses in a particularly direct way children's ability to focus on multiple dimensions; consistently correct performance requires considering all four dimensions. The task, and the hypothesized underlying ability of multiple classification, play a central role within Piaget's theory. The task also assesses analogical reasoning ability, which plays a central role in information-processing

Figure 5.1 Example of a matrix completion problem

theories (e.g., Gentner, 1989; Halford, 1993; Tomasello, 2006). Moreover, performance on matrix completion problems is predictive of school achievement, which has led to such problems being included on many intelligence tests.

Another reason for our interest in this matrix completion task was that it allowed assessment of the detailed patterning of change. The six possible answers on each problem included only one that was correct on all dimensions, but four others that were correct on three of the four dimensions (the remaining answer was incorrect on all dimensions). Thus, children could improve on one or more of the dimensions (e.g., size) by more consistently choosing alternatives on which those dimensions were correct, even if the children did not consistently choose the correct answer. Similarly, by asking why children believed that the answer they had chosen was correct, we could examine their explicit understanding of the importance of each dimension for making the correct choice.

Siegler and Svetina's (2002) study of matrix completion included seven sessions. Sessions 1–6 were presented at weekly intervals; Session 7 was presented two months after Session 6. The tasks presented in each session are described in Table 5.1.

In Session 1, six-, seven-, and eight-year-olds were presented with the matrix completion task, as well as tests of intelligence, short-term memory, and conservation knowledge. This session provided all of the data for the cross-sectional component of the study; it also provided the pretest measures for the microgenetic component.

The six-year-olds were randomly assigned to the experimental or control group. In each of the four sessions after the pretest (Sessions 2–5), children in the experimental condition were presented with 22 matrix completion problems with feedback and requests to explain why the correct answer was correct on each problem. The combination of feedback and requests to explain correct answers had been found in previous studies to promote learning on a number of tasks, including biological reasoning, geometry, number conservation, mathematical equality, and computer programming problems (Bielaczyc, Pirolli, & Brown, 1995; Chi, de Leeuw, Chiu, & LaVancher, 1994; Siegler, 1995; 2002). The combination was expected to be effective in promoting understanding of matrix completion as well. In Session 6, children in the experimental condition were presented with another 22 problems but without feedback; the goal was to assess their knowledge at the end of the instructional experience.

Table 5.1 Tasks presented to children of different ages and in different conditions in each session

	Session						
	1	2	3	4	5	6	7
6-year-olds							
Experimental	MC, C, R	MC*	MC*	MC*	MC*	MC	MC & C
Control	MC, C, R						MC & C
7-year-olds	MC, C, R						
8-year-olds	MC, C, R						

MC = matrix completion. C = conservation. R = Raven's progressive matrices test. * Feedback and self-explanation questions given.

In Session 7, matrix completion and conservation problems were presented to six-year-olds in the experimental group and to a control group that included six-year-olds who had participated in Session 1 but not in Sessions 2–6. Comparing changes in matrix completion performance between Sessions 1 and 7 allowed us to test whether the experimental condition produced changes greater than would have occurred without participation in Sessions 2–6. Comparing performance in Sessions 6 and 7 provided a measure of the stability of learning among children in the experimental group (because the two sessions were separated by two months). Examining differences between the experimental and control groups in conservation performance in Sessions 1 and 7 provided a measure of the breadth of learning (because no direct experience with conservation was provided in Sessions 2–6). Differences in conservation performance between children in the experimental and control groups in Session 7 but not Session 1 would indicate that the matrix completion experience generalized beyond the immediate task.

The combination of microgenetic and cross-sectional components within this design enabled us to compare the short-term learning within the microgenetic condition to the long term learning within the cross-sectional comparison on 10 measures of matrix completion performance: percentage of correct answers; percentage of answers that were correct on the dimensions of form, size, orientation, and color; percentage of explanations that cited each of these four dimensions; and predominant type of errors. The data also allowed two other, less direct comparisons, one of stability of learning over time and the other of generalization of learning to novel tasks. The reason why these comparisons were less direct was that the cross-sectional data did not provide information regarding stability over time or generalization across tasks, because the same children were not measured at different ages. However, because Piaget (e.g., 1964) identified stability and generalization as among the key properties that differentiate development from learning, and because individual differences in intellectual achievement tend to be positively correlated across tasks and stable over time (Brody, 1992), it seemed worthwhile to determine whether stability and generalization also are present within short-term microgenetic change.

Findings Regarding Microgenetic Changes

Changes over sessions were analyzed along five dimensions: the source, path, rate, breadth, and variability of change.

Source of Change

As shown in Figure 5.2, the combination of problem-solving practice, feedback, and self-explanations resulted in increased learning over the seven sessions. In Session 1, the experimental and control group children produced similar numbers of correct answers; in Session 7, children in the experimental group produced more correct answers. Viewed from a different perspective, number of correct answers increased between Sessions 1 and 7 among children in the experimental group but not among peers in the control group.

Variability of Change

Individual children's performance fit one of three patterns: precocious, non-learner, or learner. Some children (17%) fit the precocious pattern, which required generation of at

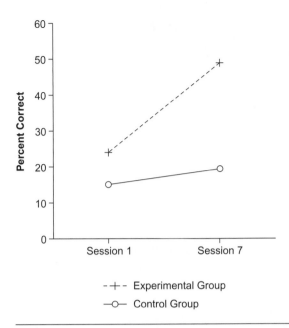

Figure 5.2 Percent correct answers on the matrix completion task in the first and last sessions among six-year-olds in the control and experimental groups

least 80% correct answers in the first session and a mean of at least 80% correct over the last three sessions. Other children (53%) fit the non-learner pattern, defined as fewer than 33% correct answers in the first session and a mean of fewer than 33% correct in the last three sessions. The remaining children (30%) fit the learner pattern, defined as fewer than 33% correct in the first session and a mean of more than 80% correct over the last three sessions. Note that these patterns were far from inherently exhaustive; if a child answered between 33% and 80% correct in either the first session or the last three sessions, the child would not have fit into any of the categories. Lending external validation to these individual difference patterns, children who fit the precocious pattern on the matrix completion task scored significantly higher on the Raven's IQ test than did those who fit the non-learner pattern, with children who fit the learner pattern in between and not differing significantly from either of the other two groups.

Path of Change

A backward trials graph (Figure 5.3) illustrated the path that led to the learners discovering how to solve matrix completion problems. In this type of graph, the 0 trial block is the point at which each child meets the criterion of discovery, in this case three consecutive correct answers on the six-choice task. Percent correct in this 0 trial block is by definition 100%. The −1 trial block refers to the three trials just before the 0 trial block, the −2 trial block refers to the three trials before that, and so on. Thus, the graph illustrates what was occurring just before the discovery and just after it.

As shown in Figure 5.3, most of children's early errors were duplicates; that is, answers that were identical to the object directly above or alongside the empty square in the 2 × 2 matrix (e.g., the small gray mouse facing left in Figure 5.1). However, about 12 trials (four trial blocks) before the discovery, the frequency of duplicate errors greatly decreased

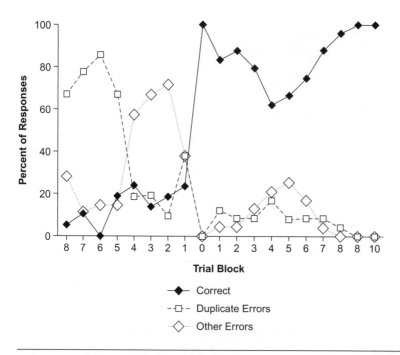

Figure 5.3 Percentage of answers that were correct, that were duplicates of an object already in the matrix, or that followed other incorrect forms on the trial blocks leading up to and following each child's discovery of the correct solution strategy

and the frequency of other errors considerably increased. Thus, children rejected the predominant incorrect approach well before they discovered the correct approach.

In the trial blocks immediately after the discovery, accuracy decreased somewhat from the 100% level during the trial block of discovery; it took about a dozen trials on average before the learners were again consistently correct (Figure 5.3). However, in all trial blocks after the discovery, percent correct was much higher than in any trial block before the discovery.

Rate of Change

Viewed from the perspective of the overall group, learning occurred gradually over the first four sessions (25%, 36%, 43%, and 50% correct in Sessions 1–4). It remained steady at around 50% in Sessions 4–7. In contrast, at the level of individual learners, change was quite abrupt. Returning to the data from the backward trials graph (Figure 5.3), percent correct increased from 20% correct on the 12 trials before each child's discovery to 78% correct on the 12 trials of that child after it (the three trials in the 0 trial block were not included in this comparison, because they were correct by definition).

Breadth of Change

Children in the experimental condition generalized their experience with the matrix completion problems to improve their conservation performance. As shown in Figure 5.4, precocious children did well on the conservation problems from the beginning, non-learners did poorly both before and after experience with the matrix completion

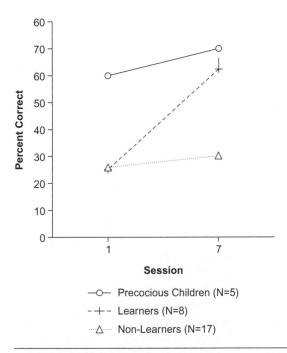

Figure 5.4 Percent correct answers of precocious children, learners, and non-learners on the conservation task in Sessions 1 and 7

problems, and learners answered inaccurately before experience with the matrix completion problems but accurately after the experience. The transfer shown by the learners was evident even after IQ was partialed out. Learning to consider multiple relevant dimensions on the matrix completion task may have led children also to consider multiple relevant dimensions on the conservation problems.

Findings Regarding Changes with Age

Consistent with Inhelder and Piaget's (1964) findings, and those of a variety of researchers since then, children's matrix completion performance improved considerably between six and eight years. Percentage of correct answers increased from 20% for six-year-olds to 48% for seven-year-olds to 78% for eight-year-olds. Percent correct answers on each of the four dimensions also increased over this age span, though the only dimension that was cited more often by children was orientation. At all ages, the same type of error – duplicate errors – predominated. Percent correct conservation answers improved from 24% correct at age six years to 62% at seven years and 74% correct at eight years.

Relations Between Short-Term and Long-Term Change

The change in percent correct answers between Sessions 1 and 7 of children in the experimental condition of the microgenetic part of the study was almost identical to that shown between six and seven years by children in the cross-sectional part. In both cases, children progressed from about 20% to 50% correct. This allowed us to compare the patterning of changes over the seven sessions with changes from six years to seven years.

Table 5.2 is a comparison of the presence or absence of microgenetic and age-related changes on 12 variables. On all but one measure, changes either were present in both microgenetic and cross-sectional comparisons or were present under neither condition. In addition, duplicate errors predominated under both conditions, and the absolute percentage of duplicate errors was nearly identical: 57% duplicate errors among six- and seven-year-olds versus 59% over the seven sessions (chance was 31%). The changes within the experimental condition of the microgenetic study also met criteria that Piaget (1964) claimed were basic characteristics of development but not of learning: transfer to related problems and stability over time. The data showing transfer to conservation were discussed earlier and are shown in Figure 5.4. The data on stability over time are best summarized by the correlation of $r = .98$ between percent correct matrix completion answers in Sessions 6 and 7, which were separated by two months. Such transfer and stability over time could not be assessed within this (or other) cross-sectional designs, but the data from the present study did indicate parallels between the observed microgenetic changes and the theoretically predicted developmental change.

To summarize, the results of Siegler and Svetina (2002) revealed striking similarities between short- and long-term changes. On five measures, changes were present in both the microgenetic and cross-sectional comparisons; on five measures, changes were absent on both measures; and the main type of error was the same on both. On only one measure were the outcomes different for cross-sectional and microgenetic comparisons. This indicates that parallels between short- and long-term changes are not just present at a general level; the parallels, at least with regard to acquisition of matrix completion, are quite specific.

MICROGENETIC AND CROSS-SECTIONAL STUDIES OF NUMERICAL MAGNITUDE REPRESENTATIONS

Another body of evidence that shows close parallels between short-term and long-term change is research on development of numerical magnitude representations. Although no single study in this area has used the microgenetic/cross-sectional design, micro-

Table 5.2 Microgenetic and age-related changes

Variable	Observed changes		Match
	Over sessions (1 to 7)	Over age (6 to 7 years)	
Total % correct	Increase	Increase	+
% Form correct	No change	No change	+
% Orientation correct	Increase	Increase	+
% Size correct	Increase	Increase	+
% Color correct	No change	No change	+
% Form cited	No change	No change	+
% Orientation cited	No change	Increase	−
% Size cited	No change	No change	+
% Color cited	No change	No change	+
Predominant error	Duplicates	Duplicates	+
Stability over time	Yes	Predicted	+
Transfer to conservation	Yes	Predicted	+

genetic and cross-sectional designs have been used to study highly similar populations with virtually identical methods. Combining these studies yields the same type of data as arise from the microgenetic/cross-sectional design.

Numerical estimation tasks have often been used to study development of numerical magnitude representations. Siegler and Booth (2005) defined numerical estimation as a process of translating between alternative quantitative representations, at least one of which is inexact and at least one of which involves a symbolically expressed (written or spoken) number. For example, numerosity estimation requires translating between a non-numerical quantitative representation (e.g., a picture of a jar of marbles) and a number (e.g., saying "there are about 320 marbles in the jar"); measurement estimation requires translating between a line length and a number of units (e.g., writing "this line is about 68 cm long"); computational estimation involves translating from an exact numerical representation (e. g. 75 × 29) to an inexact one (about 2,200); and so on.

Numerical estimation is important for both theoretical and educational reasons. Estimation tasks have proved revealing regarding theoretical issues such as the role of magnitude representations in arithmetic. Experimental manipulations designed to improve estimation also facilitate learning of novel arithmetic problems (Booth & Siegler, 2008; Siegler & Ramani, 2009). These findings indicate that arithmetic learning is not a rote associative process, but rather a meaningful one involving representations of approximate magnitudes as well as recall of exact answers. At a more applied level, early estimation skill predicts both concurrent and subsequent math achievement (Chard et al., 2005, Jordan, Kaplan, Olah, & Locuniak, 2006), and teaching children to estimate more accurately improves a wide range of other mathematical skills (Ramani & Siegler, 2008; Whyte & Bull, 2008). Thus, studying development of representations of numerical magnitudes provides a window for understanding conceptual development and relations between short- and long-term changes, as described in greater depth below.

Numerical Estimation

To study the development of numerical representations, Siegler and Opfer (2003) formulated a number line estimation task for whole number magnitudes. Since then, the task has been used in a number of studies with both whole numbers and fractions (for a review, see Siegler, Thompson & Opfer, 2009). Participants are shown a blank line with a number at each end (e.g. 0 and 100) and asked where a third number (e.g., 78) would fall on the line. They repeat this with new number lines with the same endpoints but different numbers to be estimated until the entire numerical range has been sampled.

This task is particularly revealing about representations of numerical magnitude, because it transparently reflects the ratio characteristics of the number system. Just as 80 is twice as large as 40, the distance of the estimated position of 80 from 0 should be twice as great as the distance of the estimated position of 40 from 0. More generally, estimated magnitude (y) should increase linearly with actual magnitude (x), with a slope of 1 and intercept 0, as in the equation $y = x$.

As straightforward as this linear relation between estimated and actual magnitude sounds, children's estimates often deviate systematically from it. Numerous studies of number line estimation, as well as other tasks, reveal that younger children's estimates of numerical magnitude follow a compressive function that can be approximated by Fechner's law ($y = kx (\ln x)$. Thus, young children's estimates increase logarithmically with the numbers being estimated (Booth & Siegler, 2006; Siegler & Booth, 2004; Thompson & Opfer, 2008). With increasing age and experience, the relation between actual and estimated magnitudes increasingly closely approximates the correct linear function. These findings have motivated cross-sectional, longitudinal, and microgenetic studies of changes in numerical magnitude representations, which have been highly informative regarding similarities and differences in the path, rate, breadth, variability, and sources of short- and long-term change.

Path of Change

The transition from logarithmic to linear estimation patterns occurs at different ages for different numerical ranges: between preschool and kindergarten for the 0–10 range (Bertelletti, Lucangeli, Piazza, Dehaene, & Zorzi, 2010), between kindergarten and second grade for the 0–100 range (Geary, Hoard, Byrd-Craven, Nugent, & Numtee, 2007; Siegler & Booth, 2004), between second grade and fourth or fifth grade for the 0–1000 range (Booth & Siegler, 2006), and so on. The logarithmic-to-linear transition is not unique to number line estimation – similar findings have been made on other tasks, including numerosity and measurement estimation (Booth & Siegler, 2006).

Several explanations have been advanced for the widespread use of compressive representations of numerical magnitudes. Dehaene and Mehler (1992) proposed an environmental frequency explanation; small numbers are much more frequent than larger ones, and numerical frequency decreases in a negatively accelerated fashion (with some obvious exceptions, such as 10 and 100). Siegler and Opfer (2003) proposed an evolutionary explanation – the difference between two and four pieces of food is much more important to a hungry animal than the difference between 72 and 74 pieces, so animals are more sensitive to equal size differences when magnitudes are small. Miller and Nieder (2003) proposed a neural explanation – the logarithmic pattern of behavioral responses follows straightforwardly from the responses of individual neurons to varying numbers of objects. These environmental, evolutionary, and neural explanations are not mutually exclusive; all seem useful for understanding the use of compressive representations of numbers at young ages. Experiences with counting, arithmetic, and other activities in which numbers combine linearly likely accounts for the later acquisition of linear representations.

Microgentic studies of changing numerical representations showed highly similar paths of change (e.g., Opfer & Siegler, 2007; Opfer & Thompson, 2008; Ramani & Siegler, 2008). In these studies, which examined the effects of manipulations designed to improve number line estimates, children also consistently progressed from logarithmic to linear estimation patterns. For example, in Opfer and Siegler (2007; Experiment 2), feedback at 150, the point of maximum discrepancy between the logarithmic and linear functions on 0–1000 number lines, led to large majorities of second graders moving from the logarithmic function fitting their estimation patterns better than linear or exponential patterns to the linear function providing the best fit.

Rate of Change

Cross-sectional and longitudinal studies do not ordinarily yield very useful information about the rate of change, because observations within them are usually widely spaced in time; they can establish boundaries regarding when changes usually occur, but do not indicate whether within that period individuals made a sudden change at different times from each other, or whether most children changed gradually over the entire period or some part of it. Microgenetic studies provide more directly relevant information about the rate of change under conditions in which children receive directly relevant experience.

Examination of microgenetic changes in number line estimation indicate that changes from logarithmic to linear patterns of estimates often occur very abruptly, as abruptly as a single trial (Opfer & Siegler, 2007; Opfer & Thompson, 2008; Thompson & Opfer, 2008). These changes are much more abrupt than others in related areas of mathematics, such as addition, inversion, and mathematical equality problems (Goldin-Meadow & Alibali, 2002; Siegler & Jenkins, 1989; Siegler & Stern, 1998). One reason is that the microgenetic studies of number line estimation have been conducted on relatively large numerical ranges, such as 0–100 and 0–1000, which allows children to draw direct analogies from smaller ranges (e.g., 0–10) in which they are already using linear representations to larger ranges in which they are not. Consistent with this interpretation, calling attention to these analogical relations allows children to rapidly acquire linear representations on the larger numerical ranges.

Breadth of Change

Preschoolers' knowledge of counting, number symbols, and numerical magnitudes are positively correlated, and all show substantial increases during the preschool years. Similarly broad changes occur in response to experimental interventions that improve knowledge of numerical magnitudes. For example, Ramani and Siegler (2008) presented younger and older preschoolers (four- and five-year-olds) from Head Start programs with four 15- to 20-minute sessions within a two-week period in which the children played either a number board game or a color board game. The boards were identical in almost all respects (see Figure 5.5). Both included 10 horizontally arranged, different colored squares of equal size, with the word "Start" at the left end and the word "End" at the right end. The only difference between the boards was that the number board had the numbers 1–10 listed consecutively from left to right in the colored squares, whereas the color board did not. In addition, the number board condition had an associated spinner with a "1" half and a "2" half; the color board condition had a spinner with colors that matched the colors on the squares on the board. Children chose a rabbit or a bear token and used it to mark their progress. On a pretest at the beginning of the first session, a post-test at the end of the fourth session, and a follow-up nine weeks after the fourth session, four types of numerical knowledge were assessed: counting, number line estimation, numerical magnitude comparison, and numeral identification.

As with the matrix study, the similarities in the breadth of change between long- and short-term changes were striking. With regard to changes with age, older preschoolers were more often correct than their younger classmates in numeral identification, counting, and magnitude comparison, and were more accurate on number line estimation as well. Changes over the two weeks of playing the numerical board game were highly similar. After playing the number board game for four sessions, children showed significant improvements in all of the same capabilities (Figure 5.6). Moreover, all of the gains continued to be present nine weeks after the last game playing session. The number board game also improved preschoolers' learning of subsequently presented answers to

Figure 5.5 The number board and color board used in the interventions

arithmetic problems (Siegler & Ramani, 2009). These results suggest that the benefits of playing linear numerical board games are both broad and persistent, just as was the case with the short-term changes in the matrix completion context.

Variability of Change

In Ramani and Siegler (2008), as well as other studies using the same board game (Ramani & Siegler, 2011; Siegler & Ramani, 2009), individual differences within each experimental condition showed considerable stability. Pretest, post-test, and follow-up scores of individual children were highly correlated, despite many children in the number board group improving substantially on all measures.

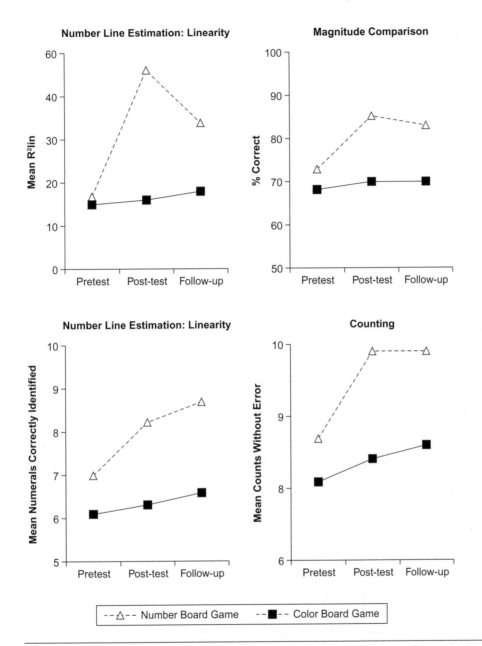

Figure 5.6 Effects of numerical board game experience on number line estimation, magnitude comparison, numeral identification, and counting (data from Ramani & Siegler, 2008)

To examine another type of variability, that which accompanies socioeconomic differences, Ramani and Siegler (2011) presented the number board game to children from low-income backgrounds and to a comparison group of children from middle-income backgrounds. The middle-income children were, on average, eight months younger than the children from low-income backgrounds, but the two groups had comparable initial knowledge of the four mathematical tasks. The path, breadth, variability, and sources of change were similar for the two groups. However, children from low-income backgrounds showed somewhat greater learning, perhaps reflecting the board game being a more novel experience for them and thus having a larger effect.

Source of Change

Microgenetic studies have allowed specification of several types of experiences that can be effective sources of short-term change in numerical magnitude representations. These include playing linear numerical board games (Ramani & Siegler, 2008), encountering linear pictorial representations of operands and answers on addition problems (Booth & Siegler, 2008), direct feedback on numerical magnitude estimates (Opfer & Siegler, 2007), and encouraging children to draw analogies between smaller and larger numerical ranges (Opfer & Thompson, 2008).

We know less about sources of the changes that occur over periods of years in the everyday environment. The fact that second graders often generate linear estimation patterns for smaller numerical ranges but logarithmic ones for larger ranges (Siegler & Opfer, 2003) suggests that experience with particular ranges of numbers is crucial to the acquisition of linear estimation patterns. But what everyday experiences with numbers could trigger the changes over years? The answers to this question no doubt vary with children's age, socioeconomic background, culture, and educational experiences, as well as with the numerical range. However, understanding how development occurs in the natural environment depends on understanding how the environment influences at least some specific developmental phenomena.

Ramani and Siegler (2008) illustrated how sources of development in the everyday environment can be studied through a combination of assessment of the relevant environment and experimental techniques. They focused on preschoolers' acquisition of representations of symbolically expressed numbers in the 0–10 range. The most obvious explanation for this development was that children learn through counting. The later that numbers occur in the counting string, the larger they are.

Empirical studies have demonstrated, however, that counting is unlikely to be the sole source of the development of knowledge of numerical magnitudes. Most three-year-olds can count flawlessly from 1 to 10, but most are highly inaccurate on a wide range of tasks that assess understanding of numerical magnitudes (Le Corre, Van de Walle, Brannon, & Carey, 2006; Schaeffer, Eggleston, & Scott, 1974; Wynn, 1990). At first, children seem to learn counting much like a song in a foreign language, rather than as a meaningful source of information.

The Ramani and Siegler (2008) study described above was based on the hypothesis that experience with number board games plays an important role in learning about numerical magnitudes in many children's everyday environments, as well as in the laboratory. Consistent with this hypothesis, preschoolers' self-reported experience with board games, but not with video or card games, correlated with numerical magnitude comparison and number line estimation accuracy (Ramani & Siegler, 2008). Also consistent with the hypothesis, kindergartners' through second graders' numerical knowledge in the 0–100 range has been found to be more highly correlated with their experience with board games than with a variety of other plausible predictors from the everyday environment, as indicated by parental reports (LeFevre et al., 2009). Studies such as these illustrate how combining experimental studies and assessments of aspects of the everyday environment relevant to gaining proficiency in specific areas can add to understanding of the sources of development.

CONCLUSIONS

The present findings present evidence that short-term and long-term change show many highly specific parallels, as well as other, more general ones. This was especially evident in the findings of Siegler and Svetina (2002). In almost all instances, a given measure either showed change over both short and long time periods or showed an absence of change over both. Stability of change, a feature said by Piaget to characterize true developmental change but not learning, could hardly have been higher than the $r = .98$ correlation observed over the two-month period within the microgenetic sample. Not only did the same type of error predominate in both microgenetic and cross-sectional data sets; the percentage of such duplicate errors was virtually identical at the end of the microgenetic sessions as among the older children.

The parallels were especially striking because the sources of change surely differed. We do not know what aspects of maturation and what experiences lead to improvements during childhood in matrix completion and number line estimation performance, but we can be reasonably sure that the relevant experiences do not ordinarily resemble the experimental procedures described in this study. This observation raises the issue: Why would cognitive change at short and long time intervals show so many parallels, even when the sources that set the changes in motion clearly differ?

One possibility is that cognitive change is analogous to physical change in the locations of inanimate objects. Consider a stone perched near the top of a mountain. Any of a variety of events may set the stone in motion – erosion of objects around it, another stone or inanimate object colliding with it, an animal kicking or stepping on it, a thunderstorm with heavy winds and rain lashing it, and so on. Once set in motion, however, the stone's motion would be similar, as long as the amount and direction of forces impacting it were similar.

Cognitive change may be similar. Any number of particular experiences and maturational changes seem likely to be sufficient to set specific cognitive changes in motion. Once they are in motion, the changes may show many similarities.

None of this is to say that different sources of change generally promote equal amounts of learning. This is clearly not the case. However, the different effectiveness of various sources of change may reflect the likelihood that they will be sufficiently strong to set the change in motion, rather than how the change will proceed once it is set in motion. Again, the analogy to the stone on the mountain may illustrate the point. The forces accompanying different sources of motion vary, and therefore the likelihood that they will set the stone in motion also will vary. However, for forces of equal strength and direction, once the stone begins to move, its subsequent motion is determined by the characteristics of the object and the landscape, rather than by the source of the motion. Analogously, given a constant task and highly similar initial knowledge states, cognitive change may show surprising similarity regardless of the source that sets the change in motion.

REFERENCES

Adolph, K. E. (1997). Learning in the development of infant locomotion. *Monographs of the Society for Research in Child Development, 62* (3, Serial No. 251).

Albali, M. W. (1999). How children change their minds: Strategy change can be gradual or abrupt. *Developmental Psychology, 35,* 127–145.

Amsterlaw, J., & Wellman, H. (2006). Theories of mind in transition: A microgenetic study of the development of false belief understanding. *Journal of Cognition and Development, 7,* 139–172.

Berteletti, I., Lucangeli, D., Piazza, M., Dehaene, S., & Zorzi, M. (2010). Numerical estimation in preschoolers. *Developmental Psychology, 41,* 545–551.

Bielaczyc, K., Pirolli, P. L., & Brown, A. L. (1995). Training in self-explanation and self-regulation strategies: Investigating the effects of knowledge acquisition activities on problem solving. *Cognition and Instruction, 13,* 221–252.

Bijou, S., & Baer, D. M. (1961). *Child development: Vol. 1: A systematic and empirical theory.* New York, NY: Appleton-Century-Crofts.

Bijou, S. W., & Ribes, E. (1996). Introduction. In S. W. Bijou & E. Ribes (Eds.), *New directions in behavior development* (pp. 9–13). Reno, NV: Context Press.

Bjorklund, D. F., Miller, P. H., Coyle, T. R., & Slawinski, J. L. (1997). Instructing children to use memory strategies: Evidence of utilization deficiencies in memory training studies. *Developmental Review, 17,* 411–441.

Booth, J. L., & Siegler, R. S. (2006). Developmental and individual differences in pure numerical estimation. *Developmental Psychology, 41,* 189–201.

Booth, J. L., & Siegler, R. S. (2008). Numerical magnitude representations influence arithmetic learning. *Child Development, 79,* 1016–1031.

Brody, N. (1992). *Intelligence* (2nd edn.). San Diego, CA: Academic Press.

Calin-Jageman, R. J., & Ratner, H. H. (2005). The role of encoding in the self-explanation effect. *Cognition and Instruction, 23,* 523–543.

Case, R. (1998). The development of conceptual structures. In W. Damon (Series Ed.) & D. Kuhn & R. S. Siegler (Vol. Eds.), *Handbook of child psychology: Vol. 2: Cognition, perception & language* (5th edn., pp. 745–800). New York, NY: Wiley.

Chard, D. J., Clarke, B., Baker, S., Otterstedt, J., Braun, D., & Katz, R. (2005). Using measures of number sense to screen for difficulties in mathematics: Preliminary findings. *Assessment for Effective Intervention, 30,* 3–14.

Chen, Z., & Siegler, R. S. (2000). Across the great divide: Bridging the gap between understanding of toddlers' and older children's thinking. *Monographs of the Society for Research in Child Development, 65,* No. 2 (Whole No. 261).

Chi, M. T. H., de Leeuw, N., Chiu, M.-H., & LaVancher, C. (1994). Eliciting self-explanations improves understanding. *Cognitive Science, 18,* 439–477

Chinn, C. A. (2006). The microgenetic method: Current work and extensions to classroom research. In J. L. Green, G. Camilli, & P. B. Elmore (Eds.), *Handbook of complementary methods in education research* (3rd edn.). Mahwah, NJ: Lawrence Erlbaum Associates.

Cole, M. (2006). Culture and cognitive development in phylogenetic, historical, and ontogenetic perspective. In W. Damon & R. M. Lerner (Series Eds.) & D. Kuhn & R. S. Siegler (Vol. Eds.), *Handbook of child psychology: Vol. 2: Cognition, perception, and language* (6th ed., pp. 636–683). Hoboken, NJ: Wiley.

Dehaene, S., & Mehler, J. (1992). Cross-linguistic regularities in the frequency of number words. *Cognition, 12,* 119–149.

Duncan, R. M., & Pratt, M. W. (1997). Microgenetic change in the quantity and quality of preschoolers' private speech. *International Journal of Behavioral Development, 20,* 367–383.

Fischer, K. W., & Bidell, T. R. (1998). Dynamic development of psychological structures in action and thought. In W. Damon (Series Ed.) & R. M. Lerner (Vol. Ed.), *Handbook of child psychology: Vol. 1: Theoretical models of human development* (5th edn., pp. 467–562). New York, NY: Wiley.

Fischer, K. W., & Bidell, T. R. (2006). Dynamic development of action and thought. In W. Damon & R. M. Lerner (Series Eds.) & R. M. Lerner (Vol. Ed.), *Handbook of child psychology: Vol. 1: Theoretical models of human development* (6th edn., pp. 313–399). Hoboken, NJ: Wiley.

Forman, E. A., & MacPhail, J. (1993). Vygotskian perspective in children's collaborative problem solving activity. In E. A. Forman, N. Minick, & C. A. Stone (Eds.), *Contexts for learning: Sociocultural dynamics in children's development* (pp. 213–229). Oxford, UK: Oxford University Press.

Gauvain, M. (2001). *The social context of cognitive development.* New York, NY: Guilford Press.

Geary, D. C., Hoard, M. K., Byrd-Craven, J., Nugent, L., & Numtee, C. (2007). Cognitive mechanisms underlying achievement deficits in children with mathematical learning disability. *Child Development, 78*, 1343–1359.

Gentner, D. (1989). The mechanisms of analogical learning. In S. Vosniadou & A. Ortony (Eds.), *Similarity and anlogical reasoning* (pp. 199–241). New York, NY: Cambridge University Press.

Gershkoff-Stowe, L., & Smith, L. B. (1997). A curvilinear trend in naming errors as a function of early vocabulary growth. *Cognitive Psychology, 34*, 37–71.

Goldin-Meadow, S. (2001). Giving the mind a hand: The role of gesture in cognitive change. In J. L. McClelland, & R. S. Siegler (Eds.), *Mechanisms of cognitive development: Behavioral and neural perspectives* (pp. 5–31). Mahwah, NJ: Lawrence Erlbaum Associates.

Goldin-Meadow, S., & Alibali, M. W. (2002). Looking at the hands through time: A microgenetic perspective on learning and instruction. In N. Granott & J. Parziale (Eds.), *Microdevelopment: Transition processes in development and learning* (pp. 80–105). Cambridge, UK: Cambridge University Press.

Graham, T., & Perry, M. (1993). Indexing transitional knowledge. *Developmental Psychology, 29*, 779–788.

Granott, N. (1998). A paradigm shift in the study of development: Essay review of *Emerging Minds* by R. S. Siegler. *Human Development, 41*, 360–365.

Halford, G. S. (1993). *Children's understanding: The development of mental models*. Hillsdale, NJ: Lawrence Erlbaum Associates.

Inhelder, B., & Piaget, J. (1964). *The early growth of logic in the child: Classification and seriation*. London, UK: Routledge.

Johnson, K. E., & Mervis, C. B. (1994). Microgenetic analysis of first steps in children's acquisition of expertise on shorebirds. *Developmental Psychology, 30*, 418–435.

Jordan, N. C., Kaplan, D., Olah, L. N., & Locuniak, M. N. (2006). Number sense growth in kindergarten: A longitudinal investigation of children at risk for mathematics difficulties. *Child Development, 77*, 153–175.

Karmiloff-Smith, A. (1992). *Beyond modularity: A developmental perspective on cognitive science*. Cambridge, MA: MIT Press.

Kuhn, D. (1995). Microgenetic study of change: What has it told us? *Psychological Science, 6*, 133–139.

Kuhn, D., & Franklin, S. (2006). The second decade: What develops (and how). In W. Damon & R. M. Lerner (Series Eds.) & D. Kuhn & R. S. Siegler (Vol. Eds.), *Handbook of child psychology: Vol. 2: Cognition, perception, and language* (6th edn., pp. 953–993). Hoboken, NJ: Wiley.

Kuhn, D., Garcia-Mila, M., Zohar, A., & Anderson, C. (1995). Strategies of knowledge acquisition. *Monographs of the Society for Research in Child Development* (Serial No. 245).

Le Corre, M., Van de Walle, G., Brannon, E. M., & Carey, S. (2006). Re-visiting the competence/performance debate in the acquisition of the counting principles. *Cognitive Psychology, 52*, 130–169.

LeFevre, J., Skwarchuk, S., Smith-Chant, B., Fast, L., Kamawar, D., & Bisanz, J. (2009). Home numeracy experiences and children's math performance in the early school years. *Canadian Journal of Behavioural Science, 41*, 55–66.

Liben, L. S. (Ed.). (1987). *Development and learning: Conflict or congruence*. Hillsdale, NJ: Lawrence Erlbaum Associates.

Miller, P. H., & Aloise-Young, P. A. (1995). Preschoolers' strategic behavior and performance on a same–different task. *Journal of Experimental Child Psychology, 60*, 284–303.

Miller, E. K., & Nieder, A. (2003). Neural correlates of categories and concepts. *Current Opinion in Neurobiology, 13*, 198–203.

Miller, P. H., & Coyle, T. R. (1999). Developmental change: Lessons from microgenesis. In E. K. Scholnick, K. Nelson, S. A. Gelman, & P. H. Miller (Eds.), *Conceptual development: Piaget's legacy* (pp. 209–239). Mahwah, NJ: Lawrence Erlbaum Associates.

Munakata, Y. (2006). Information processing approaches to development. In W. Damon & R. M. Lerner (Series Eds.) & D. Kuhn & R. S. Siegler (Vol. Eds.), *Handbook of child psychology: Vol. 2: Cognition, perception, and language* (6th edn., pp. 426–463). Hoboken, NJ: Wiley.

Opfer, J. E., & Siegler, R. S. (2004). Revisiting preschoolers' *living things* concept: A microgenetic analysis of conceptual change in basic biology. *Cognitive Psychology, 49*, 301–332.

Opfer, J. E., & Siegler, R. S. (2007). Representational change and children's numerical estimation. *Cognitive Psychology, 55*, 169–195.

Opfer, J. E., & Thompson, C. A. (2008). The trouble with transfer: Insights from microgenetic changes in the representation of numerical magnitude. *Child Development, 79*, 788–804.

Perry, M., & Lewis, J. L. (1999). Verbal imprecision as an index of knowledge in transition. *Developmental Psychology, 35*, 749–759.

Piaget, J. (1964). Development and learning. In T. Ripple & V. Rockcastle (Eds.), *Piaget rediscovered* (pp. 7–19). Ithaca, NY: Cornell University Press.

Piaget, J. (1970) *Psychology and epistemology*. New York, NY: W. W. Norton.

Pine, K. J., & Messer, D. J. (2000). The effect of explaining another's actions on children's implicit theories of balance. *Cognition and Instruction, 18*, 35–51.

Pressley, M. (1992). How *not* to study strategy discovery. *American Psychologist, 47*, 1240–1241.

Ramani, G. B., & Siegler, R. S. (2008). Promoting broad and stable inprovements in low-income children's numerical knowledge through playing number board games. *Child Development, 79*, 375–394.

Ramani, G. B., & Siegler, R. S. (2011). Reducing the gap in numerical knowledge between low- and middle-income preschoolers. *Journal of Applied Developmental Psychology, 32*, 146–159.

Rogers, T. T., & McClelland, J. L. (2004). *Semantic cognition: A parallel distributed processing approach*. Cambridge, MA: Bradford Books/MIT Press.

Schaeffer, B., Eggleston, V. H., & Scott, J. L. (1974). Number development in young children. *Cognitive Psychology, 6*, 357–379.

Schauble, L. (1990). Belief revision in children: The role of prior knowledge and strategies for generating evidence. *Journal of Experimental Child Psychology, 49*, 31–57.

Schauble, L. (1996). The development of scientific reasoning in knowledge-rich contexts. *Developmental Psychology, 32*, 102–119.

Schlagmüller, M., & Schneider, W. (2002). The development of organizational strategies in children: Evidence from a microgenetic longitudinal study. *Journal of Experimental Child Psychology, 81*, 298–319.

Siegler, R. S. (1995). How does change occur: A microgenetic study of number conservation. *Cognitive Psychology, 25*, 225–273.

Siegler, R. S. (1996). Unidimensional thinking, multidimensional thinking, and characteristic tendencies of thought. In A. J. Sameroff and M. M. Haith (Eds.), *The five to seven year shift: The age of reason and responsibility* (pp. 63–84). Chicago, IL: University of Chicago Press.

Siegler, R. S. (2002). Microgenetic studies of self-explanations. In N. Granott & J. Parziale (Eds.), *Microdevelopment: Transition processes in development and learning* (pp. 31–58). New York, NY: Cambridge University Press.

Siegler, R. S. (2006). Microgenetic analyses of learning. In W. Damon & R. M. Lerner (Series Eds.) & D. Kuhn & R. S. Siegler (Vol. Eds.), *Handbook of child psychology: Vol. 2: Cognition, perception, and language* (6th edn., pp. 464–510). Hoboken, NJ: Wiley.

Siegler, R. S., & Booth, J. L. (2004). Development of numerical estimation in young children. *Child Development, 75*, 428–444.

Siegler, R. S., & Booth, J. L. (2005). Development of numerical estimation: A review. In J. I. D. Campbell (Ed.), *Handbook of mathematical cognition* (pp. 197–212). Boca Raton, FL: CRC Press.

Siegler, R. S., & Jenkins, E. (1989). *How children discover new strategies*. Hillsdale, NJ: Lawrence Erlbaum Associates.

Siegler, R. S., & Opfer, J. E. (2003). The development of numerical estimation: Evidence for multiple representations of numerical quantity. *Psychological Science, 14*, 237–243.

Siegler, R. S., & Ramani, G. B. (2009). Playing linear number board games – but not circular ones – improves low-income preschoolers' numerical understanding. *Journal of Educational Psychology, 101*, 545–560.

Siegler, R. S., & Stern, E. (1998). A microgenetic analysis of conscious and unconscious strategy discoveries. *Journal of Experimental Psychology: General, 127*, 377–397.

Siegler, R. S., & Svetina, M. (2002). A microgenetic/cross-sectional study of matrix completion: Comparing short-term and long-term change. *Child Development, 73*, 793–809.

Siegler, R. S., & Svetina, M. (2006). What leads children to adopt new strategies? A microgenetic/cross sectional study of class inclusion. *Child Development, 77*, 996–1015.

Siegler, R. S., Thompson, C. A., & Opfer, J. E. (2009). The logarithmic-to-linear shift: One learning sequence, many tasks, many time scales. *Mind, Brain, and Education, 3*, 143–150.

Spencer, J. P., Vereijken, B., Diedrich, F. J., & Thelen, E. (2000). Posture and the emergence of manual skills. *Developmental Science, 3*, 216–233.

Thelen, E., & Smith, L. B. (2006). Dynamic systems theories. In W. Damon & R. M. Lerner (Series Eds.) & R. M. Lerner (Vol. Ed.), *Handbook of child psychology: Vol. 1: Theoretical models of human development* (6th edn., pp. 258–312). Hoboken, NJ: Wiley.

Thelen, E., & Ulrich, B. D. (1991). Hidden skills. *Monographs of the Society for Research in Child Development, 56* (Serial No. 223).

Thompson, C. A., & Opfer, J. E. (2008). Costs and benefits of representational change: Effects of context on age and sex differences in symbolic magnitude estimation. *Journal of Experimental Child Psychology, 101*, 20–51.

Thornton, S. (1999). Creating the conditions for cognitive change: The interaction between task structures and specific strategies. *Child Development, 70,* 588–603.

Tomasello, M. (2006). Acquiring linguistic constructions. In W. Damon & R. M. Lerner (Series Eds.) & D. Kuhn & R. S. Siegler (Vol. Eds.), *Handbook of child psychology: Vol. 2: Cognition, perception, and language* (6th edn., pp. 255–298). Hoboken, NJ: Wiley.

van Geert, P. (1998). A dynamic systems model of basic developmental mechanisms: Piaget, Vygotsky, and beyond. *Psychological Review, 105,* 634–677.

van Geert, P. (2002). Developmental dynamics, intentional action, and fuzzy sets. In N. Granott & J. Parziale (Eds.), *Microdevelopment: Transition processes in development and learning* (pp. 319–343). Cambridge, UK: Cambridge University Press.

Vygotsky, L. S. (1934/1962). *Thought and language.* New York, NY: Wiley.

Werner, H. (1948). *Comparative psychology of mental development.* New York, NY: International Universities Press.

Werner, H. (1957). The concept of development from a comparative and organismic point of view. In D. B. Harris (Ed.), *The concept of development: An issue in the study of human behavior* (pp. 125–148). Minneapolis, MN: University of Minnesota Press.

Whyte, J. C., & Bull, R. (2008). Number games, magnitude representation, and basic number skills in preschoolers. *Developmental Psychology, 44,* 588–596.

Wynn, K. (1990). Children's understanding of counting. *Cognition, 36,* 155–193.

Part II
Conceptual Change in the Content Areas

Part II

6

CONCEPTUAL CHANGE IN PHYSICS[1]

*David E. Brown and David Hammer, University of Illinois
at Urbana-Champaign and Tufts University*

Research on learning in physics has clearly established phenomena, often referred to as "misconceptions," of students showing conceptual difficulties with the most basic ideas, often in spite of substantial instruction (Champagne, Klopfer, & Anderson, 1980; Clement, 1982; Halloun & Hestenes, 1985; McCloskey, 1983; Peters, 1981; Posner, Strike, Hewson, & Gertzog, 1982; Trowbridge & McDermott, 1980; Viennot, 1979; Whitaker, 1983). There is widespread agreement on the following points.

- Many questions, phrased in a qualitative or "conceptual" way, remain difficult for students despite ample related instruction, including students who can solve standard, quantitative textbook questions about the same topics.
- Incorrect answers to these questions tend to cluster into a small number of alternatives.
- Students often show confidence in their incorrect answers.

For many instructors, it is a surprise to find that students can solve quantitative problems without having even a basic understanding of the ideas behind the solution methods. For example, a student may be able to apply $F = ma$ accurately to find a if given F and m, but if asked to explain what the equation means might say something like: "It means that the force of an object depends on how heavy it is and how fast it's moving." This involves alternative ways of thinking about all three variables – force as a property of an object, mass as weight, and acceleration as speed.

While there is wide consensus on the phenomena of misconceptions, there has been extensive debate regarding their underlying nature and significance. Much of the literature on conceptual change has understood *conceptions* as units of knowledge; some studies have taken the unit at a larger grain size in the form of a naïve theory. This was an early view of conceptual change, and it continues to be widely held in the physics education community. However, as we review below, current research has largely come to reject unitary views of conceptions and conceptual change. How then are we to understand these conceptual difficulties? There are multiple theoretical orientations, ranging from students' ideas as similar to theories in science to students' "ideas" as modes of discourse (see Brown & Hammer, 2008, for an extended discussion of these views). But most research on students' ideas in physics springs from two apparently contradictory theoretical perspectives – students' conceptions as coherent or students' conceptions as fragmented.

STUDENTS' IDEAS AS COHERENT – GENERATED FROM DEEPER, IMPLICIT CONCEPTIONS

While researchers taking this perspective view students' ideas as "theory-like" in some ways, the view of "theory" is that of coherent, underlying, and organizing presuppositions rather than specific theories as in science. This work draws on numerous psychological studies exploring the "naïve theories" of children, adolescents, and adults. In this use, the term "theory" denotes some level of psychological coherence, which may be at an unconscious or implicit level, not the coherence of a scientific theory that is conscious and open to scrutiny.

For example, Spelke (1991) and Baillargeon (1992) have spearheaded work focusing on the "naïve theories" of infants, well before they are able to articulate their ideas using language. Through clever experiments they determine what surprises babies, based, for example, on how long they stare at a new event. From these results they have found that babies have surprisingly adult expectations: that solid objects can't move through each other, that objects that move together are likely connected, and that inanimate objects don't move on their own. This last expectation could be called a baby's "theory of inertia" (Spelke, Katz, Purcell, Ehrlich, and Breinlinger, 1994). Such a "theory" is clearly not the carefully articulated theory of a community of scientists, but it provides an underlying, organizing basis for perception and reasoning.

The framework theory serves as something of a "nucleus" around which observations and other knowledge are organized into models in specific situations, which, as Strike and Posner (1992) argued, may be constructed on the spot. One prediction of this theory is that children's responses to classes of situations will be consistent, since they would access the same framework theory for a variety of instances. While Vosniadou has found such consistency in her work (Ioannides & Vosniadou, 2002; Vosniadou and Brewer, 1992), these results have been challenged with data showing substantially less consistency (diSessa, Gillespie, & Esterly, 2004). Clark, D'Angelo, & Schleigh (2011) replicated these studies and found a level of coherence intermediate between Ioannides and Vosniadou and diSessa et al., although closer to the results of diSessa et al.; we turn to that view now.

STUDENTS' KNOWLEDGE AS FRAGMENTED – A COLLECTION OF PRIMITIVES

The most prominent voice in this camp is Andrea diSessa and colleagues. diSessa's framework, most thoroughly presented in his 1993 monograph "Towards an Epistemology of Physics," directly challenges accounts of novices as holding "alternative frameworks" or "naïve theories." In this view, the intuitive physics of a novice "does not come close to the expert's in depth and systematicity," but the elements of that intuitive physics are the raw material for constructing expert understanding: "the development of scientific knowledge about the physical world is possible only through reorganized intuitive knowledge" (p. 108).

Rather than understanding intuitive physics as composed of intuitive theories, to be confronted, overcome, and replaced, diSessa understands it in terms of cognitive building blocks he calls "phenomenological primitives" or "p-prims." They are "phenomenological" in the sense that they are minimal abstractions from experience; they are closely tied to familiar phenomena. And they are "primitive" both in how people use them, as the obviously true ideas at the bottom level of explanation, and in their role in diSessa's model of cognitive structure as "nearly minimal memory elements, evoked as a whole . . . perhaps as atomic and isolated a mental structure as one can find" (p. 112).

P-prims work by being "cued" or "activated," and a key difference between this account and views of naïve theories is that any p-prim may or may not be activated. In this account, a student's "misconception" that force causes motion comes about as a result of a high cuing-priority for the p-prims "force as mover" and "continuous force." The former is a primitive sense of an initial force acting on an object causing it to move, such as a shove or a toss; the latter is similar but of a force continuously applied, such as a car engine.

This perspective nicely captures the contextuality observed in students' answers to questions asked in slightly different ways, as one would expect that other questions would activate different p-prims. For example, if there were a pebble on top of an ice-hockey puck, a student reasoning about the forces acting on the pebble might not see any in the direction of motion, activating only *supporting* or *guiding* to understand what the puck does to the pebble. The perspective does not, however, reject robust patterns of reasoning, such as the phenomena of misconceptions, although this account is often misread to depict intuitive physics as randomly incoherent. In fact, diSessa discusses "systematicity" at length in his monograph (1993; see also diSessa & Sherin, 1998; diSessa et al., 2004). Rather, it rejects attributing coherence as structurally encoded in the knowledge system; on this account, "systematicity" arises in a complex dynamic, to which we return below. Thus diSessa's account differs from the early views of intuitive physics, which saw students' naïve ideas as like theories in science, much as does Vosniadou's (1994) and Strike and Posner's (1992) revisionist version: While the dynamics of novices' reasoning may produce similar results to articulate, intentional theories, the structure of intuitive knowledge is not well-compared to the structure of those theories.

The differences between diSessa's account and Vosniadou's (as leading proponents of fragmented and coherence views, respectively) are more subtle. Where Vosniadou posits framework presuppositions that act as "constraints" on reasoning and intuitive modeling, diSessa posits elements that are more central in the knowledge system, and so may be cued with high priority in a wide variety of circumstances. For Vosniadou, presuppositions that differ from expert reasoning must be revised; in this sense they are structural misconceptions, albeit at an implicit rather than conscious level. For diSessa, development to expertise may require the addition of new primitives, but existing primitives change only in activation priorities, not in their semantics.

In what follows, we argue for the possibility of a synthesis across these apparently incompatible views. In particular, we suggest that these studies focus on different aspects of a complex dynamic system.

A COMPLEX DYNAMIC SYSTEMS PERSPECTIVE ON STUDENTS' CONCEPTIONS

The points of debate over conceptual phenomenology concern the extent to which students' reasoning is consistent with a core set of tacitly held ideas, and the extent to which it varies with question or context. In our view, there is strong evidence at both ends of this phenomenological spectrum. There are clearly "systematicities" in student reasoning, to use diSessa's term, that appear across a wide range of circumstances, as research since the first papers on misconceptions has documented. It is also clear "that students may change their local, situational models, move from one misconception to another, or even be internally inconsistent" (Vosniadou, 1994, p. 65), as research has amply documented as well. An adequate model of intuitive knowledge must account for the full range of established phenomena.

The field has been making progress in constructing such a model, reflected particularly in diSessa's and Vosniadou's work, and we see this progress as toward a complex dynamic systems (CDS) account of knowledge and learning. Our purpose in this section is to promote that progress. We will review the concept of a CDS, and then we will argue that a CDS perspective can integrate findings from previous work. In particular, we will argue that, couched within a CDS approach, the differences between views of students' conceptions as coherent or fragmented are not as stark as they might appear, and social and sociocultural dynamics can be seen as theoretically continuous with conceptual dynamics.

Complex Dynamic Systems

Vosniadou and diSessa are both in agreement with Strike and Posner (1992), who recommend a dynamic view of students' conceptions:

> Our view of conceptual change must therefore be more dynamic and developmental, emphasizing the shifting patterns of mutual influence between the various components of an evolving conceptual ecology.
>
> (p. 163)

The idea of a "conceptual ecology" is very much in line with a CDS view. An ecology comprises a number of interacting and interdependent organisms or agents. Structures in this ecology emerge because of the dynamic interactions of the agents, such as the relatively stable populations of various organisms. diSessa also discusses the view of students' conceptions as a complex dynamic system, using as an example the emergence of the V shape of geese flying as an example of the emergence of structure.

> Within the complex knowledge system perspective, thinking or 'concept use' is the phenomenological presentation of a complex system in operation. The system, itself, much less its pieces, looks nothing like its appearance. A familiar example is that birds flock in such a way as to give the appearance of having a leader. However, there is nothing like the concept of 'leader' in the simple rules that each bird follows. The fact of a leader might emerge from a rule like (anthropomorphism aside) 'all things equal, it's convivial to fly slightly behind and to the side of a colleague.'
>
> (diSessa, 2008, p. 52)

In a similar way, robust systematicities can emerge among the many knowledge elements that both Vosniadou and diSessa view as constituting students' naïve knowledge. Both Vosniadou and diSessa view the naïve knowledge system as dynamic in this way (Vosniadou, personal communication, 2007; diSessa, personal communication, 2007), although with some caveats, as discussed below.

A complex dynamic system has several characteristics (see Thelen and Smith, 1994, and Thelen & Bates, 2003, for more extended discussions of CDSs as well as extended arguments and evidence for their relevance in models of cognition). Consider a comparison between a CDS and a "regular thing" with enduring, static structure, such as a rock.[2]

1. *Non-linear.* Changes to a regular thing are proportional to influences on it. Double the net force on a rock, and its acceleration will double. With CDSs, at times strong influences can lead to little change (strong stabilities or "attractors" develop that are affected little by external influences), and at times weak influences can lead to substantial, often unpredictable changes (often called the "butterfly effect").
2. *Intrinsic dynamism.* Unlike a regular thing, elements of the CDS are in constant and dynamic interaction. One type of this "remaining the same but changing" is "dynamic equilibrium." Systems in dynamic equilibrium are "thing-like" in that in many respects they remain the same, but they are not "thing-like" in that the mechanisms that produce them are dynamic.
3. *Emergence.* Unlike a regular thing, which has static and fixed structures, because elements of the CDS are in constant and dynamic interaction, structures and patterns emerge as a result of these dynamics. Such structures are typically not predictable based on the individual elements of the system, and so the structures need to be studied at an appropriate grain size.
4. *Embeddedness.* CDSs often have the feature that they are embedded within CDSs at a larger scale and have CDSs at a smaller scale embedded within them. Consider the human body, for example, with its circulatory, nervous, digestive, immune, and other systems. Each can be modeled as a CDS in itself, but each of course is composed of cells, which are also CDSs, and they are all part of the larger system of the body as a whole. On a still larger scale, the nervous system of a modern-day human is a result of the dynamic processes of evolution; at still lower scales are the systems of chemical interactions. Depending on the clinical or scholarly matter at hand, it may be essential to consider more than one level of organization in understanding bodily phenomena. Unlike a change to a regular thing, which affects only the part of the thing changed (e.g., a piece taken out of a rock), a change to a CDS can affect many other embedded and embedding systems.

Non-linearity is at the heart of research on students' conceptions – the finding that even with significant influence through instruction, students' conceptual ideas often remain largely unchanged. This observation agrees with a central characteristic of a dynamic conceptual system, conceptual attractors that can be surprisingly robust. Both Vosniadou and diSessa clearly agree with the *dynamic evolution* of conceptual ideas over time as the evolution of the conceptual system is a central focus in both their frameworks. diSessa clearly agrees with *emergence* – any identifiable systematicities in student thought are the result of dynamic emergence from the complex system of knowledge elements.

Vosniadou has also come to agree with this position of dynamic emergence (personal communication, April 2007). However, emergent structures can be fleeting or highly stable. Finally, with regard to *embeddedness*, Vosniadou's view is based on the interdependence of various knowledge elements – presuppositions, mental models, ontological commitments, etc. – and she often discusses the need for social interaction in learning. diSessa is best known for his focus on the subconceptual world of p-prims, but he does also focus on larger knowledge elements, such as "coordination classes" (diSessa & Sherin, 1998). From this perspective, the disagreements between leading coherence and fragmentation advocates are not about any of these fundamental ideas of complex dynamic systems but rather concern the extent of the stability of the emergent dynamic structures.

A COMPLEX SYSTEMS PERSPECTIVE ON EXISTING AND FUTURE RESEARCH AND INSTRUCTIONAL PRACTICE

For the past 25 years, research in conceptual change has been organized primarily by the ways of thinking introduced in the early research on misconceptions and alternative frameworks: Students have ideas, sensible but incompatible with scientific expertise, and these ideas pose difficulties for constructive conceptual change.

The primary task for research, within this paradigm, is to identify those ideas. That has been a powerful organizing scheme: A researcher looking for a new, do-able, and publishable project needs only to identify a domain of science in which there has not been sufficient charting of students' misconceptions and difficulties. Existing research offers a range of methodological models for how to proceed, such as by posing problems within that domain in clinical interviews, observing students' work in classroom interactions, and designing instruments to assess conceptual understanding. The best work employs a range of these methods, such as starting with observations to find likely candidates of misunderstanding, designing clinical interviews to explore those candidates, and gathering qualitative data of the range of possible lines of reasoning. Thus the incorrect ideas discovered in observations and interviews provide ideas for item construction in the instrument, in how to pose questions and what possibilities to include in the choices for answers. (For a bibliography of several thousand articles identifying misconceptions and difficulties, see Duit, 2009).

In these respects, then, the question "What are students' misconceptions?" (or, many studies in physics ask, "What are students' difficulties?") has been extremely generative. As thinking moves on from the misconceptions paradigm, however, the need opens up for lines of inquiry that have the same fertility and generativity for research.

Our purpose in this section is to lay out a research agenda from within a complex dynamic systems paradigm, illustrating its generativity. We begin by revisiting established empirical findings, to reconsider them from within a dynamic systems perspective. We then turn to promising new areas for research.

Established Findings and Implications from a Complex Dynamic Systems Perspective

The core findings and implications from conceptual change research may all be reexpressed in terms of complex dynamic systems. We discuss several of these established findings below.

Students' Conceptual Dynamics Exhibit Conceptual Attractors

One characteristic of students' conceptual dynamics that became salient early on is that often inappropriate ideas are comparatively undisturbed by instruction (Champagne et al., 1980; Clement, 1982; Halloun & Hestenes, 1985; McCloskey, 1983; Peters, 1981; Trowbridge & McDermott, 1980; Whitaker, 1983). For example, Brown (1989) presented evidence that a conception of force as a property of objects explains much evidence from diagnostic tests focusing on the interactions of objects (e.g., a bowling ball striking a bowling pin), both before and after physics instruction. Objects that have more force exert more force. In many cases these conceptions of physical phenomena are similar even across cultures (Clark et al., 2011; Driver, Squires, Rushworth, & Wood-Robinson, 1994).

From a CDS perspective these are strong conceptual attractors, dynamically emergent stabilities. We would expect to find a range in the phenomena of stability, from momentary thoughts to long-lasting patterns of reasoning; we would expect to find patterns that tend to emerge under specific conditions and others that emerge in a wide variety of situations. This enables a dynamic perspective to embrace both the stability of students' ideas and the fluidity and contextuality of their ideas.

Instruction Must Pay Attention to Conceptual Attractors

Since the earliest articles on conceptual change, researchers have argued that instruction must pay attention to students' conceptions. A CDS perspective provides a new lens on earlier work and its implications. It predicts that learning will not be a linear accretion of knowledge, whether through instruction or through induction from experiment. Even after extensive instruction, students' reasoning may remain unchanged, as so many studies have shown. On the other hand, in some situations brief interventions can have dramatic effects (Duckworth, 1987; Mayer 1995; Clement 1989; Rosenberg, Hammer, & Phelan, 2006).

As we have noted, there is an extensive literature on instruction taking student conceptions into account (Duit, 2009), especially within physics. Reviewing this work from a complex systems perspective gives new insight into the effectiveness of this perspective.

For example, Hewson and Hewson (1983) critiqued traditional instruction as simply introducing new information without paying attention to students' existing ways of making sense of ideas related to the concept of density. They found significant improvement from encouraging students to consider their existing ideas. Minstrell (1984) found that even when he took substantial extra time to carefully outline the logical arguments for Newton's first law in a high-school physics class, most students reverted to naïve ideas later. When he involved students in activities that had them consider their naïve ideas, most correctly answered conceptual questions on Newton's first law toward the end of the year. McDermott and Shaffer (1992; Shaffer and McDermott, 1992) had similar results from helping students consider their own reasoning about electricity and electrical circuits.

In each of these cases, large interventions of one kind had little effect, and improvement resulted from changes in the kinds of interventions rather than simply the extent. From a CDS perspective, these early studies all illustrate a familiar occurrence in non-linear dynamics – the results in student learning were not proportional to the instructional "perturbation."

In each of these cases, a central aspect of the new instructional dynamic was that it engaged students in reflection about different perspectives; students became aware of different possibilities for making sense of the phenomena they were studying. White and Frederiksen (1998) focused explicitly on this aspect of their instructional design, of the role of metacognition in student learning and conceptual change, in the context of their *ThinkerTools* computational environment for middle-school students to explore forces and motion. Cheng and Brown (2012) found that with appropriate metaconceptual scaffolding, fifth-grade students were able to construct, on their own, an explanatory model close to the magnetic domain model of magnetism. In other words, the system involves not only conceptual knowledge but metacognitive knowledge as well, and we may frame White and Frederiksen's and Cheng and Brown's findings in terms of interdependencies among embedded conceptual and metacognitive stabilities.

Students' Conceptual Dynamics Exhibit Fluidity and Contextuality

While there is clear evidence of conceptual attractors, there is also clear evidence of contextual sensitivities (diSessa, 1993; Hammer, 2004; Maloney & Siegler, 1993; Mestre, Thaden-Koch, Dufresne & Gerace, 2004; Smith, diSessa & Roschelle, 1993/1994; Tytler, 1998). For example, Maloney and Siegler (1993) studied students' reasoning on a variety of kinetic energy and momentum problems to show evidence that they held multiple, conflicting conceptions, and the particular conception they applied depended on the problem they were shown. Elby (2000) showed that students were more likely to reason about graphs as though they were pictures, such as to misinterpret a velocity graph as depicting position, when the graphs contain "compelling visual attributes" such as a pointed maximum or an intersection. Parnafes (2007) observed students describing a motion as "fast" in the sense of frequency when observing a high-frequency, low-amplitude oscillation, but shifting to describing another motion as "fast" in the sense of linear velocity. Gupta, Hammer, and Redish (2010) discussed evidence of fluidity and contextuality in learners' and scientists' intuitive ontologies. Cheng and Brown (2012) found that students who were not metaconceptually scaffolded in their development of explanations of magnetic phenomena gave different explanations for different phenomena.

These studies illustrate a phenomenology of variation among different local stabilities: Ask students one question and they show one, often robust pattern of reasoning; ask them a different question or change the context, and the same students show a different pattern. This mix of stabilities and variability is quintessential to complex dynamic systems. As we have emphasized, however, the variability in complex dynamic systems is not without structure, and knowledge in pieces accounts do not present reasoning as incoherent.

Instruction can Draw on Fluidity and Contextuality

A complex systems perspective entails a view of knowledge and reasoning in terms of manifold resources that can activate in various ways at various times, rather than of unitary, systematic (mis)conceptions (Hammer, 1996, 2000). For teachers, it means thinking of student reasoning in any particular moment as possibly only a local stability, and it implies the possibility of other stabilities, of different sets of resources becoming active in other contexts. This suggests instructional strategies to help students find other possibilities in their existing knowledge, to focus attention on building from productive resources, rather than to focus primarily on eliciting and confronting wrong ideas. As well, it suggests caution in interpreting students' correct reasoning as evidence that they "got it."

The same students that have strong non-Newtonian intuitions in some contexts have strong Newtonian intuitions in other contexts (Clement, Brown, & Zietsman, 1989). Students do not only have "wrong ideas" or "misconceptions," and a constructivist understanding of learning holds that sophisticated understandings must develop from the same conceptual system that produces misconceived responses. The underlying basis of the use of analogies and models (Clement, this volume; Clement & Steinberg, 2002; Dagher, 1998; Gilbert & Boulter, 2000; Gutwill, Frederiksen, and White, 1999) is that students will have conceptual resources in one context that they can use in a different context. In other words, analogies and models may be understood in terms of drawing connections among different parts of the cognitive system, and these connections may give rise to new stabilities.

For example, students tend to think of a spring as exerting a force back on a hand that compresses it. That intuition can serve as a conceptual "anchor" for students to recognize the upward force by a table on a book, and an instructor can facilitate this connection by presenting "bridging analogies," such as a book on a bendy table (Minstrell, 1982). Brown and Clement (1989) and Brown (1993) show that this is not an abstract transfer (upward force in one context means upward force in another context), but rather that the construction of a conscious explanatory model in the table context (the table as microscopically springy) allows the attachment of appropriate intuitions to that context. When such bridging analogies and explanatory models are used in classroom instruction, students show significant gains on conceptual questions (Clement, 1993).

That analogies and models can be helpful in instruction is another strong result of the literature (for reviews see Dagher, 1998; Duit, 1991). However, the traditional view of analogy is rather static. In a "structure-mapping" account (Gentner 1983, 1989) the analogical base is construed to have a well-defined structure from the outset that is mapped to the target domain. For example, an analogy may map the structure of the solar system (the base) to an atom (the target), with a large central body and orbiting smaller bodies, with superficial features including the size and luminescence of the sun irrelevant.

From a CDS perspective, the process can be much more dynamic, a fluid recruiting of conceptual resources from different parts of the system that then interact and settle into new patterns. The structure of the base need not be so stable as to remain constant in the process; the "base" may not even exist prior to the analogy. Atkins (2004) presented a dynamic view of analogical reasoning in her analyses of several case studies. She connected the study of analogical reasoning to research on categorization, arguing that the generation of an analogy is essentially the nomination of a category, and that it is often misleading to expect a mapping from an intact, stable base to a target. As categories can be *ad hoc*, such as "things to take from your house in a fire" (Barsalou, 1987), analogies including analogical bases can be as well. Recent work on ongoing model construction, critique, and revision is consonant with this view (Clement, 1989; Clement & Steinberg, 2002; Dagher, 1998; Frederiksen, White, & Gutwill, 1999; Gilbert & Boulter, 2000; Wong, 1993a, 1993b; see also Clement, this volume, for a much more extended discussion of this area of research).

While some segments of the community have focused attention on conceptual change, other segments have focused attention on students learning science as inquiry. Research on analogies in physics classes, for example, has focused almost exclusively on instructional analogies, in the interest of promoting conceptual change, but a small number of studies have focused on understanding and promoting student abilities to generate and work with their own analogies (Atkins, 2004; Wong, 1993a, 1993b; May, Hammer, and Roy, 2006). Conceptual change and inquiry are often treated as distinct objectives (National Research Council, 1996), but a complex systems perspective would suggest they are interdependent, much as White and Frederiksen (1998) treated them in developing and analyzing the results of their *ThinkerTools* curriculum. In this way, a CDS perspective supports views of the importance of meta-level aspects of student reasoning (Hennessey, 2002; Gunstone, 1992; Andre and Windschitl, 2002; Hewson, 1985; Cheng & Brown, 2012)

Research on student epistemologies has begun to consider them as dynamic systems as well, composed of manifold "epistemological resources" that are again context-sensitive in their activation, with multiple stabilities (Hammer and Elby, 2003; Redish, 2004; Scherr and Hammer, 2009), such that students who approach learning as memorization of authoritative information in one moment may approach it as a personal construction of meaning in another. These epistemological resources may be seen in dynamic interaction with conceptual resources. For example, a stable Newtonian concept of *force* may involve a stable commitment to principled consistency in reasoning, because there are many apparent inconsistencies with that concept in unrefined intuition (Hammer, Elby, Scherr and Redish, 2005). Without a commitment to consistency, a student would experience no need to reconcile those inconsistencies (diSessa, Elby, and Hammer, 2002).

New Emphases for Research

We have discussed existing work as seen from a complex systems perspective. A fully dynamic perspective, which we argue the field is moving toward, also has a number of implications for what may be generative areas for further research.

Identifying Productive Resources

With the extensive body of literature on student difficulties and misconceptions in place, the field would also benefit from complementary research to identify possible conceptual progenitors of expert understanding in students' intuitions. In a sense, this work is already under way, as research in curriculum development to address identified student difficulties invariably involves instructional strategies of guiding students toward helpful prior knowledge (Heron, 2004a, 2004b). But relatively few studies have made it an explicit agenda to identify helpful "facets" (Minstrell, 1992, 2000) of students' prior knowledge, the "preconceptions that are not misconceptions" (Clement et al., 1989), such as how thinking about compressing springs provides useful conceptual resources for reasoning about the upward force by a table on a book, or how third graders' reasoning about what could make a toy car move can identify resources for the concept of *energy* (Radoff, Goldberg, Hammer, & Fargason, 2010). The possibilities in identifying productive resources are as rich as they have been for identifying misconceptions and difficulties.

Studying Transitions Among Multiple Stabilities

Naïve reasoning about springs and tables illustrates the phenomenon of multiple stabilities: Thinking about an object sitting on a visibly compressed spring, people think of the spring as pushing up; thinking about an object on a table, people think differently. The strategy of a bridging analogy is about facilitating a transition in student thinking from one stability to the other. We see a promising emphasis for new research in describing the dynamics of transitions from one to another, both as it happens spontaneously and as it may be facilitated by instruction.

For example, Frank (2009, 2010) studied groups of college students collaborating on a kinematics tutorial. The students had ticker-tape strips of different lengths, each with six dots that were produced by a pen making marks at a constant rate of 40 ticks per second. Frank showed that the students shifted between two different conceptual "states": In one they thought it was "obvious" that the longer strips took a longer time to make; in the other they reasoned that the longer strips moved more quickly through the machine. Frank's analysis showed multiple aspects of these different stabilities, including epistemological and physical, the latter in the way students arranged the strips of paper on the table. Similarly, Elby's work (2000) showed different patterns in students' interpretations of graphs depending on the presence or absence of eye-catching features. How subtle can the difference be and still show the correlation?

Studies of conceptual dynamics are more challenging, methodologically, than identifying misconceptions, but work of this kind has already been under way. Research in cognitive psychology began to emphasize microgenetic studies in the 1990s, trying to identify particular developmental changes as they occur, with a high density of observations "from the beginning of the change to the time at which it reaches a relatively stable state" (Siegler, 1996; see also Siegler & Svetina, this volume). That "stable state" need not be developmental, in the sense of a new, fixed part of the learner's reasoning; it might be one of multiple possible stabilities, and the research could focus on understanding the extent of those stabilities and the nature of the transitions from one stability to another.

Developing Multidimensional Accounts of Learning Dynamics

Leander and Brown (1999) discuss six dimensions of embedded dynamics they identified in a microanalysis of a 20-minute discussion in a high-school physics class. These dynamics included focal, conceptual, discursive/symbolic, institutional, social, and affective. The focal dynamics were generally unstable, with the focus of the discussion moving between a pendulum, an object on a spring, a tossed pencil, a baby on a rubber band, etc. The conceptual dynamics exhibited substantial stability within individuals, but substantial variability between individuals, leading to much "talking past each other." Discursive/symbolic modes or forms of communication varied widely between the teacher and students. Students tended to animate stories about particular situations while the teacher tended to focus on abstractions, bringing in individual situations as examples of these abstractions. Institutional stabilities and instabilities were imposed by institutional structures and policies such as grades, syllabi, standardized tests, etc. This discussion came during a test review, and this institutional stability had noticeable effects on the discussion. Social stabilities and instabilities were exhibited in interpersonal alignments and misalignments, and affective stabilities and instabilities were exhibited in various expressions of emotion such as frustration, laughter, and withdrawal.

Research on learning generally identifies a specific target of investigation, be it conceptual understanding, epistemologies, affect, or social dynamics. Educators widely recognize that these various aspects are interdependent. For example, research from an explicitly cognitive orientation often has students working in groups in order to take advantage of the social dynamics, while work from a social or sociocultural perspective will often involve students in consideration of discrepant events. In most cases it is difficult to discern the underlying theoretical orientation simply by observing the instruction. Still, there has been relatively little explicit discussion (Cobb, 1994; Roth and Duit, 2003; Vosniadou, Ioannides, Dimitrakopoulou, & Papademetriou, 2001), largely because it is difficult to conceptualize and articulate the nature of these interdependencies. A CDS perspective may help provide a theoretical framework.

Investigating Non-linear Conceptual Growth

It is easy and familiar to think about a linear relationship between effort and accomplishment. If we need to build a brick wall faster, we need to put the bricks on top of each other at a faster uniform pace. However, if students' conceptions form and are embedded within complex dynamic systems, thinking of a linear relationship between instruction and learning would not be appropriate. We might think of an analogy to population growth or to phase change rather than to adding bricks in the wall. Instructionally, this would mean expecting a period of slow growth at the outset with more rapid progress later, as ideas connect to and build on the initial conceptual understandings. This is not to say that students are not learning much at the beginning (we would argue that a great deal of learning is occurring as students begin to form initial conceptual understandings), but rather that the number of topics covered in a typical textbook is likely to be less. It would also suggest that to impose a linear rate (in terms of topics per unit of time) may not provide sufficient time for meaningful learning at the outset. This would have implications for what happens later, except for those few students who for whatever reason were already at a place in their exponential learning where their rate of learning matched the pace of instruction, and thus they were able to keep up meaningfully.

We do not know of published studies explicitly taking such an "exponential learning" perspective, but there are some indications that such an approach could be beneficial. Anecdotal accounts include Max Beberman, one of the leaders of the "New Math" movement and a skilled mathematics teacher who focused closely on students' ideas in his own instruction. He took this approach with some middle-school students and found that after one semester he was woefully behind other classes. After a year he was slightly ahead, and after two years he was far ahead of the other classes (Easley, personal communication, 1993). Don DeCoste, a former high-school chemistry teacher and current chemistry professor at the University of Illinois, obtained similar results in his own teaching. After one semester teaching high-school chemistry (and not moving on until students had a good conceptual grasp), he was well behind the other classes, but after one year he was slightly ahead (DeCoste, personal communication, 2003). Gautreau and Novemsky (1997) discuss the use of non-mathematical, conceptual physics to begin their physics instruction (van Heuvelen's 1991 Overview Case-Study physics). Even though the experimental classes did not get to practice quantitative problem solving until substantially later in the semester than comparison classes, on tests of quantitative problem solving later in the semester the experimental classes performed substantially better. Benezet (1935) delayed instruction of computational algorithms until sixth grade, focusing in the early grades instead on more conceptual aspects of mathematics such as estimation of quantities. He found the experimental students caught up to traditional students in computation after one year, but they vastly outstripped comparison students in ability to think mathematically. This lesson has gone largely unheeded in the United States. Hiebert et al. (2005) critique mathematics instruction in the United States, based on the *Third International Mathematics and Science Study*. In the US, which did poorly in this comparison, they found that 53% of the time in mathematics classes was spent on review of rather rote procedures, while in countries that performed better much less time was spent on review and much more time on introducing new conceptual material.

CONCLUSION

It has been over 30 years since seminal work on students' content area conceptions and conceptual change in physics helped define this as a central focus in physics education research (e.g., Driver & Easley, 1978; Posner et al., 1982; Viennot, 1979). Research in the area has since grown to many thousands of articles and books (Duit, 2009). As the previous discussion documents, the focus in this research has moved from early metaphors of theory change in science toward a view of students' ideas as emergent, dynamic, and embedded. Such a view helps to integrate a wide variety of findings from apparently conflicting orientations and points toward potentially fruitful future research directions in physics education. We propose the complex dynamic systems perspective not as a totally new and original approach, but rather as a perspective that we believe the field has been moving toward and that will prove generative for further development of research, theory, and practice.

NOTES

1   An earlier version, with more extended discussion in some sections, appears in Brown and Hammer, 2008. This work was supported in part by the National Science Foundation under Grant Number REC-0440113. The views expressed are those of the authors and are not necessarily shared by the Foundation.
2   Our apologies to geologists, who would view the rock, from a geological time perspective, as quite dynamic. However, from a macroscopic and human time perspective, a rock is a prototypically static and enduring entity, a "regular thing."

REFERENCES

Andre, T., & Windschitl, M. (2002). Interest, epistemological belief, and intentional conceptual change. In G. M. Sinatra & P. R. Pintrich (Eds.), *Intentional conceptual change* (pp. 173–197). Mahwah, NJ: Lawrence Erlbaum Associates.

Atkins, L. J. (2004). *Analogies as categorization phenomena: Studies from scientific discourse.* Unpublished doctoral dissertation, University of Maryland, College Park, MD.

Baillargeon, R. (1992). The object concept revisited: New directions. In C. E. Granrud (Ed.), *Visual perception and cognition in infancy* (pp. 265–315). Carnegie-Mellon Symposia on Cognition, Vol. 23. Hillsdale, NJ: Lawrence Erlbaum Associates.

Barsalou, L. W. (1987). The instability of graded structure: Implications for the nature of concepts. In U. Neisser (Ed.), *Concepts and conceptual development: Ecological and intellectual factors in categorization* (pp. 101–140). Cambridge, UK: Cambridge University Press.

Benezet, L. P. (1935). The teaching of arithmetic I, II, III: The story of an experiment. *Journal of the National Education Association, 24*(8), 241–244, *24*(9), 301–303, *25*(1), 7–8.

Brown, D. E. (1989). Students' concept of force: The importance of understanding Newton's third law. *Physics Education, 24*, 353–358.

Brown, D. E. (1993). Refocusing core intuitions: A concretizing role for analogy in conceptual change. *Journal of Research in Science Teaching, 30*(10), 1273–1290.

Brown, D. E., and Clement, J. (1989). Overcoming misconceptions via analogical reasoning: Abstract transfer versus explanatory model construction. *Instructional Science, 18*(4), 237–261.

Brown, D. E., & Hammer, D. (2008). Conceptual change in physics. In S. Vosniadou (Ed.), *International Handbook of Research on Conceptual Change*, pp. 127–154. New York, NY: Routledge.

Champagne, A. B., Klopfer, L. E., & Anderson, J. H. (1980). Factors influencing the learning of classical mechanics. *American Journal of Physics, 48*, 1074–1079.

Cheng, M. F., & Brown, D. E. (2012). *The role of metacognition in students' development of explanatory ideas of magnetism.* Paper to be presented at the annual conference of the National Association of Research in Science Teaching, Indianapolis, IN.

Clark, D. B., D'Angelo, C. M., & Schleigh, S. P. (2011). Comparison of students' knowledge structure coherence and understanding of force in the Philippines, Turkey, China, Mexico, and the United States. *Journal of the Learning Sciences, 20*, 207–261.

Clement, J. (1982). Student preconceptions in introductory mechanics. *American Journal of Physics, 50*, 66.

Clement, J. (1989). Learning via model construction and criticism: Protocol evidence on sources of creativity in science. In J. Glover, R. Ronning, and C. Reynolds (Eds.), *Handbook of creativity: Assessment, theory and research* (341–381). New York, NY: Plenum.

Clement, J. (1993). Using bridging analogies and anchoring intuitions to deal with students' preconceptions in physics. *Journal of Research in Science Teaching, 30*, 1241–1257.

Clement, J., Brown, D., & Zietsman, A. (1989). Not all preconceptions are misconceptions: Finding "anchoring conceptions" for grounding instruction on students' intuitions. *International Journal of Science Education, 11*, 554–565.

Clement, J. J., & Steinberg, M. S. (2002). Step-wise evolution of mental models of electric circuits: A "learning-aloud" case study. *Journal of the Learning Sciences, 11*(4), 389–452.

Cobb, P. (1994). Where is the mind? Constructivist and sociocultural perspectives on mathematical development. *Educational Researcher, 23*(7), 13–20.

Dagher, Z. (1998). The case for analogies in teaching science for understanding. In J. Mintzes, J. Wandersee, & J. Novak (Ed.), *Teaching science for understanding* (pp. 195–211). San Diego, CA: Academic Press.

DeCoste, D. (2003, May). Personal communication with David Brown.

diSessa, A. A. (1993). Toward an epistemology of physics. *Cognition and Instruction, 10*, 105–225.

diSessa, A. A. (2008). A bird's-eye view of the "pieces" vs. "coherence" controversy (from the "pieces" side of the fence). In S. Vosniadou (Ed.), *International handbook of research on conceptual change* (pp. 35–60). New York, NY: Routledge.

diSessa (2007, April). Personal communication with David Brown.

diSessa, A. A., Elby, A., & Hammer, D. (2002). J's epistemological stance and strategies. In G. M. Sinatra & P. R. Pintrich (Eds.), *Intentional conceptual change* (pp. 237–290). Mahwah, NJ: Lawrence Erlbaum Associates.

diSessa, A. A., Gillespie, N. M., & Esterly, J. B. (2004). Coherence versus fragmentation in the development of the concept of force. *Cognitive Science, 28*, 843–900.

diSessa, A. A., & Sherin, B. L. (1998). What changes in conceptual change? *International Journal of Science Education, 20*, 1155–1191.

Driver, R., & Easley, J. (1978). Pupils and paradigms: A review of literature related to concept development in adolescent science students. *Studies in Science Education, 5*, 61–84.

Driver, R., Squires, A., Rushworth, P., & Wood-Robinson, V. (1994). *Making sense of secondary science: Research into children's ideas.* New York, NY: Routledge.

Duckworth, E. (1987). *"The having of wonderful ideas" and other essays on teaching and learning.* New York, NY: Teachers College Press.

Duit, R. (1991). On the role of analogies and metaphors in learning science. *Science Education, 30*, 1241–1257.

Duit, R. (2009). *Bibliography: Students' and teachers' conceptions and science education.* Kiel, Germany: IPN.

Easley, J. (1993, April). Personal communication with David Brown.

Elby, A. (2000). What students' learning of representations tells us about constructivism. *Journal of Mathematical Behavior, 19*, 481–502.

Frank, B. W. (2009). The dynamics of variability in physics students' thinking: Examples from kinematics. Doctoral thesis, University of Maryland, College Park, MD.

Frank, B. W. (2010). Multiple conceptual coherences in the speed tutorial: Micro-processes of local stability. In K. Gomez, L. Lyons, & J. Radinsky (Eds.), *Learning in the disciplines: Proceedings of the 9th International Conference of the Learning Sciences* (pp. 873–880). Chicago, IL: International Society of the Learning Sciences.

Frederiksen, J. R., White, B. Y., & Gutwill, J. (1999). Dynamic mental models in learning science: The importance of constructing derivational linkages among models. *Journal of Research in Science Teaching, 36*(7), 806–836.

Gautreau, R., & Novemsky, L. (1997). Concepts first: A small group approach to physics learning. *American Journal of Physics, 65,* 418–428.

Gentner, D. (1983). Structure-mapping: A theoretical framework for analogy. *Cognitive Science, 7,* 155–170.

Gentner, D. (1989). The mechanisms of analogical learning. In S. Vosniadou & A. Ortony (Eds.), *Similarity and analogical reasoning* (pp. 199–241). New York, NY: Cambridge University Press.

Gilbert, J. K., & Boulter, C. J. (2000). *Developing models in science education.* Boston, MA: Kluwer Academic Publishers.

Gunstone, R. F. (1992). Constructivism and metacognition: Theoretical issues and classroom studies. In R. Duit, F. Goldberg, & H. Niedderer (Eds.), *Research in physics learning: Theoretical issues and empirical studies* (pp. 129–140). Kiel, Germany: IPN.

Gupta, A., Hammer, D., & Redish, R. F. (2010). The case for dynamic models of learners' ontologies in physics. *Journal of the Learning Sciences, 19*(3), 285–321.

Gutwill, J. P., Frederiksen, J. R., & White, B. Y. (1999). Making their own connections: Students' understanding of multiple models in basic electricity. *Cognition and Instruction, 17*(3), 249–282.

Halloun, I. A., & Hestenes, D. (1985). Common sense concepts about motion. *American Journal of Physics, 53*(11), 1056.

Hammer, D. (1996). Misconceptions or p-prims: How may alternative perspectives of cognitive structure influence instructional perceptions and intentions? *Journal of the Learning Sciences, 5,* 97–127.

Hammer, D. (2000). Student resources for learning introductory physics. *American Journal of Physics, Physics Education Research Supplement, 68*(S1), S52–S59.

Hammer, D. (2004). The variability of student reasoning, lectures 1–3. In E. Redish & M. Vicentini (Eds.), *Proceedings of the Enrico Fermi Summer School, Course CLVI* (pp. 279–340). Bologna, Italy: Italian Physical Society.

Hammer, D., & Elby, A. (2003). Tapping epistemological resources for learning physics. *Journal of the Learning Sciences, 12*(1), 53–91.

Hammer, D., Elby, A., Scherr, R. E., & Redish, E. F. (2005). Resources, framing, and transfer. In J. Mestre (Ed.), *Transfer of learning from a modern multidisciplinary perspective* (pp. 89–119). Greenwich, CT: Information Age Publishing.

Hennessey, M. G. (2002). Metacognitive aspects of students' reflective discourse: Implications for intentional conceptual change teaching and learning. In G. M. Sinatra & P. R. Pintrich (Eds.), *Intentional conceptual change* (pp. 103–132). Mahwah, NJ: Lawrence Erlbaum Associates.

Heron, P. R. L. (2004a). Empirical investigations of learning and teaching, part I: Examining and interpreting student thinking. In E. Redish & M. Vicentini (Eds.), *Proceedings of the Enrico Fermi Summer School, Course CLVI* (pp. 341–350). Bologna, Italy: Italian Physical Society.

Heron, P. R. L. (2004b). Empirical investigations of learning and teaching, part II: Developing research based instructional materials. In E. Redish & M. Vicentini (Eds.), *Proceedings of the Enrico Fermi Summer School, Course CLVI* (pp. 351–366). Bologna, Italy: Italian Physical Society.

Hewson, M. G., & Hewson, P. W. (1983). Effect of instruction using students' prior knowledge and conceptual change strategies on science learning. *Journal of Research in Science Teaching, 20,* 731–743.

Hewson, P. W. (1985). Epistemological commitments in the learning of science: Examples from dynamics. *European Journal of Science Education, 7*(2), 163–172.

Hiebert, J., Stigler, J. W., Jacobs, J. K., Givvin, K. B., Garnier, H., Smith, M., et al. (2005). Mathematics teaching in the United States today (and tomorrow): Results from the TIMSS 1999 Video Study. *Educational Evaluation and Policy Analysis, 27*(2), 111–132.

Ioannides, C., & Vosniadou, S. (2002). The changing meanings of force. *Cognitive Science Quarterly, 2,* 5–61.

Leander, K. & Brown, D. E. (1999). "You understand, but you don't believe it": Tracing the stabilities and instabilities of interaction in a physics classroom through a multidimensional framework. *Cognition and Instruction, 17*(1), 93–135.

Maloney, D. P., & Siegler, R. S. (1993). Conceptual competition in physics learning. *International Journal of Science Education, 15*(3), 283–296.

May, D. B., Hammer, D., & Roy, P. (2006). Children's analogical reasoning in a third-grade science discussion. *Science Education, 90*(2), 316–330.

Mayer, R. E. (1995). The search for insight: Grappling with Gestalt psychology's unanswered questions. In R. J. Sternberg & J. E. Davidson (Eds.), *The nature of insight* (pp. 3–32). Cambridge, MA: MIT Press.

McCloskey, M. (1983). Naïve theories of motion. In D. Gentner & A. Stevens (Eds.), *Mental models* (pp. 299–324). Hillsdale, NJ: Lawrence Erlbaum Associates.

McDermott, L. C., & Shaffer, P. S. (1992). Research as a guide for curriculum development: An example from introductory electricity. Part I. Investigation of student understanding. *American Journal of Physics, 60,* 994–1003.

Mestre, J., Thaden-Koch, T., Dufresne, R., & Gerace, W. (2004). The dependence of knowledge deployment on context among physics novices. In E. Redish & M. Vicentini (Eds.), *Proceedings of the Enrico Fermi Summer School, Course CLVI.* Bologna, Italy: Italian Physical Society.

Minstrell, J. (1982). Explaining the "at rest" condition of an object. *Physics Teacher, 20,* 10–20.

Minstrell, J. (1984). Teaching for the development of understanding of ideas: Forces on moving objects. In C. W. Anderson (Ed.), *Observing classrooms: Perspectives from research and practice,* Columbus, OH: Ohio State University.

Minstrell, J. (1992). Facets of students' knowledge and relevant instruction. In R. Duit, F. Goldberg, & H. Niedderer (Eds.), *Research in physics learning: Theoretical issues and empirical studies* (pp. 110–128). Kiel, Germany: IPN.

Minstrell, J. (2000). Student thinking and related assessment: Creating a facet-based learning environment. In N. S. Raju, J. W. Pellegrino, M. W. Bertenthal, K. J. Mitchell, & L. R. Jones (Eds.), *Grading the nation's report card: Research from the evaluation NAEP* (pp. 44–73). Washington DC: National Academy Press.

National Research Council. (1996). *National Science Education Standards.* Washington, DC: National Academy Press.

Parnafes, O. (2007). What does "fast" mean? Understanding the physical world through computational representations. *Journal of the Learning Sciences, 16,* 415.

Peters, P. C. (1981). Even honors students have conceptual difficulties with physics. *American Journal of Physics, 50*(6), 501.

Posner, G. J., Strike, K. A., Hewson, P. W., & Gertzog, W. A. (1982). Accommodation of a scientific conception: Toward a theory of conceptual change. *Science Education, 66,* 211–227.

Radoff, J., Goldberg, F., Hammer, D., & Fargason, S. (2010). The beginnings of energy in third graders' reasoning. In C. Singh, M. Sabella, & S. Rebello (Eds.), *2010 Physics Education Research Conference* (Vol. 1289, pp. 269–272), Portland, OR.

Redish, E. F. (2004). A theoretical framework for physics education research: Modeling student thinking. In E. Redish & M. Vicentini (Eds.), *Proceedings of the Enrico Fermi Summer School, Course CLVI* (pp. 1–63). Bologna, Italy: Italian Physical Society.

Rosenberg, S. A., Hammer, D., & Phelan, J. (2006). Multiple epistemological coherences in an eighth-grade discussion of the rock cycle. *Journal of the Learning Sciences, 15*(2), 261–292.

Roth, W.-M., & Duit, R. (2003). Emergence, flexibility, and stabilization of language in a physics classroom. *Journal of Research in Science Teaching, 40,* 869–897.

Scherr, R. E., & Hammer, D. (2009). Student behavior and epistemological framing: Examples from collaborative active-learning activities in physics. *Cognition and Instruction, 27,* 147–174.

Shaffer, P. S., & McDermott, L. C. (1992). Research as a guide for curriculum development – An example from introductory electricity. Part II: Design of instructional strategies. *American Journal of Physics, 60,* 1003–1013.

Siegler, R. S. (1996). *Emerging minds: The process of change in children's thinking.* New York, NY: Oxford University Press.

Smith, J., diSessa, A., & Roschelle, J. (1993/1994). Misconceptions reconceived: A constructivist analysis of knowledge in transition. *Journal of the Learning Sciences, 3*(2), 115–163.

Spelke, E. S., Katz, G., Purcell, S. E., Ehrlich, S. M., & Breinlinger, K. (1994). Early knowledge of object motion: Continuity and inertia. *Cognition, 51,* 131–176.

Spelke, E. S. (1991). Physical knowledge in infancy: Reflections on Piaget's theory. In S. Carey & R. Gelman (Eds.), *The epigenesis of mind: Essays on biology and cognition* (pp. 133–169). Hillsdale, NJ: Lawrence Erlbaum Associates.

Strike, K. A., & Posner, G. J. (1992). A revisionist theory of conceptual change. In R. A. Duschl and R. J. Hamilton (Eds.), *Philosophy of science, cognitive psychology, and educational theory and practice.* Albany, NY: SUNY Press.

Thelen, E., & Bates, E. (2003). Connectionism and dynamic systems: Are they really different? *Developmental Science, 6*(4), 378–391.

Thelen, E., & Smith, L. (1994). *A dynamic systems approach to the development of cognition and action.* Cambridge, MA.: MIT Press.

Trowbridge, D. E., & McDermott, L. C. (1980). Investigation of student understanding of the concept of velocity in one dimension. *American Journal of Physics, 48*(3), 1020–1028.

Tytler, R. (1998). The nature of students' informal science conceptions. *International Journal of Science Education, 20*(8), 901–927.

van Heuvelen, A. (1991). Overview, case study physics. *American Journal of Physics, 59,* 898–907.

Viennot, L. (1979). Spontaneous reasoning in elementary dynamics. *European Journal of Science Education, 1*(2), 205–221.

Vosniadou, S. (1994). Capturing and modeling the process of conceptual change. *Learning & Instruction, 4,* 45–69.

Vosniadou, S., & Brewer, W. F. (1992). Mental models of the earth: A study of conceptual change in childhood. *Cognitive Psychology, 24*(4), 535–585.

Vosniadou, S., Ioannides, C., Dimitrakopoulou, A., & Papademetriou, E. (2001). Designing learning environments to promote conceptual change in science. *Learning & Instruction, 11*(4–5), 381–419.

Whitaker, R. J. (1983). Aristotle is not dead: Student understanding of trajectory motion. *American Journal of Physics, 51*(4), 352.

White, B. Y., & Frederiksen, J. R. (1998). Inquiry, modeling, and metacognition: Making science accessible to all students. *Cognition and Instruction, 16*(1), 3–118.

Wong, E. D. (1993a). Self-generated analogies as a tool for constructing and evaluating explanations of scientific phenomena. *Journal of Research in Science Teaching, 30*(4), 367–380.

Wong, E. D. (1993b). Understanding the generative capacity of analogies as a tool for explanation. *Journal of Research in Science Teaching, 30*(10), 1259–1272.

7

CONCEPTUAL CHANGE WHEN LEARNING
EXPERIMENTAL DESIGN

Stephanie Siler, David Klahr, and Bryan J. Matlen, Carnegie Mellon University and Pittsburgh Science of Learning Center

As indicated by the other chapters in this volume, there are important cross-domain commonalities in conceptual change processes. However, some processes of conceptual change are specific to the domain in which those concepts are situated. In this chapter we describe several processes that support changes in how children think about a small, but essential, domain-general part of middle-school science instruction: the design of simple experiments (typically dubbed the "control of variables strategy" or "CVS"). Experimental design may be an interesting topic for conceptual change researchers because there are not only conceptual but also many procedural aspects involved in its mastery.

Procedurally, CVS is a method for creating experiments in which a single contrast is made between experimental conditions. Consider, for example, a procedure for creating an unconfounded experiment to determine whether or not the height of a ramp influences the distance a ball travels after rolling down the ramp. Assume that we have a pair of ramps that can vary along four dimensions: ramp height (high or low), run length (long or short), ramp surface (rough or smooth), and type of ball (golf ball or squash ball). The CVS procedure can be stated in a few simple rules: (a) Rule 1: identify the focal variable (e.g., ramp height); (b) Rule 2: contrast values for the focal variable (e.g., a high ramp and a low ramp); (c) Rule 3: ensure that all non-focal variables (e.g., ball type, ramp surface, run length) are the same across conditions.

The simplicity of this rule set would seem to make it easy to teach and learn. However, this expectation is based on the assumption that students bring to bear correct conceptions of the purpose behind these procedures: to identify the causal status of variables. If instead they bring different conceptions, instruction may not be so straightforward. Students' misconceptions about the goals of an experimentation task were reported by Schauble, Klopfer, and Raghavan (1991); rather than viewing the goal of the task as finding out whether variables are causal – i.e., adopting a "science" goal of *finding out about something*[1] – many fifth- and sixth-grade children conceived of the goal as producing desirable outcomes – i.e., they adopted "engineering" goals. Such misunderstandings of the goals of tasks that are not defined as "experiments" – but in which the given task goal is to *find out about* the effects of variables – have also been identified (e.g., Tschirgi, 1980). Thus, students' goal conceptions may initially be distinct from their conceptions of "experiments" and require integration. This issue will be discussed further later in the chapter.

In our research aimed at constructing an intelligent tutor to teach experimentation skills (e.g., Siler, Klahr, Magaro, Willows, & Mowery, 2010), we have found engineering goal orientations to be common even in middle-school children (e.g., Siler & Klahr, 2012). Thus, learning CVS may involve a crucial conceptual transition from an engineering goal to a science goal orientation toward the task. Consequently, CVS learning may involve both conceptual *and* procedural change, processes that appear to be interrelated.

In this chapter, we primarily focus on the goal orientation aspect of conceptual change in CVS. We begin by summarizing our research findings on CVS learning and goal misinterpretations to orient discussion of the nature of engineering vs. science goals in greater detail. Afterwards, we consider possible underlying causes of goal misinterpretations. Although our work was not initially motivated by considerations of theories of conceptual change, the tenacity with which some students maintained their incorrect conceptions of the instructional task – which generally led to CVS learning failures – prompted us to take these into consideration. Thus, we examine students' conceptions of CVS *vis-à-vis* specific issues that arise in conceptual change research, including the nature of the conceptual change processes during CVS acquisition and evidence of "synthesizing" CVS procedures onto intuitive conceptual knowledge. Finally, we discuss instructional strategies for inducing conceptual change in light of potential causes.

RESEARCH OVERVIEW

Our first investigation of CVS acquisition (Chen & Klahr, 1999) explored the effects of different levels of explicit instruction on the extent to which second- through fourth-graders were capable of learning CVS. Prior research suggested that children this age did not consistently apply CVS procedures (Bullock & Ziegler, 1999; Kuhn, Garcia-Mila, Zohar, & Andersen, 1995; Schauble, 1996). Several important findings emerged: (1) At least some third- and fourth-grade students could, with some instruction, learn to consistently apply the principles of CVS, (2) providing students with explicit explanations rather than relying on them to discover the strategy on their own produced better learning outcomes, and (3) even though children younger than what was previously thought were capable of learning CVS, there was still a developmental trend (i.e., second graders failed to learn CVS even when given explicit explanations and examples). When this explicit instruction was translated into a whole-classroom intervention (Toth, Klahr, & Chen, 2000), fourth-graders again demonstrated significant CVS gains. Moreover, learning from explicit instruction transferred to disparate domains (Klahr & Nigam, 2004; Matlen & Klahr, 2010), and over delays of up to three years (Strand-Cary & Klahr, 2008).

The studies summarized thus far were all conducted in schools serving populations of middle to high socioeconomic status (SES). When delivered in a low-SES school, more intensive and individualized instruction was necessary for fifth- and sixth-grade students to achieve mastery rates comparable to those of the higher-SES students (Klahr & Li, 2005). In addition, whole-classroom instruction at two low-SES fifth-grade classrooms revealed that CVS mastery rates were less than half the mastery rate of a middle-SES student population (about 33% and 77%, respectively). Such results motivated our development of the "TED" (training in experimental design) tutor, capable of adapting instruction to the needs of a diverse range of students. TED was constructed in several phases. Its earliest versions were non-adaptive, where the same material was presented to students regardless of their responses. Later versions include response-dependent instructional branching.

STUDY 1

In an initial evaluation of a non-adaptive version of the TED tutor, we compared learning and transfer rates of students from a school serving a primarily middle/high-SES and two schools serving predominnatly low-SES student populations. Students in the low-SES populations had significantly lower standardized test scores (notably, reading comprehension and science). Individual student-level data – including explanations – were collected throughout this evaluation, enabling the tracing of students' developing conceptual and procedural knowledge of CVS. Students first completed a story pretest, where they designed and evaluated experiments and explained their responses in three domains: selling drinks (Figures 7.1 and 7.2), designing rockets, and baking cookies.

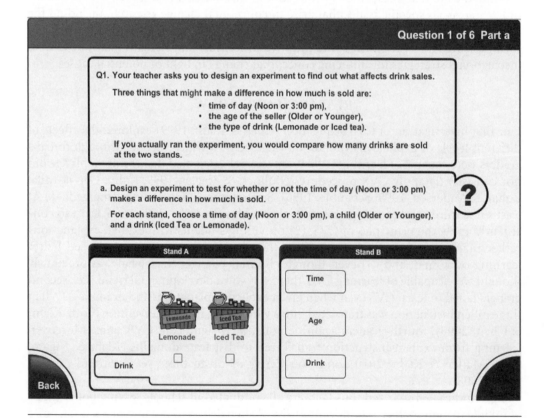

Figure 7.1 Screenshot of an experimental design question from the story pretest given in the TED tutor

Students were then introduced to a virtual ramps apparatus and its four variables[2] and completed a ramps pretest where they designed an experiment for each variable and explained their designs. Afterwards, they viewed a brief video introduction to the lesson. During instruction, students evaluated three experiments and received both feedback on their responses and explanations for why the experiments were (or were not) good ways to find out about the target variable, including the rationale for applying CVS. Afterwards, students completed a ramps post-test, identical to the ramps pretest. The next day, they completed a story post-test (identical to the story pretest) that assessed their ability to transfer CVS to the three non-instructional domains. Three weeks later they completed the story post-test.

Again, the low-SES students performed somewhat worse on the ramps post-test than the higher-SES students. However, transfer mastery rates of the low-SES students were notably lower – only about one-quarter those of the higher-SES students. To investigate why, we examined the responses students gave throughout Study 1, during human-delivered remedial tutoring sessions of students in the whole-classroom study who failed to learn CVS from the classroom instruction, and story pretest responses of third-grade students from another investigation. We realized that students often interpreted assessment and instructional questions as asking them to (a) apply engineering goals of setting up experiments to produce a desired outcome (cf. Schauble et al., 1991), *or* (b) express their beliefs about the domain-specific variables, rather than as asking about the validity of the experimental designs for determining the causal status of variables.

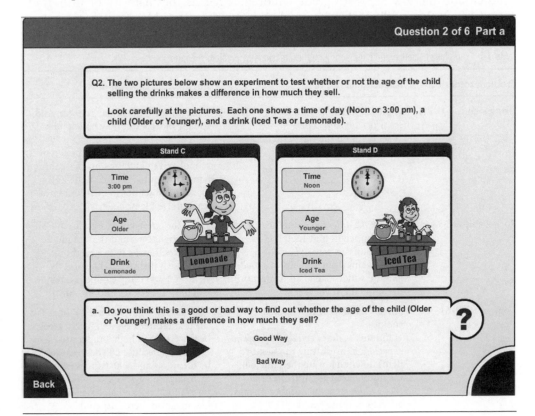

Figure 7.2 Screenshot of an experimental evaluation question from the story pretest

Age/SES-level and Goal Response

To provide further insight into possible causes of these misinterpretations, we first examine age- and SES-related trends in how students interpret the goal of the task, then discuss the nature of these misinterpretations in more detail. Students' open-ended explanations on the story pretest were coded for goal expression/application. Typical student responses are shown in Table 7.1. Response patterns included those in which students' explanations indicated: (a) only science goals and/or CVS understanding, (b) only engineering goals, and (c) both goals. That is, the pattern for students who only indicated intentions of finding out about something, including at least one variable or how conditions compare (e.g., two different drink stands, as in the first example of Table 7.1) was considered "science-only"; that of students who only indicated intentions of producing particular outcomes in their responses (e.g., of making the rockets fly straight up, examples of which are shown in Table 7.1) was considered "engineering-only"; and the pattern of students who indicated application of both goals (usually on different responses) was coded as "both goals." Responses that included only procedural explanations (e.g., "I made everything different") without explicit or implicit indication of intent were omitted from analyses, and responses indicating guessing or inability to explain were not considered to reflect any goal.

The goal response pattern of the middle/high-SES fifth-grade children (shown in Table 7.2) significantly differed from that of both the middle/high-SES third-grade children and the low-SES fifth-grade children. Whereas the majority of fifth-grade students from the middle/high-SES population (60%) indicated both goal types at least

Table 7.1 Examples of science and engineering goal expressions by problem scenario

Problem scenario	Science goal response	Engineering goal response
Drink stands (Q1&2)	"I picked different [stands] *so I could see which one did better.*" "I set them up the way I did because now *I can compare them.*"	"The hottest time of day is noon. And usually older kids know how to talk better." "At three o'clock [k]ids will be out of school and thirsty for some ice cold lemonade and . . . noon all the kids would be in school so they could not leave and get lemonade."
Rocket ships (Q3&4)	"*To see the differences* and the different height how high it goes." "I set it up this way *so I could see* what engine, way the ship was made, and the windows had an [e]ffect on the ship's flight."	"I did the curved body because the air will go right by it and the straight engines will make it go straight up." "because if it is str[a]ight it will fly str[a]ight and if the engine is down it will blow the rocket into the air."
Cookies (Q5&6)	"*I set it up to see* who likes better cookies." "I did this *so that I could compare the experiments* by putting the first two items down that were the same, but the number of eggs diff[e]rent *so that I could see if* the number of eggs affected how the people liked the cookies."	"The honey might not melt a lot as the sugar and three eggs and 350 degrees because 350 is a high temperature." "I set it up because 200 degrees would be to[o] low and 500 degrees would be to[o] high. 3 eggs would probably be to[o] much egg and alot [sic] of people like sugar on there [sic] cookie"

Table 7.2 Goal response pattern on pretest: Frequency (and percent) by SES level and grade

SES level	Mid/High	Mid/High	Low
Grade	5	3	5
Science only	6 (14%)	1 (2%)	0 (0%)
Engineering only	11 (26%)	37 (70%)	18 (86%)
Science & engineering	25 (60%)	15 (28%)	3 (14%)
Total	42	53	21

once throughout the story pretest, the majority of the younger children (70%) and the majority of fifth-grade students from the low-SES population (86%) *only* gave engineering goal explanations. (The goal response pattern of the middle/high-SES third-grade students did not significantly differ from that of the low-SES fifth-grade students.) In general, developmental as well as SES-level trends were from application of only engineering goals across pretest problems to application of both science and engineering goals. Thus, science goals appear to strengthen and/or engineering goals weaken with both age and SES level.

As noted earlier, tasks intended to activate science goals (*to find out about* something, such as causal factors) inadvertently but frequently activate engineering goals (e.g., Tschirgi, 1980; Kuhn & Phelps, 1982; Schauble, 1990; Schauble et al., 1991). We found that this tendency is rather tenacious: Even *after* Study 1 students had completed the instruction, many students held to their engineering goals (Siler & Klahr, 2012).

CHARACTERISTICS OF SCIENCE VS. ENGINEERING GOALS

Domain-specific Beliefs

What knowledge is involved in applying science *vis-à-vis* engineering goals in experimental design tasks? As previously discussed, students must understand the specific science goal underlying the task – to find out whether a variable is causal. Applying CVS in the service of this (science) goal requires identifying a variable to test, contrasting that variable's levels across conditions, and controlling other variables. CVS application within a particular domain does not depend on one's beliefs about the associated variable values. That is, any given non-focal variable can be set to any level (provided the levels are the same across conditions).

In settings where all relevant variables and their levels are explicitly defined, as is common in laboratory experiments (e.g., Chen & Klahr, 1999) and exploratory tasks (e.g., Schauble et al., 1991), it is *not* necessary to apply one's beliefs about the effects of variables.[3] And in fact, students rarely expressed their beliefs about variable effects within *any* type of science goal explanation (Siler & Klahr, 2012).

As with science goals, engineering goals are applicable across various contexts and domains (e.g., making the fastest rockets or tastiest cookies). However, in contrast to CVS science-goal applications, the specific form an engineering goal takes often necessarily depends on one's beliefs about the problem's surface features, including the specific problem scenario and associated variables. For example, the application of an engineering goal of making the fastest rocket depends on the student's beliefs about which are the better levels for each variable. In contrast, if a student wants to *find out* whether the shape of the rocket matters by designing an experiment, her beliefs about the effects of the other variables are not relevant.[4]

Three general types of engineering goals found in students' responses were "maximal-outcome," "same-outcomes," and "different-outcomes" goals (Siler & Klahr, 2012). By far the most common,[5] "maximal-outcome" goals were those attempting to maximize an outcome, such as making the fastest rocket or selling the most drinks. For example, a fifth-grade student in Study 1 set up her drink stand at noon (rather than 3pm), selected an older child seller, and chose lemonade (rather than iced tea) because "a lot of people are out earlier. I chose an older child because they can have more experience of selling stuff and I like lemonade." As shown in this example, applying maximal-outcome goals requires tailoring the design to one's beliefs about the relevant variables – specifically, beliefs about which variable values are better for producing an outcome.

Less common were "same-outcome" goals such as producing equally fast rockets or similar-tasting cookies. For example, another fifth-grade Study 1 student evaluated a non-contrastive design (where the values for each variable were the same across conditions) as good because: "if they have the same ingredients they might have the same taste." Same-outcome goals may be related to children's intuitive notions of fairness (e.g., Wollman, 1977), and were primarily found when students were asked whether a given design was a "fair way" to find out about the focal variable in the whole-classroom study. Producing the same outcomes can be done either by setting all variables the same across conditions or by "balancing" variable values so their effects "cancel each other" (e.g., by selecting the "better" value for variable 1 of condition 1 and the "better" value for variable 2 in condition 2).

The third general type of engineering goals identified were "different-outcome" goals – intentions to make outcomes differ across conditions, such as make one rocket fly faster than another or sell more drinks at one stand than another. For example, Study 1 students frequently evaluated the unconfounded experimental design testing the effect of the number of windows on a rocket's flight as "Bad" because (as one student explained) "windows would not make a difference." This goal type may be related to a misconception that only experiments showing that one or more variables have an effect are good experiments, perhaps because this is a more "exciting" outcome. Applying a different-outcome goal may require application of beliefs about variable effects, when, for example, students contrast just those variables believed to be causal or use what they believe to be the better variable values in one condition and other values in another.

Goal Explicitness

An important feature of students' science goal responses is that they usually included explicit statements of intention; phrases expressing explicit science goals are given in italics in Table 7.1. However, when students applied engineering goals, they rarely *explicitly* stated the corresponding intention of producing a specific outcome (e.g., "I am trying to make the fastest rockets"); rather, they tended to state their beliefs about the problem-specific variable values. For example, students generally did not explicitly state that they were trying to sell the most drinks. Rather, they tended to allude to the positive effects of the variable values they selected with respect to a desired outcome. In the drinks stand example in Table 7.1, the student explained that she chose noon because it is "the hottest time of day" (and people would be thirstier and buy more drinks) and chose an older child seller because "older kids [usually] know how to talk better" (and are better at persuading people to buy drinks). This may indicate that students are more aware of their intentions when applying science goals than when they apply engineering goals.

Procedural–Conceptual Relationships

When students expressed science goals, they almost always contrasted the variable(s) they were trying to find out about (Siler & Klahr, 2012). Thus, science goals appear to be tightly linked to contrasting variables. Moreover, the "same-outcome" and "different-outcome" engineering goals also demonstrate the link between students' conceptual knowledge – perhaps their understandings of "fairness" and what "good" experiments produce – and their procedural applications. That is, "fairness" interpretations typically led to non-contrastive designs and "different outcome" interpretations, which may be a consequence of misunderstanding the purpose of experiments, were related to contrastive designs.

Summary

In summary, students' science goal applications appear to be dissociated from – whereas engineering goal applications are generally associated with – domain-specific beliefs. In addition, students' intentions within science goals appear to be explicit, whereas intentions within engineering goals may be implicit. Finally, students' conceptual knowledge of task goals was often associated with their procedural applications.

CAUSES OF GOAL MISAPPLICATIONS

Why do students – especially younger and low-SES students – adopt engineering goals? One possibility is that students associate "experimenting" with achieving dramatic or exciting outcomes (Schauble et al., 1991). At the very least, students this age – and older – typically hold unsophisticated views of experimentation that include elements of both engineering and basic science goals; that is, they typically view the purpose of experiments "as producing a desirable outcome or a new fact" (Smith, Maclin, Houghton, & Hennessey, 2000). However, when "experiment" references were removed from the story pretest,[6] which students completed in non-science classrooms, almost half (45%) of low-SES fifth-grade students still gave engineering or variable-effects responses on the first item compared to 53% of low-SES fifth-grade students from the same schools who answered the original story pretest referencing "experiments" in their science classrooms. Furthermore, in a recent study comparing instruction that referenced "experimenting" with the same instruction that did not (i.e., it was framed in terms of "solving brain teasers"), students in the "experiment" framing condition were *not* significantly more likely to indicate engineering (or "variable effects") misinterpretations than students in the "brain teaser" framing condition on their first instructional responses (22% vs. 43%, respectively) (Siler, Klahr, Magaro, & Willows, 2012). Thus, use of the term "experiment" did not increase the likelihood of students applying engineering goals. However, removal of "experiment" terminology was associated with a significantly *higher* rate of science-goal responses (28% vs. 3%). This suggests that these students' conceptualizations of "experimenting" do not generally include either science or engineering goals. Correspondingly, usage of "experimenting" terminology did *not* explain why lower-SES students were more likely to adopt engineering goals.

Do students adopt engineering goals because they are unable to understand and apply science goals? Several studies have demonstrated that even young children can apply science goals in certain scenarios. For example, Sodian, Zaitchik, and Carey (1991) found that first- and second-graders can differentiate between engineering and science goal applications in simple tasks. That is, when children were presented with the problem of figuring out which of two doors – a large or a small one – would be better for determining whether a large or small mouse was stealing food (a science goal application), the majority of children chose the small door, correctly reasoning that, if the food was stolen, it had to be due to the small mouse because a larger mouse could not fit through the small door. However, when asked to ensure that the mouse – whatever its size – could get to the food (an engineering goal application), these children correctly chose the large door. Children are also able to solve similar tasks (Klahr & Chen, 2003), and other research has suggested that preschoolers can apply science goals to identify causal variables (Gopnik, Sobel, Schulz, & Glymour, 2001).

So why were the younger and lower-SES students in our studies more likely to apply engineering goals? Children may lack metacognitive awareness of the hypothetical nature of their beliefs (Vosniadou, Vamvakoussi, & Skopeliti, 2008); thus, when they read problem statements involving familiar scenarios with associated outcomes, they may not realize that their beliefs about how the variables affect the outcomes may be wrong. And if so, they are unlikely to adopt science goals – after all, it does not make sense to investigate what one (thinks one) already knows. Poor metacognitive awareness may also underlie students' lack of explicitness of intent when applying engineering goals.

Dual-process models of cognition (cf. Kahneman, 2003), which address metacognitive processes as well as elicitations of domain-specific beliefs such as those that surface in expressions of engineering goals, may further shed light on this question. These models hypothesize relationships between automatic, intuitive, associative processes – including belief elicitation – and slower, more effortful, logic-based problem-solving and metacognitive monitoring processes. In some dual-process models, these processes are assumed to run in parallel (e.g., Epstein, 1994; Sloman, 1996) and in others (e.g., Evans, 2006; Kahneman & Frederick, 2002), serially. In parallel accounts, because associative processes are faster, they generally "win the race" to consciousness even if a certain scenario also triggers higher-level reasoning processes. And, if accepted by conscious monitoring processes, this output will be applied. In serial accounts, intuitive processes are first activated and their resulting judgments are evaluated. If these are deemed inadequate, higher-level processing will step in. In yet another account of dual processing (De Neys, 2012), monitoring results from the comparison of two competing *intuitive* outputs. Only when conflicts in these outputs are detected are higher-level processes enacted.

Thus, common to all models is the monitoring/evaluating of products of intuitive processing. Because some metacognitive skills have been linked to reading comprehension (e.g., Kolic-Vehovec & Bajanski, 2007) and higher-SES students' reading comprehension scores were significantly higher than lower-SES students', the higher-SES students likely had better metacognitive/monitoring skills. Thus, differences in metacognitive skills may be one cause of the differences in expressed goal orientations.

However, this monitoring may normally be lax (Kahneman, 2003), requiring sufficiently salient cues to be triggered. On the six-item story pretest, for each of the three domains, students were first asked to design an experiment for a given focal variable before evaluating a set-up in that same domain with the same variables. Because surface features were the same in the design–evaluate question pairs, one may expect other problem features – including cues to the science-goal nature – to become relatively more salient in the second (evaluate) item (refer to Figures 7.1 and 7.2). Study 1 students were in fact significantly more likely to express science goals on the second items of question pairs. Reading achievement (a proxy for monitoring skill) and science scores were equally predictive of science-goal application on the second (evaluate) items. In contrast, only students' science achievement scores were related to science-goal expression on the first (design) items. These results suggest that general science knowledge – and possibly science goal strength and its association with experimentation – may be a factor regardless of cue strength, and that (consistent with Kahneman's assertion) metacognitive skills play a greater role as cue salience increases.

Which types of cognitive processes are likely involved in science versus engineering goal applications? Students did not take more time to formulate responses when they applied (non-CVS) science goals than engineering goals on the first story pretest item. This suggests that these applications involve the same – likely intuitive – processes. With one exception, students who expressed science goals designed maximally confounded comparisons; thus, contrasting all variables may be a common default heuristic. However, once students understand the science-goal orientation of the task, the slower, more effortful, logical thinking may come into play when learning to control variables: Study 1 students spent significantly more time designing their first unconfounded set-up than on the previous question (when they designed confounded comparisons) of the ramps pretest.

THE NATURE OF CVS DEVELOPMENT

Procedural Development

A common theoretical account of conceptual change is that conceptual knowledge often develops incrementally (Vosniadou et al., 2008). Can such additive enrichment mechanisms – in which new information is incrementally integrated with existing knowledge – account for the development of a procedural knowledge structure such as CVS? It is also conceivable that students could – in "aha!" moments – come to realize the necessity of applying CVS, perhaps by realizing its underlying logic (cf. Posner, Strike, Hewson, & Gertzog, 1982). To address this question, the ramps pretest responses of Study 1 students – in conjunction with their experimental designs – were coded for expression of CVS rules (explicated in Table 7.3). For example, responses in which students expressed the intention of testing the given focal variable, but did not contrast the focal variable, were coded as R1 only. But if the focal variable had been contrasted in the design, this response would have been credited as R1 and R2. Coding categories, in order of approaching a complete CVS explanation, are shown in Table 7.3.

Table 7.4 shows the distribution of the different types of student responses from the first to second ramps pretest question. For example, the first data cell in the table shows that eight students who gave an engineering response to the first question also gave one

Table 7.3 Explanations for ramp designs ordered by number of CVS rules expressed

Response type	Example (focal variable is starting position)	CVS rules
Engineering (ENG)	"I made them so the balls will roll fast."	None
Variable effect (VE)	"I think the shorter one will win."	None
Don't know (DK)	"I just guessed."	None
Science only (no rules)	"I designed it the way I did so I could see what happens."	None (Science only)
R1: Identify the focal variable.	"I wanted to find out about the starting position." (but starting positions are not contrasted)	R1 only
R2: Contrast the variable(s) one is testing.	"I wanted to see if the starting position and slope make a difference." (starting positions and slopes are contrasted)	R2 only
R3: Control the variable(s) one is not testing.	"The balls and slopes should be the same."	R3 only
R1/2: Contrast the focal variable.	"I did it because the balls are in different places."	R1 and R2
CVS	"Only the starting positions are different."	R1, R2, and R3
CVS + Logic (CVSL)	"Only the starting positions are different, so only they could make one ball roll farther."	R1, R2, and R3 + Why control

to the second question, and (farther down in the table) we see that five of the children who gave CVS responses on Q1 also did so on Q2. An incremental response pattern would correspond to fewer "hits" in cells as one moves farther from the diagonal (highlighted cells – which indicate consecutive responses at about the same level of sophistication). The modal response was to remain within a category. For example, eight of the 14 students who gave engineering responses on Q1 of the ramps pretest also gave engineering responses on Q2. The highlighted cells in Table 7.4 represent responses to Q1 and Q2 at roughly the same level of sophistication (e.g., comparing, testing multiple variables, and contrasting variables are approximately the same knowledge state). Response pairs to the right of the highlighted cells show Q2 responses that are progressively more sophisticated than the Q1 response (i.e., show knowledge of more CVS rules).

The student with the largest knowledge advancement could not explain his/her Q1 setup (and was assigned a "Don't know" response) but on Q2 gave a CVS (procedure only) response. Thus, this student appeared to suddenly "get" CVS. However, s/he expressed an understanding of the need to compare conditions on the story pretest (and showed implicit understanding of CVS procedure on Q3 and Q4 of the story pretest), so this "leap" in knowledge development during the ramps pretest is not as large as it appears. Overall, only 6% of students advanced more than one CVS rule between Q1 and Q2. Of students whose explanations became more sophisticated, 75% advanced no more than one rule. Thus, for the majority of Study 1 students, procedural knowledge of CVS developed incrementally when students designed experiments in the absence of feedback. That is, as shown in Figure 7.3, smaller advances were more common than larger ones, which were increasingly rare.

Table 7.4 Per-student frequency: Response to Q1 vs. Q2 on ramps pretest

Q1 Response	Ramps pretest Question 2 response												Row total
	No CVS rules or goal			Goal only	One CVS rule				Two CVS rules		Three CVS rules		
	ENG	VE	DK	SCI	SCI-R1	TMV	R2	R3	R2/R3	R1/R2	CVS	CVSL	
ENG	8	2	2	1		1							14
VE	1												1
DK	1		1				1			1	(1)		5
SCI	2	1	1	3					1				8
COMP		2		1						1			4
TMV	1												1
R2			2		1	1	7	2	1	6	1		21
R1/2	1									1	2		4
CVS				1						1	5		7
CVSL												1	1
Total	14	5	6	6	1	2	8	2	2	10	9	1	66

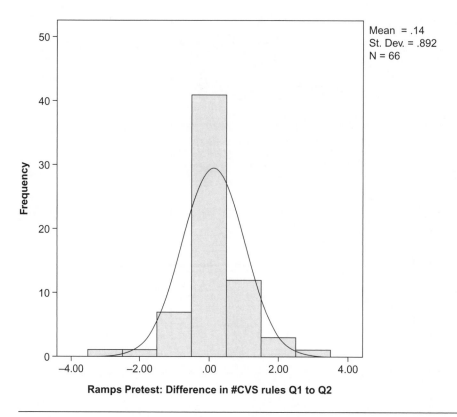

Figure 7.3 Frequency of the difference in number of CVS rules expressed from Q1 to Q2 on the ramps pretest

Knowledge Synthesis

As with conceptual change found in other domains (e.g., Vosniadou & Brewer, 1992), there was evidence that some students additively built onto their intuitive engineering-goal conceptions or "synthesized" new information (i.e., CVS rules) with their engineering goal schemas. However, such evidence was sparse. One example comes from a low-SES sixth-grade student during a remedial tutoring session following whole-class instruction in which this student had developed a "same-outcomes" misinterpretation. In tutoring, the student learned to contrast the focal variable. When asked to design a comparison to find out if the surface [of the ramp] affects how far balls roll, he set the first ramp to steep, with a rough surface, and the ball starting at the top of the ramp. He set the other ramp to steep, but with a smooth surface and the ball starting in the middle. Thus, this student correctly contrasted the focal variable (the ramp surface). When asked why he chose to use different starting positions, he responded: "Because the rough one [inaudible] probably mess the ball up, so I made it longer so it could move faster." When asked if he was trying to make one of the balls "beat the other," he responded: "No, I'm saying that if it's rough and then it's [at the top], [I want] to see if the [middle] and smooth one could get down there at the same time, because the heights will make the ball roll faster, and this one's smooth so it can roll down without messing up." Thus, he maintained his initial same-outcomes goal by varying the starting positions as well as the focal variable, so that the rough surface (which he believed would slow the ball) was paired with the top starting position (which he believed would make it roll faster), and the smooth surface was paired with the middle starting position.

As discussed in Siler and Klahr (2012), students sometimes – though rarely[7] – indicated both engineering and science goals when referencing a particular set-up. For example, one low-SES fifth-grade student explained her ramps design as follows: "I thought that you should use steep because if it was flat it wouldn't be able to roll that well. I don't know why I used fim and sif,[8] I just thought it would work. I picked the middle because it's a shorter distance and it might roll farther. And I picked the top to see if it might roll farther than the middle." This student expressed a science goal for the focal variable (starting position) after explaining her engineering-based decisions for the other variable settings. Thus, students occasionally incorporated both engineering and science goal perspectives within a single problem, without noticing the conflicting goals.

STRATEGIES FOR INDUCING CONCEPTUAL CHANGE IN CVS

As previously discussed, poorer metacognitive skills and weaker science-goal conceptions (including those of experimentation that do not include science-goal associations) may be responsible for engineering goal applications. Furthermore, conceptual change when learning CVS may involve both category shifting (from engineering to science goal orientations) and belief revision (in particular, when developing an understanding of controlling variables within a science goal orientation).

Belief Revision

As discussed in the introduction, the CVS instruction given in previous studies (e.g., Chen & Klahr, 1999; Matlen & Klahr, 2010; Strand-Cary & Klahr, 2008) has led to high rates of CVS adoption and transfer for older and higher-SES students. As previously shown, these students were more likely to adopt science-goal orientations during pretesting. Thus, instruction that includes explicit explanations of the procedural and logical aspects of CVS seems appropriate for students who understand the science-goal aspect of the task. This is further supported by a recent study (Siler, Klahr, & Price, 2012) where seventh-graders who expressed science goals on the final story pretest item benefited more from immediately entering instruction than from completing a ramps pretest prior to beginning instruction (abbreviated to control for time on task).[9]

GOAL SHIFTING

Via Novel Variable Values

We have suggested that (a) children misinterpret the task goal because surface features (such as problem variables) activate engineering goals, and (b) misinterpretations are maintained when metacognitive processes fail to detect them. We examined the effect of presenting children with both familiar and unfamiliar variables (or novel levels) to see whether unfamiliar variable levels are less likely to elicit students' engineering goals. However, this hinges on whether students monitor their understanding.

On the ramps pretest, students were asked to design one experiment for each of the four ramps variables: (Q1) the starting position, (Q2) the surface, (Q3) the ball type, and

(Q4) the slope. Two of these variables had commonly designated value names (i.e., the slope could be steep or not steep, and the starting position of the ball could be at the top or middle of the ramp). Two variables were given made-up value names (i.e., ball type was either "bab" or "lof," and the ramp surface either "sif" or "fim"). Students were *not* more likely to express science goals on questions asking them to test variables with unfamiliar values (Q2 and Q3) than on questions asking them to design experiments to test variables with familiar values (Q1 and Q4). Thus, merely presenting students with variables that had unfamiliar values did not promote shifting from engineering to science goals for fifth-grade students.

The failure to elicit science goals this way was partly due to students' assumptions about the made-up variable values' effects. For example, one low-SES Study 1 student assumed that the surfaces differed: "It has an easier surface for [ramp 1] and harder for the other," even though the surfaces differed only in color. This student also mistakenly perceived a difference in the shapes of the (actually identical) balls: "[Bab's] shape is rounder than [lof's]." Another (low-SES) student stated: "I was thinking that sif is probably fatter than fim" when explaining her design decision. These results further support poor metacognitive skills as a factor in engineering goal applications, and correspondingly, the insufficiency of this approach for inducing goal shifting.

Via Explicating Beliefs and Goals

As discussed previously and illustrated in the last section, students are often "not aware of the hypothetical nature of their beliefs" and "presuppositions that constrain their learning and reasoning" (Vosniadou et al., 2008, p. xviii). This may also apply in the case of goal shifting, where students may not be aware of the hypothetical – and possibly wrong – nature of their assumptions about variable effects underlying their engineering designs. In addition, they may not even be aware they are applying engineering goals. As noted earlier, students rarely *explicitly* stated engineering intentions when explaining their set-up choices. Would providing explicit feedback following students' engineering goal selections (on the ramps pretest) promote metacognitive awareness and improve subsequent learning?

To address this question, we took an approach similar to that used in refutational text research, where students' misconceptions are explicitly addressed and refuted (e.g., Diakidoy, Kendeou, & Ioannides, 2003; van den Broek & Kendeou, 2008). Sixth-grade students were assigned to one of the following conditions: (a) no feedback, (b) science goal feedback, or (c) "both-goal" feedback. In the science-goal feedback condition, students were reminded of the ramps pretest task goal – to design an experiment to test whether the focal variable affects how far the balls roll – and that the task was not to make the balls roll "farther, faster, or the same." Students were told the general goal of experiments – to find out whether something makes a difference – and that they would be learning how to design experiments to see whether the different parts of the ramps make a difference.

In the both-goal feedback condition, students heard the same explanations as in the science goal feedback condition. In addition, they were told that the point of an experiment was *not* to try to make a certain result, but instead to find out whether something makes a difference. Students were also told: "If you are setting up the ramps to make something you want happen, you may be using your ideas about how the different parts of the ramps work. However, you could be wrong about how the parts of the ramps work if you haven't tested the parts first. So, in order to test the parts correctly, you must NOT assume that you know how any of the parts work." Finally, as in the science-goal feedback condition, students were told that the goal of the lesson was learning how to design experiments to see whether the different parts of the ramps work. In both feedback conditions, visuals including key points (presented textually) and depictions of the ramps accompanied the audio presentation.

The effects of this manipulation were modest, at best. Students in the both-goal condition answered slightly more of the multiple-choice questions asked during the instruction correctly than students who received no feedback, and tended to answer more questions correctly than the "science-goal" condition students (but this difference was not significant). Although students in the both-goal condition also tended to design more unconfounded experiments on the ramps post-test than students in the other conditions, there were no significant pair-wise differences. Nor were there any differences on the immediate or delayed post-tests. So, though there were signs of an initial positive effect of feedback addressing both students' incorrectly applied engineering goal and the relevant task goal, this effect faded in time. This suggests that students may require more time and support to understand or realize the nature of their underlying assumptions and goals in the context of CVS instruction.

Thus, stronger interventions than the two just discussed may be necessary to induce the metacognitive processes that cause goal shifting. For example, in a task in which students were explicitly given relevant problem variables, their levels, and target outcomes by the experimenter, Schauble et al. (1991) found that fifth- and sixth-grade children from a middle-SES population shifted from engineering to science goals when the outcomes of their experiments contradicted their expectations. Thus, showing students experimental outcomes that contradict their expectations may be one such intervention that can successfully promote goal shifting in younger and lower-SES children. This is consistent with many other findings of successfully inducing conceptual change via cognitive conflict (cf. Chan, Burtis, & Bereiter, 1997; VanLehn, Siler, Murray, Yamauchi, & Baggett, 2003) and may indicate that explicit conceptual – rather than metacognitive – beliefs may be the better target for inducing conceptual change for this student population.

Another possibility, in line with Vosniadou et al.'s (2008) recommendation, is to engage students in full-class discussions with the aim of promoting goal revision. According to Vosniadou et al., such engagement "ensures that students understand the need to revise their beliefs deeply instead of engaging in local repairs" and supports students as they "engage in the conscious and deliberate belief revision required for conceptual change" (Vosniadou et al., 2008, p. 27). Alternatively, activating students' science goal conceptions may induce goal shifting, as discussed next.

Via Activating Intuitive Science-goal Knowledge

Vosniadou et al. (2008) suggested promoting conceptual change by building on students' intuitive ideas. Even young children seem to have intuitive notions of "comparing and contrasting" levels of a variable to see whether it affects an outcome (cf. Gopnik et al., 2001), which is a basic science goal that may be independent of students' conceptions of "experimentation." If they do, eliciting this notion should support a science-goal interpretation of the experimentation task. After the story pretest, as students were introduced to the ramps pretest, they were told: "In an experiment, we compare things to see if they affect the result. We need two ramps in order to do an experiment because we need to compare and contrast how far the two balls roll." If students understand "comparing and contrasting" as an intuitive science goal, we would expect to see a jump in expressions of science goals between the final question of the story pretest and the first ramps pretest item. And, in fact, there was a five-fold increase (shown in Figure 7.4) for the three fifth-grade classrooms that participated in Study 1. In contrast, the rates of science-goal expression on design items were stable within the story and ramps pretests.

Furthermore, of students who applied engineering goals on the final story pretest question, over half (56%) expressed science goals on the first ramps pretest item. Of students who *only* applied engineering goals throughout the story-problems pretest, almost half (41%) expressed science goals for the first ramps pretest item. There were no differences in the likelihood of transitioning to science goals across the three classrooms in either case. Thus, eliciting students' intuitive understanding of "comparing and contrasting" variable levels in the service of a science goal appeared to promote shifting to at least a basic science goal orientation for about half of students who appeared to be "stuck" within engineering goal orientations. This was true regardless of SES level.

In summary, inducing goal shifting by eliciting conceptual knowledge associated with science goals was more effective than attempting to promote shifting via metacognitive awareness – at least in this student population.

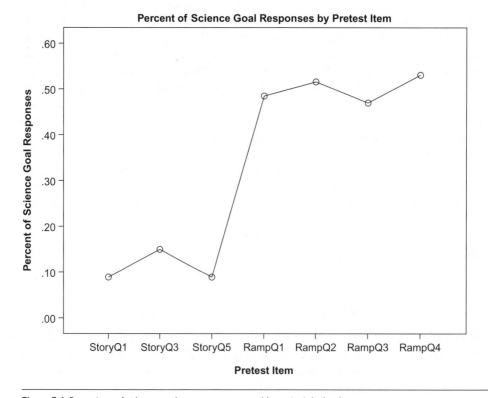

Figure 7.4 Percentage of science-goal responses expressed by pretest design item

DISCUSSION

In this chapter, we discussed the nature of students' beliefs related to experimental design, including the goals students adopt in the context of learning experimental design, how these beliefs developed, and how students' understanding of this topic may be supported. We considered whether the same processes that are associated with conceptual change in primarily conceptual domains can also account for the ways children learn this skill, which includes both conceptual and procedural components. While many other domains are rich with both procedural and conceptual information, most studies of conceptual change have focused on learning of the latter knowledge type. Few have focused on how procedural and conceptual knowledge interact. In this chapter, we showed how learning of procedural skills or lack thereof is intimately related to the learner's conceptual understanding of the task goal.

Overall, there appear to be two types of conceptual change relevant to learning CVS: belief revision and categorical shifting (cf. Chi, 2008). If children adopt science goals, then their learning of CVS resembles the type of incremental knowledge development characteristic of belief revision found in conceptual domains. That is, children appear to develop their understanding of CVS one CVS rule at a time rather than holistically.

However, some children – especially younger and lower-SES – appeared to apply engineering goals in response to pre-instructional questions asking them to design and evaluate experiments. If these orientations, or ways of interpreting the task goal, continue into instruction, students may either develop synthetic models or, more typically, fail to learn anything. Thus, conceptual change relevant to learning CVS involves "switching" from engineering- to science-goal orientations. We believe this type of conceptual change involves a type of category shifting, where children must reconceptualize the task goal from achieving an optimal outcome to creating a way to find out about variable effects. Because students in late elementary to early middle school (when CVS is typically taught) likely already have basic knowledge structures associated with pursuing science goals (cf. Sodian et al., 1991), we believe it is more a matter of eliciting this knowledge – and strengthening it through associations with "experimentation" – than developing it "from scratch." In fact, when students were presented with the (basic science-goal) notion of "comparing and contrasting" across conditions, science-goal expressions significantly increased. In addition, the relative rarity of developing synthetic models of CVS – in which students synthesize CVS rules onto their intuitive engineering goal conceptions – may be a consequence of the availability of both engineering and the target science conceptions. That is, the very rules students were learning (i.e., to contrast the focal variable) may have activated basic science goals, rendering synthetic models uncommon. Synthetic models may be more common in domains where even a minimal target framework is unlikely to be available, such as when learning emergent processes (Chi, 2005), or is not easily activated in the learning context. However, these are questions to address in future research.

Factors that likely play a role in initially understanding the task goal are students' conceptual knowledge related to experimentation – likely goal-related conceptions – and their monitoring skills. Consistent with predictions based on dual-process models of cognition (cf. Kahneman, 2003; Stanovich & West, 2000), metacognitive monitoring played a (greater) role in detecting the science-goal nature of the task in the second questions of each domain on the story post-test (where cues to the actual nature of the task were relatively more salient). A measure of monitoring skill (reading comprehension scores) and science achievement scores were correlated with goal expression on the second questions. However, only science achievement scores were related to science-goal expressions on the first items in each domain. This suggests that students' science-related conceptual knowledge – which may include conceptions of "experimenting" that include science-goal associations – is even more critical when cue salience is low.

That students who adopted engineering goals possessed weaker metacognitive skills is further suggested by their confident – though unwarranted – assumptions about the effects of completely novel variable levels. Perhaps ironically, weaker monitoring skills may have also been responsible for failures of interventions targeting these skills to promote conceptual change. Eliciting science-goal-related intuitive knowledge appears more fruitful for promoting conceptual change in these student populations.

ACKNOWLEDGMENTS

This research was supported in part by grants from the Institute of Education Sciences (R305A100404 and R305B090023), and in part by a grant from the National Science Foundation (SBE-0836012). The opinions expressed are those of the authors and do not represent views of IES or the US Department of Education. We thank Cressida Magaro and Kevin Willows for their invaluable contributions on many aspects of the project. We also thank the participating schools and teachers who allowed us to conduct research in their classrooms.

NOTES

1   Note that science goals involve intentions of finding out about something; identifying the causal status of variables is a specific type of science goal.
2   Refer to Siler et al. (2012) for screenshots of the TED tutor.
3   However, conducting an experiment in the real world, where one cannot control every possible variable, requires identifying and controlling those variables one believes might affect the outcome.
4   Assuming no interactions among variables and that none of the levels contribute to floor/ceiling effects.
5   Maximal-outcome responses accounted for 96% of middle/high-SES and 88% of low-SES students' engineering responses on the first story pretest item (Siler & Klahr, 2012).
6   For example, "design an experiment to test for whether or not the time of day makes a difference in how much is sold" was reworded as: "figure out a way to find out whether or not the time of day . . ."
7   For example, only 4% of responses indicated both goal types on the first question of the ramps pretest.
8   As discussed more later, in some evaluations, the surfaces of the ramps were made-up types ("fim" and "sif").
9   This trend was reversed for students who did not express science goals on the final story pretest item.

REFERENCES

Bullock, M., & Ziegler, A. (1999). Scientific reasoning: Developmental and individual differences. In F. E. Weinert & W. Schneider (Eds.), *Individual development from 3 to 12: Findings from the Munich Longitudinal Study.* Cambridge, UK: Cambridge University Press.

Chan, C., Burtis, J., & Bereiter, C. (1997). Knowledge building as a mediator of conflict in conceptual change. *Cognition and Instruction, 15*(1), 1–40.

Chen, Z., & Klahr, D. (1999). All other things being equal: Children's acquisition of the control of variables strategy. *Child Development, 70,* 1098–1120.

Chi, M. T. H. (2005). Commonsense conceptions of emergent processes: Why some misconceptions are robust. *Journal of the Learning Sciences, 14*(2), 161–199.

Chi, M. T. H. (2008). Three types of conceptual change: Belief revision, mental model transformation, and categorical shift. In S. Vosniadou (Ed.), *Handbook of research on conceptual change* (pp. 61–82). New York, NY: Routledge.

De Neys, W. (2012). Bias and conflict: A case for logical intuitions. *Perspectives on Psychological Science, 7*(1), 28–38.

Diakidoy, I., Kendeou, P., & Ioannides, C. (2003). Reading about energy: The effects of text structure in science learning and conceptual change. *Contemporary Educational Psychology, 28*(3), 335–356.

Epstein, S. (1994). Integration of the cognitive and psychodynamic unconscious. *American Psychologist, 49*, 709–724.

Evans, J. (2006). The heuristic-analytic theory of reasoning: Extension and evaluation. *Psychonomic Bulletin & Review, 13*(3), 378–395.

Gopnik, A., Sobel, D., Schulz, L., & Glymour, C. (2001). Causal learning mechanisms in very young children: Two, three, and four-year-olds infer causal relations from patterns of variation and covariation. *Developmental Psychology, 37*(5), 620–629.

Kahneman, D. (2003). A perspective on judgment and choice. *American Psychologist, 58*(9), 697–720.

Kahneman, D., & Frederick, S. (2002). Representativeness revisited: Attribute substitution in intuitive judgment. In T. Gilovich, D. Griffin, & D. Kahneman (Eds.), *Heuristics and biases* (pp. 49–81). New York, NY: Cambridge University Press.

Klahr, D., & Chen, Z. (2003). Overcoming the positive-capture strategy in young children: Learning about indeterminacy. *Child Development, 74*(5), 1256–1277.

Klahr, D., & Li, J. (2005). Cognitive research and elementary science instruction: From laboratory, to the classroom, and back. *Journal of Science Education and Technology, 14*(2), 217–238.

Klahr, D., & Nigam, M. (2004). The equivalence of learning paths in early science instruction: Effects of direct instruction and discovery learning. *Psychological Science, 15*, 661–667.

Kolic-Vehovec, S. & Bajanski, I. (2007). Comprehension monitoring and reading comprehension in bilingual students. *Journal of Research in Reading, 30*(2), 198–211.

Kuhn, D., Garcia-Mila, M., Zohar, A., & Andersen, C. (1995). Strategies of knowledge acquisition. In *Monographs of the Society for Research in Child Development, 60*(4).

Kuhn, D., & Phelps, E. (1982). The development of problem-solving strategies. In H. Reese (Ed.), *Advances in child development and behavior* (pp. 2–44). New York, NY: Academic.

Matlen, B. J., & Klahr, D. (2010). Sequential effects of high and low guidance on children's early science learning. In K. Gomez, L. Lyons, & J. Radinsky, (Eds.), *Proceedings of the 9th International Conference of the Learning Sciences*, Chicago, IL.

Posner, G. J., Strike, K. A., Hewson, P. W., & Gertzog, W. A. (1982). Accommodation of a scientific conception: Toward a theory of conceptual change. *Science Education, 66*, 211–227.

Schauble, L. (1990). Belief revision in children: The role of prior knowledge and strategies for generating evidence. *Journal of Experimental Child Psychology, 32*, 102–119.

Schauble, L. (1996). The development of scientific reasoning in knowledge-rich contexts. *Developmental Psychology, 32*(1), 102–119.

Schauble, L., Klopfer, L. E., & Raghavan, K. (1991). Students' transition from an engineering model to a science model of experimentation. *Journal of Research in Science Teaching, 28*(9), 859–882.

Siler, S., & Klahr, D. (2012). Detecting, classifying and remediating children's explicit and implicit misconceptions about experimental design. In R. W. Proctor & E. J. Capaldi (Eds.), *Psychology of science: Implicit and explicit processes.* New York, NY: Oxford University Press.

Siler, S. A., Klahr, D., Magaro, C., & Willows, K. (2012, March). *The effect of instructional framing on learning and transfer of experimental design skills.* Paper presented at the National Association for Research in Science Teaching (NARST) Annual International Conference, Indianapolis, IN.

Siler, S. A., Klahr, D., Magaro, C., Willows, K., & Mowery, D. (2010). Predictors of transfer of experimental design skills in elementary and middle-school children. *Proceedings of the 10th ITS 2010 Conference. Lecture Notes in Computer Science, 6095*, 198–208.

Siler. S. A., Klahr, D., & Price, N. (2012). Investigating the mechanisms of learning from a constrained preparation for future learning activity. *Instructional Science*, April.

Sloman, S. A. (1996). The empirical case for two systems of reasoning. *Psychological Bulletin, 119*, 3–22.

Smith, C. L., Maclin, D., Houghton, C., & Hennessey, M. G. (2000). Sixth-grade students' epistemologies of science: The impact of school science experience on epistemological development. *Cognition and Instruction, 18*(3), 349–422.

Sodian, B., Zaitchik, D., & Carey, S. (1991). Young children's differentiation of hypothetical beliefs from evidence. *Child Development, 62*, 753–766.

Stanovich, K. E., & West, R. F. (2000). Discrepancies between normative and descriptive models of decision making and the understanding/acceptance principle. *Cognitive Psychology, 38*, 349–385.

Strand-Cary, M., & Klahr, D. (2008). Developing elementary science skills: Instructional effectiveness and path-independence. *Cognitive Development, 23*, 488–511.

Toth, E. E., Klahr, D., & Chen, Z. (2000). Bridging research and practice: A cognitively-based classroom intervention for teaching experimentation skills to elementary school children. *Cognition & Instruction, 18*(4), 423–459.

Tschirgi, J. E. (1980). Sensible reasoning: A hypothesis about hypotheses. *Child Development, 51*, 1–10.

van den Broek, P., & Kendeou, P. (2008). Cognitive processes in comprehension of science texts: The role of co-activation in confronting misconceptions. *Applied Cognitive Psychology, 22*(3), 335–351.

VanLehn, K., Siler, S., Murray, C., Yamauchi, T., & Baggett, W. (2003). Why do only some events cause learning during human tutoring? *Cognition and Instruction, 21*(3), 209–249.

Vosniadou, S., & Brewer, W. F. (1992). Mental models of the earth: A study of conceptual change in childhood. *Cognitive Psychology, 24*, 535–585.

Vosniadou, S., Vamvakoussi, X., & Skopeliti, I. (2008). The framework theory approach to the problem of conceptual change. In S. Vosniadou (Ed.), *International handbook of research on conceptual change.* New York, NY: Routledge.

Wollman, W. (1977). Controlling variables: Assessing levels of understanding. *Science Education, 61*(3), 371–383.

8

LEARNING AND TEACHING ABOUT MATTER IN THE ELEMENTARY GRADES

What Conceptual Changes are Needed?

Carol L. Smith and Marianne Wiser, University of Massachusetts Boston and Clark University

In this chapter, we review the evidence that elementary-school students need to make major conceptual changes to develop a sound macroscopic understanding of matter that in turn supports understanding the atomic–molecular theory in middle school. We place the development of these ideas within the broader context of a *learning progression for matter*, whose beginning lies in infants' concepts of object and non-solids. We argue that this learning progression encompasses fundamental changes in a broad network of concepts – not only matter and substance, but also weight, volume, density, solid, liquid and gas – whose depth and scope have not always been clearly recognized by the science education community. Those changes are interrelated with changes in mathematical and epistemological understanding – about the validity of perceptual data unmediated by measuring instruments, the nature of numbers and measurement, and the role of theories and scientific models. We examine those conceptual changes and the difficulties they pose for students. For many students, the conceptions developed in early childhood are never revised sufficiently or even productively, suggesting that teaching about matter in elementary school needs to be rethought. We also present evidence that elementary-school students could achieve the necessary reconceptualizations with appropriate curricular support.

ASSUMPTIONS GUIDING OUR REVIEW: A LEARNING PROGRESSION CENTERED ON A SERIES OF RECONCEPTUALIZATIONS

The concept of matter develops closely with the concepts of weight, density, mass, and material. We find both individual concepts and the broader network in which they are embedded useful units of analysis. Concepts themselves are not monolithic – we see them as composed of multiple beliefs (e.g., children's early concept of weight includes "weight can be assessed by heft" and "heavier things push down on a scale more"), links to percepts (e.g., "these objects are made of the same material because they both are 'squishy'"), implicit and explicit models, etc.

In a knowledge network such as the matter network, a concept stands out as a "high-density" region – a group of highly connected components, organized around a core. For example, beliefs such as "steel objects are heavier than wood objects," "a grain of rice has weight for an ant," and "Styrofoam weighs nothing" are all implied by "weight is measured by heft." Concepts are units of thought and represent the meaning of words. As units of thought, they are applied to contexts as "packages," but different contexts foreground different parts of the concepts. The core of a concept is likely to be part of the interpretations of most contexts to which the concept is applied whereas peripheral components are foregrounded only in specific contexts (e.g., a grain of rice is heavy for an ant).

Reconceptualization always involves more than one concept because concepts take part of their meaning from each other; that is why the network is also a unit of analysis. For example, changes in the concepts of material and weight are interrelated – heft is involved in developing a concept of material, and developing an objective concept of weight depends on understanding that objects are constituted of pieces of material. Conceptual change involves movement of elements from core to periphery and vice versa (Carey, 1991, 2009): Initially, heft is the core of *weight* while its relation to amount of material is peripheral and context-dependent, whereas later the relation of weight and amount of material becomes central while heft moves to the periphery. This example also illustrates the interdependence of domain-specific content and epistemology. Heft becomes peripheral *because* students have come to appreciate that objective measurements are more precise and support lawful generalizations (e.g., about the relation of weight and volume).

Peripheral elements of concepts are crucial for conceptual change. For example "iodine vapor is visible (and so are solids and liquids)" can contribute to the reconceptualization of gases as matter, if capitalized on by instruction. We view reconceptualization as the culmination of progressive changes in beliefs that are initially peripheral to a concept, as they become more central to the concept.

We start by outlining the main elements of the matter knowledge network in early childhood. We then examine how they change as children engage with traditional curricula, focusing on profound differences that remain by the end of elementary school between students' and scientists' accounts of matter and its macroscopic behavior. We argue that students' difficulties could be alleviated by an alternative approach to teaching about matter, in which instruction (1) takes preschoolers' ideas as a starting point; (2) targets the reorganization and enrichment of portions of the knowledge network (rather than individual concepts); and (3) aims for intermediate states of knowledge that are not isolated pieces of the scientific theory, but rather integrated knowledge states that are *conceptually* closer to the scientific theory and allow meaningful interpretations of matter and its behavior. Those are the tenets of the *learning progression* (LP) approach to teaching core scientific ideas (Corcoran, Mosher, & Rogat, 2009; Smith, Wiser, Anderson, & Krajcik, 2006). We then present intervention studies that follow this approach directly or implicitly and that show students progress significantly toward a scientific understanding of matter.

PRECURSOR CONCEPTS FOR SUBSTANCE, MATTER, AND MASS IN EARLY CHILDHOOD: THEIR SIMILARITIES TO AND DIFFERENCES FROM EXPERT CONCEPTS

Precursors of Matter: Objects, Non-solids, and Substantiality

Although infants lack an explicit concept of matter, its precursors exist as concepts of object and "non-solid" (encompassing liquids and other non-rigid materials that in children's experience allow dividing, molding, or pouring). However, these precursors are separate concepts. They need to be integrated to give rise to a distinct concept of matter.

Infants have a robust concept of physical objects as bounded, solid, and permanent entities that have characteristic properties and functions (Baillargeon, 2002; Spelke, 1991). Children also think of objects as countable.

Young children view non-solids as more radically different from objects than adults do, especially scientists. Unlike objects, non-solids do not hold their shape, are not moveable without containers, keep their identity when divided into small pieces, and have completely different functions from objects. Moreover it is not obvious that all non-solids occupy space and have permanence; e.g., granular materials often "disappear" when mixed with a liquid, as do liquids when they evaporate. Further, preschoolers do not quantify non-solids: When presented with one cup of sand in one box and three individual cups of sand in another box, and asked "which box has more sand?" four-year-olds answer randomly (Huntley-Fenner, Carey & Solimando, 2002).

These precursor concepts guide young children's explorations of the physical world. For example, sensory and motor experience with objects versus non-solids entrenches the notions that the shape of (inanimate) objects is invariant and relevant to one's actions on them, whereas it is intensive properties that are invariant and relevant to one's handling of non-solids.

Embedded in the notion of both solid objects and non-solids is a notion of substantiality. Infants perceive properties such as shape, size, texture, and pliability intermodally; they expect things they see to be tangible (Bower, 1989; Spelke, 1991). But little in preschoolers' experiences contributes to enrich the notion of substantiality or to integrate solids and non-solids into a single category around it.

Precursors of Material

Preschoolers construe solids primarily as individual objects, i.e., as bounded entities with specific shape and size (Bloom, 2002; Hall, 1996). When asked, "What's that?" about an irregular shape made of wood, four-year-olds produce names of objects or shapes (Hall, 1996). Consequently, young children are often not clear about the referents of words naming solid materials and are slow to learn them (Bloom, 2000; Dickinson, 1988). Imagine an adult pointing to a blue spatula, an object for which the child does not yet have a name. "This is rubber," says the adult. The child may assume "rubber" is the name of the object, or that it refers to a property of the object. If the latter, she may associate "rubber" with flexible and non-breakable, but also with blue and having a handle. Thus, when encountering a red rubber ball the child will have a lot of semantic work to do.

In contrast, preschoolers construe non-solid samples as materials. When asked, "What's that?" of an irregular shape made of an unfamiliar aggregate or gel, four-year-olds produce names of substances or substance properties (Hall, 1996). The difference in construal is already evinced by two-year-olds, who generalize novel names of non-solid samples to samples of different shapes made of the same material, whereas they generalize novel names of solid objects to other objects of the same shape, ignoring differences in material (Soja, Carey, & Spelke, 1991).

Significantly, the first material names infants learn are for non-solids (water, milk, sand). Learning the names of non-solid materials is easier because it does not require overcoming the salient object construal.

Weight

For very young children, weight is heft and not related to the balance scale (Metz, 1993) or amount of material – small things and big pieces of materials like Styrofoam weigh nothing (Smith, Carey & Wiser, 1985). Slightly older children expect the balance scale to reflect heft: If an object is heavier than another by heft, it is expected to tilt the balance scale even if it is the same size or smaller than another object (Metz, 1993). Since weight is subjective, whether an object is heavy or not depends on who is holding it: For example, something can be light for an adult but heavy for a child (Smith et al., 1985). Finally, children say that weight changes when an object is reshaped (Piaget & Inhelder, 1974). This is consistent with a concept of weight centered on heft, since the object does not feel equally heavy before and after reshaping.

Precursors of Volume

Young children have a concept of bigness that conflates length, area, and volume and is not quantified. Sensitivity to relative length and area is present from infancy although achieving quantified concepts of length and area is difficult (Clements & Sarama, 2009; Lehrer, Jacobson, Kemeny & Strom, 1999). As to volume, children are aware that big things do not fit through small holes (Smith et al., 1985) and have known since infancy that two objects cannot simultaneously occupy the same location and that a bigger object makes a bigger bump under a blanket (Baillargeon, 2002), but those judgments are qualitative and based on direct perception and action on objects. This is very different from the concept that any object occupies a portion of 3D space that can be quantified.

In sum, the concepts reviewed above are perceptually based and consistent with young children's epistemological stance that the senses tell the truth and the world is the way it appears. For preschoolers, solids and non-solids are ontologically very different – having strikingly different characteristics, functions, and properties. Object identities are particularly important and salient for solids, impeding children's learning about the materials of which they are composed. Weight is neither quantified nor seen as an inherent property of solids and liquids; bigness is a property of objects, not the extent of a part of 3D space. The differences between those concepts and their scientific counter-parts are profound and hard to overcome.

TYPICAL CHANGES IN PRECURSOR CONCEPTS DURING ELEMENTARY SCHOOL

Material

During elementary school, children develop a material construal of solid objects and knowledge about materials. We hypothesize that this construal emerges from discovering covariations among intensive sensory-motor properties of objects. For example, the surface texture of foam objects is associated with their compressibility, and the hardness and transparency of glass objects with their breakability, irrespective of object size and shape. These empirical generalizations, however, are still about *objects*. The radical change is coming to see those properties as characterizing the *kinds of "stuff" objects are made of*. Applying a *material construal* to a solid object requires backgrounding shape, size, function, and individuality, and thinking of the object as a "chunk of material," i.e., as part of an (virtually infinite) amount of a certain material (Whorf, 1952). This supports developing the meaning of "made of" in the sense of *constituted of*, an essential component of the concept of material. The material construal of objects is part of a multifaceted ontological change about solids and non-solids – sensory-motor properties specific to materials become associated with the substantiality of liquids and solids, so that liquids and solids not only can be felt, seen, and acted upon, but that what is being felt, seen and acted upon exists in different forms – different forms of matter.

Evidence for this hypothetical course of development comes from studies using different methodologies. Krnel, Glazar, and Watson (2003) investigated the age at which material was a basis for object categorization. They asked three- to 13-year-olds to sort sets of objects, chunks, and powders made of different color wood, metal, plastic, or fabric into groups "that go together." Some five-year-olds grouped objects with chunks made of the same material (rather than by shape or color) but did not do so consistently across materials. Not until age nine did children start grouping powders with solid objects and chunks, but still not systematically across all materials. Sorting by material increased with age but even some 13-year-olds fell short of doing so systematically across all materials. Moreover, the justifications for sorting chunks with powders were predominantly color, except for the 13-year-olds who gave predominantly material justifications.

Wiser and Fox (2010) probed children's ability to differentiate between material and object-relevant properties as a basis for inferences. Kindergartners were presented pairs of nonsense objects (A and B) differing in shape and material. On *Material* trials, students were shown that A had a certain (intensive) property, e.g., getting darker when wet, while B did not. On *Object* trials, they were told, e.g., that A was "used to hold light switches." Children were then shown a second pair, one made of the same material as A and the same shape as B, and vice versa for the other, and were asked which object had the same property as A (without handling the objects). On average they were about 80% correct on both *Object* and *Material* trials, but much lower on the *Material* trials when color was not a cue.

Dickinson (1987) asked four- to 12-year-olds to put together things that were "made of the same kind of stuff" for sets including spoons, chunks, and powders made of plastic, wood, and metal, in different colors. Before sorting, children were asked to name each thing; then they were told, e.g., "This is a piece of brown plastic" or "This is a yellow plastic spoon." Only the four-year-olds failed to group spoons and chunks by material –

they sorted predominantly by color and shape and typically restricted their usage of material names to chunks. Exhaustive sorts by material (including objects, chunks, and powders of the same material) increased from age four (none) to age 12 (80%). Children were also asked whether an object (e.g., a wood airplane) was still the same object and the same "kind of stuff" after being cut into small pieces or ground into powder. All children except the four-year-olds performed well with transformations to small pieces, but the transformations to powders were much more difficult – the proportions of children who consistently answered correctly increased from 0% at age 4 to 90% at age 12.

Au (1994) tested whether three- to eight-year-old children would generalize material-relevant properties (e.g., tastes salty, turns black in the oven) and object-relevant properties (e.g., breaks a toy table) from a large chunk to a small chunk or to a pinch of powder. All children were very good with the large to small chunk transformations. The six- to eight-year-olds were also above chance, as a group, for most questions about transformations to powders, but not the younger children, except for the taste of substances they were already familiar with in powder form.

We also interviewed third, fourth, and fifth graders as part of the Inquiry Project.[1] We asked whether the little pieces that come from rubbing wood with sandpaper were wood, and whether they would burn; and whether little pieces that came from rubbing a piece of iron with a file were iron and would be attracted to a magnet. A minority of third graders, but the majority (75%) of fifth graders said "yes" to all four questions, giving evidence for a material construal – they typically said the grains were "little pieces of wood or iron" and that they would burn or be attracted to a magnet "because they were wood or iron" (Doubler et al., 2011).

Taken together these findings suggest that the material construal develops slowly through the elementary years. It emerges from a sensitivity to clusters of intensive sensory-motor properties (e.g., color, shininess, softness), which support empirical generalizations such as, "if an object is hard, smooth, and transparent, it will break if I drop it." Although young students are aware that some clusters of properties are independent of the shape and size of objects while others are not, all properties are construed as properties of *objects* and there is no distinction between intensive properties that are material-relevant and those that are not (e.g., color). They know few solid material names; those they know function as adjectives, or refer to a chunk as an object. Thus, talking about a material construal of objects in the preschool years is premature.

In contrast, knowing "this flexible, smooth, and light object is *made of* plastic" and inferring it will break "*because* it is plastic and plastic is not strong" is clear evidence for a material construal. Intensive properties are now properties of the material-as-kind-of-stuff and material names function as nouns. The development of this construal is protracted, but clearly occurring during the elementary school years.

Developing a material construal of objects is, however, different from developing a scientific concept of substance, whose identity remains invariant across phase change. In a study by Stavy and Stachel (1985), the majority (80–96%) of elementary school children said a melted candle was still wax, but many fewer thought that melted wax is flammable (32–56%); many said it was not because it was now water. Moreover, a broad range of studies (e.g., Andersson, 1990; Driver, Guesne, & Tiberghien,1985) indicate that most middle-school students do not understand conservation of substance identity across evaporation, condensation, or boiling. A recent survey of over 5,000 students (age 11–14) in England found a high prevalence of thinking that solids, liquids, and gases were three types of matter, rather than the same substance can be in three different forms (Johnson, Tymms & Roberts, 2008).

Constructing a concept of substance includes developing mutually supporting beliefs about which properties distinguish substances from each other (e.g., melting point, density, and thermal conductivity), the conservation of substance identity across phase change but not chemical reaction, and which properties can be used to establish that a solid and a liquid are the same substance. Most middle- and high-school students have difficulty with the concept of substance. Most eight- to 18-year-olds privilege historical criteria over specific properties to establish substance identity (Johnson & Papageorgiou, 2010). This works well for physical changes but makes the notion of chemical change unintelligible. In the next chapter, we consider how students can develop a more robust concept of substance that supports both the conservation of substance identity across physical changes and the creation of new substances in chemical changes.

Amount of Material

The concept of amount of material develops in concert with the concept of material in the elementary-school years. Children become increasingly successful with the classic Piagetian matter conservation[2] task (Piaget & Inhelder, 1974) in which a ball of clay is reshaped, e.g., into a pancake. Whereas preschool children typically say the amount of clay has changed (invoking size), most seven- and eight-year-olds make correct judgments.

Piaget and Inhelder originally attributed children's success to achieving concrete operations, an account that has been heavily critiqued on both theoretical and empirical grounds. We prefer to view it as a domain-specific achievement. We propose that young children fail Piaget's task because they do not apply a material construal to the ball. Clay is not yet a material in the sense of being what the ball is *made of*. Within an object construal, "more" is interpreted as referring to object properties such as size, leading to incorrect answers. Focusing on conservation as the locus of development takes attention away from the construction of the concept of material, the measure of which is amount.

The following task probes the concept of amount more directly (Figure 8.1). Children are asked: "Which plate should this very hungry puppet eat?" The total amount, number, and individual size of the pieces are varied systematically (i.e., the plate with more chocolate can have fewer bigger pieces (A) or more smaller pieces (B)). Middle-class children start successfully comparing amount around age five (Sophian, 2000).

Wiser, Frazier, and Fox (in press) used a similar paradigm to assess the material construal; i.e., the ability to see the pieces as pieces of a chunk of chocolate. A child who

Comparison A   Comparison B

Figure 8.1 Testing children's concept of amount: "Which plate should the very hungry puppet eat?"
Adapted from Figure 1 in Wiser, M., Frazier, K., & Fox, V. (in press) with kind permission from Springer Science+Business Media B.V.

applies the object construal to the plates sees a certain number of individual chocolates of a given size; he can only decide that the puppet should eat as many chocolates as it can, or bigger chocolates. Children (aged four to six, from low-income families) indeed relied on individual size or number.

We propose that an essential precursor to *material identity* and *amount of material* is a (macroscopic) *compositional model* of objects (see Figure 8.2). To construe an object as made of material X is to mentally decompose it into a certain number of pieces of material X, with the same (intensive) properties as the chunk, and to relate the pieces to the whole object. The amount of material constituting the object is the sum of those pieces. Once one has a compositional model of material, conservation of amount comes almost for free: if a chunk is conceptualized as pieces of material, reshaping it results in rearranging the pieces and therefore does not alter its amount. Indeed, children who pass the chocolate task also pass a compositional model task (see Figure 8.3) (Wiser et al., in press).

The compositional model supports the quantification and extensivity of weight, as well as understanding that material identity, amount of material, and weight do not change when an object is ground. It can also evolve into a *microscopic* compositional model, supporting the belief that pieces too small to see with the naked eye exist and have weight. Traditional curricula do not make use of it; this may be one reason few elementary-school children achieve those understandings.

Weight

The Piagetian conservation literature suggests that children around nine to 10 years typically come to understand that weight does not change when objects are divided into smaller chunks or reshaped (Piaget & Inhelder, 1974).

There may be several reasons that *weight* lags behind *amount*. For many elementary-school children, the core of weight is still felt weight, so that direct experience with adding and subtracting stuff may not provide (strong) support for their effect on weight;

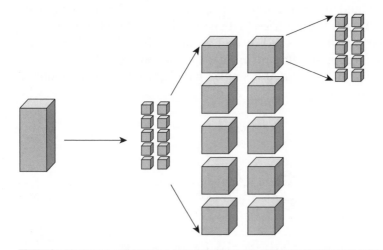

Figure 8.2 Compositional mental model of materials
Adapted from Figure 1 in Wiser, M., Smith, C., & Doubler, S. (2012) with kind permission from Sense Publishers.

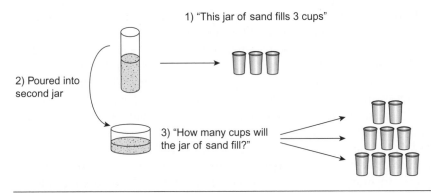

1) "This jar of sand fills 3 cups"

2) Poured into second jar

3) "How many cups will the jar of sand fill?"

Figure 8.3 Testing whether children have a compositional model of materials
Adapted from Figure 4 in Wiser, M., Frazier, K., & Fox, V. (in press) with kind permission from Springer Science+Business Media B.V.

moreover, shape transformations do affect felt weight. It is likely that experience with measuring weight with scales builds up the objectivity and extensivity of weight (which may become central for some children and remain peripheral for others). This experience could be enough to link weight to amount of material – adding material on one side of the balance scale makes it tip, removing some makes it go up – and to understand that reshaping and dividing do not change weight since nothing is added or removed. These experiences, and those in everyday life based on felt weight, lead children to formulate crude empirical generalizations – bigger things tend to be heavier than smaller things; steel things tend to be heavier than plastic things (Smith et al., 1985).

But this does not mean that children have formulated the general principle that weight is proportional to amount of matter nor differentiated weight from density. We probed third, fourth, and fifth graders' ideas about amount, weight, volume, material, and density in the recent longitudinal study that was part of the Inquiry Project. Interviews included the Piagetian ball-to-pancake task; asking whether little (visible and invisible) pieces of clay have weight or take up space; and which of two objects was made of a heavier material, calling for the differentiation of the heaviness of objects and of materials. We found that by the end of fifth grade, most Control students judged that the amount of clay and the weight of the ball and pancake were the same across reshaping. But only a minority said that tiny pieces have weight and take up space, and even fewer said that everything must weigh something. Similarly, few consistently distinguished between the heaviness of objects and the heaviness of kinds of material (Doubler et al., 2011).

Thus a concept of weight as an objective property of objects, measured with a scale, and proportional to the amount and dependent on the kind of material they are made of, appears to develop at a macroscopic level first. Only later do (a minority of) children achieve a deeper theoretical understanding of weight – that even the tiniest amount of matter has weight and that density, not weight, characterizes materials.

Precursors to Volume

During elementary school, children progress in differentiating length and area as measurable dimensions of objects but volume remains problematic (Sarama & Clements, 2009). By the end of fifth grade, most Control students in the Inquiry Project study correctly used several tools to compare the lengths of two ribbons, and the majority (67%) used tiles to compare the areas of two rectangles. However only a minority (26%) correctly used cubes to compare the volume of two rectangular blocks. In Piaget's ball-to-pancake task, most said the pancake had a greater volume – apparently confusing area with volume. Finally, 86% predicted that a heavier cylinder would make the water level rise higher than a lighter cylinder with same shape and volume (Doubler et al., 2011). Taken together, our results show the limitations of traditional curricula in developing a robust concept of volume in elementary school. Of particular relevance for the matter knowledge network, but rarely addressed in the literature, is that the volume of objects and non-solid samples is measured differently. Curry and Outhred's (2005) findings suggest that many elementary-school students may not grasp the relation between the 3D space occupied by objects (measured by "packing" solid units) and non-solid samples (measured by reading the level on a beaker). This may be related to their failure to coalesce solids and non-solids into a single ontological category, and adds to the reasons to integrate measurement into science curricula.

Precursors to Matter

Three studies investigated changes in elementary school children's judgments of what is and is not matter (Carey, 1991; Smith, Wiser, & Doubler, 2011; Stavy, 1991). Although children make some progress with age in recognizing solids, liquids, and powders as matter, they typically do not focus on weight and volume as properties they have in common, and lack a canonical concept of matter that includes gases.

Stavy (1991) asked Grades 1–7 children to explain what matter is and to judge which items were matter. Children typically explained what matter was by examples, function (something one creates something with), or structure (made from components), but no elementary children and only 10% of the seventh graders said weight and volume were properties of matter. By fifth grade, children judge solids as matter 75% of the time, but liquids or biological materials only about 50% of the time and gases only 10%. Seventh graders judged gases matter about half the time, but they often misclassified phenomena associated with matter (e.g., electricity and smell) as matter as well. Thus, even in middle school, most students lack a clear concept of matter.

Both Carey (1991) and Smith et al. (2011) asked children to sort items as matter or not matter and explain the basis of their groupings. Carey found some improvement with age: Older children were more likely to include liquids and animals (but not gases) with solids, typically offering justifications based on perception. In the Inquiry Project study, only 54% of the Control fifth graders grouped all the solids, powders, and liquids together as instances of matter. Those students typically focused on perceptual properties; only 9% mentioned that they occupy space or have weight. Only 29% included all solids and liquids with at least some gases, and only 9% included gases while excluding heat or light (Smith et al., 2011).

Given that children have explicitly been taught that air is matter on numerous occasions, these findings suggest that what they are told simply does not make sense: For them, matter is what can be seen, felt, and touched and therefore gases are not matter. Coming to believe that gases are matter in the same sense that solids and liquids are, and that all three are different from physical but non-material entities, requires an onto-logical change. Children first need to reconceptualize solids and liquids in terms of properties they share with gases; i.e., having weight and taking up space. This reconceptualization cannot be achieved without conceptual restructuring of weight, material, and volume.

Strikingly, across these three studies only a few of the older children used weight as a criterion for being matter. Without this restructuring, students who are told that gases are matter can reject the idea, fragment their understanding of matter by introducing unexplained exceptions, give matter the unconstrained meaning of "everything that exists," or accept that "solids, liquids, and gases are matter" without understanding what "matter" really is, relying on similarity to prototypes of solids, liquids, and gases to judge whether something is matter or not.

Elementary-school children do come to believe that there can be pieces of matter too small to see with the naked eye. For example, when asked by Smith, Solomon, and Carey (2005), the majority of eight-year-olds said yes, typically invoking germs or other tiny things that can only be seen with a microscope. Piaget and Inhelder (1974) found that seven- to eight-year-olds tended to be aware that dissolved little pieces of sugar were still there.

This represents progress toward scientific understanding, but students' view of matter is still anchored in perception. It does not support conservation of matter without actual or potential perceptual evidence (e.g., taste; visibility with a microscope). Even older students often fail stricter tests for conservation – they believe that if one repeatedly cuts Styrofoam into smaller and smaller pieces, the pieces disappear (Smith, 2007; Smith, Maclin, Grosslight, & Davis, 1997). Finally, this view by itself does not support conceptualizing gases as material because it is based on perception and imagined mental division, and is therefore "unidirectional." One mentally divides a chunk into little pieces, first actually and then potentially visible. But, in children's experience, gases do not start as perceptible chunks; the decomposition schema is constrained by children's ontology and applies to what is conceived as material to start with. Thus many older students fail to conserve matter in the face of perceptual evidence that it disappears and when they cannot rely on a "getting smaller and smaller" scenario (e.g., during boiling) (Johnson, 1998; Lee, Eichinger, Anderson, Berkheimer, & Blakeslee, 1993).

We have argued that traditional curricula fail to make the idea that gases are material meaningful because they do not foster the idea that any piece of matter has weight and occupies space. Additionally, curricula treat knowledge as unproblematic facts and do not engage students in theory building. Thus few students develop modeling skills or appreciate that science is the construction of ever more adequate explanatory models, developed, tested, and revised through cycles of hypothesis testing (Carey, Evans, Honda, Jay, & Unger, 1989; Grosslight, Unger, Jay & Smith, 1991). Students fail to: (a) distinguish ideas (explanations) from evidence, (b) appreciate the *conjectural* nature of hypotheses and the fact that any pattern of data can be explained in multiple ways, and (c) understand the role of models as tools in guiding hypothesis formation and inquiry. Thus, they lack an epistemological foundation for understanding the material nature of gases, and, more generally, the particulate theory as a *model* of matter.

WHAT CONCEPTUAL CHANGES SHOULD BE WORKED ON IN ELEMENTARY SCHOOL?

In the previous section, we described young children's knowledge of matter and how it evolves through elementary school with traditional instruction. Although their knowledge gets enriched and undergoes some reconceptualization, it falls short of being compatible with the scientific theory of matter. Several aspects of existing curricula can account for many students failing to fully reconceptualize matter.

Traditional curricula underestimate elementary students' capability for theory building, and for developing the epistemological resources necessary for reconceptualization. Elementary-school children are assumed to be concrete thinkers, and the goal of elementary instruction to lay the observation base for theorizing in later grades. Therefore, different topics are explored in a piecemeal fashion; measurement is taught as a set of procedures, not tied to the construction of concepts; and modeling is ignored. For example, students are *told* that solids, liquids, and gases are types of matter rather than asked to construct models to explain phenomena involving matter.

Elementary curricula also underestimate the extent and depth of the reconceptualization that lies between students' ideas and a theory of matter that supports understanding the atomic–molecular theory later on. Fostering this reconceptualization is a long-term process. It focuses on multiple relations among concepts, which can change only progressively and therefore need to be revisited several times, in different contexts, and in specific orders. Concepts are revised and new concepts developed as co-constructions of representational tools (e.g., models, measure lines, graphs) and hands-on observations.

Overview of Conceptual Changes Involved in Restructuring Macroscopic Concepts

Table 8.1 provides an overview of conceptual changes needed to develop a sound macroscopic understanding of matter. These include: (a) extending and restructuring the concepts of weight, size, material, and matter so that they are now inter-related and based on objective (measurable) properties and (b) understanding the role of measurement and models.

A number of teachers, researchers, and curriculum developers have sought to improve elementary-school children's macroscopic understandings of matter, weight, volume, or density (Lehrer, Schauble, Strom, & Pligge, 2001; Raghavan & Glaser, 1995, Smith, Snir, & Grosslight, 1992; Wiser, Smith & Doubler, 2012), and their grasp of scientific epistemology (Smith, Maclin, Houghton, & Hennessey, 2000) by engaging them in cycles of model testing and revision. Although their focus and methods vary, none relies on simple didactic instruction or unguided inquiry and all take students' initial views into account. Students systematically construct and revise representations or models with the explicit goal of accounting for key phenomena. That students progress much more with these innovative curriculum materials is important evidence that their conceptual difficulties can be addressed with more appropriate science instruction.

Lehrer et al. (2001) took a mathematically-based modeling approach to helping elementary-school students construct a concept of density. Their fifth-grade intervention worked to "reorient mathematics and science instruction around the construction, evaluation, and revision of models" (p. 39). In earlier grades, students worked on "big ideas," including developing a theory of measure applied to length and then area (Lehrer, Jaslow, & Curtis, 2003). Students created non-standard units and worked through features of "good" measurement before moving to more standard units. In the process, they developed a network of ideas about units (e.g., iteration, identical units, covering the measurement space, partitioning units to form fractional units) and about scale (e.g.,

Table 8.1 Overview of Conceptual Changes Needed in Elementary School

Concepts	Changes
Material	From material as *property of objects* to new *ontological category* (dense causal nexus explaining object properties) Change involves: • developing material construal of solid objects (including compositional mental model) • developing knowledge of objective, measurable properties of materials (e.g., density, boiling points) • distinguishing reliabilities of properties in identifying materials (unreliability of perceptual properties associated with state, greater reliability of objective properties such as melting points) • understanding material as fundamental constituent that maintains identity across state changes.
Physical quantities	From *perception-based* to *objective, measurable* quantities, interrelated in a theory of matter. Change involves: • shifting from weight as heft to measurable quantity proportional to amount of material, measured on scale • differentiating weight of objects and density of materials • shifting from size as global bigness to differentiated measurable quantities of length, area, and volume • developing an explicit theory of measure (attribute–unit relations, identical and fractional units, zero point) • understanding measures as more reliable than senses; qualities of good measures, sources of measurement error.
Matter	Developing general (ontological) concept of matter as causal nexus. Change involves: • recognizing similarities in solids and liquids as things you can see, feel, and touch • applying compositional model to solids and liquids, recognizing similarities in occupying space, having weight • differentiating states of matter from kind of material (same material can be in different states) • extending ontological category matter to include gases • understanding matter and weight are conserved across transformations, although volume and density can change.
Models	From *resemblance-based* understanding (as little pictures, replicas, or scale models) to more abstract understanding as *explanatory models* and reasoning tools that capture important relationships. Change involves: • distinguishing observation from explanation • evaluating based on explanatory power rather than resemblance • acknowledging emergent properties.

importance of a zero-point, need for appropriate precision, and inherent limitations to accuracy of measurement).

In fifth grade, students extended these ideas to construct measures of volume. They next worked with magnified rectangles to develop a mathematical expression for "same, but bigger": straight-line graphs through the origin showing the ratios of the two sides. Finally, students explored objects of different volume and material, ultimately testing their conjecture that there might be "families of materials." They built on their previous understandings of volume measure and the mathematics of similarity. They also constructed a measure of weight, made weight and volume measurements of samples of different materials, wrestled with the reliability of those measurements, and plotted their data on a coordinate graph. Their prior work with graphing families of similar rectangles led them to expect that families of objects made of the same material might be represented with lines of different slopes.

Significantly, these sustained investigations using graphical, algebraic, and tabular representations led students to conclude that materials varied in their weight/volume ratios (their density) and to use these insights to make and test novel predictions. This is noteworthy since Rowell and Dawson (1983) had shown that using straight-line graphical relations to infer the constancy of density eluded most ninth grade students. Clearly, elementary-school children have a greater capacity for mathematical abstraction than is typically encouraged in math and science instruction. Further, mathematical models are important abstraction tools that aid in developing science concepts such as density.

Our intervention studies are based on a learning progression for matter (LPM). LPM (Wiser et al., 2012) outlines a succession of conceptual changes, and learning experiences to support them, that could bridge preschoolers' precursor concepts to scientifically compatible interpretations of matter and its macroscopic-level behavior. LPM-based curricula aim to foster the conceptual changes that do not typically occur with traditional instruction (e.g., believing that any arbitrarily small piece of matter has weight and occupies space and that gases are material). They also aim to strengthen conceptual changes that do occur with traditional instruction by relating them to each other and to theoretical models. For example, explicitly using the compositional model early, and refining it over time from macroscopic to infinitely small pieces, provides a solid basis for the concept of material and conservation of amount and material identity that will make grasping mass and the conservation of matter easier in middle school. Relating weight and volume measurement to a compositional model of material provides a conceptual basis for associating weight with matter, differentiating perception-based concepts from quantified ones (e.g., heft and scale weight), and constructing a concept of density of material. If students interrelate weight and volume in a compositional model of material, they can be puzzled by phenomena where weight is invariant but volume changes (e.g., thermal expansion, phase changes). Explaining these observations helps motivate the idea that matter is composed of discrete particles separated by empty space, paving the way for the atomic model.

Below, we focus on one recent study documenting the progress elementary-school children can make with LPM-based instruction. In the previous handbook chapter (Wiser & Smith, 2008), we reviewed Smith and her colleagues' earlier studies with middle-school students that engage students in thinking about the properties of matter and with building macroscopic models that depict the interrelations among volume, mass, and density of materials (Smith et al., 1992, 1997).

TERC's Inquiry Curriculum involves a sequence of three units (of 16–18 lessons each) at Grades 3, 4, and 5, developed from LPM. In Grade 3, the concepts of material, weight, and size are foregrounded, in the context of solid objects, which afford richer and easier exploration of the relations among those concepts than non-solids. Children work with a set of same-size cubes made of different materials, which embody the relation between weight and material in the simplest way. They compare the merits of hefting versus using a scale to measure their weights, and systematize the set of properties that can be used to compare materials (one of them being the weight of the same-size cubes). They construct weight lines to represent the weights of the cubes. Going back and forth between weight lines and weight measurements integrates the numerical structure of integers into their concept of weight, contributing to its reconceptualization as an extensive property of objects. Having learned that unaided senses are neither accurate nor sensitive ways to measure weight, students are also better prepared for a guided discussion on whether very small things have weight. They imagine what happens when a piece of clay is divided into little pieces (do the little pieces continue to have weight?) and what happens if all the pieces are put back together (does their weight equal the weight of the original object?). This is a first step in developing a *compositional model of materials* and establishing that any piece of matter, however small, has weight, furthering the reconceptualization of the relation of weight and amount of material.

In Grade 4 weight, material, volume, and "heavy-for-size" are foregrounded. Students consider Earth materials – in solid, liquid, and granular form – and revisit comparing the weights of equal volumes of different materials. Students are also challenged to distinguish "heavy" and "heavy for size," predicting how samples of different materials that are the same weight will differ in volume. Students also extend their understanding of volume by devising multiple approaches to its measurement. Finally, investigating Earth materials strengthens their understanding that grinding a solid chunk into a powder does not change the identity of a material, and the concurrent distinction between a material and the state it is in – two principles expressed by the compositional model. Students also discover that weight is constant during those transformations, a first step toward conservation of mass. As a whole these activities emphasize the deep similarities between solids and liquids and support their coalescence into a new ontological category that is a precursor to the scientific concept of matter (things that have not only substantiality but also have weight, occupy space, and are made of different materials with specific "heaviness for size").

In Grade 5, weight and material remain salient while matter is introduced explicitly, and the Earth materials theme now includes the water cycle and salinity. Capitalizing on their belief that weight is an inherent property of solids and liquids, students explore the conservation of amount of material in dissolving, melting, and thawing, using weight constancy as evidence for it. They are introduced to gases in the context of evaporation and condensation and explore the materiality of air. Volume and weight now play an evidential role of the material nature of gases. Children use models to explore how things too tiny and dispersed to be visible can become visible when sufficiently aggregated. They also are introduced to a basic particulate model of matter (as computer animation) and explore the changes that occur at the particulate level during phase change.

What were the results? In a three-year comparative longitudinal study, the progress of the students who had the Inquiry Curriculum was compared to students in the same school who had their usual science curriculum. The two groups received the same two-hour interview at each grade probing their concepts of matter, material, weight, volume, and density in multiple ways. Both groups made progress on (and were near ceiling on) a few tasks – for example, standard Piagetian conservation of amount and weight tasks, tasks that assessed their ability to use scales to measure weight, and tasks that probed their understanding that ground-up solids are still the same material. However, there were striking differences between the two groups on many other tasks. Inquiry students made much more progress in understanding that little pieces of clay have weight and take up space (76% vs. 31%) and that weight and amount of material are conserved during dissolving (85% vs. 46%); differentiating weight and density (63% vs. 34%); recognizing that all solids and liquids are matter and including at least some gases (63% vs. 29%); formulating universal generalizations about weight (59% vs. 17%); and explicitly understanding that all matter occupies space or has weight (50% vs. 9%) (Doubler et al., 2011). Most Grade 5 Inquiry students showed these understandings, while only a minority of non-Inquiry students did. Of course, there is room for further improvement even for Inquiry students, and some tasks, particularly those concerned with volume measurement, remained difficult for both groups.

These studies illustrate that conceptual change occurs in the context of multiple (iterative) cycles of model construction, testing, and revision. It involves elaboration and major restructuring. Although each phase in model construction and testing is constrained by students' initial conceptual and epistemological understandings, instructional contexts can scaffold the use of conceptual resources and symbolic tools from inside and outside a given domain. Beliefs peripheral to a concept can be given prominence (e.g., the role of scales in measuring weight); implicit knowledge can be made explicit (e.g., when a sample is cut into pieces, one can mentally reconstitute the whole); empirical generalizations can be qualified and become principles (bigger things are heavier than smaller things *made of the same material*); and new symbolic representations can be constructed by integrating mathematical knowledge with data from hands-on investigations. Each new relationship is a local and meaningful modification to the knowledge network; together, they amount to its radical reorganization.

CONCLUSIONS

In this chapter, we highlighted the conceptual changes that lead to a scientific understanding of matter at the macroscopic level. Although some occur with traditional instruction (e.g., the material construal of objects and the conservation of amount of material during shape change), many do not. This is because traditional curricula do not focus on the interrelated changes involved in developing scientifically compatible concepts of weight, volume, and material or the role measurement plays in those changes. More generally, they fail to nurture the epistemological shift from perceptually-based concepts to concepts that can be quantified objectively. Thus, for most students, matter remains what can be seen, felt, and touched instead of what has weight and occupies space. They embody knowledge acquisition as the unmediated accumulation of facts instead of the construction and revision of models. Crucially missing is developing a robust (microscopic) compositional model of materials in which even very tiny pieces take up space, have weight, and retain the characteristic heaviness for size of macroscopic objects. Without these understandings, students are unprepared to discover the material nature of gases, develop a concept of substance that is differentiated from state, or understand the conservation of substance identity and matter across phase change.

In contrast, the promise of LP approaches to curricular design is that they do establish the need to foster progressive and orchestrated changes in concepts and their relations. They also establish intermediary learning goals on a conceptual basis; these learning goals are coherent states of knowledge organized around models of matter. Each provides an account of matter and its behavior that is closer to a scientific account and serves as a stepping stone for further learning. By engaging students in progressive cycles of model construction and revision – first with a macroscopic compositional model, then with a microscopic compositional model – students are better prepared both epistemologically and conceptually for later constructing a particulate model of matter that will in turn facilitate learning the atomic–molecular theory.

NOTES

1   Go to http://inquiryproject.terc.edu for description of both curriculum and research findings.
2   "Matter conservation" is actually a misnomer. What is being assessed in Piaget's task is the conservation of amount of material.

REFERENCES

Andersson, B. (1990). Pupils' conceptions of matter and its transformations (age 12–16). *Studies in Science Education, 18*(1), 53–85.

Au, T. K.-F. (1994). Developing an intuitive understanding of substance kinds. *Cognitive Psychology, 27,* 71–111.

Baillargeon, R. (2002). The acquisition of physical knowledge in infancy: A summary in eight lessons. In U. Goswami (Ed.), *Blackwell handbook of childhood cognitive development.* London, UK: Blackwell.

Bloom, P. (2002). *How children learn the meaning of words.* Cambridge, MA: MIT Press.

Bower, T. (1989). The perceptual world of the newborn child. In A. Slater (Ed.), *Infant development* (pp. 85–98). New York, NY: Psychology Press.

Carey, S. (1991). Knowledge acquisition: Enrichment or conceptual change? In S. Carey & R. Gelman (Eds.), *The epigenesis of mind* (pp. 257–291). Hillsdale, NJ: Lawrence Erlbaum Associates.

Carey, S. (2009). *The origin of concepts.* Oxford, UK: Oxford University Press.

Carey, S., Evans, R., Honda, M., Jay, E., & Unger, C. (1989). "An experiment is when you try it and see if it works": A study of grade 7 students' understanding of the construction of scientific knowledge. *International Journal of Science Education, 11,* 514–529.

Clements, D. H., & Sarama, J. (2009). *Learning and teaching early math: The learning trajectories approach.* New York, NY: Routledge.

Corcoran, T., Mosher, F., & Rogat, A. (2009). *Learning progressions in science: An evidence-based approach to reform.* Philadelphia, PA: Consortium for Policy Research in Education.

Curry, M., & Outhred, L. (2005). Conceptual understanding of spatial measurement. In P. Clarkson (Ed.), *Building connections: Theory, research and practice.* Proceedings of the 27th MERGA Conference. Sydney, Australia: MERGA.

Dickinson, D. K. (1987). The development of material kind. *Science Education, 71,* 615–628.

Dickinson, D. K. (1988). Learning names for materials: Factors constraining and limiting hypotheses about word meaning. *Cognitive Development, 3,* 15–35.

Doubler, S., Carraher, D., Tobin, R., Asbell-Clarke, J., Smith, C., & Schliemann, A. (2011). *The Inquiry Project: Final report.* Submitted to National Science Foundation DR K–12 Program, September 8.

Driver, R., Guesne, E., & Tiberghien, A. (1985). *Children's ideas in science.* Buckingham, UK: Open University Press.

Grosslight, L., Unger, C., Jay, E. & Smith, C. (1991). Understanding models and their use in science: Conceptions of middle and high school students and experts. *Journal of Research in Science Teaching, 28,* 799–822.

Hall, G. (1996). Naming solids and non-solids: Children's default construals. *Cognitive Development, 11*(2), 229–264.

Huntley-Fenner, G., Carey, S., & Solimando, A. (2002). Objects are individuals but stuff doesn't count: Perceptual rigidity and cohesiveness influences infants' representations of small numbers of discrete entities. *Cognition, 85,* 203–221.

Johnson, P. (1998). Children's understanding of changes of state involving the gas state, Part 1: Boiling water and the particle theory. *International Journal of Science Education, 20,* 567–583.

Johnson, P., & Papageorgiou, G. (2010). Rethinking the introduction of particle theory: A substance-based framework. *Journal of Research in Science Teaching, 47,* 130–150.

Johnson, P. M., Tymms, P., & Roberts, S. (2008). *Assessing students' concept of a substance* (Full research report). ESRC Society Today. Swindon, UK: Economic and Social Research Council.

Krnel, D., Glazar, S., & Watson, R. (2003). The development of the concept of "matter": A cross-age study of how children classify materials. *Science Education, 87,* 621–639.

Lee, O., Eichinger, D. C., Anderson, C. W., Berkheimer, G. D., & Blakeslee, T. D. (1993). Changing middle school students' conceptions of matter and molecules. *Journal of Research in Science Teaching, 30*(3), 249–270.

Lehrer, R., Jacobson, C., Kemeny, V., & Strom, D. (1999). Building on children's intuitions to develop an understanding of space. In E. Fennema & T. A. Romberg (Eds.), *Mathematics classrooms that promote understanding* (pp. 63–87). Mahwah, NJ: Lawrence Erlbaum Associates.

Lehrer, R., Jaslow, L., & Curtis, C. (2003). Developing understanding of measurement in elementary grades. In

D. Clements & G. Bright (Eds.), *The National Council of Teachers of Mathematics: Yearbook on learning and teaching measurement* (pp. 100–121). Reston, VA: National Council of Teachers of Mathematics.

Lehrer, R., Schauble, L., Strom, D., & Pligge, M. (2001). Similarity of form and substance: Modeling material kind. In S. Carver & D. Klahr (Eds.), *Cognition and instruction: Twenty-five years of progress* (pp. 39–74). Mahwah, NJ: Lawrence Erlbaum Associates.

Metz, K. (1993). Preschoolers' developing knowledge of the pan-balance: New representation to transformed problem solving. *Cognition and Instruction, 11*(1), 31–93.

Piaget, J., & Inhelder, B. (1974). *The child's construction of physical quantities.* London, UK: Routledge and Kegan Paul.

Raghavan, K., & Glaser, R. (1995). Model-based analysis and reasoning in science: The MARS curriculum. *Science Education, 79*(1), 37–61.

Rowell, J. A., & Dawson, C. J. (1983). Laboratory counterexamples and the growth of understanding in science. *European Journal of Science Education, 5*(2), 203–215.

Sarama, J., & Clements, D. H. (2009). *Early childhood mathematics education research: Learning trajectories for young children.* New York, NY: Routledge.

Smith, C. (2007). Bootstrapping processes in the development of students' commonsense matter theories: Using analogical mappings, thought experiments, and learning to measure to promote conceptual restructuring. *Cognition and Instruction. 25*(4), 337–398.

Smith, C., Carey, S., & Wiser, M. (1985). On differentiation: A case study of the development of the concepts of size, weight, and density. *Cognition, 21*(3), 177–237.

Smith, C., Maclin, D., Grosslight, L., & Davis, H. (1997). Teaching for understanding: A comparison of two approaches to teaching students about matter and density. *Cognition and Instruction, 15*(3), 317–393.

Smith, C., Maclin, D., Houghton, C., & Hennessey, M. G. (2000). Sixth graders' epistemologies of science: The impact of school science experiences on epistemological development. *Cognition and Instruction, 18*(3), 349–422.

Smith, C., Snir, J., & Grosslight, L. (1992). Using conceptual models to facilitate conceptual change: The case of weight/density differentiation. *Cognition and Instruction, 9*(3), 221–283.

Smith, C., Solomon, G., & Carey, S. (2005). Never getting to zero: Elementary school students' understanding of the infinite divisibility of matter and number. *Cognitive Psychology, 51,* 101–140.

Smith, C. L., Wiser, M., Anderson, C. W. & Krajcik, J. (2006). Implications of research on children's learning for standards and assessment: A proposed learning progression for matter and atomic–molecular theory. *Measurement: Interdisciplinary Research and Perspectives, 14*(1–2), 1–98.

Smith, C., Wiser, M., & Doubler, S. (2011). *Abstracting a general concept of matter among grade 3–5 students: Lessons from the Inquiry Project.* Presentation at the Jean Piaget Society Meetings, June 3, Berkeley, CA.

Soja, N., Carey, S., & Spelke, E. (1991) Ontological categories guide young children's inductions of word meaning: Object terms and substance terms. *Cognition, 38,* 179–211.

Sophian, C. (2000). From numbers to quantities: Developments in preschool children's judgments about aggregate amount. *Developmental Psychology, 36,* 724–736.

Spelke, E. (1991). Physical knowledge in infancy: Reflections on Piaget's theory. In S. Carey & R. Gelman (Eds.), *The epigenesis of mind* (pp. 257–291). Hillsdale, NJ: Lawrence Erlbaum Associates.

Stavy, R. (1991). Children's ideas about matter. *School Science and Mathematics, 91,* 240–244.

Stavy, R. & Stachel, D. (1985). Children's conception of changes in the state of matter: From solid to liquid. *Archives de Psychologie, 53,* 331–344.

Whorf, B. L. (1952). *The relation of habitual thought and behavior to language: Collected papers on metalinguistics* (pp. 27–45). Washington, DC: Department of State: Foreign Service Institute.

Wiser, M., & Fox, V. (2010). *Quantifying amount of material: A teaching intervention in pre-K and kindergarten.* Paper presented at the International Science Education Symposium on the Particulate and Structural Concepts of Matter, Athens, Greece, November 5–8.

Wiser, M., Frazier, K., & Fox, V. (in press). At the beginning was amount of material: A learning progression for matter for early elementary grades. In G. T. Tsaparlis & H. Sevian (Eds.), *Concepts of matter in science education.* Dordrecht, The Netherlands: Springer.

Wiser, M., & Smith, C. L. (2008). Learning and teaching about matter in grades K–8: When should the atomic–molecular theory be introduced? In S. Vosniadou (Ed.), *International handbook of research on conceptual change* (pp. 205–239). New York, NY: Routledge.

Wiser, M., Smith, C., & Doubler, S. (2012). Learning progressions as tool for curriculum development: Lessons from the Inquiry Project. In A. Alonzo & A. Gotwals (Eds.), *Learning progressions in sciencescience: Current challenges and future directions* (pp. 359–403). Rotterdam, The Netherlands: Sense Publishing.

9

LEARNING AND TEACHING ABOUT MATTER IN THE MIDDLE-SCHOOL YEARS

How Can the Atomic–Molecular Theory be Meaningfully Introduced?

Marianne Wiser and Carol L. Smith, Clark University and University of Massachusetts Boston

The atomic–molecular theory is one of the most important contemporary scientific theories. Its basic tenets are few and simple, offering parsimonious and elegant explanations of why and how materials differ and change phase, and enter into chemical reactions. Yet most high-schoolers display major misconceptions about the nature, behavior, and structural arrangements of atoms, and about atomic–molecular accounts of macroscopic properties and phenomena. We argue that this is not inevitable and is no reason to delay teaching the atomic–molecular theory (AMT) until high school.

Atoms are ontologically very strange: they are the sole constituents of matter but have almost none of the properties of macroscopic objects. They are not colored, hard or soft, or created or destroyed (in physical and chemical reactions). There are only about 100 different atoms, whereas the number of materials is practically infinite. The properties atoms share with objects are the most counterintuitive, given their size – occupying space and having mass. Moreover, they have properties uniquely their own: They are held together by electromagnetic forces, move at very high speed, and exist in the vacuum. Thus the discrepancy between perceived reality and how AMT accounts for it is huge. Reconciling this discrepancy calls for epistemological sophistication: not only about scientific models and their relation to observations, but also about the *emergent* nature of many macroscopic properties of matter.

Students also need objective (rather than perceptually based) concepts to make sense of AMT. For example, taking the decrease in volume when alcohol and water are mixed as supporting a discontinuous model of matter requires understanding weight and volume as objective, measurable quantities as well as the ability to evaluate competing models in light of data. Unfortunately, few students have the macroscopic conceptualization of matter, weight, and volume necessary to support a sound understanding of AMT.

Compounding those conceptual challenges is the way AMT itself is traditionally taught. Information presented to students is not rich enough for them to make sense of it, and the language and illustrations in textbooks are widely, if unwittingly, misleading.

In this chapter, we first review some important student misconceptions about atoms and molecules and analyze the reasons they develop. These reasons are often interlinked; e.g., alternative ideas about atoms may stem from students' initial ontological assumptions about matter, their naïve epistemology, and the ways these ideas are taught. Well-entrenched misconceptions tend to be those with multiple reasons.

We then propose instructional approaches that may alleviate many of these difficulties, as well as offer solutions to current debates about when and how AMT should be taught. These approaches are embedded in long-term learning progressions (LPs) – *hypotheses* about how students' understanding of core scientific concepts such as matter could undergo successive reconceptualizations and evolve meaningfully toward scientific understanding with the support of learning experiences designed and ordered to facilitate conceptual changes. What progresses is a network of "knowledge-in-use" – ideas embedded in practices (constructing models and explanations, designing investigations, measuring, and making arguments). The network progresses from *stepping stone* to *stepping stone* – coherent states of knowledge that get progressively closer, *conceptually*, to the scientific theory. Models of matter structure successive stepping stones, which also include the range of phenomena to which the models apply, the explanations they provide, and the ontological and epistemological assumptions supporting them.

MISCONCEPTIONS ABOUT ATOMS AND MOLECULES AND SOME HYPOTHESES ABOUT THEIR CAUSES

Misconceptions about the Ontology of Atoms and Molecules

Many students do not conceive of atoms as the basic constituents of matter but rather as something embedded in a material substrate (Andersson, 1990; Lee, Eichinger, Anderson, Berkheimer, & Blakeslee, 1993), as if, by themselves, they were not sufficient to be the stuff of which things are made. This extremely powerful misconception survives through college chemistry instruction (Pozo & Gomez Crespo, 2005). Many reasons conspire to cause its elaboration and entrenchment as a "molecules-in-matter" model.

First, students start by trying to map atoms and molecules onto familiar ontological categories. For many students, solid and liquids, which are visible and tangible, form an ontological category that does not include gases; gases are something else, usually more closely related to heat and electricity than to solids and liquids (Carey, 1991). This ontological commitment at the macroscopic level, in interaction with students' selective attention to classroom information, leads to misconceptions about the nature of atoms. For example, if students hear "everything has atoms – solids, liquids, and gases," they are likely to think of atoms as non-material, gas-like "specks" embedded in solids and liquids and floating in gases.

Second, students' macroscopic concepts of weight and volume also affect their beliefs about what atoms are and where they are found. For many middle-schoolers, weight and volume are, essentially, perceptual properties of objects, so that very little pieces of matter don't weigh anything or occupy space (Smith, 2007). If atoms don't weigh anything or occupy space because they are too small, they cannot be constitutive of things one can touch and see. This reinforces the need to embed atoms in "stuff."

Correlational studies support the link between holding alternative conceptions at the macroscopic level and understanding AMT as an explanatory model. Snir, Smith, and Raz (2003) showed that students who lacked sound macroscopic understandings of matter, weight, volume, and density did not retain core tenets of AMT or use them to explain macroscopic phenomena. Lee et al. (1993) showed that macroscopic and atomic–molecular misconceptions coexist in sixth graders regarding many issues (e.g., the material nature of gases, phase change, and dissolving) and that teaching that addresses misconceptions at both levels is more successful than teaching just AMT.

Third, creating new ontologies requires serious theory building; students generally lack the epistemological sophistication to realize that is what they should do (Carey, Evans, Honda, Jay, & Unger, 1989; Grosslight, Unger, Jay, & Smith, 1991). Being naïve realists and lacking sophistication in model-based reasoning, they believe that matter is *inherently* continuous since it *looks continuous* (Ben-Zvi, Eylon, & Silberstein, 1986) and develop a model consistent with that belief (Harrison & Treagust, 2002; Nakhleh, Samarapungavan, & Saglam, 2005). Instructional approaches compound the problem when they present AMT as a set of facts rather than an explanatory model.

Fourth, metaphysics also supports the "molecules-in-matter" model – vacuum between atoms violates a deeply held metaphysical principle that vacuum does not exist (Nussbaum, 1985, 1997). The need to "fill the gaps" with stuff is all the more acute because most middle-schoolers are not taught that forces hold atoms and molecules together, let alone their magnitude compared to familiar forces (Scott, 1987).

Finally, textbook illustrations also contribute to this model – a piece of substance is represented as a colored cube with black boundaries and small black spheres in it. So does language such as "Atoms *in* solids vibrate . . ." and "Molecules *escape from the water* into the air when water boils."

Many students make some progress in high school toward viewing atoms as little pieces of matter, mostly upon the introduction of the periodic table (Wiser, O'Connor, & Higgins, 1995). However, they attribute macroscopic properties to atoms (e.g., hotness, being solid or liquid), rather than understanding that those properties are *emergent*. Attributing macroscopic properties to atoms is one of the most robust misconceptions about atoms (Andersson, 1990; Ben-Zvi et al., 1986; Johnson, 1998), which deeply affects students' understanding of physical transformations. For example, many students say that molecules change size and weight upon heating and during phase change, liquefy during melting and dissolution, and disappear when liquids boil (Griffiths & Preston, 1992; Lee et al., 1993).

Undoubtedly, a naïve realist epistemology and a lack of knowledge about models are at the root of the overextension of macroscopic properties to atoms and molecules. However, it is also the case that, without information about molecular bonds, students have no way to understand how materials can be flexible without being made of flexible atoms or melt without individual atoms becoming liquid.

Misconceptions about the Difference and Relation between Atoms and Molecules

Learning about atoms and molecules is difficult not only because it involves adding a new ontology (atoms and molecules share few properties with macroscopic objects), but also because it involves making a fundamental distinction between atoms and molecules themselves. To scientists, the distinction is embedded in a rich network of beliefs and has explanatory force – e.g., atoms are conserved across chemical transformations, whereas molecules can come in and go out of existence; and pure substances, which are made of one kind of molecule, behave differently from mixtures, which are made of several kinds of molecules.

Understanding the difference between physical and chemical transformations at the atomic–molecular level is arduous. In phase change, molecules are conserved and heat affects the strength of the intermolecular forces, while in chemical reactions, atoms are conserved but molecules are not; the reconfiguration of atoms depends on intra-molecular forces. Most students do not make these distinctions and often believe, for example, that water molecules break down into hydrogen and oxygen when water boils (Osborne & Freyberg, 1985). A subtler consequence of students' epistemological short-comings and lack of information about atomic and molecular forces is their difficulty in understanding chemical reactions as dynamic interactions among molecules. In keeping with a "mixing" view of chemical reactions at the macroscopic level, some students describe molecules produced in chemical reaction as concatenating without affecting each other (Del Pozo, 2001).

Summary of the Epistemological, Ontological, and Macroscopic Knowledge that (would) make the Atomic–Molecular Theory Meaningful

Mastering AMT requires epistemological, ontological, and macroscopic knowledge that, for many students, is not in place by the time the theory is presented – nor is it acquired as they are studying it. Students need to make the ontological distinction between perceptual and physical properties and understand how they are related, rather than treat perceptual properties of matter from a naïve realist point of view. They also need to understand the nature and function of scientific models – their elements are different from the entities they account for, their value is in their explanatory power, and they represent revisable hypotheses. Students' epistemology must also include emergent properties, in order to grasp that atoms, invisible to the naked eye, can form visible matter with physical and perceptual properties they themselves do not have. The concepts used to interpret matter and its behavior at the macroscopic level should be scientifically compatible so that AMT is understandable and quickly gains credibility as it is used to account for a wide range of phenomena.

In the next sections, we highlight the complex interrelations among many aspects of knowledge to be acquired. We argue that the learning challenges posed by AMT could be lessened and the entrenchment of misconceptions prevented by organizing LP-based curricula around a series of increasingly complex models of matter: models of matter as continuous, particle models (in which no distinction is drawn between atom and molecule), and increasingly complex atomic–molecular models. These models are the nexuses of a series of stepping stones representing increasingly sophisticated knowledge about matter. Each model embodies a new coherent subset of ideas about matter, gives more depth to existing concepts, and has greater explanatory power than the previous model. Each stepping stone provides deeper explanations to a greater range of phenomena and motivates the introduction of the next model.

Three questions immediately arise: What aspects of the scientific theory of matter should students understand at the macroscopic level before they are introduced to models of matter as discontinuous? What tenets of AMT should each particle and atomic–molecular model embody? And what kinds of phenomena should each model be applied to? In the next section, we propose answers derived from current research consistent with a LP framework. Several research teams are developing matter LPs for different grade bands (e.g., Doubler et al. (2011) for Grades 3–5; Krajcik, Sutherland, Drago, & Merritt (2011) and Johnson & Papageorgiou (2010) for middle school; Stevens, Delgado, & Krajcik (2010) for Grades 7–14). They have developed and assessed curricula derived from their LPs and found impressive gains in students' understanding (e.g., Doubler et al., 2011; Krajcik, McNeill, & Reiser, 2008; Krajcik et al., 2011; Papageorgiou, Grammaticopoulou, & Johnson, 2010).

Table 9.1 provides a snapshot of three stepping stones in a broader five-level LP, synthesized in a recent paper (Rogat et al., 2011). It describes the new tenets embodied in each model, the macroscopic concepts it supports, and the range of contexts to which it applies. Although further comparative studies are needed and the benefits of concatenating curricula across grade bands need exploration, we argue that particle models are conceptually necessary in scaffolding atomic–molecular models and concepts of substance and chemical reactions. They could be introduced by the end of elementary school if an appropriate foundation is provided in prior years. Moreover, it is important to do so because they also give meaning to the materiality of gases and phase change.

INTEGRATING MACROSCOPIC AND ATOMIC–MOLECULAR UNDERSTANDINGS OF MATTER AND ITS BEHAVIOR: A LEARNING PROGRESSION VIEW

The Atomic–Molecular Theory and the Material Nature of Gases

Two milestones toward a scientific understanding of matter are believing that gases are material and that matter is discontinuous. Which understanding should be developed first? At first blush, the situation seems to involve a Catch-22.

Nussbaum (1985, 1997) and Fensham (1994) believe that the particle model should be introduced in the context of gases (rather than solids and liquids) because it is easier to believe that gases are made of tiny particles undetectable by the senses, in constant motion, and separated by a vacuum. However, learning about the particulate nature of gases will only lead to a particle model of *matter* if students already think that gases are material. Research suggests that most do not, and find this idea highly counterintuitive (Smith, 2007; Stavy, 1991). In fact, according to Pozo and Gomez Crespo (2005), students who adopt the particulate view for gases do so for the wrong epistemological and ontological reasons: It makes sense that gases are made of atoms because they share the properties of being invisible and moving on their own. This perceptual analogy leads them to infer that solids and liquids, which are visible and don't move on their own, are not made of atoms (see also Krnel, Watson, & Glasar, 1998).

Table 9.1 Overview of three stepping stones in a learning progression for matter

Grade band	Target model of matter (new assumptions)	New or revised macroscopic concepts	New contexts of application: Explaining
Grades 3–4	*Microscopic compositional model of material as continuous*[1] • Objects can be thought of as composed of tiny pieces of material that are too small to see • Each piece has weight, occupies space, and retains some characteristic properties of the material • Those pieces can be rearranged without changing the initial volume or weight of object	• Matter: any piece of solid / liquid has weight and occupies space • Liquid and solid state vs. material identity • (Scale) weight proportional to amount of material • Material; volume • Heaviness for size • Melting and freezing	• Some properties of objects • Weight stays same in reshaping, grinding, melting, and freezing • Material identity and volume stay the same in reshaping and grinding
Grades 5–6	*Basic particle model of matter*[2] • Solids and liquids consist of very tiny pre-existing particles separated by empty space. • Particles are alike for one substance, but differ, with different weights, from substance to substance • Particles have the ability to hold each other – the strength of hold differs by substance • Particles are always moving; movement increases with temperature • Particles do not change during phase change but move differently in liquids, solids, and gases and are much further apart in gases	• Material nature of gases • Distinction between air and vacuum • Evaporation, condensation • Melting and boiling points • Density • Substance as defined by properties such as melting and boiling point and density • Distinction between pure substance and mixtures	• Invisibility of gases • Volume, but not weight, changes in heating, dissolving, melting, boiling • Difference between melting/ dissolving, pure substance/ mixture • Transmission of smells • Substance identity conservation in changes in state • Different densities, boiling and melting points of different substances
Grades 7–9	*Basic atomic–molecular model (atoms as spheres)*[3] • All matter is composed of 100 different types of atoms (of different mass) that are commonly bonded together in molecules or networks • Some substances are composed of one type of atom; others of several types • Substance properties are determined by the kinds of atoms/molecules they are made of and the strength of the forces between molecules • Molecules but not atoms can come into and go out of existence	• Distinction between compound and element • Periodic Table of Elements • Chemical properties of substances (e.g., reactivity) • Chemical reaction	• Properties of substances and mixtures (more and deeper explanations) • Distinction between compounds and elements • How chemical reactions occur

[1] Adapted from Rogat et al. (2011) and Wiser, Smith, & Doubler (2012). [2] Adapted from Rogat et al. (2011) and Johnson & Papageorgiou (2010). [3] Adapted from Rogat et al. (2011), Smith, Wiser, Anderson, & Krajcik (2006) and Stevens, Delgado, & Krajcik (2010).

Should one infer that a particle model be taught first in the context of solids and liquids, and then used to explain why gases can be both material and invisible? This will not work either because it is as counterintuitive to assume that liquids and solids are discontinuous as it is to assume that gases are material. However, new understandings draw on multiple sources, some empirical and others theoretical, and develop over time. This allows a stepwise approach that capitalizes on the conceptual affinity between gases and particle models while insuring the reconceptualization of gases as material and of solids and liquids as particulate.

For example, in the LP-based Inquiry Curriculum (Wiser et al., 2012), the material nature of gases is constructed concurrently with a particle model of matter, but only *after* an ontological category of matter that includes both solids and liquids has been developed at the macroscopic level. For younger children, what solids and liquids have in common is (at best) their *substantiality* – they can be seen and touched (Wiser, Frazier, & Fox, in press). In the Grades 3 and 4 Inquiry Curriculum, deeper similarities emerge – solids and liquids have weight, occupy space, and exist as different kinds of materials with specific properties. Most crucially, any solid or liquid sample can be thought of as made of pieces so small that their individual weight and volume are undetectable with unaided senses, but add up to the weight and volume of the sample (compositional model of material). Weight is thereby reconceptualized from heft to a quantity proportional to amount of material, measured with a scale; the concepts of *volume* and *heavy for size*, a precursor to density, are also constructed.

Traditional curricula overlook the importance of this reconceptualization. Yet our longitudinal study shows that it takes place for only a minority of Grade 3–5 children in the control group. In contrast, the majority of students who worked with the Inquiry Curriculum developed new interrelated concepts of *matter, weight, volume,* and *material* that are part of a stepping stone – a coherent state of knowledge about matter at the macroscopic level that supports new interpretations of phenomena and sets the stage for learning about the material nature of gases. (See Chapter 8, this volume for more details.)

What are crucial next steps? In Grade 5, Inquiry students were exposed to puzzling new phenomena involving dissolving, melting, evaporation, and condensation, and asked, for example, "Is salt dissolved in water still there? If so, why can't we see it?" They also used a two-bottle closed system in which water slowly disappears from the bottom bottle (placed under a lamp) and slowly reappears in the upper bottle. Where did the water in the bottom bottle go? Where did the water in the upper bottle come from? These observations fostered tentative hypotheses – e.g., perhaps the salt (water) is still there, but in invisible form – that warranted further exploration. Seeing the same stuff "appear" and "disappear" strongly suggests it continues to exist in between (by analogy with macroscopic objects). Gathering relevant macroscopic empirical evidence strengthened this hypothesis. In the case of dissolving, students weighed the salt and water before and after the salt dissolved to see if weight changed or not. Other activities let them discover that air takes up space and has weight. For students who believe that matter has weight and occupies space, these investigations strongly support the hypothesis that salt continues to exist in the water, and that air and water vapor are material, like solids and liquids.

The questions remained: How can salt (air, water vapor) exist and be invisible? How did the water get from one bottle to another "unnoticed?" Without answers to those questions, empirical evidence may fail to convince students of the material nature of gases and conservation of matter. Thus the curriculum also introduced a particle model to provide plausible explanations of these phenomena. For example, water (in solid, liquid, and gas form) consists of extremely tiny particles, too small to see, which are in constant motion; heating changes the motion (and arrangement) of the particles but not the particles themselves. Air and salt are made of particles too, but different from particles of water. Particles of substances in the gaseous state, such as the air around us, are much further apart than particles of substances in the solid or liquid state. That is why air and water vapor are invisible. Gases belong to the same ontological category as solids and liquids *because* they are composed of particles which each have weight and occupy space. That these tiny particles have weight and volume is typically ignored in traditional curricula; yet it is crucial to bringing macroscopic evidence to bear on the material nature of gases and the conservation of matter during phase change and dissolving.

The Inquiry Curriculum was effective in convincing the majority of fifth graders that gases are material (Doubler et al., 2011). The construction of this understanding required combining insights from multiple sources: ideas that material objects of any size have weight and volume (originally only obvious for large scale solid samples), insights that materials can exist in very tiny bits (from applying the compositional model to solids and liquids), and the new idea these tiny bits are separated by empty space and in constant motion (consistent with observing evaporation and dissolving).

Thus the learning progression approach to teaching about gases capitalizes on the fact that a model of matter as discontinuous is easier to fit to gases than to solids and liquids, as proposed by Nussbaum and Fensham. It also ensures that it is clearly a model of *matter* (in both the student's and the scientist's sense), by making weight central to the model – solids, liquids, and gases have weight, and so do particles. Thus, integrating gases into their existing ontological category of matter and learning a particle model of matter are two faces of the same process. In a later section of the paper we discuss the explanatory power of the particle model and different forms it can take, depending on which AMT tenets it embodies.

The Atomic–Molecular Theory and Chemical Reactions

Just as there are multiple particle models, there is a hierarchy of atomic–molecular models (Stevens, Delgado, & Krajcik, 2010). What differentiates atomic–molecular from particle models is that particles of substance have structure in atomic–molecular models (particles are either atoms or collections of atoms forming molecules) and therefore can account for the formation of new substances in chemical reactions.

Whether chemical reactions should be taught before or after AMT has been a matter of debate. One view is that AMT should be motivated by extensive experience with macroscopic phenomena, most notably chemical reactions (Fensham, 1994). We strongly agree that motivating AMT is important and that extensive experience with macroscopic phenomena is essential. But we also think that the best motivation for AMT is not extensive prior macroscopic experience with chemical reactions but rather experience developing a concept of substance (Johnson, 2000, 2002). If students find chemical reactions interesting, it is usually for their "magical" side, rather than because they raise important theoretical questions (DeVos & Verdonk, 1987; Harrison & Treagust, 2002). In a constructivist framework, motivation comes from puzzling over phenomena one already understands well enough to articulate questions that will guide productive inquiry. This is particularly true of a model-based approach, in which dissatisfaction with a model's explanatory power leads to revising it so it can provide an explanation for a particular set of phenomena. Chemical reactions at the macroscopic level cannot provide that motivation unless students have a concept of substance that is sufficiently developed to determine if a new substance has been created and to articulate the most puzzling question about chemical reactions – how can *new* substances be produced?

There is little theoretical or empirical support for Johnstone's (1982) idea that the scientific concept of substance can emerge from observing patterns of chemical reactions at the macroscopic level. Students tend to map "pure substance" and "mixture" onto categories totally foreign to chemistry (Johnson, 2002). They rely on perceptual appearance (regarding homogeneous-looking substances as "pure substances" and non-homogeneous ones as mixtures) or transformational history ("pure substances" are those found in nature; mixtures are produced by "mixing" things). Such concepts and criteria cannot be used to puzzle productively about chemical reactions at the macroscopic level.

More generally, understanding how chemical transformations differ from physical transformations is difficult to achieve at the macroscopic level (Johnson, 2000; Krajcik et al., 2008). Students have difficulty, conceptually, differentiating state of matter from kind of substance (Johnson & Papageorgiou, 2010). Moreover, if they believe that substance identity is preserved during phase change, they may overextend this principle to chemical reactions. Establishing on empirical grounds that a new substance is created is arduous; it involves comparing multiple properties (e.g., densities, melting points, solubilities), each of which poses both conceptual and methodological challenges.

Does this create another Catch-22 – AMT is motivated by chemical reactions but chemical reactions don't make sense without AMT? Not within an LP framework in which concepts have multiple parts and sources (some macroscopic, some from precursor explanatory models, and some from the newly introduced model), and are constructed over an extended period of time. By the time they explore chemical reactions, students exposed to a LP-based matter curriculum could be in a position to ask meaningful questions about them, to which AMT will provide answers.

In the integrative (hypothetical) learning progression for matter outlined in Table 9.1, students start building a precursor to *substance* (the concept of material) in kindergarten and explore solid and non-solid materials throughout elementary school (Chapter 8, this volume). They develop a sense of material identity and its conservation by observing that cutting and grinding do not change properties such as smell, flammability, and "how easily" a material melts. They also learn to think of any sample as constituted of arbitrarily small pieces that retain some properties of that material. This *compositional model* helps students go beyond a historical account of material identity.

Understanding melting and freezing also develops over several years. Young students can establish, on the basis of perceptual properties such as smell, that some substances are the same in solid and liquid form (e.g., chocolate, wax, butter). As they construct an ontological category of matter which includes solids and liquids, learn that material identity is conserved across grinding, and develop the epistemological knowledge that perception is not a reliable indicator of physical properties, students become able to *meaningfully consider* that the identity of all substances could be maintained across melting and freezing.

A particle model provides a convincing explanation for the conservation of material identity across phase change, as well as strong support for the distinction between the identity of a substance and the state it is in. It also allows introducing the distinction between pure substance and mixture (pure substances are composed of only one type of particle; mixtures are composed of different particles). With this more abstract notion of substance, students can meaningfully discover that different substances have different melting and boiling points, solubilities in water, and densities.

At this point, students have a more robust concept of substance at the macroscopic and particulate levels; they also have the means to establish empirically that under some conditions new substances are produced. Their epistemological understanding of models allows them to realize their particle model cannot account for that, motivating AMT for *conceptual* reasons. A basic atomic–molecular model (in which atoms have no internal structure) accounts for the creation of new substances and provides deeper explanations for *why* different substances have different densities, boiling and melting points, and solubilities. It also provides a principled account of the difference between physical and chemical transformations, and supports the distinction between element and compound, thereby deepening the concept of substance.

To sum up: In a LP-based scenario, students' extensive and extended learning about the macroscopic properties and behaviors of materials and their using a particle model to account for physical transformations support constructing a concept of substance and ways to establish whether or not two substances differ. When they encounter chemical transformations, students are in a position to differentiate them from physical transformations and to understand that the particle model does not account for the formation of new substances and needs revising. The particle model also scaffolds understanding of a basic atomic–molecular model, which allows them to understand chemical reactions and further enriches and entrenches the concept of substance.

Johnson's findings in a three-year longitudinal study support the hypothesis that a particle model scaffolds understanding *substance* and chemical reactions. Students who did not develop the ideas that matter is discontinuous and that different substances are made of different kinds of particles did not understand the idea of chemical reaction when it was presented in Grade 9 (Johnson, 2002). The ninth graders who understood chemical reactions had a robust particle model (the model Johnson taught, which he calls Model C): Substances are constituted of particles held together by different strength attraction forces; particles of a given substance are all the same but they differ from substance to substance; particles remain invariant in phase change but their spatial arrangement and motion are different in the three states of matter. Students who held what he calls Model B – matter is made of spaced particles, and only of those particles, but particles are little macroscopic bits of the substance (i.e., particles themselves are solid, liquid, or gaseous) – did not understand chemical changes.

Most students, however, did not show a robust understanding of Model C until *after* they were also taught AMT (in Grade 9). Which portions of the Grade 9 curriculum led to this change cannot be determined from the post-unit interview design. It is possible that learning that a huge number of different molecules are all made of about 100 kinds of atoms (far fewer on earth), and that cooking gas, cells, diamonds, and milk are all constituted of molecules that contain atoms of carbon is a powerful factor in dispelling the notion that particles are little pieces of material in a particular state. Alternatively, it could be that the opportunity to review and apply Model C to explain phase change again in Grade 9 led to enhanced understanding. Unfortunately, few details of the curriculum were provided, including whether students explicitly contrasted Model B, Model C, and the atomic–molecular model. Further studies are needed to assess what elements are crucial in developing a robust understanding of Model C.

Intermediate Models as Integral to Stepping Stones

Within an LP approach, intermediate models organize the *stepping stones* toward the atomic–molecular theory targeted in high school – each gets conceptually closer to the scientific model than the previous one and scaffolds learning the next one. They do not represent pieces of the full theory but rather conceptually simpler versions of it. In interaction with hands-on experiences, each model supports the revision of core concepts (e.g., phase change, substance). At particular points of the progression, the knowledge constructed around a model allows students to formulate questions or puzzles the model cannot answer. A new model can then be presented, a more complex version of the previous one. As students apply it to a range of different phenomena, their concepts get enriched or revised, and new puzzles get articulated. The next model will explain these new puzzling phenomena as well as provide deeper explanations for the old ones.

For example, basic particle models account for the material nature of gases and the conservation of substance identity during phase change. More elaborated particle models (which include the notion of hold among particles) can support constructing new knowledge about substances that allows discovering that new substances are created in chemical reactions. This gives rise to a puzzle – where do those new substances come from? – solved by a basic atomic–molecular model, in which the particles are conceived of as being either atoms (spheres with no internal structure) or molecules (collections of atoms). Attractive forces are exerted between molecules; how molecules interact and behave is related to their forces and their energy. This model accounts for the creation of new substances via reconfiguration of atoms into new molecules. It also deepens the concept of substance as something that is made of a particular kind of atoms or molecules, can undergo physical changes, and can participate in chemical reactions. It gives a mechanistic explanation of why different substances have different physical and chemical properties, including chemical reactivity, which explains why every substance does not react with every other substance. This basic atomic–molecular model can then be elaborated to include atomic structure and intra-molecular forces. Throughout this succession of models, more and more properties of substances can be discovered and understood, phenomena (e.g., phase changes) can be interpreted at a more and more complex levels, and principles (e.g., conservation of matter) are understood at deeper levels.

The succession of models embodies a series of ontological shifts – e.g., the shift from compositional model to particle model is from a quantification model of material as continuous, in which the pieces are created by the model user, to a structural model of matter as discontinuous, in which matter is constituted of pre-existing pieces. Inherent in these ontological shifts are: greater importance of and increasingly fine-grained structure of matter, components of matter more removed from ordinary sense making, and more emergent nature of macroscopic properties of matter.

This succession of more complex models represents a "divide and conquer" approach to AMT; each model embodies a coherent, small set of AMT's tenets that can be used to broaden and deepen interpretations of matter and its behavior. "Coherent" is key and yet often ignored in traditional curricula. By "coherent," we mean that the set of tenets embodied by a model supports meaningful interpretations of the initially puzzling phenomena, and deeper interpretations of more familiar ones. Currently, there is some (productive) disagreement among LP researchers about which tenets of AMT to introduce in which intermediate model, although there is general agreement that the "traditional" particle models are too limited to be truly explanatory or even understandable by students. For example, the standard model presented in schools emphasizes movement and energy aspects, usually leaving unsaid that the particles have mass and weight. Yet weight is essential to interface the model with empirical observations at a macroscopic level. Obviously whether a set is coherent also depends on the kinds of phenomena one draws students' attention to or to which students might link the model spontaneously.

Developing each model is an extended process, spanning several grades. As in the history of science, new models are adopted as evidence accumulates and they provide more satisfying accounts to broader ranges of phenomena than previous ones. Students need time to explore a range of phenomena because different kinds of phenomena make different tenets of a model meaningful. In what order and combinations, and in what contexts, to introduce the tenets of a model is an issue that needs more research.

Snir et al. (2003) suggest working on the idea that matter is composed of discrete particles having weight and separated by empty space, before adding in particle movement. They believe one also needs to say something about forces between particles at this early time to make the model plausible – if particles are not touching, what holds things together?

Johnson and Papageorgiou (2010) also critique the standard particle model presented in middle school for focusing on the generic differences among *states of matter* rather than foregrounding differences among *substances*. Their model conveys that substances differ by representing them as having different shape. Two other tenets are introduced at the same time. One is a rich description of particles' motions: Particles are always in motion; the average energy of motion is low for particles of a substance in a solid state, medium for the liquid state and high for the gas state; heating gives particles more energy. The other tenet is that particles have the ability to "hold" each other; the strength of that hold is different for different substances. This model is explanatorily rich as well as coherent: It provides strong support for gases being material; and it can explain phase change and why different substances have different melting and boiling points (as well as why pure substances have fixed boiling and melting points whereas mixtures do not). Observing evaporation at room temperature leads to elaborating the model with the idea of energy distribution within a state. (Weight and mass are not specifically addressed.)

In the integrated and coherent Investigating and Questioning our World through Science and Technology (IQWST) curriculum developed for middle-school students by Krajcik and colleagues (Krajcik, Reiser, Fortus, & Sutherland, 2009), the particle model (introduced in the sixth grade) foregrounds that the particles of different substances are different, and that the same substance can be in any state (as in Johnson and Papageorgiou's model). They stress that the particles differ in mass and are in motion, but do not introduce inter-particulate forces or bonds. Unlike Johnson (but building on the pioneering work of Nussbaum), they explore the capacity of the model to explain the transmission of smells, a topic of interest to middle-schoolers. The number of different smells fits nicely with the idea that there is a broad range of different substances. Thus the main focus of this IQWST unit is to account *descriptively* for differences between substances and between states of matter, to distinguish between substance identity and state, to consolidate the idea that gas is a state of matter, to account for smell, and to begin exploring different properties of substances. The curriculum moves relatively quickly to the idea that particles can be atoms or molecules and to the periodic table. Like Johnson, Krajcik thinks a thorough explanation of changes of state is needed before considering chemical reactions. In Grade 7, students consider the possibility of chemical changes, and develop a macroscopic understanding of key properties of substances that will be important for detecting chemical change: density, boiling and melting points, and solubility. The atomic–molecular model introduced in the previous grade is exploited in part to give students some representational tools for describing chemical reactions and understanding how they are different from physical changes.

Ultimately, what to include in each intermediate model is an empirical question, and there are different ways to be coherent about it. The major difference between LP-minded approaches and traditional ones is that, in the former, which elements of the scientific theory to introduce at a given point, and in what form, are considered on a "need-to-know basis": What puzzles will motivate the next model, and what tenets should the next model include to provide meaningful solutions to those puzzles? In contrast, in the traditional, more "top-down" approach to curricular design, pieces of the scientific theory are introduced in an order that might make logical sense to a scientist (e.g., you need to know there are atoms before being told there are bonds between them), without sufficient attention to the cognitive consequences of those choices.

The "divide and conquer" approach to curriculum design applies to epistemological development as well. As students move from model to model, they become able to reflect on the nature and function of models, what makes a good model, and on what grounds models are revised. Progressively, the ontological distance between the explanans and explanandum grows, and so does the degree of emergence of macroscopic properties. For example, in particle models, the state of the substance is emergent but its identity is still in the particles. In the "sphere" atomic–molecular model, the identity of most substances is emergent in the sense that it depends on the combination of atoms composing their molecules, but students can hang on to some sense that "an atom of gold" is still a little speck of gold mostly with impunity. As models become more complex, however, the macroscopic properties of the substance become fully emergent, resulting from the collective spacing, arrangement, and interaction between molecules, and the properties of atoms themselves become emergent. Fortunately, students' epistemological resources can grow with those epistemological demands over a long period of time. The distinction between elements of a model and observable phenomena to be explained can start at an implicit level in early elementary school when students use the macroscopic compositional model to explain why reshaping an object does not change its weight. As they gain significant meta-knowledge about modeling, students acquire the ability to consider their own revisions to a model (Schwarz et al., 2009).

Synthetic Models

Students may introduce "erroneous" elements into a taught model early on in an attempt to reconcile it with their current beliefs and create a "synthetic" model (Vosniadou & Brewer, 1992; Vosniadou, Vamvakoussi, & Skopeliti, 2008). If the curriculum helps students confront and ultimately "kick aside" these undesirable elements no harm is done; indeed, these synthetic models may help students progress to the next stepping stone.

Whether a synthetic model is (temporarily) helpful or not is ultimately an empirical question. This was observed in Johnson's extensive three-year longitudinal study of seventh to ninth grade students, in which students were initially introduced to a particle model to explain phase change. No student initially conceptualized matter as particulate and none progressed directly to the taught model (Model C, described previously). A little more than half progressed directly to Model B (in which the particles are solid, liquid, or gas) and the majority of those then progressed to Model C. Thus, Model B appears to help some students achieve Model C. It is likely that envisioning particles separated in space allowed students to adopt the idea of inter-particulate forces and state-specific motions and to use those notions in their account of states of matter, while hanging on to the idea that particles are, literally, little pieces of macroscopic matter. At some point, students understood that different forces were enough to account for the different states and that state-specific particles were a redundant idea.

More recent short-term teaching studies with elementary-school students underscore many of these points (Johnson & Papageorgiou, 2010; Papageorgiou & Johnson, 2005; Papageorgiou et al., 2010). Most students went from non-particle models to Model B but some achieved Model C by the end of the units. These studies also confirmed that both Model B and C had explanatory power for students, although the power of Model C was much greater. Finer-grained interviews are needed to ascertain the processes by which students move to Model C. Understanding why Model B facilitates getting to it, what stops some Model B students from progressing toward it, and what allows some students to skip Model B entirely, is essential to revising the learning progression and curricula, especially given the strong correlation between holding Model C and understanding chemical reactions. We suspect that individual differences in knowledge of matter at the macroscopic level and in epistemological sophistication are involved.

More research is also needed to determine how curricula should treat the molecules-in-matter model (Johnson's Model A). Although it integrates many elements of students' knowledge and supports idiosyncratic accounts of heating and boiling, for example, it has little explanatory force from a scientific point of view (e.g., it begs the question of what the "stuff" between atoms is made of). However, its assumptions could be explicitly contrasted with some tenets of AMT and its explanatory value openly debated, thereby building a greater understanding of model building and evaluation – a point to which we will later return.

Importance of Elaborating on Concepts Progressively

Two recent longitudinal studies support a related assumption of LP approaches to teaching for lasting conceptual change: the importance of developing ideas progressively over multiple years, revisiting them and elaborating them in new contexts.

Margel, Eylon, & Scherz (2008) investigated the development of Grade 7–9 students' ideas about the structure of matter and materials as they engaged with three innovative instruction units. Grade 7 students received a unit, developed by Nussbaum, which introduced a particle model while investigating the properties of air, and debating the existence of vacuum and whether matter was continuous or particulate. Grade 8 students received a unit that introduced the distinctions between atoms and molecules and between compounds and elements, and how AMT explains the properties of materials. Grade 9 students revisited AMT and its explanations of the properties of materials while exploring the molecular structure of polymers and the relation between their structure and properties.

Over 1,000 students completed questionnaires five times between Grades 7 and 9, probing their drawings and descriptions of familiar everyday substances. Drawings were coded as depicting materials in macroscopic, particulate, or molecular terms (the distinction between Models B and C could not be scored). Overall, there was a progression from macroscopic to particulate to molecular depictions. By the end of instruction, about 85% of the students used either a particle or molecular model to represent materials (36% were able to draw molecular models). In contrast, in an earlier study, only 25% of students exposed to the traditional Israeli curriculum drew particle models after three years, with very few molecular depictions.

In the National Field trials of the IQWST curriculum involving 28 teachers and over 3,000 students, Krajcik and colleagues (2011) found improvement on all types of assessment items at every grade, with especially large effect sizes for Grades 6 and 7. Although each unit was effective for all students regardless of whether they had the prior unit, there were cumulative benefits: Students who had the sixth grade unit introducing the particle model scored higher on the seventh grade chemistry pretest than those who had not, and made greater gains on the unit on chemical reactions, supporting the assumption that a particulate model may scaffold understanding chemical reactions. Similarly, scores on the eighth grade chemistry pretest, and the amount of progress students made, were related to the number of prior years of IQWST, supporting the assumption that more coherent curricula lead to increased gains over multiple years.

CONCLUSIONS

We have analyzed the conceptual difficulties posed by AMT as it is traditionally taught. A variety of conceptual and epistemological changes are needed to bridge young children's initial understanding of matter and the atomic–molecular theory, most of them not facilitated by traditional curricula. On the basis of those analyses, and a review of innovative teaching interventions, we have made the case for a learning progression in which knowledge about matter becomes progressively more scientific while remaining coherent, first at the macroscopic, then particulate, then atomic–molecular level. We hypothesize that curricula based on this learning progression would allow students to give meaningful (and progressively deeper) explanatory accounts of broader and broader ranges of properties and behaviors of matter, as well as avoid the entrenchment of misconceptions arising within traditional instruction.

One theme in LP approaches is that engaging students in cycles of model construction and revision is at the heart of learning about matter. This gives students the opportunity to learn about both modeling and matter – a little at a time. Each new model allows students to explain a range of new phenomena, and gives them a foothold both conceptually and epistemologically for asking further questions and understanding more sophisticated models. For example, constructing a compositional model in which a sample of material is constituted of arbitrarily small pieces that have weight, occupy space, and retain some properties of the material prepares students to consider whether there can be pieces of matter too small to see, whether substance identity is maintained with melting, and even whether gases might be matter. The compositional model is part of a stepping stone toward particle models. A particle model provides coherent answers to questions about substance identity across phase changes and gives meaning to gases being matter. Adopting it involves coming to see state of matter as an emergent property. It also opens up new questions about whether and how substances could ever change. Particle models are an inherent part of stepping stones to basic atomic–molecular models which account for chemical changes, while raising further questions about the structure of atoms and the forces holding molecules together.

Learning progressions are "works in progress." They are hypothetical and revisable on empirical grounds. For example, one could decide which tenets of AMT to introduce in which intermediate models, by implementing different versions of the models in different curricula, and comparing the outcomes of the curricula to each other. However, there is general agreement on the power and promise of basing curricula on learning progressions organized around "big ideas" such as AMT. Curricula that are coherent within and between grades allow students to move from stepping stone to stepping stone, as they revisit concepts and beliefs in new contexts, progressively reconceptualizing their interpretations of the properties and behavior of matter. LP-based curricula also build epistemological sophistication not only about how models are tested and revised, but also about how much of what we see in everyday objects are properties emergent from the structural organization of atoms and molecules.

REFERENCES

Andersson, B. (1990). Pupils' conceptions of matter and its transformations (age 12–16). *Studies in Science Education, 18*, 53–85.

Ben-Zvi, R., Eylon, R., & Silberstein, J. (1986). Is an atom of copper malleable? *Journal of Chemical Education, 63*, 64–66.

Carey, S. (1991). Knowledge acquisition: Enrichment or conceptual change? In. S. Carey & R. Gelman (Eds.), *The epigenesis of mind* (pp. 257–291). Hillsdale, NJ: Lawrence Erlbaum Associates.

Carey, S., Evans, R., Honda, M., Jay, E., & Unger, C. (1989). "An experiment is when you try it and see if it works": A study of grade 7 students' understanding of the construction of scientific knowledge. *International Journal of Science Education, 11*, 514–529.

Del Pozo, R. M. (2001). Prospective teachers' ideas about the relationships between concepts describing the composition of matter. *International Journal of Science Education, 23*, 353–371.

De Vos, W., & Verdonk, A. H. (1987). A new road to reactions, Part 3: A substance and its molecules. *Journal of Chemical Education, 64*, 692–694.

Doubler, S., Carraher, D., Tobin, R., Asbell-Clarke, J., Smith, C., & Schliemann, A. (2011). *The Inquiry Project: Final report*. Submitted to National Science Foundation DR K-12 Program, September 8.

Fensham, P. J. (1994). Beginning to teach chemistry. In P. Fensham, R. Gunstone, & R. White (Eds.), *The content of science: A constructivist approach to its teaching and learning* (pp. 14–28). London, UK: Falmer Press.

Griffiths, A., & Preston, K. (1992). Grade 12 students' misconceptions relating to fundamental characteristics of atoms and molecules. *Journal of Research in Science Teaching, 29*, 611–628.

Grosslight, L., Unger, C., Jay, E., & Smith, C. (1991). Understanding models and their use in science: Conceptions of middle and high school students and experts. *Journal of Research in Science Teaching, 28*, 799–822.

Harrison, A., & Treagust, D. (2002). The particulate nature of matter: Challenges in understanding the submicroscopic world. In J. Gilbert, O. de Jong, R. Justi, D. Treagust, & J. van Driel (Eds.), *Chemical education: Towards research-based practice* (Vol. 17, pp. 189–212). Dordrecht, The Netherlands: Kluwer.

Johnson, P. (1998). Progression in children's understanding of a "basic" particle theory: A longitudinal study. *International Journal of Science Education, 20*, 393–412.

Johnson, P. (2000). Children's understanding of substances, Part 1: Recognizing chemical change. *International Journal of Science Education, 22*(7), 719–737.

Johnson, P. (2002). Children's understanding of substances, Part 2: Explaining chemical change. *International Journal of Science Education, 24*(10), 1037–1054.

Johnson, P., & Papageorgiou, G. (2010). Rethinking the introduction of particle theory: A substance-based framework. *Journal of Research in Science Teaching, 47*, 130–150.

Johnstone, A. H. (1982). Macro- and microchemistry. *School Science Review, 64*, 377–379.

Krnel, D., Watson, R., & Glazar, S.A. (1998). Survey of research related to the development of the concept of "matter". *International Journal of Science Education, 20*(3), 257–289.

Krajcik, J., McNeill, K. & Reiser, B. (2008). Learning-goals-driven design model: Developing curriculum materials that align with national standards and incorporate project-based pedagogy. *Science Education, 92*(1), 1–32.

Krajcik, J., Reiser, B., Fortus, D. & Sutherland, L. (2009). *Investigating and questioning our world through science and technology.* Ann Arbor, MI: University of Michigan.

Krajcik, J. S., Sutherland, L. M., Drago, K., & Merritt, J. (2011) The promise and value of learning progression research. In S. Bernholt, K. Neumann, & P. Nentwig (Eds.), *Making it tangible – Learning outcomes in science education.* Münster, Germany: Waxmann.

Lee, O., Eichinger, D. C., Anderson, C. W., Berkheimer, G. D., & Blakeslee, T. D. (1993). Changing middle school students' conceptions of matter and molecules. *Journal of Research in Science Teaching, 30*(3), 249–270.

Margel, H., Eylon, B., & Scherz, A. (2008). A longitudinal study of junior high school students' conceptions of the structure of materials. *Journal of Research in Science Teaching, 45*(1), 132–152.

Nakhleh, M. B., Samarapungavan, A., & Saglam, Y. (2005). Middle school children's beliefs about matter. *Journal of Research in Science Teaching, 42*, 581–612.

Nussbaum, J. (1985). The particulate nature of matter in the gaseous phase. In R. Driver, E. Guesne, & A. Tiberghien (Eds.), *Children's ideas in science.* Philadelphia, PA: Open University Press.

Nussbaum, J. (1997). History and philosophy of science and the preparation for constructivist teaching: The case of particle theory. In J. Mintzes, J. H. Wandersee, & J. D. Novak (Eds.), *Teaching science for understanding* (pp. 165–194). Boston, MA: Academic Press.

Osborne, R., & Freyberg, P. (1985). *Learning in science: The implications of children's science.* Auckland, New Zealand: Heinemann.

Papageorgiou, G., & Johnson, P. M. (2005). Do particle ideas help or hinder pupils' understanding of phenomena? *International Journal of Science Education, 27*(11), 1299–1317.

Papageorgiou, G., Grammaticopoulou, M., & Johnson, P. (2010) Should we teach primary pupils about chemical change? *International Journal of Science Education, 32*(12), 1647–1664.

Pozo, J., & Gomez Crespo, M. (2005). The embodied nature of implicit theories: The consistency of ideas about the nature of matter. *Cognition and Instruction, 23*(3), 351–387.

Rogat, A. , Anderson, A., Foster, J., Goldberg, F., Hicks, J., Kanter, D., et al. (2011). *Developing learning progressions in support of the New Science Standards: A RAPID Workshop Series,* Consortium for Policy Research in Education. New York, NY: Teachers College, Columbia University.

Schwarz, C., Reiser, B., Davis, E., Kenyon, L., Acher, A., Fortus, D., et al. (2009). Developing a learning progression for scientific modeling: Making scientific modeling accessible and meaningful for learners. *Journal of Research in Science Teaching, 46*(6), 632–654.

Scott, P. H. (1987). The process of conceptual change in science: A case study of the development of a secondary pupil's ideas relating to matter. In *Proceedings of the Second International Seminar on Misconceptions and Educational Strategies in Science and Mathematics.* Ithaca, NY: Cornell University.

Smith, C. (2007). Bootstrapping processes in the development of students' commonsense matter theories: Using analogical mappings, thought experiments, and learning to measure to promote conceptual restructuring. *Cognition and Instruction, 25*(4), 337–398.

Smith, C.L., Wiser, M., Anderson, C. W., & Krajcik, J. (2006). Implications of research on children's learning for standards and assessment: A proposed learning progression for matter and atomic–molecular theory. *Measurement: Interdisciplinary Research and Perspectives, 14*(1–2), 1–98.

Snir, J., Smith, C., & Raz, G. (2003). Linking phenomena with competing underlying models: A software tool for introducing students to the particulate model of matter. *Science Education, 87*, 794–830.

Stavy, R. (1991). Children's ideas about matter. *School Science and Mathematics, 91*, 240–244.

Stevens, S. Y., Delgado, C., & Krajcik, J. (2010). Developing a hypothetical multi-dimensional learning progression for the nature of matter. *Journal of Research in Science Teaching, 47*(6), 687–715.

Vosniadou, S., & Brewer, W. F. (1992). Mental models of the earth: A study of conceptual change in childhood. *Cognitive Psychology, 24*, 535–585.

Vosniadou, S., Vamvakoussi, X., & Skopeliti, I. (2008). The framework theory approach to the problem of conceptual change. In S. Vosniadou (Ed.), *International Handbook of Research on Conceptual Change* (pp. 3–34). New York, NY: Routledge.

Wiser, M., Frazier, K., & Fox, V. (in press). At the beginning was amount of material: A learning progression for matter for early elementary grades. In G. T. Tsaparlis & H. Sevian (Eds.), *Concepts of matter in science education.* New York, NY: Springer.

Wiser, M., O'Connor, K., & Higgins, T. (1995, April). *Mutual constraints in the development of the concepts of matter and molecule.* Paper presented at American Educational Research Association (AERA), San Francisco, CA, April 19–21.

Wiser, M., Smith, C., & Doubler, S. (2012). Learning progressions as tool for curriculum development: Lessons from the Inquiry Project. In A. Alonzo & A. Gotwals (Eds.), *Learning progressions in sciences* (pp. 359–403). Rotterdam, The Netherlands: Sense Publishing.

10

CONCEPTUAL CHANGE IN NAÏVE BIOLOGY[1]

Kayoko Inagaki and Giyoo Hatano, Chiba University

The preceding chapters have revealed that young children, at least older preschoolers, possess a naïve theory of biology. Psychologists dealing with other core domains of thought also claim that preschool children have naïve theories about the important aspects of the world; for example, they assert that preschool children have naïve psychology or a theory of mind (e.g., Perner, 1991; Wellman, 1990). However, that children have naïve theories does not mean that their theories are the same as intuitive theories lay adults possess. Because the construction of the initial theory is based on a limited database, it has to be restructured as more and more facts are incorporated into it with increasing age, unless the initial set of observed facts constitutes a representative sample of all relevant facts. Some of the innate or very early tendencies and biases that are helpful at the initial phase may be weakened or given up, as accumulated pieces of prior knowledge come to serve as constraints. This also makes conceptual change or theory change during childhood inevitable.

In this chapter, we discuss conceptual change that spontaneously occurs during childhood, and its mechanisms. More specifically, first, we discuss the nature of conceptual change as a fundamental restructuring of (conceptual) knowledge in general, and we then sketch conceptual change in the course of development of biological knowledge, primarily relying on our experimental evidence. Finally, we return to the general discussion of how conceptual change occurs.

CONCEPTUAL CHANGE AS FUNDAMENTAL RESTRUCTURING

What is Conceptual Change?

The notion of conceptual change in cognitive development has been proposed as an alternative to "enrichment views" (Carey, 1985, 1991). It denotes that conceptual development involves not just enrichment or elaboration of the existing knowledge systems but their considerable reorganization or restructuring. Conceptual change involves change in core concepts, conceptions, or conceptualizations (including rules, models, and theories). To put it differently, it concerns a large-scale restructuring of the existing knowledge system (especially conceptual knowledge in it). The knowledge systems before and after the conceptual change may sometimes be locally incommensurable (Carey, 1988); that is, some pieces of knowledge in one system cannot properly be translated into the other, as exemplified by the shift from children's undifferentiated concept of heat/temperature to adults' separate concepts of heat and temperature (Wiser & Carey, 1983).

It should be noted that conceptual change seldom occurs suddenly, just as it has taken years for concepts, conceptions, or conceptualizations to change in the history of science. The process of conceptual change tends to be slow and gradual, even if its end result is drastically different from its initial state.

Conceptual change often takes the form of theory change, because concepts and conceptions are embedded in theories; changing one core concept in a theory generates changes in related concepts and eventually leads to a change in the whole set of concepts. Theory change involves changes in causal devices or explanations, and/or large-scale changes in the range of phenomena or entities that are included. See Keil (1998, 1999) for distinct senses or conceptual change other than theory change.

TYPES OF CONCEPTUAL CHANGE

Four types of conceptual change can be distinguished with regard to the relationship between the old, pre-change knowledge system and the new, post-change system. Let us take theory change as an example. First, a new theory emerges from an old theory in the same domain, with the latter being subsumed in, or replaced by, the former. It can be described as A → A′, where A and A′ denote the old and new theory, respectively.

For example, between ages two and four to five years, the early theory of mind, which is based solely on desires and perceptions, is transformed into the "representational theory of mind," which includes beliefs as well (Gopnik & Wellman, 1994).

Second, a new theory emerges and develops from an old one within the same domain, and the latter continues to exist with its salience decreased: A → A′ & A. Sometimes the old theory is even extended by the new theory. For example, Perner (1991) claims that, although at about four years of age children's understanding of the mind changes from a "situation theory" (where mental states are construed in relation to situations) to a "representational theory" (where mental states are understood as serving representational functions), the latter does not replace the former but merely extends it; even adults may be situation theorists when possible, but they, unlike young children, can take a representational view when necessary. Subbotsky (1997) also proposed a "coexistence model of the development of fundamental structures of mind" by demonstrating that phenomenalistic forms of causal reasoning retain their power in the mind of an educated adult.

Third, a new theory emerges from an old one through differentiation, and new and old theories, representing knowledge systems in different domains, develop separately afterwards: A → A & B. One example is the emergence of a theory of matter from a theory of physics in which objects and materials from which they are made are not fully distinguished (Smith, Carey, & Wiser, 1985). Carey (1985, 1995) argued that naïve biology emerges from an intuitive psychology.

Fourth, a new theory emerges through the integration of old subtheories: A & B → C. For example, young Israeli children consider plants as neither living things nor nonliving things, but "growers" (Stavy & Wax, 1989). In contrast, they easily recognize animals as living by attending to their self-initiated movement. In other words, these young children seems to possess different theories for animals and plants. As they grow older, they acquire a theory of living things by integrating these different subtheories of animals and plants.

We consider, in the domain of biology, the second type of theory change as most tenable and the fourth type is also possible at the level of its specific theory. As we will describe in detail later, conceptual change in naïve biology takes place approximately between ages five and 10 years – within the domain. Young children tend to understand biological phenomena by relying on vitalistic causality and personifying inference, whereas older children and adults use mechanical causality and inference based on higher order biological categories. However, vitalistic causality and personifying inference continue to function as a basis of understanding and to be used as a fallback in situations where people do not think they are required to make precise and detailed predictions or explanations based on so-called scientific biology (Hatano & Inagaki, 1997).

Spontaneous Versus Instruction-based Conceptual Change

Forms of conceptual change can also be distinguished in terms of whether the change occurs spontaneously or is induced by instruction (Hatano & Inagaki, 1997; Vosniadou & Ioannides, 1998). Spontaneous conceptual change is the change that results from children's increasing experience in their physical and sociocultural environment. In other words, it occurs without systematic instruction, though schooling certainly has some general facilitative effects on it. Most of the examples referred to in the preceding section are of this form. This form of change seems to occur readily, because it is commonly found among most children growing up in highly technological societies. An additional example is the change that occurs within young children's belief–desire psychology between ages three and six; that is, from a copy-container theory of mind representing a static mind that three-year-old children are supposed to possess to an interpretive homuncular theory representing an active and constructive mind (Wellman, 1990). Cognitive developmentalists have been primarily concerned with this spontaneous conceptual change.

In contrast, researchers who are interested in science education have dealt with instruction-based conceptual change, which occurs by incorporating conceptual devices of science and thereby correcting "misconceptions" (e.g., Vosniadou &. Brewer, 1992). This instruction-based conceptual change requires laborious and effortful processes of systematic teaching to be achieved, and even with good teaching, only a limited portion of older children and adults may achieve it (e.g., Clement, 1982).

However, it should be noted that the difference between spontaneous conceptual change and instruction-based conceptual change is not in actuality so large because conceptual development during the middle elementary school years and after is directly or indirectly influenced by systematic science instruction. Even when such science education does not function well, some scientific concepts that students learned in incomplete ways may work as something like a placeholder on the students' knowledge system and contribute to restructuring it eventually. Thus conceptual change during and after the elementary school years may often be a mixture of spontaneous and instruction-based conceptual changes.

CONCEPTUAL CHANGE IN THE DOMAIN OF NAÏVE BIOLOGY

Returning to the domain of biology, we discuss conceptual change in naïve biology. Compared with lay adults' intuitive biology, young children's naïve biology has five weaknesses: (a) limited factual knowledge, (b) limited applicability of biological reasoning to classes of biological phenomena (focusing on eating, being vigorous and lively, and growing; almost neglecting, say, reproduction and etiological aspects), (c) a lack of inferences based on complex, hierarchically organized biological categories, (d) a lack of mechanical causality, and (e) a lack of some conceptual devices, such as "evolution" or "photosynthesis." During the early elementary school years, children gradually overcome weaknesses (a) and (b) through enrichment and (c) and (d) through spontaneous conceptual change. Specifically, the use of inferences based on complex, hierarchically organized biological categories and of mechanical causality requires fundamental restructuring of biological knowledge, whereas the accumulation of more and more factual knowledge and more coherent application of biological reasoning can be achieved by enrichment only.

In contrast, the acquisition of basic conceptual devices of scientific biology, such as photosynthesis or the Darwinian idea of evolution, requires instruction-based conceptual change, because children almost never acquire them without instruction, and incorporating them meaningfully into the existing body of knowledge can usually be achieved only with its restructuring. For example, one who does not know the phenomenon of photosynthesis cannot understand the basic difference between animals and plants (i.e., plants can produce nutriment themselves) and thus may construct a wrong integrative theory for animals and plants, accenting the false mapping of water for plants to food for animals. The Darwinian idea of evolution must also be difficult for children to grasp. Because naïve biology assumes living things, but not nonliving things, to be able to adjust themselves to their ecological niche or ways of life, children are ready to accept any biological entity's gradual adaptive changes over generations (Evans, 2001) and thus to form a version of the Lamarckian idea of evolution (Marton, 1989). The Darwinian idea of evolution has been fully accepted, even among biologists, since only the nineteenth century. We assume that, unlike spontaneous conceptual change in naïve theories, conceptual change through the understanding of conceptual devices is very hard to bring about, even with educational intervention, and thus occurs only among a limited portion of older children or adolescents, as described above in the case of the Darwinian idea of evolution.

In what follows, we primarily consider spontaneous conceptual change. We first sketch qualitative changes in the salient mode of inference and those in preferred causality with increasing age; that is, changes from similarity-based to category-based inference on one hand, and those from vitalistic to mechanical causality on the other. Next, we show that the pre-change and post-change modes of inference and causalities coexist even in adults, although the pre-change mode of inference and causality is no longer salient in adults' biology. It can sometimes be used as a fallback in everyday lives.

Developmental Shift from Similarity-based to Category-based Inference

In our Chapter 3 we characterized young children's biology as human-centered or personifying in nature. Our experimental demonstrations used prediction/explanation questions requiring children to construct their answers. However, we cannot use this method to examine developmental changes in modes of inference from preschoolers to adults, because in this method the change in ways of inference would be confounded with children's increased general verbal abilities with age. Thus, instead of the person analogy task, we, like Carey (1985), have adopted the task of inductive projection from humans, or the attribution of human properties. This method relies less on children's verbal ability. We considered it as admittable because personification involves both the so-called person analogy and inductive projection from humans to nonhuman entities, and the latter can be regarded as a special case of the person analogy (Inagaki & Hatano, in press).

Suppose children are asked the following attribution question, "Does X have a property Y?", where Y is a property that they know people have and that they do not know whether X has (see Figure 10.1). If children have personifying biology, they will make the following inference: First, they will judge whether X is similar to humans, as for the target property. If they judge it as dissimilar, they will answer "No" to the above question. If they perceive some similarity between humans and the target entity X, they will tend to answer "Yes" in proportion to its judged similarity, unless they make over-attribution errors for the objects. By under-attribution errors we mean that children fail to attribute a specific

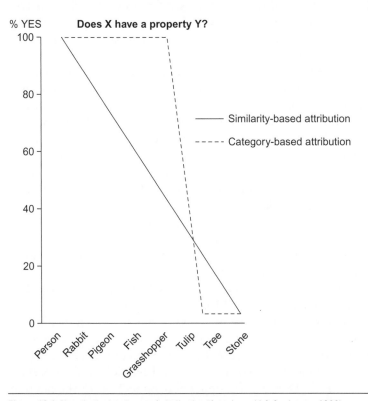

Figure 10.1 Hypothetical patterns of attribution (from Inagaki & Sugiyama, 1988)

(human) property to those objects having it, and by over-attribution errors we mean erroneous attribution of the property to those not having it.

Another apparently contrasting type of inference is a deductive attribution arrived at by relying on such higher order biological categories as mammals, vertebrates, and so on (e.g., "The grasshopper is an invertebrate and the invertebrates have no bones, so the grasshopper must have no bones"). We call it category-based attribution. This attribution generates correct responses as long as the target object is allocated to the proper category and the attributional boundary is correct. Its attributional profile is a flat pattern with a sharp break as shown in the broken line in Figure 10.1, although the location of the sharp break on the continuum may vary from uniquely human to restricted-animal to all-living-thing properties.

Carey (1985) claimed that four-year-olds attribute animal properties based on the "comparison-to-people model," whereas 10-year-olds rely little on it. To put it differently, we can expect that younger children use similarity-based inference, while older children rely on category-based attribution. How does this shift from the similarity-based to the category-based take place? More specifically, is the shift abrupt or gradual? We assume that pure similarity-based attribution progresses toward pure category-based attribution by being more and more strongly constrained by categorical knowledge, as children come to realize its usefulness through various experiences, including formal schooling. Even young children check the plausibility of similarity-based inference with factual knowledge (Inagaki & Hatano, 1987) and, though not often, with inference based on biological functions. Therefore, we can identify an "intermediate" way of attribution, which might be called a constrained similarity-based attribution; that is, inferences primarily based on similarity but constrained by categorical knowledge. The attributional profile of this intermediate way can be a variety of mixed patterns between a flat pattern with a sharp break and a gradually decreasing pattern.

However, we assume that a pattern with a decreasing part on the person/animal side and a flat part on the plant/nonliving thing side would occur most often, because children use object-specific knowledge (Inagaki & Hatano, 1987) or categorical knowledge to reject the "Yes" response obtained by projecting human properties to nonhuman entities. It is not likely that children possess object-specific knowledge that enables them to answer "Yes" when they do not project human properties to the object according to its similarity to people. This likely intermediate pattern would thus reduce over-attribution errors to plants and nonliving things more than under-attribution errors to those animals that are apparently dissimilar to humans.

We examined whether the above developmental shift from similarity-based to category-based attribution would occur through an analysis of both group data (Inagaki & Sugiyama, 1988, Experiment 1) and of individual data (Experiment 2). For the attribution of unobservable anatomical/physiological properties, we predicted, as Carey (1985) found, that there would be developmental changes from similarity-based to category-based attribution between ages four and 10.

In contrast, for mental properties, which were not taught explicitly in school biology, we predicted that there would be a delayed shift, and thus even adults might sometimes make similarity-based attributions. This is because the attribution of mental properties requires more inference than does the attribution of anatomical/physiological properties. For example, when a child is asked, "Does a grasshopper have bones?", he or she can find an answer by making an inference based on knowledge about higher order category membership and category–attribute associations. The child can reason "It is an insect, so it can't possibly have bones." However, for the question of "Does a grasshopper feel happy?" she must further consider that a brain is required to feel happy, along with whether a grasshopper has a brain. As Johnson and Wellman (1982) reported, it is fairly difficult for children to grasp associations between a brain and mental properties, especially mental properties such as having feelings and sensations.

We also predicted that intermediate patterns of attribution – that is, the constrained similarity-based attribution – would be found between the two contrasting patterns of attribution, between younger children and adults for anatomical/physiological properties, and among older children and adults for mental properties. This prediction implies that adults would be able to reduce over-attribution errors. For example, they would exclude the possibility that trees feel pain, even when they perceive them to be somewhat similar to people, because they know that plants do not have a central nervous system enabling them to have feelings.

In the first experiment, 20 participants each from five age groups were involved: four-year-olds (M = 4 years, 9 months), five-year-olds (M = 5 years, 9 months), second graders (M = 8 years, 1 month), fourth graders (M = 10 years, 2 months), and college students. Eight phylogenetically different objects were used as targets: a person, rabbit, pigeon, fish, grasshopper, tulip, tree, and stone. The objects are listed here in the order of perceived similarity to people, as established in another sample, but were presented in a random fashion in the experiment.

The participants were individually asked 10 property questions for each of the eight objects in the format, "Does X have a property Y?" The 10 properties were grouped into three types: (a) unobservable anatomical/physiological properties: having a heart, having bones, breathing, and growth; (b) unobservable mental properties: the abilities to think, feel happy, and feel pain; (c) observable properties: having eyes, the ability to move, and speaking to a person. Questions about the observable properties were included to confirm that there were no developmental differences in attribution accuracy about these properties. In fact, it turned out that the participants in all age groups had almost equally high percentages of correct knowledge about these observable properties of the target objects. All the property questions were asked about an object before the inquiry proceeded to another object.

For each of the seven unobservable property questions, we computed proportions of "Yes" response to the eight target objects, phylogenetically ordered from a person to a stone, in each age group. As shown in Figure 10.1, the category-based attribution should be a pattern consisting of a big gap (decline) and two flat parts before and after it, and the similarity-based attribution a pattern showing gradual decrease from a person to a stone. Thus we examined whether there existed a big gap (an arbitrary criterion of a difference of 40% or more between two consecutive objects) somewhere on the continuum, and whether the two parts before and after the gap were flat (i.e., all the successive differences were less than 10%). Then we classified the attributional patterns, for each property by each age group, into three types, category-based, similarity-based, and intermediate (e.g., the pattern having a big gap but only one flat part).

Results supported all three of our predictions. For the anatomical/physiological properties, there was a progression from four-year-olds' predominant reliance on similarity-based attribution to adults' predominant reliance on category-based attribution. The intermediate pattern of attribution was found between similarity-based and category-based attribution, mostly among five-year-olds, second graders, and fourth graders. One example is shown in Figure 10.2. Thus the shift seemed to occur primarily during the elementary school years. For mental properties, participants in all age groups mostly made similarity-based attributions. An illustrative example is shown in Figure 10.3.

For the above findings from the analyses of group data, there exists an alternative interpretation, which is that this apparent similarity-based pattern for a group of participants may have been generated by their disagreement on attributional boundaries. More specifically, the above shift in patterns for anatomical/physiological properties may have been due to greater variability among younger children in the category extensions or in category–attribute associations than among adults, and adults' "similarity-based" patterns for mental properties may have only represented category-based attribution with different category–attribute associations.

To exclude this alternative interpretation, we conducted Experiment 2 which examined whether the similarity-based pattern would be found within individuals as well.

Another group of five-year-olds and of college students participated in this experiment. Target objects were five members each belonging to the same higher order categories (i.e., mammals, birds, fish, insects, and plants) but differing in appearance (e.g., size), as well as a person and a stone.

Each participant was individually asked to attribute two anatomical/physiological properties (having bones and the heart) and two mental properties (feeling pain and feeling happy) to each of the above 27 objects. The question formats were the same as

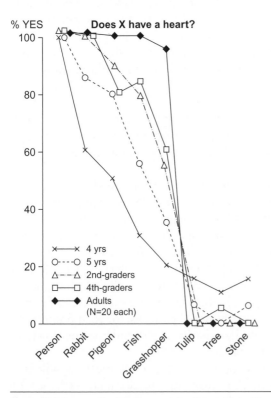

Figure 10.2 An example of developmental patterns obtained in attribution of the anatomical physiological properties (from Inagaki & Sugiyama, 1988)

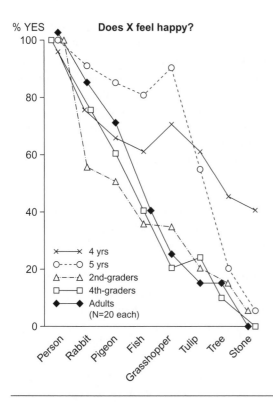

Figure 10.3 An example of developmental patterns obtained in attribution of the mental properties (from Inagaki & Sugiyama, 1988)

those of Experiment 1 described above: "Does X have a property Y?" In other words, property questions referred to the name of the target object, but did not refer to the name of the category. All the property questions were asked about an object before the inquiry proceeded to another object.

After all the property questions, the participant was required to classify into five categories all 25 of the above-described objects, excluding the person and the stone. This classification task was added in order to confirm that participants had relied on similarity-based attribution for judgment of these properties even though they were able to classify most of the objects correctly. Thus 20 five-year-olds and 20 college students who classified most of the objects correctly were used in the analyses.

We classified the responses of each participant for each property into one of three patterns; that is, category-based, similarity-based, and others (classified as neither similarity-based nor category-based). If a participant makes category-based attributions, he or she should always answer "Yes" or always answer "No" to the question of whether each of the five objects belonging to the same category has a target property. Thus, the data pattern will consist of two flat parts with a sharp break. On the other hand, if the participant makes similarity-based attributions, he or she should give "Yes" responses to some members and "No" responses to others belonging to the same category when the category is located near the boundary of "Yes" responses and "No" responses; as a result, the ratio of "Yes" responses of each category should decrease as the categories become phylogenetically farther from people.

Results of Experiment 2 confirmed our interpretation of the result obtained by analyses of group data in Experiment 1 as shown in Table 10.1. For anatomical/physiological properties, 73% of the preschoolers' patterns fit the definition of similarity-based attribution. In contrast, 90% of the adults' patterns were category-based attributions. The developmental difference in frequency of the two patterns was highly significant.

For mental properties, about half of the young children's patterns reflected similarity-based attributions, versus only 13% reflecting category-based attributions. More than 50% of adults' patterns were also similarity-based attributions; about 40% were category-based. The difference between young children and adults in ratio of similarity-based to category-based patterns was marginally significant.

The results described above clearly indicate that there exist qualitative changes in the salient mode of inference; that is, from preschoolers' use of inference based on similarity to people to older children's and adults' reliance on higher order category-based inference, and that these changes proceed gradually from preschool years to middle childhood to adult ages.

We hasten to add that we are not claiming that young children can never make inferences based on higher order biological categories. They can do so if they are urged to with some help, at least when they possess the pieces of knowledge about the higher order category membership of the target and relevant category–property relationships. However, they seldom possess such pieces of knowledge and are unlikely to rely on category-based inference spontaneously.

To paraphrase this shift, preschool children have a graded concept of living things organized in terms of their similarity to humans, but as they grow older, they come to possess a concept of living things that is divided into hierarchically organized categories, where humans are probably seen just as animals. Johnson, Mervis, and Boster (1992) obtained relevant findings for seven-year-olds, and even 10-year-olds, in their experiment, using a triad task, which required the participants to find two similar things from among, say, human/nonhuman primate/nonprimate triads. Whereas the seven- and 10-year-olds tended to treat humans as isolates by showing reluctance to acknowledge similarities between humans and nonhumans, the adults did not show such a tendency; the adults responded by basing their judgments on membership within or outside the primate category.

Interestingly, this change in the salient mode of inference is accompanied with, if not induced by, change in metacognitive beliefs and values about particular modes of inference. Hatano and Inagaki (1991) examined whether the shift from similarity-based to category-based inferences would be induced, at least in part, by a metacognitive belief about the usefulness of higher order categories; namely, the belief that category-based inference is more dependable than similarity-based inference. Children of second, fourth,

Table 10.1 Percentages of each attributional pattern in each age group

Age group	Anatomical/Physiological properties			Mental properties		
	S-based	C-based	Others	S-based	C-based	Others
5-year-olds	73	18	10	48	13	40
Adults	10	90	0	53	43	5

S-based, similarity-based attribution; C-based, category-based attribution. $N = 20 \times 2$ in each age group.

and sixth grades were required to evaluate, in a questionnaire format, a given set of reasons that were allegedly offered by same-age children in a dialogue with a teacher. That is, they were asked to judge the plausibility of three different types of reasons, each of which was preceded by a "Yes/No" judgment to such a question as, "Does an eel have bones?" or "Does a tiger have a kidney(s)?" Two of the three reasons represented similarity-based inference and category-based inference, respectively. The former referred to the target's surface similarity to people, such as, "I think a tiger has a kidney, because it is generally like a human," and the latter referred to higher order categories like "mammals," such as, "I think a tiger has a kidney, because both a human and a tiger are mammals." The other reason, clearly not category-based or similarity-based, was a distractor, for example, "I think a tiger does not have a kidney, because it is not as intelligent as a human." The same children were also given a similar attribution task as the one used in Inagaki and Sugiyama (1988).

It was found that as children grew older, the number of respondents who judged the category-based reason to be plausible and the similarity-based one to be implausible significantly increased, whereas the number of respondents who evaluated the similarity-based reason as plausible and the category-based one as implausible decreased, suggesting that children came to acquire a metacognitive belief about the usefulness of higher order categories. Moreover, even among the second-graders, those children who consistently favored category-based reasons tended to show an attributional pattern closer to the pure category-based attribution than was shown by those who favored similarity-based reasons.

Hatano and Inagaki further examined, by using indirect, "projective"-type questions, whether older students differentiated more clearly a fictitious child who gave a category-based reason from a child who gave a similarity-based reason in the rating of his or her academic talent. Another group of second, fourth, and sixth graders were given a questionnaire. It described two hypothetical pairs of children of the same grade as the students, who, in dialogue with their teacher, gave a judgment of whether rabbits and ants had a pancreas (or tigers and grasshoppers had bones) and the reason for it. The reason given by one of each pair was in fact similarity-based, and the other category-based (these labels were not given). The participating students were asked to rate how good academically the fictitious child who had given the reason would be, and how likable the child would be as a friend, on a four-point scale.

Results were as follows: The fictitious child who had allegedly given a category-based reason was rated significantly higher in academic talent than the allegedly similarity-based child in all grades. However, the older the participants, the bigger was the magnitude of the difference. That is, the older students were much more negative than the younger ones in the rating of the fictitious child who had given the similarity-based reasons. Since the likability rating for this fictitious child did not differ significantly, it is not likely that these participants always gave favorable ratings for the category-based child. These results strongly suggest that children become reluctant to use similarity to people as an inferential cue for biological attributions as they grow older. It is likely that conceptual change in modes of biological inference is enhanced by social sanctions; for instance, children may stop relying on similarity to people in order to avoid being regarded as less talented.

PROGRESSION FROM VITALISTIC TO MECHANICAL CAUSALITY

We examine how another essential element of young children's naïve biology, namely vitalistic causality, changes as they grow older. In Chapter 5 of Inagaki and Hatano (2002) we have seen that young children's naïve biology is vitalistic in nature; they tend to apply vitalistic causality to internal bodily phenomena. They consider that internal bodily phenomena are caused by activity of an internal organ having agency, and the organ's activity often involves transmission or exchange of "vital force." Since the vital force is an unspecified substance as illustrated in children's words, "vital power," "source of energy," "something good for health," and so on, vitalistic causality presumes unspecified mechanisms. Vital power seems to be a global conceptual entity that serves as a causal device in children's initial biology. It is expected that, as children learn more and more about biological phenomena including scientific words and their implications, through learning school biology, watching TV programs, or reading books, they come to acquire knowledge that enables them to specify mechanisms. In other words, the global conceptual entity of vital power is specified into a set of particular mechanisms. With this learning of specific mechanisms. children come to recognize mechanical causality (presupposing a specified mechanism) to be more reliable than vitalistic causality, and this induces the shift to mechanical causality.

To confirm this expectation, Inagaki and Hatano (1993, Experiment 2) examined whether young children's reliance on vitalistic causality would progress to the use of mechanical causality as they grow older. Not only six-year-olds but also eight-year-olds and college students participated in this study. They were asked to choose one from among three possible causal explanations for each of six bodily phenomena, such as blood circulation and respiration. The three explanations represented intentional, vitalistic, and mechanical causality, respectively. Although several of the example questions and three alternative explanations have been shown in Chapter 5 of Inagaki and Hatano (2002), we present here another example, blood circulation: "Why does the blood flow to different parts of our bodies? (a) Because we move our body, hoping the blood will flow in it [intentional causality]; (b) Because our heart works hard to send out life and energy with blood [vitalistic]; (c) Because the heart sends the blood by working as a pump [mechanical]."

As shown in Figure 10.4, the six-year-old children chose vitalistic explanations as most plausible most often (54%) and chose intentional explanations second most often (25%). In contrast, the eight-year-olds chose mechanical causal explanations most often (62%) and opted for some vitalistic ones (34%) as well, but seldom chose intentional explanations. The adults predominantly preferred mechanical explanations to explanations of the other two types.

Results of individual data analyses also confirmed this developmental change in preferred causality. Out of the 20 six-year-olds, only one chose four or more intentional explanations for the six items (we call them intentional responders), whereas nine chose four or more vitalistic explanations (vitalistic responders). Among eight-year-olds, there was only one vitalistic responder; there were 10 mechanical responders who made four or more mechanical choices; six out of nine "Others" respondents were children who chose vitalistic and mechanical explanations equally (three each), and two were children who made three vitalistic choices and two mechanical choices. Among adults, there were 19 mechanical responders and one vitalistic responder. This pattern of findings also

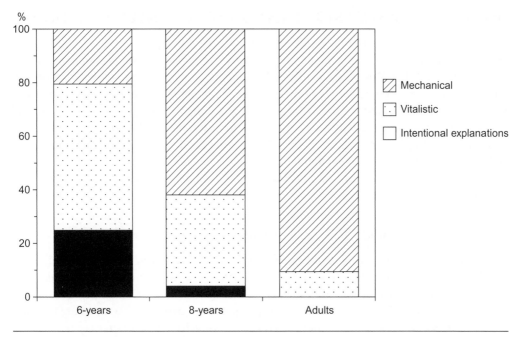

Figure 10.4 Percentages of choices for different types of casual explanations

suggests that there exists change in preferred causality from vitalistic to mechanical with increasing age.

Developmental change in preferred causality for biological phenomena is not confined to Japanese children and adults. Morris, Taplin, and Gelman (2000) who carried out a careful replication of Inagaki and Hatano's (1993) Experiment 2, confirmed this tendency among English-speaking children and adults in Australia. When asked to choose one from among three causal explanations for each of the six bodily phenomena, Australian five-year-old kindergartners showed a clear preference for vitalistic explanations over mechanical ones, whereas college students and, to a lesser extent, 10-year-old children chose the mechanical explanation most often. Results from the individual data analyses confirmed the results of the group analysis, indicating that 30% of the five-year-olds were vitalistic responders, while 48% of the 10-year-olds and 80% of the adults were mechanical responders.

Again, we would like to emphasize that the observed shift is for preferred causality, and it is premature to conclude that young children cannot rely on mechanical causality in explaining bodily processes. However, they are unlikely to be attracted by mechanical explanations because they do not have well-understood examples of specific mechanisms for bodily processes.

When the above findings on the shift in preferred causalities are combined with those on the shift in the salient mode of inference, we can conclude convincingly that there occurs conceptual change in children's naïve biology, from five years old or so through middle childhood and adulthood; from young children's personifying and vitalistic biology to older children's and adults' biology based on category-based inference and mechanical causality.

PRE-CHANGE SYSTEM STILL EXISTS IN ADULTS' INTUITIVE BIOLOGY

Is older children's and adults' intuitive biology no longer personifying at all? Is the similarity-based inference completely replaced by the category-based inference in older children and adults? Does their intuitive biology no longer rely on vitalistic causality? Answers to these questions are not affirmative. The fact that there exists a shift from similarity-based to category-based inferences does not mean that older children and adults never rely on similarity to people in their inferences. Likewise, as discussed in Chapter 5 of Inagaki and Hatano (2002), the fact that there is a developmental shift from reliance on vitalistic causality to that on mechanical causality does not denote that adults never take vitalistic views for biological understanding. We first describe the similarity-based inference in adults.

Adults' Reliance on Similarity-Based Inference

Remember that a substantial number of adults as well as older children still relied on similarity to people in attributing mental properties to various animals. As impressively indicated in Table 10.1, even adults showed the similarity-based pattern at a substantial rate (more than 50% of the time) in attributing mental properties to animate entities. This suggests that even adults sometimes rely on similarity-based inference.

This tendency is not limited to attribution of mental or psychological properties. In another experiment using reaction times (Morita, Inagaki, & Hatano, 1988), we found that college students relied on similarity-based attribution to some extent not only for mental properties but also for anatomical/physiological ones in a situation where quick responding was required. In this experiment, four pairs of animals belonging to the same category but differing in judged similarity to humans (e.g., a tiger vs. a fur seal; a tortoise vs. a snake; a penguin vs. a swallow; a mantis vs. a grasshopper) were used as targets, and four additional objects (e.g., a rose, a stone, etc.), as fillers. These four pairs were selected from 16 animals by another group of students who were required to rate them on a nine-point scale in terms of similarity to people. The former of each pair was perceived by these raters as more similar to people than the latter. First, 31 college students were told the correct higher order category that each object belongs to, and then they were required to give Yes/No responses as quickly as possible to seven property questions for each of the 12 objects (i.e., the four pairs of animals and four fillers). The property questions consisted of two unobservable anatomical/physiological properties (i.e., has bones and breathes), two mental properties (i.e., feels pain and feels sad), two observable animal properties (i.e., has a mouth and has eyes), and one human property (i.e., speaks language). Answers to these questions were to be all "Yes" for humans. There were 84 property questions altogether.

It was found that these students made more "Yes" responses to the more human-like members of the animals (e.g., a tortoise in the above example) in attributing unobservable properties. In addition, when their responses were identical within pairs, "Yes" responses were quicker for the more similar members than for the less similar ones, whereas "No" responses were slower for the more similar members than for the less similar ones (see Figure 10.5). The interaction effect was significant. This suggests that even college students use the similarity to humans as a cue when relying on category-based inference is nearly impossible because of the time pressure.

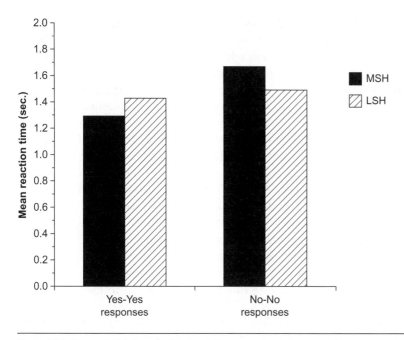

Figure 10.5 Mean reaction times for "Yes" and "No" responses to the members more similar to humans (MSH) and less similar to humans (LSH) when a participant's responses were identical pairs of animals

It is not feasible to explain the above results in terms of prototypicality; for example, that the more typical member of the pair was more readily assigned target properties shared by most members of the category. This is because the member of the pair that is more similar to humans is not always more prototypical within the category; for example, a penguin is more similar to humans, but less prototypical within the category of birds than a swallow. Moreover, some of the target properties (e.g., feeling sad) are typical of humans, and are in fact not attributed to other animals frequently.

Thus, we can summarize that the college students relied on similarity to people in attributing mental as well as unobservable biological properties under time pressure. This means that the developmental shift from similarity-based to category-based inference is only a part of the story; the similarity-based mode of inference is retained and may be used even by adults as a fallback strategy.

Adults' use of Vitalistic Causality

Inagaki and Hatano (1993) and Morris et al. (2000) revealed that older children and college students preferred more strongly mechanical causality to vitalistic causality. However, this does not necessarily mean that adults never rely on vitalistic causality in any situation. Instead, we claim, vitalistic causality is never completely superseded by mechanical causality with increasing age; rather, it may continue to work as a basis of understanding some biological phenomena and to be used in situations where people are not required to give precise and detailed answers based on scientific biology (Hatano & Inagaki, 1996, 1997). In fact, a few college students in Experiment 2 of Inagaki and Hatano (1993) seemed to use vitalistic causality as an informal or fallback mode of explanation. One student who consistently chose vitalistic explanations answered at the interview after the experiment, "We usually choose those including 'oxygen' or 'the heart works like a pump' because we have learned in school to do so. However, I chose others because they were most convincing and comprehensible to me."

Miller and Bartsch (1997), conducting a modified replication of Inagaki and Hatano's (1993) Experiment 2, found that American college students were vitalists, contrary to Inagaki and Hatano (1993); that is, these students preferred to apply vitalistic explanations for bodily phenomena as often as the six- and eight-year-olds did. Although we cannot reject a possibility that this result was an artifact produced by methodological problems in their study, as Morris et al. (2000) pointed out (instead of requiring participants to choose one from among three alternatives, they asked the participants to make a choice between intentional and vitalistic explanations, and between vitalistic and mechanical explanations), it is possible that these adults indeed preferred vitalistic explanations for bodily phenomena, because the students may have been interviewed in a situation in which answers based on scientific biology were not highly valued. It is plausible that even adults still consider vitalistic explanations reasonable for bodily phenomena and offer such explanations when they are not obliged to give an answer based on scientific biology.

We should note the fact that not only young children but also a substantial ratio of lay adults hold the idea of resistance to illness as one case of vitalism in everyday life; they believe in folk preventive medicine that advocates the importance of one's resistance to illness and that offers various specific recommendations for improving resistance. When asked what factor was considered the most important as a cause for getting a cold, about 70% of Japanese college students offered physical factors as contributing to illness susceptibility; that is, irregular daily routines or the lack of self-control of health, fatigue, deterioration of physical strength, sudden change of temperature, and so on. For example, "Bodily resistance to illness is lost due to shortage of sleep and/or fatigue," "Insufficient sleep or staying out in cold weather increases bodily susceptibility to illness," or "The body cannot adjust to sudden changes of temperature" (see Inagaki & Hatano, 1999).

We can generalize the above results as follows. Although the pre- and post-change knowledge systems are qualitatively different, there are some continuities between them (Hatano, 1994). The occurrence of conceptual change does not mean that components of the pre-change system are replaced by the post-change system and disappear completely. We claim that old components are retained as less salient fallback models or strategies in the new system. This is consistent with research findings indicating that multiple models (Yates et al., 1988) or multiple strategies (e.g., Siegler & Jenkins, 1989) coexist within the same individual. This is also in line with the claim offered by Perner (1991) as to the development of theories of mind or the claim by Subbotsky (1997) as to phenomenalistic causal reasoning. An important implication of these claims is that the post-change knowledge system of educated adults may not be as drastically different from young children's pre-change knowledge system as it appears.

Another Conceptual Change?

The qualitative changes that we have discussed so far occur in later childhood; that is, after five years of age. Considering that a great majority of investigators now believe that even preschool children possess a form of naïve biology, only those changes before five years of age can be relevant to the issue of conceptual change that has been the target of debate; namely, whether naïve biology emerges from intuitive psychology through conceptual change. Does another conceptual change take place earlier? We concentrate here on the issue of whether naïve biology emerges from naïve psychology through conceptual change.

It is true that there are some qualitative changes in children's predictions and explanations for biological phenomena approximately between ages three and five. As we reviewed in the preceding chapters, many studies have shown that five-year-old children can clearly differentiate human biological properties and phenomena from psychological ones in terms of modifiability and controllability. They also understand illness causality biologically. Around age five, children understand illness causality biologically, and can distinguish living entities including animals and plants from nonliving things and begin to recognize commonalities between animals and plants. Some studies have shown that five-year-olds can choose biological explanations presented from a number of alternative causal explanations for biological phenomena, and at times even offer biological explanations themselves.

In contrast, (a) three- and four-year-olds' predictions for biological phenomena are not highly consistent and are easily influenced by contexts or by types of question; (b) they sometimes rely on psychological causal devices as often as on biological ones for biological phenomena, whereas they seldom apply biological causality to social-psychological phenomena. However, (c) when biological and psychological causal devices are explicitly contrasted, they tend to choose the biological ones for biological phenomena.

We propose two possible interpretations for the observed change during these years. It may be that, although children as young as three possess naïve biology as well as psychology, psychological knowledge is more readily retrieved generally and thus sometimes interferes with the retrieval of its biological counterpart (as suggested above (b)). It probably takes a few years before young children clearly recognize that it is not naïve psychology but biology that can explain those bodily processes and phenomena that are needed for us to be active and lively but are beyond our intentional control. It could thus be called a kind of conceptual change, somewhat similar to a relevance shift (Keil, 1999). This interpretation is harmonious with Carey's (1985) original position, though it differs from hers in attributing a form of naïve biology to young children (based on (c) above). An alternative interpretation is that the observed change is trivial, because it is a product of the fact that three-year-olds' naïve biology is still being established. For many theories, there is some delay between acquisition and firm establishment, and such theories are unlikely to be used promptly until they are well-established. Naïve psychology as an established neighbor theory may sometimes penetrate into biological reasoning, but only until the establishment of naïve biology.

Although more studies are needed, we prefer the second interpretation, because even three-year-olds respond differently to biological and psychological phenomena unless they respond in a random fashion. In addition, they tend to choose biological causal devices for biological phenomena when these devices are given explicitly. In other words, we assume that the observed change in biological reasoning between ages three and five is not a matter of conceptual change but of a gradual construction of naïve biology.

HOW DOES CONCEPTUAL CHANGE OCCUR?

In this final section, we discuss the issue of how conceptual change occurs in general, using primarily the case of naïve biology as an example, because conceptual changes in core domains of thought are considered to be similar to each other in their mechanisms and conditions, though different in content. Although the issue of how conceptual change occurs and the specification of its mechanisms is "One of the fundamental problems of cognitive psychology today" (Vosniadou, 1994, p. 3), the available data are limited. This is partly because recent developmentalists have focused on the specification of the initial form of a naïve theory and, to a much lesser extent, on the description of the state after conceptual change, without analyzing the process of change itself (Carey, 1985; Wellman, 1990). Relying on not only findings obtained in conceptual development but also some evidence from the history of science and science education, we thus propose possible mechanisms of conceptual change and conditions for its occurrence. To put it differently, we consider primarily mechanisms and conditions of spontaneous conceptual change, but take account of findings from studies on instruction-based conceptual change or scientists' activities, when they are relevant.

The critical difference between spontaneous and instruction-based conceptual changes seems to be the extent to which a cognizer consciously recognizes incongruity in his or her existing knowledge system and to which he or she intentionally attempts to solve it. Whereas spontaneous conceptual change seems to proceed slowly but steadily without the cognizer's explicit recognition of incongruity, instruction-based conceptual change usually takes place only when students explicitly recognize the inadequacy of their conceptual knowledge by a teacher's instructional attempts to induce such recognition in them.

It is clear that in every case increased knowledge is required for conceptual change, and that the pre-change system serves as a cognitive constraint on conceptual change. In other words, conceptual change is a cognitive attempt to resume coherence of the knowledge system that has been disturbed by new pieces of information, through complex interactions of constituent elements of the current knowledge system.

Let us propose two contrasting mechanisms, one local and bottom-up; the other goal-directed and top-down. If the system includes all candidate concepts, conceptions, and conceptualizations, each of which has its own subjective truth value (i.e., how strongly it is believed to be true), conceptual change can be described as radical changes in the truth-value of a range of connected pieces of knowledge (or beliefs, these two expressions being used interchangeably). We can thus assume that one type of mechanism for conceptual change is the spreading of truth-value alteration. When new inputs change the truth-value of some pieces of knowledge, the changes bring about changes in the truth-value of other connected pieces, which may induce further changes in their neighbors. In the long run, there can be a drastic change in almost all pieces through continued spreading and recurring effects as well as further inputs to facilitate the truth-value alteration. This type of conceptual change is a bottom-up process and does not require the cognizer's conscious grasp of incongruity among beliefs and intentional attempt to reduce it. The relationships among beliefs are divided into dyadic relations with one another, each of which is characterized only in terms of whether two beliefs are roughly consonant, dissonant, or neither (one belief's being true implies the other belief's being true, false, or nothing). Here the change is gradual, takes time, and is based on a large amount of input.

The other type of conceptual change, which might be called deliberate belief revision, sometimes occurs. A representative subtype of this is similar to the process of comprehension monitoring (Markman, 1981) or repair (e.g., Ackerman, 1984; Glenberg & Epstein, 1985) in the sense that existing beliefs are consciously and deliberately rewritten (and new beliefs are introduced) in the process, in order to remove recognized inconsistencies (e.g., disconfirmed predictions based on the current set of beliefs) and make the knowledge system coherent again. In another subtype, deliberate belief revision is induced by what we call "discoordination" (Hatano, 1998); that is, the recognition that the current set of beliefs is not well connected or not powerful enough to be the basis for understanding the world. In both cases, removal of incongruity is not achieved as the accumulation of small local changes, as in the case of spreading of the truth-value alteration. It is a top-down, goal-directed process.

Instruction-based conceptual change usually takes the form of deliberate belief revision. In contrast, spontaneous conceptual change usually proceeds less consciously and less deliberately, although it is not always bottom-up. It is often initiated when a new piece of information induces unexpected incongruity. Suppose that children have a conception of birds consisting of a set of beliefs, such as "birds are flying animals," "birds are bigger than bugs," "birds lay eggs," "birds have wings," and so on. If they learn that a penguin is a bird but does not fly, it is dissonant with the first belief; or when they learn that a bat flies but isn't a bird, the target belief may become less trustworthy. As a result of these local, minor truth-value alterations and their recurring effects, children's conception of birds may change, as the flying-animals belief, being dissociated from other beliefs about birds, becomes less and less trustworthy. Alternatively, however, such incongruous pieces of information may induce a deliberate attempt to revise the conception. Of course, we human beings can ignore or tolerate incongruity to some extent, but let us suppose children are sensitive and open to the incongruous information. They may thus be tempted to modify their conception of birds, for instance, into something like, "birds are animals that have a basic body structure convenient for flying, but cannot necessarily fly."

Similarly, children who have found that similarity to people does not always lead to valid attributions, or that their peers often use and highly evaluate category-based inference, may weaken a little their belief in similarity-based inference. Alternatively, they may decide to compare similarity-based and category-based inferences systematically. Those who are afraid that vitalistic explanations are not welcome by adults (including the science teacher) and those who know some mechanical concepts and terms may shift to offering mechanical explanations either via spreading of truth-value alteration or via deliberate belief revision. We believe that spontaneous conceptual change involves a combination of the two mechanisms.

Conditions for Inducing Conceptual Change

What conditions are likely to induce conceptual change? It should be pointed out that, although accumulated knowledge is a necessary condition for conceptual change (e.g., Carey, 1985), it is not a sufficient condition. We propose three additional conditions, two cognitive requisites that seem necessary and the sociocultural context that is facilitative. Since spontaneous conceptual change occurs without systematic intervention, these conditions are usually met, but theoretically it is significant to conceptualize them explicitly.

First, some metacognitive abilities that enable one to assess and monitor incongruity within the existing knowledge system are needed for conceptual change (especially deliberate belief revision) to occur, because it is an incongruity-reducing process. In most cases, as children grow older their knowledge accumulates, and at the same time their metacognitive knowledge and skills develop. In other words, the increase of knowledge and the development of metacognitive knowledge and skills proceed hand-in-hand in normal cognitive development. Thus, the necessity of metacognitive knowledge and skills for conceptual change is often overlooked.

However, we can offer solid evidence for the importance of metacognitive ability for conceptual change by examining knowledge that individuals with the Williams syndrome have acquired. Individuals with Williams syndrome tend to talk in great detail with only superficial understanding, on one hand, and lack analytic and metacognitive knowledge and skills on the other. Johnson and Carey (1998) compared individuals with Williams syndrome, whose average verbal mental age was 11 years, with two groups of normally developing children whose average mental ages were 10 years and six years, respectively, in terms of the acquisition of general knowledge of animals (e.g., the size of their animal lexicon) and folk-biological concepts that were supposed to be normally acquired through conceptual change between ages six and 12 years (e.g., concepts of being alive or dead). They found that, although the participants with Williams syndrome performed at the level of the normal children of age 10 on the tasks concerning general knowledge of animals, their performance on the folk-biological knowledge tasks was at the level of normal six-year-olds.

Although a number of alternative interpretations could be offered, we consider this finding as strongly suggesting the role of metacognitive skills in the acquisition of knowledge through conceptual change. In the course of normal development, we assume, children use metacognitive skills more or less unconsciously, and as a result, the process of belief revision may proceed slowly and gradually because a piece of new information induces local incongruity. This may be one of the reasons why conceptual change occurring in development takes place gradually over years, as is well illustrated in the developmental shifts in a domain of biology in the previous section.

Some conceptual change observed among scientists may occur more quickly than conceptual change occurring in the course of childhood conceptual development. Scientists can carefully monitor coherence among pieces of knowledge constituting a theory and be sensitive to and respond to a small amount of disconfirmation or discoordination in their knowledge system, thanks to their advanced metacognitive abilities. A good example is the "thought experiment" including limiting case analyses, as represented by Galileo's famous thought experiment showing that heavier objects do not fall faster than lighter ones (Nersessian, 1992). Some science instruction aims at bringing about conceptual change in less time by making students aware of the incongruity in their knowledge through the presentation of contradictory evidence.

The second condition for conceptual change is that an alternative concept, conception, or conceptualization (or the set of its constituent pieces) is available at least potentially in the existing knowledge structure. As indicated above, conceptual change via a spreading of the truth-value alteration is possible only when the candidate pieces of conceptual knowledge are included in the system. The deliberate belief revision is possible only when a cognizer can think of an alternative belief. If people do not think of any alternative theory, model, or interpretation, they may stick to the old conceptual device even when predictions from it are not supported.

An alternative concept, conception, or conceptualization may be prepared gradually and slowly in development of the target naïve theory; alternatively, it can be brought in from outside the target theory by using some "borrowing" heuristics. Examples of the former case include the following.

1. Pieces of information needed to construct an alternative idea are accumulated slowly because they are not attended initially (e.g., on a balance beam, young children pay attention to the number of weights but ignore their distance from the center).
2. An idea *stays* implicit; in other words, it is "implemented" but not represented (e.g., being able to solve a concrete problem but unable to describe how to solve it).
3. An idea is available only in a particular context and has yet to be generalized (e.g., from biological understanding of illness as caused by germs only when there are obvious routes of contagion, such as coughing, to a generalized illness causality in terms of the germ theory).

Analogies and conceptual placeholders are two major "borrowing" heuristics. Conceptual change may often be triggered by an analogy that suggests an alternative view. Using analogies, people map their knowledge about the *source* to the present new case (target) so that they can make a coherent interpretation of the set of observations for the target, or even build a tentative theory.

Analogies are sometimes applied spontaneously, and other times presented by teachers and other adults. Photosynthesis is one of the difficult notions in understanding biology, because it is against the intuitive grasp of the commonality among all living things that naïve biology indicates. That plants can produce their own nutriment is usually beyond children's imagination. However, Yuzawa (1988) reported that a "production factory" analogy – processing materials with proper means, like baking bread from flour using heat – helped junior high students understand photosynthesis. Dunbar (1995) reported that scientists in real-world laboratories often rely on analogy to generate new ideas when faced with inconsistent experimental findings.

Another possibility for deriving an alternative concept, conceptions, and conceptualizations is to assume a conceptual placeholder that does not include much substantive information initially. Solomon and Johnson (2000) reported findings suggesting that conceptual change *occurs* when children are exposed to a scientific concept that can serve as a conceptual peg in a sociocultural context. Here, children of five to six years were first made aware of the inadequacy of their understanding of biological inheritance by a conversation with a teacher, and then they were given a rudimentary notion of genes and opportunities to use this notion. This intervention, though lasting only about 20 minutes, led the children to make adult-like judgments on inheritance to some extent. This strategy is often adopted in science education. However, considering that young children in highly technological societies are often presented with a scientific concept that would serve as a conceptual peg through conversation with adults, watching TV programs, reading a book with adults, and so on in everyday life, spontaneous conceptual change also could occur in a similar way in everyday life, though it would take a longer time than the instruction-based one.

Third, sociocultural contexts in which children are exposed to various, sometimes incongruous, pieces of information may make conceptual change more likely to occur. As already mentioned, children's learning that others possess different beliefs from their own may reduce the truth-value of relevant beliefs and also induce attempts to revise the beliefs. This is because, though human beings have not only confirmation biases but also tendencies to ignore incongruous information (Festinger, 1957), they cannot do so when they engage in interaction with others for an extended period of time. One of such contexts enhancing conceptual change is social interactions including group discussion. Social interactions can be sources for generating recognized inconsistencies or discoordinations in individuals' existing knowledge systems, because different perspectives are presented in the interactions, and they can also be sources for providing possible solutions. In this sense, discussion can contribute to the occurrence of conceptual change. Indeed, it has been reported that social interaction can be a powerful mechanism for inducing conceptual change among scientists (Dunbar, 1995).

However, a number of studies have revealed that even among less sophisticated thinkers, discursive interactions may induce conceptual change. For example, Hatano and Inagaki (1997) provided data to support this claim; many school-aged children (10 years of age) changed their ways of reasoning about a monkey's physical characteristics through whole-class discussion – from reasoning based on the animal's similarity to humans to reasoning based on a more sophisticated (Lamarckian) conception of evolution and specific biological taxonomy. Williams and Tolmie (2000) also reported that socially generated cognitive conflict (or inconsistencies) is effective for acquiring a more advanced conception of inheritance in their intervention study using children aged eight to 12. Their dialogue analyses indicated that the effects of group discussion could be attributed to resolution of conceptual conflict within the groups holding different conceptions.

Toward an Integrative and Moderate Model of Conceptual Change

Let us make a brief comparison with other notions of conceptual change proposed so far. In what point does our notion of conceptual change differ from others? We take the position that conceptual change, as a profound change in a child's underlying conceptual structures, can take place during childhood, and at the same time we assert that the pre- and post-change knowledge systems have some continuity. In naïve biology, for example, the pre- and post-change modes of inference or causalities coexist even among adults, though the former system becomes less salient and is used as a fallback.

How is our notion related to a newly proposed idea that children and adults differ only in shifting the relevance of already present explanatory systems (Keil, 1998, 1999)? This relevance shift notion of "conceptual change" denotes that children and adults differ not in underlying conceptual structures but in the relevance of these structures; children often possess several theories available to them early on, but they differ remarkably from adults in realizing where these theories are most relevant. It should be noted that according to this conceptualization, conceptual change is no longer clearly distinguished from enrichment. We agree with this notion of continuities in conceptual structures among young children, older children, and adults. Even preschool children possess naïve theories of core domains, such as biology and psychology, and if they are urged to do so, they may be able to reason using biological categories and relying on mechanical causality in primitive ways. However, this does not mean that all developmental differences are just quantitative, a matter of how salient a variety of competing ideas are and how adaptively they can be applied to problem situations.

In addition, we cannot ignore possibilities that instruction-based conceptual change or instructionally influenced spontaneous conceptual change can take place, especially in later cognitive development. It can produce new conceptual tools through which older children and lay adults can see the world differently than young children do. We should pay more attention to the bridge or interaction between conceptual development and instruction, as claimed and researched by Vosniadou and Ioannides (1998).

Finally, our notion of conceptual change has emphasized the sociocultural factors involved. We fully agree that an increased amount of knowledge is a necessary condition for conceptual change (e.g., Carey, 1985; Smith et al., 1985; Wiser, 1988) and that the pre-change system provides cognitive or internal constraints in conceptual change. However, the roles of other people and tools as sociocultural or interactive constraints are also very important in conceptual change. We believe that most leading investigators studying conceptual change have been too cognitive and too individualistic. The issue of motivation inducing conceptual change has also been neglected, with a few notable exceptions (e.g., Pintrich, Marx, & Boyle, 1993).

NOTE

1   This chapter is a reprint of Chapter 7 from Inagaki and Hatano (2002), *Young children's naïve thinking about the biological world.* Reprinted with permission from Kayoko Inagaki and the Taylor and Francis Group.

REFERENCES

Ackerman, B. P. (1984). The effects of storage and processing complexity on comprehension repair in children and adults. *Journal of Experimental Child Psychology, 37,* 303–334.

Carey, S. (1985). *Conceptual change in childhood.* Cambridge, MA: MIT Press.

Carey, S. (1988). Conceptual differences between children and adults. *Mind and Language, 3,* 167–181.

Carey, S. (1991). Knowledge acquisition: Enrichment or conceptual change? In S. Carey & R. Gelman (Eds.), *The epigenesis of mind: Essays on biology and cognition* (pp. 257–291). Hillsdale, NJ: Lawrence Erlbaum Associates.

Carey, S. (1995). On the origin of causal understanding. In D. Sperber, D. Premack, & A. J. Premack (Eds.), *Causal cognition: A multidisciplinary debate* (pp. 268–302). Oxford, UK: Clarendon Press.

Clement, J. (1982). Students' preconceptions in introductory mechanics. *American Journal of Physics, 50,* 66–71.

Dunbar, K. (1995). How scientists really reason: Scientific reasoning in real-world laboratories. In R. J. Sternberg & J. E. Davidson (Eds.), *The nature of insight* (pp. 365–395). Cambridge, MA: MIT Press.

Evans, E. M. (2001). Cognitive and contextual factors in the emergence of diverse belief systems: Creation versus evolution. *Cognitive Psychology, 42,* 217–266.

Festinger, L. (1957). *A theory of cognitive dissonance.* Evanston, IL: Row, Peterson.

Glenberg, A. M., & Epstein, W. (1985). Calibration of comprehension. *Journal of Experimental Psychology: Learning, Memory, and Cognition, 11,* 702–718.

Gopnik, A., & Wellman, H. M. (1994). The theory. In L. A. Hirschfeld & S. A. Gelman (Eds.), *Mapping the mind: Domain specificity in cognition and culture* (pp. 257–293). New York, NY: Cambridge University Press.

Hatano, G. (1994). Introduction. *Human Development, 37,* 189–197.

Hatano, G. (1998). Comprehension activity in individuals and groups. In M. Sabourin, F. Craik, & F. Robert (Eds.), *Advances in psychological sciences. Vol. 2: Biological and cognitive aspects* (pp. 399–418). Hove, UK: Psychology Press.

Hatano, G., & Inagaki, K. (1991). *Learning to trust higher-order categories in biology instruction.* Paper presented at the meeting of the American Educational Research Association, Chicago, IL.

Hatano, G., & Inagaki, K. (1996). Cognitive and cultural factors in the acquisition of intuitive biology. In D. R. Olson & N. Torrance (Eds.), *Handbook of education and human development: New models of learning, teaching and schooling* (pp. 683–708). Oxford, UK: Blackwell.

Hatano, G., & Inagaki, K. (1997). Qualitative changes in intuitive biology. *European Journal of Psychology of Education, 12*, 111–130.

Inagaki, K., & Hatano, G. (1987). Young children's spontaneous personification as analogy. *Child Development, 58*, 1013–1020.

Inagaki, K., & Hatano, G. (1993). Young children's understanding of the mind–body distinction. *Child Development, 64*, 1534–1549.

Inagaki, K., & Hatano, G. (1999). Children's understanding of mind–body relationships. In M. Siegal & C. C. Peterson (Eds.), *Children's understanding of biology and health* (pp. 23–44). Cambridge, UK: Cambridge University Press.

Inagaki, K., & Hatano, G. (2002). *Young children's naïve thinking about the biological world.* New York, NY: Psychology Press.

Inagaki, K., & Hatano, G. (in press). Conceptual and linguistic factors in inductive projection: How do young children recognize commonalities between animals and plants? In D. Genter & S. Goldin-Meadow (Eds.), *Language and thought in mind: Advances in the study of language and thought.* Cambridge, MA: MIT Press.

Inagaki, K., & Sugiyama, K. (1988). Attributing human characteristics: Developmental changes in over- and underattribution. *Cognitive Development, 3*, 55–70.

Johnson, C. N., & Wellman, H. M. (1982). Children's developing conceptions of the mind and brain. *Child Development, 53*, 222–234.

Johnson, K. E., Mervis, C. B., & Boster, J. S. (1992). Developmental changes within the structure of the mammal domain. *Developmental Psychology, 28*, 74–83.

Johnson, S. C., & Carey, S. (1998). Knowledge enrichment and conceptual change: Knowledge acquisition in people with Williams syndrome. *Cognitive Psychology, 37*, 156–200.

Keil, F. C. (1998). Cognitive science and the origins of thought and knowledge. In W. Damon (Ed.), *Handbook of child psychology* (5th edn., Vol. 1, R. M. Lerner (Ed.)), *Theoretical models of human development* (pp. 341–413). New York, NY: Wiley.

Keil, F. C. (1999). Conceptual change. In R. A. Wilson & F. C. Keil (Eds.), *The MIT encyclopedia of the cognitive sciences* (pp. 179–182). Cambridge, MA: MIT Press.

Markman, E. M. (1981). Comprehension monitoring. In W. P. Dickson (Ed.), *Children's oral communication skills* (pp. 61–84). New York, NY: Academic Press.

Marton, F. (1989). Towards a pedagogy of content. *Educational Psychologist, 24*, 1–23.

Miller, J. L., & Bartsch, K. (1997). Development of biological explanation: Are children vitalists? *Developmental Psychology, 33*, 156–164.

Morita, E., Inagaki, K., & Hatano, G. (1988). *The development of biological inferences: Analyses of RTs in children's attribution of human properties.* Paper presented at the 30th annual convention of the Japanese Association of Educational Psychology, Naruto, Japan [in Japanese].

Morris, S. C., Taplin, J. E., & Gelman, S. A. (2000). Vitalism in naive biological thinking. *Developmental Psychology, 36*, 582–613.

Nersessian, N. (1992). How do scientists think? Capturing the dynamics of conceptual change in science. In R. N. Giere (Ed.), *Minnesota studies in philosophy of science: Vol. 15. Cognitive models of science.* Minneapolis, MN: University of Minnesota Press.

Perner, J. (1991). *Understanding the representational mind.* Cambridge, MA: MIT Press.

Pintrich, P. R., Marx, R. W., & Boyle, R. A. (1993). Beyond cold conceptual change: The role of motivational beliefs and classroom contextual factors in the process of conceptual change. *Review of Educational Research, 63*, 167–199.

Siegler, R. S., & Jenkins, E. (1989). *How children discover new strategies.* Hillsdale, NJ: Lawrence Erlbaum Associates.

Smith, C., Carey, S., & Wiser, M. (1985). On differentiation: A case study of the development of the concepts of size, weight, and density. *Cognition, 21*, 177–237.

Solomon, G. E. A., & Johnson, S. C. (2000). Conceptual change in the classroom: Teaching young children to understand biological inheritance. *British Journal of Developmental Psychology, 18*, 81–96.

Stavy, R., & Wax, N. (1989). Children's conceptions of plants as living things. *Human Development, 32*, 88–94.

Subbotsky, E. (1997). Explanations of unusual events: Phenomenalistic causal judgments in children and adults. *British Journal of Developmental Psychology, 15*, 13–36.

Vosniadou, S. (1994). Introduction. *Learning and Instruction, 4*, 3–6.

Vosniadou, S., & Brewer, W. F. (1992). Mental models of the earth: A study of conceptual change in childhood. *Cognitive Psychology, 24,* 535–585.

Vosniadou, S., & Ioannides, C. (1998). From conceptual development to science education: A psychological point of view. *International Journal of Science Education, 20,* 1213–1230.

Wellman, H. M. (1990). *The child's theory of mind.* Cambridge, MA: MIT Press.

Williams, J. M., & Tolmie, A. (2000). Conceptual change in biology: Group interaction and the understanding of inheritance. *British Journal of Developmental Psychology, 18,* 625–649.

Wiser, M. (1988). The differentiation of heat and temperature: History of science and novice–expert shift. In S. Strauss (Ed.), *Ontogeny, phylogeny, and historical development* (pp. 28–48). Norwood, NJ: Ablex.

Wiser, M., & Carey, S. (1983). When heat and temperature were one. In D. Gentner & A. L. Stevens (Eds.), *Mental models* (pp. 267–297). Hillsdale, NJ: Lawrence Erlbaum Associates.

Yates, J., Bassman, M., Dunne, M., Jertson, D., Sly, K., & Wendelboe, B. (1988). Are conceptions of motion based on a naïve theory or on prototypes? *Cognition, 29,* 251–275.

Yuzawa, M. (1988). Understanding the meaning of the situation of a problem and a reasoning schema. *Japanese Journal of Educational Psychology, 36,* 297–306 [in Japanese with an English summary].

11

EVOLUTIONARY BIOLOGY AND CONCEPTUAL CHANGE

A Developmental Perspective

E. Margaret Evans, University of Michigan

Evolution, in a way, contradicts common sense.

(Mayr, 1982, p. 309)

Given the United States' reputation as a world leader in science, it is ironic that its scientific establishment is experiencing a public backlash. One of the most acrimonious manifestations of this backlash has been the US public's reaction to the Darwinian theory of evolution. With only 40% of the US public accepting evolutionary explanations for human origins, the US ranks second to last in acceptance rate among 34 industrialized nations. The rate in most of Europe, in contrast, ranges from 70% to 80%, whereas Japan's is 78% (Miller, Scott, & Okamoto, 2006). Explanations for this phenomenon abound, ranging from religious belief to poor scientific training to politicization. According to Mazur's (2005) analysis of several national US samples, *Christian religiosity*, especially fundamentalism, significantly outweighs other contributing factors, including educational level and political orientation. Further, after controlling for these factors, including religiosity, Mazur (2005) found that acceptance of evolutionary origins was *not* independently related to other measures of science knowledge, dogmatism (closed-mindedness), geographical locale, or ethnicity.

In this chapter, these overt largely *creationist* rejections of evolutionary origins will be linked to a parallel phenomenon, well-known to science teachers and science education researchers, which is students' misunderstanding of the mechanisms of natural selection (e.g., Bishop & Anderson, 1990). A developmental framework will be used to help explain the emergence of both sets of ideas in communities with different religious orientations and differing degrees of scientific expertise. By invoking a developmental perspective, cognitive scientists and science educators who are interested in the emergence of early scientific ideas can pinpoint the critical junctures at which commonsense, scientific, and religious reasoning meet, and trace the ensuing conceptual changes (e.g., Duschl, Schweingruber, & Shouse, 2006; Vosniadou & Ioannides, 1998; Vosniadou, Vamvakoussi & Skopeliti, 2008).

A recent approach, which differs markedly from a Piagetian developmental analysis in that it focuses on conceptual development in specific domains, aligns well with formal and informal science instruction. In this approach, human reasoning is conceptualized as a series of naïve or folk theories, which map onto fundamental domains of human knowledge, from biology to psychology to physics (Wellman & Gelman, 1998). Naïve theories provide the *commonsense* intuitions that first come to mind when humans seek everyday explanations for natural phenomena, from the workings of the human psyche to the movements of celestial objects. Conceptual change, from this perspective, may consist of the elaboration of intuitive concepts embedded in a particular explanatory framework or a more radical shift from one intuitive theory to another to explain a particular phenomenon, such as from a naïve psychology to a naïve biology (e.g., Carey, 1985). Intuitive theories are not so much discarded as reworked.

Without a detailed analysis of the processes of conceptual change within domains (e.g., Carey 2009; Siegler, 1996), Piagetian theory has little to offer in the way of improvements to subject specific learning experiences, beyond domain-general age-related changes in logical thinking. As a counterpoint to this approach, this chapter begins with a description of the intuitive conceptual barriers to evolutionary theory, followed by a developmental analysis of changes in children's and adults' reasoning about the origin of species. This cross-sectional developmental approach, utilizing an intuitive theory framework, is then augmented with an analysis of the incremental changes that occur when children (and adults) are exposed to evolutionary theory through informal learning experiences. A synthesis of the insights gained from both kinds of studies yields the broad outlines of one of several possible developmental learning progressions for an understanding of evolution. The premise of this chapter is that a domain-specific explanatory framework is necessary (if not sufficient) to clarify why evolutionary ideas are counterintuitive, and creationist ones contagious (Sperber, 1996). Without it, the public resistance to evolution can only be understood in a piecemeal fashion.

CONCEPTUAL BARRIERS TO EVOLUTIONARY THINKING: A THEORETICAL FRAMEWORK

Intuitive theories provide a conceptual framework that makes it possible for individuals to make sense of the everyday world, without any formal training (Atran, 1990; Wellman & Gelman, 1998). Intuitive reasoning works wonderfully on a day-to-day basis. It only causes difficulty when we try to understand ideas that are outside the realm of everyday experience, such as the theory of evolution. Three of the cognitive biases stemming from an everyday or intuitive biology (Medin & Atran, 2004) and psychology (Wellman & Gelman, 1998) are particularly problematic: That living things are separate, stable, and unchanging (*essentialism*) and that animate behavior is goal-directed (*teleology*) and intentional (*intentionality*). Evolutionary concepts, it is claimed, are counterintuitive precisely because they challenge this everyday understanding (Evans, 2000, 2001; Mayr, 1982), which tends to resonate better with a creationist ideology. These biases appear very early in human ontogeny (Wellman & Gelman, 1998).

Essentialism

A group of well-educated adults bursts into laughter as a leading creation scientist describes the apparently absurd idea entertained by evolutionary biologists, that whales originally walked on land (Evans, 1994/1995). On the face of it this does appear to be an odd idea: a land mammal the ancestor of an ocean dweller. What underlies this strong intuition that animal kinds are unique and cannot be transformed? Such ideas are widespread. Historians have documented them in early Western philosophers (Mayr, 1982) and they are also found in young children (Gelman & Rhodes, 2012). Psychological essentialism (Medin & Ortony, 1989), it is claimed, underlies essentialist beliefs in the unique identity of each living kind. Humans treat each living kind as if it has an underlying essence that makes it what it is. A tiger, for example, is always a tiger, even if you paint out its stripes and remove its legs; it is a deformed tiger, but a tiger, nonetheless. Essentialist beliefs may well have several functions. They appear to help us view the world as stable and unchanging, which is a very useful aspect of everyday reasoning in that we ignore the dynamic aspects of the world around us and focus on the stability. It is much easier for young children, for example, to work out what is happening in a world that is perceived as essentially the same from day to day. Everyday essentialist reasoning is, however, a significant barrier to evolutionary thinking, in which living kinds are ever changing.

Teleology

A glance at the behavior of an ant colony or a bee hive will convince most people that ant and bee activities are purposeful. These insects systematically search for food and bring it back to their home base to fuel the next generation. The human tendency to view behavior as directed toward a goal is very powerful and seen in infancy (Tomasello, Carpenter, Call, Behne, & Moll, 2005). Yet, insects, even ants, do not *reason* about goals. They aren't wondering where the next meal is coming from or how to satisfy the voracious appetites of their young. Their behavior only appears to be goal-directed; in reality, insects are responding to external environmental cues and internal signals, acquired over their evolutionary history. It is very difficult, however, to describe animal behavior without referring to its purpose or function (Keil, 1994; Kelemen 2012). Why might such teleological (or purposive) thinking be useful?

A reasonable hypothesis is that it helps people tell the difference between living and non-living things (e.g., Medin & Atran, 2004). If we see a rock plummeting down a mountain-side, we search for something that might have caused it to move. That is part of an everyday naïve physics. Conversely, if we see a cat bounding down the same terrain, we might wonder about its goal – pursuit of a rabbit, fleeing a predator? Even infants can distinguish between these two kinds of movement, one resulting from a physical cause and the other apparently satisfying a goal (Tomasello et al., 2005). The ability to detect purposeful activity is important to human survival, as it is a signal that an object is a living thing, a potential source of safety, food, or danger. Researchers hypothesize that along with essentialist reasoning, teleological reasoning forms the basis of our everyday naïve biology (Medin & Atran, 2004), appearing early in childhood (Inagaki & Hatano, 2002). This again raises a barrier to evolutionist reasoning. Evolution is adaptive in the sense that it is contingent on particular environmental conditions, but it is not directed toward the goal of adapting to those conditions.

Intentionality (Anthropomorphism)

Humans are a social species exquisitely attuned to shades of meaning. We read human minds and behaviors more easily and earlier than we read books. Unfortunately, it also leads us to assume intentions where none are meant. One child kicks another. Did he or she mean to do it? Was it intentional or accidental? Or a watchmaker creates a perfect instrument exquisitely attuned to the measurement of time (Dawkins, 1987). This artifact has been built to satisfy human goals and intentions. Creationists, it would appear, transfer this intuitive understanding of the human as an intentional manufacturer of tools, such as watches, and apply it to objects that have arisen naturally, such as the human eye. They use the artifact analogy to reason that anything as perfect as the human eye must have had a designer, a supernatural creator in this case; this is the crux of intelligent design – an anthropomorphic argument. Some researchers argue that creationism and intelligent design are so appealing because they elicit the well-honed human capacity for intentional and purposive or goal-directed reasoning – a naïve theory of mind (Evans, 1994/1995, 2000).

Counterintuitive Concepts and Evolutionary Theory

Evolutionary theory is probably one of the most counterintuitive ideas the human mind has encountered, so far. Some historians believe that is why it took such a long time before anyone could discern a natural solution to the problem of our origins, "Where did we come from?" (Mayr, 1982). That is, a solution that did not involve the direct intervention of a supernatural designer. Even when Darwin had solved the problem, it took him many years to assemble a watertight argument, one that would convince every critic (Mayr, 1988). To appreciate evolutionary arguments requires a radical conceptual change. We have to set aside or reconfigure our intuition that species were designed for a purpose, just like artifacts, and that they have unique essences. Specifically, we have to switch from a naïve psychological explanation that utilizes an anthropomorphic argument to a naturalistic explanation that eschews purpose and endorses the idea that living things can undergo radical change.

On the surface, it would seem that evolution may be too difficult for children to grasp. But we cannot assume this to be the case. An understanding of evolution does not require complex ideas that take years to acquire, such as mathematical reasoning or an understanding of genetics. Darwin and his contemporaries had no knowledge of Mendel's work on genes (Mayr, 1988). It was not until the 20th century that Darwinian evolution and Mendelian genetics were united. In the next sections, I shall describe what we know about the development of evolutionary concepts in children and describe the most typical ideas of youth of different ages, followed by a summary of the more extensive work with older students and adults.

As a caveat, I should add that the focus of this chapter is on conceptual barriers to an understanding of evolution rather than on difficulties understanding the *nature of science, per se.* Although both are important, the latter appear to be secondary rather than primary causes of the public resistance to evolution. While it is clearly the case that the public misunderstands the nature of science, that does not explain why antipathy toward the theory of evolution is stronger than to other scientific theories, such as the theory of gravity. The intuition that animals are immutable and that animate behavior is purposive increases susceptibility to a creationist world-view. For such ideas to spread with ease, the cognitive contingencies must already be in place (Sperber, 1996). Darwinian evolution, on the other hand, is notably unsettling, eliciting qualms about the place of the human in the natural world (Evans & Lane, 2011), and is more difficult to reconcile with these basic intuitions.

CONCEPTUAL CHANGE AND EVOLUTIONARY BIOLOGY: A DEVELOPMENTAL PERSPECTIVE

If human cognition is subject to constraints in the form of intuitions that increase resistance to evolutionary thinking, then the developmental evidence should provide the most powerful support for such a hypothesis. Such constraints should appear early on, change systematically over development, and persist into adulthood, even when modified by cultural input.

In sum, we should expect to see developmental change in children's understanding of evolutionary ideas that are related to children's emerging understanding of human minds and of nature. Young children should be highly resistant to the idea that animals can change and quite accepting of the idea that animate motion is purposeful (Evans, 2000). Further, the extensive work on children's theory of mind should provide evidence of changes in their everyday psychology that relate to children's understanding of intelligent design. In a series of studies that examined the early emergence of ideas about the origins of species in diverse communities, such relationships were found, though there were some surprises (Evans, 2000, 2001).

THE EMERGENCE OF IDEAS ABOUT THE ORIGIN OF SPECIES IN CHRISTIAN FUNDAMENTALIST AND NON-FUNDAMENTALIST COMMUNITIES

In the following summary of these studies, the term *Christian fundamentalist* refers to families from communities who attend churches *and* schools that endorse Biblical literalism. *Non-fundamentalist* refers to families from communities in the same locale, but who went to churches that did not endorse a literal reading of the Bible and who attended public schools. Importantly, parents from the two communities had similar educational levels and similar expectations of their children's educational attainment. Further, families from the two communities did not differ in the extent to which they endorsed musical activities and typical childhood hobbies. Consistent with their respective ideologies, however, fundamentalist families were more likely to endorse religious activities, whereas non-fundamentalist families were more likely to include fossils and nature in their preferred activities (Evans, 2001).

Children and adults from both communities were asked a series of open- and closed-ended questions about the origins of the *very first* of different kinds of animals. Given the ages of the child participants, the term "evolution" was never used. In the coding systems, the term *evolutionist* was applied to responses that endorsed the basic *macroevolutionary* concept rejected by creationist reasoners, such as Biblical literalists (Evans & Lane, 2011): that one kind of animal could be the predecessor or successor of a very different kind of animal. This is a transformationist idea. Children's responses were termed *spontaneous generationist* if they expressed a naturalistic but non-transformationist idea, implying that the very first of a species just appeared or emerged from the ground ("it came out of the ground"). Such ideas were expressed by the early Greeks (Mayr, 1982). *Creationist* ideas were those in which a supernatural power was invoked (e.g., God made it). In the results shown in Figure 11.1 (Evans, 2001), any of these ideas could be endorsed from zero to three times over three open-ended questions about the origins of humans, sun bears, and tuataras. As can be seen in Figure 11.1, children and adults from the two communities clearly differed in the extent to which they endorsed creationist and evolutionist ideas, with creationism overwhelmingly endorsed in the fundamentalist community, by all age-groups.

Overall, the results imply that five- to seven-year-olds (Young Age-Group) endorse a mixture of spontaneous generationist and creationist ideas, depending on the community of origin. In contrast, eight- to ten-year-olds (Middle Age-Group) endorse creationist ideas, *regardless* of community of origin; in fact, there was no significant difference between the communities for this age-group. By early adolescence (Older Age-Group), however, children's ideas did not differ from those of the adult members of their respective communities: evolutionist, creationist, or some mixture of the two. The pattern of endorsement in the non-fundamentalist community was very similar to that found in national samples (e.g., Gallup, 2007).

Furthermore, consistent with their robust essentialism (Gelman & Rhodes, 2012), five- to seven-year-olds responded "No" when asked the closed-ended question: Could one species have been the descendent of a completely different kind of animal? (see also

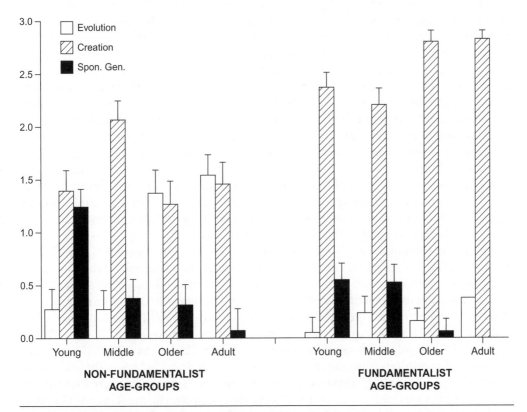

Figure 11.1 Beliefs about the origin of species in children and adults from fundamentalist and non-fundamentalist school communities, by age group (Frequency Range 0-3 + SEM)

Samarapungavan & Wiers, 1997). These young children did, however, endorse creationism at higher rates when they were explicitly presented with such ideas: Did God make them? Such results suggest that young children are susceptible to notions of intelligent design, even while they resist notions of species change. These findings were interpreted as supporting a constructive interactionist position (Wozniak & Fischer, 1993). Consistent with their intuitive cognitive biases, children spontaneously generate intuitive beliefs about origins, both natural and intentional. Community input reinforces and refines the culturally sanctioned intuitions while suppressing others, resulting in the distinctive and complex *reflective* belief systems (Sperber, 1996) of the communities at large.

What was most striking about these results was the two age-related shifts: from the mixture of spontaneous generationist and creationist ideas found in the five- to seven-year-olds to the consistent creationism of the eight- to nine-year olds; and the second shift to the endorsement of evolutionary ideas among early adolescents, at least in the non-fundamentalist communities. A series of follow-up studies examined these shifts in more detail.

Explaining the Pattern of Consistent Creationism in Eight- to Nine-year-olds

Further investigation of the pattern of reasoning of the eight- to nine-year olds in non-fundamentalist communities revealed an interesting relationship. It appeared that children in this age-group were beginning to confront existential questions, of eternity and of death, and it was this capacity that helped motivate the shift to a consistent creationism (Evans, Mull, & Poling, 2002). One of the reasons the youngest children appeared to endorse spontaneous generationist ideas was that they had failed to grasp the basic premise of the origins question: that, at one time, a particular kind of animal did not exist. In effect, some five- to seven-year-olds seemed to believe that the animals were always on earth, but someplace else where they could not be seen, such as underground. The origins questions about the *very first* of a particular kind would make little sense to a child who thought they were eternal. To test this hypothesis, in a different study 99 preschool and early school age children, who attended public schools, were asked "Have there always been 'Xs' here on this world" (*impermanence*), where X was one of three randomly presented pictures of North American mammals and three simple artifacts (Evans et al., 2002). Children responded with simple yes–no answers. As can be seen in Figure 11.2, not until children were eight to nine years of age did they consistently accept the idea of the impermanence of animals and of artifacts.

Children in the same study were also asked artificialist (Did a person make it?) and creationist (Did God make it?) questions about each of the same animals and artifacts. Replicating a pattern found among *non-fundamentalist* children in an earlier study (Evans, 2001), but using different measures, it was not until eight to nine years of age that children consistently distinguished between the creative capabilities of humans and of God (see Figure 11.3). In particular, younger non-fundamentalist children were as likely to state that God made artifacts as humans made artifacts (Evans et al., 2002). In contrast, *fundamentalist* children from the same age-group seemed precocious in that they were significantly more likely to make these distinctions. As it seems unlikely that fundamentalist adults explicitly focus on the distinctions between the capacities of God and human, the conclusion is that children make this inference unaided, perhaps based on repeated exposure to a creationist model.

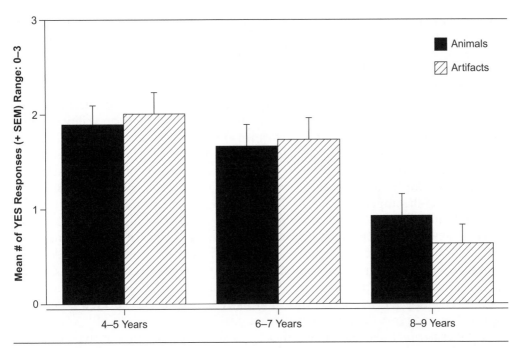

Figure 11.2 Were they always here? Children's acceptance of the permanence of animals and artifacts, by age group

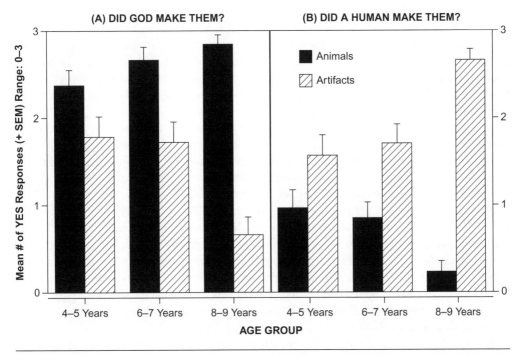

Figure 11.3 Children's responses to creationist (A) and artificialist (B) explanations for the origins of animals and artifacts, by age group

Children's emerging grasp of core existential concepts should also include death: Entities once created will not continue to exist. Although there is much variation in the age of acquisition, which depends on the measures used, a full understanding of death is often not achieved until children are seven to nine years of age (Poling & Evans, 2004; Slaughter & Lyons, 2003).

To assess whether the creationism of the children in the study was related to their understanding of existential issues and their reasoning about the human ability to create artifacts, a regression analysis was performed on a composite measure of *coherent creationism* (God made animals, God did not make artifacts): 54% of the variance was explained. Predictor variables included *coherent* artificialism (Humans make artifacts, not animals), death understanding (irreversibility, nonfunctionality, & universality), understanding the impermanence of objects, and age. Standardized regression coefficients indicated that age did not add additional variance beyond the effects of the other variables, all of which contributed variance independently of each other (Evans et al., 2002). This study suggests that children's capacity to reason about an intelligent designer is strongly related to their understanding of the human ability to create artifacts as well as their grasp of existential concepts. Once this age-related ability to reason about existential issues is in place, children are more likely to evoke the idea of God as designer, a form of *final-cause* reasoning. What else is needed?

Root-Bernstein (1984) has argued that the *final*-cause reasoning of the creationist world-view is eschewed by modern science, because science should be concerned solely with mechanistic explanations; that is, the *proximate* causes of particular phenomena. Mayr (1988) disagreed, arguing that evolutionary biology differs from the physical sciences because, in addition to proximate causes, it considers the *ultimate* or more distal causes of biological phenomena. Thus the evolutionary biologist asks both how and why questions: How does a particular organ work; that is, what is the mechanism? Why does that organ have that particular structure and function; that is, what are the evolutionary reasons – the ultimate causes? This integration of causal levels is one of the reasons that evolutionary biology appears to directly challenge a creationist world-view with theologians looking to God as the final cause of the diversity of life on earth, while biologists seek evolutionary or ultimate causes.

The focus here is on children and when they begin to make sense of these crucial distinctions. The short answer is that, as yet, not very much is known about this issue. To understand questions about *origins*, children have to integrate proximate and more distal causes into a complex causal structure. Only then can they consider *how* and *why* something came into existence (see also Abrams, Southerland, & Cummins, 2001; Southerland, Abrams, Cummins, & Anzelmo, 2001). There is plenty of evidence that young children use proximate cause reasoning (e.g., Wellman & Gelman, 1998). In the spontaneous generationist reasoning of the five- to seven-year-olds, for example, they easily explain how the animal became visible (it came out of the ground), but they do not explain how it got there in the first place. Yet the ease with which five- to seven-year-olds agreed that "God did it," when offered the opportunity to do so in closed-ended questions (Evans, 2001), suggests that they can incorporate final cause reasoning, particularly when it is provided by a reliable source (Harris & Koenig, 2006).

For younger children, however, this information is not yet integrated into a knowledge structure, in that "God did it" appears to be a loosely associated piece of information, no different from "a person did it" (Evans, 2000). Furthermore, the five- to seven-year-olds described earlier appeared to consider God as the proximate cause of the event in the sense that God directly makes objects/species in the way that people make artifacts, rather than considering the final cause, the reason why he made the object. Further evidence to support this argument is found in a follow-up study in which children were asked open-ended questions about the origins of the very first artifacts: Younger children gave single-cause answers, whereas older children were more likely to integrate different causal levels (Evans, Legare, & Rosengren, 2011; Evans, Rosengren, Szymanowksi, Smith, & Johnson, 2005). The following responses to the question, "How do you think the very first chair got here on earth?" illustrate this age-related shift:

- From the store (six years); God made it (6.8 years); Humans built it (6.8 years)
- God makes trees, so we can cut the trees down, and make chairs out of wood (8.3 years)
- God gave people the idea to make a chair (11.8 years).

Moreover, in a study (Mull & Evans, 2010) that focused on the development of a folk theory of intentionality (Malle & Knobe, 1997), it was not until eight to nine years of age that children appeared to converge on the adult theory in which proximate and distal causes are integrated. The *intentionality* inherent in an action such as that of a child knocking over a glass, for example, is interpreted differently by different age-groups. Preschoolers are likely to report that such an action occurs because of the protagonist's desires, "he wanted to knock over the glass," while five- to seven-year-olds report the immediate behavioral causes of the action, such as pushing the glass. In contrast, the eight- to nine-year olds also report more distal causes, the reasons that motivate the action, such as the knowledge, skills, and beliefs of the perpetrator: "He knew what he was doing when he pushed the glass" (Mull & Evans, 2010).

This research indicates that it is not until they about eight to nine years (or older) that children integrate an understanding of proximate cause actions with more distal mental state explanations, both of which are components of a folk theory of intentionality (Malle & Knobe, 1997). These findings could well explain why it is often not until eight to nine years of age that children begin to fully conceptualize God as intelligent designer; younger children are less likely to integrate the immediate causes of an action (he made it) with the final causes (the reasons why he made it). If the same capacity underlies the ability to reason about ultimate or evolutionary causes, then it is not too surprising that it is not until the end of the elementary school years that children typically begin to reason in evolutionary terms.

Explaining the Evolutionary Ideas of Early Adolescents

The work described so far indicates that to reason about origins, children should have confronted core existential questions and be able to integrate proximate and ultimate causes into a complex causal chain. This emerging cognitive capacity is necessary, but not sufficient. It is related, however, both to the final cause reasoning of the creationist and the ultimate cause reasoning of the evolutionary biologist. What else might predict acceptance of evolutionary ideas? In this section both microevolutionary and macro-evolutionary concepts are considered.

Clearly, exposure to a particular cultural belief system, religious or scientific, is critical. But mere exposure to Christian fundamentalist or scientific beliefs is not the only factor.

Independently of the consistency of parent beliefs about evolutionary origins, an understanding of the fossil evidence and a willingness to endorse an incorrect mechanism of change predicted preadolescents' reasoning about evolutionary origins (Evans, 2001). This mechanism included the idea that animals change in response to environmental factors (e.g., giraffes' long necks result from their habit of stretching their necks to reach into tall trees to obtain food). Even though the mechanism was incorrect, preadolescents acknowledged the critical role of environmental pressure in species change. In contrast to children from non-fundamentalist families, children from Christian fundamentalist families believed that animals would not change, because "God made it that way so it can't change" (11-year-old) (Evans, 2001). Altogether, on open-ended questions, these factors explained 76% of the variance in the frequency of preadolescents' evolutionary ideas. Predictors of the frequency of preadolescents' creationist ideas included the consistency of parent creationist ideas, attendance at a Christian fundamentalist school, and a lack of knowledge of the fossil evidence, altogether accounting for 67% of the variance.

One of the surprising findings in this study was that many of the participants had mixed beliefs, endorsing both evolutionist and creationist ideas (Evans, 2001; Evans, et al., 2011; Legare et al., 2012). Moreover, many in the non-fundamentalist community, while accepting that non-human species evolved, believed that humans were created by God. A more in-depth investigation of this finding revealed a much more nuanced acceptance or rejection of evolution than national or international surveys would allow. In this study (Evans et al., 2005), we hypothesized that an acceptance of radical within-species change, such as the metamorphosis of caterpillars into butterflies (Rosengren, Gelman, Kalish, & McCormick, 1991), would predict acceptance of evolutionary origins, because in both cases such an acceptance requires a modification of core essentialist constraints on species concepts. The relation between an acceptance of macroevolutionary change and the nature of the living kind was examined in 115 six- to 12-year-olds and their parents from both Biblical literalist and theistic evolutionist families (defined by parental belief system). Participants of all ages were more likely to accept evolutionary ideas for animals that undergo metamorphosis and were taxonomically distant from the human, in the following order: butterflies > frogs > non-human mammals > humans (Figure 11.4).

Moreover, among theistic evolutionist families, metamorphosis understanding was related to evolutionary concepts, independently of the child's age. This was not the case in Biblical literalist families, however, where older children understood metamorphosis but retained their explicit belief that each "kind" has a unique and God-given essence that cannot change. Although one implication of these studies is that teaching children about metamorphosis may provide them with the basis for modifying an early cognitive constraint, namely an essentialist bias, there is an important caveat. Metamorphosis as a model for species change introduces an inaccurate if prevalent analogy: Evolutionary change is like developmental change (Evans & Lane, 2011).

One further factor related to the spread of evolutionist and creationist ideas among members of the public is the acceptance of the human as an animal (Carey, 1985). In the same study, children were also asked whether humans, other mammals, butterflies, frogs, and artifacts were animals (Evans et al., 2005). Apart from the human, children of all ages were quite clear which were animals and which were not. For the human there was both a developmental and a community influence, with older children from theistic evolutionist families most likely to agree that the human was an animal (see Figure 11.5).

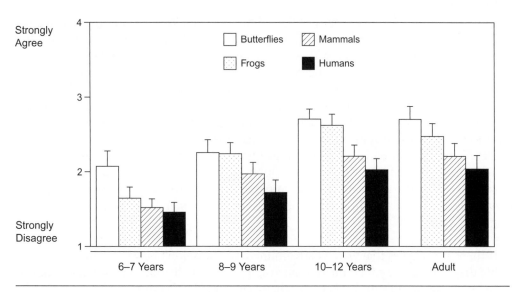

Figure 11.4 Did it evolve? Mean agreement (+SEM) for butterflies, frogs, mammals, and humans, by age group

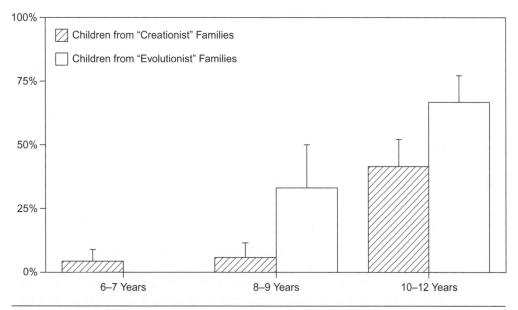

Figure 11.5 Is the human an animal? Percentage agreement among children from mostly "creationist" and mostly "evolutionist" families, by age group

Moreover, independently of other relevant factors, such as parental promotion of religious interest in the child, and the child's age, acceptance of the human as an animal was positively related to children's macroevolutionary ideas.

Early adolescents have the capacity to reason about ultimate or more distal causes. They may also accept that populations of animals undergo change. The latter acceptance is most likely to occur if their essentialist bias that species are unchanging has been modified by exposure to evidence of species change, from fossils, to metamorphosis, to adaptive variation. Moreover, many of the children who endorsed evolutionary explanations for the origin of species ideas also spontaneously invoked some kind of evolutionary cause that would explain these changes. In most cases this invoked a form of teleological reasoning, such as a need-based or developmental change in response to environmental factors, seen also in other studies with these age-groups (e.g., Abrams et al., 2001; Deadman & Kelly, 1978; Southerland et al., 2001); presumably no one taught them this, it is one that they inferred with minimal input. But there were occasional instances of something approaching a Darwinian mechanism.

Here is the response of a 10-year-old girl with no formal exposure to evolutionary theory, who had been asked about the adaptation of a novel animal called a spiggle (it looked like a mixture of a pig and a squirrel) to its newly aquatic environment –a previously dry island that had been flooded. Note the sequence of causal chains in her response (Evans, 2000):

> If there are spiggles that weren't streamlined, they wouldn't be well equipped for the life they lived so the streamlined webbed spiggles would live and – slowly the stronger webbed ones would survive and eventually all would be like this.
>
> (p. 248)

A typical response from a younger child was:

> [they] watched the fishes, copied them, one spiggle got to swim and taught the others.
> (p. 230)

Both of these responses were original. The younger child was using his understanding of human activities as goal-directed and intentional to model how spiggles could change. The 10-year-old, in contrast, thought that the spiggle population can vary (some are streamlined, some are not), and that the aquatic environment acts as a selection force, with the streamlined, webbed spiggles surviving. There is no reference to intentional or goal-directed actions. She has almost described the mechanism of natural selection.

High-school and College Students' Understanding of Evolutionary Change

The focus of this chapter, thus far, has been on concepts of species origins rather on an understanding of the processes of biological change within a population. What has been demonstrated is that by early adolescence those children who accept the idea of common ancestry, that one kind of animal could have been the descendent of a completely different kind, are also likely to endorse pre-Darwinian ideas of evolutionary change. In contrast, the main focus of the extensive body of research on high-school and college students' misunderstanding of evolution has been on evolutionary processes, in particular students' understanding of natural selection (Catley, 2006; Poling & Evans, 2004). This work has been summarized in several publications (e.g., Anderson, Fisher, & Norman, 2002; Gregory, 2009.)

What is striking about this research is the extensive documentation of the overlap between students' intuitive notions of evolutionary change and pre-Darwinian evolutionary concepts (e.g., Mayr, 1982; Shtulman, 2006), though they are certainly not identical (Evans, 2001; Kampourakis & Zogza, 2007). Students tend to focus on individual change rather than population change and utilize commonsense concepts, similar to those found in younger children: (1) that evolutionary change is need-based and adaptive, in a teleological sense, (2) that it is developmental and progressive: an emergence from an underdeveloped form, and (3) that it is not so much a dynamic process as a series of discrete events (e.g., Banet & Ayuso, 2003; Clough & Wood-Robinson, 1985; Dagher & BouJaoude, 1997; Ferrari & Chi, 1998; Nehm & Reilly, 2007). Such ideas are found at all grade levels, including science undergraduates and medical students, and are remarkably resistant to instruction (Bishop & Anderson, 1990; Brumby, 1984). Though studies of different teaching methods, some of which target students' epistemological beliefs, have yielded more promising results (e.g., Passmore & Stewart, 2002; Sandoval & Morrison, 2003; Sandoval & Reiser, 2004; Shtulman & Calabi, 2012; Sinatra, Southerland, McConaughy, & Demastes, 2003) the effects are not large. One possible explanation is that these studies include students who are uninterested in the topic and who are merely learning enough material to pass the course, not to acquire the deep understanding necessary for understanding evolutionary concepts.

Natural History Museum Visitors' Understanding of Evolutionary Change

What about a population that would be expected to have a good grasp of evolutionary theory and who have a demonstrated interest in natural history, such as natural history museum visitors? On average such visitors are more highly educated than the general population, in that 60% or more have a college education (Korn, 1995). Additionally, of course, they are interested enough in natural history to voluntarily visit such a museum, where they are likely to encounter exhibits on evolution (Diamond & Scotchmoor, 2006). As such, they would be expected to be more knowledgeable about natural history, and more accepting of evolution, than the general population. It is indeed the case that museum visitors are less likely to be creationist and more likely to accept evolutionary origins than the general population (Spiegel, Evans, Gram, & Diamond, 2006). But, just like the rest of the population, it depends on the target species. When asked about *human* origins, 28% of a sample attending three Midwest museums were creationist (Evans et al., 2010), compared with 46% in the general population (Gallup, 2007). What is more surprising is that only 34% of the same sample could be described as knowledgeable about evolution, and, even then, none of the visitors consistently invoked evolutionary reasoning across diverse species. They were more likely to invoke the intuitive essentialist, teleological, and intentional constructs described earlier (Diamond, Evans & Spiegel, 2012; Evans, et al., 2010).

These kinds of findings not only replicate those found in museum settings across the US (Macfadden et al., 2007), but are also apparent among visitors from countries where the acceptance rate of evolutionary origins is much higher. Abraham-Silver and Kisiel (2008) compared US, Canadian, English, and Australian natural history museum visitors and found that only about 30% had a reasonable grasp of natural selection. In sum, in the US and in other English-speaking countries, museum visitors exhibit the same kinds of misunderstandings of evolution found in young children and in school-age and college students, with a preponderance of intuitive explanations. The universality of these ideas is quite striking.

CONSTRUCTING DEVELOPMENTAL LEARNING PROGRESSIONS (DLPS) FOR EVOLUTION UNDERSTANDING

The detailed cross-sectional studies just described should be augmented with a different approach, such as research on the kind of incremental learning that occurs in microgenetic studies. Microgenetic research more easily lends itself to the construction of learning progressions, a detailed step-by-step description of the learning that occurs in response to particular experiences.

In response to recent calls for changes in the national science standards with a focus on core ideas, such as evolutionary theory, rather than on a sequence of disconnected topics, curriculum designers have also turned to learning progressions. For each core idea, a learning progression portrays the successive steps from students' earliest ideas, which are largely based on observation and direct experience, to progressively more sophisticated models of a particular domain (National Research Council, 2012). With these learning progressions in place, it then becomes possible to experiment with ways in which learning experiences might be modified to obtain optimal learning. For evolution, understanding much of this work remains to be done, though there are some hints as to how this learning process might unfold (see Catley, Lehrer, & Reiser, 2005). As currently constructed these learning progressions are best adapted for formal educational experiences (Duncan & Hmelo-Silver, 2009).

Given this constraint and as much learning is spontaneous, occurring in informal situations both inside and outside the home, we have recently proposed a *developmental* learning progression – DLP (Evans, Rosengren, Lane, & Price, 2012). In contrast to most formal learning progressions, the bottom anchor of a DLP explicitly reflects young children's first explanations of a particular core idea. Another feature of a DLP is that children's preexisting explanations are not so much discarded as modified as new knowledge is incorporated into their existing frameworks (see Vosniadou, Vamvakoussi, & Skopeliti, 2008). Additionally, children and adults may simultaneously engage two apparently contradictory ideas, which coexist in a variety of ways as locally coherent rather than as fragmented knowledge structures (Evans & Lane, 2011; Evans et al., 2011; Legare et al., 2012). Given this reality, proposals for DLPs should acknowledge the potentially diverse paths to an understanding of evolution. Some recent informal learning research on children's and adults' grasp of evolutionary processes illustrates one possible pattern.

As detailed in the previous sections, a consistent finding across a variety of studies is that older students describe the process of evolutionary change as one that is dependent on an individual organism's need to change to adapt to a new environment, rather than on natural selection. We argue that instead of viewing need-based reasoning as an explanation to be discarded, it can be seen instead as a key transitional step from a psychological to a more biologically feasible explanation of developmental change. As described earlier, younger elementary school children are very likely to reason that species were artificially created by a supernatural being, usually God, regardless of the beliefs of their community. In contrast, older children from non-fundamentalist families who have been exposed to information about biological change are more likely to accept the idea of evolutionary origins, even though they misunderstand the mechanism of change (Evans, 2001). Recently we have carried out a more detailed analysis of the conceptual changes that occur during this time-period, to reveal a more nuanced multistep process (Evans et al., 2012).

In a study of the effects of a museum visit on elementary school children's reasoning, children were randomly assigned to an exhibit on dinosaur–bird evolution or to an alternative exhibit (on molecules). At post-test, those five- to nine-year-olds who visited the evolution exhibit were significantly less likely than their peers, who had visited the alternative exhibit, to endorse the anthropomorphic idea that species were specially created by someone (Evans et al., 2012). When asked about the process of biological change, however, the same five- to nine-year-olds were also very likely to state that "[species X] *wanted* to change color." They used anthropomorphic reasoning, but now they referenced an intrinsic psychological process, based on desire, rather than a creative process instigated by an external agent. Older children showed a different pattern, with nine- to 14-year-olds more likely to express the idea that organisms changed because they *needed to* rather than because they *wanted to* (Evans & Lane, 2011). In this case, their need-based reasoning appeared to represent the idea that, of necessity, the organism needed to change if it were to survive in the new environment. At post-test those 9-to-14-year-olds who had visited the evolution exhibit were more likely than their peers, who had visited the alternative exhibit, to express the concepts of variation and differential survival, both components of natural selection understanding (Evans et al., 2012).

Converging evidence for the hypothesis that need-based reasoning represents an explanation that eases the transition to evolutionary understanding was also found in a separate study in which adults visited a different exhibit on evolution (Diamond et al., 2012; Spiegel et al., in press). From pre-test to post-test, adults significantly increased their endorsement of evolutionary *and* need-based explanations of biological change, while decreasing their endorsement of want-based and intelligent design explanations. Moreover, overall, there was a significant positive relationship between need-based and evolutionary explanations.

These findings support the conclusion that more sophisticated explanations of evolution are supported by need-based reasoning, provided it is disassociated from want-based reasoning (Evans et al., 2010). Moreover, the patterns of change seen both developmentally and in this informal learning research suggest that an earlier anthropomorphic (extrinsic and supernatural) explanation can, with appropriate input, yield an intuitive (intrinsic) psychological explanation, based on desire (want), which in turn yields an intuitive biological explanation, based on need. The latter, we claim, undergirds an understanding of some key components of natural selection. This is an example of one of several possible DLPs, which illustrates the two processes of conceptual change described in the introduction: (1) A shift from one explanatory framework to another, in this case from an intuitive psychology to an intuitive biology, and (2) the elaboration of intuitive concepts, in this case want- and need-based explanations. This research also suggests that exposing young elementary school children to compelling evidence for evolutionary origins (such as that for dinosaur–bird evolution) modifies their intuitive anthropomorphism and potentially increases their receptiveness to naturalistic explanations of the evolutionary process. Although in their infancy, these studies form the basis for an initial proposal for a developmental learning progression for evolution understanding (see Figure 11.6).

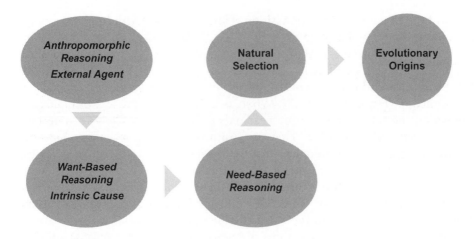

Figure 11.6 A developmental learning progression: Steps towards an understanding of evolution

CONCLUSION

The findings presented in this chapter support the position that the human mind resists evidence that contradicts a self-serving view of the world. About half of the US public embraces creationist ideas about the origins of species. Even among those members of the public who accept evolutionary origins, including common ancestry, most invoke intuitive ideas to explain species change. Moreover, only about a third of those with a demonstrated interest in natural history, such as museum visitors, grasp Darwinian evolutionary concepts. The latter patterns are found in other industrial societies as well.

As this chapter demonstrates, though, there are glimmers of hope, seen most clearly by taking a developmental perspective. The following conversation at a lunch counter between a 12-year old boy and his mother provides a prime example (Campbell, 1972 was eavesdropping; pp. 1–2):

> *Boy:* Jimmy wrote a paper today on the evolution of man, and Teacher said he was wrong, that Adam and Eve were our first parents.
> *Mother:* Well, Teacher was right. Our first parents *were* Adam and Eve.
> *Boy:* Yes, I know, but this was a *scientific* paper.
> *Mother:* Oh those scientists! *[angrily]* These are only theories.
> *Boy:* Yes I know *[was his cool and calm reply]*, but they have been factualized: they found the bones.

ACKNOWLEDGMENTS

This material is based on work supported by the Spencer Foundation and the National Science Foundation (#0411406).

REFERENCES

Abraham-Silver, L., & Kisiel, J. (2008). Comparing visitors' conceptions of evolution: Examining understanding outside the United States. *Visitor Studies, 11*(1), 41–54.

Abrams, E., Southerland, S., & Cummins, C. L. (2001). The how's and why's of biological change: How learners neglect physical mechanisms in their search for meaning. *International Journal of Science Education, 23*, 1271–1281.

Anderson, D. L., Fisher, K. M., & Norman, G. J. (2002). Development and evaluation of the conceptual inventory of the natural selection. *Journal of Research of Science Teaching, 39*, 952–978.

Atran, S. (1990). *Cognitive foundations of natural history: Towards an anthropology of science.* Cambridge, UK: Cambridge University Press.

Banet, E., & Ayuso, G. E. (2003). Teaching of biological inheritance and evolution of living beings in secondary school. *International Journal of Science Education, 25*, 373–407.

Bishop, B. A., & Anderson, C. W. (1990). Student conceptions of natural selection and its role in evolution. *Journal of Research in Science Teaching, 27*, 415–427.

Brumby, M. N. (1984). Misconceptions about the concept of natural selection by medical biology students. *Science Education, 684*, 493–503.

Campbell, J. (1972). *Myths to live by.* New York, NY: Viking Penguin.

Carey, S. (1985). *Conceptual change in childhood.* Cambridge, MA: MIT Press.

Carey, S. (2009). *The origin of concepts.* Oxford, UK: Oxford University Press.

Catley, K. M. (2006). Darwin's missing link – A novel paradigm for evolution education. *Science Education, 90*, 767–783.

Catley, K. M., Lehrer, R., & Reiser, B. (2005). Tracing a prospective learning progression for developing understanding of evolution. National Academies Committee on Test Design for K–12 Science Achievement.

Clough, E. E., & Wood-Robinson, C. (1985). How secondary students interpret instances of biological adaptation. *Journal of Biological Education, 19*, 125–130.

Dagher, Z. R., & BouJaoude, S. (1997). Scientific views and religious beliefs of college students: The case of biological evolution. *Journal of Research in Science Teaching, 34*, 429–445.

Dawkins, R. (1987). *The blind watchmaker.* New York, NY: Norton.

Deadman, J. A., & Kelly, P. J. (1978). What do secondary school boys understand about evolution and heredity before they are taught about the topics. *Journal of Biological Education, 12*, 7–15.

Diamond, J., & Scotchmoor, J. (2006). Exhibiting evolution. *Museums and Social Issues, 1*, 21–48.

Diamond, J., Evans, E. M., & Spiegel, A. N. (2012). Walking whales and singing flies: An evolution exhibit and assessment of its impact. In K. R. Rosengren, S. Brem, E. M. Evans, & G. Sinatra (Eds.) *Evolution challenges: Integrating research and practice in teaching and learning about evolution* (pp. 389–409). New York, NY: Oxford University Press.

Duncan, R. G., & Hmelo-Silver, C. E. (2009). Editorial: Learning progressions: Aligning curriculum, instruction, and assessment. *Journal of Research in Science Teaching, 46*, 606–609.

Duschl, R. A., Schweingruber, H. A., & Shouse, A. W. (Eds.). (2006). *Taking science to school: learning and teaching science in Grades K–8.* Washington, DC: The National Academies Press.

Evans, E. M. (1994/1995). *God or Darwin? The development of beliefs about the origin of species.* PhD dissertation, University of Michigan, Ann Arbor, MI.

Evans, E. M. (2000). The emergence of beliefs about the origins of species in school-age children. *Merrill-Palmer Quarterly, 46*, 221–254.

Evans, E. M. (2001). Cognitive and contextual factors in the emergence of diverse belief systems: Creation versus evolution. *Cognitive Psychology, 42*, 217–266.

Evans, E. M., & Lane, J. D. (2011). Contradictory or complementary? Creationist and evolutionist explanations of origins. *Human Development, 54*, 144–159.

Evans, E. M., Mull, M. S., & Poling, D. A. (2002). The authentic object? A child's-eye view. In S. G. Paris (Ed.) *Perspectives on object-centered learning in museums.* (pp. 55–77). Mahwah, NJ: Lawrence Erlbaum Associates.

Evans, E. M., Legare, C., & Rosengren, K. (2011). Engaging multiple epistemologies: Implications for science education. In M. Ferrari & R. Taylor (Eds.), *Epistemology and science education: Understanding the evolution vs. intelligent design controversy* (pp. 111–139). New York, NY: Routledge.

Evans, E. M., Rosengren, K., Lane, J. D., & Price, K. S. (2012). Encountering counterintuitive ideas: Constructing a developmental learning progression for biological evolution. In K. R. Rosengren, S. Brem, E. M. Evans, & G. Sinatra (Eds.), *Evolution challenges: Integrating research and practice in teaching and learning about evolution* (pp. 174–199). New York, NY: Oxford University Press.

Evans, E. M., Rosengren, K. S., Szymanowksi, K., Smith P. H., & Johnson, K. (2005, October). *Culture, cognition, and creationism.* Biennial meeting of the Cognitive Development Society, San Diego, CA.

Evans, E. M., Spiegel, A., Gram, W., Frazier, B. F., Tare, M., Thompson, S., et al. (2010). A conceptual guide to natural history museum visitors' understanding of evolution. *Journal of Research in Science Teaching, 47*, 326–353.

Ferrari, M., & Chi, M. T. H. (1998). The nature of naïve explanations of natural selection. *International Journal of Science Education, 20*(10), 1231–1256.

Gallup (2007). *Evolution, creationism, intelligent design.* Retrieved February, 2, 2008 from www.gallup.com

Gelman, S. A., & Rhodes, M. (2012). "Two-thousand years of stasis": How psychological essentialism impedes evolutionary understanding. In K. R. Rosengren, S. Brem, E. M. Evans, & G. Sinatra (Eds.), *Evolution challenges: Integrating research and practice in teaching and learning about evolution* (pp. 3–21). New York, NY: Oxford University Press.

Gregory, T. R. (2009). Understanding natural selection: Essential concepts and common misconceptions. *Evolution: Education and Outreach, 2,* 156–175.

Harris, P. L., & Koenig, M. A. (2006). Trust in testimony: How children learn about science and religion. *Child Development, 77,* 505–524.

Inagaki, K., & Hatano, G. (2002). *Young children's naïve thinking about the biological world.* New York, NY: Psychology Press.

Kampourakis, K., & Zogza, V. (2007). Students' preconceptions about evolution: How accurate is the characterization as "Lamarckian" when considering the history of evolutionary thought? *Science & Education, 16,* 393–422.

Keil, F. C. (1994). The birth and nurturance of concepts by domains: The origins of concepts of living things. In L. A. Hirschfeld & S. A. Gelman (Eds.), *Mapping the mind: Domain specificity in cognition and culture* (pp. 234–254). Cambridge, UK: Cambridge University Press.

Kelemen, D. (2012). Teleological minds: How natural intuitions about agency and purpose influence learning about evolution. In K. R. Rosengren, S. Brem, E. M. Evans, & G. Sinatra (Eds.), *Evolution Challenges: Integrating research and practice in teaching and learning about evolution* (pp. 66–92). New York, NY: Oxford University Press.

Korn, R. (1995). An analysis of difference between visitors at natural history museums and science centers. *Curator: The Museum Journal, 38,* 150–160.

Legare C. H., Evans, E. M., Rosengren, K., & Harris, P. (2012). The coexistence of natural and supernatural explanations across cultures and development. *Child Development, 83*(3), 779–793.

Macfadden, B. J., Dunckel, B. A., Ellis, S., Dierking, L. D., Abraham-Silver, L., Kisiel, J., et al. (2007). Natural history museum visitors' understanding of evolution. *BioScience, 57*(10), 875–882.

Malle, B. F., & Knobe, J. (1997). The folk concept of intentionality. *Journal of Experimental Social Psychology, 33,* 101–121.

Mayr, E. (1982). *The growth of biological thought: Diversity, evolution and inheritance.* Cambridge, MA: Harvard University Press.

Mayr, E. (1988). *Towards a new philosophy of biology.* Cambridge, MA: Harvard University Press.

Mazur, A. (2005). Believers and disbelievers in evolution. *Politics and the Life Sciences, 8* (November), 55–61.

Medin, D. L., & Atran, S. (2004). The native mind: Biological categorization and reasoning in development and across cultures. *Psychological Review, 111,* 960–983.

Medin, D., & Ortony, A. (1989). Comments on Part 1: Psychological essentialism. In S. Vosniadou & A. Ortony (Eds.), *Similarity and analogical reasoning* (pp. 179–193). Cambridge, UK: Cambridge University Press.

Miller, J. D., Scott, E. C., & Okamoto, S. (2006). Public acceptance of evolution. *Science, 313,* 765–766.

Mull, M. S., & Evans, E. M. (2010). Did she mean to do it? Acquiring a folk theory of intentionality. *Journal of Experimental Child Psychology, 107,* 207–228.

National Research Council. (2012). *A framework for K–12 science education: Practices, crosscutting concepts, and core ideas.* Committee on Conceptual Framework for the New K–12 Science Education Standards. Washington, DC: National Academies Press.

Nehm, R. H., & Reilly, L. (2007). Biology majors' knowledge and misconceptions of natural selection. *BioScience, 57,* 263–272.

Passmore, C., & Stewart, J. (2002). A modeling approach to teaching evolutionary biology in high schools. *Journal of Research in Science Teaching, 39,* 185–204.

Poling, D. A. & Evans, E. M. (2004). Are dinosaurs the rule or the exception? Developing concepts of death and extinction. *Cognitive Development, 19,* 363–383.

Root-Bernstein, R. (1984). On defining a scientific theory: Creationism considered. In A. Montagu (Ed.), *Science and creationism* (pp. 64–93). New York, NY: Oxford University Press.

Rosengren, K. S., Gelman, S. A., Kalish, C. W., & McCormick, M. (1991). As time goes by: Children's early understanding of growth in animals. *Child Development, 62,* 1302–1320.

Samarapungavan, A., & Wiers, R. W. (1997). Children's thoughts on the origin of species: A study of explanatory coherence. *Cognitive Science, 21*, 147–177.

Sandoval, W. A., & Morrison, K. (2003). High school students' ideas about theories and theory change after a biological inquiry unit. *Journal of Research in Science Teaching, 40*, 369–392.

Sandoval, W. A., & Reiser, B. J. (2004). Explanation-driven inquiry: Integrating conceptual and epistemic scaffolds for scientific inquiry. *Science Education, 88*, 345–371.

Shtulman, A. (2006). Qualitative differences between naïve and scientific theories of evolution. *Cognitive Psychology, 52*, 170–194.

Shtulman, A. & Calabi, P. (2012). Cognitive constraints on the understanding and acceptance of evolution. In K. R. Rosengren, S. Brem, E. M. Evans, & G. Sinatra (Eds.), *Evolution challenges: Integrating research and practice in teaching and learning about evolution* (pp. 46–55). New York, NY: Oxford University Press.

Siegler, R. S. (1996). *Emerging minds: The process of change in children's thinking.* Oxford, UK: Oxford University Press.

Sinatra, G. M., Southerland, S. A., McConaughy, F., & Demastes, J. W. (2003). Intentions and beliefs in students' understanding and acceptance of biological evolution. *Journal of Research in Science Teaching, 405*, 510–528.

Slaughter, V., & Lyons, M. (2003). Learning about life and death in early childhood. *Cognitive Psychology, 46*, 1–30.

Southerland, S. A., Abrams, E., Cummins, C. L., & Anzelmo, J. (2001). Understanding students' explanations of biological phenomena: Conceptual frameworks or P-Prims. *Science Education, 85*, 328–348.

Sperber, D. (1996). *Explaining culture: A naturalistic approach.* Oxford, UK: Blackwell.

Spiegel, A., Evans, E. M., Frazier, B. F., Hazel, A., Tare, M. Gram, W., & Diamond, J. (2012). Changing museum visitors' concepts of evolution. *Evolution: Education and Outreach, 5*, 43–61. DOI 10.1007/s12052-012-0399-9.

Spiegel, A. N., Evans, E. M., Gram, W., & Diamond, J. (2006). Museum visitors' understanding of evolution. *Museums & Social Issues, 1*, 67–84.

Tomasello, M., Carpenter, M., Call, J., Behne, T., & Moll, H. (2005). Understanding and sharing intentions: The origins of cultural cognition. *Behavioral and Brain Sciences, 28*, 675–735.

Vosniadou, S., & Ioannides, C. (1998). From conceptual development to science education: A psychological point of view. *International Journal of Science Education, 20*, 1213–1231.

Vosniadou, S., Vamvakoussi, X., & Skopeliti, I. (2008). The framework theory approach to the problem of conceptual change. In S. Vosniadou (Ed.), *International handbook of research on conceptual change* (pp. 3–34). New York, NY: Routledge.

Wellman, H. M., & Gelman, S. A. (1998). Knowledge acquisition in foundational domains. In W. Damon, D. Kuhn, & R. Siegler (Eds.), *Handbook of child psychology: Vol. 2. Cognition, Perception and Language* (5th ed., pp. 523–574). New York, NY: Wiley.

Wozniak, R. H., & Fischer, K. W. (1993). Development in context: An introduction. In R. H. Wozniak & K. W. Fischer (Eds.), *Development in context: Acting and thinking in specific environments* (pp. xi–xvi). Hillsdale, NJ: Lawrence Erlbaum Associates.

12

CONCEPTUAL UNDERSTANDING IN THE DOMAIN OF HEALTH

David R. Kaufman, Alla Keselman, and Vimla L. Patel,
Columbia University, National Institutes of Health, and
New York Academy of Medicine

Of all scientific disciplines, knowledge related to health sciences arguably has the greatest bearing on the daily lives of individuals. In sickness and in health, we are health consumers, regardless of our occupation, demographics characteristics and social status. As we make routine decisions about nutrition, exercise, immunization, as well as non-routine decisions about medical treatment options, we implicitly and explicitly draw upon our health knowledge. The active role of health consumers is becoming widely recognized by health care organizations and policy makers. The objective of many consumer health initiatives is to empower health consumers and enable them to act as partners in their health care (Hack, Degner, Parker, & The SCRN Communication Team, 2005). Unfortunately, lack of knowledge and a non-normative understanding of health concepts present a barrier to achieving this goal. The emphasis on educated health consumerism creates new obligations and opportunities for science and health education, and requires a good understanding of lay health knowledge and its relationship to reasoning and decision making.

Research in medical cognition has been ongoing for more than 30 years and there are relatively stable paradigms for experimental research. Health cognition is a comparatively new discipline and we are just beginning to define the central issues. Most works on lay understanding of health concepts are conducted in applied domains of public health and consumer health education. There have been comparatively few cognitive studies of conceptual change in the domain of health, especially with adults. However, general conceptual change theory has much to offer to the applied, intervention-focused consumer health research. The basic tenets of conceptual change theory suggest that: (1) individuals' prior knowledge exercises strong influence over their emergent beliefs and theories, and (2) conceptual change requires some genuine understanding, and mere knowledge accretion as a mode of learning is less likely to result in usable knowledge.

Integrating these tenets into consumer health works has the potential to enrich consumer health research and interventions. At the same time, due to its complex, "ill-structured", knowledge-rich nature, the health domain presents a fertile area for a study of science learning and conceptual change.

Medical professionals train for many years before becoming certified to practice. The vast majority of lay individuals receive minimal or no formal training in matters of health, and cannot be expected to have the extensive biomedical knowledge of health professionals. They may lack the knowledge of biomedical concepts necessary for understanding disease etiology and mechanism. For example, McGregor (2003) interviewed patients with localized prostate cancer (10 Scotland residents between the ages of 53 and 75, representing diverse educational and professional backgrounds) about their understanding of their disease. Most men had little understanding of the function of the prostate gland. They also had limited understanding of the side-effects of the possible treatments. However, while lay people may have limited biomedical knowledge, they possess many other kinds of knowledge – cultural, social, and experiential – that they draw upon in reasoning about health and diseases (Patel, Kaufman, & Arocha, 2000). Knowledge derived from these sources may be non-normative and differ significantly from the medical view. However, we will argue that this knowledge is often organized into complex causal networks, with evidence of causality grounded in narratives, memorable instances, and superficially plausible links. To the extent that these knowledge networks make logical sense given the beliefs of their holders, they are consistent and have a coherent structure. Lay individuals often possess both cultural/experiential/personal knowledge and some formal "school" knowledge of health concepts (Sivaramakrishnan & Patel, 1993). The two systems are often in conflict, and reasoning while drawing on knowledge from different sources presents a challenge. In the rest of this section, we will review research pertaining to lay understanding of health issues in indigenous and Western cultures. We will then explore the role that biomedical knowledge plays in health reasoning and the effect of conceptual change interventions on reasoning.

The studies presented in this chapter are not meant to provide an exhaustive review of the literature on lay understanding of health concepts, but rather to draw on our own research and illustrate basic trends in this literature. In doing so, we adapt a life-span approach to conceptual change in health understanding, focusing on adults to a greater extent and on children to a lesser extent than is customary in conceptual change literature. Finally, one of our basic premises is that lay understanding of health concepts has bearing on consumer health decisions and behavior. Conceptual understanding of health issues gives individuals the power to derive predictions and explanations of a wide range of health-related phenomena, which can then be applied in decision making. Such conceptual competence does not guarantee correct performance (which is affected by a broad range of other cognitive and non-cognitive factors), but provides the necessary knowledge base.

LAY HEALTH KNOWLEDGE ACROSS CULTURES

Studies of lay health theories in non-Western cultures reveal causal beliefs that are non-biological in nature. Sivaramakrishnan and Patel conducted studies of reasoning about childhood nutritional diseases by mothers in rural India. Many unschooled mothers explained symptoms of malnutrition by referring to the concept of *therai*, a toad that falls on a pregnant mother and sucks the nutrients from the fetus. Treatment for the condition involves tying a live toad in a leather pouch to the child's neck or waist. The study also demonstrated coexistence of supernatural and biological explanations. For example, after explaining the concept of *therai* and its causal role in marasmus disease (malnutrition), one of the participants added that marasmus may also be caused by worms and should then be treated by worm medicine. A similar blend of supernatural and biological causality can be observed in other studies. In her interviews with mothers of malnourished children in Pakistan, Mull (1991) showed that the majority of mothers correctly viewed diarrhea as predisposing to malnutrition. However, few mothers viewed diarrhea or the lack of food as the cause of the disease. Most explained that the condition was caused by the shadow of an unclean woman, thrown on the child or the mother. Although these explanations are obviously non-normative from the point of view of Western biomedical theories, their narrative structure is coherent, with all propositions (clauses) of the narrative tied into one causal system. They are also less dissonant with indigenous medical frameworks. For example, East Indian Ayurvedic medicine is based on the concept of "humors" that constitute the human body. Illness and health are the result of the balance or imbalance of these humors.

Combination of normative and non-normative health concepts and reliance on cultural and experiential knowledge in lay heath reasoning are not limited to non-Western cultures. Keselman and colleagues conducted a study of New York City adolescents' understanding of HIV and reasoning about HIV-related issues (Keselman, Kaufman, & Patel, 2004). Middle- and high-school students from urban schools were interviewed about their conceptual understanding of HIV. They were also asked to evaluate scenarios containing myths about HIV. On the basis of their responses to the interview, students' understanding of HIV biology was classified into three models: naïve, intermediate, and advanced. Students were assigned to models on the basis of their understanding of three factors: (1) core concept of HIV, (2) mechanism of HIV infection, and (3) disease progression. Factual knowledge that HIV is an incurable sexually transmitted disease did not affect model assignment. Of the 21 participants in the study, 11 (nine middle-school students and two high-school students) were classified at the naïve level of HIV understanding. Seven (one middle-school and six high-school students) were classified at the intermediate level, and three (high-school) students were classified at the advanced level. Students at the naïve level showed no understanding of biological concepts of a virus, infection, and immune system. Lack of awareness of hidden biological processes often led to explanations in which cause and effect had to be deduced from the "tangible" events. These included young adolescents' beliefs that HIV was caused by dirt (poor hygiene after sex), or by the sexual act itself. Adolescents' perception of causality in terms of input– output relationships may be rooted in intuitive biology that has originated during childhood attempts to make sense of the world, and survived into adulthood. In a study of adolescents' understanding of food spoilage and infectious diseases, Au and Romo (1999) recorded causal explanations that were similarly grounded in tangible relationships. Like explanations by mothers in Sivaramakrishnan and Patel's (1993) study, explanations often had narrative structure. The following quote from a seventh-grader illustrates an incorrect, but conceptually complex explanation of the HIV infection mechanism, "See, most people, like, they don't actually wash after having sex. See, if the person is dirty . . . you know, like the dirt, it goes into skin, like, it stays there for a long time, then it starts to go further in, then it starts mixing with your blood, and that's how AIDS could probably form."

In addition to personal experiences and culturally based medical practices, individuals' understanding of health issues may also be influenced by social group norms and discourse practices. For example, Bogart and Thorburn (2005) conducted a survey of African Americans' beliefs about the origin of HIV. They found that 20% of men and 12% of women somewhat agreed to strongly agreed that "HIV/AIDS is a man-made virus that the federal government made to kill and wipe out black people." Ross, Essien, and Torres (2006) found that genocidal conspiracy theories were also relatively widespread in other racial/ethnic groups. For some groups, beliefs affected health behavior: Conspiracy beliefs were associated with reduction of condom use among African American men.

THE ROLE OF CAUSALITY IN LAY CONCEPTUAL KNOWLEDGE OF HEALTH

Narrative structure of lay explanations of disease causality in Sivaramakrishnan and Patel (1993) and Keselman et al.'s (2004) studies provides some evidence about the important role that perceived causality plays in lay disease concept. More direct evidence comes from studies that involved experimental methodology. For example, Kim and Ahn (2002) conducted experiments that related lay participants' causal theories about psychiatric disorders to their categorization decisions. Participants in the studies were asked about their understanding of causal relationships among various symptoms of real and artificial mental disorders. Symptoms in participants' models were then categorized in terms of depth of cause (X, where X causes Y, which causes Z), intermediate causes (Y), and terminal effects (Z). Participants were also presented with lists of symptoms, characterizing the disorders, and asked to classify conditions as either belonging or not belonging to the disorder, when one of the symptoms was absent. For example, they were asked if the diagnosis of anorexia nervosa would hold true if the symptom "refusal to maintain minimum body weight" was absent. The findings suggest that symptoms perceived as "deeper" causes are viewed as more central to the disorders than those that are perceived as "intermediate" causes or effects. Intermediate causes are perceived as more important than effects. Finally, symptoms that were not part of the coherent causal system (causally unrelated) are seen as less central than causally connected factors.

Although Kim and Ahn's study does not mirror the real life conditions of patients (participants are given descriptions of diseases and their prior understanding of mental health issues is not considered), it has implications for health education. The study points to the flaws of interventions that provide facts without supplying well-connected causal explanations, as these accurate facts are likely to be ignored in favor of non-normative but rich concepts. Indeed, the following section will illustrate many instances where participants in interview studies reason and make decisions on the basis of incorrect but causally complex cultural/experiential theories, rather than accurate but superficial knowledge of biomedical facts.

FORMAL LEARNING AND LAY HEALTH KNOWLEDGE

In explaining diseases and reasoning about health issues, lay individuals typically draw on both their cultural/experiential knowledge and on their "school" knowledge. Attempts to resolve discrepancies between "informal" and "formal" knowledge are not easy, and often violate coherence of explanations and lead to inconsistencies in reasoning (Driver,

Asoko, Leach, Mortimer, & Scott, 1994). Studies also suggest that "formal" knowledge is more likely to be used (and to be helpful) when it has a certain depth and involves genuine understanding rather than mere knowledge of facts.

To study the effect of education on explanations of disease causality, Sivaramakrishnan and Patel (1993) interviewed 22 mothers of East Indian origins living in Canada. Five of the participants had no formal education, five had completed 10 years of secondary school, and 12 were educated in Indian universities. University-educated mothers were assumed to be familiar with Western biomedical concepts, because these studies would have been part of their university curricula. The study showed that educated mothers were more likely than their less-educated counterparts to identify dietary deficiency as a cause of malnutrition. Participants with no formal education often explained the symptoms of marasmus by referring to indigestion. Their explanations were typically coherent and consistent with an Ayurvedic framework, in which the concept of proper digestion of food is central to good health. Mothers with university education were more likely to refer to Western biomedical concepts (e.g., enzyme production) in their explanations. However, their reasoning was still largely grounded in Ayurvedic interpretation, in which all digestive problems are traced to the liver. Drawing on two medical systems also led to opportunistic and inconsistent use of concepts and contributed to the fragmentation of reasoning.

Similar to many Indian mothers in Sivaramakrishnan and Patel's studies (1993), participants in Keselman, Kaufman, and Patel's (2004) study whose HIV understanding was classified at the naïve level relied on their cultural and experiential knowledge while reasoning about HIV myths. They also used their knowledge opportunistically: If their informal/experiential knowledge did not correspond to their factual biomedical knowledge, they drew upon the experience. This is illustrated by the reasoning of a ninth grader. This student had little understanding of HIV biology, yet was able to state in the interview that he knew that there was no cure for HIV, and that he had learned this at school, in HIV education activities. Later, he was presented with a myth suggesting that HIV could be expelled from the body by urine and sweat, and recommending exercise in order to increase sweating. The student replied, "*Yeah, this is true, this is true. Cause people can stop by like that. By exercising, like they said. Like that lady, like I told you, she exercised her way out of cancer, so I think this is true, you can exercise your way out of HIV probably.*" In the absence of robust biological knowledge, experiential analogy outweighed accurate but conflicting factual knowledge.

Students at the intermediate level had greater understanding of HIV biology: they knew that HIV was a biological entity that entered the body with bodily fluids and compromised the immune system. However, because their knowledge lacked depth and was somewhat fragmented, students often could not connect these concepts into logical chains, and switched to relying on their experiential knowledge and memories of media stories, which sometimes led them to accept myths as true. In contrast, students at the advanced level had a robust understanding of HIV biology. They knew that HIV was a virus that entered the body through bodily fluids, then penetrated the T-cells of the immune system and eventually destroyed them by taking over their reproductive mechanism. These students consistently relied on biological reasoning to point to the flaws in the logic of the myths. Findings from both studies reviewed in this sub-section illustrate that the basic tenet of conceptual change theory – to be applicable to reasoning across a range of situations, knowledge needs to be sufficiently robust and coherent.

PROMOTING CONCEPTUAL CHANGE

Many public health initiatives are concerned with the challenge of facilitating behavioral change, by influencing many cognitive and non-cognitive factors that affect health behaviors (e.g., motivation, self-efficacy, perceived difficulty of the change). While we view this task as extremely important, an extensive review of behavioral change interventions is beyond the scope of this chapter. We also understand that knowledge is a necessary but not sufficient component of behavioral change. Our goal is to show that helping individuals develop a moderately deep understanding of health issues is possible, and to provide them with a knowledge base for reasoning about real or realistic situations. We then provide examples of situations in which health knowledge has been shown to positively impact health behaviors.

In a follow-up to the study of adolescents' understanding of HIV, Keselman, Kaufman, Kramer and Patel (2007) conducted a middle-school science intervention in HIV biology, which combined scientific reasoning and science writing activities. Part of the intervention involved teacher-led lectures. Students also reviewed media articles about viral diseases and developed explanations of occurrences described in the articles. Finally, students in one of the two conditions assumed the role of HIV counselors and responded to letters from fictional characters to an HIV counseling clinic. The emphasis of the intervention was on building a deeper, more meaningful, well-integrated knowledge network that could support reasoning about authentic tasks.

In the course of the intervention, many students developed reasonably robust understanding of the concepts of virus, viral transmission, and the immune system, advancing from the naïve to the intermediate model of HIV understanding. They also showed improved ability to apply their understanding to reasoning about realistic problem scenarios pertaining to HIV. Pretest and post-test assessments required students to read a letter from a fictional young woman whose friend had been diagnosed with HIV. The friendship was crumbling because the author of the letter became afraid of all types of contact with her friend, and feared sharing the friend's clean utensils and towels at her house. At the pretest, half of the students in both groups (incorrectly) acknowledged that the fear was justified. Most of them gave advice about ways to save the friendship while taking necessary precautions (e.g., using disposable utensils). At the time of the post-test, most students in the writing group pointed out that HIV could not be contracted via casual household contact, such as sharing utensils or towels. Most of them also supported their statements by providing biological explanations of reasonable conceptual depth (e.g., "You'll never get it with spit because not a lot of virus live on the spit and viruses die outside of your body"). The study suggests that a positive relationship between conceptual understanding and critical reasoning about health issues can be fostered in a classroom environment.

Although knowledge is not a sufficient condition for behavioral change, there is evidence that understanding of health concepts leads to improved health practices. Recently, much of consumer health research has focused on the study of health literacy, or "the degree to which individuals have the capacity to obtain, process, and understand basic information and services needed to make appropriate decisions regarding their health" (Nielsen-Bohlman, Panzer, & Kindig, 2004). While health literacy is a concept that is distinct from conceptual knowledge, studies suggest that health literacy is independently related to disease knowledge among patients (Gazmararian, Williams, Peel, & Baker,

2003). Studies in domains ranging from diabetes to HIV show that inadequate health literacy is related to suboptimal health practices and lower health outcome (Baker et al., 2002; Kalichman et al., 2000; Schillinger et al., 2002).

Donovan and Ward (2001) developed an intervention that aimed to facilitate patients' coping with cancer pain (RIDPAIN). The intervention was based on the recognition that the beliefs that form an individual's cognitive representation of an illness create the basis for reacting to new information and making decisions. Traditional interventions typically teach new coping skills without first addressing misconceptions in existing beliefs. Donovan and Ward argue that such interventions provide knowledge inconsistent with existing beliefs, and thus less likely to be translated into behavior.

Donovan and Ward propose a "representational approach" to patient education. Steps of their intervention are based on Leventhal's common-sense model (CSM), which proposes that individual's representation of illness has five core components: identity, cause, timeline, consequences, and cure or control (Leventhal & Diefenbach, 1991). The first step of the intervention is representational assessment, during which patients describe their beliefs about their illness along the five dimensions of the CSM. In the second step, a nurse helps patients explore their misconceptions. In the third step the nurse and the patients describe the problems associated with misconceptions, thus setting the ground for conceptual change. The fourth step involves correcting misconceptions and filling knowledge gaps with accurate information. The final step involves summarizing new information and discussing its benefits. Assessment of RIDPAIN showed that participants held a wide range of misconceptions about cancer pain management. Of the 77% of participants who participated in a follow-up two months after the intervention, 83% said the intervention had changed their understanding of pain medication, 85% said they felt more confident using pain medication, and 57% reported changes in their pain management as a result of the intervention.

At present, only a few works examine the effect of conceptual change in the domain of health as it relates to health behavior. The work in this area is distributed across a range of disciplines. Studies in science education and cognitive psychology focus on conceptual understanding and learning, but do not necessarily relate them to behavioral change. Studies in public health focus on health behavior, but treat health knowledge as a collection of facts that can be adequately assessed via survey methodology. Relating conceptual knowledge to health behavior is a challenging task, because barriers to translating knowledge into action range from non-cognitive (e.g., social support) to cognitive (e.g., deficiencies in lay reasoning). However, the requirement for educated health consumerism calls for a dialogue and an integration of knowledge amassed by the communities of science education and psychology on one hand, and health education and public health on the other.

PATIENTS' UNDERSTANDING AND MANAGEMENT OF CHRONIC ILLNESS

More than 100 million individuals suffer from chronic illness in the United States (National Academy on an Aging Society Report, 1999), and it has been reported that healthcare for people with chronic disease consumes approximately 78% of all healthcare spending in this country (Information Technology Association of America E-Health Committee, 2004). In particular, the prevalence of type 2 diabetes has increased rapidly in the past two decades and is projected to continue to grow at this rapid pace (Schulze & Hu, 2005). Patient self-management is increasingly seen as a necessary adjunct to the currently strained healthcare system (Wagner & Groves, 2002).

Recent advances in health information technologies promise to improve the quality of care and quality of life for chronically ill individuals. However, substantial challenges remain in targeting "digital divide" populations who are likely to be older, less educated, and novice computer users. There are a number of barriers that preclude chronically ill patients from employing health technologies productively (Kaufman et al., 2003). Low health literacy and the lack of adequate domain knowledge represent an impediment to adopting and maintaining a self-management program. For example, diabetes patients with inadequate health literacy were more likely to have poor control of their blood sugar and associated complications (Schillinger et al, 2002). Low health literacy can limit patient understanding of information about treatments and outcomes and is a barrier to participation in the decision-making process. Diabetes self-management necessitates a basic understanding of blood glucose regulation and metabolism. In addition to measuring their blood glucose, patients with diabetes must carefully regulate their diet, exercise, and stress levels.

Lippa and Klein (2006) studied the different ways in which people understood diabetes. They focused on three particular areas of knowledge: (1) problem detection, which involves perceiving, through experienced symptoms or through measuring blood glucose, abnormally high or low glucose values; (2) functional relationships, which involve recognizing the cause or potential cause of an abnormal value (e.g., diet, exercise, medication), and (3) problem solving, which involves taking effective action (e.g., half a glass of orange juice to ameliorate low blood glucose) to restore a glucose imbalance. The authors characterized a progression of mental models beginning with rudimentary models of self-management in which the patient was lacking a basic understanding of how to gain control. The majority of subjects possessed a "recipe model" which involves following procedures ritualistically and a basic understanding of their consequences (e.g., too much bread will raise blood sugar levels). These patients had relatively little insight into their illness and reported leaving the decision making to healthcare professionals. Such a model works fine under routine circumstances, but not under conditions of unexpected events. The "control model" involved a more sophisticated understanding of glucose regulation. These patients understood that the problem involved several interacting factors and were able to use this knowledge to guide their behavior, provide an explanatory mechanism, and facilitate prediction of future events (e.g., effects of food intake on tomorrow's blood glucose levels).

It is likely that patients with different mental models of their illness will respond differently to diabetes education and e-health initiatives. Kaufman and colleagues (2003, 2006) conducted a cognitive evaluation of older adults with diabetes use of a comprehensive telemedicine system. They documented a range of problems, many of which can be subsumed under the following three categories: (1) perceptual–motor skills, especially in relation to the use of the mouse, (2) mental models, which refer to a basic understanding of the system, and (3) health literacy, including literacy and numeracy. One of the most striking findings corresponded to problems with numeracy and representational fluency (e.g., ability to read a table or understand a chart). Kaufman et al. (2003) observed patients who had varying levels of difficulty in reading a table of their glucose and blood pressure values. Interestingly, some participants who could readily read their blood pressure values off the meter were not able to recognize a representation of the same values in a tabular form. In addition, individuals who had maintained blood glucose logs for many years were not able to understand the tabular representations in which the values are embodied in rows and cells. This limitation precluded them from effectively using the web-based record system to monitor their changes in blood pressure and blood glucose.

In order to promote health among seniors and reduce healthcare disparities, it is essential that we enable older adults and other "digital divide individuals" to use health information tools effectively. The Internet is emerging as a vital resource for consumers for health information and is increasingly serving as a mediator of health education, health-related decision making and healthcare management. However, the substantial digital divide among the elderly, especially those who are from lower SES strata, less educated, and from ethnic and racial minorities, often leaves those who are most in need with less access to health information. In response to this problem, various educational initiatives have targeted low-SES seniors with a view to training them to use online health information more productively and to become agents of change in managing their own health (Kaufman & Rockoff, 2006).

CONSUMER HEALTH VOCABULARY

The non-normative nature of lay health knowledge points to the problem of the gap between lay and professional understanding of health concepts. When lay people and health professionals use language to communicate with each other, the gulf of under-standing translates into a language gap. Studies show that both gaps contribute to misunderstandings and the loss of crucial information on both sides, and may reduced compliance with medical recommendations (Patel, Arocha, & Kushniruk, 2002; Ong, de Haes, Hoos, & Lammes, 1995; Quirt et al., 1997; Chapman, Abraham, Jenkins, & Fallowfield, 2003). This problem becomes even more prominent in the area of e-health (e.g., health-oriented Internet sites and decision support tools), which does not allow the negotiation of meaning through clarifications. Conceptual change research may guide consumer health informatics work on bridging the gap between lay and professional health terms and concepts.

In order to communicate with the lay public effectively, health professionals and designers of e-health tools need to (1) understand lay cognitive representations of health concepts and (2) know the terms that lay individuals use to refer to those concepts. One of the challenges lies in understanding the relationship between lay health terms and concepts. Depending on the nature of this relationship, the gap may be primarily terminological or primarily conceptual. In the case of a primarily terminological gap, an individual's understanding of a health concept is relatively normative, but the term used to refer to the concept is not part of any standard medical vocabulary. Examples of such non-standard terms include "high blood" as a term for hypertension and "locked bowels" as a term for constipation (Sugarman & Butters, 1985). Conceptual gaps occur when lay individuals use standard biomedical terms, but their understanding of the underlying concepts is different from that of health professionals. For example, the patient may use the term "hypertension," understanding it as "nervous" or "easily upset" (Gibbs, Gibbs, & Henrich, 1987). We can propose two hypotheses: that conceptual gaps are more difficult to detect and correct and that misunderstandings between lay individuals and health professionals are probably attributable to both conceptual and terminological gaps.

With respect to e-health communication, the crux of the problem lies in mapping lay and professional health terms and concepts in a consistent, comprehensive manner that could be converted into a computational algorithm. Compared to concept mapping, the problem of terminological matching is more manageable, and initiatives in the field of consumer health informatics are addressing the challenge. One such project is the Consumer Health Vocabulary Initiative, conducted jointly by the Decision Systems Group at Harvard Medical School and the National Library of Medicine (www.consumer healthvocab.org). The project combines computational and human review approaches in order to extract consumer health terms from the body of search queries submitted to MedlinePlus (an online health information resource of the US National Library of Medicine) and relate these terms to entries in formal biomedical vocabularies (Zeng & Tse, 2006).

The rationale for relating consumer health terms to biomedical terms is developing software tools that help lay individuals seek health information online. Search engines with access to consumer health vocabularies will connect searchers to relevant documents, even when searchers formulate their queries in non-standard terms (e.g., "clot buster" for "thrombolytic agents"). Making use of consumer health terms in consumer health materials is also likely to improve their comprehension. However, in order to meet lay individuals' health information needs and provide them with clear, comprehensible information, we need to reach beyond surface-level term familiarity, relate it to the domain of conceptual understanding.

Keselman, Kaufman, Kramer, & Patel (2007) conducted a pilot study, presenting 52 health consumers with a survey instrument, assessing surface-level and conceptual familiarity with 15 health terms. Surface-level familiarity test items assessed participants' ability to associate health terms with relevant terms at a super-category level (e.g., sphincter → muscle). Concept familiarity test items assessed the ability to associate written terms with brief phrases describing the meaning or "gists" (e.g., sphincter → a ring of muscles that opens and closes). Each multiple-choice question included four answer options: one correct answer, two plausible "distractors," and the "don't know" option. The terms varied in the frequency with which they could be found across a range of consumer health information resources. A regression model converted these frequencies into predicted "term familiarity likelihood" scores. Results showed that while familiarity likelihood scores predicted both surface-level/terminological and conceptual familiarity, conceptual familiarity scores continuously lagged behind surface level familiarity scores. The gap between surface-level and conceptual familiarity scores was greater for "easy" terms, predicted as "likely" to be familiar. While the findings of this pilot study should not be viewed as conclusive evidence, they caution developers of consumer health vocabularies against equating knowledge of terms with a genuine understanding of the underlying concept. Moreover, the nature and degree of the gap between terminological and conceptual knowledge is likely to be affected by a number of factors. Understanding these factors may be essential for developing software tools to support consumer health information seeking. The fields of cognitive psychology and science education can provide consumer health information specialists with the language and the methods for an in-depth analysis of these issues.

SUMMARY AND DISCUSSION

The current health system encourages lay individuals to be active participants in their care. Not surprisingly, many individuals are ill-prepared to take on such a role. Research presented in this chapter has been oriented toward documenting the barriers to participation. On one hand, individuals have a lifetime of experience grappling with health concepts and lay health beliefs have a certain measure of causal coherence. On the other hand, lay knowledge lacks the depth and breadth of professional understanding. An even more significant characteristic of lay knowledge is the discrepancy between formal and cultural/experiential knowledge which is apparent across cultures. Causality is not always biomedical causality, and stability of experiential and cultural beliefs may supersede accurate formal knowledge. This was in evidence in the study of middle school students' understanding of HIV and Indian mothers' understanding of childhood nutritional disorders. Culturally and socially grounded beliefs about health were shown to exert a powerful role in subjects' reasoning.

As in other domains of science (e.g., Vosniadou, 1994), health concepts can be characterized in terms of progressions of models of understanding, with more advanced models of understanding providing a better basis for critical thinking. Keselman and colleagues (2004) demonstrated that students' understanding of concepts related to HIV affected their ability to reason about myths pertaining to the cause and spread of the virus. A follow-up study demonstrated that an educational intervention targeting understanding could result in genuine conceptual change and facilitate critical reasoning and problem-solving. Strengthening the ties between biology and health sciences education could potentially achieve greater understanding in ways that public health alone could not possibly achieve.

An individual's conceptual models of disease and treatment can impact their quality of health and their ability to effectively adhere to certain regimens. It is also associated with their ability to participate effectively in various e-health initiatives. In this context, depth of conceptual understanding has real consequences and is very likely to influence health outcomes. Efforts to educate lay people in both school and medical settings are promising. Technology provides an additional resource, but many are prevented from benefiting because of the digital divide. In terms of doctor–patient communication, a vocabulary gap may also contribute to the lack of mutual understanding. Health cognition is an emerging research discipline and at present lacks a stable mature paradigms characteristic of medical cognition research. More theory-based research and interventions are needed.

REFERENCES

Au, T. K. F., & Romo, L. F. (1999). Mechanical causality in children's "folkbiology". In D. L. Medin & S. Atran (Eds.), *Folkbiology* (pp. 355–401). Cambridge, MA: MIT Press.

Baker, D. W., Gazmararian, J. A., Williams M. V., Scott, T., Parker, R. M., Green, D., et al. (2002). Functional health literacy and the risk of hospital admission among Medicare managed care enrollees. *American Journal of Public Health, 92*(8), 1278–1283.

Bogart, L. M., & Thorburn, S. (2005). Are HIV/AIDS conspiracy beliefs a barrier to HIV prevention among African Americans? *Journal of Acquired Immune Deficiency Syndromes, 38*(2), 213–218.

Chapman, K., Abraham, C., Jenkins, V., & Fallowfield, L. (2003). Lay understanding of terms used in cancer consultations. *Psycho-Oncology, 12*(6), 557–566.

Donovan, H., & Ward, S. (2001). A representational approach to patient education. *Journal of Nursing Scholarship*, *33*(3), 211–216.

Driver, R., Asoko, H., Leach, J., Mortimer, E., & Scott, P. (1994). Constructing scientific knowledge in the classroom. *Educational Researcher*, *23*(7), 5–12.

Gazmararian, J. A., Williams, M. V., Peel, J., & Baker, D. W. (2003). Health literacy and knowledge of chronic disease. *Patient Education and Counseling*, *51*(3), 267–275.

Gibbs, R., Gibbs, P., & Henrich, J. (1987). Patient understanding of commonly used medical vocabulary. *Journal of Family Practice*, *25*(2), 176–178.

Hack, T. F., Degner, L. F., Parker, P. A., & The SCRN Communication Team. (2005). The communication goals and needs of cancer patients: A review. *Psycho-oncology*, *14*(10), 831–845.

Information Technology Association of America E-Health Committee. (2004). *Chronic care improvement: How Medicare transformation can save lives, save money and stimulate an emerging technology industry.* Arlington, VA: Information Technology Association of America.

Kalichman, S. C., Benotsch, E., Suarez, T., Catz, S., Miller, J., & Rompa, D. (2000). Health literacy and health-related knowledge among persons living with HIV/AIDS. *American Journal of Preventive Medicine*, *18*, 325–331.

Kaufman, D. R., Patel, V. L., Hilliman, C., Morin, P.C., Pevzner, J, Weinstock, R. S., et al. (2003). Usability in the real world: Assessing medical information technologies in patients' homes. *Journal of Biomedical Informatics*, *36*(1&2), 45–60.

Kaufman, D. R., Pevzner, J., Hilliman, C., Weinstock, R. S., Teresi, J. Shea, S., et al. (2006). Re-designing a telehealth diabetes management program for a digital divide seniors population. *Home, Healthcare, Management & Practice*, *18*(3), 223–234.

Kaufman, D. R. & Rockoff, M. L. (2006). Promoting online health information-seeking in seniors: A community-based organizations approach. *Generations*, *30*(2), 55–57.

Keselman A., Kaufman, D. R., Kramer, S., & Patel, V. L. (2007). Fostering conceptual change and critical reasoning about HIV and AIDS. *Journal of Research in Science Teaching*, *44*(6), 844–863.

Keselman, A., Kaufman, D. R., & Patel, V. L. (2004). "You can exercise your way out of HIV" and other stories: The role of biological knowledge in adolescents' evaluation of myths. *Journal of Science Education*, *88*(4), 548–573.

Kim, N. S., & Ahn, W. (2002). The influence of naïve causal theories on lay concepts of mental illness. *American Journal of Psychology*, *115*(1), 33–65.

Leventhal, H., & Diefenbach, M. (1991). The active side of illness cognition. In J. A. Skelton & R. T. Croyle (Eds.), *Mental representations in health and illness* (pp. 247–272). New York, NY: Springer Verlag.

Lippa, K. D. & Klein, H. A. (2006). How patients understand diabetes self care. *Proceedings of the 50th Annual Meeting of the Human Factors and Ergonomic Society*, San Francisco, CA.

McGregor, S. (2003). What information patients with localised prostate cancer hear and understand. *Patient Education and Counseling*, *49*(3), 273–278.

Mull, D. S. (1991). Traditional perceptions of marasmus in Pakistan. *Social Science and Medicine*, *32*(2), 175–191.

National Academy on an Aging Society Report. (1999). *Chronic conditions: A challenge for the 21st century.* Washington, DC: Gerontological Society of America.

Nielsen-Bohlman, L., Panzer, A. M., & Kindig, D. A. (2004). *Health literacy: A prescription to end confusion.* Washington, DC: Institute of Medicine, The National Academies Press.

Ong, L. M., de Haes, J. C. J. M., Hoos, A. M., & Lammes, F. B. (1995). Doctor–patient communication: A review of the literature. *Social Science and Medicine*, *40*(10), 903–918.

Patel, V. L., Arocha, J., & Kushniruk, A. W. (2002). Patients' and physicians' understanding of health and biomedical concepts: Relationship to the design of EMR systems. *Journal of Biomedical Informatics*, *35*(1), 8–16.

Patel, V. L., Kaufman, D. R., & Arocha, J. F. (2000). Conceptual change in the biomedical and health sciences domain. In R. Glaser (Ed.), *Advances in instructional psychology* (pp. 329–392). Hillsdale, NJ: Lawrence Erlbaum Associates.

Quirt, C. F., Mackillop, W. J., Ginsburg, A. D., Sheldon, L., Brundage, M., Dixon, P., et al. (1997). Do doctors know when their patients don't? A survey of doctor–patient communication in lung cancer. *Lung Cancer*, *18*(1), 1–20.

Ross, M. W., Essien, E. J., & Torres, I. (2006). Conspiracy beliefs about the origin of HIV/AIDS in four racial/ethnic groups. *Journal of Acquired Immune Deficiency Syndromes*, *41*(3), 342–344.

Schillinger, D., Grumbach, K., Piette, J., Wang, F., Osmond, D., Daher, C., et al. (2002). Association of health literacy with diabetes outcomes. *Journal of the American Medical Association*, *288*(4), 475–482.

Schulze, M. B., & Hu, F. B. (2005). Primary prevention of diabetes: What can be done and how much can be prevented? *Annual Review of Public Health*, *26*, 445–467.

Sivaramakrishnan, M., & Patel, V.L. (1993). Reasoning about childhood nutritional deficiencies by mothers in rural India: A cognitive analysis. *Social Science & Medicine, 37*(7), 937–952.

Sugarman, J., & Butters, R. R. (1985). Understanding the patient: Medical words the doctor may not know. *North Carolina Medical Journal, 46*(7), 415.

Wagner, E., & Groves, T. (2002). Care for chronic diseases. *British Medical Journal, 325*(7370), 913–914.

Vosniadou, S. (1994). Conceptual change in the physical sciences. *Learning and Instruction,, 4*(1), 121.

Zeng, Q. T. & Tse, T. (2006). Exploring and developing consumer health vocabularies. *Journal of American Medical Informatics Association, 13*(1), 24–29.

13

CHANGING HISTORICAL CONCEPTIONS OF HISTORY

Gaea Leinhardt and Anita Ravi,
University of Pittsburgh and Alliance College-Ready Public Schools

The issue of conceptual change is not normally the framing idea for discussions about historical knowledge, reasoning, learning, or disciplinary progress. The exception is the work of Torney-Purta (1994) in which she uses the ideas of ontological shift suggested by Chi (1992) to examine the reasoning of adolescents as they include a more varied array of political and historical causes in their reasoning tasks. Unfortunately, however, the careful psychological work that she conducted is somewhat sparse from the historical point of view. If we coordinate the idea of changing ideas about what history is; that is, engage in some historical analysis, with the examination of a simple case of historical reasoning we might make some progress in the direction of considering conceptual change in history more deeply. In this chapter we start by considering a range of differing definitions of the scope and purposes of history, drawing on authors from Herodotus to Schama. These definitions range from history as a singular heroic, accurate, causal account (of, say, the Persian Wars and their causes) to history as an interpretation of conditions and perspectives that surround a particular circumstance (of, say, the role of landscape in historical memory) and back to a characterization of national identity through historical accounts. Within any of these definitions, assumptions are made such as honesty, completeness, and accuracy of the account as well as public identification of the author. We use these alternative purposes and definitions of history as the bases for an exploration of one easily understood example of an historical event, the *Boston Massacre*, and consider what challenges these issues might pose for the learner.

The Boston Massacre is often considered a defining moment for the start of the American Revolution. Yet it is a curious event, and it is unclear why this event is selected from an array of similar, and often far more powerful, moments of conflict as a major focus in the events leading up to the American Revolution. Thus, we use this event as a lens to show how the "history" has moved from heroic narrative to contentious argument surrounding ideas of law and order. We then conclude with hints at an answer to the questions of why this event and not some other one is particularly anointed. We use these discussions as a way to consider some fragments of empirical work on the ways in which students come to understand history as a constructed, contested, and authored account. We discuss Peter Lee and Roslyn Ashby's developmental account of students' beliefs about history; consider the trace of one student's learning over time in one classroom to examine the ways in which conceptual change might support the developing under-standings and competencies of the student; and show how one of several interventions to support conceptual growth (and perhaps change) seems to have succeeded.

SOME IMPORTANT DISTINCTIONS

Consider how Herodotus (writing in the mid-5th century BCE) opens his accounts of the Persian Wars:

> Herodotus of Helicarnassus hereby publishes the results of his inquiries, hoping to do two things: to preserve the memory of the past by putting on record the astonishing achievements of both the Greek and the non-Greek peoples; and more particularly, to show how the two races came into conflict.
>
> (Goold, 1920; Herodotus, 1987, 2006)[1]

There are several important elements in these sentences. First, Herodotus identifies himself in the text; he is not an anonymous committee of authors. Second, he tells us where he is from so we can infer his position with regard to the people and activities he describes; he does not just give a publisher's address. Third, he tells us why he is writing the account, namely to preserve the memory of astonishing achievements and to show HOW the conflict arose. (The reader is invited to consider Schama's (1995) *Landscape and Memory* (p. 3) and Mann's (2005) *1491* (p. ix) for similar modern actions.) Thus, Herodotus chose to cover both the events and the surrounding culture of the main actors. Herodotus, the narrator, tells us that he is responsible for his words and that he knows these things because they were told to him or he saw them. What is challenging for the student is not the history in and of itself but the presence of the historian who must also be understood. The layered and evolving nature of history is one of the hallmarks of historical thinking, as Collingwood (1946) and von Wright (1971) both pointed out.

By 400 BCE the central elements of the discipline of history were in place: identifiable authorship, stated sources, commitment to accuracy, and stated purpose for the particular account. The form of historical account was also set as distinctly narrative. None of the major branches of science can make the same claims about structure and form. Only the arts and mathematics might present such a suggestion. This means that the idea of conceptual change either of person or of field has a slightly different cast in history than it might have in other fields. To review, history is told by a specific historian with a known position *vis-à-vis* the account given, it has a purpose that is stated in any given account, and it has a commitment to accuracy. From the very earliest times, then, readers or hearers of historical accounts were aware that who was telling the tale had something to do with what was being said and why.

Simon Schama (1991) adds to this set of issues some others. In a piece in the *New York Times Magazine*, "Clio Has a Problem," he writes:

> History isn't a how-to manual full of analogies to explain whatever this week's crisis happens to be—Saddam as Hitler, Kuwait as Munich—and certainly not some care-

fully prepared tonic for self-esteem. As an irreproachable historian, R. G. Collingwood, once put it, we study what man has done to discover what man is. History is an indispensable form of self-knowledge . . . To know our past is to grow up. History's mission, then, is to illuminate the human condition from the witness of memory . . . History has always been "a debatable land" as Macaulay noted. "It lies on the confines of two distinct territories. It is under the jurisdiction of two hostile powers . . . Instead of being equally shared between its two rulers, the Reason and the Imagination, it falls alternately under the sole and absolute domination of each.

(p. 32)

In this short essay, Schama argues for a particular kind of constrained purpose in doing history and the need for narrative in historical accounts. This nuance adds to the task of the student: S/he must learn the content, the author, and the style, and must recognize the way each influences the others.

WHAT COUNTS AS HISTORY?

The non-historian often makes several naïve assumptions about history. First, everything that happened in the past counts as history. Thus, the task of history is to build a complete and neutral account of the sequence of events. The second naïve assumption is that the major "problem" for history is getting the smallest of details correct in some archeological sense. These two assumptions have some truth, since history is a domain constrained by chronology and it strives to be accurate with respect to the details of actions and actors. However, history as a domain is concerned primarily with the selection and interpretation of events and situations from the past, not simply a complete recording of all that has ever happened. Because some things are selected and other things are left unmentioned, there is an inherent interpretation. And, because there is a purposiveness there is also a sense of argumentation within any good historical narrative. Historians have an obligation to keep repositioning themselves with respect to new understandings and appreciation of different "voices" that might be salient for any given account.

What counts as history is important things that happened in the past. But what is or is not important? According to Homer, Herodotus, and Thucydides, what is important is the epic struggles of men and the personal (or god-derived) flaws that make them win or lose. The naïve learner may assume that whatever is presented is by definition important and what is not presented is not important. Modern historians have noted other things that might be important, should not be forgotten, but are at risk of being forgotten; these phenomena are more likely to be related to large amorphous social movements, such as the struggle for women's right to vote, or for labor groups to organize, or the personal and social limitations of warring factions that emerge from familial practices (see Mallon, 1983); or they may find a particular aspect of human thought significant (see Schama, 1995). The accounts of Herodotus and Thucydides focus on the ways men come into conflict and the accuracy of those accounts; there are other struggles that they chose not to discuss. Picking and choosing the events, social systems, ways of thinking, and historical actors is a part of historical activity.

The preservation of memory is also a function of history, and, in turn, what is preserved in memory becomes the fodder for history. In this sense, history can be taken to be a remembrance of the purely local because for that community it is "important."

Such local memorabilia may be associated with cultural heroes from a community. For example, there is very small museum in Puerto Rico devoted to Pablo Casals. The National Library of Wales (www.llgc.org.uk) has chosen to catalogue, in its virtual museum, the existence of a unique website dealing with issues of substance abuse worldwide, which was developed and maintained by Jim Young, alongside reproductions of the oldest Welsh Bible and the earliest book printed in Welsh (*Yny lhyvyr hwnn*). On the volcanic Western Islands of Vestmannaeyjar in Iceland one can find a small building containing various war memorabilia, swords, medals, and orders, from Icelandic soldiers of the First World War. Pablo Casals is memorialized historically as the son of a Puerto Rican mother; Jim Young is honored as a creative Welsh member of the Internet generation working for social good; the Bible (and book) written in Welsh are symbols of the preservation of the national language and its connection to both the religious and modern world; and finally the swords and medals residing in a small corner of Iceland connect a local population with a sweep of larger world events. Each example illustrates local efforts to preserve memory and commemorate local citizens' roles in the larger historical context. As Sam Wineburg (Wineburg, Mosborg, Porat, & Duncan, 2007; Wineburg, 2001) and his colleagues have pointed out, these memories, whether formally preserved or not, are often ignored or denigrated by the formal historical account – yet it is the intergenerational memories that tend to survive over time. They form the contested space surrounding a more formal account. This "memory" constitutes one of the first challenges to learning history. We "learn" history through familial tales, through modern movies set in the past, through religious texts, through museums and monuments, and through scholarly texts. The sophisticated student of history may develop the capacity of "epistemic switching" noted by Gottlieb and Wineburg (2012).

We have *multiple meanings* of history, then. One is the pure complete account, an account that permits accurate reenactment and commemoration; a second is an epic heroic tale of national identity and virtue; and a third is a contentious, argued, analytic, and interpretive account. The assertion being made in this chapter is that conceptual change in history means moving from a singular account of either of the first two to a challenged account of the third. What is challenged in the latter approach is not so much the facts of a given case but the meaning of it – when it began and ended (periodicity), how it was perceived by others at the time (vantage point), how it is authored (sourcing), and what portions of the record remain for use and interpretation (selection). The conceptual change we seek to describe for both the discipline and the learner is the movement from notions of history as story to history as the conditions and considerations that produce the "story."

WORKING THROUGH AN EXAMPLE:
THE BOSTON MASSACRE

On the night of March 5, 1770, a small conflict took place between a group of civilians in Boston and a group of British soldiers stationed there. The result was that five men were shot and killed by the British soldiers. During the 1770s there were numerous events that were similar to this one, including an event six weeks earlier in which a young boy had been killed by British troops (Zobel, 1970). Why then is this particular skirmish so important in the national consciousness that it is present in virtually every US history textbook? To begin to explore that question more carefully we need to consider some paradigmatic accounts that fit with the issues of history discussed above: the accurate reenactment account and the epic tale account.

As recently as 2005 the History Channel on US television presented a special on the Boston Massacre in which the entire focus was on whether or not Crispus Attucks was the first man to fall in the lead-up to the Revolution. Historians, doctors, and an armament specialist were all consulted and gave grave statements on camera. Careful reconstructions of the scene based on testimony from the second trial that emerged from the incident (the first trial notes having been lost), from re-firing of rifles of the day, and from medical testimony about Attucks' wounds claimed to have solved this historical "mystery." Why is that important? Crispus Attucks was of African descent, and the fact that writers of the day and later poet laureates proclaimed he was the first fallen son has a certain historical irony. In this example the tools of scientific analysis are marshaled to "prove" the accuracy of a particular historical claim. But the account overall is rather ahistorical.[2]

Two competing and conflicting national identity accounts also exist. These weave their way through US history textbooks depending on the political mood of the country over the course of the 20th century. In the first account, brave unarmed patriots confront surly occupying British troops and throw snowballs at them. The cruel British troops fire into the unarmed crowd and kill the patriots. The citizens of Boston and the surrounding communities arrange a somber and very large funeral for the fallen men, the occupying forces retreat to an island in Boston harbor, and the community ultimately honors the patriots with a monument on the Boston Commons and a brass plaque in the street where the event took place. What is noble and to be remembered is the *sacrifice for freedom*. In the second account, an unruly mob pesters, badmouths, and assaults frightened, cold, young conscripts unwillingly stationed in Boston. Although not armed with guns, the mob is armed with ice balls laced with shellfish shells and small rocks, and large wooden staves. They taunt the troops, daring them to fire, and they hit them with their staves. Accidentally the troops start to fire, church bells are rung, the mob increases in size, and the troops retreat. Both the acting governor, Hutchinson, and the military leader in charge promptly arrest the British men involved. Fearful of further mob action, the American patriot and future president, John Adams – cousin of the firebrand leader of the Sons of Liberty, Sam Adams – agrees to defend the soldiers in a court of law. Adams' sense of fairness and justice saves the day and the men are acquitted and sent home. What is to be remembered here is the value of *law* over mob rule, *and* the importance of *justice* even when it does not support personal political aims.

Both of these versions serve the purpose of history as a national identity account. Both versions are routinely presented in US history textbooks. But the historical significance of this small event and the work of historical account construction is seriously masked by all three accounts, the TV and the textbook ones. These three kinds of accounts also change as conceptions of what history is change.

What does an altered account look like? Let's consider four features that would produce a more nuanced account. First, when did this episode begin and when did it end? This issue is referred to as *periodicity*; the ambiguity surrounding the beginning and ending of a particular historical phenomenon is one location where differences in meaning may be worked out (see Lee, 2005; Lee & Ashby, 2000; Mann, 2011; and Megill, 1994). Second, what happened (most probably) and what were the reactions to it? Interpretive actions in history require fidelity to the record, not just any old story; pieces are selected in order to form the *argument* being made (Voss, 1998; Voss & Wiley, 2006). Third, who wrote the account and for what purposes? The *source* of an account, as several have noted (Britt, Rouet, Georgi, & Perfetti, 1994; Wineburg, 1991, 1994), becomes quite invisible to the student reader, who tends to read through the account like a window and does not see the purposive moves of the author. Fourth, how have we chosen to remember this event and why, and who benefits from keeping the *memory* alive (Seixas, Peck, & Poyntz, 2011)?

At first pass, the event (as contrasted to a social system or process) is perhaps the cleanest, most concrete way of describing the past: It is located in a specific time and place; particular individuals are involved; there is a narrative structure to it that gives a beginning, middle, and end; and one can speak of the impact, or significance, of the event. So one could say that the Boston Massacre took place on March 5, 1770, for example, and explicate the event from there. However, the concept of causality challenges the simple narrative details. Although the event did happen on March 5, 1770, the particular causes of this event call into question both the beginning point and the end of this conflict as well as its ramifications. Some might argue that the roots of the Boston Massacre lie in the Stamp Act riots of 1763 when, in response to British-imposed taxes on everyday paper items such as newsprint and marriage licenses, farmers and townspeople in central Massachusetts dragged a British tax collector out of his office and tarred and feathered him, initiating a series of riots in which similar behavior was repeated elsewhere in the colonies. This "mob" action in response to British policy was the first overtly violent series of events in which people lost their lives. Others might argue that the roots or beginnings of the Boston Massacre lie in the arrival of thousands of British troops in Boston in 1768. By order of the British government via the Quartering Act of 1765, Bostonians were compelled to provide housing for these soldiers. Needless to say, most refused to house the soldiers, who were seen as a hostile imposition by a distant government, and as a result, the soldiers were left to camp outdoors during some very cold Boston winters. The mere presence of 4,000 soldiers in a city of 15,000 residents led to countless conflicts and skirmishes between colonists and soldiers in the two years leading up to March 5, 1770. Still others (Beard & Beard, 1943; Zinn, 2003) might argue that this was at heart a labor dispute between the poor dockworkers and the unpaid and cold soldiers who scavenged for work and had been in a serious scuffle early on the day of March 5. Choosing one of the three "beginnings" mentioned above (or others) is essential to the construction of a historical narrative of the event. Each choice implies that relevant evidence be brought to bear in defense of that choice. The task is not to create an "accurate" account of the event *per se*, although accuracy is a primary tenet of the discipline. The task is to create a plausible argument about the causes of the Boston Massacre that takes account of historical evidence and also requires the historian to impose an order on the past by selecting relevant material to make the argument.

Making the argument about the beginning of an event also requires selecting and defending an ending point. The process of making a case for the end-point requires that the historian consider why the event has been called up in the first place – its historical purpose and standing in a particular account. If one were making the case that the Boston Massacre event was really an instance in which the rule of law was summoned to put an end to the perceived lawlessness of the "mob," then the ending to this story would lie with the trial and release of the seven British soldiers. Defended by none other than John Adams, future third president of the United States, these soldiers were found not guilty of murder. In defending the troops, Adams knew he was taking an unpopular position. But Adams was a complicated figure. He feared and hated mob violence. He believed in and respected the law. He also understood politically that if increased governance within the Colony was a goal, then it had to be shown that real law was supported and followed.

If one were making the case that the Boston Massacre was one in a series of many events in which the "common man" took matters into his own hands to protest the policies of a faraway and unresponsive government, then one could argue that the end of this type of conflict comes years after the end of the Revolution: with Shays' Rebellion in 1787. In this case, the primary conflict was between the newly formed state government of Massachusetts and a group of farmers in Western Massachusetts who were about to lose their farms due to their inability to pay taxes. These citizens felt that an undue burden was being placed on them financially by a faraway state government in Boston run primarily by merchants. Each year, their pleas to the government to help revive the local economy fell on deaf ears. In 1786 these farmers, led by Daniel Shays, protested yet another tax placed on whiskey. In 1787, on the eve of many foreclosures, Shays and several thousand followers raided the local armory in Springfield (the largest store of guns and ammunition in New England) and proceeded to do battle with soldiers representing their own state government. Although they lost the battle, their efforts were enough to initiate a constitutional convention and the creation of a new government, thus provoking the government to be responsive to those it represented (Richards, 2002).

Finally, if one were making the case that the Boston Massacre represented yet another instance in which the colonists, writ large, forced the British to reverse their policies once again (as they had done with the Stamp Act), then one could argue that the ending lies with the removal of the British soldiers to Castle Rock, an island off the coast of Massachusetts, immediately following the event. The initial arrival of 4,000 troops into the city of Boston was meant to assert a huge presence in a city that was thought to be unruly and mobbish to begin with. When the British government agreed to the removal of the troops, at the urging of Massachusetts colonial governor Hutchinson, it was prior to the trial and marked a retreat from this original intent.

Although the beginnings and endings of a particular historical account may shift, this does not mean that the account is up for grabs. Rather, what the historian selects as the beginning and end-point have particular purposes in the construction of the account *and where it sits* in the broader stream of history – in this case, where the Boston Massacre sits in the stream of events leading up to, or perhaps immediately following, the American Revolution. As the historian brings relevant accurate information to bear, it is brought with a purposeful argument in mind.

We have considered the periodicity, or beginnings and endings, of historical accounts as one feature that defines the practice and construction of history. Next we will consider describing "what happened" and how historical actors reacted at the time of the event. In the first sentence of Herodotus' *The Peloponnesian Wars*, one of his goals was "to show how the two races came into conflict." In other words, he intended to tell the story of a particular conflict, recounting "what happened." In seeking to describe accurately "what happened" before, during, and after a specific event, modern historians turn to primary accounts produced by those who witnessed or experienced the event.

Almost as soon as the Boston Massacre "ended," there was a flurry of activity on the part of many individuals to get their version of the story down on paper. As a result, multiple conflicting accounts of the event appeared almost immediately. Captain

Preston, the leader of the British soldiers and participant in the event, immediately wrote a letter to his superior officers in Britain. Several newspaper accounts were generated in local newspapers throughout the colonies. Paul Revere created an engraving of the event, which depicted the British soldiers firing on a defenseless, unarmed crowd of colonists; Sam Adams dubbed the event the "Boston Massacre," even though five people died. The Revere engraving was reproduced in newspapers across the colonies as a piece of propaganda meant to incite sympathy toward the colonists and anger toward the British soldiers. Such a flurry of written activity indicates that those who participated in the event understood its importance, especially in the context of 1770s colonial America.

There had been conflicts and skirmishes between British officials and colonists since the Stamp Act Riots. Yet the significance of this event is in the particulars: The conflict took place in front of the Boston customs house, symbol of British economic control; it involved British soldiers firing on fellow citizens; and unlike the aftermath of the Stamp Act riots, the colonial leadership stepped in to take control of how the event was played out and was perceived. The trial produced its own set of newspaper reports, both in the colonies and in Great Britain, along with three sets of court transcripts of the trial. So in seeking to describe "what happened," the historian has myriad sources at his/her disposal.

The historian (and student) must be conscious of the fact that many of those sources were authored by individuals who themselves sought to put their own spin on events: to tell their own story. In constructing a narrative of this event, then, one must be aware of how the various historical actors position themselves in relation to the event as they are telling the story from their particular perspective. Maintaining fidelity to the historical record involves taking all of these features into account: what was put down on paper, the intentions of historical actors, and how the event fit into their own schema of a path toward independence.

Just as the primary sources that constitute the raw materials of history are authored, so too are the accounts produced by historians. While historians may not introduce and position themselves outright, as Herodotus did, they are very much a part of the narratives they construct. The common reference for history in the classroom is almost always the textbook: a lengthy and weighty tome whose text appears authorless, colorless, and yet authoritative (Schama, 1991). Under such weight, and stymied by the textbook committee list at the front of the book listing 10, 15, or 20 contributors, it is easy to lose sight of how even the textbook narrative was produced by specific people in a specific time and place; that it, too, is positioned. In the work of the historian, notions of periodicity and telling "what happened" are reflective of the individual telling the story. Who we are and the times in which we live play into the structure of the historical narratives we produce. The story of the Boston Massacre as recounted by Morrison and Commager in the 1930s and 1940s or by Schlesinger in the 1960s is quite different from that of Zinn in the 1980s.[3]

So the conceptual change we seek to consider in history involves notions of periodicity, selections of materials to tell what happened, and authorship. Finally, the construction of history rests on how we have chosen to remember a particular piece of history and why (what Seixas and his colleagues, 2011 refer to as the Ethical Dimensions of History). This notion of historical memory is integral to the construction of historical accounts. In the aftermath of the Boston Massacre, once the engraving made by Revere had served the purpose of inciting ire against the British, once the trial was over, there was a concerted effort on the part of the leadership of the Revolution to, as Young (1999) argues, "erase the mob side of the Revolution." The Sons of Liberty consisted of the leaders in the colonial communities – merchants, lawyers, skilled craftsmen. Not represented in this group was the "common man" – the laborers, dockworkers, shoemakers, farmers – those who participated in the events surrounding the Boston Massacre and the Stamp Act riots. The Boston Tea Party, an event that followed the Boston Massacre, was orchestrated by the Sons of Liberty, taking their cue from the types of protest initiated by the "common man" in these earlier events.

In the tradition of heroic tales of national identity, the birth of one's nation is the cornerstone of such efforts. The History Channel documentary mentioned earlier is one example of why it matters who participated in key events leading to independence. The appearance or non-appearance of Crispus Attucks in accounts of the Boston Massacre is reflective of trends in historical memory throughout our brief history. We know that Attucks was there at the Boston customs house and that he died that day. But why focus on him? What about the other colonists who died? Because he was of African descent is one answer. He represented a class of free blacks living in the north in colonial times. There is also a question as to how involved he was with the Sons of Liberty – did this group include blacks in its membership? Attucks drops out of the story for quite a while until he is resurrected as a significant historical figure in an 1888 commemoration which memorialized his participation in the Boston Massacre conflict. He is absent from accounts of the event both before and after 1888. His resurgence in high-school textbooks coincided with a movement in the late 1970s and 80s to produce a more inclusive account of US history that looked at the contributions of many different racial and ethnic groups to the historical record. Yet reviving him in this way via textbook accounts contributed to an understanding of him as a token participant. If we are to look across all the accounts produced about this one individual, then we may begin to paint a picture of his actions and contributions to the Revolutionary effort and why he is worth remembering and studying. In looking across these varied accounts we are also in dialogue with the historical memory of him as a historical figure in the mythic event that was the birth of the nation.

We have engaged in the activity of telling and retelling, stating and challenging the story of the Boston Massacre to document how the field of history itself has shifted in significant ways. The structures of the discipline as stated by Herodotus have remained as anchors but the emphasis and the meaning have changed profoundly. Peter Seixas (2000; Seixas, Peck, & Poyntz 2011) asks whether or not we should include or exclude students from this shift – some suggest that we should start with the simple single line of story and only later add the layers of complexity. However, the historian Florencia Mallon and others have no doubt as to the requirement that students be brought into the truth of the matter from the beginning (as cited in Leinhardt, Stainton, & Virji, 1994; Reisman, 2012). We turn now to considering what this might imply for the learner.

WHAT MIGHT THIS EVOLUTION IN HISTORY MEAN FOR THE STUDENT LEARNER?

What are the challenges that these different aspects of history pose to the learner? We think that there are three challenges that are complex enough to require fairly fundamental shifts of thought on the part of the student (and teacher). First, history is authored both through the selective surviving record (some things survive and others do not, and this is not a random process) and by the deliverer of a current account, and it is in competition with the memories and beliefs of the learner (Gottlieb and Wineburg, 2012; Wineburg, 2001). Second, history is argued, interpreted, and narrated by an author while he/she is maintaining a quest for truth. Third, history is selected both in terms of beginnings and endings and in terms of inclusion and omission. The first of these challenges is to keep an eye on both the history and the historian. This duality requires a somewhat continuous juggling of perspective.

In discussing the way in which ideas of learning and conceptual change might be considered from a linked perspective between the cognitive and situative, Greeno and van de Sande (2007) introduce the idea, following MacWhinney (2005), of "perspectival understanding." They define perspectival understanding as "a cognitive arrangement of entities and some of their properties, organized in relation to each other, with a point of view. The viewer may be enmeshed in the perspective (enactive/projective) or the viewer may be viewing from the outside, representing and operating on the entities in the perspective (depictive/descriptive)" (Greeno & van de Sande, 2007, p. 14). What this would mean for the student of history is that he or she would need to include in their account of the Boston Massacre the specifics of the event itself (enactive/projective) but at the same time recognize that they had learned about these specifics from an author with a viewpoint and a position. Do teachers teach this? If they do, do students "get it?"

Our first example of efforts to embed this changed definition of history in instruction and curriculum comes from the United Kingdom's national project. Lee and Ashby (2000) were part of the national effort carried out in the United Kingdom to alter history instruction so that it included not only the substantive historical content (events and people in time) but also what the authors referred to as second-order or procedural ideas (similar efforts were launched by Peter Seixas in Canada with the Historical Consciousness project (2007), and more recently by Sam Wineburg with the Reading Like a Historian project (Reisman, 2012)). The goal of the redesign of instruction was to trace the ways that ideas about the nature of history and potential historical participation changed over time and development. In the terms of Greeno and van de Sande this means that students were being queried as to their competence and awareness of perspectival shift between the contents of an account and the purposes and authoring of the account. They must bring two different cognitive aspects into focus: the account itself, and the purpose and contestation of the account.

Lee and Ashby examined the thinking and responses of a cross-section of students ranging in age from eight to 14 in four separate panels of data. Students were given a variety of tasks in which they read two short accounts of the same historical event, such as the Roman presence in the British Isles, the collapse of the Roman Empire, or the Saxon settlement of Britain. Students were then asked questions at the end of each pair of accounts, such as the following: If two historians follow the same practices and look at the same evidence, can they disagree? If there are differing accounts of when the Roman Empire ended, how could one decide when it actually ended or would there be additional dates? Is it the case that in real history there is only one true account of what happened? (All questions have been paraphrased.) These questions all relate to what Lee and Ashby referred to as secondary historical understandings and to issues of what Greeno and van de Sande (2007), following Pickering (1995), refer to as conceptual agency. What we want to describe here is how the answers to these questions help us to understand how students do or do not address the ideas of authorship, periodicity, and argument as accounts develop or change over time.

In considering the differences in selecting the date for the end of the Roman Empire, children started with one of two positions: It was a factual problem that required getting the right history, OR it was a fundamentally unknowable problem since we can not interview or talk to people who were present at the scene, so to speak (Lee & Ashby, 2000, pp. 205–207). Some children (ages 12–13) thought that perhaps one might find the scrap of paper where someone might have written it down. (The mental picture is of someone scribbling next to the grocery list, "and today Rome fell.") Still others imagined that this was an issue of error but one that could be resolved either by splitting the difference numerically (476 and 1453) or by imagining that it was a long process. A few students (some of the older ones) believed it was an issue of criteria. One would have to decide on the criteria for what should count as a collapse of the Roman Empire and then systematically apply them.

As a follow-up to this question, Lee and Ashby asked the students how one could decide. One 14-year-old came up with several criteria: Determine when Rome stopped having an influence on the rest of the world or when the "Eastern half stopped being like the old Roman Empire" (Lee & Ashby 2000, p. 208). What is especially intriguing about this level of understanding is that it suggests that the Roman Empire itself is an historical construct, not a place or a government. That is, even if the Eastern Empire stayed intact but lost the Roman ideals of citizenship and law it could be considered to have "fallen." Lee and Ashby note a developmental trend, under the influence of instruction, in student responses that moves from seeing the history as a simple matter of greater factual detail to considering the possibilities of multiple endings (a sort of tolerance for inconsistency) to working toward a criterion-based approach. The notion of layering of the historical account is most definitely included as an instructional goal from the very beginning. Further, in including the idea of authoring, Lee and Ashby rightly connect it to the other rhetorical aspects of history construction that we identified through the discussion of the Boston Massacre.

In considering ideas of why authors might come to different conclusions or write different accounts, younger students assumed that differences lay with errors while older students saw authors as positioned and in some cases as interpreting information. The Lee and Ashby work is unique in its depth, but it echoes the earlier work of Ola Halldén (1994), in which young people's ideas about the substance and procedures of history were shown to emerge over time.

Studies of history learning in the US take place in a different context from the European one. Absent recognized, agreed-upon, national standards in history; absent the ability to purchase a rich curriculum that embodies notions of history as construction; teachers, schools, and school districts in the US are left to develop their own curricula. As such, the research we have in the US is not of the same scope and scale as the Lee and Ashby work in Great Britain. However, there are important glimmerings that emerge from studies of classroom instruction in the US. In one study of student history learning at the high-school level in the US we can see through lesson transcripts that the teacher continuously prompted students to understand that their depictive accounts shared a positional feature with respect to other historians (Leinhardt, 1993). With respect to the historian the students' ideas were enmeshed, so that the historian's voice was inherently unrecognized. Consider the following excerpt from a US history class (students were approximately 15 years old) (Leinhardt, 1993, p. 57):

T: . . . That takes me to the point of Beard [a historian] saying, that these were just self-centered men who went to Philadelphia so that they would be paid, uh, for their bonds that they had taken out during the Revolutionary War . . . Was that true? . . . Or, would you modify to some extent? . . .

S1: Yes.

T: We have a Beardian philosopher here. They are interested in themselves period . . .

S2: I would say that by, making, their own personal economy better, and stronger they would strengthen that of the whole country. And by giving themselves the opportunity they would also give the opportunity to others.

T: . . . What kind of historian's view does that coincide with? . . .

Ss: Hofstader.

T: Hofstader and also?

Ss: Commager.

In this exchange we see that the teacher is asking students to link the position of their own accounts about the planners of the Constitution with that of historians. But historians as such are not a part of the accounts that students provided either early in the school term or later. They may be able to state that Beard had an economic self-interest or interpretive stance, or that Commager had a more glorifying one; but historians' positions were not present within the students' depictive accounts either in speech or in writing. Even two months later in the term when a student, Paul, gave a lengthy description of the beginning of the Civil War, one that rested heavily on a Beardian-style interpretation of economic conditions, he told the tale as if it were unfiltered fact (Leinhardt, 1993, p. 71):

Paul: . . . And after this basically the South, the South, the South had lost all its aces. Ah, it was not going to get the ships that it needed in time to fight the war with the North to break the blockade. It had lost its card of King Cotton to begin with and as far as mediation there was now no hope of that due to the fact that the North had gained support among the English people in general.

In this exchange we hear an account that sounds uncontested; it is a simple summary of the position of the South near the beginning of the Civil War. Given that all of the students had been prompted steadily to recognize the positioned and layered feature of all of the accounts they were reading, and given the fact that Paul turned out to be one of the best of the students, it seems evident that students do not easily pick up on the idea of authoring as a notion of contested accounting.

We see more evidence of this in the work of Sam Wineburg (1991), in which he compared responses by students and historians to historical texts. The notable finding from this study and others in the same vein was that students did not use sourcing information in interpreting the texts themselves. The source information – who wrote it and from what perspective – was not seen as integral to the interpretation. Wineburg argues, however, that students cannot discuss or understand the validity of source information if they are unaware that it exists. In textbook-driven instruction, students are not taught to understand how the history they read was produced. As in the example of Paul, the responsibility for making authorship visible falls on the teacher. Likewise, in the work of Perfetti and his colleagues (Britt et al., 1994), students were shown to need a great deal of support to gradually include this kind of information in their under-standings of historical accounts. It is important to recognize that historical instruction does not always include this layer of authorship. In the United States the decision to include or exclude the contested aspects of national identity is a matter left to the discretion of the teacher. However, upper level exams such as the Advanced Placement do hold students accountable for at least some sense of both positioned authorship and an awareness of purposiveness in account construction.

The program "Reading Like a Historian" (RLH) is a document-based instructional intervention (Reisman, 2012) that is designed to address exactly this issue. In a fairly large quasi-experimental intervention considerable success was shown in getting students (nearly 250 11th graders over a six month period) to seriously investigate a historical question using a small set of documents. While there were four thinking-based goals for the program, two seemed to have been clearly met: sourcing material and reading comprehension. Thus, while we have considerable data that indicate juggling the source and content is challenging for students and does not develop spontaneously, we are beginning to see that it is at least somewhat amenable to focused instruction.

CONCLUSIONS

We can see in the episodes of student learning in the US, Canada, and Europe some of the ways in which history as a discipline has undergone a conceptual shift such that ideas of beginnings and endings, ideas of interpretation and argument, and ideas of significance and who gets to decide what is and is not, are now recognized as a legitimate part of the disciplinary practice. These secondary or procedural ideas of Lee and Ashby relate in some interesting ways to the ideas of conceptual and disciplinary agency discussed by Greeno and van de Sande (2007). These two ideas of agency refer to following the disciplinary practices and to seeing the discipline as the authoritative source in contrast to following practices that relate to the judgment, utility, and importance of actions and considering the authority to be the group engaged in the particular and local practice. Agency and perspective help to make "room" for recognition that the work of students should include the ideas of historical practice, one of which is sourcing. These concepts also suggest a need for refocusing the object of understanding to include the content of history, the historian, and the argument.

Peter Lee and Rosalyn Ashby's design experiment in history instruction and learning certainly included reference to the consideration of the historian as having a position and as building an account that supports that position, but it does not point to or make the distinction between the differing types of agency, nor does the Reisman work. The data do not yet demonstrate a strong case for conceptual change taking place in history learning *per se*, although we certainly see developmental growth; data do indicate a press toward instruction and research that reflects the shifts within the discipline itself.[4]

We have suggested in this paper that student conceptual growth or change in history is somewhat different than in other domains because it is the field itself that has undergone a conceptual shift. New elements have been considered worthy of inclusion in the field – for example, phenomena whose record is pictorial or folkloric in nature. There are new ways of organizing the field with a shift from taking extant political or social orders as given and seeing events as set down upon them, to using communication regions (the Atlantic or Pacific Rim), navigational growth, or natural occurrences as the backdrop for investigation. They are shifts in focus, assumptions, and emphasis. Such shifts also impact the particular combination of narrative and expository presentation – as suggested by our quote from Schama about imagination and reason – but not the rhetoric of argument or causality. Likewise, while the idea of authorship and its tight connection to purpose or intent has come to the foreground in recent disciplinary scholarship, it was always a vital part of the account from Herodotus (550 BCE) to Macaulay (1855/1897) to Schama (1991).

The task for the history learner is, first, to come to see their world as having histories, whether that is a social–political event, such as a war or election, or an economic and social one, such as the distribution and selection of food, or the arrangement of buildings and factories in towns and cities, or the specific sense of national character and identity. Secondly, the task is to see the presentation of those histories as purposeful and authored; and, we would add, even to see purpose and authorship when such histories are local and familial. The historical example of the Boston Massacre illustrates the nuances of how one would come to understand an historical event within this extended framework. Incorporating these practices and perspectives into classroom instruction is the goal of much of the current work.

NOTES

1   These multiple references refer to the many varieties of translations that appear for Herodotus; all contain the ideas discussed.
2   In critiquing the television history we do not mean to criticize history on television or the idea that history could expand its medium from text to video. For example, the documentary history of Ken Burns, whether it is about the Civil War, jazz, or baseball, meets the criteria of textual history and is to be applauded for its general interest, provocativeness, and educational value. Schama's TV accounts of the history of Britain likewise are engrossing and eloquent.
3   In addition, historians are in constant dialogue with their contemporary colleagues and with historians who have gone before them. For example, it would be ridiculous to put forth an argument in 2011 that the Revolution was, in fact, not so revolutionary without referencing the work of Alfred Young, who argued in 1993 that the American Revolution was not so radical, especially placed in the context of other European revolutions of the same period (the French Revolution, for example) (Young, 1993). The historian making such an argument today would need to demonstrate a command of this earlier argument and then place his/her own account/argument in this historical trajectory.
4   We have chosen not to emphasize the observed differences in history learning that surround different classes of historical topics. The different topics include event like narratives such as the Boston Massacre in contrast to the social structural elements such as Constitutional arrangements or economic systems that require a more expository development with far less agency. Events are easier to learn and teach than systems (Young & Leinhardt, 1998a, 1998b); this is consistent with Chi's (2005) assertion that emergent systems are harder to learn than more causal ones.

REFERENCES

Beard, C., & Beard, M. (1943). *The American spirit*. New York, NY: Macmillan.
Britt, M. A., Rouet, J. F., Georgi, M. C., & Perfetti, C. A. (1994). Learning from historical texts: From causal analysis to argument models. In G. Leinhardt, I. Beck, & C. Stainton (Eds.) *Teaching and learning in history* (pp. 47–84). Hillsdale, NJ: Lawrence Erlbaum Associates.
Chi, M. T. H. (1992). Conceptual change within and across ontological categories: Examples from learning and discovery in science. In R. Giere (Ed.), *Cognitive models of science: Minnesota studies in the philosophy of science* (pp. 129–186). Minneapolis, MN: University of Minnesota Press.
Chi, M. T. H. (2005). Commonsense conceptions of emergent processes: Why some misconceptions are robust. *Journal of the Learning Sciences, 14*(2), 161–199.

Collingwood, R. G. (1946). *The idea of history*. London, UK: Oxford University Press.

Goold, G. P. (Ed.). (1920). *Herodotus* (Vol. 1; A. D. Godley, Trans.). Cambridge, MA: Harvard University Press.

Gottlieb, E., & Wineburg, S. (2012). Between veritas and communitas: Epistemic switching in the reading of academic and sacred history. *Journal of the Learning Sciences, 21*(1).

Greeno, J. G., & van de Sande, C. (2007). Perspectival understanding of conceptions and conceptual growth in interaction. *Educational Psychologist, 42*(1), 9–23.

Halldén, O. (1994). On the paradox of understanding history in an educational setting. In G. Leinhardt, I. Beck, & C. Stainton (Eds.), *Teaching and learning in history* (pp. 27–46). Hillsdale, NJ: Lawrence Erlbaum Associates.

Herodotus (1987). *The history* (D. Grene, Trans.). Chicago, IL: University of Chicago Press.

Herodotus of Halicarnassus. (2006). Available at: www.livius.org/he-hg/herodotus/herodotus01.htm

Lee, P. (2005). Historical literacy: Theory and research. *International Journal of Historical Learning, Teaching, and Research, 5*(1).

Lee, P., & Ashby, R. (2000). Progression in historical understanding among students ages 7–14. In P. N. Stearns, P. Seixas, & S. Wineburg (Eds.), *Knowing, teaching, and learning history* (pp. 199–222). New York, NY: New York University Press.

Leinhardt, G. (1993). Weaving instructional explanations in history. *British Journal of Educational Psychology, 63*, 46–74.

Leinhardt, G., Stainton, C., & Virji, S. M. (1994). A sense of history. *Educational Psychologist, 29*(2), 79–88.

Macaulay, T. B. (1897). *England in 1685: Being chapter III of the history of England*. Boston, MA: Ginn & Co.

MacWhinney, B. (2005). The emergence of grammar from perspective. In D. Pecher & R. A. Zwann (Eds.), *The grounding of cognition: The role of perception and action in memory, language and thinking* (pp. 198–223). Cambridge, UK: Cambridge University Press.

Mallon, F. A. (1983). *The defense of community in Peru's central highlands*. Princeton, NJ: Princeton University Press.

Mann, C. C. (2005). *1491: New revelations of the Americas before Columbus*. New York, NY: Random House.

Mann, C. C. (2011). *1493: Uncovering the New World Columbus created*. New York, NY: Alfred A. Knopf.

Megill, A. (1994). *Rethinking objectivity*. Durham, NC: Duke University Press.

Pickering, A. (1995). *The mangle of practice*. Chicago, IL: University of Chicago Press.

Richards, L. L. (2002). *Shays's Rebellion: The American Revolution's final battle*. Philadelphia, PA: University of Pennsylvania Press.

Reisman, A. (2012). Reading like a historian: A document-based history curriculum intervention in urban high schools. *Cognition and Instruction, 33*(1), 86–112.

Schama, S. (1991, September 8). Clio has a problem. *New York Times Magazine*, 30–33.

Schama, S. (1995). *Landscape and memory*. New York, NY: Alfred A. Knopf.

Seixas, P. (2000). Schweigen! Die Kinder! or Does postmodern history have a place in schools? In P. N. Stearns, P. Seixas, & S. Wineburg (Eds.), *Knowing, teaching, and learning history* (pp. 19–37). New York, NY: New York University Press.

Seixas, P. (2007). *Theorizing historical consciousness*. Toronto, Canada: University of Toronto Press.

Seixas, P., Peck, C., & Poyntz S. (2011). "But we didn't live in those times": Canadian students negotiate past and present in a time of war. *Education as Change, 15*(1), 47–63.

Torney-Purta, J. (1994). Dimensions of adolescents' reasoning about political and historical issues: Ontological switches, developmental processes, and situated learning. In M. Carretero & J. Voss (Eds.), *Cognitive and instructional processes in history and the social sciences* (pp. 103–122). Hillsdale, NJ: Lawrence Erlbaum Associates.

von Wright, G. H. (1971). *Explanation and understanding*. Ithaca, NY: Cornell University Press.

Voss, J. F. (1998). Issues in the learning of history. *Issues in Education, 4*(2), 163–209.

Voss, J. F., & Wiley, J. (2006). Expertise in history. In K. A. Ericsson, N. Charness, P. J. Feltovich, & R. R. Hoffman (Eds.), *The Cambridge handbook of expertise and expert performance* (pp. 159–184). Cambridge, UK: Cambridge University Press.

Wineburg, S. (1991). On the reading of historical texts: Notes on the breach between school and academy. *American Educational Research Journal, 28*, 495–519.

Wineburg, S. (1994). The cognitive representation of historical texts. In G. Leinhardt, I. Beck, & C. Stainton (Eds.), *Teaching and learning in history* (pp. 85–135). Hillsdale, NJ: Lawrence Erlbaum Associates.

Wineburg, S. (2001). *Historical thinking and other unnatural acts*. Philadelphia, PA: Temple University Press.

Wineburg, S., Mosborg, S., Porat, D., & Duncan, A. (2007). Common belief and the cultural curriculum: An intergenerational study of historical consciousness. *American Educational Research Journal, 44*(1), 40–76.

Young, A. F. (1993). *Beyond the American Revolution: Explorations in the history of American radicalism.* DeKalb, IL: Northern Illinois University Press.

Young, A. F. (1999). *The shoemaker and the Tea Party: Memory and the American Revolution.* Boston, MA: Beacon Press.

Young, K. M., & Leinhardt, G. (1998a). Wildflowers, sheep, and democracy: The role of analogy in the teaching and learning of history. In J. F. Voss & M. Carretero (Eds.), *International review of history education, Vol. 2: Learning and reasoning in history* (pp. 154–198). London, UK: Woburn Press.

Young, K. M., & Leinhardt, G. (1998b). Writing from primary documents: A way of knowing in history. *Written Communication, 15*(1), 25–86.

Zinn, H. (2003). *A people's history of the United States.* New York, NY: HarperCollins.

Zobel, H. B. (1970). *The Boston Massacre.* New York, NY: W. W. Norton & Co.

14

CONCEPTUAL CHANGE AND HISTORICAL NARRATIVES ABOUT THE NATION

A Theoretical and Empirical Approach[1]

Mario Carretero, Jose A. Castorina, and Leonardo Levinas, Autonoma University; University of Buenos Aires and Consejo Nacional de Investigaciones Científicas y Técnicas; and University of Buenos Aires and Consejo Nacional de Investigaciones Científicas y Técnicas

Conceptual change has been given less empirical attention in historical knowledge than in the natural sciences. As a matter of fact, in the previous edition of this *Handbook* there was only one chapter devoted to this topic (Leinhardt & Ravi, 2008). This is clearly a consequence of the fewer cognitive studies about historical knowledge compared to those concerning natural science. However, research about history and students' knowledge has improved much in recent years and there is nowadays a clear interest in the topic. Insightful research projects have been going on, as it can be seen in previous reviews (Barton, 2008; Limón, 2002; VanSledright & Limón, 2006; Voss & Wiley, 2006).

In this chapter, the following issues will be addressed. First, a general overview of the topic of conceptual change in social and historical knowledge will be presented; in particular, establishing a relation to the specific problems and features of the latter. An important distinction will be presented concerning two different goals of history as subject matter. The so-called Romantic and Enlightened objectives mostly related to identity construction and to critical and disciplinary analysis of the past respectively. Conceptual change processes in history will be considered from this point of view, generally expecting that identity contents hinder conceptual change in history. The emphasis will be on the study of the concept of "nation," because of its pivotal role in historical accounts in numerous countries. Furthermore it is a very influential notion both in the way academic history is elaborated and the way students and adults understand historical contents in and outside school. People's concepts of their own nation will be analyzed in the context of their historical narratives. A six-features model of the processes of production–consumption of master narratives will be presented. This model is based on a comparative analysis of school historical narratives of different countries and it will be used as a framework to discuss our empirical data.

Both basic and applied educational research about conceptual change on history are still in their very first stage, and much more research will be necessary. This chapter aims to present a number of theoretical and empirical findings that will be interesting to elaborate in this area in the future: in particular, to explore the issue of capturing the process of conceptual change itself, i.e., the specific relations and tensions between prior and new knowledge. This has been one of the central problems in the study of conceptual change in general in recent decades. In this chapter we will pay attention to some differences between natural sciences contents and historical ones in relation to how prior and new knowledge are related, emphasizing the analysis of specific difficulties of prior historical knowledge.

CONCEPTUAL AND PROCEDURAL KNOWLEDGE IN HISTORY

VanSledright and Limón (2006; see also Limon, 2002) have presented a detailed analysis of the distinct types of historical knowledge. These authors distinguished between conceptual and procedural knowledge, and included two categories within the former: first- and second-order conceptual knowledge. First-order conceptual knowledge consists of conceptual and narrative knowledge that answers the "who," "what," "where," "when," and "how" of history. Examples of first-order knowledge include concepts such as "names," "dates," "democracy," and "socialism."

Second-order conceptual knowledge is the knowledge of concepts and ideas that investigators impose onto the past in order to interpret it and thus give meaning to it. This knowledge makes reference to meta-concepts, related to the epistemological conceptualizations of history. Hence, concepts such as "cause," "progress," "decadence," "proof," "primary and secondary sources," "historical context," "author perspective," and "source reliability" constitute second-order conceptual knowledge. Second-order knowledge also acts as the intersection between first-order conceptual knowledge and procedural knowledge. Concerning basically first-order concepts Barton (2008) provided a very exhaustive and detailed review of the research of recent decades. He analyzed the contribution of more than 200 papers related to students' prior ideas in history.

Procedural knowledge refers to the comprehension and application of specific practices (e.g., reasoning or solving historical problems) that researchers activate when they investigate the past and construct interpretations that result in first-order conceptual knowledge. Some examples of procedural knowledge are source evaluation, construction of cognitive maps and models, interpretation of an event within its historical context, argument elaboration, research, and document elaboration. Voss and Wiley (2006) elaborated a list of 10 cognitive activities, basically related to procedural knowledge, that a history expert must apply. These activities are divided into three larger categories: evaluation of evidence in information gathering; analysis and construction of narratives; and reasoning and problem solving.

Evidence evaluation is critical because it determines whether the "proof" in favor of one position or another, given a particular historic problem, is adequate and whether it suggests one conclusion or another. The process of evidence evaluation in history begins with data, which are frequently incomplete and even contradictory, followed by attempts to reconstruct (after the fact) the goals and causes of these data.

Studies conducted by Limón and Carretero (1999, 2000) attempted to shed light on the reasoning processes that are produced when dealing with historical problems, and how this reasoning process could eventually have an effect on conceptual change. More specifically, these authors analyzed, among other issues, selection processes, evidence evaluation, and hypothesis formulation. It was concluded that consideration of the temporal dimension and the historical contextualization of concepts constitute important skills involved in historical reasoning and problem solving. Partly, this conclusion led us to pay more detailed attention to the changing nature of historical concepts and their use; in other words, to the need to study how historical concepts have different meanings in different contexts and times. Precisely related to this question is the insightful and promising work of Koselleck (1975, 2004).

THE CHANGING NATURE OF HISTORICAL CONCEPTS

Previous research on conceptual change in history has been fruitful and clarified the different elements of cognitive processes related to historical knowledge and expertise. However, it has been based on a rather static view of historical concepts. Most previous authors have not taken into account that historical concepts have an intrinsically changing nature. We think this is of great importance in itself, and also has theoretical and applied implications. It's particularly insightful to take account of the theoretical contributions of historians themselves, as Topolski (2000) indicated. We will be considering the history of ideas elaborated by Koselleck, an essential contribution to understanding conceptual change in history.

As many history teachers know, any historical concept, for example "democracy," did not mean the same in classical Greece as it did in the French Revolution, or as it currently does. Yet underneath this very well known instructional issue lies a much more profound theoretical problem with historical concepts.

Koselleck assumes that political ideas and concepts have been decisive for the origin of modern society. Concepts may be understood as "pivots around which all arguments turn" (Koselleck, 2004, p. 65). They form a part of a discourse, a normative vocabulary that legitimizes political behavior (Iggers, 1993). Thus, historical concepts possess many diverse meanings: not only because of the passing of time, but also as in the same historical moment concepts can be used in different ways, according to different groups and interests. "The history of concepts may be reconstructed through studying the reception, or, more radically, the translation of concepts first used in the past but then pressed into service by last generations. Therefore, the historical uniqueness of speech-acts, which might appear to make any history of concepts impossible, in fact creates the necessity to recycle past conceptualizations. The record of how their uses were subsequently maintained, altered, or transformed may properly be called the history of concepts" (Koselleck, 1996, 62–63).

Koselleck emphasizes that the change in the concept of history itself is very important. The complex relationship between history understood as a *series of facts belonging to the past* and history considered as *a study of the past* is a historical process in itself. The convergence of these two meanings took place toward the 18th century. The concept "history" became a fundamental concept of society, particularly of sociability, as a fundamental concept of the social and political language – thus becoming a regulative principle of all experience and all possible expectations (Koselleck, 1975).

Koselleck's position is close to that of Gadamer (2004) concerning the importance of language. This implies an enormous influence of the verbal labels of historical concepts, but he insists that language does not fully explain historical events. Every historical event has elements that have nothing to do with language.

He argues that a concept is not just the index that captures relations; it is also one of its factors. Each concept opens some horizons of possible experiences, and closes others. Hence the history of concepts leads to discoveries that are not due solely to the empirical work. As "indexes" articulate social experiences, they also form discursive networks that transcend immediate social experiences. They are indicative of structural changes as well, and reveal the sociopolitical and historical prospective. This means that the historical concepts are factors of social change, but also set limits on the possible experience and conceivable theory. The concepts provide social actors with the tools to make sense of their actions. They make the raw experience become lived experience. In other words, changing concepts, even very old ones, come to acquire new meaning. Thus, when the term "citizen" replaces the term "establishment," these changes are anticipated and intervention takes place. The social struggle is also a fight for the concept, a sort of semantic civil war (Koselleck, 1975).

In parallel history was given a new character, as a discipline geared toward studying the processes that led to the establishment of modern nations, that is to say *national history*. The history of societies became intimately related to and even confused with political history. The concept "history" becoming a fundamental concept of society and of the description of each particular society emerged from the French Revolution, which gave rise to the age of the modern states and the corresponding national histories.

THE DYNAMIC NATURE OF HISTORICAL CONCEPTS AND THE DIFFERENT GOALS OF THE SCHOOL HISTORY CURRICULUM

According to Koselleck, the changes in historical concepts reflect the changes in historical processes. This is extremely important not only from a theoretical point of view but also in teaching history, where complex concepts – such as independence, emancipation, liberty, people, nation, state, patriotism, citizenship – need to be introduced. All concepts have a dynamic in time and a different connotation for each individual actor or protagonist group. Therefore, history teaching should take account of how students use certain historical concepts (such as nation or territory, presented below), and how the individual and the class could represent different features of the same concept, generating different meanings according to their prior knowledge and cultural experience. In the last part of this chapter, this specific contribution of Koselleck will be analyzed in terms of its relevance for both capturing the change process of historical concepts and its educational implications. Before we go more deeply into present research on the topic, let us consider an essential issue in relation to historical concepts and their teaching, which has not been taken into account by cognitive approaches. We are referring to the goals of the history curriculum. What should we teach history for? As we will see below, the answer to this question can affect in a serious way the meaning of historical concepts adopted by students.

Different researchers have considered the existence of competing objectives of school history (Barton, 2008; Wineburg, 2001). Carretero (2011) has redefined those objectives as "romantic" and "enlightened" because their features and functions stem from their respective intellectual roots in Romanticism and the Enlightenment. In other words, we claim that history is taught in any national school system attending to two different goals: to make students "love their country" (Nussbaum & Cohen, 2002) and to make them "understand their past" (Seixas, 2004).

In a romantic vein, history education is a fundamental strategy used to achieve:

(a) a positive assessment of the past, present, and future of one's own social group, both local and national;
(b) a positive assessment of the country's political history;
(c) identification with past events, characters, and national heroes.

Why should these goals of history education be considered "romantic"? There are at least two important reasons. First, because the emergence of the nation-states cannot be fully understood without the romantic ideas and their intellectual context (Hobsbawm, 1997). The idea of the nation as a specific ethnic group that is under a process of awakening, finally constituting itself as a destined community, cannot be conceived of entirely without the romantic ideal, as will be seen in the research presented later in the chapter.

In an enlightened vein there has been the goal of fostering critical citizens capable of informed and effective participation in the historical changes of both the nation and the rest of the world. This includes possible criticism of their own local or national community, or even larger political units.

In their most current manifestation in several countries, enlightened goals translate into the following disciplinary and cognitive objectives:

(a) to understand the past in a complex manner, according to age and educational level, which usually implies mastering the discipline's conceptual categories;
(b) to distinguish different historical periods, through the appropriate comprehension of historical time;
(c) to understand the complex historical multi-causality, in which individual and collective motivations interact with causal factors in a complex and sophisticated manner;
(d) to relate the past with the present and the future; this entails an important link with other social sciences and also with civic education;
(e) to approach the methodology used by historians, which allows the student to learn history in an intellectually active way and to understand historical knowledge as a depository of problems that can be solved with objectification.

These romantic and enlightened goals of history education coexisted from the very beginning of school history teaching and developed over time. The romantic goals were the most important in many countries until approximately 1960. After that, the disciplinary goals started to have an increasing importance (Carretero, 2011). When enlightened goals were included as part of the historical contents, they were considered perfectly compatible with the romantic ones. However, several studies (Carretero, Asensio, & Rodríguez Moneo, 2012; Hammack, 2011) have indicated the tension this might generate in students' minds. This chapter tries to clarify how this tension is seriously affecting the understanding of historical contents and how the romantic goals of history instruction could hinder conceptual change of historical concepts.

Based on this distinction, we think it would be possible to have a better understanding of the irreducible tension that exists between the identity-formation function and the critical function played by historical knowledge in the construction of historical narratives and concepts. But can these two goals be simultaneously achieved? Can people love their own country, and at the same time develop a critical understanding of its functioning? Serious conflicts between these two goals are expected, particularly in relation to conceptual change issues. This is because, as is very well known, the most important goal of any nation is to maintain, and not to change, the national identity of its inhabitants. In contrast, to understand the historical past of any nation in a disciplinary way would certainly imply numerous and dramatic conceptual changes. This is precisely the essence of a historian's expertise (Voss & Wiley, 2006): to produce better causal explanations, based on more advanced and complex theoretical interpretations suitably connected to empirical evidence.

THE NATION AS A POLITICAL AND HISTORICAL CHANGING CONCEPT

There are two main reasons for focusing on the concept of nation. On one hand, most school history is precisely national history, rather than history of Europe, America, or other regions and parts of the world. On the other hand, logically most of these school national histories are based on the concept of "nation." Studying how nation is represented and its possible process of change would contribute to a better understanding not only of the concept itself but of most of the historical concepts that are taught in and out of the school. In a similar vein, most of the history museums are precisely national museums (Asensio & Pol, 2012; González de Oleaga, 2012), and their narratives' main motives are based on national categories. Also, most of the historical films and TV shows are based on main national historical characters.

Now, "nation" is not only a historical but also a political concept. Its political meaning has an influence on the way it is used in history. Let us examine this issue briefly, starting with a real and meaningful anecdote about what occurred recently at a Spanish school. Like other southern European countries, Spain has received millions of immigrants in a very short period of time. In an educational context this intense immigration process is creating not only educational but also social and political problems of adjustment. This very representative social interaction in a public school near Barcelona was described in the Spanish newspaper *El Pais* (September 14, 2011; translated by Mario Carretero):[2]

> The vast majority of families repeat the enrollment of [of their children from] one course to another, but some just leave [the school]. "Here are many Moors," ... a mother justified to the director last year [unsubscribing her child]. "But you are Moroccan," he said. "Yeah, but I've been here 25 years and they just arrived." A story very similar to that of two kids from China, who last year were fighting in the playground using Chinese language. When a teacher separated them and asked for explanations [one kid said:] "Because she called me Chinese," ... "But is that what you are" [the teacher] said. "Yes, but I was born here and she was not" she replied.

The above are fascinating examples of ways of using and making meaning of the concept of nationality. In one case, we have a change from Moroccan to Spanish, and in the other case from Chinese to Spanish. But what is more interesting is that, particularly in the second case, there is a complex relationship between internal and external features of the concept. The Chinese student considers that her external features and the language she is speaking, identical to those of her classmate, are not adequate to define her national identity. We consider this as identity change or transition because she is defending the application of different features to define herself. Those features, apparently, are related to the place where she was born: Spain. And in the case of the Moroccan mother those features have to do with the number of years living in that country. Both cases refer to internal instead of external features. In other words, the protagonists are referring to symbolic or conceptual features to define their national identity, instead of physical and immediately perceptible features, such as the color of the skin and the shape of the eyes.

It could be assumed that besides the number of years living in a country, other internal features could be added to the ones necessary to define a new nationality, which implies a new concept of the nation. Thus, the previous example could be explained in terms of well known research about categories and concepts (Keil, 1992). But one of the peculiarities of the social and historical prior knowledge is its cultural and political origin. Thus, these prior ideas come very often from social representations of national historical identities, through school contents, media, etc. On the contrary, many natural scientific ideas could also have a cultural support but their origin is much more related to pure cognitive constraints.

The above illustrates what Koselleck indicates as the simultaneous use of different meanings of a political and historical concept, at the same historical moment by different persons or institutions. The child does not accept "Chinese" as the definition of her identity, because – among other causes – she considers "Spanish–Catalan" as a national concept higher in hierarchy. With the above example, and its analysis, the political meaning of the concept of nation was examined. Let us further explore the historical dimension of this key concept.

ROMANTIC VERSUS DISCIPLINARY HISTORICAL CONCEPTIONS OF NATION

Even though it is not easy to reach an agreement on the unquestionable features of nation as a concept, it is very common to find references to a common past, but also to a shared present and future. For Anthony Smith (2002), a nation is "a named human population occupying an historic territory, and sharing myths, memories, a single public culture and common rights and duties for all members" (p. 65). A distinct definition is proposed by Connor (2004): "The nation is the largest group that shares a sense of common ancestry. Corollary: The nation is the largest group that can be influenced/aroused/motivated/ mobilized by appeals to common kinship."

In historiography, we find two main approaches applied to the concept of nation. We refer to them as "romantic" and "disciplinary." Table 14.1 organizes the main characteristics of each approach. The romantic approach, also known as perennialist, is characteristic of historiography during the 18th and 19th centuries. In this approach, the nation is understood as a natural reality and national sentiment is spontaneous and innate. It is also supposed that national identities are permanent, with roots in the most remote past (Smith, 2002). In the romantic approach, nations can be found to have existed "forever," as some of the students we interviewed tended to say (Carretero & Kriger, 2011; Lopez & Carretero, 2012).

Table 14.1 Features of the romantic and the disciplinary approaches on the concept of nation (adapted from Lopez & Carretero, 2012).

Romantic approach	Disciplinary approach
The nation as a natural reality.	The nation as a social construct.
The nation as an immutable entity.	The nation as an ever-changing entity.
The nation has an antique origin, often placed in ancient times.	The rise of nations occurred in the mid-19th century.
A nation is founded on pre-modern components – territorial, cultural, and historical – which have an atemporal and immutable character.	A nation is founded on modern components: political and economic.
National identity is a natural entity, also passed on from an ancient past.	National identity is a constructed entity, originating in the mid-19th century.
The nation creates the State.	The State is what creates the nation.

In the mid-20th century, another approach was developed, known as the disciplinary or instrumentalist approach. National identities came to be seen as artificial inventions, directed by political interests (Gellner, 1978).

The disciplinary approach to the nation has become dominant in current historiography. Very few historians doubt that the nation is a modern construct, a product of the new conditions that arose after the Enlightenment and following the American and French Revolutions (Álvarez Junco, 2011; Hobsbawm, 1997; Smith, 2002).

As these authors suggest, the romantic approach creates a dual illusion, essential for any analysis of the conceptual change process of historical concepts. Despite the fact that practically no current historian doubts the constructed character of the nation and national sentiment, people still feel passionately about nations and continue to anchor their identity to the nation, expecting to somehow transcend their own brief existence. This illusion would be the source of what Billig (1995) has considered "banal nationalism." As becomes clear in the analysis of the narratives generated about the concept of the nation presented below, this banal nationalism could have the effect of preventing conceptual change in the field of history.

Within the current historiography, the nation is viewed as a modern social construct, culturally created and with an abstract and multidimensional character; it is formed by various elements whose relative importance is negotiable. However, the national narratives that are present in the teaching of history frequently reflect a romantic and essentialist conception of the nation, thus nationalizing both the events and the protagonists of the past (Carretero & López, 2010a). Both political theorists (Balibar, 1991) and historians (Braudel, 1988) consider that history has been traditionally presented in the form of a tale that creates a national continuity that begins in the remote past. This has also been affirmed by the analysis of educational researchers (Halldén, 1998).

CONCEPTIONS OF NATION IN THE CONTEXT
OF HISTORICAL NARRATIVES

Most cognitive analysis of historical thinking and expertise agrees that historical concepts are used by both experts and novices in the contexts of historical narratives (VanSledright & Limon, 2006; Wertsch, 2002; Voss & Wiley, 2006). As is well known, there has been a long and broad epistemological debate among historians and philosophers of history about the implications of narrativist approaches in historical research (Ricoeur, 1990; White, 1987). The present paper will not debate this issue, however fascinating. There is no doubt that most causal explanations by students about historical problems are of a narrative nature, whether they use abstract concepts (Halldén, 2000; Rivière, Nuñez, Barquero, & Fontela, 2000) or concrete ones (Carretero, López Manjón, & Jacott, 1997). Historical narratives have also been studied as to their contributing role in the construction process of national and cultural identities (Hammack, 2011; Wertsch, 2011). This research has shown how most of these narratives could be seriously criticized from the point of view of present disciplinary historical studies on the process of nations' formation (Berger, 2012; Foster, 2012). Even though most of these master narratives are common school historical contents, they present nations more often from a romantic point of view than from the disciplinary point of view. In this sense, master narratives, particularly in textbooks, nowadays present nations not as imagined communities (Anderson, 1983) but as real entities (see Table 14.1).

Elsewhere (Carretero, 2011, Chapter 4; Carretero & Bermúdez, 2012) we have presented a theoretical analysis of the interactive processes of production–consumption of school historical narratives. Usually production processes are related to the way cultural artifacts – history textbooks in this case – include specific historical narratives. Consumption processes have to do with the way students and people in general make sense of and appropriate those produced contents. While produced and consumed historical narratives do not share exactly the same features and elements, some kind of significant interaction is expected. Based on previous work about students' historical master narratives and their cultural and educational significance (Wertsch & Rozin, 2000) and also on our comparative analysis of history textbooks of different nations, most of them in Latin America (Carretero & Gonzalez, 2010; Carretero, Jacott & López Manjón, 2002), we have tried to establish a detailed analysis of the features of historical master narratives and the way they are related to the features of nation as a concept (see Table 14.1). In our view this could be fruitful in order to have a better understanding of the conceptual change in history. Our proposal distinguishes six common features of master historical narratives.

Exclusion–Inclusion as a Logical Operation Contributing
to Establish the Historical Subject

Historical narratives are always presented in terms of a national "we," as opposed to "they." This logical operation is performed in such a way that any positive aspect will be almost always assigned to the national "we," and any critical or negative aspect will be assigned to "the others" (Todorov, 1998). This logical operation is very critical as it determines both the main voice and the logical actions for that national subject.

Identification Processes as a Cognitive but also as an Affective Anchor

Interestingly, developmental evidence (Barrett & Buchanan-Barrow, 2005) has shown that the national distinction "we–they" is already mastered by children between six and eight years of age. Yet at that age children have no precise concept of what a nation is, particularly compared to other political units such as regions or cities. It is very probable that this emotional feature will facilitate at a very early age the formation of the nation as a concept, through a strong identification process, instead of a cognitive rational understanding. For certain, in numerous countries patriotic rituals and their historical contents play an important role in this process (Carretero, 2011: Chapter 4).

Frequent Presence of Mythical and Heroic Characters and Motives

Traditionally, one of the main differences between historical and mythical explanation is precisely the absence of time in the case of the latter (Carretero, Asensio, & Pozo, 1991; Egan, 1997). Thus, myths and mythical figures and narratives are usually beyond time restrictions. When time and its constraints are introduced, history, as a discipline, is making its appearance.

Search for Freedom or Territory as a Main and Common Narrative Theme

A number of authors (Barton & Levstik, 2004, Chapter 9) have studied how students consider the process of independence of their own nation as a historical master narrative, with the main topic of the search of freedom as the starting point of a new community. This understanding consists of very concrete and personalistic historical concepts (Halldén, 1998). Thus, it is based almost uniquely on the intention of a group of persons to be free from some domination and trying to obtain a specific territory. Usually, the territory is presented as having no differences from the present one.

Historical School Narratives Contain Basic Moral Orientations

The moral dimension of historical master narratives is quite obvious, providing tautological legitimization for the nation's main acts. Of particular importance is the right to the mentioned specific territory, which logically includes the various violent acts and political decisions devoted to achieving it.

Romantic and Essentialist Concept of Both the Nation and the Nationals

This feature implies a view of the nation and the nationals as pre-existing political entities, having a kind of eternal and "ontological" nature. As can be seen, this feature has a strong relation to the previous five, according to the general coherence of the narrative.

The main objectives of our empirical research in recent years have been to analyze 12- to 18-year-old students' and adults' concept of nation (Carretero & Castorina, 2010; Carretero & Kriger, 2011). More specifically we were interested in analyzing if their conceptions change as a result of both cognitive development and school history learning.

Our theoretical objectives were also related to examining whether both Romantic and Enlightened goals of history teaching were having an influence on students' and adults' conceptions. As stated above, our expectation was that traditional teaching of national history hinders conceptual change in historical contents instead of favoring it (Carretero, 2011).

Most of the tasks used in our investigations have to do with national foundational or national historical themes and concepts, particularly in relation to the past of both Spain and Argentina. Yet these research topics have clear similarities in other parts of the world. We will present some of our main findings as to how participants were employing the concept of nation in their narrative. Some of their uses will be related to the six narrative features previously mentioned. We will not be presenting a detailed analysis of every feature, as it can be found elsewhere (Carretero & Kriger, 2011; Carretero, López, Gonzalez, & Rodríguez-Moneo, 2012; López et al., 2012).

TWO DIFFERENT CONCEPTIONS OF THE "SPANISH RECONQUEST"

We conducted individual semi-structured interviews on the Spanish "Reconquista." This historical process refers to a period of almost 800 years during which several Christian kingdoms engaged in a series of wars on the Iberian Peninsula. Arabs dominated the Iberian Peninsula from their arrival in 711 and their victory over the then ruling Visigoths. The so-called Reconquista begins in the year 718 and culminates in 1492 with the expulsion of the Arabs from the peninsula. Besides the common-sense consideration that 800 years is too long a time for any territorial recovery, as a matter of fact Spain as a nation did not exist until the 17th century, and Spain as a modern nation-state did not exist until the 19th century (Álvarez Junco, 2011). However, this process was reinterpreted by historians over the centuries and was converted into a national endeavor, by which the monarchy was legitimized and on which the Spanish national identity was built (Ríos Saloma, 2005). It is important to mention that in terms of school history, the concept of "Reconquista" disappeared from Spanish textbooks 30 years ago. Yet this notion has had, and still has, a frequent and intense presence in everyday culture. Present historical research considers it as part of very complex developments of Christian kingdoms in the medieval Iberian peninsula.

We were interested in discovering to what extent participants understood the process of the "Reconquista." We investigated whether participants used the romantic national terms proper to 19th-century historiography – which interpreted the process as a Reconquest of the national territory – or whether, in contrast, they denationalized the event by avoiding connotations of "Reconquista" or recovery and speaking simply of conquests (see for details Carretero et al., 2012; López et al., 2012).

With respect to the sixth narrative feature, related to an essentialist concept of the nation and the nationals, the following example is very clear. It's representative of about 70% of our participants. As mentioned above, it should be taken into account that neither Spain nor the Spaniards existed before, at least, the 16th century.

> As I think about it, the Arabs arrived to the peninsula from the south . . . they began ascending all the way up and the *Spanish* started retreating . . . and then *Spain* gained strength . . . and well, the typical story of El Cid . . .
>
> (Pedro, 21 years)

The use of this essentialist concept of both the nation and the nationals is clearly and coherently supported by most of the participants, who display an explicit identification with the protagonist group of the "Reconquista" using first person plural pronouns (first and second narrative features). Importantly, this identification is of a romantic and essentialist nature, as it recognizes a common nationality between the protagonists in the historical events and the interviewed participants. A direct linkage is thereby produced between past and present, in this case founded on a supposed atemporal national identity. Also, the heroic character of the endeavor (third feature) can be seen in the following example. Ramón makes no use of any historical time category.

> Well, it ended in 92, didn't it? 1492 is when *we pushed them out of* Granada, of that I am quite certain . . . The Battle of Las Navas De Tolosa was a battle of vast importance where *we triumphed over them.* They kept giving ground and in the end they only conserved Granada, where in the end *we expelled them from* in 1492.
>
> (Ramón, 21 years old)

Also, the vast majority of participants interpreted the process of the Muslim and the subsequent Christian conquests in the Iberian Peninsula as one of loss and recovery of the national territory (fourth narrative feature). The results indicate that this romantic vision of the process is still in force and remains as the master narrative used by those trying to provide meaning to the analyzed historical event. For example:

> The Arabs invade a territory that is not theirs. During more than seven centuries they keep trying to conquer what is the entire Spanish territory, and the Spanish, when it in fact was in essence their territory before the Arabs came in, they *reconquered it again* to make it once again their own.
>
> (Juan, 25 years)

THE CONCEPT OF NATION IN THE PROCESS OF INDEPENDENCE

In Argentina, the interviews consisted of asking participants to tell about the process of independence. A picture was presented about the Independence Revolution of May 1810. It depicts the first act of political autonomy, which took place in Buenos Aires in 1810 when it was still a Spanish territory. (This event is similar to the Boston Tea Party in the United States' history narrative.) It's a very common image in history textbooks, museums, and other cultural spaces devoted to collective memory.

The interview was based on asking for a narrative about the independence process from Spain that happened, after a bourgeois revolution, in the early 19th century. Specifically, participants were asked if the people present in the pictures were Argentinians, if they were Argentinians just like present-day Argentinians, and if they felt Argentinian in the same way that present-day Argentineans feel. These three questions were necessary for exploring in detail the sixth feature presented above, i.e., a romantic and essentialist concept of both the nation and the nationals (see for details Carretero et al., 2012).

In fact, the people in the picture were not Argentinians, but Spanish colonists. Argentina did not yet exist – the official independence took place six years later – and the territory becoming independent from Spain was a very different political unit.

Argentina as a nation-state, similar to the present one but having a significantly smaller territory, did not come into existence until approximately 50 years later.

In this investigation, participants were 12, 14, 16, and 18 years old. Also a group of adults was included. All of them were middle class, lived in a medium-sized city and (had) attended public schools. Interestingly, about two-thirds of our participants considered the people depicted in the image as Argentinians.

The narrative that appears when the subjects have to justify the "Argentineness" of the people is strongly essentialist. Our participants considered the colonists to definitely be Argentineans because, as some of them expressed, Argentina and the Argentinians "always existed." It can be concluded that the historical process of becoming a member of the nation-state tends to be seen as something that is predetermined, and not a result of different political, social, and economic influences (see Table 14.1).

As Nehuen, 12 years old explains:

If they were born here, it was because they were Argentine, they were born in Argentine territory, not in Spain . . . it was here, it was owned by the Spanish, but it was an Argentine place.

Thus, it is clear that this participant is considering Argentina as a nation, even before its existence.

On the contrary, some interviews demonstrate that some subjects believe that the people depicted are not Argentine, indicating a national conception closer to the disciplinary view. For example:

Can it be said that the people in this image are Argentine? No, most of them are Spanish *[doubt]* . . . the majority were Argentine because the majority were people that . . . *[He doubts again and repeats with confidence]*. At this moment they were not Argentine. In this moment they were not Argentine because obviously, it was not Argentine, how is it possible to be American if the United States do not exist yet? What was said was quite contradictory. [So, what do you think? Were they or were they not Argentine?] And . . . they were not Argentine if Argentina did not exist. It was just a project at that moment.

(Juan, 12 years old)

Interestingly, also, some hybrid versions were found, as 16 year old Santiago explains.

[Some people argued that they were not Argentine because they were from the Spanish territory and Argentina did not exist yet; what do you think?] Even though Argentina did not exist at that moment, I think that they were Argentine because from the beginning, they rebelled against the established power . . . and they confronted it to become independent and to be Argentine; and they wanted to become Argentine . . . and if they wanted to be Argentine more than to be Spanish . . . they were Argentine in their blood.

It can be seen that this participant is careful not to take for granted the pre-existence of Argentina, but at the same time there is an essentialist use of the nation's conception. Thus, his concept is hybrid in the sense of containing a mixture of disciplinary and essentialist elements, without any awareness of their contradiction.

In the participants' answers to the three different questions asked, there were hardly any statistically significant differences. This shows that two-thirds of them considered the present Argentinians the same as the people who appeared in the picture. Let us keep in mind here that the second question asked explicitly about this possible equivalence and the third question was about a possible self-consciousness of that equivalence. In our opinion, this result indicated the extent to which the participants have an essentialist concept of both the nation and the nationals. They show a clear misunderstanding of the historical process behind any nation formation process.

Their essentialist concept of the present Argentinians prevents them from understanding that they are a result of a set of historical, political, economic, and cultural factors (see Table 14.1).

Finally, the results showed almost no statistically significant differences across groups, except in the case of the adults who demonstrated some better results. Thus, two-thirds of 12-, 14-, 16-, and 18-year-olds manifested essentialist historical concepts of the nation, showing no progress in their narratives and other features associated with them. This means that there is no conceptual change across either age and school learning experience. A surprising result, because there are six years of difference between the youngest and the oldest of our participants. Yet, in fact, if a comparison is made with research in natural sciences concepts, the result will not be surprising but will confirm the stability of many concepts in subjects' minds. Some questions can be raised about the possible reasons for such lack of change. In our opinion, common and very passive practices of history education would be very much related to this result; this issue is analyzed below.

CONCLUDING REMARKS

According to our studies it appears that the historical concept of nation is not understood in a proper historical manner. Students have a rather essentialist idea of the nation, closer to a romantic than to a disciplinary idea. This conception has essentialist features, such as an eternal territory legitimized in a tautological way. Present nations appear in the mind of citizens as immutable political objects whose historical origin is misunderstood, as if they existed "since always." The stability of these conceptions appears very clearly: No differences were found across different age groups of 12-, 14-, 16-, and 18-year-olds and adults. Also, taking into account how strong and persistent these conceptions appear, it could be assumed that they present a clear resistance to change, even though we have no data on this matter yet.

It could be maintained that the conceptual change process of the concept of nation has a number of similarities with the process taking place in a number of natural sciences concepts, as studied by numerous authors (Vosniadou, 2008). As indicated, the most striking similarity concerns the inability of both adolescents and adults to incorporate disciplinary changes in their concept of nation, which is persistently naïve, intuitive, and probably socially shared and implicit. Another similarity concerns the existence of students' hybrid mental models in both natural sciences and historical concepts. We have presented a case of such a hybrid model of the historical knowledge about the nation. We think it can be compared to the classic example found by Vosniadou and Brewer (1992) about the shape of the earth, where the students integrate astronomical conceptual elements with everyday ones. In our case, the student also integrates disciplinary elements with essentialist ones, which belong to his everyday and social experience.

On the other hand, we think there are also be some differences between conceptual change processes in historical and natural sciences concepts. These differences have to do with the epistemological nature of historical knowledge (Limón, 2002; Wineburg, 2001). They cannot be considered fully in this chapter due to space restrictions, but some of them will be mentioned. Firstly, there is an essential feature of historical knowledge in relation to time (Carretero, Jacott, Limón, López Manjón, & Leon, 1994), which is very different in the case of natural science concepts.

There is no way to make sense of the possible future without establishing a meaningful relation and dialogue among past, present, and future (Carretero & Solcoff, 2012). In other words, historical understanding implies social and political comprehension, but it adds a unique temporal dimension. This dimension has been characterized in a very insightful manner by Koselleck (2004), emphasizing the changing nature of historical concepts (consider precisely the title of one of his books, *Futures Past*). For certain, the cognitive study of conceptual change in history could benefit from his contribution about epistemology of history, as it has benefited from the contribution of Kuhn's ideas about philosophy of science.

It is commonplace to state that only through understanding the past can the present be understood. However, it is the present, understood as an effect of the past, that in fact orients historical studies. History as investigation of the past – to many historians the *construction* of the past – employing the tools of the present, is what really allows understanding. Historical concepts are defined and restructured in the course of time, and those are the very theoretical tools available to historians for analyzing the past. Therefore, the study of the changes endured by fundamental historical concepts is decisive. For example, determining the conceptual changes operating over time in the notion of "nation" tells us about the "national present" in each historical moment. Moreover, it constitutes the principal device for determining how the past has led to the actual concept of nation. In this sense, the constant changes in political maps have oriented investigating the past to figure out how new national realities were achieved.

Yet another difference exists between how change is produced in history and in the natural sciences, intimately related to the possibility for the natural sciences to design and interpret experiences. The latter is not possible in history, as its object of study is the past: something that cannot be experienced in the present. Experience and, to a great extent, the controlled experiment are the main devices through which individuals modify their theories in Kuhnian terms (Levinas & Carretero, 2010). This is not the case in history. The difference with history research is that the authority of the so-called crucial experiments is replaced by the authority of the historical fact under the form of source, document, and testimony (see above on the importance of procedural knowledge in history, which is necessary to reason about those sources; Wineburg, 2001).

Last but not least, we think there is another important difference related to the way that narratives and concepts have a very strong relation, which we still need to know in a more detailed way. This relation looks very different in the case of natural sciences knowledge, where there are no intentions, agents, motives, or other substantial elements of narrative knowledge. A theoretical proposal for analyzing school historical narratives has been presented above. One of its elements had to do precisely with the dichotomy of essentialist versus disciplinary concepts present in the narrative. But we still need to know how the different proposed features of the narratives interact with each other. For example, we do not know yet if having a disciplinary concept included in the student's narrative would affect the whole meaning of narrative, independently of the rest of the elements. In any case, we are totally persuaded that the way the concept of nation is represented by students is of central importance in the study of historical knowledge, as analyzed above. So, it may be highly probable that other historical concepts' representations would depend very much on how nation is represented.

The teaching of history in many schools across the world still needs to be seriously improved. A number of significant contributors to history education have been trying to develop new proposals. Most of them are in line with developing disciplinary historical thinking in the schools, and Peter Lee (2004) has pointed out how learning to think historically (Lévesque, 2008) often entails navigating counterintuitive ideas. Historical thinking is even described as an "unnatural process" (Wineburg, 2001), needing an epistemological switch (Gottlieb & Wineburg, 2012). This historical thinking is based on acquiring a set of skills that are characteristic of historical experts (Carretero & López, 2010b; Voss & Wiley, 2006). Some of these skills are the development of critical thinking, the understanding of historical time and change, historical causality, and source evaluation (Lee, 2005; Monte-Sano, 2010). We would like to insist also on the educational importance of a specific work on students' concept understanding and conceptual change, in line with the research presented in this paper (Camilloni & Levinas, 2002). Disciplinary history delves into the past in search of new questions and answers, and not with the goal of celebrating or justifying a glorious national past. In this way, it would be possible to develop in our students not only better historical concepts but a better historical consciousness (Seixas, 2004).

NOTES

1   This chapter was written with the support of Project 2008-1217 (National Research Agency, Argentina) and Project EDU-2010-17725 (National Research Agency, Spain), both of them coordinated by the first author. We would like express our gratitude for that support. Floor van Alphen and Alicia Barreiro provided very insightful suggestions. The first author would like also to thank to the Stanford University Humanities Center for the Bliss Carnochan Visitor Fellowship, 2011.
2   http://politica.elpais.com/politica/2011/09/14/actualidad/1315986423_800768.html (retrieved December 21, 2011).

REFERENCES

Álvarez Junco, J. (2011). *Spanish identity in the age of nations*. Manchester, UK: Manchester University Press.

Anderson, B. (1983). *Imagined communities: Reflections on the origin and spread of nationalism*. London, UK: Verso.

Asensio, M., & Pol, E. (2012). From identity to mentality conceptions: Theoretical basis for history museums. In M. Carretero, M. Asensio, & M. Rodríguez-Moneo (Eds.). (2012). *History education and the construction of national identities* (pp. 257–268). Charlotte, NC: Information Age Publishing.

Balibar, E. (1991). The nation form: history and ideology. In I. Wallerstein & E. Balibar (Eds.), *Race, nation, class: Ambiguous identities* (pp. 86–106). London, UK: Verso.

Barrett, M., & Buchanan-Barrow, E. (Eds.). (2005). *Children's understanding of society*. London, UK: Taylor & Francis.

Barton, K. C. (2008). History. In J. Arthur, C. Hahn, & I. Davies (Eds.), *Handbook of education for citizenship and democracy*. London, UK: Sage.

Barton, K., & Levstik, L. (Eds.). (2004). *Teaching history for the common good*. Mahwah, NJ: Lawrence Erlbaum Associates.

Berger, S. (2012). De-nationalizing history teaching and nationalizing it differently! Some reflections on how to defuse the negative potential of national(ist) history teaching. In M. Carretero, M. Asensio, & M. Rodríguez-

Moneo (Eds.). (2012). *History education and the construction of national identities* (pp. 33–47). Charlotte, NC: Information Age Publishing.

Billig, M. (1995). *Banal nationalism.* London, UK: Sage.

Braudel, F. (1988). *The identity of France: Vol.1. History and environment.* London, UK: Collins.

Camilloni, A., & Levinas, M. L. (2002). *Pensar, descubrir, aprender. Propuesta didactica y actividades para las Ciencias Sociales* [Thinking, discovering, learning. Teaching social sciences]. Buenos Aires, Argentina: Aique.

Carretero, M. (2011). *Constructing patriotism: Teaching history and memories in global worlds.* Charlotte, NC: Information Age Publishing.

Carretero, M., Asensio, M., & Pozo, J. I. (1991). Cognitive development, historical time representation and causal explanations in adolescence. In M. Carretero, M. Pope, R. J. Simons, & J. I. Pozo. (Eds.), *Learning and instruction, Vol. III: European research in an international context* (pp. 27–48). Oxford, UK: Pergamon Press.

Carretero, M., Asensio, M., & Rodríguez-Moneo, M. (Eds.). (2012). *History education and the construction of national identities.* Charlotte, NC: Information Age Publishing.

Carretero, M., & Bermúdez, A. (2012). Constructing histories. In J. Valsiner (Ed.), *Oxford handbook of culture and psychology* (pp. 625–646). Oxford, UK: Oxford University Press.

Carretero, M., & Castorina, J. A. (2010). *La construcción del conocimiento histórico* [The construction of historical knowledge]. Buenos Aires, Argentina: Paidos.

Carretero, M., & Gonzalez, M. F. (2010). Is the "nation" a historical concept on students' mind? Paper presented at the International Seminar "De-nationalizing History Teaching?", Autonoma University, Madrid, Spain.

Carretero, M., Jacott, L., & López Manjón, A. (2002). Learning history through textbooks: Are Mexican and Spanish children taught the same story? *Learning and Instruction, 12*, 651–665.

Carretero, M., Jacott, L., Limón, M., López Manjón, A., & Leon, J. A. (1994). Historical knowledge: Cognitive and instructional implications. In M. Carretero & J. F. Voss (Eds.), *Cognitive and instructional processes in history and social sciences* (pp. 357–376). Hillsdale, NJ: Lawrence Erlbaum Associates.

Carretero, M., & Kriger, M. (2011). Historical representations and conflicts about indigenous people as national identities. *Culture and Psychology, 17*(2), 177–195.

Carretero, M., & López, C. (2010a). The narrative mediation on historical remembering. In S. Salvatore & J. Valsiner (Ed.), *The yearbook of idiographic science: Memories and narratives in context, 2* (pp. 285–294). Rome, Italy: Firera.

Carretero, M., & López, C. (2010b). Studies in learning and teaching history: Implications for the development of historical literacy. In C. Lundholm, G. Peterson & I. Wisted (Eds.), *Begreppsbildning I ett intentionellt perspektiv. Hommage to O. Halden* [Conceptual change. An intentional perspective] (pp. 167–187). Stockholm, Sweden: University of Stockholm Press.

Carretero, M., López, C., Gonzalez, M. F., & Rodríguez-Moneo, M. (2012). Students' historical narratives and concepts about the nation. In M. Carretero, M. Asensio, & M. Rodríguez-Moneo (Eds.), (2012). *History education and the construction of national identities* (pp. 153–170). Charlotte, NC: Information Age Publishing.

Carretero, M., López Manjón, A., & Jacott, A. (1997). Explaining historical events. *International Journal of Educational Research, 27*(3), 245–253.

Carretero, M., & Solcoff, K. (2012). Comments on "After the archive: remapping memory". The relation between past, present and future as a metaphor of memory. *Culture and Psychology, 18*, 1, 14–22.

Connor, W. (2004). The timelessness of nations. *Nations and Nationalism, 10*, 35–47.

Egan, K. (1997). *The educated mind: How cognitive tools shape our understanding.* Chicago, IL: University of Chicago Press.

Foster, S. J. (2012). Re-thinking history textbooks in a globalized world. In: M. Carretero, M. Asensio, & M. Rodríguez-Moneo (Eds.), *History education and the construction of national identities* (pp. 49–62). Charlotte, NC: Information Age Publishing.

Gadamer, H. (2004). *Truth and method.* New York, NY: Continuum.

Gellner, E. (1978). *Thought and change.* Chicago, IL: University of Chicago Press.

González de Oleaga, M. (2012). Historical narratives in the colonial, national and ethnic museums of Argentina, Paraguay and Spain. In M. Carretero, M. Asensio, & M. Rodríguez-Moneo (Eds.), *History education and the construction of national identities* (pp. 239–255). Charlotte, NC: Information Age Publishing.

Gottlieb, E., & Wineburg, S. (2012). Between *veritas* and *communitas*: Epistemic switching in the reading of academic and sacred history. *Journal of the Learning Sciences, 21*(1), 84–129.

Halldén, O. (1998). Personalization in historical descriptions and explanations. *Learning and instruction, 8*(2), 131–139.

Halldén, O. (2000). On reasoning in history. In J. F. Voss & M. Carretero (Eds.), *Learning and reasoning in history* (pp. 272–278). London, UK: Routledge.

Hammack, P. (2011). *Narrative and the politics of identity: The cultural psychology of Israeli and Palestinian youth.* New York, NY: Oxford University Press.

Hobsbawm, E. (1997). *Nations and nationalism since 1780: Programme, myth, reality.* Cambridge, UK: Cambridge University Press.

Iggers, G. (1993). *Historiography in the twentieth century: From scientific objectivity to the postmodern challenge* (An expanded English version of *Geschichtswissenschaft im 20. Jahrhundert. c1993.*) Middletown, CT: Wesleyan University Press, 2005.

Keil, F. (1992). *Concepts, kinds, and cognitive development.* Cambridge, MA: MIT Press.

Koselleck, R. (1975). Geschichte, Historie (Caps. I, V–VII). In *Geschichtliche Grundbegriffe* (Vol. 2, pp. 593–595, 647–718). Stuttgart, Germany: Klett-Cotta (Spanish translation, Antonio Gómez Ramos: *historia/Historia.* Madrid, Spain: Trotta, 2004).

Koselleck, R. (1996). A response to comments on the *Geschichtliche Grundbegriffe.* In H. Lehmann & M. Richter (Eds.), *The meaning of historical terms and concepts* (pp. 59–70). Washington, DC: German Historical Institute.

Koselleck, R. (2004). *Futures past: On the semantics of historical time.* New York, NY: Columbia University Press.

Lee, P. (2004). Understanding history. In P. Seixas (Ed.), *Theorizing historical consciousness* (pp. 129–164). Toronto, Canada: University of Toronto Press.

Lee, P. J. (2005). Putting principles into practice: Understanding history. In M. S. Donovan & J. D. Bransford, *How students learn history in the classroom.* Washington, DC: National Academies Press.

Leinhardt, G., & Ravi, A. (2008). Changing historical conceptions of history. In S. Vosniadou (Ed.), *International handbook of research on conceptual change* (pp. 328–345). New York, NY: Routledge.

Lévesque, S. (2008). *Thinking historically: Educating students for the twenty-first century.* Toronto, Canada: University of Toronto Press.

Levinas, M. L., & Carretero, M. (2010). Conceptual change, crucial experiments and auxiliary hypotheses: A theoretical contribution. *Integrative Psychology and Behavioral Science, 44*(4), 288–298.

Limón, M. (2002). Conceptual change in history. In M. Limon, & L. Mason (Eds.), *Reconsidering conceptual change: Issues in theory and practice* (pp. 259–289). Dordrecht, The Netherlands: Kluwer.

Limón, M., & Carretero, M. (1999). Conflicting data and conceptual change in history experts. In W. Schnotz, S. Vosniadou, & M. Carretero (Eds.), *New perspectives on conceptual change* (pp. 137–160). Oxford, UK: Elsevier.

Limón, M., & Carretero, M. (2000). Evidence evaluation and reasoning abilities in the domain of history: An empirical study. In J. F. Voss & M. Carretero (Eds.), *Learning and reasoning in history: International review of history education* (Vol. 2, pp. 252–271). London, UK: Routledge.

López, C., & Carretero, M. (2012). Commentary: Identity construction and the goals of history education. In M. Carretero, M. Asensio & M. Rodríguez-Moneo (Eds.), *History education and the construction of national identities* (pp. 139–150). Charlotte, NC: Information Age Publishers.

López, C., Carretero, M., & Rodríguez-Moneo, M. (2013). Conquest or re-conquest? Students' conceptions of nation embedded in a historical narrative. Paper submitted.

Monte-Sano, C. (2010). Disciplinary literacy in history: An exploration of the historical nature of adolescents' writing. *Journal of the Learning Sciences, 19*(4), 539–568.

Nussbaum, M., & Cohen, D. (Eds.). (2002). *For love of country? A new democracy forum on the limits of patriotism.* Boston, MA: Beacon Press.

Ricoeur, P. (1990). *Time and narration.* Chicago, IL: University of Chicago Press.

Ríos Saloma, M.F. (2005). *De la Restauración a la Reconquista. La construcción de un mito nacional. Una revisión historiográfica. Siglos XVI–XIX* [From the Restoration to the Reconquest: The construction of a national myth. A historiographical review. 16th –19th centuries]. *España Medieval, 28,* 379–414.

Rivière, A., Nuñez, M., Barquero, B., & Fontela, F. (2000). Influence of intentional and personal factors in recalling historical texts: A developmental perspective. In J. F. Voss & M. Carretero (Eds.), *Learning and reasoning in history: International review of history education* (Vol. 2, pp. 214–226). London, UK: Routledge.

Seixas, P. (Ed.). (2004). *Theorizing historical consciousness.* Toronto, Canada: University of Toronto Press.

Smith, A. D. (2002). Dating the nation. In D. Conversi (Ed.), *Ethnonationalism and the contemporary world: Walker Connor and the study of nationalism* (pp. 53–71). London, UK: Routledge.

Todorov, T. (1998). *On human diversity: Nationalism, racism, and exoticism in French thought.* Cambridge, MA: Harvard University Press. [French edition: *Nous et les autres. La reflexion francaise sur la diversité humaine.* Paris: Seuil, 1989.]

Topolski, J. (2000). The structure of historical narratives and the teaching of history. In J. F. Voss & M. Carretero (Eds.), *Learning and reasoning in history: International review of history education* (Vol. 2, pp. 9–21). London, UK: Routledge.

VanSledright, B. & Limón, M. (2006). Learning and teaching in social studies: Cognitive research on history and geography. In P. Alexander & P. Winne (Eds.), *The handbook of educational psychology* (2nd edn., pp. 545–570). Mahwah, NJ: Lawrence Erlbaum Associates.

Vosniadou, S., & Brewer, W. (1992). Mental models of day/night cycle. *Cognitive Science, 18*(1), 122–183.

Vosniadou, S. (Ed.). (2008). *International handbook of research on conceptual change.* New York, NY: Routledge.

Voss, J. F., & Wiley, J. (2006). Expertise in history. In N. C. K. A. Ericsson, P. Feltovich, & R. R. Hoffman (Eds.), *The Cambridge handbook of expertise and expert performance* (pp. 569–584). Cambridge, UK: Cambridge University Press.

Wertsch, J. (2002). *Voices of collective remembering.* Cambridge, UK: Cambridge University Press.

Wertsch, J. (2011). Beyond the archival model of memory and the affordances and constraints of narratives. *Culture & Psychology, 17*(1), 21–29.

Wertsch, J. V., & Rozin, M. (2000). The Russian Revolution: Official and unofficial accounts. In J. F. Voss & M. Carretero (Eds.), *Learning and reasoning in history: International review of history education* (Vol. 2, pp. 39–59). London, UK: Routledge.

White, H. (1987). *The content of the form: Narrative discourse and historical representation.* Baltimore, MD: Johns Hopkins University Press.

Wineburg, S. (2001). *Historical thinking and other unnatural acts.* Philadelphia, PA: Temple University Press.

15

CONCEPTUAL CHANGE IN THE SOCIAL SCIENCES

Cecilia Lundholm and Peter Davies, Stockholm University and University of Birmingham

The research evidence base for conceptual change in social science is thin compared to the evidence base in science and mathematics education. Murphy and Alexander (2008, p. 597) suggest that this is because it is "easier to identify misconceptions of or naïve theories in biology or physics, in comparison to history or reading where 'correct' or 'scientifically-valid' positions are elusive." We accept this explanation and the implication that contesting theories within a discipline increase the difficulties in making judgments between "better" and "worse" conceptions. Disagreements over theory within a discipline draw attention to alternative value positions, and relationships between conceptual structure, values, and identity play an important role in our understanding of conceptual change in social science. To make our task manageable we restrict our attention to conceptual change in economics and environmental studies. Of course, the ideas and evidence discussed in this chapter may apply weakly, if at all, to other disciplines in social science.

Looking back, a key motivation for research on conceptual change in social science was summarized by Carretero and Voss (1994). Their argument has two main propositions. First, effective functioning and development of democratic society require an electorate that has a working understanding of the economic, political, and sociological dynamics of their world (see also Davies, 2006a; Davies & Lundholm, 2012; Lundholm, 2011). Second, for educators to play a valuable role in improving voters' understanding, teachers need a working knowledge of the range of students' prior conceptions and nature of the conceptual change for which they are aiming. In addition to these arguments, we believe there is reason to be interested in conceptual change from the perspective of the field of research in conceptual change itself, as for example Vosniadou, Vamvakoussi, and Skopeliti (2008) ask whether the theories, which have been developed to account for conceptual change, are domain general or domain specific. However, in the 18 years since Carretero and Voss published their edited volume, conceptual change in social science has remained under-researched in comparison to the many studies in natural science and mathematics. The research we summarize in this chapter reveals an emergent field in which theoretical perspectives are under construction and the evidence base is fragmentary.

The chapter first presents research on conceptual change in the domains of economics and environmental studies. Each section presents studies generated through a database search using Web of Science, ERIC, and PsycInfo, choosing abstracts in peer-reviewed journals published between January 1, 1990 and August 31, 2011. Authors used the same search words: "conception" or "conceptual change" or "concept formation" or "conceptual development" while then differing in additional words in relation to the various domains in focus: "economics" and "economic," and the words "environment" or "environmental issues" or "sustainability" or "sustainable development." As both authors work in the domains chosen, we have also added peer-reviewed work that was not picked up by the search engines, this being important since the field is very limited.

Our review of the literature suggests that while reasonable progress has been made in gathering evidence of different conceptions of key economic and environmental phenomena, few studies have examined the process of conceptual change. The exception to this judgement is found in the emerging literature (e.g., Pang & Marton 2003, 2005) on instruction based on Variation Theory. However, we do suggest that the development of conceptual structure in these subject areas is characterized by a shift from conceptions that are limited by the context of personal experience to conceptions that place economic and environmental phenomena in the context of systemic interactions in which causation is neither unidirectional nor simply linear. We also suggest that this development is accompanied by a shift away from treating personal experience as "normal" toward an appreciation of the contingency of economic and environmental phenomena on ideas and distributions of power which may reflect the dominance of particular social scientific standpoints.

CONCEPTUAL CHANGE IN ECONOMICS

Theoretical Perspectives

Qualitative distinctions between conceptions of economic phenomena have been developed in two research traditions. A series of phenomenographic studies (Dahlgren 1984, Marton & Pang, 2008, Pang & Marton 2003, 2005; Pong 1998) has suggested categories of conceptions of price, the burden of sales tax, and trade. These studies have concentrated on the conceptions held by students in secondary schools, although Dahlgren studied the conceptions of newly graduating university students. The implicit aim of these studies has been to improve teaching by helping teachers to clarify the nature of conceptual change they are aiming to achieve. The research method has been to choose an example of the phenomenon (e.g., the price of a bun in a university canteen, or the price of chickens during a bird flu epidemic) that is reckoned to be within students' everyday experience. Students are asked to explain the phenomenon with prompting through questions that do *not* offer the student the researchers' view of the phenomenon.

Categories of conceptions of economic phenomena have also been suggested by social psychologists (e.g. Berti & Grivet, 1990; Leiser & Halachmi 2006; Thompson & Siegler 2000) working largely with younger children (aged six to 12 years). These studies have aimed to reveal changes in conceptions that occur in the process of socialization and have tended to focus on students' understanding of money, banks, income and price. A typical method used by researchers in this tradition has been to present a situation to the children through pictures and to ask them what they think will happen next.

Since both research traditions have addressed conceptions of price, it is interesting to compare their conclusions. Both groups of researchers find that conceptions of price fall into the following categories: price as an intrinsic feature of a good, price as a reflection of demand, price as a reflection of supply, and price as a reflection of supply and demand. The social psychology tradition suggests that these conceptions emerge in this sequence, with a conception of price in terms of supply and demand appearing when students are aged about 12.

The phenomenographic research also suggests a similar hierarchy from "price as an intrinsic feature of a good" as the simplest conception and "price as a reflection of supply and demand" as the most complex. However, it contests the suggestion that a conception of price in terms of supply and demand is an outcome of socialization by the early teenage years. For example, Dahlgren (1984) reports that some economics graduates use a conception of price as an intrinsic characteristic of a good in everyday contexts. Pang and Marton (2005) present results from an intervention with 16–18-year-old students who had studied economics. They report that their pretest showed that no students held a conception of price as an intrinsic characteristic of a product, only 2% held a conception of price as a reflection of supply, while 44% of the students held a conception of price as a reflection of demand (only). Pang and Marton's (2005) study also suggests that differences in instruction are critical in determining whether students abandon simpler conceptions of price in their response to questions about their understanding of everyday problems.

These differences between researchers' conclusions are important because they bear upon (i) the resistance of simple conceptions of price to any instruction and (ii) the relative effectiveness of instructional strategies. In the following discussion we consider the way in which researchers' definitions of a conception of price "in terms of supply and demand" may have contributed to the apparent disagreement between the results of different studies.

First, we consider the problems that have been posed to students. The questions used in the social psychology literature present students with decisions about price to be made by an individual producer. The phenomenographic literature uses "individual producer" questions as well, but sometimes uses "market" questions instead. For example, Marton and Pang (2008, p. 544) posed the question, "Suppose you were the owner of the tuck shop. What price would you set for a hot dog?" In contrast, Pang and Marton (2005, p. 167) posed a question ending "it was surprising to find that after this move, the price of live chickens in the market did not go up but fell. Why?" The first question positions the student as a single producer deciding what price they would charge. The second question positions the student as an observer of the behavior of many producers and consumers in a market. The context of an individual producer lies more firmly within students' experience and it is also less complex than a market involving interactions between many producers. Therefore, it seems likely that at least some of the disagreement in evidence is attributable to this difference in the problems posed to students.

The distinction that Marton and Booth (1997) draw between the "internal" and "external" horizon of a conception is helpful in this regard. They use the term "external horizon" to refer to the *context* in which a phenomenon is placed, although subsequent phenomenographic research in social science has not drawn attention to this distinction. In particular, it has not recognized that a conception of price may be framed by an "external horizon" of the circumstances faced by an individual producer or the circumstances bearing upon a market comprising a number of producers and consumers. This distinction is important since economic phenomena are embedded in economic systems, and conceptions of economic phenomena are embedded in conceptions of economic systems. In this case the difference in context is a matter of scale. When the phenomenon of price is viewed "close-up" in the context of price setting by the individual producer it appears to be entirely a matter of "agency." When the limits of the context are extended to include an entire market then price appears to emerge from "structure" with individual producers subject to "market forces." More sophisticated economic models allow producers some degree of agency according to the level of competition within the market (Davies, 2011a).

The role of perceptions of the economic context in conceptions of price in supply and demand bears comparison with the distinctions between ontological states observed by Chi (2008) in her study of conceptions in science. In particular, Chi notes a progression from conceptions of scientific patterns as being outcomes of the intentions of entities to conceptions that are products of processes. This difference has been examined by Torney-Purta (1994) and by Leiser and Halachmi (2006) in conceptions in social science. However, economic theory suggests that patterns are outcomes of interactions between the intentions and expectations of sentient beings, so there might be some difference between the development of conceptual structures in science and social science on this point. We suggest that the way in which a conception of a phenomenon presumes roles for structure and agency is critical throughout social science and this is an area ripe for future research.

Second, researchers have categorized utterances as conceptions of price in terms of supply and demand with an implication of causation that they have not explored. The utterances cited thus far in the research literature refer exclusively to unidirectional causation. For example:

> Because of the bird flu crisis, many people were afraid of getting the H5N1 virus from live chickens. At the same time, live chicken hawkers also dared not buy much from the wholesalers. Thus, there were fewer live chickens in the market. However, the price did not rise but fell. As many people were scared and did not want to buy live chickens, although there were fewer chicken in the market, the price dropped instead.
>
> (Pang & Marton, 2005 p. 175)

This utterance treats causation as unidirectional: *from* supply and demand *to* price. The idea of "supply and demand" in economics suggests that causation runs not only *from* supply and demand *to* price but also *from* price *to* supply and demand. For example, an increase in price would normally be expected to increase willingness to supply and decrease willingness to buy. It is the *rate* at which supply and demand change when price changes that determines the price which eventually emerges after an *initial* change in either supply or demand (as in the market for chickens). The distinction between conceptions of causation as unidirectional/single loop or reciprocal/double loop has been carefully explored (e.g., Barbas & Psillos, 1997; Chi, 2008) in science education in terms of conceptions of electrical circuits and the circulation of blood. However, it is not self-evident that the conceptual change from unidirectional to reciprocal causation in conceptions of price is an equivalent case to these examples in science. Since there are, as yet, no studies of conceptual change in economics that address this issue, this is a matter for future research, but we can illustrate why it is a reasonable question to ask by referring to Pang and Marton's (2005) intervention study.

They describe an intervention that encouraged students to understand changes in price as an outcome of differences between the *magnitude* of a change in supply and the *magnitude* of a change in demand. This objective treats causation as running solely from supply and demand to price, and they illustrate this with three graphs (p. 179). Figure 15.1 combines these graphs in one representation.

This diagram shows Demand increasing from D to D′. It shows three alternative increases in Supply from S to S′, S″ or S‴. The increase from S to S′ is smaller than the increase in Demand from D to D′. The increase in Supply from S to S″ is the same as the increase in Demand from D to D′. The increase in Supply from S to S‴ is bigger than the increase in Demand from D to D′. The diagram shows that the change in price is related to the relative magnitude of the changes in demand and supply. However, this only works when the slopes of the demand and supply curves are the same, as they are shown in Figure 15.1. These slopes show the effect of price on demand and supply. These factors have been effectively removed by the simplification introduced in the way that this problem has been constructed. The way in which "steady states" or "equilibria" can emerge from systems with feedback loops is critical in economic reasoning. So we would expect this distinction between conceptions of causation to be evident throughout the subject. Given the evidence from science education, we may expect this shift in understanding causation to be challenging for students.

Moreover, the literature on feedback loops in science tends (e.g. Barbas & Psillos, 1997) to use examples of the form "A→B→A": there is a cycle from cause A to effect B which then also acts as a cause on A. In the case of Supply and Demand there are two reciprocal loops, coordinated by price: "B→A→B" and "C→A→C" where A is price, B is demand,

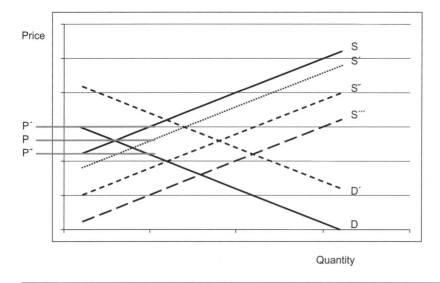

Figure 15.1 The effects of a change in quantity supplied and quantity demanded on price

and C is supply. It may be that the conceptual change toward this model of causation involves the same processes and challenges as the case described by Barbas and Psillos (1997), but it does merit further investigation.

This discussion of context and causation in conceptions of price in terms of supply and demand draws attention. The two dimensions of "price as a reflection of supply and demand" to which we have drawn attention (the economic context and the treatment of causation) are central to conceptions of economies as systems rather than just a set of individual phenomena. We therefore turn now to work that has aimed to investigate students' conceptual structure rather than their understanding of a particular phenomenon.

Kneppers, Elshout-Mohr, Van Boxtel and Van Hout-Wolters (2007) follow the concept mapping approach in their account of the structure of economic understanding. They suggest two criteria for judging the quality of a student's conceptual structure: (1) the completeness of their conceptual network and (2) the extent to which the student makes connections between their conceptual network and "practical situations." They suggest that the structure of economic understanding should be described in terms of "superordinate" concepts such as "the money cycle" and subordinate concepts such as "income" which are "part of" the superordinate concept. Although they do not describe what they mean by "the money cycle," it appears that Kneppers et al. are referring to the Keynesian notion of a "circular flow of income" in the economy. The idea of a circular flow of income (or money cycle) in the whole economy provides an external context which frames a way of understanding income in much the same way that the idea of a market frames understanding of price.

Kneppers and colleagues argue that a student's conceptual structure is incomplete when (i) subordinate concepts are missing or when the student has not established a connection between subordinate concepts or (ii) when the student has not established connections between a concept and "practical examples." They present results from an intervention which suggest that teaching that encourages students to make connections between concepts and practical examples leads to deeper understanding than teaching (through concept maps) that encourages students to fill in the gaps in their concept maps.

The visual representation of this approach through concept maps suggests that a student possesses a concept such as "income" which is independent of the way in which they connect the concept to other concepts and their everyday experience. If it is accepted that a conception is framed by the external context it assumes, then this suggestion becomes difficult to sustain. In the case of "income" the social psychology literature shows children understanding income in terms of personal and household finances. There is no "cycle" or feedback loop here. However, for the economy as a whole there is a cycle in which total expenditure becomes future income. The misapplication of ideas from a household to a whole economy is known in economics as the "fallacy of aggregation." The problems that students face in developing a systemic conception of national income may be similar to the problems noted earlier in the development of a conception of supply and demand as interaction between markets.

We now turn to an account of conceptual structure in economics that aims to take account of this difficulty. Davies (2011b) draws on the way in which, according to Variation Theory, features of a phenomenon are highlighted by particular conceptions. In the case of conceptions of price, referred to earlier, one conception highlights the feature "supply" while another conception highlights the feature "demand" as well as the feature "supply." However, we may also consider different conceptions of the phenomenon "supply." Therefore, a change in conception from "price in terms of supply" to "price in terms of supply and demand" may fall into one of three categories: (i) a change in conception of price with no accompanying change in conception of supply (component relations), (ii) a change in conception of price which is accompanied by a change in conception of supply (component reconfiguration), or (iii) a change in conception which involves a qualitative change in the perceived context in which the phenomenon is framed (as in a shift from a conception of price in terms of an individual producer to a conception of price in terms of markets). That is, the power of a conceptual change is measured in its impact on conceptual structure rather than (as in Pang & Marton, 2003, 2005) on change in the conception of a single phenomenon. Davies (2011b) illustrates the category of "theoretical reframing" with an example of change in the understanding of the context of the phenomenon of price: from the individual producer, to a single market to interaction between markets (cf. Halldén, 1990, on students' understanding of theory in biology and evolution, as students use teleological rather than causal explanations). These changes may be compared with Chi's (2008) account of ontological states in conceptions of scientific phenomena. Just as with conceptions in science, the simplest category of theoretical framing treats economic phenomena in terms of the motivation and decision-making of individual agents. However, in contrast to conceptions of science, more complex theoretical framing of conceptions of economic phenomena treats them as interactions between agency and structure, although the relative importance of agency and structure remains a central source of debate and disagreement between social scientists.

In summary, it is too early to draw firm conclusions about the development of students' economic conceptions. One early, influential study (Dahlgren, 1984) reported the persistence of a conception of price as an intrinsic characteristic of an everyday product even after an undergraduate education in economics. However, Pang and Marton (2005) report that none of the 169 16–18-year-old students in their study displayed this conception even before their intervention. We cannot yet be sure how far reported results have been affected by variation in the problems posed to students and the variation in the ways in which researchers have interpreted "price as a reflection of supply and demand." On the basis of our review of the available evidence and through drawing parallels with the literature on conceptual development in science we have suggested two dimensions of conceptions of economic phenomena that are likely to be critical to the development of students' conceptual structure. The first of these is the importance of the context in which a phenomenon is understood. Students develop conceptions of phenomena through everyday experience which exposes a very restricted set of economic relationships. Subsequent instruction often uses the same language (e.g., "supply and demand") that students have used to express their everyday understanding. However, the instructional language is intending to convey a conception using a categorically different context and this, we believe, generates substantial challenges for learners. The second dimension is the portrayal of causation within an economic conception. The equilibrium models that dominate introductory and intermediate instruction in economics embody causal relationships that operate in both directions between pairs of variables. The utterances reported so far in the research evidence seem to show students thinking of causation as unidirectional (largely from either demand or supply to price). This may indicate that developing a multi-directional understanding of causation presents a stumbling block to students, that instruction has not clearly aimed to develop a multi-directional understanding of causation or that the research process has not been exposing more sophisticated thinking. We believe that future research should investigate each of these dimensions.

Conceptual change in economics (and in other social science) entails a change in conceptual structure. We have argued that Variation Theory provides a more promising approach than concept mapping (Kneppers et al., 2007; Marangos and Alley 2007) to this problem, not least because it provides a strong connection with the evidence of qualitative differences between conceptions of particular phenomena. In particular, it would be helpful to have a body of evidence about conceptions of related phenomena (such as price and supply). As yet we have very little evidence of conceptual change in economics that is "caught in flight." Evidence of this kind is needed to judge whether it is appropriate to distinguish between conceptual change according to the depth of change in conceptual structure as suggested by Davies (2011b).

Values and Sense of Self

The relationship between sense of self and conceptual change in economic understanding is addressed in Davies and Lundholm's (2012) investigation of young people's sense of *what should be the case* – in relation to whether or not particular goods should be made available for free. This line of enquiry may be contrasted with research that has been undertaken into scientific conceptions. For example, while considerable attention has been paid to the question "What different conceptions are there of the shape of earth?", there has been no investigation of children's conceptions of what shape the earth *should be*. It is difficult to imagine the circumstances that would lead a researcher interested in instruction to pose this question. Economic phenomena are *products* of human choices, beliefs, and values and this makes them categorically different from most scientific phenomena investigated in school (e.g., the boiling point of water, tides, the life cycle of a butterfly). Prices in the former Soviet Union were not the outcomes of supply and demand because humans had decided that the economy would be run in a different way. Of course, the aim of developing students' capacity to become active citizens is an important dimension of the science curriculum in schools (e.g., in relation to understanding of climate change and healthy living). However, the distinctive relationship between phenomena, human decisions, beliefs, and values in social science means that the objective of preparation for active citizenship is more central in social science (Davies, 2006a).

The relationship between sense of self and conceptual change has featured strongly in the literature on threshold concepts (Meyer & Land, 2005) and is addressed in the literature on threshold concepts in economics (Davies, 2006b, 2011b; Davies & Mangan, 2007, 2008). This literature suggests that the development of disciplinary thought has created ideas that bind bodies of thought together. This assertion is easily recognizable as a restatement of an idea that has been prominent and powerful within the conceptual change tradition: the application of Kuhn's paradigms in the context of conceptual development. The "threshold concept" idea suggests that only a small number of conceptual changes should be understood as paradigm shifts and that these instances occur in conceptual change from one kind of disciplinary understanding to another rather than from naïve to disciplinary understanding. It is suggested that "threshold" conceptual change involves a reframing of a student's understanding of ideas from the discipline and that this kind of conceptual change is only possible when a student has become familiar with a set of disciplinary ideas.

The "threshold concept" literature also suggests that this reframing is likely to be troublesome for students because (i) it requires them to regard their previous understanding of disciplinary ideas as inadequate and (ii) it ushers in a profoundly different way of understanding a wide range of phenomena. These problems have been observed in the literature on "warm conceptual change" (Sinatra & Mason, 2008). The literature on threshold concepts has suggested that changes in students' sense of identity in relation to the discipline are closely aligned with their response to being confronted with a threshold concept. That is, coming to understand the discipline in terms of threshold concepts is proposed as critical to a sense of "thinking like an economist" while rejecting a threshold concept is likely to be associated with a rejection of a subject as a useful way of understanding everyday phenomena. This strand of research is still in its "early stages" and there is a need for research evidence on whether this suggested alignment is observed in practice.

CONCEPTUAL CHANGE ON ENVIRONMENT, SUSTAINABILITY AND SUSTAINABLE DEVELOPMENT

Theoretical Perspectives

Researchers in the field of environmental education have tended to focus on understanding of collective terms such as "environment" or "sustainability" rather than particular phenomena. For example, Loughland, Reid, and Petocz (2002) categorize the conceptions of "environment" held by young people between the ages of nine and 17. Using written answers of over 2,000 students who were asked to complete the phrase "I think the term/word environment means . . .", they applied phenomenographic analysis to identify six conceptions which they grouped in two sets (Table 15.1).

Van Petegem and Blieck (2006) used the "New Ecological Paradigm," which asks students to indicate their level of agreement with each of 16 statements. Exploratory factor analysis suggested three distinct dimensions: "limits to growth" (e.g., agreement with "We are close to having too many people on earth"); "balance of nature" (e.g., agreement with "When humans disturb nature it often produces terrible results"); and "humans over nature" (e.g., agreement with "Humans are meant to rule it over the rest

Table 15.1 Categories of students' conceptions of "environment" (Loughland et al., 2002)

Object focused
1. The environment is a place
2. The environment is a place that contains living things
3. The environment is a place that contains living things and people

Relational focus
4. The environment does something for people
5. People are part of the environment and responsible for it
6. People and the environment are in a mutually sustaining relationship

of nature"). Each of the 16 statements used in this scale presumes a relationship between the physical and the human (categories 4–6 in Loughland et al., 2002).

Shepardson, Wee, Priddy, and Harbor (2007) used a different method but achieved similar results with similar age groups. They first asked students to draw a picture of the environment and then to explain it in their own words. Second, they presented students with seven pictures and asked them to say whether they thought each showed "an environment." They suggest four categories of conception, which they refer to as distinct models (Table 15.2). The first two conceptions fall into Loughland et al.'s "object" categories, while the second two correspond to categories 4 and 5 in Loughland et al.'s "relational" categories. Shepardson et al. report that their first model was the most common with each age group. There was also little change, by age group, in the proportion of students using each model.

Walshe (2008) used concept mapping and interviews to investigate 12/13-year-olds' understanding of "sustainability." She reports that a pilot task using the word "sustainability" as the prompt was not very successful. In her main investigation Walshe asked students to produce a concept map of "sustainable *tourism*" and this prompted much more extensive diagrams. She coded students' responses using categories derived from a study (Summers, Corney, & Childs, 2004) of the conceptions of student teachers. This form of analysis counts the frequency with which elements occur in concept maps rather than attending to the structure of the concept map (e.g., in Kinchin, Hay, & Adams, 2000; Kneppers et al., 2007). The categorization grid suggested by Summers et al. is more fine-grained than the categorization suggested in any other study, although it does nest categories within two categories – "nature" and "purpose" – which appear similar to the categories "object focused" and "relational focused" suggested by Loughland et al. in 2002. Moreover, whereas Walshe categorizes "Cars and planes cause air pollution" to a category "nature: environmental" and "Don't destroy the environment for new places" to a category "purpose: preservation," both statements would be categorized as "a place modified by humans" in Shepardson et al.'s grid.

Aguirre-Bielowsky, Freeman, and Vass (2012) conducted interviews with students aged nine to 11 years in New Zealand and Mexico. They asked students "What is the environment to you?," "Do you think there are problems with the environment?" and "Why do these problems happen and can they be improved?" Their categorization of responses to the first question suggests a similar distribution of conceptions to Shepardson et al. (2007): Most students referred to the environment in purely physical terms. However, when they were prompted to suggest environmental problems, a large majority of students referred to interactions between humans and the physical environment.

Finally, Sternäng and Lundholm (2012) report an intervention study with students in a Chinese "green" school. Students took part in a role-play in which they were given information about possible effects of establishing a car factory. Two conceptions were

Table 15.2 Categories of students' conceptions of "environment" (Shepardson et al., 2007)

1. A natural place where plants and animals live
2. A place where animals, plants and humans live
3. A place which supports life
4. A place impacted or modified by humans

dominant in students' arguments during the role-play and in their reasoning after it had finished. First, they argued that the physical environment was a resource for human development (as in the fourth category in the typology suggested by Loughland et al., 2002). Second, they argued that scope for adopting policies to sustain the physical environment was dependent on achieving economic growth. This conception treats human well-being as somewhat divorced from a sustainable physical environment.

While these studies provide an emerging sense of conceptions in the field of environmental education, the variation in methods means that inferences must be very cautious. First, the literature suggests two broad categories of conceptions: those that regard environments as "objects" and those that regard environments as points of interaction with humans. It is difficult to tell from existing evidence whether or not this distinction is an artifact of the research process. This may be suggested by evidence in Aguirre-Bielowsky et al. (2012) showing that nine- to 11-year-old students who appeared to understand the environment as an object when asked "What is the environment to you?" described human–environment interactions when asked about problems with the environment. The relationship between students' conceptions of the physical environment and their social science understanding has not been a prominent theme in the literature (Lundholm, 2011). Studies of learning about environmental issues have predominantly focused on natural scientific understanding (Lundholm, 2013; Rickinson, 2001; 2006, Rickinson, Lundholm, & Hopwood, 2009), and there is a lack of social or behavioral science focus in these reviews and summaries of empirical work (cf. Sternäng & Lundholm, 2011, 2012). However, when considering causes and solutions to environmental problems such as resource depletion and degradation, the focus arguably shifts toward society and the individual.

Second, students may respond quite differently when "environment" or "sustainability" is contextualized. Shepardson et al. (2007) tried to cover this point by asking students to respond to seven different photographs showing different environments although they do not report differences between students' responses to these photographs. Walshe (2008) did find that students produced much more detailed concept maps in response to "sustainable tourism" than in response to "sustainability." Social and economic elements may be more evident in younger students' thinking about particular, familiar environments than in their responses to the word "environment."

Third, studies (Loughland et al., 2002; Shepardson et al., 2007) that have gathered data from students at different ages have found no evidence of change in conceptions as students get older. This could be interpreted evidence of any or all of (i) that a conception of the environment as a place acts as a barrier to conceptual change; (ii) teaching has typically been ineffective; or (iii) questions to students have not encouraged them to reveal the sophistication of their thinking.

Values and Sense of Self

Conceptions of interactions between humans and the physical environment are deeply imbued with students' values. They embody judgments about the value of whether environmental change should be judged solely in terms of human interest as well as judgments about the value to humans of preserving or changing physical environments. We turn now to studies which provide evidence of how students' values become evident in the process of (or resistance to) conceptual change.

First, values are revealed in students' emotions (Rickinson et al., 2009; Lundholm, Hopwood, & Rickinson, 2013). For example, a secondary school student closed her eyes, expressed unease, and disengaged from the task when viewing a video showing how the forest was cut down. Watts & Alsop (1997) provide evidence of undergraduates' disengagement associated with their dislike of, and discomfort with, instruction on nuclear power in physics.

Second, students who have committed themselves to a particular discipline may object to the way in which human/physical environment interactions are framed by another discipline. For example, one series of studies (Lundholm, 2007, 2008, 2013; Rickinson et al., 2009) reports reactions of biology undergraduates to economics lectures on the price mechanism. Students expressed frustration with what they perceived as an exclusion of "nature" from economics. One student objected to the way in which "everything has to be shown in dollars and cents when a decision is to be made, and my world view really opposes to that" (Rickinson et al., 2009, p. 52; see also Lundholm, 2007). However, these students did not abandon their economics studies, as has been reported by others (Shanahan & Meyer, 2006). The students expressing feelings of despair (as above), also saw benefits of pricing nature in relation to their environmental concerns and professional goals: gaining economical knowledge with the purpose of improving the environment.

Other studies (Lundholm et al., 2013; Rickinson et al., 2009) report students' conscious struggle with different disciplinary frames for human/environment interactions. A secondary student in geography described the subject as "a kind of opinion subject because people have different opinions about things." Biology students expressed their uncertainty about what they considered to be non-scientific approaches to environmental problems, asking questions such as "How do we distinguish and separate our viewpoints and values from 'factual' knowledge? If we don't, are we not being 'scientific'?" (Rickinson et al., 2009, p. 56).

In the terms used in our discussion of conceptual change in economics, we may describe students' anxieties and uncertainties as arising from alternative external frames, each of which encourages them to conceptualize relationships between human action and the physical environment in different ways. Rickinson et al. (2009) and Lundholm et al. (2013) observe that students' aspirations for the future may frame their thinking in a similar way. Swedish undergraduates responded in varied ways to an ecology course taken as part of a vocationally oriented degree in engineering; some considered it irrelevant to a future as an engineer, hence took a bare-minimum approach to work, while others could see it was relevant as part of an understanding that everyone in society should share (encapsulated in the Swedish concept of *allmänbildning*).

In conclusion, the research described here shows, firstly, that conceptual change (and learning processes) has not been in focus but rather descriptions and mapping of conceptions, and that there is a general lack in the research community of using learning theories. However, a few recent studies focusing on learning processes conclude that emotions and values, issues of relevance and negotiations of viewpoints are all important parts of coming to learn, and engage with, environmental content. Secondly, it is concluded that environmental and sustainability issues entail a multidisciplinary content where linkages need to be made between different subjects and fields, increasing the complexity of what is to be learnt, hence increasing learning challenges, which raises a need to further explore this aspect as well as that of understanding how students conceptually develop in these fields – societal (economics, law, politics) and natural understanding *per se*, and in conjunction.

DISCUSSION: KEY FINDINGS AND ISSUES

The body of evidence on conceptual change in social science is much smaller than that available to researchers of conceptual change in science. Few questions have been settled. There is an emerging body of evidence of conceptions of particular economic and environmental phenomena, but there has been little investigation of changes in conceptions. Moreover, conceptual change in the social science domains neglected in this chapter may occur in ways that are different from conceptual change in economics and environmental education. Therefore our summary of key findings and issues is tentative, raising more questions than answers.

First, the breadth of the perceived external context is a critical factor in conceptions of social science phenomena. Personal experience offers access to a very limited external context. A student's experience of the price of a drink they buy is restricted to their observation of selling. They do not have observational access to relationships between the seller and the market in which that seller operates. Neither do they have access to relationships between that market and other markets. Immediate experience leads students to develop a conception that sellers are generally more willing to sell at a lower price if they sell more ("bulk-buying"). A conception of sellers' behavior in the context of markets suggests that sellers will offer more for sale if the price is higher. If instruction does not directly address this problem, students try to use a "bulk-buying" idea when they are trying to deal with "market" problems.

Second, social science theories rarely accept unidirectional causation. For example, introductory economics suggests that demand and supply affect price and that price affects demand and supply. However, the conceptions of price and the environment that have been observed in students (before and after instruction) have generally been unidirectional. That is, even when instruction uses representational devices (such as supply and demand graphs) that are designed to display causation operating in two directions, this may remain opaque to students. Our analysis of the existing research base also suggests that differentiation between conceptions in social science should pay more attention to causation and context. There is a risk that lack of attention to these dimensions will exacerbate the tendency for students to adopt the formal language of a discipline while retaining more simplistic ideas developed through personal experience.

Third, students' thinking about context and causation combine to create a structure of social scientific thought: for example, a view that environmental studies means learning how to relate, and causally link, society to nature and vice versa. This entails a progression from understanding society as a "sum of all individuals" to structures (as in institutions, norms, political decision-making, legislation and economic systems), while also being able to connect and relate such understanding to nature (as in ecosystems (change) and resources). This is consistent with the suggestion that environmental learning requires an understanding of "the whole and parts" (Feng, 2012) and an increase in systemic understanding which in turn resonates with findings of learning in economics.

Fourth, social science domains consist of (often competing) bodies of thought about how societies and economies *should* be organized. *Should* universities or water be provided to people without charge? *Should* the logging of forests be subject only to private interests? So far, research has paid relatively little attention to change in conceptions about what is socially, economically, and environmentally desirable. However, we find it unsurprising that emerging evidence (e.g., Davies & Lundholm, 2012; Philip, 2011) indicates the strength of individual experience in shaping conceptions of what is "normal" in social settings. The way in which social science conceptions shape beliefs about "what ought to be" appears to be strongly associated with sense of self. We observe this, for example, in students' reactions to instruction that focuses on deforestation. These findings relate to earlier work by Sinatra and Mason (2008) and Halldén, Scheja, & Haglund (2008) on values, emotions, and metacognition on the hand, and ways that students understand and perceive the social and cultural setting on the other.

As students progress in their education they also begin to accept the value positions taken for granted in the structure of thought developed within a discipline or sub-discipline they have come to accept as their own. This tendency is evident in the environmental conceptions of older students from scientific and non-scientific disciplines. Consequently, the interdisciplinary demands typical in environmental education appear to be inherently challenging. The study of conceptual change in economics has, so far, paid little attention to instruction which aims to develop a structure of economic thought that accepts "pluralist economics," but we suspect that similar difficulties arise in this context.

Suggestions for Future Research

Murphy and Alexander (2008) stress enhancing theoretical understanding of conceptual change in discussing the results of a meta-analysis of empirical conceptual change studies, and conclude on the lack of studies in other domains than natural science. They call for a more developmental model of the conceptual change process, including younger ages, before entering into formal education, as there is a need "for a broader view of change that is not dependent on scientific domains or concepts" (p. 597). Further, they stress that "the conceptual change literature remains in need of a more developmental perspective, as well as investigations that permit the modelling of *initial conceptual formations* as much as later reformations" (p. 597; emphasis added).

We agree with the authors on the importance of enhancing our theoretical understanding of formation processes and conceptual change processes, but we would like to stress that with regard to age, there is a current "blind spot" of investigations pertaining to the ages of 16 years and beyond. This age span is particularly interesting, as this is where formal education in the social sciences domains increases – along with new experiences of social, political, and economic phenomena. This means that issues of experience, socialization, and education can and should be given central foci and be accounted for. Also, this is a time when adolescents and adults are asked to take part in democratic and societal decisions and make choices that impact on others and the future.

Furthermore, we believe the roles of values in social sciences and conceptual change research need further attention. For example, how are values understood as part of the social sciences, and how do students respond to that? What challenges arise if the disciplines are not perceived as presenting facts, but are "opinionated subjects" as shown in earlier work on students' learning in geography (Lundholm et al., 2013)? This question becomes particularly salient in the context of prominent controversies in social sciences associated with competing schools of thought. We know that epistemological beliefs are generally associated with variation in achievement and that the likelihood of a student expressing a more complex epistemological belief varies according to the social science subject they are studying. However, we know little of the interaction between episte-mological beliefs and values in the process of conceptual change in the context of competing schools of thought in social science. And how do students deal with and handle their own values, and the way theories (implicitly) address the self because content and topics in the social sciences are charging in various ways? And finally, as social science focuses on describing, explaining, and hypothesizing how societies could and should work differently, how is this understood?

REFERENCES

Aguirre-Bielowsky, I., Freeman, C., & Vass, E. (2012). Influences on children's environmental cognition: A comparative analysis of New Zealand and Mexico. *Environmental Education Research, 18*(1), 91–115.

Barbas, A., & Psillos, D. (1997). Causal reasoning as a base for advancing a systemic approach to simple electrical circuits. *Research in Science Education, 27*(3), 445–459.

Berti, A. E., & Grivet, A. (1990). The development of economic reasoning in children from 8 to 13 years old: Price mechanism. *Contributi di Psicologia, 3,* 37–47.

Carretero, M., & Voss, J. F. (Eds.). (1994). *Cognitive and instructional processes in history and the social sciences.* Hillsdale, NJ: Lawrence Erlbaum Associates.

Chi, M. T. H. (2008). Three types of conceptual change: Brief revision, mental model transformation, and categorical shift. In S. Vosniadou (Ed.), *International handbook of research on conceptual change* (pp. 61–82). New York, NY: Routledge.

Dahlgren, L. (1984). Outcomes of learning. In F. Marton, D. Hounsell, & N. Entwistle (Eds.), *The experience of learning.* Edinburgh, UK: Scottish Academic Press.

Davies, P. (2006a). Educating citizens for changing economies. *Journal of Curriculum Studies, 38*(1), 15–30.

Davies, P. (2006b). Threshold concepts: How can we recognize them? In J. H. F. Meyer and R. Land (Eds.), *Overcoming barriers to student understanding: Threshold concepts and troublesome knowledge* (pp. 70–84). London, UK: Routledge.

Davies, P. (2011a). Students' conceptions of price, value and opportunity cost: Some implications for future research, *Citizenship, Social and Economic Education, 10*(2–3), 101–110.

Davies, P. (2011b). Threshold concepts. In G. Hoyt & K. McGoldrick (Eds.), *International handbook on teaching and learning economics* (pp. 250–256). Cheltenham, UK: Edward Elgar.

Davies, P., & Lundholm, C. (2012). Young people's understanding of socio-economic phenomena: Conceptions about the free provision of goods and services. *Journal of Economic Psychology, 33*(1), 79–89.

Davies, P., & Mangan, J. (2007). Threshold concepts and the integration of understanding in economics. *Studies in Higher Education, 32*(6), pp. 711–726.

Davies, P., & Mangan, J. (2008). Embedding threshold concepts: From theory to pedagogical principles to learning activities. In R. Land, J. H. F. Meyer, & J. Smith (Eds.), *Threshold concepts in the disciplines* (pp. 37–50). Rotterdam, The Netherlands: Sense Press.

Feng, L. (2012). Teacher and student responses to interdisciplinary aspects of sustainability education: What do we really know? *Environmental Education Research, 18*(1), 31–43.

Halldén, O. (1990). Questions asked in common sense contexts and in scientific contexts. In P. L. Lijnse, P. Licht, W. De Vos, & A. J. Waarlo (Eds.), *Relating macroscopic phenomena to microscopic particles: A central problem in secondary science education* (pp. 119–130). Utrecht, The Netherlands: CD-b Press.

Halldén, O., Scheja, M., & Haglund. L. (2008). The contextuality of knowledge: An intentional approach to meaning making and conceptual change. In S. Vosniadou (Ed.), *International handbook of research on conceptual change* (pp. 509–532). New York, NY: Routledge.

Kinchin, I. M., Hay, D. B., & Adams, A. (2000). How a qualitative approach to concept map analysis can be used to aid learning by illustrating patterns of conceptual development. *Educational Research, 42*(1), 43–57.

Kneppers, L., Elshout-Mohr, M., Van Boxtel, C., & Van Hout-Wolters, B. (2007). Conceptual learning in relation to near and far transfer in the secondary school subject of economics. *European Journal of Psychology of Education, 12*(2), 115–129.

Leiser, D., & Halachmi, R. B. (2006). Children's understanding of market forces. *Journal of Economic Psychology*, *27*, 6–19.

Loughland, T., Reid, A., & P. Petocz, (2002). Young people's conceptions of environment: A phenomenographic analysis. *Environmental Education Research, 8*, 187–197.

Lundholm, C. (2007). Pricing nature at what price? A study on undergraduate students' conceptions of economics. *South African Journal of Environmental Education, 24*, 126–140.

Lundholm, C. (2008). *Contextualisation and learning in economics: An intentional perspective on the role of values.* Paper presented at the symposium Exploring "Hot" Conceptual Change: Affect, Emotions, Values, Self-Efficacy and Epistemic Beliefs at the 6th International Conference on Conceptual Change, European Association for Research in Learning and Instruction, Turku, Finland.

Lundholm, C. (2011). Society's response to environmental challenges: Citizenship and the role of knowledge. *In Factis Pax, 5*, 80–96.

Lundholm, C. (2013). Environmental learning from a constructivist perspective: Content, context and learner. In C. Russell, J. Dillon, & M. Breunig (Eds.), *Environmental education reader.* New York, NY: Peter Lang.

Lundholm, C., Hopwood, N., & Rickinson, M. (2013). Environmental learning: Insights from research into the student experience. In R. B., Brody, M. Dillon, J. Stevenson, & A. E. J. Wals (Eds.), *International handbook of research on environmental education* (pp. 242–252). London, UK: Routledge.

Marangos, J., & Alley, S. (2007). Effectiveness of concept maps in economics. *Learning and Individual Differences, 17*, 193–199.

Marton, F., & Booth, S. (1997). *Learning and awareness.* Mahwah, NJ: Lawrence Erlbaum Associates.

Marton, F., & Pang, M. F. (2008). The idea of phenomenography and the pedagogy of conceptual change. In S. Vosniadou (Ed.), *International handbook of conceptual change* (pp. 533–559). New York, NY: Routledge.

Meyer, J. H. F., & Land, R. (2005). Threshold concepts and troublesome knowledge (2): Epistemological considerations and a conceptual framework for teaching and learning. *Higher Education, 49*(3), 373–388.

Murphy, P. K., & Alexander, P. (2008). The role of knowledge, beliefs, and interest in the conceptual change process: A synthesis and meta-analysis of the research. In S. Vosniadou (Ed.), *International handbook of research on conceptual change* (pp. 583–616). New York, NY: Routledge.

Pang, M. F., & Marton, F. (2003). Beyond "lesson study": Comparing two ways of facilitating the grasp of some economic concepts. *Instructional Science, 31*, 175–194.

Pang, M. F., & Marton, F. (2005). Learning theory as teaching resource: Enhancing students' understanding of economic concepts. *Instructional Science, 33*(2), 159–191.

Philip, T. (2011). An "ideology in pieces" approach to studying change in teachers' sensemaking about race, racism, racial justice. *Cognition and Instruction, 29*, 297–329.

Pong, W.-Y. (1998). Students' ideas of price and trade, *Economic Awareness, 9*(2), 6–10.

Rickinson, M. (2001). Learners and learning in environmental education: A critical review of evidence. *Environmental Education Research, 7*(3), 207–317.

Rickinson, M. (2006). Researching and understanding environmental learning: hopes for the next ten years. *Environmental Education Research, 12*(3/4), 445–458.

Rickinson, M., Lundholm, C., & Hopwood, N. (2009). *Environmental learning: Insights from research into the student experience.* Dordrecht, The Netherlands: Springer.

Shanahan, M., & Meyer, J. H. F. (2006). The troublesome nature of a threshold concept in economics. In J. Meyer & R. Land (Eds.), *Overcoming barriers to student understanding. threshold concepts and troublesome knowledge* (pp. 100–114). London, UK: Routledge.

Shepardson, D. P., Wee, B., Priddy, M., & Harbor, J. (2007). Students' mental models of the environment. *Journal of Research in Science Teaching, 44*(2), 327–348.

Sinatra, G. M., & Mason, L. (2008). Beyond knowledge: Learner characteristics influencing conceptual change (pp. 560–582). In S. Vosniadou (Ed.), *International handbook of research on conceptual change.* New York, NY: Routledge.

Sternäng, L., & Lundholm, C. (2011). Climate change and morality: Students' conceptions of individual and society. *International Journal of Science Education, 33*, 1131–1148.

Sternäng, L., & Lundholm, C. (2012). Climate change and costs: Investigating Chinese students' conceptions of nature and economic development. *Environmental Education Research, 18*, 417–436.

Summers, M., Corney, G., & Childs, A. (2004). Student teachers' conceptions of sustainable development: The starting points of geographers and scientists. *Educational Research, 46*, 163–182.

Thompson, D. R., & Siegler, R. S. (2000). Buy low, sell high: The development of an informal theory of economics. *Child Development, 71*, 660–677.

Torney-Purta, J. (1994). Dimensions of adolescents' reasoning about political and historical issues: Ontological switches, developmental processes and situated learning. In M. Carretero and J. F. Voss (Eds.), *Cognitive and instructional processes in history and the social sciences* (pp. 103–121). Hillsdale, NJ: Lawrence Erlbaum Associates.

Van Petegem, P., & Blieck, A. (2006). The environmental worldview of children: A cross-cultural perspective, *Environmental Education Research, 12*(5), 625–635.

Vosniadou, S., Vamvakoussi, X., & Skopeliti, I. (2008), The framework theory approach to the problem of conceptual change. In S. Vosniadou (Ed.), *International handbook of research on conceptual change.* New York, NY: Routledge.

Walshe, N. (2008). Understanding students' conceptions of sustainability. *Environmental Education Research, 14,* 537–558.

Watts, M., & Alsop, S. (1997). A feeling for learning: Modelling affective learning in school science. *Curriculum Journal, 8*(3), 351–365.

16

THE FRAMEWORK THEORY APPROACH
APPLIED TO MATHEMATICS LEARNING

Xenia Vamvakoussi, Stella Vosniadou, and Wim Van Dooren,
University of Ioannina, National and Kapodistrian University of
Athens, and Katholieke Universiteit Leuven

THE CONCEPTUAL CHANGE APPROACH AND
MATHEMATICS LEARNING

The conceptual change approach to learning emerged in two different research areas, namely science education and cognitive-developmental psychology (Vosniadou, 1999). Researchers in both traditions drew on Kuhn's (1970) account of scientific change as a source of hypotheses about how concepts change in individuals in the processes of development and learning.

Science education researchers had in their hands a large body of evidence showing that students make systematic errors in science tasks. In their attempts to explain these phenomena, some researchers described students' *misconceptions* (aka *preconceptions* or *alternative conceptions*) as theories that need to be replaced by the currently accepted, correct scientific views through a process of conceptual change (Posner, Strike, Hewson, & Gertzog, 1982). Developmental psychologists, on the other hand, faced a different problem, namely evidence that challenged Piaget's account of domain-general cognitive development by showing that young children showed competency in certain domains far earlier than the Piagetian theory predicted. It was thus assumed that human cognition builds on a set of domain-specific systems of knowledge (e.g. Carey & Spelke, 1996) and cognitive development was described in terms of a radical reorganization of these initial, domain-specific knowledge structures (hence, conceptual change).

Researchers in the field of mathematics education were also faced with the phenomenon of systematic errors in mathematical tasks. Mathematics teachers typically assumed that these errors could be eradicated by drawing students' attention to them and providing the correct procedures. Their expectations, however, were repeatedly belied, as some errors "seemed to pop back up like weeds, and their attraction to students suggesting some deeper compelling quality" (Confrey & Kazak, 2006, p. 307). Despite the similarity between the problem of systematic errors in science and mathematics, the conceptual change approach prominent in the field of science education research did not gain popularity within the mathematics education research community. This may be partly due to the fact that this approach drew on the Kuhnian account of the processes of change in science, and whether this account was relevant for mathematics was in question. Indeed, mathematics has traditionally been viewed as cumulative, in the sense that that a mathematical theory, once established, is never deposed by a later theory (Crowe, 1975). Nevertheless, the question whether there are revolutions in the discipline of mathematics, inspired by the Kuhnian view (e.g., Gillies, 1992), concerned researchers interested in the philosophy of mathematics for education (e.g., Confrey, 1981). And it appears, as Greer and Verschaffel (2007) argue, that there has been a recent shift away from the view of mathematics and mathematics learning as additive to the view that mathematics is characterized by conceptual restructurings.

Another reason why the conceptual change approach may have had minimal effect on the mathematics education research community is the widespread acceptance of the constructivist idea that instruction should take account of students' existing knowledge, in particular young children's intuitive, pre-instructional knowledge, and build on it. Many instructional interventions have been developed with a view to recruiting young children's informal knowledge as a foundation for further learning. As Resnick (2006) later recognized, while such approaches may have had strong and reliable results for young children, they were far less successful for older students dealing with more advanced mathematical concepts. This unexpected result is consistent with the conceptual change approach which predicts that intuitive knowledge can sometimes stand in the way of acquiring more advanced mathematical concepts. In Resnick's own words, "What most of the intuition builders did not anticipate . . . was that intuitively grounded mathematics might, in some cases, make it harder to learn more advanced mathematical ideas" (2006, p. 174).

Finally, it should be taken into consideration that mathematics education researchers also theorized about the phenomenon of the adverse effect of prior knowledge in further learning, and such attempts were presumably considered by the community as more relevant to mathematics learning and teaching than other approaches deemed tailored to science learning and teaching (Hatano, 1996). We will examine two influential theoretical frameworks developed within the mathematics education research community in subsequent sections.

Looking at the broader area of mathematical development and learning, however, one can see that the conceptual change approach strand developed by cognitive-developmental psychologists was also applied in the case of mathematics. Researchers that adopted a domain-specificity perspective took interest in number as a distinct domain of knowledge (e.g., Carey & Gelman, 1991). A great deal of emphasis has been placed on the investigation of the origins of the number concept (for a review, see Ni & Zhou, 2005) and the spontaneous, not instruction-induced, conceptual changes that occur in the course of development (see, for example, Carey, 2009). The interaction of children's initial, pre-instructional understandings of number with new information about non-natural numbers has also been studied and it has been pointed out that initial understanding may eventually stand in the way of learning in the course of instruction (e.g., Hartnett & Gelman, 1998; Smith, Solomon, & Carey, 2005). Research in this area is focused on young children and children at the first years of their school life; consequently it is not concerned with instruction-induced conceptual change regarding more advanced mathematical concepts. As an exception, we should mention here the work of Merenluoto, Lehtinen, and their colleagues (Lehtinen, Merenluoto, & Kasanen, 1997; Merenluoto & Lehtinen, 2002) who were pioneers in considering various conceptual change perspectives coming from the cognitive-developmental strand and their relevance for explaining students' difficulties and systematic errors in a wide range of advanced mathematical notions, such as number, limit, and continuity.

In this chapter we will focus on a relatively recent attempt to apply a specific conceptual change theoretical frame, namely *the framework theory approach to conceptual change* (FTaCC) in the case of mathematics (Vosniadou & Verschaffel, 2004). The FTaCC is presented in detail in Vosniadou (this volume), so we are not going to give a full presentation in this chapter. We will highlight, however, some features that, we believe, make this frame worth considering in the broad area of mathematics learning and teaching.

The FTaCC is a domain-specific approach. It draws on and is informed by evidence coming from research in early development, notably in the domain of number, to address the issue of the structure and content of young children's informal knowledge. At the same time, it provides specific predictions about the interaction of students' prior knowledge with the information coming from instruction. More specifically, it explains students' systematic errors as the manifestation of *synthetic conceptions* that are the product of additive learning; that is, the enrichment of prior knowledge – either informal or coming from earlier instruction – with new but incompatible information. In this sense, the FTaCC builds a bridge between informal mathematics learning and learning via instruction. It also serves as a complementary perspective to domain-general views on learning, notably Piaget's theory, which has been very influential in the area of mathematics education long after it was challenged by empirical evidence in the field of cognitive-developmental psychology (Vosniadou , Vamvakoussi, & Skopeliti, 2008).

Several researchers explored the potential value of the application of the FTaCC to mathematics learning and teaching, notably in a special issue of *Learning and Instruction* (Vosniadou &Verschaffel, 2004), in an edited volume (Vosniadou, Baltas, & Vamvakoussi, 2007), and also in a Research Forum in the 30th Conference of the International Group for the Psychology of Mathematics Education which made this approach more visible to mathematics education researchers as well. This caused interest in the conceptual change perspective, which was reflected in the references to the particular framework by a number of researchers who saw it as a "representative" of the conceptual change approach research strand that can offer descriptions and explanations regarding the difficulty met in a wide range of situations wherein change is necessary (see for example, Prediger, 2008; Shinno & Iwasaki, 2008; Zazkis & Chernoff, 2008; Liljedahl, 2008). However, here we will review more extensively studies that tested specifically the predictions of the FTaCC, as well as intervention studies that investigated the value of related principles for instruction.

TESTING THE PREDICTIONS OF THE FRAMEWORK THEORY APPROACH

There are two key predictions stemming from the FTaCC. The first is that students will face difficulties and make systematic errors precisely in the cases wherein the intended knowledge is in contrast with what they already know (via either informal or formal learning). This prediction lies at the heart of the conceptual change perspective in general. The second is more specific to the FTaCC: Understanding of scientific and mathematical notions that are not compatible with what the individual already knows is not an "all or nothing" situation; rather, there are intermediate states of understanding wherein elements of prior knowledge are combined with elements of the incoming, incompatible, information to produce *synthetic conceptions*. According to this view, many so-called misconceptions in mathematics are synthetic conceptions, produced through the assimilation of new information to incompatible prior knowledge.

Many empirical studies in the domain of mathematics conducted within the conceptual change framework focus on the impact of initial understandings of number on the learning of a wide range of mathematical concepts. These initial understandings of number are tied around the ontology and properties of natural numbers and are assumed to form an explanatory framework of number that supports reasoning and learning about natural numbers – inferring the successor principle, developing computational and problem-solving strategies, etc. (see also Smith et al., 2005). The initial explanatory framework for number, however, is not compatible with information about non-natural numbers coming from instruction. It is thus predicted that students are bound to form synthetic conceptions about rational numbers as they assimilate new, incompatible, information in their pre-existing knowledge base.

Stafylidou and Vosniadou (2004) investigated the development of primary and secondary school students' understanding of the numerical value of fractions. They pointed out that, unlike what students know about natural numbers, fractions cannot be ordered in terms of their position on the counting list. In addition – unlike natural numbers, which are bounded by a smallest number (1 or 0) – fractions are not bounded by a "smallest" fraction. They also pointed to another difference that is related to symbolic notation: Each natural number is associated with one symbol (a combination of digits). On the other hand, fractions are typically symbolized as two whole numbers separated by a bar. Focusing on these three differences, Stafylidou and Vosniadou predicted – in line with the FTaCC – that students would make systematic errors in these tasks that could be interpreted as synthetic conceptions of the fraction concept. The participants (in total 200 fifth, sixth, seventh, eighth. and tenth graders) were tested via questionnaires and were asked to (a) write the smallest and biggest fraction that they could think of and explain their answers, and (b) compare and order fractions. Based on students' responses and explanations in both kinds of tasks, Stafylidou and Vosniadou were able to place 89% of them in three categories corresponding to an initial and two intermediate states of understanding. In the first category, students did not take into consideration the multiplicative relation between the numerator and the denominator and considered fractions to consist of two independent natural numbers. In the second, fractions were considered to be always smaller than the unit, again ignoring the relation between the terms of the fraction. Only in the third category were students able to take this relation into consideration. Students in the intermediate categories exhibited synthetic conceptions of fractions. One such example comes from the majority of students in the third category who, although apt to consider the relation between the terms of the fraction, still believed that fractions are bounded by a smallest and a biggest fraction.

In a series of studies, Vamvakoussi and Vosniadou (2004, 2007, 2010) focused on a major difference between natural and rational numbers: Within the natural numbers set, between any two numbers there is a finite (possibly zero) number of numbers. On the contrary, rational numbers are densely ordered; that is, between any two rational numbers there are infinitely many rational numbers. Vamvakoussi and Vosniadou hypothesized that understanding the dense ordering of rational numbers would be a slow and gradual process and that students would form synthetic conceptions of rational numbers' intervals with respect to their ordering (discrete/dense). They used one type of task, namely the question "How many numbers are there between two numbers a and b?", manipulating the type of the endpoints of the interval (natural numbers, decimals, fractions). Vamvakoussi and Vosniadou presented this task to secondary students using a number of different methodologies (i.e., individual interviews (2004), open and multiple-choice questionnaires (2007), and multiple-choice questionnaires alone (2010)). They repeatedly found that the idea of discreteness was a major constraint on students' understanding of density and that the type of the interval endpoints affected students' judgments on the number as well as the type of the intermediate numbers. For example, looking at the individual profiles of the participants of the 2011 study (549 seventh, ninth, and eleventh graders), one can see that 14% of the students consistently referred to a finite number (possibly zero) of intermediates. Another 34% referred to intervals with different ordering, depending on the interval endpoints (e.g., infinitely many intermediates between decimals, but a finite number between fractions). In addition, 11% consistently referred to infinitely many intermediates, but were reluctant to accept that, for instance, there can be decimals between fractions or fractions between decimals. The two last profiles reveal synthetic conceptions. Originally obtained with Greek students, these findings have recently been replicated with a different population, namely Flemish (Dutch-speaking Belgian) students (Vamvakoussi, Christou, Mertens, & Van Dooren, 2011).

The impact of students' initial explanatory frameworks for number on further learning has been investigated from a conceptual change perspective also in the area of algebra. In a series of studies, Christou and colleagues (Christou & Vosniadou, 2009, 2012; Christou, Vosniadou, & Vamvakoussi, 2007) investigated secondary students' understanding of the use of literal symbols in the context of algebra. They hypothesized that the development of students' understanding of the concept of variable is heavily influenced by their explanatory frameworks for number wherein natural number is the dominant type of number. They predicted that students would take literal symbols to stand mainly for natural numbers and that even when students would start to assign non-natural numbers, they would still be reluctant to accept *any* real number as substitute for variables. They expected that, instead, students would accept some types of non-natural numbers but not all types. For example, they would assign to a variable only integers, or only positive numbers, or accept decimals but not fractions, thus retaining some aspect of the natural numbers, such as the integer character, the sign, or the symbolic representation (in the sense that a number represented in fractional form resembles natural numbers less than as a decimal). They tested this hypothesis in a variety of situations (interviews, open-ended and multiple-choice questionnaires) and their findings were consistent with their predictions. Specifically, Chistou and colleagues documented a strong tendency on the part of students to assign only natural numbers to a variable. In all of their studies, students appeared very reluctant to accept that any variable can represent any type of numbers, even when the correct answer was present as an option in a multiple-choice questionnaire. For instance, in the second experiment reported in Christou and Vosniadou (2012), the participants (34 eighth and ninth graders) were presented with a set of algebraic expressions and were asked for each expression to choose among 11 alternatives any values that could *not* be assigned to the given expression. The alternatives included (positive and negative) fractions, decimals, and integers. The 12th alternative was always the correct response, namely, "No, all numbers can be assigned to it." Only 17.6% of the participants chose the correct answer regarding the expression (b). Christou and Vosniadou noted that in general it was easier for students to substitute negative whole numbers than fractional or decimal numbers – and also decimals rather than fractions – for literal symbols. The idea that a literal symbol, denoting a (real) variable, stands for a limited range of numbers points to a synthetic conception of this mathematical notion. Recently, a study with Flemish secondary students showed that, although they tend to assign only natural numbers far less frequently than their Greek peers, they still have great difficulty in consistently assigning *any* type of numbers to literal symbols (Van Dooren, Christou, & Vamvakoussi, 2010).

In the same area, namely algebra, Vlassis (2004) investigated upper secondary school students' understanding of the minus sign. She argued that understanding the role and meaning of the minus sign in the shift from natural number arithmetic to algebra requires conceptual change. She noted that in the context of arithmetic the minus sign is used to denote subtraction, whereas in the context of algebra it has multiple uses (e.g., it also is used to denote the opposite of an algebraic expression or to inverse an operation). Vlassis assumed that arithmetical presuppositions about the use of minus sign in the context of natural number arithmetic would interfere with the use of the algebraic rules required to operate with negatives and predicted that students would have difficulties in making sense of the minus sign in the second case. She interviewed 12 eighth graders who were asked to solve 16 tasks related to the reduction of polynomials, explain how they worked, and also elaborate on the meaning of the minus sign in various situations. The results indicated that many of the methods used by students to reduce the polynomials were a blend of arithmetical and algebraic methods (typically rules) that often led to errors. Moreover, no student was able to consider the multiple roles of the minus sign. All students agreed that the minus sign denotes subtraction, which is consistent with its use in the context of arithmetic. All of them believed that the minus sign at the beginning of a polynomial is always considered as the sign of a negative number, which is consistent with its use within the integers. One fourth of them considered a – mathematically "naïve" – role of the minus sign in the context of algebra, namely that it is used to split the terms of the polynomial. As Vlassis argued, these can be considered as synthetic conceptions of the minus sign.

The FTaCC has also been used in the area of geometry. Biza and colleagues (Biza, Souyoul, & Zachariades, 2005; Biza & Zachariades, 2006) focused on the concept of tangent line that is introduced in instruction in three different contexts: First as the tangent of the circle in Euclidean geometry; then as the tangent of conic sections in analytic geometry; finally, as the tangent at a point on a curve in calculus. Biza and colleagues analyzed the characteristics of the (Euclidean) circle tangent line that are not necessarily preserved in the other two contexts (i.e., that it has only one common point with the circle and that it leaves the entire circle on the same semi-plane). These can be considered as fundamental presuppositions of students' initial explanatory framework about the tangent line. Biza and colleagues hypothesized that students who have been taught about the tangent line in the context of calculus would still be constrained by these two presuppositions and thus synthetic conceptions of the tangent line would emerge. They tested this hypothesis in a pilot study with 19 first-year university students of mathematics using questionnaires and interviews (Biza et al., 2005), followed by a study with 182 participants of the same population that was conducted with questionnaires (Biza & Zachariades, 2006). The questionnaire included tasks such as recognizing and drawing tangent lines at a point on a curve. The results of both studies were consistent with the hypothesis. For instance, in the second study, about 40% of the participants assigned to the tangent line on a curve properties of the circle tangent line. About 31% generated a class of synthetic conceptions of the tangent line on a curve. These students did not apply the properties of the circle globally (i.e., for the whole graph), but locally (i.e., at a neighbourhood of the point of tangency). This class of synthetic conceptions allowed them to respond correctly to some, but not all tasks.

The studies presented here indicate that the FTaCC is a comprehensive theoretical frame that can offer persuasive explanations for students' difficulties with notions in a variety of mathematical areas (e.g., number and number systems, algebra, calculus). Moreover, as indicated by the studies by Biza and colleagues summarized above, it can deal with advanced mathematical notions, such as the tangent line at a point on a curve, where students' prior knowledge is not experience-based – as in the case of number – but is built through instruction. Last, but certainly not least, the assumptions underlying the FTaCC allow for novel predictions that lead to new results. Let us refer to the work of Christou and colleagues as an example: Prior literature regarding students' understanding of variables (see Christou & Vosniadou, 2012, for a review) had documented that students initially find it difficult to accept that a literal symbol takes its meaning in the domain of numbers – and is not, for example, merely an abbreviation of an objects' name (e.g. "h" for "height"). There was also substantial evidence that when students start to associate literal symbols with numbers, they typically believe that a variable stands for one single number, an "unknown" that has to be revealed. However, what happens after students come to understand that a literal symbol can stand for a range of numbers and not for a specific unknown number had not been investigated. Looking through the lenses of the FTaCC, Christou and colleagues predicted that there would be intermediate states of understanding and produced new empirical evidence regarding students' understanding of the notion of variable.

INSTRUCTIONAL INTERVENTIONS

An important prediction of the FTaCC is that instruction-induced conceptual change is typically a time-consuming and difficult process, because it involves the reorganization of not just one misconception or one belief but an interrelated system of beliefs and presuppositions that takes a long time to be accomplished. This implies that it takes considerable effort to plan instruction aiming at conceptual change, and that in some cases the learning gains are more modest than hoped for. Vosniadou, Ioannides, Dimitrakopoulou, & Papademetriou (2001) argued that conceptual change requires the use of many different instructional interventions and they proposed certain principles for the design of a learning environment aiming at conceptual change including (a) deep exploration of few key concepts in a field, instead of superficially covering a great deal of material, (b) paying attention to the order of acquisition of concepts involved, (c) taking students' prior knowledge into consideration, (d) facilitating metaconceptual awareness, (e) providing meaningful experiences that motivate students to put the effort necessary for conceptual change, (f) (wise) use of cognitive conflict, (g) fostering the use of models and external representations. Each one of these principles separately is not, of course, peculiar to the FTaCC, and is certainly not strange to mathematics education researchers. However, Tsamir and Tirosh (2007) argued that these principles combined offer a valuable framework for analyzing and reflecting on instructional interventions in mathematics. They in fact used this framework as a tool to retrospectively analyze and evaluate a number of interventions they had conducted with the purpose of teaching the Cantorian set theory, in particular the equivalence of infinite sets. This is a topic that presents students with many difficulties and it has been documented that they use comparison methods that are appropriate for finite, but not infinite sets – that is, they transfer their prior knowledge and experience in the domain of finite sets to infinite sets, thus this is a case where the conceptual change perspective is appropriate. Tsamir and Tirosh explained in detail how their successful instructional choices were compatible with the above principles and concluded that these recommendations could and should be used for designing learning environments for mathematics instruction aiming at conceptual change.

Van Dooren, De Bock, Hessels, Janssens, and Verschaffel (2004) also drew on these principles to design 10 experimental lessons with the purpose of remedying eighth grade students' "illusion of linearity" in the context of geometry. The illusion of linearity is a well-documented phenomenon for students of various ages and it is related to the application of linear reasoning in cases where this is not appropriate. In the context of geometry, students are typically found to believe that, for instance, if the sides of a figure are doubled to produce a similar figure, the area and volume will also be doubled. Van Dooren et al. reinterpreted this phenomenon from a conceptual change perspective, noting that children, already at a very young age, experience the wide applicability and intrinsic simplicity of linear/proportional relations. Moreover, in primary and secondary school mathematics education, extensive attention is paid to this type of relations. They assumed that by the time students meet other kinds of relations, the idea that all relations are proportional is firmly established. After implementing the series of carefully designed experimental lessons, they found that the number of linear errors dropped considerably. However, they also found that (a) some students showed no progress, (b) some students were not consistent in providing a correct response, and (c) some students started overusing non-linear reasoning. These results are consistent with the assumption that conceptual change is a slow and gradual process, and thus time and persistence is necessary in instruction for accomplishing it.

Vamvakoussi and Vosniadou (2012) drew on another suggestion stemming from the conceptual change literature, namely the use in instruction of cross-domain mapping, a particular case of analogical reasoning, which is considered an important mechanism for conceptual restructuring (see also Smith et al., 2005). Vamvakoussi and Vosniadou explored the instructional value of a cross-domain mapping between "number" and "line" for secondary school students' understanding of density. The researches were based on the findings of a pilot study showing that (a) density was more accessible to secondary school students in a geometrical context (infinitely many points on a straight line segment) compared to a numerical context (infinitely many numbers in an interval), (b) students' conceptions of the line segment were nevertheless far from that of a dense array of points, and (c) the "infinitely many intermediates" aspect of density was more accessible to students than the "no successor" aspect (although they are mathematically equivalent). They then designed a text-based intervention that attempted to build the notion of density in a geometrical context, making explicit reference to the number-to-points correspondence and using the "rubber line" bridging analogy (the line as an imaginary unbreakable rubber band) to convey the no-successor principle. The text intervention improved student performance in tasks regarding the infinity of numbers in an interval; the "rubber line" bridging analogy further improved performance, successfully conveying the idea that these numbers can never be found one immediately next to the other.

Paying attention to relations is a crucial element of analogical reasoning. In the following we summarize an intervention study that highlights the importance of emphasizing relations when presenting information to students.

Asmuth and Rips (2006) studied the interaction of deeply entrenched prior knowledge of Euclidean geometry with new information about hyperbolic geometry, one of several non-Euclidean geometries. From a conceptual change perspective, this is an interesting topic because Euclidean geometry is, in many ways, the "primary" geometry in terms of everyday experiences and also of schooling. In addition, hyperbolic geometry has both similarities and dissimilarities with Euclidean geometry. In their first experimental study, Asmuth and Rips investigated whether emphasizing the holistic properties of the system, compared to emphasizing local building blocks, would better facilitate understanding of hyperbolic geometry. They contrasted presentation of information in terms of figures (holistic approach) and in terms of lines (building-blocks approach). Students in the two conditions performed equally well at the items they were trained for, but students in the first condition were more apt to transfer what they had learned in the case of figures to the case of lines. In a follow-up experiment, Asmuth and Rips found that explicit instructions to apply what they had learned in the context of lines to the context of figures did not reliably facilitate the second condition students. They concluded that the more structured, holistic input seemed to be superior to training that focused on more specific building blocks, presumably because information is presented in a way that encourages noticing of *relations* between elements.

All in all, the intervention studies reported here point to the complexity of the issue of conceptual change in mathematics. It appears that, as predicted by the FTaCC, considerable effort in the planning of instruction and also long-term implementation are required. At the same time, these studies highlight kinds of intervention that, under appropriate conditions, may induce conceptual change in diverse mathematics domains, such as the domain of number, geometry, and advanced mathematical notions such as infinite sets.

DIFFERENT PERSPECTIVES ON THE PROBLEM OF PRIOR KNOWLEDGE IN MATHEMATICS LEARNING

In Vosniadou et al. (2008), several other approaches are compared to the FTaCC, including Piaget's account of cognitive development and diSessa's "knowledge in pieces" view on conceptual change. Here we will discuss four approaches that are relevant to mathematics learning. We first focus on two influential theoretical constructs developed in the field of mathematics education, namely the notion of *obstacle* introduced by Brousseau (2002) and the notion of *intuition* as used by Fischbein (1987, 1999). Both represent attempts to frame the problem of the adverse effect of prior knowledge on mathematics learning in general. Then we discuss two approaches that represent attempts to explore the complicated relation between prior and intended knowledge in the context of rational number learning, emphasizing the positive role of prior knowledge (Siegler, Thompson, & Schneider, 2011; Steffe & Olive, 2010).

THE NOTION OF (EPISTEMOLOGICAL) OBSTACLES TO LEARNING

Brousseau (2002) contested the traditional view of mathematics learning as additive, and drew on the Piagetian notions of accommodation and assimilation to describe the processes of learning. He used the term *obstacle* to learning to refer to "a piece of knowledge or a conception, not a difficulty or a lack of knowledge" (p. 99) which is met, used, and proved productive within a particular context but generates false responses outside this context. Any obstacle is supposed to be immune to occasional contradictions as well as the establishment of a better piece of knowledge. Brousseau was mainly concerned with two kinds of obstacles, namely those of didactical and of epistemological origin. The first are the product of instructional choices within an educational system. Brousseau offered as example the presentation of decimals as "whole numbers with a change of units" (p. 87) at the elementary level, which becomes an obstacle to students' proper understanding of the rational and real numbers. On the other hand, epistemological obstacles "are those from which one neither can nor should escape, because of their formative role in the knowledge being sought. They can he found in the history of the concepts themselves" (p. 87). Thus, Brousseau suggested that tracing down obstacles in the process of historical development of mathematical notions and comparing them with obstacles in learning manifested through recurrent errors could lead to the identification of epistemological obstacles.

Brousseau's notion of *obstacle* was used by mathematics researchers to examine several mathematical notions and the difficulties they pose to students, such as the notion of limit and function (e.g., Cornu, 1992; Sierpinska, 1987), and linearity (Modestou and Gagatsis, 2007). Eventually the notion of *obstacle* and, in particular, *epistemological obstacle* was criticized as being grounded in "recapitulationistic" views and not taking account of the sociocultural contexts within which learning takes place (e.g., Radford, 1997).

It has been pointed out that there are similarities between Brousseau's analysis of obstacles in learning and conceptual change approaches (see, for example, Prediger, 2008). We note that the obstacles in learning postulated by the FTaCC are not identical to Brousseau's epistemological and didactical objects. From an FTaCC perspective, obstacles are due to the content and structure of children's prior knowledge, as shaped within their cultural environment and by domain-specific constraints (domain-specificity being a different view on development than the Piagetian, domain-general view endorsed by Brousseau). We, of course, value the notion of didactical obstacle – in fact, studying the complex interaction of children's pre-instructional knowledge with information coming from instruction is an important aspect of our approach. There are also certain obstacles encountered in conceptual change research that can arguably be characterized as "epistemological." Consider, for example, the difficulty in conceptualizing non-natural numbers as members of the same family as natural numbers, which was prominent in the course of historical development of the notion of number and is also observed in today's students (Vamvakoussi & Vosniadou, 2010). We believe, however, that in the case of students, this obstacle is largely a didactical obstacle as well. This is because the planning of instruction is often grounded on background assumptions that appear reasonable – exactly because, in a way, they reflect aspects of the formation of the intended mathematical knowledge – but create problems in the long run. Such assumptions, for instance, may concern choices about the order and the context of presentation of mathematical notions in the curriculum. For example, an examination of Greek and Flemish mathematics curricula and textbooks (Vamvakoussi et al., 2011) showed that (a) natural numbers are presented first, in the context of typical counting activities, (b) the part–whole aspect of fractions is overemphasized, (c) fractions and decimals are treated, to a large extent, separately, and (d) the question why natural and non-natural numbers do belong to the same category despite their differences is not addressed. These choices may result in the consolidation of students' pre-instructional knowledge and experience of numbers as *counting* numbers, foster the over-generalization of natural number knowledge and strategies to non-natural numbers, and cause additional difficulty in conceptualizing natural and non-natural numbers as a unified systems of numbers.

INTUITION IN MATHEMATICS

Fischbein (1987, 1999) postulated that systematic errors are grounded in *intuitive knowledge*. In his earlier writings (e.g., Fischbein, 1987), he described intuitions as (cognitive) beliefs characterized by *self evidence*, *intrinsic certainty*, and *coerciveness*, in the sense that they are taken to be necessarily true, beyond the need for any further justification, while any possible alternatives are readily discarded as unacceptable. They are also characterized by *globality* (i.e., they allow for an immediate and integrated grasp of a situation, via the selection of features that are deemed relevant). Furthermore, intuitions are *implicit* (i.e., they are not under the conscious control of the individual). Intuitions are not isolated, unitary perceptions, skills, or beliefs. They are characterized by *extrapolativeness*, in that they provide the basis on which inferences are made that go beyond the information at hand. Finally, they are characterized by *perseverance* (i.e., once established they are robust and therefore not easily eradicated by instruction). In his latter writings, Fischbein (e.g., 1999) attributed to intuitions the role of mediators between *structural schemata* – which he defined as "behavioral mental devices which make possible the assimilation and interpretation of information and the adequate reactions to various stimuli" – and adaptive reactions, i.e., responses. In his attempt to describe how these structural schemata develop, Fischbein took a Piagetian perspective on cognitive development, postulating that every stage of development is associated with specific schemata.

Fischbein (1987) distinguished between two types of intuitions in terms of their origin: primary intuitions, which develop on the basis of everyday experience; and secondary intuitions which are the refined intuitions that, for example, a professional mathematician develops after extensive training and allow for viewing several, initially counterintuitive, notions as self-evident.

Fischbein's theoretical model of intuitions in science and mathematics has been amply expounded and discussed, and served as a theoretical framework for analyzing and interpreting students' solutions to various mathematical notions, including numbers and arithmetical operations (Fischbein, Deri, Nello, & Marino, 1985, Fischbein, Jehiam, & Cohen, 1995), infinity (Fischbein, Tirosh, & Hess, 1979), and probability (Fischbein & Schnarch, 1997). Fischbein's work on intuition also inspired the formulation of the *intuitive rules theory* (Stavy & Tirosh, 2000). Recently, the issue of intuition in science and mathematics has been placed into the more general frame of intuitive reasoning and it has been argued that the dual-process theories in cognitive psychology and their accompanying methodologies could be a valuable tool in establishing the intuitive nature of erroneous reasoning in various mathematical domains (Gillard, Van Dooren, Schaeken, & Verschaffel, 2009).

There are several similarities between Fischbein's framework on intuition and the FTaCC: They both address the issue of systematic errors in science as well as in mathematics, except that there are aspects of cognition that are not under the conscious control of the individual, and postulate that students' erroneous responses are grounded on prior knowledge organized in complex structures. However, the FTaCC takes a domain-specific perspective on the formation and development of these cognitive structures, whereas Fischbein takes a Piagetian, domain-general view. In addition, using Fischbein's terms, one could say that the framework theory approach attempts to make predictions about what happens in the shift from primary to secondary intuitions, which is the stage where information coming from instruction interacts with primary intuitions and is most relevant for an educational point of view. On the other hand, Fischbein's theoretical framework points to an important fact: People typically do not spontaneously develop the habit of reflecting on their (mathematical) beliefs, let alone question them – and there are good reasons for this (see for example, Merenluoto and Lehtinen's (2004) theoretical model describing the dynamics among cognitive, metacognitive, and motivational processes in conceptual change). Thus, instruction that aims at facilitating conceptual change should create ample opportunity for students to express and critically reflect on their beliefs – and also to help them realize that sometimes, rather than responding fast, it is better to "stop and think."

EMPHASIZING THE POSITIVE ROLE OF PRIOR KNOWLEDGE

A typical criticism of the conceptual change type of explanations regarding the phenomenon of systematic errors in mathematics and science learning is that too much emphasis is placed on the negative aspects of students' prior knowledge, while the productive aspects are neglected. This is a common idea underlying Siegler and colleagues' (2011) and Steffe and Olive's (2010) approach to the learning of non-natural numbers, in particular fractions. These researchers hold the position that the differences between natural numbers and fractions are overemphasized, as are the adverse effects of prior natural number knowledge on the learning of fractions; and that – on the contrary – crucial continuities between acquisition of understanding of whole numbers and fractions are underrated and neglected.

Let us start by saying that we don't disagree in principle with the idea that prior knowledge about natural numbers can have a productive role in further learning about non-natural numbers. The framework theory approach to learning is a constructivist approach and assumes that students will draw on what they already know about numbers to make sense of non-natural numbers (see also Vosniadou & Verschaffel, 2004). This does not exclude the possibility for positive transfer from one domain to the other.

Although we believe that spontaneous transfer on the part of students is, more often than not, on the negative side, we are nevertheless convinced that the possibility of positive transfer is worth exploring, especially when it comes to the planning of instruction. However, not every aspect of prior knowledge is appropriate as a basis for further learning. Consider for example, that the part–whole aspect of fractions is considered more accessible to students precisely because it builds on natural number knowledge – however, it severely constrains students' understanding of fractions in the long run (Moss, 2005; Stafylidou & Vosniadou, 2004). Thus we believe that investigating the aspects of prior knowledge about natural numbers that can serve as a basis for further learning, together with the conditions under which this is possible, is an important complement to the investigation of the constraining role of prior knowledge.

MEASUREMENT AS A UNIFYING ASPECT OF NATURAL AND NON-NATURAL NUMBERS

Siegler et al. (2011) proposed that numerical development is a process of progressively broadening the class of numbers that are understood to possess magnitudes that can be ordered and assigned specific location on the number line. One could hardly disagree with this assertion. However, the question that is of interest from a conceptual change perspective is whether this "progressive broadening" of the class of numbers that are understood to possess magnitudes is in fact smooth and continuous, or a process that requires reorganization of prior knowledge. This question is not explicitly addressed by Siegler and colleagues' empirical study. Indeed, the main hypothesis of the study was that understanding fraction magnitudes is crucial for understanding fractions, which in turn is important for mathematics in general. They thus predicted that understanding of fraction magnitudes would be strongly related to proficiency at fractions arithmetic and also to overall mathematical competence. They tested this hypothesis with 24 sixth graders and 29 eighth graders, whose mathematical competence, measured via a standardized math achievement test, was above the state (Pennsylvania) average. The research tasks consisted of estimating the position of fractions on the number line, comparing fractions, and solving fraction arithmetic problems (i.e., calculating the result of fraction operations). The participants were asked to solve the tasks, and also explain their strategy. Siegler and colleagues found that, indeed, understanding of fraction magnitude correlates with both arithmetic proficiency and mathematics achievement test scores. This finding importantly indicates that students who have a good understanding of fraction magnitude are good with fraction arithmetic and mathematics in general – or vice versa. On the other hand, Siegler and colleagues reported that sixth as well as eighth graders were found to use natural number strategies to deal with the tasks at hand. Quite consistently with the FTaCC, this finding indicates that students drew on their natural number knowledge and – as expected – such strategies did sometimes yield correct results, but often they didn't. For instance, in the arithmetical operations tasks, a substantial percentage of the strategies used – varying from 43% to 54% for sixth graders and from 21% to 38% for eighth graders – was based on treating numerators and denominators as if they were independent whole numbers. Siegler and colleagues argued that this finding indicates that difficulty learning about fractions stems from drawing inaccurate analogies to whole numbers, rather than from drawing such analogies *per se*, a point with which we agree. We note, however, that this finding also attests to the constraining role of natural number prior knowledge. Provided that this issue is also taken into consideration, we believe that Siegler and colleagues' proposal that measurement is the core idea around which number knowledge should be tied is promising from the point of view of instruction. This is because building on the idea that fractions are like natural numbers in having magnitudes that can be ordered and represented on the number line may facilitate students to develop a unified view of numbers, which is instrumental for more advanced number understanding (see also Kilpatrick, Swafford, & Findell, 2001; Vamvakoussi & Vosniadou, 2012).

BUILDING KNOWLEDGE OF FRACTIONS ON NATURAL NUMBER SEQUENCES

Steffe and Olive (2010; see also Steffe, 2002) ground their work in the *reorganization hypothesis*, which is summarized as follows:

> The basic hypothesis that guides our work is that children's fractional knowing can emerge as accommodations in their natural number knowing. This hypothesis is referred to as the reorganization hypothesis because if a new way of knowing is constructed using a previous way of knowing in a novel way, the new way of knowing can be regarded as a reorganization of the previous way of knowing.
>
> (Steffe & Olive, 2010, p. vii)

In particular, Steffe and Olive hypothesized that children could use *their* number sequences to construct fraction concepts and operations. We emphasize the word "their," because the term "number sequence" does not refer to the mathematical objects, but to the way that children think about them and what they can do with them (see Olive, 2001). Let us give an example of productive use of a combination of additive reasoning and counting to respond to an essentially multiplicative task: Consider the question "how many fours are there in 12?," which can also be formulated as "What fractional part of 12 is four?" One can think of a child answering this question via adding "four and four and four," keeping track of the number of fours with her fingers.

Steffe and Olive conducted a three-year teaching experiment with children who were third graders at the beginning of the intervention. They employed specially designed computer tools and exposed children to carefully designed tasks that were amenable to the use of (discrete) number sequences on continuous quantities. They made detailed qualitative analysis of the children's activity, and were able to present instances of productive and gradually more sophisticated understanding and use of number sequences to construct fractional understanding.

There is a question of interest for our discussion that cannot be answered by the data presented by Steffe and Olive: Would the participants of their teaching experiment be unaffected by natural number knowledge interference if they were exposed to different tasks, at different time, or – more importantly – in a context other than the one created by the specific computer tools they used? This said, Steffe and Olive's major contribution is in showing that *under appropriate conditions* it is possible to build fractional knowledge on natural number knowledge. Of course, this requires changes, or *reorganization*, of prior knowledge. And let us add that, from an instructional point of view, it is again measurement that is essentially at the heart of Steffe and Olive's proposal. Indeed, as

Patrick W. Thompson argues in his foreword to Steffe and Olive (2010), "it is through their number sequences that children impose segmentations on continuous quantities and reassemble them as measured quantities" (p. xiii).

CONCLUSION

In this chapter we presented the FTaCC in relation to mathematics learning and teaching. We made the case that the FTaCC adds to what we know about the complex interaction between prior and intended knowledge in various mathematical domains. This is because it not only explains a great deal of evidence on students' systematic errors, but it also generates novel predictions regarding the shift from one level of understanding to a more sophisticated one.

We compared the FTaCC to other approaches and pointed out the similarities and the differences, as well as what is, we believe, the added valued of this framework from a theoretical or an educational point of view. Finally, we chose to examine two approaches that emphasize continuities, rather discontinuities, in the process of learning. This is because we find this idea interesting from an instructional point of view. Specifically, we believe that they pose a question that is worth investigating: Would building instruction of rational numbers on the notion of measurement diminish, and to what extent, the problems of conceptual change in the shift from natural to rational numbers?

REFERENCES

Asmuth, J., & Rips, L. (2006). Conceptual change in non-Euclidean mathematics. In R. Su (Ed.), *Proceedings of the 28th Annual Conference of the Cognitive Science Society* (pp. 30–35). Mahwah, NJ: Lawrence Erlbaum Associates.

Biza, I., Souyoul, A., & Zachariades, Th. (2005). Conceptual change in advanced mathematical thinking. In M. Bosch (Ed.), *Proceedings of the Fourth Conference on European Research in Mathematics Education* (pp. 1727–1736). Sant Feliu de Guixols, Spain: CERME.

Biza, I., & Zachariades, T. (2006). Conceptual change in advanced mathematical thinking: The case of tangent line. In J. Novotná, H. Moraová, M. Krátká, & N. Stehlíková (Eds.), *Proceedings of the 30th Conference of the International Group for the Psychology of Mathematics Education* (Vol. 1, pp. 168–170). Prague, Czech Republic: PME.

Brousseau, G. (2002). *Theory of didactical situations in mathematics* (edited and translated by N. Balacheff, M. Cooper, R. Sutherland, & V. Warfield). New York, NY: Kluwer Academic.

Carey, S. (2009). *The origin of concepts*. Oxford, UK: Oxford University Press.

Carey, S., & Spelke, E. (1996). Science and core knowledge. *Philosophy of Science, 63*, 515–533.

Carey, S., & Gelman, R. (1991). *The epigenesis of mind: Essays on biology and cognition*. Hillsdale, NJ: Lawrence Erlbaum Associates.

Christou, K. P. & Vosniadou, S. (2009). Misinterpreting the use of literal symbols in algebra. In M. Tzekaki, M. Kaldrimidou, & C. Sakonidis (Eds.), *Proceedings of the 33rd Conference of the International Group for the Psychology of Mathematics Education* (Vol. 2, pp. 329–339). Thessaloniki, Greece: PME.

Christou, K. P., & Vosniadou, S. (2012). What kinds of numbers do students assign to literal symbols? Aspects of the transition from arithmetic to algebra. *Mathematical Thinking and Learning, 14*(1), 1–27.

Christou, K. P., Vosniadou, S., & Vamvakoussi, X. (2007). Students' interpretations of literal symbols in algebra. In S. Vosniadou, A. Baltas, & X. Vamvakoussi (Eds.), *Re-framing the conceptual change approach in learning and instruction* (pp. 283–297). New York, NY: Elsevier.

Confrey, J. (1981). Conceptual change analysis: Implications for mathematics and curriculum. *Curriculum Inquiry, 11*(3), 243–257.

Confrey, J., & Kazak, S. (2006). A thirty-year reflection on constructivism in mathematics education in PME. In A. Gutiérrez and P. Boero (Eds.), *Handbook of research on the psychology of mathematics education: Past, present and future* (pp. 305–345). Rotterdam, The Netherlands: Sense Publishers.

Cornu, B. (1992). Limits. In D. Tall (Ed.), *Advanced mathematical thinking* (pp. 153–166). Dordrecht, The Netherlands: Kluwer Academic.

Crowe, M. (1975). Ten "laws" concerning patterns of change in the history of mathematics. *Historia Mathematica, 2,* 161–166.

Fischbein, E. (1987). *Intuition in science and mathematics: An educational approach.* Dordrecht, The Netherlands: Reidel.

Fischbein, E. (1999). Intuitions and schemata in mathematical reasoning. *Educational Studies in Mathematics, 38,* 11–50.

Fischbein, E., Deri, M., Nello, M. S., & Marino, S. M. (1985). The role of implicit models in solving verbal problems in multiplication and division. *Journal for Research in Mathematics Education, 16,* 3–17.

Fischbein, E., Jehiam, R., & Cohen, D. (1995). The concept of irrational numbers in high-school students and prospective teachers. *Educational Studies in Mathematics, 29,* 29–44.

Fischbein, E., & Schnarch, D. (1997). The evolution with age of probabilistic, intuitively based misconceptions. *Journal for Research in Mathematics Education, 28,* 96–105.

Fischbein, E., Tirosh, D., & Hess, P. (1979). The intuition of infinity. *Educational Studies in Mathematics, 10,* 3–40.

Gillies, D. (Ed.). (1992). *Revolutions in mathematics.* Oxford, UK: Oxford University Press.

Gillard, E., Van Dooren, W., Schaeken, W., & Verschaffel, L. (2009). Dual processes in the psychology of mathematics education and cognitive psychology. *Human Development, 52,* 95–108.

Greer, B., & Verschaffel, L. (2007). Nurturing conceptual change in mathematics education. In S. Vosniadou, A. Baltas, & X. Vamvakoussi (Eds.), Reframing the conceptual change approach in learning and instruction (pp. 319–328). Oxford, UK: Elsevier.

Hartnett, P. M., & Gelman, R. (1998). Early understandings of number: Paths or barriers to the construction of new understandings? *Learning and Instruction, 8,* 341–374.

Hatano, G. (1996). A conception of knowledge acquisition and its implication for mathematics education. In L. P. Steffe, P. Nesher, P. Cobb, G. A. Goldin, & B. Greer (Eds.), *Theories of mathematical learning* (pp. 197–218). Mahwah, NJ: Lawrence Erlbaum Associates.

Kilpatrick, J., Swafford, J., & Findell, B. (2001). *Adding it up: Helping children learn mathematics.* Washington, DC: National Academies Press.

Kuhn, T. (1970). *The structure of scientific revolutions* (2nd ed.). Chicago, IL: University of Chicago Press.

Lehtinen, E., Merenluoto, K., & Kasanen, E. (1997). Conceptual change in mathematics: From rational to (un)real numbers. *European Journal of Psychology of Education, XII*(2), 131–145.

Liljedahl, P. (2008). Noticing rapid and profound mathematics teacher change. *Journal of Mathematics Teacher Education, 13,* 411–423.

Merenluoto, K., & Lehtinen, E. (2002). Conceptual change in mathematics: Understanding the real numbers. In M. Limon & L. Mason (Eds.), *Reconsidering conceptual change: Issues in theory and practice* (pp. 233–258). Dordrecht, The Netherlands: Kluwer.

Merenluoto, K., & Lehtinen, E. (2004). Number concept and conceptual change: Towards a systemic model of the processes of change. *Learning and Instruction, 14,* 519–536.

Modestou, M., & Gagatsis, A. (2007): Students' improper proportional reasoning: A result of the epistemological obstacle of "linearity". *Educational Psychology, 27*(1), 75–92.

Moss, J. (2005). Pipes, tubes, and beakers: New approaches to teaching the rational-number system. In M. S. Donovan & J. D. Bransford (Eds.), *How students learn: Mathematics in the classroom* (pp. 121–162). Washington, DC: National Academies Press.

Ni, Y., & Zhou, Y.-D. (2005). Teaching and learning fraction and rational numbers: The origins and implications of whole number bias. *Educational Psychologist, 40*(1), 27–52.

Olive, J. (2001). Children's number sequences: An explanation of Steffe's constructs and an extrapolation to rational numbers of arithmetic. *Mathematics Educator, 11*(1), 4–9.

Posner, G. J., Strike, K. A., Hewson, P. W., & Gertzog, W. A. (1982). Accommodation of a scientific conception: Towards a theory of conceptual change. *Science Education, 66,* 211–227.

Prediger, S. (2008). The relevance of didactic categories for analysing obstacles in conceptual change: Revisiting the case of multiplication of fractions. *Learning and Instruction, 18,* 3–17.

Radford, L. (1997). On psychology, historical epistemology, and the teaching of mathematics: Towards a sociocultural history of mathematics. *For the Learning of Mathematics, 17*(1), 26–33.

Resnick, L. B. (2006). The dilemma of mathematical intuition in learning. In J. Novotna, H. Moraova, M. Kratka, & N. Stehlıkova (Eds.), *Proceedings of the 30th Conference of the International Group for the Psychology of Mathematics Education: Vol. 1* (pp. 173–175). Prague, Czech Republic: PME.

Shinno, Y., & Iwasaki, H. (2008). The prescriptive role of theory of conceptual change in the teaching and learning of mathematics. In O. Figueras, J. L. Cortina, S. Alatorre, T. Rojano, & A. Sepulveda (Eds.), *Proceedings of the Joint Meeting of PME 32 and PME-NA XXX* (Vol. 4. pp. 249–256). Morelia, Mexico: PME.

Siegler, R. S., Thompson, C. A., & Schneider, M. (2011). An integrated theory of whole number and fractions development. *Cognitive Psychology, 62*(4), 273–296.

Sierpinska, A. (1987). Humanities students and epistemological obstacles related to limits. *Educational Studies in Mathematics, 18,* 371–397.

Smith, C. L., Solomon, G. E. A., & Carey, S. (2005). Never getting to zero: Elementary school students' understanding of the infinite divisibility of number and matter. *Cognitive Psychology, 51,* 101–140.

Stafylidou, S. & Vosniadou, S. (2004). The development of students' understanding of the numerical value of fractions. *Learning and Instruction, 14,* 503–518.

Stavy, R., & Tirosh, D. (2000). *How students (mis-)understand science and mathematics: Intuitive rules.* New York, NY: Teachers College Press.

Steffe, L. P. (2002). A new hypothesis concerning children's fractional knowledge. *Journal of Mathematical Behavior, 20,* 267–307.

Steffe, L. P., & Olive, J. (2010). *Children's fractional knowledge.* New York, NY: Springer.

Tsamir, P., & Tirosh, D. (2007). Teaching for conceptual change: The case of infinite sets. In S. Vosniadou, A. Baltas, & X. Vamvakoussi (Eds.), *Reframing the conceptual change approach in learning and instruction* (pp. 299–316). Oxford, UK: Elsevier.

Vamvakoussi, X., Christou, K. P., Mertens, L., & Van Dooren, W. (2011). What fills the gap between the discrete and the dense? Greek and Flemish students' understanding of density. *Learning & Instruction, 21,* 676–685.

Vamvakoussi, X., & Vosniadou, S. (2004). Understanding the structure of the set of rational numbers: A conceptual change approach. *Learning and Instruction, 14,* 453–467.

Vamvakoussi, X., & Vosniadou, S. (2007). How many numbers in an interval? Presuppositions, synthetic models and the effect of the number line. In S. Vosniadou, A. Baltas, & X. Vamvakoussi (Eds.), *Reframing the conceptual change approach in learning and instruction* (pp. 267–283). Oxford, UK: Elsevier.

Vamvakoussi, X., & Vosniadou, S. (2010). How many decimals are there between two fractions? Aspects of secondary school students' reasoning about rational numbers and their notation. *Cognition & Instruction, 28*(2), 181–209.

Vamvakoussi, X., & Vosniadou, S. (2012). Bridging the gap between the dense and the discrete: The number line and the "rubber line" bridging analogy. *Mathematical Thinking and Learning, 14*(4), 265–284.

Van Dooren, W., Christou, K. P., & Vamvakoussi, X. (2010). Greek and Flemish students' interpretation of the literal symbols as variables. In M. M. F. Pinto & T. F. Kawasaki (Eds.), *Proceedings of the 34th Conference of the International Group for the Psychology of Mathematics Education* (Vol. 4, pp. 257–264). Belo Horizonte, Brazil: PME.

Van Dooren, W., De Bock, D., Hessels, A., Janssens, D., & Verschaffel, L. (2004). Remedying secondary school students' illusion of linearity: A teaching experiment aiming at conceptual change. *Learning & Instruction, 14,* 485–501.

Vlassis, J. (2004). Making sense of the minus sign or becoming flexible in "negativity". *Learning and Instruction, 14,* 469–484.

Vosniadou, S. (1999). Conceptual change research: State of the art and future directions. In W. Schnotz, S. Vosniadou, & M. Carretero (Eds.), New perspectives on conceptual change (pp. 3–13). Oxford, UK: Elsevier Science.

Vosniadou, S., Baltas, A., & Vamvakoussi X. (Eds.). (2007). *Reframing the conceptual change approach in learning and instruction.* Oxford, UK: Elsevier.

Vosniadou, S., Ioannides, C., Dimitrakopoulou, A., & Papademetriou, E. (2001). Designing learning environments to promote conceptual change in science. *Learning and Instruction, 11,* 381–419.

Vosniadou, S., Vamvakoussi, X., & Skopeliti, I. (2008). The framework theory approach to conceptual change. In S. Vosniadou (Ed.), *International handbook of research on conceptual change* (pp. 3–34). New York, NY: Routledge.

Vosniadou, S., & Verschaffel, L. (2004). Extending the conceptual change approach to mathematics learning and teaching. *Learning and Instruction, 14,* 445–451.

Zazkis, R., & Chernoff , E. J. (2008). What makes a counterexample exemplary? *Educational Studies in Mathematics, 68,* 195–208.

17

THE BUNDLING HYPOTHESIS

How Perception and Culture Give Rise to Abstract Mathematical Concepts in Individuals

Kristen P. Blair, Jessica M. Tsang, and Daniel L. Schwartz,
Stanford University

The "bundling hypothesis" describes the development of abstract mathematical concepts through learning. We present its elements through the investigation of a single conceptual change using multiple methodologies ranging from functional magnetic resonance imaging (fMRI) to novel classroom instruction. The conceptual change of interest is the transition from natural numbers to integers, which further include zero and the negative numbers. The transition is a non-destructive conceptual change. It does not require "a radical reorganization of what is already known" about natural numbers (Stafylidou & Vosniadou, 2004, p. 504). Yet it is still a strong instance of a conceptual change, because the integers cannot be derived from the natural numbers. They depend on the additional mathematical structure of the additive inverse: $X + -X = 0$. For the integers, people need to realize a fundamentally new structure within their concept of number.

The integers present an additional conceptual challenge for learners. Negative numbers do not have a "natural" perceptual referent. In this sense, the integers are abstract. One does not hold negative objects in one's hand, and zero is arguably the prototype of abstractness – structure without substance. Nevertheless, our proposal is that people represent the increased structure of the integers by bundling in new perceptual-motor functionality not found for the natural numbers. In short, people recruit symmetry to embody the additive inverse in their representation of the integers. Without integrating symmetry into their integer representation, people can still solve integer problems by rule, but their understanding is neither deep nor flexible.

Figure 17.1 provides a schematic of the bundling hypothesis when applied to the natural numbers and the integers. The hypothesis is derivative of Case and colleagues' (Case et al., 1997) argument that a rich understanding of number depends on the integration of otherwise separate representations into a core conceptual structure. Our

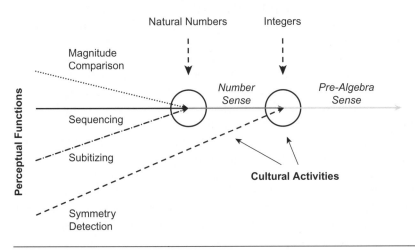

Figure 17.1 The bundling hypothesis

basic tenet is that people have perceptual-motor functions that exist prior to a full understanding of number and that are found in infants and animals. Conceptual change occurs through the integration of these functionalities, which bring new structure and possible operations to a concept.

A second tenet is that the integration is enabled by notation systems that provide a common external representation that anchors different meanings and perceptual functions (e.g., Goldstone, Landy, & Son, 2010). Notation systems also have syntactic rules that support the formal manipulation of quantities. During manipulations of the quantities, the formal rules ensure the coordination of distinct perceptually based properties, so that a change to one perceivable property is associated with changes in another. Cultural activities, such as explicit instruction, help learners notice and bind the appropriate perceptual functions through the notations to create an integrated internal representation.

For the natural numbers, Case et al. (1997) hypothesized that number sense depends on integrating different quantitative competencies that appear separately in infants as basic perceptual-motor schemes. For example, infants can discriminate the magnitudes of physical stimuli (sound, size); they can sequence their own physical movements (motor plans); and they can distinguish small discrete amounts without enumerating (subitizing). Separately, these basic schemes enable the quantitative properties of magnitude, ordinality, and cardinality, respectively. According to the bundling hypothesis, these discrete perceptual-motor uses of quantitative information are integrated through the symbolic, notational structures of mathematics. For example, the digit 5 can refer to the magnitude of a sound (five decibels); it can refer to the order of a sound (fifth); and, it can refer to the number of sounds (five taps). The notation system permits the different meanings to make contact, and articulated symbol systems have their own sets of rules that enforce the coordination for how changes to one meaning affect other meanings. For instance, adding 1 to a set of 5 (a change in cardinality) also increases the bigness of the set from 5 to 6 (a change in magnitude). Appropriate instructional activities can help people learn to coordinate and integrate the different aspects of quantity. In teaching studies, Case and colleagues found that instruction that integrates separate quantitative meanings is more effective than instruction that strengthens each meaning separately (Griffin, Case, & Siegler, 1994).

The bundling hypothesis is consistent with the basic claims of diverse developmental theories. It agrees with nativist arguments that the relevant structure finds its basis in capacities conferred by evolution (e.g., Chomsky, 1966; Spelke, 2000). It also agrees with embodied arguments that the basic building blocks of abstract understanding begin in perception and possible physical actions in the world (e.g., Glenberg & Kaschak, 2002; Lakoff & Núñez, 2000). Finally, it reconciles these tenets with the constructivist tradition that argues representations are constructed or assembled through experience (Piaget, 1952). It does this by proposing that native abilities need to be integrated to make a well-rounded concept of number. The integration allows new concepts to emerge that are more than the sum of their component parts. For example, an understanding of the natural numbers allows for more precision and flexibility in interacting with quantities than would an innate approximate magnitude system.

For the natural numbers, one could argue that the "built in" capacities of humans for perception and construction are sufficient to explain development. Even monkeys can learn to associate natural number symbols with the perceptual referents (Cantlon & Brannon, 2007), and humans may be evolutionarily hardwired for natural numerical processing in much the same way as has been argued for language processing. In contrast, the integers are a relatively new and abstract cultural innovation, with their first full expression occurring only a few hundred years ago. There is no blueprint for integer concepts in the unformed child, and there is no maturation plan for the emergence of integers. Instead, people need to exapt abilities that evolved for one type of problem to help with another. At the cortical level, Dehaene and Cohen (2007) have called this the neuronal recycling hypothesis. Brain regions that are good at specific types of computations are repurposed so they can handle (and enable) cultural demands that rely on those computations. As we present below, brain regions that support the detection of symmetry may be recycled to help with integers.

Culture provides the resources and pressures to help integrate functionality in specific ways. There are two research traditions of special importance. The first involves the abovementioned role of inscriptions and symbolic rules for organizing thought (e.g., Cole & Engeström, 1993; Lehrer & Schauble, 2000). The second involves the influence of sociocultural processes for driving specific forms of cognitive reorganization (e.g., Saxe, 1981, 1988). Vygotsky (1986), for example, proposed that culture-level "scientific" ideas help drive development through a process of internalization from the social plane to the individual plane. As discussed by Leach and Scott (2008), internalization does not mean "direct transfer"; rather the individual interprets the ideas encountered on the social plane. Quoting Vygotsky's contemporary A. N. Leontiev, "the process of internalization is not the transferral of an external activity to a pre-existing 'internal plane of consciousness': it is the process in which that plane is formed" (cited in Leach & Scott, 2008, p. 655). To understand this process, it is important to understand the building blocks that enable and constrain learning. The bundling hypothesis is an attempt to integrate the insights of developmental and sociocultural traditions to explain conceptual change.

In the case of the integers, we claim that basic perceptual-motor capacities for symmetry become bundled together with other quantitative properties through the influence of cultural inscriptions and social interactions. To support this hypothesis, we make an argument with three steps. The first step is to show that educated adults exhibit symmetry-enabled processes when reasoning about integers. This helps to demonstrate that people's understanding of the abstract integers is indeed grounded in perceptual-motor functionality. To simplify subsequent exposition, we use the term "analog" to refer to representations and processes that borrow their structure from perceptual-motor activity (Shepard & Cooper, 1986). Analog means continuous per physical experience, and it should be distinguished from syntactic or verbal rules.

The second step is to show that symmetry has been bundled with other quantitative properties of number, namely magnitude. We also show that adults have developed an analog representation of negative number magnitudes in their own right. In contrast, we find that children who have learned the integers appear to reason by rule rather than using an analog representation. This leads to the final step of our argument. Current curricula for teaching children about integers do not incorporate symmetry, which may explain why the children had not bundled symmetry into their understanding of the integers. (The adults may have learned to integrate symmetry during algebra, which requires balancing equations and interpreting quadrants in Cartesian coordinates.) Therefore, we conducted an instructional study. One condition emphasized symmetry. The students in the symmetry condition were able to solve a greater array of problems compared to students who learned in more traditional ways. This supports the claim that cultural activity, in this case instruction, helps bundle together the perceptual functions into a coordinated representation.

EVIDENCE OF SYMMETRY IN THE INTEGER REPRESENTATION

The first step in our argument involves evidence of analog representations when reasoning about integers. We begin this section with behavioral data and end with brain data. When looking for behavioral evidence of analog representations in cognitive phenomena, researchers often examine overt motor behavior. Examples include the spontaneous use of gestures while problem solving (Schwartz & Black, 1996) and the facilitation or interference of inferences by enforced gestures (Schwartz & Holton, 2000). In most cases, these studies use tasks that require some form of spatial information to achieve an answer. For example, participants may be asked about the spatial behavior of a mechanical system (Hegarty, 1992), whether a tomato can be squeezed (Klatzky, Pellegrino, McCloskey, & Doherty, 1989), or the direction of object motion (Wexler & Klam, 2001). Here, we take a different approach, because we want to show that even abstract problems can involve analog representations.

We set a number of constraints to ensure compelling evidence. First, we wanted evidence of analog representations using a task that does not display relevant spatial information or require spatial manipulation. If successful, it would constitute strong evidence of analog representations in abstract reasoning (as opposed to perceptual involvement in a perception-like task). Second, we did not want to rely on evidence of overt motoric movement, which can often be discounted as a correlate of problem solving rather than a cause. Instead, we looked for response time profiles that implicate analog representations. This methodology is characteristic of research on analog imagery (Shepard & Cooper, 1986), where people exhibit response times that indicate they are mentally rotating imagined objects.

One example of a relevant paradigm that fits these requirements comes from research on the comparison of quantitative magnitudes. In a seminal study, Moyer and Landauer (1967) had participants judge which of two natural number digits was greater (or lesser). Participants exhibited a *symbolic distance effect*: They were faster comparing digits that were quantitatively far apart (1 vs. 9) than near together (1 vs. 3). It is important to note that the digits were not further apart on the screen, so it was the implied magnitude differences that drove the results, not spatial stimuli. The symbolic distance effect is commonly interpreted as evidence for a mental number line such that magnitudes that are farther apart on the line are faster to discriminate (Restle, 1970). A related finding is the *size effect*: For pairs of natural numbers of equal separation, people are faster comparing smaller numbers (1 vs. 4) than larger numbers (6 vs. 9) (Parkman, 1971). The size effect indicates that the number line is psychophysically scaled, because smaller numbers are easier to discriminate than larger numbers. In sum, the time it takes to judge which of two positive number digits represents a greater magnitude exhibits a continuous logarithmic function. Importantly, the distance and size effects are also found when people compare physical quantities such as the loudness of two tones. Brain data indicate that a common brain region is involved in both number magnitude comparisons and physical stimuli comparisons. The intraparietal sulcus (IPS) shows parametric modulation; it is more active for the harder near-magnitude comparisons than for the easier far-magnitude comparisons whether the stimuli are digits or physical magnitudes (Ansari, Garcia, Lucas, Hamon, & Dhital, 2005; Gobel, Johansen-Berg, Behrens, & Rushworth, 2004; Kaufmann et al., 2005; Pinel, Dehaene, Riviere, & LeBihan, 2001) .

We adopted the methodological logic of the symbolic distance effect to examine whether people rely on symmetry to reason about integer problems. In our task, people saw a pair of symbolic digits, and we asked them to find the quantitative mid-point of the digits. This bisection task can be solved without imagining a number line, for example, by adding the two digits and dividing them by 2. If people exhibit evidence of symmetry in this task, it makes a strong case that people use analog representations for the abstract integers.

We predicted that people would be faster for bisection problems when the two digits were more symmetric around zero (if put on a number line). For example, people should be faster to find the mid-point of –4 and 6 compared to –2 and 8, because –4 and 6 are more symmetric with respect to zero. This would correspond to findings using visual displays that exhibit various degrees of spatial symmetry. Royer (1981) found that people are faster to judge the symmetry of a visual display as the display exhibits stronger symmetry.

Tsang and Schwartz (2009) asked adults to solve a series of bisection problems. The left side of Figure 17.2 shows the basic task, and the right side shows examples of the types of problems people received. There were perfectly symmetric problems (6 and –6) and perfectly anchored problems (0 and 12). Badland problems were as far away from either as possible (4 and –8), and nearly symmetric and nearly anchored problems were somewhere in between. People also received pure positive problems and pure negative problems that did not cross the zero boundary.

Figure 17.3 shows how long it took people to answer the bisection problems. When problems were perfectly symmetric or anchored, people were very fast, presumably because these were well-memorized number facts. Of more interest are the "tuning" curves. People became progressively faster as the digits neared quantitative symmetry

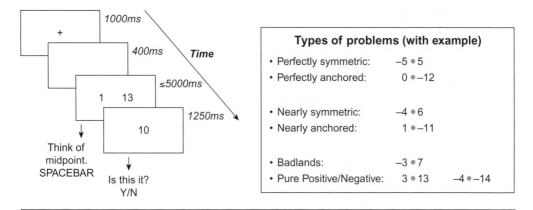

Figure 17.2 Behavioral task for detecting if people recruit symmetry for a purely symbolic task

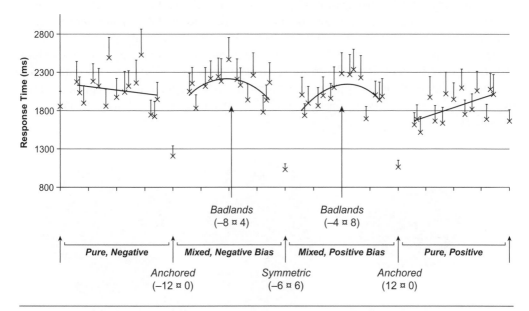

Figure 17.3 People bisect two digits faster when the digits approximate the additive inverse (symmetric) or additive identity (anchored on zero) (adapted from Tsang & Schwartz, 2009)

about zero. Although the task was purely symbolic and the digits always appeared in the same display locations, people seemed to be taking advantage of the implied quantitative symmetry. These results held whether people saw the target digits one after another instead of side-by-side, and whether they were asked to approximate the answer or told to use a formula to find the answer: $(a + b)/2$. The fact that the pattern appeared even when people used a symbolic algorithm indicates that analog symmetry is built deeply into the integer representation.

A limitation of these data is that people also responded faster as problems became more anchored (one of the digits was a neighbor of zero). Was the same underlying process responsible for the improved performance for the symmetric and anchored sides of the curve, or was the symmetry performance due to symmetry specific processes? This is where neural evidence can be useful. It may show differences in underlying process despite behavioral similarities.

Tsang, Rosenberg-Lee, Blair, Schwartz, & Menon (2010) conducted the same study in an fMRI paradigm. Figure 17.4 shows three regions that increased activity as problems became more symmetric and responses became faster. These three regions did not show increased activity as problems became more anchored, despite similar reductions in response time. Thus, the activation was not a general side-effect of faster response times, but rather, it was selective for the implied quantitative symmetry of the stimuli. The involved brain regions have also been implicated in perceptual processes involving symmetry. The left inferior LO (lateral occipital) cortex is implicated in the perception of visually symmetric stimuli (Sasaki, Vanduffel, Knutsen, Tyler, & Tootell, 2005; Tyler et al., 2005) and regions close to the right MTG (middle temporal gyrus) and nearby superior temporal regions are implicated in visual bisection tasks (de Schotten et al., 2005; Wilkinson & Halligan, 2003).

In summary, given a display of purely symbolic stimuli exhibiting no relevant spatial information (i.e., digits), people demonstrated a tuning curve that indicates sensitivity to implied symmetry. People were faster to bisect problems that were near symmetric with respect to zero (–5 and 7). Additionally, brain regions associated with perceptual symmetry became parametrically more active as problem pairs approached symmetric. Pending further evidence, it appears that people have developed internal representations of the integers that embody the integers' new structure – the additive inverse – in symmetry.

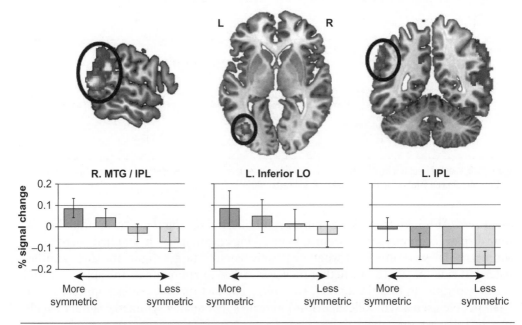

Figure 17.4 Areas of the brain that increased activation as bisection problems increased in symmetry about zero. The top panel shows the location in the brain of three areas that increased activation as the implied symmetry of the digit pairs increased (i.e., the degree to which the two digits approximated the additive inverse). The bottom panel plots the activation changes as the digit pairs became more and less symmetric. All areas of the brain are constantly active, and percentage signal change refers to the change in activity over a baseline level (adapted from Schwartz, Blair, & Tsang, 2012).

ANALOG MAGNITUDE OF THE NEGATIVE NUMBERS

The preceding section argued that people rely on symmetry to facilitate thinking about integers. This section argues that symmetry has been bundled with other properties of the integers. It does so by developing evidence of symmetry involvement when people complete a task that requires comparing magnitude rather than bisection. If people exhibit evidence of symmetry in a magnitude comparison task, it implies that symmetry has been bundled up with other properties of the integers such as magnitude.

A second issue addressed by this section is whether people represent the magnitude of negative numbers in their own right. One possibility is that people do not have a distinct analog representation of the negative numbers. Instead, people might reason about negative numbers by using their analog representation of natural number magnitude and adding a few supplementary rules (Fischer, 2003; Ganor-Stern & Tzelgov, 2008; Prather & Alibali, 2008; Shaki & Petrusic, 2005; Tzelgov, Ganor-Stern, & Maymon-Schreiber, 2009). Given the task of deciding whether –2 or –5 has a greater magnitude, people can compare positive 2 and 5, and then give the opposite answer ("5 is larger than 2, so the correct answer is that –2 is larger than –5"). Or, when asked which is the greater of –5 and 2, they can simply rely on the rule that positives are always greater than negatives. In this hybrid representation of negative numbers, the sense of magnitude comes from the positives, and people add new structure by using symbolic rules.

A second possibility is that people might represent negative magnitudes in their own right by developing a "leftward" extension of the conventional number line. Using this extended model, people could compare –2 and –5 directly.

Varma and Schwartz (2011) found that neither the first nor the second possibility is exactly right. While educated adults can reason about negative numbers by using positive numbers supplemented with rules, they also appear to have a representation of negative numbers in their own right that they can call upon, and this representation is symmetric to the positives rather than a linear extension. In contrast, 12-year-old children who are relatively new to negative numbers appear to use a hybrid model.

Varma and Schwartz asked adults and 6th-grade children to make speeded judgments about which of two digits referred to a greater amount. People saw two digits on a screen, and they had to press a button on the side of the greater digit. (For this task, participants understood that a –2 should be considered a greater amount than –5. In its own right, this is an important development, because children need to uncouple magnitude and direction for the integers; Bofferding, 2011.) People completed three major types of comparison problems: pure positive problems (e.g., 5 vs. 2), pure negative problems (e.g., –5 vs. –2), and mixed problems that spanned the zero boundary (e.g., –5 and 2).

The key evidence for an analog representation of magnitude comes from the comparison of response times for near and far problems. Near problems involved digit pairs that were three or fewer steps apart (e.g., 1 vs. 3, –5 vs. –7, –2 vs. 1). Far problems involved digits that were seven or more steps apart (e.g., 1 vs. 8, –2 vs. –9, –3 vs. 5). If people rely on an analog representation, then near comparisons should take longer than the corresponding far comparisons, per the symbolic distance effect described earlier. Again, the logic is that similar magnitudes (near) should be harder to discriminate than more distinct magnitudes (far).

Adult Representations of Negative Numbers

Figure 17.5 shows the results. We first consider the adult pattern. Both the pure positive and pure negative problems show the signature of an analog magnitude representation – near comparisons take longer than far comparisons. The striking finding involves the mixed comparisons, which showed an *inverse* distance effect (cf. Krajcsi & Igács, 2010). People were faster for near-mixed comparisons than for far-mixed comparisons. For example, people were faster to judge the larger of –1 vs. 2 than –1 vs. 7. By a pure magnitude account, the former comparison should be harder, not easier, because the digits are closer in magnitude. This suggests the adults have incorporated some additional structure into their representation of integers besides pure magnitude.

Varma and Schwartz (2011) created the mathematical model in Figure 17.6 to account for these distance effects. The model also incorporates the standard size effect: Smaller magnitudes (1 vs. 3) are compared more quickly than larger magnitudes (7 vs. 9) when they are both the same distance apart. This is why the lines are curved logarithmically – smaller numbers are further apart and more distinct in the representation.

The striking characteristic of the best fitting model (Figure 17.6) of the Varma and Schwartz data is that the negatives are a reflection of the positive numbers rather than an extension of the positive numbers. By this model, the analog representation of negative numbers is not simply an internalization of the standard number line. If it were an internalization of the number line, then near-mixed comparisons (1 vs. –2) would be harder, not easier than far-mixed comparisons (1 vs. –7) because the near-mixed comparisons would be closer to each other in the representation. Instead, the representation capitalizes on the symmetry of negative and positives about zero, which makes near-mixed comparisons easier because they are on either side of, and close to, the boundary point of zero.

The visual presentation of the model is not intended to imply that people use a picture of a sideways V when they think about integers. Rather, the model describes the structural

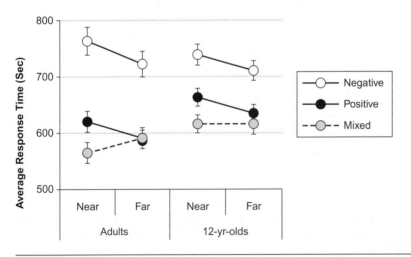

Figure 17.5 Response times for digit comparisons. Positive comparisons involved two positive digits (e.g., 2 vs. 8); negative comparisons involved two negative digits (e.g., –2 vs. –8); and, mixed comparisons involved a positive and a negative digit (e.g., –2 vs. 8). Near comparisons used digits that were within three steps of each other (–1 and –4), and far comparisons used digits that were seven or more steps apart (–1 and –8). (Adapted from Varma & Schwartz, 2011.)

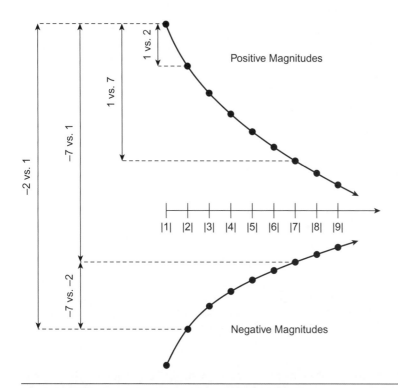

Figure 17.6 Reflection model of integer representation. Positive and negative magnitudes are reflections of one another, which embodies the additive inverse. Magnitude comparisons are a function of the projected distances between numbers, such that −2 vs. 1 is further apart than −7 vs. 1, and therefore should be answered more quickly. Comparisons of negatives versus positives should also be answered more quickly than pure positive or pure negative comparisons. The curvature of the lines indicates that people have superior resolution for comparing small magnitudes compared to large magnitudes, and therefore small magnitudes should be compared faster. (Adapted from Varma & Schwartz, 2011.)

relations that determine what is easy and hard to think about. The model posits that people have bundled the structural relation of symmetry into their analog representation of magnitude.

A second notable point of the model is that the negative magnitudes are less distinct than the positive magnitudes. In Figure 17.4, the negative magnitudes are more compressed than the positive numbers. This makes sense in that people have had much less experience with negative numbers than positive numbers. Blair, Rosenberg-Lee, Tsang, Schwartz, & Menon (2012) examined this effect using fMRI.

Participants performed a similar magnitude comparison task in an MRI scanner. Two numbers were presented on the screen and participants determined the greater or lesser number. Of particular interest was the representation of positive and negative numbers. If people have an independent representation of negative numbers that is compressed relative to positives, as predicted by the mathematical model, we would expect negative comparisons to elicit different activation in the IPS. Recall that the IPS is involved in magnitude processing.

The key analysis examined patterns of activation in the IPS for positive-only and negative-only comparisons independent of overall reaction time or activation level. A representational similarity analysis compared the spatial patterns of activation between

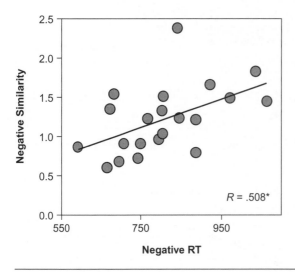

Figure 17.7 Correlation between the degree of neural overlap for near and far negative number comparisons and reaction time for solving negative comparison problems. People who exhibited larger overlap in brain regions for near and far negative comparisons were also slower to answer negative comparison problems.

near and far comparisons for positive numbers and for negative numbers. The logic is that if there is high overlap in regions of activation for the near and far problems in the magnitude processing region (IPS), then people do not have a well-differentiated magnitude representation of the numbers. In contrast, if there is less overlap in regions of activation, then people have a more differentiated representation of number magnitudes. The analysis revealed that neural responses in the IPS were more differentiated among positive numbers than among negative numbers. This helps to explain why people are slower comparing negative numbers – their representation of negative number magnitudes is less well-defined. Figure 17.7 shows that degree of neural overlap for near- and far-negative comparisons is strongly correlated with slower response times for solving negative comparison problems. These findings point to a unique, but less well-developed, magnitude representation for negative numbers, as predicted by the computational model. If individuals converted negative numbers to positive values before making magnitude comparisons there should not have been differences in the similarity for negative problems compared to positive problems, because both comparisons would involve the representation of positive magnitudes.

Immature Representations of Negative Numbers

Next, we return to the behavioral data and the children's results in Figure 17.5. The children were equally accurate as the adults (>95%). However, they show interesting differences in their response time patterns. Most notably, they do not show a distance effect for the mixed comparisons; the response times for near- and far-mixed problems are the same. Rather than consulting a magnitude representation of negative numbers, they were simply using a rule that a positive is always greater than a negative (i.e., they were only looking at the sign on the digits, and disregarding the magnitudes).

A more subtle difference is that the children were faster at making pure negative comparisons than the adults, even though they were slower for the pure positive comparisons. One interpretation of this finding is that the children were solving the pure negative comparison problems by using their well-developed natural number representation and applying a rule to flip the answer. In contrast, the adults relied on their analog representation of negative numbers. Because the adult representation of negative numbers has less resolution than the positive numbers, it took them longer than the children.

In summary, well-educated adults appear to have an independent analog representation of the negative numbers. Moreover, the overall integer representation appears to have bundled magnitude and symmetry together, with negative and positive numbers organized as a reflection of one another. The representation is not simply a copy of the standard number line seen in textbooks, but rather it takes a symmetric form that enhances the additive inverse. This representation embodies the new mathematical structure of the integer system compared to the natural numbers, but the embodiment is not a simple copy of perceptual-motor experience.

The second key finding from this study is that children were able to solve the integer problems, but they did not appear to have a distinct representation of negative numbers. Instead, they were applying symbolic rules to augment their natural number representation. This yields two points. The first is the well-known observation that people can solve mathematical problems by reference to symbolic rules and math facts without using an underlying semantic representation. This can yield much faster problem solving but, as we demonstrate below, it also leads to less flexibility and generativity. The second point involves the cross-sectional comparison of the children and the adults. The children solved the problems using an abstract rule (e.g., a positive is always greater than a negative) without reference to a representation of negative numbers. In contrast, the adults solved the problems by reference to a more perceptually derived representation. This reverses the usual concrete-to-abstract learning progression (Bruner, 1996; Piaget, 1941). With the integers, there appears to be an abstract-to-concrete shift.

Per the bundling hypothesis, we speculate that over time the symbolic representation and structure of the integers slowly enlists perceptual-motor representations. When learning integers, children already have an analog magnitude representation of natural number that exhibits perceptual-motor properties (Sekuler & Mierkiewicz, 1977). Because negative numbers and zero do not have a ready perceptual-motor basis, children initially understand them by using symbolic rules that map them to natural numbers. Over experience, the structure of the syntactic rules and their operations over integers changes the original magnitude representation of natural number to directly embody the unique properties of the integers, such as the fact that zero is a boundary between positives and negatives. By the bundling hypothesis, appropriate engagement with symbolic notations provides a mechanism for transforming perceptual-motor experiences into richer, abstract concepts.

CULTURAL SUPPORTS FOR BUNDLING SYMMETRY INTO THE INTEGERS

The first step in our support of the bundling hypothesis was evidence that people use symmetry to think about purely symbolic problems involving integers. The second step was to show that symmetry has been bundled into the other properties of number, specifically magnitude. The third step is to show that cultural organizations of representations and activities can facilitate the bundling of symmetry into the integers. To complete this theoretical demonstration, we turned our basic hypothesis and research into a practical application that improves early instruction involving the integers.

Instruction that introduces the integers usually uses a number line model, a cancellation model, or both (Bofferding, 2011; Liebeck, 1990; Gregg & Gregg, 2007). In the number line model, students are introduced to negative numbers as a leftward extension of the natural number line. Addition and subtraction with integers is modeled as movement along the number line. For example, to do addition in enVisionMATH (www. pearsonschool.com/envisionmath), students imagine standing on the first addend on the number line and facing the positive direction. Walking forward means adding a positive number and walking backward means adding a negative number. For subtraction students face the negative direction and walk forward for subtracting a positive and backward for subtracting a negative. In the number line model, integers can be thought of as positions and arithmetic can be thought of as movement or changes in position.

In the cancellation model students are encouraged to think of integers as amounts rather than distances and directions, with the negative and positive integers representing opposite quantities. Students learn that the positive and negative quantities cancel each other out, and they model arithmetic problems using a set of concrete counters (small disks). For example, for the addition problem −5 + 2, five negative (sometimes red) counters are placed in a row, two positive (sometimes yellow) counters are placed in a parallel row, and the positive and negative counters that match up cancel each other out, leaving −3 remaining as the answer. For both the number line and cancellation models, teachers may also introduce a set of rules to supplement the physical representation. For instance, given the problem 3 + (−5) students can learn to subtract the smaller number from the larger number ignoring the signs, and attach a negative sign when the original negative addend is larger than the positive addend.

Notably, these curricula do not explicitly incorporate symmetry. To find out if including symmetry would improve student learning, we conducted a study with fourth graders who had not yet learned about negative numbers. Students learned over four days in one of three instructional conditions: Jumping, Stacking, and Folding. The Jumping and Stacking conditions mapped into current instructional models and the Folding condition additionally introduced symmetry. The conditions are named for the core action students engaged in while physically modeling integer addition problems: jumping a figurine along a number line, stacking blocks on a number line, or folding the positive and negative sides of the number line together.

The purpose of the physical activities with the manipulatives was to draw student attention to the key properties of interest (e.g., folding about a symmetry point). Simply exposing students to appropriate cultural representations or phenomena is not sufficient to ensure recruitment of the appropriate mental functionality. People need to learn to notice the relevant property and operations. Any given action or perceptual stimuli has an infinite amount of information (Gibson, 1969), so it is not enough to just assume that people will pick up the relevant properties, even if they are implicit in their actions or perceptions. For example, consider the traditional number line in Figure 17.8. It exhibits a variety of properties such as ordinality and equal intervals. It also exhibits edges, curved fonts, placement on the page, arrows on the ends, and so on. It also includes symmetry

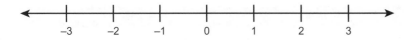

Figure 17.8 Standard representation of the integers in instruction

about zero. But, if one does not already know the symmetry of the additive inverse, it would be easy to miss it amid all the other kinds of information. Zero would be just another point on the line.

The first phase of the instruction comprised a series of instructional games using physical manipulatives that we designed to draw student attention to different ways of thinking about negatives. Figure 17.9 shows how the conditions differ when playing a simple addition game. The Jumping condition (Figure 17.9C) enacted the addition problems in each game by hopping a plastic figurine back and forth along the number line. The Stacking condition (Figure 17.9B) instead used a representation of stacked blocks. For example, for +3 + –2, students started at zero and placed three blue blocks on the positive side of the number line to represent +3. Then, working their way back toward 0, they placed two red blocks on top to represent –2. The stacked portion "canceled out," and the remaining unstacked portion was the answer, in this case 1 blue positive block. For the Folding condition (Figure 17.9A), the manipulatives included a hinge at the number zero, allowing the students to fold the number line in half. Students represented both addends on the number line at the same time, for example with three blue blocks on the positive side and two red blocks on the negative side. They then snapped the sides together by folding at zero. The blocks that matched up after folding canceled out, and the ones that did not match up were the remaining answer.

After two days of working with the manipulatives, students transitioned to computer games. The computer games maintained the differences between conditions, and they enabled students to complete more questions in the available time (students did not have to fuss with the concrete materials). With the computer games students did not engage in physical behaviors that had any sort of correspondence to manipulating the physical number line objects. Instead, the computer games showed the respective spatial representations and transformations, and students simply entered symbolic answers through discrete clicks. Over time, the computer games faded the spatial representation of the manipulatives so that students were working primarily with symbolic digits.

The study included a number of learning measures. On a simple measure of adding negative and positive digits, all the conditions improved significantly with no differences between conditions. This indicates that students learned the basic content from all three conditions. The post-test also included questions that required students to extend their understanding to new problems that they had not been taught, such as placing positive and negative fractional amounts on the number line or solving missing variable problems with integers. On these generalization items, students in the folding condition performed significantly better, indicating that they developed a more flexible understanding of integers (Figure 17.10).

Additionally, instruction influenced children's strategies for solving problems. Students in the folding condition used significantly more symmetry-based strategies, which were associated with better performance. For example, when asked to put the number 4 on a number line on which only –4 and 0 were marked, students in the symmetry condition were more likely to measure the distance from 0 to –4 with their fingers, and then measure

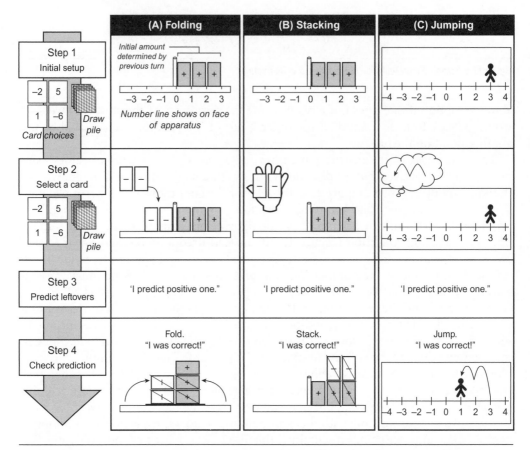

Figure 17.9 Leftovers Game schematic for each instructional condition. This is a 2–4 player card game played during the second half of the curriculum. Left column shows the steps for one turn in the game. The three panels show the corresponding actions with manipulates for the (A) Folding, (B) Stacking, and (C) Jumping conditions. The example shown is equivalent to solving the equation $3 + -2 = 1$ (adapted from Tsang, 2012).

the same distance on the right side of 0 to place positive 4. Students in the other conditions were more likely to start at 0 and draw four tick marks in the positive direction, placing the number 4 at the fourth tick mark.

Tsang (2012) also included a measure that looked for negative side-effects of the symmetry instruction. As people develop structures that are optimized for handling classes of problems, these structures may interfere with other classes of problems that would be better served by different organizations of knowledge. Evidence for this point comes from a computerized reaction time measure. A number line was shown on the screen with only the endpoints labeled. For some trials, the endpoints were symmetric (e.g., –6, 6), such that 0 would fall in the center of the line. For other trials, the endpoints were non-symmetric (e.g., –4, 8) such that zero would not be in the center of the line. One part of the number line was occluded by a green box. Students indicated whether the number 0 would fall in the area occluded by the box. Students in the jumping and stacking conditions were unaffected by whether the endpoints on the number line indicated symmetry or not. In contrast, students in the folding condition were significantly slower for the non-symmetric problems. These students had learned to rely on

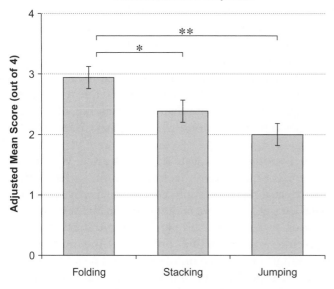

Figure 17.10 Score on generalization composite by condition (adapted from Tsang, 2012)

symmetry, and when it was not there, they had to refigure another way to solve the problem.

Ideally, people develop appropriate structure for the most prevalent and important classes of problems they will experience, and situations where that structure is an impediment are rare. This appears to be the case for symmetry and the integers. Regardless of condition, students who exhibited greater interference for the non-symmetric problems did much better on the generalization composite score that required solving novel quantitative problems. They had developed a better representation of integer symmetry, which helped them with most problems, but also hurt them on problems designed to make a symmetry orientation sub-optimal. Combined, these results indicate that students in the symmetry condition were more likely to incorporate the relationship of symmetry into their representations of integers, as evidenced by reaction time, and across conditions, students whose representations incorporated symmetry had a more flexible and generalizable understanding of the integers.

CONCLUSION

The bundling hypothesis attempts to provide a mechanistic account of how new mathematical concepts are formed. Through socially organized interaction and highly structured cultural symbol systems, distinct perceptual-motor functions get bundled together to enable new concepts with a higher-order structure. We provided a chain of evidence regarding integers that supports several of the claims within the bundling hypothesis. Adults exhibit behavior and brain activation that indicates the involvement of symmetry when finding the midpoint of a positive and negative digit. Symmetry appears to be bundling into adult sense of magnitude, because they show distinct patterns of response times when comparing the magnitudes of digits on either size of zero. Adults also exhibit a distinct neural representation of negative numbers, and adults who have more spatially distinct brain patterns of activation for negative number comparisons also show faster response times. Children who have had traditional instruction do not exhibit these patterns, but instead, they appear to rely on rules that allow them to solve problems by consulting their representation of positive numbers supplemented by rules. However, with instruction that emphasizes symmetry, children exhibit evidence of relying on symmetry when they solve visual bisection tasks. Moreover, students who have integrated symmetry into their understanding of integers are more successful at solving problems that go beyond what they have been directly taught.

There are aspects of the bundling hypothesis that were not investigated. We did not seek direct evidence on the importance of instruction that integrates the different perceptual properties into a common external representation. We have suggestive evidence but it has not been rigorously tested. In pilot work, we taught children about symmetry without making careful connections to the other properties of number (interval, magnitude, etc.). Symmetry turned into a "free-floating" property of the integers. For instance, the children never noticed that positives go on the right and negatives go on the left. We also have not conducted a pre–post intervention where we examine whether children increase the recruitment of brain regions associated with symmetry after instruction, and thus, we have not closed the loop showing that instruction causes "bundling" within the brain. We have not determined whether the involvement of symmetry makes a difference as students move to more complex topics such as algebra, which makes great use of the additive inverse.

In the meantime, if we assume that something close to the bundling hypothesis is true for the integers, are there other conceptual changes where the hypothesis would be a possible explanation? Would the bundling hypothesis help explain how people manage to find meaning and structure in other highly abstract mathematical concepts such as calculus's "instantaneous change"? Perhaps the bundling hypothesis can provide a good account of children's transition from the interval scale of natural numbers to the ratio scale of rational numbers. In addition to overcoming a simple natural number interpretation of fraction notations (e.g., Stafylidou & Vosniadou, 2004), children need to recruit a "sense of ratio." According to the bundling hypothesis, this would be found in native perceptual abilities that can provide the additional structure for rational number. There are many possible candidates, given that visual structure is often invariant of absolute size.

The bundling hypothesis is an attempt to explain how new structure arises in the mind of the learner. It is not an account of how people jump from one explanatory structure to another during a process of conceptual change, as would be the case in switching explanatory paradigms from mechanical causality to stochastic emergence (Chi, 2005). Rather, it is an attempt to answer the question of how an explanatory structure can develop in the first place. For the integers at least, it appears that culture and external representations help people bind previously discrete perceptual-motor systems into integrated conceptual structures.

REFERENCES

Ansari, D., Garcia, N., Lucas, E., Hamon, K., & Dhital, B. (2005). Neural correlates of symbolic number processing in children and adults. *NeuroReport, 16*(16), 1769–1773.

Blair, K. P., Rosenberg-Lee, M., Tsang, J. M., Schwartz, D. L., & Menon, V. (2012). Beyond natural numbers: Negative number representation in parietal cortex. *Frontiers in Human Neuroscience, 6*(7), 1–17.

Bofferding, L. C. (2011). *Expanding the numerical central conceptual structure: First graders' understanding of integers.* Doctoral dissertation, Stanford University, Stanford, CA.

Bruner, J. (1996). *The culture of education.* Cambridge, MA: Harvard University Press.

Cantlon, J. F., & Brannon, E. M. (2007). Basic math in monkeys and college students. *PLoS Biology, 5*(12).

Case, R., Okamoto, Y., Griffin, S., McKeough, A., Bleiker, C., Henderson, B., et al. (1997). The role of central conceptual structures in the development of children's thought. *Monographs of the Society for Research in Child Development, 61*, 1–295.

Chi, M. T. H. (2005). Common sense conceptions of emergent processes: Why some misconceptions are robust. *Journal of the Learning Sciences, 14*, 161–199.

Chomsky, N. (1966). *Cartesian linguistics: A chapter in the history of rationalist thought.* New York, NY: Harper & Row.

Cole, M., & Engeström, Y. (1993). A cultural–historical approach to distributed cognition. In G. Salomon (Ed.), *Distributed cognitions.* Cambridge, UK: Cambridge University Press.

Dehaene, S., & Cohen, L. (2007). Cultural recycling of cortical maps. *Neuron, 56*(2), 384–398.

de Schotten, M. T., Urbanski, M., Duffau, H., Volle, E., Levy, R., Dubois, B., et al. (2005). Direct evidence for a parietal-frontal pathway subserving spatial awareness in humans. *Science, 309*(5744), 2226.

Fischer, M. H. (2003). Cognitive representation of negative numbers. *Psychological Science, 14*(3), 278–282.

Ganor-Stern, D., & Tzelgov, J. (2008). Negative numbers are generated in the mind. *Experimental Psychology, 55*(3), 157–163.

Gibson, E. (1969). *Principles of perceptual learning and development.* New York: Appleton-Centrury-Crofts.

Glenberg, A. M., & Kaschak, M. P. (2002). Grounding language in action. *Psychonomic Bulletin & Review, 9*, 558–565.

Gobel, S. M., Johansen-Berg, H., Behrens, T., & Rushworth, M. F. (2004). Response-selection-related parietal activation during number comparison. *Journal of Cognitive Neuroscience, 16*(9), 1536–1551.

Goldstone, R. L., Landy, D., & Son, J. Y. (2010). The education of perception. *Topics in Cognitive Science, 2*, 265–284.

Gregg, J., & Gregg, D. U. (2007). A context for integer computation. *Mathematics Teaching in the Middle School, 13*(1), 46–50.

Griffin, S. A., Case, R., & Siegler, R. S. (1994). Rightstart: Providing the central conceptual prerequisites for first formal learning of arithmetic to students at risk for school failure. In K. McGilly (Ed.), *Classroom lessons: Integrating cognitive theory and classroom practice* (pp. 25–49). Cambridge, MA: MIT Press.

Hegarty, M. (1992). Mental animation: Inferring motion from static diagrams of mechanical systems. *Journal of Experimental Psychology: Learning, Memory and Cognition, 18*, 1084–1102.

Kaufmann, L., Koppelstaetter, F., Delazer, M., Siedentopf, C., Rhomberg, P., Golaszewski, S., et al. (2005). Neural correlates of distance and congruity effects in a numerical Stroop task: an event-related fMRI study. *NeuroImage, 25*(3), 888–898.

Klatzky, R. L., Pellegrino, J. W., McCloskey, B. P., & Doherty, S. (1989). Can you squeeze a tomato? The role of motor representations in semantic sensibility judgments. *Journal of Memory & Language, 28*, 56–77.

Krajcsi, A., & Igács, J. (2010). Processing negative numbers by transforming negatives to positive range and by sign shortcut. *European Journal of Cognitive Psychology, 22*, 1021–1038.

Lakoff, G., & Núñez, R. (2000). *Where mathematics comes from: How the embodied mind brings mathematics into being.* New York, NY: Basic Books.

Leach, T., & Scott, P. H. (2008). Teaching for conceptual understanding: An approach drawing on individual and sociocultural perspectives. In S. Vosniadou (Ed.) *International Handbook of Conceptual Change.* New York, NY: Routledge.

Lehrer, R., & Schauble, L. (2000). Inventing data structures for representational purposes: Elementary grade students' classification models. *Mathematical Thinking and Learning, 2*, 51–74.

Liebeck, P. (1990). Scores and forfeits: An intuitive model for integer arithmetic. *Educational Studies in Mathematics, 21*(3), 221–239.

Moyer, R. S., & Landauer, T. K. (1967). The time required for judgments of numerical inequality. *Nature, 215*, 1519–1520.

Parkman, J. M. (1971). Temporal aspects of digit and letter inequality judgments. *Journal of Experimental Psychology, 91*, 191–205.

Piaget, J. (1941/1952). *The child's conception of number.* London, UK: Routledge and Kegan Paul.

Piaget, J. (1952). *The origins of intelligence in children* (M. Cook., Trans.). New York, NY: International Universities Press.

Pinel, P., Dehaene, S., Riviere, D., & LeBihan, D. (2001). Modulation of parietal activation by semantic distance in a number comparison task *NeuroImage, 14*(5), 1013–1026.

Prather, R. W., & Alibali, M. W. (2008). Understanding and using principles of arithmetic: Operations involving negative numbers. *Cognitive Science, 32*, 445–457.

Restle, F. (1970). Speed of adding and comparing numbers. *Journal of Experimental Psychology, 83*, 274–278.

Royer, F. L. (1981). Detection of symmetry. *Journal of Experimental Psychology: Human Perception and Performance, 7*(6), 1186–1210.

Sasaki, Y., Vanduffel, W., Knutsen, T., Tyler, C., & Tootell, R. (2005). Symmetry activates extrastriate visual cortex in human and nonhuman primates. *Proceedings of the National Academy of Sciences of the United States of America, 102*(8), 3159–3163.

Saxe, G. B. (1981). Body parts as numerals: A developmental analysis of numeration among the Oksapmin in Papua New Guinea. *Child Development, 52*(1), 306–316.

Saxe, G. B. (1988). Candy selling and math learning. *Educational Researcher, 17*(6), 14–21.

Schwartz, D. L., & Black, J. B. (1996). Shuttling between depictive models and abstract rules: Induction and fallback. *Cognitive Science, 20*, 457–497.

Schwartz, D. L., Blair, K. P., & Tsang, J. (2012). How to build educational neuroscience: Two approaches with concrete instances. *British Journal of Educational Psychology Monograph Series, 8.*

Schwartz, D. L. & Holton, D. (2000). Tool use and the effect of action on the imagination. *Journal of Experimental Psychology: Learning, Cognition, and Memory, 26*, 1655–1665.

Sekuler, R., & Mierkiewicz, D. (1977). Children's judgments of numerical inequality. *Child Development, 48*, 630–633.

Shaki, S., & Petrusic, W. M. (2005). On the mental representation of negative numbers: Context-dependent SNARC effects with comparative judgments. *Psychonomic Bulletin & Review, 12*(5), 931–937.

Shepard, R. N., & Cooper, L. A. (Eds.). (1986). Mental images and their transformations. Cambridge, MA: MIT Press.

Spelke, E. S. (2000). Core knowledge. *American Psychologist, 55*, 1233–1243.

Stafylidou, S., & Vosniadou, S. (2004). The development of students' understanding of the numerical value of fractions. *Learning and Instruction, 14*, 503–528.

Tsang, J. M. (2012). Learning to see less than nothing: Symmetry in the mental representation of integers. Doctoral dissertation, Stanford University, Stanford, CA.

Tsang, J. M., Rosenberg-Lee, M., Blair, K. P., Schwartz, D. L., & Menon, V. (2010, June). *Near symmetry in a number bisection task yields faster responses and greater occipital activity.* Poster presented at the 16th Annual Meeting of the Organization for Human Brain Mapping, Barcelona, Spain.

Tsang, J. M., & Schwartz, D. L. (2009). Symmetry in the semantic representation of integers. In N. Taatgen & H. van Rijn (Eds.), *Proceedings of the 31st Annual Conference of the Cognitive Science Society* (pp. 323–328). Austin, TX: Cognitive Science Society.

Tzelgov, J., Ganor-Stern, D., & Maymon-Schreiber, K. (2009). The representation of negative numbers: Exploring the effects of mode of processing and notation. *Quarterly Journal of Experimental Psychology, 62*(3), 605–624.

Tyler, C. W., Baseler, H. A., Kontsevich, L. L., Likova, L. T., Wade, A. R., & Wandell, B. A. (2005). Predominantly extra-retinotopic cortical response to pattern symmetry. *NeuroImage, 24*(2), 306–314.

Varma, S., & Schwartz, D. L. (2011). The mental representation of integers: An abstract-to-concrete shift in the understanding of mathematical concepts. *Cognition, 121*, 363–385.

Vygotsky, L. S. (1986). *Thought and language* (A. Kozulin, Trans.). Cambridge, MA: MIT Press.

Wexler, M., & Klam, F. (2001). Movement prediction and movement production. *Journal of Experimental Psychology: Human Perception and Performance, 27*, 48–64.

Wilkinson, D. T., & Halligan, P. W. (2003). Stimulus symmetry affects the bisection of figures but not lines: Evidence from event-related fMRI. *NeuroImage, 20*(3), 1756–1764.

Part III

Conceptual Change in the
Philosophy and History of Science

18

THE PROBLEM OF CONCEPTUAL CHANGE IN THE PHILOSOPHY AND HISTORY OF SCIENCE

Theodore Arabatzis and Vasso Kindi,
National and Kapodistrian University of Athens

In this chapter we give an overview of the problem of conceptual change in 20th-century philosophy of science. The problem of conceptual change has been widely discussed in the philosophy of science since the early 1960s, when Thomas Kuhn and Paul Feyerabend, among others, launched a powerful critique of logical positivism. One of their most far-reaching theses was that scientific concepts are historical entities that evolve over time and are replaced by altogether different ones. In their view, the older concepts and their descendants refer to completely different entities. The very subject matter of scientific investigation shifts along with conceptual change. Furthermore, because of such ontological shifts, the possibility of giving an account of theory change as a rational process is undermined. In post-Kuhnian philosophy of science there has been considerable effort to come to terms with these ontological and epistemological implications of conceptual change.

THE LOGICAL POSITIVIST ANALYSIS OF CONCEPTS

The logical positivists, as they explained in their manifesto of 1929 (Hahn, Carnap, & Neurath, 1996), aimed at reaching the goal of unified science by ordering all concepts into a reductive system. The idea was that any concept, from any branch of science, had to be "statable by step-wise reduction to other concepts, down to the concepts of the lowest level which refer directly to the given" (Hahn et al., 1996, p. 331). On this lowest level there were supposed to lie concepts of "the experience and qualities of the individual psyche"; on the next, physical objects; then, other minds; and, lastly, the objects of social science (Hahn et al., 1996). The method logical positivists used to move in and deal with this hierarchical system of concepts was logical analysis, undertaken with the help of the formal logic developed by Frege and Russell at the start of the 20th century. This tool allowed logical positivists to formulate statements in a first-order formal language, that of propositional or predicate logic, which gave them the rigor, clarity, and precision they required. The aim was to move from statement to statement by tautological trans-formations representing, thus, thought and inference as a mechanical, automatically controlled process (Hahn et al., 1996, pp. 330, 331). The reason behind all this was the determination to keep metaphysics out of the scientific world-conception (Hahn et al., 1996, p. 329). The project consisted in manipulating an ordered system of concepts, arranged in statements, by means of a language that contained only structural formulae (Hahn et al., 1996, pp. 331–332). The emphasis on mere structure, mere form, and not content was thought to guarantee intersubjectivity and unity since content was considered, by definition, inexpressible and incommunicable (Schlick, 1981, pp. 137, 141). For instance, different people may have different images and impressions of particular colors but the system of colors can be represented in a publicly visible structure that can be shared by all. Let us see in more detail how they understood concepts and how they dealt with them.

Carnap (1981, p. 113) assigns to the theory of science the study, in the abstract, of the linguistic expressions of science. These expressions form statements, which form, in turn, ordered systems, the theories. The task of the philosopher is to study the relations between statements. For instance, when philosophers discuss the problem of confirmation – how scientific theories are confirmed by evidence – they consider the relations between observation statements and statements that express scientific hypotheses. When they discuss explanation – how scientists explain, for example, individual phenomena – they consider the relations between the explanans and the explanandum; that is, the relations between statements that express general laws and initial conditions on one hand (the explanans) and a statement expressing the particular event to be explained on the other. Each statement has as components terms that may express concepts. Carnap says that he prefers "terms" to "concepts" because he fears that "concepts" may be understood psychologically (1981, p. 118).

Carnap's ultimate aim was to achieve a rational reconstruction of the concepts of all fields of knowledge with the help of the formalism and logic that had been developed by Frege, Russell, and Whitehead. This task, which was shared, as we have seen, by other members of the Vienna Circle, involved the explication of concepts; that is, their clarification in the direction of greater exactness through their reduction, originally to basic concepts of sensory experience (e.g., sense data of the form "a red of a certain type at a certain visual field place at a certain time"), and later, in order to ensure a greater intersubjective agreement, through reduction to a physical basis that contained as basic concepts observable properties and relations of physical things. It should be noted, however, that Carnap's logical reconstruction was not at all concerned with the actual concepts and the empirical work of the sciences. His concepts are mere knots in a system of structural relations and have only formal, structural properties.

The different executions of this project formed the so-called received view of scientific theories conceived as an axiomatic, hypothetico-deductive, empirically uninterpreted calculus which was then interpreted observationally by means of bridge principles or correspondence rules. The idea was that there is a "theoretical scenario" involving laws, theoretical concepts, and entities, which is brought to apply, by bridge principles, to the empirical phenomena it is supposed to explain. For example, the kinetic theory of gases with its assumptions about gas molecules and the laws that govern them serves as the theoretical scenario to explain phenomena such as temperature and pressure using bridge principles which state, for instance, that the temperature of a gas (empirical concept) is proportional to the mean kinetic energy of its molecules (theoretical concept) (Hempel, 1970).

We see, then, that in the context of logical positivism, which largely shaped what is still known as philosophy of science, there is no substantive account of concepts. What mattered to Carnap and the logical positivists was to be able to manipulate signs mechanically in the effort to bring to the study of science, and, thus, to philosophy, the rigor and clarity of mathematics and logic. Their concerns were purely logical (i.e., the logical relations among statements and terms); the actual theories and concepts of science were only the occasion to exercise their logical insights. They had no ambition to influence the practice of scientists.

Conceptual change was far from their priorities, if non-existent as a matter of concern. The standard account of theories "could at best represent a theory quick frozen, as it were, at one momentary stage of what is in fact a continually developing system of ideas" (Hempel, 1970, p. 148). In theory change they'd rather speak of new laws expressed by old concepts than of new meanings of the terms used.

THE "HISTORICIST" VIEW OF CONCEPTS AND CONCEPTUAL CHANGE

The issue of conceptual change became the focus of attention in the early 1960s with the work most notably of Paul Feyerabend and Thomas Kuhn. The novel idea that these two philosophers introduced was that theory change in the sciences may involve change in the meaning of terms, in which case there is radical discontinuity in the development of scientific knowledge. The logical positivists, and those who were working in the tradition of their philosophy, did not deny that in the course of scientific development theories evolve and are modified or abandoned. They did not deny that new theoretical terms and new concepts are introduced with the advent of a new theory. But they did deny, at least implicitly, that these developments effect radical discontinuity and interfere with the meanings of the terms that are retained. The reason this possibility was not even imaginable may be sought in the confidence that logical positivists had that the observational and physicalist language which they had placed at the bottom of their formulation of theories could guarantee continuity and intersubjective validity. They had an entity idea of meaning and thought that there is a steady influx of neutral empirical content from the observation level to the abstract level of theory and into the empty syntactical shells of the theoretical terms of science.

Both Kuhn and Feyerabend had a different idea of meaning drawing upon Wittgenstein's later philosophy. Feyerabend explicitly invoked Wittgenstein when he spoke of his contextual theory of meaning (1981a, p. 74) while Kuhn (1970, p. 45) referred to Wittgenstein in connection with the notion of family resemblance.

Wittgenstein spoke of meaning as use rejecting an entity idea of meaning (the entity being a mental image, a referent in the world of objects or some kind of an abstract Platonic form). The meaning of a word is its use in language with its rules and grammar. To know the meaning of a word or, equivalently, to have the corresponding concept is to be able to use it appropriately. But the appropriate use is not given by some definition, which must be antecedently available, comprising a set of necessary and sufficient conditions that specify when and how the word ought to be employed, but rather the appropriate use is learned in practice when the users of language are exposed to concrete examples of application. The uses of a particular word on different occasions and in different contexts bear similarities to each other, "overlapping and criss-crossing," and form a family of resemblances (Wittgenstein, 2009, §66–67). Yet no common thread runs through them all and, so, no set of conditions can be used to fully define and bound a concept. As a result, concepts for Wittgenstein are normally vague and fluid with blurred edges. This does not mean, however, that they cannot be given sharp boundaries for specific purposes (Wittgenstein, 2009, §68–69) or that this rather loose understanding of concepts renders them useless or precludes the possibility of correct use.

Feyerabend was well acquainted with Wittgenstein's philosophy and used it in attacking the formal theories of explanation and reduction in the sciences. Both explanations and reductions were understood as deductive structures which meant that the terms appearing in the premises and the conclusion had to have fixed meanings that did not vary with the theories. Otherwise reduction and explanation could not go through.

Feyerabend (1981a) challenged both the deductive structure of explanation and reduction (on historical and logical grounds) and the assumption it implies of meaning invariance; i.e., the assumption that meanings are invariant with respect to the processes of explanation and reduction. He maintained that the meaning of a term is given contextually; i.e., it is dependent on "the way in which the term has been incorporated into a theory" (Feyerabend, 1981a, p. 74) and claimed that elements of many pairs of theories (concepts, principles, laws, etc) are "incommensurable and therefore incapable of mutual explanation and reduction" (Feyerabend, 1981a, p. 77). The reason is that concepts of an earlier theory cannot be defined on the basis of primitive observational terms of the theory to which a reduction is attempted, nor can there be found "correct empirical statements" to correlate corresponding terms and concepts (Feyerabend, 1981a, p. 76). Observation – and this is yet another influence of Wittgenstein's philosophy – was thought by Feyerabend, but also Hanson (1958) and Kuhn, to be theory-laden; that is, influenced and shaped by the categories and concepts of each theory. Feyerabend believed that the progress of science requires radical steps forward, so, if the meanings of terms are preserved as science develops, the much desired revolutions in the interest of knowledge will not occur. Thus, meaning invariance, according to Feyerabend, is not only incompatible with actual scientific practice but also undesirable (1981a, p. 82). Finally, in an article that was first published in 1965 (1981b, p. 98), Feyerabend maintains that there is a change of meaning "either if a new theory entails that all concepts of the preceding theory have zero extension or if it introduces rules which cannot be interpreted as attributing specific properties to objects within already existing classes, but which change the system of classes itself." This is a view that, as we will see, features prominently in Kuhn's later philosophy.

At least the initial phase of Feyerabend's criticism may be considered internal to the philosophical tradition he was combating in the sense that it focused mostly on the philosophical shortcomings and inadequacies of the models that were put forward at the time. The figure most responsible for the change of perspective and the so-called historicist turn in philosophy of science in the 1960s was Thomas Kuhn. He laid emphasis on revolutions and radical conceptual change in science and acknowledged the implications of these claims.

By studying the details of particular historical cases Kuhn came to appreciate the significance of scientific education. He realized that what binds scientists together in a specific tradition, what gives their practice its character and coherence, is not a neutral, ubiquitous, formal description of theories that is based on some intersubjectively avowed observation sentences, but exposure of students to concrete problem solutions, the paradigms or exemplars, which may vary and which function as models for further research. The process of initiation and training involves doing, rather dogmatically, "finger exercises"; that is, learning, usually through textbooks, and then imitating, particular applications of concepts, particular ways of dealing with problems, particular techniques of using instruments and doing research. The consensus in and the effectiveness of science are earned not theoretically but practically. Scientists do not need to concern themselves with abstract, explicit definitions, comprising necessary and sufficient conditions, in order to know how to apply a term. Nor do they need to reduce their practice to a set of abstract rules that capture what is essential in their field. Scientific education provides scientists with the ability, rather than the abstract knowledge of rules, to do successful research (Kuhn, 1970, pp. 43–51; cf. Kuhn, 1977).

Kuhn cites Wittgenstein and his idea of family resemblance to explain how different research problems and techniques are held together in a single tradition. They do not need to share a set of characteristics but are related between them in a network of resemblances overlapping and criss-crossing. In the case of concepts, such as, *game, chair, leaf, planet, mass, motion*, again, the idea is that one does not need to know a set of attributes, the necessary and sufficient conditions, in order to apply the corresponding term. Now, this understanding of concepts – as abilities to use terms – which is a long way from the entity account involving a seepage of meaning from an observational basis through correspondence rules to an uninterpreted calculus, implies that when there is a change in the exemplars used in teaching there is going to be a change of concepts or, what amounts to the same thing, a change in the meaning of terms.

The change of exemplars is not forced on scientists by the world as such, nor is it brought about *de novo*. Kuhn emphasizes the indispensability of commitment to the tradition built around previously upheld theories as a condition of innovation and change. This is what he calls the "essential tension" implicit in scientific research (1977, pp. 227, 236). There is, on the one hand, firm, or even dogmatic, adherence to deeply ingrained patterns of research, and, on the other, a constant pursuit of novel ideas and discoveries. Scientists are pulled in both directions: They are traditionalists and iconoclasts at the same time (Kuhn, 1977, p. 227). According to Kuhn, only if scientists are well acquainted with the problems to be tackled and the techniques appropriate for use can they be able to spot and evaluate anomalies that may arise in the course of their research. "Novelty ordinarily emerges only for the man who, knowing *with precision* what he should expect, is able to recognize that something has gone wrong" (1970, p. 65; emphasis in original). Tradition-bound research is called by Kuhn normal science. In this mode, scientists undertake to solve puzzles, that is, problems very similar to the textbook paradigms, which have solutions that are anticipated, trying more to prove their own ingenuity rather than shatter the tradition and start a new one. Yet their practice, conservative as it may be, paves the way to change, on a regular basis – in the course of normal science – but also in revolutionary moments. When anomalies persist, when they become central to the investigation and when they preclude applications that are of practical importance, scientists need to reconsider their strong commitments and inherited beliefs. They proceed, then, to reconstruct their field in an effort to assimilate new solutions and new theories. This is not always achieved in a smooth way and what usually emerges is not a cumulative result. "Because the old must be revalued and reordered when assimilating the new, discovery and invention in the sciences are usually intrinsically revolutionary" (Kuhn, 1977, p. 227). Revolutionary shifts, which Kuhn sees as displacements of the conceptual networks through which scientists view the world (1970, p. 102), are rather rare but, he also notes, "the historian constantly encounters many far smaller but structurally similar revolutionary episodes [which] are central to scientific advance" (1977, p. 226). So, scientific practice is a dynamic, developmental process punctuated occasionally by radical changes which produce theories that are incommensurable with the previous ones. This means that the new theories cannot be mapped onto the old, new relations are established between concepts and laws, and new exemplars occupy the knots in the new framework. The two systems, old and new, lack a common core or a common measure.[1] Concepts in the new context, even when they continue to be named by the terms used in the previous theories, or even when there is quantitative agreement in calculations that involve them, still are viewed by Kuhn to be markedly different. "[T]he physical referents of . . . the Einsteinian concepts are by no means identical with those of the Newtonian concepts that bear the same name. (Newtonian mass is conserved; Einsteinian is convertible with energy. Only at low relative velocities may the two be measured in the same way, and even then they must not be conceived to be the same)" (Kuhn, 1970, p. 102). The difference in the concepts of two successive theories lies in the different applications they have and the different connections they enter. There is no discussion of tracing a common meaning in some common observational content because terms in Kuhn's framework do not acquire meaning by being anchored to experience but by being taught in practice in specific applications.

EARLY RECEPTION OF THE HISTORICIST ACCOUNT OF CONCEPTUAL CHANGE

Feyerabend's and Kuhn's theses on conceptual change and incommensurability were received rather unfavorably by philosophers of science (see Suppe, 1977, pp. 200–208). The main thrust of the criticism concerned the unpalatable consequences of incommensurability. First, it was claimed that if the incommensurability thesis "were true, no theory could contradict another" (Achinstein, 1968, p. 92). For example, if the term "electron" meant different things in the context of classical electromagnetic theory and in the context of the quantum theory of radiation, then there would be no contradiction between these two theories. A second, related difficulty is that if conceptual change were as radical as portrayed by Feyerabend and Kuhn, then two incommensurable theories would not even have a common subject matter. For instance, if the concepts of Newtonian mechanics and the concepts of relativity theory referred to different entities, they could not be alternative accounts of the same domain. Third, if the principles of a theory constituted the meanings of its terms, then those principles would have to be analytic statements. That is, they would have to be devoid of empirical content. A fourth difficulty concerned the process of learning a scientific theory. If the meaning of theoretical terms were theory-dependent, then "a person could not learn a theory by having it explained to him using any words whose meanings he understands before he learns the theory" (Achinstein, 1968, p. 97).

The root of these difficulties seemed to be Feyerabend's and Kuhn's claim that scientific concepts (or, equivalently, the meanings of scientific terms) were determined by the theoretical framework in which they were embedded. Several critics stressed the obscurity of this claim and pointed out that it was not supported by a fully fledged theory of meaning. Dudley Shapere was among the sharpest early critics of Kuhn and Feyerabend. In his critical review of *The Structure of Scientific Revolutions* Shapere argued that "Kuhn has offered us no clear analysis of 'meaning' or, more specifically, no criterion of change of meaning" (Shapere, 1964, p. 390). He made a similar point against Feyerabend: "We are given no way of deciding either what counts as a part of the 'meaning' of a term or what counts as a 'change of meaning' of a term" (Shapere, 1981, pp. 41–42).

As we saw in a previous section, Feyerabend attempted to respond to this difficulty by linking meaning with classification. However, this proposal also faced problems. For instance, for a new theory to entail "that all concepts of the preceding theory have extension zero" (Feyerabend, 1981b, p. 98), a common core of meaning must be shared by the two theories (Achinstein, 1968, p. 95; Shapere, 1981, p. 52).

A different line of attack against incommensurability focused on its incompatibility with the success of translation practices. Among the most prominent critics who followed this line was Donald Davidson.[2] Davidson criticized incommensurability in a celebrated article where he denied the possibility of radically different systems of concepts or "conceptual schemes" (Davidson, 1984). He associated conceptual schemes with languages and claimed that two conceptual schemes could differ only if the languages that bear them were not intertranslatable. The difference of two conceptual schemes must, thus, have a linguistic manifestation: "two people have different conceptual schemes if they speak languages that fail of intertranslatability" (Davidson, 1984, p. 185). The impossibility of translation would preclude communication between two such speakers.

Furthermore, if there were texts written in a language incommensurable to our own, they would be impossible to translate and *ipso facto* to understand. The existence of such texts, however, is belied by the successful interpretive practice of historians, such as Kuhn himself. Kuhn has been able to decipher and convey the content of purportedly incommensurable concepts, found in past scientific texts, using the resources of contemporary language. The existence of incommensurability is called into question by that very interpretive success: "Kuhn is brilliant at saying what things were like before the revolution using—what else?—our post-revolutionary idiom" (Davidson, 1984, p. 184). Thus, "Instead of living in different worlds, Kuhn's scientists may . . . be only words apart" (Davidson, 1984, p. 189).

THE FIRST RESPONSE TO INCOMMENSURABILITY: A FLIGHT TO REFERENCE

The first attempt to come to terms with the difficulties encountered by incommensurability by developing an alternative analysis of conceptual change was made by Israel Scheffler. Scheffler accepted the holistic account of meaning, which was shared by logical positivists and their historicist critics (Scheffler, 1982, pp. 45–46). He pointed out, however, an ambiguity of the word "meaning." On the one hand, the meaning of a word is "a matter of the concept or idea expressed"; that is, it concerns "the connotation, intension, attribute, or sense associated with the word." On the other hand, the meaning of a word is "rather a matter of the thing *referred* to"; that is, it concerns "the denotation, extension, application, or reference of the word" (Scheffler, 1982, pp. 54–55; emphasis in original).

Scheffler argued "that, for the purposes of mathematics and science, it is sameness of reference that is of interest rather than synonymy [sameness of meaning], in accordance with the general principle that a truth about any object is equally true of it no matter how the object is designated" (Scheffler, 1982, p. 57). That is, a concept associated with a word may change without affecting the truth values of the statements containing the word, provided that its referent remains invariant. Furthermore, the stability of a term's referent makes possible a genuine disagreement between two users of the term who, nevertheless, associate different concepts with it. Finally, because of referential stability, conceptual change does not undermine the validity of scientific deductions. Thus, *pace* Feyerabend, Hempel's deductive–nomological model of explanation and Nagel's (1979) account of reduction *qua* deductive explanation remain applicable to actual cases of scientific explanation and scientific change (Scheffler, 1982, pp. 61–62).

Scheffler, however, did not spell out this proposal to disentangle meaning and reference in terms of a developed theory of meaning. Such a theory, which would be developed by Hilary Putnam, would have to show how the reference of a term can be fixed without invoking the full concept associated with it.

MEETING THE HISTORICIST CHALLENGE: THE CAUSAL THEORY OF MEANING

The account of meaning that Putnam developed in the early 1970s was meant to be an alternative to both the logical positivist and the historicist views of meaning. He acknowledged "that meaning change and theory change cannot be sharply separated" (Putnam, 1975c, p. 255).[3] Furthermore, theories may not describe the world correctly and, therefore, "Meanings may not fit the world; and meaning change can be forced by empirical discoveries" (Putnam, 1975c, p. 256).

Putnam explicated the notion of meaning in terms of the notions of communication and teaching. "It is a fact . . . that the use of words can be taught. If someone does not know the meaning of 'lemon', I can somehow convey it to him . . . in this simple phenomenon lies the problem, and hence the *raison d'être*, of 'semantic theory'" (Putnam, 1975d, p. 147). The meaning of natural kind terms, including those put forward in scientific theories, is not specified by a set of necessary and sufficient conditions that govern its application. Thus, it cannot be conveyed by "an analytic definition" (i.e., an analytically necessary and sufficient condition) (Putnam, 1975d, p. 146). Furthermore, the meaning of a natural kind word, say "tiger," does not involve "the totality of accepted scientific theory about tigers, or even the totality of what I believe about tigers" (Putnam, 1975d, p. 147). If that were the case, then it would be impossible to teach anyone the meaning of a natural kind term he or she does not know. Rather, to get to know the meaning of such a term one needs to learn certain "core facts" about a "normal member of the kind" (Putnam, 1975d, p. 148). This is not sufficient, however, for learning the meaning of the term in question. One needs, in addition, to become acquainted with the reference of the term; that is, with the actual entities denoted by the term.

Putnam conceded that the meaning of scientific terms is, partly, theory-dependent. He suggested, however, that the reference of those terms is fixed not by theoretical beliefs, but through our causal interaction with the world.[4] Our causal interaction with, say, electrical charges plays a double role: First, it fixes the reference of "electrical charge"; and, second, it renders the reference in question immune to any revision of our theoretical beliefs about electrical charges.

Putnam allowed for the possibility "that a concept may contain elements which are not correct" (Putnam, 1975b, p. 196). Thus, if the progress of science leads to the rejection of certain elements of a concept, its extension need not be affected: "concepts which are not strictly speaking true of anything may yet refer to something; and concepts in different theories may refer to the same thing" (Putnam, 1975b, p. 197). Different speakers need not associate the same concept with a term, say "electricity," in order to refer to the same entity. What they should share is "that each of them is connected by a certain kind of causal chain to a situation in which a *description* of electricity is given, and generally a *causal* description – that is, one which singles out electricity as *the* physical magnitude *responsible* for certain effects in a certain way" (Putnam, 1975b, p. 200; emphasis in original).

But what exactly is a concept? Putnam evaded the question and focused instead on what it means to *have a* concept. Following Wittgenstein, he suggested that possessing a concept amounts to having certain perceptual and linguistic abilities: "an organism possesses a *minimal concept* of a chair if it can recognize a chair when it sees one, and . . . it possesses a *full-blown concept* of a chair if it can employ the usual sentences containing the word *chair* in some natural language" (Putnam, 1975a, p. 3). Given that concept possession is largely a matter of linguistic skills, it follows "that a great deal of philosophy should be *reconstrued* as about language . . . In particular, all of the traditional philosophy about 'ideas', 'concepts', etc." (Putnam, 1975a, p. 9). It should, therefore, occasion no surprise that in philosophy of science the problem of conceptual change has been approached, for the most part, through linguistic categories, such as meaning and reference. Putnam, for instance, explicitly identified meaning with "what it is to have a concept of something" (Putnam, 1975a, p. 16).

Nevertheless, according to Putnam, there is an important difference between concepts and meanings. The former are possessed by individuals, whereas the latter have a social character—they are possessed by a linguistic group. Only certain people in a linguistic community, the relevant experts, have a mastery of the concepts associated with certain words. Only metallurgists, for instance, grasp fully the concept of gold. The meaning of "gold," on the other hand, is possessed collectively by a whole community (see Putnam, 1973, p. 705).

We think, however, that one still has the option to identify meanings with the concepts possessed by the relevant experts. This would imply that most of us have an inadequate mastery of the meaning of many of the words we use. But this is hardly a problem. There is no reason to pretend that a layman knows the meaning of a natural-kind term, when there are many situations in which he or she could not use this term correctly.

Moreover, Putnam argued strenuously that the concept we associate with a natural-kind term does not determine its reference. We have already seen that two speakers who associate different concepts with the same term may still refer to the same entity. Furthermore, two speakers may share the same concept and, nevertheless, refer to different things. Putnam exhibited this possibility by means of a thought experiment involving "twin earth," a fictitious planet that is identical with our earth in every respect save for the microscopic constitution of water. A speaker on earth and his counterpart on "twin earth" share the same concept of water (transparent, odorless, thirst-quenching liquid). They nevertheless refer to different things when they use the term "water." The speaker on earth refers to H_2O, whereas his counterpart refers to XYZ (Putnam, 1973, pp. 701ff.).

Putnam developed a fully fledged account of meaning and reference in a paper entitled "The Meaning of 'Meaning'" (Putnam, 1975c). To explicate the notion of meaning he introduced the notion of a stereotype associated with a natural kind, namely:

> a standardized description of features of the kind that are typical, or 'normal', or at any rate stereotypical. The central features of the stereotype generally are *criteria* – features which in normal situations constitute ways of recognizing if a thing belongs to the kind or, at least, necessary conditions (or probabilistic necessary conditions) for membership in the kind.
>
> (Putnam, 1975c, p. 230).

Thus, possessing the main characteristics of the stereotype associated with a term is necessary for being able to use that term correctly. In actual scientific practice, however, those characteristics are not used as necessary and sufficient conditions. Rather they are employed as "*approximately* correct characterizations of some world of theory-independent entities" (Putnam, 1975c, p. 237). Furthermore, stereotypes are associated with "conventional ideas, which may be inaccurate. I am suggesting that just such a conventional idea is associated with 'tiger', with 'gold', etc., and, moreover, that this is the sole element of truth in the 'concept' theory" (Putnam, 1975c, p. 250). Recalling Putnam's discussion of concept possession, we may identify stereotypes with concepts. In his more recent work, Putnam suggested a similar view.

"The Meaning of 'Meaning'" provides a novel account of meaning, according to which the meaning of a word is represented by a four-dimensional "vector" with the following components:

> (1) the syntactic markers that apply to the word, e.g. "noun"; (2) the semantic markers that apply to the word, e.g. "animal", "period of time"; (3) a description of the additional features of the stereotype, if any; (4) a description of the extension.
>
> (Putnam, 1975c, p. 269)

The semantic markers consist of those features of the stereotype that "attach with enormous centrality to the [corresponding] words . . . form part of a widely used and important *system of classification*," and are "*qualitatively* harder to revise" than the rest (Putnam, 1975c, p. 267; emphasis in original). In Putnam's view, "The centrality guarantees that items classified under these headings virtually never have to be *re*classified" (Putnam, 1975c, pp. 267–268). Furthermore, the final component of a term's meaning is its extension, which is identified by means of a (fallible) description. Since the meaning of a term includes its extension, it follows that meanings should be distinguished from concepts.

Putnam's account of meaning allows for conceptual change. The stereotype (the concept) we associate with a term may change under empirical pressure. However, conceptual change need not be accompanied by ontological shifts. Two successive scientific concepts may differ and, nevertheless, refer to the same thing(s).[5] Thus, Putnam has offered us a way to take on board some of the historicist insights about the development of the sciences without, however, succumbing to their more radical relativist and anti-realist inclinations.

Putnam's promising approach to meaning and conceptual change has also encountered difficulties. Discussing these difficulties in detail would lead us too far astray. We will just sketch one of the most important. The difficulty in question derives from the realist presuppositions of Putnam's account of meaning. As we have seen, the users of a natural kind term belong to a linguistic community which has "contact with the natural kind" (Putnam, 1975b, p. 205). There are two problems here. First, when the term in question denotes unobservable entities, such as the electron, it is unclear whether the required "contact" is available. Second, it has often been the case that words referring to putative natural kinds, such as "phlogiston" or "ether," turned out to be empty. In those cases the presumed "contact" was clearly missing. Thus, it would follow from Putnam's account of meaning that the users of those terms were not linguistically competent! Putnam realized that:

> It may seem counterintuitive that a natural kind word such as 'horse' is sharply distinguished from a term for a fictitious or non-existent natural kind such as 'unicorn', and that a physical magnitude term such as 'electricity' is sharply distinguished from a term for a fictitious or nonexistent physical magnitude or substance such as 'phlogiston'.
>
> (Putnam, 1975b, p. 206)

However, he did not seem to take into account that those who introduced and used those terms did so for similar reasons, namely to make sense of various observed phenomena. And that for some time theories based on "electricity" and "phlogiston" were equally viable accounts of their respective domains. It is unclear why our different (retrospective) judgments concerning the (non-)existence of phlogiston and electricity should lead us to different semantic stances towards the corresponding terms.

Despite its problems, Putnam's account of meaning has been one of the most articulate attempts to face the challenge that Feyerabend's and Kuhn's historicist accounts of conceptual change posed for the philosophy of science. Another such attempt was by Kuhn himself, who tried to come to terms with the difficulties faced by his early formulation of incommensurability. Kuhn's more recent work will be the subject of the next section.

KUHN'S EXPLICATION OF INCOMMENSURABILITY

Some of Kuhn's philosophical insights were an outgrowth of his experience as an interpreter of past scientific texts. One of those insights was incommensurability, which Kuhn regarded as the key notion of his philosophy of scientific development. During the 1980s and 1990s he defended this notion against the criticisms that had been raised against it, and he attempted to explicate and develop it further (Kuhn, 2000).

Two of those criticisms were particularly forceful. First, Kuhn's critics claimed that incommensurability implies incomparability and, therefore, renders rational theory-choice impossible. Second, incommensurability was construed as untranslatability and was declared to be at odds with the interpretive practices of historians of science. Kuhn rejected both of these critiques. First, he maintained that incommensurability does not imply incomparability. The term "incommensurability" was appropriated from geometry, where a comparison of incommensurable magnitudes is possible even though a particular common measure is lacking. The same is true of incommensurable theories. The fact that there is no common language (e.g., an observational language) to which the assertions of two incommensurable theories can be reduced does not preclude the possibility of comparing the theories in question in other respects.

Second, Kuhn resisted the identification of the interpretive practice of historians with a translation process. The aim of the historiographical enterprise is to understand, as opposed to translate, alien scientific texts. It is true that texts written in a language incommensurable to our own are impossible to translate. However, they are not impossible to understand, by acquiring from scratch the language in which they were written.

Having responded to criticism, Kuhn proceeded to develop a fuller account of incommensurability as a manifestation of a deeper mismatch between two linguistic structures. The language in which a scientific theory is formulated incorporates a taxonomic structure of natural kinds. These structures are subject to a no-overlap condition. That is, no entity can belong to more than one natural kind. In Kuhn's words, "There are no dogs that are also cats" (Kuhn, 2000, p. 92). The only case where this condition is not fulfilled is when one natural kind is part of another, more inclusive one. For example, cats are also mammals. Incommensurability is now conceived as the outcome of a violation of the no-overlap condition. Two incommensurable taxonomic structures contain overlapping natural kinds – kinds that have some members in common. The overlap has to be partial – the one kind must have members that do not belong to the other and vice versa. If, on the one hand, the overlap were complete then the two taxonomies would obviously coincide. If, on the other hand, there were no overlap at all, it would be possible to construct a more inclusive taxonomy incorporating each of the taxonomic structures in question. In that case incommensurability would not arise.

When, however, two taxonomies partially overlap, it is not possible to subsume both of them under a wider taxonomic framework. Any framework that would subsume one of the taxonomies in question could not accommodate the other and vice versa. Such a framework would have to include overlapping natural kinds, which are ruled out by the no-overlap condition. In the absence of such a framework no language can be found that would provide a common ground between the taxonomies in question; hence incommensurability.

Taxonomic incommensurability can now be used to reconceptualize scientific revolutions. These are episodes in the history of science where a whole taxonomic structure is replaced by its incommensurable successor, whose natural kinds partially overlap with some of the natural kinds that were hitherto in place. As a result of this overlap, the new taxonomy cannot subsume the old one.[6]

The reformulation of scientific revolutions in Kuhn's later writings goes as far as dimming the light on discontinuous change. Kuhn now speaks of two lexicons "used at two widely separated times" (Kuhn, 2000, p. 87), leaving aside and in the shadow the processes that made these lexicons possible and through which they came about. The philosopher studies two distant in time, frozen, taxonomic structures trying to detect congruence, compatibility, and overlap, whereas the historian may try to uncover the micro-processes that take place in the in-between transitional periods and by which change is effected.

The emphasis given in Kuhn's later writings to some kind of continuity rather than abrupt change is also brought out in his analogy between revolutions in science and speciation in biological evolution (Kuhn, 2000, p. 98; see also Kuhn, 1970, pp. 171–173). In both cases, a slow, steady development driven from behind is occasionally marked by episodes which yield new specialties in science and new species in nature that branch off from the trunk of knowledge or the biological tree respectively. Breakdowns of communication in science are compared to reproductive isolation of populations in nature and are taken to be signals of crises (Kuhn, 2000, p. 100). Discourse, however, among scientists across the divide of incommensurable taxonomies still goes on, Kuhn admits, "however imperfectly" (Kuhn, 2000, p. 88), by using, for instance, metaphor and other linguistic tropes.

Focus on evolution and continuity rather than revolution and discontinuity in Kuhn's later writings may not have eliminated the idea of incommensurability, which has become local, but has given rise to concerns regarding the Kuhnian project itself. Kuhn, supposedly, modified his philosophy to make more plausible the history of science which he saw as advancing through revolutions. If now evolution is substituted for revolution, "what point could there be in talking about Kuhnian revolutions at all?" (Machamer, 2007, p. 43).

A second problem concerns the notion of local incommensurability. As we saw, in order to have local incommensurability between frameworks there needs to exist partial overlap between them. Two things can be said here: First, one may maintain that partial overlap between theories is likely to hold in most cases since theories develop out of earlier ones or, in case they are contemporaneous, they develop against each other (Fine, 1975, p. 30). If this is true, then the thesis of incommensurability becomes trivialized. The second thing that can be said in relation to overlap is that instead of viewing it as a condition of incommensurability, one may view it as a means of eliminating it. Assuming certain common things – the ones falling under the area of overlap – may be of help when we try to trace and unpack the mismatching incommensurable clusters (Fine, 1975). With some effort, based on this common ground, critics say, one may access the problematic areas and achieve communication and translation. Kuhn would have conceded, we think, that a partial overlap between incommensurable taxonomic structures may provide the common ground necessary for communication, albeit not for translation.

Even if we grant that incommensurability amounts to a disparity between local areas of classificatory systems, the question remains whether there might be conceptual change that does not involve reorganization of lexical structure. Is all conceptual change a matter of taxonomic change? Kuhn's analysis of incommensurability is applicable to concepts that pick out observable objects, which can be identified by ostension. On the other hand, his analysis of the meaning of theoretical concepts (such as force, mass, charge, and field) has not been sufficiently developed. Those concepts refer to entities, properties, and processes that are not directly accessible and their meaning is learned in the context of the application of scientific laws. When those laws are revised the meanings of the concepts they contain should change accordingly. However, the source of incommensurability in such cases is rather unclear (see Nersessian, 2002).

UNDERSTANDING THE FINE STRUCTURE OF CONCEPTUAL CHANGE IN SCIENCE

Kuhn's later work on incommensurability has deepened considerably our understanding of the structure of conceptual revolutions in science. Its main drawback, as we see it, is that it focuses exclusively on the beginning and the final stages of radical conceptual change. Thus, it gives no account of the fine-grained processes of the transition between two incommensurable conceptual frameworks. This shortcoming is characteristic of most philosophical theories of conceptual change, with a few exceptions.

The most notable exception is Nancy Nersessian, who has developed a full-blown account of conceptual change in science (see, e.g., Nersessian, 1984, 1992, 1995, 2008). The problem of conceptual change, according to Nersessian, has two salient aspects. The first is about finding a representation of concepts that can capture both their synchronic characteristics and their diachronic development. Nersessian rejects the necessary and sufficient conditions view of concepts, arguing that it cannot do justice to the fact that concepts are evolving entities. If the meaning of a concept were given by a set of necessary and sufficient conditions, then the concept in question could not evolve; it could only be replaced by an altogether different one.

To highlight the continuity of conceptual change, Nersessian has proposed a representation of concepts in terms of a "meaning-schema":

> The meaning of a scientific concept is a two-dimensional array which is constructed on the basis of its descriptive/explanatory function as it develops over time. I will call this array a "meaning schema". A "meaning schema" for a particular concept, would contain, width-wise, a summary of the features of each instance and, length-wise, a summary of the changes over time.
>
> (Nersessian, 1984, p. 156).

The features that compose the meaning of a particular instance of a concept concern:

> "stuff", "function", "structure", and "causal power" ... Here, "stuff" includes what it is (with ontological status and reference); "function" includes what it does; "structure" includes mathematical structure; and "causal power" includes its effects.
>
> (Nersessian, 1984, p. 157).

This matrix-like representation of scientific concepts portrays their complex structure and their dynamic, evolving character. Furthermore, it reveals the significant continuity between successive versions of a concept (see, e.g., Nersessian, 1992, p. 36).

The second and most neglected part of the problem of conceptual change is to account for the mechanisms of concept formation and to understand how new concepts develop out of older conceptual frameworks. Nersessian insists that conceptual change cannot be adequately understood by focusing exclusively on the products of scientific theorizing; that is, on fully articulated conceptual structures. Rather, it "is to be understood in terms of the people who create and change their representations of nature and the practices they employ to do so" (Nersessian, 1992, p. 9). These practices consist in problem solving. Developing an insight of Karl Popper, who viewed the history of science as a history of problem situations, Nersessian has argued that concept formation has to be understood in the context of evolving problem situations. Problem-solving activity encompasses a rich repertoire of reasoning strategies, going well beyond induction and deduction, which have been the main preoccupation of philosophers of science. These heuristic strategies include drawing analogies, constructing visual representations, forming idealizations and abstractions, and inventing thought experiments (see Nersessian,

1992). Nersessian has argued that these strategies can be viewed as instances of model-based reasoning, which has received extensive attention in cognitive science (Nersessian, 2008).[7] On the plausible assumption that the cognitive capacities of scientists do not differ substantially from those of "ordinary" people, it becomes possible to draw on the resources provided by cognitive science to analyze the forms of reasoning employed in creative scientific work. The resulting rapprochement between history and philosophy of science and cognitive science promises to be beneficial to both parties.

Before we close let us indicate briefly how Nersessian's analysis of conceptual change may resolve one of the thorny philosophical problems that were brought to the fore by historicist philosophers of science, namely the problem of scientific rationality. Historicists and their critics thought that conceptual change undermined the rationality of scientific development. If, say, Newtonian "mass" and relativistic "mass" are not the same concepts, then how can one rationally compare Newtonian mechanics and relativity theory? This difficulty, however, is an artifact of the way the problem of conceptual change was framed; that is, as a problem concerning the relationship between the beginning and the final stages of a long process. If, on the other hand, one examines the fine structure of that process, the problem dissolves. As a matter of fact, scientists never faced a situation where they had to compare Newtonian mechanics and relativity theory. The transition from Newtonian "mass" to relativistic "mass" passed through various developments in electromagnetic theory, most notably through H. A. Lorentz's theory of electrons, all of which were rational in the sense that they were adequate responses to particular problem situations. The conceptual transition from Newtonian to relativistic physics was a gradual and reasoned process. Thus, conceptual change in science can be fully compatible with an account of science as a rational enterprise.

CONCLUDING REMARKS

One of the most salient trends in history and philosophy of science over the past 20 years has been a turn to practice. Historical and philosophical analysis has shifted away from the products of scientific activity and towards the cognitive and material practices of scientists. Nersessian's approach to conceptual change is emblematic of this practical turn. Other recent scholarship on scientific concepts has also reflected this trend, focusing on their various epistemic roles (descriptive, classificatory, explanatory, predictive, and heuristic) in theoretical and experimental practice (Feest & Steinle, 2012). Work along these lines promises to shed new light on long-standing problems in philosophy of science concerning the identity of evolving concepts and the reality of their purported referents.

ACKNOWLEDGMENT

We would like to thank Stella Vosniadou for her helpful suggestions.

NOTES

1   Kuhn acknowledges, however, that "During the transition period there will be a large but never complete overlap between the problems that can be solved by the old and the new paradigm. But there will also be a decisive difference in the mode of solution. When the transition is complete, the profession will have changed

its view of the field, its methods, and its goals" (1970, p. 85). As we will see, in his later writings, Kuhn stressed more strongly that incommensurability is only local.

2   Cf. also Scheffler (1982).

3   Interestingly, Putnam gives credit to Quine for the "realization" of the interdependence of theory and meaning.

4   Here Putnam's ideas overlapped with those of Saul Kripke (1980).

5   Conversely, as Putnam's twin earth example shows, ontological shifts need not be accompanied by conceptual change. This is in stark contrast with the cognitive-psychological literature, where ontological shifts are associated with conceptual change. Stella Vosniadou brought our attention to this point.

6   For a recent illuminating account of Kuhn's taxonomic approach to incommensurability see Andersen, Barker, and Chen (2006).

7   Space limitations prevent us from expanding on this point. We refer the interested reader to Nersessian's contribution to this volume (Chapter 21), where she gives a detailed account of the role of model-based reasoning in conceptual change.

REFERENCES

Achinstein, P. (1968). Concepts of science: A philosophical analysis. Baltimore, MD: Johns Hopkins University Press.

Andersen, H., Barker, P., & Chen, X. (2006). *The cognitive structure of scientific revolutions*. Cambridge, UK: Cambridge University Press.

Carnap, R. (1981). Logical foundations of the unity of science. In O. Hanfling (Ed.), *Essential readings in logical positivism* (pp. 112–129). Oxford, UK: Blackwell.

Davidson, D. (1984). On the very idea of a conceptual scheme. In *Inquiries into truth and interpretation* (pp. 183–198). Oxford, UK: Clarendon Press.

Feest, U., & Steinle, F. (Eds.). (2012). *Scientific concepts and investigative practice*. Berlin, Germany: De Gruyter-Verlag.

Feyerabend, P. (1981a). Explanation, reduction and empiricism. In *Realism, rationalism and scientific method* (pp. 44–96). Cambridge, UK: Cambridge University Press.

Feyerabend, P. (1981b). On the 'meaning' of scientific terms. In *Realism, rationalism and scientific method* (pp. 97–103). Cambridge, UK: Cambridge University Press.

Fine, A. (1975). How to compare theories: Reference and change. *Nous, 9,* 17–32.

Hahn, H., Carnap. R., & Neurath, O. (1996). The scientific conception of the world. In S. Sarkar (Ed.), *The emergence of logical positivism: From 1900 to the Vienna Circle* (pp. 321– 340). New York, NY: Garland Publishing.

Hanson, N. R. (1958). *Patterns of discovery*. Cambridge, UK: Cambridge University Press.

Hempel, C. (1970). On the 'standard' conception of scientific theories. In M. Radner & S. Winokur (Eds.), *Minnesota Studies in the Philosophy of Science, Vol. IV* (pp. 142–163). Minneapolis, MN: University of Minnesota Press.

Kripke S. (1980). *Naming and necessity*. Cambridge, MA: Harvard University Press.

Kuhn, T. S. (1970). *The structure of scientific revolutions*. Chicago, IL: University of Chicago Press.

Kuhn, T. S. (1977). The essential tension: Tradition and innovation in scientific research. In *The essential tension: Selected studies in scientific tradition and change* (225–239). Chicago, IL: University of Chicago Press.

Kuhn, T. S. (2000). *The road since* Structure: *Philosophical essays, 1970–1993, with an autobiographical interview*. Chicago, IL: University of Chicago Press.

Machamer, P. (2007). Kuhn's philosophical successes. In S. Vosniadou, A. Baltas, & X. Vamvakoussi (Eds.), *Reframing the conceptual change approach in learning and instruction* (35–45). Amsterdam, The Netherlands: Elsevier.

Nagel, E. (1979). *The structure of science*. Indianapolis, IN: Hackett.

Nersessian, N. J. (1984). *Faraday to Einstein: Constructing meaning in scientific theories*. Dordrecht, The Netherlands: Martinus Nijhoff.

Nersessian, N. J. (1992). How do scientists think? Capturing the dynamics of conceptual change in science. In R. N. Giere (Ed.), *Cognitive models of science, Minnesota Studies in the Philosophy of Science 15* (pp. 3–44). Minneapolis, MN: University of Minnesota Press.

Nersessian, N. J. (1995). Opening the black box: Cognitive science and history of science. In A. Thackray (Ed.), *Osiris, Volume 10: Constructing knowledge in the history of science* (pp. 194–214). Chicago, IL: University of Chicago Press.

Nersessian, N. J. (2002). Kuhn, conceptual change, and cognitive science. In T. Nickles (Ed.), *Thomas Kuhn* (pp. 178–211). Cambridge, UK: Cambridge University Press.

Nersessian, N. J. (2008). *Creating scientific concepts.* Cambridge, MA: MIT Press.

Putnam, H. (1973). Meaning and reference. *Journal of Philosophy, 70,* 699–711.

Putnam, H. (1975a). Language and philosophy. In *Mind, language and reality: Philosophical papers, Volume 2* (pp. 1–32). Cambridge, UK: Cambridge University Press.

Putnam, H. (1975b). Explanation and reference. In *Mind, language and reality: Philosophical papers, Volume 2* (pp. 196–214). Cambridge, UK: Cambridge University Press.

Putnam, H. (1975c). The meaning of 'meaning'. In *Mind, language and reality: Philosophical papers, Volume 2* (pp. 215–271). Cambridge, UK: Cambridge University Press.

Putnam, H. (1975d). Is semantics possible? In *Mind, language and reality: Philosophical papers, Volume 2* (pp. 139–152). Cambridge, UK: Cambridge University Press.

Scheffler, I. (1982). *Science and subjectivity.* Indianapolis, IN: Hackett.

Schlick, M. (1981). Structure and content. In O. Hanfling (Ed.), *Essential readings in logical positivism* (pp. 131–149). Oxford, UK: Blackwell.

Shapere, D. (1964). The structure of scientific revolutions. *Philosophical Review, 73,* 383–394.

Shapere, D. (1981). Meaning and scientific change. In I. Hacking (Ed.), *Scientific revolutions* (pp. 28–59). Oxford, UK: Oxford University Press.

Suppe, F. (1977). The search for philosophic understanding of scientific theories. In F. Suppe (Ed.), *The structure of scientific theories* (pp. 3–241). Urbana, IL: University of Illinois Press.

Wittgenstein, L. (2009). *Philosophical investigations.* Translated by G. E. M. Anscombe, P. M. S. Hacker, & J. Schulte. Revised 4th edition edited by P. M. S. Hacker and J. Schulte. Oxford, UK: Blackwell.

19

CONCEPTUAL CHANGE IN THE HISTORY OF SCIENCE

Life, Mind, and Disease

Paul Thagard, University of Waterloo

Biology is the study of life, psychology is the study of mind, and medicine is the investigation of the causes and treatments of disease. This chapter describes how the central concepts of life, mind, and disease have undergone fundamental changes in the past 150 years or so. There has been a progression from theological, to qualitative, to mechanistic explanations of the nature of life, mind, and disease. This progression has involved both theoretical change, as new theories with greater explanatory power replaced older ones, and emotional change as the new theories brought reorientation of attitudes to the nature of life, mind, and disease. After a brief comparison of theological, qualitative, and mechanistic explanations, I will describe how shifts from one kind of explanation to another have carried with them dramatic kinds of conceptual change in the key concepts in the life sciences. Three generalizations follow about the nature of conceptual change in the history of science: there has been a shift from conceptualizations in terms of simple properties to ones in terms of complex relations; conceptual change is theory change; and conceptual change is often emotional as well as cognitive.

The contention that historical development proceeds in three stages originated with the 19th-century French philosopher Auguste Comte, who claimed that human intellectual development progresses from a theological to a "metaphysical" stage to a "positive" (scientific) stage (Comte, 1970). The stages I have in mind are different from Comte's, so let me say what they involve. By the *theological* stage I mean systems of thought in which the primary explanatory entities are supernatural ones beyond the reach of science, such as gods, devils, angels, spirits, and souls. For example, the concept of fire was initially theological, as in the Greek myth of Prometheus receiving fire from the gods. By the *qualitative* stage I mean systems of thought that do not invoke supernatural entities, but which postulate natural entities not far removed from what they are supposed to explain, such as vital force in biology. Early qualitative concepts of fire include Aristotle's view of fire as a substance and Epicurus's account of fire atoms. By the *mechanistic* stage I mean the kinds of developments now rapidly taking place in all of the life sciences in which explanations consist of identifying systems of interacting parts that produce observable changes. The modern concept of fire is mechanistic: Combustion is rapid oxidation, the combination of molecules. Much more will be said about the nature of mechanistic, qualitative, and theological explanations in connection with each of the central concepts of life, disease, and mind. I will show how resistance to conceptual change derives both from (1) cognitive difficulties in grasping the superiority of mechanistic explanations to the other two kinds and (2) emotional difficulties in accepting the personal implications of the mechanistic world-view. First, however, I want to review the general importance of the topic of conceptual change for the history and philosophy of science.

HISTORY AND PHILOSOPHY OF SCIENCE

Historians and philosophers of science are concerned to explain the development of scientific knowledge. On a naïve view, science develops by simple accumulation, piling fact upon fact. But this view is contradicted by the history of science, which has seen many popular theories eventually rejected as false, including: the crystalline spheres of ancient and medieval astronomy, the humoral theory of medicine, catastrophist geology, the phlogiston theory of chemistry, the caloric theory of heat, the vital force theory of physiology, the aether (ether) theories of electromagnetism and optics, and biological theories of spontaneous generation. Rejection of these theories has required abandonment of concepts such as *humor, phlogiston, caloric,* and *aether,* along with introduction of new theoretical concepts such as *germ, oxygen, thermodynamics,* and *photon.* Acceptance of a theory therefore often requires the acquisition and adoption of a novel conceptual system.

We can distinguish different degrees of conceptual change occurring in the history of science and medicine (Thagard, 1992, 1999, p. 150):

1. Adding a new instance of a concept, for example a patient who has tuberculosis.
2. Adding a new weak rule, for example that tuberculosis is common in prisons.
3. Adding a new strong rule that plays a frequent role in problem solving and explanation, for example that people with tuberculosis have *Mycobacterium tuberculosis.*
4. Adding a new part-relation, for example that diseased lungs contain tubercles.
5. Adding a new kind-relation, for example differentiating between pulmonary and miliary tuberculosis.
6. Adding a new concept, for example *tuberculosis* (which replaced the previous terms *phthisis* and *consumption*) or AIDS.
7. Collapsing part of a kind-hierarchy, abandoning a previous distinction, for example, realizing that phthisis and scrofula are the same disease, tuberculosis.
8. Reorganizing hierarchies by *branch jumping,* that is shifting a concept from one branch of a hierarchical tree to another, for example reclassifying tuberculosis as an infectious disease.
9. *Tree switching,* that is, changing the organizing principle of a hierarchical tree, for example classifying diseases in terms of causal agents rather than symptoms.

The most radical kinds of conceptual change involve the last two kinds of major conceptual reorganization, as when Darwin reclassified humans as animals and changed the organizational principle of the tree of life to be evolutionary history rather than similarity of features.

Thus understanding the historical development of the sciences requires attention to the different kinds of conceptual change that have taken place in the non-cumulative growth of knowledge (see also Kuhn, 1970; Horwich, 1993; LaPorte, 2004; Nersessian, 1992). I will now describe the central changes that have taken place in the concepts of life, mind, and disease.

LIFE

Theology

Theological explanations of life are found in the creation stories of many cultures, including the Judeo-Christian tradition's book of Genesis. According to this account God created grass, herbs, and fruit trees on the second day, swarms of birds and sea animals on the fifth day, and living creatures on land including humans on the sixth day. Other cultures worldwide have different accounts of how one or more deities brought the earth and the living things on it into existence. These stories predate by centuries attempts to understand the world scientifically, which may only have begun with the thought of the Greek philosopher-scientist Thales around 600 BC. The stories do not attempt to tie theological explanations to details of observations of the nature of life. Thus the first sub-stage of the theological stage of the understanding of life is a matter of myth, a set of entertaining stories rather than a detailed exposition of the theological origins of life.

During the 17th and 18th centuries, there was a dramatic expansion of biological knowledge based on observation, ranging from the discovery by van Leeuwenhoek of microorganisms such as bacteria to the taxonomy by Carl Linnaeus of many different kinds of plants and animals. In the 19th century, attempts were made to integrate this burgeoning knowledge with theological understanding, including the compellingly written *Natural Theology* of William Paley (1963). Paley argued that, just as we explain the intricacies of a watch by the intelligence and activities of its maker, so we should explain the design of plants and animals by the actions of the creator. The eight volumes of the Bridgewater Treatises connected divine creation not only to the anatomy and physiology of living things, but also to astronomy, physics, geology, and chemistry. Nineteenth-century natural theology was a Christian enterprise, as theologians and believing scientists connected biological and other scientific observations in great detail with ideas drawn from the Bible. Unlike the purely mythical accounts found in many cultures, this natural-theology sub-stage of theological explanations of life was tied to many facts about the biological world.

A third sub-stage of theological understandings of life is the relatively recent doctrine of intelligent design that arose in the United States as a way of contesting Darwin's theory of evolution by natural selection without directly invoking Christian ideas about creation. Because the American constitution requires separation of church and state, public schools have not been allowed to teach Christian ideas about divine creation as a direct challenge to evolution. Hence in the 1990s there arose a kind of natural theology in disguise claiming to have a scientific alternative to evolution, the theory of intelligent design (e.g., Dembski, 1999). Its proponents claim that it is not committed to the biblical account of creation, but instead relies on facts about the complexity of life as pointing to its origins in intelligent causation rather than the mechanical operations of natural selection. American courts have, however, ruled that intelligent design is just a disguised attempt to smuggle natural theology into the schools.

Qualitative Explanations of Life

Unlike theological explanations, qualitative accounts do not invoke supernatural entities, but instead attempt to explain the world in terms of natural properties. For example, in the 18th century, heat and temperature were explained by the presence in objects of a qualitative element called caloric: the more caloric, the more heat. A mechanical theory of heat as motion of molecules only arose in the 19th century. Just as caloric was invoked as a substance to explain heat, qualitative explanations of life can be given by invoking a special kind of substance that inhabits living things. Aristotle, for example, believed that animals and plants have a principle of life (*psuche*) that initiates and guides reproductive, metabolic, growth, and other capacities (Grene & Depew, 2004).

In the 19th century, qualitative explanations of life became popular in the form of *vitalism*, according to which living things contain some distinctive force or fluid or spirit that makes them alive (Bechtel & Richardson, 1998). Scientists and philosophers such as Bichat, Magendie, Liebig, and Bergson postulated that there must be some sort of vital force that enables organisms to develop and maintain themselves. Vitalism developed as an opponent to the materialistic view, originating with the Greek atomists and developed by Descartes and his successors, that living things are like machines in that they can be explained purely in terms of the operation of their parts. Unlike natural theology, vitalism does not explicitly employ divine intervention in its explanation of life, but for vitalists such as Bergson there was no doubt that God was the origin of vital force.

Contrast the theological and vitalist explanation patterns.

- *Theological explanation pattern*
  - Why does an organism have a given property that makes it alive?
  - Because God designed the organism to have that property.
- *Vitalist explanation pattern*
  - Why does an organism have a given property that makes it alive?
  - Because the organism contains a vital force that gives it that property.

We can now examine a very different way of explaining life, in terms of mechanisms.

Mechanistic Explanations of Life

The mechanistic account of living things originated with Greek philosophers such as Epicurus, who wanted to explain all motion in terms of the interactions of atoms. Greek mechanism was limited, however, by the comparative simplicity of the machines available: levers, pulleys, screws, and so on. By the 17th century, however, more complicated machines were available, such as clocks, artificial fountains, and mills. In his 1664 *Treatise on Man*, Descartes used these as models for maintaining that animals and the bodies (but not the souls) of humans are nothing but machines explainable through the operations of their parts, analogous to the pipes and springs of fountains and clocks (Descartes, 1985). Descartes undoubtedly believed that living machines had been designed by God, but the explanation of their operations was in terms of their structure rather than their design or special vital properties. The pattern is something like the following.

- *Mechanistic explanation pattern*
  - Why does an organism have a given property that makes it alive?
  - Because the organism has parts that interact in ways that give it that property.

Normally, we understand how machines work because people have built them from identifiable parts connected to each other in observable ways.

In Descartes' day, mechanistic explanations were highly limited by lack of knowledge of the smaller and smaller parts that make up the body: Cells were not understood until the 19th century. They were also limited by the simplicity of available machines to provide analogies to the complexities of biological organisms. By the 19th century, however, the cell doctrine and other biological advances made mechanistic explanations of life much more conceivable. But it was still utterly mysterious how different species of living things came to be, unless they were the direct result of divine creation. Various thinkers conjectured that species had evolved, but no one had a reasonable account of how they had evolved.

The intellectual situation changed dramatically in 1859, when Charles Darwin published *On the Origin of Species*. His great insight was not the concept of evolution, which had been proposed by others, but the concept of natural selection, which provided a mechanism that explained how evolution occurred. At first glance, natural selection does not sound much like a machine, but it qualifies as a mechanism because it consists of interacting parts producing regular changes. (For philosophical discussions of the nature of mechanisms, see Bechtel & Abrahamsen, 2005; Bechtel & Richardson, 1993; Machamer, Darden, & Craver, 2000; Salmon, 1984.) The parts are individual organisms that interact with each other and with their environments. Darwin noticed that variations are introduced when organisms reproduce, and that the struggle for existence that results from scarcity of resources would tend to preserve those variations that gave organisms advantages in survival and reproduction. Hence variation plus the struggle for existence led to natural selection which led to the evolution of species. Over the past 150 years, the evidence for evolution by natural selection has accumulated to such an extent that it ought to be admitted that evolution is a fact as well as a theory.

Why then is there continuing opposition to Darwin's ideas? The answer is that the battle between evolution and creation is not just a competition between alternative theories of how different species came to be, but between different world-views with very different emotional attachments. Theological views have limited explanatory power compared to science, but they have very strong emotional coherence because of their fit with people's personal goals, including comfort, immortality, morality, and social cohesion (Thagard, 2005a). People attach strong positive emotional valences to the key ingredients of creationist theories, including supernatural entities such as God and heaven. In contrast, evolution by natural selection strikes fundamentalist believers as atheistic and immoral.

Although Darwin conceived of a mechanism for evolution, he lacked a mechanistic understanding of key parts of it. In particular, he did not have a good account of how variations occurred and were passed on to offspring. Explanation of variation and inheritance required genetic theory, which (aside from Mendel's early ignored ideas) was not developed until the first part of the 20th century. In turn, understanding of genetics developed in the second part of that century through discovery of how DNA provides a mechanism for inheritance. Today, biology is thoroughly mechanistic, as biochemistry explains how DNA and other molecules work, which explains how genes work, which explains how variation and inheritance work. The genomes of important organisms including humans have been mapped, and the burgeoning enterprise of proteomics is filling in the details of how genes produce proteins whose interactions explain all the operations required for the survival and reproduction of living things.

Hence what makes things alive is not a divine spark or vital force, but their construction out of organs, tissues, and individual cells that are alive. Cells are alive because their proteins and processes enable them to perform functions such as energy acquisition, division, motion, adhesion, signaling, and self-destruction. The molecular basis of each of these functions is increasingly well understood (Lodish et al., 2000). In turn, the behavior of molecules can be described in terms of quantum chemistry, which explains how the quantum-mechanical properties of atoms cause them to combine in biochemically useful ways. Thus the development of biology over the past 150 years dramatically illustrates the shift from a theological to a qualitative to a mechanist concept of life. This shift has taken place because of an impressive sequence of mechanistic theories that provide deeper and deeper explanations of how living things work, from natural selection to genetics to molecular biology to quantum mechanics. This shift does not imply that there is only one fundamental level at which all explanation should take place: It would be pointless to try to give a quantum-mechanical explanation of why humans have large brains, as the quantum details are far removed from the historical environmental and biological conditions that produced the evolution of humans. It is enough, from the mechanistic point of view, that the lower-level mechanical operations are available in the background.

In sum, theoretical progress in biology has resulted from elaboration of progressively deeper mechanisms, while resistance to such progress results from emotional preferences for theological over mechanistic explanation. Similar resistance arises to understanding disease and mind mechanistically.

DISEASE

Theology

Medicine has both the theoretical goal of finding explanations of disease and the practical goal of finding treatments for them. As for life, early conceptions of disease were heavily theological. Gods were thought to be sometimes the cause of diseases, and they could be supplicated to provide relief from them. For example, in the biblical book of Exodus, God delivers a serious of punishments, including boils, on the Egyptians for holding the Israelites captive. Hippocrates wrote around 400 BC challenging the view that epilepsy is a "sacred disease" resulting from divine action. Medieval Christians believed that the black plague was a punishment from God. In modern theology, diseases are rarely attributed directly to God, but there are still people who maintain that HIV/AIDS is a punishment for homosexuality. But even if most people now accept medical explanations of the causes of disease, there are many who pray for divine intervention to help cure the maladies of people they care about. Hence in religious circles the concept of disease remains at least in part theological.

Qualitative Explanations of Disease

The ancient Greeks developed a naturalistic account of diseases that dominated Western medicine until the 19th century (Hippocrates, 1988). According to the Hippocratics, the body contains four humors: blood, phlegm, yellow bile, and black bile. Health depends on having these humors in correct proportion to each other. Too much bile can produce various fevers, and too much phlegm can cause heart or brain problems. Accordingly, diseases can be treated by changing the balance of humors, for example by opening the veins to let blood out.

Traditional Chinese medicine, which is at least as ancient as the Hippocratic approach, is also a balance theory, but with *yin* and *yang* instead of the four humors. On the Chinese view, yin and yang are the two opposite but complementary forces that constitute the entire universe. Here is a summary.

> Like everything else, the human body and its functions are all governed by the principle of *yin* and *yang*. Remaining healthy and functioning properly require keeping the balance between the *yin* and *yang* in the body. Diseases arise when there is inequilibrium of *yin* and *yang* inside the body. This principle is central to traditional Chinese medicine, and its application dominates the diagnosis, treatment and explanation of diseases. For example, a patient's high fever, restlessness, a flushed face, dry lips and a rapid pulse are *yang* symptoms. The diagnosis will be a *yin* deficiency, or imbalance brought by an excess of *yang* over *yin*. Once the *yin–yang* character of a disease is assessed, treatment can restore the balance of *yin* and *yang*, for example by using *yin*-natured herbs to dampen and dissipate the internal heat and other *yang* symptoms.

> Whereas the Hippocratic tradition used extreme physical methods such as bloodletting, emetics, and purgatives to restore the balance of the four humors, traditional Chinese medicine uses relatively benign herbal treatments to restore the balance of *yin* and *yang*. Unlike Hippocratic medicine, which has been totally supplanted by Western scientific approaches, traditional Chinese medicine is still practiced in China and is often favored by Westerners looking for alternative medical treatments.
> (Thagard & Zhu, 2003, pp. 83–84)

Similarly, traditional Indian Ayurvedic medicine has attracted a modern following through the writings of gurus such as Deepak Chopra. On this view, all bodily processes are governed by three main *doshas*: *vata* (composed of air and space), *pitta* (composed of fire and water), and *kapha* (composed of earth and water). Too much or too little of these elements can lead to diseases, which can be treated by diet and exercise. There is no empirical evidence for the existence of the *doshas* or for their role in disease, but people eagerly latch onto Chopra's theories for their promise that good health and long life can be attained merely by making the right choices. Just as creationism survives because it fits with people's personal motivations, so traditional Chinese and Ayurvedic theories survive because they offer appealing solutions to scary medical problems.

The three balance theories described in this section are clearly not theological, because they do not invoke divine intervention. But they are also not mechanical, because they do not explain the causes of diseases in terms of the regular interaction of constitutive parts. They leave utterly mysterious how the interactions of humors, *doshas*, or *yin* and *yang* can make people sick. In contrast, modern Western medicine based on contemporary biology provides mechanistic explanations of a very wide range of diseases.

Mechanistic Explanations of Disease

Modern medicine began in the 1860s, when Pasteur and others developed the germ theory of disease. Bacteria had been observed microscopically in the 1670s, but their role in causing diseases was not suspected until Pasteur realized that bacteria are responsible for silkworm diseases. Bacteria were quickly found to be responsible for many human diseases, including cholera, tuberculosis, and gonorrhea. Viruses were not observed until the invention of the electron microscope in 1939, but are now known to be the cause of many human diseases such as influenza and measles (for a review, see Thagard, 1999).

The germ theory of disease provides mechanistic explanations in which bacteria and viruses are entities that interact with bodily parts such as organs and cells that are infected. Unlike vague notions such as *yin, yang,* and *doshas,* these entities can be observed using microscopes, as can their presence in bodily tissues. Thus an infected organism is like a machine that has multiple interacting parts. The germ theory of disease is not only theoretically useful in explaining how many diseases arise, it is also practically useful in that antimicrobial drugs such as penicillin can cure some diseases by killing the agents that cause them.

As we saw for biological explanations, it is a powerful feature of mechanistic explanations that they decompose into further layers of mechanistic explanations, Pasteur had no idea how bacteria manage to infect organs, but molecular biology has in recent decades provided detailed accounts of how microbes function. For example, when the new disease SARS was identified in 2003, it took only a few months to identify the coronavirus that causes it and to sequence the virus's genes that enable it to attach itself to cells, infect them, and reproduce. In turn, biochemistry explains how genes produce the proteins that carry out these functions. Thus the explanations provided by the germ theory have progressively deepened over the almost one and half centuries since it was first proposed. I have argued elsewhere that this kind of ongoing deepening is a reliable sign of the truth of a scientific theory (Thagard, 2007, 2012).

Not all diseases are caused by germs, but other major kinds have been amenable to mechanistic explanation. Nutritional diseases such as scurvy are caused by deprivation of vitamins, and the mechanisms by which vitamins work are now understood. For example, vitamin C is crucial for collagen synthesis and the metabolism and synthesis of various chemical structures, which explains why its deficiency produces the symptoms of scurvy. Some diseases are caused by the immune system becoming overactive and attacking parts of the body, as when white blood cells remove myelin from axons between neurons, producing the symptoms of multiple sclerosis. Other diseases such as cystic fibrosis are directly caused by genetic factors, and the connection between mutated genes and defective metabolism is increasingly well understood. The final major category of human disease is cancer, and the genetic mutations that convert a normal cell into an invasive carcinoma, as well as the biochemical pathways that are thereby affected, are becoming well mapped out (Thagard, 2003a, 2006b).

Despite the progressively deepening mechanistic explanation of infectious, nutritional, autoimmune, and genetic diseases, there is still much popular support for alternative theories and treatments such as traditional Chinese and Ayurvedic medicine. The reasons for the resistance to changes in the concept of disease from qualitative to mechanistic are both cognitive and emotional. On the cognitive side, most people simply do not know enough biology to understand how germs work, how vitamins work, how the immune system works, and so on. Hence much simpler accounts of imbalances among a few bodily elements are appealing. On the emotional side, there is the regrettable fact that modern medicine still lacks treatment for many human diseases, even ones such as cancer whose biological mechanisms are quite well understood. Alternative disease theories and therapies offer hope of inexpensive and non-invasive treatments. For example, naturopaths attribute diseases to environmental toxins that can be cleared by diet and other simple therapies, providing people with reassuring explanations and expectations about their medical situation. Hence resistance to conceptual change about disease, like resistance concerning life, is often as much emotional as cognitive. The same is true for the concept of mind.

MIND

Theology

For the billions of people who espouse Christianity, Islam, Hinduism, and Buddhism, a person is much more than a biological mechanism. According to the book of Genesis, God formed man from the dust of the ground and breathed into his nostrils, making him a living soul. Unlike human bodies, which rarely last more than 100 years, souls have the great advantage of being indestructible, which makes possible immortality and (according to some religions) reincarnation. Because most people living today believe that their souls will survive the demise of their bodies, they have a concept of a person that is inherently dualistic: People consist of both a material body and a spiritual soul.

We saw that Descartes argued that bodies are machines, but he maintained that minds are not mechanically explainable. His main argument for this position was a thought experiment: He found it easy to imagine himself without a body, but impossible to imagine himself not thinking (Descartes, 1985). Hence he concluded that he was essentially a thinking being rather than a bodily machine, thereby providing a conceptual argument for the theological view of persons as consisting of two distinct substances, with the soul being much more important than the body. Descartes thought that the body and soul were able to influence each other through interaction in the brain's pineal gland.

The psychological theories of ordinary people are thoroughly dualist, assuming that consciousness and other mental operations belong fundamentally to the soul rather than the brain. Legal and other institutions assume that people inherently have the capacity for free will, which applies to actions of the soul rather than to processes occurring in the brain through interaction with other parts of the body and the external environment. Such freedom is viewed as integral to morality, making it legitimate to praise or blame people for their actions.

Notice how tightly the theological view of the mind as soul fits with the biological theory of creation. Life has theological rather than natural origins, and God is also responsible for a special kind of life: Humans with souls as well as bodies. Gods and souls are equally supernatural entities.

Qualitative Explanations of Mind

Postulating souls with free will does not enable us to say much about mental operations, and many thinkers have used introspection (self-observation) to describe the qualitative properties of thinking. The British empiricist philosophers, Locke and Hume, claimed that minds function by the associations of ideas that are ultimately derived from sense experience. When Wilhelm Wundt originated experimental psychology in the 1870s, his observational method was still primarily introspective, but was much more systematic and tied to experimental interventions than ordinary self-observation.

Many philosophers have resisted the attempt to make the study of mind scientific, hoping that a purely conceptual approach could help us to understand thinking. Husserl founded phenomenology, an a priori attempt to identify essential features of thought and action. Linguistic philosophers such as J. L. Austin thought that attention to the ordinary uses of words could tell us something about the nature of mind. Analytic philosophers have examined everyday mental concepts such as belief and desire, under the assumption that people's actions are adequately explained as the result of people's beliefs and desires. Thought experiments survive as a popular philosophical tool for determining the essential features of thinking, for example when Chalmers (1996) uses them to argue for a non-theological version of dualism in which consciousness is a fundamental part of the universe like space and time.

Thought experiments can be helpful for generating hypotheses that suggest experiments, but by themselves they provide no reason to believe those hypotheses. For every thought experiment there is an equal and opposite thought experiment, so the philosophical game of imagining what might be the case tells us little about the nature of minds and thinking. Introspective, conceptual approaches to psychology are appealing because they are much less constrained than experimental approaches and do not require large amounts of personnel and apparatus. They generate no annoying data to get in the way of one's favorite prejudices about the nature of mind. However, they are very limited in how much they can explain about the capacities and performance of the mind. Fortunately, mechanistic explanations based on experiments provide a powerful alternative methodology.

Mechanistic Explanations of Mind

Descartes thought that springs and other simple mechanisms suffice to explain the operation of bodies, but drew back from considering thinking mechanistically. Until the second half of the 20th century, mechanical models of thinking such as hydraulic fluids and telephone switchboards seemed much too crude to explain the richness and complexity of human mental operations. The advent of the digital computer provided a dramatic innovation in ways of thinking about the mind. Computers are obviously mechanisms, but they have unprecedented capacities to represent and process information. In 1956, Newell, Shaw, and Simon (1958) developed the first computational model of human problem solving. For decades, the computer has provided a source of analogies to help understand many aspects of human thinking, including perception, learning, memory, and inference (see Thagard, 2005b, for a survey). On the computational view of mind, thinking occurs when algorithmic processes are applied to mental representations that are akin to the data structures found in the software that determines the actions of computer hardware.

However, as von Neumann (1958) noted early on, digital computers are very different from human brains. They nevertheless have proved useful for developing models of how brains work, ever since the 1950s. But in the 1980s there was an upsurge of development of models of brain-style computing, using parallel processing among simple processing elements roughly analogous to neurons (Rumelhart & McClelland, 1986). Churchland and Sejnowski (1992) and others have argued that neural mechanisms are computational, although of a rather different sort than those found in digital computers. More biologically realistic, computational models of neural processes are currently being developed (e.g., Eliasmith & Anderson, 2003). Efforts are increasingly made to relate high-level mental operations such as rule-based inference to neural structures and processes (e.g., Anderson et al., 2004). Thus neuroscience along with computational ideas inspired by neural processes provides powerful mechanistic accounts of human thinking.

Central to modern cognitive science is the concept of *representation*, which has undergone major historical changes. From a theological perspective, representations such as concepts and propositions are properties of spiritual beings, and thus are themselves non-material objects. Modern cognitive psychology reclassifies representations as material things, akin to the data structures found in computer programs. Most radically, cognitive neuroscience reclassifies representations as *processes*, namely patterns of activity in neural networks in the brain. Thus the history of cognitive science has required *branch jumping*, which I earlier listed as one of the most radical kinds of conceptual change. It is too soon to say whether cognitive neuroscience will also require *tree switching*, a fundamental change in the organizing principles by which mental representations are classified.

We saw in discussing life and disease how mechanistic explanations are decomposable into underlying mechanisms. At the cognitive level, we can view thinking in terms of computational processes applied to mental representations, but it has become possible to deepen this view by considering neurocomputational processes applied to neural representations. In turn, neural processes – the behavior of neurons interacting with each other – can be explained in terms of biochemical processes. The study of mind, like the study of life and disease, is increasingly becoming molecular (Thagard, 2003a). That does not mean that the only useful explanations of human thinking will be found at the molecular level, because various phenomena are more likely to be captured by mechanisms operating at different levels. For example, rule-based problem solving may be best explained at the cognitive level in terms of mental representations and computational procedures, even if these representations and procedures ultimately derive from neural and molecular processes.

Indeed, a full understanding of human thinking needs to consider higher as well as lower levels. Many kinds of human thinking occur in social contexts, involving social mechanisms such as communication and other kinds of interaction. Far from it being the case that the social reduces to the cognitive which reduces to the neural which reduces to the molecular, sometimes what happens at the molecular level needs to be explained by what happens socially. For example, a social interaction between two people may produce very different kinds of neurotransmitter activity in their brains depending on whether they like or fear each other.

Of course, there is a great deal about human thinking that current psychology and neuroscience cannot yet explain. Although perception, memory, learning, and inference are increasingly subject to neurocomputational explanation, there are still puzzles such as consciousness, where there are only sketches of mechanisms that might possibly be relevant. Such sketchiness gives hope to those who are opposed for various religious or ideological ideas to the provision of mechanistic explanations of the full range of human thought. From a theological perspective that assumes the existence of souls, full mechanistic explanation of thinking is impossible as well as undesirable. The undesirability stems from the many attractive features of supernatural souls, particularly their immortality and autonomy. Adopting a mechanistic view of mind requires abandoning or at least modifying traditional ideas about free will, moral responsibility, and eternal rewards and punishment (Thagard, 2010). This threat explains why the past 50 years of demonstrable progress in mechanistic, neurocomputational explanations of many aspects of thought are ignored by critics who want to maintain traditional attitudes. Change in the concept of mind, as with life and disease, is affected not only by cognitive processes such as theory evaluation, but also by emotional processes such as motivated inference. In the next section I will draw some more general lessons about conceptual change in relation to science education.

CONCEPTUAL CHANGE

Of course, there are many other important concepts in the history of science besides life, mind, and disease, and much more to be said about other kinds of conceptual change (see, for example, Thagard, 1992). But, because the concepts of life, mind, and disease are central, respectively, to biology, psychology, and medicine, they provide a good basis for making some generalizations about conceptual change in the history of science that can be tested against additional historical episodes. The commonalities in ways in which these three concepts have developed are well worth noting.

In all cases, there has been a shift from conceptualizations in terms of simple properties to ones in terms of complex relations. Prescientifically, life could be viewed as a special property that distinguished living from non-living things. This property could be explained in terms of divine creation or some vital force. In contrast, the mechanistic view of biology considers life as a complex of dynamic relations, such as the metabolism and reproduction of cells. Life is no one thing, but rather the result of many different mechanical processes. Similarly, disease is not a simple problem that can be explained by divine affliction or humoral imbalance, but rather is the result of many different kinds of biological and environmental processes. Diseases have many different kinds of causes – microbial, genetic, nutritional, and autoimmune, each of which depends on many underlying biological mechanisms. Even more strikingly, mind is not a simple thing, the non-corporeal soul, but rather the result of many interacting neural structures and processes. Thus the conceptual developments of biology, psychology, and medicine have all required shifts from thinking of things in terms of simple properties to thinking of them in terms of complexes of relations. Students who encounter scientific versions of their familiar everyday concepts of life, mind, and disease need to undergo the same kind of shift. Chi (2005) describes the difficulties that arise for students in understanding emergent mechanisms, ones in which regularities arise from complex interactions of many entities. Life, mind, and disease are all emergent processes in this sense and therefore subject to the difficult learning challenges that Chi reports in other domains.

The shift in understanding life, mind, and disease as complex mechanical relations rather than as simple substances or properties is an example of what I earlier called branch jumping, reclassification by shifting a concept from one branch of a hierarchical tree to another. The tree here is ontological, a classification of the fundamental things thought to be part of existence. Life, for example, is no longer a kind of special property, but rather a kind of mechanical process. Mind is another kind of mechanical process, not a special substance created by God. Many more mundane cases of branch jumping have occurred as the life sciences develop, for example the reclassification in the 1980s of peptic ulcers as infectious diseases (Thagard, 1999).

Most radically, the shift from theological to qualitative to mechanistic conceptions of life, mind, and disease also involved tree switching, changing the organizing principle of a hierarchical tree. From a mechanistic perspective, we classify things in terms of their underlying parts and interactions. Darwin's mechanism of evolution by natural selection yielded a whole new way of classifying species, by historical descent rather than similarity. Later, the development of molecular genetics provided another new way of classifying species in terms of genetic similarity. Similarly, diseases are now classified in terms of their causal mechanisms rather than surface similarity of symptoms, for example as infectious or autoimmune diseases. More slowly, mental phenomena such as memory are becoming classified in terms of underlying causal mechanisms such as different kinds of neural learning (Smith & Kosslyn, 2007). Thus conceptual change in the life sciences has involved both branch jumping and tree switching.

Another important general lesson we can draw from the development of concepts of life, mind, and disease is that conceptual change in the history of science is theory change. Scientific concepts are embedded in theories, and it is only by the development of explanatory theories with broad empirical support that it becomes reasonable and in fact intellectually mandatory to adopt new complexes of concepts. The current scientific view of life depends on evolutionary, genetic, and molecular theories, just as the current medical view of disease depends on molecular, microbial, nutritional, and other well-supported theories. Similarly, our concept of mind should be under constant revision as knowledge accumulates about the neurocomputational mechanisms of perception, memory, learning, and inference. In all these cases, it would have been folly to attempt to begin investigation with a precise definition of key concepts, because what matters is the development of explanatory theories rather than conceptual neatness. After some theoretical order has been achieved, it may be possible to tidy up a scientific field with some approximate definitions. But if theoretical advances have involved showing that phenomena are much more complicated than anyone suspected, and that what were thought to be simple properties are in fact complexes of mechanical relations, then definitions are as pointless at later stages of investigation as they are distracting at early stages.

My final lesson about conceptual change in the history of science is that, especially in the sciences most deeply relevant to human lives, conceptual change is emotional as well as cognitive (see also Thagard, 2010, 2012). The continuing resistance to mechanistic explanations of life, mind, and disease is inexplicable on purely cognitive grounds, given the enormous amount of evidence that has accumulated for theories such as evolution by natural selection, the germ theory of disease, and neurocomputational accounts of thinking. Although the scientific communities have largely made the emotional shifts necessary to allow concepts and theories to fit with empirical results, members of the general population, including many science students, have strong affective preferences for obsolete theories such as divine creation, alternative medicine, and soul-based psychology. Popular concepts of life, mind, and disease are tightly intertwined: God created both life and mind, and can be called on to alleviate disease. Hence conceptual change can require not just rejection of a single theory in biology, psychology, and medicine, but rather replacement of a theological world-view by a scientific, mechanist one. For many people, such replacement is horrific, because of the powerful emotional appeal of the God–soul–prayer conceptual framework. Hence the kind of theory replacement required to be bring about conceptual change in biology, psychology, and medicine is not just a matter of explanatory coherence, but requires changes in emotional coherence as well (for a theory of emotional coherence, see Thagard, 2000, 2003b, 2006a).

From this perspective, science education inevitably involves cultural remediation and even psychotherapy in addition to more cognitive kinds of instruction. The transition from theological to qualitative to mechanistic explanations of phenomena is cognitively and emotionally difficult, but crucial for scientific progress, as we have seen for the central concepts of life, mind, and disease.

REFERENCES

Anderson, J. R., Bothell, D., Byrne, M. D., Douglas, S., Lebiere, C., & Qin, U. (2004). An integrated theory of the mind. *Psychological Review, 111*, 1030–1060.

Bechtel, W., & Abrahamsen, A. A. (2005). Explanation: A mechanistic alternative. *Studies in History and Philosophy of Biology and Biomedical Sciences, 36*, 421–441.

Bechtel, W., & Richardson, R. C. (1993). *Discovering complexity.* Princeton, NJ: Princeton University Press.

Bechtel, W., & Richardson, R. C. (1998). Vitalism. In E. Craig (Ed.), *Routledge encyclopedia of philosophy* (pp. 639–643). London, UK: Routledge.

Chalmers, D. J. (1996). *The conscious mind.* Oxford, UK: Oxford University Press.

Chi, M. T. H. (2005). Commonsense conceptions of emergent processes: Why some misconceptions are robust. *Journal of the Learning Sciences, 14*, 161–199.

Churchland, P. S., & Sejnowski, T. (1992). *The computational brain.* Cambridge, MA: MIT Press.

Comte, A. (1970). *Introduction to positive philosophy* (F. Ferré, Trans.). Indianapolis, IN: Bobbs-Merrill.

Dembski, W. (1999). *Intelligent design: The bridge between science and theology.* Downers Grove, IL: InterVarsity Press.

Descartes. (1985). *The philosophical writings of Descartes.* (J. Cottingham et al., Trans.). Cambridge, UK: Cambridge University Press.

Eliasmith, C., & Anderson, C. H. (2003). *Neural engineering: Computation, representation and dynamics in neurobiological systems.* Cambridge, MA: MIT Press.

Grene, M., & Depew, D. (2004). *The philosophy of biology: An episodic history.* Cambridge, UK: Cambridge University Press.

Hippocrates. (1988). *Hippocrates, Vol. V* (P. Potter, Trans. Vol. V). Cambridge, MA: Harvard University Press.

Horwich, P. (Ed.). (1993). *World changes: Thomas Kuhn and the nature of science.* Cambridge, MA: MIT Press.

Kuhn, T. S. (1970). *The structure of scientific revolutions* (2nd ed.). Chicago, IL: University of Chicago Press.

LaPorte, J. (2004). *Natural kinds and conceptual change.* Cambridge, UK: Cambridge University Press.

Lodish, H., Berk, A., Zipursky, S. L., Matsudaira, P., Baltimore, D., & Darnell, J. (2000). *Molecular cell biology* (4th ed.). New York, NY: W. H. Freeman.

Machamer, P., Darden, L., & Craver, C. F. (2000). Thinking about mechanisms. *Philosophy of Science, 67*, 1–25.

Nersessian, N. (1992). How do scientists think? Capturing the dynamics of conceptual change in science. In R. Giere (Ed.), *Cognitive models of science* (Vol. 15, pp. 3–44). Minneapolis, MN: University of Minnesota Press.

Newell, A., Shaw, J. C., & Simon, H. (1958). Elements of a theory of human problem solving. *Psychological Review, 65*, 151–166.

Paley, W. (1963). *Natural theology: Selections.* Indianapolis, IN: Bobbs-Merrill.

Rumelhart, D. E., & McClelland, J. L. (Eds.). (1986). *Parallel distributed processing: Explorations in the microstructure of cognition.* Cambridge, MA: MIT Press/Bradford Books.

Salmon, W. (1984). *Scientific explanation and the causal structure of the world.* Princeton, NJ: Princeton University Press.

Smith, E. E., & Kosslyn, S. M. (2007). *Cognitive psychology: Mind and brain.* Upper Saddle River, NJ: Pearson Prentice Hall.

Thagard, P. (1992). *Conceptual revolutions.* Princeton, NJ: Princeton University Press.

Thagard, P. (1999). *How scientists explain disease.* Princeton, NJ: Princeton University Press.

Thagard, P. (2000). *Coherence in thought and action.* Cambridge, MA: MIT Press.

Thagard, P. (2003a). Pathways to biomedical discovery. *Philosophy of Science, 70,* 235–254.

Thagard, P. (2003b). Why wasn't O. J. convicted? Emotional coherence in legal inference. *Cognition and Emotion, 17,* 361–383.

Thagard, P. (2005a). The emotional coherence of religion. *Journal of Cognition and Culture, 5,* 58–74.

Thagard, P. (2005b). *Mind: Introduction to cognitive science* (2nd ed.). Cambridge, MA: MIT Press.

Thagard, P. (2006a). *Hot thought: Mechanisms and applications of emotional cognition.* Cambridge, MA: MIT Press.

Thagard, P. (2006b). What is a medical theory? In R. Paton & L. A. McNamara (Eds.), *Multidisciplinary approaches to theory in medicine* (pp. 47–62). Amsterdam, The Netherlands: Elsevier.

Thagard, P. (2007). Coherence, truth, and the development of scientific knowledge. *Philosophy of Science, 74,* 28–47.

Thagard, P. (2010). *The brain and the meaning of life.* Princeton, NJ: Princeton University Press.

Thagard, P. (2012). *The cognitive science of science: Explanation, discovery, and conceptual change.* Cambridge, MA: MIT Press.

Thagard, P., & Zhu, J. (2003). Acupuncture, incommensurability, and conceptual change. In G. M. Sinatra & P. R. Pintrich (Eds.), *Intentional conceptual change* (pp. 79–102). Mahwah, NJ: Lawrence Erlbaum Associates.

von Neumann, J. (1958). *The computer and the brain.* New Haven, CT: Yale University Press.

Part IV
Learner Characteristics and Mechanisms for Conceptual Change

20

BEYOND KNOWLEDGE

Learner Characteristics Influencing Conceptual Change

Gale M. Sinatra and Lucia Mason,
University of Southern California and University of Padua

For the past several decades, conceptual change researchers have demonstrated in numerous studies that learning presents unique challenges when students have their own naïve theories or preconceived notions about the world around them (see, for example, Carey, 1985; Chinn & Brewer, 1993; Spelke, 1991; Vosniadou & Brewer, 1987). These challenges distinguish conceptual change learning from knowledge acquisition conceptually and pedagogically in significant ways. Further, it is precisely these distinctions that make the area of conceptual change research fruitful for providing insights into the nature of learning itself.

Prior to the emergence of explanatory models of conceptual change, researchers studying knowledge acquisition recognized that students responded differently in learning situations when their pre-existing knowledge conflicted with the information conveyed in their textbooks and classrooms. However, this represented an interesting learning paradox. That is, how could background knowledge – well established in the psychological literature as a facilitator of learning – serve as a barrier to learning when students had everyday experiences with the phenomena? Progress on understanding the apparent paradox of background knowledge serving both as a facilitator and as a barrier to learning was modest until models of conceptual change learning were introduced (Chi, 1992; Posner, Strike, Hewson, & Gertzog, 1982; Vosniadou & Brewer, 1992).

Cognitive developmental approaches to conceptual change helped to explain how learners constructed an understanding of the natural world through both maturation and experience. Vosniadou and Brewer's (1992, 1994) classic study of children's developing conceptions of astronomical bodies illustrates how teaching young children about the shape of the earth is not simply a knowledge acquisition task. Vosniadou and Brewer (1992) demonstrated that children's conceptions of the earth are coherent, explanatory, robust, and difficult to change in favor of a scientific notion of a spherical earth. This study and dozens more demonstrated that learning about topics from the natural world requires going beyond classic knowledge acquisition; it also requires overcoming significant conceptual and affective obstacles. Models of conceptual change learning have evolved to help explain these challenges.

Early accounts of conceptual change learning documented how children's conceptions were different from those of scientists (Clough & Driver, 1985; Posner et al., 1982; West & Pines, 1985). However, these views gave little recognition to the affective, situational, and motivational factors that often play a determinative role in whether or not a new conception will be adopted. These perspectives were labeled "cold conceptual change" due to their focus on rational, cognitive factors to the exclusion of extra-rational or "hot" constructs (Pintrich, Marx, & Boyle, 1993).

Recently, however, there has been a "warming trend" in conceptual change research (Sinatra, 2005). Since Pintrich et al.'s (1993) revolutionary article "Beyond Cold Conceptual Change" there have been an increasing number of researchers characterizing conceptual change as social, contextual, motivational, and affective in nature (see for example, Dole & Sinatra, 1998; Gregoire, 2003; and Murphy & Mason, 2006). These models seek to characterize the role of hot constructs that affect conceptual change beyond those due to background knowledge.

LEARNER CHARACTERISTICS AND INTENTIONAL CONCEPTUAL CHANGE

Cognitive theory and research suggest that human cognition is organized into levels of awareness. These levels range from automatic processing of information without conscious attention (what some call algorithmic processing) to consciously aware, goal-directed, and intentional processing (for various characterization of a levels view see Stanovich, 1999). These levels of awareness represent and analyze different types of information. This structure of the human cognitive architecture allows for efficient processing given our limited resources (Bargh & Chartrand, 1999).

Learner characteristics that can act at the intentional level of awareness in conceptual change learning (Sinatra & Pintrich, 2003) include personal interest, importance, utility value, achievement goals, self-efficacy, and control beliefs according to Pintrich (1999). Following the warming trend (Sinatra, 2005), many of these characteristics have become important in recent theoretical models of conceptual change (see, for example, Dole & Sinatra, 1998; Gregoire, 2003; Murphy & Mason, 2006; Sinatra & Taasoobshirazi, 2011). Although increased attention has been paid to understanding the role these characteristics play in conceptual change in recent years, it is important to note that empirical studies investigating the relationship between these factors and knowledge revision are still relatively rare. Therefore, we discuss only factors that have been the focus of recent empirical research on conceptual change which highlight the impact of students' motivation and affect on conscious, deliberate, and self-regulated intentional knowledge change (for an extended discussion of self-regulation and intentional conceptual change see Sinatra & Taasoobshirazi, 2011). We also draw implications from this research for the interactive nature of conceptual change, and the pedagogies that support change. Other learner characteristics are reviewed in other chapters in this volume (see, for example, Murphy & Alexander, Chapter 31).

Achievement Goals

The construct of achievement goals captures the process of energizing and directing behavior in achievement situations (e.g., the classroom). Achievement goals are described as explaining the why and how of student involvement in a task or activity (Elliott & Dweck, 1988). For example, a student may have an achievement goal of understanding information for personal interest or because she deems it important to her future profession. The achievement goal of another student may be to obtain an excellent evaluation that he can proudly show to his classmates or parents. Both students involve themselves in study activities but they are oriented toward different achievement goals.

Students who adopt *mastery goals* engage in schoolwork to understand and learn. They focus on the content to be mastered and use more complex information processing strategies to help them learn. In contrast, students who adopt *performance goals* seek to demonstrate their ability and self-worth to others, or to avoid demonstrating their incompetence. Therefore, aspects of the self rather than the task become the focus of their concern. The distinction between approach and avoidance achievement goals has emerged more recently. The 2×2 achievement goal framework was proposed to include the approach–avoidance distinction within mastery goals and performance goals. So, for example, those with performance-avoidance goal orientations focus on avoiding a demonstration of low ability compared with others (Elliot, 1999, 2005).

Achievement goals have a number of well-documented effects. According to normative models of achievement goals, mastery goals are associated with deeper engagement, self-regulatory behavior, positive affect, and better learners; whereas performance goals have been associated with surface-level strategy use, lower levels of cognitive engagement, and poorer learning outcomes (Pintrich, 2000; Pintrich & Schrauben, 1992). A number of correlational studies have shown a positive relationship between self-reported use of deep processing and metacognitive strategies and mastery goals for junior high school and college students (e.g., Nolen, 1988; Wolters, Yu, & Pintrich, 1996). Experimental studies have also documented that students who are more task-focused perform better in tasks requiring deeper processing (e.g., Elliot, McGregor, & Gables, 1999; Graham & Golan, 1991). These results have been demonstrated in multiple domains. For example, research on learning in physics has demonstrated that having understanding as a goal led to deeper processing of the material (Hammer, 1994).

Although the debate regarding the relative merits of each achievement goal type is far from settled, research has indicated that there can be positive effects of performance approach goals such as task engagement, self-regulatory strategies, high aspirations, and high achievement (Senko, Hulleman, & Harackiewicz, 2011). In contrast, both mastery and performance–avoidance goals relate to negative outcomes such as low task engagement and lower achievement (Elliot & Harackiewicz, 1996; Elliot & McGregor, 2001; Mason, Boscolo, Tornatora, & Ronconi, 2013).

Until recently, few studies have documented empirically the role of achievement goals in the conceptual change process. Linnenbrink and Pintrich (2002) carried out two studies examining college students' changing understandings of projectile motion that demonstrate the role of student characteristics in conceptual change process.

Linnenbrink and Pintrich (2002) hypothesized that students who adopted a mastery goal would use more metacognitive, self-regulatory strategies, which would lead to deeper levels of engagement with the information. Deeper engagement would in turn allow students to detect discrepancies between their existing conceptions and the new information. Thus, these students would be more likely to experience conceptual change. Conversely, the researchers hypothesized that students with performance goals would be less likely to experience conceptual change because they might have difficulty admitting their existing ideas were incorrect, since they tend to focus on how they appear to others.

Results showed that adopting mastery goals was related to a change in understanding. This finding was particularly apparent for students who had low prior knowledge of the topic, revealing the potential interactive effect of these characteristics with students' knowledge. Performance goals did not promote conceptual change, but at the same time, they did not impede it.

A second study showed that mastery goals were associated with elaborative strategies, as well as with a lessening of negative affect. Linnebrink and Pintrich (2002) maintained that lowering negative affect mediated the influence of this type of achievement goal in the conceptual change process, possibly by reducing the distracting effects of anxiety on learning.

The positive influence of performance goals has been confirmed in a cross-cultural study involving American and Chinese high-school students (Qian & Pan, 2002). A significant positive correlation between performance goals and conceptual change learning indicated that students who were more inclined to change their conceptions about projectile motion were also those who focused on the self. In this study, strong performance goals sustained persistence through the demanding process of knowledge revision. More recently, it has been proposed that mastery goals coupled with performance goals can form a better achievement profile than mastery goals in combination with the absence of performance goals (Elliot, 2005). Therefore, multiple achievement goals may lead to better learning performance than a single goal (Linnenbrink & Pintrich, 2003).

Mason, Boldrin, and Vanzetta (2006) examined the effects of achievement goals on knowledge revision when students were learning about magnets. Goals were examined in relation to beliefs about the certainty, development, justification, and source of scientific knowledge. Pretest to post-test comparisons revealed a significant interaction between goals and beliefs about the nature of scientific knowledge. Students who had less advanced beliefs about scientific knowledge benefited more from reading a text if they had mastery goals than students who were less mastery-oriented. Performance goals were not associated with conceptual change.

Recently, Taasoobshirazi and Sinatra (2011) explored the role of achievement goal orientation in conceptual change in physics. Using a structural equation model, they found that approach goals had a direct effect on college students' motivation for learning physics, and students' motivation influenced both course grade and the degree of conceptual change as measured by the Force Choice Inventory (FCI), which is designed to measure physics misconceptions (Hestenes, Wells, & Swackhamer, 1992). This study demonstrates that approach goals influence conceptual change and other learning outcomes such as course grades.

Worth noting is that achievement goals may be influenced not only by students' expectations for success but also by the importance or value they attach to a particular task, activity, or subject (Eccles, 2005; Eccles & Wigfield, 2002). Students may value a task for its intrinsic enjoyment, utility (usefulness), or attainment value (importance of the task for achievement). A recent study by Johnson and Sinatra (2012) was the first to demonstrate that induced task values may promote conceptual change. The authors induced college students to adopt either a utility value or an attainment value before they read a refutation text on causes of the common cold. Findings revealed that students in the utility values condition rated their perceived engagement more highly than a control group of students not induced with a specific task value. They also demonstrated the highest degree of conceptual change of the three groups. In addition, students induced with attainment values showed greater conceptual change than those in the control group.

These studies reveal how specific characteristics of students, such as the type of goals they adopt and their mood during instruction, affect conceptual change either directly via the use of elaborative strategies or indirectly by decreased negative emotions. These studies illustrate how students' intentions, expressed through the implementation of a mastery goal, can play a pivotal role in the process of knowledge revision.

Epistemic Motivation and Beliefs

Epistemic motivation refers to motivations that are not focused on the self but rather on knowledge as an object (Kruglanski, 1989). Pintrich et al. (1993) identified epistemic motivation as one of the key learner characteristics likely implicated in the knowledge restructuring process. This characteristic is related to the broader view of motivated social cognition (Kruglanski, 1989; Kruglanski & Webster, 1996) that examines the interplay between cognition and motivation and explores the "pervasive role that affect and motivation play in attention, memory, judgment, decision making, and human reasoning, as well as highlighting the cognitive, goal-directed aspects of most motivational phenomena" (Jost, Glaser, Kruglanski, & Sulloway, 2003, p. 342).

Kruglanski and colleagues have discussed two epistemic motivations, seeking closure and avoiding closure, which can produce a wide range of effects on the knowledge construction process. Need for closure refers to the desire for definitive knowledge on a topic and the need to avoid ambiguity and uncertainty (Kruglanski, 1989, 1990). Need for closure has been shown to relate to a tendency to seize on information prematurely effectively "freezing" the decision-making process, resulting in relative closed-mindedness on the issue (Kruglanski & Webster, 1996).

In contrast, the epistemic motivation of avoiding closure refers to the need to seek new information, question current ideas, and solve discrepancies and problems. "Unfreezing" of cognition implies continued searching for information and generation and testing of hypotheses – cognitive processes that are assumed to underlie knowledge restructuring. Epistemic motivations are closely related to cognitive styles or dispositions such as actively open-minded thinking (Stanovich, 1999) and need for cognition (Cacioppo, Petty, Feinstein, & Jarvis, 1996), which have been investigated by conceptual change researchers. Sinatra and colleagues (Sinatra & Southerland, 2011; Sinatra, Southerland, McConaughy, & Demastes, 2003) have explored how college students' background knowledge, beliefs, and cognitive dispositions relate to their acceptance of scientific theories. In a series of studies, participants read passages presenting controversial theories about photosynthesis, bird evolution, and human evolution and rated their acceptance of the ideas presented in the text as well as the general scientific theories. The researchers predicted that students who held a view of knowledge as changing and who enjoyed effortful, critical, and open-minded thinking would be more likely to accept scientific theories such as human evolution than students with more static views of knowledge who were less interested in deep, critical thinking.

In all three studies, students' epistemic beliefs and thinking dispositions predicted acceptance of human evolution. Knowledge, however, was only a significant predictor of acceptance when students' level of knowledge was high (an average of nearly seven college biology courses). The researchers concluded that for students with limited biology knowledge, beliefs and dispositions serve much like epistemic motivations. That is, they play the determinative role in acceptance of emotionally laden socially embedded topics, such as human evolution. They also concluded that for knowledge to overcome motivations in decision making about scientific theories, students must undergo what Sinatra and Chinn (2011) call "epistemic conceptual change." That is, students must experience a change in how they view the very nature of knowledge to appreciate scientific concepts.

Epistemic beliefs, beliefs about the nature of knowledge and knowing (Hofer & Pintrich, 2002) have also been shown to relate to conceptual change (Mason, 2003). Qian and Alvermann (2000) indicated that epistemic beliefs can have a direct impact on the process of knowledge restructuring. They examined the relationship between high-school students' epistemic beliefs, motivational goals, and conceptual change learning. Their research showed that students who viewed knowledge as simple and certain were less likely to reason effectively and experience conceptual change (Qian & Alvermann, 1995).

Windschitl and Andre (1998) examined undergraduate introductory biology students' epistemic beliefs and their understandings of the human cardiovascular system, a topic about which many students hold misconceptions. They found that students' epistemic beliefs predicted the likelihood of conceptual change. Students who believed knowledge is changing experienced more change in their own ideas about the circulatory system than those with more static views of knowledge.

Mason (2000) investigated epistemic beliefs in relation to anomalous data in theory change on two controversial topics: One was scientific, the extinction of dinosaurs; and the other historical, the construction of the great pyramids in Giza (Egypt). The findings indicated that eighth graders' acceptance of anomalous data made the most significant contribution to their theory change. In addition, acceptance of anomalous data was associated with the belief about the stability and source of knowledge. The more students believed in changing knowledge, the more likely they were to accept anomalous data and change their theory.

Nussbaum, Sinatra, and Poliquin (2008) hypothesized that instruction in the criteria of developing a scientific argument, along with constructivist epistemic beliefs, would produce deeper intentional conceptual change. They found that college students who received argumentation instruction developed better arguments than those who did not. They also found that evaluativists, who according to Kuhn, Cheney, and Weinstock (2000) hold reasoned justifications for their knowledge, engaged more with their partners, raised more alternative ideas, solved more physics problems accurately, and demonstrated a reduction in misconceptions compared to other belief groups.

The role of epistemic beliefs in relation to text structure was investigated by Mason and Gava (2007). Eighth graders in the experimental condition read a refutation text about natural selection and those in the control condition read a normal expository text about the same topic. Findings showed that reading the refutation text and holding more advanced epistemic beliefs led to more conceptual change. Moreover, a significant interaction between the two factors advantaged students who read the refutation text and believed more in complex and uncertain knowledge.

Stathopoulou and Vosniadou's (2007) study with tenth graders also indicated that physics-related epistemic beliefs are necessary, although insufficient, for conceptual understanding in physics. Only students with strong beliefs that knowledge was changing achieved a deep understanding of Newtonian dynamics.

The interaction between epistemic beliefs, knowledge representation, and cognitive and metacognitive processing was recently examined in undergraduates when learning physics concepts from text (Franco et al., 2012). Findings revealed that when students' epistemic beliefs were consistent with the knowledge representation in the text (i.e., "rational" or "metaphorical" knowledge representation), they performed better in the use of processing strategies, text recall, and changing misconceptions than when their epistemic beliefs were inconsistent with the knowledge representations.

In sum, epistemic beliefs can promote epistemic conceptual change, particularly when brought to the level of learners' awareness (Sinatra, 2005). That is, there is emerging evidence that as students develop a view of knowledge as complex and constantly changing, they themselves become more open to changing their conceptions of scientific phenomena (Sinatra & Chinn, 2011).

Interest

Interest is one of the student characteristics identified by Pintrich et al. (1993) as a potential for motivating conceptual change. Studies on interest as a motivational variable draw a conceptual distinction between individual and situational interest (Alexander, 1997, 1998; Alexander & Murphy, 1998; Hidi & Baird, 1986; Renninger, Hidi, & Krapp, 1992). Individual interest is a relatively stable student characteristic described as an evaluative orientation towards an object or domain. In contrast, situational interest is generated by certain conditions and/or environmental stimuli such as novelty and intensity, which contribute to the "interestingness" of a situation (Schraw & Lehman, 2001).

Another type of interest that has been investigated particularly in relation to learning from text is topic interest. It can be considered as both individual and situational (Hidi, 2000). Topic interest can be an expression of individual interest when a person has positive feels about the topic, finds it of value, and seeks information about it. At the same time, it can be an expression of situational interest as it may be related to certain characteristics of the situation that trigger a person's cognitive and affective response.

The role of topic interest in learning has been demonstrated in a number of studies. It relates significantly to recall of idea units, elaborations, and main ideas, independent of preexisting knowledge (Schiefele, 1998; Schiefele & Krapp, 1996). Highly interested senior high-school students understood a text more deeply, whereas low-interest readers assimilated it superficially, regardless of their degree of prior knowledge. A study by Boscolo and Mason (2003) revealed that topic interest contribution increased relative to the degree of the learner's topic knowledge. When topic knowledge is high, topic interest may help students develop a deeper level of understanding of the text. Moreover, the beneficial effect of topic interest was evidenced in high-school students' comprehension of a dual-position text on the controversial topic of genetically modified food. Highly topic-interested readers gave more accurate and richer answers about the conflicting perspectives presented in the text than low and moderately topic-interested readers (Mason & Boscolo, 2004).

Whereas several studies have demonstrated the effect of topic interest on text comprehension, only a few have focused on the relationship between interest (individual or situational) and conceptual change. These studies have revealed that interest may not always be a resource for conceptual change. In a study of high-school students' understanding of genetics, Venville and Treagust (1998) reported some contradictory data. Students interested in the topic produced either high or very low levels of conceptual change. It should be underlined, however, that students' high interest was in human heredity and not in the microscopic aspects of genetics to be learned. Murphy and Alexander (2004) found that college students with high topic interest were less likely to alter their beliefs. The high correlation between interest and prior knowledge seen in these studies could explain the apparently contradictory findings. As pointed out by Dole and Sinatra (1998) in their model, individuals with high knowledge may show more resistance to change.

There is research demonstrating a positive effect of interest in intentional conceptual change. Andre and Windschitl (2003) conducted a series of studies on knowledge revision about electrical circuits. Conceptual understanding was positively related to interest in the subject matter, regardless of whether a traditional or conceptual change text was read. In the second study, interest contributed again to conceptual understanding of electrical circuits, significantly and independently. In the third study, a path analysis revealed that interest contributed indirectly to conceptual change through the mediated effect of prior experience. In addition, interest influenced students' post-test performance independently of its effect on experience. Topic interest can therefore affect conceptual change both directly and indirectly, through experience and knowledge (Andre & Windschitl, 2003).

In a recent study of fifth graders' conceptual change about light and vision, topic interest was examined in relation to beliefs about scientific knowledge (Mason, Gava, & Boldrin, 2008). Students read either a traditional text or a refutational text on the content to be learned, which challenged alternative conceptions and showed the value of the scientific view. Topic interest was found to be a resource for change, as highly interested students changed their alternative conceptions more often than less interested students.

The beneficial effect of interest on the knowledge restructuring process can be explained in light of the issues offered by recent literature on interest (e.g., Ainley, Hidi, & Berndorff, 2002). Interest directs the attentional resources of arousal, selective attention, and concentration. More interest in a topic is associated with increased attentional resources devoted to learning that information (Schiefele & Rheinberg, 1997). Further, cognitive resources, "liberated" by interest, can therefore be devoted to cognitive processing. All together, arousal, selective attention, and concentration sustain deep or systematic processing of the content to be learned, a key factor in intentional conceptual change.

Like goals, interest seems to have the potential to direct attention toward the information to be learned, thereby bootstrapping the conceptual change process. Some research suggests that topic interest can be a catalyst for change. And yet interest may be associated with commitment to one's current views and may create motivation to maintain one's current beliefs. This learner characteristic may be a "double-edged sword" in terms of its connection to conceptual change and well illustrates the complex interactive nature of the knowledge restructuring process. Self-efficacy is another characteristic that may play conflicting roles in knowledge restructuring.

Self-Efficacy

Self-efficacy beliefs were defined by Bandura (1986) as individuals' beliefs about their performance capabilities in particular domains. The construct does not refer to individuals' global self-concept but rather to self-judgments about functioning in general academic domains (such as mathematics or history) or specific tasks, such as solving word problems in mathematics. The predictive power of self-efficacy beliefs has been documented very extensively in multiple areas of academic achievement, from mathematical learning (Pajares & Miller, 1994) to writing (Pajares, 2003), to reading (Schunk, 2003; Shell, Colvin, & Bruning, 1995) to science learning (Pajares, Britner, & Valiante, 2000). Self-efficacy beliefs have also been shown to relate to such diverse areas as self-regulation (Zimmerman & Martinez-Pons, 1990) and career choice (Hackett, 1995).

The association of high self-efficacy beliefs with increased effort and persistence in difficult tasks, and resilience in the face of obstacles has been offered as the explanation of the potential of self-efficacy to promote learning. The activation of appropriate knowledge and strategies to process new information has also been hypothesized as the mechanism driving the self-efficacy effect (Pintrich, Marx, & Boyle, 1993; Renninger, 1992; Schunk & Pajares, 2005). Furthermore, self-efficacy is associated with positive emotional reactions. A high degree of confidence in one's own capabilities creates a feeling of calm, while low confidence is associated with anxiety (Schunk & Pajares, 2005). Adaptive cognitions, motivations, and positive affects all seem to suggest that a self-confident learner would be more likely to engage in intentional conceptual change.

Pintrich et al. (1993) cautioned, however, that there are two possible implications of the self-efficacy construct in the study of conceptual change. The first is that self-efficacy may create confidence in students' capabilities to gain a better understanding of an examined phenomenon and to learn through changing their ideas. In this case, higher self-efficacy would be facilitative of conceptual change. In contrast, the second possibility is that self-efficacy may foster a sense of confidence in students' ideas. In this case higher self-efficacy could lead to increased resistance to changing those ideas. So, confidence in one's ideas may serve as an obstacle to knowledge revision, or confidence in oneself as a learner capable of thinking and reasoning about a topic may serve as a resource for overcoming alternative conceptions.

There is very scarce empirical evidence to discern which of these two roles self-efficacy plays in the knowledge restructuring processes. In revising their well-known model describing the conditions necessary for successful conceptual change, Strike and Posner (1992) explored the influence of a student's conceptual ecology. In addition to epistemological views, motivational factors such as self-efficacy and achievement goals were also examined as part of a single factor defined as learning attitude. A significant positive correlation emerged between students' learning attitudes (which included confidence in their ability to learn science meaningfully) and conceptual change in physics, providing modest evidence in favor of the facilitative role of efficacy beliefs.

In a recent study with college students the role of self-efficacy, interest, prior knowledge, and confidence in prior knowledge has been investigated in relation to conceptual change (Cordova, Sinatra, Broughton, & Taasoobshirazi, 2011). Profiles of students were determined using k-means cluster analysis. The results revealed that students who were high relative to the other groups in self-efficacy, interest, prior knowledge, and confidence showed the least conceptual change, despite having potential for growth in their scores. The profile with the lowest scores on all constructs showed conceptual change at post-test, but also showed significant drift back to their original conceptions at delayed post-test. The most productive profile for conceptual change and maintenance of the new ideas was the mixed profile, which exhibited relatively high self-efficacy, interest, and confidence, but low prior knowledge. Similar findings about mixed student profiles were also obtained in a recent study by Linnenbrink-Garcia and colleagues (see Linnenbrink-Garcia, Pugh, Koskey, & Stewart, 2012).

The interactive nature of conceptual change learning emerges when we consider the multiple roles of self-efficacy. Both students' perceptions of their capabilities to accomplish a task and confidence in their current conceptions may impact knowledge-restructuring processes and produce different learning outcomes.

Emotions

There has been increasing interest in the role affect and emotion play in the conceptual change process. In her model of teacher belief change, Gregoire (2003) emphasizes the emotional influences on the process of change. More specifically, she explains the role anxiety and fear play when teachers encounter reform messages. When teachers receive a complex message that challenges traditional instruction in favor of a reform, they may appraise it with a feeling of anxiety. If the anxiety generated by the message is not associated with positive self-efficacy, the teacher is more likely to perceive it as a threat or avoid the message. If the message is never processed deeply, then belief change will likely not occur.

Empirical research on the influence of emotional responses on conceptual change is an emerging area of interest; however, the mechanisms underlying the impact emotion may have in knowledge restructuring is not yet clear. Linnenbrink and Pintrich (2004) posited that students' positive affect may facilitate knowledge change if it supports deep processing whereas negative emotions likely hinder knowledge revision if they lead to focus away from the content to be learned. Indeed, in one study, Linnenbrink and Pintrich (2002) showed that negative affect significantly related to lower degrees of conceptual change.

The influence of emotions on attitude and conceptual change in fifth and sixth grade students was recently investigated by Broughton, Sinatra, and Nussbaum (2011). Influenced by Pekrun and colleagues' view of academic emotions (e.g., Pekrun, Goetz, Titz, & Perry, 2002), Broughton et al. focused on learning about the controversial and emotionally charged topic of Pluto's reclassification as a dwarf-planet. They examined students' attitudes toward the reclassification of Pluto, and knowledge about the definition of planets, pre and post a refutation text intervention designed to promote change in both. They found that emotions predicted students' attitudes prior to instruction, their attitude change, as well as their conceptual change. Broughton et al. also showed that students' emotions, which were very negative prior to instruction, became less negative over the course of the intervention. They concluded that negative emotions inhibited change, but that conceptual change interventions may soften the negativity and thus open the door for further shifts in attitudes and knowledge.

Broughton, Pekrun, and Sinatra (2012) examined whether emotions were related to college students' misconceptions about controversial topics. They found that emotional intensity was positively related to the number of misconceptions students held for topics such as climate change and genetically modified food. They suggested that controversial science topics are associated with strong emotions, which vary depending on the topic and the number of misconceptions. This study highlights the unique challenges associated with promoting conceptual change on controversial topics.

In another study of emotions and conceptual change, Heddy and Sinatra (2012) used an instructional approach called Teaching for Transformative Experiences in Science (TTES; Pugh, 2002, 2011) to promote a change in college students' conceptions about natural selection. The results revealed that the TTES group experienced a significantly greater degree of conceptual change than the comparison group who received typical classroom lectures and discussion on the same topic. In regard to emotions, the TTES group reported a significant increase in their degree of enjoyment from pre to post instruction while enjoyment decreased in the comparison group. This study supports the Broughton et al. finding that conceptual change interventions can impact emotions.

When these studies are taken together, a pattern is emerging which suggests that emotions play an important role when learning in the science classroom (for a review see Sinatra, Broughton, & Lombardi, in press). Further, valence, type, and intensity of emotions vary with topic, and positive emotions appear to facilitate conceptual change, while negative emotions seem to impede it. Much more research is needed to explore these trends and test alternative hypotheses such as the potential of negative emotions to prompt deeper engagement.

A Synthesis: On the Impact of Learner Characteristics on Conceptual Change Learning

We have sought to describe what we believe to be the multifaceted and highly interactive nature of the conceptual change process, with particular emphasis on the role learner characteristics – other than knowledge – play in determining whether or not knowledge restructuring occurs. Learner characteristics tend to impact conceptual change learning when: (1) prior knowledge conflicts with to be learned information, (2) there is a high level of commitment to that knowledge, and (3) there are strong emotions associated with the content.

Learners' background knowledge is always important in any learning situation. However, in many circumstances, learners may have little relevant topic knowledge, or the knowledge they have may not conflict with the new information. For example, if a student new to chemistry is learning the symbols in the periodic table, most likely the majority of the symbols are new to her. Coming to accept that B is the chemical symbol for boron presents no difficulty, conflict, or learning challenge for our learner. However, in conceptual change learning situations, students have a great deal of relevant topic knowledge developed through years of experience. For example, if the topic is the speed with which objects of different weight fall, our learner has much relevant experience with the topic. Since she was an infant, our learner has been observing objects fall to the earth in a variety of circumstances. Some objects, such as leaves from the trees in late September, seem to float gently and slowly to the ground. Others, like ice cream from a cone on a hot July day, seem to fall to the ground in the blink of an eye. Learners bring the wealth of their prior experiences with them and this creates potential conflicts with scientific views.

Not only do learners in a conceptual change situation have relevant prior knowledge, they may also have a high degree of commitment to their ideas. For learners who have a high level of prior knowledge that differs from the new conception, learning may not be challenging if the learner has no commitment to that prior conception. So for example, it may not be difficult to accept the idea that botanists would consider a tomato to be a fruit because it grows on a vine, even though prior experience leads you to believe that it is a vegetable. If you do not have any deep commitments to the tomato's status (other than that you like them raw in your salads and cooked on your pasta), accepting a change in a tomato's scientific classification from vegetable to fruit may present little challenge.

In contrast, there are many ideas to which learners are deeply committed. The notions that the earth is flat or that objects fall to the ground at different rates may be based on naïve physics understandings and on everyday experiences ingrained over a lifetime. Strongly committed ideas are highly resistant to change in part due to this commitment, which may be highly emotionally charged (and in part due to their likely rich interconnections with other ideas). Resistance creates various barriers to learning that range from outright rejection of the new idea to deliberate revision of the conception to fit with preexisting notions (see Chinn & Brewer, 1993).

The degree of commitment to one's knowledge and beliefs and the level of emotion and affect tied to that commitment stems in part from the sociocultural context in which knowledge is embedded. Jovchelovitch (2007) describes how knowledge representations are "at once epistemic, social and personal and it is the appreciation of these three dimensions that can explain why representations are not a copy of the world outside but a symbolic construction of it" (p. 26). Jovchelovitch's (2007) perspective of "knowledge in context" reminds us of the dynamic interactive nature of knowledge construction and reconstruction and demands a multifaceted explanation of conceptual change learning that is both cognitive and social in nature.

INSTRUCTIONAL IMPLICATIONS

The multifaceted interactive nature of conceptual change, and the powerful role of learner characteristics, suggests there is a need to tailor instruction to match facets of the change process that present barriers to change. To be successful, conceptual change pedagogy must first include a determination of the full range of possible barriers to change. Instruction can then be targeted to confront barriers from multiple fronts. If learners hold misconceptions or alternative conceptions, these must be identified. The learners' level of commitment to their prior conceptions must also be determined. Next, the degree of affect and emotion tied to their prior knowledge should also be determined.

Once possible barriers are identified, instruction must be geared toward overcoming the particular barriers blocking change. Such interventions should be tailored for both the nature of the barrier and the topic. Minor conceptual misunderstandings about a tangential aspect of a phenomenon and major misconceptions about a central tenet of a scientific theory require different instructional approaches. So, for example, whereas refutation text may work to overcome a relatively minor misconception, argumentation pedagogy may be needed to promote a change in students' thinking about a controversial topic (Nussbaum & Sinatra, 2003).

As the barriers to change increase in terms of their strength or level of resistance, the nature of the instruction must also adjust to fit the level of resistance. Students' degree of commitment to their own ideas suggests that certain instructional approaches would be more successful than others. Deep commitments to an alternative conception based in naïve physics or naïve psychology and developed through extensive interactions with the physical and emotional world require pedagogical approaches that demand high engagement (Dole & Sinatra, 1998) such as experimentation, inquiry, or problem-based learning (e.g., Kolodner et al., 2003).

Emotionally based, affective commitments to deeply held personal beliefs or resistance to change due to epistemic beliefs, motivations, or dispositions toward maintaining one's views would require instruction to be "ratcheted up" to another level of engagement. In these circumstances, argumentation-based pedagogies such as collaborative argumentation (Nussbaum & Sinatra, 2003) or the use of persuasive pedagogies (Murphy, 2001; Sinatra & Kardash, 2004) may be more effective in promoting change.

The nature of the topic itself has significant implications for selecting an instructional approach as well. Some topics may be more inherently interesting than others (Schiefele, 1998). Some topics bring naïve frameworks more to the fore than others. Further, there are topics that present greater challenges for conceptual change due to the level of controversy engendered by the topic itself (Kardash & Scholes, 1996).

The classroom climate may need to be changed as well if deeply held conceptions and beliefs are to be broached pedagogically. For example, the evaluation and reward structure may need to be changed from a focus on performance goals toward promoting a mastery goal orientation. Structures and systems must be in place allowing students to feel safe to discuss alternative points of view without fear of social or academic consequences. Ultimately, students must feel unthreatened by expressing their own opinions and free to form appropriate arguments against their peers', teachers', or textbooks' espoused views.

Finally, according to Alexander's Model of Domain Learning (Alexander, Jetton, & Kulikowich, 1995), students need to move away from the acclimation stage, where they are taking their initial forays into learning about a domain, and move toward the proficiency stage where they are developing expertise before they have sufficient knowledge with which to reason (Sinatra & Chinn, 2011). Sufficient content knowledge is necessary to reason and think critically about their views and epistemic conceptual change may be prompted by content knowledge development (Sinatra & Chinn, 2011).

IMPLICATIONS FOR THEORIES OF CONCEPTUAL CHANGE

We have tried to paint a picture of the conceptual change process as complex, interactive, and at once cognitive, affective, and social. Key to understanding this multifaceted view is an examination of the role learner characteristics play in the interaction. We believe that theories and models of conceptual change learning must account for the complexity of the process. Models that are strictly cognitive or strictly social will not ultimately succeed in explaining the complexity of learning that is conceptual change.

Different theoretical perspectives on conceptual change can each be viewed as offering explanations of change at various levels of awareness, stages of development, or points along the individual-to-social continuum. A view of conceptual change as multifaceted affords an opportunity to bridge the gap between what are often seen as competing explanations of the change process. Different perspectives broaden our understanding of the nature of change itself and how knowledge restructuring can be facilitated. Ultimately, conceptual change theories and models that embrace the complexity inherent in the knowledge restructuring process will have profound implications for all forms of learning.

REFERENCES

Ainley, M., Hidi, S., & Berndorff, D. (2002). Interest, learning, and the psychological processes that mediate their relationship. *Journal of Educational Psychology, 94*, 545–561.

Alexander, P. A. (1997). Mapping the multidimensional nature of domain learning: The interplay of cognitive, motivational, and strategic forces. In M. L. Maehr & P. R. Pintrich (Eds.), *Advances in motivation and achievement* (Vol. 10, pp. 213–250). Greenwich, CT: JAI Press.

Alexander, P. A. (1998). The nature of disciplinary and domain learning: The knowledge, interest, and strategic dimensions of learning from subject-matter text. In C. Hynd (Ed.), *Learning from text across conceptual domains* (pp. 263–287). Mahwah, NJ: Lawrence Erlbaum Associates.

Alexander, P. A., Jetton, T. L., & Kulikowich, J. M. (1995). Interrelationship of knowledge, interest, and recall: Assessing a model of domain learning. *Journal of Educational Psychology, 87*(4), 599–575.

Alexander, P. A., & Murphy, P. K. (1998). Profiling the differences in students' knowledge, interest, and strategic processing. *Journal of Educational Psychology, 90*, 435–447.

Andre, T., & Windschitl, M. (2003). Interest, epistemological belief, and intentional conceptual change. In G. M. Sinatra & P. R. Pintrich (Eds.), *Intentional conceptual change* (pp. 173–193). Mahwah, NJ: Lawrence Erlbaum Associates.

Bandura, A. (1986). *Social foundation of thought and action: A social cognitive theory*. Englewood Cliffs, NJ: Prentice Hall.

Bargh, J. A., & Chartrand, T. L. (1999). The unbearable automaticity of being. *American Psychologist, 54*(7), 462–479.

Boscolo P., & Mason, L. (2003). Prior knowledge, text coherence, and interest: How they interact in learning from instructional texts. *Journal of Experimental Education, 71*, 126–148.

Broughton, S. H., Pekrun, R., & Sinatra, G. M. (2012). *Climate change, genetically modified foods, airport body scanners: Investigating students' emotions related to science topics*. Paper presented at the annual meeting of the American Educational Research Association, Vancouver, Canada.

Broughton, S. H., Sinatra, G. M., & Nussbaum, E. M. (2011). "Pluto has been a planet my whole life!" Emotions, attitudes, and conceptual change in elementary students learning about Pluto's reclassification. *Research in Science Education*. Advance online publication.

Cacioppo, J. T., Petty, R. E., Feinstein, J., & Jarvis, W. (1996). Dispositional differences in cognitive motivation: The life and times of individuals varying in need for cognition. *Psychological Bulletin, 119*, 197–253.

Carey, S. (1985). *Conceptual change in childhood*. Cambridge, MA: MIT Press.

Chi, M. T. H. (1992). Conceptual change within and across ontological categories: Examples from learning and discovery in science. In R. N. Giere (Ed.), *Cognitive models of science: Minnesota studies in the philosophy of science* (Vol. XV, pp. 129–160). Minneapolis, MN: University of Minnesota Press.

Chinn, C. A., & Brewer, W. F. (1993). The role of anomalous data in knowledge acquisition: A theoretical framework and implications for science instruction. *Review of Educational Research, 63*(10), 1–49.

Clough, E. E., & Driver, R. (1985). Secondary students' conceptions of the conduct of heat: Bringing together scientific and personal views. *Physics Education, 20*, 176–182.

Cordova, J. R., Sinatra, G. M., Broughton, S. H., & Taasoobshirazi, G. (2011, April). *Self-efficacy, confidence in prior knowledge, and conceptual change*. Paper presented at the annual meeting of the American Educational Research Association. New Orleans, LA.

Dole, J. A., & Sinatra, G. M. (1998). Reconceptualizing change in the cognitive construction of knowledge. *Educational Psychologist, 33*(2/3), 109–128.

Eccles, J. S. (2005). Subjective task value and the Eccles et al. model of achievement-related choices. In A. J. Elliot & C. S. Dweck (Eds.), *Handbook of competence and motivation* (pp. 105–121). New York: Guilford Press.

Eccles, J. S., & Wigfield, A. (2002). Motivational beliefs, values, and goals. *Annual Review of Psychology, 53*, 109–132.

Elliot, A. J. (1999). Approach and avoidance motivation and achievement goals. *Educational Psychologist, 34*(3), 169–189.

Elliot, A. J. (2005). A conceptual history of the achievement goal construct. In A. J. Elliot & C. S. Dweck (Eds.), *Handbook of competence and motivation* (pp. 52–72). New York, NY: Guilford Press.

Elliot, A. J., & Harackiewicz, J. M. (1996). Approach and avoidance achievement goals and intrinsic motivation: A mediational analysis. *Journal of Personality and Social Psychology, 70*, 968–989.

Elliot, A. J., & McGregor, H. A. (2001). A 2 × 2 achievement goal framework. *Journal of Personality and Social Psychology, 80*(4), 501–519.

Elliot, A. J., McGregor, H. A., & Gables, S. (1999). Achievement goals, study strategies, and exam performance: A mediational analysis. *Journal of Educational Psychology, 91*, 549–563.

Elliott, E. S., & Dweck, C. S. (1988). Goals: An approach to motivation and achievement. *Journal of Personality and Social Psychology, 54*, 5–12.

Franco G. M., Muis, K. R., Kendeou, P., Ranellucci, J., Sampasivam, L., & Wang, X. (2012). Examining the influences of epistemic beliefs and knowledge representations on cognitive processing and conceptual change when learning physics. *Learning and Instruction, 22*(1), 62–77.

Graham, S., & Golan, S. (1991). Motivational influences on cognition: Task involvement, ego involvement, and depth of processing. *Journal of Educational Psychology, 83*, 187–194.

Gregoire, M. (2003). Is it a challenge or a threat? A dual-process model of teachers' cognition and appraisal processes during conceptual change. *Educational Psychology Review, 15*, 147–179.

Hackett, G. (1995). Self-efficacy in career choice and development. In A. Bandura (Ed.), *Self-efficacy in changing societies* (pp. 232–258). New York, NY: Cambridge University Press.

Hammer, D. (1994). Epistemological beliefs in introductory physics. *Cognition and Instruction, 12*, 151–183.

Heddy, B., & Sinatra, G. M. (2012). *Transforming experiences and biological evolution: Facilitating deep engagement.* Paper presented at the annual meeting of the International Conference of the Learning Sciences, Sydney, Australia.

Hestenes, D., Wells, M., & Swackhamer, G. (1992). Force concept inventory. *The Physics Teacher, 30*, 141–158.

Hidi, S. (2000). An interest researcher's perspective: The effects of intrinsic and extrinsic factors on motivation. In C. Sansone & J. M. Harackiewicz (Eds.), *Intrinsic and extrinsic motivation* (pp. 309–339). San Diego, CA: Academic Press.

Hidi, S., & Baird, W. (1986). Interestingness – A neglected variable in discourse processing. *Cognitive Science, 10*, 179–194.

Hofer, B. K., & Pintrich, P. R. (1997). The development of epistemological theories: Beliefs about knowledge and knowing and their relation to learning. *Review of Educational Research, 67*(1), 88–140.

Johnson, M. L., & Sinatra, G. M. (2012). Use of task-value instructional inductions for facilitating engagement and conceptual change. *Contemporary Educational Psychology, 30*, 51–63.

Jost, J. T., Glaser, J., Kruglanski, A. W., & Sulloway, F. J. (2003). Political conservatism as motivated social cognition. *Psychological Bulletin, 129*, 339–375.

Jovchelovitch, S. (2007). *Knowledge in context.* Cambridge, UK: Cambridge University Press.

Kardash, C. M., & Scholes, R. J. (1996). Effects of preexisting beliefs, epistemological beliefs, and need for cognition on interpretation of controversial issues. *Journal of Educational Psychology, 88*(2), 260–271.

Kolodner, J. L., Camp, P. J., Crismond, D., Fasse, B., Gray, J., Holbrook, J., et al. (2003). Problem-based learning meets case-based reasoning in the middle-school science classroom: Putting learning by design-super (TM) into practice. *Journal of the Learning Sciences, 12*, 495–547.

Kruglanski, A. W. (1989). *Lay epistemics and human knowledge: Cognitive and motivational bases.* New York, NY: Plenum.

Kruglanski, A. W. (1990). Lay epistemic theory in social-cognitive psychology. *Psychological Inquiry, 1*(3), 181–197.

Kruglanski, A. W., & Webster, D. M. (1996). Motivated closing of the mind: "Seizing" and "freezing". In E. T. Higgins & A. W. Kruglanski (Eds.), *Motivational science: Social and personality perspectives.* New York, NY: Psychology Press.

Kuhn, D., Cheney, R., & Weinstock, M. (2000). The development of epistemological understanding. *Cognitive Development, 15*, 309–328.

Linnenbrink-Garcia, L., Pugh, K. J., Koskey, K. L. K., & Stewart, V. C. (2012). Developing conceptual understanding of natural selection: The role of interest, efficacy, and basic prior knowledge. *Journal of Experimental Education, 80*(1), 45–68.

Linnenbrink, E. A., & Pintrich, P. R. (2002). The role of motivational beliefs in conceptual change. In M. Limón & L. Mason (Eds.), *Reconsidering conceptual change: Issues in theory and practice* (pp. 115–135). Dordrecht, The Netherlands: Kluwer Academic Publishers.

Linnenbrink, E. A., & Pintrich, P. R. (2003). Achievement goals and intentional conceptual change. In. G. M. Sinatra & P. R. Pintrich (Eds.). *Intentional conceptual change* (pp. 347–374). Mahwah, NJ: Lawrence Erlbaum Associates.

Linnenbrink, E. A., & Pintrich, P. R. (2004). Role of affect in cognitive processing in academic contexts. In D. Y. Dai & R. J. Sternberg (Eds), *Motivation, emotion, and cognition* (pp. 57–88). Mahwah, NJ: Lawrence Erlbaum Associates.

Mason, L. (2000). Role of anomalous data and epistemological beliefs in middle students' theory change on two controversial topics. *European Journal of Psychology of Education, 15*, 329–346.

Mason, L. (2003). Personal epistemologies and intentional conceptual change. In G. M. Sinatra & P. R. Pintrich (Eds.), *Intentional conceptual change* (pp. 199–236). Mahwah, NJ: Lawrence Erlbaum Associates.

Mason, L., Boldrin, A., & Vanzetta, A. (2006). *Epistemological beliefs and achievement goals in conceptual change learning.* Paper presented at the 4th Symposium of the SIG "Metacognition" of the European Association for Research on Learning and Instruction, Stockholm, Sweden.

Mason, L., & Boscolo, P. (2004). Role of epistemological understanding and interest in interpreting a controversy and in topic-specific belief change, *Contemporary Educational Psychology, 29*(2), 103–128.

Mason, L., Boscolo, P., Tornatora, M. C., & Ronconi, L. (2013). Besides knowledge: A cross-sectional study on the relations between epistemic beliefs, achievement goals, self-beliefs, and achievement in science. *Instructional Science, 41*(1), 49–79.

Mason, L., & Gava, M. (2007). Effects of epistemological beliefs and learning text structure on conceptual change. In S. Vosniadou, A. Baltas, & X. Vamvakoussi (Eds.), *Re-framing the problem of conceptual change in learning and instruction* (pp. 165–196). Oxford, UK: Elsevier Science.

Mason, L., Gava, M., & Boldrin, A. (2008). On warm conceptual change: The interplay of text, epistemological beliefs, and topic interest. *Journal of Educational Psychology, 100*(2), 291–309.

Murphy, P. K. (2001). Teaching as persuasion: A new metaphor for a new decade. *Theory into Practice, 40*(4), 224–227.

Murphy, P. K., & Alexander, P. A. (2004). Persuasion as a dynamic, multidimensional process: A view of individual and intraindividual differences. *American Educational Research Journal, 41,* 337–363.

Murphy, P. K., & Mason, L. (2006). Changing knowledge and beliefs. In P. A. Alexander & P. H. Winne (Eds.), *Handbook of educational psychology* (pp. 305–324). Mahwah, NJ: Lawrence Erlbaum Associates.

Nolen, S. B. (1988). Reasons for studying: Motivational orientations and study strategies. *Cognition and Instruction, 5,* 269–287.

Nussbaum, E. M., & Sinatra, G. M. (2003). Argument and conceptual engagement. *Contemporary Educational Psychology, 28,* 384–395.

Nussbaum, E. M., Sinatra, G. M., & Poliquin, A. (2008). The role of epistemological beliefs and scientific argumentation in promoting conceptual change. *International Journal of Science Education, 30*(15), 1977–1999.

Pajares, F. (2003). Self-efficacy beliefs, motivation, and achievement in writing: A review of the litearature. *Reading and Writing Quarterly, 19,* 139–158.

Pajares, F., Britner, S. L., & Valiante, G. (2000). Writing and science achievement goals in middle school students. *Contemporary Educational Psychology, 25,* 406–422.

Pajares, F., & Miller, M. D. (1994). The role of self-efficacy and self-concept beliefs in mathematical problem-solving: A path analysis. *Journal of Educational Psychology, 86,* 193–203.

Pekrun, R., Goetz, T., Titz, W., & Perry, R. P. (2002). Academic emotions in students' self-regulated learning and achievement: A program of qualitative and quantitative research. *Educational Psychologist, 37,* 91–105.

Pintrich, P. R. (1999). Motivational beliefs as resources for and constraints on conceptual change. In W. Schnotz, S. Vosniadou, & M. Carretero (Eds.), *New perspectives on conceptual change* (pp. 33–50). Amsterdam, The Netherlands: Pergamon.

Pintrich, P. R. (2000). The role of goal orientation in self-regulation learning. In M. Boekaerts, P. R. Pintrich, & M. Zeidner (Eds.), *Handbook of self-regulation: Theory, research and applications* (pp. 451–502). San Diego, CA: Academic Press.

Pintrich, P. R., Marx, R. W., & Boyle, R. B. (1993). Beyond cold conceptual change: The role of motivational beliefs and classroom contextual factors in the process of conceptual change. *Review of Educational Research, 63,* 167–199.

Pintrich, P. R., & Schrauben, B. (1992). Students' motivational beliefs and their cognitive engagement in classroom academic tasks. In D. Schunk & J. Meese (Eds.), *Student perceptions in the classroom* (pp. 149–183). Hillsdale, NJ: Lawrence Erlbaum Associates.

Posner, G. J., Strike, K. A., Hewson, P. W., & Gertzog, W. A. (1982). Accommodation of a scientific conception: Towards a theory of conceptual change. *Science Education, 67*(4), 489–508.

Pugh, K. J. (2002). Teaching for transformative experiences in science: An investigation of the effectiveness of two instructional elements. *Teachers College Record, 104,* 1101–1137.

Pugh, K. J. (2011). Transformative experience: An integrative construct in the spirit of Deweyan pragmatism. *Educational Psychologist, 46,* 107–121.

Qian, G., & Alvermann, D. (1995). Role of epistemological beliefs and learned helplessness in secondary school students' learning science concepts from text. *Journal of Educational Psychology, 87,* 282–292.

Qian, G., & Alvermann, D. (2000). Relationship between epistemological beliefs and conceptual change learning. *Reading and Writing Quarterly, 16,* 59–74.

Qian, G., & Pan, J. (2002). A comparison of epistemological beliefs and learning from science text between American and Chinese high school students. In B. K. Hofer & P. R. Pintrich (Eds.), *Personal epistemology: The psychology of beliefs about knowledge and knowing* (pp. 365–385). Mahwah, NJ: Lawrence Erlbaum Associates.

Renninger, K. A. (1992). Individual interest and development: Implications for theory and practice. In K. A. Renninger, S. Hidi, & A. Krapp (Ed.), *The role of interest in learning and development* (pp. 361–395). Hillsdale, NJ: Lawrence Erlbaum Associates.

Renninger, K. A., Hidi, S., & Krapp, A. (Eds.) (1992). The role of interest in learning and development. Hillsdale, NJ: Lawrence Erlbaum Associates.

Schiefele, U. (1998). Individual interest and learning: What we know and what we don't know. In L. Hoffmann, A. Krapp, K. A. Renninger, & J. Baumert (Eds.) *Interest and learning* (pp. 91–104). Kiel, Germany: IPN.

Schiefele, U., & Krapp, A. (1996). Topic interest and free recall of expository text. *Learning and Individual Differences, 8,* 141–160.

Schiefele, U., & Rheinberg, F. (1997). Motivation and knowledge acquisition: Searching for mediating processes. In M. L. Maehr & P. R. Pintrich (Eds.), *Advances in motivation and achievement* (Vol. 10, pp. 251–301). Oxford, UK: Elsevier Science.

Schraw, G., & Lehman, S. (2001). Situational interest: A review of the literature and directions for future research. *Educational Psychology Review, 13*(1), 23–52.

Schunk, D. H. (2003). Self-efficacy for reading and writing: Influence of modeling, goal setting, and self-evaluation. *Reading and Writing Quarterly: Overcoming Learning Difficulties, 19,* 159–172.

Schunk, D. H., & Pajares, F. (2005). Competence perception and academic functioning. In A. J. Elliot & C. S. Dweck (Eds.), *Handbook of competence and motivation* (pp. 85–104). New York, NY: Guilford Press.

Senko, C., Hulleman, C. S., & Harackiewicz, J. M. (2011). Achievement goal theory at the crossroads: Old controversies, current challenges, and new directions. *Educational Psychologist, 46*(1), 26–47.

Shell, D., Colvin, C., & Bruning, R. (1995). Self-efficacy, attribution, and outcome expectancy mechanisms in reading and writing achievement: Grade-level and achievement-level differences. *Journal of Educational Psychology, 87,* 386–398.

Sinatra, G. M. (2005). The "warming trend" in conceptual change reserach: The legacy of Paul R. Pintrich. *Educational Psychologist, 40*(2), 107–115.

Sinatra, G. M., Broughton, S. H., Lombardi, D. (in press). Emotions in science education. In R. Pekrun & L. Linnenbrink-Garcia (Eds.) *Handbook of Emotions and Education.*

Sinatra, G. M., & Chinn, C. (2011). Thinking and reasoning in science: Promoting epistemic conceptual change. In K. Harris, C. B. McCormick, G. M. Sinatra, & J. Sweller (Eds.), *Critical theories and models of learning and development relevant to learning and teaching* (Vol. 1, pp. 257–282). Washington, DC: APA Publications.

Sinatra, G. M., & Kardash, C. M. (2004). Teacher candidates' epistemological beliefs, dispositions, and views on teaching as persuasion. *Contemporary Educational Psychology, 29,* 483–498.

Sinatra, G. M., & Pintrich, P. R. (Eds.). (2003). *Intentional conceptual change.* Mahwah, NJ: Lawrence Erlbaum Associates.

Sinatra, G. M. & Taasoobshirazi, G. (2011). Intentional conceptual change: The self-regulation of science learning (pp. 203–216). In B. Zimmerman & D. Shunk (Eds.), *Handbook of self-regulation of learning and performance.* New York, NY: Routledge.

Sinatra, G. M. & Southerland, S. A. (2011). *A little knowledge is a dangerous thing: Using beliefs and dispositions to make judgments about the validity of scientific theories.* Unpublished manuscript.

Sinatra, G. M., Southerland, S. A., McConaughy, F., & Demastes, J. (2003). Intentions and beliefs in students' understanding and acceptance of biological evolution. *Journal of Research in Science Teaching, 40*(5), 510–528.

Spelke, E. (1991). Physical knowledge in infancy: Reflections on Piaget's theory. In S. Carey & R. Gelman (Eds.), *Epigenesis of mind* (pp. 133–170). Hillsdale, NJ: Lawrence Erlbaum Associates.

Stanovich, K. E. (1999). *Who is rational? Studies of individual differences in reasoning.* Mahwah, NJ: Lawrence Erlbaum Associates.

Strike, K. A., & Posner, G. J. (1992). A revisionist theory of conceptual change. In R. A. Duschl & R. J. Hamilton (Eds.), *Philosophy of science, cognitive psychology, and educational theory and practice* (pp. 147–176). Albany, NY: State University of New York Press.

Stathopoulou, C., & Vosniadou, S. (2007). Exploring the relationship between physics-related epistemological beliefs and physics understanding. *Contemporary Educational Psychology, 32,* 255–281.

Taasoobshirazi, G., & Sinatra, G. M. (2011). A structural equation model of conceptual change in physics. *Journal of Research on Science Teaching, 48*(8), 901–918.

Venville, G. J., & Treagust, D. F. (1998). Exploring conceptual change in genetics using a multidimensional interpretive framework. *Journal of Research in Science Teaching, 35*, 1031–1055.

Vosniadou, S., & Brewer, W. F. (1987). Theories of knowledge restructuring in development. *Review of Educational Research, 57*, 51–67.

Vosniadou, S., & Brewer, W. F. (1992). Mental models of the earth: A study of conceptual change in childhood. *Cognitive Psychology, 24*, 535–585.

Vosniadou, S., & Brewer, W. F. (1994). Mental models of the day/night cycle. *Cognitive Science, 18*, 123–183.

West, L. H. T., & Pines, A. L. (1985). *Cognitive structure and conceptual change.* Orlando, FL: Academic Press.

Windschitl, M., & Andre, T. (1998). Using computer simulations to enhance conceptual change: The roles of constructivist instruction and student epistemological beliefs. *Journal of Research in Science Teaching, 35*(2), 145–160.

Wolters, C. A., Yu, S. L., & Pintrich, P. R. (1996). The relation between goal orientation and students' motivational beliefs and self-regulated learning. *Learning and Individual Differences, 8*, 211–238.

Zimmerman, B. J., & Martinez-Pons, M. (1990). Student differences in self-regulated learning: Relating grade, sex, and giftedness to self-efficacy and strategy use. *Journal of Educational Psychology, 82*, 51–59.

21

MENTAL MODELING IN CONCEPTUAL CHANGE

Nancy J. Nersessian, Georgia Institute of Technology

The nature and processes of "conceptual change" are problems that are of considerable interest to researchers across several disciplines occupied with developing understandings of science, learners, or cognitive development. Although the problems and methods to address them have different formulations in these areas, there is a long history in each of specifying the beginning and ending states of deep conceptual changes, such as what constitutes the nature of representational changes from Newtonian mechanics to the theory of relativity, or from a "naïve" understanding of physical phenomena to a scientific understanding provided by physics or biology, or from individual early (possibly innate) representational structures to adult community representations of a wide range of phenomena, including of other humans, during processes of cognitive development.

A major outstanding problem in all of these areas is the nature of the processes – or "mechanisms" – through which concepts and conceptual structures change. In part because of similarities in features of conceptual changes across these areas, such as ontological shifts and degrees of "incommensurability," some, myself included, have proposed that the same or related processes are at work in the several kinds of conceptual change. Clearly one would expect differences between, for example, the practices used by scientists in constructing new concepts and students learning new (for them) concepts. For one thing scientists have articulated theoretical goals and sophisticated metacognitive strategies while children and students do not. However, in conceptual change processes, a significant parallel is that each involves problem solving. One way to think of learning science, for instance, is that students are engaged in (or need to be enticed into) trying to understand the extant scientific conceptualization of a domain. In this process, learning happens when they perceive the inadequacies of their intuitive understandings – at least under certain conditions – and construct representations of the scientific concepts for themselves. The impetus for a problem solving process can arise from many sources: acquiring new information, encountering a puzzling phenomenon, or perceiving an inadequacy in current ways of understanding.

Concepts provide a means through which humans make sense of the world. In categorizing experiences we sort phenomena, noting relationships, differences, and interconnections among them. A conceptual structure is a way of systematizing, of putting concepts in relation to one another in at least a semi-coherent – or locally coherent – manner. But a conceptual structure is complex and intricate and it is not possible to entertain it in its entirety all at once. Trying to understand new experiences or how a concept relates to others can reveal heretofore unnoticed limitations and problems in the representational capabilities of current conceptual structures and even reveal inconsistencies with other parts. Although how reflectively they engage in the process differs, scientists, learners, and developing children all engage in this kind of sense-making which suggests that to a greater or lesser extent conceptual change is a reasoned "change in view" (Harman, 1986).

Thinking of conceptual change in this way focuses attention on the nature of the reasoning scientists use in solving representational problems. Creating models as systems of inquiry is central in the problem solving practices of scientists. There is a large literature in history and philosophy of science that establishes that processes of constructing and manipulating analogical, visual, and simulative models play a central role in episodes of conceptual change across the sciences. On the account of conceptual change in science I have been developing, reasoning through such models ("model-based reasoning") provides a significant means (not necessarily the *only* means) through which conceptual innovation and change occur (see, e.g., Nersessian, 1992a, 1992b, 1995, 1999, 2002b, 2008). Susan Carey (2009) has made a similar claim for conceptual change in cognitive development. Within both philosophy and cognitive science the traditional view of reasoning is identified with logical operations performed on language-like representations. In contrast to these traditional conceptions, these modeling practices of scientists are not simply aids to logical reasoning but constitute a distinct form of reasoning. Loosely construed, a model is a representation of a system with interactive parts with representations of those interactions. Models are representations of objects, processes, or events that capture structural, behavioral, or functional relations significant to understanding these interactions. What is required for something to be an instance of model-based reasoning is that: (1) it involves the construction or retrieval of a model; (2) inferences are derived through manipulation of the model; and (3) inferences can be specific or generic; that is, they can apply either to the particular model or to the model understood as a model-type, representing a class of models.

To understand how model-based reasoning leads to conceptual change requires detailed investigations both of cases of its use in conceptual change and of its basis in human cognition. This requirement stems from a "naturalist" epistemology which holds that the problem-solving practices of scientists arise out of and are constrained by basic cognitive capacities exhibited also in mundane problem solving, though of course not from these alone. The normally functioning human cognitive apparatus is capable of mental modeling, analogy making, abstraction, visualization, and simulative imagining. The sciences, through individual and collective efforts, have bootstrapped their way from these basic capabilities to the current state of play through consciously reflective develop-ment of methods of investigation aimed at gaining specific kinds of understanding and insight into nature, such as quantitative understanding. Of course, the development of these methods has been and continues to be a complex interaction among humans and the natural and sociocultural worlds in which they are embedded. Nevertheless, an important part of explaining how these investigative strategies fulfill their objectives requires examining the nature of mundane cognitive capabilities out of which they arise.

In this chapter I will focus on one capacity, that for mental modeling, in part because analogy, visualization, and simulation contribute to reasoning through mental modeling and in part because mental modeling is a central notion used in analyses of conceptual change across the literatures of studies of science, learning, and cognitive development. For an intuitive understanding of what it means to solve a problem through mental modeling, consider the situation where a large sofa needs to be moved through a door-way. The default approach to solving the problem is usually to imagine moving a mental token approximating the shape of the sofa through various rotations constrained by the boundaries of a doorway-like shape. In solving this problem people do not customarily resort to formulating a series of propositions and applying logic or to doing trigono-metric calculations. Note, too, that arriving at a problem solution is easier if it takes place in front of the doorway and the sofa, as opposed to in a furniture store and thinking about whether it is wise to purchase the sofa. In such mundane cases the reasoning performed via mental modeling is usually successful; i.e., one figures out how to get the chair through the door, because the models and manipulative processes embody largely correct assumptions about everyday real-world phenomena. In scientific problem solving, where the situations are more removed from human sensory experience and the assumptions more imbued with theory, there is less assurance that a mental modeling process will be successful. More sophisticated and explicit knowledge of constraints relating to general principles of the science and mathematical equations will play a role in constructing and manipulating the mental models.

There are four points to highlight from the mundane case that carry across in considering the case of science: (1) Humans appear able to create representations from memory that enable them to imagine being in situations purely through mental simulation; (2) the imagining processes can take advantage of affordances in the environ-ment that can make problem solving easier; (3) the predictions, and other kinds of solutions arrived at through this kind of mental simulation are often correct –or good enough – in mundane cases; and (4) when solution fails, a wide range of culturally available tools can be used, such as getting out the measuring tape and making the calculation.

Having wrestled with a considerable portion of the cognitive science literature on mental models, I have to concur with Lance Rips' observation that much use of the notion appears "muddled" (Rips, 1986), but I disagree with his conclusion that dismisses the viability of the notion entirely. A potentially quite powerful notion can be articulated and could provide a much-needed unifying framework for the study of cognition. My objective here is modest: to provide a much-needed clarification of reasoning through mental modeling; one that is consistent with the cognitive science research on mundane cases and is adequate as a cognitive basis for model-based reasoning in conceptual change, which can then be investigated further in cognitive science.

Thinking about the scientific uses has led me to extend the investigation into mental modeling to include also research on imaginative simulation in mental imagery, mental animation, and perception-based representation. Further, within traditional cognitive science, the representations and processing involved in reasoning are held to take place "in the head," and reasoning is analyzed as detached from the material environments in which it occurs. Although it is possible that simple model-based reasoning might take place only "in the head," reasoning of the complexity of that in science makes extensive use of external representations. A wide range of data establishes that many kinds of external representations are used during scientific reasoning: linguistic (descriptions, narratives, written and verbal communications), mathematical equations, visual representations, gestures, physical models, and computational models. Thus even an analysis of *mental* modeling needs to consider the relations among the internal and external representations and processes in problem solving. So, I also consider the question of what might be the nature of the mental representation used in mental modeling such as to enable that internal and external representational coupling during reasoning processes.

THE MENTAL MODELS FRAMEWORK

The notion of a "mental model" is central to much of contemporary cognitive science. In 1943, the psychologist and physiologist Kenneth Craik hypothesized that in many instances people reason by carrying out thought experiments on internal models of physical situations, where a model is a structural, behavioral, or functional analog to a real-world phenomenon (Craik, 1943). Craik based his hypothesis on the predictive power of thought and the ability of humans to explore real-world and imaginary situations mentally. We will return to Craik's own view in a later section, after first considering its contemporary legacy. Craik made this proposal at the height of the behaviorist approach in psychology, and so it received little notice. The development of a "cognitive" psychology in the 1960s created a more hospitable environment for investigating and articulating the hypothesis. A new edition of Craik's book with a postscript replying to critics in 1967 fell on more fertile ground and has since had considerable impact on contemporary cognitive science. Since the early 1980s a "mental models framework" has developed in a large segment of cognitive science. This is an explanatory framework that posits models as organized units of mental representation of knowledge employed in various cognitive tasks including reasoning, problem solving, and discourse comprehension.

What is a "mental model"? How is it represented? What kinds of processing underlie its use? What are the mental mechanisms that create and use mental models? How does mental modeling engage external representations and processes? These issues are not often addressed explicitly in the literature and where they are, there is as yet no consensus position that might serve as a theory of mental models. Thus, I have chosen the word "framework" to characterize a wide range of research. What the positions within this framework share is a general hypothesis that some mental representations of domain knowledge are organized structures containing knowledge of spatio-temporal structure, causal connections, or other relational structures.

In the early 1980s several largely independent strands of research emerged introducing the theoretical notions of "mental model" and "mental modeling" into the cognitive science literature. One strand introduced the notion to explain the effects of semantic information in logical reasoning (Johnson-Laird, 1983). Another strand introduced the notion to explain the empirical findings that in reasoning related to discourse comprehension, people seem to reason from a representation of the structure of a situation rather than from a description of a situation (so-called "discourse" and "situation" models, see Johnson-Laird, 1982; Perrig & Kintsch, 1985). Both of these strands focused on the nature of the representations constructed in working memory during reasoning and problem-solving tasks. Yet another strand introduced the notion in relation to long-term memory representations of knowledge used in understanding and reasoning, in particular, about physical systems. This literature posited the notion to explain a wide range of experimental results indicating that people use organized knowledge structures relating to physical systems in attempting to understand manual control systems and devices in the area of human – machine interactions (see Rouse & Morris, 1986, for an overview) and in employing qualitative domain knowledge of physical systems to solve problems (Gentner & Stevens, 1983). Some of the early work relating to physical systems that began with psychological studies migrated into AI where computational theories of "naive" or "qualitative" physics in particular were developed to explore issues of knowledge organization, use, access and control, such as in understanding and predicting the behavior of liquids (Hayes, 1979) or the motion of a ball in space and time (Forbus, 1983). Much of the pioneering research in third strand is represented in the edited collection, *Mental Models* (Gentner & Stevens 1983) that appeared in the same year as Johnson-Laird's (1983) monograph of the same name which brought together the working memory strands.

Research within the mental models framework is extensive and varied. As an indication of the range, research includes: AI models of qualitative reasoning about causality in physical systems (see, e.g., Bobrow, 1985), representations of intuitive domain knowledge in various areas, such as physics and astronomy (see, e.g., Vosniadou & Brewer, 1992), analogical problem solving (see, e.g., Gentner & Stevens 1983), deductive and inductive reasoning (see, e.g., Holland, Holyoak, Nisbett, & Thagard, 1986; Johnson-Laird & Byrne, 1993), probabilistic inference (Kahneman & Tversky, 1982), "heterogeneous" or "multimodal" reasoning (Allwein & Barwise, 1996), modal logic (Bell & Johnson-Laird, 1998), narrative and discourse comprehension (see, e.g., Johnson-Laird, 1982; Perrig & Kintsch, 1985), scientific thought experimenting (Nersessian, 1991, 1992c), and cultural transmission (Shore, 1997). However, a consensus view has not developed among these areas of research. The preponderance of research into mental models has been concerned with specifying the content and structure of long-term memory models in a specific domain or with respect to specific reasoning tasks or levels of expertise, and not with addressing the more foundational questions raised above.

Given that my focus is on mental modeling during reasoning processes, I consider here only psychological accounts that hypothesize reasoning as involving the construction and manipulation of a model in working memory during the reasoning process and not the accounts of the nature of representation in long-term memory, about which my account can remain agnostic. Working memory accounts of mental modeling include those concerned with reasoning and with narrative and discourse comprehension. The literatures on imaginative simulation in mental imagery, mental animation, and perception-based representation also provide insights relevant to developing an account of mental modeling. My strategy is to briefly survey the accounts in the literatures noted, then to propose a synthesis of the several threads in the research to address simulative model-based reasoning as practiced by scientists, and finally to return to the implications of all this for conceptual change.

"CRAIKIAN" MENTAL MODELING

The most influential account of mental modeling is that of Johnson-Laird. On this account, a mental model is an iconic representation that is a structural, behavioral, or functional analog of a real-world or imaginary situation, event, object, or process.

Johnson-Laird roots his view in the earlier proposal of Craik; however, his focus has been on mental modeling in the domains of deductive, inductive, and modal logics. This, coupled with his wanting to distinguish mental models from what is customarily understood as mental imagery, has led him to underplay and not develop a central insight of Craik: reasoning about physical systems via mental simulation of analog representations. To account for simulative reasoning about physical systems, and model-based reasoning in science in particular, requires more kinds of model manipulation than logical reasoning. Tacit and explicit domain knowledge of the physical system, such as causal knowledge, is needed in constructing models and creating new states and inferring outcomes via simulation.

The original Craikian notion emphasized the *parallelism* both in form and in operation in internal modeling: "By "relation-structure" I do not mean some obscure non-physical entity which attends the model, but the fact that it is a physical working model which works in the same way as the process it parallels, in the aspects under consideration at any moment" (Craik, 1943, p. 51). By this I interpret him to mean that the internal model complies with the constraints of the real-world phenomena it represents, not that it is run like a "movie in the head," which signifies vivid and detailed visual representations "running" in real time. Craik based his hypothesis on the need for organisms to be able to predict the environment, thus he saw mental simulation as central to reasoning. He maintained that just as humans create physical models – for example, physical scale models of boats and bridges – to experiment with alternatives, so too the nervous system of humans and other organisms has developed a way to create internal "'small scale model[s]' of external reality" (p. 61) for simulating potential outcomes of actions in a physical environment. I interpret his use of quotation marks around "small scale model[s]" to indicate that he meant it figuratively, and not that the brain quite literally creates, for example, an image of a small-scale boat whose motion it simulates as in a movie. He does, however, appear to mean that the representations are modal or perception-based. Mental simulation occurs, he claimed, by the "excitation and volley of impulses which parallel the stimuli which occasioned them" (p. 60). Thus the internal processes of reasoning result in conclusions similar to those that "might have been reached by causing the actual physical processes to occur" (p. 51). In constructing the hypothesis Craik drew on existing research in neurophysiology and speculated that the ability "to parallel or model external events" (p. 51) is fundamental to the brain.

Modern advocates of mental modeling also speculate that the capacity developed for simulating possible ways of maneuvering within the physical environment. It would be highly adaptive to possess the ability to anticipate the environment and potential outcomes of actions, so many organisms should have the capacity for mental simulation. Given that humans have linguistic capabilities, it should be possible to create mental models from both perception and description, which is borne out by the research on narrative and discourse comprehension that will be discussed below. Additionally, studies of expert/novice reasoning lend support to the possibility that skill in mental modeling develops in the course of learning (Chi, Feltovich, & Glaser, 1981). The nature and richness of models one can construct and one's ability to reason develops in learning domain-specific content and techniques. Thus, facility with mental modeling is a combination of biology and learning, and develops in interaction with the natural, social, and cultural realities in which one is embedded.

I next bring together research on discourse and situation models, mental imagery, mental animation, and embodied mental representation as providing evidence in support of a Craikian notion of mental modeling.

DISCOURSE AND SITUATION MODELS

Reading, comprehending, and reasoning about stories would seem to epitomize thinking with language. Yet there is a significant body of cognitive research that supports the hypothesis that the inferences subjects make from these activities are derived through constructing and manipulating a mental model of the situation depicted by the narrative, rather than by applying rules of inference to a system of propositions representing the content of the text. A major strategy of this approach is to differentiate the structure of the text from the structure of the situation depicted in the text and investigate which structure cognitive representations follow. Johnson-Laird in psycholinguistics and others in psychology, formal semantics, and linguistics have proposed that cognitive representations in the form of working memory "discourse models" or "situation models" are used in making inferences related to narratives. On this proposal, the linguistic expressions assist the reader/listener in constructing a mental model through which they understand and reason about the situation depicted by the narrative. That is, in reasoning, the referent of the text would be an internal model of the situation depicted by the text rather than a description. The central idea is that "discourse models make explicit the structure not of sentences but of situations as we perceive or imagine them" (Johnson-Laird, 1989, p. 471). The principal tenets of the theory, as outlined by Johnson-Laird, are as follows. As a form of mental model, a discourse model would embody a representation of the spatial, temporal, and causal relationships among the events and entities of the situation described by the narrative. In constructing and updating a model, the reader calls upon a combination of pre-existing conceptual and real-world knowledge and employs the tacit and recursive inferencing mechanisms of her cognitive apparatus to integrate the information with that contained in the narrative. In principle these should be able to generate the set of all possible situations a narrative could describe.

A number of experiments have been conducted to investigate the hypothesis that in understanding narrative, readers spontaneously construct mental models to represent and reason about the situations depicted by the text (van Dijk & Kintsch, 1983; Franklin & Tversky, 1990; Johnson-Laird, 1983; Mani & Johnson-Laird, 1982; McNamara & Sternberg, 1983; Morrow, Bower, & Greenspan, 1989; Perrig & Kintsch, 1985; Zwann, 1999; Zwann & Radvansky, 1998). Although no instructions were given to imagine or picture the situations, when queried about how they had made inferences in response to an experimenter's questioning, most participants reported that it was by means of "seeing" or "being in the situation" depicted. That is, the reader sees herself as an "observer" of a simulated situation. Whether the view of the situation is "spatial," i.e., a global perspective, or "perspectival," i.e., from a specific point of view, is still a point of debate, though recent investigations tend to support the perspectival account; that is, the reference frame of the space appears to be that of the body (Bryant & Tversky, 1999; Glenberg, 1997b; Mainwaring, Tversky, & Schiano, 1996).

The interpretation given these experimental outcomes is that a situation represented by a mental model could allow the reasoner to generate inferences without having to carry out the extensive operations needed to process the same amount of background information to make inferences from an argument in propositional form. The situational constraints of the narrative are built into the model, making many consequences implicit that would require considerable inferential work in propositional form. For example, consider a case where a subject is asked to move an object depicted in a model. Moving an object changes, immediately, its spatial relationships to all the other objects. In mental modeling, the reasoner could grasp this simply by means of the changes in the model and not need to make additional inferences. Such reasoning should be discernibly faster. Thus, the chronometric studies noted above provide additional experimental support that making inferences through simulation is faster than making logical inferences from propositions. Finally, reasoning through a model of a situation should restrict the scope of the conclusions drawn. For example, moving an object in a specified manner both limits and makes immediately evident the relevant consequences of that move for other objects in the situation detailed by the narrative. Further support is thus provided by demonstrations in this literature that it is much more difficult to make inferences – and some are not made at all – when participants are required to reason with the situation represented in propositional form.

MENTAL SPATIAL SIMULATION

There is an extensive literature that provides evidence that humans can perform various simulative transformations in imagination that mimic physical spatial transformations. The literature on mental imagery establishes that people can mentally simulate combinations, such as with the classic example where subjects are asked to imagine a letter B rotated 90 degrees to the left, place an upside triangle below it and remove the connecting line and the process produces an image of a heart. People can perform imaginative rotations that exhibit latencies consistent with actually turning a mental figure around, such as when queried as to whether two objects presented from different rotations are in fact the same object (Finke, 1989; Finke, Pinker, & Farah, 1989; Finke & Shepard, 1986; Kosslyn, 1980, 1994; Shepard & Cooper, 1982; Tye, 1991), and there is a correlation between the time it takes participants to respond and the number of degrees of rotation required. Further, rotational transformations of plane figures and three-dimensional models are evidenced. As Stephen Kosslyn (1994, p. 345) summarizes, psychological research provides evidence of rotating, translating, bending, scaling, folding, zooming, and flipping of images. The combinations and transformations in mental imagery are hypothesized to take place according to internalized constraints assimilated during perception (Shepard, 1988). Kosslyn also notes that these mental transformations are often accompanied by twisting and moving one's hands to represent rotation, which indicates motor as well as visual processing (see also Jeannerod, 1993, 1994; Parsons, 1994). Other research indicates that people combine various kinds of knowledge of physical situations with imaginary transformations, including real-time dynamical information (Freyd, 1987). When given a problem about objects that are separated by a wall, for instance, the spatial transformations exhibit latencies consistent with the participants having simulated moving around the wall rather than through it, which indicates at least tacit use of physical knowledge that objects cannot move through a wall (Morrow et al., 1989). This kind of knowledge is evidenced in other studies, such as those in which participants are shown a picture of a person with an arm in front of the body and then one with the arm in back; they report imagining rotating the arm around the body, rather than through it, and the chronometric measurements are consistent with this (Shiffrar & Freyd, 1990).

MENTAL ANIMATION

There is a growing literature in psychology and neuroscience that investigates the hypothesis that the human cognitive system possesses the ability for *mental animation* in problem solving tasks. This ability would be central in Craikian mental modeling. This kind of simulative model-based reasoning both in mundane thinking and in science is likely to go beyond just making spatial transformations and extend to the kinds of transformations of physical systems requiring causal and other behavioral knowledge.

Recent investigations of physical reasoning have moved beyond spatial and temporal transformations to examining the role of causal and behavioral knowledge in mental simulation. The ability to mentally animate is highly correlated with scores on tests of spatial ability (Hegarty & Sims, 1994). However, as Mary Hegarty, too, stresses, the mental representations underlying animation need not be what are customarily thought of as "mental images." Images are often taken to be vivid and detailed holistic representations, such as in a photograph or in a movie, where simulation would take place all at once. However, the imagery literature supports the notion that imagery most often is largely sketchy and schematic and that animation of an image can be piecemeal, as supported by her research.

Much of this research has its origin in thinking about diagrammatic representations in reasoning; specifically, inferring motion from static representations. It thus provides insights into the relations between internal and external representations that we will follow up on in a later section. One indication of interaction is that participants in these kinds of studies often use gestures, sometimes performed over the diagram, that simulate and track the motion (see, e.g., Clement, 1994, 2003; Goldin-Meadow, Nusbaum, Kelly, & Wagner, 2001; Hegarty & Steinhoff, 1994). Prominent research on mental animation includes Hegarty's (Hegarty, 1992; Hegarty & Ferguson, 1993; Hegarty & Just, 1989) investigations of reasoning about the behavior of pulley systems and Daniel Schwartz's (Schwartz, 1995; Schwartz & Black, 1996a, 1996b) studies focusing on gear rotations. These studies, respectively, provide evidence that people are able to perform simulative causal transformations of static figures if provided with the initial set-up of the pulleys and of the gears. Several findings are important here. Protocols of participants indicate that they do not mentally animate the pulley systems all at once as would appear to happen in the real world experience of it, but animate in segments in the causal sequence, working out in a piecemeal fashion the consequences of previous motion for the next segment. The response time for the participants in the gear problems indicates they, too, are animated in sequence, and when given only one set of gears, participants' response time was proportional to the rate of the angle of rotation. Participants perform better when given more realistic representations of gears than highly schematic ones, such as those of just circles with no cogs. In the realistic case they seem to use physical knowledge, such as friction, directly to animate the model, whereas in the schematic case they revert to more analytic strategies such as comparing the size of the angles that gears of different sizes would move through. Schwartz's research also indicates that mental animation can make use of other non-visual information such as of viscosity and gravity. When participants are well trained in rules for inferring motion, however, they often revert to these to solve the problem more quickly (Schwartz & Black, 1996b). Mental animation, on the other hand, can result in correct inferences in cases where the participant cannot produce a correct description of the animation (Hegarty, 1992). Further, people can judge whether an animation is correct even in cases where the self-produced inference about motion is incorrect (Hegarty, 1992).

Although not much research has been conducted with scientists, what there is indicates that they, too, "run" mental models in problem solving (Clement, 1994; Trafton, Trickett, & Mintz, 2005). As with the gear and pulley studies, that research provides evidence of significant interaction between the internal and external representations in the mental simulation. Though it is some distance from employing causal transformations of rotating gears or pulleys to employing the kinds of transformations requiring knowledge contained in a scientific theory, the mental animation research supports the position that the scientific practices originate in and develop out of mundane imaginative simulation abilities.

INTERNAL–EXTERNAL COUPLING

As noted previously, mental modeling is often carried out in the presence of real-world resources, including representations such as diagrams and objects such as sofas. How might the mental capability interface with relevant resources in the external world? Much of the research on this question is directed toward diagrams and other kinds of visual representations. Research by Jiajie Zhang (Zhang, 1997; Zhang & Norman, 1995), for instance, analyzes diagrams as external representations that are coupled as an information source with the individual solving problems. Recently, Hegarty has argued that the corpus of research on mental animation in the context of visual representations leads to the conclusion that internal and external representations are best seen as forming a "coupled system" (Hegarty, 2004). In considering the relation between mental modeling and external physical models I have argued that we need to conceptualize cognitive capacities as encompassing more than "natural" biological capacities (Nersessian, 2002a, 2008, 2009). "Cognitive capacities" can encompass various kinds of external representations such as text, visual representations, physical models, and computational models.

On the traditional cognitive science view, reasoning uses information abstracted from the external environment and represented internally and processed internally. External displays or various sorts of information in the world might assist working memory by, for example, co-locating information that gets abstracted (Larkin, 1989; Larkin & Simon, 1987), but all cognitive processing is internal to the individual mind. The traditional view is under challenge by several current research strands that reconstrue the notion of representation and processing such that some information remains in the environment and that processing is within the coupled system linking internal and external worlds. A major open problem for the coupled system view is an account of the nature of the cognitive mechanisms through which the internal and external worlds mesh, and this is an empirical question. On one hand, given that some mental simulation can take place in the absence of external stimuli, the mechanisms need to be such as to take stored information and process it in such a way as to allow for the possibility of making at least some of the same inferences as if the real-world stimuli were present. On the other hand, as Daniel Dennett has noted succinctly, "Just as you cannot do very much carpentry with your bare hands, there's not much thinking you can do with your bare mind" (Dennett,

2000, p. 17). Thus, even in the absence of an account of "mechanisms," there has been considerable theorizing over the past 20 years in the direction of how aspects of the environment might enter directly into cognitive processes, rather than simply scaffolding them.

Recasting cognition such that the relationship between the internal and external worlds forms a coupled cognitive–cultural system presents the challenge for cognitive science to determine the mechanisms of representation and processing that would enable this coupling. Part of this problem is to address format and processing issues with respect to the human components of the system. Here Greeno's criteria that the internal representations in mental modeling processes be such that "we interact with them in ways that are similar to our interactions with physical and – probably – social environments" (Greeno, 1989, p. 313) and thus be such that they are "acquired with significant properties of external situations and one's interactions with the situations . . . such that at least some of the properties are known implicitly in something like the way that we know how to interact with [external] environments" (p. 314) echo the earlier views of Craik. Human representations need also to be such that they interface smoothly with other system representations in problem solving processes. One plausible way for the interfacing to be smooth is for human representations to have modal aspects such that perceptual and motor mechanisms would be employed in processing.

Embodied Representation: "Perceptual" Mental Models

What might the format of the representation of a "Craikian" mental model be? Perhaps for logical reasoning it suffices that the information in a mental model is represented in amodal format. Model-based reasoning about physical systems, however, needs to allow for the possibility of simulations of physical entities, situations, and processes that go beyond manipulating amodal tokens in a spatial array, as on Johnson-Laird's account. Following Craik's notion of parallelism in the form and operation of internal modeling used in reasoning, working memory models of physical systems would be perception-based representations. Considerable knowledge would be needed to carry out such a mental simulation, not just what can be derived from perception as it is usually understood as separate from conceptual understanding. The behaviors of the parts of the model, for example, need to be connected to knowledge of how these function, although much of this can be tacit. For example, people can usually infer how water will spill out of a cup without being able to make explicit or describe the requisite knowledge. Although we have only been considering mental modeling as a working memory process, of course information from long-term memory plays a role in this process, some of which is likely to be represented in propositional form. Thus, as with mental imagery (Kosslyn, 1994), mental modeling representations need to maintain a connection to long-term memory representations, and so an account is needed of how information might be stored so as to connect to working memory representations.

In this section I draw on research on *embodied* representations to propose that there is likely to be a modal aspect to the format of the information contained in working memory representations of physical systems and also to the information to which the models are connected in long-term memory. This would be the most efficient way for the internal–external representational coupling to work.

The embodied representation research focuses on the implications of the interaction of the human perceptual system with the environment for internal representation and processing, generally. Proponents contend that a wide range of empirical evidence shows perceptual content is retained in all kinds of mental representations, and that perceptual and motor mechanisms of the brain play a significant role in many kinds of cognitive processing traditionally conceived as separate from these, including memory, conceptual processing, and language comprehension (see, e.g., Barsalou, 1999, 2003; Barsalou, Simmons, Barbey, & Wilson, 2003; Barsalou, Solomon, & Wu, 1999; Catrambone, Craig, & Nersessian, 2006; Craig, Nersessian, & Catrambone, 2002; Glenberg, 1997b; Johnson, 1987; Kosslyn, 1994; Lakoff, 1987; Solomon & Barsalou, 2004; Yeh & Barsalou, 1996).

One extensive area of embodied research concerns the representation of spatial information in mental models. This research leads to the conclusion that internal representation of spatial configurations does not provide an "outsider" 3-D Euclidian perspective – the "view from nowhere" – but provides an embodied representation that is relative to the orientation of one's body and to gravity. In early research Irwin Rock hypothesized that there is a "deeply ingrained tendency to 'project' egocentric up-down, left-right coordinates onto the [imagined] scene" (Rock, 1973, p. 17). This hypothesis is borne out by recent research (see, e.g., Bryant & Tversky, 1999; Bryant, Tversky, & Franklin, 1992; Franklin & Tversky, 1990; Glenberg, 1997a; Perrig & Kintsch, 1985). In particular, Barbara Tverksy and colleagues have found that mental spatial alignment corresponds with bodily symmetry – up–down, front–back, and gravity – depending on how the participant is oriented in the external environment. When asked to imagine objects surrounding an external central object, mental model alignment depends on whether the object had the same orientation as the observer. Arthur Glenberg argues that this bodily orientation is tied to preparation for *situated action* paralleling that which would occur in real-world situations (Glenberg, 1997b).

A second line of research focuses on concept representation. From an embodied cognition alternative, as expressed by George Lakoff and Mark Johnson, a "concept is a neural structure that is actually part of, or makes use of, the sensorimotor system of our brains" (Lakoff & Johnson, 1998, p. 20). Lawrence Barsalou has been formulating a theory (first fully articulated in Barsalou, 1999) of the human conceptual system that calls into question the traditional understanding of concept representation as amodal. A wide range of research dovetails in thinking about embodiment and representation. The work of Barsalou and colleagues is especially important because they argue for the perceptual basis of concept representation through drawing together evidence from much of that research, as well as through experiments specifically designed to test the hypothesis.

On Barsalou's account, concept representation is likely to have both modal and amodal aspects. However, the modal aspects serve the requirements of simulative mental modeling we have been discussing – both the simulation needs and the need for inter-facing between external and internal representations. There are many open questions about modal representation for which only partial solutions have been suggested, such as: How do abstract concepts become represented? How does "translation" take place across modalities? how does integration take place? How are perceptually dissimilar instances of a concept recognized and categorized? But there are many open questions about amodal representation as well, and, significantly, as Barsalou points out, there is little direct empirical evidence in favor of a fully amodal view.

In sum, the proponents of embodied cognition do make a compelling case that at the very least a more tempered conclusion is warranted in the present circumstances, and this is sufficient for our needs: "The conceptual system appears neither fully modular nor fully amodal. To the contrary, it is non-modular in sharing many important mechanisms with perception and action. Additionally it traffics heavily in the modal representations that arise in sensory-motor systems" (Barsalou, 2003, p. 527). Thus, how modal representations could contribute to various cognitive processes, such as mental modeling, merits further investigation.

CONCLUSION: MODEL-BASED REASONING IN CONCEPTUAL CHANGE IN SCIENCE

I have argued here that the capacity for mental modeling provides a cognitive basis for model-based reasoning evidenced in conceptual changes. It is a fundamental form of human reasoning that is likely to have evolved as an efficient means of navigating the environment, of anticipating situations, and of solving problems in matters of significance to existence. Humans have extended its use to more esoteric situations, such as constructing and reasoning with scientific representations. A mental model is a conceptual system representing the physical system that is being reasoned about. It is an abstraction – idealized and schematic in nature – that represents a physical situation by having surrogate objects or entities and properties, relations, behaviors, or functions of these that are in correspondence with it. Mental models embody and comply with the constraints of the phenomena being reasoned about, and enable inferences about these through simulation processes. Inferences made in simulation processes create new data that play a role in evaluating and adapting models. In reasoning processes, mental models interact with other representations – external diagrams, written equations, verbal representations such as written or oral descriptions or instructions, and gestural representations provide examples of these. The notion of interaction among internal and external resources during reasoning as "representational coupling" leads to the notion that mental models have significant modal aspects ("perceptual mental models"), though a conclusive argument cannot be made in either the modal or amodal literatures.

Simulative mental modeling can lead to potential empirical insights, as in thought experimenting (Nersessian, 1992b), by creating new states or situations that parallel those of the real world. In mundane cases at least tacit knowledge of constraints is needed, such as that the chair cannot simply pass through the wood of the door frame or that the frame of the sofa will not bend or be capable of squishing as does a cushion. In the case of science, implicit and explicit knowledge of constraints relating to general principles of the domain and mathematical equations play a role. This knowledge, such as of causal coherence and mathematical consistency, is likely to be represented in different informational formats. A cognitive science account is still needed of how conceptual, and in general, domain knowledge is utilized in mental modeling, how abstraction and model construction take place, and how the mental processes interface with the external world.

How might reasoning through mental modeling lead to conceptual change? A central problem is that given that conceptual innovation starts from existing representations, how is it possible for a genuinely novel representation to be created? In Nersessian (2008) and earlier works I have proposed that a significant method of conceptual innovation and change in science involves iterative processes of constructing, evaluating, and revising models that exemplify features of the phenomena under investigation. These models do not serve simply as aids to reasoning but provide the means through which one reasons to the new conceptual representations. The model construction and manipulation processes, which include analogical, imagistic, and simulative processes, abstract and integrate information from multiple sources specific to the problem-solving situation so as to allow for truly novel combinations to occur; that is, for a model in which heretofore unrepresented structures or behaviors emerge. The consequences of the novel combinations can be explored imaginatively, through physical realizations, and through manipulations possible by expression in other representational formats, such as mathematics and language.

Many abstractive processes enable model construction, including idealization, limiting case, and generic abstraction. These provide ways of generating and accommodating constraints from multiple domains. "Generic" abstraction, for instance, captures the idea that in reasoning it is possible to make inferences not only about the specific model, but also about the class of models at different levels of abstraction; for example, reasoning about a specific spring or reasoning about it as representative of the class of simple harmonic oscillators.

Finally, we need to consider a significant way in which conceptual change in science is unlike that in learning and cognitive development. In science it occurs not only at the individual level but also across communities. The community of physicists, for instance, experiences a conceptual change from understanding "force" as representing actions-at-a-distance to understanding it as representing continuous-action in the space between charges and bodies, or from understanding "mass" to represent an invariant quantity to understanding it to represent something that varies with speed. Most philosophical and sociological explanations of conceptual change operate at the level of how scientists choose among alternative conceptual structures or how one structure comes to replace another in a community. Thomas Kuhn, for example, in his post-*Structure* writings, repudiated his "gestalt switch" metaphor as characterizing conceptual change for precisely the reason that he argued that he intended to be addressing the level of community change while the metaphor operates at the level of individuals. However, for there to be a community phenomenon, a story needs to be told at the individual level as well. That is, what is the nature of cognitive processes used by individual scientists that generate new concepts and conceptual structures, making them available for communities to choose among? I have argued that scientists creating novel concepts and learners constructing novel (for them) concepts make use of the same cognitive processes (see also Carey, 2009). It is this story that has the potential to contribute to accounts of conceptual change in learning and in cognitive development. In this chapter I have argued that an account of reasoning through mental modeling forms a significant part of that story.

ACKNOWLEDGMENTS

This research was supported in part by grants from the National Science Foundation (DRL0109773 & DRL0450578), the National Endowment for the Humanities, and Radcliffe Institute for Advanced Study.

REFERENCES

Allwein, G., & Barwise, J. (1996). *Logical reasoning with diagrams*. New York, NY: Oxford University Press.

Barsalou, L. W. (1999). Perceptual symbol systems. *Behavioral and Brain Sciences, 22*, 577–609.

Barsalou, L. W. (2003). Situated simulation in the human conceptual system. *Language and Cognitive Processes, 18*, 513–562.

Barsalou, L. W., Simmons, W. K., Barbey, A. K., & Wilson, C. D. (2003). Grounding conceptual knowledge in modality-specific systems. *Trends in Cognitive Sciences, 7*, 84–91.

Barsalou, L. W., Solomon, K. O., & Wu, L. L. (1999). Perceptual simulation in conceptual tasks. In M. K. Hiraga, C. Sinha, & S. Wilcox (Eds.), *Proceedings of the 4th Annual Conference of the International Cognitive Linguistics Association: Vol. 3. The cultural, typological, and psychological perspectives in cognitive linguistics* (pp. 209–228). Amsterdam, The Netherlands: John Benjamins.

Bell, V. A., & Johnson-Laird, P. N. (1998). A model theory of modal reasoning. *Cognitive Science, 22*(1), 25–51.

Bobrow, D. G. (Ed.). (1985). *Qualitative reasoning about physical systems*. Cambridge, MA: MIT Press.

Bryant, D. J., & Tversky, B. (1999). Mental representations of perspective and spatial relations from diagrams and models. *Journal of Experimental Psychology: Learning, Memory, and Cognition, 25*, 137–156.

Bryant, D. J., Tversky, B., & Franklin, N. (1992). Internal and external spatial frameworks for representing described scenes. *Journal of Memory and Language, 31*, 74–98.

Carey, S. (2009). *The origin of concepts*. New York, NY: Oxford University Press.

Catrambone, R., Craig, D. L., & Nersessian, N. J. (2006). The role of perceptually represented structure in analogical problem solving. *Memory and Cognition, 34*(5), 1126–1132.

Chi, M. T. H., Feltovich, P. J., & Glaser, R. (1981). Categorization and representation of physics problems by experts and novices. *Cognitive Science, 5*, 121–152.

Clement, J. (1994). Use of physical intuition and imagistic simulation in expert problem solving. In D. Tirosh (Ed.), *Implicit and explicit knowledge* (pp. 204–242). Norwood, NJ: Ablex Publishing Corporation.

Clement, J. (2003). Imagistic simulation in scientific model construction. In D. Alterman & D. Kirsch (Eds.), *Proceedings of the Cognitive Science Society: Vol. 25* (pp. 258–263). Hillsdale, NJ: Lawrence Erlbaum Associates.

Craig, D. L., Nersessian, N. J., & Catrambone, R. (2002). Perceptual simulation in analogical problem solving. In L. Magnani & N. J. Nersessian (Eds.), *Model-based reasoning: Science, technology, values* (pp. 167–190). New York, NY: Kluwer Academic/Plenum.

Craik, K. (1943). *The nature of explanation*. Cambridge, UK: Cambridge University Press.

Dennett, D. C. (2000). Making tools for thinking. In D. Sperber (Ed.), *Metarepresentations: A multidisciplinary perspective* (pp. 17–29). New York, NY: Oxford University Press.

Finke, R. A. (1989). *Principles of mental imagery*. Cambridge, MA: MIT Press.

Finke, R. A., Pinker, S., & Farah, M. (1989). Reinterpreting visual patterns in mental imagery. *Cognitive Science, 13*, 51–78.

Finke, R. A., & Shepard, R. N. (1986). Visual functions of mental imagery. In K. R. Boff, L. Kaufman, & J. P. Thomas (Eds.), *Handbook of perception and human performance* (pp. 37.31–37.55). New York, NY: Wiley.

Forbus, K. (1983). Reasoning about space and motion. In D. Gentner & A. Stevens (Eds.), *Mental models* (pp. 53–74). Hillsdale, NJ: Lawrence Erlbaum Associates.

Franklin, N., & Tversky, B. (1990). Searching imagined environments. *Journal of Experimental Psychology, 119*, 63–76.

Freyd, J. J. (1987). Dynamic mental representation. *Psychological Review, 94*, 427–438.

Gentner, D., & Stevens, A. L. (1983). *Mental models*. Hillsdale, NJ: Lawrence Erlbaum Associates.

Glenberg, A. M. (1997a). Mental models, space, and embodied cognition. In T. Ward, S. M. Smith, & J. Vaid (Eds.), *Creative thought: An investigation of conceptual structures and processes* (pp. 495–522). Washington, DC: American Psychological Association.

Glenberg, A. M. (1997b). What memory is for. *Behavioral and Brain Sciences, 20*, 1–55.

Goldin-Meadow, S., Nusbaum, H., Kelly, S. D., & Wagner, S. (2001). Explaining math: Gesturing lightens the load. *Psychological Science, 12*(6), 332–340.

Greeno, J. G. (1989). Situations, mental models, and generative knowledge. In D. Klahr & K. Kotovsky (Eds.), *Complex information processing* (pp. 285–318). Hillsdale, NJ: Lawrence Erlbaum Associates.

Harman, G. (1986). *Change in view*. Cambridge, MA: MIT Press.

Hayes, P. J. (1979). The naïve physics manifesto. In D. Mitchie (Ed.), *Expert systems in the micro-electronic age*. Edinburgh, UK: Edinburgh University Press.

Hegarty, M. (1992). Mental animation: Inferring motion from static diagrams of mechanical systems. *Journal of Experimental Psychology: Learning, Memory, and Cognition, 18*(5), 1084–1102.

Hegarty, M. (2004). Mechanical reasoning by mental simulation. *Trends in Cognitive Science, 8,* 280–285.

Hegarty, M., & Ferguson, J. M. (1993). *Strategy change with practice in a mental animation task.* Paper presented at the Annual Meeting of the Psychonomic Society, Washington, DC.

Hegarty, M., & Just, M. A. (1989). Understanding machines from text and diagrams. In H. Mandl & J. Levin (Eds.), *Knowledge acquisition from text and picture.* Amsterdam, The Netherlands: North Holland.

Hegarty, M., & Sims, V. K. (1994). Individual differences in mental animation from text and diagrams. *Journal of Memory and Language, 32,* 411–430.

Hegarty, M., & Steinhoff, K. (1994). *Use of diagrams as external memory in a mechanical reasoning task.* Paper presented at the Annual Meeting of the American Educational Research Association, New Orleans, LA.

Holland, J. H., Holyoak, K. J., Nisbett, R. E., & Thagard, P. R. (1986). *Induction: Processes of inference, learning, and discovery.* Cambridge, MA: MIT Press.

Jeannerod, M. (1993). A theory of representation-driven actions. In U. Neisser (Ed.), *The perceived self* (pp. 68–88). Cambridge, UK: Cambridge University Press.

Jeannerod, M. (1994). The representing brain: Neural correlates of motor intention and imagery. *Brain and Behavioral Sciences, 17,* 187–202.

Johnson, M. (1987). *The body in the mind: The bodily basis of meaning, imagination, and reason.* Chicago, IL: University of Chicago Press.

Johnson-Laird, P. N. (1982). The mental representation of the meaning of words. *Cognition, 25,* 189–211.

Johnson-Laird, P. N. (1983). *Mental models.* Cambridge, MA: MIT Press.

Johnson-Laird, P. N. (1989). Mental models. In M. Posner (Ed.), *Foundations of cognitive science* (pp. 469–500). Cambridge, MA: MIT Press.

Johnson-Laird, P. N., & Byrne, R. (1993). Precis of the book, Deduction with peer review commentaries and responses. *Brain and Behavioral Sciences, 16,* 323–380.

Kahneman, D., & Tversky, A. (1982). *Judgement under uncertainty: Heuristics and biases.* New York: Cambridge University Press.

Kosslyn, S. M. (1980). *Image and mind.* Cambridge, MA: Harvard University Press.

Kosslyn, S. M. (1994). *Image and brain.* Cambridge, MA: MIT Press.

Lakoff, G. (1987). *Women, fire, and dangerous things: What categories reveal about the mind.* Chicago, IL: University of Chicago Press.

Lakoff, G., & Johnson, M. (1998). *Philosophy in the flesh.* New York, NY: Basic Books.

Larkin, J. H. (1989). Display-based problem solving. In D. Klahr & K. Kotovsky (Eds.), *Complex information processing: The impact of Herbert A. Simon* (pp. 319–342). Hillsdale, NJ: Lawrence Erlbaum Associates.

Larkin, J. H., & Simon, H. A. (1987). Why a diagram is (sometimes) worth ten thousand words. *Cognitive Science, 11,* 65–100.

Mainwaring, S. D., Tversky, B., & Schiano, D. J. (1996). Effects of task and object configuration on perspective choice in spatial descriptions. In P. Olivier (Ed.), *AAAI Symposium* (pp. 56–67). Stanford, CA: AAAI Press.

Mani, K., & Johnson-Laird, P. N. (1982). The mental representation of spatial descriptions. *Memory and Cognition, 10,* 181–187.

McNamara, T. P., & Sternberg, R. J. (1983). Mental models of word meaning. *Journal of Verbal Learning and Verbal Behavior, 22,* 449–474.

Morrow, D. G., Bower, G. H., & Greenspan, S. L. (1989). Updating situation models during narrative comprehension. *Journal of Memory and Language, 28,* 292–312.

Nersessian, N. J. (1991). Why do thought experiments work? In *Proceedings of the Cognitive Science Society, Vol. 13* (pp. 430–438). Hillsdale, NJ: Lawrence Erlbaum Associates.

Nersessian, N. J. (1992a). Constructing and instructing: The role of "abstraction techniques" in developing and teaching scientific theories. In R. Duschl & R. Hamilton (Eds.), *Philosophy of science, cognitive science, & educational theory and practice* (pp. 48–68). Albany, NY: SUNY Press.

Nersessian, N. J. (1992b). How do scientists think? Capturing the dynamics of conceptual change in science. In R. Giere (Ed.), *Minnesota Studies in the Philosophy of Science* (pp. 3–45). Minneapolis, MN: University of Minnesota Press.

Nersessian, N. J. (1992c). In the theoretician's laboratory: Thought experimenting as mental modeling. In D. Hull, M. Forbes, & K. Okruhlik (Eds.), *PSA 1992, Vol. 2* (pp. 291–301). East Lansing, MI: PSA.

Nersessian, N. J. (1995). Should physicists preach what they practice? Constructive modeling in doing and learning physics. *Science & Education, 4,* 203–226.

Nersessian, N. J. (1999). Model-based reasoning in conceptual change. In L. Magnani, N. J. Nersessian, & P. Thagard (Eds.), *Model-based reasoning in scientific discovery* (pp. 5–22). New York, NY: Kluwer Academic/Plenum Publishers.

Nersessian, N. J. (2002a). The cognitive basis of model-based reasoning in science. In P. Carruthers, S. Stich, & M. Siegal (Eds.), *The cognitive basis of science* (pp. 133–153). Cambridge, UK: Cambridge University Press.

Nersessian, N. J. (2002b). Maxwell and the "method of physical analogy": Model-based reasoning, generic abstraction, and conceptual change. In D. Malament (Ed.), *Reading natural philosophy: Essays in the history and philosophy of science and mathematics* (pp. 129–165). Lasalle, IL: Open Court.

Nersessian, N. J. (2008). *Creating scientific concepts.* Cambridge, MA: MIT Press.

Nersessian, N. J. (2009). How do engineering scientists think? Model-based simulation in biomedical engineering research laboratories. *Topics in Cognitive Science, 1,* 730–757.

Parsons, L. (1994). Temporal and kinematic properties of motor behavior reflected in mentally simulated action. *Journal of Experimental Psychology: Human Perception and Performance, 20,* 709–730.

Perrig, W., & Kintsch, W. (1985). Propositional and situational representations of text. *Journal of Memory and Language, 24,* 503–518.

Rock, I. (1973). *Orientation and form.* New York, NY: Academic Press.

Rips, L. (1986). Mental muddles. In H. Brand & R. Hernish (Eds.), *The representation of knowledge and belief* (pp. 258–286). Tuscon, AZ: University of Arizona Press.

Rouse, W. B., & Morris, N. M. (1986). On looking into the black box: Prospects and limits in the search for mental models. *Psychological Bulletin, 100*(3), 349–363.

Schwartz, D. L. (1995). Reasoning about the referent of a picture versus reasoning about the picture as a referent. *Memory and Cognition, 23,* 709–722.

Schwartz, D. L., & Black, J. B. (1996a). Analog imagery in mental model reasoning: Depictive models. *Cognitive Psychology, 30,* 154–219.

Schwartz, D. L., & Black, J. B. (1996b). Shuttling between depictive models and abstract rules: Induction and fall back. *Cognitive Science, 20,* 457–497.

Shepard, R. N. (1988). Imagination of the scientist. In K. Egan & D. Nadaner (Eds.), *Imagination and the scientist* (pp. 153–185). New York, NY: Teachers College Press.

Shepard, R. N., & Cooper, L. A. (1982). *Mental images and their transformations.* Cambridge, MA: MIT Press.

Shiffrar, M., & Freyd, J. J. (1990). Apparent motion of the human body. *Psychological Science, 1,* 257–264.

Shore, B. (1997). *Culture in mind: Cognition, culture, and the problem of meaning.* New York, NY: Oxford University Press.

Solomon, K. O., & Barsalou, L. W. (2004). Perceptual simulation in property verification. *Memory and Cognition, 32,* 244–259.

Trafton, J. G., Trickett, S. B., & Mintz, F. E. (2005). Connecting internal and external representations: Spatial transformations of scientific visualizations. *Foundations of Science, 10,* 89–106.

Tye, M. (1991). *The imagery debate.* Cambridge, MA: MIT Press.

van Dijk, T. A., & Kintsch, W. (1983). *Strategies of discourse comprehension.* New York: Academic Press.

Vosniadou, S., & Brewer, W. F. (1992). Mental models of the earth: A study of conceptual change in childhood. *Cognitive Psychology, 24,* 535–585.

Yeh, W., & Barsalou, L. W. (1996). The role of situations in concept learning. In G. W. Cottrell (Ed.), *Proceedings of the Cognitive Science Society, Vol. 18* (pp. 469–474). Hillsdale, NJ: Lawrence Erlbaum Associates.

Zhang, J. (1997). The nature of external representations in problem solving. *Cognitive Science, 21*(2), 179–217.

Zhang, J., & Norman, D. A. (1995). A representational analysis of numeration systems. *Cognition, 57,* 271–295.

Zwann, R. A. (1999). Situation models: The mental leap into imagined worlds. *Current Directions in Psychological Science, 8,* 15–18.

Zwann, R. A., & Radvansky, G. A. (1998). Situation models in language comprehension and memory. *Psychological Bulletin, 123,* 162–185.

22

ROLES FOR EXPLANATORY MODELS AND ANALOGIES IN CONCEPTUAL CHANGE

John J. Clement, University of Massachusetts

MODELS, CONCEPTUAL CHANGE, AND INITIAL TEACHING STRATEGIES

In this chapter I will review some major approaches to instruction for producing conceptual change in scientific explanatory models, including the use of analogies. While space precludes a full review here, I want to present enough research to describe some of the interesting interrelationships between analogies, models, and conceptual change. I will put more emphasis on literature from science education, since Jonassen and Easter (Chapter 30, this volume) have emphasized findings on models from educational psychology. I will concentrate on model-based, cognitive strategies for fostering conceptual change in science as an outcome in individual students. Many of these strategies will involve considering the roles that group discussions and co-construction with a teacher can play, and so some socio-cognitive processes will be included. To be sure there are other recent studies that address other social, cultural, metacognitive, and motivational factors that can have very important influences on conceptual change. However, we still need to address an enormous gap that remains at the core of conceptual change theory: We do not have an adequate cognitive model of the basic conceptual change process. Most of the "classical theory" of conceptual change in science education (Posner, Strike, Hewson, & Gertzog, 1982, Strike & Posner, 1992) is about *conditions* for change (e.g., dissonance), *effects* of change (e.g., a more plausible conception, developmental stages of conceptions), or *factors* that make it easier or more difficult (e.g., the presence of a persistent misconception). What is missing is a fuller specification of *mechanisms* of conceptual change. Many suspect that models and analogies can play a central role in conceptual change. But there is not even a consensus on a definition for the term "model" itself. And we are hard pressed to describe something as basic as the relationship between analogies and models in science learning. Historians of science such as Hesse (1966) and Harre (1972) understood that this relationship is complex and subtle in science itself, so we should expect no less in the area of student learning. Thus, there is still much work to do within the basic cognitive core of individual conceptual change theory as well as outside that core in motivational, metacognitive, and socio-cultural realms.

Conceptual Change and Mental Models

The term "conceptual change" has been used in a variety of ways. Thagard (1992) describes a spectrum of possible degrees of change, from changes in relatively surface-level details, or small revisions, to radical shifts in core concepts. A definition of conceptual change that fits well with Thagard's spectrum is learning in cases where a new knowledge structure is developed – a change that is structural or relational in character rather than a change in surface features. This could occur via the construction of a new structure or a modification or replacement of an old structure. Later in the chapter I will also advocate broadening this definition slightly to include cases where the domain of application of a structure changes significantly. I also choose to use a rather broad concept of "knowledge structure" to allow for the possibility of perceptual and motor structures as part of what is changed.

Developing a stable vocabulary with which to talk about *models* is one of the major challenges in this area. In its widest use in the literature, the term *mental model* is almost too large a category to be useful, essentially meaning any knowledge structure that represents a number of relationships between interconnected entities in a system, as opposed to a list of isolated facts. This allows a model to account for many events, making it an efficient kind of knowledge representation. Gilbert, Boulter, & Rutherford (1998) point out that models focus the user on certain features in a system. Here I will use the term "mental model" in the broad sense to mean a (mental) representation of a system that focuses the user on certain features in the system and that can predict or account for its structure or behavior (Clement, 1989). I will make some minimal assumptions about useful mental models. Useful mental models are often idealized; one might say they are always simplified, since we cannot comprehend every microscopic detail of entities in the world. This corresponds more or less to Nancy Nersessian's (Chapter 21, this volume) definition of mental model: "A mental model is a conceptual system representing the physical system that is being reasoned about. It is an abstraction – idealized and schematic in nature – that represents a physical situation by having surrogate objects and properties, relations, behaviors, or functions of these that are in correspondence with it." I want to be careful, however, to take "abstraction" here to mean something with a degree of generality – as opposed to something completely non-concrete or non-imagistic – because I want to include the possibility of schematic, imagistic mental models that are concrete in the sense of being perception-like, but that are abstract in the sense of being schematic and general. For example, different people can have mental models at different levels of depth for, say, an old-style three-speed bicycle. Some people may include a schematic image of a moving chain, bearings, and cables for brakes, internal gear shift mechanism, and gyroscopic action of the wheels, but other individuals are missing some or all of these elements (Piaget, 1930). Such a mental model is abstract in the sense of being simplified, schematic, and somewhat general, in that it applies to millions of bikes, but it may be concretely imageable. *External models*, such as diagrams, may serve to record features of a mental model, and may allow one to develop a model too complex to be stored or envisioned at once in working memory.

Scientific Models

Minimal criteria for considering a mental model to be a *scientific model* include the requirement for a certain level of precision; the requirement for a basic level of plausibility that rules out, for example, occult properties; and a requirement that, if possible, the model be internally consistent (not self-contradictory). Under this broad definition, analogies, such as thinking about water wave reflection for light reflection, or a mechanical thermostat for the body's temperature regulation system, can also be scientific models when they are used in an attempt to predict or account for the behavior or structure of the system.

Explanatory vs. Non-Explanatory Models

Harrison and Treagust (1996) discuss a pantheon of types of models, including the scale model, analogical model, mathematical model, chemical formula, theoretical model, a standard (something to be imitated), maps and diagrams. To complement this pantheon I have found it helpful to make two orthogonal distinctions to help focus this chapter on a narrower "space" of models. Along one dimension lies the familiar distinction between quantitative and qualitative models – I will focus on the latter. The other dimension requires more introduction. Historians of science, such as Campbell (1920), Hesse (1966), and Harre (1972), have developed important distinctions between empirical law hypotheses, explanatory models, and formal principles; these form the vertical dimension depicted in Table 22.1. These historians believe that hypothesized, theoretical, qualitative models (I will call these *explanatory models*), such as molecules, waves, and fields, are a kind of hypothesis separate from empirical patterns or observational descriptions of behavior. Campbell gives the example that merely being able to make predictions from the empirical gas law stating that PV is proportional to RT is not an explanatory model – it is not the same as understanding *why* the system behaves as it does in terms of an explanatory model of molecules in motion. In contrast, the explanatory elastic particle model provides a description of a hidden, non-observable mechanism that explains *how* the gas works and answers *why* questions about the causes underlying observable changes in temperature and pressure. As a special kind of scientific model, an explanatory model is not simply a condensed summary of empirical observations, but is rather a set of new theoretical terms and images that are part of the scientist's view of the world. Following Peirce, Harre and Hesse believe that an explanatory model is neither "given" in nor implied by the data. Rather it is an invention that is conjectured and then retained if it successfully explains the data. The precision of such a model can be extended by adding a mathematical description of relations between variables in the model. These distinctions helped Clement (1989) explain how experts thinking aloud could develop successful predictive knowledge at the empirical law level in Table 22.1, yet be unsatisfied that they *understood* a system at the explanatory model level.

Beyond these basic features, scientists often prefer explanatory models that are general, visualizable, simple, and that contain familiar entities (Nagel, 1961). More extensive sets of evaluatory criteria for a "good" explanatory model are discussed by Kuhn (1977) and Darden (1991). Level 4 in Table 22.1 contains *formal theoretical principles*, such as the Laws of Thermodynamics or Newton's laws, that consolidate general features of the mechanisms from the explanatory model level and state them as part of a formal

Table 22.1 Four levels of knowledge used in science

	Level	Example: Study of gases
Theories	4. Formal theoretical principles	Principles of thermodynamics
	3. Explanatory models	Colliding elastic particle model
. . .	. . .	. . .
Observations	2. Qualitative or mathematical descriptions of patterns in observations, including empirical laws	$PV = kT$ (refers to patterns of observations of measuring apparatus)
	1. Primary-level data: Observations	Measurement of a single pressure change in a heated gas

deductive system. For a discussion of studies of other kinds of models, such as graphs, charts, and maps (e.g., Lehrer & Schauble, 2003; Raghavan & Glaser, 1995), familiarity with which may be an important prerequisite for preparing young children to work with explanatory models, see Jonassen and Easter (Chapter 30, this volume).

Why Focus on Explanatory Models?

Authors such as Machamer, Darden, and Craver (2000), Campbell (1920), Harre (1972), Nagel (1961), and Hesse (1966) have argued that qualitative explanatory models (mechanisms) are at the central core of most theories, and that to develop successful explanatory models is a central goal of most sciences. Such a model is seen as the means by which a theory takes on meaning, and, if used flexibly, it gives the theory the power to explain and make predictions for new cases that the subject has not seen. On this account, significant changes that improve an explanatory model are one of the most important types, if not the most important type, of conceptual change (Lawson et al., 2000; National Research Council, 2011; Perkins & Grotzer, 2005; Windschitl, Thompson, & Braaten, 2008).

The Strategy of Presenting Models

Perhaps the most direct approach is that of *presenting* descriptions of models in a concise and clear way. For example, studies by Mayer (1989) have done this via schematic diagrams and text, finding, in many cases, that for presented explanations of mechanical systems (e.g., how car brakes work), the inclusion of a clear and simple diagram can yield a significant improvement in conceptual understanding (but usually not in factual knowledge), especially for students who have low spatial ability. Work by Hegarty, Kriz, and Cate (2003) indicates that learners can be induced to mentally animate static diagrams of dynamic processes. In a related vein, Gabel (1999) found that adding the use of physical block models of molecules to chemistry lessons increased middle school students' comprehension of chemistry reactions and principles. Such studies indicate that a focus on communicating the visual aspects of explanatory models can make a positive difference in instruction.

Other studies, however, have revealed limitations of presentation approaches. Lowe (1993) found that the mental representations derived by experts and novices from abstract technical diagrams (weather maps) depended on their ability to process the material in terms of dynamic relations between the components of the diagrams. Those who lacked prerequisite concepts did not comprehend the presented diagrams. A set of "disaster studies" in physics in the early 1980s, too numerous to review here, provided evidence that lecture presentations had not adequately dealt with the problem of persistent misconceptions, and similar results have been produced to some extent in biology and chemistry. Even though college physics students, including engineering majors, were often able to learn to solve quantitative problems using algebraic formulas, they had great difficulty with many qualitative conceptual problems. This suggests that superficial knowledge at Level 4: formal theoretical principles in Table 22.1 does not imply understanding at Level 3: explanatory models, and it highlights the sometimes unrecognized importance of Level 3 in science education.

DISSONANCE-PRODUCING APPROACHES

Dissonance Strategies

Teaching by Direct Contrast

Although I have chosen to define the concept of conceptual change more broadly, the problem of producing change in persistent misconceptions is especially interesting and challenging. In this chapter I will use the terms: *target model* or *target conception* for a scientific conception (or approximation thereof) that is to be learned in a course; *misconception* (also called an *alternative conception*) for a student's conception that is incompatible with a target conception; and *preconception* for a student's conception that is present before instruction in the course. Some misconceptions are perfectly adequate for use in daily life, but others are not, such as those affecting health issues. However, it is important not to show disrespect for students' ideas, in order to encourage their expression and examination. Some misconceptions may be articulated beliefs, others can be implicit intuitions, others can be mental models assembled upon encountering a specific situation.

The most direct attempts to deal with misconceptions have been to refer intentionally to a common misconception during instruction and to contrast it with the scientists' view. Guzzetti, Snyder, Glass, and Gamas (1993) reviewed a number of studies of refutational texts – documents in which typical misconceptions are refuted directly in juxtaposition to the scientific view – and found that, overall, there was evidence of a positive effect. A related but somewhat milder approach is to draw out students' conceptions, relate them to observations, then hold up the target model in comparison. McCloskey, Washburn, and Felch (1983) found positive effects from asking high-school mechanics students to explain their conceptions of force and motion and then contrasting these with the scientific view. This is called "contrastive teaching" by Schecker and Niedderer (1996), who believe that the student's original conception may not disappear, but that students can become aware of the difference between the two points of view.

Discrepant Events

Others have attempted to create more subtle forms of "participative dissonance" less directly, where information is provided that allows the student to discover a conflict with his or her own current model. Discrepant events are empirical experiments, data summaries, or demonstrations that provide data that could promote dissonance with students' preconceptions. Early studies reporting some success in using this technique have appeared in physics (e.g., Arnold & Millar, 1987; Rowell & Dawson, 1985; Stavy & Berkovitz, 1980), chemistry (Hand & Treagust, 1988), and biology (e.g., Dreyfus, Jungwirth, & Eliovitch, 1990), and two studies reporting significant differences in gains in favor of experimental groups are Zietsman and Hewson (1986) and Licht (1987).

Theoretically, the simplest mechanism for how dissonance may work is *replacement*. After dissonance with a misconception is produced, the conception is either discarded or suppressed. Another conception then takes its place. Chiu, Chou, and Liu (2002) reported significantly more "radical conceptual change" in experimental tutoring sessions than in a control group. In transcript analyses, they found evidence that producing cognitive dissonance in students, by having them first explain their own concepts and only then presenting conflicting evidence, appeared to be an important strategy (among others) for fostering understanding and preventing students from memorizing answers by rote. In a study of ninth graders learning about causes of the seasons, Tsai and Chang (2005) found significant gain differences in favor of groups that were encouraged to explain the seasons in their own terms (e.g., summer occurs when the earth is closest to the sun), after which they were presented with discrepant evidence (e.g., the earth is farther in the summer). Again, they interpret this as a way to prevent rote memorization, since the control group's answers were more evenly matched to the experimental group's immediately after instruction, but deteriorated on delayed post-tests, as misconceptions "reemerged."

Some authors recognize that the purpose of a discrepant event is not just to promote dissonance with existing conceptions, but also to introduce a controversial question into a class in order to promote active discussion. Working from a theory of optimal dissonance for learning motivation, Inagaki and Hatano (1977) showed that student comprehension can be heightened by asking each student to commit to a prediction for an experiment or event to be discussed. This view of the role of dissonance is more complex than a simple conflict theory.

Other Dissonance-Producing Strategies

Dissonance can come from a variety of sources in addition to discrepant events. Another source is student–student dissonance, between different students' spontaneous ideas about a predicted phenomenon (Scott, 1992). Other studies using this approach include Dreyfus et al. (1990); Niedderer and Goldberg (1996); Hewson and Hennessey (1992); Posner et al. (1982); and Jonassen and Easter (Chapter 30, this volume).

Critiques of Dissonance Strategies

Other studies, however, argue that using discrepant events alone does not always work, for several possible reasons, as follows.

- *Lack of effect of single discrepant event:* Chinn and Brewer (1998) have catalogued a variety of student reactions to discrepant information, including cases where they ignore it or do not place it in conflict with their previously stated beliefs (see also Dupin & Joshua, 1989).
- *Affective critique:* In the Dreyfus et al., study cited above, the authors noted that,

while the brighter, more successful students reacted enthusiastically to "cognitive conflicts," the unsuccessful students developed negative attitudes and tried to avoid conflicts. Stavy (1991) suggested avoiding conflict to prevent students' loss of confidence and possible regression.

- *Omission critique:* From a theoretical standpoint, using conflict strategies alone appears not to deal with building up a complex new explanatory model once the old model is called into question (Chan, Burtis & Bereiter, 1997). After dissonance is created with an initial model, can one always rely on students to simply invent a replacement model?
- *Replacement critique:* Other theoretical objections have been posed by authors such as Smith, diSessa, and Roschelle (1993), who worry that:

> Instruction designed to confront students' misconceptions head-on . . . seems destined to undercut students' confidence in their own sense-making abilities . . . In focusing only on how student ideas conflict with expert concepts, the misconceptions perspective offers no account of productive ideas that might serve as resources for learning. Since they are fundamentally flawed, misconceptions themselves must be replaced.
>
> (p. 18)

Instead, they argue for more continuous approaches to teaching that engender developmental continuity. diSessa (1988) and his colleagues, such as Hammer (1996), as well as Clement, Brown, and Zietsman (1989), and Minstrell and Krauss (2005), have also advocated an increased focus on students' useful conceptual resources, in contrast to an exclusive focus on misconceptions.

Summary

In summary, a positive characteristic of the studies favoring dissonance strategies cited above is that they embodied new recognition of the persistence of some student misconceptions, and corresponding recognition of a need to design instruction in a way that could deal with these misconceptions. Others, however, worry that such techniques on their own could be insufficient or even have negative affective consequences for some students. These controversies, despite the positive results of some dissonance studies, indicate the need for further research that investigates the effect of different types or levels of dissonance, and other strategies such as analogies.

INSTRUCTION USING ANALOGIES

Some authors have pointed to the use of analogies as a positive approach to fostering conceptual change. Joshua and Dupin (1987) found that students studying electricity showed very limited change in the belief that current is "used up" in a bulb in a DC circuit after they were confronted with what the teacher hoped would be a discrepant event: Data showing that the current was the same on each side of the bulb. However, when an analogy between electron flow in series circuits and a train running on a circular track was discussed with the students, a significant number changed to a constant-current point of view. Thus, this study pointed both to a limitation of one discrepant event and to the positive effect of an analogy.

Theoretical Potential of Analogies

Analogies are seen by some as an alternative to dissonance (Stavy, 1991) and replacement. Some useful reviews of instructional analogies already exist (Coll, France, & Taylor, 2005; Dagher, 1994, 1995; Duit, 1991), so I will focus here on studies relevant to discussing the relationship between analogies and explanatory models. Theoretically, analogies are said to tap existing knowledge in the learner that is similar enough to a target conception to allow some relational information to be transferred – to be inferred in the target (Gentner, 1989; Gorsky & Finegold, 1994; Simons, 1984; Stavy, 1991; Stepich & Newby, 1988). Analogies make explicit use of students' prior knowledge in a positive way. This represents an important shift from focusing on student prior knowledge only as problematic misconceptions. Analogy also holds out hope for efficient global change in bigger steps than a small revision, since one may be able, theoretically, to "import" a whole set of interconnected relations from the base of the analogy to the model.

Classroom Learning Trials

A number of authors have measured learning gains associated with instruction that uses analogies, including Bulgren, Deschler, Schumaker, and Lenz (2000), Glynn (1991), Mason (1994), Harrison and Treagust (1996), Treagust, Harrison, Venville, and Dagher (1996), Dupin and Joshua (1989), Podolefsky and Finkelstein (2007), Minstrell (1982), Brown (1992b, 1994) Brown and Clement (1992), and Clement (1993). Glynn (1991) introduced a six-step strategy he called a "Teaching with Analogies (TWA)" approach that includes steps for mapping similarities between the analog and target explicitly, and indicating where the analogy breaks down. When these steps are taken in interactive discussion, this strategy goes well beyond that of presenting the analogy in lecture.

Limitations of Analogies

Others, however, have advised caution on some limitations of using analogies, several of which are summarized in Table 22.2 (Else, Clement, & Rea-Ramirez, 2008; Yerrick, Doster, Nugent, Parke, & Crawley, 2003). For example, Harrison and Treagust (1996), in a study of the effectiveness of analogies used in eighth to 10th grade classrooms, write: "It appears that many students do not interpret teacher metaphors and analogies in the intended manner. Rather, they transfer attributes from the teachers' analog to the target . . . in a literal and undifferentiated sense" (p. 511). Although they found some positive effects of analogies, they found that some students preferred less accurate models of atoms over others and that many students thought that atoms were alive and divide like cells. They believe that these "dangerous" features came from analogical models used in instruction, concluding that their study "has illustrated the negative outcomes that arise when students are left to draw their own conclusions about analogical models." Duit, Roth, Komorek, and Wilbers (2001) sounded a similar theme in a study where they examined a set of ninth grade lessons on quantum and catastrophe theory phenomena in which students were encouraged to generate their own analogies. The "discuss the limitations" step in Glynn's TWA strategy described above is designed to avoid difficulty 3 in Table 22.2. However, even when that strategy is heeded, students may still make false inferences from an analogy (Else et al., 2008).

Table 22.2 Possible limitations and difficulties in using analogies in instruction

1. The base (anchor) may not be understood sufficiently.
2. The base may be too far from the target for the student to see the mapping or to see its applicability to the target.
3. The student may transfer too much from base to target ("overmapping").
4. The analogous case may not contain all of the relations needed to develop the target model.

Finding a Good Base

diSessa (1988), Clement et al. (1989), and Hammer (1996) have called for the systematic study of students' positive preconceptions, or "anchors," to address problem 1 in Table 22.2. Clement et al. (1989) found that different examples of what appears to experts to be the same physical principle varied strongly with respect to whether students could understand them as examples of the principle. This means that one may have to be quite careful in choosing examples for the base of an analogy; i.e., base examples need to be tested with students. Duit et al. (2001) confirmed this in the case of certain analogies for quantum effects where the base was poorly understood by certain students. However, Clement et al. (1989) documented that other examples are interpreted correctly by the vast majority of students and therefore can provide good starting points, or "anchors," for instruction, concluding that many preconceptions are not misconceptions. On the other hand, in areas where students have insufficiently developed anchoring intuitions about the base, those intuitions may need to be developed by real or simulated experiences. Examples are Arons' (1990) activity of having students push large objects in a low-friction environment, McDermott's (1984) use of air hoses to accelerate dry ice pucks, diSessa, Horwitz, and White's use of dynaturtle (White, 1993), and Steinberg's (2004) use of air pressure experiments to develop intuitions to be applied later to analogous electrical circuits.

Bridging Strategy

A strategy called *bridging analogies*, which uses multiple analogies, has been developed to try to overcome difficulty 2 in Table 22.2 (Brown & Clement, 1989; Clement, 1993). The strategy is used in about a dozen mechanics lessons in Camp et al. (1994). For example, they built on their tutoring study research and work by Minstrell (1982) to construct a lesson on normal forces. A common misconception in this area is that a table cannot push up on a book. Students say the table is only "in the way," serving as a "barrier" that keeps the book from falling, but do not see it as a force-producing entity. The physicist, on the other hand, views the table as elastic – deforming a tiny amount in response to the force from the book and providing an equal and opposite force upward to keep the book from falling. In the lessons, first, an *anchoring example* of a hand pushing down on a spring was used, which draws out a physical intuition in the student that is largely in agreement with accepted physical theory (most students agreeing that the spring pushes up on the hand). Then, a chain of bridging analogies was used, as shown in Figure 22.1, to gradually transfer the student's intuition, from the anchoring example to a near case of the book on a foam pad, then to the book on a thin flexible board, and finally to the far case of a book on a table. The teachers taught Socratically during this 25 minute section, posing questions about each example. This process

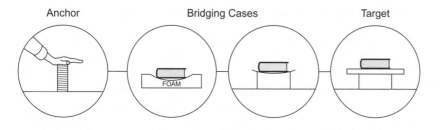

Figure 22.1 Chain of bridging analogies transferring intuition from anchor to target

exemplifies a type of change emphasized by diSessa (1988), that of changing the domain of application, or applicability conditions, of the "springiness" conception to encompass the unintuitive case of tables and other rigid objects. This prompts me to add "or significant change in the domain of application of a structure" to the definition of conceptual change given earlier.

Brown (1992b) conducted a study in which high-school chemistry students who had not had physics were asked to "learn aloud" individually as they worked through a textual presentation of the bridging analogies strategy for the book on the table lesson. Students taught with this method had significantly higher pre–post gains than students in a control group. The control group in this case read a passage of equivalent length from a well-known innovative physics textbook that presented many concrete examples of Newton's Third Law after stating the law. This passage focused on citing many examples rather than on developing bridging analogy relations and models with a few carefully selected examples. It was as if the control text were aiming to have the student induce a very general and abstract principle from a large set of unordered examples. In contrast, the superior performance of the experimental group was used to argue that the transfer of a concrete, dynamic model in a systematic, stepwise manner from the anchor toward the target is more effective.

Summary of Approaches Using Analogy

In summary, a number of studies have documented promising gains from analogy-based instruction. However, other studies have exposed various problems that can arise, as shown in Table 22.2. Identifying the conditions under which analogies succeed and fail is therefore an important problem for future research. The use of analogies is usually considered to be a strategy that is more constructive than disconfirmatory. A remaining potential general criticism of the use of analogy on its own, in addition to the criticisms in Table 22.2, is that building up a model using an analogy may do little to counteract a persistent prior misconception. Later on, the prior misconception may reassimilate the target T, causing the student to revert to their previous misconception. This suggests the strategy of combining analogies and dissonance-producing situations, discussed in the next section. In the combined strategy, in a reciprocal way, analogies might also provide one answer to the "omission critique" of dissonance approaches described in the previous major section on dissonance.

Combined Strategy: Using Analogies and Dissonance Together

Minstrell (1982), and curricula by Camp et al. (1994) and Steinberg (2004), have taken a position that embraces both the use of dissonance and the use of analogies, as summarized by the concept diagram shown in Figure 22.2. They were impressed with both (a) the depth of the persistence problem for misconceptions in many areas of physics; and (b) the importance of building on student's intuitions wherever possible (Clement et al., 1989; diSessa, 1988). This combined strategy works to resolve what I call the prior knowledge paradox: Constructivist theory tells us to build on what the student knows, but conceptual change research tells us that a significant part of what the student knows is in conflict with scientists' views. The paradox can be resolved if one recognizes that the two kinds of knowledge can coexist in students, and that one can use analogies that tap positive preconceptions to help students deal with other preconceptions that conflict with target models (misconceptions such as M1 in Figure 22.2).

For example, in Camp et al. (1994) the normal forces lesson included not only bridging analogies discussed earlier, but also a discrepant event where a light beam reflected from a mirror flat on the teacher's desk to a wall is deflected downward along the wall when a person stands on the desk. This experiment provides dissonance for students who believe that desks are rigid objects that cannot deform to provide an elastic force. In comparison with control groups, this lesson unit has shown large significant gain differences greater than one standard deviation in size, as measured by pretests and post-tests on problems that deal with students' preconceptions. Some students changed their position toward the scientific view during each major section of the lesson; e.g., after the anchor, bridge, microscopic model presentation, and discrepant event sections, leading the author to hypothesize that each technique was helpful to some subset of students (Clement, 1993). Large significant gain differences were also realized in three other topic areas in mechanics where lessons combined analogies and discrepant events (Brown & Clement, 1992; Clement, 1993).

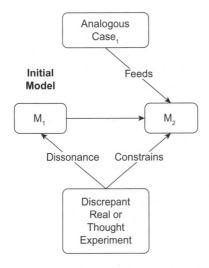

Figure 22.2 Combined strategy using analogies and dissonance together

MODEL EVOLUTION STRATEGIES

Multiple Analogies Foreshadow Model Evolution

Kuhn's (1970) description of science as going through "revolutions" was challenged by Toulmin (1972), who cited examples of historical change processes that appeared to be a more gradual kind of "evolution." Both ideas have been used as metaphors for conceptual change in students (Novak, 1977). Approaches that build up a model in stages by using successive analogies foreshadow a model evolution approach since they involve gradual improvement of the student's model. Harrison and De Jong (2005) describe the use of multiple analogies in chemistry, and Spiro, Feltovich, Coulson, and Anderson (1991) and Glynn and Duit (1995) described the use of multiple analogies to gradually build up a student's conception of biological systems such as muscle fibers or the eye, respectively. Chiu and Lin (2005) found that multiple analogies were significantly more effective than single analogies when they were complementary analogies (that spoke to different aspects of the target); when multiple analogies used were similar to each other, they were no more effective than single analogies. Podolefsky and Finkelstein (2007) found that students who were tutored on electromagnetic waves using two "layered analogies" of string and sound waves plus an abstract graph representation gave significantly more sophisticated explanations than students tutored using either the abstract representation alone or the analogies alone, indicating the desirability of coupling multiple analogies to mathematical representations.

Model Evolution Through Successive Evaluations and Modifications

This raises the issue of an evolution/revolution debate by posing the question as to whether new explanatory models should be (1) evolved incrementally, by starting from and modifying the student's own ideas, to foster engagement and ease of modification or (2) introduced all at once in order to display their coherence and superior explanatory power by contrast in a more revolutionary manner. The three contrastive teaching studies cited in the section on dissonance-producing approaches can be interpreted as advocating a more revolutionary perspective.

On the other hand, Buckley (2000) traced the work of the most successful student in a class that was given many kinds of information resources and was told to work without direct instruction on learning how the circulatory system works. She characterized this student as the one who was best able to maintain a partial, initially incomplete and faulty, explanatory model of the system – a model that became more sophisticated as new elements were incrementally added or eliminated. Not only did the student's partial model act as a central place where she added new information coherently, but new *predictions* she made from her partial model generated questions that motivated her to learn more about circulation. This paper weighs in on the side of an evolutionary approach by documenting the potential for engaging and maintaining student reasoning during learning by starting from mostly familiar concepts in a partial model and pursuing a series of implications and improvements. It is unusual in documenting a very student-directed approach that worked well for one student, but not as well for others.

Most of the teaching strategies previously described in this chapter are utilized in the diagram in Figure 22.3, which makes explicit a *model evolution* approach involving

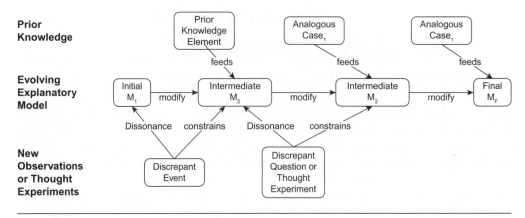

Figure 22.3 Evolution approach for teaching models

successive model evaluations and modifications. Clement and Steinberg (2002) reported on a case study in which they used detailed transcripts from tutoring sessions to acquire fine grained data on a series of substantial changes in a student's model of circuits. The middle row of Figure 22.3 shows the basic shape of the learning process. They found evidence that a cycle of small incremental steps involving dissonance and then constructive activity (including analogies) aided this student in gradually building a more complex model. For example, students who associate power in only circuits with a battery experience dissonance when they light a bulb (temporarily) by discharging a very large capacitor in a circuit with no battery. An analogy between a discharging capacitor that is releasing charge and a pressurized tire that is releasing air helps to begin building up a model that can explain this and many other phenomena. Thus, the model undergoes a *series of successive refinements*. Only two intermediate models are shown in Figure 22.3, but in practice there can be many more. Most intermediate student models in a topic area are partly correct and partly faulty. When possible the teacher may try to retain the positive pieces, and to promote conflict with each faulty piece, one step at a time, while recruiting elements from prior knowledge (often via analogy) to help repair that part of the model.

The idea of building up the student's model gradually through revisionary change is also discussed by Driver (1983), Treagust, Harrison, Venville, and Dagher (1996), Dupin and Joshua (1989), and Minstrell and Krauss (2005). It is implicit in the open discussions of lab results advocated by Wells, Hestenes, & Swackhamer (1995), who have developed ways of training physics teachers to postpone evaluation of student ideas in order to facilitate such discussions. Scott (1992) and Niedderer and Goldberg (1996) highlighted the importance of the very closely related idea of a *learning pathway* of intermediate states seen as stepping stones between preconceptions and target conceptions (see review by Niedderer, 2001). They point out that such intermediate states can develop from student ideas that are unanticipated, requiring teaching or tutoring studies, not just task analysis, to determine good pathways. Niedderer views intermediate knowledge states that appeal to many students as "attractors." For curricula resulting from such studies, Clement (2008a) distinguishes between a "planned learning pathway" specified ahead of time in a lesson plan and an "implemented learning pathway" that results from the teacher using the plan with real students adaptively. As students introduce unanticipated ideas and details, the implemented pathway is bound to be longer and somewhat different from the planned pathway. Nevertheless, the planned pathway is seen as a valuable source of focus. An extended version of this idea applied in higher level planning to multi-year time spans has been dubbed a "learning progression" in articles such as Smith, Wiser, Anderson, & Krajcik (2006) as an important principle for developing teaching standards.

Multiple Short Cycles Needed for Complex Models

Concerning Figure 22.3, Clement and Steinberg (2002) write that the small step sizes of the revisions were made possible by the careful choice on the part of the tutor of coordinated "small" analogies and "small" discrepant events. They theorize that this makes it possible for the student to participate in suggesting model revisions that are small enough to make immediate sense, allaying concerns expressed earlier about possible negative effects of too much dissonance. Brown (1992a) and Steinberg (2008) documented large gains over control groups using a curriculum on circuits of this kind, including disproportionately large confidence gains in female students. Others who have focused on the explicit development of a series of intermediate models are Gilbert et al. (1998), Gobert and Buckley (2000), and Niedderer and Goldberg (1996). In a very different context, White (1993) used a series of more than 40 short, computer simulation "hit the target" games to successfully teach, one step at a time, a qualitative appreciation of Newtonian force and motion ideas in a virtual frictionless environment.

Successive Refinement Cycles in Experts

The description in Figure 22.3 was also influenced by expert studies. On the basis of expert protocols, Clement (1989) documented examples of expert model construction occurring via an extended evolutionary cycle of model generation, evaluation, and modification, referred to as a GEM cycle. Experts engaging in theory formation and assessment cycles using analogies have also been discussed by Holland, Holyoak, Nisbett, and Thagard (1986), and Darden (1991). Nersessian (1992, 2002) documents the cyclical progressive revision process, including dissonance, engaged in by Maxwell during his construction of several visualizable models of the electromagnetic field, just prior to formulating his famous field equations.

A Dual Role for Dissonance in Model Evolution

In the following I highlight some ways in which dissonance is hypothesized to contribute to evolution.

1. *Model evaluation.* The fostering of dialectic discussions requires the careful development of a spirit of inquiry in the classroom, where students' ideas are valued. On the other hand, model evolution techniques do require model evaluation and criticism, suggesting the importance of dissonance strategies. Minstrell (1982) discusses strategies for distancing ownership of ideas away from individual students to make criticism non-threatening. Also, students have been observed using discrepant questions and thought experiments to create dissonance themselves,

although this may happen only after students are used to discussing models (Nunez-Oviedo, Clement, & Rea-Ramirez, 2007; Stephens & Clement, 2010, 2012). There is some evidence that students' preconceptions in different areas vary in how persistent they are (Gorsky & Finegold, 1994), ranging from being easily discarded (see Nunez-Oviedo & Clement, 2008; Stavy & Berkovitz, 1980; Zietsman & Hewson, 1986) to very deep-seated (see Clement, 1982, 1993; Hestenes, Wells, & Swackhammer, 1992). In low-persistence cases at least, mild forms of dissonance can be used in conjunction with other positive teaching strategies to produce model evolution. Thus, the use of dissonance to deal with misconceptions need not be associated with strong, confrontational methods (Rea-Ramirez & Clement, 1998).

2. *Positive effects of discrepant events or questions.* Clement and Steinberg (2002) point out that discrepant events can be designed not only to generate dissonance with the students' old model, but also to provide a framework of constraints for guiding construction of the new model, thereby making a positive as well as a negative contribution to conceptual change. So in Figure 22.3, the discrepant event is shown both generating dissonance with M_2 and constraining the development of M_3. Clement and Rea-Ramirez (1998) called this a "dual effect" of dissonance. In a study of ninth graders learning models of heat transfer, She (2004) found that carefully designed discrepant events or questions did help students detect problems in their existing models and also appeared to provide constraints and motivation for constructing the next step in their evolving model. Nersessian (2002) has described similar constraint-based modeling processes in her analysis of Maxwell's thought experiments, and Clement (2008c) describes such processes in experts thinking aloud. Thus instead of limiting ourselves to the choice between "confrontation" and "no confrontation," vaguely defined, there are a variety of sources of dissonance of different strengths, and this suggests intermediate strategies that should be articulated and tested. Whereas some writers have associated dissonance strategies with a replacement view of conceptual change, here dissonance is associated with model evolution instead.

Evidence from Curriculum Trials for Effective Model (and Concept) Evolution

Other studies have provided evidence that model evaluation and modification cycles can be used effectively in biology (Barker & Carr, 1989; Hafner & Stewart, 1995; Nunez-Oviedo & Clement, 2008), chemistry (Khan, Stillings, Clement, & Tronsky, 2002; Fretz et al., 2002), heat (Linn, Bell, & Hsi, 1998), electricity (Clement & Steinberg, 2002; Steinberg, 2008), thermal equilibrium (She, 2004), and mechanics (White, 1993; Zietsman & Clement, 1997). At an even more fine-grained level than intermediate *models*, Brown and Clement (1992) describe large gains over controls for mechanics lessons that teach students a set of intermediate *concepts* of inertia, such as "keeps going tendency" and "holdback tendency," before leading the students to modify and combine the concepts into a single expert concept.

Instructional Implications of Model Evolution: Teacher Directed or Student Directed?

I have said very little about how open to novel student ideas the modeling process should be, because teachers and projects vary tremendously on this dimension. Requesting student participation in the model generation, evaluation, and revision process does open up the conversation and make it more student-active and student-centered, but teachers and students using such approaches need to become comfortable with the idea of discussing intermediate models that are partially incorrect, prior to students developing a more sophisticated model. A middle position on a teacher-directed/student-directed continuum has the teacher fostering *co-construction* by stimulating inferences – as illustrated in Figure 22.4, the teacher has some input to the construction, but is also striving to stimulate student input (Hammer, 1996; Minstrell & Krauss, 2005). The ratio of student to teacher idea generation that is possible is likely to depend on what cognitive resources are available to students for each given topic and on teaching style (Williams & Clement, 2011). An extended discussion of co-construction strategies is given in Clement and Rea-Ramirez (2008).

For example, getting students to speculate on and generate models of systems such as the pulmonary system is not hard, even at the middle-school level. But students may generate a variety of ideas for model elements, some of which are at odds with the scientific view (air goes from the mouth to the heart), more or less compatible with the scientific view (air goes into your lungs), and partially correct (lungs are like hollow balloons that expand and contract). Five or 15 contributions can lead to a large variety of ideas, or what Easley (1990) called "conceptual splatter." Clement (2008b) describes the challenge this poses: A teacher must decide which idea to deal with first in order to keep students in a "reasoning zone." There is a need to set an agenda, to decide how to draw on the positive portion of the students' ideas, and this requires that teachers think on their feet, based on what models the students have generated. Nunez-Oviedo et al. (2007), and Williams and Clement (2011) have tracked how a skilled teacher can guide discussions to produce model evolution in the presence of such multiple difficulties. The skills used pose an additional challenge for teachers and teacher education. Inagaki, Hatano, and Morita (1998) suggest that one way to reduce the load on the teacher is to have students vote on a limited number of choices – those that have been researched ahead of time and shown to have many advocates – but such resources are not common at present. Electronic response systems (Dufresne, Gerace, Leonard, Mestre, & Wenk, 1996) may facilitate this.

Theoretical Implications of Model Evolution

One can extrapolate to form several theoretical hypotheses from the ideas about model evolution reviewed above: (1) While it is not likely that all science models require an evolutionary approach with many GEM cycles for learning to occur, such strategies may be especially needed whenever target models are complex or multiple misconceptions are present. (2) The intermediate steps used in model evolution are reminiscent of the "bridging analogies" approach discussed earlier. However, the intermediate steps represented in Figure 22.1 are separate analogous *cases* that are potentially observable (e.g., a book on foam rubber), whereas the intermediate models in Figure 22.3 are non-observable, explanatory *models* (e.g., more and more adequate models of what drives currents in circuits). Figure 22.1 shows a chain of analogical connections whereas Figure 22.3 shows changes in the model itself via successive modifications. Both processes have intermediate elements, but they play different cognitive roles. (3) In their call for small-step model revision starting from students' ideas, model evolution approaches support the idealistic positions of diSessa (1988), Smith et al. (1993), and Clement et al. (1989)

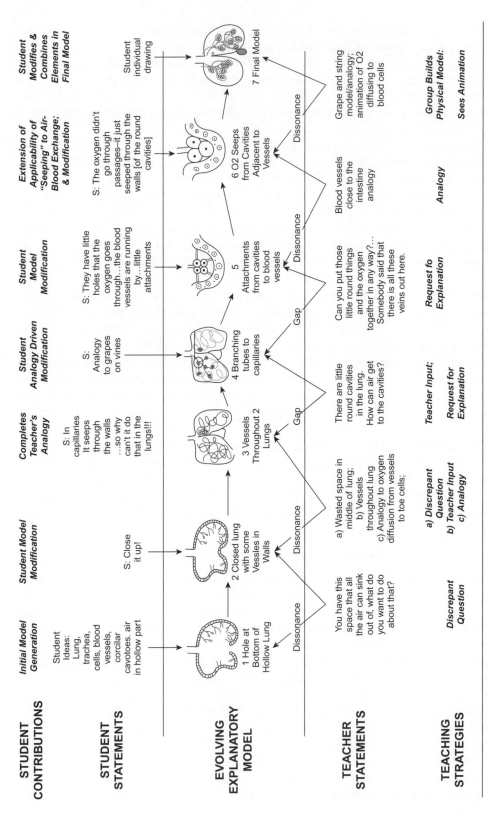

Figure 22.4 Model evolution from teacher–student co-construction

and contrast with a global replacement approach. However, model evolution in small step sizes is also an interesting idea theoretically, because it challenges the distinction between a "substantial conceptual change" (in the extreme, a "revolution") and a minor revision; a long series of small changes in a model could result, in theory, in a very substantial global change. Schwarz et al. (2009) add the process of applying, or '*Using* a model to explain, and predict phenomena' to GEM cycles and propose a learning progression describing sub-stages in elementary students' development of these processes.

As with most models, the models of piecewise conceptual change in Figures 22.3 and 22.4 (and their extensions in Williams & Clement, 2011 and Clement, 2008a, 2008b) are simplified ones. They are at a medium grain size, although they are different from and considerably more detailed than a simple conflict and replacement model. One advantage of medium grain size is comprehensibility for discussing instructional strategies with teachers. Finer grained, more systemically complex psychological models of students' conceptions are reviewed in Brown and Hammer (Chapter 6, this volume). The additional importance of making connections to form coherent "networks of ideas" in building a model is suggested by Givry and Tiberghien (2012), interpreted here as a cautionary counter to the idea of purely piecewise learning. Rea-Ramirez and Nunez-Oviedo (2008) provide evidence that evolutionary curricula and assessments that also pay attention to unit integration can be designed to aim for this.

TYPES OF CONCEPTUAL CHANGE AND THE NEED FOR MULTIPLE TEACHING STRATEGIES

Types of Conceptual Change in Explanatory Model Development

Types of conceptual change are listed in the left-hand column of Table 22.3. Dagher (1994) sorted researchers' investigations of conceptual change according to where they fell on Thagard's (1992) spectrum of types of conceptual change. I will attempt to paint a somewhat wider spectrum in an attempt to represent the variety of conceptual change types needed in instruction. In particular:

- A small change in a single feature of a model, as in Thagard's (1992) "adding a weak rule," can be considered a *minor model revision* and can sometimes be accomplished by students who have had minimal prompting.
- diSessa (1988) and Smith et al. (1993) provide examples where the content of a conception remains largely the same but the *domain of applicability is changed* or expanded significantly so that it applies to new cases.
- Gentner (1989) and Holyoak and Thagard (1989) speak of an inductive process of *abstraction* whereby a general schema can be formed by stripping away differences between two or more analogous exemplars. In a related process, Nersessian (1992) writes of scientists forming abstract models with surface features removed.
- Clement and Steinberg (2002) document examples of *major model modification*, such as the change from a focus on pressure to a focus on pressure *differences* as the cause of flows (representing voltage differences as the cause of current flow in electric circuits).
- Vosniadou and Brewer (1992) document a process of *synthesis* whereby subjects form a hybrid model that combines a prior model with a newly learned model. This

process may be related to what Collins and Gentner (1987) described as "pasting component models together" and what Clement (1994, 2008c) refers to as "compound simulation."

- Through a process of abduction, receiving a presentation (Mayer, 1989), or both, some authors believe that a new initial model can be learned by a process of *constructing a model* from known pieces or by transmission.
- Researchers have documented cases of *concept differentiation or integration* that present major challenges to students, such as the differentiation of heat from temperature (Wiser & Carey, 1983; Smith et al., 1993) or the integration of acceleration and deceleration into a single concept.
- Some researchers believe it is particularly difficult to replace a conception that has the characteristics of one philosophical/ontological category with a conception that has the characteristics of a different category; e.g., changing the conception of "heating as substance transfer" to one of "heating as energy transfer" (Chi, 1992; Thagard, 1992). They refer to *branch jumping or tree switching*.

At the top of Table 22.3 is a process that would occur on a larger time scale than an individual conceptual change, and so in some contexts it might be placed on a different dimension than the others. A paradigm shift, such as the shift from Aristotelian to Newtonian mechanics, involves deep changes in many concepts, and therefore one would not expect it to be possible via a single conceptual change, or even a few conceptual changes. Therefore a broken line is shown between it and the other processes. Students'

Table 22.3 Types of conceptual change in explanatory model development

CC process	Example of author	Outcome
Paradigm shift	Kuhn	Collection of ideas that differs drastically from original in multiple ways
———	———	———
8) Branch jumping and tree switching	Thagard, Chi	Replace concept with ontologically different type of concept
7) Fundamental concept differentiation or integration	Carey, Wiser	Fundamental concept split or concepts united
6) Construct new initial model that it has not grown out of an earlier model	Mayer	Initial model formed, with assumption
5) Synthesis or combination	Vosniadou, Collins, Gentner	Conjoined models
4) Major model revision	Clement, Steinberg	Add, remove, or change element to produce revised model
3) Abstraction	Gentner, Holyoak, Nersessian	General schema formed from exemplars
2) Change in domain of applicability	diSessa	Model with new applicability conditions and exemplars
1) Minor model revision	Rumelhart and Norman's "tuning"	Adjusted model

naïve views of mechanics are not identical to Aristotle's, and there is a question of whether the shift from naïve physics to Newtonian physics constitutes a paradigm shift, depending on whether one considers naïve physics to be a paradigm. However, there is substantial evidence that it is a huge shift that meets stiff resistance. One may need to warn students that the Newtonian view may not make sense immediately – not until they have attained a coherent critical mass of new concepts, including velocity, acceleration, force, weight, inertial mass, friction force, relative motion, vector addition of velocities, addition of forces, and net force.

Some have endeavored to draw a cut-off line in various places across Table 22.3 and to reserve the term *conceptual change* for processes above the line. I am going to resist that impulse here. All of these types could be seen as conceptual change in certain cases – that is, as a significant change in conceptual understanding. I therefore concur with the preference for including smaller changes in structure as one type of conceptual change, broadly defined. As Dagher (1994) puts it: "Limiting worthwhile conceptual change to radical conceptual change is similar to limiting worthwhile science to revolutionary science." In addition, it is possible that a series of smaller changes can add up to a large structural change, making the drawing of a sharp boundary line difficult.

Resistance to Change

It appears that change of any type in Table 22.3 could meet with more or less resistance from an existing preconception, depending on the strength of that preconception. Thus, it is possible that what looks like a small change from a philosophical or linguistic point of view (near the bottom of Table 22.3) is actually a huge change from the student's point of view. For example, the idea that air has a small, but significant, weight would seem to be a small attribute change, yet it is very counterintuitive for most middle-school students. Thagard's taxonomy itself did not deal with resistance in this sense. Chiu et al. (2002) describe how different portions of a chemistry unit varied in difficulty according to the kinds of conceptual change involved, roughly consistent with their type in Table 22.3.

Evaluation Processes

Using the GEM cycle framework as an organizer, Table 22.3 represents a dimension of *model modification* or replacement that needs to be complemented by another dimension: processes of *model evaluation*, including processes of model confirmation or disconfirmation, and model competition. Any model resulting from a conceptual change should be evaluated intuitively according to whether it makes sense, but also by more established criteria or experiments (cf. Darden, 1991). Such processes have been documented during instruction by Linn et al., (1998) and Nunez-Oviedo et al. (2007) among others. There is a school of research (stemming from linguistics) on student argumentation structures for model evaluation processes. These vary from those using more formal schemes derived from Toulmin (1972) for tracking arguments, to less formal schemes (see Duschl & Osborne, 2002). Some view argumentation as the public side of model evaluation, but others view argumentation as fulfilling different types of goals of sense-making, articulating, and persuading (Berland & Reiser, 2009; Passmore & Svoboda, 2011). Model evaluation is an important process skill that has many natural and intuitive manifestations in students (Pluta, Chinn, & Duncan, 2011), but that also needs to be refined significantly (Clement, 2008c; Hammer & Elby, 2002). Model competition processes have been documented in science by Kuhn (1970), Giere (1988), and Thagard (1992), in scientists' think-alouds by Clement (1989, 2008c), and in instruction by Linn et al. (1998), Tabak et al. (1995), Taber (2001), and Nunez-Oviedo and Clement (2008).

Need for Multiple Teaching Strategies

My own opinion, having worked on two large, model-based curriculum projects in mechanics and in the biology of respiration, is that *all types of change listed in Table 22.3 are applicable at times as descriptors of student learning processes.* Many of those types could be involved in a single unit of instruction. This view contrasts with those in the first three sections of this chapter, which focused on interventions primarily using one predominant strategy. Also, this possible variation in learning processes, from very easy to very difficult within a single unit, means that progress may be quite uneven; as a result, teachers are probably not fully prepared to appreciate the range of difficulty that can be present within a unit.

For example, the "Book on the Table" lesson, discussed earlier, aims at more than one type of conceptual change; i.e., a change in applicability conditions (expansion of the domain of exemplars for the "springiness" p-prim) and the construction of a new hidden explanatory model (molecules with springy bonds). In this lesson, one can also see evidence for several types of teaching strategies, including requests for explanation, use of analogies, use of a discrepant event, and the presentation of an explanatory model. Brown (1994) found in a tutoring study, using a lesson of this kind, that different students picked different strategies when asked what they had learned from the most. This and the recognition that there are many types of conceptual change as represented in Table 22.3 argue that using multiple teaching strategies is an important technique for reaching students. This is exemplified further in Figure 22.4, which is a highly condensed representation of two hours of instruction that depicts strategies used in a videotaped teaching session. The teacher was piloting a new curriculum unit on pulmonary respiration with a group of four middle-school students. She first asked the students to draw their initial ideas about the structure of the lungs. In the figure, the evolving student model is shown from left to right across the middle. The student contributions are across the top, while teacher statements and labeled teaching strategies are across the bottom. The teacher promoted student-active model construction with teaching strategies such as requests for explanation, discrepant questions, analogies, an animation showing O_2 diffusing to blood cells from alveoli, the teacher giving input on a feature of the model, and the exploration of a physical model (string wrapped around artificial grapes on a vine to represent blood vessels and alveoli). Throughout the process, the teacher encouraged the students to evaluate and modify their own and other students' models by revising their drawings of the lungs and alveoli. Other teachers have also used discrepant events and analogies, but this lesson unit employs a number of teaching strategies in addition to the use of discrepant events and analogy, expanding the image of conceptual change teaching depicted in Figure 22.3 to one that includes multiple methods for evaluating and modifying students' models. In some places here, the primary generator of ideas was the group of students; in other places it was the teacher. Figure 22.4 provides one image of what model evolution via teacher–student co-construction can look like, with both student and teacher inputs to the developing model, making it a social construction. Note that some evaluation strategies are seen as producing dissonance with the current model, whereas others simply speak to a gap in the model.

Tsai and Chang (2005), in their study of learning the causes of the seasons, designed their lesson around a "conflict map" diagram that shows not only discrepant information to be introduced, but also multiple kinds of evidence supporting the scientific model of the seasons. When included in a curriculum, such multiple strategy diagrams should help teachers focus on the conceptual goals and major cognitive strategies of the lesson (see also diagrams in Camp et al., 1994). Achieving focus is no mean feat when operating within the distractions of a real classroom and the somewhat unpredictable course of a large group discussion.

Figure 22.4 is organized primarily around a "major model revision" framework as the major type of conceptual change in Table 22.3 being pursued at that point in the curriculum. It is interesting that "analogy" does not appear in Table 22.3 as a type of conceptual change. Rather, it is considered here to be one of many types of teaching strategies at a finer grain size level, a sample of which is shown in the bottom row of Figure 22.4, which can facilitate the conceptual changes in Table 22.3.

Section Summary

I have posed the possibility that all of the types of conceptual change in Table 22.3 could be involved in the learning process when a student is developing the model of any complex system such as the conversion of energy in the human body. Multiple model evaluation strategies can also be important. Recognizing the possibility of model evolution and the variety of teaching strategies that can be involved in its many steps leads one to appreciate the need for multiple teaching strategies rather than simplistic one- or two-strategy models of teaching.

Comment on Process Goals

This chapter is focused on methods for achieving content goals of conceptual understanding, but this focus can quickly lead one to needing students to become engaged in scientific thinking that speaks to certain process goals. The instructional activities already described fulfill some process goals, but approaches that also emphasize process goals for their own sake would need to add additional investigation activities. It is possible that certain deep process goals, such as skills for managing self-directed inquiry cycles, are better pursued in separate types of activities from those dealing with persistent misconceptions, as opposed to trying to combine them in the same activity – a question for future research. Also, it stands to reason that specialized teaching strategies are possible for each type of conceptual change. I examine this possibility for the case of analogies in the next section.

MULTIPLE ROLES FOR ANALOGY IN DEVELOPING EXPLANATORY MODELS

An Analogy can Contribute to Building a Model

The distinction between analogies, explanatory models, and other types of models has been blurred in much of the literature, but once it is established, it makes possible a further clarification of the different types of special contributions that analogies can make to explanatory model construction. Figures 22.4 and 22.5 separate the analogous case from the explanatory model, allowing one to see analogy as participating in the revision of the student's prior model; i.e., seeing analogy as one source of ideas for improving a model rather than as identical to, or the sole source of, a model (Clement & Steinberg, 2002; Spiro et al., 1991). In this section, I will expand on this role as the most important one that analogy can play in conceptual change, and I will compare it with other roles.

One of the possible theoretical reasons for using an organizing analogy, such as air pressure for electric potential in circuits, is that it may be very efficient in producing a large conceptual change "all at once" by importing a whole relational structure from a different domain. I call this the "big bang" or "Eureka" theory of analogy in instruction. In fact, though, Clement and Steinberg (2002) found that each implication of the global air pressure analogy must be explored and examined for each type of circuit element or junction. This means that this model is still constructed in small pieces, as depicted in Figure 22.3, and each piece involves working through its own particular kind of evaluation (via dissonance) and revision cycles in the face of common difficulties. The global analogy of air pressure and flow, in this case, takes weeks to develop fully; it does not necessarily save time, but it appears to increase depth of understanding significantly (Steinberg, 2008). Not all analogies are this global and complex, but Else et al. (2008) and Harrison and Treagust (1993) have emphasized that teachers in other areas can underestimate the time and care needed to develop an analogy properly, especially for younger students. These studies indicate that analogies can be viewed inappropriately, as a "quick fix" for student learning, and that it is better to view them as a strategy for in-depth learning of a more encompassing explanatory model and to use them only when time is allocated for that.

Learning from Analogies via Enrichment vs. Abstraction

A widely accepted view considers that an analogy is beneficial because it helps the student view the target in a more abstract way. In that view, by helping the student focus on the shared relational structure between the base and the target and downplaying the significance of the actual objects and surface-level object attributes, the analogy is thought to help lend abstract relational structure to the previously poorly structured target situation (Gentner, 1983, 1989; Gick & Holyoak, 1983; Holland et al., 1986; Holyoak & Thagard,

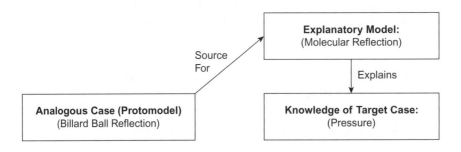

Figure 22.5 Three-element view of the relation between target, analogous case, and explanatory model

1989). The learner is left with a mental representation of the target in which objects and object attributes are less salient and abstract relational structure is more salient.

By contrast, in the successful intervention in the book on the table study described earlier (Brown & Clement, 1989), the "atomic bonds as springs" analogy appeared to help *enrich* the students' conceptions of the target situations, rather than (or at least in addition to) helping them view the situations more abstractly. In this intervention, the concrete idea of elastic springs is projected into the microscopic realm to form an explanatory model of spring-like bonds between atoms. The student learns about a new, concrete mechanism that explains what is happening inside the targeted table system. It was hypothesized that this enrichment of the target with new objects, object attributes, and causal relations (e.g., microscopic bonds, flexibility, and bending causing forces) is a very important means for conceptual restructuring. Here, the dimensions of concreteness and generality become separated; the concreteness of the imagined mechanism does not imply a lack of generality. General, schematic models can be sparse in detail but still quite concrete in being dynamically imaged. As another example, the idea of swarms of moving molecules in a gas is concretely imageable, but the model is very schematic and general in the sense of being widely applicable. The fact that this model is hidden from observation does not mean that it is not concrete. In this view, the move in Table 22.1 from the observation pattern relations at Level 2, between temperature and pressure, to the explanatory model relations at Level 3, between molecular speed and impact on the walls of the container, is not a move from concrete to non-concrete imagery; rather, it is a move from one set of concrete images at the empirical level to an additional set of concrete images at the theoretical level. In this view, analogies and models can be a source of enrichment rather than a source of abstraction.

Brown (1993) argued that analogies can help students "refocus core intuitions" by helping them to enrich their representation of the target. On the basis of in-depth interviewing data with students learning electricity via the pressure analogy, he argues that analogies can sometimes change the way the student's "core intuitions" are projected into a target domain. This can be very important for sense-making and retention, since other strong intuitions can be responsible for "unseating" newly learned target models (see Chapter 6 by Brown and Hammer in this volume).

Contrasting Diagrams

Thinking about model learning in biology offers a fresh perspective on the issue of abstraction, since abstraction is, in general, less pronounced in biology than in physics; in biology elaborated structures are a major focus. The models in the middle row of Figure 22.4 are somewhat abstract in that they are simplified, schematic representations of living organs of biomass. However, rather than seeing increasing abstraction as central to all model construction activity, in images of model evolution like those in Figure 22.4, conceptual change appears as the gradual revision and enrichment of initially simplistic models, a trend that can be considered in the opposite direction from abstraction. The use of concrete, scale models of molecules and of the solar system would seem also to work in this direction by adding more and more schematic, but concrete, structure.

On Analogies vs. Explanatory Models

It is common to make such statements as "The billiard table is an 'analog model' of the gas." That sentence is acceptable if "analog model" refers to "scientific model in the broadest sense" – in which case any constructed representation that can be used to think about the gas qualifies. But the sentence is not acceptable in the present framework if "analog model" means an *explanatory* model. A scientist's elastic-particle model of a monotonic gas is not the same as a billiard table. Certain elements have been added (tiny size, perfect elasticity, three-dimensional motion, constant motion, etc.) and subtracted (colors, external cause of motion, etc.) from the original analogous case. We do not think of there actually being billiard balls inside of gases. I would prefer to say that the *analogous case* of the pool table can be used as a starting point for developing an *explanatory model* of a gas as a swarm of elastic particles. I will call this kind of analogous case a *proto-model*. By using different names for these two entities, their relationship can be discussed, something that is not often done in the literature.

How Analogous Cases as Proto-Models can Support Explanatory Model Construction, not just Provide a Correct Prediction for a Target Problem: Harre's View

Hesse (1967) and Harre (1972) distinguish between the following.

1. An analogous case that shares only its abstract form with the target (Hesse cites hydraulic models of economic systems as one example). Such a case may happen to behave like the target case and therefore provide a way of predicting what the target will do. But it does not explain how the target works. I call this an *expedient* analogy.
2. A model that has become, in Harre's terms, a "candidate for reality," such as the elastic-particle model of a gas. In this case, a set of material – but hidden – features, in addition to the abstract form, is hypothesized to be the same in the model and the target situation. (These features are often unobservable in the target at the time.) In the elastic particle model a gas is hypothesized not only to behave like particles bouncing around, but to actually consist of something very much like tiny particles bouncing around. I refer to the latter kind of model as *explanatory*.

Thiele and Treagust (2006) observed a number of analogies that I call expedient in their study of chemistry teachers' use of analogies, such as: Activation energy is like a pole vaulter attempting a vault; and competing forward and reverse rates of a reaction is like a person walking up a down escalator. Here I call these expedient analogies because, although they are instructive, they do not introduce material elements as starting points for constructing an explanatory model.

Triangular Relation in Model Construction

An analogy can be viewed as involving two main elements: the target case and the analogous case. However, the above considerations mean that it is often desirable to take a three-element view of the relation between target, analogous case, and explanatory model, as in Figure 22.5. Pressure in a car cylinder can be explained roughly by analogy to a billiard table, but greater power comes from the development and refinement of an explanatory model, which can be thought of as our best estimate of nature's hidden mechanism in the gas. Clement (2008c) argues that such a model is neither deduced from axioms nor induced as a pattern from repeated experiences. Rather, it is abducted as a construction pieced together from various sources, including the billiards analogy, designed in such a way as to provide an explanation for the target phenomenon. As mentioned above, Clement and Steinberg (2002) tracked the learning of a high-school student as she was introduced to electric circuit concepts via an air pressure analog. There is evidence that this was a proto-model since concrete features of air pressure differences causing air flow are transferred by her to the explanatory model as a starting point for thinking about how differences in "electric pressure" (voltage) cause current flow.

Roles of Analogy

The distinctions developed in the sections above allow one to discriminate between more purposes for analogies, as shown in Table 22.4, than are commonly recognized. These analogy types have been distinguished in expert protocols in Clement (2008c), but explicit comparisons of their uses in educational contexts is a task for future research. An exception is Cheng and Brown (2010), who studied elementary students' spontaneous analogies about magnetism, finding that many were expedient analogies but only a small number were proto-models.

Using an Analog as a Proto-Model

Earlier, I raised questions about the limitations of analogies as a lone strategy, saying that it might not deal with the student's prior model M_1. Figure 22.3 depicts an improved strategy by showing how analogy can play the role of a proto-model as one source of material to help *modify* model M_2. For example, a case of lower than ambient pressure

Table 22.4 Four types and purposes of analogy

Analogous case as exemplar for induction or abstraction. *Example:* Several exemplars of acceleration may be given in order to develop the concept of acceleration. The exemplars are analogous to each other and may help students form an abstract concept of acceleration. Some may prefer to refer to this process as induction from exemplars rather than induction from analogy.

Expedient analogy. *Example:* The behavior of an LRC circuit is analogous to the behavior of a weight oscillating on a spring, including the concepts of oscillation, amplitude, and damped oscillation. But there is no deep causal connection whereby elements of one system can be used as an explanatory model for the other in the sense of a mechanism viewed as actually operating in the other.

Domain-expanding analogy. *Example:* Bridging analogies were used to expand the domain of application of the springiness idea in the book on the table lesson. (The form of this is shown in Figure 22.1.) An analogy can be formed between two examples at the same level – that is, an anchoring analogous case and a target (e.g., the spring and the table) – which can encourage a student to stretch the domain of application of a correct intuition and apply it to the target example.

Analog as proto-model. *Example:* Using billiards as a starting point for the elastic-particle model (shown in Figure 22.5) or using a camera as a starting point for developing an explanatory model of how the eye works (Glynn, 1991). Here, the anchoring, analogous case is used as a starting point, or building block, for adding to an explanatory model. The model is at a deeper, hidden, explanatory level than the observable target phenomenon, and the analogous case provides a piece of, or starting point for, developing the model. In contrast to the first type of analogy above, here the analogous case is not an exemplar of the explanatory model; e.g., a billiard table is not an exemplar of a gas.

such as a vacuum cleaner can be incorporated into an existing "pressure" model of electric potential to introduce the concept of negative voltage at one end of a battery. The intention is not to import the entire vacuum cleaner analogy into the model but primarily to contribute the "lower than ambient pressure" idea. Their use in this contributory way is not "watered down" science, because a number of historians of science have described analogies as providing contributory elements during model evolution, such as Darden (1991), Nersessian (2002), Holland, et al. (1986), Millman and Smith (1997), and Gruber (1981).

Figure 22.3 can also be used to contrast this role for analogies with that of a bridging analogy or "domain expander" illustrated in Figure 22.1. In Figure 22.1 the bridging analogies are cases that are compared with each other and the target case. In the vacuum cleaner case and Figure 22.3 the proto-model analogy is not just a case to be compared with the target circuit but contributes a sub-schema that is incorporated into the explanatory model itself.

One can now hypothesize that analogies playing the roles in Table 22.4 may contribute selectively to different processes of conceptual change shown in Table 22.3. For example, the expedient analogy of a pole vaulter might be used to introduce the idea of activation energy for a reaction, but this does not really give an *explanation* for the relationship; therefore, its contribution to explanatory modeling is marginal. A domain-expanding, bridging analogy would naturally contribute to type (2) in Table 22.3, conceptual change via changing the domain of applicability for a concept. Using analogous cases as exemplars for abstraction naturally can contribute to (3) forming a general schema by abstraction. A proto-model analog would serve as a starting point for (6) constructing a new initial model, or for adding a new component in (4), a major model modification. This mapping between types of analogies and types of conceptual change is not at present discussed in the literature, to my knowledge, and it suggests that different techniques for using analogies may be needed for different types of change. These considerations may eventually help us explain why previous studies have found mixed results in using analogies.

A Focus on Modeling as a Primary Purpose for Analogies

One thing these distinctions can buy us is focus – the ability to focus on the development of the explanatory model as the most important content goal of science instruction. The central row in Figure 22.4 represents this development. The model, as a schematic, general, and flexible knowledge structure, is a more important outcome than the knowledge of any one analogy or case. Rather than being an endpoint in themselves, analogies are seen as one of several sources of ideas for initiating or developing an evolving explanatory model. Personally, I believe this to be the way to describe the most important role of analogy in science instruction. (Zietsman & Clement, 1997 found that some *extreme cases* can play a similar role in supporting model construction. This is in opposition to the prevailing theory that the only major role of extreme cases is to provide a confident extra data point for inducing a pattern or testing a theory.)

This view is consistent with Glynn's call for teachers to be explicit about the parts of an analogy that do not map to the target. Mason (1994) documents fifth grade students' ability to discuss the shortcomings of an analogy between postmen delivering letters and the blood cells delivering oxygen to other cells, which she sees as indicative of their increasing metacognitive awareness of the purpose of an analogy. When an analogy is viewed as one stepping stone in a longer process of model evolution, the "dangerous" disanalogous aspects can become valuable points for discussion that highlight distinctive features of the explanatory model – features that *contrast* to those in the particular analogy.

Returning to the positive side of analogies, what, if anything, is transferred from an analogy to an explanatory model? Clement and Steinberg (2002) and Clement (1994, 2008c) hypothesize that it can include schema elements capable of generating dynamic imagery, citing, for example, case study evidence in which particular gestures for both pressure and flow appeared during their subject's work with the air pressure analogy and then reappeared during her work on instructional problems on circuits. They speak of this as transfer of imagery or "transfer of runnability." Hesse's idea that explanatory models involve mechanisms thought to have some material similarity to the hidden structure of the target is consistent with the idea that a central component of an explanatory model is an imagistic, or analog representation that preserves some of the structure of what it represents. The roles of imagery in analogy and explanatory model construction are important topics that I have not had space for in this chapter. They are examined in Bolger, Kobiela, Weinberg, and Lehrer (2010), Gilbert, Reiner, and Nakhleh (2008), Hegarty et al. (2003), Nersessian (2002), Clement (1994, 2008c, 2009a, 2009b), Schwartz and Heiser (2006), and Schwartz and Black (1996), among others.

In sum, analogies can play a *narrower* role in instruction for explanatory model construction than is assumed by some, in the sense that they are only one of many strategies needed for model construction (Figure 22.4). And in contrast to the prediction of the "big bang" theory of producing fast and large conceptual change via analogy, instructional analogies can require extended and careful development. Conversely, analogies can play a *wider*, more varied, more important role in instruction than is commonly assumed, in the sense that they may have more varied purposes than commonly recognized. It may be that different techniques are needed for using analogies for different purposes, such as those in Tables 22.3 and 22.4. This provides an important agenda for future research.

CONCLUSION

The tables and figures in this chapter form the basis for a summary of findings on the relationships between analogies, explanatory models, and conceptual change. From history of science, we find that hypothesized hidden mechanisms and explanatory models are a separate form of knowledge from qualitative or quantitative patterns in observations (Table 22.1). The theoretical perspective of this chapter regards explanatory models as *the qualitative core of meaning for a scientific theory* and *the center of explanatory sense-making for students.* It suggests refocusing curriculum development and instruction so that explanatory models are the central organizers for content goals. A variety of studies conclude that model presentation, dissonance, and analogy strategies can lead to positive results in conceptual change teaching under certain conditions. Figure 22.3 depicts the resulting image of model-based instruction, a kind of model evolution with inputs from both students and the teacher, that has been used in several innovative curricula, involving repeated cycles of *model evaluation and revision.* Many other strategies can be used to support *model evolution* as depicted in Figure 22.4, in a process of teacher–student co-construction. This was described as a middle road between lecture and open-ended discovery learning.

Table 22.3 portrays a *wide variety of types of conceptual change* identified by different researchers. Using these ideas, an idealized image of an approach to content-based curriculum development begins from the identification of students' positive and negative preconceptions in relation to a target model, leading to a planned *learning pathway* (shown in the central row of Figure 22.4). This prepares the way for research-based lesson or unit planning by first, identifying the type of conceptual change being sought from those in Table 22.3, for a step in the pathway, then choosing teaching strategies at a finer grain size, such as those in the bottom row of Figure 22.4, to facilitate the conceptual change. Within a lesson, maintaining class discussions or using student "voting" techniques and other ongoing assessments are ways to give the teacher enough feedback to decide how to keep students in a "reasoning zone." To succeed, these cognitive considerations need to be combined with other considerations not dealt with in this chapter, such as ways to foster: social dynamics of large and small group learning, larger integrative and motivational contexts, students learning about the nature of models and science learning, and ongoing metacognitive self assessment. A theory positing *four basic purposes for analogy* was developed on the basis of expert studies and teaching studies. Two purposes were identified as especially important for explanatory model construction: analogies used for domain expansion and analogies used as proto-models. Subsequent model revision going beyond the original analogy, however, is deemed essential. This contrasts with a view of analogy as a simple short-cut to understanding, and indicates that specialized teaching strategies may be important for different types of analogies to succeed.

Filling in other processes outlines an important agenda for future research. An initial example in this chapter is the attempt to map the four different types of analogy processes to the different types of conceptual change they can produce in Table 22.3. In future research we may be able to map other teaching strategies to different types of conceptual change. One can then imagine a form of top-down curriculum planning that could occur, starting from research on students' preconceptions and a learning pathway specifying the type of conceptual change that needs to happen at each juncture. It appears that a curriculum designer or teacher trying to decide how to teach a unit is going to encounter the need for many types of conceptual change. If we can understand what these types are, and what teaching strategies are particularly important for each, it will be a powerful advance in our theory of conceptual change instruction.

REFERENCES

Arnold, M., & Millar, R. (1987). Being constructive: An alternative approach to the teaching of introductory ideas in electricity. *International Journal of Science Education, 9*(5), 553–563.

Arons, A. B. (1990). *Teaching introductory physics.* New York, NY: Wiley.

Barker, M., & Carr, M. (1989). Teaching and learning about photosynthesis. Part 2: A generative learning strategy. *International Journal of Science Education, 11*(2), 141–152.

Berland, L. K., & Reiser, B. J. (2009). Making sense of argumentation and explanation. *Science Education, 93*(1), 26–55.

Bolger, M., Kobiela, M., Weinberg, P., & Lehrer, R. (2010). Embodied experiences within an engineering curriculum. *Proceedings of the ICLS 2010*, Chicgo, IL, Vol. 1.

Brown, D. E. (1992a). *Teaching electricity with capacitors and causal models: Preliminary results from diagnostic and tutoring study data examining the CASTLE project.* Paper presented at the annual meeting of the National Association for Research in Science Teaching, Boston, MA.

Brown, D. E. (1992b). Using examples and analogies to remediate misconceptions in physics: Factors influencing conceptual change. *Journal of Research in Science Teaching, 29*(1),17–34.

Brown, D. E. (1993). Refocusing core intuitions: A concretizing role for analogy in conceptual change. *Journal of Research in Science Teaching, 30*(10), 1273–1290.

Brown, D. E. (1994). Facilitating conceptual change using analogies and explanatory models. *International Journal of Science Education, 16*(2), 201–214.

Brown, D., & Clement, J. (1989). Overcoming misconceptions via analogical reasoning: Factors influencing understanding in a teaching experiment. *Instructional Science, 18*, 237–261.

Brown, D., & Clement, J. (1992). Classroom teaching experiments in mechanics. In R. Duit, F. Goldberg, & H. Niedderer (Eds.), *Research in physics learning: Theoretical issues and empirical studies* (pp. 380–397). Kiel, Germany: IPN.

Buckley, B. C. (2000). Interactive multimedia and model-based learning in biology. *International Journal of Science Education, 22*(9), 895–935.

Bulgren, J. A., Deschler, D. D., Schumaker, J., & Lenz, B. K. (2000). The use and effectiveness of analogical instruction in diverse secondary content classrooms. *Journal of Educational Psychology, 92*(3), 426–441.

Camp, C., & Clement, J., with the assistance of Brown, D., Gonzalez, K., Kudukey, J. Minstrell, J., Schultz, K., Steinberg, M. (1994). *Preconceptions in mechanics: Lessons dealing with conceptual difficulties.* Dubuque, IA: Kendall Hunt.

Campbell, N. (1920). *Physics: The elements.* Cambridge, UK: Cambridge University Press. Republished in 1957 as *The foundations of science.* New York, NY: Dover.

Chan, C., Burtis, J., & Bereiter, C. (1997). Knowledge building as a mediator of conceptual change. *Cognition & Instruction, 15*(1), 1–40.

Cheng, M. F., & Brown, D. E. (2010). Conceptual resources in self-developed explanatory models: The importance of integrating conscious and intuitive knowledge. *International Journal of Science Education, 32*(17), 2367–2392.

Chi, M. T. H. (1992). Conceptual change within and across ontological categories: Examples from learning and discovery in science. In R. N. Giere (Ed.), *Minnesota studies in the philosophy of science, Vol. XV: Cognitive models of science* (pp. 129–186). Minneapolis, MN: University of Minnesota Press.

Chinn, C. A., & Brewer, W. F. (1998). An empirical test of taxonomy of responses to anomalous data in science. *Journal of Research in Science Teaching, 35*(6), 623–654.

Chiu, M. H., Chou, C. C., & Liu, C. J. (2002). Dynamic processes of conceptual change: Analysis of constructing mental models of chemical equilibrium. *Journal of Research in Science Teaching, 39*(8), 688–712.

Chiu, M. H., & Lin, J. W. (2005). Promoting fourth graders' conceptual change of their understanding of electric current via multiple analogies. *Journal of Research in Science Teaching, 42*(4), 429–464.

Clement, J. (1982). Students' preconceptions in introductory mechanics. *American Journal of Physics, 50*(1), 66–71.

Clement, J. (1989). Learning via model construction and criticism: Protocol evidence on sources of creativity in science. In J. Glover, R. Ronning, & C. Reynolds (Eds.), *Handbook of creativity: Assessment, theory and research* (pp. 341–381). New York, NY: Plenum.

Clement, J. (1993). Using bridging analogies and anchoring intuitions to deal with students' preconceptions in physics. *Journal of Research in Science Teaching, 30*(10), 1241–1257.

Clement, J. (1994). Use of physical intuition and imagistic simulation in expert problem solving. In D. Tirosh (Ed.), *Implicit and explicit knowledge* (pp. 204–244). Norwood, NJ: Ablex.

Clement, J. (2008a). Six levels of organization for curriculum design and teaching. In J. Clement & M. A. Rea-Ramirez (Eds.), *Model based learning and instruction in science* (pp. 255–272). Dordrecht, The Netherlands: Springer.

Clement, J. (2008b). Student/teacher co-construction of visualizable models in large group discussion. In J. Clement & M. Rea-Ramirez (Eds.), *Model based learning and instruction in science* (pp. 11–22). Dordrecht, The Netherlands: Springer.

Clement, J. (2008c). *Creative model construction in scientists and students: The role of imagery, analogy, and mental situation.* Dordrecht, The Netherlands: Springer.

Clement, J. (2009a). The role of imagistic simulation in scientific thought experiments. *Topics in Cognitive Science, 1*, 686–710.

Clement, J. (2009b). Analogical reasoning via imagery: The role of transformations and simulations. In B. Kokinov, K. Holyoak, & D. Gentner, *New frontiers in analogy research.* Sofia, Bulgaria: New Bulgarian University Press.

Clement, J., Brown, D., & Zietsman, A. (1989). Not all preconceptions are misconceptions: Finding anchoring conceptions for grounding instruction on students' intuitions. *International Journal of Science Education, 11*, 554–565.

Clement, J., & Rea-Ramirez, M. (1998). The role of dissonance in conceptual change, *Proceedings of National Association for Research in Science Teaching*, San Diego, CA.

Clement, J., & Rea-Ramirez, M. A. (Eds.). (2008). *Model based learning and instruction in science*. New York, NY: Springer.

Clement, J., & Steinberg, M. (2002). Step-wise evolution of models of electric circuits: A "learning-aloud" case study. *Journal of the Learning Sciences, 11*(4), 389–452.

Coll, R., France, B., & Taylor, I. (2005). The role of models/and analogies in science education: Implications from research. *International Journal of Science Education, 27*(2), 183–198.

Collins, A., & Gentner, D. (1987). How people construct mental models. In D. Holland & N. Quinn (Eds.), *Cultural models in thought and language* (pp. 243–265). Cambridge, UK: Cambridge University Press.

Dagher, Z. R. (1994). Does the use of analogies contribute to conceptual change? *Science Education, 78*(6), 601–614.

Dagher, Z. R. (1995). Review of studies on the effectiveness of instructional analogies in science. *Science Education, 79*(3), 295–312.

Darden, L. (1991). *Theory change in science: Strategies from Mendelian genetics*. New York, NY: Oxford University Press.

diSessa, A. (1988). Knowledge in pieces. In G. Forman & P. B. Pufall (Eds.), *Constructivism in the computer age* (pp. 49–70), Hillsdale, NJ: Lawrence Erlbaum Associates.

Dreyfus, A., Jungwirth, E., & Eliovitch, R (1990). Applying the "cognitive conflict" strategy for conceptual change – Some implications, difficulties, and problems. *Science Education, 74*(5), 555–569.

Driver, R. (1983). *The pupils as scientist?* Milton Keynes, UK: Open University Press.

Dufresne, R. J., Gerace, W. J., Leonard, R, Mestre, J. P., & Wenk, L. (1996). Classtalk: A classroom communication system for active learning. *Journal of Computing in Higher Education, 2*(7), 3–47.

Duit, R. (1991). On the roles of analogies and metaphors in learning science. *Science Education, 75*, 649–672.

Duit, R., Roth, W. M., Komorek, M., & Wilbers, J. (2001). Fostering conceptual change by analogies: Between Scylla and Charybdis. *Learning and Instruction*, IJ(4–5), 283–303.

Dupin, J. J., & Joshua, S. (1989). Analogies and "modeling analogies" in teaching: Some examples in basic electricity. *Science Education, 73*(2), 207–224.

Duschl, R. A., & Osborne, M. (2002). Supporting and promoting argumentation discourse in science education. *Studies in Science Education, 38*, 39–72.

Easley, J. (1990). Conceptual splatter in peer dialogues in selected Japanese and U.S. first-grade mathematics classes. In L. Steffe & T. Wood (Eds.), *Transforming children's mathematics education*. Hillsdale, NJ: Lawrence Erlbaum Associates.

Else, M., Clement, J., & Rea-Ramirez, M. A. (2008). Using analogies in science teaching and curriculum design: Some guidelines. In J. Clement & M. A Rea-Ramirez (Eds.), *Model based learning and instruction in science* (pp. 215–233). New York, NY: Springer.

Fretz, E. B., Wu, H.-K., Zhang, B. H., Davis, E. A., Krajcik, J. S., & Soloway, E. (2002). An investigation of software scaffolds supporting modeling practices. *Research in Science Education, 32*(4), 567–589.

Gabel, D. (1999). Improving teaching and learning through chemistry education research: A look to the future. *Journal of Chemical Education, 76*(4) 548–554.

Gentner, D. (1983). Structure-mapping: A theoretical framework for analogy. *Cognitive Science, 7*, 155–170.

Gentner, D. (1989). The mechanisms of analogical learning. In S. Vosniadou & A. Ortony (Eds.), *Similarity and analogical reasoning* (pp. 199–241). New York, NY: Cambridge University Press.

Gick, M. L., & Holyoak, K. J. (1983). Schema induction and analogical transfer. *Cognitive Psychology, 15*, 1–38.

Giere, R. (1988). *Explaining science: A cognitive approach*. Chicago, IL: Chicago University Press.

Gilbert, J. K., Boulter, C., & Rutherford, M. (1998). Models in explanations, part 2: Whose voice? Whose ears? *International Journal of Science Education, 20*, 187–203.

Gilbert, J. K., Reiner, M., & Nakhleh, M. (Eds.). (2008). *Visualization: Theory and practice in science education*. New York, NY: Springer.

Givry, D., & Tiberghien, A. (2012). Studying students' learning processes used during physics teaching sequence about gas with networks of ideas and their domain of applicability. *International Journal of Science Education, 34*(2), 223–249.

Glynn, S. M. (1991). Explaining science concepts: A teaching-with-analogies model. In S. M. Glynn, R. H. Yeany, & B. K. Britton (Eds.), *The psychology of learning science* (pp. 219–240). Hillsdale, NJ: Lawrence Erlbaum Associates.

Glynn, S. M., & Duit, R. (1995). Learning science meaningfully: Constructing conceptual models. In S. M. Glynn & R. Duit (Eds.), *Learning science in the schools: Research reforming practice*. Mahwah, NJ: Lawrence Erlbaum Associates.

Gobert, J., & Buckley, B. (2000). Introduction to model-based teaching and learning in science education. *International Journal of Science Education, 22*(9), 891–894.

Gorsky, P., & Finegold, M. (1994). The role of anomaly and of cognitive dissonance in restructuring students' concepts of force. *Instructional Science, 22*, 75–90.

Gruber, H. E. (1981). *Darwin on man: A psychological study of scientific creativity.* Chicago, IL: University of Chicago Press.

Guzzetti, B. J., Snyder, T. E., Glass, G. V., & Gamas, W. S. (1993). Promoting conceptual change in science: A comparative meta-analysis of instructional interventions from reading education and science education. *Reading Research Quarterly, 28*(2),116–159.

Hafner, R., & Stewart, J. (1995). Revising explanatory models to accommodate anomalous genetic phenomena: Problem solving in the "context of discovery". *Science Education, 79*(2), 111–146.

Hammer, D. (1996). More than misconceptions: Multiple perspectives on student knowledge and reasoning, and an appropriate role for education research. *American Journal of Physics, 64*(10), 1316–1325.

Hammer, D., & Elby, A. (2002). Tapping epistemological resources for learning physics. *Journal of the Learning Sciences, 12*, 53–90.

Hand, B. M., & Treagust, D. (1988). Application of a conceptual conflict teaching strategy to enhance student learning of acids and bases. *Research in Science Teaching, 18*, 53–63.

Harre, R. (1972). *The philosophies of science.* Oxford, UK: Oxford University Press.

Harrison, A., & De Jong, O. (2005). Exploring the use of multiple analogical models when teaching and learning chemical equilibrium. *Journal of Research in Science Teaching, 42*(10), 1135–1159.

Harrison, A. G., & Treagust, D. (1993). Teaching with analogies: A case-study in grade 10 optics. *Journal of Research in Science Teaching, 30*(10), 1291–1307.

Harrison, A. G., & Treagust, D. F. (1996). Secondary students' mental models of atoms and molecules: implications for teaching science. *Science Education, 80*, 509–534.

Hegarty, M., Kriz, S., & Cate, C. (2003). The roles of mental animations and external animations in understanding mechanical systems. *Cognition and Instruction, 21*(4), 325–360.

Hesse, M. (1966). *Models and analogies in science.* South Bend, IN: Notre Dame University Press.

Hesse, M. (1967). Models and analogies in science. In P. Edwards (Ed.), *The encyclopedia of philosophy.* New York, NY: Free Press.

Hestenes, D., Wells, M., & Swackhammer, G. (1992). Force concept inventory. *The Physics Teacher, 30*(3), 141–158.

Hewson, P., & Hennessey, W. (1992). Making status explicit: A case study of conceptual change. In R. Duit, F. Goldberg, & H. Niedderer (Eds.), *Research in physics learning: Theoretical issues and empirical studies* (pp. 176–187). Kiel, Germany: IPN.

Holland, J., Holyoak, K., Nisbett, R., & Thagard, P. (1986). *Induction: Processes of inference, learning, and discovery.* Cambridge, MA: MIT Press.

Holyoak, K, & Thagard, P. (1989). A computational model of analogical problem solving. In S. Vosniadou and A. Ortony (Eds.), *Similarity and analogical reasoning* (pp. 199–241). New York, NY: Cambridge University Press.

Inagaki, K., & Hatano, G. (1977). Amplification of cognitive motivation and its effects on epistemic observation. *American Educational Research Journal, 14*(4), 485–491.

Inagaki, K., Hatano, G., & Morita, E. (1998). Construction of mathematical knowledge through whole-class discussion. *Learning and Instruction, 8*(6), 503–526.

Joshua, S., & Dupin, J. J. (1987). Taking into account student conceptions in an instructional strategy: An example in physics. *Cognition & Instruction, 4*(2), 117–135.

Khan, S., Stillings, N., Clement, J., & Tronsky, N. (2002). *The impact of an instructional strategy using computer simulations on inquiry skills in chemistry.* Presented at the National Association of Research in Science Teaching, New Orleans, LA, April 2002.

Kuhn, T. (1970). *The structure of scientific revolutions* (2nd edn.). Chicago, IL: University of Chicago Press.

Kuhn, T. (1977). Objectivity, value judgment, and theory choice. Reprinted in T. Kuhn, *The essential tension* (pp. 320–339). Chicago, IL: University of Chicago Press.

Lawson, A. E., Clark, B., Meldrum, E. C., Falconer, K. A., Sequist, J. M., & Kwon, Y. J. (2000). Development of scientific reasoning in college biology: Do two levels of general hypothesis-testing skills exist? *Journal of Research in Science Teaching, 37*(1), 81–101.

Lehrer, R., & Schauble, L. (2003). Origins and evolution of model-based reasoning in mathematics and science. In R. Lesh & H. M. Doerr (Eds.), *Beyond constructivism: Models and modeling perspectives on mathematics problem solving, teaching, and learning* (pp. 59–70). Mahwah, NJ: Lawrence Erlbaum Associates.

Licht, P. (1987). A strategy to deal with conceptual and reasoning problems in introductory electricity education. In J. Novak (Ed.), *Proceedings of the 2nd International Seminar Misconceptions and Educational Strategies in Science and Mathematics*, Vol. II (pp. 275–284). Ithaca, NY: Cornell University.

Linn, M., Bell, P., & Hsi, S. (1998). Using the internet to enhance student understanding of science: The knowledge integration environment. *Interactive Learning Environments*, 6(1–2), 4–38.

Lowe, R. (1993). Constraints on the effectiveness of diagrams as resources for conceptual change. In W. Schnotz, S. Vosniadou, & M. Carretero (Eds.), *New perspectives on conceptual change* (pp. 223–245). New York, NY: Pergamon.

Machamer, P., Darden, L., & Craver, C. F. (2000). Thinking about mechanisms. *Philosophy of Science*, 67, 1–25.

Mason, L. (1994). Cognitive and metacognitive aspects in conceptual change by analogy. *Instructional Science*, 22(3),157–187.

Mayer, R. E. (1989). Models for understanding. *Review of Educational Research*, 59(1), 43–64.

McCloskey, M., Washburn, A., & Felch, L. (1983). Intuitive physics: The straight-down belief and its origin. *Journal of Experimental Psychology*, 9(4), 636–649.

McDermott, L. (1984). Research on conceptual understanding in mechanics. *Physics Today*, 37, 2–32.

Millman, A. B., & Smith, C. L. (1997). Darwin's use of analogical reasoning in theory construction. *Metaphor and Symbol*, 12(3),159–187.

Minstrell, J. (1982). Explaining the 'at rest' condition of an object. *The Physics Teacher*, 20, 10–14.

Minstrell, J., & Krauss, P. (2005). Guided inquiry in the science classroom. In M. S. Donovan & J. D. Bransford (Eds.), *How students learn: Science in the classroom* (pp. 475–514). Washington, DC: National Academies Press.

Nagel, E. (1961). *The structure of science*. New York, NY: Harcourt, Brace, and World.

National Research Council; Committee on Conceptual Framework for the New K-12 Science Education Standards. (2011). *A framework for K-12 science education: Practices, crosscutting concepts, and core ideas. Social sciences*. Washington DC: The National Academies Press.

Nersessian, N. (1992). Constructing and instructing: The role of 'abstraction techniques' in creating and learning physics. In R. Duschl & R. Hamilton (Eds.), *Philosophy of science, cognitive psychology and educational theory and practice* (pp. 48–68). New York, NY: State University of New York Press.

Nersessian, N. (2002). The cognitive basis of model-based reasoning in science. In P. Carruthers, S. Stitch, & M. Siegal (Eds.), *The cognitive basis of science* (pp. 133–153). Cambridge, UK: Cambridge University Press.

Niedderer, H. (2001). Physics learning as cognitive development. In R. H. Evans, A. M. Andersen, & H. Sorensen (Eds.), *Bridging research methodology and research aims*. 5th ESERA Summer School, Gilleleje, Denmark.

Niedderer, H., & Goldberg, F. (1996). *Learning processes in electric circuits*. Paper presented at Annual Meeting of the National Association for Research in Science Teaching, St Louis, MO.

Novak, J. D. (1977). *The philosophical basis for education*. Ithaca, NY: Cornell University Press.

Nunez-Oviedo, M. C., & Clement, J. (2008). A competition strategy and other discussion modes for developing mental models in large group discussion. In J. Clement & M. A. Rea-Ramirez (Eds.), *Model based learning and instruction in science*. Dordrecht, The Netherlands: Springer.

Nunez-Oviedo, M. C., Clement, J., & Rea-Ramirez, M. A. (2007). Developing complex mental models in biology through model evolution. In J. Clement & M. A. Rea-Ramirez (Eds.), *Model based learning and instruction in science* (pp. 173–193). New York, NY: Springer.

Passmore, C. M., & Svoboda, J. (2011). Exploring opportunities for argumentation in modeling classrooms. *International Journal of Science Education*, October, 1–20.

Perkins, D., & Grotzer, T. A. (2005). Dimensions of causal understanding: The role of complex causal models in students' understanding of science. *Studies in Science Education*, 41, 117–165.

Piaget, J. (1930). *The child's conception of physical causality*. London, UK: Kegan Paul.

Pluta, W. J., Chinn, C. A., & Duncan, R. G. (2011). Learners' epistemic criteria for good scientific models. *Journal of Research in Science Teaching*, 48(5), 486–511.

Podolefsky, N., & Finkelstein, N. (2007). Analogical scaffolding and the learning of abstract ideas in physics: Empirical studies. *Physical Review Special Topics – Physics Education Research*, 3, 020104.

Posner, G. J., Strike, K. A., Hewson, P. W., & Gertzog, W. A (1982). Accommodation of a scientific conception: Toward a theory of conceptual change. *Science Education*, 66(2), 211–227.

Raghavan, K., & Glaser, R. (1995). Model-based analysis and reasoning in science: The MARS curriculum. *Science Education*, 79(1),37–61.

Rea-Ramirez, M., & Clement, J. (1998). In search of dissonance: The evolution of dissonance in conceptual change theory. *Proceedings of National Association for Research in Science Teaching*, San Diego, CA.

Rea-Ramirez, M. A., & Nunez-Oviedo, M. C. (2008). Model based reasoning among inner city middle school students. In J. Clement & M. A. Rea-Ramirez (Eds.), *Model based learning and instruction in science* (pp. 233–254). Dordrecht, The Netherlands: Springer.

Rowell, J. A., & Dawson, C. J. (1985). Equilibrium, conflict and instruction: A new class-oriented perspective. *European Journal of Science Education, 5*, 203–215.

Schecker, H., & Niedderer, H. (1996). Contrastive teaching: A strategy to promote qualitative conceptual understanding of science. In D. F. Treagust, R. Duit, & B. J. Fraser (Eds.), *Improving teaching and learning in science and mathematics* (pp. 141–151). New York, NY: Teachers College Press.

Schwartz, D. L., & Black, J. B. (1996). Analog imagery in mental model reasoning: Depictive models. *Cognitive Psychology, 30*, 154–219.

Schwartz, D. L., & Heiser, J. (2006). Spatial representations and imagery in learning. In R. K. Sawyer (Ed.), *Cambridge handbook of the learning sciences* (pp. 283–298). New York, NY: Cambridge University Press.

Schwarz, C. V., Reiser, B. J., Davis, E. A., Kenyon, L. O., Achér, A., Fortus, D., et al. (2009). Developing a learning progression for scientific modeling: Making scientific modeling accessible and meaningful for learners. *Journal of Research in Science Teaching, 46*(6), 632–654.

Scott, P. H. (1992). Conceptual pathways in learning science: A case study of the development of one student's ideas relating to the structure of matter. In R. Duit, F. Goldberg, & H. Niedderer (Eds.), *Research in physics learning: Theoretical issues and empirical studies* (pp. 203–224). Kiel, Germany: IPN.

She, H. (2004). Fostering radical conceptual change through dual-situated learning model. *Journal of Research in Science Teaching, 41*(2), 142–164.

Simons, P. (1984). Instructing with analogies. *Journal of Educational Psychology, 76*, 513–527.

Smith, C., Wiser, M., Anderson, C., & Krajcik, J. (2006). Implications of research on children's learning for standards and assessment: A proposed learning progression for matter and the atomic–molecular theory. *Measurement: Interdisciplinary Research and Perspectives, 4*(1&2), 1–98.

Smith, J. P., diSessa, A. A., & Roschelle, J. (1993). Misconceptions reconceived: A constructivist analysis of knowledge in transition. *Journal of the Learning Sciences, 3*(2), 115–163.

Spiro, R. J., Feltovich, P. J., Coulson, R. I., & Anderson, D. K. (1991). Multiple analogies for complex concepts: Antidotes for analogy-induced misconception in advanced knowledge acquisition. In S. Vosniadou & A. Ortony (Eds.), *Similarity and analogical reasoning* (pp. 498–531). Cambridge, UK: Cambridge University Press.

Stavy, R. (1991). Using analogy to overcome misconceptions about conservation of matter. *Journal of Research in Science Teaching, 28*(4), 305–313.

Stavy, R., & Berkovitz, B. (1980). Cognitive conflict as a basis for teaching quantitative aspects of the concept of temperature. *Science Education, 64*(5), 679–692.

Steinberg, M. (2004). *Electricity visualized – The CASTLE project.* Roseville, CA: PASCO Scientific.

Steinberg, M. (2008). Target model sequence and critical learning pathway for an electricity curriculum based on model evolution. In J. Clement & M. A. Rea-Ramirez (Eds.), *Model based learning and instruction in science* (pp. 79–102). Dordrecht, The Netherlands: Springer.

Stephens, L., & Clement, J. (2010). Documenting the use of expert scientific reasoning processes by high school physics students. *Physical Review Special Topics – Physics Education Research, 6*(2), 020122.

Stephens, L., & Clement, J. (2012). The role of thought experiments in science learning. In K. Tobin, C. Mcrobbie, & B. Fraser, *International handbook of science education, Vol. II.* Dordrecht, The Netherlands: Springer.

Stepich, D. A., & Newby, T. J. (1988). Analogical instruction within the information processing paradigm: Effective means to facilitate learning. *Instructional Science, 17*, 129–144.

Strike, K. A., & Posner, G. J. (1992). A revisionist theory of conceptual change. In R. Duschl & R. Hamilton (Eds.), *Philosophy of science, cognitive psychology and educational theory and practice* (pp. 147–176). Albany, NY: State University of New York Press.

Tabak, I., Sandoval, W. A., Smith, B. K., Agganis, A., Baumgartner, E., & Reiser, B. J. (1995). *Supporting collaborative guided inquiry in a learning environment for biology.* Paper presented at the Proceedings of CSCL '95: The First International Conference on Computer Support for Collaborative Learning, Bloomington, IN.

Taber, K. S. (2001). Shifting sands: A case study of conceptual development as competition between alternative conceptions. *International Journal of Science Education, 23*(7), 731–753.

Thagard, P. (1992). *Conceptual revolutions.* Princeton, NJ: Princeton University Press.

Thiele, R. B., & Treagust, D. F. (2006). An interpretive examination of high school chemistry teachers' analogical explanations. *Journal of Research in Science Teaching, 31*(3), 227–242.

Toulmin, S. (1972). *Human understanding: An inquiry into the aims of science.* Princeton, NJ: Princeton University Press.

Treagust, D., Harrison, A., Venville, G., & Dagher, Z. (1996). Using an analogical teaching approach to engender conceptual change. *International Journal of Science Education, 18,* 213–229.

Tsai, C.-C., & Chang, C.-Y. (2005). Lasting effects of instruction guided by the conflict map: Experimental study of learning about the causes of the seasons. *Journal of Research in Science Teaching, 42*(10), 1089–1111.

Vosniadou, S., & Brewer, W. F. (1992). Mental models of the earth: A study of conceptual change in childhood. *Cognitive Psychology, 24,* 535–585.

Wells, M., Hestenes, D., & Swackhamer, G. (1995). A modeling method for high school physics instruction. *American Journal of Physics, 63,* 606–619.

White, B. Y. (1993). ThinkerTools: Causal models, conceptual change, and science education. *Cognition and Instruction, 10,* 1–100.

Williams, G., & Clement, J. (2011). Multiple levels of discussion-based teaching strategies for supporting students' construction of mental models. *Proceedings of the Annual Meeting of the National Association for Research in Science Teaching,* Orlando, FL.

Windschitl, M., Thompson, J., & Braaten, M. (2008). Beyond the scientific method: Model-based inquiry as a new paradigm of preference for school science investigations. *Science Education, 92*(5), 941–967.

Wiser, M., & Carey, S. (1983). When heat and temperature were one. In D. Gentner & A. Stevens (Eds.), *Mental models* (pp. 267–297). Mahwah, NJ: Lawrence Erlbaum Associates.

Yerrick, R., Doster, E., Nugent, J. S., Parke, H. M., & Crawley, F. E. (2003). Social interaction and the use of analogy: An analysis of preservice teachers' talk during physics inquiry lessons. *Journal of Research in Science Teaching, 40*(5),443–463.

Zietsman, A., & Clement, J. (1997). The role of extreme case reasoning in instruction for conceptual change. *Journal of the Learning Sciences, 6*(1), 61–89.

Zietsman, A. I., & Hewson, P. W. (1986). Effect of instruction using microcomputer simulations and conceptual change strategies on science learning. *Journal of Research in Science Teaching, 23,* 27–39.

23

CONCEPTUAL INNOVATION AND TRANSFER

Lee Martin and Daniel L. Schwartz,
University of California, Davis, and Stanford University

Conceptual change involves building new knowledge. Changes can be small and local, like an individual's realization that whales are mammals, not fish (Chi, Slotta, & De Leeuw, 1994b), or large and society-changing, like the scientific discovery that disease is caused by germs (Thagard, 1996). People build new knowledge from a foundation of old knowledge, and for this reason, theories of transfer are pertinent to the study of conceptual change. Transfer is the use of learning gained in one context or topic to help with another. Individuals may transfer learning from school to kitchen or from algebra to chemistry. The literature on transfer shows that it is both ubiquitous, if one considers any use of existing knowledge in a new setting to be evidence of transfer (Lobato, 2003), and exceedingly rare, if one looks for the application of specified, instructed knowledge on a single transfer problem (Detterman, 1993).

Conceptual change often occurs when contextual demands necessitate the development of new knowledge. Transfer, in contrast, occurs when contextual demands necessitate the deployment of old knowledge. While these sound like opposing processes, they are in fact linked. Most conceptual change is impossible without transfer, and the transfer of knowledge to a new context imbues it with new contexts of application, thus extending (and slightly altering) the transferred knowledge.

Transfer is unique among the many approaches to conceptual change because transfer is intimately concerned with the context of cognition. Transfer research tries to explain why people can retrieve and change their ideas in some contexts, but not others. We broaden the discussion of conceptual change to include structural changes to the environment, which can feed back and change people's mental representations. To avoid diluting the term "conceptual change," we adopt the broader term *innovation*, which can refer to new ideas and new material structures.

Innovation, like conceptual change, can refer to either a process or an outcome. Innovative outcomes come at two scales. Grand innovations are those that are novel on a global scale and were previously unknown, such as the telephone and the theory of evolution. Petite innovations are local and new to a given person. Over history, many different people can achieve the same petite innovation. For example, most children learn that the amount of water in a wide glass does not change when poured into a narrow glass, even though the height changes. Although the discovery of conservation is extremely common, it is no less of an innovation for any one child.

The process of innovation – the mechanisms involved in restructuring thought or the environment – applies to both grand and petite innovations. This is important, because grand innovations are rare events, and their low frequency and unpredictability makes it hard to develop an empirically grounded account of innovation (Johnson-Laird, 1989). Because petite innovations regularly recur across people, it is possible to study the processes of these innovations. Ideally, findings from research on petite innovations can help create conditions for grand innovation. One important goal of education is to make the next generation of innovators – innovators who can make petite innovations in response to a rapidly changing world, and those who can make grand innovations that rapidly change the world.

Transfer mechanisms are relevant to the process of innovation because they enable the application of prior learning for the purposes of innovation. The main body of transfer research has not examined how mechanisms of transfer support innovation. Detterman (1993), for example, defined transfer as the "the degree to which a new behavior will be repeated in a new situation" (p. 4). Replicating a behavior is quite different from innovating a new one. Transfer research has typically focused on the transfer of prior knowledge or behavior to improve speed and accuracy on a novel task (cf. Schwartz, Bransford, & Sears, 2005). Asking how people become more efficient by repetition is different from asking how people innovate by building on prior knowledge. Nevertheless, there is research on transfer that is relevant to innovation.

The strength of the transfer literature for innovation is in its explication of how people and contexts interact to achieve an innovation (Thagard, 1996), and also, how people can fail to achieve an innovation. Transfer is a double-edged sword. People can transfer in prior learning to support change, but they can also transfer in routines that prevent change. A good example comes from children learning fractions. Children could hardly learn to compare two-out-of-three versus four-out-of-seven if they had never learned about natural numbers. At the same time, children's over-reliance on well-understood natural number schemas can interfere with a rational number interpretation (Kerslake, 1986). For example, children have difficulty understanding properties of rational numbers that differ from those of natural numbers, such as there being multiple ways to represent the same value (e.g., 1/1 and 100/100), or that there is no unique successor to a given rational number (Stafylidou & Vosniadou, 2004; Vamvakoussi & Vosniadou, 2010).

The tensions between old and new knowledge inherent in learning fractions highlight two fundamental problems of transfer for innovation. The first is the *knowledge problem*, which asks, how can new knowledge be built from existing knowledge? The second is the *inertia problem*, which asks how and why people go beyond existing routines, which may have served them well in the past, to try something new.

In the remainder of this chapter, we consider two solutions to these problems, drawn from the literature on transfer. In the first solution, *similarity transfer*, people apply well-formed concepts from one situation to explain another situation in a novel way. For example, people often use causal explanations for the "sophomore slump" in sports, where rookies who excel in their first season do worse the next year (e.g., early success led to complacency). By transferring in their knowledge of statistics, people may reconceptualize the drop in performance as an instance of regression to the mean. In the second solution, *dynamic transfer*, people do not begin with a fully formed concept, but rather they achieve a novel concept by through a process of coordination (diSessa & Wagner, 2005). For example, infants learn to coordinate the actions of looking and reaching through interactions in the environment. When these are well coordinated, they lead to the development of object permanence (Thelen & Smith, 1994).

TWO FORMS OF TRANSFER

The transfer literature has typically focused on similarity transfer, where people already possess well-formed prior knowledge developed for one situation, and they use this knowledge to understand a different situation in a new way. For example, scientists might learn to view traffic congestion in terms of their knowledge of fluid dynamics. The conceptual change does not occur to their existing knowledge of fluid dynamics; rather, they change their concept of freeway congestion. We call this similarity transfer, because the key move involves recognizing that two situations or ideas are similar, even though they may not appear so at first.

Some of the clearest and most extensively studied examples of similarity transfer for innovation come from studies of *analogical transfer* (for representative studies on analogical transfer see Gick & Holyoak, 1983; Reed, Ernst, & Banerji, 1974). Kepler developed his theory of planetary motion by drawing an analogy from the light of the sun (Gentner et al., 1997). He posited that the sun projected a force to the planets in a similar manner to the way it projected light. From there, he drew an analogy between the amount of light that reached a planet through its movement and the amount of force that kept it in place. This is an example of a grand innovation. Kepler's introduction of the concept of force explained elliptical orbits, and his theory could generatively predict orbits of new planets that were discovered, wherever they might be.

What are the requirements for a similarity transfer to take place? The first requirement is that people have well-formed knowledge in a base domain that they can eventually apply to a target domain. Many purported demonstrations of failed transfer actually were not failed transfer, as people never actually learned the source concepts or skills, so there was no way they could fail to transfer. A genuine failure of similarity transfer occurs when people have "inert knowledge" (Whitehead, 1929) – relevant knowledge that is not applied. The field has made several important discoveries about the types of experiences and knowledge structures that help people avoid inert knowledge. These include the opportunity to discern commonalities and differences using multiple examples (e.g., Gick & Holyoak, 1983; Schwartz & Bransford, 1998), explicate the general principal behind the examples (e.g., Brown & Kane, 1988), and experience the problem for which the transferable knowledge would be the solution (e.g., Bransford, Franks, Vye, & Sherwood, 1989).

A second requirement for similarity transfer is that people must detect the similarity between two situations, otherwise the knowledge from one situation will not be applied to the other. The transfer literature distinguishes between two levels of similarity. The first occurs at the level of *surface features* or "identical elements" (Thorndike & Woodworth, 1901). Chi, Feltovich, and Glaser (1981), for example, reported that undergraduates taking introductory physics classified problems by surface features (e.g., pulley problems, spring–mass problems). A focus on surface features can cause individuals to transfer the wrong ideas across problems. For example, the undergraduates would likely fail to transfer solutions across spring and pulley problems, because they see them as unrelated. They are also likely to exhibit the *negative transfer* of a solution from one pulley problem to another, even if the problems do not involve the same principles (cf., Ross, 1989). A second level of similarity involves identical relations or *deep features*. The physics graduate students in Chi et al.'s (1981) study classified problems according to the underlying principles needed to solve them. They could see when the relations between the objects within each problem involved the same principles, even if they looked quite different. When people can recognize relational or structural similarities, they are able to transfer across situations that have surface level differences. For example, they can transfer principles from pulley to (structurally similar) spring problems.

Dynamic transfer occurs when people coordinate multiple conceptual components, often through interaction with the environment, to create an innovation. For example, Blair, Tsang, and Schwartz (Chapter 17, this volume) found that the adult concept of integers (positive and negative numbers) includes symmetry, and children learn the integer system better when they learn to coordinate the negative and positive numbers using symmetry about zero. The requirements for dynamic transfer differ from those for similarity transfer. While dynamic transfer does require prior knowledge, this knowledge can be tacit and unconnected, rather than the complete, structurally complex knowledge needed for similarity transfer. While similarity transfer requires people to first notice similarities, then map across domains, dynamic transfer relies on people using the environment to coordinate conceptual components as they move toward an innovation.

An example will help to clarify the distinction between dynamic transfer and similarity transfer. Martin and Schwartz (2005) studied nine- and ten-year-old children as they learned to add simple fractions like 1/4 + 1/2. Half of the children learned using pie pieces and half learned with tile pieces, as shown in Figure 23.1. After instruction, both groups could solve the problems using their respective materials, but they could not solve the problems in their heads. For the transfer task, the children attempted similar addition problems with novel materials (e.g., beans, fraction bars).

Figure 23.2 provides a schematic of the two courses of transfer for the Tile and Pie children. The vertical dimension indicates how frequently children gave accurate verbal answers; for example, given the problem 1/2 + 1/4, they state "three-fourths." The horizontal dimension indicates how frequently the children arranged the physical materials correctly; for example, for 1/2 + 1/4, the children arrange the one-half as one of two groups of two pieces. The arrows indicate the average trajectory of learning over time for the two groups.

Figure 23.1 Pie wedges and tiles often used to teach children fractions. The pies exhibit a part–whole structure. In contrast, to turn the three tiles into three-fourths, it is necessary to impose structure, for example by adding a fourth tile to the side

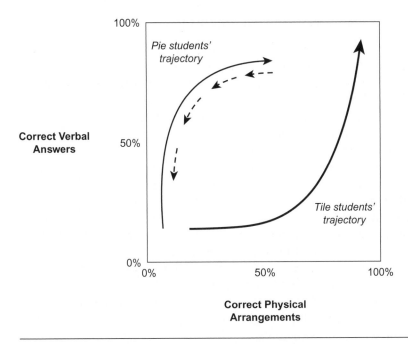

Figure 23.2 Two trajectories of transfer (adapted from Martin & Schwartz, 2005)

The Tile children showed a stable trajectory that ended in the top right corner of near-perfect verbal and physical performance. They first improved in how they structured the physical materials, before they began to give the correct verbal answers. This pattern represents a dynamic transfer, because interactions with the environment helped the children slowly coordinate their (verbal) understanding. In contrast, the Pie children did not reach high levels of accuracy on either dimension, nor were they stable: They often regressed from one trial to the next. In addition, unlike the Tile children, the Pie children were better at giving verbal answers than arranging the materials. What explains the poor performance of the Pie children? During their initial learning, they had implicitly relied on the part–whole structure of the pies, and the new materials did not exhibit the circular whole. These children could not make a dynamic transfer through interaction, because they had never explicitly learned to impose a whole to turn discrete elements into fractions. Instead of completing a dynamic transfer, they attempted a similarity transfer by trying to remember how they solved similar prior problems, and they could not use the structure of the novel materials to help them learn.

Similarity transfer, as the act of an individual mind, often has an all-or-nothing quality. In contrast, dynamic transfer is an iterative process: a sequence of near transfers that accumulate into innovations. The trajectory of the Tile students in Figure 23.2 shows that the interactive process of dynamic transfer can have the quality of trial and error and can appear inefficient. However, when coupled with the right resources, the interactions may result in a coordination that can be an innovation, in this case an understanding of parts and wholes when adding unlike fractions.

THE KNOWLEDGE PROBLEM

The knowledge problem asks, how can new ideas arise out of existing knowledge? In other words, through what processes can old concepts of one sort possibly create new concepts of another sort? Similarity transfer and dynamic transfer offer distinct solutions to this question. As described above, similarity transfer creates new knowledge by first retrieving intact, well-formed prior knowledge, and then creating a mapping to a new domain. While similarity transfer explains how people map well-formed concepts to structure new situations, it does not explain how well-formed concepts develop in the first place. Dynamic transfer attempts to answer the genesis question by showing how knowledge can be assembled, in interaction with the environment, into complex wholes.

In addition to differences in the type of prior knowledge that is "transferred in" to create new knowledge, the two forms of transfer differ in their use of the environment. In similarity transfer, the environment serves primarily as an input, providing information that can be accessed and used in cognitive processes. In particular, the world provides cues that activate intact prior knowledge. This knowledge is then applied, perhaps with some modifications, to the new situation. In dynamic transfer, the environment also plays a critical role, but in this case it serves as more than a source of information. It serves as a workspace for thought and action, where ideas can be brought together and coordinated into new structures.

A powerful example of how the environment can support the coordination of knowledge comes from the study of "split-brain" patients who have had the neural connections between the brain's right and left hemispheres surgically severed as a treatment for severe epilepsy. Although this procedure creates two highly isolated cognitive systems within a single individual, some patients who have had this procedure can function quite normally in everyday life. One reason for their success may be their ability to use the external world to coordinate thinking across hemispheres. Kingstone and Gazzaniga (1995) report that one split-brain patient almost fooled them into thinking there was covert neural communication between his two hemispheres. When they presented the words "bow" and "arrow" to opposite hemispheres (via opposite visual fields), the patient was able to produce a coordinated drawing of a bow and arrow. Although this looked like neural communication, coordination was actually occurring through the drawing surface itself, as each hemisphere had access to the emerging drawing on the page. The patient substituted the external world for neural pathways as a means to integrate two ideas.

The two forms of transfer also differ in the "critical move" that starts the process of transfer. Similarity transfer relies on noticing similarities between prior knowledge and a new domain. The critical move for similarity transfer is to see that "this is like that." Dynamic transfer relies on noticing potential coordination points among conceptual components and features of the environment. The critical move for dynamic transfer is to see that "this goes with that." We summarize these distinctions in Table 23.1.

This is not to say that similarity transfer never involves interaction with the environment. In analogical transfer, for example, people must figure out which parts of the analogy work for the target situation, a process that can involve iterations of checking, revising, and checking again (Gentner et al., 1997). But similarity transfer can occur in thought alone, while dynamic transfer relies on environmental support. In order to give a fuller picture of the nature of this interaction, we briefly outline four ways in which

Table 23.1 Similarity transfer and dynamic transfer

	Knowledge	Role of context	Critical move
Similarity transfer	Well-formed knowledge	Environment cues intact knowledge	"This is like that"
Dynamic transfer	Partial knowledge	Environment coordinates components through interaction	"This goes with that"

environments can support the coordination of component knowledge during a dynamic transfer.

Four Ways the Environment Supports Dynamic Transfer

Distributed Memory

Although purely internal mental work such as self-explanation, thought experiments, and creative visual imaginings can lead to innovations (Chi, de Leeuw, Chiu, & LaVancher, 1994a; Finke, 1990), it is nonetheless difficult. People have limited working memories, and it is hard to coordinate a jumble of concepts without distributing some of the work to the environment. The external world can store intermediate steps and structures during transfer. Architects, for example, sketch designs to help the process of conceptualizing a new design (Goel, 1995). Environmental traces also support backtracking. When the process of dynamic transfer hits a dead end, people can look at the record in the environment to backtrack as far as needed, and then try again.

Distributed memory can be a powerful support for innovation. For example, Piaget (1976) found that five- and six-year-old children could not solve Tower of Hanoi problems involving as few as two disks. Klahr and Robinson (1981) showed that, when they replaced stacking plates with nesting cups, thus embedding the hard to remember "smaller on larger" rule into the environment, six-year-old children were able to innovate solutions for problems with as many as three cups requiring as many as five moves. We suspect that an important class of metacognitive development involves learning when and how to use the environment to amplify thinking and memory in ways that lead to innovation.

Reinterpretation

Interactions with the environment generate feedback and variability that can help people shake free of initial interpretations that can block innovation.

Chambers and Reisberg (1985) studied how prior interpretations can interfere with developing new ones. They had people look at a picture that can be seen as a duck or a rabbit (e.g., Figure 23.3). Once people had an interpretation, they closed their eyes. Chambers and Reisberg then asked the people if they could come up with a second interpretation. Not a single participant over several studies could form an alternate interpretation. However, if people are allowed to open their eyes and jiggle the picture a bit, they can find the alternative interpretation.

Martin and Schwartz (2005) showed similar benefits to interactive experiences. They gave nine-year-olds plastic tiles and had them solve equivalent fraction problems such

Figure 23.3 Duck/rabbit image used in many experiments (e.g., Chambers & Reisberg, 1985)

as "What is one-fourth of eight?" Children prevented from touching the tiles tended to form whole-number interpretations, indicating one and/or four pieces as the answer. They were making a faulty similarity transfer of their well-practiced whole-number schemas to problems involving ratios. When the same children were allowed to rearrange the pieces, they were nearly four times more successful. By moving the pieces, the children began to notice mathematical grouping structures. For example, they created four groups of tiles, where each group had two tiles. The children were on their way to innovating a new understanding of rational number.

Candidate Structure

As Simon (1969) noted, complex behavior can result from either complex internal processing or a complex environment. The idea of scaffolding builds on this idea: Scaffolds build structure into the environment so that learners can engage in mature performance. People may appropriate or internalize these embedded structures, yielding petite innovations. For example, children told to use symbolic mathematics learn to predict the behavior of a balance scale more quickly than those encouraged to use natural language (Schwartz, Martin, & Pfaffman, 2005). Without the candidate structures of mathematics, the children could not coordinate the two dimensions of weight and distance. Many educators have noted the potential of technologies to provide structures for children to learn from. White (2008), for example, describes a case where students opportunistically took advantage of an unintended structure in a piece of software (the result of a programming error) to innovate a new method to solve cryptography problems.

A Focal Point for Coordination

Innovations through dynamic transfer depend on integrating knowledge. Interactivity provides a natural focal point for coordinating different sources or types of knowledge. Griffin, Case, and Siegler (1994), for example, had children play simple board games designed so that they had to coordinate ordinal and cardinal conceptions of number. Suppose a child rolls a die and gets a "6." The children have to count out six spaces to reach a particular position. As they land on each space, they pick up a chip. When they reach the final space, they have to decide if they have more chips than another student who rolled a five and ended up on the fifth space. In this example, the environment helps the child coordinate the cardinal value of the digit "6" (total amount) with its ordinal value (sixth step). Interaction can bring different pockets of knowledge into alignment.

For the children learning math, it leads to an understanding of number where ordinal and cardinal properties are related to one another.

THE INERTIA PROBLEM

We now turn to the inertia problem. A natural threat to innovation is the tendency to assimilate situations into one's pre-existing routines. People may treat new situations like old ones, instead of changing their ideas or actions. In Luchins and Luchins' (1959) classic studies of *einstellung*, or rigidity of behavior, people learned a complex method for measuring water using several jars in sequence. Once they had mastered the multi-jar method, they received simpler problems that could be solved more efficiently with only one or two jars. People transferred the complex method and never considered searching for an alternative. Instead of transferring for innovation, people often transfer for repetition. In many situations, of course, repetition is a good thing, and constant innovation would be insufferable.

In addition to fixation, there is a second source of the inertia problem. Even if people do recognize that a situation might be worth a bit of innovation, there is no guarantee that the effort to innovate will yield an innovative outcome. Moreover, the process of innovation typically requires a "productivity dip" as people become temporarily less efficient. Fullan (2001) discusses the "implementation dip" that occurs when people deploy an innovation, for example, in a business setting. The productivity dip refers to the loss of effectiveness while making the innovation itself.

An example of a productivity dip comes from the U-shaped curve in the acquisition of past tense (Ervin & Miller, 1963). Early on, children correctly use regular and irregular past tense forms, for example, "talked" and "bought" and "gave", having memorized these words on a case-by-case basis. In the next stage, children make a conceptual innovation by switching from their ad hoc system to a rule that might be summarized as, *add "-ed" to a verb to make it past tense*. At this stage, children correctly convert novel verbs into the past tense, but they also add "-ed" to irregular verbs that they previously said correctly (e.g., "buyed" or "gived"). It is only after some time that they learn to apply the past tense rule to some words and to use irregular forms for other words.

How do people overcome the inertia of their prior learning so they engage in innovation? For similarity transfer, one question is how similar the source and target domains appear to be. Researchers often distinguish *near* and *far* transfer (for factors that affect the distance of similarity, see Barnett & Ceci, 2002). When two situations share both surface features and deep features, they are highly similar, and transfer between them is considered a *near transfer*. If two situations share surface features but not deep features, transfer is inappropriate, despite the apparent similarity. Transfer in this case is called *negative transfer*. When two situations share deep features but not surface features, it can be more difficult to recognize the similarity. Transfer in this case is called *far transfer*. Innovations depend on far transfer. If the transfer were too near, then it would not illuminate a different situation in a novel way.

Another useful distinction involves *spontaneous* and *prompted* transfer. Instructors can often prompt far transfer by introducing analogies that help students innovate new (to them) concepts. For example, an instructor might use the analogy of water in a pipe to explain the invisible processes of electricity. In contrast, spontaneous transfer occurs when people make the analogy themselves without any external support. Using an analogy to help explain a concept to someone else is quite different from learners spontaneously generating the analogy on their own. Spontaneous, self-directed transfer across highly different domains or contexts is infrequent (Detterman, 1993). It took Kepler a lifetime to work out the analogy between light and gravity.

Since at least Piaget (1952), the supposition has been that efforts toward innovation, whether prompted or self-directed, are fault-driven. People detect (or are shown) an internal contradiction or an external impasse, and this causes them to search for a new way to resolve the problem. Vosniadou and Brewer (1992), for example, showed that children innovate hybrid models of the earth (e.g., a flat earth inside a round bowl) to rectify their experience of a flat world with the overheard idea that the world is round. Fault-driven accounts are consistent with the scientific practice of rectifying theories given falsifying data. Yet fault-driven transfer for innovation cannot be the complete story, as there are cases where people make a *prospective adaptation* (Martin & Schwartz, 2009) – an effort after innovation made despite no failure in performance. Elite athletes routinely step away from performance to engage in extensive *deliberate practice* (Ericsson & Lehmann, 1996), faculty take sabbaticals to learn new skills, and, as noted above, children change their concept of how to form the past tense, even though the change leads to more errors in the short term.

As we consider various solutions to the inertia problem, we anchor our discussion through a spatial metaphor. The vectors in Figure 23.4 represent a sample of the trajectories people can follow over time; they range from genuine innovation, to mere improvements in efficiency, to outright failure. Movement up the gradient represents the process of adaptation over time. The height of the gradient at any point captures the adaptiveness of the outcomes at that point in time. Adaptiveness can be gauged according to different definitions – time, cost, happiness, cultural mandates. Over time, some trajectories reach higher levels of adaptiveness that constitute innovations, while others achieve more efficient routines without yielding the long-term adaptive benefits gained by innovations. The "fault" and "productivity dip" zones indicate that people become locally less adaptive in those areas. The gradient representation is inspired by work in artificial intelligence. Higher elevations represent more innovative outcomes. However, a steeper rise is more difficult to climb, because it implies a faster rate of adaptation. The trajectories of Figure 23.4 do not cover the complete range of ways people traverse the space of innovation (different endeavors will have their own terrains), but they help to clarify different transfer solutions to the inertia problem.

In similarity transfer, people apply prior learning whole-cloth to a new situation. The challenge for similarity transfer is whether the existing knowledge and the new situation are close enough that the similarity will be noticed and leveraged. Trajectory 1 represents a spontaneous, far transfer that yields an innovation. The figure illustrates why spontaneous far transfer is rare: it depends on an unprovoked, prospective leap far beyond one's position in the space. There is no impetus to do so, unless people can prefigure the innovative outcome of the transfer. If it fails, people have learned little about the terrain over which they jumped.

Trajectory 2 represents fault-driven similarity transfer. A sequence of near transfers advances up the slope of innovation, until there is a fault that blocks further incremental progress. For example, engineers designing fruit pickers may repeatedly transfer techniques for making gentle claws to handle increasingly delicate fruit. A situation may arise that cannot be traversed by a near transfer. For example, the gentlest claws may still

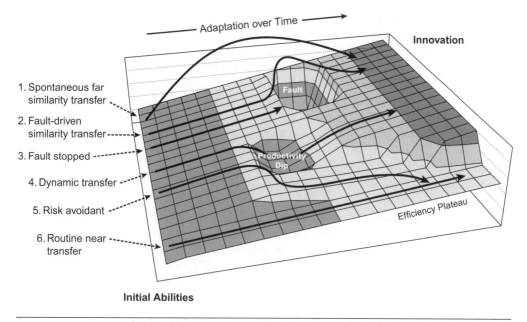

1. Spontaneous far
   similarity transfer

2. Fault-driven
   similarity transfer

3. Fault stopped

4. Dynamic transfer

5. Risk avoidant

6. Routine near
   transfer

Adaptation over Time

Innovation

Fault

Productivity
Dip

Efficiency Plateau

Initial Abilities

Figure 23.4 Trajectories of innovation (see text for explanation)

puncture tomatoes. The engineers might perseverate on making gentler claws, but the loss of adaptiveness may be too great. Instead, the engineers might intentionally search for an analogous domain, such as prior work on machines to lift boxes. They might then draw from an experience of making thicker boxes to arrive at the innovation of breeding thick skinned tomatoes. (In reality, they talked to biologists who suggested the bio-engineering solution.)

Trajectory 3 shows people stopping at the sign of a major fault. Prior knowledge fails to meet the demands of a new situation, and people disengage from the problem. This trajectory is not inherently bad, as dead ends can signal ill-conceived plans. However, people sometimes disengage when there might be other paths available given persever-ance. The transfer literature would be enriched if it examined the types of dispositions and social supports that can help people avoid the tendency to transfer in the belief that efforts to persevere are fruitless (e.g., Blackwell, Trzesniewski, & Dweck, 2007).

Trajectory 4 shows dynamic transfer. Dynamic transfer is the product of a sequence of interactions with a well-structured environment that may include tools, represen-tations, other people, and so forth. People make a number of small dynamic transfers that eventually yield the stable coordination that constitutes an innovation, as in the case of children using tiles to learn fraction problems such as "one-fourth of eight" (Martin & Schwartz, 2005). The children slowly worked through different grouping possibilities until they reached a structure that coordinated the "one," "four," and "eight" in the problem.

Dynamic transfer cannot jump across the productivity dip (or a fault) with a far transfer, as it depends on coordination with the environment for learning. Unlike fault–driven similarity transfer, people need not recognize any productivity dips that may arise. Children do not need to note their impaired performance when acquiring the past tense. Interestingly, connectionist models of past-tense acquisition are consistent with

Trajectory 4. They demonstrate that small, local, and quantitative changes of a dynamic transfer can lead to innovations – qualitative changes in how knowledge of inflectional forms is organized (e.g., Plunkett & Marchman, 1996).

Of course, there are situations where the environment is not conducive to entering the productivity dip, and people will avoid it. Children learn the past-tense rule because they are in an environment that encourages ongoing interaction and tolerates dips in efficiency. In contrast, Trajectory 5 represents a situation of high risk or pressure to perform in the short term. In this trajectory, people balk at the productivity dip, because any loss of effectiveness is problematic. One option is to stop adapting. Trajectory 5 shows the second alternative, taking a shallow gradient that does not involve a short-term loss in effectiveness. This trajectory ultimately merges with the final trajectory in our inventory.

Trajectory 6 represents a series of near similarity transfers, where people generalize and fine-tune their abilities across situations. This leads to an improvement in efficiency, but not a genuine innovation. This shallow region of the space is traversed until a plateau is reached. People achieve a level of "routine expertise" that enables them to accomplish familiar tasks in familiar and efficient ways (Hatano & Inagaki, 1986).

CAN ROUTINES SUPPORT INNOVATION?

In some contexts, innovations are neither rare nor unpredictable events. Children's development over time is characterized by continual and incremental, yet cumulatively profound changes in their thinking and understanding across a wide variety of domains. While there are numerous well-known conceptual changes that are difficult to engender (Chi et al., 1994b), conceptual change is nonetheless a commonplace event both within and across individuals. Innovations are common as well. The product cycle of Intel, for example, requires a new product release every three months (COSEPUP, 2006). This does not imply that innovations are easy to create; only that they are common. Successful learning environments and successful businesses must each have processes in place that lead to innovations in thought, in circumstances, or in processes themselves, on a fairly regular basis.

How might one create routine conditions for innovation through the processes of similarity transfer and dynamic transfer? For similarity transfer, it is difficult to imagine routines for grand innovations. Guided, petite innovations are easier to envision, as in the case when a teacher hopes to lead a student through a planned conceptual innovation. Because similarity transfer relies on creating a mapping between two distinct domains, a teacher can first ensure that students already know one domain, and then create a situation that prompts the students to think of a second domain in the same terms. For example, when teaching students about the physics of electrical current as an emergent process, a teacher might first teach students about bird flocking behavior in a computer simulation, before prompting students to map this understanding on to the study of electrical circuits.

Arranging conditions for unguided innovations with similarity transfer, where no one knows the desired outcome in advance, is more challenging. Specialists may have very precise knowledge about the topic for which an innovation would be useful, but might lack expertise in any other domains to generate candidate analogies. The analogies they can generate from other domains will not have sufficient precision and structure to map into the complexity of the situations they are trying to explain. One approach to this problem is to ensure a diverse and "well-rounded" education, comprising some level of mastery of knowledge in a variety of subject areas. Advocates of liberal arts education make the point that a narrow, overly specialized education is antithetical to innovative outcomes for just this reason.

At the group level, creation of interdisciplinary teams is a common approach to support innovation through similarity transfer. Interdisciplinary teams offer the potential for a shared knowledge base that is both diverse and well-developed. An example of this approach comes from companies that use online programs to solicit analogies from different disciplines (Feller, Fitzgerald, Hissam, & Lakhani, 2005). For example, a pharmaceutical company might post a drug compound that has side-effects it cannot explain. People from other disciplines can look at the posting, and if they can generate a solution, the company might pay them for it. For example, a mathematician might recognize a parallel between the drug problem and knot theory. Dunbar (1997) describes a second approach. He found that biology labs have computer programs that help scientists generate candidate analogies. The biologists enter specific characteristics of the biological compounds and interactions they are trying to understand, and the computer program generates homologs (i.e., other biological structures that have similar properties), and the biologist can draw the analogy between the homologs to see if they work.

Is it possible to create routines to support innovation through dynamic transfer? As we noted above, a critical aspect of dynamic transfer is the way in which the environment helps people to coordinate their thinking. As with similarity transfer, dynamic transfer driven innovations can be either guided (by a teacher) or executed independently. An example of a guided innovation comes from Schwartz, Chase, Oppezzo, and Chin (2011). They gave pairs of eighth-grade students the task of inventing density. For example, in one task, students received the worksheet shown in Figure 23.5. Each row represents a company that sends clowns to parties. The companies differ in how tightly they pack clowns onto buses, but each company is consistent from party to party (to send more clowns, they use a larger bus). The students task was to invent a crowdedness index indicating how tightly each company packed its clowns (because crowded clowns are grumpy clowns).

Notice that the task includes the four elements of environments useful for supporting innovation through dynamic transfer. Students worked in pairs and they could draw on the sheets to test out ideas, thus the task was designed to help them distribute their cognition. The different buses and companies created "contrasting cases" to help students generate alternative interpretations (e.g., the total number of clowns per bus versus the average number of clowns per bus compartment). The task required students to use the structures of mathematics to help them innovate. Rather than simply ranking the crowdedness of the three companies, students had to use the structure of mathematics to coordinate the different aspects of density (mass and volume). Finally, the visual structure of the task created a point of coordination for organizing discussions and tentative solutions.

Asking students to innovate their own solutions led to a strong concept of ratio as it is applied in physics. To demonstrate this, a second group of students learned the formula for density and practiced with the crowded clowns worksheet. This "Tell-and-Practice" condition never had an opportunity to innovate solutions. Despite the fact that both conditions received identical worksheets, with the sole difference being whether students had to innovate or practice, innovation students were three times more likely to transfer the concept of ratio to understand new problems involving the spring constant and surface pressure (both defined by ratios).

Although instruction designed around guided innovations can be highly effective, it is also important to consider how dynamic transfer can support innovation in the absence

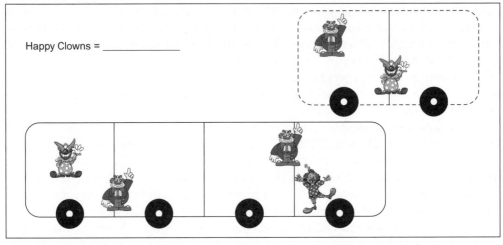

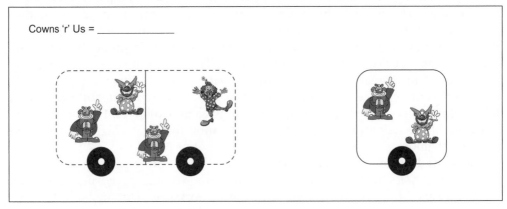

Figure 23.5 Crowded clowns task (Schwartz et al., 2011)

of a teacher or guide. We believe that one important educational outcome is teaching students how to arrange their own environments to maximize their ability to learn in interaction with the environment – in essence, to be their own guides. Martin and Schwartz (2009) looked at how differing educational experiences prepared students to complete a novel, information-dense medical diagnosis problem. Students received 12 reference cases, each indicating the symptoms and diagnosis for one patient. The students had to use the reference cases to help diagnose a series of 10 new patients. The primary question was whether the students would make representations of the reference cases to help with diagnosis; for example, creating tables or decision trees. Or, would they simply shuffle through the reference cases to diagnose each new patient? The study compared undergraduate and graduate students. The graduate students were drawn from disciplines that involved complex information management (e.g., computer science, engineering, biology), but none of them had completed diagnoses like these.

All of the graduate students made visual representations of the reference cases, and spent roughly 15 minutes before they tried to diagnose their first patient. The graduate students made a dynamic transfer. They used their general knowledge of data management to fashion representations tailored to the specifics of diagnosis, and half of them changed their representations as they became more familiar with the task. In contrast, less than 20% of the undergraduates made any sort of representation to help solve the problems, even though they knew how to do so. Instead, they began diagnosing the new patients within two minutes of receiving the reference cases. The graduate students found it worthwhile to make representations. Their experiences in school were associated with their tendency to engage in dynamic transfer and its associated productivity dip.

MEASURING INNOVATION

We conclude this chapter by considering similarity transfer and dynamic transfer as measures of learning. Similarity transfer uses a specific task structure to measure learning outcomes, which Bransford and Schwartz (1999) called sequestered problem solving (SPS). In SPS assessments of transfer, people receive a new problem without any resources or interactive opportunities to learn. The assessment detects the mastery and generality of people's learning. An SPS assessment is a useful way to detect the consequences of a completed innovation. The basic logic is that if students have made the conceptual change, then they should be able to solve the problem using that concept. However, SPS measures are not ideal for evaluating innovative experiences that create conditions for innovation, but have not yet reached fruition. When trying to detect the precursors of innovation, an alternative approach is to use preparation for future learning (PFL) assessments (Bransford & Schwartz, 1999). PFL assessments measure dynamic transfer; students have an opportunity to learn during the assessment with the support of useful external resources. In a PFL assessment, using the environment to learn during a test does not contaminate the test results or mean the student has been cheating. Instead, the assessment asks whether people can learn with the help of the environment.

For instance, Schwartz and Martin (2004) asked ninth-grade students to invent their own ways to graph and measure variability, a concept that they did not know very well. As in the study on learning density, the students worked in pairs and had visually presented contrasting cases (of high and low variability). In this case, very few students innovated conventional solutions. Was there any value in having them engage in processes of innovation, even though it did not yield an innovative outcome? After two weeks of instruction, students were divided into two conditions. Students in the Invent-a-Measure condition received raw data and tried to innovate a way to compare specific individuals from different distributions (e.g., given two groups of students who took different exams, which student got the highest relative score). No student innovated a satisfactory solution. The other half of the students was put into a Tell-and-Copy condition in which they received the same data, but they were given and then practiced a graphical procedure for solving the problems. A few days later, all students completed a long paper-and-pencil test that covered two weeks of instruction. The last problem on the test involved comparing athletes from different eras, which requires finding and using standardized scores. This was a challenging transfer problem: The students had not previously compared athletes and the target problem only provided summary statistics, whereas the students in both conditions had previously worked with raw data. Thus, it did not share surface features with the instruction.

The two instructional conditions were further subdivided into two test conditions. Half of the students in each condition had a worked example embedded in the test (the PFL condition), and the other half did not (the SPS condition). The worked example contained information on how to use standardized scores in comparison problems. Students who took this version of the test had to copy the worked example to solve an affiliated problem as part of the test, which they did quite accurately. The question was whether they would learn from the worked example and apply this learning to solve the target problem at the end of the test. Figure 23.6 summarizes the design of the study and shows the results.

As measured by the SPS assessment, the innovative experiences of the Invent-a-Measure condition did not yield any special benefits over the Tell-and-Copy condition. The PFL assessment, in contrast, was able to detect the benefits of the innovative experiences: Invent-a-Measure students learned from the worked example and did well on the target transfer problem. In contrast, the Tell-and-Copy students who received the worked example showed little benefit. These results show that innovative experiences

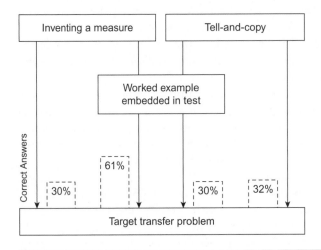

Figure 23.6 The effects of innovative experiences on SPS and PFL measures of learning (adapted from Schwartz & Martin, 2004)

can prepare students to learn, even if students never innovate the correct outcome themselves. Equally important, they show that dynamic transfer measures, which include opportunities to learn at transfer, can be more sensitive to important types of prior learning than standard similarity-based transfer measures that do not permit learning during the assessment. In this case, the PFL assessment showed that the innovation experiences prepared students for a conceptual change.

SUMMARY

Transfer is relevant to conceptual change in those situations where people build new knowledge on a foundation of old. To introduce the transfer literature, we used a series of contrasts familiar to the transfer literature: near versus far, spontaneous versus cued, positive versus negative, surface features versus deep features. We also introduced some new contrasts, because the standard transfer literature does not exhaust the ways that people use transfer to support conceptual change. In the following contrasts, the first term is part of the standard literature, whereas the second term is not: similarity versus dynamic transfer, mapping versus coordination, the knowledge problem versus the inertia problem, sequestered problem solving versus preparation for future learning. Dynamic transfer broadens the concept of transfer, because context is no longer simply input to cognitive processes, but intermingles with cognition to produce concepts and innovations. Once we broaden transfer to embrace non-cognitive variables, issues of inertia and motivation become critical to transfer. Moreover, the ways we assess transfer begin to change, because it becomes important to see how people use their context in the process of transfer. We hope these additions help make transfer more relevant to conceptual change. Conceptual change is not simply transferring old knowledge to explain a new situation – it requires going beyond old knowledge, which standard accounts of transfer cannot explain.

REFERENCES

Barnett, S. M., & Ceci, S. J. (2002). When and where do we apply what we learn? A taxonomy for far transfer. *Psychological Bulletin, 128,* 612–637.

Blackwell, L. S., Trzesniewski, K. H., & Dweck, C. S. (2007). Implicit theories of intelligence predict achievement across an adolescent transition: A longitudinal study and an intervention. *Child Development, 78,* 246–263.

Bransford, J. D., Franks, J. J., Vye, N. J., & Sherwood, R. D. (1989). New approaches to instruction: Because wisdom can't be told. In S. Vosniadou & A. Ortony (Eds.), *Similarity and analogical reasoning* (pp. 470–497). New York, NY: Cambridge University Press.

Bransford, J. D., & Schwartz, D. L. (1999). Rethinking transfer: A simple proposal with multiple implications. In A. Iran-Nejad & P. D. Pearson (Eds.), *Review of Research in Education,* (Vol. 24, pp. 61–100). Washington, DC: American Educational Research Association.

Brown, A. L., & Kane, M. J. (1988). Preschool children can learn to transfer: Learning to learn and learning from example. *Cognitive Psychology, 20,* 493–523.

Chambers, D., & Reisberg, D. (1985). Can mental images be ambiguous? *Journal of Experimental Psychology: Human Perception and Performance, 11,* 317–328.

Chi, M. T. H., Feltovich, P., & Glaser, R. (1981). Categorization and representation of physics problems by experts and novices. *Cognitive Science, 5,* 121–152.

Chi, M. T. H., de Leeuw, N., Chiu, M.-H., & LaVancher, C. (1994a). Eliciting self-explanations improves understanding. *Cognitive Science, 18,* 439–477.

Chi, M. T. H., Slotta, J. D., & De Leeuw, N. (1994b). From things to processes: A theory of conceptual change for learning science concepts. *Learning and Instruction, 4,* 27–43.

COSEPUP [Committee on Science, Engineering, and Public Policy]. (2006). *Rising above the gathering storm: Energizing America for a brighter economic future.* Washington, DC: National Academies Press.

Detterman, D. L. (1993). The case for the prosecution: Transfer as epiphenomenon. In D. K. Detterman & R. J. Sternberg (Eds.), *Transfer on trial: Intelligence, cognition, and instruction* (pp. 1–24). Norwood, NJ: Ablex.

diSessa, A. A., & Wagner, J. F. (2005). What coordination has to say about transfer. In J. P. Mestre (Ed.), *Transfer of learning from a modern multidisciplinary perspective* (pp. 121–154). Greenwich, CT: Information Age Publishing.

Dunbar, K. (1997). How scientists think: On-line creativity and conceptual change in science. In T. B. Ward, S. M. Smith, & J. Vaid (Eds.), *Conceptual structures and processes: Emergence, discovery, and change* (pp. 461–493). Washington, DC, American Psychological Association Press.

Ericsson, K. A., & Lehmann, A. C. (1996). Expert and exceptional performance: Evidence of maximal adaptation to task constraints. *Annual Review of Psychology, 47,* 273–305.

Ervin, S. M., & Miller, W. R. (1963). Language development. In H. W. Stevenson (Ed.), *Child psychology: The sixty-second yearbook of the National Society for the Study of Education, Part 1* (pp. 108–143). Chicago, IL: University of Chicago Press.

Feller, J., Fitzgerald, B., Hissam, S., & Lakhani K. R. (Eds.). (2005). *Perspectives on free and open source software.* Cambridge, MA: MIT Press.

Finke, R. (1990). *Creative imagery: Discoveries and inventions in visualization.* Hillsdale, NJ: Lawrence Erlbaum Associates.

Fullan, M. (2001). *Leading in a culture of change.* San Francisco, CA: Jossey-Bass.

Gentner, D., Brem, S., Ferguson, R. W., Markman, A. B., Levidow, B. B., Wolff, P., et al. (1997). Analogical reasoning and conceptual change: A case study of Johannes Kepler. *Journal of the Learning Sciences, 6,* 3–40.

Gick, M. L., & Holyoak, K. J. (1983). Schema induction and analogical transfer. *Cognitive Psychology, 15,* 1–38.

Goel, V. (1995). *Sketches of thought.* Cambridge, MA: MIT Press.

Griffin, S. A., Case, R., & Siegler, R. S. (1994). Rightstart: Providing the central conceptual prerequisites for first formal learning of arithmetic to students at risk for school failure. In K. McGilly (Ed.), *Classroom lessons: Integrating cognitive theory and classroom practice* (pp. 25–49). Cambridge, MA: MIT Press.

Hatano, G., & Inagaki, K. (1986). Two courses of expertise. In H. Stevenson, H. Azuma, & K. Hakuta (Eds.), *Child development and education in Japan* (pp. 262–272). New York, NY: Freeman.

Johnson-Laird, P. N. (1989). Analogy and the exercise of creativity. In S. Vosniadou & A. Ortony (Eds.), *Similarity and analogical reasoning* (pp. 313–332). New York, NY: Cambridge University Press.

Kerslake, D. (1986). *Fractions: Children's strategies and errors.* Windsor, UK: NFER-Nelson.

Kingstone, A., & Gazzaniga, M. S. (1995). Subcortical transfer of higher order information: More illusory than real? *Neuropsychology, 9,* 321–328.

Klahr, D., & Robinson, M. (1981). Formal assessment of problem-solving and planning processes in preschool children. *Cognitive Psychology, 13,* 113–148.

Lobato, J. (2003). How design experiments can inform a rethinking of transfer and vice versa. *Educational Researcher, 32,* 17–20.

Luchins, A. S., & Luchins, E. H. (1959). *Rigidity of behavior: A variational approach to the effect of einstellung.* Eugene, OR: University of Oregon Books.

Martin, T., & Schwartz, D. L. (2005). Physically distributed learning: Adapting and reinterpreting physical environments in the development of the fraction concept. *Cognitive Science, 29,* 587–625.

Martin, L., & Schwartz, D. L. (2009). Prospective adaptation in the use of external representations. *Cognition and Instruction, 27*(4), 1–31.

Piaget, J. (1952). *The origins of intelligence in children* (M. Cook., Trans.). New York, NY: International Universities Press.

Piaget, J. (1976). *The grasp of consciousness.* Cambridge, MA: Harvard University Press.

Plunkett, K., & Marchman, V. A. (1996). Learning from a connectionist model of the acquisition of the English past tense. *Cognition, 61,* 299–308.

Reed, S. K., Ernst, G. W., & Banerji, R. B. (1974). The role of analogy in transfer between similar problem states. *Cognitive Psychology, 6,* 436–450.

Ross, B. (1989). Remindings in learning and instruction. In S. Vosniadou & A. Ortony (Eds.), *Similarity and analogical reasoning* (pp. 438–469). New York, NY: Cambridge University Press.

Schwartz, D. L., & Bransford, J. D. (1998). A time for telling. *Cognition and Instruction, 16,* 475–522.

Schwartz, D. L., Bransford, J. D., & Sears, D. (2005). Efficiency and innovation in transfer. In J. P. Mestre (Ed.), *Transfer of learning from a modern multidisciplinary perspective* (pp. 1–52). Greenwich, CT: Information Age Publishing.

Schwartz, D. L., Chase, C. C., Oppezzo, M. A., & Chin, D. B. (2011). Practicing versus inventing with contrasting cases: The effects of telling first on learning and transfer. *Journal of Educational Psychology, 103*(4), 759–775.

Schwartz, D. L., & Martin, T. (2004). Inventing to prepare for learning: The hidden efficiency of original student production in statistics instruction. *Cognition and Instruction, 22*, 129–184.

Schwartz, D. L., Martin, T., & Pfaffman, J. (2005). How mathematics propels the development of physical knowledge. *Journal of Cognition and Development, 6*, 65–88.

Simon, H. A. (1969). *The sciences of the artificial.* Cambridge, MA: MIT Press.

Stafylidou, S., & Vosniadou, S. (2004). The development of students' understanding of the numerical value of fractions. *Learning and Instruction, 14*(5), 503–518.

Thagard, P. (1996). The concept of disease: Structure and change. *Communication and Cognition, 29*, 445–478.

Thelen, E., & Smith, L. B. (1994). *A dynamic systems approach to the development of cognition and action.* Cambridge, MA: MIT Press.

Thorndike, E. L., & Woodworth, R. S. (1901). The influence of improvement in one mental function upon the efficacy of other functions. *Psychological Review, 8*, 247–261.

Vamvakoussi, X., & Vosniadou, S. (2010). How many decimals are there between two fractions? Aspects of secondary school students' reasoning about rational numbers and their notation. *Cognition and Instruction, 28*(2), 181–209.

Vosniadou, S., & Brewer, W. F. (1992). Mental models of the earth: A study of conceptual change in childhood. *Cognitive Psychology, 24*, 535–85.

White, T. (2008). Debugging an artifact, instrumenting a bug: Dialectics of instrumentation and design in technology-rich learning environments. *International Journal of Computers for Mathematical Learning, 13*(1), 1–26.

Whitehead, A. N. (1929). *The aims of education.* New York, NY: Macmillan.

24

CONCEPTUAL CHANGE THROUGH COLLABORATION
Naomi Miyake, University of Tokyo

We sometimes engage in conversation about a phenomenon none of us "understands" at first and eventually find some plausible explanation, by exchanging proposals and scrutinizing them collaboratively. This chapter characterizes such a social, collaborative endeavor as a cause of conceptual change in its broader sense, proposes cognitive mechanisms for how it is possible, and relates the research on how to support such collaborative conceptual change to emerging research questions in learning sciences.

INTRODUCTION

Even though we are surrounded with many scientific facts and phenomena in our daily life, our explanatory knowledge of them could be quite superficial. When asked how a helicopter flies, we think we know the answer, until we are asked to give a detailed, step-by-step explanation. Rozenblit and Keil (2002) distinguish explanatory knowledge from knowledge about facts, procedures, and narratives, and claim that people's folk knowledge is especially elusive when we are surrounded with an environment that supports real-time explanations interactively, with visible mechanisms. Their data demonstrate that after reading experts' explanations about the phenomena, the participants' self-evaluation was more realistic. If they had had a chance to talk among themselves, with some real machines at hand, they could have changed their folk concepts to some extent, toward a scientifically deeper understanding.

Cognitive processes of comprehension have been studied mainly on individual participants. The process has also been denoted as "difficult." Among many who report on this difficulty, Clement (1982) showed that even expert physicists took a long and twisting route to reconstruct the conceptual view, after they solved the problems.

Up to the middle 1980s these processes were studied under the topics such as mental models, analogical understanding, comprehension process, and the like. The focus of research on understanding has been further sharpened by newly developed research on conceptual change, after the construct was brought to the attention of developmental researchers (e.g., Carey, 1985).

The construct contributed to refining distinctions between naïve, everyday knowledge and more scientific concepts, both in cognitive developmental research and in research in practice. The refinement also encouraged emergence of a sociocultural, collaborative approach to comprehension studies. The scope of this conceptual change research has recently grown to include instruction-induced, intentional change of scientific concepts (Sinatra & Pintrich, 2003; Vosniadou, 2003, 2007) in learning sciences.

This shift brought about a new perspective on the notorious "difficulty" of conceptual change. Such change is difficult, yet it is also true that we occasionally engage in social exchange, conversation, and collective reflection during our daily life. Greeno and MacWhinney (2006) reported an analysis of an interaction among high-school physics teachers who tried to explain why objects in the earth's gravitational field with different masses (e.g., 1 vs. 10 pounds) fall at the same speed. They depicted this shift on the amended semantic network representation as a merging of two different networks, showing how one person's conceptualization as "10 pound ball consists of 10 one-pound balls" becomes gradually integrated with others' networks, where those two masses were represented as two entirely different nodes. Schwartz (1995) also demonstrated that dyads could turn their naive external representations into abstract ones through joint work more often than individuals. It has also been known that in classroom conversation analyses, teacher's appropriation (Newman, Griffin, & Cole, 1989) and/or "revoicing" of pupils' utterances sometimes evoke discussions that lay ground for a conceptual change in children (O'Conner & Michaels, 1996; Strom, Kemeny, Lehrer, & Forman, 2001).

Taking these everyday sociocultural factors seriously, Hatano (2005) advocated that the intentional processes for conceptual change need to be studied as integration of intra-mental, individual knowledge construction and inter-mental, socioculturally constrained development. Some contributed extensive protocol analyses to explicate what happens during such integration, in comprehension activities (e.g., Miyake, 1986), as well as in learning (e.g., Roschelle, 1992).

The aim of this chapter is to give an overview on research related to mechanisms and their applications of intentional conceptual change, with particular focus on the roles of collaboration and reflection. The first section introduces descriptive research with rich protocols to document that simple conversation could lead to relatively substantial conceptual change. In the second section, two research studies will be introduced that reveal underlying mechanisms of how collaborative reflection contributes to change concepts, through detailed protocol analyses. Simply put, there are two lines of research, using different units of analyses: one focusing more on the process of convergence among the participants while the other emphasizes more of the divergent, individualistic concept formation through social interaction. Although there are some core similarities between these accounts, they yield some different predictions about collaborative processes in general and their individual outcomes in particular. In the third section, some studies on collaborative instructional designs will be introduced, including a Japanese science education practice called hypothesis–experimental–instruction and my own work using the mechanisms I explain in the second section.

EVERYDAY, COLLABORATIVE CONCEPTUAL CHANGE

In the mid 1980s, cognitive science proposed frameworks to understand the basic characteristics of human comprehension of everyday phenomena. While physics experts rely on quantitative, formal expressions, it was claimed that lay people use more qualitative, intuitive understandings, often in the forms of mental models. Those models were found to be multiple and fragmented at the beginning, progressively forming into more integrated, adaptive models (e.g., Williams, Hollan, & Stevens, 1983). It was not that the qualitative reasoning was easy, but it apparently opened up new research topics on how lay people reason.

If this kind of progressive conceptual change is a prevailing everyday phenomenon, it could occur at younger ages. Motoyoshi, an experienced daycare teacher, reports such a case (Motoyoshi, 1979). In her daycare center, it was customary for the five-year-olds to play with ice in the garden pool during the winter by stepping on it. One day, Yusuke, a boy, noticed and commented that the ice was only at the surface. They had to give up playing on it. Next day, they found there was no ice in the pool. They started to discuss how the water froze. "We don't have ice. Is it because it did not rain?" "No. I know there is ice in the pool on clear days, too." "Then why is there no ice in the pool today?" This kind of conversation led them to "experiment" by leaving water in various containers at different locations of the daycare center when they went home. The night was cold and clear. Next morning, they found the water in all the containers was frozen, confirming that rainfall did not have anything to do with freezing. They also found that some containers had thicker ice than others. Two containers with thin ice had been inside, but at this time there was no discussion about the relationship of the thinness and the location.

Next morning, three containers did not have ice, while one had a very thick ice. "Hey, why is the thickness of ice different between my container and Yuriko's? We both used the same blue plastic bucket." "Both Yoshi and Kyo used a jam jar, but only Yoshi's has ice . . ." After some pondering, one child suggested using different containers but putting them all at the same location. Next morning, there was no ice. The children became suspicious that "putting them all at one place would prevent the water from freezing," but decided to try the same setting one more day, to make sure. The water froze next morning, except for one container. The child whose container did not freeze started to cry, but the other children noticed that it had a lid on it. This encouraged them to systematically reflect on and talk about their experiences, like "when I put my container inside, the water did not freeze; when I put it outside, it froze." After this discussion, the children talked among themselves and decided to proceed much more systematically. They selected where to put their containers so that they could "test" their ideas. The next two days were too warm for the water to freeze, but the children persisted. On the third morning, six containers put outside on the north veranda of the building all had ice, while there was no ice in other containers.

All in all, the experiment lasted for nine days. The children collectively came up with many observations and reasons about why and when the water freezes.

- "The water does not freeze every day."
- "The water seems to freeze more often on cold days."
- "The water in a thin, metal container freezes into thick ice."
- "The water in a Styrofoam container does not freeze easily."
- "When we put lots of water in a bucket, only its top part freezes. The bottom could be warmer."
- "The north, darker side of the building is good for making ice."

The children felt fairly satisfied, but some continued on to invent a new game of competing to see whose ice would melt fastest by bringing the containers into the sunlight. This brought out new wonders. "The thick ice in the thin metal container melts quickly. Why?" "In a Styrofoam container, ice is hard to make, but easy to melt, strange." These findings all contradicted their "theory," causing them to think more deeply.

This episode exemplifies that some persistent, collaborative daily experiences could bring out some scientific conceptual change, even at the age of five. It is also noteworthy that the activities were both individualistic and social, strongly supported by the relationship among the independent activities of the children, as well as by the socially supportive atmosphere created by the teacher, which was crucial for the persistency of their activities. Exactly how does this socially supported conceptual change happen?

MECHANISMS FOR CONCEPTUAL CHANGE THROUGH COLLABORATIVE REFLECTION

To investigate mechanisms for collaborative conceptual change, we could use two different units for analysis. One is the pair or the group as a whole, combined unit. The other is each individual as the basic unit, to examine how the cognitive processes of each intertwine to make the whole. Adherents of the former unit often claim that the overall outcome of collaboration is "convergence." Adherents of the latter unit tend to focus more on the divergent nature of the collaborative outcome, as well as of the process. On the surface, the two approaches are contradictory. In reality, they are complementary. The former emphasizes "the pair (or the group)" as a whole to provide a uniform explanation about the "shared" (or "joint") collaborative process. The latter describes more detailed interaction by focusing on each participant's intra-mental exchange between externalized and internalized ideas of individual thoughts, which are profoundly influenced by the inter-mental exchange with other's perspectives through social interaction. In this section, I will explain these two approaches in some detail. My aim is to integrate these views and identify important characteristics when we wish to design supportive environments for collaborative conceptual change.

The Convergence-Oriented Approach

As one of the most prominent examples of the convergence-oriented approach, Roschelle (1992) proposes to integrate prior research about scientific collaboration (cf. Latour, 1986; Nersessian, 1988), social constructivist studies (cf., Newman et al., 1989), and "situated actions" in the relational theory of meaning (Barwise & Perry, 1983) in order to analyze students' convergent conceptual change. He claims that there are four primary features in the proposed process.

1. The construction of a "deep-featured" situation at an intermediate level of abstraction from the literal features of the world.
2. The interplay of metaphors in relation to each other and to the constructed situation.
3. An iterative cycle of displaying, confirming, and repairing situated actions.
4. The application of progressively higher standards of evidence for convergence.

To support this, he analyzed protocols taken from a pair of students of an urban high school, Carol and Dana (pesudonyms), while they studied the basics of Newtonian physics for the first time. They worked on a computerized scaffold called the Envisioning Machine. They were asked to manipulate the position, velocity and acceleration of the particle drawn with arrows in the "Newtonian" world (window) so that it makes the same motion as the ball in the separate, "Observable" window. Figure 24.1 schematically depicts the Newtonian window.

Their task was to figure out what would happen to the initial velocity when some acceleration is added. They worked on this task for two hours in total. Roschelle extracted five episodes from the 15-minute interaction, and analyzed their language and gestures to see whether he could identify the four features mentioned above.

Their progress through the episodes could be summarized as follows. Prior to the first episode (Episode 1), both Carol and Dana had misconceptions of "acceleration pulls the material point," a common misunderstanding among high-school students. During Episode 1 Carol changed her concept to "acceleration pulls the tip of the initial velocity" by using the "pulling metaphor." Dana converged to it in transcending to Episode 2. In Episode 3 Dana started to use the "adding metaphor," immediately shared by Carol, causing both to change their concept through Episode 4. In Episode 5, they converged to the shared "traveling along metaphor" that let them correctly solve the problem.

Now let us follow in detail exactly what is meant by "convergence" in this perspective. Shortly after they started, they could only talk about the movements in the display with ambiguous, everyday terminology, such as "lengthen" and "pull" (D for Dana; C for Carol; the numbers to the left are the line numbers of their protocol).

1. *D:* But what I don't understand is how the lengthening, the positioning of the arrow
   . . .
2. *C:* Ooh, you know what I think it is? It's like the line. Fat arrow [acceleration] is the line of where it pulls that [tip of the initial velocity line] down. Like see how that makes this dotted line [trace]. That was the black arrow [acceleration]. It [acceleration] pulls it [velocity].

Roschelle interprets this as "Carol brought the three lines to the foreground and gave them abstract interpretations as deep features – initial velocity, final velocity, and acceleration. She developed an explanation of the configuration by refer [*sic*] to the metaphor of pulling." This achieves the first feature listed above.

Up to this point, the achievement is mostly Carol's, not yet shared by the other member. This conversation continued as:

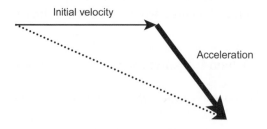

Initial velocity

Acceleration

Figure 24.1 Schematic drawings shown in the Newtonian window of the Envisioning Machine

3. *D:* You're saying this [dotted line] is the black arrow?
4. *C:* Yeah.
5. *D:* And it pulls it the other arrow [points to velocity line with mouse cursor] like
6. *C:* Like on its hinge. It pulls the other arrow on the hinge down to the tip of the black arrow.

In this follow up, Roschelle concludes that Dana "shares" her description with Carol, indicating the onset of their convergent conceptual change, or the first cycle of features 2, 3, and 4 listed above. On line 5 Dana uses the verb "pull" like Carol just did in line 2, as an indicator of her trying to construct a mental model similar to the one just proposed by Carol. Though Roschelle does not rely on this level of analysis, this gives some side-support to his argument.

Roschelle analyzed four more episodes like this, through which both Carol and Dana cyclically achieved features 2, 3, and 4 listed above. In the third episode, the two students diverged from each other in terms of their understanding about the speed of acceleration, which they successfully repaired in the fourth episode. In their fifth episode, they used the Envisioning Machine to confirm that their conception made correct predictions. The episodes and the analyses are both convincing, to the point that the collaborative endeavor led the pair, as a whole, to change their misconception of acceleration into a more scientific one. The convergence framework thus claims that collaboration induces conceptual change of a pair as the unit of analysis.

A remaining problem may be that the framework does not explain whether each individual outcome could be different from the others. Because individuals tend to diverge, Roschelle argues that the question is how convergent conceptual change could ever occur.

Roschelle claims that because Carol and Dana received no prior instruction on scientific conceptions of motion, "the means for convergent conceptual change appears incommensurate with the outcome" (p. 239)

It is clear that each influenced the other, with their language as well as with the Envisioning Machine display they created. Yet each could have gone through substantial individualistic conceptual change, in divergent forms. Each might have developed her specific concept, more abstract in quality than her initial ideas, yet with varying degrees of similarity to the target scientific concept. It might be important to analyze the collaborative process by taking each individual as the smaller unit of analysis. It would give a different explanation to the collaborative conceptual change mechanism.

The Constructive Interaction Framework

Miyake and her colleagues' work (Miyake, 1986; Shirouzu, Miyake, & Masukawa, 2002) provides an illustrative case of analyzing interaction for conceptual change with each individual as the unit of analysis. In her 1986 study, the participants were instructed to "talk together to figure out how a sewing machine makes its stitches." She used pairs of participants because one of the aims of her study was to explore a new method called "constructive interaction" to study the comprehension process in general.

Through individual-based interaction analyses, she found that the joint problem-solving situation consists of each individual's independent processes. Both the language they used and their final mental models differed from one participant to the other.

Because they work on their own problems in their own way, it is reasonable to assume they do not have easily accessible checking mechanisms to validate their solutions. She claimed that this is where the virtues of the interaction are found. Because each participant works from a different starting schema, what is obvious and natural to one may not be so to the other. This difference was often identified in her data as questions and criticisms. Studying their patterns, she concluded that the socially interactive or joint problem solving has a high potential to elicit conceptual change for each participant in different ways.

She also maintained that there is a role shift of task-doing and monitoring associated with the difference, as a possible cause for their concepts to change into more abstract scientific forms. Miyake and her colleagues expanded this view on the role-shift by examining the effects of the externalized objects and the perspectives taken on them (Shirouzu et al., 2002). Their task called for integrating various solutions to an arithmetic problem using a square sheet of paper. They found that pairs tended to reach an abstract solution more often than solos on this task. In the protocol of the pairs, they could trace the role exchange contributing to each taking a slightly broader, monitoring perspective than the other. Somewhat more detailed explanations follow.

"How Does a Sewing Machine Make a Stitch?" A Case of Finding a New Concept

When people try to understand complex physical devices such as a sewing machine, they proceed in an iterative fashion. They seem to reach several points at which they claim to "understand" the device. Each point of understanding is incomplete and requires a new level of understanding. This iterative cycle happens during each individual's conceptual change, depending on the individual's prior, experience-based understanding, as well as the goal of how deeply one needs to, or wishes to, understand the target. In order to examine this iterative process of understanding, Miyake (1986) prepared two frameworks: the function–mechanism hierarchy to identify the levels of understanding of the sewing mechanism, and another to capture the nature of the cycling of understanding and non-understanding. With these she examined whether her protocol reveals that her participants actually traced down the understanding levels by going through the understanding cycles.

The Function–Mechanism Hierarchy

The hierarchy has several levels corresponding to psychological "levels" of understanding. The term "function" refers to the description of the task performed at any given level. A functional description says, essentially, that "such and such happens," but it does not explain how. The term "mechanism" is used to describe the "how." The explanation comprises functions connected together with simple relationships. The function at one level requires the mechanism at the next lower level to explain it. The distinction of levels here is relative. Miyake used six levels because that was all that the data from her studies required.

The Level 0 function of a sewing machine is to make stitches. To achieve that function, the Level 1 mechanism has as its function the intertwining of two threads, and so on. This function–mechanism hierarchy is shown in Table 24.1.

In Level 2, the upper thread is looped entirely around the lower thread. The looping "function" creates a topological puzzle, requiring one lower level "mechanism" for the

Table 24.1 Function–mechanism hierarchy for sewing machine

Level									
0					[Stitch]				
1			[Thread comes from above]	–	[Thread 1 intertwines, can pick up thread 2]	–	[Thread 2 comes from below]		
2	[Needle makes loop of upper thread]	–	[Needle pulls down loop]	–	[Bottom thread goes through loop]	–	[Bottom thread comes from below]	–	[Needle pulls up loop]
3	[Hook catches loop]	–	[Hook pulls down loop]	–	[Loop goes around bobbin]	–	[Hook releases loop]		
4	[Bobbin is clear on front]	–	[Hook separates loop]	–	[Bobbin structure provides back space]	–	[Side 1 of loop passes bobbin back]	–	[Side 2 of loop passes bobbin front]
5	[Bobbin is on case]	–	[Case clamps on holder]	–	[Holder is held by collar]	–	[Collar is part of hook-shaft]	–	[Hook-shaft is fixed to machine]

upper thread to go around the free end of the lower thread. Determining this mechanism creates the major difficulty in understanding how the machine works.

Understanding and Non-Understanding

Miyake proposed that the process of understanding follows the function–mechanism hierarchy, with each level guiding the steps to be followed for understanding to proceed. When a function in a level n mechanism is identified and questioned, this opens up the search for a level $n+1$ mechanism. A mechanism is then proposed as a tentative solution. This proposal can be criticized, and if it passes this criticism, it is stated as confirmed. Thus, at each level, understanding proceeds through steps of identifying and questioning a function at level n, followed by searching, proposing, criticizing, and confirming the corresponding mechanism at level $n+1$. The mechanism at level $n+1$ can then be decomposed into its functions, and those one-level lower functions, when questioned, could then lead to search of a level $n+2$ mechanism.

Roughly, when one finds an explanation in a level $n+1$ mechanism for a level n function, it is felt to be understood; when a function of level n is questioned and one starts searching for its mechanisms, this gives a sense of non-understanding. Thus, going through the steps and going down the levels produces an alternation of feelings of understanding and non-understanding.

Results of the Protocol Analysis

Miyake analyzed three pairs of participants on the sewing machine interactions, Pair A, B and C (each member of the pairs will be denoted with numbers, as A1 and A2 formed Pair A). All participants reached a level 5 mechanism. In terms of the understanding process, the analyses confirmed her framework. Their senses of understanding and non-understanding alternated. Their language revealed their conceptual viewpoints that tended to be stable while they understood and tended to shift often while they did not understand. In addition, her analyses of individual protocols in terms of how each descended the levels revealed some fundamental mechanisms of both individualistic as well as socially supported constructive interaction to achieve conceptual change.

Individualistic Aspects of Interaction

While all the participants solved the task, each took a different course. They were often on different levels while exchanging proposals: For Pair A, out of their 91 turn takings, A1 and A2 were on different levels 31 times (34.1%). This discrepancy was greater at the beginning. In the first one-third when they were talking just with paper and pen, they were out of synchrony 57.7% of the time. When interviewed after the experiment, they were unaware of this discrepancy.

Their final models were different also. If we compare expressions of their Level 5 mechanisms, they were not very similar. For instance, while A1 reached a more standard model one might find in a book, A2's solution was built on an analogy with a spokeless bicycle wheel. The difference was also revealed in the drawings used by Al and A2 both during and at the very end of their interaction. When they were asked to explain how the sewing machine works at the end of the experiment, they took different points of view in their explanations – A1 a cross-sectional view, A2 a front view – even though the drawing he most often dealt with in the interaction was A1's cross-sectional view. This difference again showed up six months later, when they were asked to do this same task.

This may reflect the norm of conversation that people do not really talk to one other (e.g., Hobbs and Evans, 1980). It was also true, though, as their post-experiment interview revealed, that they felt they had talked with each other quite cooperatively, worked together to find "the" answer, and were satisfied with their achievement at the end. This was true for all pairs. Yet in actuality their solutions were different – more so than they appeared to notice themselves.

Criticisms Provide Validation Checking Mechanisms

Even when the starting and ending of interactions are individualistic, there is the virtue of working together. People interpret the problem or situation in their own ways. They find their own satisfactory solutions. The interaction provides a mechanism to validate their individualistic solutions. Because each participant works from a different starting schema, what is obvious and natural to one may not be so to the other. This leads to "criticisms."

In the sewing machine protocol, Miyake observed 41 criticisms in all. Self-criticizing accounted for only 12% of the incidents (five out of the total of 41), implying that validation checking is hard within an individual system. Criticizing the level on which both participants were working is also rare (four times). Most of the criticisms were "downward," where the person who is criticizing has less understanding than the other (22 times). It could mean that the criticizer could not understand the proposed mechanism. The important finding is, however, that these criticisms did force the other person, the one with more understanding, to keep searching for better mechanisms, or better explanations of what s/he wants to propose. Out of 22 observed downward criticisms, 10 pushed the partner to search deeper for their answers.

It seems, therefore, that criticism could occur when the two people are at different levels and have different focuses. This difference, though not even noticed, appears to stimulate both participants to search for better understanding.

Motions: The Role of the Monitors

Miyake also analyzed "motion," suggestions of a new way to approach the problem. Near the end of the Pair A interaction, A2 suggested taking off the bottom panel of the machine, so that they could get a better view of the back side of the bobbin. This suggestion "moved" them to their final conclusions.

Miyake could identify two different types of motions. Motions can be closely related to the topic under discussion at the time or can be divergent from the topic. While suggesting going back to the machine for more observation is topic-related, suggesting taking off the bottom panel is topic-divergent. When she compared members in each pair, topic-related motions were generated more by the "task-doers," or the people who were leading the problem solving at the moment. Observers who were monitoring the process tended to give more topic-divergent motions. If task-doers were more engaged with a local focus, observers could have had a more global focus, not yet being able to or not having to narrow their focus to match that of the task-doers. Topic-divergent motions might have their origins in this global focus that was not easily available to the doers. Moreover, some topic-divergent motions worked constructively. Out of the total of 17 divergent motions, six were followed by some change in the course of the problem solving. The observer can contribute by criticizing and giving topic-divergent motions, which are not the primary roles of the task-doer.

Active Use of External Resources

In another study, Miyake and her colleagues expand the notion of role-exchange and offer an explanation of how it can contribute to abstract and flexible problem solving (Shirouzu et al., 2002). They asked their participants to obtain three-fourths of two-thirds, or its reverse, of a square sheet of origami. There are mathematical and non-mathematical solutions to this problem. The mathematical solution is to solve it by calculation, while non-mathematical solutions do not involve any calculations. The participants tended to solve this non-mathematically, nearly 90% of the time.

The solution strategies adopted by the participants affected their solution paths. Let us explain this with the problem of getting two-thirds of three-fourths. When they used the non-mathematical strategy, the participants tended to follow a two-step solution of obtaining the three-fourths first and then delineating the two-thirds in the obtained three-fourths. When using a mathematical strategy, however, the participants multiplied 2/3 with 3/4 to obtain 1/2 as the answer.

Whichever strategy they took, the objective reflection on the correct answer would have the participants realize the mathematical solution, which, in this case, is quicker and requires less effort. The participants did not seem to realize this. This objective reflection can be identified by the shift of strategies from externally oriented, two-step solution path to the mathematical one. To test how objective this reflection could be, for whom, they compared the Solo participants and the Pair participants to solve the reverse problem the second time (that is, getting three-fourths of two-thirds first, then two-thirds of three-fourths second, or vice versa). When tested first to get the two-thirds of the three-fourths, and then its reverse immediately thereafter, Solos did not change their solution paths (nearly 85% stayed on, possibly showing some bias toward confirmation). In contrast, over 70% of the Pairs converted their non-arithmetic solution paths to the arithmetic one.

Shirouzu et al. interpreted these results to make the following claims. First, human beings use external resources actively, and they react to their own doings rather subjectively; that is, they actively leave traces while solving a problem, in which they only see what they expect to find in such traces. When working alone, they are not always able to assume objective perspectives. This is where having another person could contribute to changing the perspectives. Second, the roles of performing and monitoring tasks are often exchanged frequently during this collaboration. The monitor has opportunities to observe emerging events in the situation from a slightly more objective perspective than that of the doer. This perspective shift helps to produce solutions that evolve from highly individualistic and situated to more abstract and flexible alternatives. During collaboration, the abstraction is a natural outcome of the exchange between the task-doer's plans and the monitor's reinterpretation.

This set of findings should be relevant to proposing more effective design principles to promote collaboration. This mechanism offers an explanation of why there could be different learning outcomes from paired learners. It also explains why a more knowledgeable participant, or the person who preceded the other in his/her understanding, could still benefit from the interaction. This model implies that for the design of collaborative conceptual change it is important to encourage perspective exchanges and to secure ample chances for each individual learner to reflect upon the shared resources. The model is not necessarily the one widely shared among ordinary learners. They do not always grasp the value of interaction according to this model, and may complain, when put in collaborative environments without much preparation, that the more capable participants may not learn much. The model provides explanations as to why this is not so. To make a collaborative curriculum successful, sharing this piece of knowledge among the learners, teachers, and the designers as well is often the key. In the following section, we will examine some design principles of such successful classrooms.

COGNITIVE AND SOCIOCULTURAL ACCOUNTS OF CONCEPTUAL CHANGE IN THE CLASSROOM

Children form rudimentary concepts through their own everyday experiences (e.g., Inagaki & Hatano, 2002), yet such concepts need to be transformed into scientific ones, which sometimes are very different. As Vosniadou's early work on children's concepts of the earth elegantly shows (Vosniadou & Brewer, 1992), children could live with dual or multiple models, each applicable to different requirements that could happen at different situations such as school and home. Unifying these is not easy (Vosniadou and Ioannides, 1998). Early works like Roschelle's and constructive interaction suggest that carefully designed collaborative learning could provide children with chances to integrate, on their own, the everyday experience-based, self-formed "rules of thumb" with the "scientific" concepts, introduced at learning situations such as classrooms. There are some reports coming from classroom practices with sufficient levels of success cases.

Hypothesis–Experiment–Instruction

Hatano and Inagaki introduced a Japanese collaborative practice called hypothesis–experiment–instruction (HEI; Itakura, 1997) for science education. They studied this method in relation to motivation for comprehension and collective comprehension activity (Hatano & Inagaki, 1991, 2003). More recent investigations of this instruction have revealed that there is indeed some constructive interaction that occurs among the class members in HEI.

In HEI, a lesson consists of a set of strategic procedures for discussion and a "problem," whose answer is predicted and discussed by the students. An HEI "unit" consists of multiple such "problems," or experiments, carefully ordered to guide the development of scientific concepts underlying the problem set. Each student of an HEI class is expected to integrate the results of the experiments in her/his own way to formulate an individualized "hypothesis," or the rudimentary scientific concept owned by the student.

For a typical HEI problem, students follow the four steps below.

1. The teacher shows the procedure of the experiment with alternatives for the possible results. The students choose one of the alternatives, and the distribution is written down on the blackboard by the teacher.
2. Students explain and discuss their choices among them.
3. When this discussion naturally comes to an end, either the teacher or the students in small groups conduct the experiment.
4. Students write comments individually.

The <Air and Water> unit we investigated here had 11 problems, including "When an empty glass is pushed into water upside down, will the water come into the glass?" (Problem 1, P1 henceforth), "When a can of juice with just one hole on top is turned upside down, will some juice come out of it?" (P7), "What would happen if the juice can has two holes on top?" (P8), and "Will some soy sauce come out of its container if you put your finger onto the hole on its top?" (P11). Answers to P1 to P6 are consistent with daily experiences. On the contrary, situations P7 to P10 do not occur much in daily lives of children, requiring learners to answer relying on their newly formed "hypotheses" from predicting and observing the experimental results in the previous problems. The last problem, P11, can be answered by tying daily experiences with newly learned (achieved) understanding.

The data reported here come from an HEI class conducted in May and June of 2002. Twenty-one third graders learned the <Air and Water> unit through 12 lessons, taught by a highly experienced HEI teacher, who voluntarily kept records of the students' answers and discussions in hand-written notes and voice recordings. For P1 to P6, the students tended to choose the correct alternative from the beginning and stay with it after discussion. At P7, the pattern suddenly changed: Nobody chose the correct answer, even after discussion. The same phenomenon happened again at P8, yet on P9, the students recovered their performance. They were shaken again on P10, but everybody was able to predict the correct answer at the last problem, P11. The overall pattern indicated that at the end of the unit, all the children in this class somehow succeeded in forming a rudimentary concept of physical identity, at least with regards to whether the air and water could share the identical physical space or not. When we coded the contents of their utterances and comments they wrote, we found that the number of scientifically correct utterances went up sharply on P8. The average numbers of such utterances rose from 6.3 for P1 to P6 to 12.7 for P7 to P1. This shift indicates that most of the students succeeded in changing their folk theory, or rules of thumbs, based on everyday experiences into more scientifically based, theory-like understandings by bridging two different types of problems.

In order to test how and when the constructively interactive pattern occurred during the discussion, we coded the patterns of turn-taking of the 12 lessons into two categories of role-exchange, as "Individual sequence" and "Group dialogue" (Saito & Miyake, 2011). The *Individual sequence* is when the learners take turns to express their ideas in succession, as a single person's verbalization is handed down sequentially to the next person. For the *Group dialogue*, the role exchange is expected to happen socially, involving groups: In a class discussion we might observe a small group of two to three students engage in a positive discussion, exchanging roles of task-doing and monitoring among them for a while, yet at the same time this group as a whole could be identified as taking the role of *task-doing* to the whole class, whose discussion can be *monitored* by the other students in the class. We coded sequences of where two to four persons iterated their utterances, and coded these as Group dialogues. We found that the Group dialogues tended to occur often at hard-to-predict problems, as if soliciting more focused constructive interaction among the small number of students with expressable ideas, whose group dialogue was monitored by the rest of the class. During the P7 discussion, each student expressed individualistic observations, because the problem situation was new, and there were not many common focuses they could share. When they moved on to P8, after exchanging different ideas expressed in various ways, as well as observing what was the correct answer to the previous problem, some students had become able to express their rules of thumb rather abstractedly, in a top-down fashion such as "Water cannot come out because there is air outside." When this was questioned by one other student, there occurred a Group dialogue, or possibly constructive interaction, between the two, which as a whole was monitored as a Group task-doing by the rest of the class. As the situation progressed a while, another student who cared enough to think through concrete images of the juice in the can and of the water surrounding it, challenged the abstracted expression, asking for more concrete images. This created another Group task-doing, which were also monitored by the class. This "monitor-able" constructive inter-action between abstraction of and the concrete images of the set of the air–water exchange phenomena helped each class member to integrate the discussion with her/his own ideas toward the end of P9, leading them all to correct answers. It would be worth-while to point out that the children in this class were "prepared" to take part in this whole-class discussion by having shared the "same" observation across the set of experiments, and each having "similar" yet individually different "possible" expressions. This kind of analyses would reveal potential principles for designing the timing of Group task-doing of the core members and its active monitoring by the rest of the class.

If the single class in the HEI exhibited this strong tendency toward conceptual change, what are the real effects on the students who engage in a series of HEI practice? Because of the way the practice is constructed and because of the common style of classroom management, the same child often stays with the same teacher for a year to two to three years, learning all the procedures from her. These cases provide us with a chance to see the practical effects of HEI. Though not much rigorous research has been reported, there

Table 24.2 HEI and non-HEI results reported by a teacher

Grade	After HEI	HEI graduates	Non-HEIgraduates	Difference (%)
Elementary 4th	0.5 year	70.9	–	–
5th	1.5 years	77.3	–	–
6th	2.5 years	79.0	–	–
Middle 1st (7th)	3.5 years	74.4	57.5	16.9
Middle 2nd (8th)	4.5 years	81.9	67.3	14.6
Middle 3rd (9th)	5.5 years	82.2	59.8	22.4
High 1st (10th)	6.5 years	80.6	63.7	16.9
High 2nd (11th)	7.5 years	82.3	67.4	14.9

are ample episodes demonstrating the effects. One teacher who practiced the HEI for 10 years reports the sustainability of the conceptual change. He kept teaching the concept of weight in terms of the molecular construction for eight years. In the eighth year, he tested the graduates on their understanding and got the results shown in Table 24.2 (Shoji, 1988). It is not surprising to see that the 80% of the high-school students tested answered correctly the weight problem that is solvable by the students in the fourth grade. The numbers show the effects of the HEI practice because the level is ~15% lower for young adults of the same age who did not experience HEI on this "easy" problem.

THE KNOWLEDGE-CONSTRUCTIVE JIGSAW

When thinking can be made visible, it is also desirable to increase its variability. The jigsaw method (Aronson & Patnoe, 1997) helps increase the diversity of perspectives on a shared task (e.g., Brown, 1997). It is highly flexible, modifiable to facilitate many different types of collaboration. The jigsaw can, for instance, be quite dynamic, to let a college class of around 60 students collaboratively cover 20 to 30 learning materials, each representing classic research in three different domains of cognitive science. The students are supported to collaboratively read, explain, exchange, and discuss the materials to integrate them, so that each participating student would be able to verbally explain the integrated "concepts" of the target discipline, with necessary evidential pieces of knowledge from the relevant research. Knowledge integration is explicitly scaffolded by successively enlarging the scope of materials each has to cover: They start with one, exchange it with someone else and integrate those two, then exchange those two with someone else who could also explain two to integrate four, and so forth. Some assessment analyses of this type of activities have revealed (1) a fair amount of retention of the learning material concepts four to six months after the end of the course, (2) explicit knowledge integration surrounding each student's personal needs, and (3) some conscious acquisition of learning skills such as asking specific, content-driven questions (Miyake, Masukawa, & Shirouzu, 2001; Miyake & Shirouzu, 2006; Miyake, Shirouzu, & Chukyo Learning Science Group, 2005).

Lately Miyake and her colleagues have been exploring this basic jigsaw framework to let school teachers create effective constructive interaction in regular classrooms, with regular participant areas (http://coref.u-tokyo.ac.jp/en). This framework allows shifts from teacher-centric practices to learner-centered, more collaborative practices, from elementary to high schools, covering main participant areas currently taught at public schools. The newly emerging framework has been called the Knowledge-Constructive Jigsaw, which has the following characteristics.

1. Each class has a clear "question," soluble by integrating a small number of independent pieces of information, which could be found in textbooks. The students are encouraged to write down their initial answers individually, at the beginning of the class.
2. The class is divided into "expert" groups, to cover the different pieces of information.
3. One member from each expert group gathers to form a new "jigsaw" group, to exchange what they learned in the previous group, to integrate the pieces to create an answer to the question.
4. The jigsaw groups present their answers to be shared in the class.
5. The students again write down their answers individually at the end of the class.

These activities assure every student a chance to engage in constructive interaction, by becoming both a task-doer and a monitor. The activities let each student externalize his/her understandings in words, providing data for reflection and evaluation, for the teacher as well as the students. Analyses of these data have shown general success in supporting the students' scientific concept formation, and the teachers' transformation of the goals of learning (http://coref.u-tokyo.ac.jp/en), opening new hopes and challenges for studies of conceptual change.

LEARNING SCIENCES: A NEW FIELD OF RESEARCH SUPPORTING CONCEPTUAL CHANGE THROUGH COLLABORATION

Learning sciences and Computer Support for Collaborative Learning (CSCL) are emerging fields of research and practice on learning, to which the studies on conceptual change have much to contribute (Miyake, 2007; Sawyer, 2006; Stahl, Koschmann, & Suthers, 2006). They regard one of the aims of learning as serious scientific conceptual change, often attained through collaboration. The goals of such learning have also been described as achieving "adaptive" or generalizable expertise (Hatano & Inagaki, 1986).

In order to help support the new type of learning, research in these fields requires recording and analyzing the processes of learning, with greater detail for a much longer period than conventional, laboratory-based learning studies, or in usual classrooms. Currently, computers and computer-controlled recording and analyzing tools are most promising to meet such requirements (Goldman et al., 2007).

Based on theoretical research on how collaboration works, CSCL calls for such principles as making initial thoughts visible (Kali, Linn, & Roseman, 2008), scaffolding generations of different ideas and building knowledge (Bereiter, 2002; Scardamalia & Bereiter, 1994), soliciting learning-effective role exchanges by reciprocity of taking roles (Brown, 1997; Palinscar & Brown, 1984) and by using software agents (D'Mello, Graesser, Schuller, & Martin, 2011; Schwartz, Blair, Biswas, Leelawong, & Davis, 2007), and engaging learners in collaborative reflection for developing their ideas further. To design effective collaborative learning environments by implementing these requirements, computers are also quite promising tools, when coupled with carefully thought-out learning activities Remotely operable robots, for example, could provide a new tool to do a more controllable survey of how to facilitate naturalistic collaboration (Miyake, Ishiguro, Dautenhahn, & Nomura, 2011).

Short-term assessments of learning performance may not be as predictive as we would hope of cross-situational uses of concepts, skills and other achievements in the realism of longer time frames. This concern is clearly related to how outcomes from different settings of learning are, or should be, portable to other situations, dependable when the need arises to use them in different situations, and sustainable in terms of providing preparation for further learning (cf. Schwartz & Martin, 2004). A lot still needs to be done, at places where children truly learn. By supporting children to change their concepts, the researchers as well as practitioners learn how to change our own concepts of learning and teaching from experience-based collection of rules of thumb to scientifically evidenced, flexibly adaptive ones.

ACKNOWLEDGMENTS

Writing of this chapter was partly supported by CREST-SORST/JSP 2000-2008 and JSPS Grant-in-Aid 15200020 (2004–2006), MEXT Grant-in-Aid 21118001 (2009–2013). The author expresses her sincere gratitude to Giyoo Hatano, who encouraged her to write this chapter.

REFERENCES

Aronson, E., & Patnoe, S. (1997). *The jigsaw classroom: Building cooperation in the classroom,* New York, NY: Longman.

Barwise, J., & Perry, J. (1983). *Situations and attitudes,* Cambridge, MA: MIT Press.

Bereiter, C. (2002). *Education and mind in the knowledge age.* Mahwah, NJ: Lawrence Erlbaum Associates.

Brown, A. (1997). Transforming schools into communities of thinking and learning about serious matters. *American Psychologist, 52,* 399–413.

Carey, S. (1985). *Conceptual change in childhood.* Cambridge, MA: MIT Press.

Clement, J. (1982). Students' preconceptions in introductory mechanics. *American Journal of Physics, 50,* 66–71.

D'Mello, S. K., Graesser, A. C., Schuller, B., & Martin, J. (Eds). (2011). *Affective Computing and Intelligent Interaction (ACII 2011).* Berlin, Germany: Springer.

Goldman, R., Pea, R., Barron, B., & Derry, J. D. (Eds.). (2007). *Video research in the learning sciences.* New York, NY: Routledge.

Greeno, J. G., & MacWhinney, B. (2006). Perspectives in reasoning about quantities. *Proceedings of the 28th Annual Conference of the Cognitive Science Society,* 2495.

Hatano, G. (2005). *Neo-Vygotskian theory of learning: Importance of converging intra-mental and inter-mental analyses of conceptual change.* Invited talk presented at CSCL05, Taipei, Taiwan.

Hatano, G., & Inagaki, K. (1986). Two courses of expertise. In H. Stevenson, H. Azuma, & K. Hakuta (Eds.), *Child development and education in Japan* (pp. 263–272). New York, NY: Freeman.

Hatano, G., & Inagaki, K. (1991). Sharing cognition through collective comprehension activity. In B. Resnick, J. M. Levine, & S. D. Teasley (Eds.), *Perspectives on socially shared cognition* (pp. 331–348). Washington, DC: American Psychological Association.

Hatano, G., & Inagaki, K. (2003). When is conceptual change intended? A cognitive-sociocultural view. In G. M. Sinatra & P. R. Pintrich (Eds.), Intentional conceptual change (pp. 407–427). Mahwah, NJ: Laurence Erlbaum Associates.

Hobbs, J. R., & Evans, D. A. (1980). Conversation as planned behavior. *Cognitive Science, 4,* 349–377.

Inagaki, K., & Hatano, G. (2002). *Young children's naïve thinking about the biological world.* New York, NY: Psychology Press.

Itakura, K. (1997). *Kasetsu-Jikken-Jugyo no ABC, Dai 4 han* [The ABC of hypothesis–experiment–instruction: Invitation to enjoyable classes, Version 4]. Tokyo, Japan: Kasetsu-Sha. [In Japanese.]

Kali, Y., Linn, M. C., & Roseman, J. (2008). *Designing coherent science education.* New York, NY: Teachers College Press.

Latour, B. (1986). Visualization and cognition: Thinking with eyes and hands. *Knowledge and Society: Studies in the Sociology of Culture, 6,* 1–40.

Miyake, N. (1986). Constructive interaction and the iterative process of understanding. *Cognitive Science, 10,* 151–177.

Miyake, N. (2007). Computer supported collaborative learning. In R. Andrews & C. Haythornthwaite (Eds.), *The handbook of e-learning research.* Thousand Oaks, CA: Sage.

Miyake, N., Ishiguro, H., Dautenhahn, K., & Nomura, T. (2011). *Robots with children: Practices for human–robot symbiosis,* 6th ACMIEEE International Conference on Human Robot Interaction, Lausanne, Switzerland.

Miyake, N., Masukawa, H., & Shirouzu, H. (2001). The complex jigsaw as an enhancer of collaborative knowledge building. *Proceedings of European Perspectives on Computer-Supported Collaborative Learning,* Maastricht, The Netherlands, pp. 454–461.

Miyake, N., & Shirouzu, H. (2006). A collaborative approach to teach cognitive science to undergraduates: The learning sciences as a means to study and enhance college student learning. *Psychologia, 18*(2), 101–113.

Miyake, N., Shirouzu, H., & Chukyo Learning Science Group. (2005). *The dynamic jigsaw: Repeated explanation support for collaborative learning of cognitive science.* Paper presented at the 27th Annual Meeting of the Cognitive Science Society, Stresa, Italy.

Motoyoshi, M. (1979). *Watashi no seikatsu hoiku ron* [My theory of everyday daycare]. Tokyo, Japan: Frobel Kan. [In Japanese.]

Nersessian, N. J. (1988). Reasoning from imagery and analogy in scientific concept formation. *PSA: Proceedings of the Biennial Meeting of the Philosophy of Science Association, 1,* 41–47.

Newman, D., Griffin, M., & Cole, M. (1989). *The construction zone: Working for cognitive change in school.* Cambridge, UK: Cambridge University Press.

O'Conner, C., & Michaels, S. (1996). Shifting participant frameworks: Orchestrating thinking practices in group discussion. In D. Hicks (Ed.), *Discourse, learning and schooling* (63–103). New York, NY: Cambridge University Press.

Palincsar, A. S., & Brown, A. L. (1984). Reciprocal-teaching of comprehension fostering and monitoring activities. *Cognition and Instruction, 1,* 117–175.

Roschelle, J. (1992). Learning by collaboration: Convergent conceptual change. *Journal of the Learning Sciences, 2,* 235–276.

Rozenblit, L., & Keil, F. (2002). The misunderstood limits of folk science: An illusion of explanatory depth. *Cognitive Science, 26,* 521–562.

Saito, M., & Miyake, N. (2011). Socially constructive interaction for fostering conceptual change. *Proceedings of the 9th International Conference on Computer-Supported Collaborative Learning (CSCL2011),* Hong Kong, pp. 96–103.

Sawyer, K. R. (Ed.). (2006). *The Cambridge handbook of the learning sciences.* New York, NY: Cambridge University Press.

Scardamalia, M., & Bereiter, C. (1994). Computer support for knowledge-building communities. *Journal of the Learning Sciences, 3,* 265–283.

Schwartz, D. L. (1995). The emergence of abstract representations in dyad problem solving. *Journal of the Learning Sciences, 4,* 321–354.

Schwartz, D. L., Blair, K. P., Biswas, G., Leelawong, K., & Davis, J. (2007). Animations of thought: Interactivity in the teachable agents paradigm. In R. Lowe & W. Schnotz (Eds.), *Learning with animation: Research and implications for design.* New York, NY: Cambridge University Press.

Schwartz, D. L., & Martin, T. (2004). Inventing to prepare for learning: The hidden efficiency of original student production in statistics instruction. *Cognition & Instruction, 22,* 129–184.

Shirouzu, H., Miyake, N., & Masukawa, H. (2002). Cognitively active externalization for situated reflection. *Cognitive Science, 26,* 469–501.

Shoji, K. (1988). *Kasetsu-Jikken-Jugyou no ronri* [Logic of hypothesis–experiment–instruction]. Tokyo, Japan: Meiji-Tosho. [In Japanese.]

Sinatra, G. M., & Pintrich, P. R. (2003). *Intentional conceptual change,* Mahwah, NJ: Lawrence Erlbaum Associates.

Stahl, G., Koschmann, T., & Suthers, D. D. (2006). Computer-supported collaborative learning. In K. R. Sawyer (Ed.), *The Cambridge handbook of the learning sciences* (pp. 409–425). New York, NY: Cambridge University Press.

Strom, D., Kemeny, V., Lehrer, R., & Forman, E. (2001). Visualizing the emergent structure of children's mathematical argument. *Cognitive Science, 25,* 733–773.

Vosniadou, S. (2003). Exploring the relationships between conceptual change and intentional learning. In G. M. Sinatra & P. R. Pintrich (Eds.), *Intentional conceptual change* (pp. 377–406). Mahwah, NJ: Lawrence Erlbaum Associates.

Vosniadou, S. (2007). Conceptual change and education. *Human Development, 50*, 47–54.

Vosniadou, S., & Brewer, W. (1992). Mental models of the earth: A study of conceptual change in childhood. *Cognitive Psychology, 24*, 535–585.

Vosniadou, S., & Ioannides, C. (1998). From conceptual development to science education: A psychological point of view. *International Journal of Science Education, 20*, 1213–1230.

Williams, M. D., Hollan, J. D., & Stevens, A. L. (1983). Human reasoning about a simple physical system, In D. Gentner & A. L. Stevens (Eds.), *Mental models* (pp. 131–153). Hillsdale, NJ: Lawrence Erlbaum Associates.

Part V
Instructional Approaches to Promote Conceptual Change

25

TEACHING SCIENCE FOR CONCEPTUAL CHANGE
Theory and Practice

Reinders Duit, David F. Treagust, and Ari Widodo, University of Kiel, Curtin University, and Indonesian University of Education

This chapter contains two parts. In the first part, we discuss a range of theoretical perspectives giving rise to different notions of conceptual change and illustrate how researchers have conceptualized teaching and learning science from these different perspectives. In the second part, we report on studies about the awareness and implementation of these perspectives in regular science classes and document that there is still a large gap between what is known about effective teaching and learning science from conceptual change perspectives and the reality of instructional practice. Finally, we argue that more research is necessary on how teachers in regular practice can become more familiar with the key ideas of conceptual change.

THEORETICAL DEVELOPMENTS IN THE AREA OF CONCEPTUAL CHANGE

Over the past three decades, research has shown that students come to science classes with pre-instructional conceptions and ideas about the phenomena and concepts to be learned that are not in harmony with science views. Furthermore, these conceptions and ideas are firmly held and are resistant to change (Duit, 2009; Duit & Treagust, 2012). While studies on students' learning in science that primarily investigate such students' conceptions on the content level continue to be produced, investigations of students' conceptions at meta-levels, namely conceptions of the nature of science and views of learning, also have been given considerable attention since the 1980s.

The 1980s saw the growth of studies investigating the development of students' pre-instructional conceptions towards the intended science concepts in conceptual change approaches. Over the past three decades, research on students' conceptions and conceptual change has been embedded in various theoretical frames with epistemological, ontological, and affective orientations (Duit & Treagust, 2003; Taber, 2006; Zembylas, 2005).

Research on the role of students' pre-instructional ("alternative") conceptions in learning science developed in the 1970s drawing primarily on two theoretical perspectives (Driver & Easley, 1978). The first was Ausubel's (1968) dictum that the most important single factor influencing learning is what the learner already knows, and hence to teach the learner accordingly. The second theoretical perspective was Piaget's idea of the interplay of assimilation and accommodation. His clinical interview method deeply influenced research on investigating students' conceptions (White & Gunstone, 1992). By the end of the 1970s and the beginning of the 1980s preliminary conceptual change ideas addressing students' conceptions were revealed in the various studies that developed.

Conceptual change viewed as epistemology, namely when the research looks at students' learning of concepts, initially involved only an understanding of how students' conceptions evolved. Later, constructivist ideas developed by merging various cognitive approaches with a focus on viewing knowledge as being constructed. These approaches were influenced by the already mentioned Piagetian interplay of assimilation and accommodation, Kuhnian ideas of theory change in the history of science, and radical constructivism (Duit & Treagust, 1998).

As is discussed more later in this chapter, conceptual change viewed as ontology, namely how students view the nature of the conception being investigated, sought to examine the way that students viewed scientific conceptions in terms of reality. Conceptual change from an epistemological and an ontological perspective refers to students' personal views, on the nature of coming to know (what we refer to as "epistemological" in this chapter) and on the nature of reality (what we refer to as "ontological").

Other researchers were concerned that conceptual change had initially taken on an over-rational approach (Pintrich, Marx, & Boyle, 1993). Certain limitations of the constructivist ideas of the 1980s and early 1990s led to their merger with social constructivist and social cultural orientations that more recently resulted in recommendations to employ multi-perspective epistemological frameworks in order to adequately address the complex process of learning (Duit & Treagust, 2003; Tyson, Venville, Harrison, & Treagust, 1997; Zembylas, 2005).

An Epistemological Perspective of Conceptual Change

The "classical" conceptual change approach as introduced by Posner, Strike, Hewson, and Gertzog (1982) involved the teacher making students' alternative frameworks explicit prior to designing a teaching approach consisting of ideas that do not fit students' existing conceptions and thereby promoting dissatisfaction. A new framework is then introduced based on formal science that may explain the anomaly. However, it became obvious that students' conceptual progress toward understanding and learning science concepts and principles after instruction frequently turned out to be still limited. There appears to be no study which found that a particular student's conception could be completely extinguished and then replaced by the science view (Duit & Treagust, 1998). Indeed, most studies show that the old ideas stay alive in particular contexts. Usually the best that can be achieved is a "peripheral conceptual change" (Chinn & Brewer, 1993) in that parts of the initial idea merge with parts of the new idea to form some sort of hybrid concept (Jung, 1993) or synthetic model (Vosniadou & Brewer, 1992).

In the classical conceptual change model that emphasized students' epistemologies (Posner et al., 1982), student dissatisfaction with a prior conception was believed to initiate dramatic or revolutionary conceptual change and was embedded in radical constructivist epistemological views with an emphasis on the individual's conceptions and his/her conceptual development. If the learner was dissatisfied with his/her prior conception *and* an available replacement conception was intelligible, plausible, and/or fruitful, accommodation of the new conception might follow. An intelligible conception is sensible if it is non-contradictory and its meaning is understood by the student; plausible means that in addition to the student knowing what the conception means, he/she finds the conception believable; and the conception is fruitful if it helps the learner solve other problems or suggests new research directions. Posner et al. insist that a plausible conception must first be intelligible and a fruitful conception must be intelligible and plausible. Resultant conceptual changes may be permanent, temporary, or too tenuous to detect.

In this learning model, resolution of conceptual competition is explained in terms of the comparative intelligibility, plausibility, and fruitfulness of rival conceptions. Posner et al. claimed that a collection of epistemological commitments called the student's conceptual ecology (Toulmin, 1972) mediated conceptual intelligibility, plausibility, and fruitfulness. Strike and Posner (1985, pp. 216–217) expanded the conceptual ecology metaphor to include anomalies, analogies, and metaphors, exemplars and images, past experiences, epistemological commitments, metaphysical beliefs, and knowledge in other fields.

Different ways that researchers have measured students' conceptual change from an epistemological position are conceptual status and epistemological profiles.

Students' Conceptual Status

Conceptual status classifies a conception's status as intelligible, plausible, or fruitful (Hewson, 1982; Hewson & Thorley, 1989) and is particularly useful for assessing changes in students' conceptions during learning. When a competing conception does not generate dissatisfaction, the new conception may be assimilated alongside the old. When dissatisfaction between competing conceptions reveals their incompatibility, two conceptual events may happen. If the new conception achieves higher status than the prior conception, accommodation, which Hewson (1982) calls conceptual exchange, may occur. If the old conception retains higher status, conceptual exchange will not proceed for the time being. It should be remembered that a replaced conception is not forgotten and the learner may wholly or partly reinstate it at a later date. Both Posner et al. (1982) and Hewson (1982) stress that it is the student, not the teacher, who makes the decisions about conceptual status and conceptual changes. This position is in harmony with constructivist learning theory and the highly personal nature of mental models (Norman, 1983).

Studies utilizing the notion of conceptual status include that by Treagust, Harrison, Venville, and Dagher (1996), which set out to assess the efficacy of using analogies to engender conceptual change in students' science learning about the refraction of light. Following instruction by the same teacher, two classes of students, one of which was taught analogically and one that was not, were interviewed three months after instruction using an interview-about-instances protocol. Factors related to status were identified from the interview transcripts to help in the process of classifying each student's conception of refraction as being intelligible, plausible, or fruitful. Hewson and Hennessey (1992, p. 177) developed descriptors to guide this process and these were used in the research. For example, descriptors for "intelligible" included "I must know what the concept means – the words must be understandable, the words must make sense"; descriptors for "plausible" included "it first must be intelligible, it must fit in with other ideas or concepts I know about or believe"; descriptors for fruitful included "it first must be intelligible, it should be plausible and I can see it is something useful – it will help me solve problems."

Most of the evidence from this study indicated that conceptual change which meets the criteria of dissatisfaction, intelligibility, plausibility and fruitfulness is not necessarily an exchange of conceptions for others, but rather an increased use of the kind of conception that makes better sense to the student. The two groups of students performed similarly on the teacher's classroom test. However, when students' conceptions were analyzed graphically with elements of status – no status, intelligibility, plausibility, and fruitfulness – on the ordinate and test scores on the abscissa, those student in the class introduced to the analogy held conceptions of higher status than those students in the class who were not introduced to the analogy. Consequently, the application of the idea of status of a conception showed the degree to which students understood, believed, and were able to apply their scientific knowledge to otherwise unsolved problems. Nevertheless, the research showed that an increased status of a conception made possible by analogical teaching does not necessarily lead to different learning outcomes as measured on traditional tests.

Epistemological and Conceptual Profile

A different but useful way to understand student reactions to multiple conceptions or models is Bachelard's (1968) epistemological profile. People often possess more than one way for describing objects and processes and this is especially so in science. For example, mass can be described in everyday terms of "bigness," measured instrumentally using a spring balance, expressed in dynamic terms such as $F = ma$ or relativistically. Scientists use different methods depending on context, so why should not students use the same differences as they learn? What may appear to be a change in conception by a scientist or a student could simply be a contextually based preference for one conception or model over another. For instance, many secondary teachers and textbooks simultaneously use the electron shell or Bohr model when discussing atomic structure, use balls or space-filling models to explain kinetic theory, and use Lewis electron-dot diagrams for bonding.

The ability to select intelligible, plausible and fruitful representations or conceptions for a specific context is itself a measure of expertise; however, researchers need to be aware that apparent conceptual changes may in fact be context-driven choices rather than conceptual status changes. In learning settings, Mortimer and El-Hani (2013) propose the use of conceptual profiles to help differentiate conceptual changes from contextual choices.

An Ontological Perspective of Conceptual Change

Researchers who use epistemology to explain conceptual changes do not overtly emphasize changes in the way students view reality. Other researchers, however, use specific ontological terms to explain changes in the way students develop their science conceptions (Chi, Slotta, & de Leeuw, 1994; Thagard, 1992; Vosniadou, 1994). Chinn and Brewer (1993, p. 17) described ontological beliefs as being about "the fundamental categories and properties of the world," In showing that "some of the child's concepts are incommensurable with the adult's," Carey (1985, p. 269) argued for strong knowledge restructuring during childhood and Vosniadou called similar changes radical restructuring and explained that revisions to central "framework theories" (pp. 46–49) involve both ontological and epistemological changes. Chi et al. called their strongest ontological changes "tree swapping" and Thagard (1992) also has a strongest change which he calls "tree switching." Two candidates for these types of change are: heat needs to change from a flowing fluid to kinetic energy in transit, and a gene from an inherited object to a biochemical process. There are many other concepts where scientists' *process* views are incommensurable with students' *material* conceptions and the desired changes to students' ontologies are not often achieved in school science. Chiu, Chou, and Liu (2002) adopted Chi's ontological categories of scientific concepts to investigate how students perceived the concept of chemical equilibrium, arguing that "although Posner's theory is widely accepted by science educators and easy to comprehend and apply to learning activities . . . it does not delineate what the nature of a scientific concept is, which causes difficulty in learning the concept" (p. 689).

An Affective Position of Conceptual Change

The third focus of conceptual change is the affective domain, particularly involving emotions, motivation, and social aspects such as group work which has had limited attention in the epistemological position and no attention in the ontological position. Pintrich et al. (1993) proposed that a hot irrational explanation for conceptual change is as tenable as cold cognition and argued that students' self-efficacy and control beliefs, classroom social context, "individual's goals, intentions, purposes, expectations [and] needs" (p. 168) are as important as cognitive strategies in concept learning. Similarly, Solomon (1987) and Dykstra, Boyle, and Monarch (1992) claim that group factors can advantage concept learning and Vygotsky's theories (van der Veer & Valsiner, 1991) highlight the importance of social and motivational influences. Pintrich et al.'s review of the social and motivational literature highlights the importance of interest and personal and situational beliefs to students' engagement in learning activities. Indeed, they claim that teachers who ignore the social and affective aspects of personal and group learning may limit conceptual change. In a review of linking the cognitive and the emotional in teaching and learning science, Zembylas (2005) goes a step further, arguing that it is necessary to develop a "unity" between the cognitive and emotional dimensions that views emotions not only as a moderating variable of cognitive outcomes but as a variable of equal status.

Intentional Conceptual Change

Studies reported in Sinatra and Pintrich (2003) emphasized the importance of the learner, suggesting that the learner should play an active intentional role in the process of knowledge restructuring. While acknowledging the important contributions to the study of conceptual change from the perspectives of science education and cognitive developmental psychology, Sinatra and Pintrich note that the psychological and educational literature of the 1980s and 1990s placed greater emphasis on the role of the learner in the learning process. This emphasis on the impetus for change being within the learner's control forms the basis of the chapters in their text. The notion of intentional conceptual change is in some ways analogous to that of mindfulness (Salomon & Globerson, 1987, p. 623), a "construct which reflects a voluntary state of mind, and connects among motivation, cognition and learning."

Multidimensional Perspectives of Conceptual Change

Conceptual change approaches as developed in the 1980s and early 1990s contributed substantially to improving our understanding of science learning and teaching. Most studies on learning science so far have been oriented toward views of learning that are monistic to some extent. Only more recently have there been powerful developments toward admitting that the complex phenomenon of learning needs pluralistic epistemological frameworks (Greeno, Collins, & Resnick, 1997) in order to adequately address the many facets emphasized by different views of learning. In science education, there are a growing number of multi-perspectives of conceptual change which appear to be promising to improve science teaching and learning (Duit & Treagust, 1998, 2012; Zembylas, 2005). Briefly summarized, multi-perspectives of conceptual change that consider epistemological, ontological and affective domains have to be employed in order to adequately address the complexity of the teaching and learning processes.

Much of the research on conceptual change has taken a particular perspective, namely an epistemological perspective, an ontological perspective, or an affective perspective. There is ample evidence in research on learning and instruction that cognitive and affective issues are closely linked. However, the number of studies on the interaction of cognitive and affective factors in the learning process is limited. There are, for instance, many studies on the relations between interest in science and acquisition of science concepts. However, these studies are usually restricted to correlations between interest in science and cognitive results of learning. The interplay of changes of interest in science and conceptual change has been investigated in only a small number of studies. The multi-dimensional perspectives for interpreting conceptual change by Tyson et al. (1997) include, for instance, an epistemological, an ontological, and an affective domain, though the affective domain has not been fully elaborated. A fruitful outcome for future studies is to merge ideas of conceptual change and theories on the significance of affective factors. It also seems to be most valuable to view the issue of interest in science and science teaching from the perspective of conceptual change. Clearly, an important aim of science instruction is to develop interest in much the same way as to develop students' pre-instructional conceptions toward the intended science concepts.

In contrast to the approach of being committed to one theoretical perspective of conceptual change as a framework for their data analysis and interpretation, Venville and Treagust (1998) utilized four different perspectives of conceptual change to analyze different classroom teaching situations in which analogies were used to teach genetics (see also Venville, Gribble, & Donovan, 2005). The authors used Posner et al.'s (1982) conceptual change model, Vosniadou's (1994) framework theory and mental model perspective, Chi et al.'s (1994) ontological categories, and Pintrich et al.'s (1993) motivation perspective. Venville and Treagust (1998) found that each of the perspectives of conceptual change had explanatory value and contributed a different theoretical perspective on interpreting the role that analogies played in each of the classroom situations. For example, the epistemological perspective in terms of students' conceptions of genes indicated the degree of acceptance of the conception by the students. In this study, there was likely concordance with the status of the conception and different ontological models that students used to think about genes. From a social affective perspective, almost all these Grade 10 students demonstrated in interviews that they were not interested in the microscopic explanatory nature of genetics, preferring to use simple Mendelian genetics to answer questions about themselves.

THE ROLE OF COGNITIVE CONFLICT IN CONCEPTUAL CHANGE

Cognitive conflict has played a major role in various conceptual change approaches since the advent of classical conceptual change approaches in the early 1980s. As mentioned earlier, Piagetian ideas of the interplay of assimilation and accommodation have provided a powerful framework for conceptual change. Cognitive conflict plays a key role in Piagetian approaches such as the "learning cycle" (Karplus, 1977; Lawson, Abraham, & Renner, 1989) and hence also in conceptual change approaches such as "constructivist teaching sequences" (Driver, 1989; Scott, Asoko, & Driver, 1992). In these constructivist approaches, however, not only Piagetian ideas but also Festinger's theory of cognitive dissonance are referred to (Driver & Erickson, 1983). Hashweh (1986) provided a critical view of the role of cognitive conflict in learning science, arguing that various forms of cognitive conflicts have to be distinguished and that it is essential that students actually experience the conflict.

Studies on the use of cognitive conflict reveal conflicting results. Guzetti, Snyder, Glass, and Gamas (1993) carried out a meta-analysis of conceptual change approaches; approaches employing cognitive conflict strategies were found to be more efficient than studies in which this was not the case. Some studies (e.g., Limon & Carretero, 1999; Mason, 2001) report that cognitive conflict may be linked with positive learning results such that these can facilitate conceptual change, while other studies (e.g. Chan, Burtis, & Bereiter, 1997) showed that cognitive conflict may also be inefficient because even when students are confronted with contradictory information, they do not necessarily change their conceptions. In a review on the effectiveness of strategies for facilitating conceptual change within constructivist frameworks, Harlen (1999) suggested that there is no convincing evidence about the effectiveness of one strategy over the other. Vosniadou and Ioannides (1998) argued (see also Limon, 2001) that the conceptual change approaches as developed in the 1980s and early 1990s put too much emphasis on sudden insights facilitated by cognitive conflict. They claim that learning science should be viewed as a "gradual process during which initial conceptual structures based on children's interpretations of everyday experience are continuously enriched and restructured" (p. 1213). Briefly summarized, research has shown that much care is needed if cognitive conflict strategies are used for facilitating conceptual change. It is necessary not only to carefully ensure that students experience the conflict but also to consider the role of specific, usually small-scale, sudden insights within the long-lasting gradual process of conceptual change.

IMPACT OF RESEARCH ON CONCEPTUAL CHANGE IN SCHOOL PRACTICE

As outlined in the previous section, conceptual change has became a powerful domain of research on teaching and learning that developed in the early 1970s. Since this time, cognitive psychologists and science educators have worked closely together, with both domains of educational research substantially profiting from this cooperation. However, what also becomes evident in reviewing the literature is a certain polarization of researchers in the two domains such that one can read excellent research in one domain that has little reference to research in the other domain. Our intention is that the present review can help to overcome this issue of polarization.

In the research domain of conceptual change, as outlined, multidimensional theoretical perspectives allow researchers to investigate teaching and learning processes at a fine-grained level. The perspectives also provide support for the design of teaching and learning environments that usually are superior to more traditional instructional designs. In principle, there is a large potential for improving practice. However, so far the research evidence concerning the impact of teaching informed by conceptual change instructional practices in normal classes is rather limited. We address this issue in the following paragraphs.

ARE CONCEPTUAL CHANGE APPROACHES MORE EFFICIENT THAN MORE TRADITIONAL ONES?

Usually researchers who use a conceptual change approach in their classroom-based studies report that their approach is more efficient than traditional ones. Predominantly, efficiency concerns exclusively or predominantly cognitive outcomes of instruction. The development of affective variables during instruction is often not viewed as the outcome *per se*. This appears to be the case only in more recent multi-dimensional conceptual change perspectives that consider both cognitive and affective outcomes of learning as conceptual change, as discussed by Tyson et al. (1997) and Zembylas (2005).

Quite frequently individual research studies do provide convincing empirical evidence for this claim (e.g., Bryce & MacMillan, 2005; Piquette & Heikkinen, 2005), though an actual summarizing meta-analysis is not available. Previously, Guzetti et al. (1993) provided a meta-analysis that included studies that only employed a treatment–control group design and Wandersee, Mintzes, and Novak (1994) reviewed conceptual change approaches with a cautious remark that their analysis gave the impression that conceptual change approaches usually are more successful than traditional approaches in guiding students to the science concepts. However, a problem with research on conceptual change is that it is difficult to compare the success of conceptual change approaches and other approaches. Usually different approaches to teaching and learning address different aims, and hence it is only possible to evaluate whether the particular aims have been adequately met. An additional problem is that quite frequently the focus of conceptual change approaches is on particular means such as analogies (Bryce &

MacMillan, 2005). Research on instructional quality, however, has shown that usually a single intervention (such as addressing students' pre-instructional conceptions) does not lead to better outcomes *per se* (Weinert, Schrader, & Helmke, 1989). Quality of instruction is always due to a certain orchestration (Oser & Baeriswyl, 2001) of various instructional methods and strategies. Hence, conceptual change strategies may only be efficient if they are embedded in a conceptual change supporting learning environment that includes many additional features.

In summarizing the state of research on the efficiency of conceptual change approaches, there appears to be ample evidence in various studies that these approaches are more efficient than traditional approaches dominated by transmissive views of teaching and learning. This seems to be the case in particular if more inclusive conceptual change approaches based on multi-dimensional perspectives as outlined above are employed. Recent large-scale programs to improve the quality of science instruction (as well as instruction in other domains) include instructional methods that are clearly oriented toward constructivist conceptual change approaches; i.e., attempts to set constructivist principles of teaching and learning into practice (Beeth, Duit, Prenzel, Ostermeier, Tytler, & Wickman, 2003). The other characteristics of quality development approaches by Beeth et al. (2003) refer to: (1) supporting schools and teachers to rethink the representation of science in the curriculum; (2) enlarging the repertoire of tasks, experiments, and teaching and learning strategies and resources; and (3) promoting strategies and resources that attempt to increase students' engagement and interests. Clearly, these characteristics require the teachers to be reflective practitioners (Schoen, 1983) with a non-transmissive view of teaching and learning, and the students to be active, self-responsible, cooperative, and self-reflective learners. Indeed, these features are at the heart of inclusive constructivist conceptual change approaches.

TEACHERS' VIEWS OF TEACHING AND LEARNING SCIENCE

In discussing opportunities to implement science standards in the United States, Anderson and Helms (2001) point out that the major obstacle to success is that teachers usually are not well informed about the recent state of research on teaching and learning science and hold views that are somewhat limited, being predominantly transmissive and not constructivist. In many studies carried out since the 1990s (Duit, 2009), this limited view holds not only for science but also for other instructional domains (Borko, 2004). In their teacher professional development approach of content-focused coaching, West and Staub (2003) claimed that it is essential to encourage teachers to become familiar with the recent state of educational research and to help develop their views about efficient teaching and learning.

A video study on the practice of German and Swiss lower secondary physics instruction supports the above findings. In the first phase of this study, 13 German teachers participated; in the second phase, 50 German and 40 Swiss teachers were involved from a variety of randomly selected schools (Seidel, Rimmele, & Prenzel, 2005). In these two phases, lessons of each teacher were videotaped and additional data on teachers' thinking were provided by questionnaires and interviews.

Analysis of the data from both phases (Duit, Widodo and Wodzinski, 2007; Duit et al., 2005; Seidel et al., 2005) showed that most physics teachers are not well informed about key ideas of conceptual change research. Their views of their students' learning usually are not consistent with the state of recent theories of teaching and learning and appear to lack an explicit view of learning. Some of the teachers hold implicit theories that contain some intuitive constructivist issues; for instance, they want to be learning counselors, and they are aware of the importance of students' cognitive activity and the interpreting nature of students' observations and understanding. However, we also identified teachers who characterized themselves as mediators of facts and information and who were not aware of students' interpretational frameworks and the role of students' pre-instructional conceptions. These teachers mostly think that what they consider to be good instruction is a guarantee of successful learning. Considerations about the content in question predominate in teacher planning. Reflections about students' perspectives and their role in the learning process play a comparatively minor role.

Briefly summarized, two general orientations of instruction may be distinguished from the video study: (1) a focus on physics concepts with learning viewed as knowledge transmission; (2) *constructivist* – a focus on conditions necessary to support learning with learning viewed as student construction.

THE PRACTICE OF TEACHING SCIENCE IN NORMAL CLASSES

The literature on the actual practice of science instruction in normal classes is not extensive, but there are several studies that show that normal instructional practice is somewhat far from the multi-perspective conceptual change approaches outlined in this chapter. This may be expected taking into account the findings on teachers' limited views of teaching and learning science presented in the previous section. A number of studies on teachers' views also provide information on their limited practice (cf. Anderson & Helms, 2001); findings from studies that deliberately address the issue of investigating practice discussed below.

In summarizing the findings of student narratives from interpretive studies on students' experiences of school science in Sweden, England, and Australia, Lyons (2006, p. 595) pointed out that "Students in the three studies frequently described school science pedagogy as the transmission of content expert sources – teachers and texts – to relative passive recipients." It is interesting to note that students were overwhelmingly critical of this kind of teaching practice, which left them with an impression of science as being a body of knowledge to be memorized.

The seminal TIMSS Video Study on Mathematics Teaching (Stigler, Gonzales, Kawanaka, Knoll, & Serrano, 1999; Stigler, Gallimore, & Hiebert, 2000) compared the practice of instruction in the United States, Japan, and Germany. Instruction was observed to be primarily teacher-oriented, and instructional scripts based on transmissive views of teaching and learning predominated. However, it also became apparent that there are significant differences between the participating countries in the degree of constructivist-oriented teaching and learning. In Japan, for instance, students had many more opportunities for self-guided problem solving than in the other two countries. Although instruction in Japan also was teacher-controlled, students spent much of the class time solving problems using a variety of strategies. This was not the case in the German and the United States mathematics classrooms.

The TIMSS Video Study on science teaching (Roth et al., 2006) investigated the instructional scripts of science teaching in five countries: Australia, Czech Republic, Japan, The Netherlands, and the United States. Again, the predominant impression was of instructional scripts informed by traditional transmissive views of teaching and learning. However, instructional features oriented toward constructivist conceptual change perspectives, though not frequent, did occur to different degrees in the participating countries.

The video study in German and Swiss schools on the practice of physics instruction discussed above resulted in similar findings. Specifically, there was a strong teacher dominance in German physics instruction, though students worked in groups or individually for 15% of the lesson time (Duit et al., 2005). Nevertheless, in this somewhat narrow kind of classroom discourse, experiments played a significant role in instruction but students had very limited opportunities for self-organized inquiry. In Switzerland, instruction was less teacher-dominated and there were significantly more opportunities for student inquiry. But still, the orientation of instruction toward constructivist conceptual change views was limited.

In his investigation of the practice of instruction from constructivist perspectives, including deliberate analyses from the point of view of conceptual change strategies, Widodo (2004) observed that the teaching behavior of several teachers comprised various features that were characteristic of constructivist-oriented science classrooms. In these classrooms, teachers provided, for instance, cognitive activity by addressing thought-provoking questions as well as incorporating certain features of conceptual change supporting conditions such as dealing with everyday phenomena. Further, a key phase of constructivist-oriented teaching sequences (Driver, 1989), namely, elicitation of students' pre-instructional knowledge, frequently occurred, as did teachers dealing with students' conceptions, another key phase of conceptual change approaches. However, cognitive conflict was infrequent; usually, the teachers attempted to guide students step by step from their own ideas to the science views. Such attempts to elicit students' ideas and to address them were not deliberately linked. For example, after extended elicitation of what students already knew about electricity or forces, the findings usually did not play any significant role in subsequent instruction. Seldom were students' initial ideas explicitly taken into account when elaborating their conceptions. Finally, there were limited examples where students followed their own ideas in the video data, indicating that students had little voice in instruction.

Briefly summarized, the normal practice of science instruction described in the above studies was not significantly informed by constructivist conceptual change perspectives. Of course, there was a large variance within the educational culture of certain countries and also between the educational cultures of the countries. But still there is a large gap between instructional design based on recent research findings on conceptual change and what is normal practice in most of the classes observed.

CONCEPTUAL CHANGE AND TEACHER PROFESSIONAL DEVELOPMENT

Investigating teachers' views of teaching and learning science and the means to improve teachers' views and their instructional behavior through teacher professional development has become an important research domain (Borko, 2004). Two major issues are addressed in teacher professional development projects. First, teachers are made familiar with research knowledge on teaching and learning by being introduced to recent constructivist and conceptual change views and are made familiar with instructional design that is oriented toward these views. Second, attempts to link their own content knowledge and their pedagogical knowledge play a major role. The most prominent theoretical perspective applied is Shulman's (1987) idea of content-specific pedagogical knowledge, referred to as PCK (pedagogical content knowledge) (West & Staub, 2003).

The process of teacher professional development can be viewed as a set of substantial conceptual changes that teachers have to undergo. As briefly outlined above, teachers' views of teaching and learning are limited when seen from the perspective of the implemented constructivist conceptual change ideas about teaching and learning. Instead, deep changes are necessary. Learning to teach for conceptual change means "that teachers must undergo a process of pedagogical conceptual changes themselves" (Stofflett, 1994, p. 787). Hence, the conceptual change perspectives developed to analyze student learning should also be valuable frameworks for teacher learning. In fact, there have been several attempts to apply these frameworks in teacher education. Stofflett (1994) primarily draws on the classical conceptual change model by Posner et al. (1982) using the conceptual change quadriga of dissatisfaction–intelligibility–plausibility–fruitfulness to analyze the change processes in a teacher development project. A similar approach to teacher development, using the theoretical base of classical conceptual change, was proposed by Feldman (2000), who argued that because teacher practical reasoning is similar to scientific reasoning, "a model of practical conceptual change can be developed that is analogous to the conceptual change model" (Feldman, 2000, p. 606).

This classical conceptual change model by Posner et al. also provided the major orientation of a large study on professional development of biology teachers (Hewson et al., 1999a; Hewson, Tabachnick, Zeichner, & Lemberger, 1999b). Constructivist perspectives with a particular emphasis on the classical conceptual change model were observed to provide a powerful framework to design the change processes that teachers had to undergo and to analyze the characteristics of these processes. Interestingly, the changes that were initiated not only comprised teachers' views about teaching and learning but also their views of science and the nature of knowledge (Hewson et al., 1999a, p. 254): "we use the term conception of teaching science as an inclusive one that encompasses science (the nature of science, scientific knowledge, etc.), learning, and instruction, and the relationships between these three conceptions." The various analyses that were provided clearly showed that conceptual change perspectives may provide powerful frameworks not only for designing and analyzing student learning but also for teacher learning.

It is important to note, however, that attempts to explicitly employ the more recent multi-dimensional and inclusive conceptual change perspectives, as outlined in the first part of the present chapter, currently appear to be missing. Clearly, Hewson et al. (1999a, 1999b) take account of teacher change processes of various kinds, but the conceptual change perspectives applied appear to be largely concerned with teachers' epistemologies.

CONCLUSIONS

The present chapter discusses two distinct but closely connected issues concerning teaching science for conceptual change. In the first part, we provide on overview of theoretical conceptual change perspectives that have developed since the 1970s and that have been employed to design approaches that allow for teaching science more effectively than with instructional designs drawing on transmissive views of teaching and learning.

In the second part, we discuss situations where conceptual change perspectives have been put into practice in normal schools.

Concerning the first part, it becomes obvious that conceptual change has developed into one of the leading paradigms in research on teaching and learning. It is interesting to see continuous progress over the three decades since early conceptual change research occurred. As science educators, we note that science education research contributed greatly to the development of the broader research domain of conceptual change.

Very briefly summarized, we witness a development from early conceptual change perspectives based on Piagetian, Ausubelian, Kuhnian and further epistemological views. In general, the conceptual change ideas of the early 1980s were based on individualistic and somewhat radical constructivist views. Only later, in parallel with the development of constructivist ideas toward including variants of social constructivism, more inclusive views of conceptual change developed.

It is noteworthy also that the definition of what changes in conceptual change has itself changed substantially over the past three decades. Initially, the term "change" was frequently used in a somewhat naïve way – if seen from the inclusive perspectives that have since developed. The term "conceptual change" was even frequently misunderstood as exchange of the students' pre-instructional (or alternative) views for the science view. However, it became clear very soon that such an exchange is not possible. Major meanings given to the term "conceptual change" (such as status change, proposed by Hewson & Hennessey, 1992) are discussed in the first part of the present chapter. Conceptual change now denotes that learning science includes various changes of perspectives. Most of these changes of epistemological and ontological perspectives are not simple but rather difficult, as the "everyday" perspectives and the science perspectives often are not in accordance but are at best complementary.

The role given to affective issues in the process of conceptual change is also worth noting. Already the classical conceptual change approach (Posner et al., 1982) included affective issues, but only implicitly. Pintrich et al. (1993) initiated attempts to investigate the role of emotions, interests, and motivation more fully. Affective issues were, however, mainly viewed as variables moderating conceptual change. Only more recently are cognitive and affective perspectives viewed as equally important, with both having to undergo substantial conceptual changes during instruction (Zembylas, 2005). This more recent view also endows cognitive and affective outcomes of instruction with the same importance.

Instructional design oriented at conceptual change perspectives has proved more efficient than traditional design oriented toward transmissive views of teaching and learning. However, a cautious remark is needed here: A formal meta-analysis supporting this claim is so far not available, although the results of a recent large scale meta-analysis of instructional quality seem to be promising. Hattie (2009, p. 252) summarizes his findings as follows: "If the teacher's lens can be changed to seeing learning through the eyes of students, this would be an excellent beginning." Conceptual change-oriented approaches address this explicitly.

The significance of instructional design oriented at recent inclusive conceptual change perspectives for improving practices is twofold. First, rather ambitious and multifaceted conceptions of scientific literacy may be set into practice only if instructional design is informed by inclusive conceptual change perspectives. Second, as mentioned, usually such design leads to improved learning outcomes. For this reason, it appears that recent quality development approaches in science education are based on these designs (Ostermeier, Prenzel, & Duit, 2010).

In a nutshell, research on conceptual change has developed into a rich and significant domain of educational research since the 1970s. The theoretical frameworks and research methods developed allow fine-grained analyses of teaching and learning processes. The findings of research provide powerful guidance for the development of instructional design for science education that societies need.

However, there is a large gap between what is known in the research domain of conceptual change about more efficient teaching and learning and what may be set into practice in normal classes. In the second part of the present chapter, we argue that teachers usually are not well informed about actual views of efficient teaching and learning available in the research community. Most teachers hold views that are limited if seen from the recent inclusive conceptual change perspectives. At best some isolated features of these perspectives are embedded within predominantly transmissive views. Further, instructional practice is also usually far from a practice that is informed by conceptual change perspectives. Taking into account teachers' deeply rooted views of what they perceive to be good instruction, it becomes apparent that various closely linked conceptual changes in the teachers' beliefs about teaching and learning are necessary in order to commence and set recent conceptual change views into practice.

The state of theory-building on conceptual change has become more and more sophisticated, and the teaching and learning strategies developed have become more and more complex over the past 30 years. Of course, these developments are necessary in order to address the complex phenomena of teaching and learning science more and more adequately. But it appears that the gap between what is necessary from the researchers' perspective and what may be set into practice by normal teachers has increased. Maybe we have to address the paradox that in order to adequately model teaching and learning proccesses, research alienates the teachers and hence widens the theory–practice gap?

The message of the present chapter is that we should deal with this paradox. Taking account of the state of research on conceptual change as presented in the present handbook, the focus is on further developing theoretical frameworks, research methods, and more efficient conceptual change instructional strategies. However, in which way all this may become part of actual practice has been given little attention. Interestingly, the frameworks of student conceptual change – being predominantly researched so far – may also provide powerful frameworks for teacher change toward employing conceptual change ideas. While there are attempts to use this potential, more research in this field based on the recent inclusive conceptual change perspectives is most desirable.

REFERENCES

Anderson, R. D., & Helms, J. V. (2001). The ideal of standards and the reality of schools: Needed research. *Journal of Research in Science Teaching, 38*, 3–16.

Ausubel, D. P. (1968). *Educational psychology: A cognitive view.* New York, NY: Holt, Rinehart and Winston.

Bachelard, G. (1968). *The philosophy of no: A philosophy of the new scientific mind.* New York, NY: Orion Press.

Beeth, M., Duit, R., Prenzel, M., Ostermeier, C., Tytler, R., & Wickman, P.O. (2003). Quality development projects in science education. In D. Psillos, P. Kariotoglou, V. Tselfes, G. Fassoulopoulos, E. Hatzikraniotis, & M. Kallery (Eds.), *Science education research in the knowledge based society* (pp. 447–457). Dordrecht, The Netherlands: Kluwer Academic Publishers.

Borko, H. (2004). Professional development and teacher learning: Mapping the terrain. *Educational Researcher, 33,* 3–15.

Bryce, T., & MacMillan, K. (2005). Encouraging conceptual change: The use of bridging analogies in the teaching of action–reaction forces and the "at rest" condition in physics. *International Journal of Science Education, 27,* 737–763.

Carey, S. (1985). *Conceptual change in childhood.* Cambridge, MA: MIT Press.

Chan, C., Burtis, J., & Bereiter, C. (1997). Knowledge building as a mediator of conflict in conceptual change. *Cognition and Instruction, 15,* 1–40.

Chi, M. T. H., Slotta, J. D., & de Leeuw, N. (1994). From things to processes: A theory of conceptual change for learning science concepts. *Learning and Instruction, 4,* 27–43.

Chinn, C. A., & Brewer, W. F. (1993). The role of anomalous data in knowledge acquisition: A theoretical framework and implications for science education. *Review of Educational Research, 63,* 1–49.

Chiu, M.-H., Chou, C.-C., & Liu, C-J (2002). Dynamic processes of conceptual change: Analysis of constructing mental models of chemical equilibrium. *Journal of Research in Science Teaching, 39,* 713–737.

Driver, R. (1989). Changing conceptions. In P. Adey, J. Bliss, J. Head, & M. Shayer (Eds.), *Adolescent development and school science* (pp. 79–104). London, UK: Falmer Press.

Driver, R., & Easley, J. A. (1978). Pupils and paradigms: A review of literature related to concept development in adolescent science students. *Studies in Science Education, 5,* 61–84.

Driver, R., & Erickson, G. L. (1983). Theories-in-action: Some theoretical and empirical issues in the study of students' conceptual frameworks in science. *Studies in Science Education, 10,* 37–60.

Duit, R. (2009). *STCSE – Bibliography: Students' and teachers' conceptions and science education.* Kiel, Germany: IPN – Leibniz Institute for Science Education.

Duit, R., & Treagust, D. F. (1998). Learning in science: From behaviourism towards social constructivism and beyond. In B. J. Fraser & K. Tobin (Eds.), *International handbook of science education, Part 1* (pp. 3–25). Dordrecht, The Netherlands: Kluwer Academic Publishers.

Duit, R., & Treagust, D. (2003). Conceptual change: A powerful framework for improving science teaching and learning. *International Journal of Science Education, 25,* 671–688.

Duit, R., & Treagust D. F. (2012). How can conceptual change contribute to theory and practice in science education? In B. F. Fraser, K. Tobin, & C. McRobbie (Eds.), *Second international handbook of science education* (pp. 107–118). Dordrecht, The Netherlands: Springer.

Duit, R., Widodo, A., & Wodzinski, C. T. (2007). Conceptual change ideas: Teachers' views and their instructional practice. In S. Vosniadou, A. Baltas, & X. Vamvokoussi (Eds.), *Re-framing the problem of conceptual change in learning and instruction* (pp. 197–217). Amsterdam, The Netherlands: Elsevier.

Duit, R., Fischer, H., Labudde, P., Brückmann, M., Gerber, B., Kauertz, A., et al. (2005). Potential of video studies in research on teaching and learning science. In R. Pintó & D. Couso (Eds.), *Proceedings of the Fifth International ESERA Conference on Constritutions of Research to Enhancing Students' Interests in Learning Science* (pp. 829–842). Barcelona, Spain: UAB.

Dykstra, D. I., Boyle, C. F. , & Monarch, I. A. (1992). Studying conceptual change in learning physics. *Science Education, 76,* 615–652.

Feldman, A. (2000). Decision making in the practical domain: A model of practical conceptual change. *Science Education, 84,* 606–623.

Greeno, J. G., Collins, A. M., & Resnick, L. B. (1997). Cognition and learning. In D. C. Berliner & R. C. Calfee (Eds.), *Handbook of educational psychology* (pp. 15–46). New York, NY: Simon & Schuster Macmillan.

Guzetti, B. J., Snyder, T. E., Glass, G. V., & Gamas, W. S. (1993). Promoting conceptual change in science: A comparative meta-analysis of instructional interventions from reading education and science education. *Reading Research Quarterly, 28,* 116–159.

Harlen, W. (1999). *Effective teaching of science: A review of research.* Edinburgh, UK: Scottish Council for Research in Education.

Hashweh, M. Z. (1986). Toward an explanation of conceptual change. *European Journal of Science Education, 8,* 229–249.

Hattie, J. (2009). Visible learning: A synthesis of over 800 meta-analyses relating to achievement. Abingdon, UK: Routledge.

Hewson, P. W. (1982). A case study of conceptual change in special relativity: The influence of prior knowledge in learning. *European Journal of Science Education, 4,* 61–78.

Hewson, P., & Hennessey, M. G. (1992). Making status explicit: A case study of conceptual change. In R. Duit, F. Goldberg, & H. Niedderer. (Eds.), *Research in physics learning: Theoretical issues and empirical studies* (pp. 176–187). Proceedings of an International Workshop. Kiel, Germany: Institute for Science Education.

Hewson, P. W., Tabachnick, B. R., Zeichner, K.M. , Blomker, K. B., Meyer, H., Lemberger, J., et al. (1999a). Educating prospective teachers of biology: Introduction and research methods. *Science Education, 83*, 247–273.

Hewson, P. W., Tabachnick, B. R., Zeichner, K. M., & Lemberger, J. (1999b). Educating prospective teachers of biology: Findings, limitations, and recommendations. *Science Education, 83*, 373–384.

Hewson, P. W., & Thorley, N. R. (1989). The conditions of conceptual change in the classroom. *International Journal of Science Education, 11*, 541–553.

Jung, W. (1993). Hilft die Entwicklungspsychologie dem Physikdidaktiker [Does developmental psychology help the physics educator?]. In R. Duit & W. Gräber (Eds.), *Kognitive Entwicklung und naturwissenschaftlicher Unterricht* (pp. 86–107). Kiel, Germany: IPN–Leibniz Institute for Science Education.

Karplus, R. (1977). Science teaching and the development of reasoning. *Journal of Research in Science Teaching, 14*, 33–46.

Lawson, A. E., Abraham, M., & Renner, J. (1989). *A theory of instruction: Using the Learning Cycle to teach science concepts and thinking skills* (NARST Monograph Number One). Cincinnati, OH: National Association for Research in Science Teaching.

Limon, M. (2001). On the cognitive conflict as an instructional strategy for conceptual change: A critical appraisal. *Learning and Instruction, 11*, 357–380.

Limon, M., & Carretero, M. (1999). Conflicting data and conceptual change in history experts. In W. Schnotz, S. Vosniadou, & M. Carretero (Eds.), *New perspective on conceptual change* (pp. 137–160). Oxford, UK: Pergamon.

Lyons, T. (2006). Different countries, same science classes: Students' experiences of school science in their own words. *International Journal of Science Education, 28*, 591–613.

Mason, L. (2001). Responses to anomalous data on controversial topics and theory change. *Learning and Instruction, 11*, 453–484.

Mortimer, E. F., & El-Hani, C. N. (Eds.). (2013). *Conceptual profile: A theory of teaching and learning scientific concepts*. Dordrecht, The Netherlands: Springer.

Norman, D. A. (1983). Some observations on mental models. In D. Gentner & A. L. Stevens (Eds.), *Mental models* (pp. 7–14). Hillsdale, NJ: Lawrence Erlbaum Associates.

Oser, F. K., & Baeriswyl, F. J. (2001). Choreographies of teaching: Bridging instruction to learning. In V. Richardson (Ed.), *AERA's handbook of research on teaching* (4th edn., pp. 1031–1065). Washington, DC: American Educational Research Association.

Ostermeier, C., Prenzel, M., & Duit, R. (2010). Improving science and mathematics instruction: The SINUS project as an example for reform as teacher professional development. *International Journal of Science Education, 32*, 303–327.

Pintrich, P. R., Marx, R. W., & Boyle, R. A. (1993). Beyond cold conceptual change: The role of motivational beliefs and classroom contextual factors in the process of conceptual change. *Review of Educational Research, 6*, 167–199.

Piquette, J. S., & Heikkinen, H.W. (2005). Strategies reported used by instructors to address student alternate conceptions in chemical equilibrium. *Journal of Research in Science Teaching, 42*, 1112–1134.

Posner, G. J., Strike, K. A., Hewson, P. W., & Gertzog, W. A. (1982). Accommodation of a scientific conception: Toward a theory of conceptual change. *Science Education, 66*, 211–227.

Roth, K., Druker, S., Garnier, H., Chen, C., Kawanaka, T., Rasmussen, D., et al. (2006). *Teaching science in five countries: Results from the TIMSS 1999 Videostudy. Statistical Analysis Report*. Washington, DC: NCES.

Salomon, G., & Globerson, T. (1987). Skill may not be enough: The role of mindfulness in learning and transfer. *International Journal of Educational Research, 11*, 623–637.

Schoen, D. A. (1983). *The reflective practitioner*. London, UK: Temple Smith.

Scott, P. H., Asoko, H. M. , & Driver, R. (1992). Teaching for conceptual change: A review of strategies. In R. Duit, F. Goldberg, & H. Niedderer (Eds.), *Research in physics learning: Theoretical issues and empirical studies* (pp. 310–329). Kiel; Germany: IPN–Institute for Science Education.

Seidel, T., Rimmele, R., & Prenzel, M. (2005). Clarity and coherence of lesson goals as a scaffold for student learning. *Learning and Instruction, 15*, 539–556.

Shulman, L. S. (1987). Knowledge and teaching: Foundations of the new reform. *Harvard Educational Review, 57*, 1–21.

Sinatra, G. M., & Pintrich, P. R. (Eds.). (2003). *Intentional conceptual change*. Mahwah, NJ: Lawrence Erlbaum Associates.

Solomon, J. (1987). Social influences on the construction of pupils' understanding of science. *Studies in Science Education, 14*, 63–82.

Stigler, J. W., Gonzales, P., Kawanaka, T., Knoll, S., & Serrano, A. (1999). *The TIMSS Videotape Classroom Study: Methods and findings from an exploratory research project on eighth-grade mathematics instruction in Germany, Japan and the United States.* Washington DC: U.S. Department of Education.

Stigler, J. W., Gallimore, R., & Hiebert, J. (2000). Using video surveys to compare classrooms and teaching across cultures: Examples and lessons from the TIMSS video studies. *Educational Psychologist, 35*, 87–100.

Stofflett, R. T. (1994). The accomodation of science pedagogical knowledge: The application of conceptual change constructs to teacher education. *Journal of Research in Science Teaching, 31*, 787–810.

Strike, K. A., & Posner, G. J. (1985). A conceptual change view of learning and understanding. In L. West & L. Pines (Eds.), *Cognitive structure and conceptual change* (pp. 211–231). Orlando, FL: Academic Press.

Taber, K. S. (2006). Beyond constructivism: The progressive research programme into learning science. *Studies in Science Education, 42*, 125–184.

Thagard, P. (1992). *Conceptual revolutions.* Princeton, NJ: Princeton University Press.

Toulmin, S. (1972). *Human understanding: Vol. I.* Oxford, UK: Oxford University Press.

Treagust, D. F., Harrison, A. G., Venville, G. J., & Dagher, Z. (1996). Using an analogical teaching approach to engender conceptual change. *International Journal of Science Education, 18*, 213–229.

Tyson, L. M., Venville, G. J., Harrison, A. G., & Treagust, D. F. (1997). A multidimensional framework for interpreting conceptual change in the classroom. *Science Education, 81*, 387–404.

van der Veer, R., & Valsiner, J. (1991). *Understanding Vygotsky: A quest for synthesis.* Oxford, UK: Blackwell.

Venville, G., Gribble, S. J., & Donovan, J. (2005). An exploration of young children's understandings of genetics concepts from ontological and epistemological perspectives. *Science Education, 89*, 614–633.

Venville, G. J, & Treagust, D. F. (1998). Exploring conceptual change in genetics using a multidimensional interpretive framework. *Journal of Research in Science Teaching, 35*, 1031–1055.

Vosniadou, S. (1994). Capturing and modelling the process of conceptual change. *Learning and Instruction, 4*, 45–69.

Vosniadou, S., & Brewer, W. F. (1992). Mental models of the earth: A study of conceptual change in childhood. *Cognitive Psychology, 24*, 535–585.

Vosniadou, S., & Ioannides, C. (1998). From conceptual change to science education: A psychological point of view. *International Journal of Science Education, 20*, 1213–1230.

Wandersee, J. H., Mintzes, J. J., & Novak, J. D. (1994). Research on alternative conceptions in science. In D. Gabel (Ed.), *Handbook of research on science teaching and learning* (pp. 177–210). New York, NY: Macmillan.

Weinert, F. E., Schrader, F. W., & Helmke, A. (1989). Quality of instruction and achievement outcomes. *International Journal of Educational Research, 13*, 895–914.

West, L., & Staub, F.C. (2003). *Content-focused coaching: Transforming mathematics lessons.* Portsmouth, NH and Pittsburgh, PA: Heinemann and University of Pittsburgh.

White, R., & Gunstone, R. (1992). *Probing understanding.* London, UK: Falmer Press.

Widodo, A. (2004). *Constructivist oriented lessons: The learning environment and the teaching sequences.* Frankfurt, Germany: Peter Lang.

Zembylas, M. (2005). Three perspectives on linking the cognitive and the emotional in science learning: Conceptual change, socio-constructivism and poststructuralism. *Studies in Science Education, 41*, 91–116.

26

SELF-ORGANIZATION IN CONCEPTUAL GROWTH

Practical Implications

Carl Bereiter and Marlene Scardamalia, Institute for Knowledge Innovation and Technology and University of Toronto

In the famous debate between Chomsky and Piaget (Piatelli-Palmarini, 1980), which included a number of other leading philosophers and scientists, the problem of explaining conceptual growth and change proved so intractable that Fodor was led to declare:

> There literally isn't such a thing as the notion of learning a conceptual system richer than the one that one already has; we simply have no idea of what it would be like to get from a conceptually impoverished to a conceptually richer system by anything like a process of learning.

> (Fodor, 1980, p. 149)

During the next decade, however, with the increasing presence of complex systems models, conceptual growth came to be seen as one more example of self-organizing processes by which complex structures emerge from interactions among less complex ones – a process that is evident at all levels from the molecular (Kauffman, 1993) to the cultural (Dennett, 1995). Much remains to be explained about conceptual growth, but it may be said that conceptual growth has been domesticated; it has become part of a large class of phenomena amenable to explanation in terms of concepts drawn from what is broadly referred to as complexity science (Kauffman, 1995).

The self-organizing character of conceptual growth appears to be well recognized by researchers, as indicated by frequent references to it in the first edition of this *Handbook* (Vosniadou, 2008). Nevertheless, its role in both theoretical and applied work has been marginal. Complex systems theory is essentially neutral with regard to theoretical controversies in the field because, according to Brown and Hammer (2008, p. 137), it "describes the full spectrum of phenomena in the literature on conceptual change." It does not help resolve differences between "frameworks" and "knowledge in pieces" views, because both imply emergence of complex structures from diverse knowledge elements (diSessa, 2008, p. 52; Vosniadou, Vamvakoussi, & Skopeliti, 2008, p. 23). Neither is it very helpful in distinguishing spontaneous from instruction-based change (Inagaki & Hatano, 2008). Spontaneous conceptual change more easily fits into a classical dynamic systems template, but this does not mean that instruction and intentional learning lie outside the systemic processes that constitute conceptual change. The relatively neglected challenge for conceptual change theory is producing a dynamic system model in which intentions and instructional interventions are part of the process.

That complexity science should have more impact on theory than on practice is not surprising. But what effect on educational practice should it have? We omit from consideration here complexity science as subject matter in its own right and "systems thinking" as a skill objective. These are vital and challenging constituents of present-day scientific literacy (Hmelo-Silver & Azevedo, 2006; Jacobson & Wilensky, 2006), but they belong on a different ontological branch from the question of what insights drawn from complexity science may contribute to the general promotion and guidance of conceptual growth. That is the question pursued in this chapter. To clear the table for this inquiry, we may categorically reject popular notions that complexity science directly implies the superiority of "constructivist" over "instructivist" approaches. All learning involves self-organization, whether it is learning at the neuromuscular level of weight training or at the advanced cognitive level of creative problem solving. If a student slavishly taking notes during a lecture is learning something, that learning is the result of self-organizing processes in the student's brain and not of knowledge being somehow transmitted from the brain of the lecturer to the brain of the student. But such statements merely dress up well-known truths. Complexity science offers promise of going beyond this to inform educational practice under three conditions:

1. when learning goes awry or stops short of objectives, as in the persistence of naïve concepts despite instruction
2. when the desire is to go beyond the standard expectations enshrined in educational standards, achieving new levels and breadths of understanding
3. when the concern is to accommodate education to emerging societal needs for knowledge creation and innovation.

Applied research on conceptual change has dealt mainly with the first of these conditions. Through several decades of work on knowledge building in education (Scardamalia & Bereiter, 2006), however, we have been more concerned with the second and the third – with extending the range of the possible in education beyond normal expectations and with socializing students into what the OECD in numerous publications is calling an "innovation-driven society" (Organisation for Economic Co-operation and Development, 2010). "Deep understanding" and "expertise" are common terms that refer to learning that goes beyond normal expectations. Within the context of primary to tertiary education there is always a deeper level of understanding that could be pursued, and expertise is something that not only can keep growing but needs to keep growing if one is to remain an expert in a progressive field (Bereiter & Scardamalia, 1993). A conventional approach to accommodating education to the needs of an innovation-driven society takes the form of specifying cognitive skill objectives and incorporating these into curriculum standards (Johnson, 2009). The alternative pursued in knowledge-building pedagogy consists essentially of learning to innovate by innovating – a well-recognized approach in engineering and design education but one that represents a radical departure in education for understanding (Bereiter & Scardamalia, 2006, 2010).

In this chapter we first describe a complex systems model that we believe to have most practical potential in education – a model in which facts, hypotheses, intentions, feelings, and instructional inputs act as constraints on the settling of a connectionist network representing ideas. We then characterize expert learners as skillful managers of this self-organizing process, who treat learning as problem solving and are able to apply problem-solving heuristics and intuitions to it. But conceptual learning, as everyone recognizes, is a social as well as an internal cognitive process. Accordingly, we briefly consider what is involved in a classroom or a school's becoming a community organized around the pursuit of understanding.

CONCEPT ACQUISITION AS THE SETTLING OF A CONNECTIONIST NETWORK

Newly acquired concepts are emergents, arising from a self-organizing process that at a micro level (but a level still above that of brain processes) consists of ideational interactions that are uncontrollable and unknowable. And these are not the insignificant variations that all behavior exhibits (you never pick up a teacup in exactly the same way twice); they are the very essence of semantic interactions from which emerges a new organization of some part of the conceptualized world. That is the irreducible complexity of conceptual growth, when viewed from a dynamic systems perspective.

Complexity science embraces a number of models and ways of representing the activity of dynamic systems. These can range from realistic simulations, such as one where ants are depicted scurrying around on the computer screen in search of food (Resnick, 1994), to a variety of equation-based and graph-based models. We have found that for thinking about educational processes the most useful type of representation is a connectionist network in which all or some of the nodes are assigned identities as people, ideas, facts, or other meaningful entities (Bereiter, 1991). This is an approach that has proved strikingly productive in the research headed by Thagard (2000, 2006) on explanatory coherence, enabling him to model significant real events such as scientific and medical advances and the outcomes of jury trials. Such "local networks," as they are called, are to be distinguished from "distributed networks" that simulate activity at the neuronal level and typically do not have identifiable nodes except at the input and output ends; while these can do important theoretical work their relevance to conceptual growth is more distant.

As applied to concepts, local connectionist networks model the constraints that exist among propositions. These may be positive constraints such as agreement, entailment, and evidential support, or negative constraints such as contradiction and competition. These are represented by excitatory or inhibitory links between nodes representing propositions. The activation level of any particular node is determined by the sum of the positive and negative activations it receives. This activation level determines the strength of the activations it sends out, thus affecting the activation levels of the nodes to which it is connected. The network "settles" or becomes stable if and when the activation and inhibition impulses coming to each node match the existing activation level of the node, so that there is no further change. (A simplified explanation of this process, using a concrete analogy, is provided in Bereiter, 1991.) The result will be that some nodes have higher levels of activation than others and so are included in the net forming the concept at issue and some have levels that fall below some minimum and so are excluded from the concept. Except in the simplest cases, the results could not be inferred from examination of the propositions involved. Instead, the resulting concept net is an emergent of the interactions involved in the process of satisfying the positive and negative constraints and the eventual settling of the network. In Thagard's model, certain propositions identified as facts receive continuing activation from a central source, so that they are not so readily eliminated as other propositions. However, we have seen an instance of children playing with a network representing theories of dinosaur extinction, adding invented propositions until the network finally rejected the proposition that the dinosaurs are extinct.

Connectionist networks can learn through corrective feedback coming from outside the network. That is how they can learn, for instance, to distinguish male from female faces on the basis of features extracted from photographs. The system settles on one of two outputs: male or female. If it is correct, the positive and negative links of the settled network are strengthened. If it is wrong they are weakened. Gradually judgments improve. But networks can also demonstrate a kind of learning that takes place without external feedback, and this is especially interesting from the standpoint of conceptual change. Such "unsupervised" learning works on the basis of correlation rather than error correction. It can be quite effective in extracting patterns from stimuli and thus is relevant to language and concept learning (Elman et al., 1996). The change in children's explanations of dinosaur extinction referred to earlier is an example of learning without correction. The network of facts and propositions constructed by the children at first settled on a pattern corresponding to the hypothesis that volcanic eruptions and fire killed off the dinosaurs. When the students were questioned as to whether any relevant facts had been neglected, they recalled the layer of iridium found around the world. When this fact was added, the network – an implementation of Thagard's ECHO program (1989) – settled on the familiar asteroid explanation of dinosaur extinction.

HORTICULTURE AS A WEAK METAPHOR FOR SELF-ORGANIZED LEARNING

Well before complexity science came on the scene, progressive educators used a metaphor that carries a strong flavor of self-organization. It is the horticultural metaphor, which likens the teacher to a gardener and the student to a plant. It is usually contrasted with the familiar factory metaphor. The idea behind the horticultural metaphor is that teaching is a matter of assisting natural growth, which is internally regulated. You can no more manufacture learning, this metaphor suggests, than you can manufacture a cantaloupe. All you can do is provide conditions and nurturance that will support optimal development of the child or the cantaloupe, as the case may be. The horticultural metaphor is in harmony with the idea of self-organization, for the progression from seed to flower to fruit is indeed a process of self-organization, and the gardener's capacity to influence the process is severely limited. The metaphor has serious weaknesses, however. It does not accord well with two facts: first, that the main reason for having formal education in the first place is to teach things that do not come naturally – that are neither preprogrammed in the genes nor acquired through everyday experience; second, that systematic instruction, carried out as if the factory metaphor were valid, is often successful. A satisfactory model of teaching as a self-organizing process must somehow accommodate these two facts.

These strictures apply both to academic skills and to disciplinary concepts, but in this chapter we will deal only with the latter. The idea that the tilt of the earth relative to its plane with the sun determines the seasons is obviously not an idea acquired naturally through experience, and research has shown that even for people who have been exposed to modern cosmology the idea often loses out in competition with the more "natural" idea that warmth varies with closeness to the source of heat (Schoon, 1995). If taught through textbook, lecture, and demonstration, the accepted scientific explanation of seasonal change will take hold with some students, even though it fails with many others. In cases like this, where a large percentage of students fail to grasp the intended concept, it seems as if self-organization in the form of cognition settling on whatever comes most naturally is the enemy of conceptual growth. Both the horticultural metaphor and the factory metaphor fail. The education system labors to bring forth a cantaloupe, but a potato emerges instead.

BEYOND GARDENING: ON TRYING TO BECOME A CANTALOUPE

George Bernard Shaw, in his preface to *Back to Methuselah*, criticized an experiment that was supposed to demonstrate that acquired characteristics cannot be inherited. The scientist cut off the tails of mice in successive generations and found that mice continued to be born with long tails. Nonsense, said Shaw. For the experiment to prove anything, the mice would have to *want* to have short tails, just as the ancestors of today's giraffes must have wanted to have longer necks. While Shaw's quirky notion of purposeful evolution finds no support in biology, there is plenty of evidence that in conceptual growth, which is also an evolutionary process, intentions make a difference.

The most straightforward way of incorporating intentions, goals, motives, and the like into a connectionist model is to treat them as constraints. They are not hard constraints like natural laws – they can be overridden or ignored – but they can function somewhat like laws. Thagard has incorporated emotional predispositions and other personal reactions into his coherence model as constraints (2006). They play an important part in modeling decision processes that do not accord well with strict rationality, such as jury decisions that are swayed by feelings about the defendant or the accusers (Thagard, 2003). In classroom work we have introduced official standards as information for students – what the Ministry of Education expects them to learn from the unit they are working on – but understandably those are not mere items of information; they carry an authoritative weight that would not be shared by, for instance, some unknown expert's opinion about what should be learned. And yet, like a factual scientific statement, they can be overridden by a decision mechanism that tries to maximally satisfy all the relevant constraints.

The concept of constraint, as used in information and design sciences, would be a useful one for teachers to have in their repertoires. Unlike the related concept of restraint, it has a positive connotation. It is what enables constructive processes to progress, to move toward consolidation of a design or a concept. Indeed, Perkins (1981) has explained creative work as the successive addition of constraints. Thinkers need to realize that they are continually adding constraints and to consider always whether the constraint is valid and useful or whether it is lopping off branches containing alternatives that should not be prematurely eliminated. The old concept of functional fixedness (Duncker, 1945) can be understood not as a personal defect but as the adoption of deleterious constraints. Similarly, conceptual growth can be limited by unfortunate constraints, such as requiring natural phenomena to have a purpose relevant to human welfare or to a cosmic plan. Such constraints effectively put evolution beyond comprehension, but they also affect more mundane understandings, such as that of the child who opined that there is less gravity on the moon than on the earth because there aren't as many things there that need to be held down.

THE EXPERT LEARNER AS A MANAGER OF CONCEPTUAL SELF-ORGANIZATION

In a study of young children's word learning, Carey and Bartlett (1978) casually introduced a new color name into preschool activities. The new word was "chromium," and it referred to the color olive-green. (They did not use the word "olive" because it would provide a cue for those children familiar with the fruit.) The teacher would say things like "Hand me the chromium block. No, not the red block, the chromium one." In what Carey and Bartlett called "fast mapping," the children quickly caught on to the idea that "chromium" was a color, but it took some time for them to work out what that color was. According to Carey (1978), connecting the word with the intended color involved more than just linking the word to a percept; it involved reorganizing the semantic space of color concepts so as to make a place for the new concept within a network of related concepts. In contemporary terms, it involved conceptual self-organization. This idea of word learning as involving reorganization of a sometimes vast network of concepts was made explicit and implemented in latent semantic analysis (LSA), which locates concepts in a Euclidean space of hundreds of dimensions (Landauer & Dumais, 1997). Using LSA to model normal vocabulary growth, Landauer and Dumais inferred that a sizable proportion of new words (two out of the average seven words per day learned during childhood) entered a child's vocabulary not when the word was being actively processed but at some other time when spontaneous processes of semantic organization made it settle into a position relative to other words. Vocabulary growth according to this model is an eminently self-organizing process; and the model applies to a large body of findings that have followed upon Carey and Bartlett's original study (Swingley, 2010).

There is more to the "chromium" story. The preschoolers studied by Carey and Bartlett were not very successful in nailing down the new color concept. However, according to Carey (1978), the children exhibited two different strategies. In one, which we call *direct assimilation* (in acknowledgement of the process identified by Piaget), the children immediately equated chromium with green, and then gradually learned to discriminate between them. Others adopted what Carey called the "odd color, odd name" strategy. In effect, they set up a *placeholder* for the new concept (cf. Bereiter, 2010; Gelman & Brandone, 2010) and gradually attached information to it. These children made faster progress than those adopting the direct assimilation strategy. In either case acquisition of the new concept was a self-organizing process, but learning was more intentional, more under the learner's control in the case of those adopting the "odd color, odd name" strategy. They exhibited more learning expertise.

Expert learners are people unusually adept at acquiring new skills and understandings. As with most kinds of expertise, the natural contrast group is young children, who serve as all-purpose novices. (That young children may be more adept than adults when it comes to foreign language learning does not constitute a counter-example. Hard-wired excellence does not count as expertise; we do not call fish expert swimmers.) Of particular interest from the standpoint of conceptual growth is how people respond to concept-altering information.

Although differences in approaches to learning show up even with such simple tasks as learning a new color term or learning a single new concept in an already familiar domain, the difference between expert and nonexpert learning becomes much more striking when some advance in the complexity of knowledge is involved. To about 100 children ranging from first through sixth grade, Chan, Burtis, Scardamalia , and Bereiter (1992) presented a series of statements about germs or dinosaurs and asked children to think aloud after each statement. One of the text statements that proved most provocative of differences in response was the following:

> Harmful germs are not trying to be bad when they settle down in your body. They just want to live quietly, eat, and make more germs.

Responses were scaled according to five levels. The first two levels were ones at which the child did not show evidence of having assimilated the new information at all but instead responded to an isolated word or proposition by recalling old information that was cued by it. At Level 3, however, one might get a comment or paraphrase that makes it clear the passage had been taken in. For instance:

> That means they don't want to really hurt you, but they just want to live quietly and eat the food you digest and all the things that could go in your stomach and they just want to get more bacteria.

Yet at Level 3 the child shows no recognition that the statement contradicts the popular concept of germs as aggressors. At Level 4 such disparities are recognized and at Level 5 the child makes an effort to reconcile or deal with them – for instance, by considering that germs have no intelligence and thus have no idea of the effects of their actions. Level of response was positively correlated with amount learned from the texts. So were age and prior knowledge, as could be expected. However, statistical path analysis indicated that learning expertise, as indicated by response level, exerted the only significant direct effect on learning, and mediated the effects of age and prior knowledge.

In case studies of college-level students in music and medicine, expert and nonexpert learners were identified by asking instructors to pick out successful but typical students on one hand and on the other hand students whose approach to their subject resembled that of experts. Given a novel learning task in their field, the nonexpert learners manifested the *direct assimilation* approach discussed previously. Ghent (1989) presented a novel piece of piano music – a transcription of Indonesian wayang music – to a concert pianist and two piano students. In thinking-aloud protocols, one student dealt with the novel challenge by considering what the piece resembled most closely in music he was already familiar with. His answer was French Impressionism, and he proceeded immediately to play the piece in the manner of Debussy: a clear case of direct assimilation *à la* Piaget, fitting the novel into an existing schema. However, both the concert pianist and the student identified as expertlike focused on what was problematic in the new piece and worked on how to solve the problem (i.e., how to produce on the piano the percussive effect of music originally played on drums). Thus we may term their approach *learning as problem solving*. This same distinction between *direct assimilation* and *learning as problem solving* appeared in research by Tal (1992), which followed typical and expertlike medical students through a variety of tasks that arose in the regular course of their clinical training.

Problem solving is a self-organizing process almost by definition. It is goal-directed activity in which the path to the goal is not known in advance but must be discovered (Newell, 1980). If a routine procedure achieves the goal, then it is not problem solving. Most human learning and, as far as we know, all learning by non-human creatures is unproblematic – that is, it goes on without applying problem solving skills or resources to the task of learning itself. (The learning may arise from problem solving, but that is a different matter; we are talking about learners treating learning itself as a problem. This is a distinction between learning *through* problem solving and learning *as* problem solving (Bereiter & Scardamalia, 1989). There are important kinds of human learning, however, that are problematic and do not take place or do not take place efficiently without problem solving. In a study of reading comprehension strategies, using thinking-aloud techniques, Bird (Bereiter & Bird, 1985) found that one strategy used by skilled adult readers when they encountered a difficulty in text comprehension was to formulate the difficulty as a problem and then try to solve it. They also used more routine and familiar strategies such as backtracking and paraphrase. An instructional experiment intended to teach the expert strategies to school students produced significant gains in reading comprehension and there was evidence that students actually used the taught strategies – except for the problematization strategy.

In a related line of research, we asked elementary school students to imagine they were allowed an hour a day to learn anything they wished. When questioned about how they would go about their chosen learning, students generally showed a good sense of what resources and methods they would use. However, they treated learning as a straightforward process of applying routine procedures, they had little sense of how long the learning would take, they anticipated no difficulties, and when asked what they would do if they did encounter difficulties, they suggested nothing more than persistence in the routines of reading, practice, and so forth. This was in contrast to adults who, when posed the same hypothetical situation, had a more realistic sense of the amount of work and difficulty that lay ahead. In short, they saw achieving a learning objective as a problem to be solved.

An educated adult, undertaking learning in an unfamiliar field, nevertheless brings a useful body of knowledge to the task. It is knowledge about learning. Based on prior experience, the adult will know, for instance, that:

- There is probably more to be learned than they imagine at the outset.
- They may often be unable to tell what is important from what isn't, and so had better err on the side of assuming things are important.
- Words that they think they already know may turn out to have different meanings in the new discipline.
- Their initial understanding is likely to be simplistic, and so they had better be on the watch for complicating factors.

- No matter how unappealing the field might seem to them, there are intelligent people who find it fascinating, and so they should be on the watch for what it is that arouses the intellectual passions of people in the new discipline.

Naïve students, however, lacking generic knowledge about learning, will do things such as the following:

- Give no thought to how much more there is to learn, and jump to conclusions on the basis of the little they have already learned.
- Judge importance on the basis of superficial cues; e.g., assume lists are important, especially if they are numbered.
- Make subjective judgments of importance, ignoring events or statements that do not stand out as important in their own right – what Brown, Day, and Jones (1980) called the "copy–delete" strategy.
- Assume words mean what they are used to having them mean.
- Quickly construct simplistic interpretations, which are then retained in the face of contraindications.
- Dismiss whole topics as boring, without attempting to discover what might be interesting in them, while allowing themselves to be captivated by items of tangential interest.

In connectionist terms, these predispositions function as constraints that cause the process of conceptual self-organization to settle prematurely on simplistic and often incoherent concepts. Knowledge about learning of the kinds attributed to educated adults can also serve as constraints on the learning of new concepts, but these are constraints that prevent the process from premature settling and that boost the search for alternative and more complex meanings.

Of course, merely possessing declarative knowledge about learning does not guarantee that it will function to constrain concept learning. Like other relevant factual knowledge it needs continual boosting to keep it from being nullified or simply ignored. Expertise in learning means having an overarching system that ensures a privileged status for facts, both facts pertaining to the concept in question and what may be called *metacognitive facts* – facts that pertain to the learning situation as a problem space. But the boosting, which may be imagined as a continual input of energy, has to come from somewhere. For mature experts, the boosting may come from firmly established habits of mind, which influence cognition in a wide range of situations. In the classroom, boosting may come from the teacher's continual issuing of reminders about things that need to be taken into account. Not to be neglected, however, is the peer or classroom culture, which can strengthen certain constraints, weaken others, and in more general terms constitute an overarching system that can strongly influence for good or ill the self-organizing processes by which concepts develop.

CLASSROOM CULTURE ORGANIZED AROUND PURSUIT OF UNDERSTANDING

Eichinger, Anderson, Palincsar, and David (1991) analyzed an argument among a small group of Grade 6 students about whether, on a rocket trip to Mars, water should be carried in the form of a solid, liquid, or gas. The question was assigned by the teacher, with strictures that the group must reach a decision and must give reasons for their answer. After some initial discussion, a majority of the students were prepared to vote for gas, on grounds that it is lighter. However, the students took seriously the norm, emphasized throughout the trip to Mars unit, which required that students have reasons for their opinions. As a result, one student's pro-gas position was discounted because he admitted to having no reason for it. Then another pro-gas student, who was particularly attentive to the reasons given by other students, shifted to being in favor of liquid water, which then became the group's choice. The transcript of the argument makes it obvious that these were children and not model miniature adults. They turned the scientific problem into a win–lose contest, tried to score points by ridicule, and generally did not appear to take the problem very seriously. And yet the norm requiring reasons for opinions survived and ultimately led them to a scientifically reasonable conclusion that differed from where most of them had started.

The "you must have a reason" norm was part of a sustained effort by the teacher to establish a classroom culture disposed toward scientific thinking. Success in such an effort is only achieved to the extent that students themselves uphold the norms, bringing them into play without reminding by the teacher. Once this state is achieved, the boosting of norms as constraints becomes part of the normal round of classroom life and is self-maintaining.

The "you must have a reason" norm and the related norm of paying attention to both positive and negative evidence are essential to any rational controversy. A dramatic example of what can happen when such norms are absent or allowed to lapse comes from the notorious controversy in the United States about Barack Obama's place of birth. The claim that he was not actually born in the United States and therefore not a legitimate president persisted despite evidence from a legally acceptable birth certificate and newspaper announcements of his birth in the state of Hawaii. "Birthers," as the conspiracy theorists are called, questioned this evidence, demanding to see a more detailed form of birth certificate, which was eventually provided. President Obama criticized the mass media for keeping such a silly controversy alive. However, one fact that was seldom brought up and that figured hardly at all in the claims and counter-claims raging through the media is one that points to almost universal failure of the "you must have a reason" norm. The birthers offered no plausible reason for believing that Obama was not born in the United States (except for a Kenya birth certificate that was immediately revealed as a crude forgery), nor did media pundits demand a reason. As a result, the whole controversy has been carried out at a level of rationality below that of the sixth-graders we have been discussing.

A rising emphasis on argumentation (e.g., Andriessen, Baker, & Suthers, 2003) promotes classroom cultural norms that give an important place to empirical evidence, logical reasons, and openness to different viewpoints. These are norms relevant to evaluating explanations, but they do not deal with how explanations are actually produced or grasped. Consequently, their contribution to conceptual growth is limited. In terms of a distinction we have elaborated elsewhere (Bereiter & Scardamalia, 2003, 2006), they are cultural norms mainly applicable to activity in "belief mode" rather than "design mode."

What kinds of classroom cultural norms would act as favorable constraints on academic activity in design mode? Norms pertaining to the pursuit of understanding would surely rank high by any modern standard. Relevant norms would include "seek out big ideas," a norm of treating all ideas as potentially improvable, and another that figures in Scardamalia's (2002) set of 12 knowledge-building principles, "rise above." "Rise above," in the context of concept development, is synonymous with the more formal term, "synthesize." When you encounter conflicting ideas, try to create a third idea that coherently combines the strengths of the conflicting ideas. Promoting classroom cultural norms often entails concept teaching in its own right – teaching the distinction between opinions and evidence, developing the concepts of big ideas, synthesis, and what constitutes an improvement in explanatory ideas.

Cultural norms, when fully internalized, serve to shape not only classroom behavior and group cognition but personal identity as well. Young students seem readily to identify themselves as researchers or junior scientists. But such self-identification sometimes rests on a very meager set of norms. To make a difference in conceptual development, class-room norms need to have some bite – to strengthen what needs strengthening and to suppress what needs suppression.

FUN WITH IDEAS

Earlier we mentioned students playing around with propositions about dinosaur extinction until finally the software application they were using settled on the conclusion that dinosaurs were not extinct. The students were having fun, but the technology they were using was not a game or some kind of "edutainment." It was serious "thought-ware" – a version of Thagard's ECHO (1989), designed to assess coherence in a set of explanatory propositions and facts. What the students discovered was that the program could also be used for imaginative play with ideas. Young students can find a way to turn almost any activity into a game – sometimes to the detriment of educational objectives, as when they turn what should be a serious assignment into a competition to see who can finish first. Although often it is desirable to block such diversions, we want at this point to consider possibilities of turning playfulness to good account.

Of course, the value of play with ideas is already well recognized in conventional educational wisdom, with Albert Einstein almost invariably cited as the exemplar and chief proponent. It allows self-organization at the idea level to go on with relaxed constraints, which may result in the emergence of new conceptual combinations leading to conceptual growth. Not all intellectual play is play with ideas, however. Word puzzles, logical and mathematical puzzles, and games of strategy such as chess and Go may have cognitive benefits of some sort, but they do not generally involve concept development except for concepts internal to the game or puzzle type.

Play with ideas can take two distinct forms. In one form certain concepts themselves serve as constraints on a game-like system, so that achieving goals within the system requires accommodation to these constraints and thence, under favorable conditions, to actually learning the concepts. Simulation software has this character, which is mani-fested clearly in the ThinkerTools Force and Motion software (White & Frederiksen, 2000). The simulation environment operates according to Newtonian laws of motion. Challenges are presented calling for the application of forces to get a screen object to behave in a particular way, such as hitting or stopping at a designated target. However, the software provides enough flexibility that students can devise games of their own and can alter properties and physical laws to investigate the results.

The other form of play with ideas is closer to the Einstein model, featuring playful explanation. We once recorded a group of Grade 5/6 students discussing the idea that the earth is a globe. They quickly deduced that this meant people in Australia were upside down, and they found this quite amusing. Ideas flew thick and fast – that the earth was really a disk, not a globe; that people in the southern hemisphere were on the inside of the globe, not the outside; and so on over various of the naïve theories reviewed by Brewer (2008) and Vosniadou, Vamvakoussi, and Skopeliti (2008). However, one member of the group who seemed to be better informed on cosmology asserted that gravity drew things toward the center of the earth and that therefore people in the southern hemisphere were not upside down and that things dropped there fell to earth the same as they did in the northern hemisphere. He was ignored. He repeated his statements only to have them summarily dismissed. Our interpretation is that the others rejected him because he was spoiling their fun.

One invented theory that received an enthusiastic response in the group was that the earth is like a Ferris wheel, so that as it rotates the people on board remain upright. It must not be supposed that the children took this theory seriously. Although no one criticized it, its inconsistency with everyday experience is too glaring to have been overlooked. What the Ferris wheel theory illustrates is a very loose form of model-based explanation (Clement, 2008; Nersessian, 2008). The students were playing at explanatory model creation in much the way that a kitten plays at catching mice. Although direct evidence of its benefits are lacking, one is entitled to suppose that such play must have a significant and perhaps an essential role in conceptual development.

TECHNOLOGY TO SUPPORT CONCEPTUAL SELF-ORGANIZATION

Much of recent learning technology is relevant to conceptual change. This includes simulations and microworlds that enable students to explore and test ideas, as well as tools directly applicable to building conceptual models (e.g., Wilensky & Reisman, 2006). Of particular importance for collaborative concept development, however, is technology to support the kind of dialogue that transmutes information into public knowledge – that is, knowledge-building dialogue. Here the pickings are more limited. Besides the ubiquitous "threaded discourse," which generally provides no process support whatever (Hewitt, 2005), the discursive side of conceptual work in education is dominated by argumentation software (Andriessen et al., 2003). As we have noted previously, argumentation can play a significant role in concept development, but it is not the process through which conceptual advances are made. It represents the critical rather than the creative aspect of concept work. Technology to support the production and improvement of explanations rather than only their evaluation ranges from highly structured and content-laden applications such as ExplanationConstructor (Sandoval & Reiser, 2004) to open software environments, such as Knowledge Forum (Scardamalia & Bereiter, 2006), where content is brought in by the learners and knowledge-building dialogue is facilitated by affordances for linking, organizing, labeling, visualizing, and evaluating dialogue contributions.

A number of design criteria emerge for technology to support concept-developing dialogue, regardless of the extent to which the technology is content-specific versus content-independent and scripted versus structured by the users:

- The overall design of the technology should be oriented toward support of explanation through collaborative theory and model building (with such other kinds of dialogic activity as argumentation, planning, and knowledge sharing serving auxiliary purposes).
- It should be possible to connect various modes of communication (face-to-face, videoconferencing, asynchronous and synchronous discussion, text messaging, etc.) in support of a *single* coherent dialogue – coherent not merely in having a shared topic but in having followable lines of thought running through the various modes of expression and communication.
- It should be easy to build models, use multimedia to explore ideas, and bring the results of experiments, simulations, web searches, and so on into the main line of the knowledge-building dialogue.
- It should be possible to network any ideas (however they are represented) with any other ideas, for purposes of comment or synthesis.
- Without disrupting the main line of a dialogue, it should be possible to carry on a meta-dialogue, which is dialogue about the main dialogue – about its content, progress, difficulties, and so on.
- Contributions to dialogue should be tagged not only as to topic but also according to what may be broadly categorized as speech acts. Automatic tagging, using semantic analysis, could be combined with tagging by users so as to combine the strengths of both and to maximize the educational benefit from use of semantic tags.

We are not aware of any existing technology that meets these criteria. Knowledge Forum, which was designed to support knowledge-building discussion, perhaps comes closest (Scardamalia & Bereiter, 2006); but it does not fully meet any of the criteria. We are at present organizing an open source community effort to build a next-generation environment that will meet these along with more advanced design criteria.

CONCLUSION: COMPLEX SYSTEM ACCOUNTS OF CONCEPTUAL CHANGE MAY BE TRUE, BUT WHAT GOOD ARE THEY?

Complex system models of conceptual change are mathematical models, even if the mathematics is not the kind learning scientists are accustomed to. Like many other mathematical models, they may have considerable power in accounting for data, but they lack both the insight-bringing quality and the practical suggestiveness of qualitative explanations that take a narrative or "how it works" form. It seems likely that research on conceptual change will continue to deal mainly in "how it works" explanations, not unlike the descriptions we employ in everything from explaining noises in our building's plumbing to explaining why educated conservatives deny climate change. In this chapter, however, we have tried to indicate some ways that viewing conceptual change in terms of self-organizing systems may have educational benefit. These require treating the teacher or the autonomous learner as manager of a self-organizing knowledge-creating process, much like the manager of a creative design team. The manager does not control the process or guide it to a pre-determined outcome. Instead, teaching acts, intentional acts on the part of the student, and information from authoritatitve sources function as inputs to a self-organizing system, with results that are not wholly predictable. We have proposed that these inputs be regarded as non-binding constraints on the settling of a connectionist network, chosen so as to optimize even if they do not predictably deter-mine cognitive outcomes. The outputs of such a process may be thought of as conceptual artifacts (Bereiter, 2002; Paavola & Hakkarainen, 2009): ideal objects that may be represented and worked with in many different ways (Nersessian, 2008). Like other artifacts, such as computer software, these knowledge products carry an implicit version number. They represent something put out for use by a community, while design of the next version proceeds either openly or behind the scenes.

In practical terms, an important advantage of a complex systems approach is that it can assimilate rather than compete with other approaches to promoting conceptual development. Two major approaches to education for concept development are ones that feature evidence-based argumentation (Bell & Linn, 2000) and ones that focus on explanation and explanatory power (Bereiter, 2012; Clement, 2008; Thagard, 2008). It is possible to add explanation building to an evidence-oriented approach (e.g., Matuk, et al., 2012), but arguably this puts the cart before the horse. It should not be necessary to decide between these approaches, both of which have obvious merit. But a synthesis cannot be merely additive. It needs to conceptualize concept development at a higher level, which is the level that Piaget struggled toward in his genetic epistemology (Piaget, 1971) and which currently reaches its fullest realization in complex systems theory.

REFERENCES

Andriessen, J., Baker, M., & Suthers, D. (Eds.). (2003). *Arguing to learn: Confronting cognitions in computer-supported collaborative learning environments.* Dordrecht, The Netherlands: Kluwer.

Bell, P., & Linn, M. C. (2000). Scientific arguments as learning artifacts: Designing for learning from the Web with KIE. *International Journal of Science Education, 22*(8), 797–817.

Bereiter, C. (1991). Implications of connectionism for thinking about rules. *Educational Researcher, 20,* 10–16.

Bereiter, C. (2002). *Education and mind in the knowledge age.* Mahwah, NJ: Lawrence Erlbaum Associates.

Bereiter, C. (2010). *Three knowledge concepts of practical significance in education.* Paper presented at Annual Meeting of the American Educational Research Association (AERA) Denver, CO, April 30–May 4.

Bereiter, C. (2012). Theory building and education for understanding. In M. A. Peters, P. Ghiraldelli, B. Zarnic, and A. Gibbons (Eds.), *Encyclopaedia of philosophy of education.* Available at: www.ffst.hr/ENCYCLOPAEDIA/ doku.php?id=theory_building_and_education_for_understanding

Bereiter, C., & Bird, M. (1985). Use of thinking aloud in identification and teaching of reading comprehension strategies. *Cognition and Instruction, 2,* 131–156.

Bereiter, C., & Scardamalia, M. (1989). Intentional learning as a goal of instruction. In L. B. Resnick (Ed.), *Knowing, learning, and instruction: Essays in honor of Robert Glaser* (pp. 361–392). Hillsdale, NJ: Lawrence Erlbaum Associates.

Bereiter, C., & Scardamalia, M. (1993). *Surpassing ourselves: An inquiry into the nature and implications of expertise.* La Salle, IL: Open Court.

Bereiter, C., & Scardamalia, M. (2003). Learning to work creatively with knowledge. In E. De Corte, L. Verschaffel, N. Entwistle, & J. van Merriënboer (Eds.), *Powerful learning environments: Unraveling basic components and dimensions* (pp. 55–68). Oxford, UK: Elsevier Science.

Bereiter, C., & Scardamalia, M. (2006). Education for the knowledge age: Design-centered models of teaching and instruction. In P. A. Alexander & P. H. Winne (Eds.), *Handbook of educational psychology* (2nd edn., pp. 695–713). Mahwah, NJ: Lawrence Erlbaum Associates.

Bereiter, C., & Scardamalia, M. (2010). Can children really create knowledge? *Canadian Journal of Learning and Technology, 36*(1).

Brewer, W. F. (2008). Naïve theories of observational astronomy: Review, analysis, and theoretical implications. In S. Vosniadou (Ed.), *International handbook of research on conceptual change* (pp. 155–204). New York, NY: Routledge.

Brown, A. L., Day, J. D., & Jones, R. S. (1980). The development of plans for summarizing texts. *Child Development, 54,* 968–979.

Brown, D. E., & Hammer, D. (2008). Conceptual change in physics. In S. Vosniadou (Ed.), *International handbook of research on conceptual change* (pp. 127–154). New York, NY: Routledge.

Carey, S. (1978). The child as word learner. In M. Halle, J. Bresnan, & G. A. Miller (Eds.), *Linguistic theory and psychological reality* (pp. 264–293). Cambridge, MA: MIT Press.

Carey, S., & Bartlett, E. (1978). Acquiring a single new word. *Proceedings of the Stanford Child Language Conference, 15*, 17–29.

Chan, C. K. K., Burtis, P. J., Scardamalia, M., & Bereiter, C. (1992). Constructive activity in learning from text. *American Educational Research Journal, 29*, 97–118.

Clement, J. (2008). The role of explanatory models in teaching for conceptual change. In S. Vosniadou (Ed.), *International handbook of research on conceptual change* (pp. 417–452). New York, NY: Routledge.

Dennett, D. C. (1995). *Darwin's dangerous idea: Evolution and the meanings of life.* New York, NY: Simon & Schuster.

diSessa, A. A. (2008). Bird's-eye view of the "pieces" vs. "coherence" controversy (from the "pieces" side of the fence). In. S. Vosniadou (Ed.), *International handbook of research on conceptual change* (pp. 35–60). New York, NY: Routledge.

Duncker, K. (1945). On problem solving. *Psychological Monographs, 58*(5) (Whole No. 270).

Eichinger, D. C., Anderson, C. W., Palincsar, A. S., & David, Y. M. (1991, April). *An illustration of the roles of content knowledge, scientific argument, and social norms in collaborative problem solving.* Paper presented at the meeting of the American Educational Research Association, Chicago, IL.

Elman, J., Bates, E., Johnson, M., Karmiloff-Smith, A., Parisi, D., & Plunkett, K. (1996). *Rethinking innateness: A connectionist perspective on development.* Cambridge, MA: MIT Press.

Fodor, J. A. (1980). Fixation of belief and concept acquisition. In M. Piattelli-Palmerini (Ed.), *Language and learning: The debate between Jean Piaget and Noam Chomsky* (pp. 142–149). Cambridge, MA: Harvard University Press.

Gelman, S. A., & Brandone, A. C. (2010). Fast-mapping placeholders: Using words to talk about kinds. *Language Learning and Development, 6*, 223–240.

Ghent, P. (1989). *Expert learning in music.* Master's thesis, University of Toronto, Toronto, Canada.

Hewitt, J. (2005). Toward an understanding of how threads die in asynchronous computer conferences. *Journal of the Learning Sciences, 14*(4), 567–589.

Hmelo-Silver, C. E., & Azevedo, R. (2006). Understanding complex systems: Some core challenges. *Journal of the Learning Sciences, 15*, 53–61.

Inagaki, K., & Hatano, G. (2008). Conceptual change in naïve biology. In. S. Vosniadou (Ed.), *International handbook of research on conceptual change* (pp. 240–262). New York, NY: Routledge.

Jacobson, M., & Wilensky, U. (2006). Complex systems in education: Scientific and educational importance and research challenges for the learning sciences. *Journal of the Learning Sciences, 15*(1), 11–34.

Johnson, P. (2009). The 21st century skills movement. *Educational Leadership, 67*(1), 11.

Kauffman, S. (1993). *The origins of order: Self-organization and selection in evolution.* New York, NY: Oxford University Press.

Kauffman, S. (1995). *At home in the universe: The search for laws of self-organization and complexity.* New York, NY: Oxford University Press.

Landauer, T. K., & Dumais, S. T. (1997). A solution to Plato's problem: The latent semantic analysis theory of the acquisition, induction, and representation of knowledge. *Psychological Review, 25*, 211–240.

Matuk, C., McElhaney, K., Chen J. K., Miller, D., Lim-Breitbart, J., & Linn, M. (2012). *The Idea Manager: A tool to scaffold students in documenting, sorting, and distinguishing ideas during science inquiry.* Berkeley, CA: University of California.

Nersessian, N. J. (2008). Mental models in conceptual change. In. S. Vosniadou (Ed.), *International handbook of research on conceptual change* (pp. 391–416). New York, NY: Routledge.

Newell, A. (1980). Reasoning, problem solving and decision processes: The problem space as a fundamental category. In R. Nickerson (Ed.), *Attention and Performance VIII.* Hillsdale, NJ: Lawrence Erlbaum Associates.

Organisation for Economic Co-operation and Development. (2010). *The OECD Innovation Strategy: Getting a head start on tomorrow.* Paris, France: OECD.

Paavola, S. & Hakkarainen, K. (2009). From meaning making to joint construction of knowledge practices and artefacts – A trialogical approach to CSCL. In C. O'Malley, D. Suthers, P. Reimann, & A. Dimitracopoulou (Eds.), *Computer Supported Collaborative Learning Practices: CSCL2009 Conference Proceedings* (pp. 83–92). Rhodes, Greece: International Society of the Learning Sciences (ISLS).

Perkins, D. N. (1981). *The mind's best work.* Cambridge, MA: Harvard University Press.

Piaget, J. (1971). *Psychology and epistemology: Towards a theory of knowledge.* New York, NY: Viking Press.

Piatelli-Palmarini, M. (Ed.). (1980). *Language and learning: The debate between Jean Piaget and Noam Chomsky.* Cambridge, MA: Harvard University Press.

Resnick, M. (1994). *Turtles, termites, and traffic jams: Explorations in massively parallel microworlds.* Cambridge, MA: MIT Press.

Sandoval, W. A., & Reiser, B. J. (2004). Explanation-driven inquiry: Integrating conceptual and epistemic supports for science inquiry. *Science Education, 88,* 345–372.

Scardamalia, M. (2002). Collective cognitive responsibility for the advancement of knowledge. In B. Smith (Ed.), *Liberal education in a knowledge society* (pp. 67–98). Chicago, IL: Open Court.

Scardamalia, M., & Bereiter, C. (2006). Knowledge building: Theory, pedagogy, and technology. In K. Sawyer (Ed.), *Cambridge handbook of the learning sciences* (pp. 97–118). New York, NY: Cambridge University Press.

Schoon, K. (1995). The origin and extent of alternative conceptions in the earth and space sciences: A survey of pre-service elementary teachers. *Journal of Elementary Science Education, 7*(2), 27–46.

Swingley, D. (2010). Fast mapping and slow mapping in children's word learning. *Language Learning and Development, 6,* 179–183.

Tal, N. F. (1992). *Diagnostic reasoning of difficult internal medicine cases: Expert, proto-expert, and non-expert approaches.* Doctoral thesis, University of Toronto, Toronto, Canada.

Thagard, P. (1989). Explanatory coherence. *Behavioral and Brain Sciences, 12,* 435–502.

Thagard, P. (2000). *Coherence in thought and action.* Cambridge, MA: MIT Press.

Thagard, P. (2003). Why wasn't O. J. convicted? Emotional coherence in legal inference. *Cognition and Emotion, 17*(3), 361–383.

Thagard, P. (2006). *Hot thought: Mechanisms and applications of emotional cognition.* Cambridge, MA: MIT Press.

Thagard, P. (2008). Conceptual change in the history of science: Life, mind, and disease. In S. Vosniadou (Ed.), *International handbook of research on conceptual change* (pp. 374–387). New York, NY: Routledge.

Vosniadou, S. (Ed.). (2008). *International handbook of research on conceptual change.* New York, NY: Routledge.

Vosniadou, S., Vamvakoussi, X., & Skopeliti, I. (2008). The framework theory approach to the problem of conceptual change. In. S. Vosniadou (Ed.), *International handbook of research on conceptual change* (pp. 3–34). New York, NY: Routledge.

White, B. Y., & Frederiksen, J. R. (2000). Technological tools and instructional approaches for making scientific inquiry accessible to all. In M. J. Jacobson & R. B. Kozma (Eds.), *Innovations in science and mathematics education: Advanced designs for technologies of learning* (pp. 321–359). Mahwah, NJ: Lawrence Erlbaum Associates.

Wilensky, U. & Reisman, K. (2006). Thinking like a wolf, a sheep, or a firefly: Learning biology through constructing and testing computational theories – An embodied modeling approach. *Cognition & Instruction, 24*(2), 171–209.

27

THE KNOWLEDGE INTEGRATION PERSPECTIVE

Connections Across Research and Education

*Douglas B. Clark and Marcia C. Linn, Vanderbilt University
and University of California, Berkeley*

Vosniadou, Vamvakoussi, and Skopeliti (2008) discuss intersections between their framework theory perspective and other conceptual change perspectives in their chapter from the first edition of this handbook. The current chapter builds on that excellent foundation by outlining and discussing our knowledge integration perspective in light of other elemental perspectives (that emphasize the diversity of student ideas) and framework theory perspectives (that emphasize the coherence of student ideas). The goal of this chapter, as with Vosniadou et al.'s original chapter, involves moving beyond a focus on differences between conceptual change perspectives to instead focus on similarities, synergies, and affordances in hopes of better addressing core theoretical and practical questions central to learning and education.

KNOWLEDGE INTEGRATION PERSPECTIVE

An examination of the diverse, creative, and unique ideas that students formulate has led researchers to argue for a constructive process of knowledge generation and change. When students are asked to explain scientific phenomena in an abstract, de-contextualized frame, they often respond quite differently from when asked to explain an observed phenomenon. Analyzing the conceptual change processes involves explaining how students take advantage of their ideas when they encounter a new situation. Students' methods for grappling with new observations reveal that they engage in a creative process of trying to make sense of their world (Hatano & Inagaki, 2003).

Many researchers have focused on the diversity and character of student ideas. These ideas have been referred to as "misconceptions," "alternative conceptions," "beliefs," "intuitive ideas," and "constructed ideas." Any theory of conceptual change needs to explain the emergence of these views, as well as their role in conceptual change.

Researchers have compiled the varied ideas that students generate in a wide assortment of scientific domains (Pfundt & Duit, 1994). This large body of evidence has developed an image of students constructing multiple, contradictory, and fragmented ideas that stem from their interactions with the material and social world (Clark, 2006; diSessa, 1988; Howe, 2002; Linn & Hsi, 2000; Metz, 2000; Siegler, 1996). Many researchers have shown that the ideas students generate arise from observations, analogies with related events, cultural practices, or colloquial uses of language.

The knowledge integration perspective on conceptual change has emerged from a series of empirical studies. It was spurred by evidence of the impact of context on student reasoning (Linn, 1983). It celebrates the ideas students generate and views these ideas as intellectual accomplishments rather than intellectual constraints (Linn, 1995; Linn, Davis, & Bell, 2004; Linn & Hsi, 2000). Important evidence for this view comes from a longitudinal study carried out over five years that gives insight into student lifelong learning (Clark, 2006; Clark & Linn, 2003; Lewis 1996; Linn & Hsi, 2000).

This longitudinal study illustrated how students maintain conceptual ecologies involving multiple conceptual elements and ideas at various levels of sophistication, connection, and conflict. These conceptual elements and ideas include cultural and observational information and beliefs spanning both epistemological and ontological aspects of knowing and learning. Examples include, but are not limited to, nominal and committed facts, experiences, intuitive conceptions such as phenomenological primitives (diSessa, 1988), narratives, epistemological elements, mental models (Gentner & Stevens, 1983), and concepts (Carey, 1985) at various stages of development (Clark, 2006; Linn et al., 2004). As with Vosniadou et al.'s (2008) framework theory perspective and diSessa's knowledge in pieces perspective (1988), the knowledge integration perspective acknowledges that ideas can be introduced (through schooling and other experiences) that result in fragmentation, conflicts between ideas, and/or synthetic models. Learning occurs through a process of restructuring and reorganizing new and existing ideas.

Our own work (Clark, 2006; Clark & Linn, 2003; Linn & Hsi, 2000) identifies these ideas through the explanations and causal descriptions that students express in interviews and other assessments (e.g., "metal things are colder than wood things" or "the metal attracts heat"). These explanations and causal descriptions point to underlying (although often unarticulated) views that shape students' thinking, explanations, and predictions. Students use these multiple ideas to interpret the phenomena they encounter in their everyday lives. The particular ideas students consider and connect depend on contextual cues. Some connections arise from experience (e.g., metals feel cold), some connections are situation-specific and less broadly useful (e.g., cooling on the stove is different from heating), some are imported from another domain such as electricity and may or may not be useful or accurate in the new domain (e.g., glass is not a conductor of electricity so it will be a poor thermal conductor), and some have their roots in classroom instruction (e.g., metals have heavier molecules). Some connections that students make are spontaneous and ephemeral; some are much more durable and persistent. Some spontaneous ideas and connections may not persist beyond that occasion. Some ideas and connections become more established and strengthened over time, resulting in systematic predictions and explanations.

REORGANIZING AND RECONNECTING IDEAS

As students learn, they reorganize, reconnect, and sort through their ideas. Some ideas become central and pivotal as students use them as focal points around which to integrate other ideas, while other ideas are demoted in priority and centrality. Promoting ideas involves increasing the centrality of an idea in its connections to other ideas and across multiple contexts. Conversely, demoting involves decreasing the centrality of an idea in its connections to other ideas and contexts. Thus promoting and demoting involve creating and modifying connections as well as broadening or narrowing the reach of the idea. Promoting and demoting are similar to increasing and decreasing cueing and reliability priority (diSessa, 1988).

Students also combine and refine ideas between their conceptual ecologies. Integration involves creating or reinforcing the connection between two ideas (as when students identify insulation across materials). Coalescence involves a related process through which two ideas are actually merged (e.g., combining heating and cooling into a thermal equilibrium model.) Differentiation involves the reverse process, wherein one idea splits into distinct components (e.g., differentiating heat energy from temperature.) Students can also reassess and reanalyze ideas and their basic structure, as suggested by Carey (1985) with her example of Newton's realization that weight is a relation between objects rather than the property of a single object. Not all integrations, coalescences, differentiations, and reassessments necessarily result in more normative accounts from a formal scientific perspective (e.g., students may argue that metal is an insulator and a conductor). Sometimes changes made to address a specific conflict (i.e., a conflict in the student's repertoire within the given local context or explanation) may result in other local or global conflicts (i.e., a conflict between two or more ideas in a student's repertoire that are not connected within the single local context). Local and global conflicts may or may not be recognized by the student.

DISTINGUISHING IDEAS TO ACHIEVE COHERENT UNDERSTANDING

The knowledge integration framework emphasizes creating opportunities for students to distinguish among their ideas to achieve conceptual change and coherent understanding. This process can be supported in students of all ages. Linn and Eylon (2011) describe a five-year-old making sense of ideas about dinosaurs. Researchers have shown that the ideas students articulate to make sense of school and everyday situations reflect their capability to sort out confusing observations, rather than illustrating developmental constraints (e.g., Gilbert & Boulter, 2000). For example, students often argue that metal must be a naturally "colder" material because metal feels cold at room temperature. These efforts can be seen as evidence for powerful reasoning ability that can be guided by instruction (e.g., diSessa, 2008; Linn & Hsi, 2000). More specifically, when students make an effort to sort out ideas, even if the view they formulate is not supported by all the empirical data, they are engaging in the sort of reasoning that can lead to understanding.

For example, we traced the progress of a student in one study who focused on holes in materials to explain insulation and conduction (Linn & Eylon, 1996). Initially this student argued that materials with holes are poor insulators, using evidence that heat can flow through openings like doors. In later interviews, this student noted that holes like those in sweaters may have a different role. The student mentioned that holes may trap air and thus offer insulation by saying, "air pockets make heat energy not go" (Linn & Eylon, 1996, p. 599).

To promote productive distinguishing of ideas, students need to appreciate the connections among their ideas. When students distinguish between science class ideas and ideas developed by interacting with the world, they may not recognize the connections (e.g., Gilbert & Boulter, 2000). This can occur when school ideas consist of abstract principles and formulas such as "objects in motion tend to remain in motion." Curricula that do not provide much opportunity for students to explore how to use these abstract ideas in varied everyday problems can contribute to students' propensity to separate school ideas from personal experience. And, in this case, to argue that "objects in motion come to rest on the playing field."

For example, many science courses define heat and temperature in terms of units of measurement (temperature as degrees on a thermometer and heat as calories) or in terms of molecular kinetics. Students rarely study how to explain situations such as wilderness survival, predicting and measuring the temperatures of metal and wood objects that feel differently at room temperature, or estimating the cooling curves for metal and pottery objects removed from a warming oven. As a result, students have no opportunities to reconcile abstract ideas with everyday situations. Furthermore, science courses typically spend little time on connections and self-monitoring. They often isolate topics using abstract definitions, rather than showing the benefit of explanations that connect topics. Thus, typical instruction may inadvertently deter students from using their reasoning abilities to link ideas and bridge disciplines (Linn & Hsi, 2000).

Lifelong learning requires that students extend scientific ideas to new situations and new science topics. For example, students might initially study energy in isolated areas – learning how plants get and use energy, how humans get and use energy, how energy is generated and used to power an automobile, or how energy is released in an earthquake. For many students, these are quite distinct domains that never get connected. Yet sophisticated understanding of science requires combining these situations and developing a coherent or integrated view of concepts such as the nature of matter, energy, or evolution. Designers of curricula can add effective ideas such as pivotal cases or intermediate models, as we discuss later, that may prove more tractable for integration with students' everyday lives. These intermediate models can serve as a catalyst for connecting everyday and abstract formal ideas. For example, research shows that heat flow ideas were more generative for middle-school students than molecular kinetics ideas for understanding thermal equilibrium, heating and cooling, insulation and conduction, direction of heat flow, and specific heat (Linn & Muilenburg, 1996).

DESIGNING PRODUCTIVE IDEAS

Abstract scientific ideas have great power for experts wishing to organize their knowledge across varied contexts (Larkin & Reif, 1979). Efforts to identify ideas that play a similar role for students have demonstrated the value of pivotal cases or intermediate models that serve as a catalyst for connecting everyday and abstract formal ideas.

Studies demonstrate the importance of identifying pivotal cases to coalesce disparate ideas. These cases help students critique their own ideas and embrace normative views (Linn & Eylon, 2011). For example, to help students integrate the disparate idea that "metals feel cold so they must make things cold" with "metals are conductors," one teacher added a pivotal idea comparing two contexts – the beach on a hot day and the mountains on a cold day. Students were asked to compare how metal and wood objects feel in those two contexts. This pivotal case helped students integrate their ideas about the conductivity of metal and wood objects because it drew on evidence from personal experience, involved a controlled experiment, could be easily discussed with other students, and involved two familiar contexts they had not spontaneously connected.

These findings reveal a promising approach for designing inquiry activities to promote knowledge integration (Linn & Eylon, 2011). To succeed, inquiry activities need four processes: First, elicit the ideas held by the student so they can be analyzed. Second, add well-designed normative ideas that form pivotal cases to stimulate comparisons among ideas and promote normative views. Third, encourage distinguishing among ideas using valid evidence. Finally, enable reflection on the repertoire of ideas that leads to a coherent account of the scientific phenomena.

The Web-based Inquiry Science Environment (WISE) offers students and teachers units developed following this pattern. WISE has specific features that both support learning and reveal the process of knowledge integration that students follow. Inquiry activities engage learners in investigations of personally relevant questions such as "How can a picnic container be designed to keep food cold?" or "What human activities contribute to increases in greenhouse gases?" WISE features such as the Idea Basket and Explanation Builder (see Figure 27.1) support students to generate ideas, keep track of their ideas, organize their ideas, and create explanations (McElhaney, Matuk, Miller, & Linn, 2012).

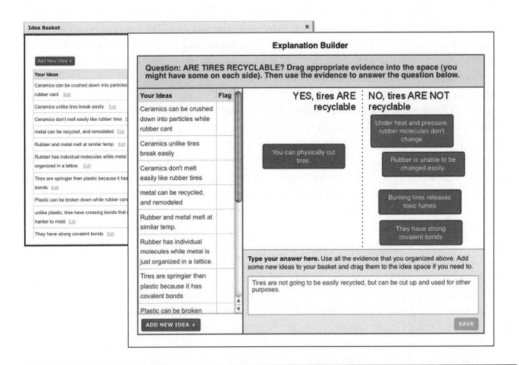

Figure 27.1 The Idea Basket and Explanation Builder support students to keep track of their ideas and organize them into arguments: WISE (http://wise.berkeley.edu)

SUMMARY: KNOWLEDGE INTEGRATION

In summary, the knowledge integration framework calls for design of inquiry science activities that capitalize on students' ability to make sense of scientific phenomena across contexts. Students generate a broad range of ideas about any scientific phenomenon. These ideas represent multiple types of explanations, vary across contexts, and may not be recognized as applying to the same topic. The knowledge integration framework takes these ideas as building blocks and mobilizes the same processes that generated them to focus instructional design and student investigations on coherent understanding. This approach is captured in the knowledge integration pattern. By inspecting their own ideas, considering new ideas, distinguishing among existing and new ideas, and reflecting on their investigations, students are encouraged to promote the most promising ideas and articulate a coherent account of the topic.

COHERENCE VERSUS FRAGMENTATION

As discussed in diSessa's (2008) chapter in the original version of this handbook, there has been a long-running debate in the conceptual change literature between framework theory perspectives and elemental perspectives on conceptual change. Much of this debate has focused on whether students' understandings in science are better characterized as a coherent unified scheme with a theory-like character (e.g., Carey, 1985; Gopnik & Wellman, 1994; Ioannides & Vosniadou, 2002; McCloskey, 1983; Vosniadou, 2002; Vosniadou & Ioannides, 1998; Wellman & Gelman, 1992; Wiser & Carey, 1983) versus an ecology of quasi-independent elements or ideas (e.g., Clark, 2006; Clark, D'Angelo, & Schleigh, 2011a; diSessa, 1988; diSessa, Gillespie, & Esterly, 2004; diSessa & Sherin, 1998; Dufresne, Mestre, Thaden-Koch, Gerace, & Leonard, 2005; Hammer & Elby, 2003; Harrison, Grayson, & Treagust, 1999; Hunt & Minstrell, 1994; Linn, 2006; Linn et al., 2004; Linn & Hsi, 2000; Minstrell, 1982; Özdemir & Clark, 2009; Parnafes, 2007; Thaden-Koch, Dufresne, & Mestre, 2006; Wagner, 2010). The comparison above simplifies the actual theoretical perspectives, which are considerably more nuanced. Proponents of framework theory perspectives, for example, do not argue that students' knowledge is theory-like to the degree that scientists' knowledge is theory-like (e.g., including meta-conceptual awareness or availability to hypothesis testing), nor do proponents of elemental perspectives propose that students' understanding involves random interactions of independent elements.

While the debate has tended to focus on the polarity of these differing positions rather than searching for commonalities, both perspectives propose systematicities in student ideas. Framework theory perspectives propose an overarching hierarchical conceptual structure with theory-like properties that constrains a student's interpretation of subordinate models and ideas. Elemental perspectives suggest that systematicities arise as elements interact with each other in an emergent manner where the combinatorial complexity of the system constrains students' interpretations of phenomena. Detailed descriptions are included in the original version of this handbook for the framework theory perspective (Vosniadou et al., 2008) and the knowledge in pieces perspective (diSessa, 2008). We would propose, as did Vosniadou et al. (2008), that the perspectives are complementary in many ways. Vosniadou et al.'s chapter, for example, highlighted several similarities between their perspective and elemental perspectives, as follows.

- Framework theory and elemental perspectives both describe systems that are "not static but constantly developing and evolving influenced by students' experience and information they receive from the culture" (p. 22).
- Neither the framework theory perspective nor elemental perspectives describe "unitary, faulty conceptions" but instead they describe "complex knowledge system[s] consisting of presuppositions, beliefs, and mental models" that "provide explanation and prediction" (p. 22).
- Framework theory and elemental perspectives both propose that "learners use additive, enrichment types of learning mechanisms to assimilate the new incompatible information to existent knowledge structures" (p. 15).
- Framework theory and elemental perspectives both propose that "the process of learning science and mathematics is slow and gradual and characterized by fragmentation, internal inconsistency and misconceptions" (p. 15) that result in "internally inconsistent responses or in the formation of synthetic models" (p. 15) when students' everyday understandings meet with formal ideas from instruction.
- The perspectives agree that accounts of knowledge acquisition should capture "the continuity one expects with development" and have "the possibility of locating knowledge elements in novices' prior knowledge that can be used to build more complex knowledge systems" (p. 22).
- The perspectives agree that accounts of knowledge acquisition should "move from single units of knowledge to systems of knowledge that consist of complex substructures that may change gradually in different ways" (p. 15).

We propose that further similarities between the perspectives emerge when we look at elements and theories through two lenses. First, it is helpful to consider a graduated spectrum for the magnitudes of influence that elements may exert on one another. Second, "zooming" out to a broader view of the conceptual landscape further clarifies common aspects of these views.

MAGNITUDE OF INFLUENCE OF IDEAS

Framework theory perspectives focus on the organizing role of a small number of key ontological and epistemological ideas (which they describe as framework theories). Students interpret observational and cultural information and beliefs (which they describe as specific theories) in light of these key ideas to create functional models for operating in the world. Vosniadou et al.'s (2008) chapter illustrated the framework theory perspective as shown in Figure 27.2.

Elemental perspectives tend to focus heavily on the interaction of many individual ideas. While elemental research has often focused on unarticulated explanatory primitives (e.g., phenomenological primitives, diSessa, 1988; diSessa & Sherin, 1998), elemental research also acknowledges the presence and role of other components in a student's conceptual ecology, which include, but are not limited to, nominal and committed facts, experiences, narratives, epistemological elements, mental models, and concepts at various stages of development and sophistication (Carey, 1985, Clark, 2006; diSessa, 2008; Linn et al., 2004). While some elemental research has examined the interaction of elements to support higher levels of systematicity (e.g., diSessa & Sherin, 1998; Thaden-Koch et al., 2006; Wagner, 2010), the primary focus of much elemental research has explored the interactions among individual ideas.

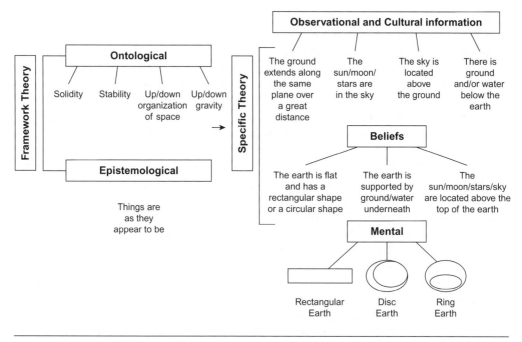

Figure 27.2 Hypothetical conceptual structure underlying children's mental models of the earth, from Vosniadou et al. (2008)

The ideas in a student's conceptual ecology have many sources and influences. Linn et al., (2004) discuss three key categories of these sources and influences in terms of deliberate efforts, cultural experiences, and interpretations of phenomena that parallel Vosniadou et al.'s (2008) typology of ideas in Figure 27.2 as well as diSessa's (1996) description of the range of components in a student's conceptual ecology. As Linn et al. (2004) explain, some ideas come from *deliberate* efforts of students to interrogate the world, such as when they plant tomatoes in sun or shade, break open a rock, or test whether objects sink. Others come from students' *cultural* experiences, such as beliefs held in their communities, family hobbies, dinner table conversations, and interactions with relatives. Some ideas are based on students' *interpretations* of the phenomena they encounter, such as when they argue that a fire is alive because it moves or consumes plants.

We can clarify the relationships between framework theory and elemental perspectives by envisioning a more extensive and graduated spectrum for the magnitudes of influence that elements may exert on one another. Framework theory suggests that elements exert high-magnitude influence on the interpretation of a "specific theory," which in turn exerts high-magnitude influence on the construction of mental models. In line with diSessa's and our own elemental perspectives, however, Vosniadou et al. (2008) propose that the connections between ideas can be disrupted through schooling or other experiences, resulting in conflicts or fragmentation in the coherence of students' explanations. All of the perspectives agree, therefore, that the influence of ideas on one another is neither necessarily unidirectional nor complete. Instead the differences are in the degree of magnitude of influence that certain ideas exert on other ideas. All of the perspectives thus acknowledge that (a) different ideas in a student's conceptual ecology exert different magnitudes of influence on other connected ideas, (b) connections, ideas, and their magnitudes of influence may change over time, and (c) this can result in inconsistencies, fragmentation, and synthetic models.

Essentially, the perspectives differ in their predictions about the scope and direction of influence of elements on one another. One main distinction resulting from this involves the degree of consistency that each perspective predicts in terms of students' explanations across contexts. None of the perspectives predict absolute consistency or randomness, but higher degrees of consistency are predicted by framework theory than by elemental theory perspectives. This distinction between perspectives focuses theoretically on the core high-magnitude ontological and epistemological ideas that organize students' thinking on scientific phenomena they encounter in their everyday lives.

Vosniadou et al. explain their perspectives on this coherence on page 16 of their chapter. Our own work suggests that students across countries and cities tend toward the middle of this scale. Thus, Özdemir and Clark (2009) studied 32 students across four age groups in Turkey; Clark et al. (2011a) studied 201 students across four age groups in Mexico, China, the Philippines, the United States, and Turkey; and Clark, Menekse, Özdemir, D'Angelo, and Schleigh (submitted) studied 78 students across four age group in two cities and across three high school tracks in Turkey. All of these studies compare interview protocols and coding methodologies developed in Ioannides and Vosniadou (2002) and diSessa et al. (2004) to analyze the consistency and types of force meanings that students of different ages expressed in interviews. All three of these studies document both systematicity and fragmentation in students' explanations of force across the interview contexts. These studies reveal fragmentation that is consistent with elemental theories. They also document the prevalence of specific ideas as posited by framework theories.

The distinction in terms of levels of consistency predicted by framework theory and elemental perspectives is strongest in terms of young students. Both framework theory and elemental perspectives predict that the introduction and reinterpretation of ideas (particularly from instruction) can fracture coherence for older learners. Framework theory perspectives propose that, prior to schooling, students' naïve framework theories will exert exceptionally high influence in constraining specific theories and mental models to the degree that young students will typically be highly consistent in their explanations across contexts, while elemental perspectives predict less consistency for young children. Even for young students in the Clark studies, consistency in responses was rather uncommon. However, methodological issues in interviewing young children have muddied explorations on this (e.g., diSessa et al., 2004). Future investigations across research groups should explore the structure and relationships of ideas that have a higher magnitude influence to refine our understanding of their import.

Essentially, framework theory perspectives have focused primarily on the relationships of ideas in terms of magnitudes of influence while elemental perspectives typically focus instead on more fine-grained descriptions and phenomena (often in the domain of physics phenomena). While research from elemental perspectives acknowledges ranges in magnitude of the influence that elements can exert on one another (e.g., Clark, 2006; diSessa, 1993), the ranges of magnitudes often appear to be relatively small compared to the range of magnitudes inherent in Vosniadou et al.'s framework theory perspective (more along the lines of a single order of magnitude rather than multiple orders of magnitude). Thus, while Vosniadou et al.'s, diSessa's, and our perspectives all predict that elements influence each other at various magnitudes, framework theory perspectives focus on the high magnitude of influence that certain elements exert on surrounding elements, while the elemental perspectives focus more on the dynamics of contradiction and fragmentation that occur when students encounter new ideas in various contexts. These contradictions and fragmentations are especially apparent when student responses are analyzed at a fine-grained level. Furthermore, at the fine-grained level, the potential benefit of encouraging comparisons of ideas becomes compelling.

ZOOMING IN AND OUT

The impact of frameworks becomes clearer as we "zoom out" to a broader view of the conceptual landscape. Essentially, while elemental perspectives acknowledge that some elements in students' conceptual ecologies are more prominent than others and exert disproportional influence on surrounding elements, these studies (e.g., Clark, 2006) are so "zoomed in" that they do not emphasize the broader relationships between elements. In contrast, studies from Vosniadou et al.'s framework theory perspective are "zoomed out" to a medium distance, highlighting a more hierarchical arrangement among elements for a single domain (e.g., Figure 27.2's representation from Vosniadou et al. of children's understanding of the shape of the earth). From the perspective of Figure 27.2, there appears to be a hierarchical up–down relationship between elements. We propose that by "zooming out" to an even greater conceptual distance at the scope of multiple domains, the relationships take on yet an additional dimension. Essentially, if we expand our focus to include not just a student's thinking about the shape of the earth but also the larger set of phenomena that the student would consider to be part of the natural world and universe, the diagram in Figure 27.2 would add many more elements at each level of magnitude (i.e., framework theories, specific theories, and mental model levels) within the various categories suggested at each of those levels (e.g., epistemological and ontological categories for framework theory elements or information and beliefs for specific theory elements).

We propose that the independent nature of the ideas at each level would become clearer in this envisioned "zoomed out" perspective if students were asked to explain several different phenomena across the domains. This type of research would reveal how students use ideas for varied, relevant phenomena (i.e., individual ideas could be marshaled for explanations of more than one phenomena or they could be marshaled independently of one another depending on the nature of the domain, explanation, and context). For example, the set of ontological, epistemological, observational, and cultural ideas and beliefs listed in Figure 27.2 would not be exclusively paired with one another for a single domain. An explanation in another related domain might draw on some but not all of these ideas and connect them to other ideas not included in Figure 27.2 to address the new question and context. Certain elements might have dramatically disproportionate influence, as suggested by framework theory perspectives, in terms of the organizing role they played and the magnitude of influence exerted. Yet individual elements could be recruited independently into configurations specific to different phenomena and contexts.

Thus we might visualize the synergies in these perspectives by looking at the relationships among element in two ways. Framework theory perspectives emphasize the magnitude of influence that an element can exert on other elements, while elemental perspectives emphasize the ways that multiple elements interact and are recruited depending on domain and context. What needs to be explained by all conceptual change perspectives is the nature of the connections between ideas that exert high-magnitude influence on other ideas in a context. Do they have any other characteristics or relationships to one another besides the fact that they each exert high influence in that context? By integrating ideas of magnitude and scope into research about conceptual ecologies we might thus better explain and model observed systematicities and fragmentation that are evidenced in data collected across studies.

LEARNING TRAJECTORIES AND PRODUCTIVE CURRICULAR SEQUENCES

The development of learning progressions builds on work in science education to establish standards for different grade levels and to define the scope and sequence for the curriculum. The learning progression efforts make hard decisions about which of the very abstract standards ought to be elaborated in the curriculum and about the expected trajectory students will follow. Learning progressions can be strengthened by incorporating core ideas about the processes of conceptual change outlined here. Specifically, the distinction between framework and elemental perspectives raises issues about learning trajectories and productive curricular sequences. From a zoomed-in view, students typically bring a wide variety of elements to science class and may follow idiosyncratic trajectories, consistent with the knowledge integration perspective. In class students generally encounter more sophisticated accounts of phenomena for the first time. The challenge and opportunity is to help students make productive connections between their everyday ideas and more formal causal and mechanistic ideas. Researchers studying learning progressions seek to characterize student progress to give structure to instruction but have to contend with the variations in student ideas.

Several research groups have begun to identify progressions of understanding in specific topic areas. The AAAS Atlas (American Association for the Advancement of Science, 2001) identifies sequences of topics and suggests appropriate grade-level goals. By identifying a sequence of accomplishments or understandings that students might achieve, researchers seek to clarify how students could progress in complex topic areas (such as genetics, force and motion, or evolution) in order to end up with generative, useful, and sound understanding of the key ideas and concepts. The success of this endeavor depends, in part, on the nature of the elements of student knowledge. If students hold very different ideas they may follow distinct paths. Finding a common instructional focus to help students advance along distinct trajectories is an exciting challenge.

As we argued for framework and elemental perspectives, characterizing learning progressions depends on "zooming out" to locate a common path to understanding a discipline. This may deter instructional designers from considering the richness and variety of ideas in students' conceptual ecologies. "Zooming in" may ultimately reveal multiple paths of conceptual change. Recent theoretical and empirical work has begun to integrate insights from conceptual change into learning progressions (e.g., Duncan & Hmelo-Silver, 2009; Lehrer, Kim & Schauble, 2007; Wilson, 2009).

Duncan, Rogat, and Yarden (2009), for example, identified a learning progression based on the big ideas in genetics. They then deconstructed the big ideas into a series of levels in their theoretical paper. They based this deconstruction on prior empirical research on learning genetics (e.g., Duncan, 2007) and on a systematic analysis of the field. Duncan et al. (2009) acknowledged that their theoretical account of the learning progression is abstract and incomplete in some ways since many of the questions relevant to this sequence have not yet been answered, but the learning progression specifies deep understanding across three levels, a goal that has rarely been achieved in textbooks and other curriculum materials. Shea and Duncan (2010) then tested the progression in a two-year long empirical investigation involving detailed analysis of interviews with students. They determined whether students expressed the ideas identified as big ideas in genetics and whether students went through the levels of understanding articulated in the learning progression. Their study explored discrepancies between the hypothesized sequence of understanding and the observed responses of individuals, while documenting the conceptual ecologies students develop and the idiosyncratic sequence of understanding that each student follows. Through this process, Duncan and colleagues illustrated how the variety of student ideas and the variation in student trajectories contributed to the actual processes of conceptual change in their learning progression.

This research on the varied paths for development of student understanding of genetics resonates with the results from our own longitudinal analysis of 50 students' conceptual change in an eighth-grade thermodynamics curriculum. We interviewed students across a semester and again preceding their 10th- and 12th-grade years to follow their subsequent progress (e.g., Clark, 2006; Lewis, 1996; Linn & Hsi, 2000).

Clark (2006), for example, first analyzed the full cohort of 50 students and then analyzed two fairly successful and two less successful students in greater detail. Clark's analyses clarify the multiple conceptual change paths, sequences, and processes through which students' understandings of thermal equilibrium evolve from disjointed sets of context-dependent ideas toward, if not achieving, greater integration, normativity, and cohesiveness. Figures 27.3 and 27.4 show how students' explanations were cataloged and coded for the connections that students made. The analyses also highlighted the centrality of certain high-magnitude ideas (which varied across students) in students' explanations and processes of reorganizing and refining the other ideas and connections within their conceptual ecologies. Clark outlined the implications of these results for curricular sequences in terms of (a) depth of coverage, (b) support for normative connection of ideas rather than simply adding more ideas, (c) increased opportunities to compare non-normative and normative ideas in contexts that cue the non-normative ideas, (d) support for multiple conceptual paths through the curriculum, (e) consideration of the pedagogical trade-offs in choosing specific accessible intermediate models, and (f) re-explanation of disruptive experientially supported ideas to support school-instructed ideas.

Our research and other recent research on conceptual change illustrates that students' learning processes involve multiple paths. Learning progressions and curricular sequences will be most successful if they "zoom in" to support these paths as well as "zooming out" to consider overall goals. To support multiple paths, curriculum designers need to make choices about which scientific models and explanations to incorporate into instruction (such as which abstractions and pivotal cases to select), as discussed briefly in the knowledge integration overview. National and international assessments demonstrate that few citizens master causal explanations for most scientific phenomena (Schmidt, Raizen, Britton, Bianchi, & Wolfe, 1997). Choosing appropriate forms of explanation is therefore challenging but critical.

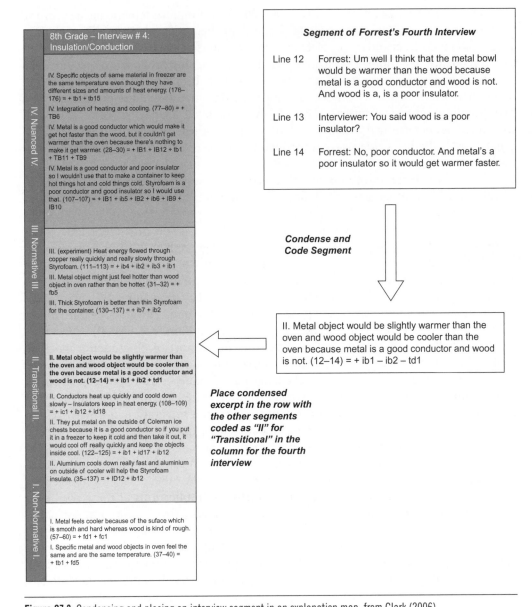

Figure 27.3 Condensing and placing an interview segment in an explanation map, from Clark (2006)

Some problems benefit from multiple explanations. White and Frederiksen (1998) report, for example, that students understand electricity better when they learn a series of explanations going from descriptive to causal. Students might start with descriptive explanations or mechanistic accounts and then learn molecular theories (Linn & Muilenburg, 1996). The molecular kinetic account of heat transfer, for example, draws on unseen processes and may be less generative than the heat flow account for students who are also struggling to understand the particulate nature of matter (Nussbaum, 1985). Furthermore, researchers have pointed out that students' descriptive views can interfere with understanding of causal or atomic explanations (Chi, 2005; Vosniadou,

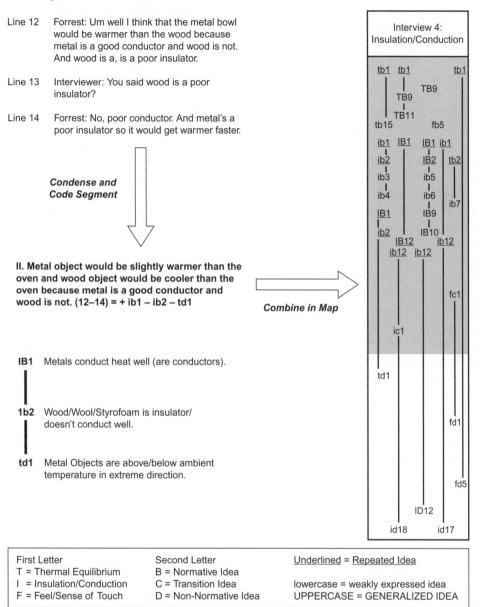

Segment of Forrest's Fourth Interview

Line 12   Forrest: Um well I think that the metal bowl would be warmer than the wood because metal is a good conductor and wood is not. And wood is a, is a poor insulator.

Line 13   Interviewer: You said wood is a poor insulator?

Line 14   Forrest: No, poor conductor. And metal's a poor insulator so it would get warmer faster.

Condense and Code Segment

II. Metal object would be slightly warmer than the oven and wood object would be cooler than the oven because metal is a good conductor and wood is not. (12–14) = + ib1 – ib2 – td1

Combine in Map

IB1   Metals conduct heat well (are conductors).

1b2   Wood/Wool/Styrofoam is insulator/ doesn't conduct well.

td1   Metal Objects are above/below ambient temperature in extreme direction.

First Letter	Second Letter	Underlined = Repeated Idea
T = Thermal Equilibrium	B = Normative Idea	
I = Insulation/Conduction	C = Transition Idea	lowercase = weakly expressed idea
F = Feel/Sense of Touch	D = Non-Normative Idea	UPPERCASE = GENERALIZED IDEA

Figure 27.4 Coding and placing an interview segment into an element map, from Clark (2006)

2007). Others argue that many causal or atomic explanations are challenging to apply to everyday events and should be added to science courses judiciously (Linn & Hsi, 2000). This research shows that students need both to distinguish between the types of explanations encountered and to learn how to make links across these explanations.

One curriculum (Linn & Hsi, 2000) addressed this goal by having students explore everyday situations and then synthesize their findings in pragmatic principles. On the topic of thermal equilibrium, for example, the curriculum focused on the following pragmatic principle: "If all the objects are in the same surround and none of them produce their own heat, then they will all come to the same temperature." Pragmatic principles like this one offer students an abstract, accessible explanation. They allow students to connect class experiments, everyday situations, and more abstract ideas about scientific phenomena.

Instructional designers need sensible ways to help students link varied types of explanations and ideas to achieve coherent understanding. Research programs have identified benchmark lessons (diSessa & Minstrell, 1998), bridging analogies (Clement, 1993), animations (Holyoak & Thagard, 1995), and argumentation and explanation approaches with simulations and games (Clark et al., 2011a, 2011b; Clark, Martinez-Garza, Biswas, Luecht, & Sengupta, P., 2012; Clark & Sampson, 2007).

Promising instructional approaches structure learning in multiple ways rather than leaving students to unguided exploration (diSessa, Hammer, Sherin, & Kolpakowski, 1991; Klahr & Nigam, 2004; Linn & Hsi, 2000). Effective instruction offers each student well-designed views of scientific phenomena such as pivotal cases or intermediate models that advance their reasoning (Edelson, 2001; Linn & Eylon, 2011; White & Frederiksen, 1998). Such instruction also ensures that students encounter multiple contexts, take advantage of social interactions, and explore alternatives (Linn & Eylon, 2011; Quintana et al., 2004). As discussed above, research on promising instructional sequences, such as the knowledge integration pattern, shows that some patterns are more effective than others in terms of helping students link explanations (Linn & Eylon, 2011; Linn & Songer, 1991). To take advantage of well-designed ideas, patterns encourage students to reflect and to monitor their own progress (Davis & Linn, 2000; Chi et al., 1994; Vosniadou et al., 2008). Productive patterns respect and leverage the many ideas students generate about scientific situations rather than trying to confront them or eradicate them (Chi et al., 1994; diSessa et al., 1991; Linn & Eylon, 2011; Siegler, 2000; Smith, diSessa, & Roschelle, 1993/1994; Vosniadou, 2002). These promising instructional ideas are captured in the knowledge integration pattern: The pattern combines the process of eliciting the full range of student ideas, adding pivotal cases or intermediate models, encouraging students to compare, contrast, and sort out ideas, and enabling students to reflect on their efforts to articulate explanations (Linn & Eylon, 2011)

CONCLUSIONS

Synthesizing Vosniadou et al.'s framework theory perspective with the knowledge integration perspective and other elemental perspectives reveals overlaps and consistencies. In particular, the explorations of this chapter emphasize how the magnitude of influence of certain ideas from framework theory perspectives can mesh well with the focus on the rich interactions within conceptual ecologies highlighted by elemental perspectives. By considering the focus of research in each theory, common findings become apparent. These synergies clarify and strengthen the accounts of conceptual change collected across studies. This synergistic perspective also supports the value of instructional sequences, such as the knowledge integration pattern, that scaffold students in refining and consolidating their conceptual ecologies around productive focal ideas (pivotal cases). Essentially, highlighting the magnitude of influence of certain ideas in students' conceptual ecologies explains systematicities in student explanations while still respecting the rich range of ideas and interactions between ideas that lead to idiosyncratic trajectories. Striking a balance between idiosyncratic and high-magnitude ideas is also central to effective design of learning progressions. This approach sheds light on the difficulties students have when grappling with the abstract formal ideas introduced in science classes.

This chapter thus elaborates on the proposition common across perspectives that variability in student ideas is a fundamentally valuable feature. Curricula designed to capitalize on the variability and the creativity of student ideas can facilitate conceptual change. The knowledge integration, framework theory, and knowledge in pieces perspectives all argue that understanding how students generate and reconcile new ideas in a specific domain governs important and essential curricular design decisions. Two areas where curricular design is particularly important involve (a) determining which new focal ideas may prove most productive for students and (b) determining sequences of instructional activities to scaffold students' integration of their ideas as they develop more coherent understandings.

Characterizing students' conceptual ecologies and adding the right ideas to those ecologies has the potential of dramatically increasing the efficiency and effectiveness of instruction. The sheer numbers of sources of ideas in students' conceptual ecologies underscores the scope of this task. The diverse range of cultural impacts combined with the broad range of students' metacognitive skills guarantees that learners will follow many different paths as they make sense of abstract school science ideas. This requires flexible curricula that support multiple paths of conceptual change. It is our claim, as is claimed by Vosniadou et al. (2008), that advancing this agenda will depend as much on exploring synergies and affordances across conceptual change perspectives as on exploring the impact of the distinctions among perspectives.

REFERENCES

American Association for the Advancement of Science (AAAS), (2001). *Atlas of science literacy*. AAAS Project 2061, Washington, DC.

Carey, S. (1985). *Conceptual change in childhood*. Cambridge, MA: MIT Press.

Chi, M. T. H. (2005). Common sense conceptions of emergent processes: Why some misconceptions are robust. *Journal of the Learning Sciences, 14*, 161–199.

Chi, M. T. H., deLeeuw, N., Chiu, M. H., & LaVancer, C. (1994). Eliciting self-explanations improves understanding. *Cognitive Science, 18*, 439–477.

Clark, D. B. (2006). Longitudinal conceptual change in students' understanding of thermal equilibrium: An examination of the process of conceptual restructuring. *Cognition and Instruction, 24*(4), 467–563.

Clark, D. B., D'Angelo, C., & Schleigh, S. (2011a). Comparison of students' knowledge structure coherence and understanding of force in The Philippines, Turkey, China, Mexico, and the United States. *Journal of the Learning Sciences, 20*(2), 207–261.

Clark, D. B., & Linn, M. C. (2003). Scaffolding knowledge integration through curricular depth. *Journal of the Learning Sciences, 12*(4), 451–494.

Clark, D. B., Martinez-Garza, M., Biswas, G., Luecht, R. M., & Sengupta, P. (2012). Driving assessment of students' explanations in game dialog using computer-adaptive testing and hidden Markov modeling. In D. Ifenthaler, D. Eseryel, & G. Xun (Eds.), *Assessments in game-based learning: Foundations, innovations, and perspectives*. New York, NY: Springer.

Clark, D. B., Menekse, M., Özdemir, G., D'Angelo, C. M., & Schleigh, S. (submitted). *Comparison of knowledge structure coherence and force meanings across sites in Turkey*. Revised and resubmitted to *Science Education*.

Clark, D. B., Nelson, B., Chang, H., D'Angelo, C. M., Slack, K., & Martinez-Garza, M. (2011b). Exploring Newtonian mechanics in a conceptually-integrated digital game: Comparison of learning and affective outcomes for students in Taiwan and the United States. *Computers and Education, 57*(3), 2178–2195.

Clark, D. B., & Sampson, V. (2007). Personally-seeded discussions to scaffold online argumentation. *International Journal of Science Education, 29*(3), 253–277.

Clement, J. (1993). Using bridging analogies and anchoring intuitions to deal with students' preconceptions in physics. *Journal of Research in Science Teaching, 30*(10), 1241–1257.

Davis, E. A., & Linn, M. C. (2000). Scaffolding students' knowledge integration: Prompts for reflection in KIE. *International Journal of Science Education, 22*(8), 819–837.

diSessa, A. A. (1988). Knowledge in pieces. In G. Forman & P. Pufall (Eds.), *Constructivism in the computer age* (pp. 49–70). Hillsdale, NJ: Lawrence Erlbaum Associates.

diSessa, A. (1993). Toward an epistemology of physics. *Cognition and Instruction, 10*(2–3), 105–225.

diSessa, A. A. (1996). What do "just plain folk" know about physics? In D. R. Olson (Ed.), *Handbook of education and human development: New models of learning, teaching, and schooling* (pp. 709–730). Oxford, UK: Blackwell.

diSessa, A. (2008). A bird's-eye view of the "pieces" vs. "coherence" controversy (from the "pieces" side of the fence). In S. Vosniadou (Ed.), *Handbook of research on conceptual change* (pp. 35–60). New York, NY: Routledge.

diSessa, A. A., Gillespie, N. M., & Esterly, J. B. (2004). Coherence versus fragmentation in the development of the concept of force. *Cognitive Science, 28*(6), 843–900.

diSessa, A. A., Hammer, D., Sherin, B., & Kolpakowski, T. (1991). Inventing graphing: Metarepresentational expertise in children. *Journal of Mathematical Behavior, 10*, 117–160.

diSessa, A. A., & Minstrell, J. (1998). Cultivating conceptual change with benchmark lessons. In J. G. Greeno & S. Goldman (Eds.), *Thinking practices* (pp. 155–187). Mahwah, NJ: Lawrence Erlbaum Associates.

diSessa, A. A., & Sherin, B. L. (1998). What changes in conceptual change? *International Journal of Science Education, 20*(10), 1155–1191.

Dufresne, R., Mestre, J., Thaden-Koch, T., Gerace, W., & Leonard, W. (2005). Knowledge representation and coordination in the transfer process. In J. Mestre (Ed.), *Transfer of learning from a modern multidisciplinary perspective* (pp. 155–215). Greenwich, CT: Information Age Publishing.

Duncan, R. G. (2007). The role of domain-specific knowledge in generative reasoning about complicated multileveled phenomena. *Cognition and Instruction, 25*(4), 271–336.

Duncan, R. G., & Hmelo-Silver, C. E. (2009). Learning progressions: Aligning curriculum, instruction, and assessment. *Journal of Research in Science Teaching, 46*, 606–609.

Duncan, R. G., Rogat, A. D., & Yarden, A. (2009). A learning progression for deepening students' understandings of modern genetics across the 5th–10th grades. *Journal of Research in Science Teaching, 46*(6), 655–674.

Edelson, D. C. (2001). Learning-for-use: A framework for the design of technology-supported inquiry activities. *Journal of Research in Science Teaching, 38*(3), 355–385.

Gentner, D., & Stevens, A. L. (1983). *Mental models.* Hillsdale, NJ: Lawrence Erlbaum Associates.

Gilbert, J. K., & Boulter, C. J. (2000). *Developing models in science education.* Dordrecht, The Netherlands: Kluwer.

Gopnik, A., & Wellman, H. M. (1994). The theory theory. In L. A. Hirschfeld & S. A. Gelman (Eds.), *Mapping the mind: Domain specifity in cognition and culture* (pp. 257–293). New York, NY: Cambridge University Press.

Hammer, D., & Elby, A. (2003). Tapping students' epistemological resources. *Journal of the Learning Sciences, 12*(1), 53–91.

Harrison, A. G., Grayson, D. J., & Treagust, D. F. (1999). Investigating a grade 11 student's evolving conceptions of heat and temperature. *Journal of Research in Science Teaching, 36*(1), 55–87.

Hatano, G., & Inagaki, K. (2003). When is conceptual change intended? A cognitive–sociocultural view. In G. M. Sinatra & P. R. Pintrich (Eds.), *Intentional conceptual change* (pp. 407–427). Mahwah, NJ: Lawrence Erlbaum Associates.

Holyoak, K. J., & Thagard, P. (1995). *Mental leaps: Analogy in creative thought.* Cambridge, MA: MIT Press.

Howe, A. (2002). *Engaging children in science.* Upper Saddle River, NJ: Merrill Prentice Hall.

Hunt, E., & Minstrell, J. (1994). A cognitive approach to the teaching of physics. In K. McGilly (Ed.), *Classroom lessons: integrating cognitive theory and classroom practice* (pp. 51–74). Cambridge, MA: MIT Press.

Ioannides, C., & Vosniadou, S. (2002). The changing meanings of force. *Cognitive Science Quarterly, 2*(1), 5–62.

Klahr, D., & Nigam, M. (2004). The equivalence of learning paths in early science instruction. *Psychological Science, 15*(10), 661–667.

Larkin, J. H., & Reif, F. (1979). Understanding and teaching problem solving in physics. *European Journal of Science Education, 1*, 191–203.

Lehrer, R., Kim, M., & Schauble, L. (2007). Supporting the development of conceptions of statistics by engaging students in modeling and measuring variability. *International Journal of Computers for Mathematical Learning, 12*(3), 195–216.

Lewis, E. L. (1996). Conceptual change among middle school students studying elementary thermodynamics. *Journal of Science Education and Technology, 5*(1), 3–31.

Linn, M. C. (1983). Content, context, and process in adolescent reasoning. *Journal of Early Adolescence, 3*, 63–82.

Linn, M. C. (1995). Designing computer learning environments for engineering and computer science: The Scaffolded Knowledge Integration framework. *Journal of Science Education and Technology, 4*(2), 103–126.

Linn, M. C. (2006). The knowledge integration perspective on learning and instruction. In R. K. Sawyer (Ed.), *The Cambridge handbook of the learning sciences* (pp. 243–264). New York, NY: Cambridge University Press.

Linn, M. C., Davis, E. A., & Bell, P. (Eds.). (2004). *Internet environments for science education.* Mahwah, NJ: Lawrence Erlbaum Associates.

Linn, M. C., & Eylon, B.-S. (1996). Lifelong science learning: A longitudinal case study. In G. Cottrell (Ed.), *Proceedings of CogSci96* (pp. 597–600). Mahwah, NJ: Lawrence Erlbaum Associates.

Linn, M. C., & Eylon, B.-S. (2011). *Science learning and instruction: Taking advantage of technology to promote knowledge integration.* New York, NY: Routledge.

Linn, M. C., & Hsi, S. (2000). *Computers, teachers, peers: Science learning partners.* Mahwah, NJ: Lawrence Erlbaum Associates.

Linn, M. C., & Muilenburg, L. (1996). Creating lifelong science learners: What models form a firm foundation? *Educational Researcher, 25*(5), 18–24.

Linn, M. C., & Songer, N. B. (1991). Teaching thermodynamics to middle school students: What are appropriate cognitive demands? *Journal of Research in Science Teaching, 28*(10), 885–918.

McCloskey, M. (1983). Intuitive physics. *Scientific American, 248*(4), 122–130.

McElhaney, K. W., Matuk, C. F., Miller, D. I., & Linn, M. C. (2012). Using the Idea Manager to promote coherent understanding of inquiry investigations. *The future of learning: Proceedings of the 10th International Conference of the Learning Sciences,* Sydney, Australia.

Metz, K. E. (2000). Young children's inquiry in biology: Building the knowledge bases to empower independent inquiry. In J. Minstrell & E. Van Zee (Eds.), *Inquiring into inquiry learning and teaching in science* (pp. 3–13). Washington, DC: American Association for the Advancement of Science.

Minstrell, J. A. (1982). Explaining the "at rest" condition of an object. *The Physics Teacher, 20*, 10–14.

Nussbaum, J. (1985). The particulate nature of matter in the gaseous phase. In R. Driver, E. Guesne, & A. Tiberghien (Eds.), *Children's ideas in science* (pp. 124–144). Milton Keynes, UK: Open University Press.

Özdemir, G., & Clark, D. B. (2009). Coherence of Turkish students' understanding of force. *Journal of Research on Science Teaching, 46*(5), 570–596.

Parnafes, O. (2007). What does fast mean? Understanding the physical world through representations. *Journal of the Learning Sciences, 16*(3), 415–450.

Pfundt, H., & Duit, R. (1994). *Bibliography: Students' alternative frameworks and science education* (4th ed.). Kiel, Germany: Institute for Science Education.

Quintana, C., Reiser, B. J., Davis, E. A., Krajcik, J., Fretz, E., Golan, R. D., et al. (2004). A scaffolding design framework for software to support science inquiry. *Journal of the Learning Sciences, 13*(3), 337–386.

Schmidt, W. H., Raizen, S. A., Britton, E. D., Bianchi, L. J., & Wolfe, R. G. (1997). *Many visions, many aims: A cross-national investigation of curricular intentions in school science.* Dordrecht, The Netherlands: Kluwer Academic Publishers.

Shea, N., & Duncan, R. (2010). Validation of a learning progression: Relating empirical data to theory. In K. Gomez, L. Lyons, & J. Radinsky (Eds.), *Learning in the disciplines: Proceedings of the 9th International Conference of the Learning Sciences* (Vol. 1, pp. 532–539). Chicago, IL: International Society of the Learning Sciences.

Siegler, R. S. (1996). *Emerging minds: The process of change in children's thinking.* New York, NY: Oxford University Press.

Siegler, R. S. (2000). The rebirth of children's learning. *Child Development, 71*(1), 26–35.

Smith, J. P., diSessa, A. A., & Roschelle, J. (1993/1994). Misconceptions reconceived: A constructivist analysis of knowlege in transition. *Journal of the Learning Sciences, 3*(2), 115–163.

Thaden-Koch, T. C., Dufresne, R. J., & Mestre, J. P. (2006). Coordination of knowledge in judging animated motion. *Physical Reveiw Special Topics – Physics Education Research, 2*(2), 020107.

Vosniadou, S. (2002). On the nature of naïve physics. In M. Limón & L. Mason (Eds.), *Reconsidering conceptual change: Issues in theory and practice* (pp. 61–76). Dordrecht, The Netherlands: Kluwer Academic Publishers.

Vosniadou, S. (2007). The conceptual change approach and its re-framing. In S. Vosniadou, A. Baltas, &

X. Vamvakoussi (Eds.), *Re-framing the conceptual change change approach in learning and instruction.* Oxford, UK: Elsevier.

Vosniadou, S. (Ed.). (2008). *International handbook of research on conceptual change.* New York, NY: Routledge.

Vosniadou, S., & Ioannides, C. (1998). From conceptual development to science education: A psychological point of view. *International Journal of Science Education, 20*(10), 1213–1230.

Vosniadou, S., Vamvakoussi, X., & Skopeliti, I. (2008). The framework theory approach to the problem of conceptual change. In S. Vosniadou (Ed.), *International handbook of research on conceptual change.* New York, NY: Routledge.

Wagner, J. F. (2010). A transfer-in-pieces consideration of the perception of structure in the transfer of learning. *Journal of the Learning Sciences, 19,* 443–479.

Wellman, H. M., & Gelman, S. A. (1992). Cognitive development: Foundational theories of core domains. *Annual Review of Psychology, 43,* 337–375.

White, B. Y., & Frederiksen, J. R. (1998). Inquiry, modeling, and metacognition: Making science accessible to all students. *Cognition and Instruction, 16*(1), 3–118.

Wilson, M. (2009). Measuring progressions: Assessment structures underlying a learning progression. *Journal of Research in Science Teaching, 46*(6), 716–730.

Wiser, M., & Carey, S. (1983). When heat and temperature were one. In D. Gentner & A. L. Stevens (Eds.), *Mental models* (pp. 267–298). Hillsdale, NJ: Lawrence Erlbaum Associates.

28

PROMOTING CONCEPTUAL CHANGE THROUGH INQUIRY

*Clark A. Chinn, Ravit Golan Duncan, Michael Dianovsky,
and Ronald Rinehart, Rutgers University*

Many instructional approaches to conceptual change in science aim to promote conceptual change through inquiry. By *inquiry*, we refer to practices of developing and/or evaluating conceptions based on evidence (National Research Council, 1996). Inquiry approaches to conceptual change encourage students to develop and adopt scientific concepts through the use of evidence. For example, students who think that matter can be created out of nothing or destroyed may be placed in an inquiry environment in which they design experiments and gather data to investigate whether various kinds of physical, state, and chemical changes produce changes in mass. The designers of this inquiry environment hope that, through their investigations, learners will conclude that mass and matter are conserved during ordinary physical and chemical changes, thus adopting a very different conception of matter.

In this chapter, we examine a broad range of issues related to inquiry-based approaches to promoting conceptual change. The outline of the chapter is as follows. (1) We discuss core features of inquiry-based approaches to conceptual change and distinguish them from alternative approaches. (2) We survey a range of prominent exemplars, examining some of the empirical evidence bearing on their efficacy. (3) Building on our discussion of these exemplars, we discuss key issues in developing a theory of conceptual change through inquiry. (4) We examine three practical and theoretical challenges to achieving conceptual change through inquiry. (5) Finally, we discuss principles of instructional design that make inquiry-based instruction more effective in promoting conceptual change.

The chapter focuses primarily, although not exclusively, on the domain of science. Most of the research on inquiry methods of promoting conceptual change has been conducted in the domain of science. Although educators have developed and tested inquiry methods in domains such as history, the focus in these studies is typically more on improving competence in historical reasoning rather than on promoting conceptual change in how learners understand historical periods or events. However, there has been research on inquiry-based methods of learning economics. Thus, our review encompasses some investigations in the social sciences.

Mathematicians and mathematics educators also write of mathematical inquiry. Although mathematical inquiry can involve testing ideas against real-world examples, normative methods of mathematical reasoning require more formal, logical proofs and do not attempt to explain a body of evidence (Weber, 2008). The issues raised by these forms of inquiry go beyond our scope in this manuscript. Nonetheless, we note that some studies of learning statistics involve students examining the properties of data from real-world datasets (e.g., Cobb, McClain, & Gravemeijer, 2003). Thus, learning involving inquiry based on evidence also occurs in some domains of mathematics education.

WHAT IS INQUIRY-BASED INSTRUCTION?

Although definitions of inquiry may vary from scholar to scholar, what is central to most is a focus on developing and justifying explanations, with a strong emphasis on explaining evidence. Philosophers and historians of science have found that scientists use fit with evidence as a core criterion for developing and evaluating theoretical explanations (e.g., Longino, 2002). Scientists use other criteria as well, such as elegance and parsimony, fit with established theories, and internal coherence (Kuhn, 1977; Newton-Smith, 1981). Thus, a broader definition of scientific inquiry that better accords with scientific practices would be that inquiry involves developing and justifying explanations based on rational criteria such as fit with evidence and internal coherence, with evidential fit playing a particularly central role. Among science educators, Stewart and Hafner (1991) and Pluta, Chinn, and Duncan (2011) have emphasized the use of a broad range of criteria in scientific inquiry.

Inquiry in many of the social sciences, such as psychology, also involves developing and justifying explanations based on evidence. In domains such as history and archaeology, evidence still plays a central role, but scholars in these disciplines have disputed whether explanations in the sense of general scientific explanations are a goal of inquiry (Wylie, 2002). Rather, the goal often seems to be something more like developing rich contextual narratives that cohere with the known evidence (Roth, 1998).

We have argued that explanation and evidence are central to inquiry, but not all instructional methods that make use of explanations and evidence are inquiry-based methods. Consider the following:

- A biology textbook chapter on evolution explains evolutionary theory and discusses many specific pieces of evidence in support of the common descent of species.
- A physics teacher demonstrates principles of gravity by showing that a feather and a comb fall at the same rate in a vacuum.
- Physical science students learn about the conservation of matter and then conduct experiments confirming that mass is conserved through a variety of chemical and physical changes.

In each of these cases, evidence is used, but students are not engaged in inquiry because they are never expected to develop explanations or evaluate whether possible explanations are correct or not. Rather, students are told the explanatory model or principle, and the evidence is used as illustrations of this. In contrast, a hallmark of inquiry is that there is a period of uncertainty in which students are grappling with the evidence, trying to decide how to interpret it, and deciding which explanation is best. Evidence is used as a tool of inquiry, not as an illustration of a just-taught principle.

Recent work in science education has begun to frame inquiry in terms of the *practices* of inquirers (e.g., Kang & Lundeberg, 2010). In this view, to engage in inquiry is to engage in scientific practices of developing questions, devising how to answer these questions, designing studies, gathering data, analyzing and interpreting data, developing theoretical models, comparing and choosing between alternative theoretical models using appropriate criteria, communicating findings and theories to others, and engaging in reasoned argumentation about the merits of different proposals. Each of these general practices comprises more specific practices. For example, choosing between alternative models may include doing searches for relevant evidence, evaluating the quality of the evidence, cataloging the findings, and weighing the different findings against each other. Scientists in different fields often engage in different practices. For example, the research design practices of experimental microbiologists (focused on designing properly controlled experiments) will differ from the research design practices of paleontologists (often involving non-experimental evaluations of the fossil record).

Some might argue that students are engaged in inquiry only when they are engaged in all of these types of practices, from choosing questions to communicating findings. However, scientists themselves do not always engage in all these practices. For example, a scientist may sign onto a grant project that has been conceived and framed by another scientist, engaging in most types of practices but never choosing questions or devising the overall research plan (Samarapungavan, Westby, & Bodner, 2006). We think most would agree that this scientist is nonetheless engaged in scientific inquiry.

Whether an instructional curriculum should be counted as inquiry or not is a judgment call, and depends on the range of inquiry practices that are invoked by the curriculum. In this chapter, inquiry-based instruction refers to instruction that engages students in a range of inquiry practices, but not necessarily the full range of all practices. We will examine the efficacy of such instruction in promoting conceptual change.

EXEMPLARS OF INQUIRY-BASED INSTRUCTION FOR PROMOTING CONCEPTUAL CHANGE

In this section, we discuss three exemplars of inquiry-based instruction designed to promote conceptual change. Through these exemplars, we aim to provide a sense of some of the common characteristics of inquiry-based instruction designed to promote conceptual change.

PRACCIS

In our own research, we have developed PRACCIS (Promoting Reasoning and Conceptual Change in Science), a middle-school life-science program based on model-based instructional practices embedded in an inquiry-oriented setting (Chinn & Buckland, 2012; Chinn, Duschl, Duncan, Pluta, & Buckland, 2008; Pluta et al., 2011). The goal of PRACCIS is to foster conceptual change in content understanding together with growth in reasoning. Modeling practices are the centerpiece of PRACCIS because one of the primary activities of scientists is to construct and evalaute models (National Research Council, 2007).

Each lesson is guided by a set of driving questions (Krajcik & Blumenfeld, 2006), such as "Why do organisms have the traits that they have?" or "How do new species arise?" Students consider and weigh two or more alternative models and use evidence to judge which explanations are best. For example, when learning about Mendelian patterns of inheritance, students are presented with several models that represent common misconceptions about inheritance. According to one model, children get 50% of their traits from their mother and the other 50% from their father. From this model students can make predictions and then check those predictions against evidence. They also weigh this model against several alternatives, only one of which provides a good fit with all the evidence the students are examining.

To assess these models, students collaboratively generate their own evidence or reflect on evidence that has been generated for them. PRACCIS employs both "first-hand" evidence that students gather and "second-hand" evidence (Hapgood, Magnusson, & Palincsar, 2004) presented in the form of short research reports rewritten at a seventh-grade level; thus, students learn the important scientific practice of reading others' research as well as practices of gathering their own data. In addition, group work and class discussions are designed to foster dialogic practices of argumentation, so that students engage in reasoned argumentation about the fit of models with evidence. Students also learn to write cogent, elaborated arguments in support of their reasoning.

PRACCIS employs a variety of scaffolds to aid students' inquiry. One prominent scaffold is the use of class-developed public criteria to make epistemic judgments. For example, students develop criteria for judging the goodness of models (e.g., good fit with evidence, explains *all* the evidence, showing clear labels, telling step-by-step processes) and for judging the quality of scientific research (e.g., good comparisons, good measures, adequate sample size). Classes refine these criteria throughout the year. The criteria constitute class norms that students formulate and are then accountable to. This scaffold cues students to core criteria used by scientists to evaluate models and studies.

A second central scaffold is the model–evidence link scaffold (see Figure 28.1). This scaffold directs students (a) to draw lines between evidence and models (indicating the particular kind of relationships the student identifies, including evidence that supports, strongly supports, contradicts, and is irrelevant to one or more models) and (b) to provide elaborated reasons for the kind of link they selected. This scaffold is designed to focus students' attention on using evidence to evaluate theories. In addition, by asking students to distinguish between evidence that *strongly supports* a model, as opposed to only *supporting* the model, the scaffold encourages students to reflect on the quality of evidence as well. Thus, these PRACCIS scaffolds seek to engage students in key practices of science.

IQWST

Our second exemplar of inquiry-based instruction designed to promote conceptual change in science is Investigating and Questioning our World through Science and Technology (IQWST) (Krajcik, McNeill, & Reiser, 2008). The IQWST project built on an earlier project by the Center for Learning Technologies in Urban Schools (LeTUS) (Singer, Marx, Krajcik, & Clay-Chambers, 2000).

As in PRACCIS, the LeTUS materials are standards- and project-based science curricula focused on core topics in middle school science (e.g., chemical reactions, natural

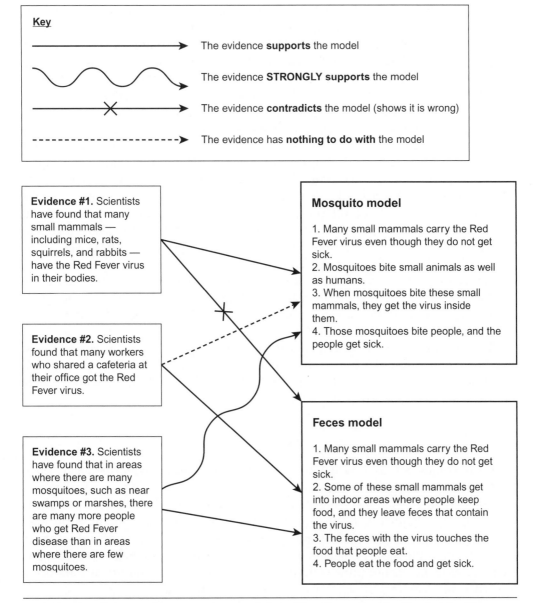

Figure 28.1 A scaffold using different types of arrows to indicate different types of model–evidence relationships

selection, ecosystems, etc.). These curriculum units engaged students in extended inquiries around driving questions such as "What is the quality of air in my community?" The LeTUS curricula also feature technology tools to support students' domain-specific investigations. For example, the Finches software (Sandoval & Reiser, 2004) supports students' interactions with a large database of scientific data about the finches of the Galapagos Islands. Students can pose queries to the database to determine the role of various traits and behaviors of finches on their differential survival after a catastrophic drought event.

An evaluation study in 18 schools with 37 teachers and over 5000 students revealed significant learning gains on Michigan's state standardized assessment in science for students who completed at least one LeTUS unit, compared to non-LeTUS students in the same schools (Geier et al., 2008). The effect size for the first cohort ranged between 0.28 and 0.53; the effect size dropped somewhat for the second cohort (0.17–0.37), which included significantly more schools following a substantial scale-up effort.

IQWST extended the LeTUS development efforts in several ways, including incorporating a stronger and more integrated focus on scientific practices and building coherent progressions that focus on core ideas and practices in science to support student learning across the grade band (Krajcik et al., 2008). IQWST also emphasizes the importance of engaging students with core scientific practices (Krajcik & Sutherland, 2009). Specifically, IQWST curricula develop the practices of (a) modeling; (b) data gathering, organization, and analysis; (c) constructing evidence-based explanations; and (d) designing investigations (Shwartz, Weizman, Fortus, Krajcik, & Reiser, 2008). The focus on scientific practices includes the performance of the practice itself as well as the epistemological understandings of the goals and forms of the practice (meta-knowledge of the practice). Simple versions of these practices are introduced in the sixth grade units, and they are revisited in growing sophistication throughout the seventh and eighth grade units, within and across the disciplinary units (McNeill & Krajcik, 2008; Merritt, Shwartz, & Krajcik, 2008; Shwartz et al., 2008).

The IQWST materials have been implemented in urban, suburban, and rural settings. Published studies from this project show significant learning gains for both content and scientific practices (McNeill & Krajcik, 2008; McNeill, Lizotte, Krajcik, & Marx, 2006; Merritt et al., 2008; Shwartz et al., 2008).

Smithtown

Smithtown (Shute & Glaser, 1990, 1991) is an intelligent tutoring system designed to help learners gain content knowledge in economics through inquiry. Learners conduct economic simulations in the fictional location of Smithtown. The goals are for students to develop better inquiry skills and gain content knowledge of basic economics principles including supply, demand, equilibrium, surpluses, and shortages. The software analyzes the behaviors of the learner interacting with the system and then supplies feedback. The feedback system does not provide hints about the economics concepts that are being learned. Instead, its suggestions focus only on inquiry strategies.

Scaffolding for developing good inquiry skills is also built into Smithtown. The learner's choice of variables to manipulate is constrained to some degree by the software. The combination of the feedback system and the option to manipulate variables enables learners to begin to view economic concepts such as price, supply, and demand as variables to be manipulated and as core economic concepts.

In a pretest–post-test study of 30 undergraduates, Shute and Glaser (1990) showed that learning gains in economics concepts were approximately equal for undergraduates using the Smithtown software and for undergraduates enrolled in a traditional introductory economics course. Given that inquiry-based instruction simultaneously pursues both reasoning and content goals, it will often be an acceptable outcome if students learn an equal amount of content in inquiry-based instruction as in traditional instruction, as long as they also make gains in reasoning, which would not be made in traditional curricula that do not teach reasoning.

Other Prominent Inquiry Programs

Space does not permit a detailed inventory of the many inquiry-based approaches to promoting conceptual change. Here we mention just a few other programs that have documented learning gains from program use. ThinkerTools is an inquiry-oriented, computer-based physics curriculum in which students learn about and engage with scientific models to learn both about force and motion and about scientific inquiry (White & Frederiksen, 1998). The Genetics Construction Kit employs computer simulations to foster the development of normative models of genetic inheritance (Stewart, Cartier, & Passmore, 2005). Linn and her colleagues (e.g., Linn, Davis, & Bell, 2004a) have developed an array of Internet-based modules to promote learning and reasoning on a broad range of science topics. Other programs have addressed topics such as evolution (e.g., Passmore & Stewart, 2002), density (e.g., Smith & Unger, 1997), and heat (e.g., Wiser & Amin, 2001).

TOWARD A THEORY OF LEARNING THROUGH MODEL-BASED INQUIRY

In this section, we discuss two foundational theoretical issues related to processes of learning through model-based inquiry: (1) the interdependent processes of achieving two aspects of conceptual change: understanding and belief, and (2) the interdependent processes of promoting growth in both content knowledge and reasoning. We argue that theories of learning through model-based inquiry must come to grips with the issues raised by both sets of processes.

Promoting Understanding and Belief

Achieving conceptual change involves both understanding the new ideas and believing them (Chinn & Samarapungavan, 2001, 2009; Ohlsson, 2009). Sometimes belief and understanding may move in lockstep; sometimes they diverge. One topic on which divergence often occurs is evolution. A student may understand what evolutionary biologists say about how evolutionary processes operate but not believe that evolution actually occurs, instead believing that God created each species through an act of special divine creation. Similarly, Chinn and Samarapungavan (2001) reported that some middle-school students learning about molecules may understand the idea that matter is composed of molecules with empty spaces between them but insist that they do not believe this to be true.

A counterargument to the claim that belief and understanding are distinct is that, if one truly understands a set of ideas, one will believe them. On this view, a creationist who *says* that she understands evolutionary theory but does not believe it does not really understand evolutionary theory; if she did understand the theory and all the evidence for it, she would believe it. However, on our view, this stretches the meaning of the term *understanding* well beyond reasonable usage. If understanding requires belief, then no one could ever say that they understand historical doctrines and theories now viewed as false – such as Lamarckian views of evolution or the belief that the earth is flat. Thus, we contend that it is possible to gain a reasonable understanding of a theory without believing it.

This issue is important because interventions that promote understanding may fail to promote belief, and vice versa. For example, in research with their Smithtown system, Shute and Glaser (1990) reported that some students gained an understanding of the economic principles that governed Smithtown in the computer simulation but did not believe that the simulation properly captured the way real economies operate; thus, Smithtown succeeded in promoting understanding but, with its purely simulated evidence, failed to promote new beliefs about the actual world.

In contrast, consider students working within learning environments that successfully foster an appreciation of what the core practices of science are and how these processes reliably produce knowledge. These students may, on this basis, readily believe theories such as evolution and global warming without understanding them very well because they believe that these theories were generated using practices of science that they find credible.

On some topics, such as evolution, there is controversy over whether belief is a proper target of instruction (due to a concern for attacking deeply held religious beliefs in a pluralistic democratic society) (e.g., Smith & Siegel, 2004). We will not endeavor to untangle the thorny ethical problems in this chapter, but we will note that there are many topics in which educators clearly seem to intend to promote both belief and under-standing as part of conceptual change. Medical schools expect that doctors will not only understand what they have learned about topics such as the role of vitamins in health but will also believe it, so that they treat patients according to this understanding and not according to crackpot theories unsupported by any evidence. Engineering schools expect their students to believe as well as understand the principles of safe bridge design and therefore to design bridges according to these principles.

A virtue of inquiry-based methods of promoting conceptual change is that they are well positioned to promote both belief and understanding. In presenting students with a nontrivial base of evidence, they have the potential to render new explanations plausible as well as understandable. A student who has seen and reflected on a great deal of evidence supporting evolutionary theory will have more grounds for believing the theory than a student who has seen little evidence. Further, model-based inquiry environments are likely to promote deeper understanding of evidence than might be achieved by cursorily reading it. Inquiry-based methods can promote belief in new ideas because of a deeper grasp of evidence. A student who has extensively grappled with evolutionary evidence showing many, many gradations in eye evolution, and also showing the usefulness of very primitive eyes, will find creationist claims that the eye is useful only in its current whole form to be wrong, and will be more likely to appreciate the plausibility of the evolutionary claims. Chinn and Brewer (1993) provided evidence that deeper processing of data is more likely to yield belief change.

Deeper reflection on evidence also can promote better understanding of new ideas. For example, Schwartz and Martin (2004) examined students learning about standard deviation and its uses in solving real-world problems. They contrasted students who engaged in a discovery task of trying to answer questions about data that required understanding of spread or variation with students who spent the same amount of time receiving instruction on standard deviations. All students later received additional instruction on standard deviations. Even though students who worked with the data failed to discover the standard deviation formula, they learned more from the subsequent instruction than students who had not engaged in discovery. Schwartz and Martin (2004) theorized that working with data leads students to notice key dimensions of the domain that are relevant to the principles they will be learning – dimensions such as how spread out the numbers are, what the number of observations are, and so on.

Nathan (2012) has proposed more generally that students learn more if they work with concrete phenomena in order to master more abstract ideas, rather than just being presented with the abstract ideas. Applying Nathan's proposal to working with evidence, we suggest that deep reflection on evidence helps students notice key data patterns that require explanation. Thus, students may appreciate that an explanatory model needs to have a particular component to explain particular data that they have seen; this appreciation simultaneously promotes understanding and belief (or acceptance). For example, a student who has seen data showing that male guppies with brighter colors sire more offspring will be more likely to appreciate the need for processes of sexual selection to be included among models of natural selection, and they will also see some clear evidence that supports the position that sexual selection occurs.

Promoting Both Content Understanding and Growth in Reasoning

Most of the inquiry methods we have discussed aim to promote growth in both content understanding and reasoning competence. For instance, IQWST targets both conceptual understanding of topics such as evolutionary theory and reasoning competence in areas such as argumentation, model evaluation, and model revision. We contend that, during inquiry-based instruction, students simultaneously undergo foundational changes in their explanatory conceptions in the domain (e.g., in students' theories of heat or economics) and foundational changes in reasoning processes (e.g., practices of testing hypotheses and reasoning from evidence) (Chinn & Samarapungavan, 2009).

In the philosophy and history of science, Thomas Kuhn argued that, in times of revolutionary scientific change, rival theories are incommensurable with each other in two distinct ways (Kuhn, 1977; Zammito, 2004). The first type of incommensurability is between the concepts and principles of the rival theories. The extreme version of content incommensurability posits that the concepts and principles of rival theories can be so different that one set of concepts cannot even be translated into the terms of the other. When many conceptual change researchers emphasize that students must learn new concepts that are fundamentally different from their prior conceptions, they are advocating to some degree a view that the old and new concepts are incommensurable.

The second type of Kuhnian incommensurability is in the methods and standards used to decide which of two rival theories is correct. Kuhn (1962) observed, for example, that for many years following the widespread adoption of the Copernican theory of planetary motion, the supplanted Ptolemaic view continued to give more precise predictions of planetary and stellar movements. Thus, it wasn't fit with the evidence alone that led astronomers to accept Copernican theory; other factors such as elegance, simplicity, and future promise also played a role. But who is to say that it is more or less rational to favor elegance as opposed to evidential fit, or vice versa? This is a question about what one values in an explanation. There can be fundamental differences in what one values in an explanation, in what one counts as evidence, in what one views as reliable methodologies, and so on. These differences in standards of how to reason might be so great that it is impossible for the rivals to ever come to agreement.

We argue that, in inquiry-based instruction, conceptual change often involves *both* kinds of foundational changes – changes in both conceptions and standards and practices of reasoning. Indeed, we argue that learning to reason can itself be viewed as a form of conceptual change. We discuss two lines of evidence for this position below: (1) evidence for fundamental changes in more domain-general forms of reasoning, and (2) evidence for fundamental changes in epistemic stances.

Fundamental Changes in Domain-General Reasoning

Fundamental changes in reasoning may occur in more domain-general processes used in inquiry practices. One line of evidence in support of this claim comes from developmental research addressing the development of reasoning about evidence during the school years. Some of this research indicates that young students and even adults may struggle to consistently differentiate theories from the evidence that supports them (e.g., Kuhn, 1989, 1991). When asked to give putative evidence for a cause, even some adults appear unable to do more than re-describe the theory in different words, as if that counts as evidence for the theory. Thus, at the level of general reasoning, there is reason to think that children and even some adults may lack a concept of evidence that resembles that of scientists.

There is also evidence for foundational shifts in standards for judging what makes a good explanatory model. For example, Pluta et al. (2011) found that only a quarter of seventh graders spontaneously mentioned anything connected with evidence when listing characteristics of good scientific models or explanations. Buckland, Chinn, Pluta, and Duncan (2009) have documented major shifts in some students' preferred explanatory criteria as students engage in model-based inquiry, from a focus on aesthetic aspects of models (e.g., how nice they look) to a focus on evidential criteria. Cartier (2000) found that 83% of high school students learning from a nine-week genetics course employing the Genetics Construction Kit shifted from a stance that models need not cohere with other models and ideas to the stance that models need to cohere with one another, representing a major change in the way students conceived of the role of models in scientific inquiry. Thus, there is evidence that students undergo foundational changes in their ideas in their standards for evaluating models during instruction.

To summarize, there are concepts related to evidence, theory, the criteria for evaluating theories, and their complex interconnections that undergo fundamental change during inquiry. Thus, at the same time students are using evidence to develop new domain explanations, they are reconstituting their very notions of what evidence is and what good explanations are. Much research on inquiry-based methods demonstrates an explicit awareness of this by measuring changes in both. However, there is as yet little systematic work showing how these changes interface with each other.

Changes in Epistemic Stances

Chinn and Buckland (2011) have argued that there are major differences between experts and nonexperts at the general level of epistemic stances. By epistemic stances, we are referring to a network of cognitions related to a variety of closely interrelated phenomena including knowledge and the processes of achieving knowledge (see Chinn, Buckland, &

Samarapungavan, 2011). Focusing on the domain of theories of speciation, they argued that evolutionary biologists and creationists (including creationists who advocate "intelligent design") differ fundamentally in their epistemic aims, beliefs, and practices. Among 13 categories of differences analyzed by Chinn and Buckland (2011) are the following:

- *Core aims of inquiry.* Evolutionary scientists have as their primary aim explaining empirical data. Creationists set as their foremost aim attesting to the truth of the Bible and spreading that truth to others.
- *Explanations.* Evolutionary scientists develop more and more elaborated explanations, which both explain a growing body of empirical findings and cohere with other scientific theories. In contrast, creationists focus on explanations consistent with scriptural texts, which they view as primary sources of truth in case of any disagreements with scientific claims.
- *Human capacities.* Scientists believe that humans, through reason, can gain knowledge of the world, even though doing so is fraught with difficulties. But for many creationists, human reason cannot be trusted due to "original sin" and "the fall of mankind." Thus, empirical inquiry is not epistemically trustworthy.

Moving from a creationist to a scientific worldview involves changing not only one's explanatory beliefs about how species came to exist. It also involves foundational changes in epistemic beliefs and practices. The belief that something is more likely to be true if it is supported by a broad base of empirical research is incommensurable with the belief that truth is determined by consistency with sacred scriptures. Thus, conceptual change in the domain of evolution involves truly foundational changes in both reasoning and content.

There is considerable evidence that many people have, more generally, naïve epistemic commitments that are at odds with those of science. For instance, many adolescents and adults indicate a belief that knowledge is simple rather than complex, whereas in many domains, scientific and social scientific theories can be regarded as complex (Chinn et al., 2011). Thus, it may be generally the case that adopting more sophisticated reasoning practices requires some major changes in epistemic practices and beliefs.

In summary, inquiry-based instruction can be regarded as involving two kinds of conceptual change: change in the explanatory conceptions in the target domain and change in the conceptual categories and practices that guide reasoning. There is a need for theorizing that more clearly recognizes the difficulty of using evidence to improve content knowledge when students are applying nonnormative reasoning practices for coordinating explanations and evidence.

THEORETICAL AND PRACTICAL CHALLENGES

In previous sections, we discussed exemplars of inquiry-based methods for promoting conceptual change and some of the cognitive and social processes by which inquiry-based methods might effect change. In this section, we turn to three sets of challenges that have been raised against these methods: (1) theoretical challenges based on cognitive load theory, (2) practical concerns over time, efficacy, and ease of implementation, and (3) the underdetermination of theories by evidence.

Theoretical Challenges Based on Cognitive Load Theory

In a paper that instigated much discussion, Kirschner, Sweller, and Clark (2006) argued that constructivist approaches to learning are ineffective because they assume learning processes that are incompatible with the fundamental facts of human cognitive architecture. Kirschner et al. (2006) argued that, because learners' working memories are overloaded when they try to manage all the complex tasks of solving problems in a constructivist environment, they lack the space in working memory to make connections to information in long-term memory and thus create enduring new long-term memories. Kirschner et al. (2006) argued that more direct forms of instruction, such as studying worked examples, are more compatible with human cognitive architecture.

Kirschner et al.'s argument focused generally on methods of learning that ask students to discover ideas with the teacher providing minimal guidance; they appear to have assumed that all constructivist approaches to instruction rely on such discovery learning. An implication of their argument is that inquiry-based methods will fail due to overloading working memory. As students attempt to coordinate multiple pieces of evidence and multiple models, their working memories will be overtaxed, and they will learn little.

The challenges raised by Kirschner et al. have stimulated many responses in the literature (e.g., Hmelo-Silver, Duncan, & Chinn, 2007; Schmidt, Loyens, Van Gog, & Paas, 2007; Tobias & Duffy, 2009). The first category of response is empirical. The general claim that constructivist, problem-based, or inquiry-based approaches to instruction are ineffective in the classroom fails on empirical grounds. One line of evidence concerns problem-based curricula in medical schools and other settings. Hmelo-Silver et al. (2007), Schmidt et al. (2007), and Schmidt, Van Der Molen, Te Windel, and Wijnen (2009) reviewed research showing that problem-based learning is more effective than traditional methods of instruction at achieving many valued outcomes (such as the ability to solve real-world problems). Thus, the general claim that constructivist methods such as problem-based learning are ineffective founders on empirical grounds.

More specifically, two recent reviews of research comparing inquiry-based instruction to other forms of instruction in science classes similarly found that the inquiry-based instruction showed positive effects. In a systematic review of 138 science education studies, Minner, Levy, and Century (2010) concluded that inquiry-based instructional practices – especially those that engage students actively in the learning process through scientific investigations – increase conceptual understanding in comparison to instruction that is not inquiry-based. Schroeder et al. (2007) conducted a meta-analysis of research on the effects of specific science teaching strategies on student achievement. The effect size for the use of inquiry strategies was 0.65. Just as research on problem-based learning demonstrates that, empirically, constructivist approaches to instruction are effective, the Minner et al. and Schroeder et al. reviews demonstrate that inquiry-based instruction promotes learning in a subject – science – in which many if not most studied topics involve conceptual change.

A second category of responses to the Kirschner et al. (2006) arguments addresses Kirschner et al.'s equating of constructivist or inquiry-based instruction with minimally guided discovery learning. There is indeed a wide body of research showing that unguided discovery learning is ineffective (e.g., Mayer, 2004); to our knowledge, no contemporary advocates of inquiry-based instruction favor unguided or minimally guided discovery learning. On the contrary, as we discussed earlier, the instruction in inquiry-based instruction is heavily scaffolded in ways that support both reasoning and conceptual understanding. For example, Smith and Unger's (1997) instructional research on teaching density engages students in reasoning with a dots-to-boxes scaffold. The scaffold constrains students to work on and revise a generally accurate explanatory model and does not require students to discover a theory from scratch. The various forms of scaffolding prevent students from getting lost in dead ends of inquiry, and they reduce the cognitive load needed to reason about evidence and revise explanatory models accordingly (Hmelo-Silver et al., 2007).

On theoretical grounds, inquiry-based methods have two advantages that many other methods (such as studying worked examples or reading clear expository presentations) lack. First, as we have already discussed, inquiry-based methods encourage deep, detailed processing of evidence, which can be critical to promoting both belief and understanding. Second, well-designed inquiry-based methods may have motivational advantages. Many inquiry environments incorporate hands-on experiments and computer-based simulations, which students may find interesting. There is evidence that the opportunity to engage in reasoned argumentation about competing positions also enhances engagement and motivation (Chinn, 2006; Chinn & Clark, 2013). Although there is a danger that poorly scaffolded inquiry environments are too difficult for students, thus undermining motivation by reducing self-efficacy, a central goal of most designers is to scaffold effectively so that students experience success.

Practical Concerns: Efficiency and Efficacy

Inquiry-based curricula typically take a great deal of instructional time, often substantially more time than traditional instruction. Critics may argue that there are too many curriculum topics to cover to allow so much time to be devoted to each topic. Further, critics argue, managing inquiry-oriented classrooms is very challenging, and many teachers may fail to implement it successfully (e.g., Kirschner, 2009). A second, related concern is that inquiry curricula invite students to make their own judgments about what explanations are supported by the evidence. As a consequence, many students may opt not to adopt the normative models that are the targets of inquiry-based curricula. For example, instead of adopting the normative model of supply and demand, students may develop an alternative, non-normative model and never learn or adopt the normative model.

Inquiry-based proponents readily acknowledge that inquiry-based instruction is time-intensive and that some students may not arrive at the normative models. But the alternatives are even less successful (Minner et al., 2010; Schroeder, Scott, Tolson, Huang, & Lee, 2007). Research on conceptual change was spurred in part by the discovery that students in traditional curricula were leaving their classes with numerous alternative conceptions; even students who are successful in classes often continue to hold many non-normative views that persist unchanged through instruction (Eylon & Linn, 1988). Thus, although inquiry-based methods developed to date are far from perfect, many of the possible alternatives appear to be worse. Further, although even inquiry proponents agree that it is challenging to learn to teach well via inquiry, the fact that inquiry-based instruction has proved to be more effective than non-inquiry-based alternatives indicates that enough teachers are successful with it that it is a practical form of instruction.

The Theory Underdetermination Problem

A third challenge to inquiry-based methods is the theory underdetermination problem (see Zammito, 2004). Some philosophers and sociologists of science have argued that theories are underdetermined by data, which means that for any body of evidence taken to support Theory X, a proponent of a rival Theory Y could rationally interpret the available evidence to support that theory just as well. The proponent of Y might argue that some of the evidence supporting Theory X is methodologically flawed, claim that other evidence should be regarded as irrelevant, and reinterpret other evidence to support the theory. Extreme proponents of the underdetermination thesis are, ultimately, relativists who think that, for any body of evidence, one could interpret that evidence in a manner that supports a contrary theory equally well or better.

It is beyond the scope of this chapter to recount all the arguments that can be advanced for or against underdetermination. We agree with Laudan (1990) and many others (e.g., Kitcher, 1993; Zammito, 2004) that the rationality of science is not threatened by underdetermination arguments. However, although underdetermination may not be a fatal threat to rational theory choice in science, it may be a fundamental problem for rational choice in the science classroom. Consider, for example, a high-school inquiry unit on geology that asks students to use evidence to decide whether continental drift is occurring. Chinn and Samarapungavan (2008) argued that, in such a unit, students' theory choices would be severely underdetermined by the data available to them. The data that convinced scientists were highly technical (e.g., data involving evidence of magnetic reversals in the earth's crust), whereas the data that are readily understood by middle-school or high-school students are the same data that were *not* persuasive to many scientists of the 19th century (e.g., data about similar fossils and rock formations on the west coast of Africa and the east coast of South America). Similarly, what persuades scientists to adopt a theory is often a vast, interlocking tapestry of evidence, whereas science classes (even allowing extensive time) can only address in depth a few pieces or lines of evidence. Any one or two pieces of this evidence might be explained away rationally in a science classroom context, but it would prove impossible to do so coherently for the whole body of evidence, which is mutually reinforcing and often contains many lines of independent support. Without access to the full body of evidence, students may rationally discount the data they see and thus fail to adopt the normative model. We have observed such issues with underdetermination in our own PRACCIS project (Chinn et al., 2012).

There is no easy solution to the problem of underdetermination of theories in the science classroom. One method is to foster shared norms of evaluating evidence so that students do not discount evidence unreasonably. However, much more research on this important topic is needed.

PRINCIPLES OF DESIGNING INQUIRY ENVIRONMENTS THAT PROMOTE CONCEPTUAL CHANGE AND GROWTH IN REASONING

In the final section of this chapter, we provide a very brief overview of some of the instructional methods that designers of inquiry environments have found effective in promoting conceptual change. Roughly, these can be divided into methods that focus especially on reasoning and methods that focus primarily on conceptual understanding.

Design Features Focused on Improving Reasoning

Designers of inquiry environments are interested in promoting growth in reasoning both as a valued learning outcome in its own right and as a means to promote conceptual change. If students are reasoning from evidence to develop explanations, they are more likely to accept the normative scientific conceptions if they reason more effectively. Better reasoning is thus a route to conceptual change. Most of the instructional techniques designed to improve reasoning attempt to increase metacognitive awareness of reasoning processes.

Scaffolds Focused on Epistemic Practices

Designers have developed a range of scaffolds designed to engage students in the epistemic practices of science. One of these is *accountable talk* (K-12 Alliance & WestEd, 2007), which introduces students to question stems such as "One reason why _____ is _____," "I disagree with _____ because _____," and "What is the biggest (strength/weakness) of this study?" Using these stems, students learn to engage in the kinds of thinking processes used by experts in the field they are studying.

Prompts can also direct students to use the desired processes. In a study with middle-school students, Davis (2003) found that general prompts such as "What are you thinking now?" were more effective at promoting effective reasoning than were more specific prompts such as "When we critique evidence, we need to _____." However, many projects have achieved success with the latter kind of prompt as well (e.g., Linn, Davis, & Bell, 2004b). More research is needed on the conditions under which different kinds of prompts are most effective.

Herrenkohl & Guerra (1998) reported success with having students adopt cognitive roles during class discussions. Different groups of students took responsibility for each role, which consisted of (1) making a prediction and building a theory, (2) summarizing results of investigations, and (3) relating the results to the prediction and theory. These promoted class discussions at a much higher level than when no such roles were used.

Focus on Epistemic Categories and Distinctions

A number of scaffolds embedded in inquiry environments are designed to focus students' attention on key epistemic categories and to foster learning of key epistemic distinctions. For example, the diagrams illustrated earlier in Figure 28.1 are designed to direct students' attention and discourse to distinguishing between models and evidence and to distinguish between different degrees of strength of support. Similarly, the class criteria discussed earlier as part of the PRACCIS and IQWST projects are intended to draw students' attention and discourse to critical standards used by scientists to evaluate scientific models.

Establishing Disciplinary Norms

Many recent inquiry projects have emphasized the importance of establishing disciplinary norms in the classroom and holding students accountable to these norms. The question stems we discussed earlier show students how to engage in reasoned argumentation, but there must also be a shared commitment to use these norms in individual, group, and class work. When students collaborate in the development of class criteria for what counts as a good model, then teachers can ask them to be accountable to the criteria that they themselves have developed and agreed to (Chinn et al., 2012).

White and Fredericksen (1998) showed that having students set goals and evaluate their own group performance improved student outcomes – both in reasoning and in conceptual understanding – in their ThinkerTools curriculum focusing on forces and motion. In subsequent work, they have had students take ownership of these evaluations by helping to develop and refine the evaluative criteria (Shimoda, White, & Frederiksen, 2002).

Argumentation

Most inquiry environments designed to promote conceptual change in classroom settings are explicitly geared to promote argumentation as a core disciplinary discourse of the classroom. The focus is not on argumentation as interpersonal disagreement but on collaborative, shared reasoning about problems by giving arguments and counter-arguments to work out an explanation that best explains a body of evidence. Chinn and Clark (2013) have provided an overview of instructional methods that make argumentation more productive.

Motivational Components

Effective inquiry environments include many features designed to enhance motivation (Blumenfeld, Kempler, & Krajcik, 2006). These include hands-on experiments, work with engaging computer simulations, and instruction centered around an interesting "driving question," as we discussed earlier. By focusing on authentic problems and reasoning skills, the designers seek to enhance the relevance of the instruction. Students have considerable autonomy in carrying out inquiry; such autonomy is believed to enhance motivation. However, there is a need for motivational researchers, who have typically studied traditional instructions, to investigate how further to enhance motivation in inquiry environments.

Design Features Focused on Conceptual Understanding

Finally, we turn to design features of inquiry environments that are focused especially on conceptual understanding.

Building on Students' Prior Conceptions

Most current designers of inquiry environments aim not only to take students' prior conceptions into account but to identify conceptions that can be built upon. Some scholars have termed these productive prior conceptions *conceptual resources* (Smith, diSessa, & Roschelle, 1993/1994). Wiser and Amin (2001) explicitly took this approach when they treated students' preinstructional views of heat and temperature not as incorrect ideas but as correct perceptual ideas that needed to be refined and contrasted with the normative scientific models of heat. Similarly, the PRACCIS evolution unit recruits students' rich knowledge of variation in humans and other species they are familiar with to help build up notions of variation within species.

Simplification

Almost all inquiry environments severely constrain the problem space by simplifying the task faced by students. This is accomplished in a variety of ways: Students may be given a limited range of theories to consider. The amount of evidence that they examine is far less than that available to real scientists or social scientists. Evidence is simplified in various ways: Scientific reports are shortened and rewritten in language that students can more readily understand. Technical jargon is often minimized. Databases and simulations come with tools that make important aspects of the data salient to students. The tasks are often broken down into subsets that are more readily handled by students. In all of these ways, designers aim to help students achieve challenging tasks at an appropriate developmental level (Quintana et al., 2004).

As an example, Sandoval and Reiser (2004) developed a tool to guide (and constrain) the form of natural selection explanations that students developed by working to explain why finch populations on a Galapagos Island decreased during a drought. The students are required to fill in slots that specify the selective pressure, the change that introduced the selective pressure, the organisms that are more likely to survive and those more likely to die, and several other components. On their own, students might come up with a diverse range of explanations; this scaffold channels their reasoning to focus on desired aspects of the space of explanatory options.

Scaffolding the Coordination of Multiple Representations

In many fields of science, there is a need to coordinate multiple representations. For example, there are three main levels of chemical representations in chemistry: microscopic, macroscopic, and symbolic. Studies have shown that students have difficulties understanding symbolic and microscopic representations (Wu, Krajcik, & Soloway, 2001). One reason for these difficulties is that symbolic and microscopic representations are abstract and invisible to students, and the microscopic entities engage in different processes and have different properties than macroscopic entities have (Chi, 2005). Students have difficulty translating one type of representation to another and need scaffolding in order to see the relationship between the three types of chemical representations. Many interventions, particularly technologically based interventions, are designed to help students see how different representations map onto each other.

CONCLUSIONS

In this chapter we have discussed inquiry-based methods of promoting conceptual change. We have described exemplars of this method and noted evidence for its efficacy in promoting conceptual change. We have argued that theoretical accounts of learning through inquiry should attend to changes in understanding and belief, as well as accounting for how foundational changes in reasoning and content knowledge occur simultaneously. Despite theoretical and practical challenges, the empirical support for the use of inquiry methods is strong. In part, this is probably because inquiry-based methods engage students in deep processing of evidence-theory linkages, which promotes conceptual change. Finally, we have discussed a range of commonly used techniques that have been used to scaffold reasoning and conceptual content in inquiry-based environments.

The use of these techniques helps constrain the task so that learners will not be overwhelmed and can succeed at learning.

ACKNOWLEDGMENT

This material is based on work supported by the National Science Foundation under Grant No. 9875485. Any opinions, findings, and conclusions or recommendations expressed in this material are those of the author(s) and do not necessarily reflect the views of the National Science Foundation.

REFERENCES

Blumenfeld, P. C., Kempler, T. M., & Krajcik, J. C. (2006). Motivation and cognitive engagement in learning environments. In R. K. Sawyer (Ed.), *The Cambridge handbook of the learning sciences* (pp. 475–488). Cambridge, UK: Cambridge University Press.

Buckland, L. B., Chinn, C. A., Pluta, W. P., & Duncan, R. G. (2009, April). *Model evaluation criteria in inquiry classrooms*. Paper presented at the annual meeting of the American Educational Research Association, San Diego, CA.

Cartier, J. L. (2000). *Research report 99-1: Using a modeling approach to explore scientific epistemology with high school biology students*. Madison, WI: University of Wisconsin-Madison.

Chi, M. T. H. (2005). Commonsense conceptions of emergent processes: Why some misconceptions are robust. *Journal of the Learning Sciences, 14*, 161–199.

Chinn, C. A. (2006). Learning to argue. In A. M. O'Donnell, C. E. Hmelo-Silver, & G. Erkens (Eds.), *Collaborative learning, reasoning, and technology* (pp. 355–383). Mahwah, NJ: Lawrence Erlbaum Associates.

Chinn, C. A., & Brewer, W. F. (1993). The role of anomalous data in knowledge acquisition: A theoretical framework and implications for science instruction. *Review of Educational Research, 63*, 1–49.

Chinn, C. A., & Buckland, L. A. (2011). Differences in epistemic practices among scientists, young earth creationists, intelligent design creationists, and the scientist creationists of Darwin's era. In R. Taylor & M. Ferrari (Eds.), *Epistemology and science education: Understanding the evolution vs. intelligent design controversy* (pp. 38–76). New York, NY: Taylor & Francis.

Chinn, C. A., & Buckland, L. A. (2012). Model-based instruction: Fostering change in evolutionary conceptions and in epistemic practices. In K. S. Rosengren, E. M. Evans, S. K. Brem, & G. M. Sinatra (Eds.), *Evolution challenges: Integrating research and practice in teaching and learning about evolution* (pp. 212–232). Oxford, UK: Oxford University Press.

Chinn, C. A., Buckland, L. A., & Samarapungavan, A. (2011). Expanding the dimensions of epistemic cognition: Arguments from philosophy and psychology. *Educational Psychologist, 46*, 141–167.

Chinn, C. A., & Clark, D. B. (2013). Learning through collaborative argumentation. In C. E. Hmelo-Silver, C. A. Chinn, C. K. K. Chan, & A. M. O'Donnell (Eds.), *International handbook of collaborative learning* (pp. 314–332). New York, NY: Routledge.

Chinn, C. A., Duschl, R. A., Duncan, R. G., Pluta, W. J., & Buckland, L. A. (2008). A microgenetic classroom study of learning to reason scientifically through modeling and argumentation. *ICLS 2008: Proceedings of International Conference of the Learning Sciences*, Utrecht, The Netherlands.

Chinn, C. A., Rinehart, R., Drescher, C, Duncan, R. G., Dianovsky, M., & Buckland, L. A. (2012, April). *Standards for evaluating evidence in arguments*. Paper presented at the annual meeting of the American Education Research Association, Vancouver, Canada.

Chinn, C. A., & Samarapungavan, A. (2001). Distinguishing between understanding and belief. *Theory into Practice, 40*, 235–241.

Chinn, C. A., & Samarapungavan, A. (2008). Learning to use scientific models: Multiple dimensions of conceptual change. In R. A. Duschl & R. E. Grandy (Eds.), *Teaching scientific inquiry: Recommendations for research and implementation* (pp. 191–225). Rotterdam, The Netherlands: Sense Publishers.

Chinn, C. A., & Samarapungavan, A. (2009). Conceptual change—Multiple routes, multiple mechanisms: A commentary on Ohlsson (2009). *Educational Psychologist, 44*, 47–57.

Cobb, P., McClain, K., & Gravemeijer, K. (2003). Learning about statistical covariation. *Cognition and Instruction, 21*, 1–78.

Davis, E. A. (2003). Prompting middle school science students for productive reflection: Generic and directed prompts. *Journal of the Learning Sciences, 12*, 91–142.

Eylon, B., & Linn, M. C. (1988). Learning and instruction: An examination of four research perspectives in science education. *Review of Educational Research, 58*, 251–301.

Geier, R., Blumenfeld, P., Marx, R. W., Krajcik, J., Fishman, B., & Soloway, E. (2008). Standardized test outcomes for students engaged in inquiry-based science curriculum in the context of urban reform. *Journal of Research in Science Teaching, 45*, 922–939.

Hapgood, S., Magnusson, S. J., & Palincsar, A. S. (2004). Teacher, text, and experience: A case of young children's scientific inquiry. *Journal of the Learning Sciences, 13*, 455–505.

Herrenkohl, L. R., & Guerra, M. R. (1998). Participant structures, scientific discourse, and student engagement in fourth grade. *Cognition and Instruction, 16*, 431–473.

Hmelo-Silver, C. E., Duncan, R. G., & Chinn, C. A. (2007). Scaffolding and achievement in problem-based and inquiry learning: A response to Kirschner, Sweller, and Clark (2006). *Educational Psychologist, 42*, 99–107.

K-12 Alliance & WestEd. (2007). Accountable talk toolkit. Available at: http://msopage.weebly.com/uploads/3/8/5/1/3851505/203_accountable_talk_toolkit_10-09.pdf

Kang, H., & Lundeberg, M. A. (2010). Participation in science practices while working in a multimedia case-based environment. *Journal of Research in Science Teaching, 47*, 1116–1136.

Kirschner, P. A. (2009). Epistemology or pedagogy, that is the question. In S. Tobias & T. M. Duffy (Eds.), *Constructivist instruction: Success or failure?* (pp. 144–157). New York, NY: Routledge.

Kirschner, P. A., Sweller, J., & Clark, R. E. (2006). Why minimal guidance during instruction does not work: An analysis of the failure of constructivist, discovery, problem-based, experiential, and inquiry-based teaching. *Educational Psychologist, 41*, 75–86.

Kitcher, P. (1993). *The advancement of science: Science without legend, objectivity without illusions.* New York, NY: Oxford University Press.

Krajcik, J. S., & Blumenfeld, P. C. (2006). Project-based learning. In R. K. Sawyer (Ed.), *The Cambridge handbook of the learning sciences* (pp. 317–333). Cambridge, UK: Cambridge University Press.

Krajcik, J., McNeill, K. L., & Reiser, B. J. (2008). Learning-goals-driven design model: Developing curriculum materials that align with national standards and incorporate project-based pedagogy. *Science Education, 92*, 1–32.

Krajcik, J. S., & Sutherland, L. M. (2009). *IQWST materials: Meeting the challenges of the 21st century.* Paper presented at the NRC Workshop on Exploring the Intersection between Science Education and the Development of 21st Century Skills. Washington, DC: National Academies Press.

Kuhn, D. (1989). Children and adults as intuitive scientists. *Psychological Review, 96*, 674–689.

Kuhn, D. (1991). *The skills of argument.* Cambridge, UK: Cambridge University Press.

Kuhn, T. S. (1962). *The structure of scientific revolutions.* Chicago, IL: University of Chicago Press.

Kuhn, T. S. (1977). *The essential tension: Selected studies in scientific tradition and change.* Chicago, IL: University of Chicago Press.

Laudan, L. (1990). Demystifying underdetermination. In C. W. Savage (Ed.), *Scientific theories* (Vol. 14, pp. 267–297). Minneapolis, MN: University of Minnesota Press.

Linn, M. C., Davis, E. A., & Bell, P. (2004a). Inquiry and technology. In M. C. Linn, E. A. Davis, & P. Bell (Eds.), *Internet environments for science education* (pp. 3–27). Mahwah, NJ: Lawrence Erlbaum Associates.

Linn, M. C., Davis, E. A., & Bell, P. (Eds.). (2004b). *Internet environments for science education.* Mahwah, NJ: Lawrence Erlbaum Associates.

Longino, H. E. (2002). *The fate of knowledge.* Princeton, NJ: Princeton University Press.

Mayer, R. E. (2004). Should there be a three-strikes rule against pure discovery learning? The case for guided methods of instruction. *American Psychologist, 59*, 14–19.

McNeill, K. L., & Krajcik, J. (2008). Scientific explanations: Characterizing and evaluating the effects of teachers' instructional practices on student learning. *Journal of Research in Science Teaching, 45*, 53–78.

McNeill, K. L., Lizotte, D. J., Krajcik, J., & Marx, R. W. (2006). Supporting students' construction of scientific explanations by fading scaffolds in instructional materials. *Journal of the Learning Sciences, 15*, 159–191.

Merritt, J., Shwartz, Y., & Krajcik, J. (2008). Middle school students' development of the particle model of matter. *ICLS 2008: Proceedings of International Conference of the Learning Sciences,* Utrecht, The Netherlands.

Minner, D., Levy, A. J., & Century, J. (2010). Inquiry-based science instruction: What is it and does it matter? Results from a research synthesis years 1984 to 2002. *Journal of Research in Science Teaching, 47*, 474–496.

Nathan, M. J. (2012). Rethinking formalisms in formal education. *Educational Psychologist, 47*, 125–148.

National Research Council. (1996). *National science education standards.* Washington, DC: National Academy Press.

National Research Council. (2007). *Taking science to school: Learning and teaching science in grades K-8.* Washington, DC: National Academies Press.

Newton-Smith, W. H. (1981). *The rationality of science.* Boston, MA: Routledge & Kegan Paul.

Ohlsson, S. (2009). Re-subsumption: A possible mechanism for conceptual change and belief revision. *Educational Psychologist, 44,* 20–40.

Passmore, C., & Stewart, J. (2002). A modeling approach to teaching evolutionary biology in high schools. *Journal of Research in Science Teaching, 39,* 185–204.

Pluta, W. J., Chinn, C. A., & Duncan, R. G. (2011). Learners' epistemic criteria for good scientific models. *Journal of Research in Science Teaching, 48,* 486–511.

Quintana, C., Reiser, B. J., Davis, E. A., Krajcik, J., Fretz, E., Duncan, R. G., Kyza, E., Edelson, D. C., & Soloway, E. (2004). A scaffolding design framework for software to support science inquiry. *The Journal of the Learning Sciences, 13*(3), 337–386.

Roth, P. A. (1998). Narrative explanations: The case of history. *History and Theory, 27,* 1–13.

Samarapungavan, A., Westby, E. L., & Bodner, G. M. (2006). Contextual epistemic development in science: A comparison of chemistry students and research chemists. *Science Education, 90,* 468–495.

Sandoval, W. A., & Reiser, B. J. (2004). Explanation-driven inquiry: Integrating conceptual and epistemic scaffolds for scientific inquiry. *Science Education, 88,* 345–372.

Schmidt, H. G., Loyens, S. M. M., Van Gog, T., & Paas, F. (2007). Problem-based learning *is* compatible with human cognitive architecture: Commentary on Kirschner, Sweller, and Clark (2006). *Educational Psychologist, 42,* 91–97.

Schmidt, H. G., Van Der Molen, H. T., Te Windel, W. W. R., & Wijnen, W. H. F. W. (2009). Constructivist, problem-based learning does work: A meta-analysis of curricular comaprisons involving a single medical school. *Educational Psychologist, 44,* 227–249.

Schroeder, C. M., Scott, T. P., Tolson, H., Huang, T.-Y., & Lee, Y.-H. (2007). A meta-analysis of national research: Effects of teaching strategies on student achievement in science in the United States. *Journal of Research in Science Teaching, 44,* 1436–1460.

Schwartz, D. L., & Martin, T. (2004). Inventing to prepare for future learning: The hidden efficiency of encouraging original student production in statistics instruction. *Cognition and Instruction, 22,* 129–184.

Shimoda, T. A., White, B. Y., & Frederiksen, J. R. (2002). Student goal orientation in learning inquiry skills with modifiable software advisors. *Science Education, 86,* 244–263.

Shute, V. J., & Glaser, R. (1990). A large-scale evaluation of an intelligent discovery world: Smithtown. *Interactive Learning Environments, 1,* 51–77.

Shute, V. J., & Glaser, R. (1991). An intelligent tutoring system for exploring principles of economics. In R. E. Snow & D. Wiley (Eds.), *Improving inquiry in social science: A volume in honor of Lee J. Cronbach* (pp. 333–366). Hillsdale, NJ: Lawrence Erlbaum Associates.

Shwartz, Y., Weizman, A., Fortus, D., Krajcik, J., & Reiser, B. (2008). The IQWST experience: Coherence as a design principle. *Elementary School Journal, 109,* 199–219.

Singer, J., Marx, R. W., Krajcik, J., & Clay-Chambers, J. (2000). Constructing extended inquiry projects: Curriculum materials for science education reform. *Educational Psychologist, 35,* 165–178.

Smith, C., & Unger, C. (1997). What's in dots-per-box? Conceptual bootstrapping with stripped-down visual analogs. *Journal of the Learning Sciences, 6,* 143–181.

Smith, J. P., III, diSessa, A. A., & Roschelle, J. (1993/1994). Misconceptions reconceived: A constructivist analysis of knowledge in transition. *Journal of the Learning Sciences, 3,* 115–163.

Smith, M. U., & Siegel, H. (2004). Knowing, believing, and understanding: What goals for science education? *Science & Education, 13,* 553–582.

Stewart, J., Cartier, J. L., & Passmore, C. M. (2005). Developing understanding through model-based inquiry. In N. R. Council (Ed.), *How students learn: History, mathematics, and science in the classroom.* Washington, DC: National Academies Press.

Stewart, J., & Hafner, R. (1991). Extending the conception of "problem" in problem-solving research. *Science Education, 75,* 105–120.

Tobias, S., & Duffy, T. M. (Eds.). (2009). *Constructivist instruction: Success or failure?* New York, NY: Routledge.

Weber, K. (2008). *Students' difficulties with proof.* Mathematical Association of America. Available at: www.maa.org/t_and_l/sampler/rs_8.html

White, B. Y., & Frederiksen, J. R. (1998). Inquiry, modeling, and metacognition: Making science accessible to all students. *Cognition and Instruction, 16,* 3–118.

Wiser, M., & Amin, T. (2001). "Is heat hot?" Inducing conceptual change by integrating everyday and scientific perspectives on thermal phenomena. *Learning and Instruction, 11*, 331–355.

Wu, H.-K., Krajcik, J. S., & Soloway, E. (2001). Promoting understanding of chemical representations: Students' use of a visualization tool in the classroom. *Journal of Research in Science Teaching, 38*, 821–842.

Wylie, A. (2002). *Thinking from things: Essays in the philosophy of archaeology.* Berkeley, CA: University of California Press.

Zammito, J. H. (2004). *A nice derangement of epistemes: Post-positivism in the study of science from Quine to Latour.* Chicago, IL: University of Chicago Press.

29

REPRESENTATION CONSTRUCTION TO SUPPORT CONCEPTUAL CHANGE

Russell Tytler and Vaughan Prain,
Deakin University and La Trobe University

ENCOURAGING AND GUIDING CONCEPTUAL CHANGE

Despite extensive contributions to this field over the past 20 years, the fundamental issue of identifying and enacting effective instructional processes to achieve student mastery of concepts remains an ongoing concern in science education research (Taber, 2011; Treagust & Duit, 2008; Tytler & Prain, 2010; Vosniadou, 2008b). This pedagogical challenge persists for various reasons. Recent claims about the formation of concepts and the nature of conceptual learning from (a) cognitive science perspectives (diSessa, 2008) and (b) semiotic and discursive frameworks (Jewitt, 2008; Lemke, 2004; Mercer, 2008; Prain & Tytler, 2012; Tobin, 2008) challenge past accounts of causal mechanisms for this learning. Further, a growing range of contextual factors and cognitive/affective processes has been identified as influencing student learning generally, and science in particular (Barsalou, 2008; Jakobson & Wickman, 2008; Klein, 2006; Wells, 2008). At the same time, science learning outcomes based on conceptual change approaches continue to fall short of systemic expectations (Duit, 2009), suggesting the need for new, or modified, or more widely adapted successful classroom practices.

In this chapter we describe an approach incorporating pragmatist, semiotic, socio-cultural, and cognitive science perspectives that addresses each of these concerns by focusing on student engagement in sequences of representational challenges to support conceptual growth. We consider that this focus on guided development of students' representational resources and competence (a) provides strong student motivation to reason about science concepts, and (b) offers a theoretically justifiable and highly practical way to support and direct student conceptual mastery. We view our approach as a form of guided inquiry that is compatible with model-based reasoning orientations, but also provides precise strategies to focus on and support student conceptual learning. We put a case that guided construction of representations productively constrains students' reasoning and learning of science concepts and processes. Finally, we explore the theoretical implications of this work for the conceptualization of the conceptual change process. First, however, we review other current pedagogical approaches to characterize further what is both complementary and distinctive about our own approach.

CONCEPTUALIZING CHANGE MECHANISMS AND PROCESSES

The traditional cognitivist account of concepts as mental models within individual minds (Posner, Strike, Hewson & Gertzog, 1982) led to the view that student conceptual change or growth could occur if teachers problematized students' initial explanations/ conceptions as a basis for guided inquiry and rational acceptance of target models. However, even these early accounts of concepts recognized that they were more than just mental propositions to be held or changed in the mind. Concepts were also to be understood as "strings, images, episodes, and intellectual and motor skills" (White & Gunstone, 1992, p. 5), suggesting that conceptual understanding also entailed practices, inquiry, applications, and making connections between ideas, artifacts, representations and contexts. There is increasing recognition within conceptual change research of the contextual and sociocultural factors influencing learning. This recognition underpinned early conceptual change schemes (e.g., Cosgrove & Osborne, 1985; Driver & Oldham, 1986) incorporating student questions and open classroom discussion. A growing body of research into classroom practice, sitting broadly within the conceptual change framework, focuses on discourse and the teacher's role in managing classroom talk (e.g., Mortimer & Scott, 2003). There have also been calls for more research into classroom talk to support conceptual change (Mercer, 2008).

Various researchers have attempted to integrate conceptual change and sociocultural views. For instance, Vosniadou (2008b) noted that "conceptual change should not be seen as only an individual, internal cognitive process, but as a social activity that takes place in a complex socio-cultural world." In explaining how her conceptual change perspective differed from cultural studies views, Vosniadou (2008a) claimed that mental models and model-based reasoning were crucial to explaining the creation of artifacts and the capacity of humans to develop and modify theories about the natural world. In this way, "a globe as a cultural artifact is nothing more than a reified mental model of the earth viewed from a certain perspective" (Vosniadou, 2008a, p. 281). Our own approach focuses explicitly on the symbolic and material artifacts and representations through which scientific models are generated, justified, refined, and communicated by learners.

Research on student model-based reasoning through inquiry is a major strand in theorizing the mechanisms and processes of conceptual change (Clement, 2000; Gilbert & Boulter, 2000; Harrison & Treagust, 2000; Justi & Gilbert, 2003; Lehrer & Schauble, 2006a; Vosniadou, 1994). Advocates of this approach claim that the process of constructing, critiquing, testing and revising models arising from inquiry into science topics is the key mechanism for promoting student conceptual growth. Other approaches broadly within this perspective have focused variously on enabling features of technology-enhanced inquiry (Gerard, Varma, Corliss, & Linn, 2011), model-building through problem-solving tasks (Lee, Jonassen, & Teo, 2011), and increased student attention to representational resources for meaning-making (Taber, 2011).

Our own approach is broadly consistent with these strategies, but entails a systematic explicit focus on students being challenged to generate, interpret, refine, and justify representations as a key practical step in learning science concepts. In developing our case we focus on key affordances or enablers of different representational modes to support students' reasoning around models. Our broad orientation continues a pragmatist tradition of inquiry into problem-solving through dialogue, debate, and logical proof, where inquiry is focused on resolving practical questions assumed to have identifiable causes (Dewey, 1996; Peirce, 1931–1958; Wittgenstein, 1972). Our perspective is also consistent with current cognitive science accounts of thinking and learning processes that stress the role of context, perception, activity, motor actions, identity, feelings, embodiment, analogy, metaphor, and pattern-spotting in cognition (see Barsalou, 2008; Klein, 2006; Sinatra, 2005). Here knowledge is viewed as more implicit, perceptual, concrete, and variable across contexts, rather than as purely propositional, abstract, and decontextualized.

SEMIOTIC AND SOCIOCULTURAL PERSPECTIVES ON LEARNING

There is a substantial literature arguing that learning and knowing in science should be seen as a process of enculturation into the discursive practices of science (Lave & Wenger, 1991), where these practices are substantially shaped around a set of discipline-specific and generic literacies used in science to build and validate knowledge (Moje, 2007). Learning concepts in science involves students switching between verbal, written, visual, and mathematical (graphs, tables, equations) and 3D representational modes, and coordinating these to generate explanations (Greeno & Hall, 1997; Hubber, Tytler, & Haslam, 2010; Lehrer & Schauble, 2006a; Prain, Tytler, & Petersen, 2009; Waldrip, Prain, & Carolan, 2010). From this perspective, students are expected to generate and coordinate multi-modal representational resources to develop explanations and solve problems. Thus, explicit discussion of the form and function of scientific representations becomes a key aspect of teaching and learning in science (Ainsworth, 2006, 2008; Lemke, 2004), enabling students to understand the value and use of conventions in this work. Achieving meta-representational competence (diSessa, 2004) as a goal of science education means that students need to understand (a) the key characteristics of effective representational practices, (b) the selective nature of representations, and (c) how they are coordinated to develop persuasive solutions (Gilbert, 2005; Kozma & Russell, 1997, 2005; Kozma, Chin, Russell, & Marx, 2000). A growing modeling literature identifies the power of refinement of explanatory models through classroom negotiation to achieve this goal (Clement & Rea-Ramirez, 2008).

Further studies have verified the defining, rather than supporting role played by representations in generating knowledge and solving problems (Ainsworth, Prain & Tytler, 2011; Klein, 2001; Tytler, Haslam, Prain, & Hubber, 2009). This perspective is consistent with pragmatist accounts of the material nature of knowledge (Peirce 1931–1958; Wittgenstein, 1972), and the way representations actively shape knowing and reasoning. This implies that classroom teaching and learning processes need to focus on the representational resources used to instantiate scientific concepts and practices (Moje, 2007).

From sociocultural perspectives, learners need to participate in authentic activities with these cultural resources/tools to learn effectively (Cole & Wertsch, 1996; Vygotsky, 1978, 1981a, 1981b). A further literature in science education argues the need for students to actively construct representations in order to become competent in scientific practices and to learn through participating in the reasoning processes of science (Ford & Forman,

2006). Sociocultural accounts of the value of this practice focus on the potential for increased student engagement in a learning community (Greeno, 2009; Kozma & Russell, 2005). From a cognitive perspective, Bransford and Schwartz (1999) sought to reconceptualize the learning gains and potential for transfer when students generated their own representations. Rather than argue that students developed transferable domain knowledge from this activity, they claimed that student construction of representations led to the development of problem-solving skills that could be applied in new contexts.

Researchers in classroom studies in this area (Cox, 1999; Greeno & Hall, 1997; Lehrer & Schauble, 2006a, 2006b; Tytler, Peterson & Prain, 2006; Waldrip, Prain, & Carolan, 2010) have noted the importance of teacher and student negotiation of the meanings evident in verbal, visual, mathematical, and gestural representations in science. They claimed that students benefited from multiple opportunities to explore, engage, elaborate, and re-represent ongoing understandings in the same and different representations. Greeno and Hall (1997) argued that different forms of representation supported contrasting understanding of topics, and that students needed to explore the advantages and limitations of particular representations. As noted by Cox (1999), representations can be used as tools for many different forms of reasoning such as for initial, speculative thinking, to record observations, to show a sequence or process in time (see also Ainsworth et al., 2011), to sort information, or predict outcomes. Students need to learn how to select appropriate representations for addressing particular needs, and be able to judge their effectiveness in achieving particular purposes.

Distinguishing Representations from Models

Drawing on Peirce's (1931–1958) triadic model of semiotics or meaning-making systems, we view representations as signs that stand for something for an interpreter. Distinctions here are made between a concept (for example, the scientific idea of force), its representation in a sign or signifier (arrows in diagrammatic accounts of force), and its referent, or the phenomena to which both concept and signifier refer (examples of the operation of force on objects in the world). Learners are expected to recognize the differences between an idea, the different ways this idea can be represented and used, and the phenomena to which it refers. Coming to know what "force," "electricity," or "states of matter" mean both as concepts and as words in science must entail understanding and using the appropriate representational resources to make cognitive links between appropriate phenomena and theoretical, scientific accounts of this phenomena. Therefore learning about new concepts cannot be separated from learning both how to represent these concepts and what these representations signify in particular contexts for specific purposes. Demonstrating an understanding of the meaning of the words "sound waves," for instance, involves being able to coordinate a range of wave diagrams, time-sequenced representations of air particle movement, and pressure variation, and to know when, why and how to use these representations for particular purposes as required in specific contexts.

All models can be classified as representations. However, not all representations are models. For example, student exploratory talk, gestures, drawings, enactments, and manipulation of artifacts can function as representations of emerging ideas and insights rather than as evidence of resolved models. We therefore view representations as a very broad range of symbolic and material resources and artifacts for supporting students' reasoning processes, where they can function as both process markers and products of understanding.

An Approach to Learning and Teaching through Representation Construction

Associated with theoretical development of a pragmatist, semiotic perspective on conceptual change (Prain et al., 2009; Tytler, Peterson, & Prain, 2006; Tytler & Prain, 2010; Tytler, Prain, & Peterson, 2007), we worked through a series of research projects with classroom teachers to develop pragmatically a pedagogy that would reflect these unfolding views, culminating in working closely with a small number of teachers over a three year period to develop, refine, and evaluate a set of teaching and learning principles. This research involved video capture and analysis of classroom sequences in key science conceptual areas identified in the literature as involving particular challenges. The principles reflect a view of quality learning as induction into the epistemic practices of the science community, with student construction of scientific representations understood as a crucial strategy for acquiring an understanding of the literacies of science as well as their underpinning epistemologies and purposes.

The principles are described below, together with an illustrative case description of a teaching sequence.

1. *Teaching sequences are based on sequences of representational challenges that involve students constructing representations to actively explore and make claims about phenomena.*
   a. *Teachers clarify the representational resources underpinning key concepts:* Teachers need to clearly identify big ideas, key concepts, and their representations at the planning stage of a topic in order to guide refinement of representational work.
   b. *A representational need is established:* Students are supported, through exploration, to identify the problematic nature of phenomena and the need for explanatory representation, before the introduction of canonical forms.
   c. *Students are supported to coordinate representations:* Students are challenged and supported to coordinate representations across modes to develop explanations and solve problems.
   d. *There is a process of alignment of student constructed and canonical representations:* There is interplay between teacher-introduced and student-constructed representations where students are challenged and supported to refine, extend and coordinate their understandings.
2. *Representations are explicitly discussed:* The teacher plays multiple roles, scaffolding the discussion to critique and support student representation construction in a shared classroom process.
   a. *The selective purpose of any representation:* Students need to understand that multiple representations are needed to work with aspects of a concept.
   b. *Group agreement on generative representations:* Students are guided to critique constructed representations, aiming to achieve group resolution.
   c. *Form and function:* There is explicit focus on representational function and form, with timely clarification of parts and their purposes.
   d. *The adequacy of representations:* Students and teachers engage in a process of ongoing assessment of features of representations including coherence, clarity, and persuasiveness.

3. *Meaningful learning involves representational/perceptual mapping:* Students experience strong perceptual/experiential contexts, encouraging constant two-way mapping/reasoning between observable features of objects, potential inferences, and representations.
4. *Formative and summative assessment is ongoing:* Students and teachers focus on the adequacy and coordination of representations.

These principles involve a learning process for teachers as well as students. The clarification of the relation between concepts and representational resources, and the epistemological shift entailed in moving from a view of science knowledge as consisting of resolved, declarative concepts to one in which knowledge is seen as contingent and expressed through representational use, involve significant challenges.

To illustrate the approach we will draw on a previously reported teaching and learning sequence (Hubber et al., 2010) that focuses on force and motion, involving students in Year 8 (13-year-olds).

Introducing Representations of Force

The representational focus places stringent demands on clarifying what knowledge is to be pursued, and what will count as evidence of understanding. The planning process began with the researchers and teachers identifying the big ideas or key concepts associated with force. Students' alternative conceptions reported in the literature were discussed, and became key resources for guiding planning decisions.

An examination of the chapter on "forces" in the student textbook, traditionally used to structure this unit, showed a "run through" of many different types of force, represented by arrows superimposed on complex and often dramatic photographs of force phenomena. The force arrow convention, not discussed as such in the text, was felt to be central to the representational conventions associated with problem-solving in this area, so the initial lessons in the sequence focused on exploring representations of force, leading to the scientific conventions. The idea that a force arrow is a representation convention rather than a resolved and idealized reality was initially challenging for teachers, who needed support to think their way through this approach. This epistemological shift became important, however, in guiding the exploratory and open discussions that occurred throughout the sequence.

Lyn's sequence was broadly representative of the approach of the three teachers involved in this particular unit, who met regularly to share ideas and experiences and plan. The sequence consisted of a series of challenges in which students constructed representations to clarify force and motion processes, develop explanations, or solve problems. These were often reported on in the public space of the classroom, providing an opportunity for Lyn to question and negotiate the adequacy of the representations and move students toward an appreciation of canonical forms. Lyn began the sequence by developing in students an understanding of the term "force", assisting them to construct meaning for force through their everyday language, and gathering these through the intermediate vocabulary of *push* or *pull*.

A noticeable feature of the teachers' and students' communication during this unit were the gestures that became an important part of describing and validating what was being represented in words or diagrams. Gestures were used to indicate pushes or pulls or lifting forces, to mime the size of forces, and to indicate direction and points of application of forces. Following Roth (2000), we see gesture as a natural form of pre-linguistic and re-representational meaning in the public space.

Lyn then explored with the students various ways in which an everyday action or series of actions involving forces could be represented in a two-dimensional form on paper. The students were given the one minute task of changing the shape of a handful-sized lump of plasticine, and following this task, they were to represent in paper form their actions. The representations constructed by the students, some of which are shown in Figure 29.1, were discussed and evaluated within a whole-class discussion. One representation, posted on the whiteboard, which had a sequenced series of figures with annotations (Figure 29.2, Image A), was unanimously accepted as providing clarity of explanation of the actions.

For the next stage of the sequence Lyn introduced diagrams using the scientific convention of representing forces as arrows. She discussed with the students the benefits in adding arrows, to represent pushes and pulls, to John's drawings to enhance the explanations (Figure 29.2, Image B). The students were then given the task of re-representing their explanations of changing the shape of the plasticine in pictorial form using arrows. Figure 29.3 shows two students' responses.

The completion of this task produced different meanings of the use of arrows, leading to a teacher-guided discussion which included distinguishing between the arrow representation as a force or as a direction of motion, and distinguishing between different types of arrows, such as curved or straight, thick or thin, many or few.

This provided the opportunity for Lyn to introduce the scientific convention of representing forces as straight arrows, with the base of the arrow at the application point of the force. The students were then encouraged to apply this convention to various everyday situations. For example, students were each given an empty soft-drink bottle and asked to represent the forces needed to twist off the bottle cap, and asked to use the arrow convention to represent a gentle and a rough stretch (Figure 29.4).

This introductory sequence is illustrative of a number of the representation construction principles, particularly how activity sequences are built that involve students constructing rather than practising and interpreting representations. The representation construction task is built on a need to communicate a sequence of shaping forces using verbal and visual and gestural modes, and leads to the canonical arrow form through a process of explicit discussion of representational form and function (Is it clear? Could we

Student 1   Student 2

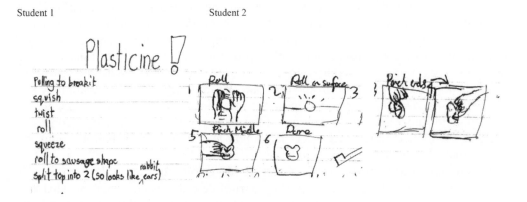

Figure 29.1 Student representations of manipulating plasticine

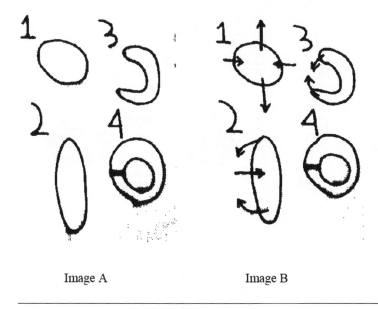

Image A   Image B

Figure 29.2 Reproduction of video images of John's representations

Student 1   Student 2

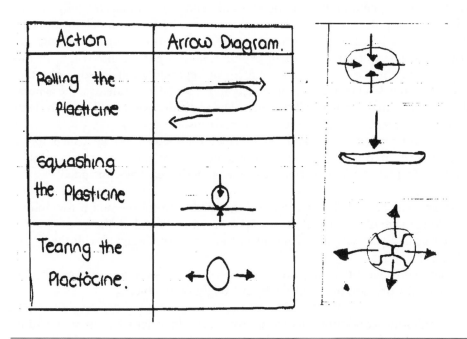

Figure 29.3 Students' use of arrows

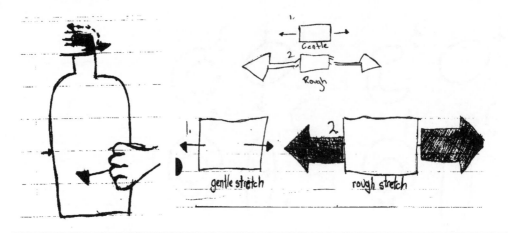

Figure 29.4 Student exploration of the arrow representation of force

reproduce the sequence?), and of the adequacy of student representations. This process of public negotiation in which students agree on effective representations of the shaping process leads to an alignment of student and canonical representations. The teacher, at particular points, introduced arrow notations in response to a felt representational need.

The approach could be seen as a particular form of guided inquiry in which teachers introduce tasks that open up representational needs, and intervene strategically to scaffold students' development of representational resources. It also has much in common with other conceptual change approaches, including exploration of prior learning, and the development of explanation through exploration and guided discussion, In this particular version, however, there is a close focus on representational resources rather than directly on high-level concepts, and there is ample scope for students to be generative and creative within the structured sequence. The end point is not fixed, with students free to produce different versions of the canonical forms.

Concepts about gravity, weight and mass formed the focus of the next stage in the teaching sequence, preceded by probing of students' prior ideas. Several modes of representations formed the structure of the challenge activities. These included:

- role-plays with large balls representing the earth and moon, and a toy animal simulating the gravitational effects on a person on earth and on the moon
- comparing everyday language conventions for the term "weight" with the term's scientific meaning
- a student-constructed spring force measurer and construction of a graph that connects the extension of the spring to the weight of an object.

Unlike a traditional conceptual change approach, in which activities are designed to directly challenge "alternative conceptions" and establish a scientific perspective through a rational evaluative process, this approach treats understanding as the capacity to utilize the representational conventions of science in thinking and communicating about phenomena, and hence focuses on building up students' representational resources, and their understanding of the role of representation in learning and knowing.

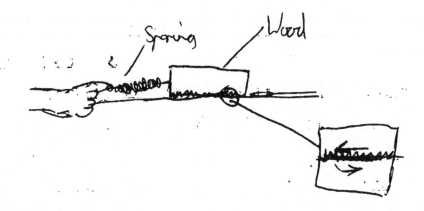

Figure 29.5 Representation of friction

The next stage of the teaching sequence focused on frictional effects. Students were asked to imagine, on a magnified scale, the surface of an object as it slides along a flat surface (Figure 29.5). Students used multiple representational modes to report on the design and conduct of an investigation into factors that affect friction on everyday objects, such as sports shoes.

Friction is thus understood through the coordination of modes, including arrow representations, detailed microscopic mechanisms, and gestures, aligned with and explanatory of tactile perceptual experiences. Each of these provides a selective, partial view of the phenomenon of friction.

The challenge "can you draw it for me", or "can you represent that" became increasingly common for teachers in this study, and accepted and responded to by students.

A bridging analogy (Clement, 1993) was used by Lyn to introduce the idea of contact forces. Figure 29.6 shows two students' interpretation of that discussion. In classical conceptual change theory, these bridging analogies are seen as props that help span the gap between naïve and scientific conceptions. From a representation construction perspective they are representational resources that are made available to students, which help them to coordinate meaning across different aspects of the phenomenon.

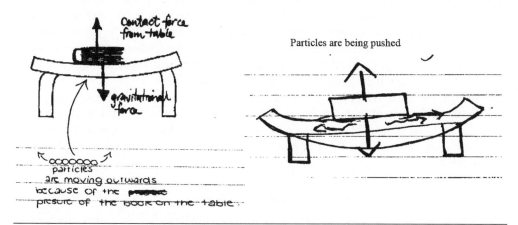

Figure 29.6 Student representation of contact forces

Understanding of contact forces involves the flexible coordination of macroscopic and microscopic representations (see Gilbert, 2005 on this point) to create a coherent explanatory narrative.

Quality of Learning Deriving from this Approach

In this research we collected substantial informal evidence of quality learning. The teachers noted that their students engaged more in class, discussed at a higher level, and performed better in their workbooks (Hubber et al., 2010). Examination of these workbooks demonstrated high levels of conceptual thinking, and pretest and post-test results were uniformly encouraging. Analysis of astronomy test results showed stronger outcomes than in previous studies using comparable methods (Hubber, 2010). A significant outcome of the explicit discussion and evaluation of representations was a sharper understanding, for teachers as well as students, of the role of representations/models in knowledge building in science. These findings raise the question: What are the key features of this representation construction approach that lead to quality learning? We can find some leads to this in the research literature.

Productive Constraint in Representational Construction

Constructing a representation is constrained productively by its purpose, context, and the various physical and conventional resources available for any particular type of representation. For instance, when making a drawing of a process, students are constrained by the physical space available, the conventions they can deploy and their form/function limitations, the need to achieve specificity of detail, and the requirement of unambiguous communication. All these constraints have the potential to encourage students to engage with functional concerns with conventions to serve succinctness and adequacy in explanatory accounts. The representation-maker is compelled to be specific in selection of details, to engage with issues of emphasis, layout, adequacy, communicability to self, and fitness for purpose in ways that interpreting existing texts does not foreground. Thus, the constraints offered by particular representational modes and tasks enable reasoning and learning precisely because of the specific ways they channel attention, and force choices by the person or group constructing the representation. For example, when making a video explanation of a scientific process, students are productively constrained by the need to synchronize sound, text and image to make their representational case coherent to themselves and others. Students also need to understand the partial nature of representations, where each representation serves to focus attention on a specific aspect of a problem, and that generating an explanatory account involves coordinating various representations, each bringing a complementary perspective.

Drawing on Gibson's (1979, p. 5) view of "affordances" as productive constraints within the environment that support an individual's intentions, we argue that particular material and symbolic tools offer specific affordances as students construct and refine representations to make and clarify claims about science topics or processes (Prain & Tytler, 2012).

Epistemological Dimensions of Productive Constraint

There is growing acceptance that the representational tools of science are crucial resources for speculating, reasoning, contesting explanations, theory-building, and communicating to self and others. For Nersessian (2008, pp. 77–78), model-based reasoning by scientists is explicitly enabled through the productive constraints that operate in the way knowledge is represented, including spatial, temporal, topological, causal, categorical, logical, and mathematical constraints on this representation. These constraints also enable a diverse range of reasoning processes, including making abstractions (limiting the case, making generalizations), using simulations, evaluating particular cases (identifying the extent of fit between representation and purpose, and between representation and features of the phenomena, the explanatory power of a new case), and judging the coherence and adequacy of a claim or claims.

This construction and justificatory work can serve a very wide range of cognitive purposes and reasoning functions. Cox (1999) noted that representations can be used as tools for many different forms of reasoning, such as initial, speculative thinking, as in constructing a diagram or model to imagine how a process might work, or to find a possible explanation, or see if a verbal explanation makes sense when re-represented in 2D or 3D. They can also be used to record precise observations, to identify the distribution of types, to show a sequence or process in time, to predict outcomes, sort information, and to work out reasons for various effects. Ford and Forman (2006) argued that reasoning in science needs to have a purpose and that active generation and evaluation of representations in pursuit of investigations captures the nature of science knowledge building practices in ways that formal reasoning schema do not. When students focus on the purposes, adequacy, claims, and applications of representations to particular contexts, they are engaging in crucial aspects of learning or coming to know in science, where representational work functions as a tool for knowing and making claims in this field. Also, as noted by Cazden (1981), following Vygotsky (1978), students' learning capacities are often in advance of their demonstrated developmental level, and students therefore benefit from opportunities to perform representational tasks before they have achieved full competence in these tasks.

AN ILLUSTRATIVE CASE OF REPRESENTATION AFFORDANCE TO SUPPORT REASONING

The description below summarizes the events in one lesson of a sequence of seven lessons on evaporation, each lesson of which posed a problem for students to explore and represent, based on molecular ideas. Prior to this lesson students had been challenged to demonstrate a variety of places in the school where water is found and to represent water in visible and invisible forms. Students in that lesson speculated on the idea of molecules of water in the air, and the class was challenged to suggest investigations to "prove" that this might be true. In the lesson described, the molecular representation is introduced and refined. The description in Table 29.1 is structured to show the different *representations* that are introduced in key teacher moves, and sample student responses.

In brief, the lesson begins with a video presentation of puddle evaporation, and the teacher question "what is actually going on?" (Move 1) is used to introduce the notion of molecules through a role play. The teachers (Malcolm and Lauren are co-teaching a composite Grade 5/6 class of 50 children) then take the activities through a sequence of representational moves and challenges to open up, negotiate, and come to some agreement concerning the different molecular representations of the states of matter and the

Table 29.1 Lesson 3 sequence illustrating the role of multimodal representations

Representation	Teacher and student reasoning moves
1. Video of puddle evaporating	The video voiceover refers to heat energy turning water into water vapour. Malcolm asks: "What is actually going on?"
2. Role play	Malcolm: "I want you to imagine you are water molecules, in the solid state, I want you to move to show me what you would look like".
	Students discuss whether they should move.
	5A: Hold my hand.
	5T: Why? Because we need some sort of shape and also move.
	6M: No, each one sort of moves – *[pushes the other student and moves to and fro]*
3. Malcolm jiggles to simulate vibration	Malcolm confirms that molecules move and jiggles his body to simulate vibration.
4. Use of role-play to have students simulate solid, liquid, gas	Malcolm leads question–response discussion where he establishes the greater movement in liquids (students model a liquid compared to solid) and increased spacing for gas (students scatter round the hall and continue to vibrate).
5. Drawing challenge: show solids, liquids, gases	Malcolm asks them to think about the difference between water molecules in solid, liquid and gas phases: "You have bodily moved, very well . . . how would you indicate that in a diagram?" Figure 29.7 shows a typical drawing.
6. Malcolm uses beads now to model a focus on individual molecules responding to an energy source – vibrates them – some spill	Malcolm: Come back again to that gas molecule . . . when we had that heat source, that energy coming in, is this what happens? A student comes to the container, picks up a bead and moves his hand in a haphazard motion above the head. The teacher challenges this by demonstrating dispersal by shaking beads out – models randomness of distribution. Lauren: Which molecules are the first ones to go? Students: Top ones . . . Ones that had started moving faster . . . More heated ones . . . Ones that get more energy.
7. Bead demonstration to focus on individual molecules	Malcolm: Okay, let us give these molecules, beads, a human form [picks up a bead and points to it]. Here is George, he is here vibrating in water as a solid, then there is more energy he moves more in a liquid state, and then here is Molly . . .
8. Drawing challenge: Malcolm models storied drawing on board	Malcolm: Tell me a story about one water molecule, about what happens to it. Let's do it in four frames. Remember, label, say why is he here, what does he actually need? [Students work on their diagram narrative]

evaporative process. The lesson ends with a review of the key features of the molecular model, expressed verbally.

The sequence illustrates the ways in which representations are critical to learning and reasoning and knowing in science. The public and individual coordination of representations in a variety of modes, around the molecular model, is very apparent as the teacher

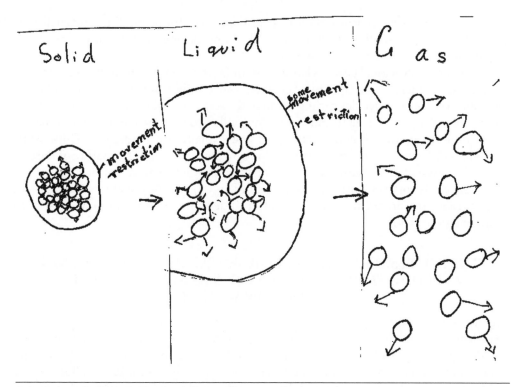

Figure 29.7 Student drawing of molecules in the solid, liquid, and gas states

introduces each in turn and challenges students to extend and explore these in developing a molecular explanation of changes to matter in a range of contexts. The centrality of semiotic resources is clearly displayed in students' reasoning. The pedagogy is built around a process of representational weaving as students are challenged to transform representations across modes, in constructing an increasingly complete picture of the molecular model.

Critically from our perspective, we can identify productive constraint as a characteristic of each representational resource – each representation constrains what can be imagined about the process of evaporation. For instance, the role-play (moves 2–4) places constraints on molecular size and number, and focuses attention on spacing and movement. In so doing it opens up possibilities for exploration of the affordances of the representation, which in this case were taken up by the students and teacher (moves 2 and 3). In this sequence the group of students were confronted with the question of how they linked and whether they should remain still or move. Their decision to move could be seen as a case of embodied, speculative reasoning. In this case as with all these representational challenges, students are driven by the role play to discern and integrate different features of the representation. This, in Schwartz and Bransford's (1998) terms, amounts to the discernment of features of the representational problem space – how might we imagine molecules behaving? In Cazden's (1981) terms, the students are being required to perform before they are competent. The drawings (move 5) provided a strong visual sense of the difference in spacing for the three states, and forced consideration of molecular size across the three phases. This, with the students' drawings in move 8, requires them to make choices and coordinate and discern the possibilities and challenges posed by the representation (needing to think about spacing, number, size, speed, time sequencing, and how to represent these).

The focus on individual beads (George and Molly, move 7) and the narrative story line (8) was used to focus on the individual energetics governing evaporation at the molecular level, and a sense of molecules cycling through the states of water. Move 7 shifts the focus from molecular assemblage to individual molecules, forcing new representational co-ordination requirements and opening up the explanatory landscape. Thus, while students had latitude in constructing their drawings and role plays, the nature of the task and the representation funneled attention in a productive way. We have discussed elsewhere (Ainsworth et al., 2011) the particular arguments for visual representation as a resource for reasoning, and the variation in student drawings illustrating considered representational choices.

THE EPISTEMIC CASE FOR REPRESENTATION CONSTRUCTION AS PRODUCTIVE CONSTRAINT IN SCIENCE KNOWLEDGE BUILDING PRACTICES

We also claim that the principles guiding our classroom practice are central to the knowledge-building processes of science itself, thus providing a legitimate induction into this domain. The role of representation, including visualization, is understood as central to current knowledge production practices (Gooding, 2004; Latour, 1999). Elkins (2011, p. 149) notes that much research in science is concerned with generating and analyzing images, with fields such as biochemistry and astronomy being "image obsessed." A con-siderable body of research also confirms the central role of representational manipulation in generating, integrating and justifying ideas in historical scientific discoveries, and thus in contributing to this knowledge production. Gooding's (2004, p. 15) account of Faraday's work on conceptualizing the interaction of electricity, magnetism, and motion highlights the central role of representational refinement and improvisation in develop-ing "plausible explanations or realisations of the observed patterns." Faraday's develop-ment and modification of representations were critical to clarifying and instantiating his theoretical understandings. Latour (1999) argues that making sense of science involves understanding the process by which data are transformed into theory through a series of representational "passes," each of which transforms data in a chain linking ideas with evidence, through to publication. Nersessian (2008, p. 69), in examining cases of inno-vation in science using studies of Faraday and Maxwell and more recent work, argued that model-based reasoning is critically important to the generation of new theory and that the productive interaction of models is the key to this process.

There is also a growing agreement that classroom science should be organized to enact these processes to provide authentic induction into science learning (Duschl & Grandy, 2008). A long tradition in science education has sought to integrate the processes and products of science into a coherent set of science education practices. However, at various times a process or product focus has been in the ascendancy, largely treated separately, and conceptualized as distinct. Thus "working scientifically" strands address measure-ment in science, the nature of investigable questions, and such issues as appropriate design built on levels of sophistication of variables control. The argumentation perspec-tive (Osborne, 2010) looks at the way evidence is used to select between alternative positions and how knowledge claims are justified with evidential backings that can withstand alternative positions. These perspectives have tended to explore the crucial justificatory aspects of science knowledge building, the public process by which scientists claim their work as verified against possible alternative findings. While students need to understand this process of public challenge and justification and defense as the way scientific knowledge is established within the community, these processes do not deal with the complex ways in which knowledge is generated in the first place. There is also a need for learning in science to focus on the processes by which knowledge is built.

To capture the scientific generation of knowledge in classrooms, we argue there is a need to foreground representational generation, coordination and transformation rather than mainly focus on formal aspects of "scientific method" and argumentation. Duschl and Grandy (2008) argued that attempts to define a general inductive rule for specifying the scientific method have been a failure and that we must see scientific methods as contextual, local, and contingent. They claim that there have been three phases to understanding the nature of science: (1) logical positivism (the received view) that underpins traditional versions of scientific method, (2) paradigm shifts/conceptual change views that admit social processes, and (3) model-based science with acknowledgment of the centrality of language, representation, and communication. We view student representational construction as a way to enact new pedagogies appropriate to these new understandings of the relationships between process, product and language in learning science.

PERSPECTIVES ON CONCEPTUAL CHANGE IMPLIED BY THIS APPROACH

This representation construction approach to teaching and learning science offers a promising, coherent pedagogical approach to student conceptual learning/conceptual change. Pedagogically, it sits within the broad spectrum of modeling approaches to conceptual change, but with a major focus on representation construction rather than interpretation. The approach has much in common particularly with the classroom work of Lehrer and Schauble (2006a, 2006b) and Clement and Rea-Ramirez (2008), which also feature representational challenge and negotiation.

In practice, we have found that teachers' initial responses to the approach are very positive, since it aligns well with a view of student activity and engagement as a key to learning. At a deeper level, however, the approach implies, and inspires in teachers, a shift in perspective on the task of learning science, and the nature of what is learnt.

Theoretical developments in the social constructivist tradition (e.g., Driver, Asoko, Leach, Scott, & Mortimer, 1994; Mortimer & Scott, 2003) match classroom processes aimed at the development of shared understandings, with a conceptual change perspective on outcomes based in traditional cognitive versions of knowing. While our own work can be seen in this tradition, it raises important questions about learning and knowing in science. The first question concerns the nature of reasoning that students need to engage in to learn science. We have argued that recent work in cognitive science places much more importance on informal modes of reasoning, in contrast to the formal logic that tends to be emphasized in traditional conceptual change accounts of science learning, and expectations that rational appraisal of inadequate conceptions can drive the learning process.

The second question concerns the nature of concepts as drivers of learning and knowing in science. From a sociocultural, pragmatist semiotic perspective, learning in science is seen as a process of enculturation into the discursive practices of the scientific community. In this sense, the focus of learning is primarily on the particular representational practices, and representations, that are core to developing explanations in any conceptual area. The task then becomes one of building students' representational resources with respect to engaging with these practices. From this perspective, conceptual understanding involves being able to work with and coordinate representations to develop explanations and solve problems. This contrasts with traditional verbal definitions of concepts that dominate textbooks and curriculum outcome statements. The question therefore concerns the nature of a "concept." In the conceptual change literature, this question is far from resolved (Taber, 2011; Vosniadou, 2008b).

A pragmatist perspective considers the meaning of terms to be instantiated in cultural practices, and argues they should not be idealized beyond these practices. In this spirit, we contend that it is fruitful to think of concepts, which are core entities within the language practices of experts discussing learning and knowing in science, as privileged linguistic markers through which conversations in the domain can productively proceed. Thus, while understanding sound waves implies a capability to select and coordinate a range of verbal, mathematical and visual representations, the conceptual term is useful for someone who has achieved such a capability, to converse with others with similar capabilities ("understanding") without the need for further explication (until questions might be raised about instances, in which case the representational system will be called into play to clarify).

Privileging of "concepts" performs a very valuable function in enabling flexible movement around the conceptual space in an area, and acting as a marker in high-level discursive practices. Concepts are used as organizing entities to shape learning sequences. The danger is that if we ascribe to a concept an idealized, resolved mental existence (rather than recognize it as standing for a range of representational practices), we run the danger of misrepresenting the learning task. To "achieve" a concept is a question of the degree of mastery of a range of relevant representational practices. We argue that the learning issues identified so thoroughly in the conceptual change literature are fundamentally representational issues, and the learning task involved in achieving the required shifts needs to be conceived of in terms of building students' requisite representational resources.

Thus, to the question of "what is a concept?" we would respond, referring to Wittgenstein (1972), that it should be viewed as a language form used by experts for effective communication, referring to a range of discursive (representational) practices that may include formal category lists, verbal strings, arrays of representations including metaphors and analogies and the ways these are selected and coordinated to solve problems, as well as personal aspects such as historical narratives and analogies. From this perspective, concepts have both public and personal aspects. They are not resolved entities despite the tight linguistic forms often used to define them.

The other aspect of this work that provides a significant way forward for science classroom practice is the fresh way it interprets and aligns with the epistemic practices of science. The approach, and the theoretical perspective underpinning it, aligns with significant contemporary research directions on science epistemic practices that emphasize the contextual and cultural nature of knowledge production (Duschl & Grandy,

2008; Nersessian, 2008), and the key role of representational practices in generating and justifying theory (Latour, 1999; Pickering, 1995). Compared to more idealized versions of the nature of science (NOS) which focus on relations between theory and evidence viewed through a Kuhnian lens of socially determined paradigm shifts (Kuhn, 1970), this pragmatist semiotic perspective provides a more grounded education for students in the way it models the chains of representational transformation that characterize theory-building from evidence in science, and discussions about the adequacy and the role of models to represent natural phenomena. Thus, there is a natural alignment here between the processes and the conceptual products of science, and classroom practices and practices in science.

REFERENCES

Ainsworth, S. (2006). DEFT: A conceptual framework for learning with multiple representations. *Learning and Instruction, 16*(3), 183–198.

Ainsworth, S. (2008). The educational value of multiple representations when learning complex scientific concepts. In J. K. Gilbert, M. Reiner, & M. Nakhlel (Eds.), *Visualization: Framework and practice in science education* (pp. 191–208). New York, NY: Springer.

Ainsworth, S., Prain, V., & Tytler, R. (2011). Drawing to learn in science. *Science, 333,* 1096–1097.

Barsalou, L. (2008). Grounded cognition. *Annual Review of Psychology, 59,* 617–645.

Bransford, J., & Schwartz, D. (1999). Rethinking transfer: A simple proposal with multiple implications. *Review of Research in Education, 24,* 61–100.

Cazden, C. (1981). Performance before competence: Assistance to child discourse in the zone of proximal development. *Quarterly Newsletter of the Laboratory of Comparative Human Cognition, 3,* 5–8.

Clement, J. (1993). Using bridging analogies and anchoring intuitions to deal with students' preconceptions in physics. *Journal of Research in Science Teaching, 30*(10), 1241–1257.

Clement, J. (2000). Model based learning as key research area for science education. *International Journal of Science Education, 22*(9), 1041–1053.

Clement, J., & Rea-Ramirez, M.A. (2008). *Model based learning and instruction in science.* Secaucus, NJ: Springer.

Cole, M., & Wertsch, J. V. (1996). Beyond the individual–social antinomy in discussions of Piaget and Vygotsky. *Human Development, 39,* 250–256.

Cosgrove, M., & Osborne, R. (1985). Lesson frameworks for changing children's ideas. In R. Osborne & P. Freyberg (Eds.), *Learning in science: The implications of children's science* (pp. 101–111). Auckland, New Zealand: Heinemann.

Cox, R. (1999). Representation construction, externalized cognition and individual differences. *Learning and Instruction, 9,* 343–363.

Dewey, J. (1996). Essays. In L. Hickman (Ed.), *Collected work of John Dewey, 1882–1953: The electronic edition.* Charlottesville, VA: InteLex Corporation.

diSessa, A. (2004). Metarepresentation: Native competence and targets for instruction. *Cognition and Instruction, 22*(3), 293–331.

diSessa, A. (2008). A bird's eye view of the "pieces" vs "coherence" controversy (from the "pieces" side of the fence). In S. Vosniadou (Ed.), *Handbook of research on conceptual change* (pp. 35–60). New York, NY: Routledge.

Driver, R., & Oldham, V. (1986). A constructivist approach to curriculum development in science. *Studies in Science Education, 13,* 105–122.

Driver, R., Asoko, H., Leach, J., Scott, P., & Mortimer, E. (1994). Constructing scientific knowledge in the classroom. *Educational Researcher, 23*(7), 5–12.

Duit, R. (2009). *Bibliography – Students' and teachers' conceptions and science education.* Kiel, Germany: IPN.

Duschl, R., & Grandy, R. (2008). Reconsidering the character and role of inquiry in school science: Framing the debates. In R. Duschl & R. Grandy (Eds.), *Teaching scientific inquiry: Recommendations for research and implementation* (pp. 1–37). Rotterdam, The Netherlands: Sense Publishers.

Elkins, J. (2011). Visual practices across the university: A report. In O. Grau (Ed.), *Imagery in the 21st century* (pp. 149–174). Cambridge, MA: MIT Press.

Ford, M., & Forman, E.A. (2006). Refining disciplinary learning in classroom contexts. *Review of Research in Education, 30,* 1–33.

Gerard, L., Varma, K., Corliss, S., & Linn. M. (2011). *Review of Educational Research, 81*(3), 408–448.

Gibson, J. (1979) *The ecological approach to visual perception.* Boston, MA: Houghton Mifflin.

Gilbert, J. (Ed.). (2005). *Visualization in science education.* New York, NY: Springer.

Gilbert, J., & Boulter, C. (2000). *Developing models in science education.* Dordrecht, The Netherlands: Kluwer Academic Publishers.

Gooding, D. (2004). Visualization, inference and explanation in the sciences. In G. Malcolm (Ed.), *Studies in multidisciplinarity* (Vol. 2, pp. 1–25). Amsterdam, The Netherlands: Elsevier.

Greeno, J. (2009). A framework bite on contextualizing, framing, and positioning: A companion to Son and Goldstone. *Cognition and Instruction, 27*(3), 269–275.

Greeno, J. G., & Hall, R. P. (1997). Practicing representation: Learning with and about representational forms. *Phi Delta Kappan, 78*, 361–367.

Harrison, A., & Treagust, D. F. (2000). Learning about atoms, molecules, and chemical bonds: A case study of multiple-model use in Grade 11 chemistry. *Science Education, 84*(3), 352–381.

Hubber, P. (2010). Year 8 students' understanding of astronomy as a representational issue: Insights from a classroom video study. In D. Raine, L. Rogers, & C Hurkett (Eds.), *Physics community and cooperation: Selected contributions from the GIREP-EPEC & PHEC 2009 International Conference* (pp. 45–64). Leicester, UK: Lulu, the Centre for Interdisciplinary Science, University of Leicester.

Hubber, P, Tytler, R., & Haslam, F. (2010). Teaching and learning about force with a representational focus: Pedagogy and teacher change. *Research in Science Education, 40*(1), 5–28.

Jakobson, B., & Wickman, P.-O. (2008). The roles of aesthetic experience in elementary school science. *Research in Science Education, 38*, 45–65.

Jewitt, C. (2008). Multimodality and literacy in school classrooms. *Review of Research in Education, 32*, 241–267.

Justi, R., & Gilbert, J. K. (2003). Models and modelling in chemical education. In J. K. Gilbert, O. de Jong, R. Justi, D. F. Treagust, & J. H. van Driel (Eds.), *Chemical education: Towards research-based practice* (pp. 47–68). Dordrecht, The Netherlands: Kluwer.

Klein, U. (2001). Introduction. In U. Klein (Ed.), *Tools and modes of representation in the laboratory sciences.* Boston, MA: Kluwer Academic Publishers.

Klein, P. (2006). The challenges of scientific literacy: From the viewpoint of second-generation cognitive science. *International Journal of Science Education, 28*(2–3), 143–178.

Kozma, R., Chin, E., Russell, J., & Marx, N. (2000). The roles of representations and tools in the chemistry laboratory and their implications for chemistry learning. *Journal of the Learning Sciences, 9*(3), 105–144.

Kozma, R., & Russell, J. (1997). Multimedia and understanding: Expert and novice responses to different representations of chemical phenomena. *Journal of Research In Science Teaching, 34*(9), 949–968.

Kozma, R., & Russell, J. (2005). Students becoming chemists: Developing representational competence. In J. Gilbert (Ed.), *Visualization in Science Education* (pp. 121–145). New York, NY: Springer.

Kuhn, T. S. (1970). *The structure of scientific revolutions* (2nd edn.). Chicago, IL: University of Chicago Press.

Latour, B. (1999). *Pandora's hope: Essays on the reality of science studies.* Cambridge, MA: Harvard University Press.

Lave, J., & Wenger, E. (1991). *Situated learning: Legitimate peripheral participation.* Cambridge, UK: Cambridge University Press.

Lee, C., Jonassen, D., & Teo, T. (2011). The role of model building in problem solving and conceptual change. *Interactive Learning Environments, 19*(3).

Lehrer, R., & Schauble, L. (2006a). Cultivating model-based reasoning in science education. In K. Sawyer (Ed.), *Cambridge handbook of the learning sciences* (pp. 371–388). Cambridge, UK: Cambridge University Press.

Lehrer, R., & Schauble, L. (2006b). Scientific thinking and science literacy. In W. Damon & R. Lerner (Eds.), *Handbook of child psychology* (6th edn., Vol. 4). Hoboken, NJ: Wiley.

Lemke, J. (2004). The literacies of science. In E. W. Saul (Ed.), *Crossing borders in literacy and science instruction: Perspectives on theory and practice* (pp. 33–47). Newark, DE: International Reading Association/National Science Teachers Association.

Mercer, N. (2008). Changing our minds: A commentary on "Conceptual change": a discussion of theoretical, methodological and practical challenges for science education. *Cultural Studies in Science Education, 3*, 351–362.

Moje, E. (2007). Developing socially just subject-matter instruction: A review of the literature on disciplinary literacy learning. *Review of Research in Education, 31*, 1–44.

Mortimer, E., & Scott, P. (2003). *Meaning making in science classrooms.* Milton Keynes, UK: Open University Press.

Nersessian, N. (2008). Model-based reasoning in scientific practice. In R. Duschl & R. Grandy (Eds.), *Teaching scientific inquiry: Recommendations for research and implementation* (pp. 57–79). Rotterdam, The Netherlands: Sense Publishers.

Osborne, J. (2010, April). Arguing to learn in science: The role of collaborative, critical discourse. *Science, 328,* 463–466.

Peirce, C. S. (1931–1958). *Collected papers of Charles Sanders Peirce. 8 Volumes* (Eds. C. Hartshorne, P. Weiss, & A. W Burks, Vols. 1–6; A. W. Burks, Vols. 7–8). Cambridge, MA: Harvard University Press.

Pickering, A. (1995). *The mangle of practice: Time, agency and science.* Chicago, IL: University of Chicago Press.

Posner, G. J., Strike, K. A., Hewson, P. W., & Gertzog, W. A. (1982). Accommodation of a scientific conception: Toward a theory of conceptual change. *Science & Education, 66*(2), 211–227.

Prain, V., & Tytler, R. (2012). Learning through constructing representations in science: A framework of representational construction affordances. *International Journal of Science Education, 34*(17), 2751–2773.

Prain, V., Tytler, R., & Petersen, S (2009). Multiple representation in learning about science. *International Journal of Science Education, 31*(6), 787–808.

Roth, W.-M. (2000). From gesture to scientific language. *Journal of Pragmatics, 32*(11), 1683–1714.

Schwartz, D., & Bransford, J. (1998). A time for telling. *Cognition and Instruction, 16*(4), 475–522.

Sinatra, G. (2005). The "warming trend" in conceptual change research: The legacy of Paul R. Pintrich. *Educational Psychologist, 40*(2), 107–115.

Taber, K. (2011). Review of "International handbook of research on conceptual change". *Science and Education, 20,* 563–576.

Tobin, K. (2008). In search of new lights: Getting the most from competing perspectives. *Cultural Studies of Science Education, 3*(2), 227–230.

Treagust, D., & Duit, R. (2008). Conceptual change: A discussion of theoretical, methodological and practical challenges for science education. *Cultural Studies of Science Education, 3*(2), 297–328.

Tytler, R., Haslam, F., Prain, V., & Hubber, P. (2009). An explicit representational focus for teaching and learning about animals in the environment. *Teaching Science, 55*(4), 21–27.

Tytler, R., Peterson, S., & Prain. V. (2006). Picturing evaporation: Learning science literacy through a particle representation. *Teaching Science, 52*(1), 12–17.

Tytler, R., & Prain, V. (2010). A framework for re-thinking learning in science from recent cognitive science perspectives. *International Journal of Science Education, 32*(15), 2055–2078.

Tytler, R., Prain, V., & Peterson, S. (2007). Representational issues in students learning about evaporation. *Research in Science Education, 37*(3), 313–331.

Vosniadou, S. (1994). Capturing and modeling the process of conceptual change. *Learning and Instruction, 4,* 45–69.

Vosniadou, S. (2008a). Bridging culture with cognition: A commentary on "Culturing conceptions: From first principles". *Cultural Studies of Science Education, 3,* 277–282.

Vosniadou, S. (2008b). Conceptual change research: An introduction. In S. Vosniadou (Ed.), *Handbook of research on conceptual change.* New York, NY: Routledge.

Vygotsky, L. S. (1978). *Mind in society.* Cambridge, MA: Harvard University Press.

Vygotsky, L. (1981a). *Thought and language* (revised and edited by A. Kozulin). Cambridge, MA: MIT Press.

Vygotsky, L. (1981b). The instrumental method in psychology. In J. Wertsch (Ed.), *The concept of activity in Soviet psychology* (pp. 134–143). Armonk, NY: M. E. Sharpe.

Waldrip, B., Prain, V., & Carolan, J. (2010). Using multi-modal representations to improve learning in junior secondary science. *Research in Science Education, 40*(1), 65–80.

Wells, G. (2008). Learning to use scientific concepts. *Cultural Studies of Science Education, 3*(2), 329–350.

White, R. T., & Gunstone, R. F. (1992). *Probing understanding.* London, UK: Falmer.

Wittgenstein, L. (1972). (G. E. M. Anscombe, Trans.). In G. E. M. Anscombe & R. Rhees (Eds.), *Philosophical investigations* (2nd edn.). Oxford, UK: Basil Blackwell.

30

MODEL BUILDING FOR CONCEPTUAL CHANGE

David Jonassen and Matthew A. Easter, University of Missouri

PREMISE: MODELING FOR CONCEPTUAL CHANGE

Conceptual change is most meaningful when it is intentional (Dole & Sinatra, 1998). In order for intentional conceptual change to occur, according to Luque (2003), learners must be aware of a need to change and be able to know what to change; learners must want to change, making change as a personal goal; and learners must be able to self-regulate the process of change; that is, be able to plan, monitor, and evaluate the process (self-regulation prerequisite). The question that pervades much of the work described in the book is, "how do we engage and encourage intentional conceptual change?"

Vosniadou (1992, 1994), like many researchers, believes that conceptual change arises from interaction between experience and current conceptions during problem solving. Nersessian (1999) agrees that conceptual change results most consistently from extended problem solving or some higher-order cognitive activity. However, an unanswered question is what kind of problem solving is necessary for engaging conceptual change. Jonassen (2000) described several dimensions of problem solving (structuredness, complexity, abstractness, and dynamicity). Based largely on a continuum of problems from well structured to ill structured, he also identified several different kinds of problems (algorithms, story (word) problems, rule-using problems, troubleshooting, diagnosis-solution, strategic performance, policy problems, design problems, and dilemmas). What we need to know is: Which kinds of problems best engage conceptual change processes? How complex and dynamic should those problems be? Does conceptual change result more consistently from embedding problems in rich contexts?

The answers to these questions can be found not in empirical evidence, but in principles of conceptual change. Conceptual change requires conceptual engagement (Dole & Sinatra, 1998). Learners tend to interact with information that is comprehensible, coherent, and plausible in light of their existing theories. The degree to which learners interact with new information lies on a continuum from low cognitive engagement to high metacognitive engagement. When learners are not cognitively engaged, they are processing information shallowly. *Conceptual change requires high cognitive engagement.*

In order to restructure what they know, learners must become self-regulated and effort-ful, analyzing and synthesizing new information. At the highest level of engagement, according to Dole and Sinatra (1998), learners think deeply about arguments and counterarguments related to the message, resulting in the strongest likelihood of conceptual change. These are skills that are more consistently required of ill-structured problems rather than well-structured problems (Hong, Jonassen, & McGee, 2003); however, a great deal of empirical research is needed to isolate the problem-solving factors that more readily encourage intentional conceptual change.

The premise of this chapter is that using computer technologies to construct qualitative and quantitative models of phenomena being studied is among the most conceptually engaging tasks that students can undertake in schools, and it has significant potential for engaging and assessing conceptual change as well as supporting different kinds of problems solving. After discussing different roles for models and explicating a rationale for building models to engage conceptual change, we describe how computer formalisms can be used as cognitive tools (aka Mindtools; Jonassen, 1996, 2000, 2006) for representing different kinds of knowledge. We conclude by describing some cognitive and motivational factors that could impact modeling for conceptual change.

WHAT ARE MODELS?

There are numerous kinds of models that can be used to represent phenomena in the world or the mental models that learners construct to represent them. Mathematicians and scientists most often refer to computational models using mathematical formalisms (e.g., calculus, differential equations, Bayesian probabilities); however, these data models are only one kind of model. Harris (1999) describes three kinds of models: data models, theoretical models, and experimental models. Theoretical models are abstract represen-tations of systemic elements or factors, while experimental models are designed to test the theoretical models. Experimental models are more specific than theoretical, including directives for action; specifications of the size of sample populations; definitions of experimental variables and test statistics; and measures for comparing hypotheses and observed values. Their purpose is to predict or specify the kind of data that we are looking for and to specify analytical techniques for linking data to questions. From another perspective, Lehrer and Schauble (2003) describe a continuum of model types including physical models, representational systems (grounded in resemblance between the model and the world), syntactic models (summarizing essential functioning of system), and hypothetical–deductive models (formal abstractions). Whatever they are, models qualita-tively, functionally, or formally resemble the real objects under study (Yu, 2002).

HOW ARE MODELS USED?

Historically, much of the modeling research has focused on mathematization as the primary modeling formalism. Representing phenomena in formulas is the most succinct and exact form of modeling. However, most contemporary researchers argue that qualitative models are just as important as quantitative. Qualitative representation is a missing link in novice problem solving (Chi, Feltovich, & Glaser, 1981; Larkin, 1983). When students try to understand a problem in only one way, especially when that way conveys no conceptual information about the problem, they do not understand the underlying systems they are working in. So, it is necessary to help learners to construct a qualitative as well as a quantitative model of the problem. Qualitative models both constrain and facilitate the construction of quantitative representations (Ploetzner & Spada, 1998).

Modeling is fundamental to human cognition and scientific inquiry. Modeling helps learners to express and externalize their thinking; visualize and test components of their theories; and make materials more interesting. Models function as epistemic resources (Morrison & Morgan, 1999). We must first understand what we can demonstrate in the model before we can ask questions about the real system.

EXTERNAL AND INTERNAL MODELS

Models are conceptual systems consisting of elements, relations, operations, and rules governing interactions that are expressed using external notation systems and that are used to construct, describe, or explain the behavior of other systems (Lesh & Doerr, 2003). The models that are constructed by learners using equations, diagrams, and computer programs represent the models that exist in the minds of learners. That is, there are models in the mind (mental models) and there are models in the world that are constructed by learners. Both of these kinds of models reflect phenomena in the world. The relationship between internal and external models is not well understood, but there is good reason to believe that there is a dynamic and reciprocal relationship between internal mental models and the external models that students construct. The mental models provide the basis for external models. The external models in turn constrain and regulate internal models, providing the means for conceptual change. In this chapter, we argue for the construction of external, syntactic models using different technology-based modeling tools, because each tool imposes a different set of structural or rhetorical constraints (syntaxes) that enable student to tune their internal models.

The ability to form mental models is a basic characteristic of the human cognitive system, and these mental models are essential for conceptual development and conceptual change (Vosniadou, 2002a). When solving problems, learners may construct models and apply those models to solving problems rather than by applying logical rules (Vandierendonck & deVooght, 1996). As soon as problems are presented, learners construct an initial model and integrate new information into the model in order to make the model look and function like the problem. The mental models that learners construct are generally believed to retain the structure of the world that they are representing. Mental models, according to Norman (1983), are the internal representations that humans develop of themselves and the objects they interact with in the world. Mental models are developed inductively as we interact with objects for the purpose of reasoning about causality in physical systems (deKleer & Brown, 1981). These models often result in analogical, incomplete, or even fragmentary representations of how those objects and the system they are in work (Farooq & Dominick, 1988). Johnson-Laird (1983) believes that "human beings understand the world by constructing models of it in their minds" that are structural analogs of real-world or imaginary situations, events, or processes. They embody representations of the spatial and temporal relations and causal structures connecting the events and entities depicted.

Stronger or more radical forms of conceptual change require significant restructuring of mental models. Model building is critical to this kind of conceptual change.

Conceptual change is task-dependent (Schnotz, Vosniadou, & Carretero, 1999). The task that most engages and supports the construction and reorganization of mental models is the use of a variety of tools for constructing physical, visual, logical, or computation models of phenomena. Building representational and interpretive models using technologies provides learners with the opportunities to externalize and restructure their mental models. When students discover conceptual anomalies or inconsistencies in their own conceptual structures by modeling them, they are more likely to revise and restructure them. In order to recognize and resolve perturbations or anomalies, learners must use experimentation or some other high-engagement process such as modeling to compare rival conceptions (Dole & Sinatra, 1998).

MODEL USING VS. MODEL BUILDING

We learn from models by using them and by building them (Morgan, 1999). What we can learn from using models, however, depends on the extent to which we can transfer the things we learn from manipulating the model to our theory of the real world. Learning from building models involves finding out what elements fit together in order to represent the theory or the world or both. Modeling requires making certain choices, and it is in these choices that the learning process lays. "We do not learn much from looking at a model — we learn a lot more from building the model and from manipulating it" (Morrison & Morgan, 1999, pp. 11–12).

Despite the cognitive benefits of building models, technology-based learning environments more often exemplify model using. Models are commonly used as the cognitive engine in software. Most intelligent tutoring systems possess learner models, expert or domain models, and tutoring models. Models also provide the cognitive engine in microworlds, such as Geometric Supposer, SimCalc, and others. In microworlds, the model is implicit in the exploratory options provided by the software, but the model is not explicitly demonstrated. Learners interact with these black-box systems in order to infer the propositions embedded in the model in order to test hypotheses. Research shows that interacting with model-based environments can result in development and change of mental models (Frederiksen & White, 1998; Mellar, Bliss, Boohan, Ogborn, & Tompsett, 1994). Model using has certain cognitive limitations. For example, the model is immutable. Not only do learners have no access to the model, but also they cannot change it in order to change the assumptions of the system being modeled.

The major premise of this chapter is that building models using different qualitative and quantitative formalisms embedded in different classes of modeling software is among the most conceptually engaging classroom activities possible and has the greatest potential for engaging and encouraging conceptual change process (Nersessian, 1999). Building explicit models externalizes or reifies mental models or personal theories, thereby fostering conceptual change. The multiple formalisms afforded by different modeling tools enable learners to construct syntactically different models. Comparing and contrasting those models is an essential process in comprehension. Other essential characteristics of models include the separation of a model and its referent, assessment of the fit of the model to its referent, the conventionalization of the external representations used in the model, and the incorporation of models into disciplinary practice (Lehrer & Schauble, 2003). Perhaps the most important characteristic that Lehrer and Schauble cite is the evaluation of competing alternative models; that is, the comparison of two or more models for their relative fit to the world. Comparing and evaluating models requires understanding that alternative models are possible and that the activity of modeling can be used for testing rival models. That process is at the heart of conceptual change. "Inquiry takes on new meaning when one moves from identifying simple relationships and principles in existing expert models to producing a model of one's own that describes and predicts the behavior of a system" (Windschitl, 2000, pp. 89–90). Interacting with model-based environments certainly can result in conceptual change. However, the models that learners build mediate between personal theories and related objects or phenomena in the world. When discrepancies between the models learners build and scientifically valid understandings occur, learners must revise their models, which reflects concomitant changes on learners' mental models. Therefore, building models is among the most conceptually embedded and engaging tasks that students can undertake, and building models of problems being solved enhances problem solving, which in turn enhances conceptual change. Although building models of all kinds (physical, computational, or virtual) can engage and support conceptual change, this chapter will focus on the use of computer-based modeling tools.

RATIONALES FOR MODELING

Constructing technology-mediated models of phenomena is among the most conceptually engaging tasks that students can undertake. Modeling engages and supports conceptual change and also provides measurable evidence of conceptual change. The conceptual reasons for constructing models to support meaningful learning and mental model construction include the following.

- Model building is a natural cognitive phenomenon. When encountering unknown phenomena, humans naturally begin to construct personal theories about those phenomena that are represented as models.
- Modeling is essentially constructivist – constructing personal representations of experienced phenomena.
- Modeling supports hypothesis testing, conjecturing, inferring, and a host of other important cognitive skills.
- Modeling requires learners to articulate causal relationships, the cognitive basis for most scientific reasoning.
- Modeling is among the most conceptually engaging cognitive activities that can be performed, resulting in conceptual change.
- Modeling results in the construction of cognitive artifacts (externalized mental models).
- When students construct models, they own the knowledge. Student ownership is important to meaning-making and knowledge construction.
- Modeling supports the development of epistemic beliefs. Epistemologically, what motivates our efforts to make sense of the world? According to Wittgenstein (1953), what we know is predicated on the possibility of doubt. We know many things, but we can never be certain that we know them. As already described, comparing and evaluating models requires understanding that alternative models are possible and that the activity of modeling can be used for testing rival models (Lehrer & Schauble, 2003).

Modeling Different Kinds of Knowledge Using Computer-based Modeling Tools

If model building externalizes mental models, then learners should learn to use a variety of tools to model a variety of phenomena in a variety of ways. Each tool provides a different formalism for representing mental models in different ways (Jonassen, 2000). In this section, we briefly describe how different kinds of knowledge can be represented using different modeling tools. Most of these models are what Lehrer and Schauble (2000) refer to as syntactic models. These are formal models, each of which imposes a different syntax on the learner that conveys a relational correspondence between the model and the phenomena it is representing. The purpose of syntactic models is to summarize the essential function of the system being represented.

Semantic Models

The primary use of modeling has been in the math and science domains. Middle-school and high-school students use computer-based modeling tools such as databases or concept mapping tools to construct their models of domain knowledge. Modeling the underlying semantics or structural knowledge (Jonassen, Beissner, & Yacci, 1993) in any domain is necessary but not sufficient for comprehending any domain. More complete comprehension also requires causal and experiential understanding (described later). For example, Figure 30.1 illustrates a semantic model of the molar conversion process in chemistry that was produced using the concept-mapping tool, Inspiration (many other concept-mapping tools exist). That model illustrates all of the important stoichiometric concepts such as mole and atomic mass and the semantic relationships between them (measures/measured by). As students study domain content in a course, concept-mapping tools provide them with a semantic structure for representing their domain knowledge. In a meta-analysis of concept-mapping studies, Horton, McConney, Gallo, and Woods (1993) showed that concept mapping supports knowledge acquisition. Comparing your semantic network with others often results in conceptual change as students see how other models represent and structure the same ideas (Chularut & DeBacker, 2004), a formidable strategy for engaging conceptual change. Therefore, concept mapping is predictive of different forms of higher order thinking. Concept mapping has been significantly related to formal reasoning in chemistry (Schreiber & Abegg, 1991) and in biology (Briscoe & LeMaster, 1991; Mikulecky, 1988). Concept maps help in organizing such knowledge by integrating information into a progressively more complex conceptual framework.

In addition to concept maps, semantic models can also be constructed by students using database management systems and hypermedia construction tools (Jonassen, 2006). Databases are organized by data structures that are defined by fields and records. Those data structures constrain the ways that students interconnect ideas. Hypermedia (hypertext), on the other hand, generally has a more open associative structure that can be defined by students in various ways.

Causal Models

The reason why linking is so important to concept mapping is that linked pairs of concepts define propositions. The most important propositions to conceptual change and to scientific reasoning are causal propositions. Causal reasoning is second only to concept categorization as the most pervasive cognitive process in everyday life, as humans

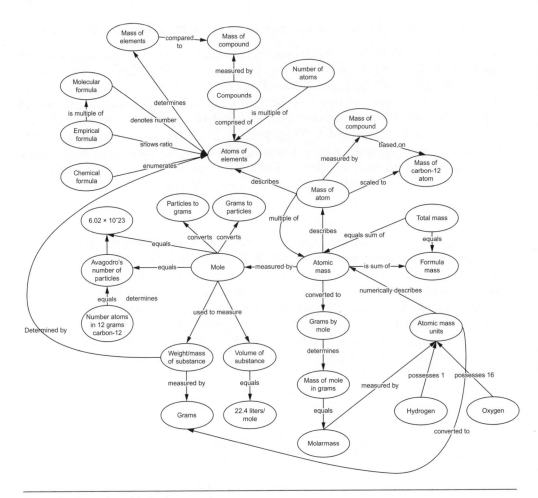

Figure 30.1 Semantic model of molar conversion process

and other animals rely primarily on observable empirical cues to understand and predict causal sequences (Rehder, 2003). Causal reasoning is required for making predictions, drawing implications and inferences, and explaining phenomena. The cognitive process that underlies all thinking is causal reasoning (Carey, 1995; Keil, 1989).

Another impediment to comprehending causal domains is the oversimplification of causal relationships in those domains. Students tend to focus on quantitative and molar-level depictions of causality. However, causal relations are usually more complex than learners understand. They need to be able to articulate covariational attributes of causal relationships, including direction, valency, probability, duration, responsiveness, as well as mechanistic attributes, including process, conjunctions/disjunctions, and necessity/sufficiency (Jonassen & Ionas, 2006).

Learners can use a variety of tools, such as spreadsheets, expert system shells, and systems modeling tools to construct dynamic testable models of phenomena (Jonassen, 2000, 2006). These tools enable learners to represent both qualitative and quantitative representations of dynamic phenomena. Conceptual change in science domains is too frequently impeded by an exclusive use of quantitative representations of problems and the absence of conceptual representations. Qualitative and quantitative representations are complementary. Ploetzner, Fehse, Kneser, and Spada (1999) showed that when solving physics problems, qualitative problem representations are necessary prerequisites to learning quantitative representations. Qualitative representation is a missing link in novice problem solving (Chi et al., 1981; Larkin, 1983). When students try to understand a problem in only one way, especially when that way conveys no conceptual information about the problem, students do not understand the underlying systems they are working in. So, it is necessary to support conceptual understanding in students before solving problems by helping them to construct a qualitative representation of the problem as well as a quantitative one. Qualitative problem representations both constrain and facilitate the construction of quantitative representations (Ploetzner & Spada, 1998).

Building expert systems is a knowledge modeling process that enables experts and knowledge engineers to construct conceptual models (Adams-Webber, 1995). The expert system rule base in Figure 30.2 simulates the process of calculating molar conversions in chemistry. This is a purely qualitative representation of the process that focuses on the reasoning processes entailed.

Causal relationships aggregate into functional systems. That is, rather than focusing on discrete causal relationships, learners must understand how those relationships cohere

---

Context 'This knowledge base is intended to simulate the processes of calculating molar conversions.'

D1: 'You know the mass of one mole of sample.'
D2: 'You need to determine molar (formula) mass.'
D3: 'Divide sample mass by molar mass.'
D4: 'Multiply number of moles by molar mass.'
D5: 'You know atomic mass units.'
D6: 'You know molar mass.'
D7: 'Divide mass of sample by molar mass and multiply by Avogadro's number.'
D8: 'Divide number of particles by Avogadro's number.'
D9: 'Convert number of particles to moles, then convert moles to mass.'
D10: 'Convert mass to moles using molar mass, and then convert moles to molecules using Avogadro's number.'
D11: 'Convert from volume to moles) divide volume by volume/mole), and then convert moles to moles by multiplying by Avogadro's number.'

Q1: 'Do you know the number of molecules?'   A 1 'yes'   2 'no'
Q2: 'Do you know the mass of the sample in grams?'   A 1 'yes'   2 'no'
Q3: 'Do you know the molar mass of the element or compound?' A 1 'yes'   2 'no'
Q4: 'Do you know the number of moles of the sample?' A 1 'yes'   2 'no'
Q5: 'Do you want to know the number of molecules?'   A 1 'yes'   2 'no'
Q6: 'Do you want to know the mass of the sample in grams?' A 1 'yes'   2 'no'
Q7: 'Do you want to know the molar mass of the compound?' A 1 'yes'   2 'no'
Q8: 'Do you want to know the number of moles of the sample?' A 1 'yes' 2 'no'
Q9: 'Do you know atomic mass units?'   A 1 'yes'   2 'no'
Q10: 'Do you know the volume of a gass?'   A 1 'yes'   2 'no'

Rule 1: IF q2a1 AND q8a1 THEN D2
Rule 2: IF (d1 OR q3a1) AND q2a1 AND q8a1 THEN D3
Rule 3: IF q4a1 AND q3a1 AND q6a1 THEN D4
Rule 4: IF q3a1 THEN D1
Rule 5: IF q3a1 THEN D5
Rule 6: IF q9a1 THEN D6
Rule 7: IF qq3a1 AND q2a1 AND q5a1 THEN D7
Rule 8: IF q1a1 AND q8a1 THEN D8
Rule 9: IF q1a1 AND q6a1 THEN D9
Rule 10: IF q2a1 AND q5a1 THEN d10
Rule 11: IF q10a1 AND q1a1 THEN d11

Figure 30.2 Excerpt from expert system rule base on stoichiometry

into systems. For example, while a sneeze may be a key causal agent in catching a cold, the system of viral transmission is much more complex than that. Students' mental models must explicate the casual factors that mediate that relationship. Germs are dispersed through the air by the sneeze, some of which attach to host cells. The virus injects its genetic material into the host cell. That genetic code is copied into the host cell, breaking out of it and invading other cells, all of which sets off complex immunological reactions, including the distribution or mast cells to the site of the infection, the release of histamines causing inflammation of the tissue causing more immune cells to be delivered to fight off the infection. If learners cannot adequately articulate and model these systems of complex causal processes, their understanding is overly simplified. Building models of systems that convey causal relationships supports the construction of internal conceptual frameworks necessary for transferable problem solving.

There are a variety of computer-based tools for modeling systems. Based on systems dynamics, tools such as Stella, PowerSim, and VenSim are sophisticated tools for modeling systems. These tools enable learners to construct systems models of phenomena using a graphic interface. Systems modeling tools enable students to construct models of actual problems. For example, Figure 30.6 illustrates how systems modeling tools, such as Stella, can be used to model actual stoichiometry problems (described semantically in Figure 30.2 and procedurally in Figure 30.3). After constructing the model of a molar conversion process in Figure 30.3, the students were able to run the model in order to test the accuracy of the model. The graph resulting from the test is illustrated in the lower part of Figure 30.3. Students must then interpret the results. If the results are not consistent with predictions, then the student may revise the model. This iterative testing and revising of the model to ensure that it predicts theoretically viable outcomes is one of the most conceptually engaging processes possible. When expected values do not result from the model, learners are faced with a cognitive conflict that they must resolve.

Very little research has directly addressed the effects of systems modeling on conceptual change. In a 2006 study, fifth grade students in Singapore who modeled problems associated with the water cycle using Model-It performed better on a knowledge test that also significantly predicted problem-solving performance (Lee, 2006). Model-It is a systems modeling tool that is similar to but simpler than Stella. It was designed for use by middle-school students. Rather than entering formulae into the model, students use a relationship editor to select the most accurate relationship among variables. Figure 30.4 shows one of the models that students constructed. Students' mental models were induced from the justification portion of the knowledge test. Students who constructed models of the process using Model-It generated fewer nonsensical conceptual models after modeling, more textbook repetition models, and more syntactic models where students attempted to synthesize disparate pieces of information (Lee, 2006). The students who produced syntactic and scientifically viable models were also better problem solvers. This study confirmed the interrelationships among modeling, problem solving, and conceptual change.

Experiential Models

The most meaningful forms of knowledge are based on our experiences. The most common means for representing and conveying those experiences are stories, which are the oldest and most natural form of sense making. Stories are the "means [by] which human beings give meaning to their experience of temporality and personal actions"

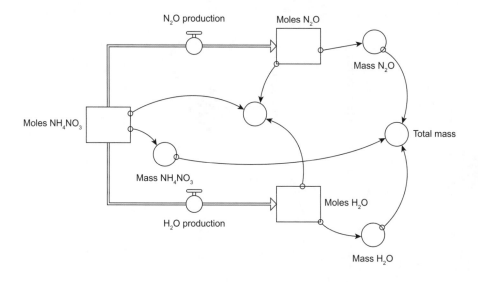

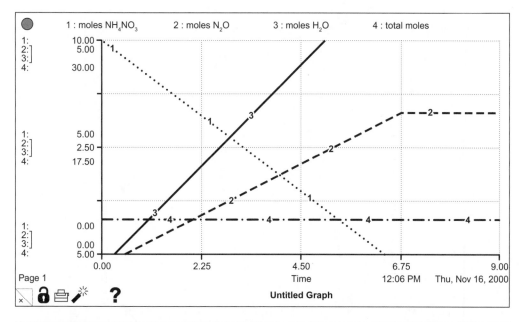

Figure 30.3 Systems model of a molar conversion problem

(Polkinghorne, 1988, p. 11). Stories can function as a substitute for direct experience. Some researchers believe that hearing stories is tantamount to experiencing the phenomenon oneself (Ferguson, Bareiss, Birnbaum, & Osgood, 1991). Therefore, we have experimented extensively with collecting stories about experiences.

The cognitive theory describing how stories are recalled and reused is case-based reasoning (CBR). An encountered problem (the new case) prompts the reasoner to retrieve cases from memory, to reuse the old case (i.e., interpret the new in terms of the old), which suggests a solution (Aamodt & Plaza, 1994). If the suggested solution will not work, then the old and/or new cases are revised. When their effectiveness is confirmed,

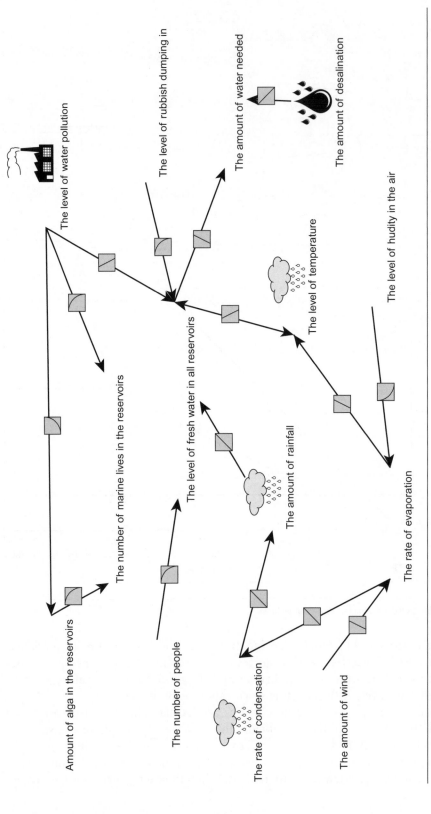

Figure 30.4 Systems model built by fifth grader

then the learned case is retained for later use. Cases or stories are reminded and retrieved by indexing them to previous cases; that is, what does the current situation have in common with previously stored cases?

Students can support their conceptual change by modeling people's experiences; that is, collecting stories about their experiences. The most effective tool for capturing and indexing stories in order to model experiences is the database. Learners collect stories via interviews, surveys, magazines, or news reports. The database in Figure 30.5 recounts one of many stories that were collected by students studying the conflict in Northern Ireland. The database contains stories that have been indexed by topic, theme, context, goal, reasoning, religion, etc. When students analyze stories in order to understand the issues, they better understand the underlying complexity of a phenomenon in terms of the diverse social, cultural, political, and personal perspectives reflected in the stories. Because those stories often contain elements that result in cognitive conflict, conceptual change is often inevitable. Encountering this diversity of beliefs provides anomalous data that entail the need to change one's conceptual models of the world. Having collected stories, learners must decide what the stories teach them, so the stories must be indexed. Indexes are used to retrieve stories when needed and to compare and contrast experiences and their conceptual frameworks. Indexing requires the learners to identify relevant dimensions of the stories, such as context, goals, or lessons learned. Databases facilitate this learning process by allowing students to search or sort on any field to locate similar cases or results.

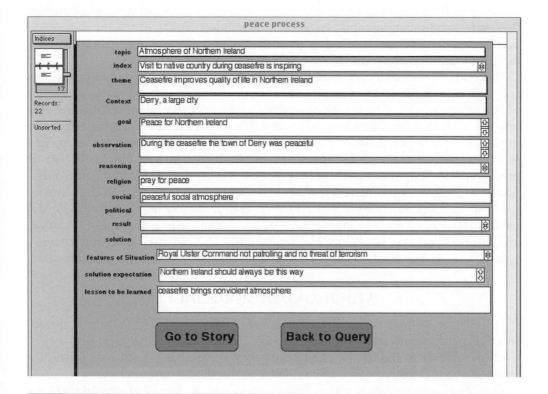

Figure 30.5 Record from database of stories about Northern Ireland

Reflective Models (Cognitive Simulations)

"Cognitive simulations are runnable computer programs that represent models of human cognitive activities" (Roth, Woods, & People, 1992, p. 1163). They attempt to model mental structures and human cognitive processes. "The computer program contains explicit representations of proposed mental processes and knowledge structures" (Kieras, 1990, pp. 51–52). Building cognitive simulations attempts to reify mental constructs for analysis and theory building and testing; that is, to manifest theories and models of human mental functioning. So, rather than studying about cognitive phenomena, students construct simulation models of those phenomena. Theories of cognition all rely on constructs that may or may not exist. Cognitive simulations provide a medium for testing those theories in a computational model. Cognitive simulations may be constructed using expert systems or systems dynamics tools. Jonassen and Wang (2003) experimented with having a seminar class develop an expert system to simulate different metacognitive reasoning processes. The design and development process was highly iterative, involving extensive discussions and very intense self-reflections about our own preferred methods. The students who participated in constructing the cognitive simulation made significantly more contributions to the seminar discussion and had stronger opinions about the material.

In a seminar on conceptual change, students built models of the different theories of conceptual change that we were comparing. The instructor and students collaboratively built systems models of different theories, including cognitive structures, synthetic meaning, cognitive conflict (see Figure 30.6), revisionist theory, paradigm shifts, and ontology shifts. By constructing models of the different theories of conceptual change, they were able to manifest and assess their own understanding of the theories. While building models of each theory, they reconciled their naïve personal theories with the different theoretical accounts.

When we ran the model in Figure 30.6, we had to adjust the delay for new experiences and the time frame in order to manifest a rational restructuring performance. If the rate of new experiences is too high, they cannot be accommodated, let alone restructured. The importance of the rate of new anomalous experiences was a discovery that resulted from our modeling experiences. Realizing that such a model is always incomplete, the process of constructing it required intensive negotiation about which factors in the change process are most important and how the process of conceptual change looks in an operationalized form. Reifying different theories of conceptual change supported comparison–contrast thinking, an essential skill in conceptual development. We also realize that viewers of the model and its runtime performance will take issue with some of the factors and assumptions that we made. The opportunity to negotiate those differences of opinion would likely result in conceptual changes for all engaged in the negotiations.

WHICH KIND OF MODELING?

In this chapter, we have demonstrated a variety of computer-based tools (e.g., spreadsheets, expert systems, systems modeling tools, concept maps, databases) that may be used by students to model the phenomena they are studying. Each tool fosters the representation of different kinds of knowledge, and each tool imposes its own syntax, so the quality of representation within that tool depends on the affordances of that tool. Throughout this chapter, we have also cited a few studies that have demonstrated the

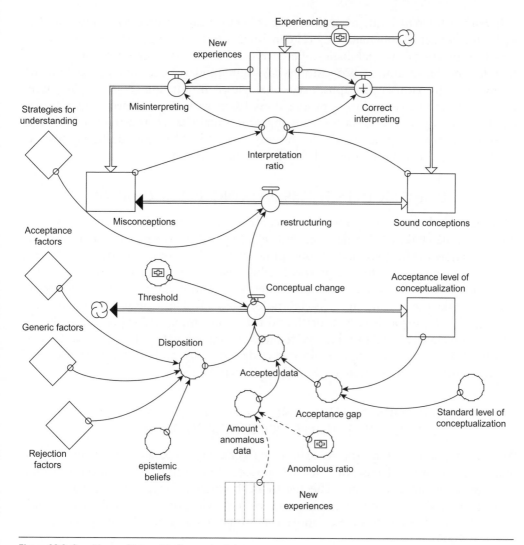

Figure 30.6 Cognitive conflict model of conceptual change

effects of different modeling activities on conceptual change, although none of that research is systematic enough to provide advice on which tools are most effective in fostering difference kinds of conceptual change. In a study taking place over an entire semester, Jonassen (1993) showed that students who constructed concept maps in one class and expert systems in another class improved both the organization and the coherence of their knowledge structures, as measured by Pathfinder Networks, an accepted method for assessing mental models. The concept-mapping group produced more hierarchically structured nets than did the expert system group, indicating that the formalism embedded in the tool has an effect on knowledge structures that learners constructed.

Advice about which tools are most effective for engaging different kinds of conceptual change is based on largely theoretical arguments. Thagard (1992) provides perhaps the best rubrics for assessing conceptual change in models in the form of explanatory coherence. Different kinds of explanatory coherence can be used to analyze models, including deductive coherence (logical consistency and entailment among members of set of propositions), probabilistic coherence (probability assignments), and semantic (similar meanings among propositions). Within models, assessors would look for symmetry, explanatory value, appropriate analogies, contradictions, competition among propositions, and acceptability of propositions. Extensive work is needed to operationalize these or any other criteria for assessing conceptual change as a result of different modeling activities. Numerous studies are easy to conceive. A major question ("how can models be used to assess conceptual change?") is addressed next.

USING MODELS TO ASSESS CONCEPTUAL CHANGE

Although the theoretical accounts of conceptual change are replete (Limon & Mason, 2002; Schnotz et al., 1999; Sinatra & Pintrich, 2003), there is very little literature that addresses how to effectively assess conceptual change. The dominant methods that are used include analyzing student protocols while engaged in problem-solving activities (Hogan & Fisherkeller, 2000), structured interviews (Southerland, Smith, & Cummins, 2000), and the use of concept maps (Edmundson, 2000). The analysis of interview and conversation protocols is very difficult and time-consuming and is plagued with reliability problems. Throughout this chapter, we have argued that the models that students construct while representing domain knowledge, systems, problems, experiences, and thought processes can be used to assess their conceptual change.

FACTORS INFLUENCING THE EFFECTIVENESS OF MODEL BUILDING FOR CONCEPTUAL CHANGE

Although we have made a strong case for using technology-mediated model building for fostering conceptual change, we must acknowledge that both cognitive and motivation processes could impact just how effective model building is for conceptual change. This latter focus on motivation represents a more "hot" view of conceptual change while the former could be considered a more traditional "cold" view of conceptual change (Sinatra, 2005).

Cognitive Factors Influencing Modeling for Conceptual Change

Cognitive Load and Modeling

A disadvantage of model building is that it places enormous demands on working memory. Construction of models places heavy cognitive load on learners. Sweller and his colleagues (Mwangi & Sweller, 1998; Tarmizi & Sweller, 1988; Ward & Sweller, 1990) found that integrating textual and diagrammatic information describing the same problems placed heavier demands on working memory, known as the split-attention effect. Requiring students to integrate multiple sources of information, a fundamental requirement of most modeling tools, is more difficult and will likely impede many learners from constructing models. Mitigating this effect will require better-developed mental models for the tools along with extensive practice.

Contradictions and Modeling

Any activity system has potential contradictions that may impede work flow and learning (Engeström, 1987). That is, elements of any activity system (subject, goal, object, division of labor, and so on) using modeling tools may contradict each other. Because of the difficulty in producing models and integrating them in classroom activity systems, the outcomes of such activities may be compromised. As an empirical example of this notion, Barab, Barnett, Yamagata-Lynch, Squire, and Keating (2002) used activity theory as an analytical lens for understanding the transactions and pervasive tensions that characterized course activities. They discovered substantive contradictions between the use of a simulation tool, which the students enjoyed and were engaged by, and learning of the astronomy content, which was the goal of the teacher. Not only does modeling require cognitive commitment, but it must also be carefully integrated into other lesson activities.

Fidelity and Modeling

Many tacit misconceptions prevail about models. One is the identity hypothesis. Although one goal in building models is to reify ideas and phenomena, the models themselves are not, as many people tacitly believe, identical to the phenomena themselves. Models are representations of interpretations of phenomena in the world, not the objects themselves. All models are at best inexact replicas of the real phenomenon.

Another misconception of models relates to their stability. Models are usually synchronic representations of dynamic processes. Phenomena change over time, context, and purpose. Models often do not. Assuming that models are literal and immutable representations of phenomena will surely lead to misconceptions.

Phenomena in the world are typically far more complex than anything that can be represented by any model. Modeling always involves certain simplifications and approximations that have to be decided independently of the theoretical requirements or data conditions (Morrison & Morgan, 1999).

As long as we recognize these limitations of models that we build, then we should avoid overstating the meaning of them.

Motivational Factors Influencing Modeling for Conceptual Change

Self-Efficacy and Modeling

Both Pintrich (1999) and Sinatra (2005) noted that self-efficacy could have a complex relationship with conceptual change. Self-efficacy is the belief in one's ability to successfully complete a given task, and high self-efficacy leads to confidence in one's abilities to complete tasks (Bandura, 1986). On one hand, confidence in one's ability could encourage engagement in challenging tasks that often promote conceptual change; however, confidence in one's ability could also lead to confidence in current conceptions and inhibit the conceptual change process (Pintrich, 1999; Sinatra, 2005). Therefore, high self-efficacy could be important for engaging the student in the challenging, cognitively engaging task of modeling. Students with low self-efficacy might not engage in the modeling task at all, or if they do engage, quickly decrease efforts or disengage when only middling models are achieved. Any of these actions would likely thwart the impact of modeling for conceptual change, and such students would benefit from smaller, less difficult modeling tasks that could foster successes and build self-efficacy. Most of these assertions about modeling and self-efficacy are theoretical, but Sins, van Joolingen, Savelsbergh, and van Hout-Wolters (2008) did find students with high self-efficacy engaged in more deep processing during a collaborative computer modeling task. As we have noted, deep processing is often a hallmark of the conceptual change process.

Self-efficacy could impact the effectiveness of a modeling task, but the opposite of this relationship might also be true. A student has to put forth a lot of effort to evaluate and create models, and we can reasonably assume that this will create a high sense of efficacy for the student with a lot confidence in their constructed model. Yet what happens if their model contains misconceptions? Many theories of conceptual change (Chinn & Brewer, 1993; Dole & Sinatra, 1998; Strike & Posner, 1992) note that adherence to existing conceptions will impair the conceptual change process, and high confidence in one's misconstructed model could certainly lead to adherence toward both the externally constructed model and the internal mental model that it represents. This could result in a resistance to conceptual change about the misconceptions in the model, and it highlights the need for instructors to closely scaffold and observe students' model construction in order to correct any misconceptions before they are too entrenched in the model.

Classroom Structures and Modeling

Students with mastery achievement goals will be focused on learning the material and improving their own performance while students with performance goals will be more concerned with others' views of their performance (Elliot & Church, 1997). Since mastery achievement goals have often been associated with deeper processing and self-regulation, Pintrich (1999) believed that they would help foster conceptual change. There is some research to suggest that this is indeed the case. Linnenbrink and Pintrich (2002) found that mastery goal orientations were related to conceptual change regarding physics. This relationship may also be relevant to model building, as Sins et al. (2008) found that mastery goals were positively related to deeper processing and achievement for a cooperative, model building task.

Although little research has been conducted to investigate how and why student motivation such as achievement goals changes (see Turner & Patrick, 2008), research involving classroom goal structures has generally suggested that teachers can influence the achievement goals that students adopt. For instance, Wolters (2004) found that students who perceived their classrooms as mastery-oriented were more likely to report having individual mastery achievement goals, and similar results were reported by Urdan (2004) in two separate studies. Theory and research would suggest that mastery-oriented approaches to modeling would be most beneficial for conceptual change. Such approaches would likely include focusing students on understanding the content they are modeling and on improving their own modeling skills as opposed to competing with others students' models or judging their models by comparing them to other students'. This is not to say that performance-approach goals (i.e., demonstrating one's competence to others) would inhibit modeling or the conceptual change process, but research of their impacts on learning is less clear and typically depends on the underlying processes (e.g., fear of failure versus need for achievement) informing the students' achievement goal (Elliot, 2006).

CONCLUSIONS ABOUT MODELING FOR CONCEPTUAL CHANGE

In this chapter, we have argued that model building is a powerful and engaging method for fostering and assessing conceptual change. Conceptual change requires the reorganization of personal conceptual knowledge that may transpire over long periods of time or more radically while trying to accommodate anomalous information. Building models of knowledge, problems, systems, experiences, or thought processes reifies the conceptual entities requiring reorganization. Because running models often provides anomalous data, the reconciliation of the model in order to achieve expectations of theoretical standards forces learners into conceptual change. As a relatively under-researched activity, many issues regarding model building remain. Research is needed to determine which kinds of models (domain knowledge, problems, systems, experiences, or cognitive simulations) or which kinds of modeling tools are more likely to result in more complete or meaningful conceptual change. Which tools learners can more readily adopt is largely a function of individual differences in cognition. Also, because mental modes are dynamic and multimodal, consisting of structural knowledge, procedural knowledge, executive or strategic knowledge, spatial representations, personal reflection, and even metaphorical knowledge (Jonassen & Henning, 1999), which kinds of tools afford the best representation of conceptual understanding is not known. In addition, cognitive and motivational factors need to be considered when both implementing models and researching their effectiveness. Modeling provides rich research opportunities in the effects of knowledge representation on conceptual change.

REFERENCES

Aamodt, A., & Plaza, E. (1994). Case-based reasoning: Foundational issues, methodological variations, and system approaches. *Artificial Intelligence Communications, 7*(1), 39–59.

Adams-Webber, J. (1995). Constructivist psychology and knowledge elicitation. *Journal of Constructivist Psychology, 8*(3), 237–249.

Bandura, A. (1986). *Social foundations of thought and action: A social cognitive theory.* Englewood Cliffs, NJ: Prentice Hall.

Barab, S. A., Barnett, M., Yamagata-Lynch, L., Squire, K., & Keating, T. (2002). Using activity theory to understand the contradictions characterizing a technology-rich introductory astronomy course. *Mind, Culture, and Activity, 9*(2), 76–107.

Briscoe, C., & LeMaster, S. U. (1991). Meaningful learning in college biology through concept mapping. *American Biology Teacher, 53*(4), 214–219.

Carey, S. (1995). On the origin of causal understanding. In D. Sperber, D. Premack, & A. J. Premack (Eds.), *Causal cognition: A multidisciplinary debate* (pp. 268–302). Oxford, UK: Clarendon Press.

Chi, M. T. H., Feltovich, P. J., & Glaser, R. (1981). Categorization and representation of physics problems by experts and novices. *Cognitive Science, 5*, 121–152.

Chinn, C. A., & Brewer, W. F. (1993). The role of anomalous data in knowledge acquisition: A theoretical framework and implications for science education. *Review of Educational Research, 63*, 1–49.

Chularut, P., & DeBacker, T. K. (2004). The influence of concept mapping on achievement, self-regulation, and self efficacy in students of English as a second language. *Contemporary Educational Psychology, 29*, 248–263.

deKleer, J., & Brown, J. S. (1981). Mental models of physical mechanisms and their acquisition. In J. R. Anderson (Ed.), *Cognitive skills and their acquisition.* Hillsdale, NJ: Lawrence Erlbaum Associates.

Dole, J. A., & Sinatra, G. M. (1998). Reconceptualizing change in the cognitive construction of knowledge. *Educational Psychologist, 33*, 109–128.

Edmundson, K. M. (2000). Assessing science understanding through concept maps. In J. J. Mintzes, J. H. Wandersee, & J. D. Novak (Eds.), *Assessing science understanding: A human constructivist view* (pp. 19–40). San Diego, CA: Academic Press.

Elliot, A. J. (2006). The hierarchical model of approach–avoidance motivation. *Motivation and Emotion, 30*, 111–116.

Elliot, A. J., & Church, M. (1997). A hierarchical model of approach and avoidance achievement motivation. *Journal of Personality & Social Psychology, 70*, 461–475.

Engeström, Y. (1987). *Learning by expanding: An activity-theoretical approach to developmental research.* Helsinki, Finland: Orienta-Konultit.

Farooq, M. U., & Dominick, W. D. (1988). A survey of formal tools and models for developing user interfaces. *International Journal of Man–Machine Studies, 29*, 479–496.

Ferguson, W., Bareiss, R., Birnbaum, L., & Osgood, R. (1991). ASK systems: An approach to the realization of story-based teachers. *Journal of the Learning Sciences, 2*(1), 95–134.

Frederiksen, J. R., & White, B. Y. (1998). Teaching and learning generic modeling and reasoning skills. *Journal of Interactive Learning Environments, 55*, 33–51.

Harris, T. (1999). A hierarchy of model and electron microscopy. In L. Magnani, N. J. Nersessian, & P. Thagard (Eds.), *Models are used to represent reality.* New York, NY: Kluwer Academic/Plenum Publishers.

Hogan, K., & Fisherkeller, J. (2000). Dialogue as data: Assessing students' scientific reasoning with interactive protocols. In J. J. Mintzes, J. H. Wandersee, & J. D. Novak (Eds.), *Assessing science understanding: A human constructivist view* (pp. 96–129). San Diego, CA: Academic Press.

Hong, N. S., Jonassen, D. H., & McGee, S. (2003). Predictors of well-structured and ill-structured problem solving in an astronomy simulation. *Journal of Research in Science Teaching, 40*(1), 6–33.

Horton, P. B., McConney, A. A., Gallo, M., & Woods, A. L. (1993). An investigation of the effectiveness of concept mapping as an instructional tool. *Science Education, 77*, 95–111.

Johnson-Laird, P. N. (1983). *Mental models: Towards a cognitive science of language, inference, and consciousness.* Cambridge, MA: Harvard University Press.

Jonassen, D. H. (1993). Changes in knowledge structures from building semantic net versus production rule representations of subject content. *Journal of Computer Based Instruction, 20*(4), 99–106.

Jonassen, D. H. (1996). *Computers in the classroom: Mindtools for critical thinking.* Columbus, OH: Merrill/Prentice Hall.

Jonassen, D. H. (2000). *Computers as mindtools for schools: Engaging critical thinking.* Columbus, OH: Merrill/Prentice Hall.

Jonassen, D. H. (2006). *Modeling with technology: Mindtools for conceptual change.* Columbus, OH: Merrill/Prentice Hall.

Jonassen, D. H., Beissner, K., & Yacci, M. (1993). *Structural knowledge: Techniques for assessing, conveying, and acquiring structural knowledge.* Hillsdale, NJ: Lawrence Erlbaum Associates.

Jonassen, D. H., & Henning, P. (1999). Mental models: Knowledge in the head and knowledge in the world. *Educational Technology, 39*(3), 37–42.

Jonassen, D. H., & Ionas, I. G. (2006). Learning to reason causally. *Educational Technology Research & Development, 54*(4).

Jonassen, D. H., & Wang, S. (2003). Using expert systems to build cognitive simulations. *Journal of Educational Computing Research, 28*(1), 1–13.

Keil, F. C. (1989). *Concepts, kinds, and cognitive development.* Cambridge, MA: MIT Press.

Kieras, D. (1990). The role of cognitive simulation models in the development of advanced training and testing systems. In N. Frederickson, R. Glaser, A. Lesgold, & M. G. Shafto (Eds.), *Diagnostic monitoring of skill and knowledge acquisition.* Hillsdale, NJ: Lawrence Erlbaum Associates.

Larkin, J. H. (1983). The role of problem representation in physics. In D. Gentner & A. L. Stevens (Eds.), *Mental models* (pp. 75–98). Hillsdale, NJ: Lawrence Erlbaum Associates.

Lee, C. B. (2006). *Capturing and assessing conceptual change in problem solving.* Doctoral dissertation, University of Missouri, Columbia, MO.

Lehrer, R., & Schauble, L. (2000). Modeling in mathematics and science. In R. Glaser (Ed.), *Advances in instructional psychology: Volume 5. Educational design and cognitive science* (pp. 101–159). Mahwah, NJ: Lawrence Erlbaum Associates.

Lehrer, R., & Schauble, L. (2003). Origins and evolution of model-based reasoning in mathematics and science. In R. Lesh & H. M. Doerr (Eds.), *Beyond constructivism: Models and modeling perspectives on mathematics problem solving, teaching, and learning* (pp. 59–70). Mahwah, NJ: Lawrence Erlbaum Associates.

Lesh, R., & Doerr, H. M. (2003). Foundations of a models and modeling perspective on mathematics teaching, learning, and problem solving. In R. Lesh & H. M. Doerr (Eds.), *Beyond constructivism: Models and modeling perspectives on mathematics problem solving, teaching, and learning* (pp. 3–33). Mahwah, NJ: Lawrence Erlbaum Associates.

Limon, M., & Mason, L. (2002). *Reconsidering conceptual change: Issues in theory and practice.* Amsterdam, The Netherlands: Kluwer.

Linnenbrink, L., & Pintrich, P. R. (2002). The role of motivational beliefs in conceptual change. In M. Limon & L. Mason (Eds.), *Reconsidering conceptual change: Issues in theory and practice* (pp. 115–135). Dordrecht, The Netherlands: Kluwer Academic.

Luque, M. L. (2003). The role of domain-specific knowledge in intentional conceptual change. In G. M. Sinatra, & P. R. Pintrich (Eds.), *Intentional conceptual change.* Mahwah, NJ: Lawrence Erlbaum Associates.

Mellar, H., Bliss, J., Boohan, R., Ogborn, J., & Tompsett, C. (1994). *Learning with artificial worlds: Computer-based modelling in the curriculum.* London, UK: Falmer Press.

Mikulecky, L. (1988). *Development of interactive programs to help students transfer basic skills to college level science and behavioral sciences courses.* Bloomington, IN: Indiana University (ERIC Document No. ED 318469).

Morgan, M. S. (1999). Learning from models. In M. S. Morgan & M. Morrison (Eds.), *Models as mediators: Perspectives on natural and social science* (pp. 347–388). Cambridge, UK: Cambridge University Press.

Morrison, M., & Morgan, M. S. (1999). Models as mediating instruments. In M. S. Morgan & M. Morrison (Eds.), *Models as mediators: Perspectives on natural and social science* (pp. 10–37). Cambridge, UK: Cambridge University Press.

Mwangi, W., & Sweller, J. (1998). Learning to solve compare word problems: The effect of example format and generating explanations. *Cognition & Instruction, 16,* 173–199.

Nersessian, N. J. (1999). Model-based reasoning in conceptual change. In L. Magnani, N.J. Nersessian, & P. Thagard (Eds.), *Models are used to represent reality.* New York, NY: Kluwer Academic/Plenum Publishers.

Norman, D. A. (1983). Some observations on mental models. In D. Gentner & A. Stevens (Eds.), *Mental models* (pp. 15–34). Hillsdale, NJ: Lawrence Erlbaum Associates.

Pintrich, P. R. (1999). Motivational beliefs as resources for and constraints on conceptual change. In W. Schnotz, S. Vosniadou, & M. Carretero (Eds.), *New perspectives on conceptual change* (pp. 33–50). Amsterdam, The Netherlands: Pergamon.

Ploetzner, R., Fehse, E., Kneser, C., & Spada, H. (1999). Learning to relate qualitative and quantitative problem representations in a model-based setting for collaborative problem solving. *Journal of the Learning Sciences, 8*(2), 177–214.

Ploetzner, R., & Spada, H. (1998). Constructing quantitative problem representations on the basis of qualitative reasoning. *Interactive Learning Environments, 5,* 95–107.

Polkinghorne, D. (1988). *Narrative knowing and the human sciences.* Albany, NY: State University of New York Press.

Rehder, B. (2003). Categorization as causal reasoning. *Cognitive Science, 27*(5), 709–748.

Roth, E. M., Woods, D. D., & People, H. E. (1992). Cognitive simulation as a tools for cognitive task analysis. *Ergonomics, 35*(10), 1163–1198.

Schnotz, W., Vosniadou, S., & Carretero, M. (1999). *New perspectives in conceptual change.* Amsterdam, The Netherlands: Pergamon.

Schreiber, D. A., & Abegg, G. L. (1991, April). *Scoring student-generated concept maps in introductory college chemistry.* Paper presented at the Annual Meeting of the National Association for Research in Science Teaching, Lake Geneva, WI (ERIC Document No. 347055).

Sinatra, G. M. (2005). The "warming trend" in conceptual change research: The legacy of Paul R. Pintrich. *Educational Psychologist, 40*(2), 107–115.

Sinatra, G. M, & Pintrich, P. R. (2003). The role of intentions in conceptual change learning. In G. M. Sinatra, & P. R. Pintrich (Eds.), *Intentional conceptual change.* Mahwah, NJ: Lawrence Erlbaum Associates.

Sins, P. H. M., van Joolingen, W. R., Savelsbergh, E. R., & van Hout-Wolters, B. (2008). Motivation and performance within a collaborative computer-based modeling task: Relations between students' achievement goal orientation, self-efficacy, cognitive processing, and achievement. *Contemporary Educational Psychology, 33*(1), 58–77.

Southerland, S. A., Smith, M. U., & Cummins, C. L. (2000). "What do you mean by that?" Using structured interviews to assess science understanding. In J. J. Mintzes, J. H. Wandersee, & J. D. Novak (Eds.), *Assessing science understanding: A human constructivist view* (pp. 72–95). San Diego, CA: Academic Press.

Strike, K. A. & Posner, G. J. (1992). A revisionist theory of conceptual change. In R. A. Duschl & R.J. Hamilton (Eds.), *Philosophy of science, cognitive psychology, and educational theory and practice* (pp. 147–176). New York, NY: State University of New York Press.

Tarmizi, R. A., & Sweller, J. (1988). Guidance during mathematical problem solving. *Journal of Educational Psychology, 80,* 424–436.

Thagard, P. (1992). *Conceptual revolutions.* Princeton, NJ: Princeton University Press.

Turner, J. C., & Patrick, H. (2008). How does motivation develop and why does it change? Reframing motivation research. *Educational Psychologist, 43,* 119–131.

Urdan, T. (2004). Using multiple methods to assess students' perceptions of classroom goal structures. *European Psychologist, 9*(4), 222–231.

Vandierendonck, A., & deVooght, G. (1996). Evidence for mental-model-based reasoning: A comparison of reasoning with time and space concepts. *Thinking and Reasoning, 2*(4), 249–272.

Vosniadou, S. (1992). Knowledge acquisition and conceptual change. *Applied Psychology, 41*(4), 347–357.

Vosniadou, S. (1994). Capturing and modeling the process of conceptual change. *Learning and Instruction, 4*(1), 45–70.

Vosniadou, S. (2002a). On the nature of naïve physics. In M. Limon & L. Mason (Eds.), *Reconsidering conceptual change: Issues in theory and practice* (pp. 61–76). Dordrecht, The Netherlands: Kluwer Academic Publishers.

Ward, M., & Sweller, J. (1990). Structuring effective worked examples. *Cognition & Instruction, 7,* 1–39.

Windschitl, M. (2000). Supporting the development of science inquiry skills with special classes of software. *Educational Technology: Research & Development, 48*(2), 81–95.

Wittgenstein, L. (1953). *Philosophical investigations* (G. E. M. Anscombe, Trans.) Oxford, UK: Blackwell.

Wolters, C. A. (2004). Advancing achievement goal theory: Using goal structures and goal orientations to predict students' motivation, cognition, and achievement. *Journal of Educational Psychology, 96*(2), 236–250.

Yu, Q. (2002). Model-based reasoning and similarity in the world. In L. Magnani & N. J. Nersessian (Eds.), *Model-based reasoning: Science, technology, and values.* New York, NY: Kluwer Academic/Plenum Publishers.

Part VI
Reflections

Part VI

31

SITUATING TEXT, TALK, AND TRANSFER IN CONCEPTUAL CHANGE

Concluding Thoughts

P. Karen Murphy and Patricia A. Alexander,
The Pennsylvania State University and University of Maryland

In order to foster conceptual change through instruction, we need to design curricula and instruction that on the one hand try to reduce the gap between initial knowledge and the to-be-acquired information so that students can use their usual constructive, enrichment types of mechanisms successfully. On the other hand we also should try to develop in students the necessary metaconceptual awareness, epistemological sophistication, hypothesis testing skills and top-down, conscious and deliberate mechanisms for intentional learning that will help them understand the problem of conceptual change and deal with it in the best possible way. In other words, instruction-induced conceptual change requires not only the restructuring of students' naïve theories but also the restructuring of their modes of learning and reasoning. In order to accomplish these changes substantial cognitive effort and sociocultural support are necessary.

(Vosniadou, Vamvakoussi, & Skopeliti, 2008, p. 28)

In their chapter on the framework theory approach in the first edition of this *Handbook*, Vosniadou and colleagues signaled many of the themes that run through the present volume, and open the door to critical arenas of inquiry and intervention that merit deeper exploration as theory and research on conceptual change move forward. For this concluding chapter, we have been asked to comment on the insights offered herein by international scholars representing different theoretical orientations toward conceptual change, as well as diverse methodologies and varied disciplines. For that reason, we pick up the gauntlet Vosniadou et al. have thrown down by accepting their challenge to consider certain keys to the "restructuring of [students'] modes of learning and reasoning" (Vosniadou, 2008b, p. xx). In so doing, it is our hope that students will come to form richer, more evidence-based concepts that foster future learning and development rather than the relatively shallow or misconstrued notions that become barriers to intellectual growth not solely in mathematics and science, but in all academic domains.

Specifically, it is our intention to forward three areas for empirical study and for explicit classroom interventions that mirror the trends and recommendations that the contributing scholars address in this compilation. Those areas are text, talk, and transfer. With regard to "text," we examine the research on quality materials written to effectively inform students or to confront accepted ideas, thereby potentially prompting cognitive dissonance among readers (Allen, 1991). In terms of "talk," we consider the manner of critical–analytic discourse that has been shown to promote deeper reflection among students and counter-tendencies to deal superficially with academic content (Murphy, Wilkinson, Soter, Hennessey, & Alexander, 2009). Finally, in association with "transfer," we delve into the topic of relational reasoning that holds promise for disrupting students' tendency to deal with information in a piecemeal and isolated fashion and for assisting them in attending to salient attributes of ideas, tasks, or contexts (Alexander & the Disciplined Reading and Learning Research Laboratory [DRLRL], 2012). Such meaningful "patterning" is offered as a critical step to the use and transfer of conceptual understanding to new or varied problems and contexts. Through this combined focus on instructive or persuasive materials, quality classroom talk, and ways of thinking, we intend to stimulate new ideas about learning and reasoning that Vosniadou et al. (2008) demand in the service of conceptual change.

GUIDING PREMISES

Before we consider the individual areas of text, talk, and transfer, we want to posit certain premises that frame our orientation toward conceptual change and to our analysis of contributions to this *Handbook*. We make no claims that others will or should accept these premises, although we would contend that there is ample empirical evidence to support each. Rather, we only see it as fair to position ourselves ontologically and epistemologically with regard to what we see as the nature of conceptual change and to the effort required to address misconstrued but deeply held beliefs about the world or about academic domains.

Naïve or Misconceived Ideas are Unavoidable Outcomes of Human Learning and Development

When speaking about cognitive development, John Flavell (1979) observed that we do not have to teach children to think; thinking comes naturally. Of course it is another matter entirely when we are describing effective thinking or the effective monitoring of one's cognitive endeavors. Effective cognition or metacognition requires concentrated effort and the support of others who are more knowledgeable and capable. There are no assurances that effective cognition or metacognition simply happens in the course of human development.

Much the same can be said about naïve or misconceived ideas, what some have called "misconceptions." If individuals are learning and developing naturally, they will have misconceived or misconstrued notions. No one – from the child acclimating to the world to the expert immersed in a field of study – is immune. Misconceived ideas not only are unavoidable but they also may well be necessary stepping stones to more mature, evidence-based understandings. Moreover, as Perkins and Simmons (1988) argued decades ago, it would seem that the type of the malformed ideas might be associated with one's level of expertise.

Further, it would appear that misconceived notions are not random occurrences. Instead, functioning minds operating within given sociocultural environments are likely to share certain misunderstanding about the world or about the domains that are central to human learning. Perhaps it is the "primitive" perceptions (diSessa, 1993) that guide individuals toward such shared misunderstandings or it is the mental models that they form as a consequence of the incomplete and misleading interactions they have with the world (Vosniadou & Brewer, 1992). Or perhaps – or most likely – it is some reasonable combination of both (diSessa, Chapter 2, this volume). Whatever the causal mechanisms, it is not a mark of failure as a learner that one manifests misconstrued or "naïve" ideas about some object, phenomenon, or construct. What becomes of concern is when such notions persist even in the face of formal education meant to dissuade such thinking; when those we expect to be "educated" generally or within some specified field "reveal" their conceptual naïveté when their understandings are brought to light.

Naïve or Misconceived Ideas Represent a Certain Interplay Between Knowing and Believing

So, why do some abandon their less expert ways of perceiving or set aside more naïve mental models in the face of compelling evidence or effective instruction, while others continue to wallow in misconceptional bliss? One explanation may lie in the intricate interplay of knowing and believing that unfolds across situations and over time – an interplay we regard as central to all conceptual development and conceptual change. In essence, most of what we know conceptually is continuously shifting and modulating, even if that conceptual frame has the tendency to retain some of its basic form (Murphy, 2007). Those in conceptual change research recognize this fact and do not generally attempt to deal with run-of-the-mill, everyday, and non-invasive conceptual change. Rather, they focus on the matter of concepts that *should* undergo significant and systematic change as a consequence of formal education or relevant disciplinary experiences, but seemingly do not.

To understand this conceptual resistance or the persistence of naïve and misconceived ideas, we find it helpful to think about the interplay between various manifestations of knowing and believing that this process of conceptual change may entail. We find concern for this interplay noted throughout this volume (Chinn, Duncan, Dianovsky, & Rinehart, Chapter 28, this volume), especially when discussions of epistemic beliefs are brought to the forefront (Brown & Hammer, Chapter 6, this volume). For our purposes, we also find it informative to consider the manner of concepts or "mis-concepts" that arise at differing stages of knowledge/belief change. Thus, we can draw on the belief and knowledge components of Murphy's (2007, 2009) Characteristics of the Learner and Argument Integration Model (CLAIM) to illustrate how varied forms of misconceived ideas may exist at each of her stages.

Although we offer a more extensive discussion of the CLAIM later in the chapter, it is fruitful to focus specifically on the interplay of individuals' beliefs and knowledge and their relation to conceptual change and misconceptions. As represented in Figure 31.1,

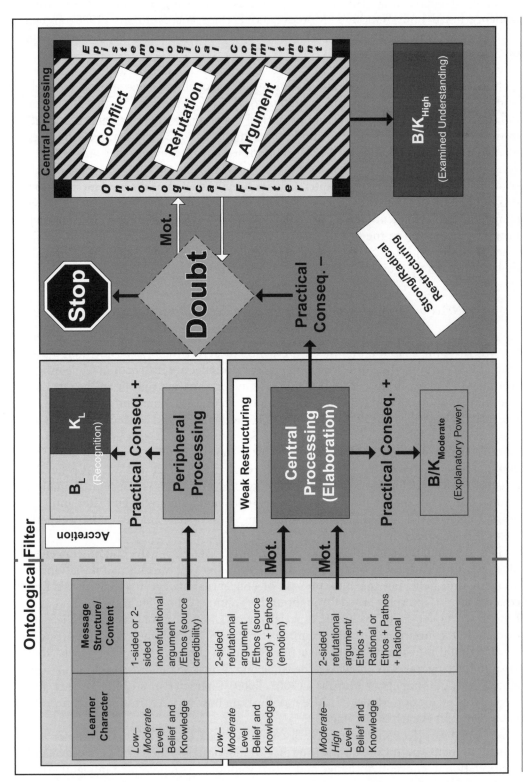

Figure 31.1 Characteristics of the Learner and Argument Interaction Model (CLAIM; Murphy, 2009)

there are likely those underdeveloped or ill-formed conceptualizations that exist in the recognition stage of change where beliefs are rather tacit and unexamined and knowledge is fragmented or superficial and non-scrutinized. Those misconceived notions that exist within this stage may, thus, persist as a consequence of low motivation, limited formal knowledge, *or* lack of strategic engagement (Perkins & Simmons, 1988). More importantly, however, misconceived notions are likely attributable to the lack of thoughtful reconciliation between one's beliefs and knowledge. Indeed, numerous studies suggest that beliefs and knowledge are initially acquired from diverse sources (Alexander & Dochy, 1995), and as a result may not be cognitively activated or compared in working memory (Nersessian, Chapter 21, this volume). This likely contributes to what some in this volume refer to as local inconsistencies (Chinn et al., Chapter 28, this volume).

Although misconceived ideas can still be identified among those in the stage of explanatory power, beliefs and knowledge are now more closely aligned then they were at the recognition level. Concomitantly, however, beliefs around a concept have become more engrained, knowledge more entrenched, or the affective valence toward those understandings more intense. At this point, it could be that the power of the beliefs obscures the knowledge that would contribute to conceptual restructuring, or that the evidence has strengthened the individuals' inaccurate understanding, or the affective valence associated with current conceptions dampens the desire to question what one believes or knows. Consequently, more rooted but misconceived ideas hold their ground. At this stage, it becomes clear that closer alignment between what one believes and knows is important but not sufficient for alleviating misconceptions, particularly those that are deeply rooted within one's conceptual schema.

But even those who achieve the stage of examined understanding, including those of us who research conceptual change, are not immune to misconceived ideas even in our domains of expertise. Granted, such flawed understandings at this stage – where beliefs and knowledge are closely interconnected, clearly explicated, well scrutinized, and affectively very high – are not apt to be numerous or pedestrian in nature. But where these misconceived ideas exist, as Perkins and Simmons's (1988) label of "Gordian misconception" suggests, they are often highly integrated into the very fabric of one's disciplinary or domain understanding and, therefore, potentially more challenging to restructure than those found at any other stage. For that reason, we refer to misconceived ideas at this stage as entrenched. As we will discuss later, changes to these highly interconnected topical beliefs and knowledge require deep, meaningful and often emotionally difficult change.

Naïve or Misconceived Ideas Occur in all Realms of Knowledge and Performance

As others (Carretero & Voss, 1994) and we have noted (Murphy & Alexander, 2008), misconceptions are not the privileged domain of science and mathematics, as might appear to be the case. All fields of human knowledge come with their own unique cases of misconceived ideas – from history to biology or from art to geometry. What, after all, is lore if not the shared but undocumented notions of some sociocultural group? Within the *Handbook*, we see the acknowledgment of the pervasiveness of misconceived ideas with chapters devoted specifically to history (Carretero, Castorina, & Levinas, Chapter 14, this volume) and the social sciences (Lundholm & Davies, Chapter 15, this volume). Even in light of this acknowledgment, this *Handbook*, as with the prior volume

(Vosniadou, 2008a), continues to emphasize misconceptions or misconceived knowledge in scientific and mathematical domains, as Lundholm and Davies (this volume) note.

The concern for the overrepresentation of science and mathematics is not a problem solely of these domains but legitimately must be placed on the doorstep of those engaged in social science research – a point on which we concur with Carretero et al. (this volume). It may well be that the nature of the misconceived ideas within the social sciences will be qualitatively different from those in the traditional sciences. We see the potential for deeply held but misguided beliefs about the very nature of these domains or about the manner of justification required to support a claim or "prove" a position. There is ample evidence, for instance, that many view the learning of history as simple memorization of names and dates (VanSledright, 2002), or presume that the multiplicity of potential explanations for historical events and the lack of absolute certainty means that any reasonable explanation qualifies as an answer (Maggioni, Fox, & Alexander, 2010). Such broad and pervasive notions *about* a field can potentially have far more serious consequences to students' learning and development than the misconstrued ideas about any particular concept *within* a field.

Because Naïve or Misconceived Ideas are Complex and Multifaceted by Nature, the Approaches to Addressing Them Must be Likewise Complex and Multifaceted

Returning to the challenge that Vosniadou et al. (2008) set before us, we reject the notion that simple solutions to the complex and multifaceted problems of naïve and misconceived beliefs exist – as do they. As we learn from the *Handbook* contributors, reasons that misconceived ideas take hold in the first place – even weak ones – are numerous. Those reasons can be cognitive, metacognitive, social, cultural, or motivational; they can reflect the nature of the discipline or domain itself; they may be a consequence of inadequate or inappropriate instructional practices; or simply a feature of human nature. Thus, to presume that the pathway to resolution of these conundrums can be singular or straightforward is misguided in our judgment.

That does not mean that educators are incapable of promoting deeper or more learned understandings – there is too much evidence to the contrary. It does suggest that some amalgamation of the suggestions offered herein will be required if we are to confront pre-existing beliefs; augment limited, fragmented, or distorted understandings; provide strategic and metastrategic guidance; and enhance learner motivation and affect toward learning and academic development. In the following discussion, we build on several of the themes that populate this *Handbook* to forward what we see as three areas where this amalgamated approach to enhanced conceptual development seems possible: text, talk, and transfer.

TEXT

As has been the case in our research (e.g., Murphy, 1998), we want to herald the promise of text in altering students' beliefs and knowledge. Indeed, like Chambliss and Garner (1996), we contend that the power of text is in its ability to stand still, affording readers repeated and sustained opportunities to examine it for veracity and truth. By *text* we are referring to any meaningful, nonverbal representation including connected discourse, diagrams, display, or models (Guzzetti, Synder, Glass, & Gamas, 1993; Murphy &

Alexander, 2004). Despite the fact that support for such a perspective can easily be found in the broader literature, text holds less sway among the contributors to this volume. A quick search of the chapters of this volume revealed that less than half of the authors (*n* = 13 chapters) even use the word *text*, and a relative minority of those authors have been proponents of text as a vehicle for initiating conceptual change among learners. Rather, the majority of the authors mentioning *text* did so in a less than positive fashion, and this negativity appeared to strongly correlate with the nature of the text being discussed.

Specifically, authors were negative about school texts more often in the form of text-books (Siler, Klahr, & Matlen, Chapter 7, this volume). In some cases, school texts were determined to be limited in their affordances and likeness to the phenomena being learned (e.g., Jonassen & Easter, Chapter 30, this volume) or inadequate in terms of their effectiveness as a pedagogical tool for promoting conceptual change (Duit, Treagust, & Widodo, Chapter 25, this volume).

For example, in discussing the shortcomings of traditional curriculum in teaching atomic theory, Wiser and Smith (Chapter 9, this volume) contend that the content of the textbook is simply not rich enough for the students to make sense of the phenomena and that the illustrations are, at best, confusing. Tytler and Prain (Chapter 29, this volume) forward similar contentions regarding the lack of affordances in textbooks, such as vague symbols to represent scientific phenomena (e.g., arrow used to represent force). Some authors suggested that school texts often forward a singular perspective as though there are no other alternatives (Carretero et al., Chapter 14, this volume) or are written in a language that is, for all intents and purposes, foreign to the reader (Arabatzis & Kindi, Chapter 18, this volume). Still others highlight the fact that texts take on a particular meaning within a particular context (Halldén, Scheja, & Haglund, Chapter 4, this volume) or that the usefulness of text in learning scientific knowledge is dependent on the time of its introduction (Kaufman, Keselman, & Patel, Chapter 12, this volume).

The lack of enthusiasm regarding the role of text in conceptual change likely has a number of causes. For example, Sinatra and Broughton (2011) suggest that the decline in interest in and use of text as a catalyst for conceptual change may be due to the inconsiderate nature of exposition (e.g., low comprehensibility or coherence breaks) commonly found in science textbooks, the lack of prior knowledge requisite for reading and processing the texts (Arabatzis & Kindi, Chapter 18, this volume), or the alignment with external curricular demands or instructional trends (e.g., inquiry-oriented pedagogy; Jonassen & Easter, Chapter 30, this volume).

Importantly, we agree with Carretero et al. (Chapter 14, this volume), Halldén et al. (Chapter 4, this volume) and others (Kaufman et al., Chapter 12, this volume) that particular factors appear to mediate the effectiveness of text-based conceptual change. We would contend that contemporary research has shed light on the factors that mediate the power of text in promoting learners' conceptual change (e.g., Nersessian, Chapter 21, this volume) and that the worth of text as a vehicle for inducing conceptual change should be reconsidered. Toward that end, we endeavor to offer an overview of some of the factors that appear to mediate text-based conceptual change, as well as how these factors interact with each other to promote conceptual change. Among the factors mediating the effectiveness of text in promoting conceptual change discussed here are: the nature of the text (Sinatra & Broughton, 2011), characteristics of the learner (Sinatra & Mason, Chapter 20, this volume), and the conceptual change goal (e.g., weak to radical restructuring). To understand the interaction of these factors, we draw on the extant research in text-based learning, persuasion, and conceptual change, as well as Murphy's CLAIM (Murphy, 2009).

Nature of the Text: Type, Features, Structure, and Content

The nature of a given text can be discussed in terms of its type, features, structure, and content. *Text type* refers to the purposes, intentions, or intended outcomes of a text (Alexander & Jetton, 1996). While some texts are written in order to tell a story (i.e., narrative text), others describe or elaborate events, activities, or ideas in a relatively objective fashion with the purpose of informing readers (i.e., informational/expository text), and still others are written to alter the perspectives of readers or move them to act through the presentation of positions or claims and supporting evidence (i.e., argument/persuasive text).

While the organization of exposition can be generally straightforward, many have referred to this type of text as "inconsiderate" (Anderson & Armbruster, 1984). That is, structural patterns can vary from paragraph to paragraph (e.g., compare/contrast versus cause/effect), and the texts are often found to be information-dense and uninteresting (Sinatra & Mason, Chapter 20, this volume). The inconsiderate nature of expository text has no doubt contributed to its constrained effectiveness as a tool for conceptual change (Wiser & Smith, Chapter 9, this volume). By comparison, argument or persuasive texts have been shown to be particularly effective at altering the beliefs and knowledge of the reader; that is, promoting conceptual change (Murphy & Mason, 2006). The term "refutational text" is often used to refer to a kind of argument or persuasive text in which the author has the intention of altering students' misconceptions regarding a specific belief, topic, or concept (Murphy & Mason, 2006).

Empirical evidence suggests that the comprehensibility, interestingness, and understandability of a text influence the extent to which students process or engage the text (Andiliou, Ramsay, Murphy, & Fast, 2012). Similarly, the structure and content of the arguments influence the persuasiveness of a text (Sinatra & Broughton, 2011). At least three distinct argument-based text structures have been studied in the extant literature: one-sided, two-sided nonrefutational, and two-sided refutational texts (Allen et al., 1990). A *one-sided* text presents a single viewpoint, as is common in many textbooks (Carretero et al., Chapter 14, this volume). In contrast, a *two-sided nonrefutational* text presents two conflicting positions, yet keeps a neutral perspective (Guzzetti et al., 1993). This type of text is akin to point–counterpoint texts also commonly found in textbooks. Finally, a *two-sided refutational* text presents two opposing stances, but discounts one in favor of the other. The refutational text often referred to in the conceptual change literature is a kind of two-sided refutational text in which the "misconception" serves as the alternative perspective that is refuted or discredited based on commonly accepted scientific evidence. Findings from numerous empirical studies and meta-analyses (e.g., Allen, 1993) on argument-based text structure suggest that two-sided refutational texts are more effective than either two-sided nonrefutational or one-sided texts in changing readers' views and in correcting misconceived ideas (Guzzetti et al., 1993). These findings seem to parallel the perspectives and experiences of many of the contributors in this volume.

The content of a persuasive text is also important in changing learners' understandings. Aristotle described three means of persuasion that are supplied by the content of an oral or written argument. Those are (a) gaining the confidence of the listener through the personal character of the speaker as portrayed in speech or text (i.e., ethos); (b) tapping of the proper attitude in the hearer (i.e., pathos); and (c) the argument itself (i.e., logos). The *ethos* (i.e., author credibility) and *pathos* are particularly important text characteristics for learners with limited topic knowledge (Murphy & Alexander, 2004) or for those who minimally or peripherally process the message (Petty & Cacioppo, 1986). As Carey (1994, p. 35) noted, ethos and pathos have reciprocal effects:

> one effect of *ethos*, as well as inducing a degree of trust, is also to produce a feeling of goodwill in the audience towards the speaker, so that the projection of the appropriate character achieves more subtly the effect sought by explicit appeals for a favorable hearing.

Such a finding is nicely illustrated in the Broughton, Sinatra, and Nussbaum (in press) study in which the credibility of the source of the text diminished students' negative emotions over Pluto's demotion from planet status. Finally, strong, causal arguments are more likely to alter students' understandings than weak, data-driven arguments (Chambliss & Garner, 1996).

Characteristics of the Learner and Argument Interaction

As discussed, what makes texts meaningful is how learners interact with them; that is, how the characteristics of learners (e.g., beliefs, knowledge, or motivation) lead learners to interact with the features, structure, and content of the text. Within this volume, Sinatra and Mason have presented an exceptional review of learner characteristics and the role they play in the conceptual change process. Many of the points Sinatra and Mason raise generalize to text-based conceptual change. As such, we will not revisit those issues herein. Rather, we want to overview one contemporary model (i.e., CLAIM, Murphy, 2009), which depicts the learner with text, as well as the anticipated outcomes of such interaction (see Figure 31.1). The model is rooted in the pragmatist philosophy of Charles Peirce (1958), as well as the levels of processing (Lockhart & Craik, 1990) and dual processing models (Petty & Cacioppo, 1986) from psychology. Foundational to the model is Peirce's notion that our beliefs (or initial knowledge) served as habits of action. Behavior is driven by one's beliefs, and as one acts on those beliefs, the habits become strengthened and entrenched; that is, as long as the practical consequences of behaving in accordance with the habit are positive. However, when the practical consequence of one's habits is negative, then doubt ensues and the individual is forced to consider the viability of maintaining those habits. Importantly, Peirce maintained that individuals are intolerant of doubt and will quickly seek out a new belief. Also, the more entrenched the belief, the more severe the practical consequences have to be for change to take place.

Equally foundational from the cognitive and social psychology literature is the principle that acquisition of understanding proceeds along a continuum from sensory perception (i.e., Recognition Level) to levels associated with pattern discernment (i.e., Explanatory Power Level) and, finally, to semantic/associative stages of enrichment (i.e., Examined Understanding Level). Specifically, from the levels of processing model, Murphy (2007) draws on the principle that individuals can acquire representations with very little cognitive effort (i.e., peripheral processing based on text cues or heuristic strategies), but that well-integrated, examined understandings are the result of sustained cognitive processing in which individuals integrate the understanding within larger cognitive semantic and associative structures (i.e., elaboration, Petty & Cacioppo, 1986).

It is the integration of learner characteristics with text characteristics that predicts the alterations or modifications of learners' understandings (i.e., conceptual change). At the Recognition Level, learners' beliefs and knowledge are generally superficial, partial, or fragmented (i.e., low to moderate), and when reading non-refutational text, the learner can readily process the message peripherally based on some textual cue (e.g., credibility of the source or length of the text). This type of interaction will generally strengthen learners' prior understandings or allow for the partial acquisition of additional representations. Paralleling Carey's (1985) notion of accretion, this type of growth does not imply additional depth of processing, but rather the maintenance or strengthening of the initial impression or the acquisition of a new representation. An example can be seen in students' understandings of the day/night cycle. Having witnessed the sun low in the morning sky, students enter school with a very strong belief that the sun "rises" in the morning. It is not that students have deeply processed this understanding, but rather that the recurrence of the event on a daily basis has strengthened their belief. Given the minimal processing, it is highly probable that students can acquire inconsistent belief and knowledge, both across and within respective concepts (e.g., Chi, Chapter 3, this volume).

Changing the structure and content of the text will likely lead the same learners to deeper, more meaningful processing and conceptual change. Empirical findings suggest that learners with low to moderate levels of beliefs and knowledge on a topic who are exposed to a two-sided refutational text from a credible source are more likely to engage the text and elaborate the arguments (Andiliou et al., 2012). The same could be said of learners with moderate to high levels of knowledge and beliefs on a given topic. What seems to differentiate these two groups of learners is that learners with low to moderate levels of beliefs and knowledge are more persuaded when the two-sided argument evokes their emotion, whereas the learners with relatively higher levels of belief and knowledge are more persuaded by rational, non-emotive arguments (Murphy, 2001). Through the process of engaging and elaborating upon the text-based arguments the learner will find either consistency or inconsistency between the arguments and their own perspectives. If there is consistency, then the practical consequences of maintaining their beliefs and knowledge are positive and the individual will likely gain the ability to explain their understandings in greater detail. This level of change parallels Carey's (1985) notion of weak restructuring. The beliefs and knowledge of learners become less fragmented and affectively charged.

If learners' beliefs and knowledge fail to align with those presented in the text, then they will need to assess the practical consequences of maintaining their current understandings (Murphy, 2007). If the practical consequences are substantive, then learners will begin to doubt their understandings. Motivated learners will exert additional cognitive effort in an attempt to deeply explore and modify their perspectives. In some cases, this will lead to a state of examined understanding in which learners either can justify their prior understandings or have modified them in a meaningful way so as to align with the new beliefs and knowledge.

This sophisticated level of examination would be associated with Carey's (1985) weak restructuring and radical restructuring and likely involves the consternation often associated with the reformulation of fundamental understandings. In essence, when students continue to engage deeply with the understandings they acquired at the Explanatory Level, there is the possibility that they will encounter information, data, or even discourse that is either inconsistent or puzzling in relation to their prior understandings (e.g., anomalous data; Chinn & Brewer, 1993). It is the discord that propels students toward Examined Understanding, and as individuals progress through this level, they struggle to make sense of their experiences given a particular contextual environment (Mason, 2001). We hold that Murphy's model provides initial guideposts for researchers and practitioners interested in altering the conceptions of learners with text. Further, as we will suggest in the next section, the road to Examined Understanding can be enriched through topic- and text-specific classroom discussions.

TALK

Talk can be an extremely powerful mechanism in belief and knowledge acquisition and change (Anderson, Chinn, Waggoner, & Nguyen, 1998). As nicely illustrated in several of the chapters in this volume, talk can be used: (a) to explain complex theoretical models through the use of analogies (Clement, Chapter 22); (b) as a means to better understand biological concepts (Inagaki & Hatano, Chapter 10); (c) to strengthen small group collaborations and enable students to acquire representational understandings (Miyake, Chapter 24); to enable students to modify external representations into abstract ones (Tytler & Prain, Chapter 29); or, (d) as a venue for dissecting and digesting large group lectures in medicine (Martin & Schwartz, Chapter 23).

Similarly, Chinn and colleagues (Chapter 28, this volume) document a particularly strong example of talk as a tool for change. Chinn et al. have successfully created a middle-school intervention, Promoting Reasoning and Conceptual Change in Science (PRACCIS), that combines model-based instructional practices with an inquiry orientation and embraces discourse as a tool for conceptual change and reasoning (Chinn, Buckland, & Samarapungavan, 2011). Each lesson is guided by a set of big questions; students weigh and consider possible explanatory models and alternatives, and use evidence to judge which explanations are best. Importantly, dialogue and discussions are central in the group's determination of the viability of the models and the quality and viability of the supporting evidence. Thus, discourse is fundamental to establishing epistemic and ontological judgments regarding evidence and the possible explanatory models.

The fact that several chapters highlight the power of talk (i.e., teacher to student or student to student) in the change process is not at all surprising to us. Indeed, recognition of the power of talk dates back to ancient Greek philosophy and the Socratic dialogues (Murphy, Wilkinson, & Soter, 2010). Acknowledgment of the role of talk in learning and conceptual change can also be traced to the contemporary belief and knowledge literature. For example, Alexander and colleagues (e.g., Alexander & Dochy, 1995) conducted numerous studies exploring students' and teachers' perceptions of the relations between beliefs and knowledge and found that students perceived their friends and "talking" with friends or others as credible and as strong catalysts for belief change – perhaps a more important catalyst than their teacher.

In terms of this *Handbook*, what was surprising to us was the lack of linkages to literacy research where the role of discourse in learning has been explored for decades. One notable exception in this volume is the abovementioned program of research by Chinn and colleagues. Indeed, the discourse component of PRACCIS appears to share characteristics with Collaborative Reasoning (Anderson et al., 1998), a text-based discourse approach designed to enhance the argument and reasoning of participants through the co-construction of meaning and weighing of evidence. Similar results were evidenced in research conducted by Mason (2001). In her naturalistic study, Mason was attempting to use Collaborative Reasoning (Anderson et al., 1998) as a way for students to enhance their understandings of a series of science experiments.

In particular, students in the Mason (2001) study were charged with the task of observing experiments and taking fields notes, then in small groups the students were encouraged to discuss their observations and generate interpretations of what they were observing. In one experiment, the children observed mold growing on cheese over several days. Over time the mold spots became larger, but the surface area of the cheese appeared to stay the same. In discussing these observations many of the students expressed varying opinions on what was happening, and through discussions were able to either enhance their understandings and justifications or modify them altogether. Mason (2001, p. 318) nicely explains the transcript.

> The development of argument through claims, oppositions, justifications, and counterpositions required the participants to activate crucial cognitive procedures by continuously appealing to experience, facts, specific prior knowledge, hypothetical counterevidence.

Our sense is that this is the kind of deep, meaningful change so earnestly sought by researchers in conceptual change studies – change that mirrors learning as described in the Examined Understanding Level of CLAIM (Murphy, 2009).

As such, it seems to us that there is much to be gleaned from the text-based literacy research on classroom discussions that can be readily applied to discourse practices aimed at conceptual change. Of particular importance to conceptual change are approaches to discussion whose purpose is to enhance the critical–analytic thinking skills of participating students (e.g., *Collaborative Reasoning*, Anderson et al., 1998 or *Philosophy for Children*, Sharp, 1995). To better understand the nature of the critical–analytic approaches to discussion, Wilkinson and colleagues conducted a meta-analysis of relevant empirical studies (Murphy et al., 2009) and an analysis of discourse (Soter et al., 2008) of the various approaches to discussion. Based on their findings, Wilkinson, Soter, and Murphy (2010) created the *Quality Talk* discussion approach – an approach to discussion that combines key features from the various critical–analytic approaches.

Quality Talk discussions vary substantially from typical or traditional classroom discussions or recitations. Research suggests that the teacher typically talks for a disproportionate amount of time during discussions (Cazden, 2001). In traditional classroom discourse, the teacher *initiates* a topic by asking a question; the student *responds*; and, the teacher *evaluates* the student's response (IRE; Mehan, 1979). *Quality Talk* stands in stark contrast to an IRE approach and comprises four components including an ideal instructional frame, discourse elements, teacher modeling and scaffolding, and a set of pedagogical principles (Wilkinson et al., 2010). The *instructional frame* represents a set of conditions that Wilkinson et al. consider fundamental for promoting rich, meaningful talk about text including shared control between teacher and students, where the teacher has control over choice of text and topic, but students have interpretive authority and control of turns. There is an emphasis on both knowledge gathering and students' relevant lived experiences. Importantly, a moderate degree of affective and knowledge-driven engagement is necessary for students to interrogate or query text in search of its underlying arguments, assumptions, or beliefs (i.e., epistemic engagement).

The second component of the model emphasizes the *discourse elements* teachers must recognize and promote during productive talk about text in order to foster critical–analytic thinking (Wilkinson et al., 2010). Among those discourse elements are: asking authentic questions that invite a range of responses, building on students' contributions (i.e., uptake), and asking questions to elicit high-level thinking (i.e., generalization, analysis, and speculation) (Nystrand, Wu, Gamoran, Zeiser, & Long, 2003). Wilkinson et al. (2010) also encourage the use of questions to elicit extra-textual connections by students (i.e., affective, intertextual, and shared knowledge connections; Edwards & Mercer, 1987), elaborated explanations (Chinn, O'Donnell, & Jinks, 2000), engagement in exploratory talk (Mercer, 2000), and the use of words that signal reasoning (Wegerif, Mercer, & Dawes, 1999). Empirical evidence has shown that over time students internalize ways of talking about text and begin using them to support their own thinking and that of their peers (Jadallah et al., 2011).

Teacher modeling and scaffolding, the third component, refers to ways in which teachers initiate students into productive talk about a text (Wilkinson et al., 2010). As suggested by Chinn et al. (Chapter 28, this volume), promoting critical–analytic thinking requires temporary support from teachers in the early stages of discussions. Such support comes in the form of particular teacher moves including summarizing, modeling, prompting, or challenging. Each of these moves can be used to highlight specific knowledge claims, their justifications, and how students can become critical consumers of what they read (Slotta & Chi, 2006).

The fourth component, the *pedagogical principles*, refers to understandings about pedagogy and language that appear to be essential to fostering a classroom culture of dialogic inquiry (Wilkinson et al., 2010). These norms are discussed in depth in Wilkinson et al. (2010) and include understandings regarding the importance of collectively established ground rules for discussion, the role of a big question, and the importance of a rich, interesting text that permits a variety of interpretations, opinions, or positions and about which students have some prior knowledge. The ultimate goal is for students to take responsibility for co-constructing their own interpretations and responses to text – a goal that aligns quite nicely with CLAIM. Indeed, *Quality Talk* discussions typify the kind of discourse that we believe will propel students to the level of Examined Understanding within CLAIM (Murphy et al., 2010) and conceptual change.

TRANSFER

As with many contributors to this volume (e.g., Vamvakoussi, Vosniadou, & Van Dooren, Chapter 16) and the broader conceptual change literature (Greeno, 1999; Mayer, 1999), we bemoan the lack of transfer, especially positive transfer evidenced by individuals whose education and experiences promise better (Thagard, Chapter 19, this volume). Nonetheless, like Martin and Schwartz (Chapter 23, this volume), we contend that: "People build new knowledge from a foundation of old knowledge, and for this reason, theories of transfer are pertinent to the study of conceptual change." In their informative chapter, Martin and Schwartz put a novel spin on the debate about transfer or the typical foci within the literature. That is to say, they do not attend primarily or exclusively to the cognitive aspects of transfer, but instead concentrate on structural modifications to the learning environment that they argue "can feed back and change people's mental representations;" what they term *innovation*.

What we want to highlight from the Martin and Schwartz chapter on "Conceptual Innovation and Transfer" is the distinction they systematically draw between *similarity* transfer and *dynamic* transfer. We then want to use that distinction as a platform to discuss the role of relational thinking and its value to conceptual change. Core to the notion of similarity transfer that Martin and Schwartz describe are at least two requirements. For one, the focus is on the mind and individuals' ability to discern commonality across situations and contexts in order to utilize what is already known and to acquire deeper understandings. The other is the state of individuals' existing knowledge. Specifically, according to Martin and Schwartz, similarity transfer is predicated on individuals' ability to reason analogically on the basis of well-formed conceptual understanding. Clement (this volume) and Thagard (this volume) strike a related theme as they home in on analogies as mechanisms to prime deeper understanding and the subsequent use of that understanding in varied situations and context (i.e., transfer).

In contrast to similarity transfer, Martin and Schwartz offer dynamic transfer, which demands the coordination of multiple conceptual components triggered by environmental affordances. Further, they differentiate between the "complete, structurally complex knowledge needed for similarity transfer" and the often tacit and unconnected knowledge the results in dynamic transfer. While Martin and Schwartz cast dynamic transfer as a form of person–environment interaction not evident in similarity transfer, we see the issue somewhat differently. For one, person–environment interaction marks all manner of transfer, whether similarity or dynamic in form. The point of contrast has more to do with the weight placed on person or environment in each act (or form) of transfer. We appreciate the work of researchers such as Martin, Schwartz, and others (diSessa, this volume) who remind us of the power of learning environments and their affordances. But even in the case of similarity transfer, the environment is inevitably at work.

Moreover, as several of our guiding premises suggest, we do not see "complete, structurally complex knowledge" as a reasonable expectation in general and thus, we do not see it as a feasible precursor to similarity transfer or any case of transfer. Certainly, as analogical reasoning researchers have made evident, sufficient source knowledge is essential for mapping from source to target to occur (Dunbar & Blanchette, 2001). But sufficient knowledge does not equate to complete knowledge. Thus, we do not concur with Martin and Schwartz's argument that "complete, structurally complex" knowledge is a defensible requisite for transfer – similarity or otherwise.

There are two principal concerns that we want to bring to the foreground. First, there appears to be an overly simplified debate between the "pieces" and "coherence" adherents within the conceptual change literature that has raged for more than a quarter of a century. Second, conceptual change and transfer researchers have come to view the person–environment association almost exclusively in terms of analogical reasoning. With regard to the first concern, we were encouraged by the presence of the two opening chapters of this *Handbook*, authored by two of the most identifiable proponents of these two positions: diSessa (pieces; Chapter 2) and Vosniadou (coherence; Chapter 1). In both of these chapters, the presence of the other viewpoint is at least acknowledged. Nonetheless, despite diSessa's contention that he was seeking a "sensible resolution" to this ongoing debate, we would characterize both these opening salvos as examples of two-sided refutational texts. Yes, the other view is acknowledged and its seeming merits noted, but the objective of the discourse appeared to be to document the primacy of the researcher's own perspective.

It seems to us that a resolution to this conundrum is achievable and we believe that the resolution might arise from reconsidering the interplay of percept and concept in human learning and development (James, 1911/1996; Peirce, 1955). While percepts are the *in situ* impressions that are formed from our immediate interactions with the world, such percepts are innumerable and likely flawed, with little need for justification due to their alignment with environmental affordances (Murphy, 2007). In contrast, concepts are more generalized and enduring impressions *in mente* that manifest some degree of internal coherence. It is fruitless to question the value of one over the other. Percepts and concepts are in constant flux and continual interaction with one another. Conceptual change could not proceed without either, as William James (1911/1996, p. 74) so eloquently argued:

> We thus see clearly what is gained and what is lost when percepts are translated into concepts. Perception is solely of the here and now; conception is of the like and unlike, of the future, of the past, and of the far away . . . Who can decide off-hand which is absolutely better, to live or to understand life? We must do both alternately, and a man can no more limit himself to either than a pair of scissors can cut with a single one of its blades.

The only thing we would add to James's statement is that both percepts and concepts – both the pieces and coherence sides of the conceptual change debate – would benefit from a deeper examination of the relational reasoning processes that foster the immediate, *in situ* impressions *and* the more enduring *in mens* models that arise.

Further, we aver that analogical reasoning is foundational to knowledge transfer (Alexander & Murphy, 1999). Yet the bases for transfer and for conceptual change more broadly do not rest solely on seeing similarities within informational arrays. Rather, both transfer and conceptual change have a great deal to do with attending and perceiving and, thereby, forging meaningful perceptual–conceptual couplings founded on varied forms of relations – what we and others have defined as relational reasoning (Alexander & the DRLRL, 2012).

Specifically, when individuals engage deeply with information – a requisite for either conceptual learning or transfer – they may notice similarities within that information or between what they already know and what they presently discern (analogical reasoning). In contrast, they may recognize how the information they are encountering deviates in some non-trivial way from the prior patterns (concepts) they had internalized (anomalous reasoning). The work of Chinn and colleagues (Chinn & Malhotra, 2002) has established the role that anomalous reasoning plays within scientific learning and development. There is also the potential that the information presented stands in direct contrast or opposition to what is known (antithetical reasoning). The research on refutational or persuasive texts previously discussed bears witness to the influence that antithetical reasoning can have on students' comprehension and conceptual learning (Murphy & Mason, 2006).

Finally, within the research of Chi (Chapter 3, this volume) and others (Carey, 1985), we find reference to another manifestation of relational reasoning, where individuals recognize the incompatibility of two ideas (antinomous thinking). Thus, something cannot simultaneously be alive and dead, even and odd, or plant and animal. The rules that bound particular concepts exclude information that violates those rules. Yet it would appear that students often fail to discern such incompatibility and, thus, seem capable of holding to ideas that are not only somewhat conflicting, but also truly incompatible. While the research on antinomous reasoning is the least researched among the four aforementioned processes, we were encouraged to find that the very notion of conceptual change forwarded by Vosniadou et al. (2008, p. 3) speaks directly to such thinking ability. Specifically, when discussing the foundational writings of Kuhn (1962) and Carey and the concept of incommensurability, Vosniadou et al. write that: "Conceptual change according to Carey (1991) requires the re-assignment of a concept to a different ontological category or the creation of new ontological categories."

On the heels of the prior discussion of text and talk, we regard this treatment of transfer via relational reasoning as timely for several reasons. For one, it reminds us that quality texts and quality talk serve little purpose unless learners attend to the information communicated and perceive the valuable content that resides therein. More importantly, it is essential not only to attend to and perceive the relevant information conveyed via quality texts and talk, but also to examine that information in juxtaposition to existing conceptions or to the notions presented elsewhere. Finally, as has been repeatedly documented with the wealth of literature on analogical reasoning and conceptual learning, including Clement (this volume) and Thagard (this volume), such depth of thinking and reflection cannot be assumed to develop well without instructional intervention and support. That is, various manifestations of relational reasoning should be treated as valued metastrategies and made components of any conceptual change intervention.

CODA

As we bring this commentary to a close, we want to return to the quotation that opened it and to the challenges that still face all of us committed to students' learning and development – and, thus, to conceptual change. There is no question that "substantial cognitive effort and sociocultural support" (Vosniadou et al., 2008, p. 28) will be required if we are to: confront the inadequate educational materials and instructional approaches that contribute to weak or malformed understandings; promote metaconceptual awareness and epistemic competence; and transform typical modes of conceptual operation into those marked by critical analytic thought and relational reasoning. We remain optimistic that these challenges can be met and we look to the diverse and stellar community of conceptual change scholars represented in this volume to serve in the vanguard of this revolution.

REFERENCES

Alexander, P. A., & the Disciplined Reading and Learning Research Laboratory (2012). Reading into the future: Competence for the 21st century. *Educational Psychologist, 47*(4), 259–280.

Alexander, P. A., & Dochy, F. J. R. C. (1995). Conceptions of knowledge and beliefs: A comparison across varying cultural and educational communities. *American Educational Research Journal, 32*, 413–442.

Alexander, P. A., & Jetton, T. L. (1996). The role of importance and interest in the processing of text. *Educational Psychology Review, 8*(1), 89–121.

Alexander, P. A., & Murphy, P. K. (1999). Nurturing the seeds of transfer: A domain-specific perspective. *International Journal of Educational Research, 31*, 561–576.

Allen, M. (1991). Meta-analysis comparing the persuasiveness of one-sided and two-sided messages. *Western Journal of Speech Communication, 55*, 390–404.

Allen, M. (1993). Determining the persuasiveness of message sidedness: A prudent note about utilizing research summaries. *Western Journal of Communication, 57*, 98–103.

Allen, M., Hale, J., Mongeau, P., Berkowits-Stafford, S., Stafford, S., & Shanahan, W. (1990). Testing a model of message sidedness: Three replications. *Communication Monographs, 57*, 274–291.

Anderson, R. C., Chinn, C., Waggoner, M., & Nguyen, K. (1998). Intellectually stimulating story discussions. In J. Osborn & F. Lehr (Eds.), *Literacy for all: Issues in teaching and learning* (pp. 170–186). New York, NY: Guilford Press.

Anderson, T. H., & Armbruster, B. B. (1984). Studying. In P. D. Pearson, R. Barr, M. L. Kamil, & P. Mosenthal (Eds.), *Handbook of reading research: Vol. I* (pp. 657–679). White Plains, NY: Longman.

Andiliou, A., Ramsay, C., Murphy, P. K., & Fast, J. (2012). Weighing opposing positions: Examining the effects of intratextual persuasive messages on students' knowledge and beliefs. *Contemporary Educational Psychology, 37*(2), 113–127.

Broughton, S. H., Sinatra, G. M., & Nussbaum, E. M. (in press). "Pluto has been a planet my whole life!" Emotions, attitudes, and conceptual change in elementary students learning about Pluto's reclassification. *Research in Science Education.*

Carey, C. (1994). Rhetorical means of persuasion. In I. Worthington (Ed.), *Persuasion: Greek rhetoric in action* (pp. 26–45). New York, NY: Routledge.

Carey, S. (1985). *Conceptual change in childhood.* Cambridge, MA: MIT Press.

Carey, S. (1991). Knowledge acquisition: Enrichment or conceptual change? In S. Carey & R. Gelman (Eds.), *The epigenisis of mind: Essays on biology and cognition* (pp. 257–291). Hillsdale, NJ: Lawrence Erlbaum Associates.

Carretero, M., & Voss J. F. (1994). *Cognitive and instructional processes in history and the social sciences.* Hillsdale, NJ: Lawrence Erlbaum Associates.

Cazden, C. B. (2001). *Classroom discourse: The language of teaching and learning* (2nd edn.). Portsmouth, NH: Heinemann.

Chambliss, M. J., & Garner, R. (1996). Do adults change their minds after reading persuasive text? *Written Communication, 13*(3), 291–313.

Chinn, C. A., & Brewer, W. F. (1993). The role of anomalous data in knowledge acquisition: A theoretical framework and implications for science education. *Review of Educational Research, 63*, 1–49.

Chinn, C. A., Buckland, L. A., & Samarapungavan, A. (2011). Expanding the dimensions of epistemic cognition: Arguments from philosophy and psychology. *Educational Psychologist, 46*(3), 141–167.

Chinn, C. A., & Malhotra, B. A. (2002). Children's responses to anomalous scientific data: How is conceptual change impeded? *Journal of Educational Psychology, 94*, 327–343.

Chinn, C. A., O'Donnell, A. M., & Jinks, T. S. (2000). The structure of discourse in collaborative learning. *Journal of Experimental Education, 69*, 77–97.

diSessa, A. A. (1993). Toward an epistemology of physics. *Cognition and Instruction, 10*(2–3), 105–225.

Dunbar, K., & Blanchette, I. (2001). The in vivo/in vitro approach to cognition: The case of analogy. *Trends in Cognitive Sciences, 5*, 334–339.

Edwards, A. D., & Mercer, N. (1987). *Common knowledge: The development of understanding in the classroom.* New York, NY: Methuen.

Flavell, J. H. (1979). Metacognition and cognitive monitoring: A new area of cognitive–developmental inquiry. *American Psychologist, 34*, 906–911.

Greeno, J. C. (1999). Commentary: Alternative perspectives on transfer and transfer studies. *International Journal of Educational Research, 31*, 645–654.

Guzzetti, B. J., Snyder, T. E., Glass, G. V., & Gamas, W. S. (1993). Promoting conceptual change in science: A comparative metaanalysis of instructional interventions from reading education and science education. *Reading Research Quarterly, 28*, 117–159.

Jadallah, M., Anderson, R. C., Nguyen-Jahiel, K., Miller, M., Kim, I.-H., Kuo, L.-J., et al. (2011). Influence of a teacher's scaffolding moves during child-led small group discussions. *American Educational Research Journal, 48*(1), 194–230.

James, W. (1996). *Some problems of philosophy: A beginning of an introduction to philosophy*. Lincoln, NE: University of Nebraska Press. (Original published in 1911.)

Kuhn, T. (1962). *The structure of scientific revolutions*. Chicago, IL: University of Chicago Press.

Lockhart, R. S., & Craik, F. I. M. (1990). Levels of processing: A retrospective commentary on a framework for memory research. *Canadian Journal of Psychology, 44*, 87–112.

Maggioni, L., Fox, E., & Alexander, P. A. (2010). The epistemic dimension of competence in the social sciences. *Journal of Social Science Education, 9*(4), 15–23.

Mason, L. (2001). Responses to anomalous data and theory change. *Learning and Instruction, 11*, 453–483.

Mayer, R. E. (1999). Multimedia aids to problem-solving transfer. *International Journal of Educational Research, 31*, 611–623.

Mehan, H. (1979). *Learning lessons: Social organization in the classroom*. Cambridge, MA: Harvard University Press.

Mercer, N. (2000). *Words and minds: How we use language to think together*. London, UK: Routledge.

Murphy, P. K. (1998). *Toward a multifaceted model of persuasion: The interaction of textual and learner variables*. Unpublished doctoral dissertation, University of Maryland, College Park, MD.

Murphy, P. K. (2001). What makes a text persuasive? Comparing students' and experts' conceptions of persuasiveness. *International Journal of Educational Research, 35*, 675–698.

Murphy, P. K. (2007). The eye of the beholder: The interplay of social and cognitive components in change. *Educational Psychologist, 42*, 41–53.

Murphy, P. K. (2009, June). *Toward examined understanding: Rethinking the role of belief in academic development*. Invited address presented at the Scientific Meeting on Cognitive Flexibility and Epistemic Beliefs, Marche-en-Famenne, Belgium.

Murphy, P. K., & Alexander, P. A. (2004). Persuasion as a dynamic, multidimensional process: A view of individual and intraindividual differences. *American Educational Research Journal, 41*, 337–363.

Murphy, P. K., & Alexander, P. A. (2008). The role of knowledge, beliefs, and interest in the conceptual change process: A synthesis and meta-analysis of the research. In S. Vosniadou (Ed.), *International handbook of research on conceptual change* (pp. 583–616). New York, NY: Routledge.

Murphy, P. K., & Mason, L. (2006). Changing knowledge and changing beliefs. In P. A. Alexander & P. Winne (Eds.), *Handbook of educational psychology* (2nd ed., pp. 305–326). Mahwah, NJ: Lawrence Erlbaum Associates.

Murphy, P. K., Wilkinson, I. A. G., & Soter, A. O. (2010). Instruction based on discussion. In R. Mayer & P. A. Alexander (Eds.), *Handbook of research on learning and instruction* (pp. 382–407). New York, NY: Taylor & Francis.

Murphy, P. K., Wilkinson, I. A. G., Soter, A. O., Hennessey, M. N., & Alexander, J. F. (2009). Examining the effects of classroom discussion on students' high-level comprehension of text: A meta-analysis. *Journal of Educational Psychology, 101*, 740–764.

Nystrand, M., Wu, A., Gamoran, A., Zeiser, S., & Long, D. A. (2003). Questions in time: Investigating the structure and dynamics of unfolding classroom discourse. *Discourse Processes, 35*(3), 135–198.

Peirce, C. S. (1955). Two notes: On motive, on percepts. In J. Buchler (Ed.), *The philosophical writings of Peirce*. New York, NY: Dover.

Peirce, C. S. (1958). The fixation of belief. In P. P. Wiener (Ed.), *Charles S. Peirce: Selected writings* (pp. 91–112). New York, NY: Dover.

Perkins, D. N., & Simmons, R. (1988). Patterns of misunderstanding: An integrative model for science, math, and programming. *Review of Educational Research, 58*, 303–326.

Petty, R. E., & Cacioppo, J. T. (1986). The elaboration likelihood model of persuasion. In L. Berkowitz (Ed.), *Advances in experimental social psychology* (Vol. 19, pp. 123–205). New York, NY: Academic Press.

Sharp, A. M. (1995). Philosophy for children and the development of ethical values. *Early Child Development and Care, 197*, 45–55.

Sinatra, G. M., & Broughton, S. H. (2011). Bridging reading comprehension and conceptual change in science education: The promise of refutation text. *Reading Research Quarterly, 46*(4), 374–393.

Slotta, J. D. & Chi, M. T. H. (2006). The impact of ontology training on conceptual change: Helping students understand the challenging topics in science. *Cognition and Instruction, 24*(2), 261–289.

Soter, A. O., Wilkinson, I. A. G., Murphy, P. K., Rudge, L., Reninger, K. B., & Edwards, M. N. (2008). What the discourse tells us: Talk and indicators of high-level comprehension. *International Journal of Educational Research, 47*(6), 372–391.

VanSledright, B. (2002). *In search of America's past: Learning to read history in elementary school*. New York, NY: Teachers College Press.

Vosniadou, S. (Ed.). (2008a). *International handbook of research on conceptual change*. New York, NY: Routledge.

Vosniadou, S. (2008b). Conceptual change research: An introduction. In S. Vosniadou (Ed.), *International handbook of research on conceptual change* (pp. xiii–xxviii). New York, NY: Routledge.

Vosniadou, S., & Brewer, W. F. (1992). Mental models of the earth: A study of conceptual change in childhood. *Cognitive Psychology, 24*, 535–585.

Vosniadou, S., Vamvakoussi, X., & Skopeliti, I. (2008). The framework theory approach to the problem of conceptual change. In S. Vosniadou (Ed.), *International handbook of research on conceptual change* (pp. 3–34). New York, NY: Routledge.

Wegerif, R., Mercer, N., & Dawes, L. (1999). From social interaction to individual: An empirical investigation of a possible socio-cultural model of cognitive development. *Learning and Instruction, 9*, 493–516.

Wilkinson, I. A. G., Soter, A. O., & Murphy, P. K. (2010). Developing a model of Quality Talk about literary text. In M. G. McKeown and L. Kucan (Eds.), *Bringing reading research to life* (pp. 142–169). New York, NY: Guilford Press.

CONTRIBUTORS

EDITOR

Stella Vosniadou
National and Kapodistrian University of Athens (Greece)

CHAPTER AUTHORS

Patricia A. Alexander
University of Maryland (USA)

Theodore Arabatzis
University of Athens (Greece)

Carl Bereiter
University of Toronto (Canada)

Kristen P. Blair
Stanford University (USA)

David E. Brown
University of Illinois, Urbana-Champaign
(USA)

Mario Carretero
Autónoma University, Madrid and
Facultad Latinoamericana de Ciencias
Sociales (Argentina)

Jose A. Castorina
University of Buenos Aires and Consejo
Nacional de Investigaciones Científicas y
Técnicas (Argentina)

Michelene T. H. Chi
Arizona State University (USA)

Clark A. Chinn
Rutgers, The State University of
New Jersey (USA)

Douglas B. Clark
Vanderbilt University (USA)

John J. Clement
University of Massachusetts at Amherst
(USA)

Peter Davies
University of Birmingham (UK)

Michael Dianovsky
Rutgers, The State University of
New Jersey (USA)

Andrea A. diSessa
University of California at Berkeley
(USA)

Ravit Golan Duncan
Rutgers, The State University of
New Jersey (USA)

Reinders Duit
IPN – Leibniz Institute for Science
Education (Germany)

Matthew A. Easter
University of Missouri (USA)

E. Margaret Evans
University of Michigan (USA)

Liza Haglund
Stockholm University (Sweden)

Ola Halldén
Stockholm University (Sweden)

David Hammer
Tufts University (USA)

Kayoko Inagaki
Chiba University (Japan)

David Jonassen
University of Missouri (USA)

David R. Kaufman
Columbia University (USA)

Alla Keselman
National Institutes of Health (USA)

Vasso Kindi
University of Athens (Greece)

David Klahr
Carnegie Mellon University (USA)

Gaea Leinhardt
University of Pittsburgh (USA)

Leonardo Levinas
University of Buenos Aires and Consejo
Nacional de Investigaciones Científicas y
Técnicas (Argentina)

Marcia C. Linn
University of California at Berkeley
(USA)

Cecilia Lundholm
Stockholm University (Sweden)

Lee Martin
University of California, Davis (USA)

Lucia Mason
University of Padova (Italy)

Bryan J. Matlen
Carnegie Mellon University (USA)

Naomi Miyake
The University of Tokyo (Japan)

P. Karen Murphy
Pennsylvania State University (USA)

Nancy N. Nersessian
Georgia Institute of Technology (USA)

Vimla L. Patel
New York Academy of Medicine (USA)

Vaughan Prain
La Trobe University (Australia)

Anita Ravi
Alliance College-Ready Public Schools
Los Angeles, CA (USA)

Ronald Rinehart
University of Pittsburgh (USA)

Marlene Scardamalia
University of Toronto (Canada)

Max Scheja
Stockholm University (Sweden)

Daniel L. Schwartz
Stanford University (USA)

Robert S. Siegler
Carnegie Mellon University (USA)
Beijing Normal University (China)

Stephanie Siler
Carnegie Mellon University (USA)

Gale M. Sinatra
University of Southern California (USA)

Carol L. Smith
University of Massachusetts at Boston
(USA)

Matija Svetina
University of Ljubljana (Slovenia)

Paul Thagard
University of Waterloo (Canada)

David F. Treagust
Curtin University (Australia)

Jessica M. Tsang
Stanford University (USA)

Russell Tytler
Deakin University (Australia)

Xenia Vamvakoussi
University of Ioannina (Greece)

Wim Van Dooren
Katholieke Universiteit Leuven
(Belgium)

Ari Widodo
FPMIPA UPI (Indonesia)

Marianne Wiser
Clark University (USA)

INDEX

Note: Page numbers followed by 'f' refer to figures and followed by 't' refer to tables.